Corporate Financial Reporting and Analysis

Text and Cases

FOURTH EDITION

Corporate Financial Reporting and Analysis

Text and Cases

David F. Hawkins

Lovett-Learned Professor of Business Administration
Graduate School of Business Administration
Harvard University

IRWIN/McGraw-Hill

New York • San Francisco • Washington, D.C. • Auckland • Bogotá
Caracas • Lisbon • London • Madrid • Mexico City • Milan
Montreal • New Delhi • San Juan • Singapore
Sydney • Tokyo • Toronto

Irwin/McGraw-Hill

A Division of The **McGraw·Hill** Companies

CORPORATE FINANCIAL REPORTING AND ANALYSIS: TEXT AND CASES

This book is printed on acid-free paper.

1 2 3 4 5 6 7 8 9 0 DOC/DOC 9 0 9 8 7

ISBN 0-256-08147-6

Publisher: *Jeff Shelstad*
Editorial coordinator: *Martin Quinn*
Marketing manager: *Heather L. Woods*
Project manager: *Karen J. Nelson*
Production supervisor: *Karen Thigpen*
Designer: *Larry J. Cope*
Compositor: *GAC/Shepard Poorman*
Typeface: *10/12 Times Roman*
Printer: *R. R. Donnelley & Sons Company*

http: //www.mhcollege.com

Library of Congress Cataloging-in-Publication Data

Hawkins, David F.
    Corporate financial reporting and analysis : text and cases /
David F. Hawkins. — 4th ed.
        p.   cm.
    Includes index.
    ISBN 0-256-21895-1 (alk. paper)
        1. Corporations—Accounting.   2. Corporation reports.
3. Financial statements.   I. Title.
HF5686.C7H35   1997
658.15′12—dc21   97-6227

To Barbara, Whitney and Lauren

Preface

This text–case book is based on the very successful Analysis of Corporate Financial Reports second-year MBA course taught at the Harvard Graduate School of Business Administration. The course is based on the assumption that success in the business world as a manager, investor, grantor of credit, or public accountant requires in part an appreciation of the interplay between a company's corporate strategy and its corporate financial reporting policies and practices.

Corporate financial statements can represent genuine managerial performance or they can represent an illusion of performance, either good or bad. Corporations have leeway in how they report their financial condition and results of operations. Despite progress in eliminating undesirable reporting practices, areas remain in which alternative practices are equally acceptable for reporting essentially identical business transactions. The profits and reported financial condition of the reporting company will vary depending on which alternative is used.

Those who can use corporate financial statements to tell the difference between real and illusory performance have a considerable advantage in making business decisions of all kinds. For example, corporate managers who understand the relationship between corporate financial reporting and business policy, as well as how other managers can influence profits through the judicious use of alternative accounting practices, are more likely to succeed than their less knowledgeable competitors. Ignorance of the options, uncertainties, and ambiguities of the practices underlying the preparation of corporate financial statements can lead investors and creditors to make poor decisions. On the other hand, unless those practicing public accountancy understand how investors use financial data, know how to identify and interpret the motives of managers issuing financial reports, and recognize the relationship between business strategy, and financial reporting decisions, they run the risk of not satisfactorily fulfilling their third-party responsibility to the issuers and users of corporate financial statements. In short, an intimate knowledge of the subtleties of financial accounting and the ability to apply appropriate financial analysis techniques can be critical to the success of many of those who participate in our business system.

This book shows financial statement users how to analyze financial reports so as to identify the economic realities of the reporting corporation. To accomplish this end the book provides the reader with an understanding of the current state of financial reporting practices; the way in which the corporate financial statements influence our economic system; the significant consequences of corporate financial data for the people who depend on their credibility; and the methods by which competent statement users interpret the data contained in corporate financial reports. It is not a book on accounting methodology.

The subject matter is approached from a variety of points of view. Foremost are the interests of those closest to the corporation, namely, the management communicating the financial data, existing and potential stockholders, financial analysts using corporate financial statements for investment recommendations, the grantors of trade and commercial credit, and the independent certified public accountant responsible for expressing an opinion on the fairness of the corporate financial statements issued by management.

Textual Material

The first chapter of this book represents background material. Its purpose is to familiarize the reader with (1) some of the fundamental issues in corporate financial reporting and analysis and (2) some of the key institutions that influence corporate financial reporting standards and practices.

Each of the subsequent chapters consists of text and selected case studies. Each chapter deals with a particular financial reporting and/or financial analysis topic. The split of pages between text and cases is about even. Thus, unlike in a number of other casebooks, there should be sufficient textual material in this book to satisfy the professional user seeking to gain a better understanding of fundamentals and current practices in the area of corporate financial reporting and analysis. Such readers might include corporate executives, bankers, financial analysts, and individual investors.

International Standards

One particular chapter should be mentioned. Because of its importance in today's business world, the International Accounting Standards issued by the International Accounting Standards Committee are covered in Chapter 27.

Uses of Financial Data

Every chapter includes a discussion of financial statement analysis and interpretation practices relevant to that chapter. In Part Four, however, three chapters are devoted exclusively to financial analysis topics. These three chapters cover the fundamentals of financial analysis that the reader will need to interpret the case data presented in later chapters.

A Clinical Approach

The case studies have been prepared as a basis for discussion of the topics covered in the related text. They have not been selected to illustrate either appropriate or inappropriate handling of financial reporting situations. To decide what is appropriate action is the purpose of the case discussion.

Most of the cases require a decision on the part of the student. Typically, the student is asked to assume a role with a real sense of the professional and personal involvement of (1) top management responsible for issuing financial data to the public in a particular situation or (2) a statement user responsible for making recommendations based on the data.

To make the management decision realistically, the student must identify the administrative burdens of the decision maker, the opportunities for creative action, and the manager's responsibilities. In particular, the student must be concerned with how financial reporting relates to other areas of top management concern, such as corporate strategy, stockholder relations, the market price of the company's stock, dividend policy, and capital structure. In addition, the student must think through the implications for the company of actions that investors, the company's independent auditor, the regulatory authorities, and others might take as a result of the company's financial reporting decision.

In cases where the student is asked to apply financial analysis techniques directly to obtain insights into the reporting company for security valuation purposes, the student should relate these insights to security valuation practices and, as well, assume the responsibility of making a competent recommendation to others who must rely upon the analyst's recommendations.

Seldom will there be a simple, easy answer to the problems posed. Discussion of the case studies within a decision-making framework should give students an appreciation of:

- The "real world" difficulties in resolving financial reporting and analysis issues.
- The role of judgment in the selection of appropriate accounting practices and analytical techniques.
- The evolutionary state of accounting principles and analysis practices.
- The significance and limitations of financial accounting data for corporate decision-making purposes and security valuations.
- The need for managers to involve themselves in the financial reporting process.
- The vital communication function that financial reports play in our economic system.
- The difficulties encountered in trying to develop an integrated statement of a basic theory of accounting that is both acceptable to accounting theoreticians and at the same time responsive to the subtleties of our complex economic system.
- The relationship between the accounting systems and reports management uses for management control and financial reporting purposes.
- The continuing need for the business, financial analysts, and accounting professions to develop a useful and acceptable set of accounting principles that eliminates the differences in accounting practices not justified by different circumstances.

Non-U.S. Company Cases

A number of cases involve non-U.S. companies. Experience has shown that discussion of these cases enhances the student's understanding of U.S. accounting practices and the alternative ways a company's

financial statements might be viewed for decision-making purposes.

Reading Plan

The cases and chapters included in this book have been used in many undergraduate and graduate accounting and financial analysis courses at both the introductory and advanced levels. In each of these courses the order and manner in which the materials were used varied according to students' prior background in the field and the instructor's course objectives. Consequently, it is unlikely that the materials included in this book could be put together in an order that would meet the needs of all readers and courses.

It is suggested that each reader skim the table of contents before reading the text and determine where to begin and in what order the chapters should be covered. For example, readers with limited or no prior understanding of financial accounting and financial analysis probably should read the chapters in the order presented. On the other hand, a reader with considerable exposure at the introductory level might just skim the first eight chapters and begin reading seriously at Chapter 10.

Acknowledgments

A number of people have helped in the preparation of this book and the Harvard Business School's financial accounting and analysis courses, from which the book draws heavily. Walter Frese provided the pedagogical and corporate-reporting–philosophy foundation for both the book and the course upon which it is based. Two of my colleagues—Robert Madeira and Mary Wehle—were responsible for many of the original course materials that were subsequently incorporated into the book. The difficult and frustrating task of controlling the manuscript in its many drafts was ably accomplished by Beverly J. Outram. My wife Barbara provided both the inspiration and continuing support required to squeeze out of our busy family and professional lives the time needed to complete the manuscript. In addition, I wish to thank the President and Fellows of Harvard College for their permission to reproduce the case and textual materials copyrighted in their name, as well as my current and former colleagues at the Harvard Business School who have granted me permission to use case materials prepared by them, in particular, Amy Hutton, Krishna Palepu, Peter Wilson, Mary Barth, Thomas Piper, William Bruns, Norman Bartczak, Charles Christenson, and Robert Simons.

David F. Hawkins

Contents

PART NINE

Special Reporting and Analysis Issues

23 Foreign Activities   789

24 Disaggregated Business Disclosures   812

25 Interim Period Reports   839

26 Contingencies   852

27 International Accounting Standards and Transnational Financial Analysis   870

PART ONE Corporate Financial Reporting and Analysis Environment

CHAPTER

1

Introduction

Corporate Financial Reporting and Analysis deals with the selection of corporate financial reporting strategies and practices by managers, the preparation of financial statements by accountants, and interpretation by financial statement users of corporate financial reports issued by business enterprises when reporting to parties outside of the business.

The function of corporate financial reports is to provide a continual history, expressed in money terms, of the economic resources and obligations of a business enterprise and of the economic activities that affect them. These items and any changes in them are identified and measured in conformity with financial accounting principles that are generally accepted at the time the statements are prepared. The typical output of this process are the statement of financial position, the income statement, and the statement of cash flows.

Those involved in the issuance and use of corporate financial reports should have a basic understanding of the institutions involved in the setting of accounting standards and the regulation of the financial reporting process as well as the fundamental issues that underlie much of the controversy that is generated by the process of proposing, adopting, and implementing accounting standards in response to changes in the business, social, political and economic environments. This knowledge will be useful in identifying the motivations of those advocating changes in particular accounting standards; appreciating the limitations of corporate financial report data; and understanding the respective roles of those involved in the corporate financial reporting process.

Professor David F. Hawkins prepared this note as the basis for class discussion.
Copyright © 1995 by the President and Fellows of Harvard College. Harvard Business School teaching note 195–242.

Authorities

The adequacy of financial statements is judged in terms of the relevance and reliability of the data provided to the interested parties. These are difficult standards to define, and there is considerable disagreement as to their definition in particular instances. Nevertheless, a great number of financial accounting conventions, concepts, principles, and standards of disclosure have evolved and been supported by recognized accounting authorities. These authorities include the Financial Accounting Standards Board (FASB), the American Institute of Certified Public Accountants (AICPA), and the Securities and Exchange Commission (SEC).

One of the early actions of the SEC was to rule that companies under its jurisdiction be audited by independent public accountants. Although the SEC was given the power to establish accounting rules by the Securities Exchange Acts of 1933–1934, very early in its existence the commission made it known that it expected the private sector to assume the main part of this activity. For many years, with few exceptions, the accounting profession carried out this responsibility through the AICPA's Accounting Principle Board (APB) and its predecessor, the Committee on Accounting Procedures (CAP). However, in 1973 the accounting profession voluntarily gave up its central role in developing generally accepted accounting principles to a newly created independent private body called the Financial Accounting Standards Board (FASB). At that time, the SEC indicated that it would continue its policy of leaving the determination of accounting rules primarily to a responsible private body and that it would support the FASB in much the same way as it had worked with the AICPA's earlier rule-making bodies. Today, the SEC is encouraging the FASB to work with other national accounting standards-setting bodies and the International Accounting Standards Committee (IASC) toward a goal of harmonizing global accounting standards.

Financial Accounting Standards Board

The FASB consists of seven full-time members with specific terms of appointment from the fields of public accounting, industry, government, and education. They are selected by the trustees of the Financial Accounting Foundation (FAF). Assisting the board members is a full-time research staff, as well as individuals who are invited to join ad hoc task forces to resolve specific issues, and an appointed Financial Accounting Standards Advisory Council (FASAC). This broadly representative advisory council meets periodically and advises the FASB on agenda topics and priorities, suggests members for task forces, and consults on numerous other technical and administrative matters.

The standard-setting process of the FASB begins with placing an accounting problem on the board's technical agenda. Next, a board member is assigned to prepare, with staff assistance, a preliminary definition of the problem and a bibliography of the significant literature on the subject. Once this step is completed, the assembled materials are reviewed by the FASB and a task force is appointed to continue work on the project. This task force (consisting of at least one member of the board who serves as chairperson, members of the advisory council, and other persons with expertise in some aspects of the problem) is responsible for preparing a neutral and comprehensive discussion memorandum on the agenda item. This document outlines alternative solutions to the problem and the arguments and implications relative to each.

Upon completion of the required research and the discussion memorandum, the FASB initiates a procedure to establish financial accounting standards taking into consideration the interests and points of view of all concerned parties. This process begins with the issuance of a notice of a public hearing on the problem and the simultaneous publication of the discussion memorandum. At the public hearings, oral reports and written papers are solicited and presented. After the public hearing, an exposure draft of a proposed Financial Accounting Standards Board (FASB) is prepared. An affirmative vote of at least five of the seven FASB members is required before a draft statement can be released to the public. Next, after a public comment exposure period of at least 60 days, the FASB reviews the exposure comments, and if the required five out of seven votes are obtained, it issues a final draft of the statement.

The FASB also issues Interpretations covering the application of specific aspects of its standards as well as Emerging Issues Task Force (EITF) abstracts. These abstracts are summaries of the proceedings of the EITF. This 13-person group is charged with the early identification of emerging issues affecting financial reporting and of problems in implementing authoritative pronouncements. A consensus by this group on a particular issue is accepted by the SEC, FASB, and AICPA.

Securities and Exchange Commission

The SEC is responsible for administering the Securities Acts of 1933 and 1934. These acts give the SEC the power to set accounting standards and to require specific kinds of financial disclosure by corporations covered by the acts. The commissioners are appointed by the President of the United States. The commission's budget is approved by Congress.

The Securities Act of 1933 deals primarily with the registration of securities in public offerings. Under this act, the SEC is concerned with the adequacy and validity of the information disclosed to investors in the registration statements filed with the commission by corporations and the prospectuses furnished to investors by sellers of securities. The commission does not pass judgment on the merits of the securities offered.

The Securities Exchange Act of 1934 regulates the trading in securities. This act requires among other things that corporations registered with the commission periodically file reports on their operations and conditions. These reports are available to the public and most companies will provide them free to interested parties upon request. The principal reports are Forms 10-K (annual reports), 10-Q (quarterly reports), and 8-K (reportable events).

The SEC issues pronouncements on accounting matters which registered companies must adopt. These may set new disclosure requirements, state the SEC's interpretation of a specific accounting standard, or describe the SEC's response to a common accounting problem encountered during the review of filings by corporations. These releases are concerned more with disclosure problems than with setting accounting principles. The commission, through its office of the chief accountant, maintains a close liaison with the FASB. The SEC exerts a strong influence on the FASB's decisions, since the FASB is powerless to enforce them if the SEC does not require corporations filing with it to follow a FASB proposal.

American Institute of Certified Public Accountants

The AICPA's Accounting Standards Executive Committee (AcSec) is the senior technical committee authorized to speak for the institute in the area of financial accounting. The institute's Auditing Standards Committee (AuSec) performs a similar function in the field of auditing.

Periodically the AICPA publishes "Statements of Position" (SOPs) on accounting principles and procedures, and guides related to industry accounting and auditing. These pronouncements are advisory to the institute's members rather than authoritative. However, in areas not covered by FASB pronouncements, the FASB and SEC have indicated that the SOPs are useful guides and should be followed as long as they do not conflict with other existing official FASB pronouncements. Furthermore, the FASB has adopted certain of these SOPs and guides.

International Accounting Standards Committee

The IASC is an independent private sector body supported by the accounting bodies in over 80 countries. It is located in London, United Kingdom. The IASC works for the global improvement and harmonization of accounting standards and procedures related to the presentation of financial statements. Currently, it is the recognized body for the development of International Accounting Standards (IAS). Adoption of IAS is voluntary. A number of countries have adopted IAS and others, such as Mexico, have indicated that IAS should be followed by local companies if they cover areas not dealt with by local standards.

Basic Issues

The basic purpose of financial accounting and financial statements is to provide timely, relevant, and reliable quantitative financial information about a business enterprise. There is little argument about this general objective. However, the implementation of the objective in practice involves considerable controversy.

Historical Cost vs. Current Values

A fundamental controversy underlying much of the ferment over accounting practices is the question of whether or not accounting measurements should reflect the historical cost of an asset or liability or some measures of its "current value," which may be measured in a variety of different ways. The FASB while generally adhering to the historical cost concept in its decision, nevertheless has adopted a number of fair value based standards (i.e., what a willing seller and buyer would pay) in the area of financial instrument accounting and disclosure. The issue is should these decisions be measured or modified and should fair value or some other valuation basis other than historical cost accounting be extended to other areas of accounting, such as operating property, plant and equipment and income-producing real estate. In the latter situation, many real estate companies provide supplemental disclosure of current value of their real estate holdings. In this case current value of an asset is the amount it can be sold for in the open market or can be used as a basis for borrowing. The current value of a liability is the amount at which it can be liquidated at the reporting date.

Cookbook vs. General Standards

There are two basic approaches to standard setting: Issue detailed rules or standards that set forth accounting principles in the form of general principles.

The tendency of the FASB has been to publish accounting standards with detailed implementation requirements and guidelines. This approach to standard setting has been characterized as a "cookbook" approach. It is the result of a need on the part of practicing public accountants, for guidance in the application of accounting standards, investors seeking uniform accounting by companies to facilitate intercompany comparisons, and a general belief that this approach will produce financial statements that are fair to all who rely upon them. Without detailed standards, the supporters of this approach claim, some managements will take advantage of the lack of guidance to issue misleading statements that will lower the confidence of statement users in all financial statements.

The supporters of the proposition that accounting principles should embody principles rather than detailed rules claim accounting rules cannot cover every situation. As a result, there will always be some situations that rules will miss but which would be covered by a well stated general principle.

Disclosure vs. Recognition

Financial data can be communicated through corporate financial reports in two ways: By recognition on the face of financial statements or disclosed in the notes accompanying financial statements. Those supporting recognition argue if financial data are important enough to be disclosed it ought to be on the face of the financial statements. In their view, disclosure is not a substitute for recognition. Others argue disclosure is a satisfactory interim step toward ultimate recognition in cases involving recognition and measurement controversy. It also permits experimentation and reduces the risk of adopting an inappropriate recognition accounting principle.

Expanding the Accounting Model

Some critics of the current accounting model believe it is too limited and have explored the possibility of extending the traditional role of accounting to include the measurement and disclosure of a corporation's social contribution. Others have experimented with accounting systems and concepts that would communicate to management and interested outsiders better data on a corporation's investment in and utilization of human resources. Both of these activities have from time to time generated considerable controversy as to how appropriate it is for accountants to undertake such responsibilities, how relevant the data would be, what methods to use to measure costs and benefits, and what interest management and the public would have in the data generated.

The supporters of social contribution accounting argue that business is only part of a larger social system. As the public increasingly accepts this view of society, it judges each social unit, such as a business, in terms of its contribution to the whole society. As a result, the public needs access to data that permits evaluation of a corporation in terms of both its income responsibility to shareholders and its contribution to society as a whole. It is logical and reasonable some argue that accounting, because of its interests in corporate measurements and disclosure, should assume a role of informing the public of the social-responsibility activities of corporations.

Human resource accounting advocates believe that accounting communication currently does not deal adequately with one of a corporation's most important resources, namely, its human resources. These resources are developed at a considerable cost to corporations, and a corporation's policies for developing and acquiring employees may be vital to its success. Traditional accounting, however, treats expenditures to acquire, develop, and hold human resources as expenses rather than as assets; rarely identifies and discloses the extent of these expenditures; and makes no effort to evaluate the effectiveness or value of a corporation's human resources. Those interested in human resource accounting are experimenting with different financial and nonfinancial measurements and disclosures of corporate human resources with the goal of incorporating these data in accounting communications.

To date, those proposing expanding the scope of current corporate financial reports have had relatively little success in influencing practice.

Tax Accounting

The accounting rules for determining taxable income are independent (with one major exception) of the accounting rules governing corporate financial reports. Failure to recognize this fact can lead to misunderstanding the cash flow implications of corporate financial reporting decisions, the true nature of corporate tax accounts, and the relationship between tax and book reporting strategies.

A firm's taxable income is established by accounting rules established by the Internal Revenue Service (IRS). These rules are similar to generally accepted accounting principles used in the normal course of its business. However, the tax code allows companies to deviate from these public reporting rules in specific areas when calculating taxable income without having to change the corporate financial reports issued to stockholders. As a result, in such areas as fixed asset accounting, a company can maintain two sets of accounting data: one for determining the current tax payments to the government, another for preparing the statements for public reporting purposes.

From time to time, it is advocated that there should be closer, if not complete, agreement between the income figures determined for taxation and for financial reporting purposes. This position fails to recognize that the objectives of financial and tax accounting are different. Financial accounting's objective is to present fairly the results of operations and the financial condition of a company to its stockholders and other interested parties external to the firm, such as employees and creditors. Tax accounting's objective is to raise tax revenues and to carry out the government's economic, political, and social policies. For example, tax surcharges and investment credits are adopted to influence the growth of the economy. The tax provision permitting rapid amortization of certain pollution control facilities is an example of congressional concern with the ecological problem of pollution. In addition, some tax accounting practices are based on administrative practicalities. For example, a basic tax concept is that the timing of a tax liability should be influenced by when the taxpayer can most readily pay and the government can most readily collect. Clearly, this concept is at odds with the accrual concept of financial accounting, which says income should be recognized when it is earned.

Tax accounting is only covered in subsequent notes to the extent necessary to understand the recognition and disclosure issues it raises in corporate financial reports for statement issuers and users.

Management Accounting

While this book focuses on *financial* accounting—the goal of which is to provide stockholders and other parties external to the firm with useful financial information about the company, it is important that statement users understand the influence on management behavior of another closely related system of accounting designed to provide management with useful financial information for running the business. This is the internally oriented system known as *management* accounting.

A company's management accounting system need not conform to the generally accepted accounting principles that govern its financial accounting. In practice, however, these two accounting systems are usually closely related. One of the principal functions of management accounting is to measure the performance of the various units of a company against a set of performance standards. These performance measures are selected to motivate unit managers to achieve these standards through actions that collectively will move the company toward the realization of its overall corporate objectives. Since generally accepted accounting principles will be used to measure the total corporate progress, there must be a link between the two systems. There is no sense in motivating unit managers to achieve results that look good for internal accounting purposes but poor when translated into external accounting terms. Also, if a company's rules for maintaining the internal and external systems are different, the company must maintain two sets of books to record its business transaction. This can be very expensive. Therefore, to reduce accounting costs, most companies collect and record their basic management accounting data according to financial accounting rules.

While most companies use essentially the same accounting principles for management and financial accounting purposes, a number of companies have explicitly decided not to adopt this practice. Their rationale is that adopting some of the company's external reporting practices internally might introduce an undesirable behavior bias in the decisions of unit managers. This practice raises a disturbing question: How can a company justify the use of a generally accepted principle for external reporting if it is not useful for internal purposes, either because it motivates managers to follow undesirable operating policies, provides top management with misleading measures of performance, or fails to reflect the company's real progress and prospects?

Financial Reporting Decisions

One of the dual perspectives adopted in this book is that of the manager responsible for the development of a corporate financial reporting strategy for a business enterprise.

The process of analyzing and resolving financial reporting policies, strategies, and practice issues is similar to that followed in other business decision-making situations, except that the decision maker must usually work within the constraints of generally accepted accounting principles. Typically, the business executive is faced with a problem which has more than one possible solution. The task is to choose the best possible course of action. This can be done intuitively or through careful, systematic consideration and weighing of the anticipated consequences, or through some combination of these two approaches. Whatever the approach used, the manager must eventually make a decision.

The evaluation of the alternative courses of action can be facilitated by developing "yardsticks" or criteria, weighted by their relative importance. For any particular problem, these criteria can be used to distinguish between acceptable and unacceptable solutions and to rank the acceptable solutions in a relative order of attractiveness.

In the case of financial reporting problems, the decision criteria are usually developed from an analysis of the company's overall strategic objectives and its operating and financial plans to achieve these objectives. This is done by answering these questions: Given the company's objectives and operating plans, what characteristics must the financial reporting policy satisfy if it is to measure and communicate clearly the extent of the realization of these plans? What are the implications for the company's financial reporting policies of the characteristics of the company's particular operations, relations with external groups, competitors' policies and plans, industry, financial structure, and management? Answers to these questions require a detailed analysis of such areas as the company's operations and financing plans and requirements, the stock market's evaluation of similar companies, the company's business environment, and the public interest and regulatory requirements that may be relevant.

The identification and correct definition of the financial reporting problem to be solved is a critical stage in the decision-making process. Unless this is done well, the decision maker may tackle the wrong issue or solve only part of the problem, which may produce a more unsatisfactory situation. In most accounting situations, at least the accounting part of the problem is fairly evident. How clearly and fully one is able to state the managerial dimensions of the problem will depend in large part on the quality of the strategic, operating, and environmental analysis described above.

Financial reporting problems usually involve the selection of accounting principles to handle a specific item. These problems involve at least six interrelated considerations:

1. Which generally accepted principle or principles are the most appropriate?
2. As a result of financial reporting decisions, what other adjustments, if any, must be made in a particular mix of generally accepted accounting principles that collectively constitute the company's financial reporting policy?
3. What operating or financial bias will this decision have on management's future business decisions or policies?
4. How will this decision contribute to the real or apparent achievement of management's objectives?
5. Is the decided upon course of action ethically and legally acceptable?
6. How should the resolution of this accounting policy application be communicated to the public?

The second question of the above list recognizes that a company's earnings per share and financial image are the net result of applying accounting policy decisions to a variety of individual transactions. Therefore, a change in one part of this mix may necessitate changes in other parts to achieve the overall effect management is seeking.

The alternative solutions to financial reporting problems usually reflect a choice between generally accepted accounting principles. Therefore, to fully appraise and consider the full range of possible solutions in any particular situation, the decision maker must be familiar not only with accounting principles but also the conditions justifying the usage of particular generally accepted principles and the theoretical and practical arguments for and against each.

Once the criteria, the problem, and the possible solutions are identified, the decision maker must sift through the facts available to extract those that are relevant to the problem. Some of these facts are measurable and others are not, but all must be related to the possible solutions. When the advantages and disadvantages of each solution are clear, the decision maker must then use judgment to decide which one of the possible solutions has the greatest net advantage.

There is often no right answer to financial reporting problems, or even an answer to which everyone will agree. The decision maker must make the best decision with the facts available, knowing that other people may interpret or weigh the same facts differently and reach quite different conclusions. Decision making under these circumstances is a complicated and difficult task, fraught with uncertainty and testing ethical considerations.

Financial Analysis

The second perspective adopted in this book is that of the users of financial statements. The general purpose financial reports issued by business enterprises are used for a variety of purposes by many individuals who have no direct involvement in the management of the reporting company. A dominant common interest of many of these external statement users is the ability of a business to generate future earnings and positive cash flows. Yet, the primary focus of the financial reports that they examine is information about the company's past earnings, cash flows, and financial condition.

Financial statement analysis helps to bridge this gap between the historical financial accounting data provided and the users' future-oriented earnings and cash flow interests. Financial statement techniques make it possible for statement users to penetrate the historical accrual accounting data to develop an understanding of an enterprise's past, present, and continuing ability to generate earnings and cash flows. This understanding is gained by applying techniques and standards that focus on evaluating management's operating and financial performance, identifying past cash receipts and payments, assessing the quality of a company's earnings, identifying "red flags" that suggest emerging problems, estimating the level of business and financial risk, measuring potential borrowing power, and confirming or rejecting earlier predictions or assessments.

Financial statements are prepared with knowledgeable statement users in mind. Consequently, accounting knowledge and skill in financial analysis is necessary to appreciate fully the content of financial statements and to use the data effectively for decision-making purposes in such diverse activities as granting credit, buying securities, negotiating mergers, extending trade credit, and conducting business research. The mechanical or arithmetic dimension of financial analysis is fairly simple and straightforward and not difficult to master. More difficult is developing the ability to interpret the significance of the quantitative and qualitative data that financial analysis generates in the form of ratios, trends, and quality assessments. This ability comes with experience, an understanding of the business being analyzed, a thorough knowledge of corporate financial reporting practices, and a full appreciation of the technical and business aspects of the purpose for which the analysis is being performed. In addition, the skillful analyst possesses such traits as ability to recognize irregularities, inquisitiveness, skepticism, diligence, and a willingness to consult with others with more specialized knowledge.

Managers signal through financial reporting decisions and financial transactions changes in corporate policies and expectations. For example, a major corporate restructuring change may be a signal that management intends to radically change the way the company is managed, its cost structure, and business focus. A dividend increase may signal that management is confident that the company's future cash flows and profits will remain high enough to support continued payment of dividends at the new level. A major challenge for statement users is to determine through financial statement analyses if management's use of financial reporting and financial transactions to signal future corporate prospects represent reasonable expectations or are attempts by management to mislead.

Finally, statement users use corporate financial reports to monitor the actions of managers in their role as agents of stockholders responsible for enhancing stockholder values. When using financial reports for this purpose, statement users are seeking through financial analysis to identify managerial alignment or conflicts of interests with those of stockholders, management's actions detrimental or supportive of stockholders' interests, and management's stockholder value enhancing or dissipating actions.

PART TWO

Corporate Financial Reporting Fundamentals

Basic Accounting Concepts

Corporate financial reporting does not rest on one generally accepted unified theory of accounting. Rather, financial accounting and disclosure decisions reflect a number of basic conventions or concepts which are more or less commonly accepted as useful guides to selecting appropriate accounting policies. These conventions have grown out of the experiences of accountants and business executives in devising ways to measure and communicate the results of operations and financial conditions of corporations, as well as from the theoretical works of accounting scholars. In practice, accounting conventions seem to be utilitarian. Their acceptance stems from their usefulness to those making decisions that involve accounting data. This usefulness is determined by whether the convention is compatible with the legal, social, and economic conditions, needs, and concepts of the time. Clearly, as these factors change over time, so must accounting conventions.

The Financial Accounting Standard Board (FASB) has developed a framework of accounting fundamentals on which the financial accounting and reporting standards it issues are based. The five operative Statements of Financial Accounting Concepts issued to date are:

- "Objectives of Financial Reporting by Business Enterprises" (No. 1);
- "Qualitative Characteristics of Accounting Information" (No. 2);
- "Objectives of Financial Reporting by Nonbusiness Organizations" (No. 4);
- "Recognition and Measurement in Financial Statements of Business Enterprises" (No. 5);
- "Elements of Financial Statements" (No. 6).[1]

---

[1]This statement replaced "Elements of Financial Statements of Business Enterprises" (No. 3).

Professor David Hawkins prepared this note as the basis for class discussion rather than to illustrate either effective or ineffective handling of an administrative situation.

Unlike a Statement of Financial Accounting Standard, a Statement of Financial Accounting Concepts does not establish a generally accepted accounting principle. They are intended to serve the public interest by setting the objectives, qualitative characteristics, and other concepts that guide selection of economic events to be recognized and measured for financial reporting and their display in financial statements or related means of communicating information to those who are interested. Concepts Statements guide the Board in developing sound accounting principles and provide the Board and its constituents with an understanding of the appropriate content and inherent limitations of financial reporting. The FASB's five concepts Statements are the most authoritative source of fundamental accounting concepts available.

Significance to Users

Those who use financial statements might be tempted to dismiss the subject matter covered in this chapter (and other chapters in this series on accounting fundamentals) as being primarily of interest to managers, accountants, and bookkeepers. This would be a mistake. Financial statements are presented on the assumption that the reader understands the basics of accounting and finance. Therefore, knowledge of corporate reporting fundamentals is required to be a literate reader of financial statements.

The basic accounting conventions and definitions determine the character and scope of data used for statement analysis. Because no one set of conventions governs accounting, financial statements include amounts that are arrived at by a variety of valuation procedures based on cash, economic, financial, and accrual concepts of measurement. A statement user who does not appreciate an accounts valuation bases can easily misinterpret financial statements.

The amounts shown against accounts listed in financial statements indicate that some event with financial consequences met the definition of the accounting transaction. Statement users must be able to distinguish between financial consequences included and those not included in financial statements. A knowledge of basic accounting concepts is helpful in this regard. For example, a company may be involved in a lawsuit that might result in an adverse judgment. For most statement users, this is a significant event. Someone unfamiliar with accounting's liability definition might assume that a prudent company would recognize a liability for the amount of a possible adverse judgment. However, if no reasonable estimate of the judgment amount can be determined, the accounting definition of a liability requires that no liability be recorded. A statement user familiar with accounting definitions would be aware of this possibility. Such an analyst would ask: "Is a provision for damages included or not included in the liabilities?" and then diligently seek out the answer to the question.

Financial statement analysis is usually undertaken for a specific decision, such as buying a security, determining a bond rating, or valuing a company. Statement users have to be careful when they incorporate financial statement data in their analyses leading up to such decisions. Frequently, the conventions of accounting result in financial statement data that are actually irrelevant for these decisions although they may appear to be relevant. For example, the market value of the properties of a company being considered for potential acquisition is important economic data for determining an acquisition price. Market price data related to properties will not be found in financial statements. Yet, there is something that could be misinterpreted as data relevant to property valuation, namely, the net book value (original cost less accumulated depreciation) of the company's properties. A statement user who is ignorant of the historical cost convention may unwittingly use these accounting values for the more relevant economic values. One who is aware of accounting conventions is not likely to fall into the trap of thinking the accounting data are something other than what they intend to represent.

One of the purposes of financial analysis is to determine if the accounting conventions incorporated in a particular company's financial statements are reasonable reflections of the company's circumstances. Knowledge of the basic conventions is necessary to make an appropriate test. For example, an important accounting convention is "the going concern" assumption. Because a company issues financial statements with no indication that the auditors question the company's continued existence, analysts should not assume that the issuer will in fact be in existence in the near future. As we will see later, an important use of financial analysis is to ferret out companies approaching financial difficulties and possible bankruptcy on the basis of data contained in the company's most recent statements, which were issued on the going concern assumption.

Those who analyze financial statements should know when to seek assistance from others more expert in accounting. To know when to call on others, analysts must know their own limitations. This requires a conscious effort to determine the gaps and limits in one's knowledge of the substance and scope of the basic accounting conventions. You cannot identify what you do not understand well until you have a broad sense of the subject in which you are testing the limits and depth of your own understanding.

Basic Concepts

This chapter briefly describes a number of basic conventions. Some may argue that certain conventions should be combined or dropped. Others might try to break the list into categories that distinguish between postulates and principles. Many of these proposals will have merit, but the purpose of this list is simply to cover the basic conventions that seem to be accepted to some degree in outstanding books on this subject and in basic concepts statements issued by such groups as the FASB and the American Accounting Association.[2]

Each of these conventions is discussed in greater detail in later chapters that focus on the relevant conventions for each accounting principle.

---

[2]The American Accounting Association is a professional association whose members are mostly academic accountants.

Business Entity

The business entity convention is that financial statements refer to a business entity that is separate and distinct from its owners. What happens to its owners' affairs is irrelevant. The principal reason for this convention is that it defines the accountant's area of interest and sets limits on the possible objectives and contents of financial reports.

The boundaries of the business entity are sometimes difficult to establish. Typically, the accountant defines these boundaries in terms of the firm's economic activities and administrative control rather than legal relationships. For example, consolidated financial statements present the financial condition and results of operations of different entities with common ownership in a single set of statements, thus treating the various entities as a single economic unit, even though they consist of several legal entities. Here the accountant is trying to present useful statements that look beyond legal relationships to the underlying economic and managerial relationships. The legal considerations are relevant only insofar as they define or influence economic activities and managerial control.

An alternative approach is to define the boundaries of the accounting entity in terms of the economic interests of the statement users rather than the economic activities of the unit. In practice, accounting reports may reflect to some degree this concept of the entity.

The entity concept applies equally to incorporated, unincorporated, small, and big businesses. In the case of incorporated, widely held, and publicly owned companies, such as General Motors, it is not difficult to separate the affairs of the business and its owners. However, in the case of small unincorporated businesses where the owners exert day-to-day control and personal and business assets are intermingled, the definition of the business entity is more difficult for financial—as well as managerial—accounting purposes.

Going Concern

Unless evidence suggests otherwise, those preparing accounting statements for a business entity assume it will continue operations into the foreseeable future. This convention reflects the normal expectation of management and investors. To avoid misleading readers of financial statements, the statements of business entities with limited lives must clearly indicate the terminal date and type of liquidation involved (i.e., receiver's statements, etc.). Otherwise, the reader will assume that the accounts are based on the presumption that the enterprise has an indefinitely long life.

Accounting emphasizes and reflects the continuing nature of business activity. For example, the accountant expects that in the normal course of business the company will receive the full value of most of its accounts receivable. Accordingly, these items are recorded at their face value, less some deductions for anticipated bad debts, rather than at current liquidation value. Similarly, expenditures for finished goods inventories are recorded as assets, since the accountant assumes the inventories will be disposed of later in the normal course of operations. The continuity assumption does not imply, however, that the future will be the same as the past.

The going concern convention leads to the corollary that individual financial statements are part of a continuous, interrelated series of statements. This further implies that data communicated are tentative.

Not all accounting theorists support the common interpretation of the continuity convention. One author claims that the continuity assumption underlying accounting is misleading since it is a prediction rather than an assumption. Another views the firm as being in a continual state of orderly liquidation.

Monetary

Accounting is a measurement process dealing only with events that can be measured in monetary terms. This convention reflects the fact that money is the common denominator used in business to measure the exchange value of goods, services, and capital. Obviously, financial statements should indicate the money unit used.

The monetary convention leads to one of the limitations of accounting. Accounting, for example, does not record or communicate factors such as the state of the president's health, the attitude of the labor force, or the relative advantage of competitive products. Consequently, the most important aspect of a business may not be reflected in the financial statements.

Another potential limitation of the monetary convention is that it fails to distinguish between the purchasing power of monetary units in different periods. This can become a significant problem in trying to interpret financial statements during periods of high rates of inflation. For example, expenses may include dollars spent currently as well as dollars spent in earlier periods when the dollar purchased more goods and services.

Accounting Period

For decision-making purposes, managers and investors need periodic "test readings" of the progress of their business. Accounting recognizes this and breaks the flow of business activity into a series of reporting or fiscal periods. These periods are usually 12 months in length. Most companies also issue quarterly statements to stockholders. For management use, statements covering shorter periods such as a month or week may be prepared. Regardless of the length of the period, the statements must indicate the period covered.

The success of a business can be determined accurately only upon liquidation. Consequently, the periodic financial statements are at best estimates, subject to change as future events develop.

Breaking business activity into a series of discrete segments creates a number of accounting problems. For example, given the uncertainties surrounding the life of an asset and its scrap value, how should the cost of the asset be allocated to specific periods? How should the income and costs associated with long-term contracts covering several accounting periods be treated? Such questions must be resolved in the light of the particular circumstances. There is no easy, general solution. The accountant and business executive must rely upon their experience, knowledge, and judgment to arrive at the appropriate answer.

The timing of the accounting period will depend upon the nature of the business. For most companies, the accounting period runs from January 1 to December 31. Some companies use a different period, usually because their yearly business cycle does not conform to the calendar year. For example, the annual statements of department stores are more revealing if their fiscal period ends January 31. This is a time when inventories are low and the December holiday selling peak is over.

Consistency

The consistency convention requires that similar transactions be reported in a consistent fashion from period to period. Clearly, comparison of interperiod results would be difficult if a company changed its depreciation policy each year. The consistency concept is not inflexible, however. Changes in accounting policies are appropriate when justified by changing circumstances.

Accountants place considerable emphasis on consistency. When expressing an audit opinion, the accountant notes whether or not the statements were prepared "on a basis consistent with that of the preceding year." If changes were made, the auditor notes these in the audit opinion and insists that the nature and impact of these changes be fully disclosed.

The consistency concept does not necessarily mean that accounting practices are uniform among affiliated business units or even within a single company. One unit may value inventory on the so-called LIFO basis, whereas another may use the FIFO basis. Similarly, a single unit might use both methods to value different parts of its inventory. In either case, the policy should be disclosed and consistently followed.

The consistency concept does not imply uniformity in the treatment of particular items among different independent companies. Indeed, one characteristic of American accounting practice is the diversity of accounting methods among different companies, all of which meet the criterion of "generally accepted accounting principles."

Historical Cost

For accounting purposes, business transactions are normally measured in terms of the actual prices or costs at the time they were acquired. This convention applies to both the initial recording and subsequent reporting of transactions. While agreeing with the need to record historical costs initially, some influential accountants argue that accounting would be "more useful" if, under certain conditions, estimates of current and future values were substituted for historical costs. The extent to which cost and value should be reflected in the accounts is central to much of the current accounting controversy.

The market value of assets may change with time. Typically, accounting does not recognize these changes in value. The cost of assets shown on financial statements seldom reflects the assets' current market value. Some believe that the historical cost convention flows from the going concern concept, which implies that since the business is not going to sell its fixed assets as such, there is little point in revaluing assets to reflect current values. For practical reasons, the accountant prefers the reporting of actual original costs to less certain estimates, which are more difficult to verify. By using historical costs, the accountant's already difficult task is not further complicated by the need to keep additional records of changing market values.

There is little disagreement among theorists that accounting should record the original cost value of a transaction initially. However, not all believe that this value should be used to measure expenses, to determine income, or value assets over time. For example, one proposal is that fixed assets be reported at their replacement cost and that the expense related to their use be based on this value. Another suggestion is that appraisals of current market values ought to be the basis for recording asset values. A third alternative suggestion is that the current cash equivalent value be used. The proponents of these recommendations argue that the going concern assumption does not necessarily depend on historical costs as the basis for accounting measurement; appraisal or replacement costs may be determined in just as an objective fashion as historical costs; and the data communicated to statement users is more useful for such purposes as valuing securities or appraising management's use of the firm's resources.

While accounting is still based on historical costs, these proposals are slowly beginning to influence corporate reporting. For example, the FASB now requires certain financial instruments to be accounted for at their fair value, which in most cases is the financial instrument's market value.

In practice, there have been a number of modifications to the historical cost concept. For example, under special conditions inventory may be reported at market values if it is less than historical cost. Assets acquired for stock are recorded at the estimated market value of the stock exchanged. Mutual funds and pension funds whose assets consist almost entirely of securities report the market value of their investments, taking the unrealized gain or loss into income at the end of each reporting period. Similarly, donated assets may be carried at their appraised value at the time of acquisition. The definition of the content of cost, irrespective of whether the historical cost convention or one of the alternative proposals is used, poses some problems. Issues arise as to what cost elements should be included in the cost of assets created by the company rather than bought from outsiders. Or, if an asset is acquired through a swap, the value to be placed on the asset given up or received may be unclear.

Realization

For accounting purposes, revenue is realized during the period when services or goods are exchanged for a valuable consideration, or when the revenue amount can be verified with a reasonable degree of objectivity. In practice, no one test, such as sale or delivery, has proven satisfactory, given the diversity of industry's production, sale, and credit practices. The application of the realization concept depends upon the circumstances of each case.

Some authorities claim revenue is earned during the operations process, rather than, say, entirely at the time of sale. They argue that all activities related to production and sales contribute to the final product and, hence, to revenue. Accordingly, they state that accounting should recognize revenue in proportion to the costs accumulated to date of such activities. In practice, one method of accounting for long-term construction contracts over several accounting periods does this by permitting revenues to be recognized in the proportion the estimated progress bears to the total job, provided it is anticipated that the contract can be completed and the profit originally estimated can be obtained. In the absence of firm contracts or reasonable certainty as to the course of future events, accounting practice does not normally recognize revenue during production.

Some accounting theorists advocate that revenue should be recognized when asset values change from accretion, such as occurs when timber grows or whiskey ages. This view is similar to that proposed by the production supporters, but it does not require a transaction to occur before revenue is recognized. In contrast, accretion revenue would be recognized through the production process by comparing inventory values at different points in time. This view of revenue may be acceptable in economic theory, but it is generally rejected in accounting practice because of the difficulty in determining asset values prior to sales and the tentative nature of such figures.

Matching of Costs and Revenues

Accounting income or profit is the net result of the accountants trying to match the related costs and revenues of one period. This process can be described as matching "effort and accomplishments," where costs measure effort and revenues measure the related accomplishments. Often this ideal cannot be achieved, since costs cannot be easily identified with specific current or anticipated revenues.

Matching costs and revenues may require deferring recognition of expenses and revenues to future periods. For example, cash may be spent today to obtain subscriptions to a magazine that will provide subscribers with copies for the next five years. In this case, the accountant will defer recognizing the cash outlay as an expense until the magazines are due and the expected revenues are earned. At this time, the costs and the revenues would be matched. In the meantime, however, the unexpired cost would be reported as an asset (i.e., capitalized). Whether or not costs should be deferred and, if deferred, over what time period, are difficult questions to resolve in practice.

The matching process is usually achieved through application of the accrual method of accounting rather than the cash method. The cash method of accounting records cash receipts and disbursements and focuses on changes in the cash account. The accrual method seeks to measure changes in owner's equity during the accounting period. Revenues are realized from noncapital transactions that result in an increase in owner's equity. In contrast, expenses are expired costs which are associated with the period, or the period's revenues that decrease owner's equity. The difference between revenues and expenses is net income for the period. These changes in owner's equity may not necessarily result in changes in the cash account. For example, a $100 sale on credit will increase accounts receivable and owner's equity. The accrual method recognizes the fact that the service has been performed and a valuable asset created. If a cash method was being used, no record of the event would be made until the customer's $100 cash was received.

The accrual method also leads to the accounting practice of recognizing costs as expenses when they expire (i.e., lose their future benefit generation value) rather than when they are incurred. In addition, the accrual method requires that costs be recognized as incurred when the firm receives goods and services, even though the actual billing or payment date is sometime in the future.

Dual Aspect

The dual aspect convention recognizes that someone has a claim on all the resources owned by the business. The resources are called "assets."

The creditors' claims against these assets are usually referred to as "liabilities." The owners' claims are called either "stockholders' equity," "owners' equity," or "proprietorship." Consequently, since the total assets of the business are claimed by somebody, it follows that:

$$\text{Assets} = \text{Liabilities} + \text{Stockholders' Equity}$$

Assets represent probable future, measurable economic benefits which the reporting entity has acquired through a current or past transaction. Assets include such items as cash, inventories, and buildings. An asset can represent an expected future economic benefit for several reasons:

1. The asset may be used to acquire other assets. Cash is the principal example of an asset that derives its value from its purchasing power.
2. The asset represents a claim upon another entity for money—for example, accounts receivable, which are amounts owed to the company for credit sales.
3. The asset can be converted to cash or a money claim. Finished goods inventories that will be sold in the normal course of business are an example.
4. The asset has potential benefits, rights, or services which will result in the entity earning something from its use in some future accounting period. Such assets include items like buildings and raw materials.

The term *liabilities* may be defined as probable future sacrifices of measurable economic benefits arising from the entity's obligations to convey assets or perform services to a person, firm, or another organization at some time in the future. These obligations require future settlement and represent claims of a nonownership nature on the entity's assets. Accounts payable to trade creditors, bonds payable, and taxes payable are examples of liabilities.

Liabilities also include so-called deferred credits. These do not represent clear-cut claims on the entity. They result from the need to recognize some expenses currently in order to get a "proper" matching of costs and revenues. To offset the expense item, a reserve balance is reported as a liability. Examples of deferred credits are reserves set up currently for tax expenses that may or may not be paid in the future but which accounting standards require to be recognized now.

Stockholders' or owners' equity is thought to represent ownership interest in the entity. It is a residual item. It is the excess of the entity's total assets over its liabilities.

Clearly, the measurement of owners' equity in the accounting equation represents no problem once liabilities and assets have been defined and measured. The problem arises in describing the nature of this residual amount. Certainly, it is not the market value of the firm to the owners. Some of the principal theories as to the nature of ownership equity are discussed below.

The *proprietary theory* regards the proprietor as the focus of interest in the accounting equation. Assets are owned by the proprietor, and liabilities are the proprietor's obligations. The basic accounting equation is:

$$\text{Assets} - \text{Liabilities} = \text{Proprietorship Interest}$$

The proprietorship interest implies that liabilities are negative assets, since the proprietor is thought to own all of the assets and the goal of accounting is to determine the net value of these assets to the proprietor.

The entity theory regards the business entity as separate from the wealth and personalities of its owners. The business assets of the entity are the entity's assets, and against these assets are equity claims by creditors and owners, who are regarded as the principal beneficiaries of the business activities. This view of the entity is probably a better description of the typical corporate–investor relationship than the proprietorship theory. The entity theory's basic accounting equation is:

$$\text{Assets} = \text{Equities}$$

The enterprise theory regards the business–owner relationship in a similar fashion to the entity theory, except that beneficiaries of business activities are not limited to creditors and owners. It regards the entity as being operated for the benefit of society as a whole. As a result, the capital contributed and earnings retained in a business are thought of as benefiting more than just the stockholders, since the capital may produce benefits for society. Thus, society has an interest in the so-called net worth of a company.

A few accounting authors argue that the traditional accounting equation should be changed to reflect current thinking in finance and business. One such approach suggests that contemporary financial accounting practice is becoming increasingly concerned with maintaining a continuing record of capital invested in an enterprise from the double perspective of both sources and uses of funds, with funds broadly defined as all financial resources. This focus, it is argued, is in line with modern financial theory and practice, which tends to view assets as funds invested within the business, and liabilities and net worth as financial resources obtained from sources external to the firm. As a result, the balance sheet can be regarded as a report, at an instant of time, of both the status of funds obtained from sources external to the business and the items in which these funds (and those generated by drawing down other assets) are invested. This point of view regards earnings retained in the business as stockholders' reinvested profits; as such they represent an external source of funds.

Those who support this point of view express the dual aspect of transactions in terms of sources and uses of funds. Since for each use of funds there must be a matching source and for each source a use, the basic accounting equation suggested is:

Items in which capital is invested (assets) = External sources of capital (equities)

Accounting systems are designed to record events in terms of their influence on assets, liabilities, or owners' equity. Every event has a dual aspect. For example, assume Jane Smith invested $5,000 in a new business; the accounting entry would recognize the $5,000 asset of the business and Jane Smith's claim upon this asset:

Asset, $5,000 = Stockholders' equity, $5,000

Now, if the company borrowed $1,000 from the bank, the firm's accounting statement would be:

Assets		Liabilities and Stockholders' Equity	
Cash	$6,000	Bank loan payable	$1,000
		Stockholders' equity	5,000
Total	$6,000	Total	$6,000

Cash has increased $1,000 and so has the bank loan payable account. Next, assume the business used $2,000 of its cash to acquire some inventory; the new statement would be:

Assets		Liabilities and Stockholders' Equity	
Cash	$4,000	Bank loan payable	$1,000
Inventory	2,000	Stockholders' equity	5,000
Total	$6,000	Total	$6,000

The cash account is reduced by $2,000 and the inventory balance increased by a similar sum. Thus, the double-entry system requires two entries for each event. Other systems are possible, but the double-entry system is the most widely used.

Reliability of Evidence

Accountants recording events rely as much as possible upon objective, verifiable documentary evidence, in contrast to the subjective judgments of a person who may be biased. Acceptable evidence includes such items as approved sales or purchase invoices. This desire to base decisions on objective evidence is one of the principal supports of the historical cost convention, although, as noted earlier, some of the proponents of alternative approaches believe these approaches can be objective also.

In practice, accountants do not apply the absolute standard of objective, verifiable evidence. Many major decisions, such as allocation of costs between periods, must be based on reasonable estimates after considering all the relevant facts. In many instances, it is not feasible for an auditor to verify the recording of every event. As a result, auditors base their opinions in large part upon an assessment of management's internal controls, which are the procedures adopted by management to safeguard assets, check the reliability and accuracy of data, and encourage adherence to operating policies and programs.

The definition of what constitutes an objective measurement is not a settled matter. At least four different approaches can be identified among accounting writers. One author defines an objective measurement as being impersonal and outside the mind of the person making the measurement. Another thinks of it as based on the consensus of qualified experts. A third considers a measurement objective if it is based on verifiable evidence. The fourth approach rates objectiveness in terms of the narrowness of the statistical dispersion around the mean measurement from results obtained by different measurers. The narrower the dispersion, the less subjective is the mean considered to be.

A convention closely related to the reliability convention is the standard proposed by some that accounting statements should be free from bias, meaning that the facts have been impartially determined and reported and contain no built-in bias.

Disclosure

The disclosure convention requires that accounting reports disclose enough information that they will not mislead careful readers reasonably well informed in financial matters. Special disclosure is made of unusual items, changes in expectations, significant contractual relations, and new activities. The disclosure can be in the body of the financial statements, the auditor's opinion, or the notes to the statements.

Conservatism

The conservatism convention prescribes a degree of skepticism in assessing the prospects that incompleted transactions will be concluded successfully. In practice, this means that in deciding between permissible accounting choices, some added weight should be given to whichever choice leads to the lowest asset or highest liability figures and that more stringent requirements must be imposed for recognizing revenues and gains as components of earning than for recognizing expenses and losses.

If not carefully applied, this convention can lead to abuses that result in unnecessary or dishonest understatements. Also, by understating income in one period, income in another period may be overstated. Thus, the application of this convention requires considerable judgment.

A number of accounting theorists reject conservatism as a legitimate accounting convention. In their opinion, it leads to a deliberate misstatement and as such has no place in accounting. They also believe that statement issuers should provide unbiased data so that statement users can evaluate the risks of, say, investing in the issuer company. If conservatism is applied, issuers allow their evaluations of risk to substitute for the user's independent evaluation, which might have been different from the issuer's if unbiased data had been available to the user. Finally, they argue that the convention of conservatism is capricious in practice. There are no uniform approaches to its application.

Materiality

Accounting standards apply only to material and significant items. Inconsequential items can be dealt with expediently. However, in applying this convention, care must be taken to ensure that the cumulative effect of a series of immaterial items does not materially alter the total statements. Whether or not an item is immaterial depends on judgment and the particular circumstances. One common test of materiality is: Would the decision of a reasonably well-informed user of the statements be altered if the item was treated differently? If the decision would change, the item is material.

Substance over Form

In order to reflect economic activities, accounting emphasizes and reflects the economic substance of events, even though the legal form may differ from the economic substance and suggest a different treatment.

Limitations

The conventions of accounting define the scope and character of information contained in financial statements. Rarely is the whole answer to an analytical question contained in the financial statements. Statement users should always be conscious of this fact. In most cases, data beyond the scope of the financial statement must be obtained to complete a competent analysis.

Application

The application of these conventions in specific instances is left to the judgment of managers and their accountants. The relative importance of these conventions changes from decision to decision. Also, in one instance, two or more conventions may be in conflict. The problem facing the accountant or business executive is to select those conventions most relevant to the statements. Whether or not a convention leads to a feasible solution will also determine its relevance.

Cape Cod Novelty Shop

As part of an industry profitability study being conducted for the state of Massachusetts, Paul Stone submitted to the Research Division of a local business school the most recent annual profit and loss statement for his small retail novelty shop shown in **Exhibit 1.** Stone and his wife operated the store, which was located on Cape Cod, a popular Massachusetts summer resort, with the minimum of outside help. During the off-season, Stone supplemented his income with a variety of part-time jobs.

On writing to Mr. Stone for supplementary information, the division learned that of the net profit of $10,627 shown on his statement, Mr. Stone had withdrawn $4,500. He did not make a charge for his own services as manager, but up to a few years ago he had been employed in a similar capacity in another store at a salary of $10,400 a year. Mr. Stone stated that he owned his store building, which had a rental value of $3,900 a year. From the balance sheets submitted for this firm, the division computed the net worth of the business exclusive of real estate to be $98,677.98. Interest on this sum at 6%, which Mr. Stone stated to be the local rate on money market type accounts, amounted to $5,920.

On the basis of these additional data, the division adjusted the profit and loss statement for the Stone store and sent it back as shown in **Exhibit 2.**

After receiving this adjusted profit and loss statement, Mr. Stone wrote the following letter to the division:

Dear Sirs:

I have received a copy of my most recent profit and loss statement as adjusted by you, and I am at a loss to understand some of the changes you have made.

For instance, the statement which I sent you showed a net profit of $10,627 but the copy which you have returned to me shows a net merchandising loss of $5,851. I notice that you

Professor David F. Hawkins prepared this case as the basis for class discussion rather than to illustrate either effective or ineffective handling of an administrative situation.
Copyright © 1995 by the President and Fellows of Harvard College. Harvard Business School case 196–042.

EXHIBIT 1   Cape Cod Novelty Shop Profit and Loss Statement

Gross sales	$104,850.48	
Less: Returns and allowances to customers	4,500.00	
Net sales		$100,350.48
Net inventory of merchandise at beginning of year	$ 50,258.79	
Plus: Purchases of merchandise at billed cost	74,762.67	
Inward freight, express, and parcel postage	428.61	
Gross cost of merchandise handled	$125,450.07	
Less: Cash discounts taken	1,276.95	
Net cost of merchandise handled	$124,173.12	
Less: Net inventory of merchandise at end of year	55,245.84	
Net cost of merchandise sold		68,927.28
Gross margin		$ 31,423.20
Expenses:		
Total salaries and wages	$ 9,480.39	
Advertising	1,702.56	
Boxes and wrappings	556.41	
Office supplies and postage	1,220.73	
Taxes, insurance, repairs, and depreciation of real estate	2,616.30	
Heat, light, and power	515.79	
Taxes	342.00	
Insurance	863.31	
Depreciation of store equipment	660.00	
Interest on borrowed capital	178.80	
Miscellaneous expense	1,533.63	
Income taxes	1,125.30	
Total expenses		20,795.22
Net profit		$ 10,627.98

---

have charged $10,400 as my salary. I do not draw any regular salary from the business, and since I am in business for myself I consider that I am not working for a salary but for profits. Also you have shown a rental expense of $3,900. Since I own the building, I consider that the item of rent is adequately taken care of by the expenses incurred in connection with the building, such as taxes, insurance, and so on. Furthermore, you have shown an expense of $5,920 for interest on owned capital. I have worked hard to put this business in a position where I would not have to borrow money, but if I have to charge interest on my own capital, I do not see where I am any better off, according to your version of affairs, than if I were continually in debt to banks and wholesalers.

In short, it seems to me that your adjustments to my statement amounts merely to shifting money from one pocket to another and calling it salary, rent, or interest, as the case may be; whereas what I am really interested in is the profit that I make by being in business for myself rather than working for someone else. It seems to me that if I carried your apparent line of reasoning to its extreme, I would include the annual increase in the value of my building and business goodwill as part of the store's income.

An explanation from you will be appreciated.

Yours very truly,
Paul Stone

EXHIBIT 2   Cape Cod Novelty Shop Profit and Loss Statement
Merchandise Statement

Gross sales		$104,850.48	
Less: Returns and allowances to customers . . .		4,500.00	
Net sales			$100,350.48	100.00%
Net inventory of merchandise at beginning of year	$ 50,258.79		
Plus: Purchases of merchandise at billed cost . .	74,762.67		
Inward freight, express, and parcel postage	428.61		
Gross cost of merchandise handled	$125,450.07		
Less: Cash discounts taken	1,276.95		
Net cost of merchandise handled	$124,173.12		
Less: Net inventory of merchandise at end of year	55,245.84		
Net cost of merchandise sold		68,927.28	68.69
Gross margin		$ 31,423.20	31.31%

Expense Statement

Proprietor's salary		$ 10,400.00	9.92%
All other salaries and wages		9,480.39	9.45
Total salaries and wages		$ 19,880.39	19.37%
Advertising		1,702.56	1.70
Boxes and wrappings		556.41	0.55
Office supplies and postage		1,220.73	1.21
Rent		3,900.00	3.89
Heat, light, and power		515.79	0.51
Taxes		342.00	0.34
Insurance		863.31	0.86
Depreciation of store equipment		660.00	0.66
Interest on borrowed capital	$ 178.80		
Interest on owned capital	5,920.68		
Total interest		$ 6,099.48	6.08
Miscellaneous expense		1,533.63	1.53
Total expenses		$ 37,274.30	36.70%

Net Gain (Loss) Statement

Net merchandising loss		$ 5,851.10	5.58%
Interest and rentals earned:			
Interest on owned capital invested in the business		$ 5,920.68	
Rent of owned store building	$3,900.00		
Less: Expense on owned store building (taxes, insurance, repairs, depreciation, interest on mortgages)	2,616.30	1,283.70	
Total interest and rentals		7,204.38	
Net gain		$ 1,353.28	
Provision for federal and state income taxes . .	$ 1,125.30		
Withdrawals	4,500.00	5,625.30	
Deficit for the year		$ (4,272.02)	

Questions

1. Did Mr. Stone make a profit from his novelty business during the current year? How much, if any? How may the difference between Mr. Stone's computation of profits and that of the Division of Research be explained? _____

2. Was Mr. Stone a successful business executive? _____

3. Should Mr. Stone have sold his novelty business? _____

4. What were the incentives which motivated Mr. Stone? _____

Primary Financial Statements

The typical corporate annual report to stockholders contains three primary statements: a statement of financial position, a statement of net income, and a statement of cash flows. Occasionally, a fourth statement showing the changes in owners' equity is also presented. These statements are presented on a comparative basis with previous years' results.

In practice, there are many variations in the titles, form, content, and coverage of these statements. For example, they may be for a parent company alone or for a consolidated entity representing the parent and its subsidiaries. Irrespective of their title or whether they are annual or interim statements, the function of these basic statements is to communicate useful quantitative information of a financial nature about a business to stockholders, creditors, and others interested in reporting the company's financial condition, results of operations, and cash flows.

This chapter describes the purpose and content of the typical statement of financial position (balance sheet) and income statement and the basic bookkeeping debit–credit mechanisms used to record the transactions summarized by these statements. The statement of changes in owners' equity is discussed also. The chapter also expands upon some of the definitions and concepts discussed in the previous chapter. The cash flow statement is covered in a later chapter.

Statement Analysis

A knowledge of the debit–credit mechanism for recording accounting data and the accepted formats for financial statements is important to those who analyze financial statement data.

Professor David F. Hawkins prepared this note as the basis for class discussion.

Financial analysts must understand the debit–credit mechanism because the clue as to what is going on in a company is often revealed by the account that represents the other side of the transaction rather than by the account that is of direct interest. For example, a company's sales growth may be the primary focus of an analyst's interest. Sales may appear to be growing at a spectacular rate. Yet the "sales" account is only one part of the accounting transaction. The analyst who knows that the offsetting entry to sales is accounts receivable will instinctively look at this second account. By examining the accounts receivable, the analyst may discover the company's sales are growing because it is extending extremely generous credit terms to customers of doubtful credit quality. In the light of this finding, the analyst may not be very impressed with the company's sales growth rate.

Sometimes companies use the terms "debit" and "credit" in their reports to stockholders to describe the results of some event. Unless the statement user understands the technical application of these terms, the user may be misled. For example, a company's income tax obligation may change because of a modification to its accounting practices for tax purposes. In its discussion of this event, its management may note that the accounting change resulted in a "credit to taxes payable." A naive statement reader may believe a "credit" is a good event, meaning lower taxes. This would be a wrong conclusion, because in accounting jargon a credit to a liability account, such as taxes payable, means an increase in that account balance. A statement user who understood the debit–credit mechanism would interpret correctly management's accounting language. Taxes payable increased.

A knowledge of bookkeeping helps identify account balances that are dependent on management's estimates and judgments. These are the so-called adjusting entries, such as the charging of depreciation expense and the establishment of a bad debt reserve. These accounts are of particular interest to financial analysts because an irresponsible management may manipulate them to achieve a desired end result. For these accounts, the financial analyst must make a judgment as to whether management's assertions are reasonable. This is not an easy task, but it must be done. Otherwise the financial analyst may be fooled by a dishonest management. To the extent that a statement user is unfamiliar with the adjusting entries required by bookkeeping to complete a set of financial statements, the likelihood of being misled by an unscrupulous management increases.

The general format of the three basic financial statements has become fairly standard. Statement users should be familiar with this format and its common variations. This knowledge helps financial analysts to identify unusual features in financial statement presentations which might indicate a need for extra thoroughness in conducting the statement analysis. Familiarity with the standard formats can also expedite the location of required data and make the analytical process more efficient.

Statement Objectives

According to the FASB's *Statement of Accounting Concepts No. 1*, "Objectives of Financial Reporting by Business Enterprises," the objective of the three basic financial reports is to provide:

1. Information that is useful to present and potential investors and creditors and other users in making rational investment, credit, and similar decisions. The information should be comprehensible to those who have a reasonable understanding of business and economic activities and are willing to study the information with reasonable diligence.

2. Information to help present and potential investors and creditors and other users in assessing the amounts, timing, and uncertainty of prospective cash receipts from dividends or interest and the proceeds from the sale, redemption, or maturity of securities or loans.

3. Information about the economic resources of an enterprise, the claims to those resources (obligations of the enterprise to transfer resources to other entities and owners' equity), and the effects of transactions, events, and circumstances that change resources and claims to those resources.

4. Information about how an enterprise obtains and spends cash, about its borrowings and repayment of borrowings, about its capital transactions (including cash dividends and other distributions of enterprise resources to owners), and about other factors that may affect an enterprise's liquidity or solvency.

5. Information about how management of an enterprise has discharged its stewardship responsibility to owners (stockholders) for the use of enterprise resources entrusted to management.

6. Explanations and interpretations to help users understand financial information provided.

For pragmatic reasons, these objectives are focused on information for investment and credit decisions. Relevance, reliability, and costliness are criteria that should be used in evaluating and selecting accounting information for disclosure.

General Requirements

All financial statements must carry the name of the reporting company, the dates of the period covered, and an indication of whether or not the statements and accompanying footnotes are audited. Unless otherwise indicated, it is presumed that the statements are for a going concern. However, as noted in the previous chapter, in practice this assumption should not be accepted literally in all cases, since reporting companies' future prospects for survival over the long run vary greatly. In addition, companies under the jurisdiction of the Securities and Exchange Commission should not publish statements that differ from those required to be filed with the Commission on an annual and interim basis.

Financial statements should present data that can be understood by users of the statements in a form and with terminology compatible with the users' range of understanding. In practice, this requirement assumes that users have some basic familiarity with the business activities of the reporting entity, the financial accounting process, and the technical language used in financial statements.

Another basic requirement is that the comparative statements issued by a company be truly comparable. This requires that (1) the format of the statements be identical, (2) the same items from the underlying accounting records are classified under the same captions, (3) the accounting principles followed in preparing the statements are not changed (or if so, that the changes and their effects are disclosed), (4) changes in the circumstances of the enterprise are disclosed, and (5) the comparative reporting periods are of equal length.

Other requirements include: the statements must be complete for the periods covered; the data must be communicated soon enough after the close of the accounting period to be useful to the statement users; the disclosure of all data relevant to the users' needs must be adequate; and a summary of the accounting principles must be presented.

Statement of Financial Position

The statement of financial position or balance sheet purports to present data related to a company's financial condition as of a specific time, based on the conventions and generally accepted principles of accounting. Balance sheets for the current and prior accounting periods are shown for comparative purposes.

The amounts shown on these statements are the balances at the date of the statement. Typically these amounts, except for monetary items, such as cash, accounts receivable, and accounts payable balances, may have little financial significance. For example, inventory may be stated at a cost that does not come close to approximating the actual investment in the inventory. Similarly, the net asset value reported for plant and equipment may be only a small fraction of the cash value of the asset. This situation occurs because of the historical cost convention and the preoccupation of accounting with the measurement of income. As a result, in practice, the statement of financial position is increasingly regarded as a step between two income statements that shows what residual balances remain in the accounts after current income has been determined. Statement users are expressing concern that much of the data in balance sheets may be of little significance to investors seeking to analyze the financial status of a company.

Balance sheets do not all follow the same precise format or use the same account titles. However, within reasonable limits of flexibility the items on a balance sheet are typically grouped in the following general categories:

Assets		*Liabilities and Owners' Equity*	
Current assets	$xxx	Liabilities:	
Long-term investments	xxx	Current liabilities	$xxx
Fixed assets	xxx	Long-term liabilities	xxx
Other assets (sometimes divided into noncurrent, prepaid and deferred charges, and intangible assets)	xxx	Other liabilities (sometimes divided into deferred credits and accumulated provisions)	$xxx
		Total liabilities	xxx

(continued)

Assets	*Liabilities and Owners' Equity*	
	Owners' Equity:	
	Capital stock	xxx
	Other paid-in capital	xxx
	Retained earnings	xxx
	Total Owners' Equity	$xxx
	Total Liabilities and	
Total Assets . . . . $xxx	Owners' Equity	xxx

The totals of the amounts listed in each of three major categories of the statement of financial position conform to the basic accounting equation.

$$\text{Assets} = \text{Liabilities} + \text{Owners' Equity}$$

Assets

Assets are probable future economic benefits obtained or controlled by an entity as a result of current or past transactions or events. These resources may be considered to have future economic benefits for a variety of different reasons. For example, some expenditures, such as capitalized[1] franchise acquisition expenditures, are called assets because they are expected to contribute to the generation of income in future accounting periods. Some assets, such as accounts receivable, represent resources that can readily be converted into cash. Other resources, such as the land owned by the business, are called assets because they represent valuable property rights. Assets are typically carried at a value equal to their original cost or net realizable value, whichever is lower. Monetary assets such as cash and accounts receivable are carried at the equivalent of the cash value expected to be realized in the normal course of business. Certain securities are reported at their market value.

Illustration A presents the asset section of a major corporation's consolidated balance sheet. Assets are divided into four categories common to many statements—current assets, investments, property, and other assets. Although they are not shown here, the notes to the statements provided additional information relevant to understanding the data in the asset section of the statement. For example, the method used to determine inventory values and the company's depreciation accounting policy were disclosed.

Illustration A will be used to explain briefly the nature of the assets accounts found on most balance sheets. A fuller explanation of these items is presented in subsequent chapters.

Current Assets

Current assets include cash and other assets that are reasonably expected to be realized in cash or sold or consumed during the normal operating cycle of the business, or

---

[1]An expenditure is said to be capitalized when it is recorded as an asset rather than an expense.

ILLUSTRATION A   Asset Section of a Major Corporation's Consolidated Balance Sheet, December 31, 1997 (in thousands)

ASSETS

Current Assets:

Cash:	$ 39,274
U.S. government and other marketable securities	3,722
Notes and accounts receivable (less estimated losses, $4,251,000)	165,288
Inventories	193,795
Prepayments and other current assets	9,979
Total Current Assets	$ 412,058

Investments:

Investments in jointly owned companies, at equity	$45,758
Other, at cost or less	9,739
Total Investments	$ 55,497

Property:

Land, buildings, machinery, and equipment etc. (at cost)	$1,199,489
Less: Accumulated depreciation and depletion	594,085
Net Property	$ 605,404

Other Assets:

Excess of cost of investments in consolidated subsidiaries over equities in net assets	$11,165
Deferred charges	10,629
Total Other Assets	$ 21,794
TOTAL ASSETS	$1,094,753

ILLUSTRATION B

Normal Operating Cycle Illustrated

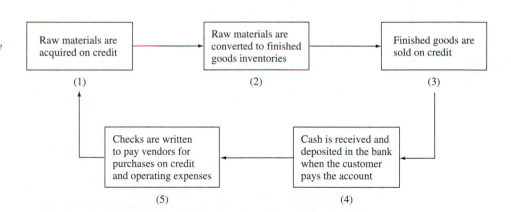

within one year if the operating cycle is shorter than one year. The operating cycle can be represented as that period during which the series of events described in **Illustration B** occur in sequence.

For most companies the operating cycle is less than 12 months. However, there are some notable exceptions. For example, one large bowling equipment manufacturer sold bowling alley equipment in return for long-term notes with payment schedules ranging up to seven years. These notes receivable from customers were classified as a current asset on the grounds that the company's "normal operating cycle" was seven years, since it took that long to complete all of the events related to each sale. Other more common examples of industries with operating cycles longer than one year are the distilling and tobacco industries. Their inventories must age for a long period before being offered for sale. In other cases, such as land development companies, no distinction is made between current and noncurrent assets, since the period during which land is held for sale can be very long and the period over which the purchase price is paid by the buyer of the land even longer.

Current assets include cash, accounts receivable, marketable securities, and inventories. Cash is shown at its face value and includes cash on hand, undeposited checks at the date of the balance sheet, cash in banks, and checks in transit to banks. (Checks written by the company but not yet deposited and charged to the company's bank account are treated as if they had been deposited.)

Sometimes corporations invest surplus cash in *marketable securities*. Typically these securities, as in **Illustration A,** are short-term obligations of the United States government. Depending on the intent of the holder, marketable securities are presented at either their current market price or original price.

Notes and accounts receivable represent the claims against customers generated by credit sales for amounts still due to the company. The balance of such an account includes only billings for services performed on or before the balance sheet date. The amount presented in the balance sheet is net of the company's estimated losses from uncollectible accounts. The procedures used to estimate these amounts are described in a later chapter.

Inventories include tangible items that will be sold directly or included in the production of items to be sold in the normal course of operations. The inventory account shown in **Illustration A** probably includes three types of inventory: a finished goods inventory, consisting of products ready for sale; a work-in-process inventory, consisting of products in various stages of production; and a raw materials and supplies inventory, consisting of items that will enter directly or indirectly into the production of finished goods.

Inventories are carried at cost, unless their utility is no longer as great as their cost. The so-called lower-of-cost-or-market rule to determine if the carrying value of inventories should be written down below cost is covered in a later chapter. This same chapter also discusses the alternative methods for determining the cost value of inventories shown on the balance sheet. These methods include the first-in, first-out method, which values the inventory on the balance sheet date using recent costs; and the last-in, first-out method, which uses the old costs to value the asset inventory.

The current asset category may include other accounts which will be realized during the normal operating cycle. Examples are unbilled costs on construction contracts performed by contractors for customers, prepaid insurance and expenses where the benefits to be derived from the prepayment extend beyond the current accounting period, and tax refunds receivable. Even though they do not result in a conversion into cash, prepaid expenses are listed among current assets. This practice is followed because these expenditures are expected to be recovered in cash through sales during the next 12 months or the benefits from the expenditures are to be received during the next 12 months.

It is customary to list current assets in their descending order of liquidity. For example, in **Illustration A** cash is listed first, marketable securities next, and then accounts receivable. Marketable securities precede accounts receivable because, of the two items, marketable securities can more easily be turned into cash by management. For a similar reason, inventories are listed after accounts receivable but before prepayments.

Investments

Investments made in other companies are carried on the consolidated balance sheet as noncurrent items when the investing company's objective is one of control, affiliation, or some continuing business relationship with the company, and when the circumstances of the investment do not require the subsidiary to be consolidated. These investments may be common stock, debt securities, or long-term advances. It is not customary to state the market value of such noncurrent investments, since it is assumed there is no present intention to sell the securities. Depending on the circumstances, these securities may be carried at their original cost or at an amount equal to the investing company's original cost plus its proportional share of the subsidiary's retained earnings. This latter approach is called the equity method. Later chapters explain the cost and equity methods in greater detail.

Illustration A shows two types of long-term investments and their valuation basis: *investments in joint ventures*, valued according to the equity method; *other*, valued by the cost method at their original cost or less.

Property

Long-lived tangible assets, such as equipment acquired to produce goods for sale, are referred to as "fixed assets." Assets in this category are *land*, *buildings*, *machinery*, *equipment*, and any other long-lived tangible items used in the company's operations. Land is always stated at its original cost. The other assets are stated at their original cost less depreciation, rather than at their replacement value or current market value.

Depreciation represents the allocation of the cost of fixed assets due to use and obsolescence. An annual charge for depreciation is included in the expenses of current operations. The amount of this depreciation expense is related to the anticipated useful life of the asset, which may be computed on the basis of either expected years of service or actual use (i.e., hours of operation, units produced, etc.). The accumulated amount of depreciation expense related to the fixed assets still carried on the books of the company is presented on the balance sheet in an account called "accumulated depreciation." Sometimes the term "allowance for depreciation" is used.

A later chapter discusses the various depreciation methods in detail. The two principal approaches to depreciation are the straight-line and accelerated methods. Straight-line depreciation allocates the cost of a fixed asset, less any estimated salvage value, equally to operations over the life of the asset. Accelerated depreciation methods charge a greater proportion of an asset's total depreciation to operations during the early years of its life than during the latter years.

It is customary, as presented in **Illustration A** under the caption *property*, to show both the original cost and the depreciated book value of the fixed assets available for use in operations. The difference between these two amounts, accumulated depreciation, is shown as a deduction from the total original cost of the fixed assets to arrive at the net book value of the assets. This net book value, called "net property" in **Illustration A,** seldom reflects the current market value of the asset. It is simply the balance left in the property accounts of the company's accounting records after deducting the related accumulated depreciation charges.

Illustration A refers to "accumulated depreciation and depletion." The term *depletion* relates to investments in natural resources, whereas the term *depreciation* is associated with plant and equipment investments. Depletion is the amount of a company's investment in natural resources that is charged to operations over the period during which these resources are extracted or exhausted. Accumulated depletion is the cumulative total of these charges related to the natural resource investments still available to the company for the generation of future revenues. Depletion is often charged on a units-of-production basis.

Other Assets

Items included in the "Other Assets" category include intangible assets and deferred charges. Assets that fall into this category are patents, trademarks, copyrights, and franchises. To be recorded, these assets must be created or acquired through a business transaction. Intangible assets are carried at cost initially and then charged to operations in a systematic manner over their useful life. A later chapter covers the topic of intangible assets in greater detail.

Illustration A lists an *intangible* asset labeled "excess of cost of investments in consolidated subsidiaries over equities in net assets." The popular name for this item is "goodwill." It arises when a company purchases another company for a price in excess of the fair market value of its net assets. Goodwill, this difference between the purchase price and the net asset values acquired, must be charged to operations over a period of not more than 40 years. However, the actual period used varies greatly from company to company. The accounting for business acquisitions and goodwill is covered in a later chapter.

Deferred charges are similar to prepaid expenses, since both are payments or accruals recognized before the balance sheet date that properly should be charged to operations subsequent to that date. However, it is important to distinguish between them, since prepaid expenses are a current asset and deferred charges are assigned to the other-asset category. Prepaid expenses relate to amounts paid for services yet to be received, which are properly related to future revenues. In contrast, deferred charges represent amounts paid for services already received by the business but not yet charged to operations. For example, the prepayment of the premiums on a three-year insurance policy is a prepaid expense, since the insurance protection has yet to be received. In addition, since the benefit of the insurance is to be received over the next three years, it should be charged against income over this period. In contrast, preoperating expenditures for opening a new store that are expected to produce benefits beyond the current period may be considered a deferred charge, since the company has already received the preopening service. However, in order to determine income in accordance with the matching convention, the company has elected to hold off expensing this item until the future benefits are received.

Liabilities

Liabilities are probable future sacrifices of economic benefits arising from the entity's present obligations to transfer assets or perform services to other entities at some time in the future as a result of past transactions or events.

Typically, where liabilities relate to specific assets, it is not acceptable to show the liability as a deduction from the asset. For example, the mortgage on a building is shown on the right-hand or liability side of the balance sheet and the asset "building" is listed on the left-hand side.

The accounting concept of liabilities is broader than liabilities in the popular sense of legal debts and obligations. The accounting concept includes certain deferred credits that do not involve a debtor–creditor relationship. For example, for accounting purposes, the seller's profit on a sale and leaseback transaction is not recognized in the income statement as a gain at the time of the sale. The required treatment is to list the profit as a deferred credit on the right-hand side of the balance sheet and allocate this amount to the income statement as a reduction to lease rentals over the life of the lease. This practice leads to a better matching of costs and revenues.

Illustration C presents an example of the right-hand side of a major corporation's consolidated balance sheet, the liabilities and owners' equity section. Taken together, **Illustrations A** and **C** comprise this company's entire balance sheet with the exception of the related notes.

Current Liabilities

Current liabilities are defined as (1) those liabilities that the company expects to satisfy with either assets classified as current in the same balance sheet or by creating other current liabilities; (2) all obligations arising from operations directly related to the company's operating cycle; or (3) those liabilities expected to be satisfied during the following year. The one-year rule is widely considered to be the cutoff between current and noncurrent liabilities. However, if the enterprise's operating cycle is longer than 12 months, an exception is made to this rule and the operating cycle period may be used.

Current liabilities include the current portion (due within 12 months) of notes payable to banks, amounts owed to trade creditors, wages earned by employees but not paid to them, and funds received in advance for services not yet rendered. The order of

ILLUSTRATION C   **Liability and Owners' Equity Section of a Major Corporation's Consolidated Balance Sheet, December 31, 1997 (in thousands)**

Liabilities and Owners' Equity

Current Liabilities:

Notes payable—banks	$ 59,504
Current maturities of long-term debt	7,953
Accounts payable and accruals	113,953
Domestic and foreign taxes on income	19,700
Total Current Liabilities	$ 201,110

Long-term Debt:

11⅝% of sinking fund debentures	$ 125,000
10½% term loan	42,088
Other	26,666
Total Long-term Debt	$ 193,754

Deferred Credits:

Deferred income tax	$ 36,186
Other	19,752
Total Deferred Credits	$ 55,938

Accumulated Provisions:

Product warranties	$ 10,356
Foreign operations	543
Total Accumulated Provisions	$ 10,899
Total Liabilities	$ 461,701

Capital and Retained Earnings:

Cumulative preferred stock—unauthorized 5,000,000 shares, no shares issued	—
Common stock—authorized, 50,000,000 shares, par value $2.50 each; issued, 21,721,988 shares	$ 212,850
Earnings retained for use in the business	462,972
Less: Common stock in treasury, 1,245,420 shares at cost	(42,770)
Total Capital and Retained Earnings	$ 633,052
Total Liabilities and Owners' Equity	$1,094,753

presentation followed in the current liability section of **Illustration C** is typical of many balance sheets.

The captions of the various current liabilities listed in **Illustration C** are almost self-explanatory. *Notes payable to banks* represent the company's obligations to banks arising from short-term borrowing arrangements. The amount shown as the *current maturities on long-term debt* is a portion of the long-term debt's principal that must be repaid during the next 12 months. *Accounts payable* represent the claims of trade creditors for goods and services provided on an open account basis. If these trade obligations were evidenced by a note or similar written promise to pay, they would be included with notes payable. The *accruals* combined with the accounts payable in **Illustration C** might include items such as wages owed to employees or deposits owed to customers on returnable containers not yet returned. The taxes owed as of the balance sheet date that will be paid to various taxing authorities during the next 12 months are included in the obligations listed as *domestic and foreign taxes on income*.

Long-Term Liabilities

Long-term liabilities are all of an enterprise's noncurrent liabilities. They are often subdivided on the balance sheet into several different categories. For example, the long-term liabilities shown in **Illustration C** are presented in three groups—long-term debt, deferred credits, and accumulated provisions.

Long-term debt represents debt obligations of a company that will mature beyond one year's time. These obligations are recorded at their principal value. However, in the case of long-term debt, such as bonds and debentures issued at a discount or premium, the discount or premium is shown as an adjustment to the principal amount. In the case of bank loans, the principal value is the amount owed the banks. The current interest on these obligations is charged to operating income as the interest obligation is incurred. A later chapter discusses the accounting for long-term debt in greater detail.

Deferred Credits

Deferred credits are the opposite of deferred charges. They are unearned revenues, such as subscriptions collected in advance of providing the service; or deferred profits, such as the deferral of profit on a sale-and-leaseback transaction. Another important class of deferred credits results from charges required by generally accepted accounting principles to current or past income in advance of the actual expenditure or obligation being incurred, such as the deferred credit resulting from income tax allocation requirements (see below). Some deferred credits, such as subscriptions received in advance, are obligations; whereas others, such as deferred sale-and-leaseback profits, are not.

Illustration C shows a significant deferred credit: namely, the deferred income tax item.

Deferred income tax represents the amount of the company's potential income tax obligation that the company has deferred from past periods to future periods by reporting lower profits for taxation purposes than for book purposes. This results from following different accounting practices for book and tax reporting.

Accumulated Provisions

Accumulated provisions are estimates of future expenditures, asset impairments, or liabilities that have been accrued by a charge to income. **Illustration C** presents two examples of accumulated provisions.

The two examples of accumulated provisions shown in **Illustration C** are contingencies for future losses. In both cases, the estimated loss from the future contingencies has already been charged to income in anticipation of the event. The offsetting accounting entry was made to the related liability account. When the actual loss occurs, it will be charged to this liability account. Loss contingencies are discussed further in a later chapter.

Product warranties are obligations incurred in connection with the sale of goods or services that may require further performance by the seller after the sale has taken place. To record the correct profit from a sale, it is necessary to recognize as a current expense all of the past, current, and future costs associated with each sale at the time the sale revenue is recorded. Warranty obligations are future costs of current sales. Because of the uncertainty surrounding claims that may be made under warranties, warranty obligations fall within the definition of a contingency. The amount shown in **Illustration C** for this item should be a reasonable estimate of the probable future warranty costs associated with recorded sales.

The *provision for foreign operations* represents the recognition by management that an event has occurred that will probably lead to some identifiable losses overseas. The provision was set up by a charge to income. When the actual extent of the losses is known, they will be charged to the liability account. Any actual losses in excess of the amount set aside in the liability account will be charged to income directly.

Owners' Equity

Owners' equity sections of the balance sheet represent the residual financial interest of the owners in an enterprise. It is the balance that remains after deducting the total liabilities of the enterprise from its total assets. For most companies the residual owners' interest determined in this fashion is rarely equal to or even close to the actual market value of that interest.

Illustration C presents the owners' equity for our example company under the caption "Capital and Retained Earnings." Other terms used to describe the owners' equity are "net worth," "net assets," and "stockholders' equity." A later note covers equity capital transactions.

The *capital* section of the balance sheet lists (1) the amount and type of capital stock authorized, (2) the number of shares issued, (3) the net amount received by the company for the issued stock, and (4) the number of shares and acquisition costs of the company's own stock held by the company. **Illustration C** shows that the company's stockholders have authorized five million shares of preferred stock, but none have been issued. The authorized number of shares represents the maximum number of shares the company may sell under the terms of its charter. Thus, the principal source of company's capital from stock issues was the 21.7 million shares of $2.50 par-value common stock sold at various times to the public for a total consideration of $212 million.

Rather than showing, as in **Illustration C,** the value of the total consideration received from the issuance of common stock, an alternative approach is to value the common stock account at the par value of the securities issued. Then, if the company sells any of this stock for more than its par value, this excess is shown in an account labeled "Capital Received in Excess of Par Value of Stock Issued." This account appears immediately below the common stock account.

The *retained earnings* account represents the balance of net income of the enterprise from the date of incorporation, after deducting distributions of dividends to shareholders. Translation gains and losses resulting from restating the local currency-denominated balance sheets of foreign subsidiaries into dollars may also be included in this account or as a separate line item. In addition, under some circumstances, such as when stock dividends are declared, transfers may be made from retained earnings to the capital stock accounts.

Data related to issued stock reacquired by the issuing company are presented in the *treasury stock* account. This stock is carried at its acquisition cost. It is always presented as a deduction from owners' equity. Accounting regards only the stock actually in the hands of the stockholders as outstanding stock.

Income Statement

The results of operations of a business for a period of time are presented in the income statement.[2] For comparative purposes statements for the current and two preceding accounting periods are presented.

From the accounting system's point of view, the income statement is subordinate to the balance sheet. The income statement simply presents the details of the changes in the retained earnings balance sheet account due to profit-directed activities. In contrast to this accounting perspective, most users of financial statements regard the income statement as a more important source of information than the balance sheet because net income more directly influences equity stock prices and dividend payments.

Elements

The elements of a business's profit-directed operations and their net results can be represented by the equation:

$$\text{Revenues} - \text{Expenses} = \text{Net Income (Net Loss)}$$

The income statement presents the details of this expression. Also included in the income statement are gains and losses arising from peripheral or incidental transactions that change the net assets of a company and are included in the determination of net income as required by generally accepted accounting principles.

Revenue (i.e., sales) is defined in *Concepts Statement No. 6* as:

Inflows or other enhancements of assets of an entity or settlements of its liabilities (or a combination of both) from delivering or producing goods, rendering services, or other activities that constitute the entity's ongoing major or central operations.

---

[2]Common alternatives are: "statement of profit and loss," "statement of earnings," and "statement of operations."

Not all increases in assets or decreases in liabilities are included in revenue. For example, the receipt of cash from a bank loan does not result from profit-directed activities and does not change owners' equity. It is not revenue. This transaction increases an asset (cash) and a liability (bank loans payable). In contrast, a cash sale of inventory in the normal course of business is revenue. It increases the asset cash and changes the owners' equity account, Retained Earnings. If the goods are sold at a profit, Retained Earnings will increase by the after-tax amount of the profit.

Different concepts of revenue can be found in accounting theory. This diversity reflects the lack of common agreement as to the nature of revenue. One approach regards revenues as an inflow of assets derived from the sale of goods and rendering of services. An opposite concept, the so-called outflow approach, considers revenue to the goods and services created by a business that are transferred to customers.

Expenses are the goods and services of a business that are used in the process of creating revenues. In this process the expenditures incurred for the business's goods and services are said to have expired. Some of these expenditures, like administrative costs, may be incurred and expire in the same accounting period. Others, like inventory, may be incurred in one period, held as unexpired costs on the balance sheet, and then expensed as expired costs in a later period when the inventory transfers to the customer.

Concepts Statement No. 6 defines expenses as:

> Outflows or other using up of assets or incurrences of liabilities (or a combination of both) from delivering or producing goods, rendering services or carrying out other activities that constitute the entity's ongoing major or central operations.

Like revenues, expenses can only result from profit-directed activities that change owners' equity. The reduction of inventory as the result of a sale is an expense, since the net result of this operating transaction is a change in the owners' equity account, Retained Earnings. The purchase of inventory on credit is not an expense. It does not change owners' equity. The purchase increases the asset inventory and the liability trade payables.

Although the payment of dividends reduces owners' equity, it is not an expense. This transaction reduces cash and the owners' equity Retained Earnings account, but it is not a profit-directed activity. It is a distribution of capital.

Net Income.   The FASB could not reach agreement among its members on a definition of "net income." Accordingly, in *Statement of Financial Accounting Concepts No. 5*, "Recognition and Measurement in Financial Statement of Business Enterprises," it advanced two concepts related to income that encompassed all of the various net income concepts advocated by individual board members. These concepts were labeled "earnings" and "comprehensive income." According to *Concepts Statement No. 5*:

> Statements of earnings and of comprehensive income together reflect the extent to which and the ways in which the [owners'] equity increases or decreases from all sources other than transactions with owners during a period. . . .
>
> The concept of earnings . . . is similar to net income in present practice. . . .

Earnings is a measure of entity performance during a period. It measures the extent to which asset inflows (revenues and gains) associated with cash-to-cash cycles substantially completed during the period exceed asset outflows (expenses and losses) associated, directly or indirectly, with the same cycles. . . .

Comprehensive income is a broad measure of the effects of transactions and other events on an entity, comprising all recognized changes in equity (new assets) of the entity during a period from transactions and other events and circumstances except those resulting from investments by owners and distributions to owners.

The board's concept of earnings differs from the net income figure resulting from current practice. It excludes certain accounting adjustments to prior periods that are now included in net income. The board's conceptual framework includes these accounting adjustments in comprehensive income. Recognized holding gains and losses are also excluded from earnings and included in comprehensive income. The board expects practice will move toward its earnings concept through a gradual evolutionary process.[3] A later chapter discusses the many problems associated with income recognition. Particular aspects of expense measurement are discussed in a number of different notes.

Basic Conventions

Four basic conventions discussed in an earlier note influence the preparation of the income statement. These are the accrual concept, the accounting period concept, the realization concept, and the matching concept. Each will be reviewed here briefly.

The *accrual concept* relates revenues and expenses to changes in owners' equity, not cash. Statements prepared on this basis recognize and report the effects of transactions and other events on the assets and liabilities of a business in the time period to which they relate, rather than only when cash is received or paid. Accordingly, for example, wage expense is recognized when labor services are performed, not when the workers are paid.

The *accounting period* is the segment of time covered by the income statement. All events affecting income determination during this period should be measured and recorded in the company's accounting records and assigned to this period for income determination purposes. The accounting period is bounded by a beginning and ending balance sheet. The income statement relates to the changes in owners' equity from one balance sheet date to another due to profit-directed activities.

In practice, the *realization or recognition concept* is interpreted to mean that revenue is generally recognized when the following conditions are met: (1) the earnings process is complete or virtually complete; (2) an exchange has taken place; (3) the amount of income is determinable and its collection is reasonably assured; and (4) reasonable estimates can be made of related future costs. For example, interest revenue from loans to others is recognized as time passes, since that, assuming the borrower is solvent, is the critical event dictating the timing and amount of interest receivable.

---

[3] In mid-1997 the FASB proposed adding a comprehensive income figure and display to the required financial statements.

The *matching concept* recognizes that some costs have a presumed direct association with specific revenues or time periods. This is a process of associating cause and effect. It is through this matching process that income is determined.

Expenditures and Expenses

A troublesome accounting problem is determination of whether a purchase results in an asset or an expense. An expenditure occurs whenever an asset or service is purchased. At the moment of the transaction, all expenditures for purchases can be thought to result in assets. These assets will then become expenses if they (a) are directly or indirectly related or associated with the revenue of the period, or (b) suffer a loss during the period in their future revenue-generating capacity, such as in the case of assets destroyed by fire or patents carried as assets in prior periods that become worthless due to the development of a new technology.

Statement Format

A common order of items in the income statement is:

1. Revenues (sales for the period).
2. Cost of sales (the manufacturing or acquisition costs of the goods sold during the period).
3. Gross profit or margin (the difference between revenues and cost of sales; item 1 less item 2).
4. Operating expenses (the selling, administration, and general expenses associated with operating the company's principal business activity during the period).
5. Operating income (item 3 less item 4).
6. Nonoperating revenues (revenues derived from sources other than operations during the period, such as interest on the temporary investment of excess cash).
7. Nonoperating expenses (expenses not directly related to the principal business activity and the financial cost of borrowed money).
8. Provision for taxes (the income tax expense).
9. Income before extraordinary items (item 5 plus item 6 less item 7 and item 8).
10. Extraordinary items. (These are infrequent, abnormal gains or losses that are clearly not related to the company's normal operations or business activities. These items are shown net of their related tax effect. A later chapter discusses extraordinary items.)
11. Net income (item 9 plus or minus item 10).

A more complicated statement is presented when a company makes a change in an accounting principle or discontinues a part of its operations. The cumulative effect

ILLUSTRATION D   Example: A Major Corporation's Single-Step Income Statement

Statement of Earnings for the Year Ended December 31, 1997

Net sales	$1,962,487,755
Cost and expenses:	
Cost of products sold	$1,445,785,281
Selling, advertising, general, and administrative expenses	182,507,421
Interest and debt expense	7,581,233
	$1,635,873,925
Earnings before provision for taxes	$ 326,613,830
Provision for federal and state taxes on income	176,569,000
Net income	$ 150,044,830

of an accounting principle change is reported net of taxes as a single item after extraordinary items but before net income. The profit or loss net of taxes of an operation that a company intends to discontinue is shown separately before extraordinary items but after income from continuing operations.

An alternative form of income statement is shown in **Illustration D.** This statement omits the gross and operating profit calculations. It is known as a single-step statement. Each of the items on this statement will be discussed briefly.

The *net sales* figure represents the company's net sales during the calendar year 1997. It is derived by deducting from gross sales any sales returns, allowances, and discounts. The gross sales amount is the invoice price of the goods and services sold. Sales returns and allowances result from the credit given to customers for sales returns or defective goods. Sales discounts are discounts granted to customers for prompt payment of amounts owed to the seller. Sometimes this item is shown as a sales expense rather than as a reduction of gross sales. Discounts from list price granted to members of the seller's trade do not enter into the accounting records. These sales are recorded as the actual invoice price.

Cost of products sold is the manufactured cost or, in the case of merchandising companies, the purchase price of the goods sold during the period. The manufactured cost includes the cost of direct labor, raw materials, and manufacturing overhead. The amount of cost of goods sold expense matched with current revenues will depend in large part on the company's inventory valuation practices, since any current expenditures for products not included in cost of products sold must be assigned to the inventory account.

Selling, general, and administrative expenses are all of the expenses incurred for these activities during the accounting period. Generally these expenditures are not assumed to have a lasting value beyond the current period. Therefore they are related directly to the current accounting period for income determination purposes.

Interest and debt expenses are financial charges. It is customary to segregate these items from operating expenses. This approach assumes that users of the statements wish (1) to identify and evaluate the cost of financing operations and (2) to determine whether or not management's return from operations is adequate, given the financing costs.

Earnings before provision for taxes are the basis for determining the company's tax expense. It should be remembered that this amount most likely will be different from the taxable income shown on the company's tax return. Two common reasons for this difference are that some cost items included in the income statement are not recognized for tax purposes, and that some revenue items recognized currently to determine book income are deferred to future periods for tax purposes.

Provisions for federal and state taxes on income will, for most companies, consist of two parts: the taxes actually payable based on the income shown in the current tax return and the taxes recognized for book purposes for which there is no current tax liability. This latter type of accounting expense is the source of the changes in deferred tax liability discussed earlier.

Net income is the final figure on the statement. It represents the net impact of profit-directed activities on owners' equity after considering all items of profit and loss recognized during the period.

Interrelationship

The items on the income statement and the balance sheet are interrelated. For example, when a credit sale is made, revenues and accounts receivable both increase. In addition, the sale causes finished goods inventory to decline and cost of goods sold to increase, and the increased tax expense related to the profit on the sale causes taxes payable to increase. Therefore, in order to gain a full appreciation of any item on one statement, it is necessary to examine also the related items on the other.

Changes in Owners' Equity

The income statement alone does not present all of the changes in owners' equity during an accounting period since it relates only to profit-directed activities. Therefore, to describe the changes due to capital additions and distributions, an additional statement or disclosure is sometimes required of the changes in owners' equity, which presents changes in both the retained earnings and the capital stock accounts.

The Retained Earnings account is the link between the net income figure and the owners' equity. The Retained Earnings balance at the end of the period is derived as follows:

1. Beginning retained earnings (the balance at the beginning of the accounting period).
2. Net income (shown in the income statement for the period—add to 1).
3. Dividends paid to common stockholders. (Subtract from sum of 1 and 2.)
4. Ending retained earnings (the amount appearing in the balance sheet at the end of the period—equal to item 1 plus item 2 less item 3).

Other Considerations

Notes to Financial Statements

Financial statements are inevitably accompanied by notes disclosing such information as the company's accounting policies, changes in these policies, details of account balances, off-balance sheet obligations and risks, fair value of certain financial instruments and contingent liabilities. These notes are an integral part of the statements and should be read before relying on the accounting figures.

The notes also include summary data related to the operating parts of the business and their geographical locations.

Auditor's Report

The auditor's report accompanying financial statements should always be read in conjunction with the statements. It is important for anyone using the statements to know the auditor's appraisal of the statements.

Financial statements are the direct responsibility of the management and directors of the reporting company. Although the company's public auditor may assist and advise management in its preparation of the statements, management alone is responsible for their contents. Management is not compelled to follow the auditor's advice. However, the auditor does have a responsibility to state whether he or she agrees with the fairness of the financial presentation. In practice, it is this duty of the auditor to state exceptions that brings reluctant managements to accept auditors' recommendations in cases where differences of opinion exist between management and auditors. A later chapter discusses in greater detail the nature of the auditor's opinion and the basis for reaching this opinion.

Interim Statements

Most corporations publish condensed income statements for the quarter and the year to date on a comparative basis with the same periods during the previous year. Companies also present in their quarterly reports a condensed balance sheet as of the end of the quarter.

As will be explained in a later chapter, considerable caution should be exercised when using quarterly statements. They are unaudited and are based on numerous estimates.

Forecasts

Companies seldom include forecasts of sales and net income for future periods in their public reports.

It has been advocated by some that annual reports should disclose in summary form the reporting companies' budgeted results for the next annual period. It is argued that these data would provide stockholders with a better basis for evaluating management's planning capabilities and how well management achieved its objectives for the reporting period. In addition, it would put the current results into better perspective.

The accounting profession has not encouraged this type of reporting because of the problems associated with auditing forecasts objectively. Managements have also been reluctant to publish these forward-looking data, considering forecast data to be competitive data that should not be revealed publicly. Also, management is concerned that a *failure* to achieve the forecast might lead to stockholder litigation.

However, under certain circumstances, the SEC encourages the publication of forecasts. The AICPA has published guidelines for preparing these forecasts and the auditor's role in communicating them to the public.

Summary of Financial Results

In addition to the financial statements covered by the auditor's opinion, annual reports typically include two sets of summary financial statistics. First, inside the front cover, and opposite the chief executive officer's letter to the stockholders that inevitably begins the text of the report, selected statistical data on a comparative basis are often shown, related to such items as current earnings per share, sales volume, dividends per share, return on investment, net income as percentage of sales, and the ratio of current assets to current liabilities. Second, usually following the notes to the financial statements, a five- or ten-year statistical summary is presented. The basic data included in this summary are often similar to that covered in the statistical presentation at the beginning of the report. Additional statistics presented may include such data as the number of employees, the number of common shares outstanding, and the preferred dividends paid per share.

These statistical summaries are not covered by the auditor's opinion. However, for companies under the jurisdiction of the SEC these disclosures should not be materially different from the data presented in the audited statements.

Management Discussion and Analysis

The SEC also requires management to include in annual reports an analysis of the current and past few years' results. This presentation is known as the "Management Discussion and Analysis" (MD&A) section of the financial report. Statement users should read the MD&A carefully. It contains management's views on the company's operations, liquidity, and ability to cope with inflation. Also presented are explanations of changes in circumstances and a listing of unusual events and their consequences. The MD&A tends to follow a consistent format. Statement users should regard changes in its format as a red flag signaling a conscious decision by management to change the format, possibly to exclude or obscure some unfavorable information.

Text

Most annual reports include textual material describing the companies' policies, activities, plans, and problems. A thorough reading of this material is essential for anyone trying to determine the significance of the communications contained in the financial statements.

Appendix A

Basic Accounting Mechanics

So far the effect of individual transactions in terms of their impact on the balance sheet and income statement have been discussed with little concern for accounting mechanics. **Appendix A** presents a summary of the systematic procedures used by accountants to record and summarize transactions. These procedures are called bookkeeping. The objective of this material is to help the reader without prior accounting training learn how to reduce, in an efficient manner, a complex set of business facts to the comprehensible set of relationships expressed in financial statements.

Accounts

Accountants use a series of accounts to record transactions. These accounts correspond to the items shown on the financial statements. The simplest form of account, and the one we will use, is a T-account. The Cash account of a company might look like this:

Cash

(Increases)		(Decreases)
Beginning balance at beginning of		
accounting period	$100,000	$ 3,000
	5,000	8,000
	20,000	40,000
	10,000	
	$135,000	$51,000
New beginning balance at end of		
accounting period	$ 84,000	

All of the increases in cash are shown on one side. All of the decreases are recorded on the other. The new balance is determined by (1) adding all of the amounts listed on the increases and decreases side and (2) subtracting one total from the other.

Debit–Credit Mechanism

Each accounting transaction has two parts. This dual aspect convention, discussed in an earlier chapter, is reflected in the statement, "The payment by a customer of an accounts receivable increases cash and reduces accounts receivable." This statement uses layman's language to describe what occurred. The accountant would describe this transaction in terms of the debit–credit mechanism.

The accountant uses the term *debit* (Dr.) to describe that part of a transaction that

1. Increases an asset account.
2. Decreases a liability account.
3. Decreases an owners' equity account.
4. Decreases a revenue account.
5. Increases an expense account.

The term *credit* (Cr.) is used to describe that part of the transaction that

1. Decreases an asset account.
2. Increases a liability account.
3. Increases an owners' equity account.
4. Increases a revenue account.
5. Decreases an expense account.

The reader is encouraged to memorize these debit–credit rules rather than to try to determine their algebraic relationship to the basic accounting equation: Assets = Liabilities + Owners' Equity.

Here are some examples of the debit–credit terminology used to describe transactions:

1. A company borrows $10,000 cash from the bank. The accounting effect of the transaction is
   Dr. Cash 10,000
       Cr. Bank Notes Payable 10,000
2. The company repays the loan. The accountant would describe the transaction as:
   Dr. Bank Notes Payable 10,000
       Cr. Cash 10,000

The words *debit* and *credit* have no meaning in accounting other than the following: debit means the amount is entered on the left-hand side of the T-account; credit means the amount is entered on the right-hand side of the T-account. The words carry no moral judgment. Depending on the

ILLUSTRATION A–1

Debit–Credit Rules

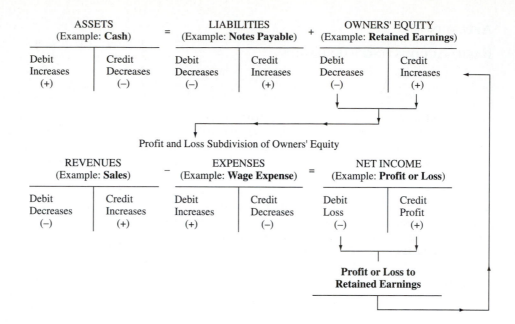

account involved, they can be "desirable" or "undesirable" from the company's point of view.

Illustration A–1 shows the relationship between T-accounts and the debit–credit mechanism. The reader should note that because debit and credit are used to signify the left and right sides of the T-account, the side used to record an increase or a decrease depends on the account. For example, increases in assets are recorded on the left or debit side, whereas increases in liabilities are listed on the right or credit side.

An Example

The following problem will be used to illustrate the steps in the process used to prepare financial statements.

Climax Industries, Inc., a new company started on January 1, 1997, sold at the beginning of the year 10,000 shares of common stock for $50,000. The company bought for cash $20,000 worth of raw materials and processing equipment worth $10,000. The equipment was expected to last 10 years. During the year the company had sales of $45,000, of which $5,000 was still owed by customers at year-end; consumed $15,000 worth of raw materials; spent $10,000 cash on wages; and paid $5,000 cash for administration, rent, and selling activities. During the year the company also bought $15,000 of raw materials for which it still owed $5,000 at the end of the year. Dividends of $2,000 were declared and paid at year-end.

The company anticipates it will have no bad debts. Your assignment is to prepare an income statement for the period and a balance sheet as of the end of the year. (Disregard taxes.)

The first step is to *analyze* the transactions and record them in the debit–credit form. This is called *journalizing original entries*. It is purely mechanical. Here are the journal entries. To help you understand the debit–credit decision better, each account will be labeled *A* if it is an asset account, *L* if it is a liability account, and *OE* if it is an owners' equity account. For the purpose of this exercise the revenue and expense accounts will be treated as subdivisions of owners' equity.

1. To record the sale of capital stock for cash:
   Dr. Cash (A) 50,000
      Cr. Capital Stock (OE) 50,000

2. To record the initial purchase of raw materials for cash:
   Dr. Raw Materials Inventory (A) 20,000
      Cr. Cash (A) 20,000

3. To record the purchase of processing equipment for cash:
   Dr. Processing Equipment (A) 10,000
      Cr. Cash (A) 10,000

4. To record the sales during the period:
   Dr. Cash (A) 40,000
   Accounts Receivable (A) 5,000
      Cr. Sales (OE) 45,000

5. To record the period's wage expense:

   Dr. Wage Expense (OE) 10,000
       Cr. Cash (A) 10,000

6. To record the period's administration, rent, and selling expense:

   Dr. Administration, Rent, and Selling
   Expense (OE) .5,000
       Cr. Cash (A) 5,000

7. To record the purchase of raw materials during the year:

   Dr. Raw Materials Inventory (A) 15,000
       Cr. Cash (A) 10,000
           Accounts Payable (L) 5,000

8. To record dividend declaration and payment:

   Dr. Retained Earnings (OE) 2,000
       Cr. Cash (A) 2,000

9. To record the Raw Materials Inventory withdrawals during the year:[a]

   Dr. Raw Materials Expenses (OE) 15,000
       Cr. Raw Materials Inventory (A) 15,000

10. To record the processing equipment's depreciation expense (see below for the debit–credit treatment of the "contra asset" account accumulated depreciation):

    Dr. Depreciation Expense (OE) 1,000
        Cr. Accumulated Depreciation (L) 1,000

This last journal entry is called an adjusting entry. There is no transaction with parties outside the entity to prompt the recording of the event or to determine the amounts. These entries are made at the end of the period. They are the adjust-

---

[a]The ending inventory can be calculated as follows:

Beginning inventory	$20,000
Plus: Purchases	15,000
Less: Withdrawals	15,000
Ending Inventory	$20,000

ments to assets or liabilities previously recorded that are required to achieve a periodic matching of costs and revenues. Many of these entries require considerable judgment to determine the amounts involved. In this case management estimated the equipment would last 10 years. Based on this estimate one-tenth of the asset's costs was expensed this year.

Using the scheme of T-accounts similar to those in **Illustration A–1,** the next step is to *post* the journal entries to the appropriate T-accounts. The results of this process are shown in **Illustration A–2.** The numbers beside each amount refer to the journal entries describing the transaction.

Illustration A–2 shows the accumulated depreciation account under the "liabilities" caption. The debit–credit mechanism treats this account as a liability. However, for statement purposes it is shown as a deduction, or a contra account, to the asset "Processing Equipment."

The next step is to calculate the *ending balances* in the asset and liability accounts, *close out* the expense and revenue accounts to the net income account, and then close the balance in this account to retained earnings. Here are the required journal entries to reduce the revenue, expense, and net income accounts to zero:

11. To close the revenue account:

    Dr. Revenues 45,000
        Cr. Net Income 45,000

12. To close the expense account:

    Dr. Net Income 31,000
        Cr. Expenses 31,000

13. To close the net income account:

    Dr. Net Income 14,000
        Cr. Retained Earnings 14,000

Now the statements can be prepared. **Illustration A–3** presents the company's income statement combined with a statement of changes in retained earnings. **Illustration A–4** presents the balance sheet of Climax Industries, Inc.

ILLUSTRATION A–2   T-Accounts for Climax Industries, Inc., Example

| ASSETS | LIABILITIES | + | OWNERS' EQUITY |

ASSETS
Cash

+	−
50,000(1)	20,000(2)
40,000(4)	10,000(3)
	10,000(5)
	5,000(6)
	10,000(7)
	2,000(8)
90,000	57,000
33,000	

Raw Materials

+	−
20,000(2)	15,000(9)
15,000(7)	
35,000	15,000
20,000	

Processing Equipment

+	−
10,000(3)	0
10,000	

Accounts Receivable

+	−
5,000(4)	0
5,000	

LIABILITIES
Accounts Payable

−	+
0	5,000(7)
	5,000

Accumulated Depreciation*

−	+
0	1,000(10)
	1,000

OWNERS' EQUITY
Capital Stock

−	+
0	50,000(1)
	50,000

Retained Earnings

−	+
2,000(8)	14,000(13)
2,000	14,000
	12,000

Retained Earnings Subdivisions

REVENUES		−	EXPENSES		=	NET INCOME	
−	+		+	−		−	+
	45,000(11)		10,000 (5)	31,000(12)		31,000(12)	45,000(11)
45,000(11)	45,000(4)		5,000 (6)			14,000(13)	
			15,000 (9)			45,000	45,000
			1,000(10)				
			31,000	31,000			

ILLUSTRATION A–3   Climax Industries, Inc., Statement of Earnings and Changes in Retained Earnings, for the Year Ended December 31, 1997

Sales		$45,000
Cost of goods sold:		
Raw materials	$15,000	
Direct labor	10,000	
Manufacturing depreciation	1,000	26,000
Gross profit		$19,000
Selling, rent, and administration		5,000
Net income		$14,000
Less: Common stock dividends declared ..		2,000
Additions to income retained in the business		$12,000

ILLUSTRATION A–4   Climax Industries, Inc., Statement of Financial Condition, December 31, 1997

Assets		*Liabilities and Owners' Equity*	
Current Assets:		Current Liabilities:	
Cash	$33,000	Accounts payable	$ 5,000
Accounts receivable	5,000	Long-term liabilities	—
Raw materials inventory	20,000	Total Liabilities	$ 5,000
Total Current Assets	$58,000		
Property (at cost):		Owners' Equity:	
Processing equipment	$10,000	Capital stock	$50,000
Less: Accumulated depreciation	1,000	Retained earnings	12,000
Net property	$ 9,000	Total Owners' Equity	$62,000
		Total Liabilities and	
Total Assets	$67,000	Owners' Equity	$67,000

Marion Boats, Inc.

Fred Cunningham was a fire truck salesman for many years, while Bill, his brother, worked as a book salesman for a major publishing house. Although they had done fairly well financially, they wanted to "be their own bosses," so they decided to go into business together.

They agreed that selling small fishing and recreational boats would be a good line for them to go into as both had been interested in fishing and boating for many years. Also, the small town of Marion, Mississippi, where they lived, did not have any boat dealerships. The nearest dealer was some 95 miles away.

After some searching, they chose a suitable site for their proposed operation. It was situated at a popular local dock. A dilapidated building which had been condemned by the local authorities stood on the site.

At this point in time, the brothers decided to incorporate the business. The services of a lawyer were obtained to draw up the legal papers and to handle all aspects of the execution of the incorporation. The fee for this service was $800, and each of the brothers paid half of it.

On October 1, 1995, Fred purchased 1,800 shares of the company's stock for $72,000, and Bill purchased 500 shares for $20,000. The payment for legal services was considered part of these investments, so the actual cash received by the new company was $91,200. Further purchases of the company's shares could be made only at the prevailing book value per share at the time of the purchase and only if both parties agreed to the transaction. If either brother wished at any time to sell his shares back to the company, this transaction would also be conducted at the prevailing book value of the shares. The brothers also agreed that they should each receive salaries of $24,000 per year at all times during which they were engaged in the company's business on a full-time basis. Both knew this amount was less than they could earn in

Professor David F. Hawkins prepared this case as the basis for class discussion rather than to illustrate either effective or ineffective handling of an administrative situation. Copyright © 1995 by the President and Fellows of Harvard College. Harvard Business School case 196-041.

other jobs, but they realized a small salary was needed at this time to ensure that the dealership could pay its bills on time.

On November 1, 1995, with the aid of a $40,000 bank loan and $32,000 of the company's money, Fred purchased the property which had been selected. The same day, he left his job to devote his full attention to the new enterprise.

First, Fred arranged to have the old building demolished. A cursory examination revealed there was nothing of any significance that could be salvaged, except for some building stone. Mr. Mahoney, the wrecker, agreed to clear the site for $7,000, provided he could have the stone. Otherwise, he would want $9,000. Fred was convinced he could get a better price for the stone, so he instructed Mr. Mahoney to clear the site and store the stone in a corner of it. This work was started immediately and completed before Christmas. Mr. Mahoney agreed to defer collection of payment until May 31, 1996.

In the meantime, Fred got in touch with a large boat manufacturer, Sport Boats, Inc., who had previously indicated interest in the projected dealership. Fred asked Sport Boats for financial help to construct the buildings needed to carry on business. Sport Boats agreed to provide all the financing needed for the building through a loan repayable in 10 equal annual installments, provided Marion Boats sold only Sport Boats models. The loan carried an interest rate of 10% per year, payable from April 1, 1996. The first repayment, including interest, would fall due on March 31, 1997.

On December 31, 1995, Sport Boats sent a check for $40,000 to get Marion Boats started. Fred deposited the check in the business's bank account. The remainder of the loan would be forthcoming when the building was completed.

Next, Fred arranged through a consulting architect for several construction companies to bid for the job. The lowest bidder was the Birkett and Snell Company. They agreed to construct the specified building for $124,000. On the advice of his architect, however, Fred decided to accept the Holmes Brothers Construction Company bid of $140,000; the architect believed Birkett and Snell was less reliable than Holmes in meeting promised completion dates.

The construction was started immediately, Holmes promising completion by the end of March 1996. Progress payments on certificates from the architects were to be made at the end of January, the end of February, and the date of completion in amounts of $40,000, $40,000, and $60,000.

During early 1996, Fred tried to obtain some orders for boats which he planned to deliver directly to customers from Sport Boats's warehouse in Cleveland. Fred had some success with the model he had recently bought himself. Between January 1 and March 30, Fred sold 17 of this model at an average cash cost to Marion of $9,000. Nothing was paid to Sport Boats for these boats during the period. These 17 sales realized $183,600, whereof $58,000 represented trade-in allowances, $112,000 in cash, and the rest was outstanding at March 30. Fred sold all the trade-in boats for $54,800 cash before March 31. Previously, Bill and Fred agreed that the latter should receive $40 for every new boat sale as compensation for using his private boat as a display model.

At the end of March, the building was completed. However, there was an additional charge of $2,400 for materials, which Marion had to pay according to the provisions of the building contract. At the same time, the architect's bill for $2,600 arrived.

Fred sent the progress payments to the builder as previously arranged, making the

January payment with $40,000 of the company's money and the February payment with the Sport Boats loan. On March 31, the last $60,000 progress payment and the $2,400 materials surcharge were paid. The $40,000 bank loan plus interest of $2,000 was repaid by check on March 30.

On March 30, Bill quit his job with the publishing house and joined Marion on a full-time basis. At Bill's request, it was agreed that financial statements would be prepared, to allow the two brothers to see where they stood at the end of March. Sport Boats asked that a portion of the amount of the dealership owed the manufacturers for boats be regarded as payment due to the dealership under the building contract, and Fred accepted this arrangement on behalf of Marion. The two brothers agreed that they would invite Mr. William Hurley, an accountant who was a mutual friend of theirs, to prepare the accounts.

Questions

1. As Mr. Hurley, prepare journal entries to record the events that have taken place in the business up to March 31, 1996. _____
2. From these journal entries, prepare a balance sheet as of March 31, 1996, and an income statement for the operating period to that date. _____
3. Based on your financial statements, what is the value of each brother's equity in the company? _____
4. Using the cash account data, prepare a statement showing the sources and uses of cash during the period from the formation of the business until March 31, 1996. _____

CASE

3-2

Superior Clamps, Inc.

Peter Fuller was the inventor of a metal hoseclamp for automobile hose connections. Having confidence in its commercial value, but owning no surplus funds of his own, he sought among his friends and acquaintances for the necessary capital to put it on

Professor David F. Hawkins prepared this case as the basis for class discussion rather than to illustrate either effective or ineffective handling of an administrative situation.
Copyright © 1995 by the President and Fellows of Harvard College. Harvard Business School case 196–040.

the market. The proposition which he placed before possible associates was that a corporation should be formed with capital stock consisting of 60,000 shares of $1 par value stock, that he be given 32,000 shares for his patent, and that the remaining 28,000 shares be sold for cash. Fullers' patent had 16 years of the 17-year legal life remaining.

The project looked attractive to a number of the individuals to whom the inventor presented it, but the most promising among them—a retired manufacturer—said he would be unwilling to invest his capital without knowing what uses were intended for the cash to be received from the proposed sale of stock. He suggested that the inventor determine the probable costs of experimentation and of special machinery, and prepare for him a statement of the estimated assets and liabilities of the proposed company when it was ready to begin actual operations. He also asked for a statement of the estimated transactions for the first year of production and sales operations, together with an analysis of the operating results indicated by those expectations. This information would be based on the studies the inventor had made of probable markets and costs of labor and materials. It would include a listing of resulting assets and liabilities; a statement of expected sales, expenses, and profits; and an explanation of the expected flow of cash over the course of the year.

After consulting the engineer who had aided him in constructing his patent models, Fuller drew up the following list of data relating to the transactions of the proposed corporation during its period of organization and development.

1. Probable selling price of 28,000 shares of stock, $36,000.
2. Probable cost of incorporation and organization of Superior Clamps, Inc., $1,650, which includes estimated officers' salaries during development period.
3. Probable cost of developing special machinery, $26,000. This sum includes the cost of expert services, materials, rent of a small shop, and the cost of power, light, and miscellaneous expenditures.
4. Probable cost of raw material, $1,000, of which $600 is to be used in experimental production.

Fuller drew up the first of the statements desired by his prospective associate in the following manner:

Probable Assets and Liabilities of the Superior Clamps, Inc. When Ready to Begin Actual Operations

Assets		*Liabilities and Owners' Equity*	
Patent	$32,000	Common stock at par	$60,000
Machinery	26,000	Plus: premium on stock	8,000
Organization costs	1,650	Capital paid in	68,000
Experimental costs	600		
Raw materials and supplies	400		
Cash	7,350		
Total assets	$68,000	Total liabilities and proprietorship	$68,000

With this initial part of his assignment completed, the inventor set down the following estimates as a beginning step in furnishing the rest of the information desired.

1. Expected sales, $56,000, all to be received in cash by the end of the first year following completion of organization and initial experimentation.

2. Expected additional purchases of raw materials and supplies during the course of this operating year, all for cash, paid by end of year, $18,000.

3. Expected help from the banks during year—loans, including $100 interest, to be repaid before close of year—$4,000.

4. Expected payroll and other cash expenses and manufacturing costs for the operating year, $28,000 (of which $6,000 is to be for selling and administrative expenses).

5. Expected inventory of raw materials and supplies at close of period, at cost, $3,600.

6. No inventory of unsold process or finished stock expected as of the end of the period. All goods to be sold "on special order"; none to be produced "for stock."

7. All experimental and organization costs, previously capitalized to be charged against income of the operating year.

8. Estimated depreciation of machinery on hand at start of operations, $2,600, based on a 10-year life. (However, Fuller was aware of a plastic hoseclamp being developed by a major corporation that might make his product and the equipment used to produce it obsolete in about four years' time. If this occurred, Fuller thought that it might be possible to convert the special machinery into general-purpose equipment at a cost of several thousand dollars.)

9. Machinery maintenance, cash, $150.

10. New machinery and equipment to be purchased very near the end of the operating year for cash, $2,000.

11. Profit distributions in the form of dividends, $6,000.

The above transaction data were for the most part cumulative totals, and should not be interpreted to mean that the events described were to take place in the precise order or sequence indicated.

Question

Prepare the information wanted by the retired manufacturer.

CHAPTER 4

Intercorporate Equity Investments

Frequently, corporations acquire equity interests in other corporations ranging from a few shares of capital stock to 100% ownership. Sometimes the assets or net assets, rather than the stock, are acquired. The reasons for these investments vary from temporary short-term investments of excess funds to permanent investments made to gain control. At the time these investments are contemplated or announced, in order to understand the financial statement implications for the investor company, experienced managers and financial analysts prepare pro forma financial statements for the investor company reflecting the investment. This requires a good grasp of the accounting for intercorporate investments, consolidated statements, and business combinations.

A parent company statement shows the investor company's equity interest in its investee companies as an investment. A consolidated statement presents the financial position and results of operations of a parent company and the affiliates it controls, as if the group was a single economic unit. Parent company financial statements are prepared for internal purposes but only consolidated financial statements are published. How an equity investment is accounted for in a consolidated statement depends on the nature of the investment.

In mid-1995 the FASB was reconsidering the criterion for requiring consolidation of subsidiaries and the nature of consolidated financial statements.

Ownership Interests of Less than 20%

Presentation of investments representing less than a 20% interest in an investee company on the investor company's balance sheet, and their effect upon current income, depends upon whether the investment is made for temporary, short-term reasons or for

Professor David F. Hawkins prepared this note as a basis for class discussion.

the purpose of creating some longer-term relationship, and whether the equity securities involved are marketable.

Marketable Equity Securities

Marketable equity securities held for trading purposes are marked-to-market at the end of each accounting period and unrealized gains and losses are included in periodic income. Equity securities classified as trading securities are those equity securities intended to be held for short periods of time. Typically the entity buys and sells these securities expecting to make a profit on the difference between retail and dealer, or bid and asked prices, rather than on price changes during the period securities are held.

Marketable equity securities not classified as trading securities are classified as "securities available for sale." Equity securities held for sale are accounted for at market, but unrealized gains and losses are a direct adjustment to owners' equity.

Other Than Investment

Nonmarketable securities and ownership interests of less than 20% acquired for corporate purposes other than trading or sale purposes are typically reported using the cost method. Initially, the stock acquisition is recorded by debiting an asset investment account for the investment cost, which includes the purchase price plus all incidental acquisition costs such as broker's commissions. Dividends received as a distribution of earnings subsequent to acquisition are recognized at the time of receipt as dividend income. "Other than temporary" declines in values of the security are recognized and charged to income.

Ownership Interests of More than 20%

Ownership of a voting interest of 20% or more is accounted for by the equity method on the statements of the investor company. The cost method can only be used in the case of 20% plus interests if the investor company lacks the ability to significantly influence the investee's affairs.

As explained later, investor interests in excess of 20% may be reported in consolidated statements using the equity method or on a fully consolidated basis depending on the circumstances.

Cost and Equity Methods Illustrated

An investor corporation initially records the acquisition of an equity interest in an investee by charging the cost of the stock purchased to an investment account. Cost is the cash price paid or if property is exchanged, its fair value. Subsequent to the initial investment, depending on the investment characteristics the investment may be recorded by the investee using either (1) the cost method or (2) the equity method.

ILLUSTRATION 1   Cost and Equity Methods of Accounting for Intercorporate Investments

Transaction	Investor Owns Less than 20%: Cost Method			Investor Owns More than 20%: Equity Method		
1. Investor acquires part of investee company's stock for $200,000	Dr. Investment Cr. Cash	200,000	200,000	Dr. Investments Cr. Cash	200,000	200,000
2. Investee reports $40,000 earnings	No entry			Dr. Investments Cr. Income	32,000[a]	32,000
3. Investee pays $20,000 in dividends	Dr. Cash Cr. Dividend Income	3,800[b]	3,800	Dr. Cash Cr. Investments	16,000[c]	16,000
4. Investee reports $30,000 loss	No entry			Dr. Income Cr. Investments	24,000[d]	24,000

[a]$40,000 × 0.80 (assumes 80% ownership).
[b]$20,000 × 0.19 (assumes 19% ownership).
[c]$20,000 × 0.80 (assumes 80% ownership).
[d]$30,000 × 0.80 (assumes 80% ownership).

Illustration 1 summarizes the accounting entries in the investor's books applying the cost and equity methods.

The *cost method* maintains the separate legal distinction between corporate entities. This method gives no recognition in the investor company's financial statements to the investee company's earnings or losses. The investment account includes only the amounts invested in the investee by the investor corporation. Dividends from the investee are credited to income.

After the initial acquisition cost has been entered in the investor's investment account, the *equity method* subsequently adds or subtracts from this amount the investor's proportional share of the changes in the investee's retained earnings. The investment account increases as the investor's share of the investee's reported earnings is credited to an income account. Dividends received from the investee reduce the investment account. As a result of these entries, the investment account reflects initial cost plus or minus the investor's share of the change in the investee's retained earnings subsequent to acquisition.

An investor's share of losses of an investee may equal or exceed the carrying amount of an investment accounted for by the equity method plus advances made by the investor. The investor ordinarily would discontinue applying the equity method when the investment (and net advances) is reduced to zero and would not provide for additional losses unless the investor has guaranteed obligations of the investee or is otherwise committed to provide further financial support for the investee. If the investee subsequently reports net income, the investor should resume applying the equity method only after its share of that net income equals the share of net losses not recognized during the period the equity method was suspended.

Ability to Influence.   The equity method can only be used if the investor has significant influence over the investee company's financial and operating policies. Whether or not an investor has the ability to exercise significant influence over the operating and financial policies of an investee could be difficult to determine in practice. In order to achieve a reasonable degree of uniformity a direct or indirect investment of 20% or more in the voting stock of an investee leads to the presumption that in the absence of contrary evidence an investor has the ability to exercise a significant influence over an investee.

If, despite a holding of more than 20% of an investee's voting stock, an investor can present evidence suggesting that the presumption of ability to influence is not warranted, the investor can use the cost method to account for the investment. Such a situation may arise in the case of an investor company that owns more than 20% of an investee but for antitrust reasons has entered into an agreement with the government not to participate in the investee's affairs. There are some investor companies that have used the equity method to account for their investments in companies where their equity interest was less than 20% of the investee's voting stock. Usually in these cases, the investor has significant board representation.

Consolidated Financial Statements

Consolidated financial statements treat majority controlled affiliated corporations as though they were a single economic unit even though the affiliated companies are legally separate entities. The financial information of each controled affiliate is combined as if the corporations involved were merely departments or divisions of a larger corporation. The consolidating procedure cancels out on work sheets all offsetting reciprocal pairs of assets and liabilities, revenues and costs, and investment and equity accounts which appear on the statements of affiliated corporations. For example, a parent may lend its subsidiary $100,000. This will appear as a loan receivable on the parent's statements. It will be carried as a loan payable on the subsidiary's books. When the statements of the two companies are consolidated, these items will be eliminated. Similarly all such transactions involving intercompany investments and gains and losses on intercompany transactions are reversed on the work sheets so that only events involving the economic unit and outside parties will show on the consolidated statements.

Consolidation

Control.   In general, to include an investee company in its consolidated financial statements the parent must have ownership and management control over the investee company. Prior to 1997, control was defined as "more than a 50%" voting interest and the parent–subsidiary relationship was not hampered or threatened by currency, dividend, legal, or political restrictions. In late 1995 the FASB proposed to do away with the 50% plus voting interest consolidation criterion and require a controlling entity to consolidate all of the entities it controls unless control is temporary at the time the entity becomes a subsidiary. In its proposal the FASB defined control as the power of an entity to use or direct the use of the individual assets of another entity in essentially the same way as the controlling entity can use its own assets. The FASB was expected to issue a new standard along the lines of its proposal in 1997.

Accounting Concepts Peculiar to Consolidated Statements

Most items appearing on consolidated financial statements are comparable to those found on parent company statements. There are four items which are peculiar to consolidated statements: minority interest, goodwill, consolidated net income, and consolidated retained earnings.

Minority Interest.   Financial statements prepared for single corporations do not distinguish between the individuals or groups owning a single class of capital stock. In the case of consolidated statements, if the parent does not own 100% of the capital stock of a subsidiary, that part of ownership equity not owned by the parent is presented separately on the consolidated balance sheet and identified as minority interest. After total net income for the affiliated group is determined, a deduction is made for that part of the subsidiary's earnings applicable to the minority ownership. Thus, the minority interest shown on the consolidated balance sheet consists of the minority interest's pro rata share of net worth or capital contribution plus accumulated earnings less any dividends paid.

Minority interest is listed on balance sheets between total liabilities and owners' equity. This practice conforms to the view that consolidated financial statements should be prepared from the point of view of the parent company which exercises controlling ownership over its subsidiaries.

The FASB's 1995 proposal takes a different point of view. It is based on the point of view that consolidated financial statements should be prepared from the point of view of the consolidated entity. Under this approach minority interest is included in consolidated owners' equity.

Goodwill.   The intangible asset goodwill is recognized only when a business is acquired through a purchase transaction at a price greater than the fair value of the net assets.[1] When a parent acquires an interest in a subsidiary under these circumstances, this excess of investment is not separated on the parent's statements. It remains as an unidentified part of the parent's total investment in the subsidiary, which is listed as an asset.

When the subsidiary giving rise to the goodwill is consolidated, the investment account on the parent's balance sheet must be offset against the subsidiary's equity accounts. If there is an excess of investment over the subsidiary's net assets at acquisition, goodwill results, and it must be descriptively recognized as an asset on the consolidated balance sheet. Negative goodwill arises when net assets are purchased for less than their value. On consolidation negative goodwill is recorded as a deferred credit to income.

Consolidated Net Income.   Consolidated income statements present the total net income during the period for the affiliated group as if it were operating as a single corporation. To achieve this, all intercompany transactions giving rise to gains or losses are eliminated. Also those earnings applicable to minority ownership are deducted from consolidated net income. The resulting consolidated net income consists

---

[1]The nature and handling of both positive and negative goodwill will be treated in greater detail in a subsequent chapter.

of parent company earnings plus the parent's share of subsidiary earnings for the period arising from external transactions.

The FASB's 1995 proposal would not deduct earnings applicable to minority interest in the measurement of consolidated net income. Rather, it would be included with an indication of the net income applicable to controlling and noncontrolling interests.

Consolidated Retained Earnings.   Consolidated retained earnings include all of the retained earnings of the parent plus the parent's share of the subsidiary's retained earnings from the date of acquisition. Also, dividends paid by subsidiary companies to the parent have been eliminated, since they are merely transfers of cash within the consolidated entity.

Proportional Consolidation

Proportional or proportionate consolidation is used frequently outside of the U.S.A. but seldom used by U.S. corporation in consolidated statements to present joint venture interests. Proportional consolidation includes the joint venture's account balances in the consolidated statements in proportion to the interest of the reporting company in the joint venture. For example, if a company held a 50% interest in a joint venture under proportional consolidation 50% of each of the joint venture's balances would be included in the consolidated statements.

The FASB's 1995 proposal would not permit the use of proportional consolidations.

Equity Method Adjustments

The difference between consolidation and the equity method lies in the details reported in the financial statements, not in the stockholders' equity and income determination. Therefore, the equity method is applied in such a way as to produce the same stockholders' equity and net income as would be the case in consolidation. Accordingly, to achieve this result using the equity method, intercompany profits and losses are eliminated from income until realized by the investor or investee as if the investee company were consolidated. Similarly, when the cost of the investor company's investment is greater than its underlying equity in the investee's net assets, this difference affects the determination of the amount of the investor's share of earnings or losses of the investee, as if it were a consolidated subsidiary. If the investor is unable to relate the difference to specific accounts, the difference should be considered goodwill and amortized.

Consolidation Procedures

The act of consolidation occurs only on the worksheet used for assembling the consolidated data, not in the accounts or records of the parent or subsidiary corporations. The parent and subsidiary's accounting records and financial statements are based upon the principal that each company is a separate legal entity.

Confusion in consolidating procedures is minimized if one bears in mind constantly that (1) consolidating, adjusting, and eliminating entries are never recorded in the accounts of the affiliated group and (2) each periodic or annual consolidation is made as if it were the initial consolidation.

A common procedure for preparing consolidated financial statements involves the following steps:

1. Arrange vertically in parallel columns on a worksheet the unconsolidated statements of the parent and of the subsidiaries to be consolidated, as shown in **Illustration 2.**

2. Make any preconsolidating adjustments necessary to bring consistency into the statements. For example, a worksheet adjustment would be required if an affiliate had forwarded cash to another affiliate in payment of a debt but the other affiliate had not yet received the cash as of the closing date. In this case, the statement of the affiliate to whom the cash was sent would be adjusted as if the cash had actually been received. All intercompany relationships such as these must be reconciled and brought into agreement before eliminations can be made. The receipt of cash such as $10,000 for payment of accounts receivable by the parent from the subsidiary is shown as adjustment 1 in the illustration.

3. Eliminate intercompany assets and liabilities. All debtor–creditor relationships between affiliates to be consolidated are offset on the worksheet. This is achieved by making worksheet entries which cancel the asset of one affiliate against the liability of another affiliate. The effect of these eliminations is reversal of transactions that created the intercompany assets and liabilities in the accounts of affiliates. For example, if a subsidiary borrowed $175,000 from its parent, the subsidiary would enter the transaction on its books by debiting Cash $175,000 and crediting Loans Payable $175,000. The parent's records will reflect an entry debiting Loans Receivable $175,000 and crediting Cash $175,000. On the consolidating worksheet the eliminating entry will debit Loans Payable and credit Loans Receivable each for $175,000. (See adjustment 2.) This entry, involving accounts from the statements of different corporations, has the effect of reversing the entries made on the books of the affiliates, but no entries to Cash are necessary because assets and liabilities of all affiliates will be combined. As noted earlier, all eliminating entries are made only on the consolidating worksheets and are not entered in the accounts of the individual corporations.

4. Eliminate (or cancel out) any intercompany revenue against the appropriate costs or expenses. Adjustment 3 shows the entries reversing $150,000 of intercompany sales. This entry assumes none of the goods sold to the subsidiary are still in its inventory account.

5. Eliminate the effect of dividends declared by a corporation to another member of the affiliated group. (None shown in **Illustration 2.**)

ILLUSTRATION 2   Consolidation Working Papers (in thousands)

	Parent	Subsidiary	Adjustments Debits		Adjustments Credits		Consolidated Statement
Assets							
Cash	$ 400	$ 20	(1)	10			$ 430
Accounts receivable	700	125			(1)	10	815
Inventory	1,200	275					1,475
Investment in subsidiary	400				(6)	400	—
Note due from subsidiary	175	—			(2)	175	—
Plant and equipment (net)	300	200					500
Goodwill			(6)	240	(7)	30	210
Other assets	25	10					35
Total assets	$3,200	$630					$3,465
Liabilities							
Accounts payable	$ 200	$100					$ 300
Notes payable	400	30					430
Loans payable—bank	1,000	25					1,025
Loans payable—parent		175	(2)	175			—
Total liabilities	$1,600	$330					$1,755
Minority interest	—	—			(4)	60	60
Common stock	$1,000	$200	(4)	40			1,000
			(6)	160			
			(4)	20			
Retained earnings	600	100	(6)	0			
			(7)	30			650
Total owner's equity	$1,600	$300					$1,650
Total liabilities, minority interest and owner's equity							$3,465
Income Statement							
Sales	$1,200	$475	(3)	150			$1,525
Costs of goods sold	800	125			(3)	150	775
Gross margin	$ 400	$350					$ 750
Selling expense	$ 50	$ 75					$ 125
Operating expense	75	125	(8)	10[b]			210
Total expense	$ 125	$200					$ 335
Minority interests	—	—	(5)	30[a]			30
Net income	$ 275	$150					$ 385

[a]Single entry (see p. 71 for explanation).
[b]Single entry (see p. 72 for explanation).

6. Eliminate from the accounts all intercompany profits or losses which may be cumulatively included in asset accounts of the purchaser and in equity accounts of the seller. The gains or losses of prior periods of affiliation as well as those of the current period must be canceled.

Illustration 2 does not include an example of this kind of adjustment. If such an adjustment is required, however, it might be handled as follows: Assume the parent had sold three years earlier to its subsidiary a machine for $20,000, including the parent's $2,000 profit, and the subsidiary was depreciating this machine over 10 years, the adjustment would be:

a. To eliminate the profit on the intercompany sale from the gross carrying value of the assets of the subsidiary and the retained earnings of the parent:

        Dr. Retained earnings (parent)   2,000
            Cr. Plant and equipment (sub)........................   2,000

b. To eliminate the depreciation expense based on the intercompany profit of $2,000 included in the subsidiary's fixed asset account. This requires $200 (or $2,000/10 years) to be deducted from this year's depreciation expense and an elimination from the subsidiary's beginning retained earnings of $400 representing the last two years' depreciation charged by the subsidiary on the intercompany profits included in its asset base.

        Dr. Accumulated depreciation (sub)   600
            Cr. Depreciation expense (sub)   200
            Retained earnings (sub)   400

7. Eliminate the investment account of the parent in those subsidiaries being consolidated and adjust those subsidiaries' equity accounts for any minority interests that may be present. The minority interest is equal to the minority stockholders' proportional share of the subsidiary's *current* or year-end net worth. It is assumed there is a 20% minority interest.

The computation of the minority interest is:

        Dr. Minority interest (in subsidiary):
            Common stock .... 20% × $200 = $40
            Retained earnings .... 20% × $100 = 20
                Cr. Minority interest......................... $60

The adjusting entries in **Illustration 2** (number 4) are:

        Common stock (sub)   40
        Retained earnings (sub)   20
            Minority interest   60

The above entries are to year-end balance sheet balances. A further adjusting entry must be made to show the minority interest in the subsidiary's net income [($150 × 20%) = $30]. This is achieved by a single entry (number 5). The offsetting entry is already included in number 4's adjustment to year-end retained earnings.

If the parent's investment in the subsidiary exceeded its proportional share of the subsidiary's equity capital and retained earnings accounts at the *acquisition date*, an adjustment will also be required to determine the goodwill amount on the consolidated statements. To illustrate assume the $400 "investment in subsidiary" balance shown in **Illustration 2** represents an 80% interest in the subsidiary's equity and the subsidiary's retained earnings were zero at the time the investment was made because prior to this time it had been the practice of the investee to pay out all of its profits in dividends. Also, assume that the asset and liability values on the subsidiaries' books approximate their fair market values.[2]

The goodwill at date of acquisition calculation is:

Investment (parent)		$400
Common stock (sub), 80% × 200	$160	
Retained earnings (sub), 80% × $0	0	160
Goodwill		$240

The adjusting entries in **Illustration 2** (number 6) are:

Dr. Common stock (sub)	160	
Retained earnings (sub)	0	
Goodwill	240	
Cr. Investment in Subsidiary (parent)		400

The goodwill account, if positive, is usually labeled descriptively as "excess of cost over net assets of acquired companies" and presented as an asset on the consolidated balance sheet. A negative balance is identified as "excess of net assets of acquired companies over cost." The amount of positive or negative goodwill is amortized as a charge against income over a period not to exceed 40 years.

In the case of **Illustration 2,** the amortization of the goodwill in the consolidated statement involves (1) a write-down of the goodwill asset by an amount equal to the sum of the annual charges to date, (2) an increase in the operating expense by the annual charge (and a decrease in profits by the amount of this charge), and (3) a decrease in retained earnings by the cumulative effect of the goodwill charges to profits. Thus, assuming a 24-year write-off period, the goodwill balance shown on **Illustration 2** would be decreased by $30 [($240/24) × 3]; retained earnings would decline by $30 (prior two-year charges plus current year charge); operating profits would decrease by $10 (current year charge); and operating expenses would increase by $10.

The adjusting debit–credit entries to recognize goodwill amortization in **Illustration 2** (number 7) are:

Dr. Retained earnings	30	
Cr. Goodwill		30

The above debit–credit procedure for handling goodwill is not technically correct. It was done in this fashion because **Illustration 2** focuses on the consolidating process. The goodwill amortization adjusting entries should have been made to the parent's statements prior to consolidation by a $30 credit to investment in subsidiary, a $20 debit to retained earnings, and a $10 debit to operating expenses. Because this procedure was not followed, to achieve the correct consolidated income figures, a single-entry debiting operating expenses $10 must be made (number 8).

---

[2]Goodwill is computed after adjusting the acquired company's assets and liabilities to their fair market value.

8. Combine all remaining statement amounts for all affiliates being considered. The balances can then be arranged in the traditional financial statement form, modified for the four concepts peculiar to consolidation described previously.

Financial Analysis Considerations

Typically, consolidated financial statements provide those wishing to appraise a company's total performance and financial risk with much more relevant data than if the user had to work with the individual statements of the parent company and its subsidiaries. In the latter case, the user would have no way to appraise the extent to which individual company statements were distorted by intercompany transactions. Simply combining the individual company reports would not suffice. The distortions would still exist. Consolidating statements eliminates this problem.

The underlying assumption that consolidated financial statements are more meaningful than separate statements for affiliated companies needs to be qualified. Since consolidated financial statements ignore the separate legal character of affiliated corporations, information concerning any of the individual companies included in the consolidated statements cannot be obtained from the statements. For example, creditors and investors cannot evaluate the profitability or financial condition of any single corporation within the group on the basis of the consolidated statements. The analyst is unable to associate the assets and liabilities of the consolidated group with any of the individual corporations. Similarly, consolidated statements are of limited value to a minority stockholder interested in a subsidiary company.

In order to find information about the individual companies comprising the consolidated and unconsolidated company group, users should examine the notes to the consolidated statements where summary statements for significant consolidated and unconsolidated entities may be presented, locate published copies of individual company reports with public minority stockholders, check credit reference services for data, and, if regulated, obtain copies of the company reports from the regulatory authorities.

While using consolidated statements, it is wise to keep several points in mind. First, there may be restrictions on the ability of consolidated subsidiaries to pass cash up to the parent. This may occur if the subsidiary has borrowed money directly. If such restrictions exist, some of the consolidated cash flows might not be available for dividends or reinvestment in other subsidiaries. Restricted cash flow is less valuable than unrestricted cash flow.

Second, the equity method includes the income of unconsolidated investee companies in the consolidate income, but none of the investee companies' sales, expenses, or balance sheet items are included in the consolidated statements. This can distort the significance of certain financial ratios. For example, if the unconsolidated entities' income is included in consolidated net income but their sales are excluded from consolidated sales, the ratio of consolidated net income to consolidated sales may not represent management's ability to generate profit from sales. Similarly, the level of financial safety indicated by the ratio of consolidated net income to consolidated net interest expense will be distorted since the unconsolidated entities' interest expense is not included in the consolidated interest expense, but their income is included in consolidated income. Tax rates will also be distorted since equity income is an aftertax figure that is included in the consolidated profit before tax calculation.

These distortions can be overcome in several ways. One is to exclude equity method income of unconsolidated entities from consolidated net income where its inclusion might lead to misleading financial ratio impressions based on consolidated financial ratios. If the unconsolidated entities' net income is excluded from consolidated income, it may also be appropriate in some cases to exclude the asset account investments in unconsolidated entities and adjust retained earnings when calculating ratios that include consolidated total assets and owners' equity. Another approach is to combine the unconsolidated entities' statements with the consolidated statements.

Care must be exercised in using consolidated statements. Financial ratios may not make a lot of sense if a consolidated entity's business is very different from the other businesses included in the consolidated statements. For example, operating ratios based on data in a consolidated income statement for a finance company and a manufacturing company would be meaningless. The revenue items and the appropriate mix of assets and liabilities of each company are not compatible. In some cases, however, a consolidated balance sheet might be very useful for assessing the combined company's level of financial risk, particularly if a consolidated finance subsidiary primarily finances the group's accounts receivable.

The third point to keep in mind when using consolidated statement data for analysis purposes is that while the consolidated sales and expense are not adjusted for any minority interests, minority net income is deducted from the total income of the affiliated companies before arriving at consolidated net income. This deduction is made to determine the net income available to the parent company stockholders. For a ratio analysis focusing on evaluating management's operating performance, such as measuring management's ability to generate profits from sales activities, the consolidated profit before the minority interest deduction is the appropriate figure. It reflects management operating activities and is not influenced by ownership arrangements.

Finally, when incorporating data from consolidated statements into a financial analysis, it is important to remember that equity income related to unconsolidated entities whose financial policies can be influenced by the parent company is more valuable than income related to uncontrolled investee companies. The element of influence gives the parent the ability to determine how the cash flows associated with the equity income will be used.

CASE
4-1

Productos Azteca (A)

In 1933, Javier Ortiz, after inheriting a large fortune, established Productos Azteca, in Madrid, Spain, to manufacture textile products. Between 1933 and 1991, the company prospered and expanded. In 1991, its operations included two foreign and one domestic textile subsidiaries, a private bank, a real estate leasing subsidiary, an electronic company, a finance company, and a farm equipment company. Productos Azteca or one of its subsidiaries established each of these companies and owned substantially all of their outstanding common stock.

In mid-1991, David Ortiz, president and principal stockholder of Productos Azteca, learned that the Royal Decree 1815/1991 would require "full consolidation" for financial reporting purposes. David Ortiz was concerned that this possible accounting development might hurt his plan to make a small public offering sometime in the next few years to a limited number of investors of some of his Productos Azteca common stock. Several members of the Ortiz family thought a wider market holding of their stock would simplify the valuation of their holdings in the company for estate purposes. In 1991, Productos Azteca had outstanding, and in the hands of the Ortiz family, one million shares of common stock.

To date, for internal reporting purposes, Productos Azteca carried its subsidiaries on the parent company's financial statements as an "investment." The investment was measured using the cost method. Productos Azteca had never prepared consolidated statements. David Ortiz believed that he was better able to manage the group of companies by treating each company separately, rather than as a group or even part of a group of companies.

Professor David Hawkins prepared this case as the basis for class discussion rather than to illustrate either effective or ineffective handling of an administrative situation.
Copyright © 1994 by the President and Fellows of Harvard College. Harvard Business School case 194–072.

Mr. Ortiz realized for the purposes of the stock offering he would have to present the company's financial statements on a consolidated basis. However, he was not sure which subsidiaries he would have to consolidate.

In line with Javier Ortiz's often articulated belief that "every tub should stand on its own bottom," it had been the company's practice to reinvest the earnings of its subsidiaries in the subsidiary creating the earnings, to minimize intercompany investment and operating transactions, and to satisfy the needs of Productos Azteca's stockholders for dividends from the current earnings of the parent. To date, the parent had never received dividends from its subsidiaries. For income tax purposes, the company submitted unconsolidated returns. Intercompany transactions were immaterial.

Textile Companies.   Productos Azteca owned three subsidiaries in the textile area: Tejidos de Calidad; Bull Dog Linens Proprietary, Ltd.; and Mohawk Products (Australia), Ltd. Tejidos de Calidad was formed in 1939 to manufacture blankets in Barcelona, Spain. Bull Dog Linens, the company's British subsidiary, was created in 1953 to produce fine linen goods for the British and European markets. Bull Dog's two plants were located in Manchester and Liverpool. During the recent years, repeated labor troubles had plagued Bull Dog Linens. The Australian subsidiary, Mohawk Products (Australia), was formed in 1985 to operate a small specialty textile mill near Sydney, Australia.

Private Banking Company.   In 1939, following a national credit crisis, Javier Ortiz created Banco Union to make private loans to his employees, their relatives, and the many local tradespeople who relied upon the Productos Azteca mill and its employees for their livelihood. Over the years, new companies moved into the mill's neighborhood and the local population increased considerably. Throughout this period, Banco Union expanded its private banking business to include some of these new arrivals.

Since it had been founded, Banco Union had held all of Productos Azteca's cash balances. However, it had never loaned money to its parent or its subsidiaries. This "no loan" practice followed Javier Ortiz's promise to the customers and regulatory authorities that the finance company would avoid conflict-of-interest situations such as lending money to its parent or any of the parent's subsidiaries. As a result, whenever Productos Azteca or its subsidiaries needed financing they obtained it from external sources.

Farm Equipment Company.   In 1937, Javier Ortiz's youngest daughter married John Atkins, the British-born sales vice president for one of the largest farm equipment manufacturers in the country. As a wedding present, Mr. Ortiz used Productos Azteca's cash to buy at a distress price the company's eastern Spanish franchise to distribute and sell the company's products. He made Atkins president of the new company, Controladora Granjas. John Atkins quickly developed an effective system of subdistributors, and the company made progress, despite the unfavorable state of the farm economy.

In early 1938, the franchise became worthless when the franchiser went bankrupt. Aware of the growing threat of war in Europe, John Atkins bought the assets of the franchiser at book value, with the expectation that in the event of war, Controladora Granjas could manufacture tanks and small arms profitably. Productos Azteca guaranteed the loans to finance this acquisition. Accordingly, during World War II, the company manufactured farm equipment, tanks, and small arms, and its wartime profits were used to extinguish the acquisition loans.

Finance Company.   In early 1988, Controladora Granjas created a wholly owned finance subsidiary, Financiera Consolidada, to finance the company's credit sales to dealers. Beginning in 1987, Controladora Granjas had begun a major program to increase both the number of its dealers and their inventory levels. As part of this program, the company sold equipment to its dealers on extremely favorable credit terms. In turn, Controladora Granjas sold its dealers' accounts receivable at a discount to Financiera Consolidada. As part of this arrangement, the banks lending to Financiera Consolidada forced Controladora Granjas to agree to take back any dealer receivable falling in default.

Electronics Company.   In early 1990, Productos Azteca bought a patent covering a new technique for manufacturing electronic interconnect systems. In order to exploit this patent, Productos Azteca established a new company called Electron. Within six months, the company was in business and rapidly developed a market for its product.

Real Estate.   Electron leased its building from Alternativa, Bienes Raices, a wholly owned subsidiary of Electron. In 1991, the real estate company did not have any other business. Sometime in the future, however, David Ortiz planned to extend the company's activities in the real estate area to include some form of non-Productos Azteca business.

Exhibit 1 presents the profits after taxes of Productos Azteca and its subsidiaries for the period 1982–1991E, inclusive. Exhibit 2 shows condensed balance sheets for Productos Azteca and its subsidiaries as of December 31, 1991E and 1990, respectively.

In addition to Productos Azteca's current holdings, Ortiz was contemplating a 3.1% investment in CESPA, a large publicly traded Spanish company. This would be the group's first major investment in a public company. CESPA's projected 1991 earnings and dividends were Pta 15.8 billion and Pta 3.6 billion, respectively.

EXHIBIT 1   Productos Azteca and Subsidiaries Profits after Taxes, 1982–1991E
(100 millions of peseta)

	1991E	1990	1989	1988	1987	1986	1985	1984	1983	1982
Productos Azteca	4.2	4.5	4.1	4.5	3.2	3.1	5.0	4.7	4.8	4.2
Tejidos de Calidad	2.9	3.2	3.1	2.9	1.9	1.4	2.9	2.8	2.7	2.6
Banco Union	0.5	0.4	0.3	0.2	0.1	0.1	0.2	0.1	0.2	0.1
Controladora Granjas	2.8	2.9	3.9	1.9	(0.4)	(1.0)	3.4	3.7	3.6	2.4
Bull Dog Linens	(0.4)	(0.6)	0.4	0.7	0.6	0.4	0.5	0.4	0.1	0.1
Mohawk (Australia)	2.5	1.9	1.3	(0.6)	0.8	0.9	(0.4)			
Financiera Consolidada	0.2	0.2	0.2	0.1						
Electron	(0.6)	(1.5)								
Alternativa, Bienes Raices	0.1	0.0								

Exhibit 2 **Productos Azteca and Subsidiaries Condensed Balance Sheets**
(100 millions of peseta)

December 31, 1990

	Productos Azteca	Tejidos de Calidad	Banco Union	Controladora Granjas	Bull Dog Linens	Mohawk (Australia)	Financiera Consolidada	Electron	Alternativa, Bienes Raices
Assets									
Cash	3.8	2.3	4.9	1.7	0.9	1.2	0.7	0.8	0.1
Accounts (loans) receivable	8.7	5.4	77.0	-0-	1.4	4.0	30.7	1.8	-0-
Investments in subsidiaries (cost method)	36.0	-0-	-0-	2.5	-0-	-0-	-0-	0.5	-0-
Other assets	81.3	69.2	10.2	48.4	7.1	12.5	2.3	6.8	3.2
Total assets	129.8	76.9	92.1	52.6	9.4	17.7	33.7	9.9	3.3
Equities									
Accounts payable (deposits)	5.7	5.8	81.2	3.1	1.3	2.0	-0-	2.1	-0-
Other current liabilities	8.7	2.7	2.3	3.6	0.7	1.8	0.7	4.3	0.3
Long-term debt[a]	-0-	-0-	-0-	-0-	-0-	5.0	30.0	-0-	2.5
Capital stock[a]	50.0	10.0	3.5	8.5	4.0	5.0	2.5	5.0	0.5
Retained earnings	65.4	58.4	5.1	37.4	3.4	3.9	0.5	(1.5)	0.0
Total equities	129.8	76.9	92.1	52.6	9.4	17.7	33.7	9.9	3.3

December 31, 1991E

	Productos Azteca	Tejidos de Calidad	Banco Union	Controladora Granjas	Bull Dog Linens	Mohawk (Australia)	Financiera Consolidada	Electron	Alternativa, Bienes Raices
Assets									
Cash	4.2	2.1	5.2	1.4	0.7	1.3	0.6	0.7	0.1
Accounts (loans) receivable	9.2	5.2	76.9	-0-	1.5	4.3	32.3	1.9	-0-
Investment in subsidiaries (cost method)	36.0	-0-	-0-	2.5	-0-	-0-	-0-	0.5	-0-
Other assets	80.7	72.7	12.7	51.3	6.7	15.0	2.2	6.5	3.1
Total assets	130.1	80.0	94.8	55.2	8.9	20.6	35.1	9.6	3.2
Equities									
Accounts payable (deposits)	4.9	6.2	83.3	2.7	1.5	2.3	-0-	3.7	-0-
Other current liabilities	7.7	2.5	2.4	3.8	0.4	1.9	0.7	3.0	0.2
Long-term debt	-0-	-0-	-0-	-0-	-0-	5.0	31.2	-0-	2.4
Capital stock[a]	50.0	10.0	3.5	8.5	4.0	5.0	2.5	5.0	0.5
Retained earnings	67.5	61.3	5.6	40.2	3.0	6.4	0.7	(2.1)	0.1
Total equities	130.1	80.0	94.8	55.2	8.9	20.6	35.1	9.6	3.2

[a]Original investment

EXHIBIT 3   Summary of Royal Decree 1815/1991

Consolidated financial statements should normally be prepared on a fully consolidated basis. Subsidiaries can be excluded from consolidation if:

- It is immaterial to presenting a true and fair view of the group.
- Conditions exist that restrict the parent company's ability to exercise its right to the subsidiary's assets or management of the company.
- Including the subsidiary in the consolidated accounts would be too costly or would unduly delay publication of the group accounts.
- The subsidiary is for sale or the parent intends to sell it.
- The subsidiary's activities are so different that its inclusion in the group accounts on a full consolidation basis would be contrary to the purpose of consolidated accounts.

Companies excluded from consolidation because their activities are so different must be included in consolidated accounts using the equity method if the parent has considerable influence over the excluded subsidiary. A voting interest of 20% or more is assumed to give the parent considerable influence over the excluded subsidiary. For excluded companies listed on the Stock Exchange, an ownership of a 3% voting interest is sufficient to require use of the equity method. In the care of jointly owned companies, the equity method or proportionate consolidation may be used to include the joint venture in the group accounts.[1]

---

[1]Begona Gine Merchausti, "The Spanish Accounting Framework," *European Accounting Review*, 1993, 2, 379–386.

A summary of Royal Decree 1815/1991 is presented in **Exhibit 3.**

Questions

1. Under the existing Spanish accounting principles, what consolidation policy should Mr. Ortiz adopt if he issued public statements for Productos Azteca? How would adopting these standards change the company's financial statement? Give examples. What would be the principal differences between these statements and statements prepared using the FASB's consolidation accounting standard? _____

2. Assuming that you are not constrained by any accounting principles, what subsidiaries do you think Mr. Ortiz ought to include in the consolidated statements presented in the prospectus given to potential outside investors? _____

3. Do you think it makes sense for the FASB to require consolidation of all controlled investee companies? _____

4. Assume the company sold 50% of its stock in Mohawk (Australia) to a joint venture partner. How should Productos Azteca's joint venture interest be reflected in the Productos Azteca consolidated statements? Would you change your decision if the joint venture was jointly controlled? If Productos Azteca had sole control? _____

CASE
4-2

Productos Azteca (B)

Royal Decree 1815/1991 required "full consolidation" for financial reporting by Spanish companies. David Ortiz, president and principal stockholder of Productos Azteca, a Spanish operating and holding corporation, was concerned about this new law's impact on his plans for a small public issue of his company's common stock. Currently, Productos Azteca only prepared parent company statements. The cost method was used to account for the parent company's various subsidiaries in these statements.

David Ortiz was unfamiliar with consolidation accounting. In order to understand the accounting mechanics and financial ratio implications of consolidated statements, David Ortiz asked his chief accountant to prepare a short presentation illustrating the preparation of consolidated statements.

Illustrative Case

The chief accountant intended to use the following case example to illustrate consolidation accounting.

> Company P purchased 80% of the outstanding capital stock of Company S from individual stockholders for 290 million pesetas, cash on January 1, 1987. On this date, the retained earnings of Company S were 30 million pesetas.
>
> Company S was primarily, but not exclusively, engaged in marketing goods purchased from Company P. Company S's purchases from Company P during the year 1991 were 1,200 million pesetas. The inventory held by Company S at the beginning or the close of the year did not include any merchandise acquired from Company P. On December 31, 1991, the balance due to Company P for these intercompany purchases was 280 million pesetas.
>
> All plant and equipment owned by Company S was acquired for cash from Company P on January 1, 1989, and has been depreciated on the basis of its estimated life of 10 years, using the straight-line method without salvage value. In 1989, Company P recorded a $50 million profit on the sale of these fixed assets to its subsidiary.

Professor David F. Hawkins prepared this case as the basis for class discussion rather than to illustrate either effective or ineffective handling of an administrative situation.
Copyright © 1994 by the President and Fellows of Harvard College. Harvard Business School case 194–073.

EXHIBIT 1   Company P and Subsidiary Company S Working Papers for Consolidated Statements for the Year Ended December 31, 1991
(millions of pesetas; parentheses indicate deductions)

	Company P	Company S	Adjustments and Eliminations Dr.	Cr.	Consolidated Statements
Income Statement					
Sales	1,500	1,800			
Cost of sales	(900)	(1,400)			
	600	400			
Depreciation	(40)	(20)			
Operating expenses	(440)	(290)			
Net income from operations	120	90			
Dividend income	24				
Minority net income					
Goodwill amortization					
Net income	144	90			
Retained Earnings Statement					
Retained earnings, Jan. 1, 1991					
Company P	248				
Company S		70			
Net income (as above)	144	90			
Dividends:					
Company P	(72)				
Company S		(30)			
Retained earnings December 31, 1991	320	130			
Balance Sheet					
Cash	110	150			
Accounts receivable (net)	375	410			
Inventories	310	75			
Plant and equipment	885	200			
Less: accumulated depreciation	(265)	(60)			
Investment in Company S (at cost)	290				
Goodwill					
Total	1,705	775			
Accounts payable	385	345			
Minority interest					
Capital stock:					
Company P	1,000				
Company S		300			
Retained earnings (as above)	320	130			
Total	1,705	775			

A 10% cash dividend was declared and paid by Company S on its outstanding capital stock on July 1, 1991.

Financial statements of Company P and of Company S are presented in vertical form on the accompanying worksheet (**Exhibit 1**) to facilitate assembly of information for consolidation statements.

Using this illustrative case and ignoring taxes the chief accountant intended in his presentation to David Ortiz to:

1. Complete the worksheet and prepare
    a. A consolidated income statement.
    b. A consolidated retained earnings statement.
    c. A consolidated balance sheet.
2. Compare the financial condition of Company P on an unconsolidated basis with that presented by the consolidated statements. His planned comparison included computations of
    a. Working capital (current assets–current liabilities).
    b. Total assets.
    c. Long-term capital.
    d. Any other ratios he thought significant.
3. Compare the profitability of Company P on an unconsolidated basis with that shown by the consolidated statements.
4. Discuss with David Ortiz the significance of consolidated statements to
    a. A stockholder of Company P.
    b. A minority stockholder of Company S.

To simplify the presentation the chief accountant decided to assume that Company P used the cost method to account on its book for Company S. This was consistent with Productos Azteca's present accounting policy. A 26-year goodwill amortization period was also assumed.

Question

1. Complete the chief accountant's illustrative presentation.

Statement of Cash Flows

CHAPTER

5

The Statement of Cash Flows provides information on the changes in the cash position of a company over some period of time. An attractive characteristic of this financial statement is that it works with a tangible variable—cash. This is in contrast with the income statement, which measures performance using accrual accounting.

Each financial statement provides unique information relevant to the analysis of a firm's present and future health. The Statement of Cash Flows is especially helpful in assessing questions where cash flows are important. These include the following:

- Firm's ability to meet its current and long-term cash obligations.
- Firm's needs for external financing and the use of its long-term debt.
- Analysis of credit proposals.
- Valuation of firms.
- Bankruptcy assessments.
- Ability of the firm's operations to generate cash.

The statement tries to achieve these objectives by requiring firms to summarize the transactions affecting their cash and cash equivalents[1] into operating, investing and financing activities. The separation of operating activities from the other activities provides a potent new accounting number for the manager and the financial analyst to examine: the cash flow from operations (CFO). Differences between net income and CFO, both in levels and trends, can provide valuable information on the firm's quality of earnings as well as its strategies in funding its capital needs. Two different methods are available to present a summary of transactions related to operating activities: the *indirect method* and

---

Doctoral Candidate Antonio Dávila revised this note under the supervision of Professor Robert Simons. It is based on an earlier note by Visiting Professor Bala G. Dharan.
Copyright © 1995 by the President and Fellows of Harvard College. Harvard Business School teaching note 196–108.

[1]See **Exhibit 1** for the definition of cash used by FASB.

EXHIBIT 1   Definition of Cash and Cash Equivalents

The FASB, in Statement No. 95, provides fairly rigid criteria for what constitutes cash and cash equivalents, the basic unit of the statement of cash flows, in order to achieve consistency and comparability (i.e., in order to facilitate comparisons over time and across companies). Cash and cash equivalents are defined as short-term, highly liquid investments that are both readily convertible to cash and have original maturities of three months or less. Examples:

- Investments in government securities such as U.S. treasury bills and treasury bonds, with maturities of 3 months or less at the time of purchase.
- Commercial paper, money market funds, and international currency accounts.

    The following are not considered cash equivalents:

- Investments in corporate equity and debt securities, even if they are readily marketable.
- Government securities with more than three months of maturity at the time of purchase, even if they have less than three months of maturity at balance sheet date. (This rule seems illogical, but it is consistent with the historical cost system.)
- Securities held by financial institutions in their *trading accounts* rather than cash management accounts.

---

the *direct method.* The first one reconciles net income with CFO, while the second provides a summary of transactions affecting the cash of the company with no reference to the income statement. Both, however provide identical answers.

It is important to notice that *noncash* transactions are excluded from the cash flow statement. For example, conversion of long-term debt into equity would not be reported in the statement of cash flows since no cash is involved. The company would instead append a note detailing such transactions.

The Statement of Cash Flows is a required statement in most countries. The various formats used throughout the world are all based on the same underlying principles, and the differences are easily mastered once the basic skills to understand the statement are developed.

In the next section the three parts of the Statement of Cash Flows are presented:

- Cash from operating activities (*indirect* and *direct* methods).
- Cash from investing activities, and
- Cash from financing activities.

The following section takes a closer look at the indirect and direct methods of presenting cash flow from operating activities. Then, we review the preparation of the cash flows from investing activities and from financing activities. The final section provides some background on various techniques used to analyze this financial statement.

Basic Structure of the Statement of Cash Flows

We can think of the cash flow statement as an expanded version of the company's cash account, specially formatted to separate all entries into one of three types of activities: operating, investing, and financing. The cash flow statement thus highlights whether the cash came from (or went to) operating activities, investing activities or financing activities. Each of these groups of activities is described below:

Operating.   Activities primarily related to the firm's ongoing ability to generate cash from operations and the resultant changes in its operating working capital items. This would include information on cash receipts from customers for sales and services and cash payments related to vendors, employees, taxes, and interest. This information is presented using either the direct or the indirect method as described in the next section. Interest payment is classified as operating cash flow even though the underlying borrowing and repayment are financing cash flows.[2] The "bottom line" from the "operating" section of the cash flow statement gives the cash from operations (CFO) variable.

Investing.   Activities primarily related to changes in noncurrent assets. This includes information on capital expenditures to acquire assets and proceeds from sale of noncurrent assets. Because of the attempt to restrict the cash flow statement to cash transactions, capital expenditures (or purchase of entities) not involving the cash account may not be fully disclosed here[3], and the financial analyst or the manager must look elsewhere for supplementary information on noncash transactions. Only the cash payments made at the time of purchase or soon before or after are considered investing cash flows. Moreover, the subsequent principal payments made on loans used to buy assets are considered financing cash flows.

Financing.   Activities primarily related to changes in borrowings and owners' equity. This includes information on cash proceeds from issuing equity and short-term or long-term debt, and cash outflow due to repurchase of stocks and payment or repurchase of bonds. Dividend payment is a financing cash flow.[4] Short-term borrowings such as bank loans are considered financing cash flows even though they appear in the current liability section and thus are part of working capital.

Computing Cash Flow from Operations

Cash flow from operations can be computed and reported using one of two equivalent procedures. Under the *indirect method,* the company starts with net income and shows the additions and subtractions that are needed to remove the effects of accruals on income in order to get the cash flow from operations. This method also highlights how changes in operating (current) assets and liabilities such as inventory and accounts payable can affect cash flows and company performance. Under the *direct method,* the company tries to provide information to answer basic cash flow questions such as:

---

[2]Interest payments are classified as either operating or financing flows in different countries.

[3]For example, acquiring a company through an exchange of shares will not appear in the Statement of Cash Flows because no cash is involved in the transaction.

[4]Here again, dividends are reported as either operating or financing cash flows in different countries.

How much cash did we get from customers during the period covered? How much cash did we pay to our vendors and employees? How much did we pay in taxes and interest? The resulting cash flow data are easy to interpret, especially for a novice or a nonfinancial manager. However, many companies argue that investors benefit more from the indirect method's format since it focuses on explaining the differences between net income (which is closely followed) and cash flow from operations. Many companies also argue that a reconciliation between net income and cash flow from operations is more informative to an investor or manager trying to understand the quality and usefulness of the income number.

Despite the simplicity of the direct method format, most companies continue to prepare and report the cash flow statement using the indirect method. In a recent survey of 600 companies, 585 used the indirect method and only 15, or 2.5 percent, used the direct method.[5] In addition to the arguments presented above, a practical reason for the failure of the direct method to catch on may be that, under FASB Statement No. 95, companies using the direct method must also present data under the indirect method. By contrast, companies using the indirect method do not have to present supplementary data under the direct method.

An illustration of the indirect and direct methods is given in **Exhibit 2.**[6] Under the **indirect method,** companies start with the reported net income and adjust it for various accrual items that did not produce or consume cash. More specifically, the following accrual-related adjustments are made to net income:

1. Add back expenses and losses that did not use cash, and subtract revenues and gains that did not produce cash. Examples in **Exhibit 2** are:

   • Depreciation is added back because it is an accounting item that did not require the use of cash and yet is deducted in computing the net income. A similar reasoning is used for goodwill amortization.

   • Premium amortization is subtracted because it is a noncash income-increasing account.

   • Gain on sale of noncurrent asset is subtracted because the gain itself is a noncash accrual item. Instead, the actual cash proceeds from the sale are reported in the investing section of the cash flow statement.

2. Add back decreases in operating current assets and increases in operating current liabilities, and subtract increases in operating current assets and decreases in operating current liabilities. (As noted earlier, changes in short-term debt are considered financing cash flows and are excluded from these adjustments.) Examples in **Exhibit 2** are:

   • Decrease in inventory is added back because this portion of cost of goods sold did not involve a cash transaction this period. In other words, this amount was transferred from inventory to cost of goods sold without any

---

[5]*Accounting Trends and Techniques,* American Institute of Certified Public Accountants (1993).
[6]**Exhibit 3** presents the complete Statement of Cash Flows for the example used as illustration.

EXHIBIT 2   Illustration of Indirect and Direct Methods of Computing CFO

Income statement

Sales	$2,214,500
Cost of goods sold	(931,100)
Depreciation	(200,000)
Goodwill amortization	(103,800)
Selling and general expenses	(420,000)
Gain on sale of assets	19,900
Interest expense (including premium amortization of $3,500)	(88,500)
Income tax expense	(170,000)
Net income	$ 321,000

Additional data on changes in operating working capital items (from the balance sheet, see **Exhibit 3**):

Increase in accounts receivable	$ 37,700
Increase in accounts payable	$ 9,900
Decrease in inventory	$ 7,400
Increase in tax payable	$ 2,000
Increase in prepaid expenses	$ 16,800

Cash Flow from Operating Activities (CFO)

Indirect method:

Net Income	$ 321,000
Noncash adjustments:	
Depreciation	200,000
Goodwill amortization	103,800
Premium amortization	(3,500)
Decrease in inventory	7,400
Increase in accounts payable	9,900
Increase in tax payable	2,000
Increase in accounts receivable	(37,700)
Increase in prepaid expenses	(16,800)
Gain on sale of assets	(19,900)
Cash flow from operations	$ 566,200

Direct method

Collection from customers (2,214,500 − 37,700)		$2,176,800
Payment to suppliers (931,100 − 7,400 − 9,900)		(913,800)
Other operating payments (512,000 + 16,800)	(528,800)	
Income tax payment (170,000 − 2,000)	(168,000)	
Cash flow from operations	$566,200	

Note how the direct method items are computed by regrouping the reconciliation items in the indirect method with the appropriate income statement items.

---

cash expenditure, so it needs to be "added back" to net income to get the cash flow for the period.

- Increase in accounts payable is added back because the cash payments to vendors (implied in the cost of goods sold number) is overstated by this amount.

- Increase in accounts receivable is subtracted because this portion of sales of the period has not yet been collected.

Some other common additions and subtractions made to net income related to noncurrent assets and liabilities are:

- Amortization of intangibles (add).
- Bad debt expense (add).
- Amortization of bond discount (add) or premium (subtract).
- Increase in deferred tax liability (add) or asset (subtract).
- Loss on sale of noncurrent assets (add).
- Undistributed profits of subsidiaries accounted for using the equity method (subtract).
- Special charges for restructuring or asset impairment (add).

Alternatively, under the **direct method,** companies calculate CFO by disclosing major classes of cash receipts and payments, including the following:

- Cash collected from customers.
- Cash paid to suppliers and employees.
- Interest and dividends received.
- Interest paid.
- Other operating cash receipts and payments.
- Income taxes paid.

Even though some companies have argued that the direct method is hard to implement and is procedurally more complex than the indirect method, the direct method items listed above can be easily computed by rearranging the various adjustment lines reported under the indirect method, as shown below:

- Cash collected from customers = Sales − Increase in accounts receivable.
- Cash paid to suppliers and employees = Cost of sales (before depreciation) + Increase in inventory − Increase in accounts payable − Increase in wages payable.
- Interest paid = Interest expense − Increase in interest payable − Decrease in bond discount + Decrease in bond premium.
- Other operating cash flows = Selling and general expense + Increase in prepaid expense − Increase in accrued liabilities.
- Income taxes paid = Tax expense − Increase in tax payable − Increase in deferred tax liability.

Computing Cash Flow from Investing and Financing Activities

With CFO from operations now computed, cash flows from investing and financing activities can be computed and reported using a procedure similar to the one used in the direct method. The idea is to provide a summary of the various cash transactions involving primarily noncurrent assets and borrowings and owners' equity.

Exhibit 3 presents the complete Statement of Cash Flows for the example that is being used as illustration. In this example, cash flow from investing activities includes the actual cash proceeds from the sale of equipment. The other accounting adjustments related to this transaction do not appear because they do not involve cash. The journal entry in the company's accounting records is:

EXHIBIT 3   Illustration of How Balance Sheet Differences Are Accounted for on a Statement of Cash Flows

	Beginning Balance	Ending Balance	Difference	Where to Trace in the Statement of Cash Flows
Assets				
Cash		$ 107,300	$ 53,300	Outcome of SCF
Accounts receivable	$ 372,600	410,300	37,700	CFO
Inventory	324,400	317,000	(7,400)	CFO
Prepaid expenses	0	16,800	16,800	CFO
PP&E	1,945,400	2,100,300	154,900	See note 1
Account depreciation	(800,400)	(905,400)	(105,000)	See note 1
Goodwill	875,300	771,500	(103,800)	CFO
Total assets	$2,771,300	$2,817,800		
Liabilities and Owners' Equity				
Accounts payable	$ 43,800	$ 53,700	$ (9,900)	CFO
Taxes payable	0	2,000	(2,000)	CFO
Notes payable	290,200	300,300	(10,100)	Financing activities
Bonds payable	1,100,000	900,000	200,000	Financing activities
Premium on bonds	54,000	50,500	3,500	CFO
Common stock	500,000	520,000	(20,000)	See note 2
Retained earnings	783,300	991,300	(208,000)	See note 3
Total liabilities and owners' equity	$2,771,300	$2,817,800	0	

Statement of Cash Flows (SCF)

Operating activities
Cash from operating activities (from Exhibit 2) . . . . $ 566,200

Investing activities
Sale of equipment   70,000
Purchase of equipment . . . .   (300,000)
Cash from investing activities . . . . $(230,000)

Financing activities
Proceeds from notes payable . . . . $ 10,100
Repayment of bonds . . . .   (200,000)
Dividend payment . . . .   (93,000)
Cash from financing activities . . . . $(282,900)

Increase in cash . . . . $ 53,300

EXHIBIT 3   (Continued)

Additional Information Needed to Prepare the Statement of Cash Flows.

1. Fixed Assets and Depreciation

(a) Sale of noncurrent asset. An asset with a purchase price of $145,100 and accumulated depreciation of $95,000 was sold for $70,000 for a gain of $19,900. The entry is:

Dr. Cash	$70,000	
Accumulated depreciation	$95,000	
Cr. Property, plant and equipment		$145,100
Gain on sale of equipment		$19,900

(b) Purchase of equipment: $300,000. (This information, as well as the data used above, will not be available from the balance sheet data alone, and must be obtained from company records.)

Property, plant and equipment	$300,000
Cash	$300,000

(c) Depreciation expense = $200,000 (from income statement)

(d) Balance sheet changes can be reconciled as follows:

$$\text{PP\&E} = \$300,000 \text{ (purchases)} - \$145,100 \text{ (sale)} = \underline{\$154,900}$$

$$\text{Accumulated depreciation} = \$200,000 - \$95,000 = \underline{\$105,000}$$

($200,000 is depreciation expense and $95,000 is reduction in accumulated depreciation related to the disposal of asset)

2. Common stock

Stock dividends issued with a market value of $20,000.* The balance sheet entry is:

Dr. Retained earnings	$20,000	
Cr. Common stock (par value and additional capital)		$20,000

3. Retained earnings can be reconciled as follows:

Net income	$321,000	(from income statement)
Cash dividends*	(93,000)	
Stock dividends	(20,000)	
	$208,000	

---

*This information is also not in the balance sheet and income statement, and must be obtained from company records.

Cash	$70,000	
Accumulated depreciation	$95,000	
Property, plant and equipment		$145,100
Gain on sale of equipment		$19,900

Adjustments to accumulated depreciation and to property, plant and equipment are not recorded in the Statement of Cash Flows. Only the "gain on sale of equipment" appears in the *indirect* method under CFO because it is a noncash accrual adjustment that is included in net income.

Purchase of equipment in the amount of $300,000 is the other cash flow related to investing activities. Were the firm to finance the purchase of the equipment through a loan from a bank, the cash flow statement would reflect two transactions, a cash inflow from the bank reported in cash flows from financing activities, and a cash outflow for the payment of the equipment.

Cash flow from investing activities (**Exhibit 3**) reflects an increase in notes payable as a source of cash, which means that the company obtained cash from the issue of notes payable. It also records the use of cash to repay bonds and the payment of cash dividends. The $20,000 stock dividend is not reported in the statement because the transaction does not involve any cash. The journal entry is:

> Dr. Retained earnings $20,000
>   Cr. Common stock $20,000

The summary measure at the bottom of the Statement of Cash Flows is the change in cash for the year, which is just the addition of the cash generated (used) by the three types of activities. This measure is equal to the change in the cash account presented in the balance sheets (**Exhibit 3**).

Financial Analysis Using the Cash Flow Statement

A careful analysis of the cash flow statement can provide valuable information on the company's operating strategies, in addition to information on the quality of its earnings. A key question is whether the capital expenditure needs of the company are being met by its internal cash flow generation. For example, PepsiCo in 1994 had $3.72 billion of cash flow from operations and had $2.25 billion of capital spending. It also paid out $540 million in cash dividends to its shareholders. Its cash flow from operations was thus more than adequate to fund its entire capital spending and dividend needs. The difference between cash flow from operations and needed capital expenditure is sometimes known as free cash flow. In contrast to PepsiCo, fast-growing companies and companies with less profitable operations would often have negative free cash flows, necessitating the need for additional borrowings or equity issues to keep the company going. The cash flow from operations can also indicate whether the company has adequate cash flows to meet its interest obligations and other fixed commitments. Indeed, many academic studies have found cash flow from operations to be a useful predictor of bankruptcy.

Some commonly cited financial ratios based on cash flow from operations are:

- Cash Flow per Share (CFPS) = (CFO − Preferred dividends)/Weighted common shares.
- Cash Flow Return on Investment (CFROI) = CFO before interest and taxes/ Total investments. For after-tax CFROI, multiply the ratio by 1 minus tax rate.
- Cash Flow Return on Equity (CFROE) = CFO/Average stockholders' equity.

Cash Flow ROI, or CFROI, is a better performance yardstick than earnings-based ROI to evaluate the cash-flow–generating capacity of individual business units within a company and to select new projects. The denominator of CFROI is the cumulative cash invested, not the accrual-based total asset measure used in the traditional ROI. Another performance yardstick based on CFO is net cash contribution, computed by subtracting from CFO an estimated cost of equity capital. It is thus similar to the concept of residual income or economic value added (EVA). Net cash contribution is particularly useful when comparing companies or projects that have very different debt-equity mixes.

What should the financial analyst or the manager look for in analyzing the cash flow statement? In general, the relationship between earnings and CFO provides valuable information on the quality of reported earnings. For example, the following situations might call for further investigation of the quality of earnings:

- CFO is large, but it is due to inventory reductions or one-time nonoperating items. This suggests that the current cash flow level is not sustainable.
- Earnings and CFO are both positive, but CFO is less than earnings. This raises questions about the accruals that went into the computation of earnings. Items to look for would include unusual nonoperating transactions such as the gain on sale of noncurrent assets.
- Earnings increased relative to last year, but CFO decreased. Here again, earnings growth might have been achieved by means of nonoperating activities such as sale of assets, or by means of accounting changes.
- Dividends are less than earnings but more than CFO. This suggests that the current dividend level might not be sustainable. If new debt is being issued to pay for the dividends, future operating costs would also be higher.

Any changes in the relationship between assets and liabilities can also be discerned from the cash flow statement. For example, the analyst might want to know whether the company is financing its acquisitions with short-term debt or long-term debt. The cash flow statement also provides, unlike the balance sheet, the gross changes in noncurrent assets and liabilities. Thus an analyst might be able to evaluate whether the company is redeploying its assets or changing its business strategies by examining the relationship between noncurrent assets acquired and assets disposed. The balance sheet would only provide the net changes and thus would not reveal the underlying changes in the company's operations.

Northrop Corporation
Statement of Cash Flow

When I first started my career, I viewed myself as a doctor whose purpose was to explain to my patients (shareholders) how their stock was faring. Over time, however, I have come to think of myself as a lab technician. Like a lab technician, I provide Northrop's reports to doctors (financial analysts) who, in turn, report to patients (shareholders). Also, like a lab technician, I want to help financial analysts interpret Northrop's reports by highlighting certain items in the Management Discussion and Analysis section of our annual report (MDA) and by providing new items whenever possible. I am particularly concerned that users and standard-setters frequently confuse the roles of the Statement of Cash Flow (SCF), income statement, and balance sheet and as a result fail to realize the full potential of the SCF in analyzing liquidity and financial flexibility.

Jack Wear, *Director of Financial Reporting and Accounting Policy*

Cash is critical to aerospace companies. Inventory, receivables, and deferred taxes are very important for Northrop and progress payments over inventories is a really big thing! Government inventories and receivables suck up cash and cash flow projections are tough because it is difficult to forecast when deferred taxes will come due. I have my own cash-flow model that is based on numbers from the SCF, balance sheet, and income statement. I use the model's cash flow projections to help predict stock price changes. By analyzing trends in cash flows, I also assess financial flexibility. Will the company have to finance when debt is tight? Will their

This case was prepared by Professor G. Peter Wilson as the basis for class discussion rather than to illustrate either effective or ineffective handling of an administrative situation. The generous assistance of Jack Wear, Northrop's director of financial reporting and accounting policy, is gratefully acknowledged.

balance sheet and cash flow be healthy enough to secure dividends? Will their interest expense increase and kill their earnings?

Cai von Rumohr, *aerospace analyst, Cowen & Company, Boston.*

The key thing in this industry is cash flow, but it is hard to get a handle on. Using numbers from income statements, balance sheets and SCFs, I build an old-fashioned cash flow model. The model accounts for trends in various financial ratios that help me determine when contract payments are forthcoming. A good chunk of cash flow depends on whether the company is meeting contract performance milestones. If progress payments over total inventory is increasing, then the trend in meeting milestones is stable or improving. I use my model to forecast cash balances so that I can estimate future debt levels. I use these forecasts, in turn, to predict interest expense which enters my earnings per share forecast.

Anonymous aerospace analyst at a leading investment firm

Northrop Corporation

Northrop Corporation is an advanced technology corporation that designs and manufactures military aircraft, commercial aircraft subassemblies, missiles and electronic systems. The majority of the company's 1991 sales of $5.69 billion comprised aircraft and aircraft structures. Northrop's major customer is the United States government; its largest single program is the B-2 stealth bomber. The company participated significantly in the U.S. defense build-up of the 1980s, when its revenues doubled and employment increased more than 55 percent. With the end of the Cold War and the shrinking of the defense budget, the company's external environment has changed. Said its 1991 annual report:

> We now are formally and methodically exploring the various directions that we see opening for us in the coming years. . . . at the conclusion of the presently planned B-2 program for 20 operational aircraft, we expect Northrop to have an aerospace business foundation of $3 billion to $4 billion annually on the strength of our present programs and core competencies alone. We expect our financial resources to grow. And we can foresee an equity base able to support more than $2 billion of additional financing, if necessary, to make investments in new technologies, new programs or new businesses to secure our long-term future, inside and outside the defense industry.

Northrop is prime contractor for the B-2. Northrop, the U.S. Air Force, and this nationwide B-2 industrial team were awarded the 1991 Collier Trophy for "the greatest achievement in aeronautics or astronautics in America." As principal subcontractor to McDonnell Douglas Corporation, Northrop produces the center and aft fuselage, twin vertical tails and associated subsystems for the F/A-18, the multi-role attack fighter used by the U.S. Navy and Marine Corps as well as other nations' air forces. The company's F-5 fighter is the most widely used American supersonic aircraft in the world, used in some 30 countries. More than 2,600 F-5s were produced in more than 20 configurations, of which nearly 1,700 are still flying. The Northrop T-38 supersonic jet trainer has been in service for nearly 30 years and its reliability, versatility and safety will enable it to serve as the Air Force's standard basic trainer for another 20 years.

Northrop has been principal subcontractor on Boeing's 747 jetliner since the program began in 1966, building the 153-foot-long fuselage section, cargo and passenger doors and other components. The company expects this program to continue well into the next century. Northrop is also a leader in unmanned vehicle systems, including a stealthy cruise missile now under development, as well as in electronic countermeasures, guidance and navigation systems, sensors, and precision instruments. One program employing its advanced acoustic sensor technologies is a "brilliant" submunition under development called BAT, designed to find and destroy moving tanks and other armored vehicles.

Financial Reporting Awards

Between 1982 and 1987, Northrop won outright or shared the Financial Analysts Federation's award for excellence in corporate reporting in the aerospace industry. While it has not won since, the clarity of its financial reports was again complimented by the awarding committee. In September 1990, and again in 1991 the *Institutional Investor* ranked Northrop's annual report as the best in the Aerospace industry, praising it for providing five years of data and for having an excellent Management Discussion and Analysis (MDA).

Focus on Cash Flow

While Northrop has received kudos from Wall Street for providing honest financial information, analysts find the company a challenge. Over half of Northrop's sales are usually from classified programs and, thus, it is extremely difficult to forecast its financial performance. Wall Street's sensitivity to the exposures associated with classified contracts was amplified in 1988 and 1989 when Northrop sold Wilcox Electric Unit and Northrop Services Inc. and rumors circulated that it might sell its corporate headquarters in Los Angeles. When some analysts suggested that these sales were signals that Northrop needed cash, President and Chief Executive Officer, Kent Kresa, responded:

> We are pruning operations outside our core businesses of aircraft and electronics design and manufacturing. From 1980 to 1985 our employment expanded 56%, a gain of 17,000 workers. Capital outlays and corporate debt built up rapidly as we won new programs that required significant investment while the government imposed company-funded cost sharing. Because we could not explain investments in classified activities, the financial community saw the impact on our operating results as negative surprises.
>
> Northrop's commitment to the future is paying off: the company's indebtedness has peaked at $955 million and should tail off in the near future and disappear in the 1990's. If the same progress payment rate had applied in 1987 as in 1983, its debt would have been $300 million less.[1]

---

[1]*Aviation Week,* May 23, 1988.

Northrop's short-term debt increased dramatically between 1984 and 1987, leaving some analysts concerned that Northrop might get caught in a cash squeeze. Shortly thereafter, the company converted a considerable portion of its short-term debt to long-term by making a private placement of $550 million. At that time, they could have issued additional equity but as Dean Witter aerospace analyst William N. Deatheridge stated, "Jack Campbell [Northrop's senior vice president and chief financial officer] would never stand for an equity or convertible financing. Issuing new equity would dilute the ownership of present shareholders in the bonanza due from the B-2 program."[2]

As the decade was ending and defense budgets were tightening, Northrop's Chairman of the Board, Thomas V. Jones stated, "Northrop is the one company the government will turn to for high-quality, minimal cost systems that will work for the user."[3] In March 1988, one analyst expressed a common view about Northrop, "If management can bring in its current programs, they will earn so much money they will turn out to resemble a bank more than a manufacturing company."[4]

In February, 1992, Phil Friedman of Morgan Stanley said of Northrop, "The company has done an excellent job of reducing its debt . . . For the year, net debt fell by over $400 million, and year-end debt-to-equity of 32% was a vast improvement from 79% at the end of 1990. We expect the debt reduction to continue at a slower pace (about $200 million in 1992), due to strong profitability, depreciation in excess capital spending, and aggressive working capital management."[5]

---

[2]*Ibid.*
[3]*Ibid.*
[4]*Ibid.*
[5]Morgan Stanley, U.S. Investment Research, Feb. 24, 1992.

Questions

1. Compare Northrop's cash from operations and earnings for the years 1987–1991 (See Exhibit 1). What are the major reasons why they differ? _____

2. What information is provided in Northrop's direct SCF? What information is provided in their indirect SCF (or reconciliation)? What is the difference? Which do you prefer and why? _____

3. Prepare a total cash flow statement for 1987–1991. To simplify this task, start with cash from operations and do not spend too much time classifying items. What did you learn about Northrop? How are they financing working capital growth? How are they financing dividends? Has their financial flexibility changed during these five years? What other information would you like to have to make this judgment? _____

4. Jack Wear is concerned that analysts are not taking advantage of Northrop's unique direct SCF format. Do you agree? _____

EXHIBIT 1

$ in millions

Year ended December 31	1991	1990	1989	1988	1987
Operating Activities					
Sources of Cash:					
Cash received from customers					
Progress payments	$2,646.7	$2,618.1	$2,324.0	$2,099.2	$1,794.4
Other collections	3,050.5	2,976.8	2,829.7	3,459.6	3,847.2
Interest received	11.5	2.4	2.8	2.4	1.7
Income tax refunds received	3.1	1.1	.2	2.2	.2
Shareholder litigation settlement	9.0				
Other cash receipts	3.7	17.1	19.3	2.3	3.5
Cash provided by operating activities	5,724.5	5,615.5	5,176.0	5,565.7	5,647.0
Uses of Cash:					
Cash paid to suppliers and employees	4,986.5	5,220.6	4,967.0	5,302.7	5,635.2
Interest paid	85.0	97.1	122.1	150.2	40.7
Fines from settled litigation	10.2	17.0			
Settlement of accrued product support					27.7
Income taxes paid	31.8	13.6	8.0	13.1	9.7
Other cash payments	1.6	1.1	.3	2.7	.9
Cash used in operating activities	5,115.1	5,349.4	5,097.4	5,468.7	5,714.2
Net cash provided by (used in) operating activities	609.4	266.1	78.6	97.0	(67.2)
Investing Activities					
Additions to property, plant and equipment	(117.4)	(121.2)	(186.8)	(254.2)	(294.4)
Proceeds from sale of property, plant and equipment	2.6	252.1	14.3	12.0	29.9
Proceeds from sale of subsidiaries and affiliates			1.1	67.3	
Proceeds from sale of direct financing leases			21.9		
Dividends from affiliate, net of investments	.1	.1		20.7	
Other investing activities	(8.4)	(2.3)	4.8	6.2	2.3
Net cash provided by (used in) investing activities	(123.1)	128.7	(144.7)	(148.0)	(262.2)
Financing Activities					
Borrowings under lines of credit		750.0	783.0	971.0	954.6
Repayment of borrowings under lines of credit		(920.0)	(659.0)	(1,413.6)	(565.9)
Proceeds from issuance of long-term debt				550.0	1.0
Principal payments of long-term debt/capital leases	(400.3)	(.3)	(.4)	(1.4)	(2.8)
Proceeds from issuance (repurchase) of stock	.6				(1.1)
Dividends paid	(56.4)	(56.3)	(56.4)	(56.4)	(56.2)
Net cash provided by (used in) financing activities	(456.1)	(226.6)	67.2	49.6	329.6
Increase (decrease) in cash and cash equivalents	30.2	168.2	1.1	(1.4)	.2
Cash and cash equivalents balance at beginning of year	172.9	4.7	3.6	5.0	4.8
Cash and cash equivalents balance at end of year	$ 203.1	$ 172.9	$ 4.7	$ 3.6	$ 5.0

EXHIBIT 1   **$ in millions**

Year ended December 31	1991	1990	1989	1988	1987
Reconciliation of Net Income (Loss) to Net Cash Provided by (Used in) Operating Activities					
Net income (loss)	$ 200.8	$ 210.4	$ (80.5)	$ 104.2	$ 94.2
Adjustments to reconcile net income (loss) to net cash provided (used):					
Depreciation and amortization	171.3	186.6	220.6	240.8	246.8
Common stock issued to employees	4.1	3.7	5.1	4.8	5.3
Amortization of restricted award shares	1.7	1.3	4.9	3.4	4.1
Loss (gain) on disposals of property, plant and equipment	6.1	(103.0)	8.6	(.6)	(11.2)
Cumulative effect on prior years of changes in accounting principles for					
Income taxes	(20.3)			(135.1)	
Retiree health care and life insurance benefits	87.7				
Non-cash retiree benefit cost (income)	13.5	(53.3)	7.3	2.7	
Amortization of deferred gain on sale/leaseback	(2.9)	(2.3)			
Loss (gain) on sale of subsidiaries and affiliates			6.8	(12.7)	
Gain on sale of direct financing leases			(12.9)		
Undistributed income of affiliates				(4.3)	(3.8)
Decrease (increase) in					
Accounts receivable	1,058.2	(1,085.4)	(1,209.0)	(1,034.4)	(750.4)
Inventoried costs	122.6	49.7	(85.9)	(5.1)	26.6
Prepaid expenses	(7.9)	.4	(4.3)	5.0	(3.4)
Refundable income taxes		8.1	1.2	(9.3)	
Increase (decrease) in					
Progress payments	(1,054.0)	1,204.2	1,137.5	790.4	292.6
Accounts payable and accruals	115.8	(211.2)	54.2	64.0	46.3
Provisions for contract losses	(99.5)	(41.0)	59.9	145.6	(58.9)
Deferred income taxes	.1	93.3	(34.0)	(41.7)	50.2
Income taxes payable	12.9	6.2	.8	(20.5)	(8.4)
Other non-cash transactions	(.8)	(1.6)	(1.7)	(.2)	2.8
Net cash provided by (used in) operating activities	$ 609.4	$ 266.1	$ 78.6	$ 97.0	$ (67.2)

PART THREE

Role of Certified Public Accountants' Opinion in Corporate Reporting and Analysis

Independent Auditor's Report

The financial statements published by management are usually accompanied by a signed auditor's report. It means that a member of a licensed profession, who is morally bound to exercise competent independent judgment, has examined management's financial statements to the extent necessary and stakes his or her professional reputation upon the opinion that the financial statements do or do not present fairly the financial position, results of operations, and cash flows of the company. The criteria used to judge the professional competence of the audit are "generally accepted auditing standards." The criteria for forming an opinion on the fairness of the statements taken as a whole are "generally accepted accounting principles."

The auditor's report expresses a professional opinion. For many years, it was customary for auditors to use the phrase "we hereby certify" in their reports on financial statements. Even today the term "auditor's certificate" is used interchangeably with "auditor's report." This outdated terminology may be partly responsible for the confusion as to the nature of the auditor's work. The professional auditor may well be certified by a state licensing board, but the auditor does not certify financial statements.

Statement users must rely heavily on the auditor's opinion since they cannot independently verify management's assertions, estimates, and judgments embodied in financial statements. Consequently, it is important that statement users know what an audit report does and does not mean, as well as the procedures used by auditors to reach their opinions on financial statements. Auditor's opinions are very helpful to statement users when they are prepared by competent auditors who feel a responsibility to those who must rely upon their work and management's representation. Occasionally, audit examinations are conducted by incompetent auditors, and their opinions can be very misleading. To protect themselves against these auditors, experienced statement analysts seldom

Professor David Hawkins prepared this note as a basis for class discussion.
Copyright © 1995 by the President and Fellows of Harvard College. Harvard Business School teaching note 195–184.

accept the auditor's opinion as sufficient assurance without first making their own assessment of the company's quality of earnings, management's accounting estimates and judgments, and reporting company's ability to meet maturing financial obligations. In addition, astute statement users are aware of corporate conditions that are likely to lead to financial statement fraud. When they encounter these conditions, statement users must exercise caution when relying on the auditor's opinion.

The Auditing Profession

The characteristics which make the auditor opinion on published financial statements useful are independence and competence. The role of the auditor will continue to be significant only to the extent that the public continues to attribute these qualities to the profession of public accountancy.

Auditors have a code of professional conduct prepared by the AICPA that sets high standards of ethical behavior in the conduct of their professional activities. Auditors adhering to this code should act in a way that serves the public interest, honors the public trust, and displays professional independence and competence.

From the public's point of view, independence is perhaps the most important of the auditor's characteristics. A basic conflict arises in an audit engagement because the client whose financial statements are examined pays for the auditor's services. To be independent, professional auditors must be prepared to give higher priority to their responsibilities to third-party readers of financial reports than to their continued services to a particular client. This attitude of public responsibility and service is an essential characteristic of a profession and distinguishes it from commercial enterprise. By achieving this sense of public responsibility, public accountants have earned the right to call auditing a profession.

Competence is the second characteristic which the auditor must achieve, maintain, and apply with due care. Professional accountants offering services to the public must comply with the licensing requirements of the states in which they practice. Public accountancy boards are appointed by the state to administer each state's public accounting regulations. Those who wish to become certified public accountants must pass an examination given by each state board, that is prepared and graded by the American Institute of Certified Public Accountants (AICPA). These licensing requirements protect the public interest by restricting the practice of public accountancy to those who have a demonstrated proficiency in auditing and accounting.

The AICPA is a national organization whose members are subject to a code of professional ethics adopted voluntarily and enforced by the group. Training and professional development programs are sponsored continually. The institute has, as the voice of the accounting profession, assumed the position of leadership in the development of auditing standards. Its publications include the *Journal of Accountancy, Statements on Auditing Standards, Guides, Statements of Position*, and many technical and professional books and pamphlets.

Auditors, as members of a profession, have a legal responsibility to their clients and to third parties who might be injured by shortcomings in an auditor's opinions. As a general rule, the client may recover damages from auditors who have been negligent in the performance of their examinations, and third parties may claim damages arising because of auditor's fraud, negligence, or failure to adhere to professional standards.

The professional accountant offers services to the public in a number of areas related to financial reporting and management. Traditionally, the certified public accountant is best known as an auditor who reviews the accounting statements and records of business firms and renders an opinion on them. The work of the professional accountant also includes preparation of tax returns and counseling in related matters, installation of accounting systems, and management consulting services. The following comments are concerned only with auditing.

The Auditor's Report

The auditor's report is addressed to the directors and stockholders of the client corporation. An example of an audit report is presented in **Illustration 1**. Each word and phrase of this report has been carefully chosen to describe concisely the examination and to state the opinion to which the examination has led.

ILLUSTRATION 1   Report of Independent Public Accountant

To the Stockholders and Board of Directors, Occidental Petroleum Corporation:

We have audited the accompanying consolidated balance sheets of OCCIDENTAL PETROLEUM CORPORATION (a Delaware corporation) and consolidated subsidiaries as of December 31, 1992 and 1991, and the related consolidated statements of operations, nonredeemable preferred stock, common stock and other stockholders' equity, and cash flows for each of the three years in the period ended December 31, 1992 (included on pages 33 through 58). These financial statements are the responsibility of the Company's management. Our responsibility is to express an opinion on these financial statements based on our audits.

We conducted our audits in accordance with generally accepted auditing standards. Those standards require that we plan and perform the audit to obtain reasonable assurance about whether the financial statements are free of material misstatement. An audit includes examining, on a test basis, evidence supporting the amounts and disclosures in the financial statements. An audit also includes assessing the accounting principles used and significant estimates made by management, as well as evaluating the overall financial statement presentation. We believe that our audits provide a reasonable basis for our opinion.

In our opinion, the financial statements referred to above present fairly, in all material respects, the financial position of Occidental Petroleum Corporation and consolidated subsidiaries as of December 31, 1992 and 1991, and the results of their operations and their cash flows for each of the three years in the period ended December 31, 1992, in conformity with generally accepted accounting principles.

As discussed in Note 4 to the consolidated financial statements, the Company has adopted Statement of Financial Accounting Standard No. 106 and No. 109 effective January 1, 1992.

ARTHUR ANDERSEN & CO.
Los Angeles, California

January 29, 1993 (except with
respect to the matters
discussed in Note 18, as to
which the date is February 18,
1993)

The first paragraph of the standard audit report is called the "introductory paragraph." It indicates that the financial statements were audited, management is responsible for the financial statements, and the auditor's responsibility is to provide an opinion only on the financial statements specifically identified in the auditor's report.

The second paragraph is referred to as the "scope" paragraph. It states the audit was conducted in accordance with generally accepted auditing standards, which are a set of authoritative auditing standards issued by the AICPA, and outlines the auditor's basis for forming an opinion on the financial statements. It should be noted that the auditor's objective as stated in this paragraph is to provide reasonable assurance, not a guarantee, that the financial statements taken as a whole are free of material misstatement.[1]

The third or "opinion" paragraph presents the auditor's conclusions as a result of the audit. The phrase used to open the paragraph, "in our opinion," implies that the auditor is reasonably sure of his or her conclusions. The following phrases "present fairly" and "in conformity with generally accepted accounting principles" are linked as representing a single concept as to what constitutes a fair presentation.

The phrase "present fairly" means that the opinion applies to the statements taken as a whole. The auditor does not imply that any single item on the statements is exact or precisely correct. Instead, the auditor attests that the statements as a whole are a complete disclosure and free from any material bias or misstatement.

The "generally accepted accounting principles" referred to in the opinion are those accounting standards established by the Financial Accounting Standards Board (FASB).

Forms of the Audit Report

The auditor's opinion can be expressed in four different forms: (1) an unqualified opinion; (2) a qualified ("except for") opinion; (3) an adverse opinion; and (4) a disclaimer of opinion. The choice of the form of opinion is part of the auditor's responsibility for applying informed judgment in all matters concerning the audit.

The auditor's standard opinion presented earlier in **Illustration 1** is referred to as an unqualified opinion. The auditor made no reservations and stated no conditions precedent to the opinion about the fairness of management's financial statements. In most audit engagements, conditions which might lead to nonstandard wording in the opinion can be eliminated by agreement between the auditor and the client to extend the auditing procedure or revise the financial statements.

A qualified opinion includes the phrase "except for" and a statement indicating that there was a material restriction on the scope of the auditor's work, or a material departure from generally accepted accounting principles. There are a number of reasons why this nonstandard wording might be required. The client's unwillingness to

---

[1]Misstatements are material if they are significant enough to make a difference in the decision of a reasonable financial statement user.

permit some essential auditing procedure, such as confirming accounts receivable or observation of the taking of inventories, would require qualification of the auditor's opinion. The auditor's failure to agree with the propriety of an accounting method or a presentation on the financial statements would also result in a qualification.

An adverse opinion is a completely negative expression by the auditor about the fairness of the financial statements. It indicates the auditor has concluded that departures from generally accepted accounting principles are so material that the financial statements do not fairly present the company's financial position, results of operations, and cash flows. This type of report is rarely published; an engagement leading to an adverse opinion would probably be terminated prior to its completion.

The disclaimer opinion is a pronouncement by the auditor that scope restrictions are so pervasive that the auditors cannot form an opinion.

The Auditor's Work

Auditors use a variety of techniques to examine the financial statements of a company. The techniques applied in carrying out an "audit program" can be grouped into four categories: internal analysis, inspection, external communication, and analytical review. These standards relate to planning and supervision, evaluation of the internal control system, and evidential matter.

The Audit Plan

After appraisal of the company's situation, the auditor prepares an audit plan, which schedules audit procedures and indicates the extent to which they will be applied during the course of the audit. This formalized plan of audit procedures serves several vital needs. First, it enables the auditor to anticipate time and manning requirements. Second, it permits effective assignment of assistants and facilitates the coordination of their efforts. Third, the audit program serves as a master list of the audit procedures used for indexing of working papers prepared during the examination. Audit firms have developed standard "checklist" programs to ensure that no essential procedure is omitted. Each audit will require program modifications to fit the requirements of the investigation. The program is subject to constant revision as the audit progresses and new circumstances come to light during the examination. In this sense, the audit plan is not in final form until the entire audit is completed and the auditor's report has been drafted.

Since the audit is essentially an examination of the financial statements, it is logical that investigations of the financial accounts are, in general, accomplished in the order of their appearance on the balance sheet and on the income statement. However, the interrelationship of the accounts makes it impractical to audit any single segment of the client's operations without recognizing the effect upon other accounts. For example, the examination of accounts receivable will directly relate to cash receipts, income recognition, and finished goods shipment. Therefore, the audit proceeds by investigation of various areas of functional activity rather than of individual account balances.

Evaluation of Internal Controls

Early in the examination, the auditor must make a study of the organization's internal controls. The system of internal controls includes all measures instituted by management (1) to ensure accuracy and dependability of financial data; (2) to protect assets from improper or inefficient use; and (3) to control and evaluate operations.

The extent to which the auditing procedures to be required by the auditor will depend almost entirely upon the adequacy of the system of internal controls. The evaluation of internal controls continues throughout the entire course of the audit. Financial and administrative procedures are investigated by inquiry and observation. Usually the results of this essential part of the examination are summarized in a separate report to management, together with recommendations for improved internal controls. The auditor's evaluation of internal controls is the basis for determining the reliability of the resulting financial statements. If the internal controls are weak, the amount of evidential matter the auditor requires to reach an opinion on the financial statements will be greater than if the internal controls are judged to be strong.

Auditing Procedures

A comprehensive view of auditing procedures would require detailed consideration of the many groups of accounts which make up the financial statements. Auditing procedures can be classified by the types of investigative activities employed by the auditor: (1) internal analysis, (2) inspection, (3) external communication, and (4) analytical review. Each of these is considered briefly to describe the varied techniques the auditor uses to form an opinion of management's financial statements.

Testing and sampling are employed extensively throughout the audit procedure. It would be impractical (and probably impossible) for the auditor to examine and review all records and activities of a business entity. The auditor's judgment, supplemented to an increasing extent by formal sampling methods, is the basis for determining testing procedures.

Internal Analysis.   A major part of the auditor's time is devoted to an analysis of the company's internal financial records. Internal analysis to verify mathematical accuracy is minimized by the presence of effective internal controls. Many of the accounts are analyzed for an independent verification of changes and balances. For example, receivable and payable accounts may be analyzed and listed for subsequent investigation. Plant asset and security investment accounts are analyzed to show necessary details of balances. Supporting business documents such as purchase invoices, checks issued, and cash remittance receipts are traced and compared to the accounting entries. The client's employees may assist with clerical work, but the auditor's independence must be maintained by close supervision and verification.

Inspection.   Auditors make extensive visual inspections of their client's properties to satisfy themselves that assets are properly presented. Cash on hand is counted and securities are inspected for reconciliation with records. Physical inventories taken by the client's employees are observed by the auditor. Plant assets may be inspected at least to a limited extent. These inspections and observations must be coordinated with the client's business operations and with preparation of appropriate analyses of the financial accounts.

External Communication.   The auditor should communicate directly with individuals, businesses, and institutions having dealings with the audit client. These external communications or confirmations aid the auditor in verifying relationships independently of the client's records. Information is requested from outsiders only with the client's approval and cooperation. Confirmations might be obtained (1) from banks, to verify balances of cash on deposit and amount of indebtedness; (2) from trade creditors; (3) from customers; (4) from corporate transfer agents and registrars; (5) from sinking fund trustees; (6) from public warehouses; (7) from others, such as appraisers and attorneys. In addition, the auditor may use specialists to confirm management's assertions that involve technical considerations beyond the auditor's competence. Typically, these direct communications with third parties produce highly credible evidence for the auditor in forming an independent opinion.

Analytical Review.   An analytical review of the relationships between data shown by the financial records and revealed during the audit examination adds significantly to the auditor's degree of satisfaction with the resulting financial statements. It is in this general area that the ingenuity and imagination of the auditor become especially important. For example, comparisons of the client's current bad debt losses with those of prior periods and with those for other businesses in the industry provide insights into the adequacy of the client's current bad debt provisions. Analysis of changes in departmental gross profit percentages and inventory turnover may help substantiate the recorded income and inventory levels. Comparisons of income from securities with records of security ownership adds assurance that financial statements present consistent data. Property tax payments will corroborate property ownership.

Audit Committee

Corporations appoint audit committees of their board of directors. These committees usually consist of outside directors. Their function is to monitor the corporation's corporate reporting practices, review the work of the company's auditors as to audit scope and results, and watch over the quality and appropriateness of the company's internal controls.

Detecting Financial Statement Fraud

Auditors cannot be relied upon to detect every case of financial statement fraud. Neither can statement users expect to catch fraudulent statements that go undetected during an auditor's examination. The best protection for statement users is always to be alert to the possibility of statement fraud and to be aware of the conditions likely to encourage it. Then, when these conditions are encountered and an analysis of the company's statements produces an uneasy feeling on the part of the user that something is wrong, that statement users should begin to suspect statement fraud is a possibility and act accordingly.

In most cases of revealed financial statement fraud one or more of the following conditions existed:

- The chief executive officer managed by setting ambitious simple financial objectives, such as a compound earnings growth rate of 25% per year.
- The chief executive officer had a low regard for the financial and accounting functions.
- The nonmanagement members of the board of directors played a passive role in the board and company affairs.
- The management believed accounting choices and actions are a legitimate means to achieve the corporate goals.
- In the past the company had used questionable accounting that, while legitimate, nevertheless stretched the rules.
- The company had a rapid growth in earnings that was becoming harder to sustain because of internal weaknesses, market changes, or competitive development.
- The company and its chief executive's future survival was very dependent on maintaining a high earnings growth rate.
- Management repeatedly issued optimistic statements about the company's future.
- The company had weak internal controls.
- Management was in the hands of a single dominant person.
- Questionable related party transactions were entered into.

Statement users should not assume because the chief executive officer appears to be honest that everyone else in the organization is honest and therefore the probability of financial statement fraud is remote.

The chief executive officer is not always the individual responsible for committing the statement fraud. It can occur at lower levels in the organization, such as in the case of a factory manager responsible for sales shipping to nonexistent customers at year-end in order to meet an annual sales goal. Such actions may go undetected because of weak internal controls and lax auditing.

To appreciate properly the significance of findings generated by financial statement analysis, an analyst must understand the business of the company whose statement is being analyzed. Auditors exercising due professional care are expected also to have a thorough understanding of the client's business. Statement users should be able to assume that this is the case, but it may be a dangerous assumption. Not all independent auditors have the required level of knowledge of their client's business. In these cases the audit plan may be deficient. It may not be responsive to the company circumstances. Also, the auditor may tend to rely too much on management assurances as to estimates, judgments, and values incorporated in the financial statements. Under these circumstances management may be tempted to commit financial statement fraud. Knowledge of the reporting company's business is a prerequisite for a competent audit and analysis. It also reduces the probability of becoming the victim of statement fraud.

Whether the audit firm is big or small, audit opinions should be relied upon with some degree of caution. The best advice is to test the results of your analysis against your knowledge of the business and, if something seems troublesome, out of line with expectations, irregular, or not understandable, act accordingly. Do not wait to find out for sure if you are right or wrong. It may be too late by then.

CASE

6-1 Elevator Service, Incorporated

Elevator Service, Inc., was engaged in servicing and repairing elevator equipment. Maintenance service contracts were the major source of revenue. Substantial repair jobs furnished the remainder of the company's revenue. Annual sales were approximately $10 million, and there were about 150 employees engaged in service and repair work.

The company had not been previously audited. Your public accounting firm has been engaged to conduct the annual audit You have been assigned to review and test the cash receipts and disbursements procedures and to make suggestions for improvements where the internal accounting controls appear to be deficient.

The company's accounting staff consists of:

1. Cashier.
2. Assistant cashier, who also posted the detail accounts receivable ledger.
3. Bookkeeper.
4. Assistant bookkeeper.
5. Billing and job cost clerk.
6. Two general clerks—filing, general office work, incoming and outgoing mail.
7. Secretary.
8. Messenger.

The vice president, who is engaged mostly in the technical end of the business, is also the treasurer. You are favorably impressed with the caliber of the staff, who appear to carry out their duties efficiently.

Professor David Hawkins prepared this case as the basis for class discussion rather than to illustrate either effective or ineffective handling of an administrative situation. This case is based on materials originally prepared by F. R. Madera.
Copyright © 1996 by the President and Fellows of Harvard College. Harvard Business School case 197–004.

The following is a brief summary of the procedures as you have recorded them in your notes:

Cash Receipts

a) All incoming remittances were received by check.

b) Incoming mail was opened by one of the general clerks.

c) Clerk prepared two tapes of checks as a means of control: one tape of checks accompanied by remittances advices and another of checks for which remittance advices were not received. On the latter tape, the clerk noted against each item the name of the customer for the information of the accounts receivable ledger clerk in posting collections. Tapes were delivered to the ledger clerk, who was also the assistant cashier.

d) Clerk delivered checks to the cashier, who endorsed them, prepared bank deposits, agreed amount with tapes, and made the cash receipts entry, which was supported by the tapes and remittance advices received from customers.

Cash Disbursements

a) Invoices were processed for payment by assistant bookkeeper; invoices were matched up with receiving reports (received directly from receiving department) and with copies of purchase orders as to quantity, description, and price; invoices were matched with freight and trucking charges (if any); mathematical accuracy of invoices was checked; work done was not initialed for by the assistant bookkeeper.

b) On the 10th and 25th of the month (or on discount date), invoices were assembled by vendor and vouchered for payment by the assistant bookkeeper, who also kept the accounts payable ledger. Amounts vouchered were entered in the accounts payable ledger.

c) The vouchers with documents attached were sent to the cashier, who prepared the checks and entered them as disbursements.

d) Checks and vouchers with attached documents were sent by the cashier to the vice president-treasurer; she reviewed the vouchers and supports, initialed the vouchers, signed the checks (one signature only on checks), and sent them back to the cashier. The vouchers and support documents were not canceled with a dated paid stamp or by machine.

e) As the recording of checks was time consuming, the cashier abbreviated somewhat by using initials only instead of full names for some companies (e.g., TCSI for Technical Control Systems, Inc.). Apparently, some of the larger suppliers emphasized initials on their invoices and letterheads, and they had no difficulty cashing checks prepared in this manner.

f) Upon occasion, a representative of the company was required to visit certain suppliers to expedite shipments of sorely needed material for jobs. For psychological reasons, it was decided that the request for early shipments would be aided by the presentation of a check in payment of past orders, and therefore certain checks were secured from the mail clerk before mailing.

Questions

1. On the basis of the foregoing information, what recommendations would you make for improvement in internal accounting controls over cash receipts and disbursements. _____

2. Based on your appraisal of the company's internal controls, what audit steps would you undertake to examine cash receipt and disbursements and related areas? _____

Eagle Tools, Incorporated

Eagle Tools, Inc., manufactured a line of small hand tools and machines. Your public accounting firm audits the company's books, and you have been assigned responsibility for the inventory items.

Eagle's perpetual inventory records were maintained for raw materials and finished goods, showing quantities and dollar amounts; general ledger control accounts were maintained for raw materials and finished goods. No work in process records were maintained, since the production time of each of the company's lines was generally one day. The cost of raw materials put into process and productive labor was charged directly to the finished goods account.

Charges to the raw material perpetual records were made from vendors' invoices and receiving reports. Credits for materials put into production were based on material requisitions, priced at weighted average cost.

A lot (or production) order was issued for the manufacture of quantities to be produced of each type of tool or machine, and a requisition was prepared for the required amount of raw materials to produce the quantity of finished product ordered. Labor tickets prepared by shop workers showed lot order number, hours worked, and units processed. These time tickets were extended for labor charges by the cost clerk; the hours were agreed with time-clock cards. Daily production line inspection counts

Professor David Hawkins prepared this case as the basis for class discussion rather than to illustrate either effective or ineffective handling of an administrative situation. This case is based on materials originally prepared by F. R. Madera.
Copyright © 1996 by the President and Fellows of Harvard College. Harvard Business School case 197–007.

were made by the timekeeper of finished products, and the quantities were agreed by the cost clerk with the production reported by the shop workers. A summary by lot orders was made by the cost clerk of materials, labor charges, and quantities produced, and the totals were charged to the perpetual records of finished products. A new weighted average was computed each time a production order was completed, and this new average was used by the cost clerk to calculate the cost of the sales made under shipping reports.

Requisitions for additional raw materials to replace items spoiled in manufacture and an estimate of labor spent on the spoiled materials were charged to shop overhead (spoilage account), with an offsetting credit to finished goods.

Monthly trial balances of the perpetual stock records of raw materials and finished products were reconciled monthly by the bookkeeper with the general ledger control accounts. Overhead was apportioned to inventory at year-end only (December 31), based on the relation of overhead for the year to direct labor costs for the year.

Because Eagle experienced heavy production demands during the month of December and business was relatively slow in late summer, a complete physical inventory was taken at September 30, after shutting down production and clearing all in-process work. Your accounting firm had generally found the inventory to be carefully taken and the perpetual records to be reasonably accurate. Shipping and receiving cutoffs were properly recorded. The physical inventory at the interim date was priced as follows:

1. Raw material at the latest weighted average cost of purchases.
2. Finished goods at the latest weighted average cost per unit (material and labor only).

Question

1. Your audit tests have satisfactorily established the reasonableness of the company's inventory as at the interim date. What audit test do you suggest to determine that the inventories in the company's financial statements at the year-end are reasonably stated?

International Oil

International Oil Company, a medium-sized integrated oil company, maintained three large sales divisions in the United States and three small sales divisions outside the United States. In addition, a separate sales division in the head office handled all large special sales and direct refinery shipments.

Divisions in the United States sold both at retail and wholesale. Retail accounts receivable arose through sales on credit cards. There were some 115,000 active credit card accounts. There were about 30,000 wholesale accounts and 200 general sales (special and refinery shipment) accounts. The accounts receivable and annual sales by divisions are summarized below (all *dollar* amounts are in thousands):

| | Accounts Receivable | | | | Annual Sales | |
| | Retail | | Wholesale | | | |
	No. of Accounts	*Amount*	*No. of Accounts*	*Amount*	*Retail*	*Wholesale*
Divisions in United States						
No. 1	50,000	$ 700	10,000	$2,500	$10,000	$20,000
No. 2	35,000	500	10,000	2,000	7,000	18,000
No. 3	30,000	450	8,000	1,500	5,000	15,000
Divisions outside United States						
No. 4			800	250		3,000
No. 5			1,000	400		4,000
No. 6			200	100		1,000
Special division			200	3,000		35,000
Total	115,000	$1,650	30,200	$9,750	$22,000	$96,000

The company's system of internal accounting control at the three U.S. divisions was satisfactory, the accounting staff at each of the sales divisions being sufficiently large to permit adequate segregation of duties. The company maintained a staff of internal auditors at each of the U.S. divisions.

Professor David Hawkins prepared this case as the basis for class discussion rather than to illustrate either effective or ineffective handling of an administrative situation. This case is based on materials originally prepared by F. R. Madera.

The number of employees at each of the sales divisions outside the United States was small, and a certain amount of overlapping of duties existed. The company auditors did not regularly visit these divisions, their last visit having been about five years ago.

The company used the cycle method of billing retail accounts; that is, the accounts were divided into five groups of cycles, the billings of which were staggered throughout the month, one cycle being billed every five days. Trial balances of past-due accounts only were run for each cycle immediately before the cycle billing, and current billings were entered on these trial balances in one amount to balance to the controls maintained for each cycle. The cycle controls were balanced monthly with the divisional ledger.

Wholesale accounts were segregated by area, and separate controls were maintained for each marketing area, of which there were between 60 and 100 in each division.

The number of transactions in the special sales division was relatively small, and the internal accounting control was considered adequate. The company auditors did not examine the records of this division.

The company maintained a credit section at each of the sales divisions, and the head office credit department controlled and supervised the divisional credit sections and received for review copies of all divisional trial balances.

Early in the year, the chief internal auditor submitted his proposed program of circularized (confirmation) of accounts receivable as of an interim date. The program was similar to those of the past five years:

1. No work would be undertaken at any of the divisions outside the United States or at the special sales division.

2. Retail accounts: 100 accounts at each U.S. division would be circularized by use of the positive form of confirmation (i.e., the customer would be requested to confirm the balance shown in the confirmation letter, regardless of whether or not the balance was correct). The chief auditor explained that only a token number of retail accounts would be circularized because (1) the credit risk was well spread, (2) it was his experience that most replies were unsatisfactory because of cycle billing, and (3) he considered a test of a significant portion of the accounts to be impracticable.

3. Wholesale accounts: 5% of the wholesale accounts at each U.S. division would be circularized by use of the positive form. The chief internal auditor maintained records of the ledgers circularized each year, so that over a period of years all ledgers would be circularized. The ledgers which he selected each year included some from each of the people responsible for maintaining the individual ledgers.

4. Accounts written off: 25% of the accounts written off in the preceding two years would be circularized. This work would include examination of the credit files of accounts circularized.

5. Second requests would be mailed to all regular wholesale accounts failing to reply at the end of one month if such accounts had not then been paid in full. Second requests would not be mailed on accounts written off. Confirmation requests returned unclaimed would be remailed if another address could be determined.

6. All incoming mail for a period of 10 days would be opened and remittances received noted for subsequent tracing to individual accounts.

7. All postings to wholesale accounts for a two-day period would be checked.

8. A report summarizing the results of the circularization would be prepared and furnished to you for review. The internal auditors' working papers would also be made available to you.

Questions

1. The work of the internal auditors is considered satisfactory by the external auditor. On that basis, to what extent should the independent certified public accountant circularize accounts receivable in the examination for the year ending December 31? _____

2. In reviewing the work of the internal auditors, what points would you keep in mind? _____

3. Do you recognize any situations in the facts stated that might call for recommendations to International? What might customers' replies disclose that could prove helpful to management? _____

CASE

6-4

Precision Instrument Corporation

Precision Instrument Corporation sold a line of high-temperature measuring instruments (pyrometers). The principal users of the equipment were steel mills and various metal extraction companies, and Precision's small sales force had concentrated almost exclusively on establishing good relations with these customers. Occasional inquiries

Professor David Hawkins prepared this case as the basis for class discussion rather than to illustrate either effective or ineffective handling of an administrative situation. It is based on materials originally prepared by J. M. McInnis and J. R. Yeager.
Copyright © 1996 by the President and Fellows of Harvard College. Harvard Business School case 197–003.

EXHIBIT 1   **Precision Instrument Corporation, Financial Data as of December 31**
(dollar figures in thousands)

| | Audited Results | | | | Unaudited |
	1990	1991	1992	1993	1994
Inventories related to pyrometers	791	806	909	805	627
Working capital	933	1,021	1,165	1,155	819
Net assets	1,889	1,965	1,995	1,926	1,549
Net sales of pyrometers	2,881	2,475	2,025	996	583
Other sales (net)	—	—	—	—	115
Net income (loss)..............................	108	77	67	(91)	(376)

---

and orders came from other sources, such as scientific laboratories, but the company had never actively solicited these markets.

The device in its present form had been developed and put into production in the early 1980s. Essentially, it utilized principles which had been known for almost a hundred years, but until recently the accuracy attainable had fallen short of the requirements of modern industry. The company had introduced no new products until the last quarter of 1994. Effectively, the company had not faced any serious competition in its market area until 1990 and had maintained a stable sales level of around $3 million until that time.

During 1990, a competing product had been introduced to the market. Operating on completely different principles, this device performed substantially the same job as Precision's product and gave similar levels of accuracy. The only major differences were in the useful life (five years) and its purchase price, each of which was about half of those of the Precision product. The lower purchase price was a telling sales advantage, and Precision's sales had suffered accordingly. **Exhibit 1** gives some of the financial data of Precision Instrument Corporation from 1990 through 1994.

By 1991, the management of Precision realized that without a new product to bolster its faltering sales volume, the company was facing a serious predicament. They therefore began a search for an additional product which would be suited to the competences of the company. In 1992, they approached an inventor, who held patents for just such a product, with a view to buying the patents. After some negotiation, a mutually satisfactory price was reached, and, as part of the agreement, the inventor agreed to join the company and lead the additional development work which was required before a commercial product was ready for marketing.

On top of the cost of the patents and the development expenses, the company was faced with substantial start-up costs and investment in inventories. The company's financial resources, already adversely affected by the lagging sales of pyrometers, were inadequate without an injection of fresh capital. The company's capital stock was closely held by members of top management and a few of their friends and family members. None of these people was willing to contribute any further capital.

Management believed that the recent poor operating results made it unwise to seek fresh equity capital at that time, and they therefore decided that a bank loan was the only feasible course of action. It did not prove any easy matter to find a bank willing to make the required loan, but eventually the capital was obtained from a bank. In extending the loan, the bank imposed several restrictions upon the management of Precision, one of these being that a minimum working capital level of $800,000 should be maintained. By the end of 1994, with the sales of pyrometers still falling and the new product only just introduced to the market, the company was close to defaulting on the requirements of the working capital covenant.

In the 1994 audit, the public accountant was satisfied with all the accounts except for the valuation of the inventories related to pyrometers. Most of this inventory was in good condition and had been carefully handled and stored. A few items of purchased parts had become obsolete, and management had written them down. This represented an insignificant adjustment, however, and the bulk of the inventory was still reported on the company's books at cost. The auditor was not concerned about the physical condition of the inventory, but he had serious reservations as to the marketability of the product, and therefore the realization of the investment through profitable sales. In approaching management on this matter, the auditor was aware that a large adjustment would throw the company into default on its loan covenant concerning working capital.

The auditor, Mr. Bill Adams, arranged a meeting with the president of Precision Instrument Corporation, Mr. Tom Fairmuir, in order to discuss the 1994 financial statements. Part of the meeting is recorded below:

Mr. Adams: Everything seems to be in fine order except for your valuation of inventories relating to pyrometers, Tom. Now we discussed this matter briefly a few days ago and you expressed the opinion that there would be no material loss of value in the inventories and that you would in fact be able to sell it all in the normal course of business. Since then I have examined your record of sales orders, and at present you have only $58,000 worth of open orders on your books, compared with $65,000 worth at the beginning of the year. Your billings by quarters for the past year were fairly stable: $149,000 first quarter, $136,000 second quarter, $141,000 third quarter, and $157,000 in the final quarter.

I have also read several articles in trade publications, such as this one in *Steel Monthly,* which seem to indicate that your type of pyrometer is at a technical as well as an economic (in terms of purchase price) disadvantage.

Frankly, it appears to me that you are going to be left with a lot of inventory which will have to be marked down very significantly to sell it.

Mr. Fairmuir: Now hold it, Bill, things are not so bleak as that. In fact, we have plans for our pyrometers which will return the sales volume to its previous level, or close to it. Look at these letters, Bill. These are inquiries concerning substantial orders, and we have been receiving such inquiries at a greatly increased rate recently. If this continues, and I have no doubt that it will, and even half of them become firm orders, we shall be selling pyrometers in 1995 at twice the 1994 level.

You know we hired a new sales manager this year? Well, he has reorganized our sales force and is beginning to get results. At the same time, we have gone over our production process and reduced the manufacturing cost of our lines by some 10 percent. No doubt you noticed that our cost of goods figures, which have been stable at about 60 percent of selling price for several years, were lower for the past two or three months. We expect to improve on that further in 1995. Of course this gives us some price flexibility when we are faced with a competitive situation. So you see, I have good reason to predict better results in the future.

Mr. Adams: What exactly has the new sales manager done?

Mr. Fairmuir: He reorganized the sales territories and reassigned the salespeople so that we should get greater market penetration. He released a couple of employees who have clearly not been pulling their weight and hired a couple of bright young people to replace them. The main thing is that he has done wonders for the morale of the sales force.

In addition, he has identified new markets and is helping the salespeople to break into these markets.

Mr. Adams: Why don't we look at the prospects market by market, Tom? You had sales of only $62,000 to steel mills in 1994. It seems as if the steel mills market is almost defunct, wouldn't you agree?

Mr. Fairmuir: It has certainly declined. However, some of our salespeople have built up a good relationship with their customers in the steel industry and we expect this to produce a certain loyalty. We should keep a small part of the business, say, billings of about $50,000 a year.

Then in the other metal extraction industries we know that our product has some distinct competitive advantages, such as its ruggedness and lower maintenance costs. With the new emphasis on selling, we expect that our customers will be well aware of these advantages, and the downward sales trend should be reversed this year. On this basis, we expect 1995's sales to this market to be at least $400,000 and to increase further in the future.

Mr. Adams: But look, Tom, that means an increase over this year's sales, bucking a strong downward trend. I can't base my opinion on your optimism, you know.

Mr. Fairmuir: Well, look at this market which we think has great potential— scientific laboratories. We are going to place advertisements in some of the engineering journals and pay direct sales calls to many of the labs in our market areas, those who do a lot of high-temperature work. We anticipate yearly sales of $200,000 to $300,000 in this market.

And, finally, we have set up a contract with a representative in Washington to handle our line of government sales. She has already got some orders for us, and she seems certain that we can build up a stable volume of some $300,000 a year. Several government agencies are testing our product at the moment. If we get our equipment specified for installation into government facilities, we shall have a large continuing market.

Mr. Adams: So you expect sales of about $1 million this year, twice 1994's sales?

Mr. Fairmuir: No, not right away. But we are confident of substantially reversing the trend of recent years and eventually, say, in two years or so, building our sales up at least $1.5 million for pyrometers. For 1995, we predict sales of about $800,000.

Mr. Adams: We look at this from my point of view. I have a professional responsibility to give an opinion on your company's financial statements and I cannot base my opinion on your predictions. I have to go on historic facts and reasonable expectations. The historic facts are that sales of pyrometers have been falling and you have only a small volume of open orders on your books.

You have a substantial inventory, the value of which can only be realized through the sale or pyrometers. Any other representation of these facts would mislead the reader of the statements.

Mr. Fairmuir: I agree with you on that, and in my opinion, we *will* realize the value of our inventory through normal sales. I could not contemplate a write-down in the value of the inventory. For one thing, it would not be right to do so since it would be misleading in valuing our assets. And for another, it could easily lead to a difficult situation with the bank and, at worst, lead to liquidation of the company. True, we have experienced a few bad years. But we are fighting back, and I am confident we shall save our pyrometer line. And also our new line will start to contribute to profits this coming year.

The discussion continued for some time and became fairly heated. Finally, Mr. Adams terminated the discussion in order to consider the question further. He arranged a meeting with Mr. Fairmuir for three days later, at which time the two men agreed they would come to a decision as to whether or not the value of the inventory should be written down. Mr. Adams was concerned as to what opinion he should issue on Precision's 1994 financial statements.

Questions

1. What further steps should Mr. Adams take in preparing for the coming meeting with Mr. Fairmuir? _____

2. Putting yourself in Mr. Fairmuir's position, what steps would you take in preparing for the meeting? If Mr. Adams insists that the value of the inventory be written down, what would you do? _____

3. Do you think that the value of the inventory should be written down? If so, how should the adjustment be made? _____

4. If the inventory was not written down by management, how would you, as auditor, phrase your opinion if you believed a write-down was appropriate? _____

PART FOUR

Basic Financial Statement Analysis Techniques

Financial Statement Analysis

Financial statement analysis involves the use of simple mathematical techniques, an understanding of accounting and an appreciation of business strategy to gain insights into the reporting corporation's history, current position and future prospects through an examination of the corporation's financial statement. The results of these analyses can play an important role in credit decisions, valuing securities, analyzing competitors, and appraising managerial performance. This chapter introduces some of the basic tools of financial statement analysis. A knowledge of these techniques is essential to appreciate fully the communication aspect of financial reports. The valuation and rating of debt securities and its related financial analysis techniques are discussed in a later chapter. In addition, many of the ratios discussed in this chapter are also covered in greater detail in other chapters dealing with accounting issues and transactions that are the specific focus of a ratio.

A Business Analysis

Competent financial statement analysts approach their task as if it was a business analysis. Accordingly, before beginning a financial statement analysis they first identify the reporting company's strategy, predict the possible consequences of this strategy, and assess whether it is appropriate for the company.

This initial step is useful for several reasons. First, it helps the analyst avoid the problem of "not seeing the forest for the trees." That is, it reduces the probability that the analyst will become focused to such an extent on the details of the analysis that a larger and more critical view of the company is missed. Second, it gives the analysis a

Professor David F Hawkins prepared this note as the basis for class discussion.
Copyright © 1994 by the President and Fellows of Harvard College. Harvard Business School teaching note 195–177.

focus that facilitates the forming of relevant interpretations of the data and analytical results. Third, it provides a framework for presenting the results of the financial statement analysis in a meaningful and coherent communication.

Strategy identification and analysis is a complex task that is beyond the scope of focus or this chapter. Readers should look elsewhere for an understanding of this topic, but look they should because an understanding of alternative strategies models and the optimum strategies under a given set of conditions should help analysts to appreciate better the significance of the historical, comparative and projected financial statement statistics developed by their analysis. For example, in some instances the financial analysis may indicate that the company has adopted the optimum strategy for its circumstances. This revelation may explain why the trends and ratios are what they are. It may provide also some clues as to what the future strategy of the company might be, which would, in turn, imply certain trends and ratios. Alternatively, the analysis might indicate that the optimum strategy is not being followed. This could raise questions as to why the optimum strategy is not being followed, which may result in the identification of some unique characteristics of the company that suggest the theoretical best strategy is not appropriate. Or, if the company indeed is following a suboptimizing strategy, a knowledge of the theoretical consequences of this action may improve the analyst's ability to forecast the consequences of the actual strategy.

Financial Reporting Bias

A company's financial reporting decisions influence its financial statement data. Accordingly, before subjecting financial statement data to any ratio or other type of detailed analysis, experienced analysts assess where and how management's financial reporting decisions may have biased the financial statement data. In particular the analyst examines the financial statements and accompanying notes looking for business transactions and management's accounting principle elections, account caption decisions, format choices, and measurement judgments that might bias the data or the analyst's perception of the data. If the analyst concludes the financial statement data have been materially biased by management, the analyst may attempt to eliminate the bias by adjusting the raw data.

Financial Ratio Analysis

Financial ratios are the fundamental analytical tools for interpreting financial statements. Financial ratio analysis mathematically relates items in the financial statements in a meaningful manner. The analyst evaluates these results against the particular characteristics of the company and its industry. The astute analyst seldom expects answers from this process. Rather, the analyst hopes it will provide clues as to where to focus subsequent analysis that may involve such investigation techniques as company visits, supplier and customer interviews, library searches, and credit bureau report reviews.

Financial ratios fall into four classes: ratios appraising *liquidity,* ratios measuring *solvency,* ratios evaluating *funds management,* and ratios measuring *profitability.* The categories indicate that different ratios may be more helpful than others for particular purposes. Therefore, rather than calculating ratios indiscriminately, the experienced analyst begins by considering the kinds of insights that will be helpful in understanding the problem faced. The analyst then calculates those ratios that best serve his or her purpose. To get the most meaningful results, the analyst compares these ratios over a period of several years against some standard; examines in depth major variations from this standard; and cross checks the various ratios against each other.

The balance sheet and income statement of The Ampex Corporation, a retailing business, will be used to illustrate some of the more common ratios (see **Illustrations A** and **B**).

ILLUSTRATION A   **Ampex Corporation, Comparative Balance Sheets, December 31, 1996, and 1997**
(in thousands of dollars)

Assets	*1996*	*1997*
Current assets:		
Cash	$ 20	$ 30
Accounts receivable (net)	95	95
Inventory	130	110
Total current assets	$245	$235
Fixed assets:		
Land	$ 10	$ 10
Building and equipment (net)	120	100
Total fixed assets (net)	$130	$110
Other assets:		
Goodwill and organization costs	$ 10	$ 10
Total assets	$385	$355
Liabilities and Stockholders' Equity		
Current liabilities:		
Accounts payable	$ 50	$ 40
Estimated income taxes payable	10	10
Total current liabilities	$ 60	$ 50
Fixed liabilities:		
Mortgage bonds, 10 percent	$ 50	$ 50
Total liabilities	$110	$100
Stockholders' equity:		
Convertible preferred stock, 5 percent	$ 20	$ 20
Common stock (10,000 shares outstanding)	50	50
Retained earnings	205	185
Total stockholders' equity	$275	$255
Total liabilities and stockholders' equity	$385	$355

ILLUSTRATION B   Ampex Corporation Condensed Income Statement, 1997
(in thousands of dollars)

Gross sales	$11,516	100.66%
Less: Returns and allowances	10	0.66
Net sales	$ 1,506	100.00%
Less: Cost of goods sold	1,004	66.67
Gross profit	$ 502	33.33%
Operating expenses[a]	400	26.56
Operating profit	$ 102	6.77%
Interest	5	0.33
Profit before taxes	97	6.44%
Income tax expense	47	3.12
Net income	$ 50	3.32%
Less: Preferred dividends	1	0.07
Common dividends	29	1.93
Change in retained earnings	$ 20	1.32%

[a]Includes lease rental costs of $30,000 and depreciation of $10,000.

Liquidity Ratios

A corporation's liquidity is measured by its ability to raise cash from all sources, such as bank credit, sale of redundant assets, and operations. Liquidity ratios have a narrower focus. They help statement users appraise a company's ability to meet its current financial obligations using its existing cash and current assets. These ratios compare current liabilities, which are the obligations falling due in the next 12 months, and current assets, which typically provide the funds to extinguish these obligations. The difference between current assets and current liabilities is called "working capital." (Ampex's 1997 year-end working capital is $185,000 ($245,000 − $60,000).

Current Ratio

$$\frac{\text{Current assets}}{\text{Current liabilities}} = \frac{\$245,000}{\$\ 60,000} = 4.1$$

The meaningfulness of the current ratio as a measure of liquidity varies from company to company. Typically, it is assumed that the higher the ratio, the more protection the company has against liquidity problems. However, the ratio may be distorted by seasonal influences, slow-moving inventories built up out of proportion to market opportunities, or abnormal payment of accounts payable just prior to the balance sheet date. Also, the nature of some businesses is such that they have a steady, predictable cash inflow and outflow, and a low current ratio is appropriate for such a business.

Acid-Test or Quick Ratio

$$\frac{\text{Quick assets}}{\text{Current liabilities}} = \frac{\$115,000}{\$\ 60,000} = 1.9$$

The acid-test or quick ratio measures the ability of a company to use its "near-cash" or quick assets to immediately extinguish its current liabilities. Quick assets include those current assets that presumably can be quickly converted to cash at close to their book value. Such items are cash, investments in securities, and accounts receivable. Like the working capital ratio, this ratio implies a liquidation approach and does not recognize the revolving nature of current assets and liabilities.

Solvency Ratios

Solvency ratios generate insight into a company's ability to meet long-term debt payment schedules. There are a number of ratios that compare stockholders' equity or operating profits to the amount and cost of funds provided by creditors. All of these ratios are designed to give some measure of the extent to which operating cash flows and asset values provide protection to creditors should a company incur losses.

Times Interest Earned

$$\frac{\text{Operating profit (before interest expense)}}{\text{Long-term debt interest}} = \frac{\$102,000}{\$5,000} = 20.4 \text{ times}$$

This coverage ratio is calculated on a pretax basis, since bond interest is a tax deductible expense. The ratio in the example implies that operating profits cover interest payments 20 times. This indicates the extent to which operating profits can decline without impairing the company's ability to pay the interest on its long-term debt.

Some analysts prefer to use operating profit plus noncash charges as the numerator of this ratio. This modification indicates the ability of the company to cover its cash outflow for interest from its funds from operations. For example, the only so-called noncash charge in the Ampex income statement is depreciation; that is, no cash outflow results from incurring this expense. Adding the company's $10,000 depreciation expense to operating profit changes the numerator to $112,000 and increases the coverage to 22 times.

Coverage ratios can be computed for preferred stock dividends and other fixed charges, such as lease rentals. The *preferred-stock-dividend-coverage* ratio is calculated on an after-tax basis, since preferred stock dividends are not a tax deductible expense. For example, the Ampex preferred-stock-dividend-coverage ratio is:

$$\frac{\text{Net income}}{\text{Preferred stock dividends}} = \frac{\$50,000}{\$1,000} = 50 \text{ times}$$

A coverage ratio for all of a company's fixed charges is called the *times-fixed-charges-earned* ratio. The denominator of this ratio includes such items as lease rentals, interest, and preferred dividends converted to a pretax basis. The numerator is operating profit before these charges. The times-fixed-charges-earned ratio for Ampex is:

$$\frac{\text{Operating profit before fixed charges}}{\text{Lease rentals, interest, preferred dividends}} = \frac{\$132,000}{\$34,000} = 3.9 \text{ times}$$

Sometimes depreciation is added to the numerator.

Debt-to-Equity Ratios.   The relationship of borrowed funds to ownership funds is an important solvency ratio. Capital from debt and other creditor sources is more risky for a company than equity capital. Debt capital requires fixed interest payments on specific dates and eventual repayment. If payments to a company's creditors become overdue, the creditors can take legal action which may lead to the company being declared bankrupt. Ownership capital is less risky. Dividends are paid at the discretion of the directors, and there is no provision for repayment of capital to stockholders. It is generally assumed that the more ownership capital relative to a debt a company has in its capital structure, the more likely it is that the company will be able to survive a downturn in business that may force other more financially-leveraged companies into bankruptcy. An excessive amount of ownership capital relative to debt capital may not necessarily indicate sound management practices, however. Equity capital is typically more costly than debt capital. Also, the company may be foregoing opportunities "to trade on its equity," that is, borrow at a relatively low interest rate and earn a greater rate of return on these funds. The difference between these two rates can increase earnings per share without having to increase the number of common shares outstanding.

There are a number of debt-to-equity ratios. Four of the most common are:

$$\frac{\text{Total liabilities}}{\text{Total assets}} = \frac{\$110,000}{\$385,000} = 28.6\% \text{ or } 0.286 \text{ to } 1$$

This ratio indicates the proportion of a company's total assets financed by short- and long-term credit sources.

$$\frac{\text{Long-term debt}}{\text{Capitalization}} = \frac{\$ 50,000}{\$325,000} = 15.4\% \text{ or } 0.154 \text{ to } 1$$

This measure, which excludes current liabilities, reflects management's policy on the mix of long-term funds obtained from ownership and nonownership sources. The term "capitalization" includes all of a company's long-term debt and equity capital.

$$\frac{\text{Total liabilities}}{\text{Stockholders' equity}} = \frac{\$110,000}{\$275,000} = 40\% \text{ or } 0.4 \text{ to } 1$$

This ratio is another way of measuring the relative mix of funds provided by owners and creditors.

$$\frac{\text{Total assets}}{\text{Stockholders' equity}} = \frac{\$385,000}{\$275,000} = 1.4$$

The *total leverage* ratio relates total assets to stockholders' equity. This ratio is an indication of the degree to which management has financed the company's asset investments with nonownership capital. A 1.4 ratio means that for every dollar of owners' equity, $0.40 of nonownership funds has been used to fund the company's assets.

Ampex appears to have an adequate cushion of ownership funds against losses from operations, decreases in the book value of assets, and downturns in future cash flows.

Funds Management Ratios

The financial situation of a company turns in large measure on how its investments in accounts receivable, inventories, and fixed assets are managed. As a business expands its sales, it is not uncommon to find that the associated expansion of these three items is so great that despite profitable operations the company is short of cash. In such situations, the management of vendor credit becomes critical. It is a source of capital which should expand along with the increased sales.

Receivables to Sales

$$\frac{\text{Accounts receivable (net)}}{\text{Net sales}} = \frac{\$\ \ \ 95,000}{\$1,506,000} = 6.3\%$$

In the absence of an aging of accounts receivable (classification of outstanding receivables by days since billing) or other detailed credit information, the receivables-to-sales ratio, computed over a number of years, can give a crude indication of the trend in a company's credit policy. In those cases where a company sells for cash and credit, only credit sales should be used in the denominator. Receivables include accounts receivable, trade receivables, and trade notes receivable. The rather low receivables-to-sales percentage for Ampex is indicative that this retailer's sales most probably include a high proportion of cash sales.

Average Collection Period

$$\frac{\text{Accounts receivable}}{\text{Net sales}} \times \text{Days in the annual period} = \text{Collection period}$$

$$6.3\% \times 365 \qquad\qquad\qquad = 23 \text{ days}$$

A two-step method to get the same result is:

1. Calculate the average daily sales:

$$\frac{\text{Net sales}}{\text{Days}} = \frac{\$1,506,000}{365 \text{ days}} = \$4,126 \text{ per day}$$

2. Calculate the day's sales represented by receivables:

$$\frac{\text{Accounts receivable}}{\text{Net sales per day}} = \frac{\$95,000}{\$\ \ 4,126} = 23 \text{ days}$$

To appraise the quality of accounts receivable, the average collection period can be related to the typical credit terms of the company and its industry. A collection period substantially longer than either of these standards might indicate credit management problems, resulting in an increasing amount of funds being tied up in this asset. On the other hand, a significantly shorter collection period than is typical in the industry might mean that profitable sales to slower paying customers are being missed.

Average Accounts Payable Period

$$\frac{\text{Accounts payable}}{\text{Purchases}} = \frac{\$\ \ \ 50,000}{\$1,024,000} = 4.9\%$$

Similar tests can be made of accounts payable to see how well they are managed. In this case, the accounts payable are compared to the purchases for the period (cost of goods sold plus inventory changes). The two-step calculation of the average day's payables is made as follows:

1. Calculate the average daily purchases:

$$\frac{\text{Purchases}}{\text{Days}} = \frac{\$1,004,000 + \$20,000}{365 \text{ days}} = \$2,805 \text{ per day}$$

2. Calculate the day's purchases represented by payables:

$$\frac{\text{Accounts payable}}{\text{Purchases per day}} = \frac{\$50,000}{\$\ 2,805} = 18 \text{ days}$$

The day's-payables ratio becomes meaningful when compared to the credit terms given by suppliers to the object company's industry. If a company's average day's payables is increasing, it may mean trade credit is being used increasingly as a source of funds. If the payables period is less than the average for the industry, it may indicate that management is not using this source of funds as much as possible. If it is longer, it may mean the company is overdue on its payables and is using this source of funds beyond the normal trade limits.

Rarely is the purchases figure available to people outside of the company. Consequently, the analyst has to approximate this amount. In merchandising situations, like the Ampex illustration, estimating purchases is fairly straightforward since a retailer's inventory value and cost of goods sold is the price paid to suppliers for the goods. Therefore, a retailer's outside purchases are equal to its cost of goods sold figure, adjusted for inventory changes.

In manufacturing situations, estimating outside purchases is not such an easy task. The cost of goods sold expense includes direct labor, raw materials, and some manufacturing overheads. If the raw materials portion of the cost of goods sold and inventories figures are available, they can be used to calculate an approximation of the raw materials purchases, which in most cases represents the minimum level of purchases.

Another difficulty is that the accounts payable figure may include payables incurred for other than items included in cost of goods sold. As a result of this problem and the other measurement problems, this ratio is usually not regarded as a particularly reliable indicator of the use of trade credit.

Inventory Turnover

$$\frac{\text{Cost of sales}}{\text{Average inventory}} = \frac{\$1,004,000}{\$\ \ 120,000} = 8.4 \text{ times}$$

The inventory-turnover ratio indicates how fast inventory items move through a business. It is an indication of how well the funds invested in inventory are being managed. The analyst is interested in two items: the absolute size of the inventory in relation to the other funds needs of the company and the relationship of the inventory to the sales volume it supports. A decrease in the turnover rate indicates that the absolute size of the inventory relative to sales is increasing. This can be a warning signal, since funds may be tied up in this inventory beyond the level required by the sales volume, which may be rising or falling.

Average inventory is used in the denominator because the sales volume is generated over a 12-month period. The average inventory is obtained by adding the opening inventory and closing inventory balances and dividing the sum by two.

If the cost of goods sold figure is not available, an approximation of the inventory-turnover rate can be obtained by using the sales figure in the numerator. If profit margins have remained fairly steady, then this sales-to-average-inventory ratio can provide, over a period of years, an indication of inventory management trends.

By dividing the turnover rate into 365 days, the analyst can estimate the average length of time items spent in inventory:

$$\frac{365 \text{ days}}{\text{Inventory turnover}} = \frac{365}{8.4} = 43 \text{ days}$$

If the company uses the so-called last-in, first-out (LIFO) inventory valuation method, the inventory balance must be converted to its equivalent value based on either the first-in, first-out (FIFO) or average cost inventory valuation method. This is accomplished by adding the LIFO reserve to the FIFO inventory balance reported on the balance sheet. The LIFO reserve figure can be found in the inventory note accompanying the financial statements.

Asset Turnover

$$\frac{\text{Net sales}}{\text{Average assets}} = \frac{\$1,506,000}{\$ \ 370,000} = 4.07 \text{ times}$$

The asset turnover ratio is an indicator of how efficiently management is using its investment in total assets to generate sales. High turnover rates suggest efficient asset management.

Fixed Asset Turnover

$$\frac{\text{Net sales}}{\text{Average net fixed assets}} = \frac{\$1,506,000}{\$ \ 120,000} = 12.6 \text{ times}$$

A similar turnover ratio can also be calculated for fixed assets. It provides a crude measure of how well the investment in plant and equipment is being managed relative to the sales volume it supports. The usefulness of this measure is reduced considerably because book values seldom approximate market values or are comparable from company to company due to different depreciation policies.

Capital or Investment Turnover

$$\frac{\text{Net sales}}{\text{Average total capital}} = \frac{\$1,506,000}{\$\ \ 315,000} = 47.8 \text{ times}$$

A ratio similar to the inventory and asset turnover ratios can also be calculated for a firm's total capital investment.

Profitability Ratios

Analysts look at profits in two ways: first, as a percentage of net sales; second, as a return on the funds invested in the business.

Profit Margin.   Profit margins relative to net sales can be evaluated in a number of different ways.

Net Margin

$$\frac{\text{Net income}}{\text{Net sales}} = \frac{\$\ \ \ \ 50,000}{\$1,506,000} = 3.32\%$$

Net income as a percentage of net sales measures the total operating and financial ability of management, since net profit after taxes includes all of the operating and financial costs of doing business.

Pretax Margin

$$\frac{\text{Pretax margin}}{\text{Net sales}} = \frac{\$\ \ \ \ 97,000}{\$1,506,000} = 6.44\%$$

Pretax income as a percentage of net sales measures management's ability to generate profits before recognizing taxes related to those profits. This figure is of interest because changes in the tax code or actions by management that impact the company's tax rate can result in more or less of the pretax profits flowing down to net income.

EBIT

$$\frac{\text{Earnings before interest and taxes}}{\text{Net sales}} = \frac{\$\ \ 102,000}{\$1,506,000} = 6.77\%$$

The ratio of net profit before taxes and interest to net sales is indicative of management's operating ability. Interest is excluded because it relates to financing policy rather than operation efficiency.

Gross Margin

$$\frac{\text{Gross profit}}{\text{Net sales}} = \frac{\$\ 502,000}{\$1,506,000} = 33.3\%$$

Gross profit (sales minus cost of sales) as a percentage of sales is an indication of the management's ability to mark up its products over their cost.

In addition to these ratios, it is often informative to express all of these expense items as a percentage of net sales (see **Illustration B**). This is called a common-size statement. Common-size statements can also be prepared for balance sheets using total assets as the base.

Return on Investment.   The relationship between profitability and investment is considered the key ratio by many analysts. It provides a broad measure of management's operating and financial success. Several different return-on-investment ratios are commonly used.

Pretax Operating Return on Total Assets

$$\frac{\text{Profit before taxes and interest}}{\text{Average total assets}} = \frac{\$102,000}{\$370,000} = 27.6\%$$

This ratio gauges how well management has managed the total resources at its command, before consideration of taxes and credit costs. It focuses on the earning power of the assets and is not influenced by how they are financed. Average total assets is used as the denominator since profit is earned over a 12-month period.

Return on Total Assets

$$\frac{\text{Net income}}{\text{Average total assets}} = \frac{\$\ 50,000}{\$370,000} = 13.5\%$$

This variation measures the return on total assets after recognition of taxes and financing costs.

Return on Total Capital

$$\frac{\text{Net income}}{\text{Average total capital}} = \frac{\$\ 50,000}{\$315,000} = 15.9\%$$

Another ratio measuring return on investment equates investment with total long-term capital (equity capital plus long-term liabilities). This ratio indicates how well management has managed the permanent funds at its disposal. The ratio can be computed on a before- or after-tax basis. If interest is paid on long-term liabilities, then this amount is sometimes added to the net income figures, since it relates to the financial management of those items.

Return on Stockholders' Equity

$$\frac{\text{Net income}}{\text{Average stockholders' equity}} = \frac{\$\ 50,000}{\$265,000} = 18.9\%$$

The return on net worth percentage measures the return on ownership capital after all taxes and interest payments. It is perhaps the most common return-on-investment figure published by financial services.

Return on Tangible Net Worth

$$\frac{\text{Net income}}{(\text{Average net worth} - \text{Average intangible assets})} = \frac{\$50,000}{(\$265,000 - \$10,000)} = 19.6\%$$

This modification measures the return on net worth less the intangible assets, such as goodwill and capitalized organization costs. The principal use of this ratio is to present a more conservative measure of the investment base. The $10,000 deduction from net worth in the above equation is Ampex's investment in goodwill.

Linking Ratios

Statement users can often gain greater insight into a company's returns on capital, assets, and net worth by linking together selected financial ratios.

For example, how a company achieves its return on total capital can be explained in terms of its capital turnover and net margin by using the following equation:

$$\text{Capital turnover} \quad \times \text{After-tax profit margin} = \quad \text{Return on capital}$$

$$\frac{\text{Net sales}}{\text{Average total capital}} \times \frac{\text{Net income}}{\text{Net sales}} = \frac{\text{Net income}}{\text{Average total capital}}$$

$$4.78 \text{ times} \quad \times \quad 3.32\% \quad = \quad 15.95\%$$

This formula indicates that a business return on investment can be improved by increasing the sales volume per dollar of capital, by generating more net income per dollar of sales, or by some mix of these two factors. Thus, the performance of a firm earning 2% on sales with a capital turnover of 10 times can be equivalent to that of another company with a profit margin of 10% and an investment turnover of 2 times. Both have the same return on investment, 20%.

A number of other ratios are closely related. For example, a greater appreciation of the relationship between profitability, asset turnover, and return on total assets can be obtained as follows:

$$\text{After-tax profit margin} \times \quad \text{Asset turnover} \quad = \text{Return on total assets}$$

$$\frac{\text{Net income}}{\text{Net sales}} \times \frac{\text{Net sales}}{\text{Average total assets}} = \frac{\text{Net income}}{\text{Average total assets}}$$

$$3.32\% \quad \times \quad 4.07 \text{ times} \quad = \quad 13.5\%$$

ILLUSTRATION C   Analysis of Ampex Corporation's Return on Stockholders' Equity

---

Pretax profit margin	×	Asset turnover ratio	×	Total leverage ratio	×	Tax retention rate	=	Return on stockholders' equity
$\dfrac{\text{Pretax profits}}{\text{Net sales}}$	×	$\dfrac{\text{Net sales}}{\text{Average assets}}$	×	$\dfrac{\text{Average assets}}{\text{Average stockholders' equity}}$	×	$(1 - \text{Tax rate})$	=	$\dfrac{\text{Net Income}}{\text{Average stockholders' equity}}$
6.44%	×	4.07	×	1.40	×	$(1 - .48)$	=	19.1%

Pretax return on assets
(6.44% × 4.07 = 26/2%)

Pretax return on stockholders' equity
(6.44% × 4.07 × 1.40 = 36.7%)

Return on stockholders' equity
(6.44% × 4.07 × 1.40 × .52 = 19.1%)

An analysis of the causes of changes in the level and quality of the company's return on stockholders' equity can be facilitated by the use of the equation presented in **Illustration C,** which incorporates the Ampex Corporation data and ratios. The average, rather than ending, stockholders' equity and total asset values are used to compute the total leverage ratio because the equation is being used to explain the variables contributing to the company's return on average stockholders' equity.

The only new ratio introduced in **Illustration C** is the so-called *tax retention* ratio, which measures the percentage of pretax profits retained by the company after payment of income taxes. This ratio is expressed as 1 minus the book tax rate, which is the percentage of the book tax expense to the pretax profits. The equation demonstrated in **Illustration C** is often referred to as the Du Pont equation after the name of the company that first used it extensively to analyze the performance of its divisions, subsidiaries and investee corporations.

A similar set of ratios which have more meaning when examined together are the components of the current ratio. For example, an examination of the relationship between the inventory turnover period and the receivables and payables periods demonstrates how changes in these working capital items influence a company's working capital financing requirements.

Some Refinements.   In practice, there are a number of minor refinements to the basic Du Pont equation.

Some users of the expanded equation preferred to use long-term capital, rather than total liabilities, in the turnover and leverage ratios on the grounds that they are interested in how a company uses its "permanent" capital. If capital is defined as long-term liabilities plus owners' equity, the ratios used in the Du Pont equation are:

$$\text{Turnover} = \frac{\text{Sales}}{\text{Capital}}$$

$$\text{Leverage} = \frac{\text{Capital}}{\text{Owners' equity}}$$

A few analysts use the pretax income plus interest charges, rather than income before income taxes, as the numerator in the margin ratio. When a company's interest charges are large relative to pretax income, these analysts are interested in what is described as "pure" operating margin figure and "pure" return on assets ratio. The ratios to adjust the Du Pont equation are:

$$\text{Pretax margin} = \frac{(\text{Pretax income} + \text{Interest})}{\text{Sales}}$$

$$\text{Return on assets} = \frac{(\text{Pretax income} + \text{Interest})}{\text{Assets}}$$

To convert the pretax margin before interest deduction to the margin based on the reported pretax income figure, the following ratio has to be inserted into the expanded equation after the pretax before interest margin:

$$\text{Ratio to adjust pretax before interest margin to pretax margin} = \frac{\text{Pretax income}}{(\text{Pretax income} + \text{Interest})}$$

A Warning

Financial ratio analysis has many limitations. It can easily mislead the unsophisticated analyst. To be a useful analytical tool it must be used wisely.

First, ratio analysis deals only with quantitative data. It does not look at qualitative factors such as management's ethical values, the quality of the management, or the workers' morale. These are important considerations which should be taken into account when evaluating a company.

Second, management can take certain short-run actions prior to the statement dates to influence the ratios. For example, a company with a better than 1:1 current ratio can improve this ratio by paying off current liabilities just prior to the balance sheet date.

Third, comparison of ratios between companies can be misleading because of differences in accounting practices in such areas as depreciation, income recognition, and intangible assets. For this reason, analysts often put companies on a comparable accounting basis before making ratio comparisons.

Fourth, different definitions of common ratios are used by different analysts. This can lead to misleading comparisons and interpretations.

Fifth, because accounting records are maintained in historical dollars, a change in the purchasing power of the dollar due to inflation can distort the comparability of the ratios computed for different time periods. For instance, in periods of inflation the ratios comparing sales and net income to assets and equity may be biased upwards.

Sixth, a ratio standing alone has no significance. What constitutes an appropriate ratio for a company is determined by its industry, management strategy, and the state of the general economy. For example, meat packers have high inventory-turnover ratios and jewelry stores have low inventory-turnover ratios. To conclude one ratio is good and the other bad is a mistake. Ratios results must be evaluated in their business context.

Finally, ratios based on published financial statements show relationship as they existed in the past. The analyst interested in the future should not be misled into believing that the past data necessarily reflect the current situation or future expectations.

Common Stock Ratios

Financial statement analysis and equity valuation models incorporate a number of ratios relating the market value of common stocks to financial statement–related items, such as earnings, net book value, and dividends.

Earnings per Share

The most straightforward computation of earnings per share is for companies with fairly simple capital structures, like Ampex. In these situations, the calculation is:

$$\frac{\text{(Net income − Preferred stock dividends)}}{\text{Average number of common shares outstanding}} = \frac{\$50,000 − \$1,000}{10,000} = \$4.90 \text{ per share}$$

This earnings per share figure is known as "basic earnings per share."

Preferred stock dividends, if any, are deducted from net income before calculating basic earnings per share because this portion of the net income is not available to common stockholders. The denominator is the weighted average number of shares determined by the portion of time within a reporting period common shares have been outstanding to the total time in that period.

The number of earnings-per-share figures a company must report will vary with the complexity of its capital structure. The accounting rules for computing earnings per share require that companies with complex capital structures present with equal prominence two types of earnings-per-share amounts on the face of the income statement: one, basic earnings per share; the other, diluted earnings per share. Basic earnings per share is the amount of earnings attributable to each share of common stock outstanding. Diluted earnings per share is the amount of current earnings per share reflecting the maximum dilution that would result from conversions and exercises, of convertible debt, warrants, options and other issues with contingent rights to common stock that individually, in the future, may decrease earnings per share and in the aggregate might have a dilutive effect. It is always dangerous to use earnings-per-share figures without knowing which definition is being used.[1]

Typically, financial analysts eliminate nonrecurrent items from a single-year analysis of companies. In single-year analysis, financial analysts tend to want to know whether or not the current earnings are in line with the "normal" or continuing earnings of the company. Consequently, extraordinary items, discontinued operations, adjustments for new accounting principle adoptions, unusual items such as material refunds of overpaid taxes are excluded from these analyses.

In long-run analyses of historical data, financial analysts tend to include in income every profit and loss item, unless it is quite unrelated to normal operations. This practice recognizes that many of these so-called unusual items are elements of profit and loss that would have been included in income if the accounting period had been longer than, say, one year. In this latter case, the tax refund excluded from the single-year analysis would be included. An example of items typically excluded from long-term analyses would be gains from pension plan terminations.

Price-Earnings Ratio

Assuming the price for the Ampex stock is $40, the company's price-earnings ratio is:

$$\frac{\text{Market price per share}}{\text{Earnings per share}} = \frac{\$40.00}{\$\ 4.90} = 8.2 \text{ times}$$

Since the stock market is responsive to anticipated earnings-per-share estimates, the price-earnings ratio is often quoted using the company's projected next year's earnings-per-share figure. Typically, the net income figure before extraordinary items is used by analysts to compute this ratio. Also, as noted above, the potential shares issuable to holders of potentially dilutive securities is included in the earnings-per-share calculation.

The reciprocal of the price-earnings ratio gives the so-called *capitalization rate* applied by investors to the company's earnings per share.

$$\frac{\text{Earnings per share}}{\text{Market price per share}} = \frac{\$\ 4.90}{\$40.00} = 12.2\%$$

---

[1]The detailed rules for calculating earnings per share are covered in a later chapter.

Book Value per Share

Book value per share is the relationship between a company's stock price and its net assets, expressed on a per common share basis. Assuming the Ampex's stock price is $40, the company's price to book value ratio is:

$$\frac{\text{Market price per share}}{\text{Net assets per common share}} = \frac{\$40.00}{\$25.50} = 1.57 \text{ times}$$

The book value per common share ratio excludes the preferred stock portion of stockholders' equity.

Dividend Yield

Dividend yield is the relationship between a company's dividend and its stock price. In situations where interim cash dividends have been increased at the last payment date, the current dividend rate converted to a yearly basis is sometimes used for the numerator:

$$\frac{\text{Cash dividends per share}}{\text{Price per share}} = \frac{\$\ 2.90}{\$40.00} = 7.3\%$$

Stock dividends are not included in this calculation. The *payout ratio* is the percentage of net income paid out in cash dividends:

$$\frac{\text{Cash dividends}}{\text{Net income}} = \frac{\$29.00}{\$50.00} = 58\%$$

Growth Analysis

Past and expected growth rates of a corporation's sales, profits, and dividends are a major focus of many financial statement analyses. Investors are interested because of the close relationship between equity stock values and the projected growth rate and the expected volatility of earnings and dividends. Creditors examine past growth records in order to predict the future level of funding required to finance changes in accounts receivables, inventories, and productive assets. Corporations scrutinize growth rates of themselves and their rivals in order to ascertain how well they are doing on a comparative basis, to detect potential weaknesses in their competitors, and to predict future competitive behavior.

Typically, the analysis of growth characteristics and growth rates involves three major steps: First, a quantitative measurement of the rate of growth of the variables being examined. This quantification may range from a simple index number series to a complex mathematical equation describing the trend pattern inherent in the data. Second, the identification of the various sources of the growth. This phase involves both quantitative and qualitative assessments of the sources of growth as well as an analysis of the relationship of these various sources to each other, the operating and financial characteristics of the firm, and the external environment during the period under review. Third, the use of the preceding analyses in combination with projections such as projected industry growth rates, managements' announced capital expansion plans, other analysts' forecast of future levels of growth to develop forecast growth rates and to speculate on the possible financial and operating consequences of the projected growth rates.

Sustainable Growth Rate Equation

Historical and pro forma growth rate analyses use a convenient mathematical expression known as the sustainable growth rate equation. This equation demonstrates if a company does not issue new equity, its potential maximum earnings growth rate will be a function of its rate of return on equity and dividend payout policy.

For example, assume that a company had earnings of $10 million during the year just ended; a net worth of $100 million at the beginning of that year; and a permanent dividend payout policy of 50%. Thus, during the year just ended, the company earned 10% on its beginning net worth; retained $5 million of earnings, and ended the year with an equity of $105 million. If the past year's 10% return on beginning equity is repeated during the next year, the company's earnings will grow to $10.5 million, i.e., 10% of this year's beginning net worth of $105 million. This 5% earnings growth rate will be repeated annually as long as the company continued to earn 10% on each year's beginning net worth and pays out 50% of its earnings in dividends.

The relationship between future earnings growth, return on beginning equity, and dividend payout policy described in this example is captured in more general terms in the sustainable growth rate equation

$$g = \text{ROE} \times (1 - \frac{D}{E})$$

where:

g = Annual net income growth rate or sustainable growth rate.

ROE = Rate of return on beginning-of-year net worth, including preferred stock.

$\frac{D}{E}$ = Dividends payout ratio, i.e., annual common and preferred dividends (D) divided by annual earnings (E).

$(1 - \frac{D}{E})$ = Earnings retention rate, i.e., $1 -$ the dividend payout ratio.

By observation, it can be seen from the above equation that a future earnings growth rate cannot be greater than a company's return on beginning equity, i.e., g = ROE, when dividends are zero. In addition, should a company wish to maintain a given earnings growth rate, it can do so by a variety of combinations of payout ratio and return on equity levels. For example, should the company in the above example find that its projected return on beginning equity had slipped to, say 8%, it would have to adjust its payout ratio downward to 37.5% if it wished to maintain its 5% earnings growth rate in the future $[.08 \times (1 - .375) = .05]$.[2]

Basis of Comparison

The results of financial statement analysis take on real meaning when compared to a standard appropriate to the company's stage of development, seasonal pattern, and industry and management plans. The selection of a relevant standard is always difficult.

The management of a company can use its budget as a basis of comparison. These are rarely available to the outside analyst. Therefore, the statement user must seek other sources. By comparing a company's current results as shown in its financial reports to similar data in past reports, the analyst can get some indication of how much "better" or "worse" things are compared to the past.

Important sources of average data for a particular industry are the investor reference services' publications. Another source of comparison bases are the publications of the various trade associations. Often, these publications report selected financial data for industries broken down by sales volume and asset categories. These data can be used to highlight variations from the typical company situation.

Another source of standards can be ratios computed from the data in the annual reports of companies in the same industry. This type of external comparison, when used with good judgment, can indicate the relative quality of the company's operating performance and financial management compared to its competitors.

Experienced financial analysts rarely rely on any one standard. They use several standards. They also look at a variety of related ratios and know from experience that they must have a good appreciation of the particular company's business before drawing conclusions based upon financial statement analysis.

Transnational Financial Statement Analysis

In a global economy financial statement users are increasingly faced with the need to read, analyze and understand financial statements issued by companies located in many countries. This activity is known as transnational financial statement analysis. In this setting the task of the analyst is complicated because the analysts must deal with financial statements that are often based on unfamiliar accounting rules, are expressed in a foreign language and currency, and present financial data in an unfamiliar format. Underlying these differences may be cultural, tax and legal conditions peculiar to the reporting company's country that influence a company's attitudes toward financial reporting principle and disclosure decisions.

---

[2]A later chapter discusses the sustainable growth rate equation and growth rate analysis in greater depth.

Formats

Statement formats can vary considerably from country to country. For example, some income statement formats show expenses by function (wages) while others classify expenses by type (production wages, selling wages, etc.). Some balance sheets show assets by increasing order of liquidity while others list assets in the reverse order. Classification of items within financial statements can also differ. For example, current liabilities in Germany may be liabilities maturing over the next four years whereas one year is the cut-off point in the United States of America. Transnational financial analysts deal with the multi-format problem by either learning to work with different formats, recasting foreign financial statements to their domicile country's format or recasting all financial statements to a standard format developed by the analyst.

Language

Few statement users have the multi-language skills required to feel comfortable dealing with financial statements presented in languages other than their own. Some companies recognized this problem and publish their financial reports in several languages. In some cases statement users employ translators. Translations can be helpful, but often the translation is prepared by accountants who know accounting but are not good translators or by translators who are not accountants. In either case this can lead to confusing and misleading translations. Statement users must be alert to this problem. Other solutions include using accounting lexicons to translate foreign accounting terms or limiting the analysis to the financial statement data in standard investor reference books. These two solutions often result in the analyst using summary data without a full understanding of the company's true condition or the accounting policy decisions.

Different Terminology

Transnational financial analysts must become familiar with accounting terminology differences. Some of these differences are easy to deal with as one term can be directly substituted for the other. For example, turnover is the British equivalent for what is called sales in the United States of America. Other differences are more difficult to handle. For example, the term *exceptionnel* in a French financial report might mean the item is either an unusual or an extraordinary item. In these cases, close reading of the financial statement is required to determine the exact meaning of the term.

Currencies

Typically companies issue financial statements expressed in the currency of the parent company's country. Financial ratios are unaffected by the reporting currency, except in the case where a company for the convenience of foreign readers restates its reporting currency financial statements into other currencies. These so called convenience statements are prepared by multiplying all items in the statements by the period end exchange rate. Analysts using these data must be careful to not be misled by distortions in period to period comparisons and trend analyses caused by changes in exchange rates. If the analyst wants to use convenience reports to analyze trend data, then the data must be scaled to eliminate the exchange rate effect. This can be done by using a consistent exchange rate over time. The best way to avoid being misled by convenience statements is to use the original reports to calculate trend data. This approach has the added advantage of giving the analyst the same view of the reporting company as its management, who is most probably measuring itself and managing the company based on the original statements.

Accounting Principles

There is considerable diversity of accounting standards around the world. For example, some countries, such as the Republic of Ireland, permit revaluation of property, others, such as the United States of America, insist on valuing it at its original purchase price, while others, such as Mexico, require the cost of property be adjusted for inflation. Some countries, such as the United Kingdom, allow purchased goodwill to be charged directly to owner's equity, while others, such as Sweden, require it to be recorded as an asset and then charged to income over time.

How these differences are handled in financial analyses depends on the intended use of the analysis and the analyst's comfort level in dealing with different accounting models and rules. If the analyst is analyzing different companies within a single country or a single company over time, in most cases a satisfactory financial ratio analysis can be prepared using the financial statements data as reported regardless of the accounting rules employed. Accounting diversity becomes a major problem in comparative analysis of financial statements from different countries with dissimilar accounting standards. In this situation the analyst usually recasts the financial statement data to make it comparable using a common accounting basis, such as the analyst's home country accounting standards or an accounting model of the analyst's own creation. Since restatement to a common basis is often difficult to accomplish and inevitably leads to at best rough approximations of comparable data, analysts tend to focus on reconciling only those accounting differences responsible for material differences in the original comparative data.

Disclosure

The extent of financial disclosure by corporations can vary considerably between countries and within some countries between listed and private companies. When confronted with the need to analyze a company with a low level of financial disclosure, such as a Swiss company not using International Accounting Standards, the analyst has little choice than to seek the missing information from noncompany sources, such as local investment bankers, competitors, retired employees and others familiar with the company. This will increase the financial analysis cost, but it may give the analyst a valuable advantage over less diligent analysts who are simply content to analyze the limited financial data provided by the company.

Tax Code

In some countries, such as Germany, the tax code requires in a large number of instances identical accounting be used in financial statements if certain tax accounting rules are elected for tax reporting purposes. In other countries, such as the United States of America, companies are not bound except in a limited number of cases by such tax code requirements. Transnational analysts must be aware of situations where tax return accounting elections may have a significant distorting influence on financial statements. The financial statements may not reflect the economic realities of the reporting company, since the goal of tax management is usually to minimize taxable income and tax accounting rules are adopted by governments to achieve revenue, social and economic objectives.

Legal

In many countries corporate reporting practices are governed by company legislation. Typically, this legislation provides some overarching requirements for financial reporting and, in some cases, may specify specific accounting practices. For example, the United Kingdom's 1985 Companies Act requires that financial statements provide a "true and fair" view of the company's state of affairs and of the profit or loss. Such legislation may provide companies with an opportunity to depart in their financial reports from their local generally accepted accounting principles. Such departures may be very useful to statement users, since the data may represent management's best judgment of the company's true state of affairs. In contrast, in other cases, such as the statutory reporting requirements of France, company legislation spells out in great detail and severely restricts company accounting principle elections and classification practices. These requirements have been imposed on corporations to facilitate national economic planning by the government and are not likely to lead to useful financial reports for other purposes. Fortunately, French corporations have more flexibility in the presentation of consolidated financial statements for public reporting purposes.

Cultural

A country's accounting culture or traditions can influence the way in which local accounting standards are employed in practice. For example, German accounting has a long history of being credit oriented with the result that prudence is encouraged in financial reports. That is, assets tend to be understated, liabilities tend to be overstated and disclosure clearly limited. In contrast, United Kingdom accounting has for a long time been geared more to the information needs of public equity investors who want transparent financial reports that reflect the current economic realities of the reporting company. Given these different perspectives on accounting, it is very likely that a German company and a British company could apply the same accounting standard to an identical transaction and end up with very different accounting results. Transnational financial analysts need to be aware of these accounting cultural differences so that they do not fall into the trap of assuming the same accounting rules necessarily lead to comparable accounting data.

Efficient Markets

A branch of financial economics research known as efficient markets research has reached these following conclusions that may be relevant to the field of financial analysis and equity valuation: The major equity markets are efficient in that security prices typically reflect all of the publicly available accounting and nonaccounting data. Inside information gives the holder of it an advantage over other investors until it is used. Financial statement data are used in investment decisions. The market is able to "look through" most accounting differences to distinguish real economic changes from the apparent changes reported by using different accounting alternatives. Finally, in the long run security markets reflect economic reality.

Efficient market researchers believe these findings may have a number of implications for the field of financial analysis. Since financial analysis techniques and its results are widely known, the value of using known analytical tools must already be impounded in security prices. Therefore, if financial analysis is to be beneficial, it must be helpful in predicting future results or have some novel quality. However, once these techniques and the data they produce become public, the advantages of the predictor and innovator will be quickly lost.

Another finding suggested by the research into the role of accounting data in equity markets is that companies using the more liberal accounting practices tend to have the higher market risk, as measured by the volatility of a stock's price relative to some index of the volatility of the market as a whole. Since companies that have liberal accounting often have weak operating and financial characteristics, some believe this market activity reflects the underlying corporate economics rather than the accounting practices. This belief is consistent with the efficient market theories.

Finally, it should be noted that the research to date has reached mixed conclusions on the relationship between accounting information, stock prices, and investment returns.

Critical Skill

An understanding of financial analysis is essential to those who use and issue corporate financial statements. Issuers who hope to use financial statements to influence others will be more likely to succeed if they know how statement users analyze financial data. On the other hand, financial statement users will be less likely to respond naively to financial data if they know how to analyze it correctly. Through research we are learning more each day about how around the world statement users analyze financial statements and how the results of these analyses are used. Anyone interested in corporate financial reporting should follow efficient markets research efforts of financial economists on a current basis, as today's knowledge in this area is fast being made obsolete.

CASE

7-1

Assessing a Company's Future Financial Health

Assessing the long-term financial health of a company is an important task for outsiders considering the extension of credit and for insiders in their formulation of strategy. History abounds with examples of firms that embarked upon overly ambitious programs and subsequently discovered that their portfolio of programs could not be financed on acceptable terms. The outcome frequently was the abandonment of programs in midstream, at considerable financial and organizational cost to the company, its vendors, its employees, or its creditors.

The key issue in assessing the long-term financial health of a company is whether or not the corporate system of goals, product-market strategies, investment requirements, and financing capabilities are in balance.

> At any given period every enterprise has a defined business mission which is realized in its established competitive positions in particular product markets. Corporate strategy centers on these competitive positions. This strategy may include a harvesting mode for a few mature and relatively unprofitable business units. But for most of the firm's product markets it is designed to maintain an existing market position or expand that position against primary competitors. Competitive strategy therefore dictates that the firm grow at least as rapidly as aggregate industry demand grows. The firm's targeted growth rate of sales must meet (or exceed) the expected growth rate of the industry.[1]

Thus, the starting point for assessing a firm's long-term health must be a thorough investigation of (1) management's goals for the company and for each of the product markets; (2) the strategy planned for each product market; (3) the likely response of competitors; and (4) the market, competitive, and operating characteristics of each

This case was prepared as the basis for class discussion rather than to illustrate either effective or ineffective handling of an administrative situation.
Copyright © 1991 by the President and Fellows of Harvard College. Harvard Business School case 292–019.
[1]Gordon Donaldson, *Managing Corporate Wealth* (New York: Praeger, 1984), pp. 64–65.

149

FIGURE A

*Factors in determining a
financing plan*

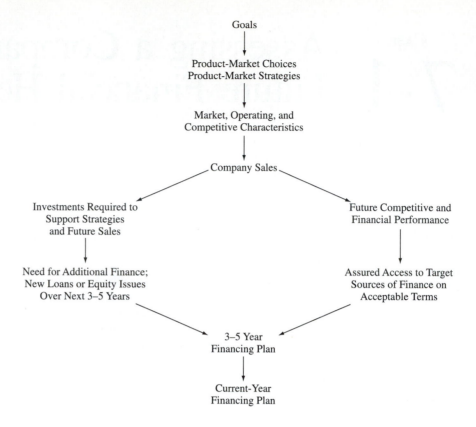

product market. The analyst is well-advised to devote substantial time exploring these
areas as the entire financial system of the company is driven by the economic and
competitive environment of its established product markets. The firm's strategy and
sales growth in each of its product markets will heavily determine the investments in
assets needed to support these strategies; and the effectiveness of the strategies, combined with the response of competitors, will strongly influence the firm's competitive
and financial performance and its resultant access to funds to finance the investments
in assets.

The following are some of the questions that seem important in assessing a company's future financial health. The sequencing of the question's corresponds to that
suggested by **Figure A.**

   1. What are management's goals for the company?
   2. In which product markets does management plan to compete?
      (a) What are management's goals in the various product markets?
      (b) What is the strategy in each product market?
   3. What are the market, competitive, and operating characteristics of each
      product market?
      (a) What is the growth of primary demand in each product market? Are
          sales seasonal? Cyclical?

(b) What are the strategies of the company's competitors?

(c) What are the company's operating policies?

(d) What are the main market, competitive, and operating risks?

4. What volume and nominal sales growth are likely for the company's units, individually and collectively?

5. What investments must be made in accounts receivables, inventory, and plant and equipment to support the various product market strategies? What will happen to the level of total assets over the next 3–5 years?

6. What is the outlook for profitability?

(a) What is the trend in reported profitability?

(b) What are the underlying financial accounting practices?

(c) Are there any hidden problems, such as suspiciously large levels or buildups of accounts receivable or inventories relative to sales?

(d) Is the level of profitability sustainable, given the outlook for the market and for competitive and regulatory pressures? (**Figure B** summarizes market and industry factors that can adversely affect a firm's future performance.)

7. Will the company need to raise additional finance over the next year, or over the next 3–5 years, to carry out strategically important programs?

(a) Does the company have a seasonal financing need? If so, how large is it and what will be the perceptions of suppliers of finance at the time of the need?

(b) Does the company have a long-term need for additional finance? If so, how large is it and what will be the perceptions of suppliers of finance at the time of the need?

(c) Will the company have a need for additional finance if it encounters adversity?

8. How soundly is the company financed, given its level of profitability, its level of business risk, and its future need for additional finance? (Access

FIGURE B

Sources of downward pressure on above-market returns

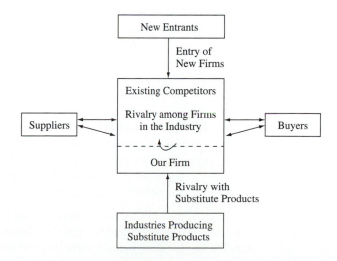

to target sources of finance depends on future competitive and financial performance and on the soundness of the company's existing financial structure.)
(a) How current is the company in the payment of its suppliers?
(b) Is the company close to its borrowing limit according to restrictive covenants?
(c) Is the company within its capacity to service the debt? What is the maturity structure of existing debt?
(d) Are there any hidden problems such as unconsolidated subsidiaries with high debt levels or large contingent or unfunded liabilities?

9. Does the company have assured access on acceptable terms to external sources of funds in amounts needed to meet its seasonal, long-term, or adversity needs?
   (a) Can the company raise equity funds?
      (1) Is there a market for the shares?
      (2) How many shares could be sold?
      (3) At what price could the shares be sold?
      (4) Would management be willing to issue new shares?
   (b) Can the company raise long-term debt?
      (1) Who are the target suppliers?
      (2) What are their criteria for lending?
      (3) How well does the company meet these criteria?
      (4) How much additional long-term debt can the company raise on acceptable terms?
   (c) Can the company raise short-term debt?
   (d) Does the company have assets that could be sold to raise funds? How quickly could they be sold?

10. Are the company's goals, product-market choices and strategies, investment requirements, financing needs, and financing capabilities in balance? (**Figure C** diagrams the interrelation of these management and financial considerations.)

11. Will the company's goals, strategies, investment requirements, financing needs, and financing capabilities remain in balance if the firm is struck by adversity?
   (a) What are the main regulatory, competitive, and operating risks? What combination of them might reasonably be expected to occur?
   (b) How would management respond in strategic and operating terms?
   (c) What would the implications be for future financing needs? For future financial performance?
   (d) Will it be possible to raise the finance needed on acceptable terms, given the financial suppliers' perceptions of the firm's strategic, competitive, and financial performance?

Clearly, many of these questions cannot be answered by only using the information contained in a company's published financial statements. Many require an understanding of (1) future industry structure and competitive behavior; (2) the competitive

FIGURE C

Testing for system balance

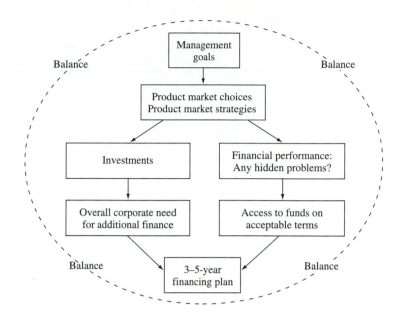

and operating characteristics of the business; (3) the long-term goals and plans of management; (4) the lending criteria of various segments of the capital markets; and (5) the soundness of management. Analysis of the published financial statements and their footnotes is only *one part* of a complete analysis of a company's future financial health.

It is also clear that the evaluation of a firm's financial health can vary substantially, depending on the perspective of the individual making the evaluation. A bank or supplier considering the extension of seasonal credit may consider a company a very safe bet, whereas a long-term lender dependent on the health and profitability of the company over a 15-year period may be very nervous.

The remainder of this case provides familiarity with the financial ratios that can be useful in answering some of the preceding questions. **Exhibits 1** and **2** provide financial statements for 1986 and 1990 for a hypothetical company. The following section (Financial Ratios and Financial Analysis) presents four types of financial ratios and then asks a series of questions concerning the financial statements in Exhibits 1 and 2. Use the equations to answer the questions and fill in the blank spaces in the text. Your analysis of the statements should also answer two overall questions:

1. Has the financial condition of the company changed during the four-year period?
2. What are the most significant changes, as indicated by the financial ratios?

Financial Ratios and Financial Analysis

The two basic sources of financial data for a business entity are the income statement and the balance sheet. The income statement summarizes revenues and expenses over a period of time, e.g., for the year ending December 31, 1990. The balance sheet is a

Exhibit 1   **Magnetronics, Inc., Consolidated Income Statements for Years Ending December 31, 1986, and 1990**
(thousands of dollars)

	1986	1990
Net sales	$32,513	$48,769
Cost of goods sold	19,183	29,700
Gross profit	13,330	19,069
Operating expenses	10,758	16,541
Interest expenses	361	517
Income before taxes	$ 2,211	$ 2,011
Federal income taxes	1,040	704
Net income	$ 1,171	$ 1,307

Exhibit 2   **Magnetronics, Inc., Consolidated Balance Sheets at December 31, 1986, and 1990**
(thousands of dollars)

	1986	1990
Cash	$ 1,617	$ 2,020
Accounts receivable	5,227	7,380
Inventories	4,032	8,220
Current assets	10,876	17,620
Net fixed assets	4,073	5,160
Total assets	$14,949	$22,780
Notes payable, banks	$ 864	$ 1,213
Accounts payable	1,615	2,820
Accrued expenses and tax	2,028	3,498
Current liabilities	$ 4,507	$ 7,531
Long-term debt	2,750	3,056
Stockholders' equity	7,692	12,193
Total liabilities and stockholders' equity	$14,949	$22,780

list of what the business owns (its assets), what it owes (its liabilities), and what has been invested by the owners (owners' equity) at a specific point in time, e.g., *at* December 31, 1990.

From the figures found on the income statement and the balance sheet, one can calculate the following types of financial ratios:

1. Profitability ratios.
2. Activity ratios.

3. Leverage ratios.
4. Liquidity ratios.

How Profitable is the Company? Profitability Ratios.   One measure of the profitability of a business is profit as a percentage of sales, as determined by the profitability ratio equation:

$$\frac{\text{Net profit after taxes}}{\text{Net sales}}$$

The information necessary to determine a company's profits as a percentage of sales can be found in the company's _____ .

1. Magnetronics' profit as a percentage of sales for 1990 (see Exhibit 1) was $ _____ divided by $ _____ , or _____ %.
2. This represented an ( ) *increase/decrease* from _____ % in 1986.
3. The deterioration in profitability resulted from an *increase/decrease* in cost of goods sold as a percentage of sales, and from an *increase/decrease* in operating expenses as a percentage of sales. The only favorable factor was the decrease in the _____ .

Management and investors often are more interested in the return earned on the funds invested than in the level of profits as a percentage of sales. Companies operating in businesses requiring very little investment in assets often have low profit margins but earn very attractive returns on invested funds. Conversely, there are numerous examples of companies in very capital-intensive businesses that earn miserably low returns on invested funds, despite seemingly attractive profit margins.

Therefore, it is useful to examine both the level and the trend of the company's operating profits as a percentage of total assets. To increase the comparability across companies within the same industry, it is useful to use profit before taxes and before any interest charges (earnings before interest and taxes, or EBIT). This allows the analyst to focus on the profitability of operations, without any distortion due to tax factors or the method by which the company has financed itself.

4. Magnetronics had a total of $ _____ invested in assets at year-end 1990 and earned before interest and taxes $ _____ during 1990. Its operating profit as a percentage of total assets is calculated as follows:

$$\frac{\text{Profit before interest and taxes}}{\text{Total assets}}$$

In 1990 this figure was _____ %, which represented an *increase/decrease* from the _____ % earned in 1986.

From the viewpoint of the shareholders, an equally important figure is the company's return on equity. Return on equity is calculated by dividing profit after tax by the owners' equity:

$$\frac{\text{Profit after taxes}}{\text{Owners' equity}}$$

It indicates how profitably the company is utilizing shareholders' funds.

5. Magnetronics had \$ _____ of owners' equity and earned \$ _____ after taxes in 1990. Its return on equity was _____ %, an *improvement/ deterioration* from the _____ % earned in 1986.

Are There Any Hidden Problems? Activity Ratios. The second basic type of financial ratio is the activity ratio. Activity ratios indicate how well a company employs it assets. Ineffective utilization of assets results in the need for more finance, unnecessary interest costs, and a correspondingly lower return on capital employed. Furthermore, low activity ratios or a deterioration in the activity ratios may indicate uncollectible accounts receivables or obsolete inventory or equipment.

"Total asset turnover" measures the company's effectiveness in utilizing its total assets and is calculated by dividing total assets into sales:

$$\frac{\text{Net sales}}{\text{Total assets}}$$

1. Total asset turnover for Magnetronics in 1990 can be calculated by dividing \$ _____ into \$ _____ . The turnover had *improved/deteriorated* from _____ times in 1986 to _____ times in 1990.

It is useful to examine the turnover ratios for each type of asset, as the use of total assets may hide important problems in one of the specific asset categories. One important category is accounts receivables. The average collection period measures the number of days that the company must wait on average between the time of sale and the time when it is paid. The average collection period is calculated in two steps. First, divide annual credit sales by 365 days to determine average sales per day:

$$\frac{\text{Net sales}}{\text{365 days}}$$

Then, divide the accounts receivable by average sales per day to determine the number of days of sales that are still unpaid:

$$\frac{\text{Accounts receivable}}{\text{Average sales per day}}$$

2. Magnetronics had \$ _____ invested in accounts receivables at year-end 1990. Its average sales per day were \$ _____ during 1990 and its average collection period was _____ days. This represented an *improvement/deterioration* from the average collection period of _____ days in 1986.

A third activity ratio is the inventory turnover ratio, which indicates the effectiveness with which the company is employing inventory. Since inventory is recorded on the balance sheet at cost (not at its sales value), it is advisable to use cost of goods sold as the measure of activity. The inventory turnover figure is calculated by dividing cost of goods sold by inventory:

$$\frac{\text{Cost of goods}}{\text{Inventory}}$$

3. Magnetronics apparently needed $ _____ of inventory at year-end 1990 to support its operations during 1990. Its activity during 1990 as measured by the cost of goods sold was $ _____ . It therefore had an inventory turnover of _____ times. This represented an *improvement/deterioration* from _____ times in 1986.

A fourth and final activity ratio is the fixed asset turnover ratio which measures the effectiveness of the company in utilizing its plant and equipment:

$$\frac{\text{Net sales}}{\text{Net fixed assets}}$$

4. Magnetronics had net fixed assets of $ _____ and sales of $ _____ in 1990. Its fixed asset turnover ratio in 1990 was _____ times, an *improvement/deterioration* from _____ in 1986.

5. So far, we have discussed three measures of profitability: they are (a) _____ (b) _____ and (c) _____ . We have also discussed four activity ratios which measure the effectiveness with which the company is utilizing its assets: they are (d) _____ (e) _____ (f) _____ and (g) _____ .

6. The deterioration in Magnetronics' operating profits as a percentage of total assets between 1986 and 1990 resulted primarily from _____ _____ _____ _____ .

How Soundly is the Company Financed? Leverage Ratios. The third basic type of financial ratio is the leverage ratio. The various leverage ratios measure the relationship of funds supplied by creditors and the funds supplied by the owners. The use of borrowed funds by profitable companies will improve the return on equity. However, it increases the riskiness of the business and, if used in excessive amounts, can result in financial embarrassment.

One leverage ratio, the debt ratio, measures the total funds provided by creditors as a percentage of total assets:

$$\frac{\text{Total debt}}{\text{Total assets}}$$

Total debt includes both current and long-term liabilities.

1. The total debt of Magnetronics as of December 31, 1990, was $ _____ or _____ % of total assets. This represented an *increase/decrease* from _____ % as of December 31, 1986.

The ability of Magnetronics to meet its interest payments can be estimated by relating its earnings before interest and taxes (EBIT) to its interest payments:

$$\frac{\text{Earnings before interest and taxes}}{\text{Interest charges}}$$

This ratio is called the times interest earned ratio.

2. Magnetronics' earnings before interest and taxes were $ _____ in 1990, and its interest charges were $ _____ . Its times interest earned was _____ times. This represented an *improvement/deterioration* from the 1986 level of _____ times.

A similar ratio to the times interest earned ratio is the fixed charge coverage ratio. This ratio recognizes that lease payments under long-term contracts are usually as mandatory as interest and principle payments on debt. The ratio is calculated as follows:

$$\frac{\text{EBIT} + \text{Lease payments}}{\text{Interest charges} + \text{Lease payments}}$$

3. Magnetronics had annual lease payments of $760. Its fixed charge coverage in 1990 was _____ times.

A fourth and final leverage ratio is the number of days of payables ratio. This ratio measures the average number of days that the company is taking to pay its suppliers of raw materials. It is calculated by dividing annual purchases by 365 days to determine average purchases per day:

$$\frac{\text{Annual purchases}}{\text{365 days}}$$

Accounts payable are then divided by average purchases per day:

$$\frac{\text{Accounts payable}}{\text{Average purchases per day}}$$

to determine the number of days of purchases that are still unpaid.

It is often difficult to determine the purchases of a firm. Instead, the income statement shows cost of goods sold, a figure that includes not only raw materials but also labor and overhead. Thus, it often is only possible to gain a rough idea as to whether or not a firm is becoming more or less dependent on its suppliers for finance. This can be done by relating accounts payable to cost of goods sold,

$$\frac{\text{Accounts payable}}{\text{Cost of goods sold}}$$

and following this ratio over time.

4. Magnetronics owed its suppliers $ _____ at year-end 1990. This represented _____ % of cost of goods sold and was an *increase/decrease* from the _____ % at year-end 1986. The company appears to be more/less prompt in paying its suppliers in 1990 than it was in 1986.

5. The deterioration in Magnetronics' profitability, as measured by its return on equity, from 15.2% in 1986 to 10.7% in 1990 resulted from the combined impact of _____ _____ and _____ _____ .

6. The financial riskiness of Magnetronics *increased/decreased* between 1986 and 1990.

How Liquid is the Company? Liquidity Ratios.   The fourth basic type of financial ratio is the liquidity ratio. These ratios measure a company's ability to meet financial obligations as they become current. The current ratio, defined as current assets divided by current liabilities,

$$\frac{\text{Current assets}}{\text{Current liabilities}}$$

assumes that current assets are much more readily and certainly convertible into cash than other assets. It relates these fairly liquid assets to the claims that are due within one year—the current liabilities.

1. Magnetronics held $ _____ of current assets at year-end 1990 and owed $ _____ to creditors due to be paid within one year. Its current ratio was _____ , an *improvement/deterioration* from the ratio of _____ at year-end 1986.

The quick ratio or acid test is similar to the current ratio but excludes inventory from the current assets:

$$\frac{\text{Current assets} - \text{Inventories}}{\text{Current liabilities}}$$

Inventory is excluded because it is often difficult to convert into cash (at least at book value) if the company is struck by adversity.

2. The quick ratio for Magnetronics at year-end 1990 was _____ , an *improvement/deterioration* from the ratio of _____ at year-end 1986.

The Case of the Unidentified Industries

The preceding exercise suggests a series of questions that may be helpful in assessing a company's future financial health. It also described several ratios that are useful in answering some of the questions, especially if the historical trend in these ratios is examined.

However, it is also important to compare the actual absolute value with some standard to determine whether the company is performing well. Unfortunately, there is

EXHIBIT 3   Unidentified Balance Sheets

	Company				
	A	*B*	*C*	*D*	*E*
Balance Sheet Percentages					
Cash	7.3%	.8%	13.5%	7.2%	11.3%
Receivables	22.5	5.4	5.8	60.3	10.9
Inventories.	8.3	2.8	35.8	8.7	61.5
Other current assets	4.6	.1	4.1	7.3	2.7
Property and equipment (net)	35.0	83.0	23.6	4.3	8.3
Other assets	22.3	7.9	17.2	12.2	5.3
Total assets	100.0%	100.0%	100.0%	100.0%	100.0%
Notes payable	2.4%	1.8%	4.5%	50.8%	5.5%
Accounts payable	7.9	3.2	14.6	15.2	14.3
Other current liabilities	14.7	2.2	10.6	5.7	10.5
Long-term debt	19.3	29.6	15.8	22.7	9.2
Other liabilities	17.9	17.8	8.5	1.3	2.5
Owners' equity	37.8	45.4	46.0	4.3	58.0
Total liabilities and equity	100.0%	100.0%	100.0%	100.0%	100.0%
Selected Ratios					
Net profits/net sales	.04	.16	.014	.01	.05
Net profits/total assets	.05	.06	.07	.01	.06
Net profits/owners' equity	.12	.13	.15	.13	.12
Net sales/total assets	1.2	.38	5.6	2.1	1.5
Collection period (days)	71	52	3	106	23
Inventory turnover	12	11	12	23	1.2
Total liabilities/total assets	.62	.55	.54	.96	.42
Long-term debt/owners' equity	.51	.65	.34	5.3	.16
Current assets/current liabilities	1.7	1.3	2.0	1.0	2.9
Quick ratio	1.4	.9	.8	.9	.8

no single current ratio, inventory turnover, or debt ratio that is appropriate to all industries, and even within a specific industry, ratios may vary significantly among companies. The operating and competitive characteristics of the company's industry greatly influence its investment in the various types of assets, the riskiness of these investments, and the financial structure of its balance sheet.

Try to match the five following types of companies with their corresponding balance sheets and financial ratios, as shown in **Exhibit 3**:

1. Electric utility
2. Japanese trading company
3. Retail jewelry chain
4. Automobile manufacturer
5. Supermarket chain

In doing the exercise, consider the operating and competitive characteristics of the industry and their implications for (1) the collection period, (2) inventory turnover,

(3) the amount of plant and equipment, and (4) the appropriate financial structure. Then identify which one of the five sets of balance sheets and financial ratios best matches your expectations.

CASE
7-2

First Investments, Inc.: Analysis of Financial Statements

In March 1995, Fred Aldrich, a summer trainee with the First Investments, Inc., was called into the office of the head of investment analysis section of the trust department. The following conversation took place:

> Fred, here are the 1994, 1993, and 1985 Basic Industries Company's financials (**Exhibit 1**) and a 10-year summary (**Exhibit 2**). Our trust department has owned this stock since the early 1980s. As you know, our portfolio people place a lot of emphasis on the quality of a company's earnings and the return on owners' equity in making stock selections. Well, they are worried. The 1994 Basic Industries annual report shows a decline in the return on owners' equity. Now, they want us to comment on the way that the company has achieved its return on equity over the last 10 years, starting with 1985. I would like you to prepare this analysis. I suggest you forget the strike years of 1989 and 1990. Also, concentrate on what happened in the 1993–1994 period. I hope the analysis will include a direct comparison of the quality of 1985 and 1994 returns on stockholders' equity and the other key financial ratios for these two years. Finally, you should know that the company has not changed its accounting policies and practices materially over the last decade. The only changes have been due to new standards issued by the FASB, but these have not materially distorted the comparative data.

Professor David F. Hawkins prepared this case as the basis for class discussion rather than to illustrate either effective or ineffective handling of an administrative situation.

Copyright © 1996 by the President and Fellows of Harvard College. Harvard Business School case 197–010.

EXHIBIT 1 **Basic Industries Company and Consolidated Affiliates: Statement of Current and Retained Earnings (as reported) for the Years 1994, 1993, and 1985**
(in millions)

	1994	1993	1985
Sales of products and services to customers...............	$13,413.1	$11,575.3	$6,213.6
Operating Costs:			
Employee compensation, including benefits	$ 5,332.0	$ 4,709.7	$2,440.8
Materials, supplies, services, and other costs	6,966.7	5,690.5	3,063.4
Depreciation......................................	376.2	334.0	188.4
Taxes, except those on income	123.0	113.5	51.6
Increase in inventories during the year.................	(270.8)	(227.2)	(176.1)
	$12,418.1	$10,620.5	$5,568.1
Operating margin	$ 995.0	$ 954.8	$ 645.5
Other income	185.8	183.7	72.1
Interest and other financial charges	(180.1)	(126.9)	(27.4)
Earnings before income taxes and minority interest	$ 1,000.7	$ 1,011.6	$ 690.2
Provision for income taxes	(382.4)	(418.7)	(352.2)
Minority interest in earnings of consolidated affiliates	(10.2)	(7.8)	17.1
Net earnings applicable to common stock	$ 608.1	$ 585.1	$ 355.1
Dividends declared	(291.2)	(272.9)	(216.7)
Amount added to retained earnings	$ 316.9	$ 312.2	$ 138.4
Retained earnings at January 1	2,683.6	2,371.4	1,246.0
Retained earnings at December 31....................	$ 3,000.5	$ 2,683.6	$1,384.4

Basic Industries Company and Consolidated Affiliates: Statement of Financial Position (as reported) December 31, 1994, 1993, 1985 (in millions)

	1994	1993	1985
Assets			
Cash	$ 314.5	$ 396.8	$ 289.9
Marketable securities	57.3	25.3	353.3
Current receivables	2,593.8	2,177.1	1,062.5
Inventories......................................	2,257.0	1,986.2	1,136.9
Current assets	$ 5,222.6	$ 4,485.4	$2,842.6
Investments	1,004.8	869.7	241.0
Plant and equipment...............................	2,615.6	2,360.5	1,037.0
Other assets	526.1	608.6	180.0
Total assets	$ 9,369.1	$ 8,324.2	$4,300.6

EXHIBIT 1   (Continued)

	1994	1993	1985
Liabilities and Equity			
Short-term borrowings	$ 644.9	$ 665.2	$ 120.6
Accounts payable	696.0	673.5	376.2
Progress collections and price adjustments accrued	1,000.5	718.4	300.5
Dividends payable	72.8	72.7	58.7
Taxes accrued	337.2	310.0	318.3
Other costs and expenses accrued	1,128.1	1,052.6	392.6
Current liabilities	$ 3,879.5	$ 3,492.4	$1,566.9
Long-term borrowings	1,195.2	917.2	364.1
Other liabilities	518.9	492.1	221.0
Total liabilities	5,593.6	4,901.7	2,152.0
Minority interest in equity of consolidated affiliates	$ 71.2	$ 50.1	$ 41.4
Preferred stock	—	—	—
Common stock	$ 465.2	$ 463.8	$ 455.8
Amounts received for stock in excess of par value	414.5	409.5	266.9
Retained earnings	3,000.5	2,683.6	1,384.5
	$ 3,880.2	$ 3,556.9	$2,107.2
Deduct common stock held in treasury	(175.9)	(184.5)	—
Total shareowners' equity	$ 3,704.3	$ 3,372.4	$2,107.0
Total liabilities and equity	$ 9,369.1	$ 8,324.2	$4,300.6

EXHIBIT 2 Basic Industries Company and Consolidated Affiliates: 10-Year Financial Highlights as Reported in 1994 Annual Report

(dollar amounts in millions; per share amounts in dollars)

	1994	1993	1992	1991	1990	1989	1988	1987	1986	1985
Summary of Operations										
Sales of products and services	$13,413.1	$11,575.3	$10,239.5	$9,425.3	$8,726.7	$8,448.0	$8,381.6	$7,741.2	$7,177.3	$6,213.6
Materials, engineering, and production costs	10,137.6	8,55.2	7,509.6	6,962.1	6,423.6	6,346.1	6,251.1	5,779.4	5,311.0	4,449.2
Selling, general & administrative expenses	2,280.5	2,105.3	1,915.2	1,726.2	1,754.2	1,615.3	1,482.1	1,320.9	1,234.3	1,118.9
Operating costs	$12,418.1	$10,620.5	$9,424.8	$8,688.3	$8,177.8	$7,961.4	$7,733.8	$7,100.3	$6,545.3	$5,568.1
Operating margin	$995.0	$954.8	$814.7	$737.0	$548.9	$486.6	$647.8	$640.9	$632.0	$645.5
Other income	185.8	183.7	189.2	152.0	106.8	98.7	86.3	91.4	72.4	72.1
Interest and other financial charges	(180.1)	(126.9)	(106.7)	(96.9)	(101.4)	(78.1)	(70.5)	(62.9)	(39.9)	(27.4)
Earnings before income taxes and minority interest	$1,000.7	$1,011.6	$897.2	$792.1	$554.3	$507.2	$663.6	$669.4	$664.5	$690.2
Provision for income taxes	(382.4)	(418.7)	(364.1)	(317.1)	(220.6)	(231.5)	(312.3)	(320.5)	(347.4)	(352.2)
Minority interest	(10.2)	(7.8)	(3.1)	(3.2)	(5.2)	2.3	5.8	12.5	21.8	17.1
Net earnings	$608.1	$585.1	$530.0	$471.8	$328.5	$278.0	$357.1	$361.4	$338.9	$355.1
Earnings per common share	$3.34	$3.21	$2.91	$2.60	$1.81	$1.54	$1.98	$2.00	$1.88	$1.97
Dividends declared per common share	$1.60	$1.50	$1.40	$.38	$1.30	$1.30	$1.30	$1.30	$1.30	$1.20
Earnings as a percentage of sales	4.5%	5.1%	5.2%	5.0%	3.8%	3.3%	4.3%	4.7%	4.7%	5.7%
Earned on average shareowners' equity	17.2%	18.1%	18.0%	17.6%	13.2%	11.5%	15.4%	16.5%	16.2%	18.0%
Cash dividends declared	$291.2	$272.9	$254.8	$249.7	$235.4	$235.2	$234.8	$234.2	$234.6	$216.7
Shares outstanding—average (in thousands)	182,120	182,051	182,112	181,684	181,114	180,965	180,651	180,266	180,609	180,634
Shareowner accounts—average	547,000	537,000	536,000	523,000	529,000	520,000	530,000	529,000	530,000	521,000
Market price range per share	65-30	75-7/8-55	73-58-1/4	66-1/2-46-1/2	47-1/4-30-1/8	49-1/8-37	50-1/4-40-1/8	48-41-1/4	60-40	60-1/8-45-1/2
Price-earnings ratio range	19-9	24-17	25-20	26-28	26-17	32-24	5-20	29-21	32-21	31-23
Current assets	$5,222.6	$4,485.4	$3,979.3	$3,639.0	$3,334.8	$3,287.8	$3,311.1	$3,207.6	$3,013.0	$2,842.6
Current liabilities	3,879.5	3,492.4	2,869.7	2,840.4	2,650.3	2,366.7	2,104.3	1,977.4	1,883.2	1,566.8
Total assets	9,369.1	8,324.2	7,401.8	6,887.8	6,198.5	5,894.0	5,652.3	5,205.3	4,768.1	4,300.6
Shareowners' equity	3,704.3	3,372.4	3,084.6	2,801.8	2,553.6	2,426.5	2,402.1	2,245.3	2,128.1	2,107.2
Plant and equipment additions	$671.8	$598.6	$435.9	$553.1	$581.4	$530.6	$514.7	$561.7	$484.9	$332.9
Depreciation	376.2	334.0	314.3	273.6	334.7	351.3	300.1	280.4	233.6	188.4
Employees—average worldwide	404,000	388,000	369,000	363,000	297,000	410,000	394,000	385,000	376,000	333,000
—average United States	307,000	304,000	292,000	291,000	310,000	318,000	305,000	296,000	291,000	258,000

Basic Industries is a diversified multinational corporation with major shares in various electrical related markets.

Questions

Complete the assignment given to Fred Aldrich.

CASE
7-3

Identify the Industries

Common sized balance sheets of thirteen firms are presented in **Exhibit 1** along with some useful ratios. These companies were chosen because they consist of primarily one major business segment and the relationships between balance sheet items, profit, and operations are fairly typical of these industries. The companies involved are: (In alphabetical order)

1. A profitable major airline.
2. A regional bank.
3. A major consumer products manufacturer.
4. A defense contractor.
5. An upscale department store chain.
6. A discount department store chain.

Research Associate Barbara Seal prepared this case under the supervision of Professor Sharon M. McKinnon of Northeastern University and William J. Bruns, Jr. as the basis for class discussion rather than to illustrate either effective or ineffective handling of an administrative situation.

7. A grocery store chain.

8. A for-profit hospital chain.

9. A hotel chain.

10. A major international oil company.

11. A home and personal security provider.

12. A temporary office personnel agency.

13. A major regional utility company.

Question

The financial statement dates are noted at the top of each column. Use the ratios, common sized statements, and your knowledge of business conditions at the time these data were generated to identify the companies.

Exhibit 1

	Dec.90 A	Feb.90 B	Dec.90 C	Jan.91 D	Dec.90 E	Jun.90 F	Aug.90 G	May90 H	Jan.91 I	Dec.90 J	Dec.90 K	Dec.90 L	Dec.90 M
Cash and marketable securities	1.6	0.8	25.5	1.3	0.1	0.9	3.9	2.2	0.1	2.2	11.7	5.2	49.0
Receivables	10.9	2.5	68.6	30.2	6.4	10.0	17.3	7.9	2.7	12.8	43.4	7.7	36.8
Inventories	7.3	21.6	—	23.6	3.5	0.9	2.3	12.0	51.0	42.4	4.2	0.7	—
Other current assets	1.1	0.9	—	2.2	0.2	2.1	3.3	5.7	2.5	1.4	8.3	1.2	2.8
Total current assets	20.9	25.8	94.1	57.3	10.2	14.1	26.8	27.7	56.3	58.9	67.6	14.8	88.6
Plant & equipment	71.5	39.4	1.8	42.4	83.9	74.7	57.9	58.8	41.4	25.0	2.9	66.0	8.5
Investments	5.0	—	—	—	—	—	—	—	—	—	—	—	—
Goodwill	—	15.0	—	—	—	4.3	—	2.0	—	—	26.4	—	2.4
Other noncurrent assets	2.6	19.8	4.0	0.3	5.9	6.9	15.3	11.6	2.3	16.1	3.0	17.5	0.5
Total noncurrent assets	79.1	74.2	5.9	42.7	89.8	85.9	73.2	72.3	43.7	41.1	32.4	85.2	11.4
Total Assets	**100.0**	**100.0**	**100.0**	**100.0**	**100.0**	**100.0**	**100.0**	**100.0**	**100.0**	**100.0**	**100.0**	**100.0**	**100.0**
Accounts payable	17.8	15.8	88.9	10.7	4.4	9.9	3.7	15.8	23.3	10.0	2.2	9.0	4.1
Notes payable	6.9	0.3	—	7.9	5.1	0.9	—	3.1	3.5	23.3	—	—	—
Current portion of L/T debt	—	1.1	—	0.5	2.6	0.4	0.9	2.4	0.1	0.0	—	0.8	—
Other current liabilities[a]	2.6	10.1	5.6	9.9	3.6	14.2	20.1	14.3	8.2	18.1	42.4	2.7	19.7
Total current liabilities	27.4	27.3	94.4	29.0	15.6	25.4	24.8	35.7	35.0	51.4	44.5	12.5	23.9
L/T debt	8.8	57.3	0.5	25.2	35.6	16.3	18.2	20.9	6.5	0.8	31.8	27.3	—
Other noncurrent liabilities	26.2	10.2	0.2	2.4	19.1	22.1	12.6	18.8	11.4	1.3	—	12.2	—
Total liabilities	62.3	94.7	95.2	56.6	70.4	63.8	55.5	75.4	52.9	53.5	76.3	52.1	23.9
Preferred stock	0.0	0.3	—	—	7.3	0.3	0.4	—	—	—	2.4	—	—
Common stock	3.2	0.0	0.3	7.9	22.3	2.3	11.6	9.0	1.0	1.1	0.0	6.6	7.2
Additional paid-in-capital	—	5.6	2.3	—	—	12.2	—	—	3.6	3.4	8.2	0.6	0.3
Retained earnings	50.5	-0.6	2.4	35.5	—	29.9	32.5	46.5	42.5	41.7	13.2	50.6	70.0
Adjustments to retained earnings[b]	2.8	—	-0.2	—	—	-0.2	-0.1	-6.2	—	0.3	0.0	—	0.3
Treasury stock	-18.8	-0.0	-0.0	—	—	-8.2	—	-24.7	—	—	—	-9.9	-1.4
Total stockholders' equity	37.7	5.3	4.8	43.4	29.6	36.2	44.5	24.6	47.1	46.5	23.7	47.9	76.1
Total Liabilities & Stock Equity	**100.0**	**100.0**	**100.0**	**100.0**	**100.0**	**100.0**	**100.0**	**100.0**	**100.0**	**100.0**	**100.0**	**100.0**	**100.0**
Selected Ratios													
Current ratio	0.76	0.95	1.00	1.98	0.65	0.56	1.08	0.78	1.61	1.15	1.52	1.18	3.71
Inventory turns (X)	7.9	8.9	N.M.[c]	4.5	10.1	N.M.	N.M.	8.8	4.4	2.8	N.M.	N.M.	N.M.
Receivables collection period	30	3	N.M.	45	41	31	51	15	3	31	51	48	41
Net sales/total assets	1.320	2.638	0.109	1.521	0.418	1.188	1.233	1.960	2.863	1.514	3.093	0.584	3.313
Net profits/net sales	0.043	0.001	-0.064	0.040	0.092	0.035	0.064	0.059	0.040	0.060	0.011	0.100	0.048
Net profits/total assets	0.057	0.001	-0.007	0.061	0.042	0.042	0.079	0.116	0.113	0.091	0.035	0.058	0.160
Net profits/net worth	0.152	0.022	-0.143	0.140	0.107	0.116	0.177	0.471	0.241	0.196	0.147	0.122	0.211

Notes: [a]Other Current Liabilities primarily consists of unearned revenues.
[b]Adjustments to Retained Earnings primarily consists of foreign translation adjustments.
[c]N.M. means that the ratio is not meaningful, even if calculable, for this company.

⎯⎯⎯⎯⎯⎯⎯⎯⎯⎯⎯⎯⎯⎯⎯⎯⎯⎯⎯

CASE 7-4 Scranton Furniture Company

In March 1992, Richard Allan, an assistant credit analyst for the Scranton Furniture Company, was concerned about changes in two of Scranton's accounts in Minnesota—Lloyd's, Inc., of Minneapolis and The Emporium department store in St. Paul. He therefore brought the credit folders of these two customers to the attention of Watt Ralphson, the credit manager of Scranton Furniture. The Scranton Furniture Company had its headquarters in Scranton, Pennsylvania, and manufactured a limited line of high-quality home furniture for distribution to department stores, independent home furnishing retailers, and regional chains.

Lloyd's retailed quality home furnishings from four locations—one in the downtown section of Minneapolis and the others in nearby suburban areas. Sales were somewhat seasonal, with a slight downturn in the midsummer months and a slight upturn during the December holiday season. Lloyd's sales were approximately 75% for cash or credit cards and 25% on six-month installment terms. Installment terms called for 25% down and the balance in equal monthly payments over a six-month period.

Lloyd's had been established as a partnership and was later incorporated. In June 1991, two of the four original partners sold their shares in the company to the two remaining owners.

Lloyd's had been a customer of Scranton Furniture for over 30 years and had previously handled its affairs in a most satisfactory manner. The Emporium was a comparatively new customer of Scranton's, having established an account in 1983. A medium-sized department store in downtown St. Paul, The Emporium was well-known for its extensive lines of home furnishings. Its account with Scranton had been satisfactory through 1991.

Both accounts were sold on terms of 2%, 10, net 30, and although not discounting, had been paying invoices promptly until December 1991. Ralphson had previously established a $50,000 limit on Lloyd's and an $85,000 limit on The Emporium.

Professor David Hawkins and Professor Norman J. Bartczak, Columbia University, prepared this as the basis for class discussion rather than to illustrate either effective or ineffective handling of an administrative situation.

Scranton Furniture advertised its lines nationally and attempted to maintain intensive coverage of its trading areas by distributing through stores strategically located within a particular marketing area. Beginning in 1990, activity in the furniture market had become sufficiently spotty that quality of product and service were not the only bases for competition among manufacturers for outlets. Credit terms and financing of dealers became equally important, thus, the Scranton Furniture Company, in Ralphson's words, was "backed into the position of supporting numerous customers in order to maintain adequate distribution for its products."

Because of this requirement for the extension of fairly liberal credit, Ralphson had adhered strictly to a policy of obtaining current reports on the financial status of customers. These reports, obtained as annual balance sheets and profit and loss statements for customers that were considered satisfactory risks, were supplied directly by the customers. Under certain circumstances, wherein Scranton was working very closely with a particular customer who was trading actively on a small investment, Ralphson received quarterly and at times monthly financial statements in order "to keep on top" of the credit situation.

In early March 1992, Richard Allan received the annual reports of Lloyd's and The Emporium. After reviewing these statements and checking the accounts receivable ledger for both customers, Allan felt that the accounts should be reviewed by Ralphson. Accordingly, he furnished Ralphson with the information found in **Exhibits 1** through **5.**

When reviewing the accounts, Ralphson kept in mind that 1991 had not been a particularly good year for retail furniture stores. It was generally known that stores such as The Emporium, carrying low-priced furniture lines, were the first to suffer the declines which had come in the late summer and early fall. This situation was followed by signs of a relaxing demand for furniture of higher quality and higher price toward the end of 1991. The drop in volume and the subsequent price-cutting hit the profit margins of some retailers to such an extent that the losses in the latter part of the year in some cases equaled, or more than offset, profits gained in the earlier part of the year.

In the early months of 1992, the "softness" of the furniture business continued. Although there was no severe drop in the buying of furniture at the retail level, retail stores reduced orders of new lines and reorders of established lines in January, February, and March, because of a general feeling that there had been considerable "overbuying" by consumers which would result in a subsequent downturn in retail sales.

EXHIBIT 1   Aging of Scranton Furniture's Accounts Receivable Balances Owed by Lloyd's and The Emporium as of March 31, 1992

	Prior	*December*	*January*	*February*	*March*	*Totals*
Lloyd's		$34,819	$5,480	$21,146	$ 6,168	$ 67,613
The Emporium..............	$2,285[a]	29,304	6,153	26,112	54,749	118,603

[a]Represents invoice on disputed shipment; customer claimed damaged merchandise.

EXHIBIT 2   Lloyd's, Inc. Balance Sheets as of January 31, 1990–1992
(dollars in thousands)

	1/31/90	*1/31/91*	*1/31/92*
Assets			
Cash	$ 85	$ 65	$ 50
Accounts receivable, net	1,385	1,565	1,610
Inventory	1,825	1,820	1,825
Total current assets	$3,295	$3,450	$3,485
Land	355	355	355
Buildings, fixtures, and equipment	1,355	1,370	1,575
Less: Accumulated depreciation	190	290	395
Net buildings, fixtures, and equipment	$1,165	$1,080	$1,180
Investments	65	65	65
Due from stockholders	—	215	290
Deferred charges	40	20	20
Total assets	$4,920	$5,185	$5,395
Liabilities and Net Worth			
Accounts payable	$ 865	$ 870	$ 925
Notes payable—employees	70	80	80
Estimated federal income tax	65	—	—
Current maturities on long-term debt	155	360	220
Miscellaneous accruals	220	205	65
Total current liabilities	$1,375	$1,515	$1,290
Notes payable—bank[a]	545	900	875
Mortgage notes payable	2,260	2,250	2,630
Preferred stock—5% noncumulative	190	190	190
Common stock	360	360	360
Additional paid-in capital	—	—	115
Retained earnings (deficit)	190	(30)	(65)
Total liabilities and net worth	$4,920	$5,185	$5,395

[a]Secured by pledged accounts receivable.

Throughout the country, orders for shipment in March were down about 30% from February; February had itself shown a drop of about 10% from January. Thus, credit managers among furniture manufacturing concerns were placed in the unhappy position of trying to please sales managers who wanted to maintain volume, while they were aware that the shipment of furniture to customers who had already overextended their financial positions was potentially dangerous in such a period.

EXHIBIT 3   Lloyd's, Inc. Income Statements for Years Ending January 31, 1990–1992 (dollars in thousands)

	1/31/90	*1/31/91*	*1/31/92*
Gross sales	$11,720	$9,600	$9,160
Less: Returns and allowances	1,050	1,115	730
Net sales	$10,670	$8,485	$8,430
Cost of goods sold	6,460	5,125	5,100
Gross profit	$ 4,210	$3,360	$3,330
Operating expenses	3,570	3,090	3,045
Operating profit	$ 640	$ 270	$ 285
Other income	400	65	85
Net profit after other income	$ 1,040	$ 335	$ 370
Other deductions	290	345	405
Net profit (loss) before tax	$ 750	$ (10)	$ (35)
Income and other tax expense	345	—	—
Net profit (loss)	$ 405	$ (10)	$ (35)
Dividends paid	$ 210	$ 210	$ —

EXHIBIT 4   The Emporium Balance Sheets as of January 31, 1990–1992 (dollars in thousands)

	1/31/90	*1/31/91*	*1/31/92*
Assets			
Cash	$ 565	$ 740	$ 475
Notes and accounts receivable[a]	5,450	5,500	5,305
Inventory	5,480	5,370	4,925
Tax carryback claim	—	—	445
Total current assets	$11,495	$11,610	$11,150
Fixed assets, net	1,370	1,465	1,325
Leasehold improvements, net	3,480	3,590	3,460
Cash value life insurance	285	280	275
Investments	55	55	55
Notes receivable—officers and employees	105	110	140
Prepaid and deferred items	140	145	155
Total assets	$16,930	$17,255	$16,560
Liabilities and Net Worth			
Notes payable—Industrial Finance Corporation[a]	$ 5,380	$ 5,310	$ 4,300
Accounts payable	2,305	2,440	2,660
Miscellaneous accruals	630	590	680
Total current liabilities	$ 8,315	$ 8,340	$ 7,640
Common stock and additional paid-in capital	3,420	3,420	3,420
Retained earnings	5,195	5,495	5,500
Total liabilities and net worth	$16,930	$17,255	$16,560

[a]Receivables pledged to secure 30-day renewable notes to Industrial Finance Corporation

EXHIBIT 5   The Emporium Income Statements for Years Ending January 31, 1990–1992
(dollars in thousands)

	1/31/90	1/31/91	1/31/92
Gross sales	$32,125	$31,265	$28,970
Less: Returns and allowances	2,925	2,870	2,215
Net sales	29,200	28,395	26,755
Cost of goods sold	18,105	17,850	18,385
Gross profit	11,095	10,545	8,370
Operating expenses	9,080	8,995	9,780
Operating profit (loss)	$ 2,015	$ 1,550	$(1,410)
Adjustments:			
Elimination—reserves for inventory losses	—	—	870
Reduction—bad debt reserve	—	—	105
Tax carryback	—	—	445
Federal income and other tax expense	925	650	—
Net profit before dividends	$ 1,090	$ 900	$ 10
Dividends paid	725	600	5
Net profit to retained earnings	$ 365	$ 300	$ 5

Questions

1. What do you think is happening at Lloyd's and The Emporium? _____

2. What financial ratios and questions raised in your analysis of the two companies' financial statements support your opinions? _____

CHAPTER 8

Quality of Earnings Analysis

Investors use accounting earnings to price stocks because it is thought that the level of earnings and changes in earnings signal relevant information about a company's current and future ability to generate economic value that other investors will recognize and price appropriately. Knowledgeable investors have long recognized that not all dollars of reported profit are equal when it comes to representing a corporation's current economic progress and signaling future levels of economic achievement. Investors aware of this difference carefully examine the sources of reported and projected earnings to assess the degree to which they can be taken at their face value as reliable economic value creation indicators. This examination and assessment has been labeled quality of earnings analysis.

The phrase "earnings quality" and the related earnings quality analysis techniques are seldom encountered outside of the global securities industry. Most of those who use the phrase would predict that if two comparable companies in the same industry had the same projected earnings growth rate, the company with the higher "earnings quality" would have the higher price-to-earnings multiple. However, few of these same individuals would agree on a definition of "quality of earnings," use the concept in similar fashion, or undertake an analysis of earnings quality in the same way. This should not be surprising given the number of different ways quality of earnings analysis enters into the stock evaluation process. Some investors use earnings quality as a gauge of management's bias toward prudence. Others focus on the accounting quality of the *change* in earnings from one accounting period to another in order to appreciate the role played by accounting decisions and practices in the earnings change. Some examine earnings quality in order to assess what portion of earnings is potentially available in distributable cash; this last analysis reflects on investment interest in a

Professor David Hawkins prepared this note as the basis for class discussion.

company's present and potential dividend-paying practices. Still others use earnings quality as part of their assessment of the riskiness of a stock. Another use of quality of earnings analysis by those in and outside of the investment field is to identify accounting "red flags" which may suggest that the character of the company is changing, its accounting figures are potentially misleading, or extra care should be taken in analyzing its statements.

Quality of Earnings Concept

Financial analysts who focus on earnings quality seem to believe that high-quality earnings-per-share companies have these characteristics: A consistent conservative accounting policy that results in a prudent measurement of the company's financial condition and net income. A pre-tax income stream that is derived from recurring, rather than one-time, transactions related to the basic business of the company. Sales that quickly convert to cash after being recorded for accounting purposes. A net income level and growth rate that is not dependent on a lowering of the tax rate through means which may be vulnerable to future tax code changes or place detrimental constraints on the company's use of the tax savings or deferrals. A debt level that is appropriate for the business and a capital structure that has not been manipulated to produce earnings-per-share effects. Earnings that are not materially inflated by unrealized inflation or currency gains. Earnings trends that are stable, predictable, and indicative of future earnings levels. The fixed assets used in the generation of earnings are well maintained and up to date. The income figure presented is relevant to the user's objective.

Low-quality earnings-per-share companies have the opposite characteristics.

Key Determinants

Based on an analysis of what financial analysts consider as high- and low-quality earnings suggests that the factors shown in **Illustration A** and their relationship to the absolute level and the annual change in earnings per share seem to be relevant to this assessment.

When using the framework presented in **Illustration A,** it is important to realize that there is no agreed-upon way that the various elements listed affect stock values.

ILLUSTRATION A

Quality of earnings determinants

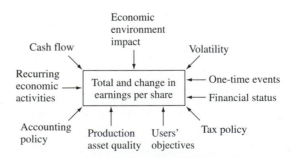

Also, there are no commonly agreed-upon standards to follow in rating the relative importance individually or in combination that the various elements bear on the quality assessment. Finally, the significance of the elements can change as the economy's prospects change and as the individual investor's preferences for risk shift.

The factors that enter into the quality of earnings assessment are similar to those used by analysts to quantify and classify the sources of the year-to-year changes in a company's earnings per share.

Financial and Operating Considerations

Earnings quality involves more than just income statement considerations. As indicated in **Illustration A,** certain financial and operating characteristics can contribute to a higher or lower quality of earnings ratings.

A company's degree of operating leverage reflects the extent to which fixed costs are a part of the firm's total cost structure. The higher the percentage of fixed costs, the higher the degree of operating leverage and the greater are the potential earnings variations caused by changes in the level of operations. The more variable are the earnings of a company, the lower will be the quality rating of those earnings and the more risk associated with them by investors.

Also, as a company's variable costs as a percentage of sales decrease, it is harder to match expenses to revenues for income determination purposes because the relationship between revenues and the costs spent to generate revenues is not easy to establish. The tendency of companies with this cost structure is to capitalize expenditures rather than expense them when they experience operating problems. When this occurs, earnings quality declines.

In the case of capital asset–intensive firms, adequate maintenance of capital assets is a key earnings quality rating factor. If capital assets are insufficiently maintained or are growing obsolete, the earnings tend to be overstated in terms of the ability of a company to be competitive and maintain the efficiency of operations. Such earnings are considered to be of low quality.

Financial characteristics, such as financial leverage, liquidity position, and availability of financing, affect the quality of earnings ratings also. As financial leverage increases, it may become increasingly more difficult to obtain additional debt financing and when accomplished, it may be at a higher interest rate than the present debt. As the fixed interest charges increase, earnings have a tendency to be more volatile and, hence, of a lower quality.

Funds must be available for future growth, and the source of these funds bears directly on earnings quality. If a company is unable to finance its growth at reasonable and affordable costs, it may not be able to maintain its growth rate, and its earnings stability may be jeopardized.

Liquidity is a key factor in assessing a company's ability to meet its current obligations. Although liquidity may not bear directly on current reported earnings, a company that cannot meet its financial obligations will most likely have to resort to actions that will result in a greater level of uncertainty and risk being attached to future earnings. Also, earnings of nonfinancial institutions that include a high percentage of interest income are also considered to be low quality.

Industry

Industry analysis must be undertaken when looking at the quality of a company's earnings. Accounting and financial practices acceptable in one industry may not be so in another. For example, capitalization of interest on borrowings related to construction activities is acceptable to many investors in the utility field because future rates should reflect the recovery of this cost. In contrast, even though it is a generally accepted accounting principle requirement, interest on construction accounting is less acceptable in the industrial sector because the future recovery of the capitalized cost is less certain.

Political and environmental factors related to the industry also affect earnings quality. Typically, these factors are not controllable by management. For example, earnings from companies that operate in foreign countries with economic and political instability may be rated low quality because of the risk of nationalization and restrictions that the host country may place on earnings repatriation. Other government regulations such as price and wage controls may also adversely impact earnings stability and, hence, earnings quality.

Relationship to Earnings Multiples

An examination of the foregoing quality of earnings characterizations suggests why "the higher quality of earnings, the higher the price-earnings multiple" prediction of those who used this phrase is not surprising. The first reason is purely mathematical. The others relate to the investor's investment goals and the variables considered relevant to these goals.

First, many of the characteristics of earning quality relate to accounting practices. With respect to these accounting considerations, if two companies are similar in all respects, except that one uses more "liberal" accounting than the other, the one with the more "conservative" accounting will typically show lower earnings and a more prudent balance sheet. However, efficient market theory suggests that the stock market will see through the accounting differences and place a similar stock price value on the two companies. If this is so, then simple arithmetic dictates that the company with the more conservative lower earnings will have a higher total market value to earnings multiplier than the company with the more liberal higher earnings, since a smaller earnings figure will be divided into the market value that is common to the two firms.

Second, a number of the qualities attributed to high- or low-quality earnings relates to volatility and uncertainty. It is widely held that the stock market abhors uncertainty, and the typical expression of this sentiment is a low price-earnings multiple. Therefore, since high-quality earnings are associated with companies having highly predictable earnings with low volatility, experience suggests that earnings-oriented investors would tend to give such companies a higher price-earnings multiple than similar companies with uncertain and volatile earning prospects.

Third, some of the characteristics of earnings quality seem to be related to the company's current and potential dividend-paying ability or the closeness of the earnings figure to distributable cash which, besides being available for dividends, can be

reinvested in the business to finance new assets or to reduce obligations. Again, it is not difficult to understand how those who have a dividend-oriented investment strategy might define earnings quality in these terms and assign higher earnings multiples to companies whose reported earnings closely reflect actual distributable cash.

Fourth, earnings quality seems to be defined by some as the closeness of the earnings to what is considered "economic reality." This is a very subjective assessment, but those who suggested this definition apparently feel capable of making it. Assuming that "economic reality" can be appraised, it is not surprising that higher quality earnings would be valued more than low-quality earnings which may be the result of accounting manipulations solely.

Finally, "understandability" is sometimes suggested as a criterion for judging the relative quality of an earnings figure or earnings history. Common sense suggests that confronted with two companies with identical earnings figures and earnings projections, the investor would value more highly the company with the earnings stream that lent itself more easily to a straightforward analysis and understandability.

Assessing Quality

While there is no absolute scale that can be used to measure degrees of earnings quality, it is possible conceptually to distinguish between the extremes of high- and low-quality earnings. Earnings classified as high quality are regarded at the levels they are reported at as credible and reliable indicators of a corporation's ability to generate economic values in the past, now, and in the future. In contrast, a low quality designation means the earnings as presented in a corporation's financial statements are potentially misleading as to its past, current, or future economic prospects.

It is important to note that the emphasis in the definition of high- and low-quality earnings is on the reliability of the information about economic values communicated by the reported earnings. There is no relationship between the level or direction of change in economic values included in this definition. A company may have high-quality earnings and declining economic value. Conversely, a company could report low-quality earnings and increasing economic value. The emphasis is on the degree to which the reported earnings "tells it like it is."

Earnings quality analysis focuses on making two assessments. These are to identify a company's:

- Absolute level of earnings quality on the high/low scale; and
- Changes in its earnings quality over time.

The absolute earnings assessment usually enters into the determination of the appropriate price/earnings multiple to assign to a company's earnings. Changes in earnings quality are usually interpreted to indicate a positive or negative change in the company's economic value due to a change in operating and/or financial circumstances and prospects that are not reflected in its reported earnings figures.

Typically, earnings quality assessments are interpreted as follows:

- **A high earnings** quality figure suggests an earnings figure that is a good indicator of the company's current condition and prospects, and a management with a realistic view of its business.
- **A low level** of earnings quality indicates the earnings figure may overstate the company's true economic value, mask a weak situation, or indicate that management does not have a realistic view of its company's true state of affairs and prospects.
- **A decline in earnings quality** suggests the company's current circumstances and prospects are weakening relative to past levels, and that management is using low quality earnings tactics to generate earnings figures in an attempt to suggest to the world that "things are better than they really are!"
- **An increase in earnings quality** indicates that management is developing a more realistic view of its circumstances, and that the company's ability to generate earnings through economic value improving activities rather than relying on low-quality earnings practices has improved.

These interpretations of earnings quality rest on three very important assumptions about management behavior:

- Managers prefer to report high-quality earnings.
- If managers cannot reach the highest level of earnings quality, they prefer to report earnings of at least the same quality as their industry leader.
- Irrespective of the level of earnings quality, managers prefer to maintain or improve their current level of earnings quality.

Earnings quality assessments are made using a variety of standards. For example, they may be made at various points in time relative to:

- The analyst's/investor's own scale of earnings quality;
- The security market's apparent current scale of earnings quality;
- The company's past earnings quality; and
- The quality of earnings of the company's industry leader.

Each of these standards plays an important role in interpreting the results of earnings quality assessments. For example, since there is no general agreement as to how to scale earnings quality, each individual must develop his or her own sense of what constitutes high and low earnings quality and the various quality points in between. Each individual's standard is used to measure the degree of earnings quality of a company standing alone. The security market's current earnings quality standards appear to shift over time. Sometimes the market tolerates a particular level of earnings quality and at other times it responds adversely to this same level. Keeping track of the market's current standard helps investors know how to translate their earnings quality assessments into predictions of security price behavior.

A company's past earnings quality is an important standard against which to calibrate current earnings quality. Changes in quality are usually interpreted as signals that changes have taken place in the company's operating and financial circumstances and prospects.

Finally, changes in a company's earnings quality relative to the earnings quality of the industry leader are typically interpreted as indicating the company's ability to compete with the industry leader has changed.

Two Common Applications

Quality of earnings analysis is used extensively by investors who specialize in selling stocks short and those who favor investing in growth stocks. In both cases, the investor is trying to identify earning quality declines where the reported earnings are still meeting the stock market's consensus earnings expectations. The shortseller is interested in the stocks of such companies because they are often good candidates for a short sale. The growth investor is looking for a sell signal to get out of the stock before others realize the company is in trouble.

Sometimes in the pursuit of extra profit growth, investors who detect an earnings quality decline in situations where the reported earnings are still meeting consensus growth expectations ignore the earnings quality decline signal. They assume that the reporting company's current earnings momentum will continue and less knowledgeable investors will push the stock price even higher. This can be a costly move. All too often earnings quality declines are quickly followed by reported earnings below consensus expectations. When this occurs investors tend to dump the stock and it is usually too late to execute an orderly sale at attractive prices.

The Signals

Investors using quality of earnings analysis to uncover clues as to when they should sell short or sell growth stocks look for managerial actions that:

- Do not lower the current earnings quality, but may be used if necessary in the future to meet earnings expectations through lowering the quality of earnings.
- Lower the quality of current earnings while meeting consensus expectations.

Not Now, but Later

Actions that do not lower current earnings quality, but have the potential to be used in future periods to lower earnings quality while meeting consensus expectations are not sell signals. They are a warning to be vigilant.

The message is that the company has taken steps to use, if necessary, lower earnings quality techniques to meet earnings expectations. Future circumstances may be favorable to the company and they may not have to lower earnings quality. On the other hand, if circumstances are unfavorable, the earnings expectations can be met by lowering earnings quality using the vehicles already in place.

Two particular actions that may indicate getting ready to lower the quality of future earnings are:

- Made acquisitions late in the current year using the purchase method; and/or

- Set up during the current year off balance sheet financing arrangements that could be used to hide future potential accounts receivable build-ups.

These acts did not lower earnings quality in the current year, but they could be used to hype next year's earnings through lowering earnings quality.

In the case of growth companies that make acquisitions in the current year, investors should ask: Was this a meaningful acquisition viewed from the point of view of business strategy? If there are any doubts on this score, then be alert to the possibility that the acquisition may result in lower next year earnings quality.

Here's how: An acquisition accounted for by the purchase method made in its current year has little effect on current results and none on the first three quarters of the current year. The next year story is very different. The acquisition impacts every quarter during the next year. If the next year quarterly earnings growth comes in large measure because of the prior year's dubious acquisition, earnings quality has declined.

Investors should be wary of growth companies that set up accounts receivable off balance sheet financing arrangements during the current year that were not used in the current year to hide earnings quality declines because management did not encourage customers through these financing arrangements to load up on inventories. That is, management did not pull sales in from future periods to the current period and call the results growth.

In the next year, however, these financing arrangements may be used to hype current sales and to hide the fact that accounts receivable are growing at a faster rate than sales. If this occurs, management will no doubt point out that the arrangements are longstanding and there is nothing unusual about their use. It may be best to assume what was true in the prior year may not be true in the current year.

Current Signals

A common reason for examining the quality of a company's current earnings is to detect "red flags" that may indicate changes in a company's fortunes which may or may not yet be reflected in the price of the company's stock or be readily apparent from the key financial measures of performance or financial condition. When doing quality of earnings analysis to determine if the quality of the current earnings of a publicly traded company has declined from prior periods, the focus should be on looking for sources of low quality earnings that at the margin make the difference between the company earning or not earning the stock market's consensus expectation. In making this analysis, it is important to remember that red flags are not necessarily indicative of a declining or undesirable situation. Red flags identification is the beginning of an analysis, not the end.

A list of accounting quality-related red flags and the possible type of problems they may suggest are:

- An audit report that is unusually long; contains unusual wording; mentions material uncertainties; is dated later than is customary; or indicates a change in auditors. These red flags may indicate that management and their public accountants disagree over how certain transactions should be accounted for. Typically, this disagreement is over transactions that involve a high degree of uncertainty as to their ultimate outcome.

- Reductions of managed costs, such as advertising, in total or relative to sales. These costs are often reduced to help a company reach its profit goal. When this occurs, a question should be raised as to whether or not the long-run interests of the corporation are being endangered.

- Changes in accounting policies, accounting estimates, or the application of existing accounting policies toward a more liberal application. The accounting change may signal a change in the economics of the firm or simply be a change to create a higher earnings growth rate.

- An increase in accounts receivable that is out of line with the past experience. The company may be using credit to create sales in order to reach an earnings objective. These sales may be to higher–credit risk customers, pulled into the current year from the next year or creating financial problems for the seller.

- Extension of trade payable that is out of line with past experience or longer than the normal trade credit period. Companies at balance sheet dates like to have their trade payables appear current.

- An unusual increase in intangible asset balances. The company may be capitalizing expenditures because income is insufficient to absorb the expenditures as expenses of the current period.

- Onetime sources of income, such as the sale of nonproductive assets like the company's headquarters building. The sale at a profit may be made to close the gap between actual and forecast profits.

- Decline in gross margin percentages. Price competition may be hurting the company, its costs may be out of control, or the company's product mix may be changing.

- Reduction of reserves by direct charges or reversals. The direct charges suggest that the contingency for which the reserve was created occurred or the company needs to reverse the reserve to create profits.

- Reliance on income sources other than the company's core business. The company's strategy may be failing.

- Selective use of pooling of interests accounting to avoid recording goodwill.

- Business combination accounting is being used to give the illusion of growth.

- Underreserving for future losses. Fully reserving may lead to covenant problems. Management may have an unrealistic, optimistic view of the future.

- Unusual increase in borrowings. The company may be having trouble financing its activities from internally generated funds.

- Increase in the deferred tax portion of the tax expense. The company may be making its accounting for public purposes more liberal, or the pre-tax profit for tax purposes may be falling, which may be a better measure of the company's actual performance trend.

- Increase in the unfunded pension liability reported in the notes or on the face of the balance sheet. The funding of pensions may be becoming more difficult, which suggests a cash flow problem.
- Low cash and marketable securities balances at year-end. The company may be using its cash to reduce payables so as to improve its current ratio on a one-shot basis.
- Peak short-term borrowings at year-end or at a time during the year that is different from the past. The company may have borrowed funds to support the use of credit to get sales up at year-end, or the nature of the business is changing from its traditional pattern.
- Slowdown of inventory turnover rate. Sales, inventory, or production problems may be developing.

Most of these sources of declining earnings quality can be detected by a careful reading of financial statement notes, management discussion and analysis presentation, and simple financial ratio analysis. However, statement users must be aware that managers know they are searching for "red flags." Consequently, managers might attempt to conceal their company's deteriorating condition by taking steps to avoid having their financial statements signal their company's true condition. For example, in countries where full consolidation of all subsidiaries is not required, to avoid a build-up of accounts receivable on consolidated statements, accounts receivable might be sold to an unconsolidated finance subsidiary. Accounts receivable might be sold to third parties. In reality these so-called sales may be little more than loans. Or, customer loans might be guaranteed by the vendor so customers can raise cash and pay off their payables to the vendor. Similarly, period-end inventory levels can be reduced by delaying until after the period end to replace sold inventories. In making a quality of earnings assessment, it is useful to remember that some managers attempting to foist lower quality earnings onto investors usually present what appear on the surface to be plausible reasons for their actions. Investors should be wary of too easy acceptance of management's story. A healthy streak of cynicism is good protection against the misleading story.

Lowering the Cost

Quality of earnings analysis is potentially a high cost analytical activity. Investors lower this cost by concentrating on company situations that experience has taught are the most likely to find a lowering of earnings quality. These characteristics include:

- The company has achieved a significant market share and is growing faster than the industry. The bigger the share, the more difficult it is to grow faster than the industry.
- Business combinations are frequently entered into. Both purchase and pooling of interests accounting are used to avoid goodwill charges and to manage the growth rate. Eventually, all the good acquisitions have been made and only the marginal companies are left.

- Management has a history of using accounting decisions to achieve earnings expectations.
- The auditors are fired. Auditors don't give up clients easily. Most probably the auditor refused to go along with management's attempt to lower earnings quality.
- The company has grown rapidly. It is difficult to put in place strong internal controls during periods of rapid growth. Poor or even fraudulent business practices are hard to detect and discourage.
- Management's growth strategy comes down to meeting earnings per share goals at the apparent expense of other business considerations. The temptation is to meet the earnings goals irrespective of the means used and the potential future damage to the business.
- The company is doing too well to believe. Sales, profits, and cash balances are soaring upward. This may be all the result of creative inventory shifting and holding. A typical arrangement of this kind often boils down to generous supplier financing to a distributor and off–balance-sheet customer financing arranged by the distributor. When business at the ultimate buyer's end slows down, the whole scheme unravels and today's miracle company fast becomes tomorrow's disaster.

Other Applications and Measurements

In addition to its "red flag" usage, the quality of earnings concept is used in a variety of other ways. Some of those applications and a few of the efforts to measure earnings quality are discussed below.

Management Appraisal

One application involves a checklist of accounting policies to perform a penalty point by penalty point analysis of a company's accounting policies over the last three years. This formal system assigns penalty points to accounting policies that the analyst considers "liberal." For example, if a company uses straight-line depreciation, it receives one penalty point. The more penalty points a company accumulates, the lower its earnings quality. The penalty point scores are used to rank companies within their industry according to accounting quality, gain an understanding of the role of accounting in generating earnings, and the bias of management toward prudence. This last application of the earnings concept is based on the hypothesis that the selection of accounting principles by management reflects in part the character of the management.

Relative Quality

The ranking of companies by their relative accounting practices quality is thought to be a useful exercise by some analysts. Those who use earnings quality in this manner believe that by keeping track of the relative earnings quality of the companies in an industry, you can detect changes in the relative earnings quality. Sometimes this may be a tip-off that the relative strengths of the companies are changing. Little in the way of formal research backs up this assertion, however.

Adjusted or Not Adjusted

Once they have identified the accounting rules used by management to determine earnings and the related balance sheet items, some analysts adjust the financial reports to conform to either the analyst's view of the appropriate accounting for the firm's circumstances or the accounting practices of the industry leader which often in practice has the most conservative accounting practices in the industry. The further the reported earnings are away from the adjusted earnings, depending on the direction, the lower or higher the earnings quality rating.

Most analysts, however, make no attempt to adjust the reported figures when valuing stocks. They make their adjustments to the price-earnings multiple if they believe earnings are over- or understated relative to some accounting standard of the analyst.

Volatility and Risk

One dimension of earnings quality is the volatility of earnings over time. Since lower volatility (i.e., a more stable earnings stream) implies less investment risk, low volatility is often associated with high-quality earnings.

A Useful Tool

Those who evaluate earnings quality recognize that it is a subjective process, which at best can only be a crude evaluation technique. Also, they acknowledge that when assessing whether an earnings figure is "high," "acceptable," or "low" quality, the unique circumstances of the reporting company must be taken into account. In addition, they would agree that the quality of a company's earnings is only one factor to consider in the total investment quality appraisal of a stock. Nevertheless, those who try to evaluate earnings quality find it is a useful analytical tool, particularly when used for "red flag" identification purposes and as one of the rating factors in stock investment quality ratings schemes.

The News Corporation Limited: Quality of Earnings Analysis

The News Corporation (NYSE:NWS) is an international Australia-based media conglomerate run by its largest shareholder, Mr. Rupert Murdoch. Mr. Murdoch expanded News Corporation aggressively during the eighties through a series of large media property acquisitions. It is our contention that Mr. Murdoch overpaid for many of these assets, in some cases significantly so. As a result, News Corporation is now an extremely highly leveraged company with what we believe to be a recurring very negative cash flow. Although the News Corporation has recently filed a flurry of public offerings and announced a series of deals all designed to reduce debt, we believe that these deleveraging attempts are far too little given the breadth of News Corporation's problems. As our cash flow analysis will show, debt may not even be reduced much, if at all.

Our opinion is that viewed realistically, the shares of News Corporation could be worthless. Even giving News Corporation the benefit of every doubt (including what we believe to be questionable accounting practices), we feel its shares are absurdly overpriced at current levels. . . . News Corporation's common equity should rightly be priced as nothing more than a risky warrant—a $1 to $2 security. . . .

The News Corporation Limited
Living on Borrowed Time,
Kynikos Associates, Ltd,
November 25, 1991[1]

Professor David F. Hawkins prepared this case as the basis for class discussion rather than to illustrate either effective or ineffective handling of an administrative situation.
Copyright © 1993 by the President and Fellows of Harvard College. Harvard Business School case 194–006.

[1]Kynikos Associates, Ltd was a major U.S. hedge fund. The excerpts quoted are from a Kynikos report prepared by James S. Chanos and Jeffrey R. Perry.

The Company

In November, 1991, The News Corporation Limited (the "Company" or "News Corporation") was a diversified international communications company principally engaged in the production and distribution of motion pictures and television programming, television broadcasting, publishing of newspapers, magazines and books, publication of promotional freestanding inserts, and commercial printing. News Corporation's activities were conducted principally in the United States, the United Kingdom, and Australia and the Pacific Basin. Principal businesses based in the United States included Twentieth Century Fox Film Corporation, the Fox Broadcasting Company national television program distribution service, seven Fox Television Stations located in major cities, the HarperCollins global book publishing group, *TV Guide,* and the publishing of promotional free-standing inserts. News Corporation, through Twentieth Century Fox Film Corporation (the activities of which include the production and syndication of television programming) and Fox Broadcasting Company (which offers a national television program distribution service through 138 television station affiliates across the United States), constituted the only vertically integrated company in the United States broadcast television industry providing such products and services. In the United Kingdom, News Corporation operated the largest commonly owned group of newspapers, consisting of five national newspapers including *The Times, The Sunday Times* and *The Sun,* and was the principal shareholder of British Sky Broadcasting Limited, which together with its subsidiary Sky Television plc, owned and operated a six-channel direct-to-home satellite television broadcasting service. In Australia, News Corporation published approximately 100 newspapers, which constituted the largest commonly owned group of newspapers in Australia. News Corporation was also engaged in magazine publishing and commercial printing in Australia and owned a 50% interest in Ansett Australia, which was one of Australia's two major domestic airlines. It also owned a 50% interest in a joint venture which was primarily engaged in the leasing of commercial jet aircraft to airlines worldwide. In Hong Kong, News Corporation owned a 50% interest in the daily and Sunday *South China Morning Post* newspapers, which had the highest circulation and advertising revenues of any English language daily and Sunday newspapers in that colony.

Summary Financial Data

Generally accepted accounting principles in Australia ("A-GAAP") differs from generally accepted accounting principles in the United States ("US-GAAP") with respect to News Corporation's results of operations in a number of significant respects. A comparison of the results for fiscal 1989, 1990 and 1991 (see Exhibit 1 for details) and the unaudited results for the three months ended September 30, 1990 and 1991 (see Exhibit 2 for details) under both A-GAAP and US-GAAP is as follows (in millions):

	Year Ended June 30,			Three Months Ended September 30,		
	1989	*1990*	*1991*	*1990*	*1991*	*1991 (in US$)*
Operating Profit						
A-GAAP	A$1,394	A$1,363	A$1,558	A$334	A$420	US$329
US-GAAP	A$1,021	A$ 861	A$1,253	A$255	A$335	US$262
Net Income (Loss)						
A-GAAP	A$1,164	A$ 343	A$ (393)	A$ 55	A$106	US$ 83
US-GAAP	A$ 988	A$ 270	A$ (305)	A$ 10	A$ 38	US$ 30

As more completely described and quantified in Note 19 of **Exhibit 1** the major differences in each of the fiscal years were: (a) the amortization of intangible assets (both for acquired subsidiaries and equity investees), (b) the treatment of interest on convertible notes, and (c) the differences in the recorded net investment of sold properties (revalued for A-GAAP, but not for US-GAAP).

In fiscal 1989, new business start-up costs were expensed for US-GAAP purposes and in fiscal 1990, these previously capitalized start-up costs were fully expensed for A-GAAP purposes. Additionally, in 1991, costs related to certain banking arrangements were expensed for A-GAAP as Abnormal Items while, for US-GAAP, certain of these costs were deferred and amortized with the remainder charged to interest expense.

In each of the fiscal years presented, certain items which were presented as Abnormal Items under A-GAAP, were reclassified for US-GAAP purposes as components of Operating Profit. These items included new business start-up costs, costs associated with staff reductions and contingency expenses. In addition, the Company's share of earnings of partnerships included in operating profits under A-GAAP is included in equity earnings under US-GAAP.

Subsequent Events

Subsequent to the issuance of its 1991 annual report, the Company decided to sell 55% of Pacific Magazines and Printing Limited through a rights issue. The anticipated net proceeds were A$655 million of which A$300 million was additional debt assumed by the new entity. Pacific Magazines and Printing Limited was a company established to hold the Company's Australian magazine and commercial printing businesses. The Company anticipated a gain would be realized for this transaction. In October and November 1991, two wholly owned subsidiaries of the Company issued A$230 (US$180 million) of exchangeable preference shares. The Company was also preparing concurrent offerings of US$400 million of Senior Notes and US$404 million of ordinary shares. The estimated aggregate net proceeds of the three transactions of about A$1.85 billion was to be used to reduce debt and working capital and fund other requirements.

EXHIBIT 1   **The News Corporation Limited and Subsidiaries—Consolidated Statements of Operations[a]**
(A-GAAP in thousands except per share amounts)

	Year Ended June 30		
	1989	*1990*	*1991*
Revenues	A$7,813,212	A$8,763,284	A$10,970,543
Costs and Expenses			
Operating	4,897,792	5,668,003	7,108,015
Selling, general and administrative	1,343,620	1,504,044	2,019,410
Depreciation and amortization	177,399	228,165	285,560
	6,418,811	7,400,212	9,412,985
Operating profit	1,394,401	1,363,072	1,557,558
Other income (expense)			
Equity in pre-tax earnings (losses) of associated companies	84,552	(18,865)	(37,404)
Interest expense (net of interest income of A$66,600, A$78,874 and A$68,839)	(876,607)	(951,487)	(1,169,793)
Other	38,117	36,506	59,660
Income before income tax expense, minority interest and abnormal items	640,463	429,226	410,021
Income tax expense			
The News Corporation Limited and subsidiaries	60,154	7,887	10,479
Associated companies	25,743	3,883	8,151
	85,897	11,770	18,630
Income before minority interest and abnormal items	554,566	417,456	391,391
Minority interest in subsidiary companies	58,0780	135,174	70,070
Income before abnormal items	496,496	282,282	321,321
Abnormal items (net of tax)			
The News Corporation Limited and subsidiaries	695,984	33,738	(619,256)
Associated companies	(28,854)	27,285	(94,941)
	667,130	61,023	(714,197)
Net income (loss)	A$1,163,626	A$ 343,305	A$ (392,876)
Earnings (loss) per share			
Income before abnormal items	A$ 1.58	A$ 1.02	A$ 1.11
Abnormal items	1.94	0.19	(2.20)
Net income (loss)	A$ 3.52	A$ 1.21	A$ (1.09)

[a]See notes to consolidated statements (selected notes only reproduced)

EXHIBIT 1   **(continued) The News Corporation Limited and Subsidiaries—Consolidated Balance Sheets**[a]

(A-GAAP in thousands except per share data)

	June 30,	
	1990	*1991*
Assets		
Current assets		
Cash	A$ 160,083	A$ 201,862
Receivables		
Trade—net of allowance	1,557,264	1,673,742
Other	277,670	398,484
Inventories	1,291,610	828,926
Prepaid expenses and other	150,138	171,992
Total current assets	3,436,765	3,275,006
Investments		
Equity in associated companies	1,746,514	2,246,314
Other investments	1,702,865	753,132
Total investments	3,449,379	2,999,446
Property, plant, and equipment—net of accumulated depreciation . . .	3,460,850	3,249,018
Other assets		
Excess of cost over net assets acquired	572,247	499,734
Publishing rights, titles, and television licenses	13,340,542	12,395,690
Long-term receivables	522,794	502,170
Inventories	1,058,774	1,626,882
Deferred tax assets	89,181	73,710
Prepaid expenses and other	211,111	226,523
Total other assets	15,794,649	15,324,709
Total assets	A$26,141,643	A$24,848,179
Liabilities and Stockholders' Equity		
Current liabilities		
Current maturities of long-term debt		
Loans	A$ 404,235	A$ 185,635
Bank loans	2,549,002	563,623
Accounts and other payables	2,991,818	3,005,662
Accrued liabilities	183,003	209,779
Income taxes payable	121,622	120,877
Total current liabilities	6,249,680	4,085,576

Exhibit 1   (continued)

	June 30,	
	1990	*1991*
Noncurrent liabilities		
Loans	1,333,607	1,096,363
Bank loans..	6,246,375	8,830,547
Accounts and other payables	735,205	900,650
Income taxes payable	145,862	143,947
Deferred income taxes	53,694	54,237
Other	40,425	29,553
Total noncurrent liabilities	8,555,168	11,055,297
Commitments and contingencies		
Stockholders' equity		
Ordinary shares A $0.50 par value 1,000,000,000 shares authorized; issued and outstanding 268,467,701—1990 and 268,468,101—1991	134,234	134,234
Convertible Notes A $18.00 par value, issued and outstanding 67,064,199—1990 and 67,063,799—1991	1,257,454	1,257,447
Special Dividend Shares 25 pence par value 49,814,000 shares authorized; issued and outstanding 30,864,373—1990 and 1991 ..	17,347	17,347
Reserves and retained earnings	8,187,867	7,571,600
Redeemable preference shares	1,406,851	376,982
Minority interest in subsidiaries.........................	333,042	349,696
Total stockholders' equity	11,336,795	9,707,306
Total liabilities and stockholders' equity	A$26,141,643	A$24,848,179

[a]See notes to consolidated financial statements (selected notes only reproduced)

EXHIBIT 1   **(continued) The News Corporation Limited and Subsidiaries—Consolidated Statements of Cash Flows**[a]
(A-GAAP in thousands except per share data)

	Year Ended June 30		
	1989	*1990*	*1991*
Operating Activity:			
Net income (loss)	A$1,163,626	A$ 343,305	A$ (392,876)
Adjustment for noncash and nonoperating activities			
Distribution in excess of equity earnings or (undistributed equity earnings) in associated companies	73,864	(361)	144,423
Depreciation and amortization	177,399	228,165	285,560
Employee and sundry provisions	21,975	36,473	(34,948)
Investment provisions and write-offs	—	229,108	67,747
Net (gain) loss on sale of assets	(862,420)	(439,759)	175,095
Override costs—expensed	—	—	193,189
Minority interest in subsidiary companies	(947)	(7,094)	40,533
Change in related balance sheet accounts—net of disposition and acquisition effects:			
Receivables	(7,418)	(36,742)	92,791
Inventories	(220,394)	(226,890)	(391,364)
Payables	16,349	556,369	345,650
Cash provided by operating activity	362,034	682,574	525,800
Investing and other activity:			
Property, plant, and equipment	(620,506)	(1,767,958)	(723,841)
Investments	(5,275,346)	(1,002,761)	(317,466)
Proceeds from sale of noncurrent assets	2,552,705	924,415	1,090,301
Sale of minority interest in a subsidiary	—	189,175	
Other	(56,200)	(35,158)	(12,697)
Cash provided by (used in) investing activity	(3,399,347)	(1,692,287)	36,297
Financing activity:			
Issuance of debt	2,566,376	2,357,740	987,956
Repayment of debt	(591,385)	(857,095)	(941,966)
Issuance of ordinary shares and convertible notes	16,249	—	—
Special dividend shares redeemed	—	(11,716)	
Preference capital redeemed	(86,406)	(849,068)	(357,980)
Issuance of preference capital	1,193,660	398,925	—
Dividends paid	(30,465)	(29,815)	(15,139)
Override costs—paid	—	—	(193,189)
Other	1,539	—	—
Cash provided by (used in) financing activity	3,069,568	1,008,971	(520,318)
Net increase (decrease) in cash	32,255	(742)	41,779
Opening cash balance	128,570	160,825	160,083
Closing cash balance	A$ 160,825	A$ 160,083	A$ 201,862
Cash paid:			
Interest (net of amount capitalized)	A$ 943,207	A$1,030,361	A$1,238,632
Income tax	50,832	36,974	43,197
Noncash transactions:			
Proceeds from sale of assets	A$ —	A$ 254,939	A$ 65,317
Preference shares exchanged	—	—	699,369

[a]See notes to consolidated financial statements (selected notes only reproduced)

Exhibit 1   (continued) The News Corporation Limited and Subsidiaries— Selected Notes to Consolidated Financial Statements

---

Note 1—Basis of Presentation and Significant Accounting Policies (partially reproduced)
The consolidated financial statements and notes thereto of The News Corporation Limited and its subsidiaries (the Group) have been prepared in accordance with accounting principles generally accepted in Australia (A-GAAP) and are presented in Australian dollars (A$).

A-GAAP differs in certain significant respects from accounting principles generally accepted in the United States (US-GAAP). The significant differences and the approximate related effect on the consolidated financial statements are set forth in Note 19.

(a) *Underlying Principles of Consolidation*
The consolidated financial statements have been prepared on a basis consistent with previous years and in accordance with conventional historical cost principles, except for certain revaluation of investments, property, plant and equipment, publishing rights, titles and television licenses. Unless otherwise shown, valuations are Directors' valuations.

The consolidated financial statements include all subsidiaries (companies in which the Group holds more than half of the issued ordinary share capital). Accounts of foreign subsidiary companies presented in accordance with overseas accounting principles are, for consolidation purposes, adjusted to comply with Group policy and generally accepted accounting principles in Australia. . . .

(d) *Other Assets*
Publishing Rights, Titles and Television Licenses
These assets are stated at cost or valuation. No amortization is provided on publishing rights and titles since, in the opinion of the Directors, they do not have a finite useful economic life. Although television licenses in the United States are renewable every five years, the Directors have no reason to believe that they will not be renewed and, accordingly, no amortization has been provided.

Excess of Cost Over Net Assets Acquired
Excess of cost over net assets acquired is amortized on a straight-line method over 20 years. . . .

(i) *New Business Start-Up Costs*
Costs incurred in the development of major new activities are capitalized until the operations are commenced on a commercial basis. Thereafter these costs are amortized over the period that benefits are expected to be received.

EXHIBIT 1   (continued)

For the period to August 31, 1989, the investment in the development of Sky Television plc., a new multi-channel broadcasting service, was capitalized. The investment was to be amortized over the shorter of five years or the period benefits were expected to be received. In June 1990, the Directors after considering the size and nature of the investment in Sky determined it would be proper to charge the capitalized development cost of Sky to operating profit in the 1990 financial year. This decision was made notwithstanding that Sky was performing in accordance with its long-term strategic business plan. Accordingly, A$284.4 million of capitalized development cost was written off as an abnormal item in the 1990 consolidated statement of operations. . . .

(k) *Reserves*

(i) *Capital*

(a) Capital redemption reserves represent amounts transferred from revenue reserves equivalent to the value of shares redeemed. Distribution of these reserves is restricted to effect a stock split or stock dividend.

(b) Share premium reserves are the excess subscription price for shares over their par value. Distribution of these reserves is restricted to effect a stock split, stock dividend or the absorption of specific share issue costs.

(c) Capital reserves consist of the total of all profit and losses related to the sale of noncurrent assets transferred from retained earnings. These reserves are freely distributable.

(d) Asset revaluation reserves are the excess of the valuations of investments, property, plant and equipment and publishing rights, titles and television licenses over their net book values at the date of revaluation. . . .

(l) *Revaluation of Assets*

Amounts shown "at valuation" in respect of investments (Note 5), property, plant and equipment (Note 6) and publishing rights, titles and television licenses (Note 7) comprise the historical cost of the revalued assets plus the revaluation increment. Increments in a class of assets are taken to the asset revaluation reserve. Decrements are offset against previous increments relating to the same class of assets, or charged against profit.

(m) *Reclassifications*

Gains and losses arising outside a Company's normal trading activities were considered extraordinary items for the fiscal year ended June 30, 1989. In accordance with ASRB 1018 these gains and losses are now considered abnormal items. Certain reclassifications have been made to the fiscal 1989 and 1990 consolidated financial statements to conform with the fiscal 1991 presentation.

Note 2—Dispositions and Acquisitions (not reproduced)

EXHIBIT 1   **(continued)**

Note 3—**Receivables** (not reproduced)
Note 4—**Inventories**

	June 30, (in thousands)	
	1990	*1991*
Current:		
Raw materials and printing materials	A$ 283,766	A$ 173,969
Finished goods	445,231	288,964
Work in progress	63,496	78,302
Television program rights	385,370	228,349
Completed television and film product	112,844	58,423
Other	903	919
	A$1,291,610	A$ 828,926
Noncurrent:		
Film costs in process	A$ 302,200	A$ 487,032
Finished goods	156,324	281,490
Completed television and film product	292,630	597,694
Television program rights	307,620	260,666
	A$1,058,774	A$1,626,882

Note 5—**Investments**
Cost and quoted value of listed equity shares are as follows:

	June 30 (in thousands)		
	1989	*1990*	*1991*
Cost and valuation	A$1,123,326	A$1,107,383	A$433,625
Revalued increment (decrement)	16,916	(1,641)	(3,795)
Cost	1,140,242	1,105,742	429,830
Quoted value	1,069,673	1,298,328	357,370
Net unrealized gains (losses)	A$ (70,569)	A$ 192,586	A$ (72,460)
Gross unrealized gains	A$ 115,680	A$ 314,166	A$ 17,447
Gross unrealized (losses)	A$ (186,249)	A$ (121,580)	A$ (89,907)

EXHIBIT **1   (continued)**

Note 6—Property, Plant and Equipment (in thousands)
Property, plant and equipment consists of the following:

	June 30, (in thousands)	
	1990	*1991*
Land:		
At professional valuation	A$ 26,477	A$ 18,579
At valuation	780	780
At cost	186,016	196,946
	213,273	216,305
Buildings:		
At professional valuation	20,841	13,121
At valuation	3,522	3,478
At cost	428,826	477,648
	453,189	494,247
Less depreciation	63,033	62,834
	390,156	431,413
Leasehold premises:		
Land at professional valuation	111,055	107,021
Land at cost	15,978	15,474
Buildings at professional valuation	49,721	51,043
Buildings at cost	596,085	721,022
	772,839	894,560
Less amortization	33,466	38,426
	739,373	856,134
Plant and motor vehicles:		
At cost	2,866,395	2,493,634
Less depreciation	748,347	748,468
	2,118,048	1,745,166
Total	A$3,460,850	A$3,249,018

Note 7—Publishing Rights, Titles and Television Licenses

	June 30, (in thousands)	
	1990	*1991*
At cost	A$ 1,508,061	A$ 1,479,238
At valuation	11,832,481	10,916,452
	A$13,340,542	A$12,395,690

Publishing rights, titles and television licenses are revalued triennially. On June 30, 1990, in accordance with the Group's accounting policy, the Directors in office at that time revalued the Group's publishing rights, titles and television licenses, with the exception of those rights, titles, and licenses acquired during the year. The film library, distribution rights and trade names of the Twentieth Century Fox Film Group were not revalued.

EXHIBIT 1   (continued)

The Directors' valuation at June 1990 was based on advice from two firms of independent appraisers. The publishing rights, titles and television licenses at valuation June 1990 include the original cost and the revaluation increment. When valuations have resulted in incremental values being attributed to those rights, titles and licenses, the Directors adopted valuations that resulted in the incremental revaluation being 70% of the net difference between the original cost and the advised total valuation. Where book values of the publishing rights, titles and television licenses were greater than the valuation, the decrement was treated in accordance with the Group's accounting policies.

The primary valuation technique used was a methodology based on the maintainable revenues of the publishing rights, titles and television licenses. This incorporates multiples which take account of the market factors particular to the rights, titles and licenses and which reflect the composition of the revenues and profitability, the loyalty of readership, the risk attaching to the advertising revenue and the potential for future growth. The results derived using the primary methodology have been supported by an extensive review of market transactions in the United States of America, the United Kingdom, Australia and Hong Kong.

Note 8—Loans Payable (not reproduced)

Note 9—Bank Loans (not reproduced)

Note 10—Pensions (not reproduced)

Note 11—Income Taxes (not reproduced)

Note 12—Noncurrent Accounts Payable (not reproduced)

Note 13—Commitments and Contingencies (partially reproduced)

Income tax would arise if certain fixed assets, investments and mastheads were to be disposed of at their revalued amount. As there is no present intention to dispose of any of these assets, the Directors believe it would be misleading to record any amount against this contingency.

The Group has an approximate 50% interest in the Ansett Worldwide Aviation Services ("AWAS") aircraft leasing business. The business is conducted through partnerships and through incorporated entities. The principal operating entities of AWAS are Ansett Worldwide Aviation, U.S.A., a Nevada general partnership ("AWA"), and Ansett Worldwide Aviation Limited ("AWAL"), a Hong Kong corporation. AWA and AWAL enter into long-term operating lease arrangements for aircraft which are sub-leased to airline operators. Typically, head leases range between 10 and 20 years (10 years where AWAL is the lessee and 20 years where AWAL is the lessee), while sub-leases range between 5 and 10 years. Under sub-leases currently in effect, annual receipts under such sub-leases exceed annual rental payments under the relevant head leases. Where a sub-lease expires before a head lease, AWA and AWAL may negotiate a replacement sub-lease or, subject to limited conditions, terminate the relevant head lease. In connection with head leases entered into by AWA, the Group, as a partner in AWA, has joint and several liability for amounts due under such head leases.

Exhibit 1   (continued)

Note 13 (continued)
The Group's approximate 50% share of the future lease rentals with respect to lease arrangements entered into by AWA is:

	(in thousands)		
	Sublease income	*Head lease expense*	*Net lease rental*
Operating lease rentals:			
Not later than one year	A$101,455	A$ 71,390	A$ 30,065
Later than one year, not later than two years	104,615	76,869	27,746
Later than two years, not later than five years	278,322	228,334	49,988
Later than five years, not later than ten years	116,246	410,402	(294,156)
Later than ten years	—	667,001	(667,001)
Total	A$600,638	A$1,453,996	A$(853,358)

The shortfall in net lease rentals of A$853 million will only arise if sub-leases are not renegotiated and aircraft cannot be re-leased or sold. At June 30, 1991, because of the Group's joint and several liability for amounts due under head leases entered into by AWA, in the event that the other general partners in AWA fail to meet their respective obligations with respect to such head leases, the Group would be contingently liable for 100% of the head lease obligation of A$2,908 million.

Note 14—Redeemable Preference Shares (not reproduced)

Note 15—Minority Interest in Subsidiaries (not reproduced)

Note 16—Abnormal Items

	Year Ended June 30, (in thousands)		
	1989	*1990*	*1991*
The News Corporation Limited and Subsidiaries:			
Disposal of noncurrent assets, net of tax of A$155.1 million—1989, A$40.5 million—1990, and A$114.0 million—1991	A$703,360	A$ 403,043	A$(287,044)
New business start-up and termination costs	—	(284,354)	—
Provision against investments and contingencies	—	(74,341)	(67,747)
Redundancies, net of tax benefits of A$0.5 million—1990, and A$1.7 million—1991	—	(10,139)	(65,244)
Override costs	—	—	(193,189)
Other	(7,376)	(471)	(6,032)
	A$695,984	A$ 33,738	A$(619,256)
Associated Companies (net of tax benefit of A$17.0 million—1989, tax expense of A$3.5 million—1990, tax benefit of A$13.0 million—1991):			
Foreign exchange fluctuation on long-term debt	(24,272)	12,409	(12,477)
Disposal of noncurrent assets including the write-down of investments	—	15,018	(65,578)
Other	(4,582)	(142)	(16,886)
	(28,854)	27,285	(94,941)
Total abnormal items	A$667,130	A$ 61,023	A$(714,197)

EXHIBIT 1   (continued)

Note 17—Industry and Geographic Segment Data (not reproduced)

Note 18—Stockholders' Equity (not reproduced)

Note 19—United States Generally Accepted Accounting Principles

The following consolidated condensed statements of operations, balance sheets and statements of cash flows are presented in accordance with US-GAAP. The significant differences between US-GAAP and A-GAAP are described in notes (a) through (j); to the statements and a reconciliation of income and stockholders' equity between A-GAAP and US-GAAP follows the notes.

Consolidated Condensed Statements of Operations (in millions of Australian Dollars except per share amounts)

	Year ended June 30,		
	1989	*1990*	*1991*
Revenues	A$ 7,752	A$ 8,691	A$10,919
Costs and expenses	(6,397)	(7,430)	(9,196)
Depreciation and amortization	(334)	(400)	(470)
Operating profit	1,021	861	1,253
Other income (expense)			
Equity in net earnings (losses) of associated companies	76	24	(127)
Interest, net	(829)	(913)	(1,172)
Other	1,020	481	(48)
Total other income (expense)	267	(408)	(1,347)
Income (loss) before income taxes and minority interest and extraordinary item	1,288	453	(94)
Income tax expense	(266)	(113)	(187)
Minority interest	(58)	(135)	(70)
Income (loss) before extraordinary item	964	205	(351)
Extraordinary item	24	65	46
Net income (loss)	A$ 988	A$ 270	A$ (305)
Earnings per share:			
Income (loss) before extraordinary item	A$ 2.96	A$ 0.63	A$ (1.09)
Extraordinary item	0.07	0.20	0.14
Net income (loss)	A$ 3.03	A$ 0.83	A$ (0.95)

EXHIBIT 1   (continued) Consolidated Condensed Balance Sheets (in millions of Australian Dollars)

	June 30,	
	1990	*1991*
Assets		
Current assets		
Cash	A$ 160	A$ 202
Receivables	1,835	2,072
Inventories	1,292	829
Other	150	172
Total current assets	3,437	3,275
Investments	2,437	1,946
Property, plant and equipment—net of accumulated depreciation	3,315	3,113
Other assets		
Excess of cost over net assets acquired	661	601
Publishing rights, titles, and television licenses.......................	8,312	7,318
Long-term receivables.............................	523	502
Inventories	1,059	1,627
Other	286	452
Total other noncurrent assets	10,841	10,500
Total assets	A$20,030	A$18,834
Liabilities and Stockholders' Equity		
Current liabilities		
Current maturities of long-term debt	A$ 2,953	A$ 749
Accounts payable	2,713	2,391
Other	584	776
Total current liabilities	6,250	3,916
Noncurrent liabilities		
Long term debt	7,580	9,927
Accounts payable—noncurrent	735	1,070
Other	254	242
Total noncurrent liabilities	8,569	11,239
Redeemable preference shares....................................	1,407	377
Minority interest in subsidiaries	333	350
Stockholders' equity..	3,471	2,952
Total liabilities and stockholders' equity	A$20,030	A$18,834

Exhibit 1   (continued) Consolidated Statement of Cash Flows (in millions of Australian Dollars)

	Year ended June 30,		
	1989	*1990*	*1991*
Operating Activity:			
Net income (loss)	A$ 988	A$ 270	A$ (305)
Adjustment for noncash and nonoperating activities:			
Distributions in excess of equity earnings in associated companies	115	53	183
Depreciation and amortization	334	400	470
Employee and sundry provisions	22	134	(35)
Investment provisions and write-offs	—	229	68
Net (gain) loss on sale of assets	(992)	(516)	36
Override costs—expensed	—	—	41
Minority interest in subsidiary companies	(1)	(7)	41
Change in related balance sheet accounts	(58)	159	65
Cash provided by operating activity	408	722	564
Investing and other activity			
Property, plant and equipment	(621)	(1,768)	(724)
Investments	(5,275)	(1,003)	(317)
Proceeds from sale of noncurrent assets	2,553	924	1,090
Other	(56)	154	(12)
Cash provided by (used in) investing activity	(3,399)	(1,693)	37
Financing activity			
Issuance of debt	2,566	2,358	988
Repayment of debt	(591)	(857)	(942)
Preference capital redeemed	(86)	(849)	(358)
Issuance of preference capital	1,194	399	—
Dividends and convertible note interest paid	(78)	(69)	(54)
Override cost—paid	—	—	(193)
Other	18	(12)	—
Cash provided by (used in) financing activity	3,023	970	(559)
Net increase (decrease) in cash	32	(1)	42
Opening cash balance	129	161	160
Closing cash balance	A$ 161	A$ 160	A$ 202

A description of the Australian generally accepted accounting principles (A-GAAP) which differ significantly in certain respects from United States generally accepted accounting principles (US-GAAP) follows:

(a) Revaluation of Assets
Property, plant and equipment, publishing rights, titles, television licenses and investments have been revalued at an amount in excess of cost. The major portion of such revaluations was ascribed to publishing rights. Accounting principles generally accepted in the United States do not permit the revaluation of assets in excess of cost.

The gain on the sale of revalued assets under A-GAAP is the difference between the carrying amount of the revalued asset (including revalued increments) and the proceeds of sale. Under US-GAAP the gain is the difference between the carrying value based on historical cost and the proceeds of sale.

Exhibit 1 (continued)

Note 19—(continued)

The revaluation of a class of assets under A-GAAP allows the netting of increments and decrements, with the resultant net increment taken directly to reserves. Under US-GAAP any permanent decrement in the value of an asset is expensed.

(b) Intangible Assets

Amounts paid on the acquisition of publishing rights, titles, and television licenses are not amortized and the excess of cost over net assets acquired is amortized over 20 years. Under US-GAAP, intangible assets are amortized to income over a period not exceeding 40 years. For the purpose of the US-GAAP, these intangible assets are being amortized on a straight line method principally over 40 years.

(c) Investments in Associated Companies

The equity method of accounting for associated companies has been adjusted to reflect the approximate effect of applying US-GAAP to their consolidated financial statements. The Group's investment exceeds its equity in the underlying net assets of these investees. Amortization is not provided on this amount. Under US-GAAP the difference between the cost of these investments and the underlying equity in their net assets is considered an intangible asset and is amortized over a period not to exceed 40 years.

Ordinary shares and convertible notes of the Group are owned by associated companies. These shares and notes are included as part of the Group's investment in associated companies. Under US-GAAP the Group's interest in these shares and notes is eliminated and presented as a reduction of stockholders' equity.

Under US-GAAP, the Group's share of earnings of partnerships in which the Group has invested is included in equity in net earnings (losses) of associated companies. Such amount is included in operating profits for A-GAAP purposes. Under A-GAAP profits are recognized upon the sale and leaseback of aircraft. Under US-GAAP such amounts are recognized over the lease term.

(d) Extraordinary Item and Abnormal Items

The tax benefit realized from a loss carryforward is reflected as a reduction of income tax expense. Under US-GAAP such tax benefits are treated as an extraordinary item.

Under US-GAAP classification of items as abnormal is not permitted. Accordingly, abnormal items have been reclassified to operating (start-up costs, redundancies and contingencies), other income (disposals of noncurrent assets), interest expense, net (Override costs) and prepaid expenses (Override costs)—(see (i).

(e) Preference Shares

Preference shares subject to mandatory redemption are included in stockholders' equity. Under US-GAAP preference shares subject to mandatory redemption would not be included in stockholders' equity. Preference shares are classified on the balance sheet above stockholders' equity.

Exhibit 1   (continued)

Note 19—(continued)

(f) Minority Interest in Subsidiaries

Minority interest in subsidiaries is included in stockholders' equity. Under US-GAAP minority interest is classified on the balance sheet above stockholders' equity.

(g) Convertible Note Interest

The required semi-annual payment on the Group's convertible notes is presented as interest in the statements of operations. Under US-GAAP amounts paid on equity securities are classified as dividends. Accordingly, the semi-annual payments are included in cash provided by operating activities under A-GAAP and financing activities under US-GAAP.

(h) New Business Start-up Costs

Costs incurred in the development of major new activities are capitalized until the operations have commenced on a commercial basis. Thereafter these costs are amortized over the period that benefits are expected to be received. Under US-GAAP these costs are charged to operating income in the period incurred.

(i) Refinancing Costs

Costs associated with the February 1991 Override were charged to abnormal items. Under US-GAAP, the related period costs are charged to expense with the remainder capitalized and amortized over the three year life of the agreement.[2]

(j) Recently Issued Pronouncements

(i) The Financial Accounting Standards Board issued Statement of Financial Accounting Standards No. 96, "Accounting for Income Taxes" ("FASB 96"), in December 1987 with implementation deferred to fiscal year 1993. Further deferral of the effective dates of FASB 96 to fiscal 1994 is currently addressed in the Financial Accounting Standards Board exposure draft dated June 17, 1991. The Group has not decided when it will adopt and has not yet determined the effect of adopting the new standard.

(ii) The Financial Accounting Standards Board issued Statement of Financial Accounting Standard No. 106, "Employers' Accounting for Postretirement Benefits Other Than Pensions" ("FASB 106") in December 1990. The Group is currently required to adopt FASB 106 no later than fiscal 1994, although earlier implementation is permitted. While the Group has not decided when it will adopt the new standard, it has determined that the effect is immaterial.

---

[2]In February 1991, News Corporation extended the maturities of certain nonpublic debt through a new three-year banking agreement at a cost of A$193.2 million, which was treated as an abnormal item during 1991.

Exhibit 1   (continued)

The application of accounting principles generally accepted in the United States, as described above, would have had the following approximate effect on consolidated net income and stockholders' equity.

	Year ended June 30, (in Millions of Australian Dollars)		
	1989	*1990*	*1991*
As reported in the consolidated statements of operations	A$1,164	A$ 343	A$(393)
Items increasing (decreasing) reported income before extraordinary items:			
Amortization of publishing rights, titles, and television licenses . . .	(165)	(184)	(216)
Amortization of excess of cost over net assets acquired	7	12	12
Equity in earnings of associated companies	(41)	(53)	(38)
Interest on convertible notes	48	39	39
Gain on sale of revalued assets	130	76	139
Revaluation of noncurrent assets	—	(98)	—
New business start-up costs	(155)	134	—
Refinancing costs	—	—	152
Benefit from the utilization of tax loss carryforwards netted against income tax expense	(24)	(64)	(46)
Net increase (decrease) in reported income before extraordinary items	(200)	(138)	42
Approximate income (loss) before extraordinary items in accordance with accounting principles generally accepted in the United States . .	964	205	(351)
Approximate extraordinary items in accordance with accounting principles generally accepted in the United States	24	65	46
Approximate net income (loss) in accordance with accounting principles generally accepted in the United States	A$ 988	A$ 270	A$(305)

	June 30, (in millions of Australian Dollars)	
	1990	*1991*
Stockholders' equity as reported in the consolidated balance sheets	A$11,337	A$ 9,707
Items increasing (decreasing) reported equity:		
Amortization of publishing rights, titles and television licenses	(513)	(674)
Amortization of excess of cost over net assets acquired	75	87
Revaluation of assets	(4,537)	(4,441)
Associated companies reserve	(1,011)	(1,050)
Reclassification of redeemable preference shares	(1,407)	(377)
Reclassification of minority interest in subsidiaries	(333)	(350)
Refinancing costs	—	152
Other	(140)	(102)
Net (decrease) in reported stockholders' equity	(7,866)	(6,755)
Approximate stockholders' equity in accordance with accounting principles generally accepted in the United States	A$ 3,471	A$ 2,952

EXHIBIT 2   **The News Corporation Limited and Subsidiaries—Note 8 to Unaudited Consolidated Financial Statements for the Three Months Ended September 30, 1990 and 1991**
(partially reproduced).

A description of the Australian generally accepted accounting principles (A-GAAP) which differ significantly in certain respects from United States generally accepted accounting principles (US-GAAP) is included in Note 19 to the audited financial statements (see **Exhibit 1**).

The application of accounting principles generally accepted in the United States, as described above, would have had the following approximate effect on consolidated net income and stockholders' equity.

	For the three months ended September 30, (in millions)	
	1990	*1991*
As reported in the consolidated statements of operations	A$ 55	A$ 106
Items increasing (decreasing) reported income before extraordinary items:		
Amortization of publishing rights, titles and television licenses	(52)	(61)
Amortization of excess of cost over net assets acquired	3	3
Equity in earnings of associated companies	(1)	(2)
Interest on convertible notes	9	10
Gain on sale of revalued assets	(4)	—
Refinancing costs	—	(18)
Benefit from the utilization of tax loss carryforwards netted against income tax expense	(18)	(9)
Net (decrease) in reported income before extraordinary items	(63)	(77)
Approximate income (loss) before extraordinary items in accordance with accounting principles generally accepted in the United States	(8)	29
Approximate extraordinary items in accordance with accounting principles generally accepted in the United States	18	9
Approximate net income in accordance with accounting principles generally accepted in the United States	A$ 10	A$ 38

	For the three months ended September 30, 1991 (in millions)
Stockholders' equity as reported in the consolidated balance sheets	A$9,886
Items increasing (decreasing) reported equity:	
Amortization of publishing rights, titles and television licenses	(736)
Amortization of excess of cost over net assets acquired	91
Revaluation of assets	(4,442)
Associated companies reserve	(1,052)
Reclassification of redeemable preference shares	(380)
Reclassification of minority interest in subsidiaries	(364)
Refinancing costs	135
Other	(123)
Net (decrease) in reported stockholders' equity	(6,871)
Approximate stockholders' equity in accordance with accounting principles generally accepted in the United States	A$3,015

continued from page 187

Kynikos Associates Report

The 16-page Kynikos report, "The News Corporation Limited Living on Borrowed Time," closed with the following conclusions:

> Earlier this year News Corporation ADRs traded as low as $5⅜. In our view, little has changed fundamentally in this story since that time. Indeed, we believe that five dollars per ADR may even be overstating the value of News Corporation's equity at this time. In summary, we would make the following points:
>
> 1. News Corporation is burning cash at an alarming rate (A$2 billion + last year alone). As noted earlier, the company cannot explain this cash outflow.
> 2. While News Corporation is reporting profits, we believe that these are merely book entries made possible by the lax standards in entertainment and publishing accounting. On a cash basis, we believe that it is entirely possible that News Corporation is losing money from operations. This would explain the increase in net debt last year, even after massive asset sales.
> 3. A low tax rate and large amounts of capitalized interest further reduce, in our opinion, the quality of News Corporation's reported earnings. A comparison of the company's earnings as reported under U.S. GAAP versus Australian GAAP illustrates this clearly.
> 4. The off–balance-sheet liabilities at News Corporation are unquantifiable, and indeed, in many cases unknown, but they could have a materially negative impact on the company if recognized.
> 5. Despite our accounting and cash flow concern, we would point out that even if one believes that News Corporation's reported operating profits reflect true economic reality, its shares are overpriced. Specifically, on a comparable company valuation basis, News Corporation's ADRs should trade about $8.

In our minds, the News Corporation creditors are closer to being on the right track. Two series of publicly traded News Corporation bonds, guaranteed by the parent company, currently trade at yields to maturity of 14½% and 15½% respectively. In addition, Twentieth Century Fox Film (one of News Corporation's best divisions) has bonds outstanding that currently yield about 13½%. News Corporation must really need new cash to even contemplate a new junk bond offering at these rates.

While the high-yield debt community considers News Corporation debt to be a very risky investment, stock market investors are currently valuing the common equity of the company at over US$4.6 billion! In fact, News Corporation's bondholders are expressing, through the pricing mechanism, a significant concern that they will not be made whole, while stock market investors believe there is tremendous residual value for the equity.

To conclude, we believe that shares in News Corporation represent nothing more than warrants on any residual value to the common equity of this company. As such, we believe that the ADRs should trade at the appropriate warrant valuation, certainly in the low single digits. Indeed, we doubt whether there is any value to the common equity, since, as explained above, it appears that News Corporation is selling assets and securities in the public market simply to fuel the tremendous cash outflow from operations. In sum, recent security issuances and the stock price notwithstanding, we believe that in the end News Corporation clearly paid too much to acquire properties in the 1980s and, as such, is at best living on borrowed time.

Questions

1. How do you rate the accounting quality of News Corporation's A-GAAP financial reports? Are the company's US-GAAP financial data higher quality? _____ Illustrate your answer to both questions with specific examples.

2. Do you agree with Kynikos Associates' cash flow, earnings quality and valuation conclusions? _____ Cite specific case data to support your conclusions.

CASE

8-2 Kendall Square Research Corporation (A)

Kendall Square Research Corporation (KSR) was founded in 1986 by Henry Burkhardt III and Steve Frank, another computer designer. KSR was the third computer company cofounded by Burkhardt, the first two having been Data General Corporation and Encore Computer Corporation. At KSR, Burkhardt chose a radical design for a supercomputer that would make the machines attractive for both government and university laboratories and for commercial users. The company delivered its first machine to the Oak Ridge National Laboratory in the fall of 1991, and Kendall Square Research reported that it reached break-even volume before the end of 1992.

Professor William J., Bruns, Jr. prepared this case as the basis for class discussion rather than to illustrate either effective or ineffective handling of an administrative situation.
Copyright © 1994 by the President and Fellows of Harvard College. Harvard Business School case 194–068.

EXHIBIT 1   Excerpts from 1992 Annual Report of Kendall Square Research Corporation

---

Management's Discussion and Analysis of Financial Condition and Results of Operations

Introduction

The Company was incorporated in February 1986 and sold its first computer system in September 1991. As of December 26, 1992, the Company had sold 22 systems, of which 11 were sold to customers in the United States and 11 to customers in Europe. Several of these customers have enlarged the size of their system configuration since initial installation. The Company's revenue for the fiscal year ended December 26, 1992 was $20.7 million. The Company has not been profitable on an annual basis since its inception and no assurance can be given that the Company will be able to operate on a profitable basis. As of December 26, 1992, the Company's accumulated deficit was approximately $69.7 million.

The Company's future operating results will depend on many factors, including the demand for the Company's products for both technical and commercial applications, the level of competition faced by the Company and the ability of the Company to develop and market new products and control costs. The Company's sales and marketing strategy contemplates sales of its computer systems for both technical and commercial applications. To date, however, all of the computer systems have been sold for technical applications.

Results of Operations

Years ended December 28, 1991 and December 26, 1992

The Company does not believe that the year-to-year comparison of various items of expense as a percentage of revenue is meaningful due to the significant growth in the Company's revenue from 1991 to 1992.

From its beginning KSR funded its development and the design of its products through private placements of its equity and debt securities and an initial public stock offering in April 1992. A subsequent stock offering in April 1993, brought the total financing of the start-up to about $150 million, more than $80 million of which had come in two offerings of stock to the public. Shares in the first of the public offerings had more than doubled in price in less than 18 months. By October 1993, the market capitalization of the shares was about five times estimated 1993 sales and 45 times estimated 1993 earnings.[1]

From the time of its first sale, some critics questioned the criteria used by KSR to determine when revenue would be recognized. The company recognized revenue on product sales upon written customer acceptance of the product. Acceptance often occurred before the configuration of a particular system was finalized or any payment had been received from a customer. Kendall Square Research fully disclosed its policy on revenue recognition in its financial reports to shareholders. (See **Exhibit 1** for excerpts from the 1992 Kendall Square Research Corporation Annual Report to Shareholders.)

continues on page 219

---

[1]Dorfman, John R., and William M. Bulkeley, "Heard on the Street: Supercomputer Maker Kendall Square's Effort to Crack Business Markets Has Some Skeptics," *The Wall Street Journal,* October 11, 1993, p. C2.

EXHIBIT 1   (continued)

Revenue

Revenue increased from $904,000 to $20,729,000. The Company shipped its first computer system in September 1991 and recorded its first revenue in the third quarter of 1991. The Company recorded revenue growth in each of the four quarters in 1992 as it increased the number of systems shipped. There can be no assurance that the Company will continue to achieve quarterly revenue growth in future periods. See "Quarterly Results." Sales to customers in Europe accounted for approximately 44% of revenue in 1992.

Cost of Revenue

Cost of revenue increased from $332,000 to $9,189,000, or from 37% to 44% of revenue. These expenses include actual material, labor, and indirect costs associated with the manufacture of systems for which revenue has been recognized. The Company does not believe that the year-to-year comparison is meaningful due to the low level of revenues in fiscal 1991 as well as the allocation of certain start-up manufacturing costs in 1991 to other operating costs.

Research and Development

Research and development expenses decreased by 11% from $15,786,000 to $14,113,000. Additionally, in 1992 the Company capitalized $3,506,000 of costs attributable to software license fees and software development. No such costs were capitalized in 1991. The Company increased research and development staffing levels from 79 to 115 persons from 1991 to 1992. In order to establish a competitive position and to develop new and enhanced products, the Company intends to continue to devote substantial resources to research and development. The Company expects that research and development expenses will fluctuate from quarter to quarter but will generally increase over time.

Selling, General and Administrative

Selling, general and administrative expenses increased by 63% from $6,441,000 to $10,475,000. These expenses were comprised primarily of selling and marketing expenses, reflecting significant increases in sales, marketing, and support staffing levels from 49 to 66 persons from 1991 to 1992. These expenses are expected to continue to increase as the Company expands its selling and marketing efforts.

Other Operating Costs and Expenses

Other operating costs in 1991 of $850,000 resulted from costs incurred in the establishment of the Company's manufacturing facilities and procedures and other initial manufacturing costs, including depreciation of test equipment. The manufacturing facilities and procedures became operational during the fourth quarter of 1991. There were no such costs incurred in 1992.

Other Income (Expense), Net

The Company recorded other income of $326,000 in 1992, compared to other expense of $2,000 in 1991. Interest income increased by 104% from $380,000 to $775,000 which was partially offset by an 18% increase in interest expense from $382,000 to $449,000. The Company's average cash and investments balances were higher in 1992 than in 1991 as a result of the receipt of proceeds from convertible debt financings and the Company's initial public offering. All of the convertible debt was converted into shares of common stock upon the closing of the Company's initial public offering on April 3, 1992.

EXHIBIT 1   (continued)

To date, inflation has not had a material impact on the Company's revenue or results of operations.

Years ended December 29, 1990, and December 28, 1991

Revenue

Revenue for the year ended December 28, 1991, of $904,000 resulted from the Company's first shipment and customer acceptance of one KSR1-20 system. There were no shipments in the year ended December 29, 1990.

Cost of Revenue

Cost of revenue of $332,000 includes actual material, labor, and indirect costs associated with the manufacture of systems for which revenue was recognized.

Research and Development

Research and development expenses increased by 49% from $10,575,000 to $15,786,000. This increase resulted primarily from materials and other costs incurred in the design and development of product prototypes, as well as an increase in research and development staffing levels from 77 to 79 persons from 1990 to 1991.

Selling, General and Administrative

Selling, general and administrative expenses increased by 108% from $3,099,000 to $6,441,000. These expenses were comprised primarily of selling and marketing expenses, reflecting an increase in sales, marketing and support staffing level from 24 to 49 persons from 1990 to 1991. These expenses were incurred as part of the Company's strategy to market its computer systems concurrently with its development efforts.

Other Operating Costs and Expenses

Other operating costs increased by 134% from $363,000 to $850,000. This increase resulted from costs incurred in the establishment of the Company's manufacturing facilities and procedures and other initial manufacturing costs, including depreciation of test equipment.

Other Income (Expense), Net

The Company recorded other expense of $2,000 in 1991 compared to other income of $687,000 in 1990. The Company had more proceeds from private equity and convertible subordinated debt financings in 1990 available for investment than in 1991 and earned higher average interest rates thereon. Additionally, interest expense was higher in 1991 as a result of higher capital lease obligations and the issuance in 1991 of $12,820,000 in convertible subordinated notes.

Quarterly Results

The following table presents unaudited quarterly financial information for the four fiscal quarters ended December 26, 1992. This information has been prepared by the Company on a basis consistent with the Company's audited consolidated financial statements and includes all adjustments (consisting only of normal recurring adjustments) which management considers necessary for a fair presentation of the results for such periods. The operating results for any quarter are not necessarily indicative of the results for any future period.

EXHIBIT 1   (continued)

	3 Months Ended			
	March 28, 1992	June 27, 1992	Sept. 26, 1992	Dec. 26, 1992
			(in thousands)	
Revenue	$ 1,954	$ 2,297	$ 5,310	$11,168
Cost of revenue	896	1,058	2,466	4,769
Gross profit	1,058	1,239	2,844	6,399
Cost and expenses:				
Research and development	3,407	4,312	3,444	2,950
Selling, general and administrative	1,890	2,160	2,859	3,566
	5,297	6,472	6,303	6,516
Loss from operations	(4,239)	(5,233)	(3,459)	(117)
Other income (expense):				
Interest income...........................	30	348	249	148
Interest expense	(323)	(61)	(40)	(25)
	(293)	287	209	123
Net income (loss)...........................	$(4,532)	$(4,946)	$(3,250)	$ 6

Revenue in the first full year of shipments demonstrated successive quarterly growth, highlighted by fourth quarter revenue of $11,168,000 from the sale of systems to 13 new customers. The Company sold systems to eight new customers during the first three quarters of the year. Gross profit was approximately 54% of revenue throughout the first three quarters and improved to approximately 57% in the fourth quarter as revenues increased more rapidly than fixed costs. Research and development expenses increased in the second quarter primarily due to the shifting of development efforts to new products. The reduction in fourth quarter expenses was attributable to the capitalization of certain patents and trademarks and to increased capitalization of software development costs. Selling, general and administrative expenses reflect the increasing investment in the expansion of sales offices in Europe and the United States, staffing increases in sales, marketing and support staffing level and marketing programs. Interest income increased in the second quarter as a result of the investment of the proceeds from the Company's initial public offering. Interest expense in the first quarter was primarily attributable to the outstanding convertible debt, which was converted into shares of common stock early in the second quarter. The balance of the year reflects the interest expense on capital leases.

Selected Consolidated Financial Data

The following data has been derived from financial statements audited by Price Waterhouse, independent accountants. The consolidated balance sheet at December 28, 1991 and December 26, 1992 and the related consolidated statements of operations, of stockholders' equity and of cash flows for the three years ended December 26, 1992 and the notes thereto appear elsewhere in this Annual Report.

Exhibit 1   (continued)

	Year Ended				
	December 31, 1988	*December 30, 1989*	*December 29, 1990*	*December 28, 1991*	*December 26, 1992*
	(in thousands except per share data)				
Statement of Operations Data:					
Revenue				$ 904	$ 20,729
Cost of revenue				$ 332	$ 9,189
Gross profit				572	11,540
Costs and expenses:					
Research and development	$ 6,348	8,253	10,575	15,786	14,113
Selling, general, and administrative	902	2,494	3,099	6,441	10,475
Other operating costs and expenses			363	$ 850	
	7,250	10,747	14,037	23,077	24,588
Loss from operations	(7,250)	(10,747)	(14,037)	(22,505)	(13,048)
Other income (expense), net	499	425	687	$ (2)	$ 326
Net loss	(6,751)	(10,322)	(13,350)	(22,507)	(12,722)
Pro forma net loss per share[a]	(2.31)	(2.92)	(2.77)	(3.90)	(1.22)
Weighted average shares outstanding[a]	2,925	3,531	4,814	5,712	10,171

	Year Ended				
	December 31, 1988	*December 30, 1989*	*December 29, 1990*	*December 28, 1991*	*December 26, 1992*
	(in thousands)				
Balance Sheet Data:					
Working capital	$ 7,112	$5,471	$10,674	$ 4,463	$33,473
Total assets	10,298	9,226	15,959	13,129	48,733
Long-term capital lease obligations		114	942	892	599
Stockholders' equity[a]	9,316	7,523	12,812	6,408	40,427

[a]Assumes the conversion of all outstanding shares of all series of convertible preferred stock and convertible subordinated notes outstanding prior to the closing of the Company's initial public offering on April 3, 1992 into common stock. See Notes 1 and 4 of Notes to Consolidated Financial Statements.

Exhibit 1   (continued)

Price Range of Common Stock

The Company's common stock is traded in the Over-the-Counter market on the National Association of Securities Dealers, Inc. Automated Quotation ("NASDAQ") National Market System under the symbol "KSRC." The following table sets forth the range of high and low sale prices for the common stock for the periods indicated, as reported on the NASDAQ National Market System. Quotations represent prices between dealers and do not reflect retail mark-ups, markdowns or commissions. There was no market for the Company's common stock prior to its initial public offering effective on March 27, 1992.

Price Range of Common Stock

	High	Low
First quarter	$12	$11
Second quarter	13¼	7½
Third quarter	11½	7½
Fourth quarter	19½	5½

As of February 10, 1993, there were approximately 1,500 individual participants in security position listings for the Company's common stock.

Report of Independent Accountants

To the Board of Directors and Stockholders of
Kendall Square Research Corporation

In our opinion, the accompanying consolidated balance sheet and the related consolidated statements of operations, of stockholders' equity and of cash flow present fairly, in all material respects, the financial position of Kendall Square Research Corporation and its subsidiaries at December 26, 1992 and December 28, 1991, and the results of their operations and their cash flows for each of the three years in the period ended December 26, 1992, in conformity with generally accepted accounting principles. These financial statements are the responsibility of the Company's management; our responsibility is to express an opinion on these financial statements based on our audits. We conducted our audits of these statements in accordance with generally accepted auditing standards which require that we plan and perform the audit to obtain reasonable assurance about whether the financial statements are free of material misstatement. An audit includes examining, on a test basis, evidence supporting the amounts and disclosures in the financial statements, assessing the accounting principles used and significant estimates made by management, and evaluating the overall financial statement presentation. We believe that our audits provide a reasonable basis for the opinion expressed above.

Price Waterhouse
Boston, Massachusetts
February 8, 1993,
except as to Note 4, which is as of April 1, 1993

Exhibit 1   (continued) Consolidated Balance Sheet

	December 28, 1991	December 26, 1992
	(in thousands, except share and per share data)	
Assets		
Current assets:		
Cash and cash equivalents	$ 4,035	$ 7,392
Short-term investments		10,372
Accounts receivable	804	13,328
Inventories	4,316	8,939
Prepaid expenses and other current assets	1,137	1,149
Total current assets	10,292	41,180
Fixed assets, net	2,635	3,108
Software development cost, net		3,451
Other assets, net	202	994
	$13,129	$48,733
Liabilities and Stockholders' Equity		
Current liabilities:		
Accounts payable	$ 2,885	$ 3,001
Accrued payroll costs	1,019	1,575
Other accrued expenses	612	2,047
Deferred revenue	428	196
Current portion of long-term capital lease obligations	885	888
Total current liabilities	5,829	7,707
Long-term capital lease obligations	892	599
Stockholders' equity:		
Convertible preferred stock	50,098	
Convertible subordinated notes, converted into common stock upon the closing of the initial public offering	13,029	
Common stock. $.01 par value; 35,000,000 shares authorized; 375,578 and 11,356,517 shares issued at December 28, 1991 and December 16, 1992, respectively	4	114
Additional paid-in capital	215	109,987
Accumulated deficit	(56,938)	(69,660)
	6,408	40,441
Less 1,263 shares of common stock held in treasury, at cost		(14)
Total stockholders' equity	6,408	40,427
Commitments (Note 7)		
	$13,129	$48,733

The accompanying notes are an integral part of the financial statements.

EXHIBIT 1   (continued) Consolidated Statement of Operations

	Year Ended		
	December 29, 1990	December 28, 1991	December 26, 1992
	(in thousands, except per share data)		
Revenue		$ 904	$ 20,729
Cost of revenue		332	9,189
Gross profit		572	11,540
Costs and expenses:			
Research and development	$ 10,575	15,786	$ 14,113
Selling, general and administrative	3,099	6,441	10,475
Other operating costs and expenses	363	850	—
	14,037	23,077	24,588
Loss from operations	(14,037)	(22,505)	(13,048)
Other income (expense):			
Interest income	755	380	775
Interest expense	(68)	(382)	(449)
	687	(2)	326
Net losses	$(13,350)	$(22,507)	$(12,722)
Unaudited pro forma net loss per share assuming conversion of convertible preferred stock and convertible subordinated notes (Note 1)	$ (2.77)	$ (3.90)	$ (1.22)
Weighted average shares outstanding	4,814	5,712	10,171

The accompanying notes are an integral part of the financial statements.

EXHIBIT 1   (continued) Consolidated Statement of Cash Flows Increase (Decrease) in Cash and Cash Equivalents

	Year Ended		
	December 29, 1990	*December 28, 1991*	*December 26, 1992*
		(in thousands)	
Cash flows from operating activities:			
Cash received from customer		$ 527	$ 8,533
Cash paid to suppliers and employees	$(13,538)	(23,192)	(36,231)
Interest received	636	530	681
Interest paid	(68)	(173)	(177)
Net cash used for operating activities	(12,970)	(22,308)	(27,194)
Cash flows from investing activities:			
(Purchase) sale of short-term investments	(2,888)	2,888	(10,372)
Payment for capitalized software development costs			(3,506)
Purchase of fixed assets	(1,561)	(710)	(879)
Proceeds from sale of fixed assets	242		
Net cash provided for (used for) investing activities	(4,207)	2,178	(14,757)
Cash flows from financing activities:			
Proceeds from sale and leaseback of equipment	961		
Principal payments on capital lease obligations	(325)	(666)	(1,156)
Issuance of convertible subordinated notes		12,820	6,451
Debt issuance costs			(288)
Issuance of convertible preferred stock	18,817	3,059	
Convertible preferred stock issuance costs	(195)	(47)	
Initial public offering of common stock			44,000
Initial public offering issuance costs			(3,964)
Proceeds from exercise of common stock options, warrants, and employee stock purchases	17	64	279
Repurchase of common stock			(14)
Net cash provided by financing activities	19,275	15,230	45,308
Net increase (decrease) in cash and cash equivalents	2,098	(4,900)	3,357
Cash and cash equivalents, beginning of period	6,837	8,935	4,035
Cash and cash equivalents, end of period	$ 8,935	$ 4,035	$ 7,392

The accompanying notes are in integral part of the financial statements.

EXHIBIT 1   **(continued) Consolidated Statement of Cash Flows (continued)—Reconciliation of Net Loss to Net Cash Used for Operating Activities**
(in thousands)

	Year Ended		
	December 29, 1990	*December 28, 1991*	*December 26, 1992*
Net loss	$(13,350)	$(22,507)	$(12,722)
Adjustments to reconcile net loss to cash used for operating activities:			
Depreciation and amortization	1,526	1,786	2,115
Gain on sale of fixed assets	(114)		
Interest accrued on convertible subordinated notes		209	277
Change in assets and liabilities:			
Increase in accounts receivable		(804)	(12,524)
Increase in inventories		(4,316)	(5,411)
Increase in prepaid expenses and other current assets	(860)	(81)	(12)
(Increase) decrease in other assets	(183)	10	(792)
Increase (decrease) in accounts payable	(161)	2,190	116
Increase in accrued payroll costs	107	509	556
Increase in other accrued expenses	65	268	1,435
Increase (decrease) in deferred revenue		428	(232)
Net cash used for operating activities	$(12,970)	$(22,308)	$(27,194)

The accompanying notes are an integral part of the financial statements.

EXHIBIT 1   (continued)

Notes to Consolidated Financial Statements

Note 1: Nature of Business and Summary of Significant Accounting Policies

Kendall Square Research Corporation (the "Company") was incorporated on February 4, 1986. The Company develops, manufactures, markets, and supports a family of high performance, general purpose parallel computer systems for a broad range of mainstream applications, including numerically intensive computation, on-line transaction processing and database management and inquiry.

Principles of consolidation   The consolidated financial statements include the accounts of the Company and its wholly-owned subsidiaries. All significant intercompany transactions are eliminated in consolidation.

Fiscal year   The Company's fiscal year ends on the last Saturday of December.

Cash equivalents and short-term investments   The Company considers all highly liquid debt instruments purchased with original maturities of three months or less to be cash equivalents. Short-term investments, which include treasury bills with original maturities of greater than three months, are recorded at cost which approximates market.

Revenue recognition   The Company recognizes revenue from product sales upon written customer acceptance. Warranty costs are accrued as product sales revenue is recognized.

Inventories   Inventories are stated at the lower of cost or market. Cost is determined by the first-in, first-out (FIFO) method.

Fixed assets   Fixed assets are recorded at cost and depreciated by use of the straight-line method over their estimated useful lives. Repair and maintenance costs are expensed as incurred.

Software development costs   Certain software development costs incurred subsequent to the establishment of technological feasibility are capitalized and amortized under straight-line and units-shipped methods over the lesser of the estimated economic life of the products or three years commencing when the products are available for general release. Amortization of software development costs is included in cost of revenue and in 1992 totaled $55,000.

Note 2: Inventories
Inventories consist of the following (in thousands):

	December 28, 1991	December 26, 1992
Raw materials and manufactured assemblies	$1,337	$4,808
Work in process	1,906	1,272
Finished goods	1,073	2,859
	$4,316	$8,939

Deposits on inventory purchases at December 28, 1991 and December 26, 1992 totaled $543,000 and $164, respectively, and are included in prepaid expenses and other current assets.

Note 3: Fixed Assets
Fixed assets consist of the following (in thousands):

EXHIBIT 1   (continued)

	Useful Life in Years	December 28, 1991	December 26, 1992
Computer equipment and purchased software..........	3	$ 7,151	$ 8,916
Office furniture and equipment	3–5	778	1,274
	Lease term	345	617
Leasehold improvements		8,274	10,807
Less accumulated depreciation and amortization		(5,639)	(7,699)
		$ 2,635	$ 3,108

The Company incurred capital lease obligations of $1,757,000, $844,000, and $866,000 in 1990, 1991, and 1992, respectively. Accumulated depreciation on equipment under capital leases totaled $1,229,000 and $2,219,000 at the end of 1991 and 1992, respectively.

In 1992, inventories totaling $788,000 were transferred to fixed assets.

The Company has a $2,600,000 lease line with a commercial lender for the leasing of fixed assets. At December 26, 1992, the Company has $1,734,000 available under the lease line.

Note 4: Stock Option and Purchase Plans

During 1991, the board of directors adopted the 1991 Stock Option Plan (the "Plan") under which it may issue both incentive and nonqualified stock options. The exercise price of incentive stock options will be no less than the fair market value of the common stock on the date of grant. The Plan allows for a maximum of 1,211,250 common shares to be granted under options over a ten-year period expiring in 2001. The options generally vest between three to five years. Options for the purchase of 210,625 common shares vest in seven years, however, the vesting may be accelerated based on the Company achieving certain revenue levels. All options to date have been issued at fair market value. At December 26, 1992, options for 181,492 shares were available for future grants. On February 8, 1993, the board of directors, subject to stockholder approval, authorized an increase of an additional 1,500,000 shares issuable under the Plan.

A summary of activity in the Plan is as follows:

	Incentive Stock Options		Nonqualified Stock Options	
Incentive Stock Options	*Number of Shares*	*Option Price*	*Number of Shares*	*Option Price*
Balance at December 30, 1989	320,421	$.16–$1.60	48,750	1.60
Granted	50,656	1.60– 4.00		
Exercised	(22,646)	.16– 1.60		
Canceled	(32,031)	.80– 1.60		
Balance at December 29, 1990	316,400	.80– 4.00	48,750	1.60
Granted	91,500	4.00– 9.00	23,125	4.00
Exercised	(42,916)	.80– 4.00		
Canceled	(77,772)	.80– 4.00		
Balance at December 28, 1991	287,212	.80– 9.00	71,875	1.60–4.00
Granted	432,099	9.00–11.00		
Exercised	(26,986)	.80– 4.00	(4,125)	1.60
Canceled	(22,946)	1.60–11.00	—	
Balance at December 26, 1992	669,379	.80–11.00	67,750	1.60–4.00

EXHIBIT 1   (continued)

At December 26, 1992, options for the purchase of 149,384 shares were exercisable.

On December 14, 1991, the Company's board of directors adopted the 1991 Employee Stock Purchase Plan (the "Purchase Plan") which provides for the issuance of up to 262,500 shares of common stock to participating employees of the Company through a series of four six-month offerings, beginning May 1, 1992. The Purchase Plan covers substantially all employees, subject to certain limitations. Each employee may elect to have up to 11% of base pay withheld and applied toward the purchase of shares in such offering. The price at which the shares of common stock may be purchased in an offering is 85% of the fair market value of the common stock on the date such offering commences or the date such offering terminates, whichever is lower. In 1992, 33,395 shares were purchased under the Purchase Plan.

The Company has reserved 1,412,892 shares of common stock for issuance upon the exercise of warrants (Note 4) and for use in the Plan and Purchase Plan.

Note 6: Income Taxes

Certain items of expense, primarily research and development, are recognized for income taxes in different periods than for financial reporting purposes. Certain research and development costs are capitalized for tax reporting purposes. Beginning in 1992, the Company is amortizing these costs over a period of 60 months. At December 26, 1992, unamortized research and development costs totaled $34,100,000.

At December 26, 1992, the Company has net operating loss carryforwards of approximately $64,100,000 and $26,500,000 for financial and tax reporting purposes, respectively. The net operating loss carryforwards expire through 2007. In addition, the Company has research and development tax credit carryforwards which expire through 2007 of approximately $2,900,000 available to offset future regular income tax liabilities. Under the Internal Revenue Code, certain substantial changes in the Company's ownership could result in an annual limitation on the amount of the carryforwards which could be utilized.

Note 8: Major Customers and Export Sales

Sales to one and three major customers accounted for $904,000 and $7,763,000, or 100% and 37% of revenue, for 1991 and 1992, respectively. In 1992, revenue from European customers totaled $9,173,000.

Note 10: Line of Credit

The Company has a bank line-of-credit which provides for borrowings of up to $2,500,000. Borrowings under the line-of-credit bear interest at the bank's base rate plus 2%. In the event that the Company's quarterly net income exceeds $250,000, borrowings under the line of credit may increase to $5,000,000 and the interest will decrease to the bank's base rate plus æ%. All borrowings are secured by accounts receivable and inventories. At December 26, 1992, there were no borrowings outstanding under the line of credit.

Kendall Square Research and Supercomputing[2]

Kendall Square Research recognized at its founding that a key to its success would be its ability to deliver more computing power at lower cost per computation than its

---

[2]This section is based on information taken from the 1992 Annual Report of Kendall Square Research Corporation.

competitors. Its approach was based on linking many low-cost minicomputers and dividing the computer task among them, rather than building larger mainframe computers or trying to improve programming and software to wring more performance from the computer architectures that were available. The concept of massively parallel processing had first surfaced in the 1980s, and several competitors felt that it had tremendous potential.

A large scale parallel computer was potentially faster and less expensive than traditional mainframes or available supercomputers. In addition to lower cost per computation or transaction, large scale parallel computers were theoretically scalable; bigger and more powerful machines could be assembled merely by adding processors and the memory and input and output devices to support them. However, as processors were added, programming became more difficult and cumbersome.

Kendall Square's founders believed that a highly successful parallel computer could succeed only if it could take advantage of the library of applications and languages that were already standard in the mainframe and supercomputer worlds. Their goal was to develop a standards-based multi-user system which could run multiple applications simultaneously, so that a sufficiently powerful system could serve an entire technical or business enterprise. Their ideal system would even be able to run scientific and business applications at the same time.

The technology which was needed to develop such a computer did not exist in 1986 when KSR was founded. For six years Kendall Square scientists and engineers invested in chip development technology that they hoped would turn their insight into a working computer. By 1992 they were sure they had succeeded. They had developed a large scale parallel computer which combined the power of massively parallel, distributed memory machines with the familiar shared-memory programming environment of conventional mainframes. The KSR1 family of computers was designed for high performance computing requirements typical of scientific environments, for decision support and complex database query applications, and for on-line transaction-intensive environments such as automatic teller machines or airline reservation systems.

The KSR1 family of systems scaled from 16 to 1088 processors. A $975 thousand model with 16 processors could handle 1,200 transactions per second, a measure of commercial computer speed. Scalability allowed users to add computer resources in incremental and cost-effective steps without changes in software and without performance degradation. Therefore, a customer could add to an installation at a later date without the need to replace all software or to reprogram operating systems. While the scaling up of processors in massive parallel processing computer systems was not fully reliable, reports from users of KSR machines seemed to support the company's contention that they scale up more effectively than those of some other competitors.

In 1993 supercomputers with massively parallel processing were more commonly found in scientific applications than in commercial applications. One reason for this was the tendency for supercomputers to crash as users pushed their limits. In scientific applications users were often willing to sacrifice reliability for performance, but most commercial applications required computers to work reliably for months at a time. The business market for supercomputers had been estimated to be about $31 billion, far larger than the scientific and research market, which had been estimated to be about $4 billion.[3] In 1992, Kendall Square signed contracts with Neodata, a direct-mail company working with Electronic Data Systems (EDS), and AMR, the parent company of American Airlines, to work together to develop systems using KSR computers.

Revenue Recognition at Kendall Square Research Corp.

Critics of the revenue recognition practices used by KSR claimed that the company was far too liberal in what it called a sale of a machine or system. They cited cases in which laboratories had ordered or received equipment which was subsequently accepted but for which there was no prospective funding, or for which research grants had been requested but not yet granted. In such cases there was no assurance that the research grant would be received, and even if it was, certain there could be significant delays before the customer would pay KSR.

Other analysts thought that the liberal accounting practices used by KSR were not uncommon in the computer industry, but such practices were less visible in the financial statements of more mature companies such as IBM or Digital Equipment Corporation. These analysts pointed out that terms requiring payment in six or nine months, after a customer had received a grant from a government agency—often very slow payers—were not unusual. Such terms might be appropriate for the typical university or research laboratory that were the base of early KSR users.

> Terms of Kendall's supercomputer deliveries were often extremely attractive to researchers. For example, Edward Lazowska, chairman of the department of computer science at the University of Washington, said that it has two KSR1 computers with a total of 60 processors. He said, "We paid $1 million for half of it, and the rest was a loan of equipment against future grants." Kendall . . . treated the entire shipment as a sale.
>
> William Goddard, a physicist at the California Institute of Technology, said he paid for 32 processors in September 1992 using a National Science Foundation grant. He liked it so much that last spring he wanted to double the size of the system and applied for more grant money. Kendall shipped him the computer immediately, but he and Kendall are still waiting for the grant award. "I'm committed to buying it," he said. "I am applying for two very large grants."[4]

Other contracts included one for $1.5 million that could be cancelled if the second of two phases was not completed. Still others involved distributors that had the right to cancel the contract if a customer could not be found.

A second sales practice added to the concerns of critics of KSR's accounting policies. Some users purchased machines with fewer processors than were eventually thought to be needed. In these cases the processors purchased were booked as revenue and accounts receivable, but KSR had delivered additional processors to the customer for installation and use by the customer. The additional processors remained on KSR's balance sheet as inventory pending the customer's decision to keep the processors, apply

---

[3]Dorfman and Bulkeley, loc. cit.

[4]Bulkeley, William M., "Kendall Square . . . " *The Wall Street Journal,* December 2, 1993, p. A3.

for grants to buy them, or to otherwise make arrangements to pay for the loaned processors.

As a result of these practices revenues recognized had exceeded cash collected from customers by significant amounts. Some critics thought this indicated that revenue was being recognized too early. Other observers thought this was normal for a new, growing company in the process of ramping up sales.

Of additional concern was the practice of KSR giving research grants to some users of its systems. Such grants had been reported to range between $5 thousand and $50 thousand or more. Mr. Burkhardt was reported to have agreed that grants ". . . sometimes do run into substantial amounts, but are legitimate expenses to foster software development, not disguised sales incentives. . . ."[5]

Kendall Square Research in 1993

In August, 1993, *The Wall Street Journal* reported:

> **WALTHAM, Mass** Kendall Square Research Inc. is "quite comfortable" with analysts' estimates that it will earn 45 cents to 50 cents a share for the year, President Henry Burkhardt said.
>
> Mr. Burkhardt also said he is comfortable with estimates that revenue for the year will top $60 million, up from $20.7 million. And he said he is comfortable with third-quarter earnings estimates of nine cents to 13 cents a share. For the year-earlier quarter, Kendall Square reported a net loss of 29 cents a share on revenue of $5.3 million.[6]

---

[5]Ibid.

[6]"Kendall Square Agrees With Profit Estimates for Quarter and Year," *The Wall Street Journal,* August 13, 1993, p. B5A.

Questions

1. Evaluate the revenue recognition policies used by Kendall Square Research. Do they conform to generally accepted accounting principles with respect to:
   a. The timing of revenue recognition.
   b. The amount of revenue recognized.
   c. The matching of costs and expenses to revenue.

2. The rapid growth in sales expected by Kendall Square Research managers will strain the company's ability to finance their expansion. How, if at all, should this fact affect the ways in which management chooses accounting principles and a reporting strategy? _____

CASE
8-3

National Electric Corporation

In mid-February 1993, Janet Blair, a portfolio manager for a large mutual fund, held a significant investment in National Electric Corporation (National) in her equity stock portfolio. She was undecided as to whether to increase or decrease her holding of the company's stock. If she shared the enthusiasm as to the company's future prospects expressed by the company's chairman, she would be inclined to accumulate more National shares. On the other hand, if a quality of earnings type of appraisal of the company's 1992 financial statements indicated the 1992 results had been achieved by a lowering of the company's earnings quality, most probably she would significantly reduce her National position.

1992 Earnings Revisions

On January 30, 1993, National reported net income for 1992 of $161.9 million or $1.82 a share. This represented a drop of 19% from net income of $198.7 million or $2.24 a share in 1991. Sales, however, were up 12% in 1992 to a record $5.7 billion from $5.1 billion.

The dramatic drop in earnings at National surprised some on Wall Street. Until late October 1992 most analysts were projecting 1992 earnings to exceed the record earnings reported in 1991. Much of their optimism was based on statements by National's chairman, D. C. Burke, who had seen National's sales double and its earnings quadruple in his 10 years as chief executive. As late as August 29, 1992, Burke expected a good year for National. At that time, analysts were projecting 1992 earnings for National of between $2.35 and $2.50 a share.

During an August 29 interview Burke stated that he was "relatively satisfied with a growth of 10% a year" in sales. He added, however, "I'm not satisfied with our

Professors David F. Hawkins and Norman Bartczak of Columbia University prepared this case as the basis for class discussion rather than to illustrate either effective or ineffective handling of an administrative situation.
Copyright © 1994 by the President and Fellows of Harvard College. Harvard Business School case 195–159.

profit margin, which has been running around 4%. I think it should be 5%." Burke indicated that the company would be "working very hard" in the third quarter in an effort to better the $49.7 million, or $.55 per share earned in the third quarter of 1991.

On October 10, 1992, National announced third-quarter earnings of $44.1 million or $.50 per share. Although this was 11.3% less than third-quarter earnings in 1991, Burke attributed most of this profit decline to National's Power Systems Group where shipments of turbines and generators had lagged the entire year. Material shortages and production scheduling problems caused by regulatory and financing delays in constructing new power stations were cited as the reason for the decline in shipments. According to John W. Snyder, president of the Power Systems Group, "this is business which is only deferred and not lost." He expected with the strengthening economy that shipments would start to rebound during the fourth quarter. After National's announcement of its third quarter earnings, analysts pared their earnings projections for the year to be flat—approximately the same as the $2.24 per share in 1991.

On December 20, 1992, Wall Street was again taken by surprise by National. In a dramatic reversal from his earlier optimism, Burke announced that he expected National's fourth-quarter net income to be about half of 1991's $53.6 million or $0.61 per share, and profits to be down for the full year. He noted that the downward trend stemmed from heavy losses in four subsidiaries. Excluding the four loss operations, he added, 1992 results would have exceeded 1991's record net income.

Once again, analysts revised their estimates of National's full year 1992 earnings, this time to between $1.80 and $1.85 per share. On January 30, 1993, National announced 1992 earnings of $1.82 per share.

In an interview with a leading finance weekly, Burke commented on National's 1992 results:

> We simply took on more projects than we had competent management to handle. What we didn't evaluate was the risk of a new business in new locations with a lot of new managers. And when things went wrong, we didn't control the costs. . . . I will be riding herd a lot harder this year. I'm sure of that," says Burke. . . . In Spain the management at its electrical parts company has been sacked and Burke has tightened the auditing procedures.
>
> All in all, Burke expects some write-offs, but smaller ones, for 1993, and no bad surprises. Earnings for the year should be up slightly. "We've got the organization structure to grow with," Burke says. "This year we'll do better than $6 billion sales"—a gain of nearly 20%.
>
> By Burke's own doing, National's top executives, himself included, must step aside at age 65. That means that 1993 will be his last year on the corporate throne. He leaves no doubt that he intends to end his generally productive reign on a prosperous note. Which includes trying to get his stock up.

Company Operations, 1993

As of February 1993, National's core business activity was the manufacture and sale of equipment and appliances for the generation, transmission, utilization, and control of electricity.

Included among National's products were practically all electrical and much related mechanical equipment required by power companies, railroads, city transit systems, and industrial plants; steam and gas turbines; propulsion and electrical equipment for the marine industry; electrical and electronic systems, instrumentation and other equipment for the aerospace industry; and consumer products. National developed, designed, and furnished a limited range of nuclear power plant equipment for the generation of electricity.

National supplied products to the construction industry. It also engaged on a joint venture basis in land development and sales, conventional construction activities, conventionally and federally financed real estate and housing development, and the operation and management of rental properties.

National owned and operated four television stations and its Educo subsidiary offered various educational services and materials to the nation's schools, sold language instruction courses, and developed and administered various training and management skill development programs. In the area of leisure time activities, National's subsidiaries bottled and distributed various soft drink brands in important market areas; manufactured, assembled, and sold wristwatches and other timepieces; marketed and sold, principally by mail, discounted videotapes and various related items; leased and rented automobiles on both a direct basis and through franchisees in locations across the United States, in Canada, and in the Caribbean; and operated resort hotels.

National Credit Corporation (NCC) engaged in the extension of credit in transactions secured by real or personal property or both and in leasing transactions including leverage leasing.

National manufactured household appliances which were sold to independent distributors and dealers through a sales organization of National.

National engaged in the distribution of electrical and other products outside the United States, primarily those manufactured by National. Such distribution was accomplished through a wholly-owned subsidiary and through company representatives and independent distributors. National also had a number of subsidiaries outside the United States, the majority of which engaged in the manufacture and sale of electrical generation, transmission, utilization and control equipment, and consumer products.

National was subjected to a high degree of competition (including price, services, warranty, and product performance) for sales of heavy equipment, primarily from larger companies, and for sales of household appliances and smaller types of equipment from both larger and numerous smaller competitors.

Management Incentives

National's management incentive compensation plan disclosure stated:

> Under Article XVI of the by-laws, as amended by the stockholders, a special committee of the Board of Directors is empowered to authorize the payment of additional compensation to executive and supervisory officers of the Corporation and its subsidiaries for any year in which cash dividends of at least $.25 per share on the corporation's Common Stock are

paid, in amounts which in the aggregate do not exceed 5% of the consolidated net income for that year before deducting taxes on income and before any provision for incentive payments under the by-law plus any unused amount that may be carried forward from previous years for which the full amount of payments permitted by the by-law shall not have been made. Payments may be made in cash, in Common Stock of the Corporation, or both. On awards payable in deferred installments in Common Stock, the by-law authorizes the payment of amounts equivalent to the dividends which are paid during the period of deferment on a like number of outstanding shares. Such amounts equivalent to the dividends are used to purchase additional shares to be held for delivery on the same terms and conditions applicable to the other shares covered by the awards.

Janet Blair

To lower the time cost of her analysis of National's earnings quality, Blair decided to focus on the company's last two years of operations. Accordingly, she reviewed selected financial data for 1991–1992, in particular the company's quarterly results, quarterly stock prices, and selected daily stock prices information (**Exhibit 1**). In order to put this company's 1991–1992 results into perspective, she prepared a summary of selected company financial and nonfinancial data for the 1983–1992 period (**Exhibit 2**). Next she read the 1991 and 1992 chairman's letter to the stockholders (selected portions reproduced in **Exhibits 3** and **4,** respectively). Then, as preparation for reading the financial statement Blair reviewed note 1, "Significant Accounting Principles and Policies," to the company's 1992 financial statements (**Exhibit 5**). Because she was focusing on the changes in the company's quality of earnings since its 1991 annual report, Blair elected to exclude the company's 1990 financial statements and related disclosures from her analysis. In addition, because the company's consolidated financial statements included NCC on a fully consolidated basis she considered financial ratios based on this primary statement meaningless. (For example, see the company's consolidated statement of position at December 31, 1992 and 1991 shown in **Exhibit 6**). Accordingly Blair further decided to limit the analysis to the NCC and National financial statements presented as supplemental disclosures in the 1992 annual report (**Exhibits 7, 8, 9,** and **10**). The supplemental National financial statements accounted for NCC on an equity method basis.

In her review of the notes to the 1992 financial statements, Blair noted the following National-related disclosures for the period 1991–1992 under the these captions (1990 data omitted).

Consolidated Statement of Capital

Common stock held in treasury amounted to 798,453 shares at December 31, 1992, and 364,778 shares at December 31, 1991.

During 1992, a systematic plan for reacquisition of common stock of the Corporation was begun. All the shares will be used to supply the various plans under which common stock is distributed to employees.

Exhibit 1   Financial Data, 1991–1992 ($000,000, except per share amounts)

Quarterly Income Statement Information	First	Second	Third	Fourth	Year
1991					
Sales	$1,180.0	$1,260.0	$1,230.0	$1,420.0	$5,090.0
Net income	42.8	52.6	49.7	53.6	198.7
Earnings per share	$ 0.48	$ 0.60	$ 0.55	$ 0.61	$ 2.24
1992					
Sales	$1,270.0	$1,410.0	$1,390.0	$1,630.0	$5,700.0
Net income	40.8	53.4	44.1	23.6	161.9
Earnings per share	$ 0.46	$ 0.60	$ 0.50	$ 0.26	$ 1.82

Quarterly Stock Price Information	Daily Average Volume	High	Low	Close
1991				
First	53,700	$48.25	$43.00	$47.75
Second	40,100	54.785	47.75	50.75
Third	61,900	52.50	38.375	42.50
Fourth	66,600	46.25	39.875	43.00
1992				
First	61,300	47.375	35.25	38.125
Second	56,400	38.375	31.125	35.00
Third	50,400	38.875	31.375	36.75
Fourth	112,500	39.875	24.25	25.375

Selected Daily Stock Price Information Date	Volume	High	Low	Close
08/28/92	29,000	$34.625	$34.25	$34.375
08/29/92	73,200	34.75	34.25	34.375
08/30/92	96,700	34.875	34.125	34.75
10/09/92	67,500	39.875	39.25	39.25
10/10/92	68,700	39.50	36.625	36.625
10/11/92	549,500	34.375	33.75	33.75
12/20/92	38,100	33.00	32.00	32.25
12/21/92	573,900	24.875	24.25	24.375
01/29/93	71,500	23.625	23.25	23.375
01/30/93	114,200	23.75	22.875	23.50
01/31/93	112,100	24.00	22.75	23.00
02/15/93	57,500	21.875	21.25	21.75
02/19/93	81,500	22.75	21.75	21.75

EXHIBIT 2 Ten-Year Summary of Selected Statistics, 1983–1992[a]

	1992	1991	1990	1989	1988	1987	1986	1985	1984	1983
Per common share data										
Earnings	$1.82	$2.24	$2.08	$1.53	$1.89	$1.74	$1.60	$1.55	$1.41	$1.02
Dividends	0.972	0.936	0.90	0.90	0.09	0.90	0.80	0.70	0.625	0.60
Book value	22.37	21.56	20.09	17.76	17.01	16.01	15.04	14.12	13.36	12.84
Stock price: high–low	$47–$24	$55–$38	$49–$33	$35–$27	$36–$27	$40–$30	$40–$28	$34–$20	$32–$29	$23–$15
Common shares outstanding	88,320	88,300	83,603	82,219	81,418	79,005	77,875	77,177	75,516	74,560
Common stockholders	168	161	156	163	166	168	175	188	190	197
Employees	194	184	180	186	163	155	147	139	128	125
Financial position										
Current assets	$2,607,778	$2,172,488	$2,029,542	$2,041,477	$1,404,543	$1,352,900	$1,313,600	$1,280,500	$1,097,100	$1,042,300
Accounts receivable	1,308,232	1,016,191	952,149	911,467	720,630	688,800	564,725	472,263	438,257	434,783
Inventories	983,911	866,901	895,365	975,954	766,829	715,315	763,097	727,313	585,074	539,705
Total assets	4,407,665	3,843,291	3,537,851	3,358,167	2,477,612	2,271,400	2,075,300	1,931,600	1,711,500	1,606,600
Current liabilities	1,502,225	1,095,473	962,325	1,139,818	694,969	587,782	459,283	538,710	357,597	278,048
Accounts payable	405,307	351,045	297,235	288,296	132,631	131,090	126,921	143,291	102,663	92,656
Short-term debt	475,301	208,346	182,070	431,061	228,311	149,700	66,000	143,900	15,000	15,000
Long-term debt	671,727	629,109	641,247	620,980	382,142	404,409	426,586	240,574	241,991	258,848
Stockholders' equity	$1,996,137	$1,930,119	$1,776,818	$1,487,417	$1,389,330	$1,276,574	$1,189,409	$1,103,089	$1,037,918	$983,951
Capital expenditures	$202,414	$224,721	$200,018	$207,411	$173,700	$206,400	$145,400	$111,700	$73,000	$52,800
Income										
Sales	$5,702,310	$5,086,621	$4,630,530	$4,313,410	$3,924,286	$3,664,050	$3,216,347	$2,851,396	$2,630,339	$2,486,843
Depreciation	115,161	103,240	90,913	87,015	76,944	73,000	63,641	65,442	69,019	65,895
Net income	161,928	198,667	175,256	126,999	154,920	139,052	125,874	121,371	108,314	77,868
Preferred dividends	1,158	1,158	1,158	1,158	1,191	1,410	1,510	1,541	1,548	1,548
Common dividends	$85,567	$81,966	$74,380	$71,748	$69,832	$68,937	$60,384	$51,936	$45,564	$43,509

[a]National Credit Corporation (NCC) accounted for on an equity method basis to facilitate comparisons of post and pre FAS 94 periods. FAS 94 required consolidation of all controlled subsidiaries, including NCC. Prior to its adoption of FAS 94 NCC was accounted for on an equity methods basis in National's consolidated financial statements.

Exhibit 3   Selected Portions of Chairman's 1991 Letter to Stockholders

---

To Our Stockholders:

January 31, 1992

Again I can say, "It was the most successful year in National history."

The Company, excluding National Credit Corporation's revenues, in 1991 achieved record sales for the 10th straight year, topping the $5 billion mark for the first time. We achieved record earnings despite some problems in the economy which prevented even better results. And while new marks were being set, National was building a strong base for continued success in years ahead.

We invested nearly $225 million in new and improved plants and laboratories, adding facilities in the United States and overseas. With 60 manufacturing plants in this country and 40 in 19 other countries of the world, National is better prepared to serve the needs of customers and society than ever before. Our sales to countries outside the United States from both our domestic and worldwide facilities exceeded a billion dollars for the first time. This means your Company is accelerating its drive to meet the needs of people in all parts of the world—and to build commercial success in so doing.

These things were achieved despite such problems in the economy as the delayed upturn in capital spending by industry, delays in licensing new electric power plants and continued uncertainties in the minds of businesspeople and consumers.

I am encouraged by the performance of our four operating groups. The Consumer Product Groups showed improvement in sales and earnings which we expect will continued as a result of aggressive marketing of quality products and better cost control.

The Power System Group established another outstanding sales and earnings record. With the largest backlog of orders in its history and with exciting projects ahead, Power Systems shows excellent prospects for strong performance throughout the rest of the 90s and beyond. . . .

In January, our Directors raised the quarterly dividend to 24.3 cents.

For the future the four operating groups will emphasize strategic planning which plots the National course through the balance of the 90s and, in some cases, well into the second decade of the next century. Backing up such planning is the continued support of research and development. We will increase research expenditures in 1992. Emphasis will also be placed on productivity improvement with capital expenditures for plants and equipment again at about the 1991 level.

Plans to keep National moving with vigor in the future also involve organization. Early in 1991 we announced the "step-down-at-65" program which assures that the top seven positions in the Company will be filled by competent young executives, and releases the talents and experience of the former top executives for programs of long-range significance to society and to National.

The past 10 years have seen your Company move into the mainstream of technological and social progress, encountering as it goes the problems which always accompany change. But solving people's problems is exactly where a company such as ours can make its greatest contribution to the good of mankind.

On the cover of this report are the words of Albert Einstein: "Concern for man himself and his fate must always form the chief interest of all technical endeavors." National could find no better guideline for its future course.

D. C. Burke
Chairman

EXHIBIT 4   Selected Portions of Chairman's 1992 Letter to Stockholders

To Our Stockholders:

January 30, 1993

While the steady growth in National's sales excluding NCC's revenues continued during 1992 and order backlogs reached a record of $7.8 billion, our earnings progress was interrupted by heavy losses in four subsidiaries and several joint ventures, abnormally low scheduled shipments of power equipment and continuing cost problems in our major appliance business. The result was a disappointing drop of 42 cents a share from 1991 earnings.

The losing subsidiaries, which are receiving close attention and undergoing vigorous corrective action, included operations engaged in low-income housing, water quality control, the direct mail-order business and our electrical parts company in Spain.

Intensive assessment to determine the appropriate course of action with respect to these subsidiaries and our troubled joint venture activities is continuing, and decisive action will be taken during 1993. The potential for successful operation of our Spanish electrical parts subsidiary in the European Community justifies further efforts to reach a profitable level.

Because these loss operations have had such a disproportionate effect on our overall results, we have instituted a tighter, centralized management system to prevent such areas of weakness from developing into major problems in the future. Each group president is still in charge of their operations, but our new more sensitive system will help detect and solve problems more rapidly and effectively.

One of the 1992 problems was the low level of power equipment shipments. While incoming orders for power equipment were at a record high, the effect of depressed order levels in several prior years resulted in relatively low shipments in 1992. Added production expense and investment to prepare for increased shipments ahead also reduced the profit contribution of the Power Systems Group. We look for deliveries to improve moderately, starting in the second quarter of 1993. . . .

To summarize 1993, although National experienced a difficult time in several of its noncore businesses, it moved ahead as planned in most of its core operations whose prospects for both the near and long-term future have steadily brightened. National's management is confident that we can resume the progress that marked our past decade of profitable growth. We expect this progress to begin slowly in 1993 but to gain momentum as the year progresses.

D. C. Burke
Chairman

Exhibit 5   Note 1, 1992 Annual Report

Significant Accounting Principles and Policies

The major accounting principles and policies followed by the corporation are presented below to assist the reader in evaluating the consolidated financial statements and other data in this report.

Consolidation   The Consolidated financial statements represent the adding together of all affiliates—companies that the corporation directly or indirectly controls, either through majority ownership or otherwise. Results of associated companies—companies that are not controlled but are 20% to 50% owned—are included in the financial statements on a "one-line" basis.

Financial statement presentation   Financial data and related measurements are presented in the following categories.

- **National.** This represents the adding together of all affiliates other than National Credit Corporation, Inc. (NCC), which is presented on a one-line basis.
- **NCC.** NCC and its respective affiliates are consolidated in the NCC columns and constitute its business.
- **Consolidated.** These data represent the adding together of National and NCC.

The effects of transactions among related companies within and between each of the above-mentioned groups are eliminated.

The assets, liabilities income and expense amounts of non-U.S. subsidiaries are translated at current exchange rates. The effects of translation are included in stockholders' equity.

Sales are recorded as products are shipped on substantially all contracts. The percentage-of-completion method is used for orders with durations generally in excess of five years and for certain construction projects where this method of accounting is consistent with industry practices. In accordance with these practices, Long-Term Contracts in Process are stated at cost plus estimated profits recognized to date. Costs related to long-term contracts are also accumulated in Inventories, Recoverable Engineering and Development Costs (Government Contracts), and Progress Payments to Subcontractors. In accordance with terms of the particular contracts, progress billings are made to customers and are shown in total as Progress Billing on Contracts. The amounts of long-term contracts in process do not exceed realizable value.

NCC's revenues from operations (earned income). Income on all loans is recognized on the interest method. Accrual of interest income is suspended when collection of an account becomes doubtful, generally after the account becomes 90 days delinquent.

Financing lease income, which includes residual values, is recorded on the interest method so as to produce a level yield on funds not yet recovered. Unguaranteed residual values included in lease income are based primarily on periodic independent appraisals of the values of leased assets remaining at expiration of the lease terms.

Operating lease income is recognized on a straight-line basis over the terms of underlying leases.

Origination, commitment and other nonrefundable fees related to funding are deferred and recorded in earned income on the interest method. Commitment fees related to loans not expected to be funded and line-of-credit fees are deferred and recorded in earned income on a straight-line basis over the period to which the fees relate. Syndication fees are recorded in earned income at the time related services are performed unless significant contingencies exist.

Inventories. The cost of the inventories of the consolidated companies is determined principally by the LIFO method. Inventories not on LIFO are valued at current standard costs, which approximate actual, or average cost. In accordance with the practice of the corporation and of the electrical manufacturing industry generally, inventories include items which are not realizable within one year.

EXHIBIT 5   Note 1, 1992 Annual Report

Depreciation on plant and equipment acquired since January 1, 1988, is provided for on the straight-line method. Plant and equipment acquired prior to 1988 is depreciated using accelerated methods. Accelerated depreciation methods using guideline lines are used for federal income tax purposes.

Deferred income taxes are provided for timing differences between financial and tax reporting, principally related to long-term contracts in process, product guarantees and depreciation.

Deferred federal income taxes are not provided on the undistributed earnings of certain subsidiaries (located outside the United States) when such earnings have been indefinitely reinvested or will be remitted in the form of a tax-free liquidation.

Research and development costs are recorded as expenses when incurred.

Recognition of losses on financing receivables and investments. NCC maintains an allowance for losses on financing receivables at an amount that it believes is sufficient to provide adequate protection against future losses in the portfolio. When collateral is formally or substantively repossessed in satisfaction of a loan, the receivable is written down against the allowance for losses to estimated fair value and transferred to other assets. Subsequent to such transfer, these assets are carried at the lower cost or estimated current fair value. This accounting has been employed principally for highly leveraged transactions (HLT) and real estate loans.

Intangible assets. Goodwill is amortized over a 40 year period.

EXHIBIT 6   Consolidated Statement of Financial Position ($000)

Assets	At December 31, 1992	At December 31, 1991
Cash and marketable securities	$135,309	$145,209
Financing receivables, less unearned finance charges and allowance for losses	954,690	805,283
Customers receivables	1,343,444	1,027,192
Inventories..	983,911	866,901
Prepaid and other current assets	191,400	152,169
Investments	79,055	98,551
Plant and equipment, net	1,327,013	1,215,209
Other assets...	299,549	274,187
Total assets	$5,314,371	$4,584,701
Liabilities and Stockholders' Equity		
Short-term loans	$1,075,993	$708,446
Accounts payable—trade	455,307	393,245
Accrued payable and payroll deductions	178,154	159,913
Income taxes currently payable	19,182	29,091
Deferred current income taxes	150,009	116,941
Other current liabilities...............................	285,272	236,247
Non-current liabilities................................	85,100	82,601
Deferred non-current income	78,000	43,687
Long-term debt	851,727	779,109
Subordinated debt	70,000	40,000
Minority interest	69,490	65,302
Stockholders' equity:		
Capital..	775,223	784,408
Retained earnings	1,220,914	1,145,711
	$5,314,371	$4,584,701

EXHIBIT 7   Supplemental NCC Statements of Financial Position and Income

Balance Sheet	*At December 31, 1992*	*At December 31, 1991*
Cash	$6,020,000	$5,982,000
Financing receivables, less unearned finance charges and allowance for losses	1,021,376,000	855,940,000
Other assets (net)	21,976,000	3,939,000
Total assets	$1,049,372,000	$865,861,000
Short-term loans and other liabilities	$665,692,000	$550,606,000
Long-term debt	180,000,000	150,000,000
Subordinated debt	70,000,000	40,000,000
Subordinated debt due parent	26,800,000	40,100,000
Capital[a]	34,500,000	24,500,000
Retained earnings	72,380,000	60,655,000
Total liabilities and stockholders' equity	$1,049,372,000	$865,861,000

[a]$10,000 National contribution in 1992.

Statement of Income	*Year Ended December 31, 1992*	*Year Ended December 31, 1991*
Total earned income	$123,225,000	$95,496,000
Less:		
Operating expense	34,350,000	27,863,000
Interest	65,778,000	37,821,000
Income and other taxes	8,978,000	13,965,000
Net income	$ 11,725,000	$15,847,000

EXHIBIT 8   **Supplemental National Statements of Income and Retained Earnings ($000, except per share amounts)**

Income	Year Ended December 31, 1992	Year Ended December 31, 1991
Income		
Sales	$5,702,310	$5,086,621
Equity in income from non-consolidated subsidiaries and		
joint venture companies	3,868	25,702
Other income	70,662	57,771
	$5,776,840	$5,170,094
Cost and expenses:		
Cost of sales	4,423,557	3,877,876
Distribution, administration, and general	868,706	783,116
Depreciation	115,161	103,240
Interest	76,940	56,699
Other costs	12,236	10,000
Income taxes	115,000	137,167
Minority interest in net income of consolidated		
subsidiaries	3,312	3,329
	$5,614,912	$4,971,427
Net income	$ 161,928	$ 198,667
Net income per common share	$ 1.82	$ 2.24
Retained Earnings		
Retained earnings at beginning of year	$1,145,711	$1,028,892
Plus:		
Net income	161,928	198,667
Pooling of interests adjustments	—	1,276
Less:		
Dividends paid on preferred stock	1,158	1,158
Dividends paid on common stock	85,567	81,966
Retained earnings at end of year	$1,220,914	$1,145,711

EXHIBIT 9   **Supplemental National Statement of Financial Position ($000)**

Assets	At December 31, 1992	At December 31, 1991
Current assets:		
Cash and marketable securities	$ 129,289	$ 139,227
Customer receivables	1,308,232	1,016,191
Inventories.	983,911	866,901
Prepaid and other current assets	186,346	150,169
Total current assets	$2,607,778	$2,172,488
Investments	185,935	183,706
Plant and equipment, net	1,324,913	1,213,390
Other assets	289,039	273,707
Total assets	$4,407,665	$3,843,291
Liabilities and stockholders' equity		
Current liabilities:		
Short-term loans	$ 475,301	$ 208,346
Accounts payable—trade	405,307	351,045
Accrued payrolls and payroll deductions	175,154	157,113
Income taxes currently payable	19,182	29,091
Deferred current income taxes	140,009	116,441
Other current liabilities.	287,272	233,437
Total current liabilities	$1,502,225	$1,095,473
Non-current liabilities.	87,131	81,101
Deferred non-current income	80,955	42,187
Long-term debt	671,727	629,109
Minority interest	69,490	65,302
Stockholders' equity:		
Capital	775,223	784,408
Retained earnings.	1,220,914	1,145,711
Total liabilities and stockholders' equity	$4,407,665	$3,843,291

Exhibit 10   Supplemental National Statement of Cash Flows ($000)

	Year Ended December 31, 1992	Year Ended December 31, 1991
Net income	$ 161,928	$ 198,667
Income charges (credits) not affecting cash:		
Depreciation	115,161	103,240
Deferred income taxes	64,424	23,600
Minority interest in net income of consolidated subsidiaries	3,312	3,329
Equity in income from non-consolidated subsidiary and		
investee companies	(3,868)	(25,702)
Customer receivables	(292,041)	(66,042)
Inventories..................................	(117,010)	(3,937)
Prepaid and other current assets	(36,117)	658
Accounts payable—trade	54,262	53,810
Other	85,475	53,062
Cash flow from operations	$35,526	$340,685
Expenditures for new and improved facilities	(202,414)	(224,721)
Increase in investment (net)	(14,273)	(17,683)
Other (net)	(41,607)	(10,529)
Cash used for investing activities	($258,294)	($252,932)
Increase in short-term loans	$ 266,955	$ 26,276
Increase in long-term debt	69,185	27,913
Issuance of common stock to employees	26,278	29,825
Dividend payments	(86,725)	(83,124)
Purchase of common stock for treasury	(36,296)	(645)
Reduction of long-term debt	(26,567)	(40,051)
Cash provided from (used for) financing activities	212,830	(39,806)
Increase (decrease) in cash and cash equivalents during year	$ (9,938)	$ 47,946
Cash and cash equivalents at beginning of year	139,227	91,281
Cash and cash equivalents at end of year	$ 129,289	$ 139,227

Income Taxes

	Year Ended December 31, 1992	Year Ended December 31, 1991
Income Taxes Currently Payable		
Federal	$ 13,209	$ 81,494
State	8,598	15,083
Non-U.S..	28,769	16,990
	$ 50,576	$113,567

Income Taxes Deferred

Federal	54,932	21,100
State	8,000	2,500
Non-U.S.	1,492	—
	$ 64,424	$ 23,600
Total	$115,000	$137,167

Deferred tax expenses results from timing differences in the recognition of revenue and expense for tax and financial statement purposes. The source of these differences for the years 1992 and 1991, and the tax effect of each follow:

Income Taxes Deferred	*1992*	*1991*
Excess of tax over book depreciation	$32,840,000	$18,123,000
Difference between financial and tax reporting on long-term contracts in process	22,273,000	11,656,000
Provision for warranty costs not deductible for tax purposes until incurred	(2,422,000)	(8,583,000)
Other miscellaneous timing differences	11,733,000	2,404,000
Total	$64,424,000	$23,600,000

There are cumulative undistributed earnings of $180 million from certain non-U.S. subsidiaries which have been reinvested for an indefinite period of time and, therefore, no deferred federal taxes have been provided. Cumulative undistributed earnings were $120 million in 1992.

The federal income tax returns of the Corporation and its wholly-owned subsidiaries are closed through December 31, 1989, and it is believed that adequate provisions for taxes have been made through December 31, 1992.

FASB Statement 96, "Accounting For Income Taxes" is effective for fiscal years beginning after December 15, 1992.

Inventories

	1992	*1991*
Inventories—valued principally on LIFO method[a] (58% valued on LIFO method)	$1,106,842,000	$ 896,414,000
Recoverable engineering and development costs (government contracts)	40,093,000	54,937,000
Long-term contracts in process	858,994,000	800,469,000
Progress payments to subcontractors	542,894,000	424,878,000
	2,548,823,000	2,176,698,000
Less: progress billing on contracts	1,564,912,000	1,309,797,000
Total	$ 983,911,000	$ 866,901,000

[a]The excess of current cost (principally at current standards) over the cost of inventories valued on the LIFO basis was $163 million at December 31, 1992, and $152 million at December 31, 1991.

Other Current Assets

Customer receivables are net of doubtful account allowances of $34 million for 1993 and $23 million for 1991.

Plant and Equipment, at Cost

Plant and Equipment	1992	1991
Land and buildings	$ 758,056,000	$ 702,671,000
Machinery and equipment	1,555,609,000	1,424,404,000
Construction in progress................................	99,486,000	92,005,000
	2,413,151,000	2,219,080,000
Less: accumulated depreciation	1,088,238,000	1,005,690,000
Total	$1,324,913,000	$1,213,390,000

Short-Term Bank Loans

Short-term bank loans amounted to $475 million on December 31, 1992, and $208 million on December 31, 1991. These were the maximum amounts of borrowings outstanding during the respective years. The average aggregate short-term borrowings outstanding during 1992 totaled $280 million.

Contingencies

At December 31, 1992, National was contingent guarantor of customers' notes sold to banks and other liabilities aggregating $154 million and of notes payable and other borrowing of non-consolidated joint venture companies in the amount of $83 million.

Audit Opinion

Finally, Blair noted that the Corporation had received a "clear opinion" from its auditors on its 1992 and 1991 financial statements.

Questions

1. What is your assessment of the quality of the company's $1.82 earning per share for 1992? _____
2. What signs do you see that the company may or may not be experiencing operating or financial difficulties? _____

CHAPTER 9

Growth Rate Analysis

A corporation's value is determined in large part by its projected sales, earnings, and dividend growth rates, which in turn are a function of its projected industry growth rate, competitive position, and corporate strategy. Growth rate analysis uses financial ratio analysis, quality of earnings analysis, and selected statistical techniques to analyze corporate financial reports in order to project growth trends and to identify possible changes in the operating, financial, and strategic characteristics of corporations.

Because of the importance of corporate growth rates to corporate success and valuation, the growth rate of a corporation's sales, profits, and dividends is a major focus of many financial statement analyses: Investors are interested because of the close relationship between equity stock values and projected growth rate and the expected volatility of earnings and dividends. Creditors examine past growth records in order to predict the future level of funding required to finance changes in accounts receivables, inventories, and productive assets. Corporations scrutinize growth rates of themselves and their rivals in order to ascertain how well they are doing on a comparative basis, to detect potential weaknesses in their competitors, and to predict future competitive behavior.

Typically, the analysis of growth characteristics and growth rates involves three major steps: First, a quantitative measurement of the rate of growth of the variables being examined. This quantification may range from a simple index number series to a complex mathematical equation describing the growth pattern inherent in the data. Second, the identification of the various sources of the growth. This phase involves both quantitative and qualitative assessments of the sources of growth as well as an analysis of the relationship of these various sources to each other, the operating and financial characteristics of the firm, and the external environment during the period under review. Third, the use of the preceding analyses in combination with other data,

Professor David Hawkins prepared this note as the basis for class discussion.

Copyright © 1995 by the President and Fellows of Harvard College. Harvard Business School teaching note 195–179.

such as projected industry growth rates or management's announced capital expansion plans, to forecast future levels of growth and to speculate on the possible financial and operating consequences of the projected growth rates.

Appendix A presents some common quantitative approaches to the description, measurement, and projection of growth rates.

Optimum Strategies

Given its market share and industry growth rate, business strategy studies indicate that a company can optimize its market value if it adopts certain pricing strategies, cost structures, financing practices, and dividend policies. An understanding of these optimum strategies should help analysts to appreciate better the significance of the historical, comparative, and projected financial statement statistics developed by their analysis of growth situations. For example, in some instances the financial analysis may indicate that the company has adopted the optimum strategy for its circumstances. This revelation may explain why the trends and ratios are what they are. It may provide also some clues as to what the future strategy of the company might be, which would, in turn, imply certain trends and ratios. Alternatively, the analysis might indicate that the optimum strategy is not being followed. This could raise questions as to why the optimum strategy is not being followed, which may result in the identification of some unique characteristics of the company that suggest the theoretical best strategy is not appropriate. Or, if the company indeed is following a suboptimizing strategy, a knowledge of the theoretical consequences of this action may improve the analysts' ability to forecast the consequences of the actual strategy.

Excluding acquisitions, a corporation's optimum operating and financing strategy is in large measure determined by the growth rate of its industry or product lines, its market share, and its financing options. One model for optimum strategies using four market share–industry growth rate combinations is presented below. These optimum strategies are based on the premise that the company with the largest market share is its industry's low cost producer.

High Market Share–High Industry Growth Rate.   A company in this situation should be seeking to consolidate its market share before the industry growth rate slows down as the market matures. During the high growth–consolidation phase, the company with the largest market share may be able to generate enormous cash flows because of its market position. However, it will also consume cash in large amounts. In fact, it is suggested that unless the company's return on assets is at least equal to the industry unit growth rate plus the rate of inflation, it will need to raise cash from external sources if it wishes to retain its market share. As a result, since such a high return is often difficult to achieve, companies in this situation nearly always employ high levels of financial leverage, sell equity frequently, and pay nominal dividends, if any.

Super industry growth rates do not last forever. As the growth rate subsides, cash requirements to finance growth subside also. If the company can maintain its high market share during this growth slowdown phase, it should be able to earn high profit levels relative to its smaller competitors and generate an excess cash flow, which can be used to improve liquidity, reduce debt, and increase dividends or finance new growth opportunities.

The stock market value of these companies during their super growth phase is based on the expectation that as growth slows down, the company will pay substantial dividends from its excess cash flow. Unfortunately, in practice this does not always occur. All too often a management, seeing its company's growth rate declining, tries to maintain the old level by investing in expensive, futile marketing programs to further increase market share; diversifies to industries that it does not understand; or spends huge sums on research in the vain hope of finding the next super growth product or technology.

High Market Share—Mature Industry with Low Growth Rate.   A company in this position usually has a return on assets that is greater than its industry growth rate. Therefore, it is able to generate excess cash, reduce its borrowings, buy back its stock, and pay dividends without impairing its market share and growth potential.

Those with the highest market share may try to use their borrowing capacity to finance programs to increase their market share and to raise their return on equity. However, there is a point where it becomes so expensive to increase market share that the investment cannot be justified by the potential rewards.

Low Market Share—Low Industry Growth Rate.   Companies in this situation are candidates for liquidation, since any profits earned must be reinvested to maintain market share in a situation which promises little future growth. Liquidation could be achieved through sale or by letting the company's market share deteriorate over time and paying out dividends to stockholders from profits and funds freed by asset reductions.

Low Market Share—New Industry with Potentially High Growth Rate.   Companies in this position have very uncertain futures and an enormous need for cash. Permanent market shares have not yet been established and the fight for share requires considerable investment, since everyone wants to end up with the dominant share. Also, since the industry has a high growth potential, capital must be invested to keep up with the projected growth rate. If a company cannot acquire a strong market share position and keep up with the industry's growth rate, a company should consider withdrawing from the industry.

Exceptions

While it is generally true that on the average, companies with high market shares have higher pre-tax returns on investment than do firms with lower market shares and that low market share companies face serious business obstacles when competing with high-share companies, there are some low market share companies that are notable exceptions to these observations. These exceptions are companies that have formed the best fit between the opportunities in the competitive environment and the company's particular strengths, skills, and resources. Typically, low-share companies that are able to find the best fit and earning high returns on investment are those that think small, have an outstanding chief executive leadership whose influence pervades the entire organization, use research funds selectively and efficiently, carefully segment their markets, and most importantly, exploit those segments where the company has a comparative advantage. This market segmentation may be by stages of production, manufacturing policies, prices, products, customers, and services.

Other Strategies

Corporations can pursue a variety of strategies with a domestic or multinational scope beyond those discussed to date. Some companies follow niche strategies where they seek to develop a specialty product or market position which others, for one reason or another, do not duplicate. When successful, this strategy can generate high rates of return and strong positive cash flows. Other companies may be locked into a business because the exit barriers, such as loss on disposal of assets or management pride, are high. Their strategy may be to liquidate the business through operations. Conversely, some companies are protected because their industry's entry barriers are high. These companies may adopt strategies designed to exploit this advantage. Private label strategies are pursued by others. These companies manufacture products that others will sell under their own label. This strategy's key to success is extremely low manufacturing costs and fast response to customer needs. Another strategy followed by some companies is to make the company attractive to potential buyers. For example, a company courting leveraged buyout proposals, whereby a buyer finances the acquisition primarily with borrowing secured by the company's own assets and debt capacity, may build up substantial cash balances, eliminate all of its debt, and focus on developing those businesses with persistent cash flows.

Financial Strategies

A company's capital structure and dividend policies are an integral part of its business strategy. For example, a company may set market share and growth rate objectives but be unable to finance the attainment of these objectives from internally generated funds after payment of dividends. In this case, some of the choices that the company may consider to finance the strategy are: issue new equity, borrow capital, reduce or eliminate dividends, or some combination of these choices. Alternatively, the company may consider adopting less ambitious market objectives that are consistent with its existing and potential financial resources.

The key to whether or not a company may consider alternatives to its present financial policies or modify its market objectives is the relationship between the projected corporate growth rate, return on stockholders' equity, and the company's profit retention rate, which is one minus the company's dividend payout ratio. If the return on equity times the profit retention rate is lower than the corporate growth rate objectives, the growth rate objectives may have to be lowered or a company's financial policies changed in such a way as to raise the needed capital from external sources.

Sustainable Growth Rate Equations

The financial and operating dimensions of growth rate analyses can be summarized and related to each other through the use of a convenient mathematical expression known as the "sustainable growth rate equation." This equation is based upon the fact that if a company does not issue new equity, its potential maximum earnings growth rate will be a function of its rate of return on equity and dividend payout policy.

For example, assume that a company had earnings of $10 million during the year just ended; a net worth of $100 million at the beginning of that year; and a permanent dividend payout policy of 50%. Thus, during the year just ended, the company earned 10% on its beginning net worth; retained $5 million of earnings, and ended the year with an equity of $105 million. If the past year's 10% return on beginning equity is repeated during the next year, the company's earnings will grow to $10.5 million, i.e., 10% of this year's beginning net worth of $105 million. As long as market conditions permit, this 5% earnings growth rate may be repeated annually as long as the company continues to earn 10% on each year's beginning net worth and pays out 50% of its earnings in dividends.

The relationship between future earnings growth, return on beginning equity, and dividend payout policy described in this example is captured in more general terms in the sustainable growth rate equation which is,

$$g = ROE \times \left(1 - \frac{D}{E}\right)$$

where:

g = Annual net income growth rate or sustainable growth rate.

ROE = Rate of return on beginning-of-year net worth, including preferred stock.

$\frac{D}{E}$ = Dividends payout ratio, i.e., annual common and preferred dividends (D) divided by annual earnings (E).

$\left(1 - \frac{D}{E}\right)$ = Earnings retention rate, i.e., 1 − the dividend payout ratio.

By observation, it can be seen from the above equation that a future earnings growth rate cannot be greater than a company's return on beginning equity, i.e., g. = ROE, when dividends are zero. In addition, should a company wish to maintain a given earnings growth rate, it can do so by a variety of combinations of payout ratio and return on equity levels. For example, should the company in the above example find that its projected return on beginning equity had slipped to, say 8%, it would have to adjust its payout ratio downward to 37.5% if it wishes to maintain its 5% earnings growth rate potential in the future [.08 × (1 − .375) = .05].

If the sustainable growth rate equation is further reduced from the form presented above, as shown below, the sustainable growth rate is equal to the annual change in retained earnings divided by the year's beginning net worth.

$$g = \frac{E\left(1 - \frac{D}{E}\right)}{OE} = \frac{\Delta RE}{OE}$$

where:

g = Sustainable growth rate.
E = Annual earnings.
D = Annual dividends.
ΔRE = Change in retained earnings during the year.
OE = Net worth at beginning of the year.

Actual versus Indicated

In practice, a company's annual earnings growth rate may differ for at least four reasons from the rate indicated by the sustainable growth rate calculation. The first two reasons are fairly obvious: the actual return on equity and the actual payout ratio may differ from the ones used in the equation. The other two reasons require some explanation.

The sustainable growth rate is a maximum potential rate of growth. If a company's industry is growing slower than the company's potential growth rate and the company cannot increase its market share, then the industry growth rate becomes the sustainable growth rate.

Also, as noted earlier, the sustainable growth rate computation assumes a company's only source of new equity is retained earnings. If new equity is sold, then a company's earnings in the year in which the equity is sold will be derived from both the equity retained in the prior year and the new capital. This can result in a one-year earnings growth that is greater than the original projected growth rate.

Sources of Growth

Because of the key role of the return on equity, the sustainable growth rate analysis is expanded in practice to include those variables that influence a company's return on equity. A company's return on equity is a common element in both the DuPont equation and the sustainable growth rate equation. Therefore, the two equations can be combined and the sources of earnings growth explained in the expanded equation as follows:

$$\frac{\text{Pre-tax profit}}{\text{Sales}} \times \frac{\text{Sales}}{\text{Assets}} \times \frac{\text{Assets}}{\text{Equity}} \times (1 - \text{Tax Rate}) \times (1 - \text{Payout}) = g$$

or

Pre-tax margin $\times$ Turnover $\times$ Leverage $\times$ Tax retention
$\times$ Profit retention = Sustainable growth rate

Up to this point, we have discussed sustainable growth rate primarily in terms of sustainable *earnings* growth rates. However, it should be noted that the g computed is also the sustainable growth rate for *dividends*, since the payout ratio is assumed to remain constant. This means that dividends will grow at the same rate as earnings.

If a company maintains the same ratios for the variables in the growth equation from one period to another, its assets, liabilities, owner's equity, sales, profits, and dividends will all grow at the indicated sustainable growth rate. However, if the ratio level of any of the variables changes, the actual growth rate of the variables will be different from the indicated growth rate at the beginning of the year, even if at the end of the year the sustainable growth rate figure is unchanged.

The linking of the DuPont model to the sustainable growth rate equation through their common element, return on equity, results in a much more powerful analytical equation for those interested in growth analysis than the sustainable growth rate equation standing alone. The sustainable growth rate equation indicates what the potential growth rate might be, but it says nothing about the risks associated with this indicated growth rate. The marrying of this equation to the DuPont equation provides some perspective on how the growth was achieved and, in doing so, gives some perspective on the risk associated with the growth rate.

The expanded equation can be broken down into two parts—those ratios that relate to operations and those that relate to financial considerations. The "operating" ratios are sales turnover and pre-tax profit margin. Those interested in growth analysis typically like to see a company's growth and return on investment coming from the operations area since it relates to the ongoing economic activity of the company. In contrast, growth derived from the use of financial means such as financial leverage and tax rate management is less desirable since there is a limit to how much leverage and tax rate management can be used to achieve growth. Also, these sources of equity returns and growth depend on groups outside the company. In addition, more leverage increases the risk of earnings volatility. In general, an increasing reliance on these financial ways to achieve a higher return on equity suggests a lowering of the quality of returns on equity and a potentially more uncertain or volatile growth rate.

Earnings-per-Share Growth

Management frequently adopts earnings-per-share growth objectives. The attainment of this objective is influenced by the linkage between debt policy, payout ratio, market-determined interest rates, and return on new investments. In order to understand the relationship of these variables to earnings-per-share growth, sometimes the sustainable growth equation is recast to focus on the analysis of earnings-per-share growth.

The following growth equation is a common earnings-per-share form of the sustainable growth rate equation. It is based on the assumption that next year's earnings per share will be equal to this year's earnings per share plus the profits on both the earnings retained and the incremental debt made possible by the retained earnings, after deducting the cost of the incremental debt:

$$eps_{t+1} = eps_t + eps_t(b)(r) + eps_t(b)(D/E)(r - i)$$

where:

b = Portion of earnings retained (1 − dividend payout ratio).
r = After-tax rate of return on incremental asset investment.
D/E = Debt to equity ratio (at book).
i = After-tax interest rate.

To illustrate, assume that this year's earnings per share is $2, the company pays out 50% of its profits in dividends; the after-tax rate of return on incremental asset investment is 10%; the debt to equity ratio is two times; and the after-tax cost of debt is 5%. Using the above equation, next year's earnings-per-share should be $2.20:

$$\underbrace{\$2.20}_{\substack{\text{Next year's} \\ eps}} = \underbrace{\$2.00}_{\substack{\text{This year's} \\ eps}} + \underbrace{\$2.00(.5)(.10)}_{\substack{\text{Incremental profit} \\ \text{on earnings retained}}} + \underbrace{\$2.00(.5)(2)(.10 - .05)}_{\substack{\text{Incremental profit on} \\ \text{incremental debt}}}$$

This basic equation can be rearranged and the rate of growth in earnings per share (*g*) can be calculated directly as follows:

$$g = br + (b)(D/E)(r - 1)$$

Alternatively, if the analyst wished to compute the profit retention rate needed to reach a specific earnings-per-share growth rate, the equation is:

$$b = \frac{g}{[r = D/E(r - i)]}$$

Analysis of Income Changes

In contrast to the growth equation analyses previously discussed, which focus on the operating and financial causes of the *rate of growth*, growth analysis also involves an identification and examination of the sources of a company's *dollar growth in earnings*. This dollar-oriented analysis is similar to an earnings quality analysis. It develops answers to the question: "What accounted for the dollar change in earnings from one period to another?" The answer to this question is presented frequently in terms of the dollar contribution to the change in earnings from these six variables: accounting; environment; infrequent and/or unusual transactions; tax rate; capital structure transactions; and operations.

An *accounting source* of earnings change may arise from a change in an accounting principle, estimate or the way in which a principle is implemented. For example, a decision to use longer depreciation lives in the current period could be a source of earnings growth over the prior period, since the prior period's income will be based on the old depreciation schedule. The "Accounting Changes" notes to financial statements usually identifies and gives the dollar value of these sources of earnings change.

Environmental sources of earnings change include all of those domestic and international economic changes that influence earnings, other than interest rates. Typically these are: changes in the business cycle or the economy and/or the industries of the company, shifts in foreign exchange rates, and changes in the rate of inflation. It is difficult to relate net income changes to changes in the business cycle in general and/or the industries of a company. Often, the analyst has to be content to make such statements as: "Income improved due to an improvement in the economy." However, no matter how crude the final figure related to this source of earnings change, the analyst should try to gauge the relative significance of this influence. For example, the impact on earnings of shifts in foreign exchange rates are reported in the management analysis and discussion and notes section of financial reports. In the case of inventories of LIFO companies, one impact of inflation is captured in the change in the LIFO reserve. The extent of the impact on profit changes of using historical cost depreciation in periods of inflation may be crudely estimated by computing how much the historical depreciation of a company falls short of its replacement cost depreciation determined by applying inflation rate measurements to the historical cost figures.

Infrequent and/or unusual transactions may occur in one period and not another and as such are a source of earnings change. Examples of such transactions are extraordinary items and infrequent or unusual items included in income before extraordinary items, such as write-down of inventories or the gain on the sale of equipment.

Tax rate sources of earnings change are reflected directly in a change in the tax rate between two periods. The current income before taxes times the prior period's tax rate less the net income reported for the current period measures this influence. The tax expense note should provide clues as to what caused the company's book tax rate to change.

Capital structure derived changes in income include such transactions as: the conversion of debt securities to common stock, which changes the interest charged to income, and the reacquisition and extinguishment of debt securities, which changes the interest expense and may generate a gain or loss on the transaction.

Operating sources of income changes are those changes that can be identified with the basic ongoing business of the company. These include such sources of income change as market share shifts, changes in the cost structure, different product mixes, and new product price schedules.

Real versus Nominal

Most financial trend data are expensed in nominal dollars. Nominal dollars reflect the purchasing power of the period. These data are not adjusted for changes in the purchasing power of the dollar during the period covered. It may be useful, particularly in high inflation rate periods, to adjust the nominal data for price level changes.[1]

Additional Analysis

This chapter has focused on the analysis and measurement of corporate growth, particularly sales, income, and dividend growth. The first task of the analyst is to identify the company strategy being followed, project the consequences of this strategy, and assess whether or not it is the best one for the company. In approaching this task the

---

[1]A later chapter discusses the various techniques for converting nominal dollar financial data to a real or price-level–adjusted basis.

analyst should remember that most businesses do not have the advantage of a high market share; they must devise a specific strategy that leads to their best performance irrespective to their position. The market share–industry growth rate classification scheme may be helpful in performing the analysis, but because it represents such a high level of abstraction, it should not be substituted for a precise, specific, and far-ranging description of the company's strategy. This statement should define the markets in which a business competes, the products that it sells, their performance and price characteristics, and the ways in which they are produced, sold, and financed.

The analyses described in the chapter focus on explaining the rate of growth or the change in dollar levels of growth variables being examined. These may be helpful in understanding both the strategy and its success. However, to fully appreciate the impact of growth on a company, additional detailed financial analyses should be undertaken of the key variables that (1) contribute to growth, such as capital structure changes; and (2) are influenced by growth, such as working capital needs. In addition, the operating segment data disclosed in financial reports should not be neglected. It may provide important insights into product strategy, which is the core of most business strategies.

While this chapter has dealt primarily with the analysis of past growth, it should not be forgotten that the objective of analyzing past growth is typically to forecast future growth. The insights gained through the analysis of the past can be helpful in projecting future growth, but they are seldom enough to project future growth rates and patterns with confidence. These insights must be combined with relevant economic and industry forecasts and an appreciation of management's stated future plans.

The chapter has also concentrated on sales, earnings, and dividend growth rate analysis. This is appropriate since these variables are typically the focus of this type of analysis. To concentrate on these variables without considering their related balance sheet implications of growth can be a mistake, however. When projecting sales, earnings, and dividends, the related future balance sheets must also be projected to identify possible balance sheet constraints to growth, such as illiquidity, possible balance-sheet–related risks, such as excessive debt, and possible balance sheet opportunities, such as excess cash.

In addition to the financial ratio and earnings quality analysis of growth rates covered in this chapter, in some instances the analysis of growth rates can be enhanced by using statistical techniques such as index numbers, moving averages, histograms, measurements of means and standard deviations, graphs, ratio charts, regression analysis, probability distributions, expected values and time series analysis. Most standard books on statistical analysis provide clear explanations of these statistical tools. Those planning to become truly competent analysts of financial statement data should consult these books and become familiar with their contents. Appendix A of this chapter briefly reviews some of these statistical approaches to measuring, analyzing, and projecting growth rates.

APPENDIX A

MEASUREMENT OF GROWTH

There are a variety of different ways to describe and measure growth of some variables, such as sales or profit, over a period of time. Some of the more common approaches are presented briefly below.

Index Numbers

Simple index numbers express the relative changes in a variable over time relative to a base value, which is expressed as 100.

A simple index number is computed from a single series of data which extends over a period of time. One time period is designated as the base, and the item for this base is taken as 100. The other data items in the series are then expressed as percentages of this base. **Illustration A–1** illustrates the steps involved in constructing a simple index number series (choosing a base period, dividing each item by the base figure, and multiplying the result by 100).

Index numbers are useful in measuring changes in growth over a period of time relative to the base. As seen from **Illustration A–1**, Company A's sales in 1995 are 269% of sales in 1990 as compared to Company B's 165% change in sales from 1990 to 1995. To express the percentage change in sales in any period, take the index number of that period relative to the index in the period being compared. To illustrate, the increase in sales from Company A from 1993 to 1994 is 11.2% (248 ÷ 223 = 1.112). Other advantages include comparison of changes in series of data that may be expressed in a variety of units and description of typical seasonal or cyclical business patterns.

Arithmetic versus Compound Growth Rate

Growth rate may also be measured by plotting observations on a simple graph. In **Illustration A–2**, annual sales starting at $100 million in 1990 and rising by $10 million for the next five years are plotted along the vertical or Y-axis against time expressed in years along the horizontal or X-axis.

Caution must be used in calculating growth rate from a simple graph such as the one in **Illustration A–2**. Using the arithmetic process will produce a different result than when the compounding process is used. In the arithmetic process, to measure the rate of change when the figure is a straight line as in **Illustration A–2**, the slope of the line must be calculated. This slope represents the change in Y (i.e., rate of growth) per unit change in X. Thus, for any two years on the straight line in **Illustration A–2**, this ratio or slope would be 10; that is, for every year on the X-axis, sales in millions of dollars as measured on the Y-axis grow by 10. This rate is constant.

The compounding process works differently. Let us assume we want to find the compound growth rate in sales over the five-year period 1990–1995. The end value in 1995 of $150 million is equal to the beginning value in 1990 of $100 million times a growth factor $(1 + g)^n$, where g is a growth rate (equivalent to an interest rate) and n represents the number of time periods involved. The following equation can be used to calculate g:

$$S_n = S_0(1 + g)^n$$

where:

S_n = End sales amount.
S_0 = Beginning sales amount.
g = Growth rate (or interest rate).
n = Number of time periods involved.

There are present value tables that may be used to aid in the calculation of the compounding rate. Also, most hand-held calculators include this capability. Using present value

---

ILLUSTRATION A–1   Simple Index Numbers: Sales of Company A and Company B, 1990–1995

Year	Sales in Millions of Dollars		Sales Growth Rate Index (1990 = 100)	
	Company A	Company B	Company A	Company B
1990	40.0	395	100	100
1991	51.3	402	128	102
1992	64.7	479	162	121
1993	89.3	501	223	127
1994	99.2	549	248	139
1995	107.4	650	269	165

ILLUSTRATION A–2

Sales 1990–1995
($ millions)

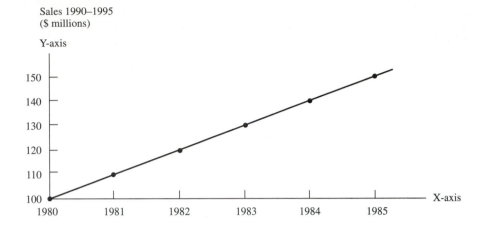

tables and the data given in **Illustration A–2**, we can calculate g in the following way. First, since the tables are present value tables, the above equation should be stated in terms of the beginning amount S_0.

$$S_0 = S_n(PVIF)$$

where:

PVIF = Present value interest factor.

Then, by substituting the data given (S_0 = $100 million, S_n = $150 million, n = 5 years), find the time period in the left column of present value tables showing the value of a dollar received n years hence at i interest rate (5 years) and move right until the value .667 (S_0/S_n) is reached. Reading up from the approximate position of .667 on the table, we find the rate to be approximately 8.5%. This may be substituted in the original equation.

Averages

Another basic tool used to measure the annual growth rate of a series of data, such as sales, is the average of the series. Some of the most common averages used are the arithmetic mean, median, mode, and moving average.

The *mean* of a series of values is the sum of the variables divided by the number of values. The formula $\bar{X} = \Sigma X/n$ is used to determine the mean from a series of data where:

$\bar{X}$ *(read "X bar")* = Mean of the variable X.
Σ = "Sum of."
n = Number of values.

For example, the mean of series 10, 17, 27, 34, 50 would be $138 \div 5 = 27.6$.

When the values to be averaged are of differing degrees of importance, they may be weighted by multiplying each value by a numerical weight based on its relative importance. The total is then divided by the sum of the weights, and the result is termed a *weighted mean*.

The *median* of a set of data is the middle value in order of size if there is an odd number of observations or the mean of the two middle values if the number of observations is even. The median may be more reliable than the mean in samples where extreme deviations occur.

The *mode* is that value which occurs most often or around which there is the greatest degree of clustering. The mode is used when a problem specifically requires the most common value as an average.

A *moving average* is simply an average for a specified period of time, moved up a unit at a time, and the oldest unit included in the average calculation dropped. For example, a three-month moving average is a three-month average moved up a month at a time and the data for the oldest month in the preceding three months dropped. A moving average can be calculated to include high and low seasonal months or business cycles during the year. To do so, one might use a 12-month moving average. Seasonal influences can thus cancel each other out and what remains is the smoothed trend or cycle. In this way, seasonal influences may cancel out while the trend remains. Since this is an average, however, there is no data for the beginning and ending period, which can make prediction of future trends difficult. An example of a three-month moving average is shown in **Illustration A–3**.

ILLUSTRATION A–3   Three-Month Moving Average

Time Period	Percent Growth Rate for Each Time Period	Three-Month Total for Calculation Purposes	Average for Three Months
t_0–t_1	2.0		
t_1–t_2	4.0		
t_2–t_3	3.0	9.0	3.00
t_3–t_4	4.5	11.5	3.83
t_4–t_5	3.5	11.0	3.67
t_5–t_6	5.0	13.0	4.33
t_6–t_7	7.0	15.5	5.17
t_7–t_8	9.0	21.0	7.00
t_8–t_9	6.0	22.0	7.33
t_9–t_{10}	11.0	26.0	8.67
t_{10}–t_{11}	10.5	27.5	9.17

Dispersion

When measuring growth rates over time, it is useful to consider the range of the values so as to put the growth rate into perspective. *Dispersion* is the term used to define this range or variation of a set of values, and the purpose of measuring dispersion is to try to determine the nature and cause of the variation in order to be able to control the variation.

Frequently distribution charts may be used to summarize and present data that will be useful in measuring dispersion. The histogram is one useful approach to presenting a frequency distribution. It is a set of vertical bars whose areas are proportional to the frequencies presented. The height of each bar shows the frequency per unit width. The tallest bar represents the modal class which has the greatest frequency of occurrence. On either side, the bars get smaller, which shows that the farther the figure is from the modal class, the smaller is the frequency of occurrence. **Illustration A–4** shows a histogram.

A smooth curve can be drawn to approximate the frequency distribution for a population of continuous data. Thus, a frequency is provided for every value on the X axis rather than just one value per class interval as in a histogram. If a smooth curve were drawn over the data in **Illustration A–4** to show a general nature of the distribution, we would most likely have a normal or bell-shaped curve as in **Illustration A–5.** The area under any part of the curve corresponds to the number of values in that range.

Dispersion is the scatter or variation of a set of values, and the following are measures of dispersion: the range, the quartile deviation, the mean deviation, and the standard deviation. The measurements are all particularly useful when looking at an array of growth rates, for example, in attempting to determine how variable a particular company's growth may be within an industry, or how variable a particular year's growth may have been for a single company.

The *range* is simply the difference between the largest and smallest values of a variable. The range can be unreliable and misleading if the two extremes are erratic and no indication is given of the intervening values.

The *quartiles* are the three points which divide a frequency distribution into four relatively equal parts. The quartile range $Q_3 - Q_1$ includes the middle half of the items, and the quartile deviation, Q, half this range, is as follows:

$$Q = \frac{(Q_3 - Q_1)}{2}$$

where:

$Q_1$1 separates lowest-valued quarter of total number of values from the second quarter

Q_2, usually the median, separates the second quarter from the third quarter

Q_3 separates the third quarter from the top quarter.

Quartiles are commonly used as measures of dispersion in reporting operating statistics of companies in a particular industry.

The *mean* or *average deviation* is the mean of the absolute deviations of all the values in a distribution from a central point, usually the arithmetic mean or the median. It is a simple measure of variability. It takes every item into account and is less affected by extreme deviations than the range.

The formula for the mean deviation (measured from the arithmetic mean) is:

$$MD = \frac{\Sigma |X - \bar{X}|}{n}$$

where:

MD = Mean deviation.

| | = Means that the signs of the value of X are ignored (absolute values are used).

$X - \bar{X}$ = Deviations of any value X from the arithmetic mean $\bar{X}$.

n = Number of values.

The *standard deviation* is also based on the deviation of all values from $\bar{X}$ but is much better adapted to further statistical

ILLUSTRATION A–4

Histogram: Sales in millions of dollars for 350 companies

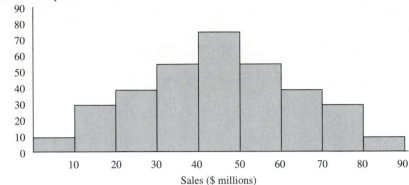

Number of companies

Sales ($ millions)

analysis than the above measures of dispersion. It is calculated by first finding the variance and then extracting the square root of the variance. The variance is found by squaring the deviations of each value from the arithmetic mean, summing the squares, dividing the sum by $(n - 1)$, when n is the number of items in the sample. The formula below has been found to provide the best estimate of the standard deviation:

$$v = \frac{\Sigma(X - \bar{X})^2}{n - 1} \qquad s = \sqrt{\frac{\Sigma(X - \bar{X})^2}{n - 1}}$$

where:

v = Variance.
s = Standard deviation.
$X - \bar{X}$ = Deviations of any value X from the arithmetic mean $\bar{X}$.
$\Sigma(X - \bar{X})^2$ = Sum of the squared deviation.
n = Number of items in the sample.

In the frequency distribution, the midpoint of each class is used to represent every value in that class. The above formula then becomes:

$$s = \sqrt{\frac{\Sigma f(X - \bar{X})^2}{n - 1}}$$

where:

$X - \bar{X}$ = Deviations of the class midpoint X from the mean $\bar{X}$.
f = Frequency in that class.

Using the data from **Illustration A–4**, the histogram, and approximating a mean of $\bar{X}$ of $45 million, we can calculate the standard deviation as in **Illustration A–6**.

The standard deviation is a measure of dispersion about the mean in a sample. In this case, the $17.51 million is equal to one standard deviation. What this means is that typically in a normal distribution, the proportion of items falling within one, two, or three standard deviations of the mean are as follows:

$\bar{X} \pm 1$ standard deviation(s) includes 68.27% of the items

$\bar{X} \pm 2$ standard deviation(s) includes 95.45% of the items

$\bar{X} \pm 3$ standard deviation(s) includes 99.73% of the items

where:

$\bar{X}$ = Mean
$\pm$ = Plus or minus

Graphs and Ratio Charts

Graphs and charts may also be used to show changes in data for purposes of growth rate calculation and projection. Caution must be used in charting and graphing material, however. Arithmetic scales show absolute changes in data but do not show the relative or percentage changes, which are often of more importance. Ratio charts show ratios in their true proportion. Equal ratios or percentages cover equal spaces on the vertical scale. This type of scale is preferable to the arithmetic scale when the relative changes in two series of data are being compared.

A ratio chart is plotted on semilogarithmic paper as opposed to arithmetic graph paper. In a semilog chart, the natural numbers are plotted on the vertical scale at distances from

ILLUSTRATION A–5

Normal bell-shaped curve for a population of continuous data

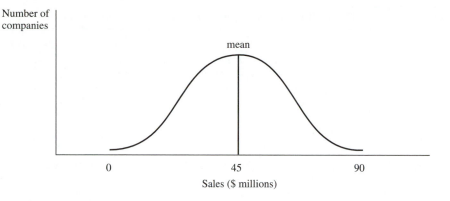

the bottom line that are proportional to their logarithms. The horizontal axis shows time on the usual arithmetic scale.

On a ratio scale, data series of disparate size or those not expressed in the same units may be compared because the slopes of the curves register percentage changes which may be compared. The slope of a line on a ratio chart indicates the percentage change between two points of time. Thus, when comparing two curves or sets of data, relative growth can be determined by comparing their slopes. A curve sloping downward represents a decreasing percentage growth rate; a straight line represents a constant growth rate; and a curve sloping upward represents an increasing growth rate.

ILLUSTRATION A–6   Computation of Standard Deviation $\bar{X} = 45$

Sales in Millions of Dollars (Class Midpoint) X	Number of Companies (Frequency) f	Absolute Deviation from Means (Millions of Dollars) $(X - \bar{X})$	$(X - \bar{X})^2$	$f(X - \bar{X})^2$
5	5	40	1,600	8,000
15	25	30	900	22,500
25	40	20	400	16,000
35	65	10	100	6,500
45	80	0	0	0
55	65	10	100	6,500
65	45	20	500	18,000
75	15	30	900	13,500
85	10	40	1,600	16,000
Total	350			107,000

$$s = \sqrt{\frac{107{,}000}{350 - 1}} = \sqrt{\frac{107{,}000}{349}} = \sqrt{306.59} = 17.51$$

Regression Analysis and Correlation

In looking at a company's statistical data and growth rates, it is often useful to be able to estimate the degree of closeness with which two or more variables are associated and to be able to measure the average amount of change in one variable associated with a unit increase in the value of another variable. When only two variables are involved, the analysis used is simple regression or correlation. When more than two variables are being used, the process is called multiple regression or correlation. For purposes of this chapter, only simple regression analysis will be discussed.

Caution must be used, however, when measuring correlation between variables. Because two variables are correlated does not imply that one is the cause of the other. Generally, if two variables X and Y are correlated, any of the following statements might be correct: (1) X causes Y; (2) Y causes X; (3) X and Y influence each other continuously or intermittently; (4) X and Y are both influenced by a third factor Z; or (5) the correlation is due simply to chance.

The most simple way to express the relationship between two variables is a straight line. The formula for a straight line is $Y = a + bX$, where:

Y = Dependent variable (here, growth rate).
X = Independent variable (here, time).
a = Constant equal to Y when X = 0.
b = Slope of the line or increase in Y for each unit increase in X; it is also called the regression coefficient when the regression equation is linear.

On a scatter diagram, the regression line may be determined by estimation, since the predicted value of Y is roughly the average of the observations, or by the least squares method. Using the least squares method will give the best possible fit to the data involved; that is, will best estimate

ILLUSTRATION A–7   Arithmetic Straight Line Fitted by Least Squares

Time Period	Sales in Millions of Dollars Y	Periods from Beginning X	$(X - \bar{X})$	$(Y - \bar{X})$	$(X - \bar{X})(Y - \bar{Y})$	$(X - \bar{X})^2$
t_0-t_1	2.0	0	−5	−3.95	19.75	25
t_1-t_2	4.0	1	−4	−1.95	7.8	16
t_2-t_3	3.0	2	−3	−2.95	8.85	9
t_3-t_4	4.5	3	−2	1.45	−2.90	4
t_4-t_5	3.5	4	−1	2.45	−2.45	1
t_5-t_6	5.0	5	0	0.95	0	0
t_6-t_7	7.0	6	1	1.05	1.05	1
t_7-t_8	9.0	7	2	3.05	6.10	4
t_8-t_9	6. 0	8	3	0.05	0.10	9
t_9-t_{10}	11.0	9	4	5.05	20.20	16
$t_{10}-t_{11}$	10.5	10	5	4.55	22.75	25
Sum	65.5	55	0	9.75	81.25	110

Therefore $Y = 2.255 + 0.739X$

$$\bar{X} = \frac{55}{11} = 5$$

$$\bar{Y} = \frac{65.5}{11} = 5.95$$

$$b = \frac{81.25}{110} = 0.739$$

$$a = 5.95 - (0.739)(5.0)$$

$$= 2.255$$

---

the total observations. It is called least squares method because it minimizes the sum of the squared deviations from the line more than any other straight line would do. (The deviations below the regression line should be equal to those above, which means that their total value should be zero.) These deviations are vertical measures along the Y-axis. The straight line passes through the overall mean of the data.

To find the values of a and b in the equation $Y = a + bX$, use the following equation, where n = number of pairs of data in the sample.

$$a = \frac{\Sigma Y}{n} - \frac{b\Sigma X}{n} = \bar{X} - b\bar{X}$$

$$b = \Sigma(X - \bar{X})(Y - \bar{Y})\Sigma(X - \bar{X})^2$$

where:

$$\bar{X} = \frac{\Sigma X}{n}$$

$$\bar{Y} = \frac{\Sigma Y}{n}$$

Illustration A–7 shows these computations, using the data from **Illustration A–3**. The method is simplified in trend analysis by choosing an odd number of time periods and placing the X origin at the midpoint in time. In this way, the negative X values cancel out the positive so that the sum of all Xs = 0. Thus, the time variable is measured as a deviation from its mean. The constant a is the arithmetic mean of the series and b becomes a simple ratio.

Using any two time periods and calculating Y for each, a straight line can be drawn through the data arrayed on a graph that best approximates the given data.

Thus, the regression line gives an estimate of Y for any value X and the regression coefficient b gives the average change in Y for a unit change in X. There is a measure called the coefficient of determination (r^2) which is a relative measure of the relationship between two variables and ranges

ILLUSTRATION A–8

Probability distribution

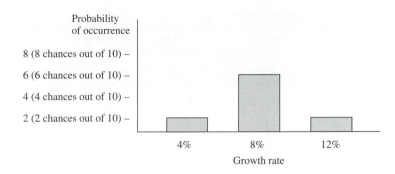

Probability
of occurrence

8 (8 chances out of 10) –

6 (6 chances out of 10) –

4 (4 chances out of 10) –

2 (2 chances out of 10) –

            4%   8%   12%

Growth rate

from 0 (no correlation) to 1 (perfect correlation). It may be defined as the proportion of the total variance in the dependent variable (*Y*) which is explained by the independent variable (*X*).

Curvilinear Regression

Sometimes the situation may call for a curved relationship rather than a straight line; or a curve may actually fit the data better than a straight line. Visual inspection of a scatter diagram can usually determine this. In this case, a curvilinear measure of regression should be used rather than the straight-line method. A regression curve may be fit by drawing a free-hand curve or estimate, by fitting a parabola by least squares, or by transforming the available data into logarithms or other functions and then fitting a linear equation to these functions. Choosing the functional form of the equation is the key to fitting a mathematical curve.

Forecasting and Probability Distribution

Up to this point, the various mathematical and statistical tools described have been used to analyze historical performance and trends. Regression and correlation have been considered merely as descriptions of the relationship between variables. Managers, investors, and analysts, however, are usually interested in the results of such measures to be able to control future variation or to predict new values of the dependent variable from the original available data.

Future growth rate may be projected using some of the above-mentioned statistical tools in the following ways:

1. Index numbers may be projected relative to a chosen base period using historical data, and from these projections percentage changes in sales, growth, or whatever is being measured may be predicted.

2. Arithmetic and/or compound growth rate analysis using the straight line methods as in Illustration A–2. may be used to predict future sales levels and growth rates.

3. Averages may be used primarily to summarize historical data but are often used as a base for or starting point for further statistical analysis for purposes of projection.

4. Dispersion analysis becomes useful for computation of standard deviation which is then used in future projection analysis.

5. Graphs and ratio charts are useful in illustrating historical trends from which future predictions may be made visually.

6. And finally, regression analysis is used to estimate historical data to fit a straight line from which future trends may be projected.

One of the ways in which future growth rate may be estimated using the statistical measures described is through the use of a probability distribution, which is similar to a frequency distribution. A probability of occurrence must be assigned to each possible growth rate figure in the array to be used. The probabilities may be based on historical data or the estimates of a competent person. A simple distribution may look like the one in **Illustration A–8**. Growth rate is plotted on the *X*-axis, and the probability of occurrence is assigned to each possible outcome. The sum of the probabilities must equal one (i.e., .2 + .6 + .2 = 1).

The expected value or mean of the distribution is found by multiplying each outcome by its probability and summing as in **Illustration A–9**. The equation for expected value is:

$$X = \sum_{t=1}^{n} (G_t P_t)$$

**ILLUSTRATION A–9   Calculating the Expected Value of a
Probability Distribution**

Probability of Occurrence	×	Growth Rate	=	Expected Value
0.2		4%.		.8%
0.6		8		4.8
0.2		12		2.4
		Expected value =		8%

---

where:

G_t = Growth rate associated with time period t.

P_t = Probability of occurrence of the tth outcome.

X = Expected value or weighted average of the possible outcomes, weighted by the probability of each occurring.

For example, using the data from **Illustration A–9**, there are three occurrences or time periods n, the respective growth rates G_t are 4%, 8%, and 12%, and the probability of each occurring P_t is .2, .6, and .2, respectively (i.e., 2 chances out of 10, 6 chances out of 10, etc.). The growth rates weighted by their respective probabilities are then summed as in **Illustration A–9**, and the result is the expected value X. Since there is an unlimited number of possibilities, and not merely three as shown above, the distribution would be a continuous curve. Let us assume that the distribution is "normal," that is, the curve is bell shaped (see **Illustration A–10**). The tighter the curve, that is, the closer the end points are to the mean, the less we expect the actual growth to be from the expected growth rate. The standard deviation is used as a measure of the tightness of a

probability distribution. Thus, the smaller the standard deviation, the tighter is the probability distribution and the closer those projecting expect the actual growth rate will be to the expected value in the distribution.

The standard deviation for a probability distribution is defined as:

$$s = \sqrt{\sum_{t=1}^{n} (\bar{X} - X_t)^2 \, P(X_t)}$$

where:

s = Standard deviation.

$(\bar{X} - X_t)$ = Deviation from the mean.

$P(X_t)$ = Probability of any occurrence.

The above formula is for a probability distribution where the random variable (usually represented as the X-axis) has distinct values and no intermediate values. This may be contrasted to a distribution which has continuous values over a range.

Using the set of growth rates from **Illustration A–11** and the above formula, the standard deviation can be calculated as in **Illustration A–11**.

ILLUSTRATION A–10

*Normal distribution—
bell-shaped curve*

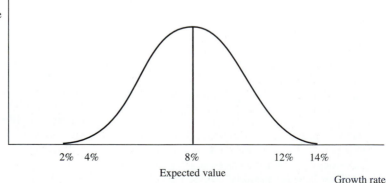

ILLUSTRATION A–11   Calculation of Standard Deviation for a Probability Distribution, (figures in percentages)

$\bar{X}$	$-$ X_t	$=$ $(\bar{X}-X_t)$	$(\bar{X}-X_t)^2$	$(\bar{X}-X_t)^2 P(X_t)$	
8	4	4	16	16 (.02)	= 3.2
8	8	0	0	0 (.6)	= 0
8	12	−4	16	16 (.2)	= 3.2
					6.4 = sum

$\sqrt{6.4} = 2.53 =$ Standard deviation

Based on **Illustration A–9**, we expect that the actual observed growth rate should fall between 5.47% and 10.53%, over 68.27% of the time (one standard deviation).

Sometimes two different probability distributions can have the same standard deviation but different expected value or means. The percentage deviation from the mean of one distribution may be much higher or lower than of the other. To determine this percentage deviation from the mean in a situation where the standard deviation may be misleading, or where the absolute measures of dispersion are not comparable because two different sets of data are expressed in different units, we use a measure of relative dispersion called the coefficient of variation. This measure is obtained by dividing the standard deviation s by the expected mean $\bar{X}$.

$$v = \frac{s}{\bar{X}} = \text{Coefficient of variation}$$

The coefficient of variation is thus a relative measure of the relationship between two variables. The smaller the number, the tighter, or less variable to the mean, is that probability distribution.

The prediction of future growth may require that the analyst determine the probability that a certain growth rate will occur. To do this, one must calculate the area under the curve (in a normal distribution).[1] Assume the expected growth rate to be 8% as in the above example and the standard deviation to be 2.53% as calculated in **Illustration A–11**. For purposes of illustration, let us find the probability that the growth rate of the firm being studied will be between 10.5% and 12%.

_____
[1]A normal distribution assumes symmetry around the mean.

First, we must standardize the distribution using the Z variable, which represents the number of standard deviations from the mean of our outcome of interest.

$$Z = \frac{X - \bar{X}}{s}$$

where:

Z = Number of standard deviations from the mean.
X = Outcome of interest (growth rate).
$\bar{X}$ = Expected mean.
s = Standard deviation.

We already know that the probability of the growth rate falling between 5.4% and 10.53% is 68.2% since this is within one standard deviation from the mean of 8%. Thus, the probability of the rate falling between 8% and 10.53% is 34.14% (68.27/2). We now need to find the probability of the actual growth rate falling between 8% and 12%.

$$Z = \frac{12\% - 8\%}{2.53\%} = \frac{4\%}{2.53\%} = 1.58$$

Once we have determined the value of Z, the number of standard deviations from the mean of our outcome of interest, we must use a table found in any standard book on statistics for the area under the nominal curve. Each item in the table is that proportion of the total area under a normal curve which lies under the segment between the mean Z value (Z standard deviations from the mean).

For example, for our Z value of 1.58, we would find 1.58 in the left column of the standard table and move right horizontally to the .08 column. The area indicated is .4429. Since we know the area between 8% and 10.5% (rounded) is .3414 (half of 68.27%), we must subtract that from .4429.

$$.4429 - .3414 = .1015$$

This means that the probability of the growth rate falling between 8,0% and 10.5% is 34.14%; between 8% and 12% is 44.29%; and finally, between our values of interest 10.5% and 12%, it is 10.15%.

Time Series Analysis

The tools of regression analysis may be used on monthly or yearly data, but caution must be used. Time series are probability samples and are subject to trends, cycles, and seasonality as well as to purely random movements. Extreme highs and lows may influence the regression line and, hence, distort the results. Time series analysis usually consists of the following steps: fitting a secular trend curve, measuring seasonal variation, and analyzing cyclical-irregular residuals. Secular trend is measured to appraise recent trends, for long-term forecasting, and to eliminate trends due to isolate cycles. A trend curve is fit by using graphic methods or the method of least squares to fit a mathematical curve. Seasonal variation is measured in much the same way as the secular trend component, while cyclical and irregular movements are usually treated as a residual in combined form.

There is a wide variety of statistical tools, measurements, and techniques to present and to analyze historical data and to project and predict the future. In the prediction of future data, it is important that past trends be correctly presented and estimated and that regression lines, for example, when used, fit the observed data as closely as possible. However, as noted above, the results can be misleading. In general, the more historical observations that are available, the better will be the total picture of historical trend as well as the better will be the mathematical projections.

Butler Lumber Company

After a rapid growth in its business during recent years, the Butler Lumber Company in the spring of 1991 anticipated a further substantial increase in sales. Despite good profits, the company had experienced a shortage of cash and had found it necessary to increase its borrowing from the Suburban National Bank to $247,000 in the spring of 1991. The maximum loan that Suburban National would make to any one borrower was $250,000, and Butler had been able to stay within this limit only by relying very heavily on trade credit. In addition, Suburban was now asking that Butler secure the loan with its real property. Mark Butler, sole owner and president of the Butler Lumber Company, was therefore looking elsewhere for a new banking relationship where he would be able to negotiate a larger and unsecured loan.

Mr. Butler had recently been introduced by a friend to George Dodge, an officer of a much larger bank, the Northrup National Bank. The two men had tentatively discussed the possibility that the Northrup Bank might extend a line of credit to Butler Lumber up to a maximum amount of $465,000. Mr. Butler thought that a loan of this size would more than meet his foreseeable needs, but he was eager for the flexibility that a line of credit of this size would provide. After this discussion, Mr. Dodge had arranged for the credit department of the Northrup National Bank to investigate Mr. Butler and his company.

The Butler Lumber Company had been founded in 1981 as a partnership by Mr. Butler and his brother-in-law, Henry Stark. In 1988 Mr. Butler bought out Mr. Stark's interest for $105,000 and incorporated the business. Mr. Stark had taken a note for $105,000, to be paid off in 1989, to give Mr. Butler time to arrange for the financing necessary to make the payment of $105,000 to him. The major portion of the funds needed for this payment was raised by a loan of $70,000, negotiated in late 1988. This

This case was prepared as the basis for class discussion rather than to illustrate either effective or ineffective handling of an administrative situation.
Copyright © 1991 by the President and Fellows of Harvard College. Harvard Business School case 292–013.

loan was secured by land and buildings, carried an interest rate of 11%, and was repayable in quarterly installments at the rate of $7,000 a year over the next 10 years.

The business was located in a growing suburb of a large city in the Pacific Northwest. The company owned land with access to a railroad siding, and two large storage buildings had been erected on this land. The company's operations were limited to the retail distribution of lumber products in the local area. Typical products included plywood, moldings, and sash and door products. Quantity discounts and credit terms of net 30 days on open account were usually offered to customers.

Sales volume had been built up largely on the basis of successful price competition, made possible by careful control of operating expenses and by quantity purchases of materials at substantial discounts. Much of the moldings and sash and door products, which constituted significant items of sales, were used for repair work. About 55% of total sales were made in the six months from April through September. No sales representatives were employed, orders being taken exclusively over the telephone. Annual sales of $1,697,000 in 1988, $2,013,000 in 1989, and $2,694,000 in 1990 yielded after-tax profits of $31,000 in 1988, $34,000 in 1989, and $44,000 in 1990.[1] Operating statements for the years 1988–1990 and for the three months ending March 31, 1991, are given in **Exhibit 1**.

Mr. Butler was an energetic man, 39 years of age, who worked long hours on the job. He was helped by an assistant who, in the words of the investigator of the Northrup National Bank, "has been doing and can do about everything that Mr. Butler does in the organization." Other employees numbered 10 in early 1991, five of whom worked in the yard and drove trucks and five of whom assisted in the office and in sales.

As part of its customary investigation of prospective borrowers, the Northrup National Bank sent inquiries concerning Mr. Butler to a number of firms that had business dealings with him. The manager of one of his large suppliers, the Barker Company, wrote in answer:

> The conservative operation of his business appeals to us. He has not wasted his money in disproportionate plant investment. His operating expenses are as low as they could possibly be. He has personal control over every feature of his business, and he possesses sound judgment and a willingness to work harder than anyone I have ever known. This, with a good personality, gives him a good turnover; and from my personal experience in watching him work, I know that he keeps close check on his own credits.

All the other trade letters received by the bank bore out this opinion.

In addition to owning the lumber business, which was his major source of income, Mr. Butler held jointly with his wife an equity in their home. The house had cost $72,000 to build in 1979 and was mortgaged for $38,000. He also held a

---

[1]Sales in 1986 and 1987 amounted to $728,000 and $1,103,000, respectively; profit data for these years are not comparable with those of 1988 and later years because of the shift from a partnership to a corporate form of organization. As a corporation, Butler was taxed at the rate of 15% on its first $50,000 of income, 25% on the next $25,000 of income, and 34% on all additional income above $75,000.

	1988	1989	1990	1st Qtr 1991
Net sales	$1,697	$2,013	$2,694	$ 718[a]
Cost of goods sold				
Beginning inventory	183	239	326	418
Purchases	1,278	1,524	2,042	660
	$1,461	$1,763	$2,368	$1,078
Ending inventory	239	326	418	556
Total cost of goods sold	$1,222	$1,437	$1,950	$ 522
Gross profit	475	576	744	196
Operating expense[b]	425	515	658	175
Interest expense	13	20	33	10
Net income before taxes	$ 37	$ 41	$ 53	$ 11
Provision for income taxes	6	7	9	2
Net income	$ 31	$ 34	$ 44	$ 9

[a]In the first quarter of 1990 sales were $698,000 and net income was $7,000.

[b]Operating expenses include a cash salary for Mr. Butler of $75,000 in 1988, $85,000 in 1989, $95,000 in 1990, and $22,000 in the 1st quarter of 1991. Mr. Butler also received some of the perquisites commonly taken by owners of privately held businesses.

$70,000 life insurance policy, payable to his wife. She owned independently a half interest in a house worth about $55,000. Otherwise, they had no sizeable personal investments.

The bank gave particular attention to the debt position and current ratio of the business. It noted the ready market for the company's products at all times and the fact that sales prospects were favorable. The bank's investigator reported: "Sales are expected to reach $3.6 million in 1991 and may exceed this level if prices of lumber should rise substantially in the near future." On the other hand, it was recognized that a general economic downturn might slow down the rate of increase in sales. Butler Lumber's sales, however, were protected to some degree from fluctuations in new housing construction because of the relatively high proportion of its repair business. Projections beyond 1991 were difficult to make, but the prospects appeared good for a continued growth in the volume of Butler Lumber's business over the foreseeable future.

The bank also noted the rapid increase in Butler Lumber's accounts and notes payable in the recent past, especially in the spring of 1991. The usual terms of purchase in the trade provided for a discount of 2% for payments made within 10 days of the invoice date. Accounts were due in 30 days at the invoice price, but suppliers ordinarily did not object if payments lagged somewhat behind the due date. During the last two years, Mr. Butler had taken very few purchase discounts because of the

EXHIBIT 2   Balance Sheets at December 31, 1988–1990, and March 31, 1991 (thousands of dollars)

	1988	1989	1990	1st Qtr 1991
Cash	$ 58	$ 49	$ 41	$ 31
Accounts receivable, net	171	222	317	345
Inventory	239	325	418	556
Current assets	$468	$596	$776	$ 932
Property, net	126	140	157	162
Total assets	$594	$736	$933	$1,094
Notes payable, bank	$ —	$146	$233	$ 247
Notes payable, Mr. Stark	105	—	—	—
Notes payable, trade	—	—	—	157
Accounts payable	124	192	256	243
Accrued expenses	24	30	39	36
Long-term debt, current portion	7	7	7	7
Current liabilities	$260	$375	$535	$ 690
Long-term debt	64	57	50	47
Total liabilities	$324	$432	$585	$ 737
Net worth	270	304	348	357
Total liabilities and net worth	$594	$736	$933	$1,094

shortage of funds arising from his purchase of Mr. Stark's interest in the business and the additional investments in working capital associated with the company's increasing sales volume. Trade credit was seriously extended in the spring of 1991 as Mr. Butler strove to hold his bank borrowing within the $250,000 ceiling imposed by the Suburban National Bank. Balance sheets at December 31, 1988–1990, and March 31, 1991, are presented in **Exhibit 2**.

The tentative discussions between Mr. Dodge and Mr. Butler had been about a revolving, secured 90-day note not to exceed $465,000. The specific details of the loan had not been worked out, but Mr. Dodge had explained that the agreement would involve the standard covenants applying to such a loan. He cited as illustrative provisions the requirement that restrictions on additional borrowing would be imposed, that net working capital would have to be maintained at an agreed level, that additional investments in fixed assets could be made only with prior approval of the bank, and that limitations would be placed on withdrawals of funds from the business by Mr. Butler. Interest would be set on a floating-rate basis at 2 percentage points above the prime rate (the rate paid by the bank's most creditworthy customers). Mr. Dodge indicated that the initial rate to be paid would be about 10.5% under conditions in effect in early 1991. Both men also understood that Mr. Butler would sever his relationship with the Suburban National Bank if he entered into a loan agreement with the Northrup National Bank.

Questions

1. What is Mr. Butler's growth strategy? _____ How does he plan to make sales, keep his costs as low as possible, and use his capital? _____

2. How successful has Mr. Butler been in achieving his growth strategy? _____ The following ratios might be useful in answering this question: percentage increase in sales by years; percentage change in net income by years; annual net income divided by average net worth (one half of the sum of beginning net worth plus ending net worth); and profit as a percentage of sales.

3. How have the financial and operating characteristics of Mr. Butler's business changed over the periods covered by the financial statements presented in the exhibits? _____

4. How has Mr. Butler financed his business growth in recent years? _____

5. What has Mr. Butler done with the financial resources he has obtained? _____

6. Would you give Mr. Butler the additional loan he requests? _____ *Hint:* If you forecast his December 31, 1991, annual balance sheet, you will have no problem answering this question. The preceeding ratios you computed in questions 2 and 3 can be used for this purpose. You should forecast every account in the balance sheet, except the Notes Payable–Bank account. This account balance will be the number that makes the assets equal to the sum of the liabilities and owners' equity.

7. What changes do you recommend Mr. Butler make in his operating and financial strategy? _____ How might your suggestions change his financial needs and return on stockholders' equity (annual net income divided by average owners' equity)? _____

CASE
9-2

The Home Depot, Inc.

The difference between a company with a concept and one without is the difference between a stock that sells for 20 times earnings and one that sells for 10 times earnings. The Home Depot is definitely a concept stock, and it has the multiple to prove it—27–28 times likely earnings in the current fiscal year ending this month. On the face of it, The Home Depot might seem like a tough one for the concept-mongers to work with. It's a chain of hardware stores. But, as we noted in our last visit to the company in the spring of '83, these hardware stores are huge warehouse outlets—60,000 to 80,000 feet in space. You can fit an awful lot of saws in these and still have plenty of room left over to knock together a very decent concept.

And in truth, the warehouse notion is the hottest thing in retailing these days.

The Home Depot buys in quantum quantities, which means that its suppliers are eager to keep within its good graces and hence provide it with a lot of extra service. The company, as it happens, is masterful in promotion and pricing. The last time we counted, it had 22 stores, all of them located where the sun shines all the time.

Growth has been sizzling. Revenues, a mere $22 million in fiscal '80, shot past the quarter billion mark three years later. As to earnings, they have climbed from two cents in fiscal '80 to an estimated 60 cents in the fiscal year coming to an end [in January 1985].

Its many boosters in the Street, moreover, anticipate more of the same as far as the bullish eye can see. They're confidently estimating 30% growth in the new fiscal year as well. Could be. But while we share their esteem for the company's merchandising skills and imagination, we're as bemused now as we were the first time we looked at The Home Depot by its rich multiple. Maybe a little more now than then.[1]

The above report appeared on January 21, 1985, in "Up & Down Wall Street," a regular column in *Barron's* financial weekly.

Company Background

Bernard Marcus and Arthur Blank founded The Home Depot in 1978 to bring the warehouse retailing concept to the home center industry. The company operated retail "do-it-yourself" (DIY) warehouse stores which sold a wide assortment of building materials and home improvement products. Sales, which were on a cash-and-carry basis, were concentrated in the home remodeling market. The company targeted as its customers individual homeowners and small contractors.

The Home Depot's strategy had several important elements. The company offered low and competitive prices, a feature central to the warehouse retailing concept. The Home Depot's stores, usually in suburbs, were also the warehouses, with inventory stacked over merchandise displayed on industrial racks. The warehouse format of the stores kept the overhead low and allowed the company to pass the savings to customers. Costs were further reduced by emphasizing higher volume and lower margins with a high inventory turnover. While offering low prices, The Home Depot was careful not to sacrifice the depth of merchandise and the quality of products offered for sale.

To ensure that the right products were stocked at all times, each Home Depot store carried approximately $4,500,000 of inventory, at retail, consisting of approximately

---

[1]Reprinted with permission from *Barron's*, January 21, 1985.

This case was prepared by Professor Krishna Palepu as the basis for class discussion rather than to illustrate either effective or ineffective handling of an administrative situation.

25,000 separate stock-keeping units. All these items were kept on the sales floor of the store, thus increasing convenience to the customer and minimizing out-of-stock occurrences. The company also assured its customers that the products sold by it were of the best quality. The Home Depot offered nationally advertised brands as well as lesser known brands carefully chosen by the company's merchandise managers. Every product sold by The Home Depot was guaranteed by either the manufacturer or by the company itself.

The Home Depot complemented the above merchandising strategy with excellent sales assistance. Since the great majority of the company's customers were individual homeowners with no prior experience in their home improvement projects, The Home Depot considered its employees' technical knowledge and service orientation to be very important to its marketing success. The company pursued a number of policies to address this need. Approximately 90% of the company's employees were on a full-time basis. To attract and retain a strong sales force, the company maintained salary and wage levels above those of its competitors. All the floor sales personnel attended special training sessions to gain thorough knowledge of the company's home improvement products and their basic applications. This training enabled them to answer shoppers' questions and help customers in choosing equipment and material appropriate for their projects. Often, the expert advice the sales personnel provided created a bond that resulted in continuous contact with the customer throughout the duration of the customer's project.

Finally, to attract customers, The Home Depot pursued an aggressive advertising program utilizing newspapers, television, radio, and direct mail catalogues. The company's advertising stressed promotional pricing, the broad assortment and depth of its merchandise, and the assistance provided by its sales personnel. The company also sponsored in-store demonstrations of do-it-yourself techniques and product uses. To increase customers' shopping convenience, The Home Depot's stores were open seven days a week, including weekday evenings.

Fortune magazine commented on The Home Depot's strategy as follows:

> Warehouse stores typically offer shoppers deep discounts with minimal service and back-to-basics ambiance. The Home Depot's outlets have all the charm of a freight yard and predictably low prices. But they also offer unusually helpful customer service. Although warehouse retailing looks simple, it is not: As discounting cuts into gross profit margins, the merchant must carefully control buying, merchandising, and inventory costs. Throwing in service, which is expensive and hard to systematize, makes the job even tougher. In the do-it-yourself (DIY) segment of the industry—which includes old-style hardware stores, building supply warehouses, and the everything-under-one-roof home centers—The Home Depot is the only company that has successfully brought off the union of low prices and high service.[2]

The Home Depot's strategy was successful in fueling an impressive growth in the company's operations. The first three Home Depot stores, opened in Atlanta in 1979, were a quick success. From this modest beginning, the company grew rapidly and

---

[2]Reprinted with permission from *Fortune*, February 1988, p. 73.

went public in 1981. The company's stock initially traded over-the-counter and was listed on the New York Stock Exchange in April 1984. Several new stores were opened in markets throughout the sunbelt and the number of stores operated by The Home Depot grew from 3 in 1979 to 50 by the end of fiscal 1985. As a result, sales grew from $7 million in 1979 to $700 million in 1985. Exhibit 1 provides a summary of the growth in the company's operations. The company's stock price performance during 1985 is summarized in Exhibit 2.

Industry and Competition

The home improvement industry was large and growing during the 1980s. The industry sales totaled approximately $80 billion in 1985 and strong industry growth was expected to continue, especially in the do-it-yourself (DIY) segment, which had grown at a compounded annual rate of 14% over the last 15 years. With the number of two–wage-earner households growing, there was an increase in families' average disposable income, making it possible to increase the frequency and magnitude of home improvement projects. Further, many homeowners were undertaking these projects by themselves rather than hiring a contractor. Research conducted by the Do-It-Yourself Institute, an industry trade group, showed that DIY activities had become America's second most popular leisure-time activity after watching television.

The success of warehouse retailing pioneered by The Home Depot attracted a number of other companies into the industry. Among the store chains currently operating in the industry were Builders Square (a division of Kmart), Mr. HOW (a division of Service Merchandise), The Home Club (a division of Zayre Corp.), Payless Cashways (a division of W. R. Grace), and Hechinger Co. Most of these store chains were relatively new and not yet achieving significant profitability.

Among The Home Depot's competitors, the most successful was Hechinger, which had operated hardware stores for a long time and recently entered the do-it-yourself segment of the industry. Using a strategy quite different from The Home Depot's, Hechinger ran gleaming upscale stores and aimed at high profit margins. As of the end of fiscal 1985, the company operated 55 stores, located primarily in southeastern states. Hechinger announced that it planned to expand its sales by 20 to 25% a year by adding 10 to 14 stores a year. A summary of Hechinger's recent financial performance is presented in Exhibit 3.

The Home Depot's Future

While The Home Depot had achieved rapid growth every year since its inception, fiscal 1985 was probably the most important in the company's seven-year history. During 1985 the company implemented its most ambitious expansion plan to date by adding 20 new stores in eight new markets. Nine of these stores were acquired from Bowater, a competing store chain which was in financial difficulty. As The Home Depot engaged in major expansion, its revenues rose 62% from $432 million in fiscal

1984 to $700 million in 1985. However, the company's earnings declined in 1985 from the record levels achieved during the previous fiscal year. In fiscal 1985, The Home Depot earned $8.2 million, or $0.33 per share, as compared with $14.1 million or $0.56 per share in fiscal 1984.

EXHIBIT 1

The Home Depot, Inc. Summary of Performance during Fiscal Years 1981–85

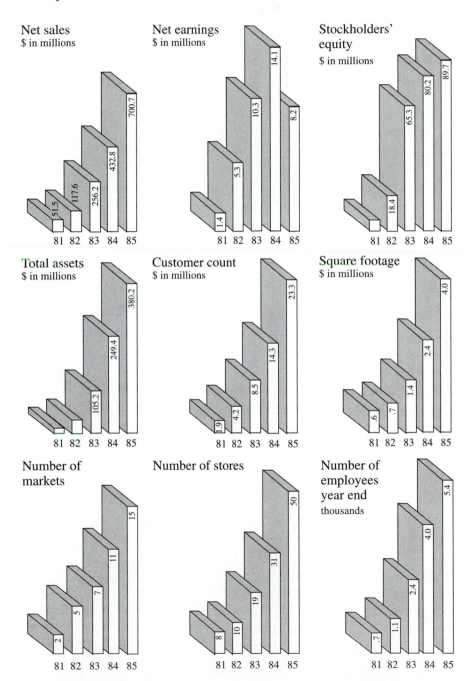

EXHIBIT 2   The Home Depot's Common Stock Price and Standard & Poor's 500 Composite Index from January 1985 to February 1986

Date	Home Depot Stock Price	S&P 500 Composite Index
1/2/85	$17.125	165.4
2/1/85	16.375	178.6
3/1/85	19.000	183.2
4/1/85	17.000	181.3
5/1/85	18.000	178.4
6/3/85	16.125	189.3
7/1/85	13.000	192.4
8/1/85	12.625	192.1
9/2/85	11.875	197.9
10/1/85	11.375	185.1
11/1/85	10.750	191.5
12/2/85	11.000	200.5
1/2/86	12.625	209.6
2/3/86	13.125	214.0
Cumulative Return:	−23.4%	29.4%

The Home Depot's β = 1.3 (Value Line estimate).

EXHIBIT 3   The Home Depot, Inc.—Summary of Financial Performance of Hechinger Company

Part I—Hechinger's Financial Ratios

	Year Ending		
	February 1, 1986	*February 2, 1985*	*January 28, 1984*
Profit before taxes/sales (%)	7.80	9.40	9.80
× Sales/average assets	1.48	1.72	2.02
× Average assets/average equity	2.21	2.12	1.79
× (1 − average tax rate)	0.62	0.55	0.54
= Return on equity (%)	15.80	18.90	19.10
× (1 − dividend payout ratio)	0.93	0.95	0.95
= Sustainable growth rate (%)	14.70	18.00	18.10
Gross profit/sales (%)	29.30	30.10	32.10
Selling, general and administrative expenses/sales (%)	21.60	21.10	22.90
Interest expenses/sales (%)	2.10	1.30	0.70
Interest income/sales (%)	2.20	1.70	1.30
Inventory turnover	4.50	4.50	4.40
Average collection period* (days)	32.00	33.00	35.00
Average accounts payables period** (days)	58.00	61.00	63.00

*Assumed 365 days in the fiscal year.

**Payables also include accrued wages and expenses.

Purchases are computed as cost of sales plus increase in inventory during the year. Assumed 365 days in the fiscal year.

EXHIBIT 3 **(continued) The Home Depot, Inc.—Summary of Financial Performance of Hechinger Company**

Part II: Hechinger's Cash Flow

	Year Ending		
(Dollars In Thousands)	*February 1, 1986*	*February 2, 1985*	*January 28, 1984*
Cash Provided from Operations			
Net earnings	$ 23,111	$ 20,923	$ 16,243
Items not requiring the use of cash or marketable securities			
Depreciation and amortization	6,594	4,622	3,429
Deferred income taxes	1,375	2,040	1,515
Deferred rent expense	2,321	2,064	1,463
	33,401	**29,649**	**22,650**
Cash Invested in Operations			
Accounts receivable	4,657	7,905	7,954
Merchandise inventories	17,998	8,045	20,596
Other current assets	4,891	3,760	1,304
Accounts payable and accrued expenses	(6,620)	(12,099)	(9,767)
Taxes on income—current	285	3,031	(575)
	21,211	**10,642**	**19,512**
Net Cash Provided from Operations	**12,190**	**19,007**	**3,138**
Cash Used for Investment Activities			
Expenditures for property, furniture and equipment, net of disposals, and other assets	(36,037)	(25,531)	(16,346)
Cash Used to Pay Dividends to Shareholders	**(1,550)**	**(1,091)**	**(868)**
Cash Provided from Financing Activities			
Proceeds from public offering of 8 1/2% Converted Subordinated Debentures, net of expenses	—	85,010	—
Proceeds from public offering of common stock net of expenses	28,969	—	13,439
Proceeds from sale and leaseback transactions under operating leases	—	8,338	6,874
Increase (decrease) in long-term debt	—	(4,750)	6,366
Decrease in short-term debt	—	—	(318)
Exercise of stock options including income tax benefit	180	674	611
Decrease in capital lease obligations	(311)	(280)	(254)
	28,838	**88,992**	**26,718**
Increase in Cash and Marketable Securities	**$ 3,441**	**$ 81,377**	**$ 12,642**

Bernard Marcus, The Home Depot's chairman and chief executive officer, commented on the company's performance as follows:

> Fiscal 1985 was a year of rapid expansion and continued growth for The Home Depot. Feeling the time was ripe for us to enhance our share of the do-it-yourself market, we seized the opportunity to make a significant investment in our long-term future. At the same time, we recognized that our short-term profit growth would be affected.

The Home Depot's 1985 annual report (Exhibit 4) provided more details on the firm's financial performance during the year.

As fiscal 1985 came to a close, The Home Depot faced some critical issues. The competition in the do-it-yourself industry was heating up. The fight for market dominance was expected to result in pressure on margins, and industry analysts expected only the strongest and most capable firms in the industry to survive. Also, The Home Depot had announced plans for further expansion that included the opening of nine new stores in 1986. The company estimated that site acquisition and construction would cost about $6.6 million for each new store, and investment in inventory (net of vendor financing) would require an additional $1.8 million per store. The company needed significant additional financing to implement these plans.

Home Depot relied on external financing—both debt and equity—to fund its growth in 1984 and 1985. However, the significant drop in its stock price in 1985 made further equity financing less attractive. While the company could borrow from its line of credit, it had to make sure that it could satisfy the interest coverage requirements (see Note 3 in Exhibit 4 for a discussion of debt covenant restrictions). Clearly, generating more cash from its own operations would be the best way for Home Depot to invest in its growth on a sustainable basis.

EXHIBIT 4   The Home Depot., Inc.—Abridged Annual Report for Fiscal Year 1985

A Letter to Our Shareholders:

Fiscal 1985 was a year of rapid expansion and continued growth for The Home Depot. Feeling the time was ripe for us to enhance our share of the do-it-yourself market, we seized the opportunity to make a significant investment in our long-term future. At the same time, we recognized that our short-term profit growth would be affected.

The Home Depot intends to be the dominant factor in every market we serve. The key to our success has been that upon entering a new market, we make a substantial commitment—opening multiple stores, providing excellent customer service, creating highly visible promotions, and growing the entire market. We turn the novice into a do-it-yourselfer and enable the expert to do more for less money.

From shortly before the end of fiscal 1984 to the close of fiscal 1985, The Home Depot entered eight new markets—Dallas, Houston, Jacksonville, San Diego, Los Angeles, Shreveport, Baton Rouge and Mobile—in a period of approximately 13 months. In that time, the number of Home Depot stores rose dramatically, from 22 to 50, including 9 stores acquired in the Bowater acquisition which had not been in our original plan. Twenty of these stores were opened during the past fiscal year alone. During this time span, we have become the only national warehouse retailing chain serving markets across the Sunbelt.

This expansion program required a tremendous investment of capital expenditures and inventory, as well as in personnel. As a result, our net

---

EXHIBIT 4   (continued)

---

earnings declined from record levels achieved during the previous fiscal year. In fiscal 1985, The Home Depot earned $8,219,000, or $.33 per share, as compared with $14,122,000, or $.56 per share, in fiscal 1984. However, as The Home Depot engaged in this major thrust forward, it also increased its market share and market presence as revenues rose 62% from $432,779,000 in fiscal 1984 to $700,729,000 in fiscal 1985.

Despite our significant investments, we still continue to be in a very strong financial condition. In December, The Home Depot replaced a prior $100 million bank credit line with an eight-year decreasing revolving credit agreement of $200 million. In addition, we are pursuing sale-and-lease-back negotiations for an aggregate of approximately $50 million for ten of our stores. These sources of additional funds, along with internally generated cash flow, will provide us with an ample financial foundation to continue to underwrite our growth over the next several years.

We are also quite proud that The Home Depot achieved its substantial gain in sales and market share in what turned out to be a very difficult year for our industry and retailing in general. The do-it-yourself "warehouse" industry, which we pioneered only a few short years ago, has recently attracted many competitors, some of whom have already fallen by the wayside, having mistaken our dramatic success as a path towards easy profits. Now the industry is faced with a situation when only the strongest and most capable will survive. As this process continues, we expect to encounter additional cost competition in the fight for market dominance. However, with our strengths—both financial and our successful ability to develop a loyal customer base—we are confident that The Home Depot will emerge an even stronger company.

We have never doubted The Home Depot's ability to be a leader in our business. We have the market dominance, the superior retailing concepts and the necessary foundation of experienced management. Further, we have the determination to maintain our position.

Looking at some of our markets individually, clearly our most difficult environment has been in Houston, where the oil-related economy is undergoing painful contractions combined with particularly fierce industry competition. This has caused our newly-opened stores to operate at a sub par level. In Dallas/Fort Worth, the stores we acquired at the end of fiscal 1984 have not yet generated the profits we expect. Such difficult market conditions demand a flexible reaction both in merchandising and operations. Recognizing the future potential of both of these markets, our management team is addressing the issues and feels confident that the final outcome will be positive.

In the other markets entered this year, the situation has been considerably more positive. There, our stores are experiencing growth much closer to our historical patterns.

In support of our California and Arizona operations, a west coast division was inaugurated to facilitate a timely response to the demands of that marketplace. With management personnel in place, this division is now responsible for the merchandising and operations of all stores in the western states.

Other highlights of the past year's activities include the progress we have made in expanding our management team, and the computer systems we installed into our operations to enhance our efficiency.

During the year, we completed the store price look-up phase of our management information system. This facilitates tracking individual items' sales through our registers, resulting in a more concise method of inventory reorder and margin management with the information now available.

During the coming year we will be testing a perpetual inventory tie-in with our price look-up system, eliminating pricing of our merchandise at the store level. The latter is being tested in several stores presently and hopefully will be expanded to include all of our stores by year end. This will have a significant effect on labor productivity at the store level.

The Home Depot is always looking for ways in which to do things better, priding ourselves on our flexibility and ability to innovate and to react to changing conditions. Whether it is a matter of developing a state-of-the-art computer system, reevaluating our store layouts or adapting to fast-changing markets and new types of merchandising, flexibility has always been a Home Depot characteristic.

EXHIBIT 4   (continued)

In fiscal 1986, The Home Depot will continue to expand, but at a much more moderate pace. We plan to open 9 new stores. These stores will be in existing markets except for the two locations in the new market of San Jose, California.

When we open stores in existing markets, sharing advertising costs and operational expenses, we achieve a faster return than stores in new markets. With this in mind, in January 1986, we withdrew from the Detroit market and delayed the opening of stores in San Francisco. These stores were targeted for a substantial initial loss in earnings that would have been necessary to achieve market dominance. From our standpoint, these new markets would have had the combined effect of diluting our personnel and negatively affecting our earnings.

It has always been Home Depot's philosophy to maintain orderly growth and achieve market dominance as we expand to new markets. Indeed, growth for growth's sake has never been and never will be our objective. We intend to invest prudently and expand aggressively in our business and our markets only when such expenditures meet our criteria for long-term profitability.

We are quite optimistic about our company's future—both for fiscal 1986 and for the years to follow. Essential to this optimism is the fact that The Home Depot has consistently proven that we can grow the market in every geographical area we enter. Simply, this means that we do not have to take business away from hardware stores and other existing home-improvement outlets, but rather, to create new do-it-yourselfers out of those who have never done their own home improvements.

Our philosophy is to educate our customers on how to be do-it-yourselfers. Our customers have come to expect The Home Depot's knowledgeable sales staff to guide them through any project they care to undertake, whether it be installing kitchen cabinets, constructing a deck, or building an entire house. Our sales staff knows how to complete each project, what tools and material to include, and how to sell our customers everything they need.

The Home Depot traditionally holds clinics for its customers in such skills as electrical wiring, carpentry, and plumbing, to name a few. Upon the successful completion of such clinics, our customers are confident in themselves and in The Home Depot. This confidence allows them to attempt increasingly advanced and complex home improvements.

Concerning our facilities, Home Depot's warehouse retailing concept allows us to carry a truly fantastic selection of merchandise and offer it at the lowest possible prices. Each of our stores ranges from about 65,000 to over 100,000 square feet of selling space, with an additional 4,000 to 10,000 square feet of outdoor selling area. In these large stores, we are able to stock all the materials and tools needed to build a house from scratch, and to landscape its grounds. With each store functioning as its own warehouse, with a capacity of over 25,000 different items, we are able to keep our prices at a minimum while providing the greatest selection of building materials and name brand merchandise.

For the majority of Americans, their home is their most valuable asset. It is an asset that consistently appreciates. It is also an asset in need of ongoing care and maintenance. By becoming do-it-yourselfers, homeowners can significantly enhance the value of their homes. We at The Home Depot have found that by successfully delivering this message, we have created loyal and satisfied customers. And by maintaining leadership in our markets, we have established a sound basis on which to build a future of growth with profitability.

The Home Depot management and staff are dedicated to the proposition that we are—and will remain—America's leading do-it-yourself retailer.

Bernard Marcus
Chairman and
Chief Executive Officer

Arthur M. Blank
President and
Chief Operating Officer

Consolidated Statements of Earnings

	Fiscal Year Ended		
	February 2, 1986 (52 weeks)	*February 3, 1985 (53 weeks)*	*January 29, 1984 (52 weeks)*
Net sales (note 2)	**$700,729,000**	$432,779,000	$256,184,000
Cost of merchandise sold	**519,272,000**	318,460,000	186,170,000
Gross profit	**181,457,000**	114,319,000	70,014,000
Operating expenses:			
Selling and store operating expenses	**134,354,000**	74,447,000	43,514,000
Preopening expenses........................	**7,521,000**	1,917,000	2,456,000
General and administrative expenses	**20,555,000**	12,817,000	7,376,000
Total operating expenses	**162,430,000**	89,181,000	53,346,000
Operating income	**19,027,000**	25,138,000	16,668,000
Other income (expense):			
Net gain on disposition of property and equipment (note 7)	**1,317,000**	—	—
Interest income...........................	**1,481,000**	5,236,000	2,422,000
Interest expense (note 3)....................	**(10,206,000)**	(4,122,000)	(104,000)
	(7,408,000)	1,114,000	2,318,000
Earnings before income taxes	**11,619,000**	26,252,000	18,986,000
Income taxes (note 4)	**3,400,000**	12,130,000	8,725,000
Net Earnings	**$ 8,219,000**	$ 14,122,000	$ 10,261,000
Earnings per common and common equivalent share (note 5)................................	**$ .33**	$ .56	$ .41
Weighted average number of common and common equivalent shares	**$ 25,247,000**	25,302,000	24,834,000

The Home Depot, Inc.

Consolidated Balance Sheets

	February 2, 1986	February 3, 1985
Assets:		
Current Assets:		
Cash, including time deposits of $43,374,000 in 1985	**$9,671,000**	$52,062,000
Accounts receivable, net (note 7)	**21,505,000**	9,365,000
Refundable income taxes	**3,659,000**	—
Merchandise inventories	**152,700,000**	84,046,000
Prepaid expenses	**2,526,000**	1,939,000
Total current assets	**190,061,000**	147,412,000
Property and Equipment, at Cost (note 3):		
Land	**44,396,000**	30,044,000
Buildings	**38,005,000**	3,728,000
Furniture, fixtures, and equipment	**34,786,000**	18,162,000
Leasehold improvements	**23,748,000**	11,743,000
Construction in progress	**27,694,000**	14,039,000
	168,629,000	77,716,000
Less accumulated depreciation and amortization	**7,813,000**	4,139,000
Net property and equipment	**160,816,000**	73,577,000
Cost in Excess of the Fair Value of Net Assets Acquired, net of accumulated amortization of $730,000 in 1985 and $93,000 in 1984 (note 2)	**24,561,000**	**25,198,000**
Other	**4,755,000**	3,177,000
	$380,193,000	$249,364,000

Consolidated Balance Sheets (continued)

	February 2, 1986	*February 3, 1985*
Liabilities and Stockholders' Equity		
Current Liabilities:		
Accounts payable	**$53,881,000**	$32,356,000
Accrued salaries and related expenses	**5,397,000**	3,819,000
Other accrued expenses	**13,950,000**	10,214,000
Income taxes payable (note 4)	**—**	626,000
Current portion of long-term debt (note 3)	**10,382,000**	287,000
Total current liabilities	**83,610,000**	47,302,000
Long-Term Debt, Excluding Current Installments (note 3):		
Convertible subordinated debentures	**100,250,000**	100,250,000
Other long-term debt	**99,693,000**	17,692,000
	$199,943,000	$117,942,000
Other Liabilities	**861,000**	1,320,000
Deferred Income Taxes (note 4)	**6,687,000**	2,586,000
Stockholders' Equity (note 5)		
Common stock, par value $.05. Authorized: 50,000,000 shares; issued and outstanding—25,150,063 shares at February 2, 1986 and 25,055,188 shares at February 3, 1985	**1,258,000**	1,253,000
Paid-in capital	**48,900,000**	48,246,000
Retained earnings	**38,934,000**	30,715,000
Total stockholders' equity	**89,092,000**	80,214,000
Commitments and Contingencies (notes 5, 6 and 8)	**$380,193,000**	$249,364,000

Consolidated Statements of Changes in Financial Position

	Fiscal Year Ended		
	February 2, 1986	*February 3, 1985*	*January 29, 1984*
Sources of Working Capital:			
Net earnings	**$ 8,219,000**	$ 14,122,000	$10,261,000
Items which do not use working capital:			
Depreciation and amortization of property and equipment	**4,376,000**	2,275,000	903,000
Deferred income taxes	**3,612,000**	1,508,000	713,000
Amortization of cost in excess of the fair value of net assets required	**637,000**	93,000	—
Net gain on disposition of property and equipment....	**(1,317,000)**	—	—
Other	**180,000**	77,000	59,000
Working Capital Provided by Operations	**15,707,000**	18,075,000	11,936,000
Proceeds from disposition of property and equipment....	**9,469,000**	861,000	3,000
Proceeds from long-term borrowings	**92,400,000**	120,350,000	4,200,000
Proceeds from sale of common stock, net	**659,000**	814,000	36,663,000
	$18,235,000	$140,100,000	$52,802,000
Uses of Working Capital:			
Additions to property and equipment...............	**$99,767,000**	$ 50,769,000	$16,081,000
Current installments and repayments of long-term debt ..	**10,399,000**	6,792,000	52,000
Acquisition of Bowater Home Center, Inc., net of working capital of $9,227,000 (note 2):			
Property and equipment	**—**	4,815,000	—
Cost in excess of the fair value of net assets acquired	**—**	25,291,000	—
Other assets, net of liabilities	**—**	(913,000)	—
Other, net	**1,728,000**	2,554,000	252,000
Increase in working capital	**6,341,000**	50,792,000	36,417,000
	$18,235,000	$140,100,000	$52,802,000
Changes in Components of Working Capital:			
Increase (decrease) in current assets:			
Cash	**(42,391,000)**	$ 29,894,000	$13,917,000
Receivables, net..............................	**15,799,000**	7,170,000	1,567,000
Merchandise inventories	**68,654,000**	25,334,000	41,137,000
Prepaid expenses	**587,000**	1,206,000	227,000
	42,649,000	63,604,000	56,848,000
Increase (decrease) in current liabilities:			
Accounts payable.............................	**21,525,000**	10,505,000	17,150,000
Accrued salaries and related expenses	**1,578,000**	(93,000)	**2,524,000**
Other accrued expenses	**3,736,000**	2,824,000	341,000
Income taxes payable	**(626,000)**	(657,000)	406,000
Current portion of long-term debt	**10,095,000**	233,000	10,000
	36,308,000	12,812,000	20,431,000
Increase in Working Capital	**$ 6,341,000**	$ 50,792,000	36,417,000

Selected Financial Data

	Fiscal Year Ended				
	February 2, 1985	*February 3, 1985*[1]	*January 29, 1984*	*January 30, 1983*	*January 31, 1982*
Selected Consolidated Statement of Earnings Data:					
Net sales	**$700,729,000**	$432,779,000	$256,184,000	$117,645,000	$ 51,542,000
Gross profit	**181,457,000**	114,319,000	70,014,000	33,358,000	14,735,000
Earnings before income taxes and extraordinary item . .	**11,619,000**	26,252,000	18,986,000	9,870,000	1,963,000
Earnings before extraordinary item	**8,219,000**	14,122,000	10,261,000	5,315,000	1,211,000
Extraordinary item—reduction of income taxes arising from carryforward of prior year's operating losses . .	—	—	—	—	234,000
Net earnings .... $	**8,219,000**	$ 14,122,000	$ 10,261,000	$ 5,315,000	$ 1,445,000
Per Common and Common Equivalent Share:					
Earnings before extraordinary item .... $	**.33**	$ .56	$ .41	$ .24	$ .06
Extraordinary item	—	—	—	—	.01
Net earnings .... $	**.33**	$ .56	$ .41	$ .24	$ .07
Weighted average number of common and common equivalent shares	25,247,000	25,302,000	24,834,000	22,233,000	21,050,000
Selected Consolidated Balance Sheet Data:					
Working capital	**$106,451,000**	$100,110,000	$ 49,318,000	$ 12,901,000	$ 5,502,000
Total assets	**380,193,000**	249,364,000	105,230,000	33,014,000	16,906,000
Long-term debt	**199,943,000**	117,942,000	4,384,000	236,000	3,738,000
Stockholders' equity........................	**89,092,000**	80,214,000	65,278,000	18,354,000	5,024,000

[1] 53-week fiscal year, all others were 52-week fiscal years.

Management Discussion and Analysis of Results of Operations and Financial Condition

The data below reflect the percentage relationship between sales and major categories in the Consolidated Statements of Earnings and selected sales data of the percentage change in the dollar amounts of each of the items.

	Fiscal Year[a]			Percentage Increase (Decrease) of Dollar Amounts	
	1985	*1984*	*1983*	*1985 v 1984*	*1984 v 1983*
Selected Consolidated Statements of Earnings Data:					
Net sales	**100.0%**	100.0%	100.0%	**61.9%**	68.9%
Gross profit	**25.9**	26.4	27.3	**58.7**	63.3
Cost and expenses:					
Selling and store operating	**19.2**	17.2	17.0	**80.5**	71.1
Preopening	**1.1**	.4	.9	**292.3**	(21.9)
General and administrative	**2.9**	3.0	2.9	**60.4**	73.8
Net gain on disposition of property and equipment	**(.2)**	—	—	**—**	—
Interest income	**(.2)**	(1.2)	(.9)	**(71.7)**	116.2
Interest expense	**1.4**	.9	—	**147.6**	3,863.5
	24.2	20.3	19.9	**92.9**	72.6
Earnings before income taxes	**1.7**	6.1	7.4	**(55.7)**	38.3
Income taxes	**.5**	2.8	3.4	**(72.0)**	39.0
Net earnings	**1.2%**	3.3%	4.0%	**(41.8%)**	37.6%
Selected Consolidated Sales Data:					
Number of customer transactions	**23,324,000**	14,256,000	8,479,000	**63.6%**	68.1%
Average amount of sale per transaction	**$30.04**	$30.36	$30.21	**(1.1)**	.5
Weighted average weekly sales per operating store	**$342,500**	$365,500	$360,300	**(6.3)**	1.4

[a]Fiscal years 1985, 1984, and 1983 refer to the fiscal years ended February 2, 1986, February 3, 1985, and January 29, 1984, respectively. Fiscal 1984 consisted of 53 weeks while 1985 and 1983 each consisted of 52 weeks.

Results of Operations

For an understanding of the significant factors that influenced the Company's performance during the past three fiscal years, the following discussion should be read in conjunction with the consolidated financial statements appearing elsewhere in this annual report.

Fiscal Year Ended February 2, 1986, Compared to February 3, 1985

Net sales in fiscal year 1985 increased 62% from $432,779,000 to $700,729,000. The growth is attributable to several factors. First, the Company opened 20 new stores during 1985 and closed one store. Second, second-year sales increases were realized from the three new stores opened in 1984 and from the nine former Bowater Home Center stores acquired during 1984. Third, comparable store sales increases of 2.3% were achieved despite comparing the 52-week 1985 fiscal year to the sales of the 53-week 1984 fiscal year, due in part to the number of customer transactions increasing by 64%. Finally, the weighted average weekly sales per operating store declined

6% in 1985 due to the significant increase in the ratio of the number of new stores to total stores in operation—new stores have a lower sales rate than mature stores until they establish market share.

Gross profit in 1985 increased 59% from $114,319,000 to $181,457,000. This increase was due to the increased sales and was partially offset by a reduction in the gross profit margin from 26.4% to 25.9%. The reduction is primarily due to lower margins achieved while establishing market presence in new markets.

Cost and expenses increased 93% during 1985 and, as a percent of sales, increased from 20.3% to 24.2%. The increase in selling and store operating, preopening expenses and net interest expense is due to the opening of 20 new stores, the costs associated with the former Bowater Home Center stores, and the related cost of building market share. The large percentage of new stores which have lower sales but fixed occupancy and certain minimum operating expenses tends to cause the percentage of selling and store operating costs to increase as a percentage of sales. The net gain on disposition of

(continued)

property and equipment is discussed fully in note 7 to the financial statements.

Earnings before income taxes decreased 56% from $26,252,000 to $11,619,000 resulting from the increase in operating expenses to support the Company's expansion program. The Company's effective income tax rate declined from 46.2% to 29.3% resulting from an increase in investment and other tax credits as a percentage of the total tax provision. As a percentage of sales, earnings decreased from 3.3% in 1984 to 1.2% in 1985 due to the increase in operating expenses as discussed above.

Fiscal Year Ended February 3, 1985, Compared to January 29, 1984

Net sales in fiscal 1984 increased 69% from $256,184,000 to $432,779,000. The growth was attributable to several factors. First the Company opened three new stores during fiscal 1984. Second, the Company had sales of $9,755,000 from the nine former Bowater Home Center stores acquired on December 3, 1984. Third, second-year sales increases were realized from the nine stores opened during fiscal 1983. Fourth, comparable store sales increases of 14% were due in part to 53 weeks in fiscal 1984 compared to 52 weeks in fiscal 1983 and in part to the number of customer transactions increasing by 63%. Finally, excluding the sales of the former Bowater Home Center stores, the weighted average weekly sales per operating store increased 6% to $383,500 in fiscal 1984.

Gross profit in fiscal 1984 increased 63% from $70,014,000 to $114,319,000. This net increase was due to the increased sales and was partially offset by a reduction in the gross profit margin from 27.3% to 26.4%. The reduction in the gross profit percentage is largely the result of the purchase of a high proportion of promoted merchandise by customers in the second quarter.

Costs and expenses increased 73% during fiscal 1984. As a percent of sales, costs and expenses increased from 19.9% to 20.3% due to increased selling, store operating, general and administrative expenses. This planned increase was in preparation of the Company's future expansion. Interest expense increased significantly as a result of the issuance of substantial debt during fiscal 1984 to fund the Company's expansion. These increases were partially offset by reduced preopening expenses and increased interest income resulting from temporary investment of the proceeds of the debt financing.

Earnings before income taxes increased 38% from $18,986,000 to $26,252,000 resulting from the factors discussed above. Such pretax earnings, however, were reduced by a loss from the Bowater stores of approximately $1,900,000 from date of acquisition (December 1984) to year end. The Company's effective income tax rate increased slightly from 46.0% to 46.2% resulting principally from less investment and other tax credits as a percentage of the total tax provision. As a percentage of sales, earnings decreased from 4.0% in

fiscal 1983 to 3.3% in fiscal 1984. The decline is a result of the company's reduced gross profit percentage and increases in the operating expenses discussed above.

Impact of Inflation and Changing Prices

Although the Company cannot accurately determine the precise effect of inflation on its operations, it does not believe inflation has had a material effect on sales or results of operations. The Company has complied with the reporting requirements of the Financial Accounting Standard Board Statement No. 33 in note 10 to the financial statements. Due to the experimental techniques, subjective estimates and assumptions, and the incomplete presentation required by this accounting pronouncement, the Company questions the value of the required reporting.

Liquidity and Capital Resources

Cash flow generated from existing store operations provided the Company with a significant source of liquidity since sales are on a cash-and-carry basis. In addition, a significant portion of the Company's inventory is financed under vendor credit terms. The Company has supplemented its operating cash flow from time to time with bank credit and equity and debt financing. During fiscal 1985, $88,000,000 of working capital was provided by the revolving bank credit line, $4,400,000 from industrial revenue bonds, and approximately $15,707,000 from operations. In addition, during fiscal 1985, the Company entered into a new credit agreement for a $200,000,000 revolving credit facility with a group of banks.

The Company has announced plans to open nine new stores during fiscal 1986, two in the new market of northern California and the balance in existing markets. The cost of this store expansion program will depend upon, among other factors, the extent to which the Company is able to lease second-use store space as opposed to acquiring leases or sites and having stores constructed to its own specifications. The Company estimates that approximately $6,600,000 per store will be required to acquire sites and construct facilities to the Company's specifications and that approximately $1,700,000 will be required to open a store in leased space plus any additional costs of acquiring the lease. These estimates include costs for site acquisition, construction expenditures, fixtures and equipment, and in-store minicomputers and point-of-sale terminals. In addition, each new store will require approximately $1,800,000 to finance inventories, net of vendor financing. The Company believes it has the ability to finance these expenditures through existing cash resources, current bank lines of credit which include a $200,000,000 eight-year revolving credit agreement, funds generated from operations, and other forms of financing, including but not limited to various forms of real estate financing and unsecured borrowings.

(continued)

Notes to Consolidated Financial Statements

1. Summary of Significant Accounting Policies

Fiscal Year
The Company's fiscal year ends on the Sunday closest to the last day of January and usually consists of 52 weeks. Every five or six years, however, there is a 53-week year. The fiscal year ended February 2, 1986 (1985) consisted of 52 weeks, the year ended February 3, 1985 (1984) consisted of 53 weeks, and the year ended January 29, 1984 (1983) consisted of 52 weeks.

Principals of Consolidation
The consolidated financial statements include the accounts of the Company and its wholly owned subsidiary. All significant intercompany transactions have been eliminated in consolidation. Certain reclassifications were made to the 1984 balance sheet to conform to current year presentation.

Merchandise Inventories
Inventories are stated at the lower of cost (first-in, first-out) or market, as determined by the retail inventory method.

Depreciation and Amortization
The Company's buildings, furniture, fixtures, and equipment are depreciated using the straight-line method over the estimated useful lives of the assets. Improvements to leased premises are amortized on the straight-line method over the life of the lease or the useful life of the improvement, whichever is shorter.

Investment Tax Credit
Investment tax credits are recorded as a reduction of Federal income taxes in the year the credits are realized.

Store Pre-opening Costs
Noncapital expenditures associated with opening new stores are charged to expense as incurred.

Earnings per Common and Common Equivalent Share
Earnings per common and common equivalent share are based on the weighted average number of shares and equivalents outstanding. Common equivalent shares used in the calculation of earnings per share represent shares granted under the Company's employee stock option plan and employee stock purchase plan.

Shares issuable upon conversion of the 8½% convertible subordinated debentures are also common stock equivalents. Shares issuable upon conversion of the 9% convertible subordinated debentures would only be included in the computation of fully diluted earnings per share. However, neither shares issuable upon conversion of the 8½% nor the 9% convertible debentures were dilutive in any year presented, and thus neither were considered in the earnings per share computations.

2. Acquisition
On December 3, 1984, the Company acquired the outstanding capital stock of Bowater Home Center, Inc. (Bowater) for approximately $38,420,000 including costs incurred in connection with the acquisition. Bowater operated nine retail home center stores primarily in the Dallas, Texas metropolitan area. The acquisition was accounted for by the purchase method and, accordingly, results of operations have been included with those of the Company from the date of acquisition. Cost in excess of the fair value of net assets acquired amounted to approximately $25,291,000, which is being amortized over forty years from date of acquisition using the straight-line method.

The following table summarizes, on a pro forma, unaudited basis, the estimated combined results of operations of the Company and Bowater for the years ended February 3, 1985, and January 29, 1984, as though the acquisition were made at the beginning of fiscal year 1983. This pro forma information does not purport to be indicative of the results of operations which would have actually been obtained if the acquisition had been effective on the dates indicated.

	Fiscal Year ended	
	February 3, 1985	*January 29, 1984**
	(Unaudited)	
Net sales	$482,752,000	$274,660,000
Net earnings	9,009,000	6,913,000
Earnings per common and common equivalent share	.36	.28

*Includes the operations and pro forma adjustments from the date of inception of Bowater's operations in August, 1983.

(continued)

3. Long-Term Debt and Lines of Credit

Long-term debt consists of the following:	February 2, 1986	February 3, 1985
8½% convertible subordinated debentures, due July 1, 2009, convertible into shares of common stock of the Company at a conversion price of $26.50 per share. The debentures are redeemable by the Company at a premium from July 1, 1986, to July 1, 1995, will retire 70% of the issue prior to maturity. Interest is payable semi-annually.	$ 86,250,000	$ 86,250,000
9% convertible subordinated debentures, due December 15, 1999, convertible into shares of common stock of the Company at a conversion price of $16.90 per share. The debentures are redeemable by the Company at a premium from December 15, 1986, to December 15, 1994. An annual mandatory sinking fund of $2,000,000 per year is required from 1994 to 1998. Interest is payable semi-annually	14,000,000	14,000,000
Total convertible subordinated debentures	100,250,000	100,250,000
Revolving credit agreement. Interest may be fixed for any portion outstanding for up to 180 days, at the Company's option, based on a CD rate plus 3/4%, the LIBOR rate plus 1/2% or at the prime rate	88,000,000	—
*Variable Rate Industrial Revenue Bond (see note 7)	10,100,000	10,100,000
*Variable Rate Industrial Revenue Bond, secured by a letter of credit, payable in sinking fund installments from December 1, 1991 through December 1, 2010	4,400,000	—
9⅜% Industrial Revenue Bond, secured by a letter of credit, payable on December 1, 1993, with interest payable semi-annually	4,200,000	4,200,000
*Variable Rate Industrial Revenue Bond, secured by land, payable in annual installments of $233,000 with interest payable semi-annually	3,267,000	3,500,000
Other	108,000	179,000
Total long-term debt	210,325,000	118,229,000
Less current portion	10,382,000	287,000
Long-term debt, excluding current portion	$199,943,000	$117,942,000

*The interest rates on the variable rate industrial revenue bonds are related to various short-term municipal money market composite rates.

Maturities of long-term debt are approximately $10,382,000 for fiscal 1986 and $234,000 for each of the next four subsequent years.

During the fiscal year ended February 2, 1986, the Company entered into a new unsecured revolving line of credit for a maximum of $200,000,000, subject to certain limitations, of which $88,000,000 is outstanding at year-end. Commitment amounts under the agreement decrease by $15,000,000 on July 31, 1990, by $20,000,000 each six months from that date through January 31, 1993, by $35,000,000 on July 31, 1993, and with the remaining $50,000,000 commitment expiring on January 31, 1994. Maximum borrowings outstanding within the commitment limits may not exceed specified percentages of inventories, land and buildings, and fixtures and equipment, all as defined in the Agreement. Under certain conditions, the commitments may be extended and/or increased. An annual commitment fee of 1/4% to 3/8% is required to be paid on the unused portion of the revolving line of credit. Interest rates specified may be increased by a maximum of 3/8 of 1% based on specified ratios of interest rate coverage and debt to equity.

Under the revolving credit agreement, the Company is required, among other things, to maintain during fiscal year 1985 a minimum tangible net worth (defined to include the convertible subordinated debentures) of $150,000,000 (increasing annually to $213,165,000 by January 3, 1989), a debt to tangible net worth ratio of no more than 2 to 1, a current ratio of not less than 1.5 to 1, and a ratio of earnings before interest expense and income taxes to interest expense, net, of not less than 2 to 1. The Company was in compliance with all restrictive covenants as of February 2, 1986. The restrictive covenants related to the letter of credit agreements securing the industrial revenue bonds and the convertible subordinated debentures are no more restrictive than those under the revolving line of credit agreement.

(continued)

Interest expense in the accompanying consolidated statements of earnings is net of interest capitalized of $3,429,00 in fiscal 1985 and $1,462,000 in fiscal 1984.

4. Income Taxes

The provision for income taxes consists of the following:

	Fiscal Year Ended		
	February 1, 1986	*February 3, 1985*	*January 29, 1984*
Current:			
Federal	$ (578,000)	$ 9,083,000	$ 6,916,000
State	66,000	1,539,000	1,096,000
	(212,000)	10,622,000	8,012,000
Deferred:			
Federal	3,306,000	1,464,000	713,000
State	306,000	44,000	—
	3,612,000	1,508,000	713,000
Total	$3,400,000	$12,130,000	$ 8,725,000

The effective tax rates for fiscal 1985, 1984, and 1983 were 29.3%, 46.2%, and 46.0%, respectively. A reconciliation of income tax expense at Federal statutory rates to actual tax expense for the applicable fiscal years follows:

	Fiscal Year Ended		
	February 2, 1986	*February 3, 1985*	*January 29, 1984*
Income taxes at federal statutory rate, net of surtax exemption	$5,345,000	$12,076,000	$8,734,000
State income taxes, net of federal income tax benefit	363,000	855,000	592,000
Investment and targeted jobs tax credits	(2,308,000)	(800,000)	(747,000)
Other, net	—	(1,000)	146,000
	$3,400,000	$12,130,000	$8,725,000

Deferred income taxes arise from differences in the timing of reporting income for financial statement and income tax purposes. The sources of these differences and the tax effect of each are as follows:

	Fiscal Year Ended		
	February 2, 1986	*February 3, 1985*	*January 29, 1984*
Accelerated depreciation	$2,526,000	$1,159,000	$713,000
Interest capitalization	855,000	349,000	—
Other, net	231,000	—	—
	$3,612,000	$1,508,000	$713,000

(continued)

5. Leases

The Company leases certain retail locations, office, and warehouse and distribution space, equipment, and vehicles under operating leases. All leases will expire within the next 25 years; however, it can be expected that in the normal course of business, leases will be renewed or replaced. Total rent expense, net of minor sublease income for the fiscal years ended February 2, 1986, February 3, 1985, and January 29, 1984 amounted to approximately $12,737,000, $6,718,000, and $4,233,000, respectively. Under the building leases, real estate taxes, insurance, maintenance, and operating expenses applicable to the leased property are obligations of the Company. Certain of the store leases provide for contingent rentals based on percentages of sales in excess of specified minimums. Contingent rentals for fiscal years ended February 2, 1986, February 3, 1985 and January 29, 1984 were approximately $650,000, $545,000 and $111,000.

The approximate future minimum lease payments under operating leases at February 2, 1986 are as follows:

Fiscal Year

1986	$ 16,093,000
1987	16,668,000
1988	16,345,000
1989	16,086,000
1990	16,129,000
Thereafter	171,455,000
	$252,776,000

7. Disposition of Property and Equipment

During the fourth quarter of fiscal year 1985, the Company disposed of certain properties and equipment at a net gain of $1,317,000. The properties represented real estate located in Detroit, Houston, and Tucson, and the equipment represented the trade-in of cash registers of current generation point of sale equipment. Under the terms of the Detroit real estate sale, the purchaser will either assume the bond obligations of the Company of $10,100,000 after February 2, 1986 or pay the Company the funds disbursed under the bonds in order for the Company to prepay the total amount outstanding. Included in accounts receivable at February 2, 1986, is $13,800,000 related to these transactions.

8. Commitments and Contingencies

At February 2, 1986, the Company was contingently liable for approximately $5,300,000 under outstanding letters of credit issued in connection with purchase commitments.

The Company has litigation arising from the normal course of business. In management's opinion, this litigation will not materially affect the Company's financial condition.

9. Quarterly Financial Data (Unaudited)

The following is a summary of the unaudited quarterly results of operations for fiscal years ended February 2, 1986, and February 3, 1985:

	Net Sales	Gross Profit	Net Earnings	Net Earnings per Common and Common Equivalent Share
Fiscal Year Ended February 2, 1986:				
First Quarter	$145,048,000	$ 36,380,000	$ 1,945,000	$.08
Second Quarter	174,239,000	45,572,000	2,499,000	.10
Third Quarter	177,718,000	46,764,000	1,188,000	.05
Fourth Quarter	203,724,000	52,741,000	2,587,000	.10
	$700,729,000	$181,457,000	$ 8,219,000	$.33
Fiscal Year Ended February 3, 1985:				
First Quarter	$ 95,872,000	$ 25,026,000	$ 3,437,000	$.14
Second Quarter	119,068,000	29,185,000	3,808,000	.15
Third Quarter	100,459,000	27,658,000	3,280,000	.13
Fourth Quarter	117,380,000	32,450,000	3,597,000	.14
	$432,779,000	$114,319,000	$14,122,000	$.56

(continued)

AUDITORS' REPORT

The Board of Directors and Stockholders,
The Home Depot, Inc.:

We have examined the consolidated balance sheets of The Home Depot, Inc. and subsidiary as of February 2, 1986, and February 3, 1985, and the related consolidated statements of earnings, stockholders' equity, and changes in financial position for each of the years in the three-year period ended February 2, 1986. Our examinations were made in accordance with generally accepted auditing standards, and, accordingly, included such tests of the accounting records and such other auditing procedures as we considered necessary in the circumstances.

In our opinion, the aforementioned consolidated financial statements present fairly the financial position of The Home Depot, Inc. and subsidiary at February 2, 1986, and February 3, 1985, and the results of their operations and the changes in their financial position for each of the years in the three-year period ended February 2, 1986, in conformity with generally accepted accounting principles applied on a consistent basis.

PEAT, MARWICK, MITCHELL & CO.
Atlanta, Georgia
March 24, 1986

Questions

1. Evaluate Home Depot's growth strategy. Do you think it is a viable strategy in the long run? _____
2. Analyze Home Depot's financial performance during the fiscal years 1983–85. (You may use the ratios and the cash flow analysis in Exhibit 3 in this analysis.) Compare Home Depot's performance in this period with Hechinger's performance.
3. How productive were Home Depot's stores in the fiscal years 1983–85? _____ (You may use the statistics in Exhibit 1 in this analysis.) How can the company improve its store productivity? _____
4. If the company maintains its operating performance at the fiscal 1985 level, do you think it can implement its growth plans? _____ What changes, if any, should the company make in its strategy? _____
5. What is your overall assessment of Home Depot's future prospects? _____

PART FIVE

Measurement and Analysis of Income

Revenue Recognition

This chapter focuses on the timing of revenue recognition and the other key element of the net income measurement process, namely the simultaneous matching with specific revenues those expenses that relate directly or jointly to the same transaction or events, such as matching the cost of inventory sold to the related sales revenue. Other elements of the net income measurement process are covered in later chapters. These involve the recognition of expenses, such as interest, that relate to specific periods of time, or expenses such as depreciation that are not directly related to either specific asset expiration or periods of time.[1]

Concepts Statement No. 6 defines revenues as:

Inflows or other enhancements of assets of an entity or settlements of its liabilities (or a combination of both) from delivering or producing goods, rendering services, or other activities that constitute the entity's ongoing major or central operations.

Concepts Statement No. 6 defines gains and losses as follows:

Gains are increases in equity (net assets) from peripheral or incidental transactions of an entity and from all other transactions and other events and circumstances affecting the entity except those that result from revenues or investments by owners.

Losses are decreases in equity (net assets) from peripheral or incidental transactions of an entity and from all other transactions and other events and circumstances affecting the entity except those that result from expenses or distributions to owners.

---

[1]Statement users wishing to understand the income recognition practices of specific industries should refer to the numerous AICPA Statement of Positions and Industry Accounting Guides that discuss the specialized accounting principles and practices of various industries.

Professor David F. Hawkins prepared this note as the basis for class discussion.

Recognition

Two conditions must be met before revenue and gains can be recognized. These two prerequisites are labeled (a) realized or realizable and (b) earned, with sometimes one and sometimes the other being the more important. Concepts Statement No. 5 states:

> Revenues and gains generally are not recognized until realized or realizable. Revenues and gains are realized when products (goods or services), merchandise, or other assets are exchanged for cash or claims for cash. Revenues and gains are realizable when related assets received or held are readily converted to known amounts of cash or claims to cash.
>
> Revenues are not recognized until earned. . . . Revenues are considered to have been earned when the entity has substantially accomplished what it must do to be entitled to the benefits represented by the revenues.

No one accounting rule or practice covers all revenue recognition situations. Nevertheless, an analysis of revenue recognition practices seems to indicate that revenue is typically recognized when the event that reduces the risk of ultimately receiving a determinable amount of revenue is reduced to a minimum level considered prudent by those issuing and using financial statements. This point in the earnings process is referred to as the critical event. Depending on the circumstances, the critical event can be anywhere in the chain of business events from production through the receipt of cash from the sale of goods or services, and, in some cases, to the fulfilling of warranty obligations. Determining this critical event in novel situations can require management judgement which must be exercised in the light of a thorough, objective analysis of the particular circumstances and the generally accepted accounting principles applicable to analogous situations.

There can be disagreement as to the nature of the critical event and what is prudent. As a result, recognition rules, even for very compatible exchanges within industries, can vary. For example, some companies within the same industry, such as the computer industry, might recognize in current income all shipments made prior to midnight on the last day of the accounting period that are billable to customers within the next 30 days. Other computer companies use the midnight cutoff, but include in the current period all shipments that will be installed in the next 14 days. Still others use the midnight cutoff criterion coupled with a requirement that all of the paperwork related to the shipment be materially completed.

While the generation of net income in most situations seems to turn on the timing of revenue recognition, the final measurement of net income must also include a consideration of the past, current, and estimated future costs related to the revenue recognized. In practice, management appears to tolerate slightly more uncertainty in the recognition of costs than it does in the case of revenues. However, if the total amount of revenue from a transaction is certain and the eventual costs of obtaining the revenue are fairly uncertain, the revenue should be deferred and held back from the income statement until the costs are more certain. To do otherwise might be misleading and imprudent. Again, this is a management decision, involving responsible and careful consideration of the particular facts.

Revenue Recognition Methods

The recognition of income varies from the time of production, in the case of certain mining operations, to the actual receipt of cash, in some installment sale situations. These variations fall into seven revenue recognition categories:

1. Recognition at the time services are rendered or goods shipped (i.e., sales method).
2. Recognition at the time the sale price is collected (i.e., installment sales method).
3. Recognition at the time the product is completed, but before delivery (i.e., production method).
4. Recognition proportionally over the performance of a long-term contract (i.e., percentage-of-completion method).
5. Recognition at the completion of a long-term contract (i.e., completed contract method).
6. Recognition after the buyer's cumulative cash payments exceed the seller's total costs (i.e., cost recovery method).
7. Recognition at time of delivery if the sale is made and cash is received prior to delivery or production (delivery method).

Sales.   The time of sale is the most common revenue recognition method. Typically, the act of invoicing, accompanied by delivery or consignment to a common carrier, is considered to constitute a sale for accounting purposes, rather than the legal criterion of title passing. In recognition of the fact that the cash eventually received from sales will fall short of the invoiced sale prices, a number of estimate deductions are made directly from the gross sales figure. These include: allowance for returns, warranty or service guarantees, and cash discounts. Allowances for bad debts are usually reported as an expense rather than a revenue deduction. Also, cash discounts for prompt payment are sometimes deducted from a customer's account at the time of sale, and then any discounts not taken are reported as a separate revenue item.

Installment Sales.   An installment sale involves a down payment and a specified series of payments over time. Depending on the circumstances, the gross profit from such sales must be recognized in one of two ways: at the time of sale, or proportionally as the cash payments are received. This latter approach is known as the installment method. It is rarely used for financial reporting purposes. APB Opinion 10 is very emphatic that "unless the circumstances are such that the collection of the sale price is not reasonably assured," the installment method of recognizing income is not acceptable for financial reporting purposes. The sale method must be used.

Production.   In some industries a sale or the collection of cash is not the critical event in the recognition of income. For example, in the case of a number of extractive industries, there is a market that stands ready to take their product at a going firm price. The company has merely to make the decision as to when and where it will convert its inventory of products into a sale. For such companies, production is the critical event in the recognition of income.

Long-Term Contracts.   There are two methods for recognizing income from contracts covering a long period of time: the completed contract method and the percentage-of-completion method. FASB Statement No. 56 states that the percentage-of-completion method is the preferable method and that persuasive evidence to the contrary is necessary to overcome this presumption.

The percentage-of-completion method is the preferable accounting for long-term contracts in circumstances in which reasonably defendable estimates of future revenues and costs can be made and in which all the following conditions exist:

1. Contracts executed by the parties include provisions that clearly specify the enforceable rights regarding goods and services to be provided and received by the parties, the consideration to be exchanged, and the manner and terms of settlement.
2. The buyer can be expected to satisfy his or her obligation under the contract.
3. The contractor can be expected to perform his or her contractual obligation.

The percentage-of-completion method recognizes income as the work on the contract progresses. The income recognized is the percentage of estimated total income

1. That incurred costs to date bear to estimated total costs after giving effect to costs to complete based upon most recent information; or
2. That may be indicated by such other measures of progress toward completion as may be appropriate having due regard to work performed.

Under this method current assets may include costs and recognized income not yet billed, with respect to certain contracts; and liabilities, in most cases current liabilities, may include billings in excess of costs and recognized income with respect to other contracts.

When the current estimate of total contract costs indicates a loss, in most circumstances provision should be made for this loss on the entire contract. If there is a close relationship between profitable and unprofitable contracts, such as in the case of contracts which are parts of the same project, the group may be treated as a unit in determining the necessity for a provision for loss.

There are two principal advantages to the percentage-of-completion method. First, periodic income is recognized currently rather than irregularly as contracts are completed. Second, the status of the uncompleted contracts is provided through the current estimates of costs to complete or of progress toward completion.

The principal disadvantage of the percentage-of-completion method is that in order to accrue current income, it is necessary to make estimates of ultimate costs. Typically, these are subject to the uncertainties frequently inherent in long-term contracts.

The completed contract method recognizes income only when the contract is completed or substantially so. Accordingly, costs of contracts in process and current billings are accumulated, but there are no interim charges or credits to income other than provisions for losses. A contract may be regarded as substantially completed if remaining costs are not significant in amount.

When the completed contract method is used, it may be appropriate to allocate general and administrative expenses to contract costs rather than to periodic income. This may result in a better matching of costs and revenues than would result from treating such expenses as period costs, particularly in years when no contracts were completed. It is not so important, however, when the contractor is engaged in numerous projects, and in such circumstances it may be preferable to charge those expenses as incurred to periodic income. In any case there should be no excessive deferring of overhead costs, such as might occur if total overhead was assigned to abnormally few or abnormally small contracts in process.

Although the completed contract method does not permit the recording of any income prior to completion, provision should be made for expected losses in accordance with the well-established practice of making provision for foreseeable losses. If there is a close relationship between profitable and unprofitable contracts, such as in the case of contracts which are parts of the same project, the group may be treated as a unit in determining the necessity for a provision for losses.

When the completed contract method is used, an excess of accumulated costs over related billings should be shown in the balance sheet as a current asset, and an excess of accumulated billings over related costs should be shown among the liabilities, in most cases as a current liability. If costs exceed billings on some contracts, and billings exceed costs on others, the contracts should ordinarily be segregated so that the figures on the asset side include only those contracts on which costs exceed billings, and those on the liability side include only those on which billings exceed costs. It is suggested that the asset item be described as "costs of uncompleted contracts in excess of related billings" rather than as "inventory" or "work in process," and that the item on the liability side be described as "billings on uncompleted contracts in excess of related costs."

The principal advantage of the completed contract method is that it is based on final results, rather than on estimates for unperformed work which may involve unforeseen costs and possible losses.

The principal disadvantage of this method is that it does not reflect current performance when the period of any contract extends beyond more than one accounting period. Under these circumstances, it may result in an irregular pattern of income recognition.

Interim billings should not be used as a basis for recognizing income, since considerations other than those acceptable as a basis for the recognition of income frequently enter into the determination of the timing and the amounts of interim billings.

Cost Recovery.   The cost recovery method is seldom used. This method does not recognize any gross profit from the sale until the cumulative total of the payments received equals the cost of the item sold. FASB Statement No. 5, "Accounting for Contingencies," indicates that it is used only where receivables are collectible over an extended period of time and, because of the terms of the transaction or other conditions, there is no reasonable basis for estimating the degree of collectibility.

Delivery.   In some situations cash is received before a service is performed or a product is delivered. In these cases revenue is recognized rateably as the service is performed or the product delivered.

Nonmonetary Transactions

Typically, sale transactions involve the exchange of cash, other monetary assets or liabilities[2] for nonmonetary assets or services. The monetary element of such exchanges generally provides an objective basis for measuring the cost of the goods and services received by an enterprise as well as the gain or loss on the business.

However, some business transactions do not involve monetary items, such as when a company exchanges inventory for equipment. Since there is no monetary element in the transaction, the determination of the value to assign to the nonmonetary asset transferred, or the amount of gain or loss on the transaction, is not clear.

In general, the accounting for nonmonetary transactions should be based on the fair values of the assets or services involved which is the same basis as that used in transactions that involve monetary elements. The fair value of a nonmonetary asset transferred to or from a business in a nonmonetary transaction can be determined in a number of ways. These include (1) reference to the estimated realizable values in cash transactions involving the same or similar assets; (2) quoted market prices for the same or similar assets; (3) independent appraisals; and (4) management estimates, if adequate evidence to support the estimate is available. If one of the parties to the nonmonetary transaction could have elected to receive cash rather than a nonmonetary asset, then the amount of cash that might have been received could be considered as evidence of the fair value of the nonmonetary asset.

Right of Return

Products sold with a buyer's right-to-return privilege should only be recorded as sales with appropriate accruals for expected returns or losses when all these conditions set forth in FASB Statement No. 48, "Revenue Recognition When Right of Return Exists," are met:

1. The seller's price to the buyer is substantially fixed as determinable at the date of sale.

---

[2]Monetary assets and liabilities are assets and liabilities whose amounts are fixed in terms of units of currency by contract or otherwise, such as notes payable and cash.

2. The buyer has paid the seller, or the buyer is obligated to pay the seller and the obligation is not contingent on resale of the product.

3. The buyer's obligation to the seller would not be changed in the event of theft or physical destruction or damage of the product.

4. The buyer acquiring the product for resale has economic substance apart from that provided by the seller.

5. The seller does not have significant obligations for future performance to directly bring about resale of the product by the buyer.

6. The amount of future returns can be reasonably estimated.

Sales revenue and cost of sales that are not recognized because these conditions are not met can be recognized when either the return privilege expires or the conditions are met.

Product Financing Agreements

Sometimes companies attempt to generate sales revenue through transactions that in essence agree to repurchase the buyer's unsold inventory at a price equal to the original sale price plus carrying and financing costs. The FASB in Statement No. 49, "Accounting for Product Financing Arrangements," required that such transactions be accounted for as borrowing rather than sales.

Inappropriate Interest Rates

Sometimes the seller of property, goods, or services may receive in exchange a note with a face value that does not reasonably represent the present value of the consideration given or received in the exchange. This situation may arise if the note is noninterest bearing or has a stated interest rate which is different from the rate of interest appropriate for the debt at the date of the transaction. Unless in these circumstances the note is recorded at its present value,[3] rather than the stated amount, the sales price and profit to the seller and cost to the buyer are misstated, and interest income and interest expense in subsequent periods are also misstated.

APB Opinion No. 21, "Interest on Receivables and Payables," sets forth the appropriate accounting in these cases. It requires that the receivable or payable be recorded on the balance sheet at its face value with an adjustment to arrive at its discounted value. Then, the interest income or expense is the market rate, which is the interest actually received or paid plus a portion of the adjustment amount shown on the balance sheet.

---

[3]The present value amount is the future cash payments required by the note discounted at the appropriate market interest rate.

Accounting for Bad Debts

Revenues are ordinarily accounted for at the time a transaction is completed, with appropriate provision for uncollectible amounts. This section presents alternative procedures used by businesses in recognizing and reporting losses from uncollectible receivables.

Every enterprise extending credit to customers sustains some losses from bad debts. An account receivable becomes a bad debt when all reasonable expectation of collection is exhausted. The amounts of bad debt loss to the business firm will depend upon such factors as the type of customer served, policies regarding investigative procedures prior to granting credit, and policies employed in the collection of receivables. In spite of efforts to minimize these losses, it is impossible to predict customer payments with certainty, and some accounts will remain uncollectible. Bad debt losses can be avoided only if a firm receives payment in cash at the time of sale.

There are two basic reasons for recognizing bad debt losses in the financial records. First, the determination of net income based upon the proper matching of revenue and expense must include these unavoidable losses. Second, the valuation of receivables in the balance sheet requires consideration of these losses to present a realistic estimate of the anticipated funds that will flow from the collection of receivables.

Accounting for bad debt losses can be accomplished by either of two methods: (1) the direct write-off method or (2) the bad debt estimation method.

Direct Write-Off Method

The direct write-off method of accounting for bad debt expense ignores the possibility of any bad debt loss until individual accounts receivable prove to be uncollectible. No advance provision is made for doubtful accounts. Under this method, the bad debt expense represents the amount of receivables which have actually become uncollectible during the operating period.

When an account receivable is considered uncollectible, the following entry is made:

Bad Debt Expense	xxx	
Accounts Receivable (customer A)		xxx

This entry has the effect of charging an asset account (Accounts Receivable) directly to an expense account (Bad Debt Expense) and gives this method its descriptive name.

If subsequent events prove that an account previously written off can be collected, the entry required to reinstate the receivable is:

Accounts Receivable (customer A)	xxx	
Bad Debts Recovered (or Bad Debt Expense)		xxx

At the close of the accounting period, Bad Debts Recovered must be recognized as revenue while Bad Debts Expense is deducted in the determination of net income. Alternatively, recoveries and expenses might be netted.

The direct write-off method has two severe limitations. First, the bad debt expense may be deducted from the revenue of an accounting period subsequent to the original sale. Hence, it fails to properly match income and expense of a particular operating period. Second, current assets in the balance sheet may be overstated, since no recognition is given to the probable uncollectibility of some part of the receivables. For these reasons, the direct write-off method is not widely used by businesses of significant size. However, its simplicity makes it a popular method among very small businesses.

Also, in those cases where a reasonable estimate of the anticipated bad debts cannot be made, FASB Statement No. 5 requires that the direct write-off method be used.

Bad Debt Estimation Method

Matching of revenue and expense and a realistic valuation of accounts receivables is achieved by including an estimate of bad debt expense in the financial statements. The estimated amount of bad debt losses which will eventually result from sales of an accounting period is treated as an expense of the period. That part of the estimated loss which cannot be identified with particular receivables is deducted from total receivables on the balance sheet to show the expected amount to be collected eventually.

The special feature of the bad debt estimation method is the creation of the asset valuation account deducted from receivables. This contra-asset account, called Allowance for Doubtful (or Uncollectible) Accounts, is increased as estimated bad debt expense is recorded and decreased by recognition of actual bad debt losses.

There are several different approaches to the estimation of bad debt expense. Bad debt losses for a business enterprise can usually be estimated with a high degree of accuracy based upon its own experience of actual bad debt losses over a period of time or upon the experience of similar businesses. For estimating purposes, this experience can be related on a percentage basis to (1) sales for a period or operations or (2) the amount of receivables at the close of the operating period. Either of these approaches will, over a period of time, theoretically result in proper charges to income and proper valuation of receivables.

Percentage of Sales.   The estimate for bad debt losses may be expressed as a percentage of sales. For example, historical experience might indicate that actual bad debt losses averaged 2% of sales. This rate for estimating bad debt losses might be applied in successive operating periods until actual experience suggests that the rate be adjusted upward or downward to achieve greater accuracy. Frequently the rate is determined on the basis of a sale figure adjusted by eliminating cash sales and sales returns, in recognition that bad debts result only from net credit sales to customers.

Percentage of Receivables.   The estimate for bad debt losses may be expressed as a percentage of receivables at the close of an accounting period. For example, prior experience might indicate that on the average 5% of the balance of receivables subsequently proves uncollectible. In each operating period sufficient bad debt expense might be charged to maintain the Allowance for Doubtful Accounts at 5% of receivables until actual experience requires revision of this rate.

To obtain greater accuracy in estimating uncollectibility, an analysis grouping accounts receivable by "age" from date of sale may be prepared. Since older accounts are more likely to be uncollectible, separate consideration of each group of accounts might suggest that the provision for uncollectibility should be equal, for example, to 1% of receivables 0 to 30 days old, 3% of receivables 31 to 60 days old, and 25% of receivables over 60 days old.

Accounting Entities for Bad Debt Estimation Method.   The following accounting entries are typically required to handle estimated and actual bad debt losses under the estimation method.

   1. To record estimated bad debt expense:

Dr. Bad Debt Expense	xxx	
Cr. Allowance for Doubtful Accounts		xxx

This entry is usually made only at the close of the accounting period immediately before financial statements are prepared. The amount of the entry will be either (1) the amount of bad debt expense computed as a percentage of sales or (2) the amount necessary to bring the Allowance for Doubtful Accounts to a computed percentage of receivables.

   2. To write off an account determined to be uncollectible:

Dr. Allowance for Doubtful Accounts	xxx	
Cr. Accounts Receivable (customer A)		xxx

In this entry, specific uncollectible receivables are identified with the bad debt expense previously recognized on an estimated basis.

   3. To recognize collectibility of a receivable previously written off:

Dr. Accounts Receivable (customer A)	xxx	
Cr. Allowance for Doubtful Accounts		xxx

This entry will reflect the amount expected to be collected from the customer. Reinstatement of the receivable previously written off is accomplished so that a complete history of dealings with customers is maintained in the accounts receivable records. The actual collections on the reinstated account will then be recorded as though the account had never been written off.

Financial Statement Presentation

Bad debt expenses recorded on the basis of an estimate is reported as an expense on the income statement. Usually this expense is classified as selling expense or as administrative expense, depending upon where the firm assigns responsibility for the granting of credit.

The allowance for doubtful accounts is subtracted from the total of the related receivables in the current asset section of the balance sheet. This net amount represents the expected cash proceeds from subsequent collection of the receivables.

FASB Statement No. 5 requires that the bad debt estimation method be used when the amount of the anticipated bad debts can be reasonably estimated.

Warranties and Service Guarantees

Some merchandise is sold with a warranty against defects or a service guarantee, which when fulfilled is usually paid in labor and materials rather than cash. These items are similar to bad debts in that the future expense and accompanying liability are unknown at the time of sale. Therefore, initially, they must be estimated. If the amount of the future warranty cost can be reasonably estimated, FASB Statement No. 5 requires that future warranty costs be recorded at the time a sale is made. If a reasonable estimate cannot be made, the warranty costs must be recognized as they are actually incurred in future accounting periods.

The accounting for warranty or service guarantees is analogous to bad debt accounting. The estimated expense is recognized at the time of the sale and an offsetting liability is established. This liability is then reduced when the cost of the guarantee or warranty is paid. Sometimes the estimated costs are shown as a revenue offset instead of an expense.

Realization Controversy

Accounting practice has relied heavily on the realization principle as a guide to recognizing income. With the exceptions discussed earlier, this principle states that income generally arises at the point of sale. A number of accounting authors do not accept this concept and its related practices as an essential feature of accounting. They claim it lacks analytical precision and places undue emphasis on the act of selling, which is only one point in a company's total economic activity.

The critics of the realization concept believe the proper function of accounting is measurement of the resources of specific entities and of changes in these resources. These changes are attributable to the whole process of business activity. Accordingly, the principles of accounting should be directed toward fulfilling this function. In the critics' opinion, changes in resources (income) should be classified among the amounts attributable to:

1. Price level changes which lead to restatement of capital, but not to revenues and expense.
2. Changes in the current value of assets beyond the effect of price level changes.

3. The recognition through sales and other operating-related transfers of net realizable value which leads to revenue or gain.

4. Other causes, such as the accretion or discovery of previously unknown natural resources.

This approach requires the use of price level accounting and current values of assets rather than the presently more accepted historical cost principle.

The supporters of the realization principle argue that it is difficult to determine the fairness and reasonableness of appraisals. In addition, they believe it is not prudent to recognize gains before they are realized.

Analytical Considerations

Evaluation of periodic net income is a critical part of most financial analyses. To complete this analytical task competently requires a thorough understanding of how a company generates and recognizes revenues, since the accounting revenue recognition rules adopted by management determine in large part the timing and measurement of net income.

The most important fact to remember always when analyzing revenues and their related profits is that revenues, other than cash sales, are recorded typically using the accrual accounting bookkeeping entry.

Dr. Accounts Receivable xxx
    Cr. Sales xxx

If the analyst keeps this bookkeeping entry in mind, the analyst will never fall into the trap of thinking the flow of revenues and their related profits recorded by accountants are cash flows. As the above entry indicates, the offsetting entry to record a sale is to accounts receivable, which is one step away from cash. Until the cash is received, the company has to continue financing the cost of the item sold. If the receivable is due well into the future, this could be expensive. Also, if the customer's credit is weak, the anticipated cash payment may never be received.

Analysts should never assume that a company is healthy because its accounting revenues and profits appear to be robust. This could be an illusion. The sales could be accounting fictions that do not have future beneficial cash flow consequences.

Usually, an accounts receivable aging and cash flow analysis will uncover these situations. In carrying out these analyses it is important to track down off–balance-sheet financing and recording of receivables and revenues, since the cash flow analysis will be limited to consolidated financial statement cash flow, revenues, and income data. These consolidated data will not capture fully off–balance-sheet transactions, such as guaranteeing customer borrowings to pay off payables due the guarantor, that may be used to boost consolidated cash flow and income.

Understanding how a business actually generates sales and ultimately collects cash is fundamental to revenue and income analysis. It is the actual business transactions, not their accounting representations, that generate the cash flows that determine this economic value of individual assets and of the business as a whole. Financial analysis is a tool that helps statement users penetrate the accounting data to develop insights into these actual flows and to determine the appropriateness of the company's revenue and income recognition rules, given the company's underlying cash flow generating process.

An analyst concerned with revenues is usually trying to understand the market share, seasonal, and cyclical pattern of a company's cash flow from sales as well as possible future trends in this pattern. While statement analysis can be used to track past flows and make statement projections of possible future flows, the analyst must go beyond financial statement data to develop an appreciation of the underlying business factors that determine actual cash flows. This requires an understanding of the nature of a company's products as well as who buys them, why they are bought, where they are bought, how they are bought, and when they are bought. This knowledge can be used to determine the company's critical marketing, distribution, and product development success factors, which in turn are useful for focusing analytical attention on how well the company is executing those actions that are key to the generation of revenues and operating cash flows. This company-specific knowledge will also help the analyst to appreciate the impact on cash flows and revenues of seasonality, economic cycles, exchange rate shifts, inflation, new regulations, changing customer purchasing patterns, and competitive behavior. This understanding should be used to explain the results of the financial analysis of past financial statement data and to project cash flows and revenues based on an environmental, business, and financial analysis appreciation of the determinants of the company's revenues and cash flows.

An understanding of a business's earnings process is necessary to appraise the appropriateness of management's selection of revenue recognition rules. To make proper earnings quality appraisal, the analyst must be familiar with the details of the company's recognition rules, the nature of the possible alternative rules rejected, and the range of income recognition methods in the company's industry. The two key questions are: Is management's designation of the "critical act" appropriate? Are the recognition methods consistent with this designation?

Analysts should form their own judgments as to what constitutes this critical act. Sometimes they will find conservative managers designating the critical act as one occurring much later in the earnings process than those designated by other managers in their industry, or even than the analyst's selection. Typically these conservative companies are not a problem. The companies to worry about are those that seem to be aggressively recognizing income relative to the generally acknowledged leading companies in the industry and the analyst's designated critical act. Because the timing of revenue recognition is so influential in the measurement of net income, aggressive recognition practices carry a heavy negative weighting in assessing earnings quality. They are also a red flag suggesting that other aggressive accounting practices may be followed. In addition, premature recognition of income can precipitate later adverse earnings reports because subsequent unanticipated events may lead to related accounts receivable being written off as the costs to complete the earnings process rise unexpectedly or the receivables prove to be uncollectible.

When income is recognized before the earnings process is completed, provision must be made for some future costs or revenue adjustments, to reflect the nature of the earnings process yet to be completed. The costs, such as warranty expense, and revenue adjustments, such as provisions for returns and allowances, are based on management estimates. Analysts should check these estimates carefully as managers tend to overstate these items in highly profitable years and understate them in times of difficulty. Adjustment to gross sales as a percentage of net or gross sales should always be calculated. Similarly, the revenue-related expenses based on management estimates should be tracked as a percentage of net sales. In both cases the question should be asked: Does this percentage figure make sense given the circumstances?

Statement readers should be aware of the various actions management can take in the short run to pump revenues up to hide a deteriorating situation. These include accelerating work on contracts accounted for by the percentage-of-completion method; advancing the statement date of goods not originally due to be received by the customer until a later period in return for not requiring payment until after the original payment date; overloading the channels of distribution; guaranteeing third party loans to customers so that customers can place an order they normally might defer because of funding problems; and swapping sales with firms in similar difficulties. In reality shipments generated in these ways are little more than shipping inventories to someone else's warehouse and calling it a sale.

Normally these actions are hard to detect. The best indicator of these dubious sales-boosting maneuvers is unusual changes in the inventory and accounts receivable levels relative to sales. For example, if receivables rise faster than sales in one quarter and there is no discernible reason for this relationship, sales may have been pulled into that quarter from future periods or goods sold to questionably creditworthy customers. Similarly, if the prior quarter's reports indicate excessive inventories and these excess inventories apparently disappear in the current quarter, sales-boosting tactics that have little lasting value may have been engaged in to move the excessive inventories and to cover up indications of poor production controls and planning.

Analysts focusing on revenues should always look at the liability side of the balance sheet. It is where deferred revenues and income are presented. This is an important source of revenue information, because under some circumstances the recognition of income may be deferred to the future, even though the company has already received cash or a note from the transaction. This occurs when a magazine sells subscriptions. These deferred revenue and income items can be an important source of future revenues and income and should be traced over time to see how management uses them for balance sheet, cash flow, and earnings management purposes.

D.C. Electrical, Inc.

On March 7, 1987, the board of directors of D.C. Electrical, Inc. ("D.C.") approved a proposal from First Bank N.A. whereby First Bank would be D.C.'s agent bank on a two-bank $5 million reducing revolving credit agreement having a maturity of seven years and D.C.'s lead bank on a contemplated two-bank $6 million line of credit.

On March 30, 1987, D.C. signed the reducing revolving credit agreement with First Bank and Third Pennsylvania Bank N.A. (the "Banks"). The Banks also established lines of credit in favor of D.C. not to exceed $4 million and $2 million respectively, bearing interest at First Bank's Base Rate (important terms of the agreement are provided in **Exhibit 1**). The total provided by the Banks aggregates $11 million and is available on the unsecured basis to D.C. and its subsidiaries for working capital needs. This arrangement replaced D.C.'s $5 million unsecured line of credit with National Bank N.A. of which $4 million was available for general working capital purposes and the remaining $1 million was available on a short-term, specific transactional basis, at the discretion of National.

On March 31, 1987, D.C. borrowed $5 million under the reducing revolving credit agreement.

Company Background

Founded in 1925, D.C. became a public company in 1978 and since 1978 it has experienced rapid growth. As early as 1987, D.C. has become one of the U.S.'s largest

Professors David F. Hawkins of the Harvard Business School and Norman J. Bartczak of Columbia Business School prepared this case as the basis for class discussion rather than to illustrate either effective or ineffective handling of an administrative situation.

EXHIBIT 1   **Excerpts From D.C. Electrical Inc.'s March 30, 1987 Credit Agreement with First Bank N.A. and Third Pennsylvania Bank N.A.**

Bank credit decision   D.C. represents and warrants that the balance sheets of D.C. and its subsidiaries as at March 31, 1986, and the related statements of income, retained earnings, and changes in financial position of the fiscal year then ended, copies of which have been furnished to each of the Banks, fairly present the financial condition of D.C. and its subsidiaries as at such date and the results of operations of D.C. and its subsidiaries for the period ended on such dates, all in accordance with generally accepted accounting principles consistently applied, and since March 31, 1986, there has been no material adverse change in such condition or operations. . . .

Commitments   Until July 1990 each Bank's commitment under the reducing revolving loan agreement is $2.5 million. From July 1, 1990 each Bank's commitment is reduced by $125 thousand per quarter until July 1, 1993. From July 1, 1993 each Bank's commitment is reduced by $250 thousand per quarter until the Termination Date. . . .

Working capital covenant   D.C. and its subsidiaries shall maintain:

(i) An excess of consolidated current assets over consolidated current liabilities (excluding deferred income taxes) of not less than $22 million to and including March 31, 1987 rising in $500 thousand increments each year thereafter to a maximum of $25.5 million after March 31, 1993.

(ii) A ratio of consolidated current assets to consolidate current liabilities of not less than 1.3 to 1.0.

(iii) A ratio of consolidated current assets to consolidated current liabilities (excluding deferred income taxes) of not less than 2.7 to 1.0.

Net worth covenant   D.C. and its subsidiaries shall maintain an excess of consolidated total tangible assets over consolidated total liabilities of not less than $14 million to and including March 31, 1987. The excess shall increase by $1 million increments each annual period after March 31, 1987 to a maximum of $21 million after March 31, 1993.

Dividend restrictions   D.C. and its subsidiaries will not, without the written consent of the Banks, declare and pay cash dividends to its stockholders, except for those declared out of 66-2/3% of net income of D.C. and its subsidiaries arising after March 31, 1987 and within the 12-month period immediately preceding the date of computation and computed on a cumulative consolidated basis. This provision is applicable to the next quarterly cash dividend scheduled to be paid in August 1987. It is not applicable to the dividend declared prior to the signing of the agreement namely the 16¢ per share dividend declared February 5, 1987 and payable May 25, 1987 to stockholders of record April 26, 1987.

Debt covenant   D.C. and its subsidiaries will not, without the written consent of the Banks, create or suffer to exist any Debt maturing in excess of one year from the date of determination, if immediately after giving effect to such Debt and the receipt and application of any proceeds thereof, the ratio of the aggregate amount of such Debt of D.C. and its subsidiaries, on a consolidated basis, to (x) the total tangible assets less (y) total liabilities would be greater than 1.0 to 1.0.

---

electrical construction and contracting firms participating in all sectors of construction other than single family housing.

D.C. is active in the following business sectors: public and institutional construction; industrial plant construction, expansion and modernization; commercial construction of all kinds; public utility plants and distribution facilities; and space and military projects.

During the last five fiscal years the approximate percentages of D.C.'s gross contract income attributable to the various categories of its business were as follows:

	Fiscal Year Ended March 31				
	1982	*1983*	*1984*	*1985*	*1986*
Public and institutional	23%	43%	40%	39%	40%
Industrial	28	11	14	19	22
Commercial	30	15	15	21	20
Utilities	17	27	27	14	14
Space and military	2	4	4	7	4
Total	100%	100%	100%	100%	100%

Typical projects include interior and exterior illumination; automation and instrumentation systems; pollution control systems; natural gas, fossil fuel, and nuclear power plants and distribution systems; highway, bridge and tunnel control systems; hospital facilities; traffic and cargo handling systems; and mass transit systems.

D.C.'s business is performed under contracts obtained by competitive bidding or by negotiations based on plans and specifications submitted by the owner or general contractor. It employs more than 2,600 people and operates 19 branches in the continental United States and two branches overseas.

Types of Contracts

Although the terms of individual contracts may vary substantially, D.C.'s business is generally performed under two basic types of contracts:

Fixed Price Contracts.   The greater share of D.C.'s work is done pursuant to contracts where it receives a fixed sum for the project or a fixed amount per unit of work performed, which is intended to cover D.C.'s costs and overhead and to return a profit.

Cost Plus Contracts.   To a lesser extent, and generally in cases where final plans and specifications for the work are not available to establish a fixed bid, D.C. contracts on a cost plus basis. Under these contracts it is reimbursed for its costs, and receives a fee which may be a fixed amount or a percentage of cost.

Fixed price contracts generally involve greater risks for D.C. but also have greater potential profit margins. Cost plus contracts customarily insulate it from the risk of cost increases. For the five years ended March 31, 1986, the percentages of contract income derived from fixed price contracts were 83% in 1982, 84% in 1983, 74% in 1984, 75% in 1985, and 85% in 1986. The balance of contract income in each year was derived from cost plus contracts.

Practically all of D.C.'s business is obtained by competitive bidding or negotiation based on plans and specifications submitted to it by the owner or general contractor. Competitive bidding generally is limited to contractors who have qualified for inclusion on the customer's bid list. Such qualification depends on, among other things, the contractor's financial responsibility, its ability to perform the work, and its record of on-time completions. Standard company estimating procedures are followed for submitting a fixed contract price or fixed unit price. Where the plans and specifications are not sufficiently definitive to permit reliable estimates, the cost plus contract is utilized with the fee portion negotiated or bid to the customer. D.C. assumes the risk of losses on contracts if its cost estimates prove to be incorrect. In addition, contract specifications may be inaccurate or projects may be deferred or delayed by customers or other contractors, in which case additional costs and expenses may be incurred by D.C. for which it must seek recourse through negotiation or litigation. When the customer requests, D.C. furnishes surety bonds for the performance of its work and the payment of its suppliers and personnel. D.C. has never defaulted on a contract nor required its surety company to complete a project or perform any obligation to a customer.

Operations

While D.C. generally contracts for its own account, it has participated in joint ventures with other electrical contractors, where the joint venture enters into a subcontract with the general contractor. It generally acts as manager of these joint ventures, for which it receives a management fee. It has also participated in joint ventures with building contractors in other trades, where the joint venture acts as the general contractor. These joint ventures have been principally in connection with the construction of automated bulk mail facilities. As a participant in a joint venture, D.C. is jointly and severally obligated with each of its joint venturers for the performance of the joint venture's contract with the customer. D.C. has recently reduced its participation in joint ventures with building contractors in other trades.

Under almost all of D.C.'s contracts, payment is made by the general contractor or owner monthly, or sometimes more frequently, based upon the percentage or stage of completion of the job. Usually a percentage of the amount which is due is retained by the general contractor or owner until completion and acceptance of the project. (See ''Accounting for Contracts'' in Note 1 of the Notes to Consolidated Financial Statement.)

No material part of the business of D.C. is seasonal. Due to its diversity in various sectors of the construction industry, it has not experienced cyclical variations in its total contract income even though sectors of the construction business are cyclical. Major fixed price contracts generally require 18 to 30 months to complete.

Domestic

D.C. conducts its business in the continental United States through 19 branch offices. The following table sets forth the approximate percentages of gross contract income by geographical region during the last five fiscal years:

	Fiscal Year Ended March 31				
Region	*1982*	*1983*	*1984*	*1985*	*1986*
Mid-Atlantic	27%	27%	26%	32%	30%
Southern	26	29	31	31	26
Mid-Western	20	20	18	14	21
Northeastern	27	24	25	22	20
Western	—	—	—	1	3
Total	100%	100%	100%	100%	100%

International

D.C. International Corp. was incorporated as a wholly owned subsidiary in August 1984 to engage in contracting activities in foreign countries. Its contract income for the fiscal year ended March 31, 1985, was $853,000, of which $653,000 was attributable to one materials supply contract which is substantially completed and on which D.C. realized a nominal profit. The general and administrative expenses of this subsidiary, including the cost of bids during the start-up period, accounted for its loss after tax benefit of $582,000 ($.43 per share) in that fiscal year. Activities prior to April 1, 1985 were not significant.

D.C. expected that international operations will become a material part of its business. It is intended that operations will be conducted primarily in developing nations and difficult climates and, accordingly, weather conditions, actions of foreign governments, fluctuations in local currencies, transportation difficulties, shortages of labor or materials, civil strife and other factors may subject D.C. to more substantial risks of loss than those present in its domestic activities. A guaranty of performance is generally required under fixed price contracts, both domestic and foreign. While domestic contracts traditionally call for surety bonds issued against the general credit of D.C., foreign contracts often require a financial guaranty by a bank in the foreign country backed by a letter of credit which may involve a deposit of collateral in addition to the general credit of D.C.

A substantial amount of overseas work was awarded to D.C. late in the fourth quarter of fiscal 1986 consisting mainly of two contracts, one for approximately $22 million with a U.S. general contractor for the U.S. Corps of Engineers for construction of housing, water wells, medical support facilities, and hospital air conditioning in Saudi Arabia. D.C.'s contract covers the electrical, mechanical, and utilities work involved in the project which is being constructed for, and funded by, the Saudi Arabian government. The guaranty of D.C.'s performance was furnished by surety bonds. The other major foreign contract involves the construction of a hotel in El Salvador.

Competition

D.C. is one of the largest electrical contractors in the United States based on published contract awards. The electrical contracting industry is characterized by intense competition. D.C. competes with many large and small firms, both union and non-union, as well as with certain large general contractors which have their own electrical contracting capability. Competition for large contracts and contracts with respect to specialized electrical installations, while limited to fewer concerns (including D.C.), is still active.

Management and Ownership

Executive Officers Name, Age	Position	Current Rate of Remuneration
Edward P. Johnson, Sr., Age 77	Chairman of the board, chief executive officer, joined D.C. in 1945	$250,200
J. A. Martin, Age 65	President, chief operating officer, joined D.C. in 1949	226,200
Nicholas J. Grady, Age 65	Executive vice president, chief administrative officer, joined D.C in 1964	202,200
Edward P. Johnson, Jr. Age 46	Senior vice president, International, joined D.C. in 1965	166,200
R. A. Clay, Age 34	Vice president—finance, treasurer, joined D.C. in 1969	Less than 100,000
Joseph J. McCarthy, Age 60	Secretary, general counsel, joined D.C. in 1976	149,200

Board of Directors Name	Occupation	Director Since	Common Shares Beneficially Owned
Edward P. Johnson, Sr.	Chairman and chief executive officer of D.C.	1949	218,283
John A. Martin	President and chief operating officer of D.C.	1966	188,515
Joseph J. McCarthy	Secretary and general counsel of D.C.	1977	3,736
Arthur S. Friedman	Member, Tanner & Friedman, P.C., attorney at law	1978	6,754
Nicholas J. Grady	Executive vice president and chief administrative officer of D.C.	1980	5,089
Edward P. Johnson, Jr.	Senior vice president, international of D.C.	1982	144,729
Francis Lyman Hine	Chairman and director of Meta-Glas Systems Corp.; vice president and director National Glass Plastics Corp.	1983	0

Principal Shareholders and Sale of Shares

On July 27, 1986, D.C. offered to sell 400,000 shares of common stock. The offering came to market at $9 per share and consisted of 140,000 new shares and 260,000 shares from selling shareholders. The following table, from the offering prospectus, sets forth certain information with respect to the selling shareholders and D.C.'s principal shareholders:

Name	Owned as of May 31, 1986		No of Shares to be Sold	Owned after the Offering	
	No. of Shares	Percentage of Outstanding		No of Shares	Percentage of Outstanding
Edward P. Johnson, Sr.	302,283	22%	84,000	218,283	15%
John A. Martin	272,515	20	84,000	188,515	13
Trust Company Bank, Edward P. Johnson, Jr., and Arthur S. Friedman, as trustees under trust agreement dated July 5, 1978	288,739	17	84,000	144,729	10
Joseph J. McCarthy	5,736	—	2,000	3,736	—
Richard L. Senior III	3,841	—	2,000	1,841	—
James K. Shannon	6,306	—	2,000	4,306	—
Robert H. Shepherd	3,841	—	2,000	1,841	—

The actual number of new shares sold to the public was 155,000. The net proceeds to D.C of the sale were $1,256,900.

Financial Information

Disagreement on Accounting Matter

On March 7, 1987 (the same day on which D.C. approved First Bank's proposal), D.C.'s board of directors engaged Walter A. Elcock & Company as the independent accounting firm to conduct the audit of D.C.'s financial statements for the fiscal year ending March 31, 1987. Elcock was engaged in place of Peabody & Company who audited D.C.'s financial statements initially for the fiscal year ended March 31, 1979, and each fiscal year thereafter, through and including the fiscal year ended March 31, 1986.

On March 22, 1987, D.C. filed a Form 8-K "Current Report" with the Securities and Exchange Commission reporting a disagreement between D.C. and Peabody & Company (its former accountants) as to the application of D.C.'s percentage-of-completion method of accounting on foreign contract in the third quarter ended December 31, 1986. Details of the disagreement are provided in **Exhibit 2.**

Quarterly Information

D.C. Electrical, Inc. Quarterly Data (Dollars in thousands, except per share amounts)

Fiscal 1977	I 6/30/86	II 9/30/86	III 12/31/86	IV 3/31/87
Contract income	$29,514	$34,478	$32,025	NA[a]
Net income	650	735	863	NA
Net income per share	.48	.50	.57	NA
Dividends per share	.14	.15	.16	.16
Market price: High	9.75	9.75	11.125	12.25
Low	7.75	8.25	8.50	10.00

[a]Not available on March 31, 1978.

EXHIBIT 2   Excerpts from Form 8-K "Current Report" filed with S.E.C. on March 22, 1987

D.C. Electrical, Inc. ("D.C.") engaged Elcock & Company to perform limited reviews with reporting by them to the Company's Board of Directors. In connection with such reviews for the three-month periods ended September 30, 1986 and December 31, 1986 there was disagreement relating to the recognition of a material amount of income under a foreign fixed price contract. In these respective three-month periods contract costs included and contract profit, based on costs incurred to date to total estimated costs, was recognized on (i) the costs of materials shipped overseas which were on the project site but not yet installed, (ii) the costs of materials which were in transit to the project site, and (iii) the cost of expendable capital equipment purchased for the project and included in the original estimate of total contract costs. The question of including such costs first arose in November 1986 with respect to the second quarter ended September 30, 1986 and was resolved to Elcock & Company's satisfaction with D.C. excluding the applicable costs in question. However, D.C. maintained the correctness of its accounting procedures for review in the then current quarter ending December 31, 1986.

As a result of the review for the quarter ended December 31, 1986, Elcock & Company expressed the opinion that D.C. in respect of the specific foreign contract should not recognize income on the basis of the relationship of incurred costs to date to estimated total costs, since in their view the unusually high costs of materials and the relatively limited installation effort created an imbalance in the "incurred costs" which did not reflect a fair basis for determination of the percentage of completion of the contract, for which the major installation effort is not scheduled until subsequent to March 31, 1987.

They recommended that, in the specific case of the contract in question, performance could more properly be reflected by determining percentage of completion on the basis of the relationship of labor hours expended to date to total estimated labor hours. They suggested that an approximately equivalent result would be obtained were income to be recognized on a "cost incurred" basis by excluding from such costs all materials not at the job site, by including as costs only the proportionate periodic depreciation applicable to capital assets to be utilized during the life of the contract, and by recognizing 50% of the anticipated contract profit relative to the costs of materials delivered to the job site but not yet installed.

Elcock & Company, in a meeting with the Board of Directors on February 5, 1987, informed D.C. that should the presently known fact pattern relating to the specific contract in question remain unchanged, they would not be able to express an unqualified opinion on the March 31, 1987 consolidated financial statements since, in their opinion, the accounting which D.C. proposed to follow during such fiscal year for the recognition of profit on that contract is not in accordance with generally accepted accounting principles. That opinion was reaffirmed by letter dated February 14, 1987 to the Chairman of the Board of Directors.

D.C. has not made the adjustments requested by Elcock & Company since, in its opinion, the adjustments are inconsistent with the substance of the transaction. It was anticipated that the purchase of materials and shipment to the foreign project site would be required before installation efforts could commence. The costs of the materials, delivery, and freight have been established by fixed price contracts with suppliers obtained by D.C. To exclude the requested portion of the incurred costs would, in D.C.'s opinion, be a departure from the procedure by which D.C. recognizes income and in its opinion would not result in a more meaningful allocation of income to the fiscal periods involved. Independent accounting opinion from Peabody & Company has been obtained concurring with D.C.'s accounting treatment.

Elcock & Company's reports on the financial statements for the fiscal years ended March 31, 1985 and 1986 did not contain any adverse opinion or disclaimer of opinion or qualifications as to uncertainty, audit scope or accounting principles.

Recent Financial Statements

The 1986 Report to Shareholders from D.C. management is reproduced in Exhibit 3. A condensed version of D.C.'s 1986 Annual Report and fiscal 1987 third quarter (12/31/86) 10-Q (financial report to the S.E.C.) are provided in **Exhibit 4.**

EXHIBIT 3   **July 7, 1986, Report to Shareholders from D.C. Electrical, Inc.
Management in 1986 Annual Report**

TO OUR STOCKHOLDERS

D.C. Electrical set new records in earnings and volume in fiscal 1986. That performance accompanied by a record backlog at year end was achieved in a period when the nation's overall construction industry continued to be beset by recession.

Contract income reached $109,900,000 up 14% (of which one-fourth of the increase was due to the acquisition of Systems Electric Company Inc.) from last year's record of $96,000,000. Earnings per share increased to $1.81 up 16% from $1.56. Net income compared with last year was $2,463,000 to $2,147,000 an increase of 15%.

Backlog of $100,000,000 as we began fiscal 1987 was 37% ahead of last year's record $73,000,000.

Cash dividends totalled $.47, an increase of 34% from the previous year. This reflects the policy of the Board to declare quarterly cash dividends in relation to D.C.'s earnings, financial condition, and other factors.

Even as the country began to throw off the most troublesome of the recent recessions and real activity such as industrial production and employment began to move up, the construction industry this year remained depressed.

Nationally, construction expenditures in 1985 fell from the previous year. Real unit volume decreased even more. In the private sector, cautious attitudes discouraged new capital investment. In the public sector, the problems of our major cities had a negative impact on raising funds for construction programs. As a result, competition intensified for fewer available jobs.

D.C. did well in this environment for a number of reasons. The Company continued to obtain contracts for projects of increasing size and complexity. Gains in contract income were recorded in energy/utilities, environmental controls work, water treatment, public transit, and the institutional sectors. These types of projects required major commitments of resources that tended to limit the number of qualified bidders.

The mix of our contracts also contributed to our growth and stability. As major joint venture projects, begun a few years ago, were completed, they were more than balanced by new joint venture projects and sub-contracts for the Company's own account.

Market recognition of D.C.'s technical capabilities and management experience benefited us.

Productivity gains by the Company kept job costs under control. The depressed state of the construction industry, generally, made ample supplies of materials and skilled workers available, which resulted in good job movement. Another factor in our improved performance was the contribution to profit from the new branches. New domestic branches opened since FY 1983 have helped to contribute to our return on stockholders' equity as well as to our contract volume and backlog. Expansion has given us additional geographic diversity by providing new centers for business in the West, Midwest, and Northeast in addition to our traditional presence in the Middle Atlantic States and the South. At this time we have 19 domestic branches operating, including the New Orleans branch recently opened in the South.

In international operations, D.C. International Corp., a wholly owned subsidiary, received a major contract for overseas construction late in the fourth quarter. This subsidiary, created in August 1984, should begin to make a contribution to profit during the present fiscal year.

D.C.'s contract income shows growing regional diversity for the past five years.

Current Year

For D.C. to date in fiscal 1987, business has been good based on contracts awarded. Major contract awards have been made for energy projects, environmental pollution and wastewater treatment control facilities, and industrial expansion and renovation. We have recently received a contract in commercial construction involving a major office structure. In the public sector, while government activity has increased, projects for the most part are of limited size.

Overseas, the race by the non-industrial nations to achieve self-sufficiency through industrialization and to raise living standards in line with those of the established industrial nations, offers excellent opportunities for this Company.

EXHIBIT 3   (continued)

D.C., of course, must continue to be able to operate at efficient costs and to maintain standards of performance as we grow and extend our operations around the country and the world. This is not an easy task. However, our selectivity in the projects we undertake and the contractors we work with remain the keystone of our operating policy. In addition, we intend to continue tight controls over every aspect of our business, wherever it may be.

Financial Condition

The Company's financial position at year end was strong. Dividends were increased again for the current fiscal year by the Board of Directors. The quarterly dividend payable August 25, 1986 to stockholders of record July 26, 1986 goes from 12¢ in the preceding quarter to 14¢ per common share. Complete details of the financial developments for fiscal 1986 are found in the Financial Review.

Edward P. Johnson, Sr.   John A. Martin
Chairman   President

Financial Review

Operating achievements continued to have a positive effect on D.C.'s financial strength resulting in the third dividend increase in as many years. Some of the other noteworthy developments included:

Sales for the year increased to $109,900,000 from $96,000,000 a year earlier, an increase of 14% (of which increase approximately one-fourth is attributable to the acquisition of Systems Electric Company, Inc., January 31, 1985).

Earnings per share were $1.81 compared with $1.56 a year earlier, a 16% advance.

Direct costs were kept under control as gross margins improved to 16% compared with 13.4% a year earlier. Along with material cost controls, this, in part, reflects a return to a more stable materials market, ample availability of labor and continued increased job productivity.

General and administrative costs as a percentage of contract income (exclusive of joint venture income) increased to 12.2% in fiscal 1986 from 11.1% a year earlier. In fiscal 1986, approximately $1,380,000 of general and administrative costs were attributable to the Company's international subsidiary which began to seek contracts in fiscal 1985; excluding this item the above percentage of 12.2% would have been 10.8%.

Cash dividends increased to $.47 per share from $.35 per share in fiscal 1986. The Board of Directors on May 5, 1986 voted a payment of $.14 payable in the second quarter of fiscal 1987.

Cash and certificates of deposit were $4,447,000 of which $3,600,000 is currently in certificates of deposit. However, interest income on this available cash was reduced during the year as the rate of return on the certificates declined.

The current ratio (excluding deferred income taxes) was 2.7 to 1 in fiscal 1986 compared with 2.9 to 1 in the prior year.

Short-term notes payable to banks for working capital purposes at year end were $1,000,000. The Company's unsecured line of credit, at prime rates, currently remains at $4,000,000.

Richard A. Clay
Vice President–Finance

EXHIBIT 4   **Condensed Version of D.C. Electrical Inc.'s Fiscal 1986 Annual Report and Fiscal 1987 Third Quarter Report**

D.C. Electrical, Inc. Consolidated Statement of Income and Retained Earnings—Five Years Ended March 31, 1986, and Nine Months Ended December 31, 1985, and 1986 ($ in thousands)

	Year Ended March 31,					(Unaudited) Nine Months Ended December 31,	
	1982	1983	1984	1985[g]	1986[h]	1985	1986
Contract income[a]	$ 63,433	$ 70,489	$ 79,187	$ 96,036	$ 109,911	$ 78,710	$ 96,017
Cost and expenses[a, b, c, d]							
Direct contract	55,131	60,247	68,205	83,197	92,311	66,164	81,047
General and administrative	5,927	6,626	7,171	8,243	11,649	8,857	9,922
Depreciation	464	396	347	377	515	355	444
Minority interests in profit of consolidated joint ventures	—	—	—	—	289	—	418
	61,521	67,370	75,723	91,817	104,764	75,375	91,831
	1,911	3,119	3,465	4,219	5,148	3,334	4,186
Interest income (expense), net	(89)	(78)	(13)	253	(18)	48	(113)
Income before income taxes and extraordinary charge	1,822	3,041	3,451	4,472	5,130	3,383	4,073
Provision for income taxes:[e]							
Current	—	—	95	30	87	—	—
Deferred	900	1,555	1,781	2,325	2,667	1,727	1,822
	900	1,555	1,781	2,325	2,667	1,727	1,822
Income before extraordinary charge	922	1,486	1,670	2,147	2,463	1,656	2,251
Extraordinary charge[f]	(395)	—	—	—	—	—	—
Net income	528	1,486	1,670	2,147	2,463	1,565	2,251
Retained earnings—beginning of year	2,312	2,484	3,730	5,123	6,790	6,790	8,612
Stock dividends	(356)	(240)	—	—	—	—	—
Cash dividends	—	—	(277)	(481)	(641)	(477)	(662)
Retained earnings—end of year	$ 2,484	$ 3,730	$ 5,123	$ 6,790	$ 8,612	$ 7,968	$ 10,201

EXHIBIT 4   (continued)

	1982	1983	1984	1985[g]	1986[h]	(Unaudited) Nine Months Ended December 31, 1985	1986
			Year Ended March 31,				
Per share of common stock:[i]							
Income before extraordinary charge	$ .66	$ 1.06	$ 1.20	$ 1.56	$ 1.81	$ 1.21	$ 1.55
Extraordinary charge[f]	(.28)	—	—	—	—	—	—
Net income	$ .38	$ 1.06	$ 1.20	$ 1.56	$ 1.81	$ 1.21	$ 1.55
Cash dividends..................	$ —	$ —	$ .20	$ .35	$ .47	$ .35	$ .45
Shares of stock used to calculate earnings per share of common stock[i]	$1,396,489	$1,397,071	$1,386,405	$1,376,980	$1,363,541	$1,363,882	$1,451,874

[a]The consolidated statement of income includes the Company's proportionate share of the operations of joint ventures in which it does not have a majority share (generally 20% to 50%) as follows:

	1982	1983	1984	1985	1986
			Year Ended March 31,		
Contract income	$11,167,000	$15,227,000	$17,654,000	$21,737,000	$14,484,000
Direct contract costs................	9,676,000	13,712,000	15,208,000	18,434,000	11,822,000
Equity in joint venture income..........	$1,491,000	$1,515,000	$2,446,000	$3,303,000	$2,662,000

[b]Pension expense was approximately $1,700,000, $1,900,000, $2,375,000, $3,126,000, and $4,088,000 for the years ended March 31, 1982, 1983, 1984, 1985, and 1986, respectively, for employees covered by union pension plans and, commencing in 1984, for salaried employees under a Company plan.

[c]The amounts of bonuses and profit-sharing costs under an informal discretionary plan were $283,000, $364,000, $677,000, $519,000, and $634,000 for the years ended March 31, 1982, 1983, 1984, 1985, and 1986, respectively.

[d]The provision for doubtful accounts was $82,000, $404,000, $59,000, $117,000, and $10,000 in 1982, 1983, 1984, 1985, and 1986, respectively.

[e]The provisions for income taxes exceed the amount of tax determined by applying the U.S. federal statutory income tax rate to income before income taxes, principally due to the inclusion of state income taxes in the provision.

[f]In March 1982, the Company incurred an extraordinary net loss of $395,000, after related tax benefits of $555,000.

[g]The outstanding capital stock of D.C. Midwest, Inc. (formerly Systems Electric Co., Inc.) was acquired by Company, Inc. as of January 31, 1985, for cash and notes of $573,000 in a transaction accounted for as a purchase. If D.C. Midwest had been combined for the entire year ended March 31, 1985, contract income and net income on a pro-forma basis, using D.C. Midwest's year ended September 30, 1984, would have been $107,848,000 and $1,261,000 ($.92 per share), respectively. D.C. Midwest had contract income of $2,830,000 for its six months ended March 31, 1985, and a net loss of $835,000. The net loss includes a $950,000 charge to operations prior to its acquisition as a result of D.C. Midwest's former parent having provided guaranty of performance on a joint venture entered into in 1982.

[h]D.C. International Corp., incorporated in August 1984, engages in contracting activities outside the United States and through May 1986 has been awarded several significant contracts. For fiscal 1986, D.C. International's contract income was $853,000 and its loss, after-tax benefit, was $582,000 ($.43 per share). Activities prior to fiscal 1986 were not significant.

[i]Net income per share of common stock has been computed on the basis of the weighted average number of shares outstanding during the periods, including applicable equivalent shares under the stock option plan, adjusted for the 5% stock dividend in 1982 and the 3% stock dividend in 1983. Warrants to purchase 20,079 shares, which expired in August 1984, were not considered as common stock equivalents since such treatment would be anti-dilutive for the years ended March 31, 1982, 1983 and 1984. Certain other options were not considered as common stock equivalents since they would be anti-dilutive or have an immaterial effect on net income per share.

[j]The amounts of material and supplies inventory were $314,000, $463,000, $473,000, $573,000, $1,085,000 and $813,000 at March 31, 1981, 1982, 1983, 1984, 1985 and 1986, respectively.

EXHIBIT 4   **(continued) D.C. Electrical, Inc. Consolidated Balance Sheets—March 31, 1985, March 31, 1986, and December 31, 1986 ($ in thousands)**

	March 31, 1985	*March 31, 1986*	*(Unaudited) December 31, 1985*	*(Unaudited) December 31, 1986*
Assets				
Current assets:				
Cash	$ 3,116	$ 4,447	$ 3,220	$ 3,888
Contract receivables, including unbilled				
retainage due after one year (Note 1) . .	17,673	23,213	18,748	28,942
Less allowance for doubtful accounts . . .	490	490	490	590
Net contract receivables	$17,183	$22,723	$18,258	$28,352
Equity in unconsolidated joint venture				
(Note 6)	3,726	3,945	5,503	5,444
Material and supplies inventory	1,085	813	689	726
Other	293	178	151	159
Total current assets	$25,403	$32,106	$27,821	$38,569
Property and equipment, at cost:				
Land and buildings	1,486	1,922	1,922	2,477
Furniture, machinery and equipment	4,484	5,162	5,025	5,591
	$ 5,970	$ 7,084	$ 6,947	$ 8,068
Less accumulated depreciation	3,491	3,912	3,938	4,311
Net property and equipment	$ 2,479	$ 3,172	$ 3,009	$ 3,757
Other assets	449	621	560	1,229
Total assets	$28,330	$35,899	$31,390	$43,555
Liabilities and Stockholders' Equity				
Current liabilities:				
Note payable to bank (Note 5)	$ 970	$ 1,000	$ 1,000	$ 4,000
Accounts payable	4,855	6,168	4,919	7,180
Accrued liabilities	1,495	1,743	240	922
Advance payments on uncompleted				
contracts	1,131	2,349	2,517	1,752
Installment obligation	250	300	300	300
Minority interest in consolidated joint				
ventures	—	289	150	407
Total current liabilities before deferred				
income taxes	$ 8,701	$11,849	$ 9,126	$14,561
Deferred income taxes (Note 4)	9,270	11,710	10,997	12,527
Total current liabilities	$17,971	$23,559	$20,123	$27,088

EXHIBIT 4   (continued)

	March 31, 1985	March 31, 1986	*(Unaudited)* December 31, 1985	*(Unaudited)* December 31, 1986
Noncurrent liabilities:				
Accrued deferred compensation	230	342	272	459
Mortgages payable, generally over a 25-year period	53	424	53	479
Other (primarily non-current deferred income taxes)	300	—	—	1,094
Total non-current liabilities	$ 583	$ 766	$ 325	$ 2,032
Stockholders' equity (Note 7):				
Common stock, $.50 par value; 1,399,782 shares issued at March 31, 1985, and 1986, and December 31, 1985, 1,554,782 shares issued at December 31, 1986	700	700	700	777
Capital in excess of par value	2,470	2,464	2,464	3,640
Retained earnings (Note 6)	6,790	8,612	7,968	10,201
	$ 9,960	$11,775	$11,132	$14,619
Less cost of shares in common stock in treasury; 35,616 shares at March 31, 1985, 37,696 at March 31, 1986, and 35,796 shares at December 31, 1985, 34,571 shares at December 31, 1986 . .	183	202	190	183
Total stockholders' equity	$ 9,777	$11,574	$10,942	$14,435
Total liabilities and stockholders' equity . . .	$28,330	$35,899	$31,390	$43,555

See accompanying notes.

EXHIBIT 4 **(continued) D.C. Electrical, Inc. Consolidated Statement of Changes in Financial Position—Five Years Ended March 31, 1986 and Nine Months Ended December 31, 1985 and 1985 ($ in thousands)**

	Year Ended March 31,					(Unaudited) Nine Months Ended December 31,	
	1982	*1983*	*1984*	*1985*	*1986*	*1985*	*1986*
Source:							
Income before extraordinary charge.....................	$ 922	$1,486	$1,670	$2,147	$2,463	$1,656	$2,251
Charges against income not involving capital in the current period:							
Depreciation....................................	464	396	347	377	515	355	444
Deferred compensation	—	—	76	93	113	—	—
Other	20	—	—	—	—	—	—
Working capital provided from operations, excluding extraordinary charge	$ 1,407	$1,882	$2,094	$2,617	$3,090	$2,011	$2,695
Working capital provided from extraordinary charge (net extraordinary charge—$395,000 charges not involving the use of working capital—$522,000)....................	127	—	—	—	—	—	—
Increase in long-term debt	2,000	1,000	—	355	400	—	1,266
Proceeds from sale of common stock....................	—	—	—	—	—	—	1,272
Proceeds from disposal of interests related to real estate partnership	2,525	—	—	—	—	—	—
Exercise of stock options	—	—	—	—	18	—	—
Disposition of property and equipment	18	26	33	8	34	—	—
Sale of treasury stock	18	—	—	—	—	—	—
Decrease in other assets	—	111	—	—	—	—	—
	$ 6,096	$3,019	$2,126	$2,981	$3,542	$2,011	$5,233
Application:							
Cash dividends....................................	$ —	$ —	$ 277	$ 481	$ 641	$ 477	$ 662
Property and equipment	168	318	345	1,749	1,241	884	1,028
Reduction in long-term liabilities......................	1,549	910	575	2	329	258	—
Purchase of treasury stock	—	63	30	90	43	—	—
Investment and long-term receivables	980	—	—	—	—	—	—
Increase in other assets.............................	2	—	119	136	173	126	609
	$ 2,697	$1,291	$1,346	$2,458	$2,427	$1,745	$2,299
Increase in working capital...........................	$ 3,398	$1,728	$ 780	$ 523	$1,116	$ 266	$2,934

316 *D.C. Electrical, Inc.*

EXHIBIT 4 (continued)

	Year Ended March 31,					(Unaudited) Nine Months Ended December 31,	
	1982	*1983*	*1984*	*1985*	*1986*	*1985*	*1986*
Changes in components of working capital:							
Increase (decrease) in current assets:							
Cash	$ 554	$ 858	$1,027	$ 193	$1,332	$ 104	$ (559)
Contract receivables	(2,277)	1,727	1,005	4,624	5,540	1,075	5,629
Equity in unconsolidated joint ventures	1,294	(18)	1,142	656	219	1,777	1,499
Material and supplies inventory	149	10	100	512	(272)	(396)	(87)
Other	184	(137)	138	18	(115)	(152)	(19)
	$ (96)	$2,441	$3,412	$6,002	$6,704	$2,418	$6,463
Increase (decrease) in current liabilities:							
Notes payable to banks	($1,900)	$ (500)	$ —	$ 970	$ 30	$ 30	$3,000
Accounts payable	(1,445)	109	271	1,638	1,313	64	1,012
Accrued liabilities	144	(752)	720	(174)	248	(1,255)	(831)
Advance payments on uncompleted contracts	(639)	52	282	544	1,218	1,386	(597)
Installment obligation	—	—	—	250	50	50	—
Long-term debt due within one year	1	272	(291)	—	—	—	—
Minority interests in consolidated joint ventures	—	—	—	—	289	150	118
Deferred income taxes	345	1,532	1,648	2,251	2,440	1,727	817
	($3,494)	$ 713	$2,631	$5,480	$5,588	$2,152	$3,529
Increase in working capital	$ 3,398	$1,728	$ 780	$ 523	$1,116	$ 266	$2,934

See accompanying notes.

EXHIBIT 4   (continued)

---

1. SUMMARY OF SIGNIFICANT ACCOUNTING POLICIES

Consolidation.   The consolidated financial statements, from which appropriate eliminations have been made for intercompany transactions, include the accounts of D.C. Electrical Inc., its wholly-owned subsidiaries, D.C. Midwest, Inc. (formerly Systems Electric Co., Inc.) and D.C. International Corp.; and joint ventures in which the Company has a majority share. Other joint ventures (in which the Company's share is generally 20% to 50%) are accounted for on the equity method and contract income and costs and expenses in the consolidated statement of income include the Company's proportionate share of these items from such ventures.

Accounting for contracts.   Income from contracts, including joint venture contracts, is recorded on the percentage-of-completion method utilizing engineering estimates when experience is sufficient to project final results with reasonable accuracy. Under this method there is included in income that proportion of the total contract price which the cost of the work completed bears to the total estimated cost of each contract. When a loss is anticipated on a contract the entire amount of the estimated loss is provided for in the current period. Contract receivables have been adjusted by the following amounts to reflect income on the percentage-of-completion method:

At March 31,

1982	1983	1984	1985	1986
($193,000)	$211,000	($594,000)	($341,000)	($2,260,000)

Pursuant to industry practice, unbilled contract retainage is classified as a current asset and approximately $2,200,000 relates to contracts with anticipated completion dates after March 31, 1987. The following amounts of unbilled retainage are included in contract receivables:

At March 31,

1982	1983	1984	1985	1986
$2,923,000	$3,204,000	$3,404,000	$4,862,000	$6,841,000

Income from contracts is determined for federal and state income tax purposes under the completed contract method. Deferred income taxes, arising principally from the difference in contract accounting for book and tax purposes, relate to items included in current assets and accordingly are classified as a current liability.

Material and supplies inventory.   Inventory is stated at the lower of cost, determined on the first-in, first-out method, or market.

Depreciation, amortization, and maintenance and repairs.   Depreciation is determined principally on the straight-line basis, over estimated useful lives of 25 to 40 years for buildings and 3 to 10 years for furniture, machinery, and equipment.

The cost of ordinary maintenance and repairs and minor renewals of property and equipment are charged to income. Major replacements or renewals are capitalized and the items replaced are retired.

Upon sale or retirement of property and equipment, the cost and accumulated depreciation are removed from the respective accounts and any gain or loss is included in income for the year.

Pensions.   There is a non-contributory pension plan for salaried employees and also defined contributions are made to pension plans for employees covered under union agreements. There is no liability for past service costs for employees under the union plans. Pension costs for the salaried employees' plan are accrued and funded currently, including amortization of past service costs over 30 years.

Exhibit 4 **(continued)**

2. ACQUISITION

See Note (g) to Consolidated Statement of Income for the acquisition of D.C. Midwest, Inc. (formerly Systems Electric Co., Inc.) as of January 31, 1985.

3. FOREIGN OPERATIONS

See Note (h) to Consolidated Statement of Income for information with respect to foreign operations.

4. INCOME TAXES

On the basis of its tax returns, the Company has net operating loss carryforwards at March 31, 1986 of approximately $2,200,000. These carryforwards, resulting from the difference in contract accounting for book and tax purposes (see Note 1), are available to reduce taxable income generally during fiscal years ending through March 31, 1991.

In addition, there are pre-acquisition operating loss carryforwards for tax purposes of approximately $1,000,000 attributable to D.C. Midwest which can be used only against its separate taxable income and which generally expire ratably over fiscal years ending in 1988. Approximately $430,000 of such operating losses have been recognized by D.C. Midwest since date of acquisition for financial accounting purposes resulting in a tax benefit of $215,000 which has been credited in consolidation to the cost of property and equipment at date of acquisition of D.C. Midwest.

Based upon anticipated future activities, the Company estimates the cash outlay for income taxes in 1987 will exceed income tax expense in that year by approximately $2,500,000. Such excess has been estimated on assumptions as to future events which are expected to result in future recognition for tax purposes of gross profits from completion of contracts which have been previously recognized for financial accounting purposes on the percentage of completion basis.

5. NOTE PAYABLE TO BANK

This consists of borrowings under a $4,000,000 unsecured line of credit with a bank, entered into in May 1985, of which $3,000,000 is available for general working capital purposes and the remaining $1,000,000 is available on a short term, specific transactional basis at the discretion of the bank. Additionally, a $300,000 limit is available under the line to be used for letters of credit issued on behalf of the Company's subsidiary, D.C. International Corp. Outstanding letters of credit under this provision reduce the amount available under the working capital portion of the line. The line bears interest at a rate equal to the bank's published "prime" rate. There is no formal compensating balance arrangement with the bank, but it is understood that the Company will maintain balances at the bank in an amount deemed sufficient by the bank; such amount has not been defined in terms of dollars or percentage of credit in use or available.

6. UNCONSOLIDATED JOINT VENTURES

Condensed combined balance sheet data for these joint ventures are shown below at March 31, 1986:

Assets, principally current, including $1,250,000 unbilled receivables	$13,555,000
Current liabilities	3,822,000
Total venture equity (Company share—$3,945,000)	$ 9,733,000

EXHIBIT 4   (continued)

At March 31, 1986, retained earnings of the Company include undistributed joint venture income, less applicable income taxes, from these ventures of approximately $1,050,000.

7. STOCKHOLDERS' EQUITY

The Company has agreements with two key officers that in the event of their death it will purchase shares at market value, of the Company's common stock held by their respective estates up to an aggregate of $1,125,000. The Company presently carries insurance policies on the lives of these officers in the face amount of $1,125,000.

The Company's "Qualified Stock Option Plan" for officers and key employees provides for five year options at 100% of fair market value at date of grant. The options become exercisable as to 25% of the granted shares each year on a cumulative basis, commencing one year after grant, except exercisable shares not exercised after three years expire.

8. PENSION COSTS

The actuarially computed present value of vested benefits at the most recent valuation date exceeded the pension fund and accruals at March 31, 1986 by approximately $700,000 for the salaried employees' plan. The unfunded past service cost under the plan based on information as of the valuation date was estimated to be $1,040,000.

9. RENEGOTIATION

Certain of the Company's contracts are subject to renegotiation. In the opinion of management no excess profits have been realized.

Questions

1. Before beginning your analysis of the company's long-term contract accounting and the company's financial statement data, try to understand the kind of company D.C. Electrical is and the nature of the industry in which it operates. What are the key success factors in this industry? _____ How do companies in this industry earn a profit? _____

2. What is the company's strategy? _____ How successful does management believe the company has been in the past? _____ Will be in the future? _____

3. Do the financial statements reflect management's views? _____

4. How liquid is D.C. Electrical? _____ How do you rate the quality of its earnings? _____ Does the company's funds flow statement reflect your views?[1] _____ Would an alternative format capture your perception of the company's liquidity and earnings quality? _____

5. Would you be willing to increase D.C. Electrical's line of credit from $5 to $11 million? Why? _____

---

[1]Note that D.C. Electrical published a changes-in-financial-position statement in 1986.

CASE

10-2

Accounting for Frequent Fliers

By 1991, almost all U.S. airline companies offered frequent flier programs to their passengers. Under these programs, passengers could become members of a program where the miles they flew would be recorded and accumulated to earn free future flights. The proliferation and growth of frequent flier programs created concerns about the proper way to account for and report them in financial reports. The airlines, the Securities and Exchange Commission (SEC), the American Institute of Certified Public Accountants (AICPA), and the Financial Accounting Standards Board (FASB) had each voiced concerns about measuring the expenses and reporting airlines' obligations under frequent flier programs.

The percentage of revenue passenger miles (the number of miles flown by revenue passengers including free-flight–award passengers; computed by multiplying the number of revenue passengers by the miles they have flown) flown under free travel awards was less than 5% for all U.S. airlines combined. However, on some routes for some airlines (U.S. mainland to Hawaii, for example) the percentage of revenue passenger miles represented by free flights exceeded 12%. And there was some evidence that the problem was growing.

Background of Frequent Flier Programs

American Airlines first introduced frequent flier programs in 1981. Initially the program was meant to be a promotional gimmick designed to attract more customers. The program's immediate success in generating repeat business shocked the industry. This success forced other carriers to introduce their own free mileage programs, each promising better and better rewards to customers who would sign up. Through agreements with hotels, auto rental companies, and financial institutions, airlines made it possible for program participants to earn free miles by choosing where to stay, what auto to rent, or what credit card to use. By 1988, frequent flier programs were so popular that

Susan S. Harmeling, MBA '91, prepared this case under the supervision of Professor William Bruns as the basis for class discussion rather than to illustrate either effective or ineffective handling of an administrative situation.

airlines owed more than 3 million round-trip domestic tickets to their free mileage program members. These tickets amounted to a minimum of 5.4 billion free miles according to one published report.

The question was how, when, and whether participants would use their free miles. The worst scenario for the airline industry would have all their free fliers cashing in over a short period of time, taking up revenue-producing seats on many flights. In 1984, for example, Pan Am forced frequent fliers to use their awards or lose them, and the result was chaos at the check-in counter and a $50 million revenue loss. By 1991, all airlines limited the number of free travel award seats on some flights and used "blackout" dates during peak holiday travel periods when very limited or no free travel awards could be used. However, controls such as these had to be used cautiously to avoid diluting the promotional value of the programs. Members of a program who had earned a free flight but who then found it hard to schedule could easily switch their allegiance to another airline.

The Accounting Issue

By 1990, all the major airlines offered similar frequent flier programs. Members of a program would receive miles credited to their accounts based on the actual miles flown on the particular airline. In some cases, additional bonus miles were credited to members flying first or business class and, in certain circumstances, for flying certain routes or during periods when special promotions were offered.

The use of free mileage from frequent flier programs represented between 2% and 6% of total revenue passenger miles for each airline offering such awards in 1990. Based on the issuance of free travel awards to qualified members, coupled with program characteristics and the use of "blackout" dates during peak holiday periods, airlines generally did not consider the liability of free travel awards to be material.

In contrast, the airlines' auditors were concerned that growth of the programs might eventually force airlines to change the way in which they accounted for free miles. As more and more tickets were being given away, and as paying passengers were being replaced on flights by free fliers, a "new reality" might soon have to be reflected on the balance sheet and income statement.

The AICPA considered new rules that would likely force the airlines to change their accounting practices in 1988. When they did not take action, many observers thought the FASB might take up the problem, but the FASB did not add the issue to its agenda. Ultimately, the SEC issued a rule that required the airlines to disclose in their filings with the SEC, beginning in 1991, the number of free trips taken by frequent flier participants.

United Air Lines, Inc.

One of the largest frequent flier programs was that of United Air Lines (United). Travel awards redeemed in 1990 by members of the United's program totaled 1.2 million free trips, an increase of 200,000 over the prior year. By early 1991, United had enrolled more than 13.3 million members in its frequent flier program and was adding 130,000 new members each month. **Exhibits 1** and **2** contain some disclosures of financial and flight data taken from the 1990 Annual Report and Form 10K filed with the SEC by United in early 1991.

EXHIBIT 1   United Air Lines, Inc. Statement of Consolidated Financial Position (in thousands, except share data)

	December 31,	
	1990	*1989*
Assets		
Current assets:		
Cash and cash equivalents	$ 221,401	$ 465,181
Short-term investments	973,695	957,312
Receivables, less allowance for doubtful accounts (1990—$13,129; 1989—$11,719)	912,663	888,015
Aircraft fuel, spare parts, and supplies, less obsolescence allowance (1990—$57,406; 1989—$55,493)	322,866	248,581
Prepaid expenses	209,435	178,711
	2,640,060	2,737,800
Operating property and equipment:		
Owned—		
Flight equipment..	5,677,428	5,217,535
Advances on flight equipment purchase contracts	641,281	427,616
Other property and equipment	1,747,415	1,537,401
	8,066,124	7,182,552
Accumulated depreciation and amortization	(3,565,590)	(3,557,440)
	4,500,534	3,625,112
Capital leases—		
Flight equipment..	420,452	420,452
Other property and equipment	100,337	101,015
	520,789	521,467
Accumulated amortization	(272,394)	(248,117)
	248,395	273,350
	4,748,929	3,898,462
Other assets:		
Intangibles, less accumulated amortization (1990—$55,023; 1989—$42,074)	128,884	175,780
Deferred income taxes	49,193	71,022
Other	426,755	323,628
	604,832	570,430
	$7,993,821	$7,206,692

Notes are omitted.

Exhibit 1   (continued)

	December 31,	
	1990	*1989*
Liabilities and Shareholders' Equity		
Current liabilities:		
Short-term borrowings	$ 447,260	$ 446,276
Long-term debt maturing within one year	61,607	60,928
Current obligations under capital leases	27,174	22,863
Advance ticket sales	842,665	660,639
Accounts payable	552,780	596,435
Accrued salaries, wages, and benefits	675,547	585,983
Accrued aircraft rent	380,775	181,997
Accrued income taxes	86,945	62,656
Other accrued liabilities	682,514	606,046
	3,757,267	3,223,823
Long-term debt	**887,749**	945,667
Long-term obligations under capital leases	**361,246**	388,419
Other liabilities and deferred credits:		
Deferred pension liability	367,958	363,781
Deferred gains on sale and leaseback transactions	922,862	655,657
Other	24,493	62,945
	1,315,313	1,082,383
Redeemable preferred stock:		
5½% cumulative prior preferred stock, $100 par value	**1,590**	2,067
Common shareholders' equity:		
Common stock, $5 par value; authorized, 125,000,000 shares; issued, 23,467,880 shares in 1990 and 23,419,953 shares in 1989	117,339	117,100
Additional capital invested	52,391	47,320
Retained earnings	1,620,885	1,526,534
Unearned compensation	(8,053)	(14,538)
Common stock held in treasury — 1,582,900 shares in 1990 and 1,585,400 shares in 1989	(111,906)	(112,083)
	1,670,656	1,564,333
Commitments and contingent liabilities		
	$7,993,821	$7,206,692

Notes are omitted.

EXHIBIT 1 (continued)

	Year Ended December 31,		
	1990	*1989*	*1988*
Operating Revenues:			
Passenger	$ 9,633,627	$8,536,000	$7,723,139
Cargo	592,872	521,274	509,639
Contract services and other	810,978	736,361	748,965
	11,037,477	9,793,635	8,981,743
Operating Expenses:			
Salaries and related costs	3,549,981	3,158,414	2,837,599
Aircraft fuel	1,811,417	1,352,511	1,179,571
Commissions	1,718,902	1,335,537	1,101,755
Depreciation and amortization	559,585	516,989	518,387
Purchased services	658,781	614,834	572,933
Rentals and landing fees	829,311	574,425	408,228
Aircraft maintenance materials and repairs	388,139	348,602	293,522
Food and beverages	241,583	213,693	193,367
Advertising and promotion	203,215	200,711	206,493
Personnel expenses	202,176	185,000	158,351
Other	910,663	828,379	846,609
	11,073,754	9,329,096	8,316,815
Earnings (loss) from operations	(36,277)	464,539	664,928
Other deductions (income):			
Interest expense	192,228	221,186	245,306
Interest capitalized	(71,323)	(51,884)	(30,983)
Interest income	(122,615)	(120,913)	(100,873)
Equity in earnings of Covia Partnership	(16,220)	(45,441)	(87,460)
Gain on sale of Covia Partnership interests	—	—	(393,006)
Net gains on disposition of property	(285,846)	(106,422)	(13,989)
Other, net	103,131	29,502	57,145
	(200,645)	(73,972)	(323,860)
Earnings from continuing operations before income taxes	164,368	538,511	988,788
Provision for income taxes	69,903	214,330	388,874
Earnings from continuing operations	94,465	324,181	599,914
Discontinued operations:			
Earnings from discontinued operations, less income taxes	—	—	457
Gain on sales of discontinued operations, less income taxes	—	—	523,929
Net earnings . . . . $	94,465	$ 324,181	$1,124,300
Net earnings per share:			
Continuing operations . . . . $	4.33	$ 14.96	$ 20.20
Discontinued operations	—	—	17.67
Net earnings . . . . $	4.33	$ 14.96	$ 37.87

Notes are omitted.

EXHIBIT 2   Selected Operating Statistics for United Air Lines, Inc.

	Year Ended December 31				
	1990	*1989*	*1988*	*1987*	*1986*
Revenue Aircraft Miles (millions)[a]	597	552	543	553	507
Revenue Aircraft Departures	654,555	621,111	626,809	670,790	627,943
Available Seat Miles (millions)[b]	114,995	104,547	101,721	101,454	91,409
Revenue Passenger Miles (millions)[c]	76,137	69,639	69,101	66,348	59,312
Revenue Passengers (thousands)	57,598	54,859	56,175	55,089	50,419
Average Passenger Journey (miles)	1,322	1,269	1,230	1,204	1,176
Average Flight Length (miles)	912	888	866	824	807
Passenger Load Factor[d]	66.2%	66.6%	67.9%	65.4%	64.9%
Breakeven Load Factor[e]	66.5%	63.0%	62.2%	63.0%	64.1%
Average Yield Per Revenue Passenger Mile[f]	12.6¢	12.2¢	11.1¢	10.3¢	10.0¢
Cost Per Available Seat Mile[g]	9.6¢	8.9¢	8.2¢	7.9¢	7.7¢
Average Price Per Gallon of Jet Fuel	80.4¢	63.6¢	56.0¢	57.8¢	56.2¢
Average Fare Per Revenue Passenger	$167.26	$155.60	$137.48	$124.45	$118.17
Average Daily Utilization of Each Aircraft (hours: minutes)[h]	8:14	8:09	8:29	9:04	8:46

[a]"Revenue aircraft miles" means the number of miles flown in revenue producing service.

[b]"Available seat miles" represents the number of seats available for passengers multiplied by the number of miles those seats are flown.

[c]"Revenue passenger miles" represents the number of miles flown by revenue passengers including frequent flier awards.

[d]"Passenger load factor" represents revenue passenger miles divided by available seat miles.

[e]"Breakeven load factor" represents the number of revenue passenger miles at which operating earnings would have been zero (based on the actual average yield) divided by available seat miles.

[f]"Average yield per revenue passenger mile" represents the average revenue received for each mile a revenue passenger is carried.

[g]"Cost per available seat mile" represents operating expenses divided by available seat miles.

[h]"Average daily utilization of each aircraft" means the average air hours flown in service per day per aircraft for the total fleet of aircraft.

Questions

Part 1. The cost of United's frequent flier program

    a. What are the various methods United might use to measure the costs of its frequent flier program? _____ What are the potential differences in dollars of the cost measured by each method? _____

    b. What method should United use to measure the cost of its frequent flier program? _____ Estimate the cost of the program using this method. Show all calculations and indicate the assumptions you make.

    c. If you were the chief financial officer (CFO) of United, how would you determine if continuing the frequent flier program would be beneficial to United? _____

Part 2. Financial disclosure for United's frequent flier program

    a. Do you believe that United should account in its published financial statements for the frequent flier program or is "disclosure" in public filings with the SEC sufficient? _____ Why? _____

b. In either case, what is it that should be accounted for or disclosed? _____ Why? _____

c. What possible ways might United choose to account for the program in its published financial statements if it chooses to do so? _____

d. How do you believe United should account for the program in its published financial statements? _____ Explain and support your chosen method and why you rejected other approaches. Show by some means (such as journal entries, T accounts, or pro forma statements) how your chosen method would be applied and all of the accounts that would be affected by the accounting you believe to be best.

e. If you were CFO of United, what would you do? _____

Patten Corporation

Forget Florida. Today's underdeveloped land hype centers on good old New England. The affluent young and upwardly mobile lust not for perpetual sunshine but for "unspoiled" woodland and farmland plots close to Boston, Providence or New York. An urban yearning for the bucolic.

Who's there to sell wide-open spaces to cramped but credit worthy city dwellers? Patten Corp., a $35 million installment land sales company based in Stamford, VT. A nice business? So it seems. In 1986 Patten's reported net per share was $1.40, vs. 47 cents in 1985. In the first six months of fiscal 1987, Patten's property sales rose 110%, while reported earnings increased 53%. Patten's stock—recently listed on the Big Board—jumped from a split adjusted $4 a share in early 1986 to around $19 in late December.

Trouble is, Patten's earnings suffer serious shrinkage when scrutinized. And the asset side of the company's balance sheet looks a bit bloated. Patten records 100% of its land sales as revenues, even though it typically receives just 10% to 50% of the amount in cash. Therefore, the quality of its earnings is suspect.[1]

_____

[1]Excerpts from "Old Game, New Twist," *Forbes*, January 12, 1987. Reprinted with permission. The magazine issue became available on the newsstands in the last week of December 1986.

This case was prepared by Professor Krishna Palepu as the basis for class discussion rather than to illustrate either effective or ineffective handling of an administrative situation.
Copyright © 1987 by the President and Fellows of Harvard College. Harvard Business School case 188–027.

When during the last week of December 1986, the above comments were published in *Forbes* magazine, Patten's share price dropped from $18.250 to $15.875 in
frenzied trading on the New York Stock Exchange, representing a loss of approximately $19.5 million dollars in the market value of the company's stock.

Business Method and Performance

Patten Corporation acquired large undeveloped rural properties, subdivided these
properties into parcels averaging approximately 15 acres, and sold them. The company's primary customers were residents of metropolitan areas who sought to own
rural land for vacation or retirement home sites and investment. Most of the land that
the company purchased and resold was two to five hours driving time from major
metropolitan areas such as Boston, Hartford, New York City, and Philadelphia.

Acquisition of Land

The Company employed a staff of approximately 46 acquisition specialists in its 13
regional offices. The acquisition staff in each office systematically contacted all major
property owners and real estate brokers in its territory. Patten's objective was to
develop strong relationships with property owners and brokers so that it would be the
first party to see a property when it became available for purchase.

Once an appropriate property was located, Patten entered into a purchase agreement with the seller. Generally, the company agreed to make a small down payment
and to pay the balance on closing after all necessary governmental approvals were
obtained. The time between execution of a purchase agreement and closing was usually two to six months. By requiring that all regulatory approvals be obtained prior to
closing and by making only a small down payment upon signing purchase agreements,
the company held a large number of properties under contract without expending
significant amounts of cash.

After contracting for, but prior to acquiring a property, the company completed a
survey, designed a subdivision plan, conducted soil tests if feasible, reviewed applicable environmental and zoning laws and regulations, and received all necessary regulatory approvals to permit subdivision and sale of the property. After acquisition, Patten
made only minor improvements and rarely built on or otherwise developed the land it
sold. Because of the extended escrow period, the company would turn over its properties rapidly, with the period from acquisition to resale generally being one to twelve
weeks. This strategy to reduce the time it actually owned any given property minimized the market risk associated with holding real estate.

Marketing of Land

Patten's marketing activities were targeted by geography and customer demographics.
To sell parcels of land from a property, the company usually advertised in major
newspapers in metropolitan areas located within a two to five hour drive of the

property. When a property contained a large number of parcels, the company also conducted a direct mail campaign using brochures describing available parcels.

The company's advertisements and direct mail campaigns were designed to cause prospective customers to call for more information. A sales representative answered each call, discussed the property with the prospective purchaser, attempted to ascertain the customer's needs and whether an available parcel would be suitable for that person, and arranged an appointment for the customer to visit the property. Patten offered no premiums or other inducements for such visits.

Patten's typical customer was 38 years old with an annual income of $30,000–50,000, married, and owned a home. The company attempted to match the profile of its sales representatives to its customer profile because it felt that sales success depended on a high degree of trust and personal identification that developed between the customer and the company representative during the customer's visit. The typical Patten sales representative was 36 years old, earned an annual income of $40,000, was married, and owned a home.

The company's marketing strategy was very successful. In 1986, the sales staff converted 25% of initial customer calls to appointments to visit properties, and 45% of customers who made a visit purchased a property. Patten attributed its marketing success to its careful targeting of customers and its strategy of ensuring that, before visiting the properties offered by the company, the customers had:

- Taken the time to look for land offers in a newspaper;
- Made a long distance call to receive additional information on an advertisement of interest;
- Made an appointment to visit a property without the offer of any premiums, gifts, or other inducements;
- Driven anywhere from 2 to 5 hours to view the property.

After deciding to purchase a parcel of land, the customer entered into a contract and paid Patten a deposit equal in most cases to 10% of the purchase price. The closing usually occurred within two to four weeks after payment of the deposit. Upon closing, the company delivered to the buyer a warranty deed and a recent survey of the property.

During fiscal 1986, 90% of the parcels were sold at prices ranging from $5,000 to $40,000, and the average sales price of all parcels sold was $19,327. This price represented an average price per acre of $1,282, as compared with an average acquisition cost to Patten of $579 per acre.

Customer Financing

Patten offered up to 90% financing of the purchase price of a parcel to all qualified customers. The company viewed its customer financing offer as a marketing tool because it removed the difficulty most customers would have in obtaining financing to purchase undeveloped land in an area often outside their home state. In 1986, 21% of Patten's customers paid cash for their property, while 79% used the company's financing.

In general, customers who utilized Patten's financing paid 10–50 percent of the purchase price in cash, and the balance was represented by promissory notes. Notes were secured by first mortgages on the parcels sold. Rates of interest charged by the company on notes from customers were approximately 4–5% over the prime rate. The company's own borrowing cost usually was 0.5–2 percent above prime. As a result, the company's portfolio of notes receivable, which amounted to $18.6 million at the end of 1986, was an important source of income to the company. Since customer financing was an important marketing tool and a source of stable interest income, the company had plans to increase the proportion of sales which it financed.

Before granting financing, Patten performed substantially the same type of credit review of the customer as a lending institution would undertake. The company considered the delinquency and default rate on its notes receivable to be low by industry standards. In approximately 90% of default cases, the company forgave the note in exchange for title to the parcel.

Recent Performance

Patten's well-focused land acquisition and marketing strategy led to the company's rapid growth in recent years. The company's sales grew from $11.2 million in fiscal 1984 to $33.3 million in 1986. During the same period, the reported profits grew from $0.47 million (40 cents per share) to $3.95 million ($1.40 per share). In November 1985 the company went public and was listed on the New York Stock Exchange.

The success of Patten's land retailing strategy has attracted considerable attention and favorable comments from financial analysts. For example, Kurt Fenerman and Terence York, analysts with Drexel Burnham Lambert Inc., stated in their November 1986 report on Patten:

> Patten is in the midst of a dramatic earnings expansion driven by an exciting retailing concept. The management team is young and aggressive. Growth is fueled by both existing and new (regional) offices. Inventory turnover remains very high by design, reducing risk. Profit margins are the highest of any stock we follow, and are rising. If there is risk to our earnings estimates, which have already been raised five times this year, it is that they are too low.[2]

As a result of investors' favorable assessment of the company's performance and future prospects, Patten's stock price rose rapidly in 1986. In 1986 the company split the stock two-for-one in response to the rapid stock price increase.

The Accounting Controversy

Since only a small portion of Patten's revenues were from cash sales, how to record the noncash sales was an important financial reporting policy decision. The company recorded a sale of real estate and recognized revenue when a minimum of 10% of sales

---

[2]Excerpts from "Research Abstracts: Patten Corporation" by Kurt A. Fenerman and Terence M. York, Drexel Burnham Lambert Inc. November 4, 1986.

EXHIBIT 1   Patten Corporation Abridged Annual Report for 1986
Financial Highlights

	1986	1985	% Change
	(000's omitted except per share data)		
Operating Results			
Revenues:			
Sales of Real Estate	$33,263	$18,549	79
Interest Income	1,694	645	163
Total Revenues	34,957	19,194	82
Pre-Tax Income[a]	8,810	2,272	288
Net Income	3,951	852	364
Net Income Per Common Share	1.40	.47	198
Weighted Average Number of Common and Common		1,820	55
Equivalent Shares Outstanding	2,829		
Financial Position			
Current Assets	$15,353	$6,777	127
Current Liabilities	8,467	5,440	56
Working Capital	6,886	1,337	415
Total Assets	35,304	13,985	152
Shareholders' Equity	14,848	2,289	549
Operating Ratios			
Gross Profit Margin	54.8%	48.2%	14
Pre-Tax Margin	25.2%	11.8%	114
Net Margin	11.3%	4.4%	157
Long-Term Debt/Total Capital[b]	28.5%	53.0%	46
Return on Beginning Equity	172.6%	59.3%	191
Return on Average Total Assets	16.0%	7.5%	113

[a]Income before income taxes and minority interests.
[b]Includes long-term debt, equity interests of minority shareholders in subsidiaries, and shareholders' equity.

proceeds was received and collectability of the balance was reasonably assured. The excess of sales price over legally binding deposits received was recorded as contract receivables or notes receivable. All related costs were recorded when a sale was recorded. Patten's 1986 Annual Report (Exhibit 1) provides more details on the company's revenue recognition and other accounting policies.

Accounting Rules

Under Generally Accepted Accounting Principles (GAAP) for retail land sales (as sated in Statement No. 66 of the Financial Accounting Standards Board), Patten's revenue recognition method was considered appropriate if *all* of the following conditions were met:

1. The buyer signs a legally bound contract for the land purchase, and a nonrefundable down-payment of 10% or more of the sales price.

EXHIBIT 1   (continued)

Letter to Shareholders

Fellow Shareholders:

It is my pleasure to report that the year ended March 13, 1986 was one of exceptional achievement and profitability for Patten Corporation.

The Company's revenues reached $35 million, up 82.3% over 1985 revenues of $19.2 million. Net income rose to $3,951,000 or $1.40 per share, from $852,000 or $.47 per share.

Fourth quarter revenues of $9.7 million were 146% ahead of $4 million for the same period last year. Net income rose 33X to $1,053,000 or $.27 per share, from $32,000 or $.02 per share.

Your Company has never been in a better financial position. As a result of the initial public offering of Patten Corporation Common Stock in November 1985 and fiscal 1986 net income, shareholders' equity grew to $14.8 million from $2.3 million. Working capital reached a record $6.9 million and total assets were up 152% to an all-time high of $35.3 million.

Revenues increased 99% in the five offices that were opened throughout 1985 and 1986.

Vertical & Horizontal Expansion

Among the factors contributing to the Company's strong financial performance were faster-than-expected growth in our existing offices, unusually dry weather, and the addition of 15 qualified acquisition professionals, bringing the acquisition staff to 46.

During 1986, a total of five new offices opened in Concord, New Hampshire; Bangor, Maine; York, Pennsylvania; Montpelier, Vermont; and Brooklyn, Connecticut. Continuing geographic diversification allows a more varied product mix and lessens the effect of seasonal fluctuations.

In addition to our ongoing program of gradual geographic and new market expansion, each regional office continues to develop its own specialized market area and products. After successful testing in 1986, each office will increase its residential and bulk acreage sales efforts in 1987, in addition to maintaining its significant rate of growth in the sale of large country parcels and specialized products.

The Bangor, Maine office is currently successful in marketing 40-acre parcels, while Sleepy Hollow Lake, New York continues to specialize in small lake-front parcels within a 2½-hour drive of New York City. Our York, Pennsylvania office is in a strategic location for providing the 3-million-person Philadelphia-Baltimore-District of Columbia market with properties in Maryland, Virginia, West Virginia, and Pennsylvania.

The Patten People

Each Patten office is headed by a regional president with bottom-line responsibility for acquisition and sales teams throughout his area. We have continued to strengthen our management team at all levels through advancement, training, and a rigorous recruiting program.

Michael Sanders joined the Company as Executive Vice President of Acquisitions and comes to us with 12 years experience in the acquisition of rural properties. He will oversee our continuing geographic expansion and work with the regional presidents on the development of acquisition managers.

On May 1, 1986, Jeffrey B. Lavin, C.P.A., joined Patten Corporation to serve as the Company's Chief Financial Officer, and will be working closely with the Executive Vice President of Finance and the regional presidents to coordinate financial planning and control. He has ten years of public accounting experience.

Joseph R. O'Brien, Gary P. Sumner and Raymond A. Lamoureaux were promoted to regional presidents of the Bangor, Maine; York and Stroudsburg, Pennsylvania; and Brooklyn, Connecticut offices, respectively. Each of these men has worked for the Company for several years.

Exhibit 1   (continued)

In Memphis, William J. Britton brought 25 years of real estate experience, including extensive knowledge of the Tennessee market, when he joined the Patten team to spark our expansion into the mid-south. His appointment and the promotions to regional president illustrate Patten's balanced approach to strengthening its management team.

A Commitment to Conservation

Since year-end, we established the Patten Environmental Trust, a non-profit corporation designed to protect the environment through the creation of forever-wild areas. We believe that the free enterprise approach to land conservation will be the most effective in the long run. The formation of this Trust is a reflection of the unique spirit, attitudes, and commitments that have made Patten Corporation the leader in its market.

Looking Ahead

There is every reason to believe that the exceptional achievement and performance of Patten Corporation will continue.

- At least 16 offices should be open by the end of 1987. Since the end of 1986, we expanded operations to the mid-south market by opening an office in Memphis, Tennessee.
- While new offices will contribute to our success in 1987, most of our growth in the next fiscal year will continue to come from our established offices where we expect to further increase the quality of our acquisition of sales staffs.
- On March 31, 1986, the Company held options on 33,366 acres of land at an aggregate purchase price of $17.7 million, as compared with $11.2 million four months earlier, placing the Company in the strongest inventory position in its history.
- The average selling price of a parcel in 1986 rose 68% to $19,300 from $11,500 a year earlier. We believe this is a reflection of our improving pricing policies and product mix.
- Several sales managers are now ready to assume responsibility for new offices. It is our goal to prepare a minimum of six managers for this role within the next twelve months.

In May of 1986, Patten Corporation successfully completed an offering of $30 million of 7¼% convertible subordinated debentures to the public through Drexel Burnham Lambert, Incorporated, First Albany Corporation and Morgan Keegan and Company, Inc.

This offering provides us with funds to increase working capital to support expansion of the Company's business, to increase the amount of customer mortgages retained by the Company, and to open new offices.

We appreciate your support and confidence since our initial public offering on November 21, 1985. The results of the past year, and those we expect in the future, would not be possible without the continued, dedicated efforts of our employees and the support of our customers and Shareholders.

Sincerely,

Harry S. Patten, President
Chairman, Board of Directors
May 21, 1986

Financial Statistics

(000's omitted except in per share & operating data)

Operating Results for the Years Ended March 31,	*1986*	*1985*	*1984*	*1983*	*1982*
Revenues					
Sales of Real Estate	$33,263	$18,549	$11,186	$ 4,315	$ 2,822
Interest Income	1,694	645	293	111	84
Total Revenues	34,957	19,194	11,479	4,426	2,906
Income from Operations	8,658	2,006	1,459	732	105
Income Before Income Taxes and					
Minority Interests	8,810	2,272	1,557	842	282
Provision for Income Taxes	4,184	971	729	338	94
Net Income	3,951	852	475	386	188
Net Income per Common Share	1.40	.47	.26	.21	.10
Weighted Average Number of Common and					
Common Equivalent Shares Outstanding . . .	2,829	1,820	1,820	1,820	1,820
Financial Position on March 31,					
Current Assets	$15,353	$ 6,777	$ 4,604	$ 2,055	$ 1,464
Current Liabilities	8,467	5,440	3,532	1,072	1,151
Working Capital	6,886	1,337	1,072	983	313
Total Assets	35,304	13,985	8,635	3,490	2,246
Long Term Debt	5,908	3,414	2,070	700	236
Shareholders' Equity	14,848	2,289	1,437	962	576
Operating Ratios					
Gross Profit Margin	54.8%	48.2%	46.4%	51.9%	47.2%
Net Margin	11.3%	4.4%	4.1%	8.7%	6.5%
Long-Term Debt/Total Capital (a)	28.5%	53.0%	53.7%	38.8%	29.1%
Return on Beginning Equity	172.6%	59.3%	49.3%	67.0%	48.4%
Return on Average Total Assets	16.0%	7.5%	7.8%	13.5%	9.5%
Operating Data					
Average Sale Price per Parcel	$19,327	$11,521	$10,310	$10,396	$ 6,006
Number of Parcels Sold	1,721	1,610	1,085	415	470
Total Acres Sold	25,935	14,084	10,537	5,706	6,928
Number of Offices at End of Period	13	8	6	3	1

(a) Includes long-term debt, equity interests of minority shareholders in subsidiaries and shareholders' equity

Price Range of Common Stock The Company's Common Stock is traded in the Over-The-Counter market under the symbol "PATN." The following table sets forth the range of high and low bid quotations per share of Common Stock from the initial public offering of Common Stock on November 21, 1985 through February 3, 1986, as reported by the National Association of Securities Dealers Automated Quotation ("NASDAQ") System, and the range of high and low sale prices since February 4, 1986, as reported on the NASDAQ National Market System. Quotations represent prices between dealers and do not reflect retail mark-ups, mark-downs or commissions and, for periods prior to February 4, 1986, may not represent actual transactions.

Fiscal 1986:	*High*	*Low*
Third Quarter (from November 21)	10⅝	9⅞
Fourth Quarter (through February 3)	15⅛	10¼
Fourth Quarter (from February 4)	20	14½

The Company has not paid any cash dividend on its Common Stock to date and does not intend to pay dividends in the foreseeable future. As of April 16, 1986, there were 358 holders of record of Common Stock.

(continued)

Management's Discussion and Analysis

Fiscal 1986 vs. Fiscal 1985

Sales of real estate increased by $14.7 million, or 79.3%, from $18.5 million to $33.3 million. This increase was primarily attributable to an increase in the total acres sold from 14,084 to 25,935, and an increase in the average sale price per parcel from $11,521 to $19,327. The number of parcels sold increased from 1,610 to 1,721. Sales by existing offices (offices open during all of fiscal 1985 and 1986) increased 99% from $12.8 million to $25.5 million. Sales also increased due to the opening of regional offices in Bangor, Maine and Concord, New Hampshire. In addition, the Company opened a new office in Stroudsburg, Pennsylvania to replace an office in Milford, Pennsylvania. The Company sold 4,441 acres in bulk parcels (100 acres or more) resulting in $2.7 million of bulk acreage sales in fiscal 1986 as compared with no such sales in the prior year. The number of regional offices was 13 and 8 at March 13, 1986 and 1985, respectively.

Interest income increased from $645,000 to $1.7 million. This was due primarily to an increase in the amount of notes receivable retained by the Company, as well as an increase in the total amount of notes receivable originated by the Company.

Gross margin on sales of real estate improved from 48.2% to 54.8% as a result of the Company's ability to increase the sale prices of parcels without reducing sales volume, and to allocate certain fixed acquisition expenses over a greater volume of properties sold. In addition, the financial resources provided by the Company's initial public offering in November 1985 increased the Company's ability to make acquisitions.

Selling, general and administrative expenses increased by $3.6 million, or 52.3%, from $6.7 million to $10.3 million primarily due to the expansion of the Company's operations, resulting in an increase in advertising, marketing and selling expenses of $784,000, or 26.1%. In addition, as a result of increased sales volume, personnel costs and other variable expenses increased. Selling, general and administrative expenses decreased as a percentage of total revenues from 35.1% to 29.3%, primarily reflecting increased sales volume.

Interest expense rose from $846,000 to $1.0 million. This reflects an increase in the amount of borrowings outstanding, partially offset by a decrease in the weighted average interest rates on borrowings.

The effective income tax rate increased from 42.7% to 47.5%, reflecting a lower proportion of investment tax credits and surtax exemptions relative to income before income taxes.

Net income increased $3.1 million, or 364%, from $852,000 to 3.9 million. The increase in earnings is primarily due to increased revenues, improved gross margins, and lower selling, general and administrative expenses as a percentage of total revenues.

Fiscal 1985 vs. Fiscal 1984

Sales of real estate increased by $7.3 million, or 66%, from $11.2 million to $18.5 million. This increase was primarily attributable to the opening of an additional regional office at Sleepy Hollow Lake, New York. Sales in existing offices (offices open during all of both fiscal 1984 and 1985) increased from $9.3 million to $11.0 million, or 19%. The number of parcels sold increased from 1,085 to 1,610, and the average sale price per parcel increased from $10,310 to $11,521. The number of regional offices was eight and six at March 31, 1985 and 1984, respectively.

The Company also broadened the types of real estate parcels available for sale to include water-view property, such as ocean-front, lake-front and fishing rivers, and primary home sites. In fiscal 1985, the Company was involved in selling a large volume of lake-front parcels at Sleepy Hollow Lake in New York, the majority of which were less than one acre.

Interest income increased from $293,000 to $645,000. This was due primarily to an increase in the amount of notes receivable originated by the Company.

Gross margin on sales of real estate improved from 46.4% to 48.2%, primarily as a result of an increased proportion of sales of higher-margin and higher-priced lake-front and ocean-view properties.

(continued)

Selling, general and administrative expenses increased by $3.0 million, or 82%, from $3.7 million to $6.7 million and increased as a percentage of total revenues from 32.3% to 35.1%, primarily reflecting increased advertising, marketing and sales costs incurred in part in connection with the development of a new direct mail program. Selling, general and administrative expenses also increased as a result of the addition of acquisition and marketing personnel and increased salaries.

Interest expense increased from $321,000 to $846,000, reflecting an increase in the amount of borrowing outstanding. The weighted average interest rates on borrowing outstanding during the periods did not vary materially.

The effective income tax rate declined from 46.8% to 42.7%, primarily reflecting a higher proportion of investment tax credits and surtax exemptions relative to income before income taxes.

Net income increased to $852,000 from $475,000, reflecting the opening of additional regional offices, increased revenues, and improved gross margins.

Liquidity and Capital Resources

The Company's capital resources are provided from both internal and external sources. These funds support the Company's operations, including the acquisition and holding of land, and allow it to offer financing to its customers.

The Company typically advances only a small down payment when signing a contract to acquire property. At March 31, 1986, the Company had contracted to purchase approximately $17.7 million of property against which it had made down payments of $499,000. In most cases, the Company is not required to advance the full purchase price until all regulatory approvals for the subdivision and sale of land have been obtained and certain other conditions have been satisfied. The Company further reduces its capital requirements by marketing and selling properties promptly, with the period from acquisition to sale generally being one to 12 weeks.

The Company finances a substantial portion of its sales (approximately 64% of its sales in fiscal 1986) and pledges or holds the related notes it receives. As of March 31, 1986, approximately $18.6 million of notes receivable were held by the Company. Approximately 47% of these notes were pledged as collateral for the Company's bank loans, with the Company being entitled to borrow amounts totaling 70–80% of the outstanding principal of pledged notes. Until the end of calendar 1985, the Company sold the notes it did not hold to banks at face amount, and receives as interest income the difference between the coupon rate on the notes sold (Usually 4–5% over the banks' prime lending rate) and the banks' prime lending rate plus 3%. The Company was required to guarantee the repayment of each note sold to banks, although in some cases the Company was only required to guarantee the repayment of a note until one-half of the term of the note expired or one-half of the amount due on the note was paid, whichever occurred later. As of March 31, 1986, the Company was subject to contingent liabilities under such guarantees of approximately $10.9 million. The determination to pledge rather than to sell notes receivable is made by the Company in part, as discussed below, to defer income taxes. The Company has increased, and intends to continue increasing, the proportion of its sales which it finances and intends to retain or pledge rather than sell the receivables generated. The Company continues to have the ability to sell a substantial portion of its notes if required for liquidity purposes.

(continued)

Cash flow provided by the Company's operations (which includes net income plus non-cash deductions from net income) was $1.7 million, $2.5 million and $8.8 million for the years ended March 31, 1984, 1985 and 1986, respectively. However, as a result of increasing sales and the Company's mortgage financing activities over the three-year period, net funds used for the Company's operations were $2.4 million, $856,000 and $9.3 million, respectively. The increase in funds used for operations during fiscal 1986 was due primarily to the Company's decision to finance a greater percentage of customer purchases and to hold all of the notes receivable it originated. Notes receivable retained by the Company totaled $2.6 million, $4.0 million and $13.6 million for the years ended March 31, 1984, 1985 and 1986, respectively. The Company's growth in its real estate operations and its mortgage financing activities have been funded through cash flow generated from operations, borrowings under secured and unsecured lines of credit, sales of notes receivable to banks and the approximately $7.2 million of net proceeds from the public offering of 850,000 shares of its Common Stock in November 1985. The Company increased the aggregate amounts available under its lines of credit from $6.5 million at March 31, 1984 to $16.4 million at March 31, 1986, approximately 65% of which required the security of existing real estate mortgage notes and inventory. At March 31, 1986, approximately $6.1 million remained available for additional borrowings under such lines of credit.

A portion of the Company's liquidity is provided through the use of the installment sale method of reporting income from property sales for income tax purposes, the effect of which is to defer income taxes, thereby increasing available cash. Under current tax law, the Company is able to pledge its installment notes receivable to secure loans from banks without accelerating the tax liability attributable to such notes. Legislative proposals have been made which, if they were to become effective, would require the Company to accelerate the tax liability attributable to its installment notes upon their pledge to banks and prevent the Company from continuing to increase its liquidity in this manner.

Based upon its current financial condition and credit relationships, the Company believes that it has, or can obtain, adequate financial resources to satisfy its liquidity and capital requirements for the foreseeable future at anticipated rates of growth.

Effects of Inflation

Management believes that inflationary increases in costs of sales and operations can normally be absorbed by increases in the price of properties sold. To date, inflationary effects have had little impact on the Company.

Consolidated Balance Sheet

	March 31,	
Assets	*1986*	*1985*
Current assets:		
Cash	$ 1,578,361	$ 658,016
Contracts receivable	2,939,417	1,078,813
Notes receivable, current portion (Notes 2 and 5)	1,328,374	693,161
Inventory (Notes 4 and 5)	7,172,050	2,921,722
Due from officers and other related parties (Note 8)	1,016,998	1,125,770
Other current assets	1,318,126	299,498
Total current assets	15,353,326	6,777,030
Property and equipment, net (Notes 3 and 5)	2,716,147	1,087,820
Notes receivable (Notes 2 and 5)	17,234,488	5,746,639
Due from officers and other related parties (Note 8)	—	373,296
Total assets	$35,303,961	$13,984.785
Liabilities and Shareholders' Equity		
Current liabilities:		
Accounts payable	$ 1,277,173	$ 588,297
Accrued liabilities	383,631	176,430
Income taxes payable (Note 7)	253,632	10,848
Notes payable (Note 4)	5,487,592	3,719,982
Current portion of long-term debt (Note 5)	1,065,223	944,611
Total current liabilities	8,467,251	5,440,168
Long-term debt (Note 5)	5,908,498	3,413,837
Deferred income taxes (Note 7)	6,080,531	2,103,107
Commitments and contingencies (Notes 6 and 10)		
Equity interests of minority shareholders in subsidiaries (Note 11)	—	738,564
Shareholders' equity (Notes 4 and 11):		
Preferred Stock, $.01 par value, 1,000,000 shares authorized: none		
issued and outstanding at March 31, 1986 and 1985	—	—
Common Stock, $.01 par value, 10,000,000 shares authorized:		
3,900,000 shares issued and outstanding at March 31, 1986 and		
1,820,000 at March 31, 1985	39,000	18,200
Capital in excess of par value	8,586,958	—
Retained earnings	6,221.723	2,270,909
Total shareholders' equity	14,847,681	2,289,109
Total liabilities and shareholders' equity	$35,303,961	$13,984,785

Consolidated Statement of Income

	Years Ended March 31,		
	1986	*1985*	*1984*
Revenues			
Sales of real estate (Notes 6 and 8)	$33,262,613	$18,548,630	$11,185,870
Interest income	1,693,923	645,335	293,238
	34,956,536	19,193,965	11,479,108
Cost and Expenses			
Cost of real estate sold (Notes 6 and 8)	15,028,396	9,606,072	5,993,651
Selling, general and administrative expense	10,258,788	6,736,083	3,705,471
Interest expense	1,011,513	846,074	320,953
	26,298,697	17,188.229	10,020,075
Income from operations	8,657,839	2,005,736	1,459,033
Other income (Note 8)	151,847	266,5670	98,298
Income before income taxes and minority interests	8,809,686	2,272,296	1,557,331
Provision for income taxes (Note 7)	4,184,086	970,583	729,424
Income before minority interests	4,625,600	1,301,713	827,907
Minority interests in earnings of subsidiaries	674,786	449,341	353,259
Net income	$ 3,950,814	$ 852,372	$ 474,648
Net income per common share	$ 1.40	$ .47	$ .26
Weighted average number of common and common equivalent shares used to calculate net income per common share	2,829,303	1,820,000	1,820,000

Consolidated Statement of Shareholders' Equity
(Note 11)

	Years Ended March 31		
	1986	*1985*	*1984*
Class A Preferred Stock, no par value			
Balance beginning of period	—	—	—
Issuance of stock dividend on April 9, 1985	$2,289,000	—	—
Exchange for Common Stock, $0.1 par value, on			
November 21, 1985	(2,289,000)	—	—
Balance end of period.	—	—	—
Preferred Stock, $.01 par value			
Balance beginning of period	—	—	—
Balance end of period.	—	—	—
Common Stock, no par value			
Balance beginning of period	—	—	$ 3,627
Transfer to Common Stock, $.01 par value, for			
retroactive effect of reincorporation in Massachusetts			
on October 8, 1985	—	—	(3,627)
Balance end of period.	—	—	—
Common Stock, $.01 par value			
Balance beginning of period	$ 18,200	$ 18,200	—
Transfer from Common Stock, no par value, and			
retained earnings for retroactive effect of			
reincorporation in Massachusetts on October 8, 1985,			
and for exchange of Class A Preferred Stock on			
November 21, 1985	—	—	$ 18,200
Shares issued for acquisition of minority interests	12,300	—	—
Shares issued in public offering.	8,500	—	—
Balance end of period	$ 39,000	$ 18,200	$ 18,200
Capital in Excess of par value			
Balance beginning of period	—	—	—
Excess of book value of minority interests acquired over			
par value of Common Stock, $.01 par value, issued			
for acquisition of minority interests	$1,410,645	—	—
Shares issued in public offering.	7,176,313	—	—
Balance end of period.	$8,586,958	—	—
Retained Earnings			
Balance beginning of period	$2,270,909	$1,418,537	$ 958,462
Issuance of stock dividend on April 9, 1985	(2,289,000)	—	—
Transfer to Common Stock, $.01 par value, for			
retroactive effect of reincorporation in Massachusetts			
on October 8, 1985	—	—	(12,284)
Exchange of Class A Preferred Stock for Common			
Stock, $.01 par value, on November 21, 1985	2,289,000	—	(2,289)
Net income for the period.	2,950,814	852,372	474,648
Balance end of period	$6,221,723	$2,270,909	$1,418,537

340

Patten Corporation

Consolidated Statement of Changes in Financial Position

	Years Ended March 31,		
	1986	*1985*	*1984*
Operations			
Net income	$ 3,950,814	$ 852,372	$ 474,648
Add (deduct) items not affecting cash:			
Depreciation	246,923	230,122	135,989
Deferred income taxes	3,977,424	933,686	693,155
Minority interests in earnings of subsidiaries	674,786	449,341	353,259
Cash payments on notes receivable	1,493,406	948,591	656,773
Proceeds from sale of notes receivable to banks	5,751,952	4,932,513	3,280,280
Notes receivable originated during the period	(19,368,420)	(8,909,141)	(5,840,366)
Increase (decrease) in:			
Accounts payable and accrued liabilities	896,077	100,324	509,183
Income taxes payable	242,784	(21,355)	23,896
Decrease (increase) in:			
Contracts receivable	(1,860,604)	113,749	(441,689)
Inventory	(4,250,278)	(330,029)	(2,173,230)
Other current assets	(1,018,628)	(156,419)	(113,168)
Net funds used for operations	(9,263,764)	(856,246)	(2,441,270)
Investments			
Purchase of property and equipment, net	(1,875,250)	(284,042)	(823,873)
Decrease (increase) in amount due from officers and other related parties, net	482,068	(1,606,608)	—
Decrease in investment in affiliates	—	—	39,087
Acquisition of equity interests of minority shareholders in subsidiaries	(1,422,945)	—	—
Other, net	9,595	(30,667)	(101,666)
Net funds used for investments	(2,806,532)	(1,921,317)	(886,452)
Financing			
Addition to short-term borrowings	1,767,610	1,291,817	1,869,396
Addition to long-term debt	4,209,243	2,030,384	1,714,781
Reduction in long-term debt	(1,593,970)	(148,453)	(126,330)
Issuance of common stock	8,607,758	—	—
Net funds provided by financing	12,990,641	3,173,748	3,457,847
Increase in cash	$ 920,345	$ 396,185	$ 130,125

Notes to Consolidated Financial Statements

1. Significant Accounting Policies

Principles of Consolidation

The financial statements include the accounts of Patten Corporation (the Company) and all majority owned subsidiaries. All intercompany transactions are eliminated.

Business

The Company acquires large underdeveloped rural properties, subdivides these properties into parcels, and markets and sells the parcels to persons living in metropolitan areas. Generally, the Company makes only minor improvements and rarely builds on or otherwise develops the land it sells. In fiscal 1986 the Company began a program of acquiring large properties for bulk acreage sales.

Inventory

Inventory is stated at the lower of cost or market, with cost being determined on a specific cost basis considering relative fair values. Cost includes cost of real estate, improvements and capitalizable purchase costs.

Property and Equipment

Property and equipment are recorded at cost. Depreciation is computed on both the straight-line and accelerated methods based on the estimated useful lives of the related assets.

Contracts Receivable and Revenue Recognition

The Company records a sale of real estate and recognizes revenue when a minimum of 10% of the sales proceeds has been received and collectability of the balance can be reasonably assured. The excess of sales price over legally binding deposits received is recorded as contracts receivable. All related costs are recorded when the sale is recorded. The amount of delinquent contracts receivable at March 31, 1986 is not material.

Income Taxes

Deferred income taxes are provided for those items of revenue and expense which are recognized for financial reporting in different periods than for income tax purposes. Investment tax credits are accounted for as a reduction of the provision for income taxes in the year in which they arise.

Net Income per Common Share

Net income per common share was determined by dividing net income by the weighted average number of common shares and, in fiscal 1986, common equivalent shares outstanding during each period after giving retroactive effect to the common stock dividends as of April 9, 1985 and August 21, 1985, the exchange of common shares pursuant to the reincorporation of the Company in Massachusetts on October 8, 1985, and the issuance of 228,900 shares of Common Stock, $.01 par value, in exchange for 1,000 shares of Class A Preferred Stock on November 21, 1985. The common equivalent shares reflect the dilutive impact of shares reserved for outstanding stock options and common stock purchase warrants. (See Note 11.)

Presentation

The format of the statement of changes in financial position for the years ended March 31, 1985 and 1984 has been changed to conform to the 1986 presentation.

2. Notes Receivable

The weighted average interest rate on notes receivable is approximately 13.8% and 14.2% at March 31, 1986 and 1985, respectively. The interest rates on these notes at March 31, 1986 range from 9.5% to 19%. As of March 31, 1986, the amount of outstanding notes receivable held by the Company which were delinquent, with delinquency defined as notes receivable with payments more than 30 days past due, was approximately 0.6% or $104,000. Notes receivable are shown net of an allowance for possible losses on notes receivable of $10,000, in the accompanying consolidated balance sheet as of March 31, 1986. The amount of notes receivable written off in the years ended March 31, 1986, 1985 and 1984 was not material.

(continued)

Installments due on notes receivable during each of the five fiscal years subsequent to March 31, 1986 are as follows:

March 31, 1987	$ 1,328,374
March 31, 1988	1,412,710
March 31, 1989	1,504,613
March 31, 1990	1,491,521
March 31, 1991	1,462,209
Thereafter	11,363,435

3. Property and Equipment

Property and equipment consist of the following:

	March 31,	
	1986	*1985*
Land and buildings	$ 383,500	$ 196,000
Building improvements	543,948	377,930
Office equipment, furniture and fixtures	577,752	252,491
Aircraft	1,362,034	454,174
Vehicles	432,642	226,313
	3,299,876	1,506,908
Accumulated depreciation	583,729	419,088
	$2,716,147	$1,087,820

4. Notes Payable

The Company has borrowings with various banks which are used to finance inventory purchases and the carrying of notes receivable and to fund operations.

Significant financial data related to the Company's notes payable to banks are as follows:

	Years Ended March 31,		
	1986	*1985*	*1984*
Total lines of credit available	$8,400,000	$9,500,000	$6,000,000
Borrowings outstanding at end of period	$4,891,586	$3,418,521	$2,211,739
Weighted average interest rate on borrowings outstanding at end of period	10.5%	12%	12%
Average amounts outstanding during the period	$4,090,262	$2,930,345	$1,514,156
Maximum amount borrowed during the period	$5,078,045	$3,481,521	$2,211,739
Weighted average interest rate during the period (determined by dividing interest expense on notes payable to banks by average borrowings of notes payable to banks)	11%	12%	11.8%

All line of credit arrangements may be withdrawn at the option of the banks. There are no significant compensating balance requirements or legal restrictions as to the withdrawal of funds. Under the terms of certain of these line of credit arrangements, the Company is prohibited from the payment of dividends on its outstanding Common Stock and is required to maintain working capital of $1,300,000 or more, a current ratio of at least 1 to 1 and a debt to equity ratio not greater than 5.5 to 1.

(continued)

In addition, at March 31, 1986 and 1985, $596,006, and $238,461, respectively, is owed to unaffiliated individuals from whom the Company purchased property. The notes evidencing the borrowings are secured primarily by the property purchased, with the balance being paid off as such property is sold by the Company. The interest rates on these notes at March 31, 1986 range from 10% to 12%.

In May of 1985, the Company arranged for a $500,000 term loan to refinance a portion of the current notes payable. Accordingly, $500,000 of notes payable at March 31, 1985 have been classified as long-term in the accompanying consolidated balance sheet.

5. Long-Term Debt

Long-term debt consists of the following:

	March 31,	
	1986	*1985*
Mortgage notes secured by certain inventory, property and equipment with interest rates ranging from 8% to 14% fixed and prime plus 1½% variable. Maturities range from 1987 to 1999.	$ 491,983	$ 631,711
Notes payable under long-term available lines of credit of $8,000,000 secured by mortgages held by the Company with total outstanding principal balances aggregating $7,386,000 and $3,251,223 at March 31, 1986 and 1985, respectively. Interest rates are variable ranging from prime (9%) plus 1% to prime plus 2% with the total principal scheduled for repayment through March 1996 (see debt covenants in Note 4).	5,363,467	2,641,125
Notes secured by various equipment with interest payable at rates ranging from 8.5% to 14% fixed and prime plus 1% variable. Maturities range from 1986 through 1989.	951,033	415,728
Notes secured by irrevocable letters of credit issued by a commercial bank with interest rates ranging from 9% to 10%. Maturities range from 1988 to 1992. Total letters of credit outstanding to secure such obligations amount to $302,310 at March 31, 1986.	167,238	169,884
Notes payable refinanced to long-term, bearing interest at prime plus 1½%, due May 1986	—	500,000
	6,973,721	4,358,448
Less current maturities	1,065,223	944,611
Long-term debt	$5,908,498	$3,413,837

Installments due on long-term debt during each of the five fiscal years subsequent to March 31, 1986 are as follows:

March 31, 1987	$1,065,223
March 31, 1988	886,153
March 31, 1989	702,512
March 31, 1990	479,123
March 31, 1991	462,472
Thereafter	3,378,238

6. Agent Agreement

During the year ended March 31, 1985, the Company entered into an agreement under which the Company acted as sole agent for the sale of subdivided land owned by another party. Under the terms of the agreement, the Company received 50% of the sales proceeds for each lot as compensation. The Company also had an option to acquire any remaining unsold lots at specified prices provided that less than 80% of the total lots were sold. The Company was obligated to acquire all remaining unsold lots when 80% of the total lots were sold.

(continued)

Sales of real estate and cost of real estate sold for the year ended March 31, 1985 include $3,339,990 and $1,652,200, respectively, in order to recognize the substance of the above agreement. On April 17, 1985, the Company acquired the remaining unsold lots at a cost of $584,450. All lots were sold during the year ended March 31, 1986.

7. Income Taxes

The provisions for income taxes consist of the following:

	Years ended March 31,		
	1986	*1985*	*1984*
Federal			
Current	$ 47,758	$ 21,303	$ 13,189
Deferred	3,366,762	757,427	555,675
State			
Current	158,496	15,594	23,080
Deferred	611,070	176,259	137,480
	769,566	191,853	160,560
Total	$4,184,086	$970,583	$729,424

The reason for the differences between the provision for income taxes and the amount which results from applying the federal statutory tax rate of 46% to income before income taxes and minority interests are as follows:

	Years Ended March 31,		
	1986	*1985*	*1984*
Income tax expense at statutory rate	$4,052,456	$1,045,256	$716,372
Increase in income tax expense due to inclusion of state taxes	415,566	103,601	86,702
Investment tax credits	(258,593)	(100,781)	(40,455)
Impact of graduated federal tax rates	(116,831)	(77,493)	(33,195)
Other	91,488	—	—
	$4,184,086	$ 970,583	$729,424

The sources of deferred income taxes were as follows:

	Years Ended March 31,		
	1986	*1985*	*1984*
Recording of sales for financial reporting purposes when at least 10% of the proceeds are received while the sales are not recorded for tax purposes until actual closing and title passage	$ 525,982	$ 20,541	$ 64,463
Installment sales treatment of notes receivable for tax purposes	3,344,304	898,206	606,511
Excess of depreciation for tax purposes over that for financial reporting purposes	107,546	14,939	22,181
	$3,977,832	$933,686	$693,155

(continued)

8. Related Party Transactions

The Company performed various management services for related entities which are owned in part by an officer and shareholder of Patten Corporation and one of which is owned in part by a director. Such fees amounted to $60,200, $89,700 and $130,000 for the years ended March 31, 1986, 1985 and 1984, respectively, and are reflected as other income in the consolidated statement of income.

The Company pays maintenance costs for certain facilities to a corporation owned by an officer and shareholder of Patten Corporation. Total maintenance expense of $55,000, $78,000 and $41,000 for the years ended March 31, 1986, 1985 and 1984, respectively, was incurred under this agreement.

Since June 1984, the Company has acted as general partner in a partnership which manages two rental properties. As a result of various consulting activities with this partnership, net fees of $3,500 and $172,294 were earned and are reflected as other income in the consolidated statement of income for the years ended March 31, 1986 and 1985, respectively.

During the years ended March 31, 1986 and 1985, the Company sold certain parcels of land to entities controlled by related parties. The consolidated statement of income for the years ended March 31, 1986 and 1985 includes sales of real estate of $153,903 and $872,243, respectively, and cost of real estate sold of $130,782 and $546,513, respectively, associated with these sales. At March 31, 1986 and 1985, the Company held 10% demand notes receivable totaling $575,770 and $681,221, respectively, from these related parties.

In October 1985, the Company sold its regional office building in Bangor, Maine to a general partnership of which the regional managers of the Bangor office and Harry S. Patten are the sole general partners. The sales price amounted to $132,500 which equaled book value of the property. Subsequent to the sale, the Company has rented the office building from the partnership. The total rent expense paid by the Company for the Bangor office through March 31, 1986 was $5,200.

Effective on April 1, 1984, the Company sold its 51% interest in Patten Southeast Corporation to Harry S. Patten for $25,296, representing the book value of such interest. Prior to April 1, 1984, the Company conducted real estate acquisition and sales activities in South Carolina through Patten Southeast Corporation. The Company determined to sell its interest in Patten Southeast Corporation, which no longer engages in the purchase of real estate, but continues to hold mortgages on properties it sold. At March 31, 1986 and 1985, Patten Southeast Corporation owed $331,189 and $258,989, respectively to the Company.

During the fiscal years 1986, 1985 and 1984, the Company made interest-free demand loans to Harry S. Patten in the amounts of $642,628, $1,255,120 and $736,926, respectively. All of such loans have been repaid in full to the Company.

As a result of the above transactions and certain other advances to and from officers and other related parties, the consolidated balance sheets include the following:

	March 31, 1986 Current	March 31, 1985	
		Current	Noncurrent
Accounts receivable from officers and other related parties......................................	$1,049,652	$1,178,815	$439,548
Accounts payable to officers and other related parties ...	(32,654)	(53,045)	(66,252)
	$1,016,998	$1,125,770	$373,296

(continued)

9. Supplementary Income Statement

Supplementary income statement information is as follows:

	Years Ended March 31		
	1986	*1985*	*1984*
Advertising costs	$1,562,423	$1,511,921	$ 691,751
Taxes, other than payroll and income taxes	$ 547,747	$ 195,407	$ 210,306

10. Commitments and Contingent Liabilities

At March 31, 1986, the Company had contracted to purchase approximately $17.7 million of property against which it had made down payments of $499,000. In most cases, the Company is not required to advance the full purchase price until all regulatory approvals for the subdivision and sale of land have been obtained and certain other conditions have been satisfied.

The Company and its subsidiaries have discounted notes receivable in conjunction with property sales. In the event of default of future payment by a property owner, the Company and its subsidiary that discounted the note would have direct responsibility for satisfying any outstanding balance. In each case, a security interest in the property securing the note is maintained; accordingly, the Company may repossess the property to satisfy the note. No material losses have occurred in the past as subsequent disposition of repossessed properties has created a gain due to inflationary effects on price and the equity that returns to the guarantor in the event of default. Of the total of all loans acquired by the bank and outstanding at March 31, 1986, approximately 5% were over 30 days' delinquent as of March 31, 1986. As of March 31, 1986, the Company's contingent liability was approximately $10,950,000.

11. Shareholders' Equity, Minority Interests, Stock Option Plan and Warrants

As of April 9, 1985, the Company's Board of Directors authorized a stock dividend on its outstanding 795,550 shares of Common Stock of 1,000 shares of Class A 8% Redeemable Preferred Stock (liquidation preference $2,289,000) and 795,550 shares of Common Stock to Harry S. Patten, its sole shareholder at that time (such share amounts and all other share amounts discussed in these financial statements reflect the stock dividend, reincorporation and exchange transactions discussed below in this Note 11). Transfer restrictions were imposed on all stock of the Company requiring that shareholders who desire to transfer any stock of the Company must first offer such stock to the Company at a formula price. The formula price for the Common Stock is its net book value as of the close of the month ended next prior to the date of the offer. The formula price for the Class A 8% Redeemable Preferred Stock is its liquidation value.

As of August 21, 1985, the Company's Board of Directors declared a 59.11% Common Stock dividend on each share of its issued and outstanding Common Stock on that date.

As of September 1, 1985, the Company acquired the minority interests in seven of its subsidiaries in exchange for an aggregate of 1,230,000 shares of the Company's Common Stock. In each case, the owner of the minority interest in the subsidiary was the regional manager in charge of operations of such subsidiary. One owner of a minority interest was issued 50,000 shares of Common Stock which are held in escrow contingent upon future earnings of the subsidiary. The number of shares of the Company's Common Stock issued to each regional manager in exchange for the minority interest was determined by negotiations among such regional managers and the Company. The value of the shares of the Company's Common Stock exchanged for such minority interests was based on the book value of the minority interests ($1,422,945 as of September 1, 1985).

This transaction has resulted in the Company owning 100% of these subsidiaries. Consolidated financial statements of the Company subsequent to September 1, 1985 include all of the net income of these subsidiaries. Previously issued financial statements of the Company included all of the assets, liabilities, revenues and expenses of these subsidiaries, but only the Company's proportionate share of equity and net income of the subsidiaries. Assuming the acquisition had been made as of April 1, 1984, pro forma consolidated net income and net income per common share would have been as follows:

(continued)

	Years Ended March 31	
	1986	*1985*
Net income	$4,625,600	$1,301,713
Net income per common share	$1.37	$.43
Weighted average number of common and common equivalent shares used to calculate net income per common share	3,368,394	3,050,000

On October 8, 1985, the Company reincorporated in Massachusetts by merging into a wholly-owned subsidiary which was organized on September 18, 1985. In connection with this reincorporation and merger, each share of the Company's Common Stock was exchanged for 10,000 shares of Common Stock, $.01 par value, and each share of its Class A 8% Redeemable Preferred Stock was exchanged for one share of Class A Preferred Stock.

On November 21, 1985, the Company exchanged the 1,000 shares of its Class A Preferred Stock held by Harry S. Patten for 228,900 shares of its Common Stock, $.01 par value. Such exchange was based on a liquidation preference of $2,289 per share of preferred stock, as provided in the Company's Articles of Organization, and the public offering price of the Company's Common Stock. At the same time, the Company's Articles of Organization were amended to eliminate the restrictions on the transfer of the Company's capital stock.

As a result of the above transactions, $14,573 has been transferred to Common Stock, $.01 par value, from retained earnings in the accompanying Statement of shareholders' equity as of March 31, 1984.

All references to numbers of shares of Common Stock and per share amounts have been adjusted to reflect the stock dividend of 795,550 shares as of April 9, 1985 and the 59.11% stock dividend authorized by the Company's Board of Directors on each share of the Company's Common Stock outstanding as of August 21, 1985, pursuant to which each share of Common Stock outstanding was exchanged for 10,000 shares of Common Stock.

By consent of the sole Shareholder and Directors of the Company on September 30, 1985, the Company adopted an employee incentive stock option plan. Under the plan, options may be granted at prices not less than the fair market value on the date of grant. On November 20, 1985, the Board of Directors granted options to purchase an aggregate of 145,500 shares of the Common Stock of the Company to 53 employees, at an exercise price of $10.00 per share. The options expire in 1995. As of March 31, 1986, no options have been exercised under the plan, and no options were exercisable. As of March 31, 1986, 225,000 shares of Common Stock were reserved for issuance under the plan. As of March 31, 1986, 176 employees of the Company were eligible to participate in the plan and 53 employees were actually participating in the plan.

On November 21, 1985, the Company issued five-year warrants to purchase up to an aggregate of 50,000 shares of Common Stock at $12.00 per share. The warrants may be exercised as to all or any less number of shares of Common Stock commencing on November 21, 1986.

On November 21, 1985, the Company sold 850,000 shares of Common Stock in an initial public offering. Net proceeds to the Company amounted to $7,184,813.

12. Quarterly Financial Information (Unaudited)

Summarized quarterly financial information (in 000's except for per share information) for the years ended March 3, 1986 and 1985 is as follows:

(continued)

	Three Months Ended			
	June 30, 1985	Sept. 30, 1985	Dec. 31, 1985	March 31, 1986
1986				
Sales of real estate	$6,223	$10,728	$7,262	$9,050
Interest income	278	322	423	671
Gross profit	3,451	6,099	3,809	4,876
Net income	479	1,537	882	1,053
Net income per common share	.26	.69	.27	.27

	Three Months Ended			
	June 30, 1984	Sept. 30, 1984	Dec. 31, 1984	March 31, 1985
Sales of real estate	$2,048	$ 6,480	$6,304	$3,717
Interest income	118	138	153	236
Gross profit	766	3,387	3,040	1,750
Net income	(150)	565	406	32
Net income per common share	(.08)	.31	.22	.02

Report of Independent Certified Public Accountants

Board of Directors and Shareholders
Patten Corporation

We have examined the accompanying consolidated balance sheet of Patten Corporation at March 31, 1986 and 1985 and the related consolidated statements of income, changes in financial position and shareholders' equity for each of the three years in the period ended March 31, 1986. Our examinations were made in accordance with generally accepted auditing standards and, accordingly included such tests of the accounting records and such other auditing procedures as we considered necessary in the circumstances.

In our opinion, the statements mentioned above present fairly the consolidated financial position of Patten Corporation at March 31, 1986 and 1985 and the consolidated results of operations and changes in financial position for each of the three years in the period ended March 31, 1986, in conformity with generally accepted accounting principles applied on a consistent basis during the period.

ARTHUR YOUNG & COMPANY

Worcester, Massachusetts
April 22, 1986

2. The seller's collection experience on similar prior sales indicates that at least 90% of the receivables will be collected in full. A down-payment of 20% or more is an acceptable substitute for the experience test.

3. The seller's receivable for the property sold is not subject to subordination of new loans taken by the buyer.

4. The seller is not obliged to construct amenities or other facilities, or complete any improvements for lots which have been sold.

Patten's revenue recognition policy was not valid if one or more of the above tests were not met. When that occurred, several accounting alternatives were available, all of which recognized revenues less rapidly. For example, if all criteria except the last one were met, sales and profits could be recognized by the percentage-of-completion method, in proportion to the work performed over time by the seller. If only the first criterion was met, revenues and profits could be recognized under the installment sales method, in proportion to the cash payments received from the buyer.

Patten's management was responsible for judging which of the above accounting alternatives was appropriate given the company's business circumstances. Management was also responsible for estimating an allowance to cover potential defaults on any receivables recognized. The company's management was expected to use its knowledge of the industry, the firm's business strategy, and the characteristics of its customers in making these judgments. The firm's auditors were responsible for verifying the appropriateness of the managers' accounting choices and bad debt estimates.

Forbes Criticism

In the article "Old Game, New Twist," cited at the beginning of the case, *Forbes* magazine criticized Patten's accounting as aggressive. The article explained:

> Of Patten's customers, 80% buy their land on time, signing notes that obligate them to pay off loans at an adjustable interest rate, currently 12.5%. Patten includes these notes receivable among its assets and records them at face value. In 1986 this amounted to more than $17 million. Patten allows for possible losses on the notes, but for a laughably small amount: $10,000. Delinquency rates have been low so far, but that's often true in the early stages of these installment land deals.
>
> Patten's accounting techniques are, to put it mildly, aggressive. The company says it actually received 35% of reported revenues as cash down payments in 1986. That's $12.2 million. But subtract the company's costs and expenses from this figure—just the costs of real estate sold, for example, amounted to $15 million and it becomes clear that Patten is operating on a negative cash flow. This explains why Patten has such a heavy debt load: 70% of total capitalization.
>
> Negative cash flow and go-go accounting have burned some nasty holes in investors' pockets over the years. Remember Punta Gorda Isles, a Florida land sales and development company? Its stock traded as high as 16 in 1981, before its similarly obscured negative cash flow came to light. Now the shares languish at 2. Then there is Thousand Trails, a company that sold lifetime campground members. It was hot in 1984, following three years of 40% annual revenue growth. Trails' stock climbed to 29 a share. Soon, however, membership sales evaporated. The stock recently traded around 2½.[3]

Patten's Response

In response to the criticism by *Forbes,* Patten issued a press release defending the company's revenue recognition policy. In this press release, Donald Dion Jr., executive vice president and treasurer of Patten Corporation, stated, "Our financial statements and accounting policies have been audited by Arthur Young & Company, a 'Big

---

[3]Reprinted with permission.

Eight' public accounting firm. Arthur Young & Company has issued an unqualified opinion on our financial statements for each of the past four years."

Dion also stated that the delinquency rate has always been low in the company's 20-year history with mortgage notes customers. "The delinquency rate on our mortgage note portfolio has been low throughout inflationary periods and recessions," he said. "Over the past five years, losses on our mortgage note portfolio have not been material."

The company also attempted to allay investors' concerns raised by the *Forbes* article through a series of meetings with security analysts. The "Heard on the Street" column of *The Wall Street Journal* commented on investor reaction to Patten's efforts[4]:

> Patten Corp, a land sales company whose rapid growth made it the third-best–performing stock on the New York Stock Exchange last year, has held analysts' meetings in Boston, New York and San Francisco this week to counter a negative news report about its finances. The good news is that the stock went up 1⅝ during the course of the meetings, closing yesterday at 18¾. The bad news is that there are still plenty of questions about Stamford, VT-based Patten's growth prospects.

---

[4]Excerpts from "Patten Summons Analysts to Dispel Doubts, but Its Growth Prospects Remain," "Heard on the Street," Randall Smith, *The Wall Street Journal*, January 29, 1987. Reprinted with permission.

Questions

1. Evaluate Patten's business strategy.
2. If Patten recognized revenue when it received cash rather than on the accrual basis it currently uses, what items in the company's 1986 income statement and balance sheet would change, and by how much? _____ (Note: In answering this question, assume that the ratio of cost of real estate sold to sales remains the same under the two revenue recognition methods.)
3. In your opinion, does the recognition of revenues on a cash basis reflect Patten's performance better or worse than the company's present accounting method? _____ Do you think the accounting rules justify Patten's current revenue recognition policy? _____ Do you agree with *Forbes'* criticism of Patten's revenue recognition policy? _____
4. What advice would you give Mr. Dion about the steps he may take to increase investors' confidence in Patten's reported financial results? _____

Extraordinary and Unusual Items, Discontinued Operations, and Accounting Changes

CHAPTER

11

One of the oldest and most persistent controversies in accounting and financial analysis is how extraordinary items, unusual gains or losses, the effects of an accounting change, and a decision to discontinue part of a company's operations should enter into the determination of periodic net income for financial reporting, management evaluation, and security valuation purposes.

Income statements are used by financial analysts to measure past corporate performance and as a basis for estimating future performance and assessing future cash flow prospects. Therefore, what items are included or omitted in the income statement for analytical purposes, where in the statement these items are presented, and management's discretion in deciding these questions are all important to statement issuers and users.

Unusual gains or losses include such diverse events as the sale of a plant, the loss of property from an unexpected hurricane, a one-time payment as a result of successful litigation, a gain or loss on the early extinguishment of debt, and the settlement of a prior year's tax liability for an unexpectedly higher or lower amount than anticipated. Some of these items are designated as unusual items and others—if they are both infrequent and unusual in nature—are labeled *"extraordinary"* items. *The discontinuance of a business segment* accounting problem arises when, for example, a company sells a division or closes down a segment of its business. *Accounting changes* include decisions to switch from one accounting principle to another, such as a change from accelerated to straight-line depreciation, and revisions of accounting estimates, such as the extension of depreciation lives from 10 to 12 years.

APB Opinion No. 30 is the most authoritative guide to the accounting for extraordinary, unusual, and infrequently occurring events and transactions. It also covers the

Professor David Hawkins prepared this note as the basis for class discussion.
Copyright © 1995 by the President and Fellows of Harvard College. Harvard Business School teaching note 195–185.

Illustration 1   Income Statement Format (amounts in thousands)

Revenues..		$100
Expenses..		80
Gain from unusual sources...		3
Income from continuing operations....................................		$23
Loss on discontinued operations:		
Income from operating discontinued segment...........................	$10	
Loss on disposal of discontinued segment.............................	12	2
Income before extraordinary items and effect of a change in accounting principles		$21
Extraordinary loss	$ 6	
Cumulative effect on prior years of a change in accounting principles	2	8
Net income		$13

---

accounting for discontinued operations. *APB Opinion No. 20* is the principal source of accounting authority on accounting changes. In addition, a number of other APB *Opinions* and FASB *Statements* touch on these accounting issues.

Current Presentation

Much of the controversy over how to account for unusual and extraordinary items, discontinued operations, and accounting changes involve questions of how these items should be defined and where in the income statement these items should be recorded and presented. The income statement format for presenting these items is shown in **Illustration 1.**

Two Points of View

The format shown in **Illustration 1** reflects an evolution in accounting for net income toward the so-called "all-inclusive" concept of the income statement. Others argue that the alternative approach referred to as "current operating performance" concept is preferable. Those holding the extreme version of this point of view would include only the revenue and expense items related to continuing operations shown in **Illustration 1** in net income. All of the other items would be treated as adjustment to owners' equity. The major arguments for the all-inclusive concept are:

1. The annual income statements over the life in an enterprise should, when added together, represent total net income.
2. Omitting certain items from the income statement invites income statement manipulation and income smoothing.

3. It is simple to prepare and leads to borderline cases being treated in a consistent manner by all companies.

4. Past income statements are of limited value in forecasting future results. Therefore, the inclusion of unusual and extraordinary items in income does not diminish their predictive value to statement users.

5. Including all items in income protects statement users against overlooking material extraordinary items.

6. If all items are included in income statements, users can use their judgment to decide which items should be omitted.

The major arguments of those favoring the current operating performance concept are:

1. Including unusual items in current income may be so distorting as to lead to unsound judgments with respect to the current earnings performance of a company.

2. It leads to an income figure that is more representative of what a company is able to earn from its usual or typical operations.

3. Not all statement users are trained to eliminate distorting extraordinary and unusual items included in an income figure determined using the all-inclusive concept.

4. Management and their independent accountants are in a better position than statement users to decide which distorting items should be excluded from income.

5. Comparisons with the income of prior years and other comparisons are easier.

To date, the FASB and SEC recommendations primarily reflect the all-inclusive point of view. The current operating performance concept has also been accepted in part, since the recommendations of these bodies have provided for an identification of the nonrecurring and unusual items in the income statement.

Financial analysts and investors often restate net income determined after inclusion of unusual items to a current operating performance basis for the purpose of valuing equity securities. They believed it is a better indicator of a company's future earnings potential.

Extraordinary Items

APB Opinion No. 30 concluded that all items of profit and loss should be included in the determination of net income, with the exception of items which are essentially adjustments to the results reported in prior periods. In addition, the APB recommended that extraordinary items, net of their related tax effect, should be segregated from the operating-related results in the income statement.

APB Opinion No. 30 adopted the point of view that an event or transaction should be presumed to be a usual and ordinary activity or event for the reporting entity unless the evidence clearly justifies its classification as an extraordinary item. *Opinion No. 30* defines an extraordinary item as an event or transaction that is both unusual and infrequent. It defines these qualities as follows:

1. Unusual nature—the underlying event or transaction should possess a high degree of abnormality and be of a type clearly unrelated to, or only incidentally related to, the ordinary and typical activities of the entity, taking into account the environment in which the entity operates.
2. Infrequency of occurrence—The underlying event or transaction should be of a type that would not reasonably be expected to recur in the foreseeable future, taking into account the environment in which the entity operates.

Since the environment in which the reporting company operates must be taken into account, judgment is required to determine whether or not an item is extraordinary. For example, an event or transaction may be unusual in nature for one entity but not for another, because of differences in their respective industries, locations, or extent of government regulation. Similarly, because the probabilities of an unusual occurrence differ in different environments, a specific transaction of one company may not meet the Opinion's definition of infrequency of occurrence, whereas a similar transaction of another company might. The fact that an unusual or infrequent event is beyond the control of management or significant financially does not automatically make it extraordinary.

The APB anticipated that extraordinary items would be rare. Gains or losses directly resulting from a major casualty or an expropriation are examples of extraordinary items cited in the *Opinion*.[1]

The *Opinion* specifically noted that the following gains and losses should *not* be reported as extraordinary items, because they are usual in nature and may be expected to recur as a consequence of customary continuing business activities:

1. Write-down or write-off of receivables, inventories, equipment leased to others, deferred costs, or other intangible assets.
2. Gains or losses from exchange or translation of foreign currencies, including those relating to major devaluation and revaluations.
3. Gains or losses on disposal of a segment of a business.
4. Other gains or losses from sale or abandonment of property, plant, or equipment used in the business.
5. Effects of a strike, including those against competitors and major suppliers.
6. Adjustment of accruals on long-term contracts.

Extraordinary items are reported in comparative statements, as shown in **Illustration 2.**

---

[1] Any portion of the losses from such events which would have resulted from a proper valuation of assets on a going concern basis should be excluded from the extraordinary item.

ILLUSTRATION 2   Illustrative Comparative Statement Presentation (amounts in thousands)

	1997	*1996*
Income before extraordinary items	$10,130	$ 7,990
Extraordinary items, net of applicable income taxes of $1,880,000 in 1997 and $500,000 in 1996....................................	(2,040)	(1,280)
Net income	$ 8,090	$ 6,710

Immaterial extraordinary items may be included in the net income without the extraordinary item label. *APB Opinion No. 30* discussed materiality as it related to extraordinary items as follows:

> The effect of an extraordinary event or transaction should be classified separately in the income statement if it is material in relation to income before extraordinary items or to the trend of annual earnings before extraordinary items, or is material by other appropriate criteria. Items should be considered individually and not in the aggregate in determining whether adjustments of opening balances in retained earnings or of net income of prior periods will be overlooked by the reader.

Unusual Events and Transactions

One of the potential major criticisms of *APB Opinion No. 30* is that many material transactions or events that are of an unusual nature or infrequent occurrence, but not both, may be included in the determination of income before extraordinary items. In the opinion of some statement users this requirement may obscure the profits from the continuing underlying business operations of the business, which is a figure many believe is very relevant to appraising the future prospects of a company. To counter this criticism, *APB Opinion No. 30* required that such transactions or events should be reported as a separate component of income from continuing operations on the face of the statement, or, alternatively, disclosed in the notes of the statement. These items should not be reported net of taxes.

Discontinuance or Disposal of a Business Segment

APB Opinion No. 30 set forth accounting rules for discontinued business operations, whether by sale or abandonment. For the purposes of the *Opinion,* a discontinued operation was defined as the operations of a segment of a business that has been sold, abandoned, spun off, or otherwise disposed of or, although still operating, is the subject of a formal plan for disposal. A segment of business is a component of an entity whose activities represent a separate major line of business or class of customer.

A segment may be in the form of a subsidy, a division, or a department. It may also be a joint venture or nonsubsidiary investee, provided the entities are clearly distinguishable operationally and physically from the investor entity.

APB Opinion No. 30 conclude that the results from continuing operations should be reported separately from discontinued operations and not as an extraordinary item. Accordingly, operations of a segment that has been or will be discontinued should be reported separately on a net of tax basis as a component of income before extraordinary items and the cumulative effect of accounting changes (if applicable) in the following manner:

(Amounts in thousands)

Income from continuing operations before income taxes	$5,000	
Provision for income taxes	2,000	
Income from continuing operations		$3,000
Discontinued operations:		
Income (loss) from operations of discontinued Division A less applicable income taxes of $500	500	
Loss on disposal of Division A including provision of $300 for operating losses during phase-out period (less applicable income taxes of $100)	400	100
Net income		$2,900

In addition, the statement of prior periods should be restated to disclose the results of operations of the disposed segment, less applicable income taxes, as a separate component of income before extraordinary items.

The measurement date of the gain or loss from a disposal of a business segment is the date when the management with the authority to approve the action commits itself to a formal plan to dispose of the segment. If a loss is anticipated on the disposal, the anticipated loss should be provided for in the accounting period that includes the measurement date. If a gain is expected, it should be recognized when it is realized, which ordinarily is the time of the disposal. Should the plan of disposal be expected to be carried out over several accounting periods, any estimated income or losses from the projected operations of the segment during these periods should be considered at the measurement date in determining the anticipated gain or loss.

All expected losses from future operations between the measurement and disposal date should be included in the gain or loss computation. If income is projected during this period, it should be included in the computation up to the amount of any projected losses. Income in excess of the projected losses should be recognized when realized. In addition to any projected income or losses from the operating segment, the gain or loss from the disposal should include only those costs and expenses subsequent to the measurement date that are directly associated with the decision to dispose of the segment, such as severance pay and employee relocation expenses. Finally, should the estimate of the disposal loss included in the measurement date period later prove faulty, the revised estimates of the loss should be included in the determination of income in the period of the revised estimate.

Accounting Principle, Estimate, and Entity Changes

The net income and financial condition of a company may change from one period to another because of accounting changes. This will affect the usefulness of historical data for trend analysis. It may also obscure poor managerial performance. Therefore, users of financial statements must be aware of (1) how changes in accounting are reflected in financial statements and (2) when and how to adjust accounting data to make the presentation comparable from one period to another.

The treatment of accounting changes is determined primarily by *APB Opinion No. 20* "Accounting Changes" and its subsequent amendments. The *APB Opinion* covers: (1) changes in accounting principles, (2) changes in accounting estimates, and (3) reporting a change in the definition of the entity issuing the financial statements. These are considered to be accounting changes. In addition, the *Opinion* deals with reporting corrections of errors in previously issued financial statements, which is not considered to be an accounting change, however.

In general, *APB Opinion No. 20* requires that:

1. The cumulative effect of an accounting principle change is reported in the period of the change.
2. Changes in accounting estimates are accounted for prospectively.
3. Changes in the reporting entity require that restatement of all prior period statements presented to conform to the new reporting entity.
4. A correction of an error in the previously issued financial statement is reported as a prior period adjustment.

APB Opinion No. 20 and several subsequent FASB *Statements* contain exceptions to the general rule for accounting principle changes. These exceptions will be discussed after the review of the general rules.

Principle Changes

A change in accounting principle comes with the adoption of a generally accepted accounting principle that is different from the one used previously to report a particular kind of transaction. The *Opinion* notes that an accounting principle change includes not only changes in accounting principles and practices but also changes in the method of applying them.

Common examples of an accounting change include a shift from accelerated to straight-line depreciation and a change from reporting income on an installment basis to the sale method.

A characteristic of these changes is that each involves a choice between two or more generally accepted accounting principles.

A change in accounting principles does not occur when:

1. An accounting principle is adopted initially in recognition of events or transactions occurring for the first time or which were previously immaterial

2. An adoption or modification of an accounting principle is required by a change that is clearly different in the substance of events or transactions from those previously occurring.

Whenever an accounting principle is changed, the statements of the period in which the change is made must include (1) the current annual charge or credit for the item according to the new principle as an element of the operating income, and (2) an adjustment to the current period's net income equal to the cumulative effect on the period's beginning retained earnings of applying the new accounting principle retroactively. This cumulative amount, which is the difference between the recomputed amount and the amount originally recorded, is shown after extraordinary items. In addition, pro forma net income figures, based on a retroactive adjustment of the prior periods' statements to reflect the new principle, should be included for each period presented in the statements. Thus, the current comparative statement presents both actual and pro forma results.

Cumulative Effect.   The cumulative effect of changing to a new accounting principle is shown in the income statement between the captions "extraordinary items" and "net income," but it should not be considered as an extraordinary item. This item is shown net of its related tax effect.

In addition, both the gross amount and the per share amount of the effect of an accounting principle change must be disclosed. The per share data on the face of the statement should also include the per-share amount of the cumulative effect of the accounting change.

The data for prior periods included in the comparative statements are not adjusted for the accounting change. It is the same as stated previously in the prior years' annual reports.

Pro Forma Effects.   In addition to current period's actual net income (including the cumulative effect) shown in the face of the statements income before extraordinary items and net income on a pro forma basis, computed as if the newly adopted accounting principle had been applied to all periods presented, should be disclosed. These data should also be on a per-share basis.

In addition to the direct effects of the change, the pro forma income figure should include adjustments for any nondiscretionary items that are based on either income before taxes or net income. Such nondiscretionary items may be profit sharing expenses or royalties based on income. In these cases, if the accounting principle change resulted in a different income figure than reported previously, these income-based expense items would automatically be different. In computing the pro forma data, all related tax effects should be recognized.

Disclosure is required of the adjustments made to prior years' income before extraordinary items and net income to determine the pro forma amounts. In addition, if only an income statement for the current period is presented, the actual and pro forma amounts for the current and immediately preceding periods should be disclosed.

Which Income Number?   Users of financial statements should base their evaluation of a company on both the net income and pro forma net income figure. Of the two,

---

ILLUSTRATION 3 **Reporting an Accounting Principle Change**

	1997	*1996*
Income before extraordinary item and cumulative effect of a change in accounting principle	$1,200,000	$1,100,000
Extraordinary item (description)	(35,000)	100,000
Cumulative effect of prior years (to December 31, 1996) of changing to a different depreciation method	125,000	—
Net income	$1,290,000	$1,200,000

---

however, the pro forma figures are usually the better indicator of future earnings, since the current year's net income figure includes the one time cumulative debt or credit and the prior year's net income was determined using the old accounting method. The footnote related to these presentations should always be examined since it will explain (1) the nature and effect of the accounting principle change; and (2) the computation of the pro forma figures. There is no requirement that this footnote disclosure be repeated in subsequent periods.

The situation assumed in **Illustration 3** is: The ABC Company decided in 1997 to adopt the straight-line method of depreciation for plant equipment. The straight-line method will be used for new acquisitions as well as for previously acquired plant equipment for which depreciation has been provided on the accelerated method.

Amortization Method Changes. Long-lived assets are charged to income through a process which, depending on the type of asset involved, is called depreciation, depletion, or amortization (all of which are referred to as amortization in this note). Sometimes changes are made in the amortization method for classes of similar identifiable assets. In such cases, if the new method is adopted for all newly acquired assets of a particular class (and the old method is used for the previously recorded asset in that class), there is no need to adjust income figures shown on the face of the statements. That is, no cumulative effect is included and no pro forma data are presented. Such data are presented only if the new method of amortization is applied to the previously recorded assets.

When an amortization method change is not applied to previously recorded assets, the nature of the change and its effects on income and related per-share data should be disclosed.

Amounts Not Determinable. If it is impossible to compute the cumulative effect of beginning retained earnings, the effect on the change on the current period's results should be disclosed. In addition, an explanation should be given for omitting the cumulative effect and the pro forma amounts.

If the pro forma amounts cannot be determined for individual prior periods, the cumulative effect should nevertheless be computed and included in an adjustment to current income. The reason for not showing the pro forma amounts should be explained.

Special Retroactive Restatements.   Restatements of all prior periods presented to reflect the retroactive application of a newly adopted accounting principle is required by *APB Opinion No. 20,* as amended, in five special cases. These are:

1. A change from the LIFO method of inventory pricing to another method.
2. A change in the method of accounting for long-term construction-type contracts.
3. A change to or from the full cost method of accounting, which is used in the extractive industries.
4. An initial public offering of securities.[2]
5. A change from retirement–replacement–betterment accounting to depreciation accounting for railroad tract structures.

Restatement is achieved by:

a. Including in each statement for the periods presented an amount based upon the new principle. This replaces the amount determined by the old method in all periods preceding the current one.
b. Adjusting each period's beginning retained earnings for the cumulative effect of the change up to that point in time.

Interim Statements.   If an accounting principle change is made in the first interim period of a fiscal year, the cumulative effect of the change should be included in the first period's statement. Accounting changes of this type made during the accounting year should be presented as if the change had been made in the first interim period of the year. That is, the current period should not include the cumulative effect. However, the year-to-date figures and first interim period should be restated to conform to this restatement.

Justification.   If a new accounting principle is adopted, the change must be justified on the ground that it is preferable. The burden of justifying other changes rests with the entity proposing the change.

The nature, effect on income, and justification for an accounting change should be disclosed in the footnotes to the statements of the period in which the change is made. In addition, similar data related to accounting changes must be filed with the SEC along with a letter from the company's auditor stating that the new principle is preferable to the old one.

---

[2]Accounting changes made in anticipation of an initial public distribution of stock are exempt from the general requirement of *APB Opinion No. 20.* Typically, closely held private companies follow different accounting practices than they would use if they were publicly held. Since these old practices are likely to be discontinued once the initial public distribution is made, it is more useful to investors for such companies to adopt their new accounting principles and estimates retroactively in connection with initial public stock offerings.

This exemption is available only once. It is also available only when a company first issues its financial statements for any one of the following purposes: (a) obtaining additional equity capital from investors; (b) affecting a business combination; or (c) registering securities.

Consistency.   Financial reporting presumes that once an accounting principle is selected, it will be applied consistently from one period to another to account for similar events and transactions. This makes statements comparable and enhances their usefulness and intelligibility.

Changes in Accounting Estimates

The preparation of financial statements requires estimating the effects of future events, such as the life of a piece of equipment or the amount of future warranty expenses related to current sales. Since the future cannot be predicted accurately, it is desirable that the accounting estimates be revised as more experience is acquired or additional information is obtained.

Sometimes it is difficult to distinguish between a change in the accounting principle and a change in an accounting estimate. For example, a company may decide to write off all of its deferred plant preoperating costs immediately, because it now seems unlikely that the related plant will become a profitable commercial venture. Thus, the new accounting method is adopted in part because the estimate of the investment's future benefits has changed. The principle and estimate changes are inseparable. Changes of this type are considered to be changes in estimates for the purposes of applying *APB Opinion No. 20.*

Prospective Treatment.   *APB Opinion No. 20* requires that the effect of a change in accounting estimate be recorded prospectively in financial statements. That is, the estimate change should be accounted for in (a) the period of the change if the change affects that period only or (b) the period of the change and future periods if the change affects both. The statements of prior periods must not be restated on a direct or pro forma basis to reflect accounting estimate changes.[3]

Disclosure.   The effects on income before extraordinary items, on net income, and on related share amounts of an estimate change that affects future periods should be disclosed. Unless the information is material, disclosure is not necessary of estimates made each period in the ordinary course of accounting for such items as uncollectable accounts or inventory obsolescence.

Changes in the Entity

A change in the reporting entity occurs when the definition of the reporting entity with its group of companies represented in the current period's statement is different from the entity represented in the immediately prior period's statement. This situation results from (a) presenting consolidated or combined statements in place of individual company statements; or (b) changing the specific subsidiaries in the group of companies for which consolidated or combined financial statements are presented.

---

[3]The only exception occurs when the change meets all the conditions for a prior period adjustment.

Changes in the reporting entity should be made by restating the financial statements of all prior periods presented in order to provide the financial information of all periods for the new reporting entity.[4]

The nature, the effect on income figures and related share amounts, and the reasons for a change in the reporting entity should be disclosed for all periods presented. Subsequent statements need not repeat this disclosure.

Materiality

The basis for *materiality* determinations is defined for the purposes of *APB Opinion No. 20* as being any effect of a change, or a combined effect of changes, that materially affect (a) income before extraordinary items and net income or (b) the trend of earnings.

This basis for determining materiality conforms closely to the investor's interest in statements. Investors focus on both net income and the change in income from one period to another. Items that are immaterial relative to total income may be very relevant when compared to the amount of change in income from the prior period.

More recently, the *FASB Statement of Financial Accounting Concepts No. 2,* "Qualitative Characteristics of Accounting Information," defined material as:

> The magnitude of an omission or misstatement of accounting information that, in the light of surrounding circumstances, makes it probable that the judgment of a reasonable person relying on the information would have been changed or influenced by the omission or misstatement.

A change that does not materially affect the current status, but is reasonably certain to have material effects on later periods, should be disclosed in the period of change.

Correction of an Error

Errors in financial statements result from mathematical mistakes, mistakes in the application of an accounting principle, or oversight or misuse of facts that existed at the time the statements were prepared. (In contrast, a change in estimate results from new information or subsequent developments which provide better insight or improved judgment.) A change to a generally accepted accounting principle from one that is not generally accepted is considered to be a correction of an error.

An error in the statement of a prior period discovered subsequent to its issue should be reported as a prior period adjustment. That is, the beginning retained earnings of each period presented should be adjusted for the error. If the error relates to any of the income figures presented, these should be adjusted for the related amount of the error.

The nature of the error and its effect on the statements should be disclosed in the period in which the error was discovered and corrected. Future statements need not repeat this disclosure.

---

[4]A later chapter describes the accounting for change in the reporting entity due to a business combination.

Financial Analysis

The typical issue that confronts statement users when they encounter unusual items, discontinued operations, extraordinary items, and accounting change situations is whether these items should be included or excluded from their financial ratios, cash flow, and earnings quality assessments that include a profit component. While the resolution of this issue depends upon the company's circumstances and the objective of the financial analysis, some general practices have evolved. These are described below.

In most cases, unusual items that qualify for extraordinary item accounting treatment are excluded from current appraisals of management performance and earnings projections based on current and past statements. These exclusions are justified by management's inability to control the event giving rise to the extraordinary items and the nonrecurring, unusual, and unexpected nature of the item. In contrast, cash flow effect, if any, of an extraordinary item is always included in analyses of a company's cash flow. Extraordinary items have cash flow benefits and disadvantages that can impact the total current and anticipated resources of a company, its ability to meet financial commitments, and the value of its stock. Standing alone, extraordinary items are usually excluded from earnings quality assessments. If a company reports extraordinary items frequently or has the potential to report them frequently, however, this characteristic is regarded as a negative earnings quality consideration. The earnings surprise aspect of extraordinary items merits this rating, irrespective of whether the company reports extraordinary gains or losses.

Unusual events not classified as extraordinary items for accounting purposes are often excluded from single-year appraisals of management, but are nearly always included in long-term management performance evaluations and earnings projections based on past earnings data. This treatment reflects the operating nature of the item and also the fact that by recording an unusual operating item, management is indicating that prior period operating results may have been over- or understated in the light of current knowledge. Like extraordinary items, the cash flow effect of unusual nonextraordinary items is always included in cash flow appraisals. Unusual items given rise to losses are usually considered to be a negative quality-of-earnings factor. It indicates the company's earlier earnings may have been overstated, and the same bias may still be present in current and prospective earnings. Unusual gains leave the opposite impression. While this may seem to suggest they should be regarded as a positive factor, they are not, primarily because statement users generally don't like positive or negative surprises. Furthermore, unusual gains may be a red flag signaling that management is realizing gains in an attempt to mask declining operating earnings.

Income from continuing operations is used by most statement users to predict future income levels, since by definition any income or losses reported for discontinued operations is not expected to continue once the operation responsible is discontinued in future periods. While following this practice, statement users should always be mindful that some so-called discontinued operations have continued to operate over many accounting periods beyond the announcement date of management's intention to discontinue them. Because of this experience and management's responsibility to manage the operation until discontinued, the results of discontinued operations are usually included in current appraisals of management until the discontinued operation is in fact discontinued. Since discontinued operations impact cash flows, they are included in cash flow analysis. Discontinued operations involving losses are regarded as a negative earnings quality factor until discontinued. Discontinued operations involving potential gains are normally treated like one time income sources and as such are regarded as a low-quality source of earnings.

The effects of accounting changes are usually excluded from management appraisals in the year of change, since the accounting change typically has little, if any, economic substance. However, most statement users seem to use the actual reported income for the prechange year as well as the change year in making earnings projections based on past earnings data. Their rationale is that since management often makes accounting changes to maintain past earnings trends, the trend line rather than actual earnings is the more important piece of data for projection purposes. Also, in the future, to maintain historical growth rates management will continue to make accounting changes that cannot be predicted in the current period.

While past periods are not usually restated for prediction purposes, statement users ought to restate past earnings to the new accounting basis to understand why it was not used in the past. Projecting the restated data can also be helpful in understanding some future implications of the accounting change.

Since accounting changes are usually made only for reporting purposes and not for tax reporting, they typically do not have any cash flow effect. Therefore, they often do not enter into cash flow analyses.

In most cases, accounting changes result in lower quality earnings, since the shift is from a conservative to a more liberal accounting method. Since most companies making accounting changes retain their tax method, which is usually a more conservative approach than their book method, statement users often examine the deferred tax effect of the differences between the tax and the new and old book methods to get a sense of dollar effect of the shift away from conservatism.

Finally, the reported dollar effect of retaining the old accounting method should always be identified in both the year of change and the following year. In most instances, the reason for the change is higher profits or an improved balance sheet ratio, rather than the reason stated to meet the *APB Opinion No. 20* accounting change criteria.

For analysis purposes, extraordinary items, unusual gains, and discontinued business profits are usually excluded from those ratios incorporating profits that are designed to measure a company's ability to sustain a level of performance over time, such as debt coverage ratios and measures of return on capital. The inclusion of these items is thought to distort future profits implied by the current measurement, and, in the case of gains, to overstate current performance. Unusual and (if the discontinued business is still being operated) discontinued business losses are usually included in these ratios. This practice reflects the conservative bias of prudent analysts. Since accounting changes seldom have any economic or cash flow substance, care must be taken not to interpret ratios incorporating the profit figures inflated by the accounting change as indicators of an improved situation.

Agro Feed Products, Incorporated

In April 1995, David Strange, president, Agro Feed Products, Inc. (AGF) said: "We believe it is clearly in the best interest of the stockholders to discontinue AGF's feed business, to sell the assets of the Feed Division and release capital funds for operations that offer greater opportunities for profit and growth." In late May, the company's audit committee met to review the accounting issues facing AGF's top management as a result of the decision to discontinue the Feed Division.

In addition, the audit committee planned to review at this meeting the accounting for several other major events that had occurred during the last quarter of the company's fiscal year. These were: the write-off of a foreign subsidiary's inventories as a result of a new government regulation banning the use of a certain food preservative; the decision of management to extend the depreciation life of some domestic depreciable assets; the out-of-court settlement of a claim against the company; an uninsured loss arising from the destruction by a tornado of a major AGF grain storage facility in Kansas; and the gain on the sale of land acquired earlier for possible future plant sites.

The Company

In 1995, AGF was a large convenience foods manufacturer with diversified interests in specialty chemicals, electronics, materials testing equipment, and related fields. Sales for the fiscal year ended May 31, 1994, exceeded $575 million and net earnings after taxes were almost $13 million for the same period. (See **Exhibits 1** and **2** for financial statements.) The company's operations included flour mills, terminal elevators, flour

Professor David F. Hawkins prepared this case as the basis for class discussion rather than to illustrate either effective or ineffective handling of an administrative situation.
Copyright © 1996 by the President and Fellows of Harvard College. Harvard Business School case 197–006.

EXHIBIT 1   **Agro Feed Products, Inc., Consolidated Balance Sheet at May 31 (in thousands)**

	1994	1993
Assets		
Cash	$ 12,541	$ 15,211
Accounts receivable (net)	44,825	42,515
Inventories	69,513	55,879
Total current assets	$126,879	$113,605
Miscellaneous cost chargeable to future periods	8,767	7,268
Land, buildings, and equipment (net)	124,780	121,048
Miscellaneous assets	2,816	2,790
Goodwill, patents, trade names, and other intangibles	4,646	3,970
Total assets	$267,888	$248,681
Liabilities and Equity		
Notes payable	$ 7,250	$ —
Accounts payable and accrued expenses	29,611	22,597
Accrued taxes	12,833	12,513
Thrift accounts of officers and employees	3,665	3,539
Dividends payable	277	277
Total current liabilities	$ 53,636	$ 38,926
Long-term debt	45,444	45,200
Other liabilities	4,837	4,959
Total liabilities	$103,917	$ 89,085
Stockholders' equity:		
Preferred stock, 5% cumulative	$ 22,147	$ 22,147
Common stock	46,276	45,123
Retained earnings	95,787	92,658
Treasury stock	(239)	(332)
Total stockholders' equity	$163,971	$159,596
Total liabilities and equity	$267,888	$248,681

and food packaging plants, and chemical and electronic installations throughout the United States and in a number of foreign countries.

AGF was incorporated in 1971 to acquire several grain-handling and milling firms in the Midwest. Numerous acquisitions in related areas were made in the years following. During its early years, the company was essentially a holding company; but in 1985, most of the subsidiary corporations were dissolved and the firm became an operating company. Rapid expansion followed as the company integrated vertically and developed brand-name consumer goods including breakfast cereals, cake mixes, and similar products based upon its basic milling activities. Livestock feed products were an integral part of operations throughout most of the company's history.

Increased competition and declining profit margins for food manufacturing caused AGF to seek more rapid growth by diversification into chemicals, electronics, oil-seed processing, and for a short time into small household appliances. Sales increased only

Exhibit 2   Agro Food Products, Inc., Consolidated Income Statement for the Fiscal Year Ended May 31 (in thousands)

	1994	1993
Sale of products and services	$575,512	$537,818
Costs:		
Cost of products and services sold, exclusive of items shown below	$431,060	$405,256
Depreciation	8,427	7,681
Interest	2,989	2,502
Contribution to employees' retirement plan	2,779	2,435
Selling, general and administrative expenses	105,966	97,582
Federal and other taxes on income	11,459	10,847
Total costs	$562,680	$526,303
Earnings for the year	$ 12,832	$ 11,515

modestly in the 1980s and profits moved erratically. AGF found itself competing for sales in industries that were dominated by large companies and where, again, margins were very low or even nonexistent. This was the case for a number of years in the company's Feed Division.

The company also sought to reach wider markets on an international scale. In 1982, productive and marketing facilities were constructed in Canada for several food products. In the early 1980s, small acquisitions were made in Central and South America, in Pakistan, and in Europe. Most of these international ventures were wholly owned subsidiaries, but a few were joint enterprises with firms in foreign nations. The nature of these foreign operations varied from food product marketing and raw material processing to electronic activities.

The company's 1994 sales volume was distributed among the major segments of the company as follows: consumer foods, $260 million; flour, $161 million; feed, $78 million; specialty products, $28 million; chemicals, $15 million; and electronics, $33 million.

Change in Management and Company Policy

In December 1994, several important changes were made in the AGF top management. David Strange, who had come to the company from a top management position in the food industry, was named president. Several new vice presidents and divisional managers were also announced about this time.

The change in management was followed by a change in corporate policy directed toward improved profitability and growth through concentration in the areas of convenience foods and specialty chemicals. Early in 1995, in response to a stockholder's question, "Where is the company's profit potential?" management published its succinct answer in *AGF News,* a quarterly publication directed to stockholders: "Our combined chemical and electronic business was still less than 10% of total sales in the last fiscal year. We expect growth in these areas, but our greatest profit potential is in packaged convenience food products." A consumer food research facility was completed, and expenditures for research and development and for advertising were increased markedly. Management believed that development and marketing for new convenience food products would bring the desired higher sales and wider profit margins. norm

All areas of the company's activities were reorganized to conform to this new policy. For example, several further changes were made in the organization and personnel of the company's Electronic Group, which had been created a year earlier to combine all electronic, mechanical, aerospace, and related operations into a single unit. In line with these changes, management was considering the discontinuance of several of its electronic operations at a later date.

Decision to Liquidate the Feed Division

For several years, the entire operation of the Feed Division of AGF had been under study. Management could not see any means of changing operations to make a satisfactory return on investment in the future, despite efforts to build needed volume in the highly competitive, low-margin feed industry through extensive expansion into poultry, broiler, and turkey growing operations. Prices of broilers and turkeys during most of fiscal year 1995 were below the cost of production. In addition, many direct feed customers, suffering from the same depressed prices, were unable to buy in normal volumes and some could not meet their financial obligations. Increasing bad debt losses from uncollectible receivables added to the company's operating losses in this area.

Feed Division operating losses had been substantial for several prior years, and losses for the fiscal year to end May 31, 1995, were expected to be $5 million before tax credits of $2.3 million.[1] Total company sales and profits were expected to be significantly lower than those reported in the 1995 fiscal year.

The decision to begin liquidation of the Feed Division was made and announced in April 1995. An orderly withdrawal extending over a two- or three-year period was planned. During this period, all plant facilities of the division were to be sold. Operations were to be continued into the 1996 fiscal accounting period, but only to honor existing firm contracts which were to require several months for completion. The division's employees were to be transferred and absorbed into other AGF operations or to be terminated with benefits in line with existing company policies.

Reporting the Feed Division Liquidation to Stockholders

The controller was asked by the audit committee to prepare a projection of the amounts involved in the Feed Division liquidation. This report did not include the 1995, $5 million pre-tax operating loss of the division. His report was submitted to the

---

[1]The estimated operating losses of the division between the measurement date April 1995 and May 31, 1995, included in this amount were $1 million before a tax credit of nearly $500,000.

EXHIBIT 3   Agro Food Products, Inc., Projection of Estimated Costs and Losses Arising from Feed Division Liquidation as of May 31, 1995

Accounts receivable charged off between measurement date (April 1995) and end of fiscal year	$5,110,461	
Less: Bad debt allowance provided from operations to date	3,644,536	
	$1,465,925	
Estimated future additional uncollectible receivables	570,000	$ 2,035,925
Losses and write-down of land, building, and equipment:		
Recorded between measurement data and end of fiscal year	$1,465,425	
Estimated additional losses in future dispositions	6,867,608	8,333,033
Costs and expenses related to discontinuance of operations:		
Incurred between measurement date and end of fiscal year	$2,294,559	
Estimated future liquidation costs, including fiscal year 1996 operations to satisfy existing contracts	2,803,073	5,097,632
Total		$15,466,590
Less income tax credits[a]		11,027,752
Total after income tax credits		$ 4,438,838

---

[a]Income tax credits will be claimed against actual tax liability when expenses are incurred or when properties are sold. Loss carryover provisions in the tax law will provide full benefit for losses not used currently. Tax credits include benefit of write-off of Feed Division goodwill not carried on books as an asset. This goodwill resulting from acquisitions of feed companies in earlier years was written off the books, but a deduction for income taxes was not allowable until the liquidation of feed operations.

AGF audit committee in late May. The controller's projections were made to May 31, 1995, and gave recognition to the operations and partial liquidation transactions that were expected to occur both prior to and after that date. A summary of his detailed report is shown in **Exhibit 3.**

The analysis pointed out that neither the timing nor the method of reporting the liquidation in the annual report to stockholders would have any effect upon income tax reporting. The estimated total book loss of more than $15 million was significantly reduced by computed tax benefits, to a projected net loss of $4,438,838.

The loss on liquidation was significant in amount in comparison to both net income and financial size.

Other Agenda Items

In addition to the Feed Division liquidation accounting issues, the audit committee had to consider five other accounting items on its agenda.

In early March 1995, after several years of litigation, the French courts up-held a government ban on the use in food products of certain preservatives that were thought to cause cancer. This ruling required the company to destroy all of its existing inventories containing the banned preservatives and recall the affected products from the marketplace. The estimated cost of this action was $500,000 after tax credits. It was expected that the recall program would be completed by May 31, 1995. In addition, it was anticipated that in the near future other Common Market governments might follow the lead of the French government. To avoid any possible trouble in these other Common Market countries, AGF had stopped using the banned preservative in all of the other Common Market countries. The estimated after tax cost of reformulation and testing associated with the switch in preservatives was $300,000. The after-tax legal and other costs incurred in contesting the government's ban were $500,000 in 1994 and $75,000 in 1995.

During the fourth quarter of fiscal year 1995, the AGF management decided to use a 13-year depreciation life for a certain class of equipment used extensively in the company's food operations. Previously, this class of equipment had been depreciated on a 10-year basis. This decision applied only to equipment purchased after March 1995. This decision increased the fourth-quarter after-tax profits by $200,000 over what they would have been if a 10-year life had been used.

In April 1995, AGF reached an out-of-court settlement with a consumer protection group which had brought a class action against the company on behalf of a number of individuals who claimed an AGF product had been injurious to their health. This action, which had been in litigation since 1980, was settled for an after-tax cost of $250,000. Originally, the plaintiffs for the class had sought $100 million in damages. Since the company could not reasonably estimate what their ultimate loss might have been from this claim, no provisions for this possible loss had been made in prior years. This $250,000 settlement was not covered by insurance.

In the fourth quarter of fiscal 1995, an unseasonal and unusually severe tornado destroyed AGF's central grain facility in Kansas. The company estimated that its after-tax loss from this catastrophe was $135,000 more than AGF would recover from its facilities insurance claim.

Soon after the new management took over control of the company, it conducted a survey to identify redundant and surplus assets that might be sold to raise funds to finance the company's operations. Among the assets identified as potential candidates for sale were several pieces of industrial land purchased as possible factory or distribution center sites. After several months of trying, AGF sold two of these sites in May 1995 for an after-tax gain of $750,000.

During the prior three quarters of fiscal year 1995, the company had not reported any unusual items, extraordinary items, discontinued operations, or accounting changes in its interim financial statements.

Some Considerations

The terms of the sizable long-term note indebtedness of AGF placed a restriction upon the payment of dividends to common stockholders. In general, dividends paid or declared after May 31, 1994, could not exceed 85% of consolidated net earnings since that date. At May 31, 1994, $30,411,380 of retained earnings was free from this restriction.

Management was very much aware of its position in the competitive environment in which it operated. Selected information for several firms in the milling and consumer foods industries is shown in **Exhibit 4.**

In mid-April 1995, the market price of AGF's common stock had dropped to $28 after being in the middle $30s in the last few months of 1994. Although sales for the six months ended November 30, 1994, had exceeded those of the corresponding period for the previous year, earnings per share had declined to $0.55 from $0.75 for

EXHIBIT 4   Selected Industry Data[a]

	Sales[b]	Net Income after Taxes[a]	Earnings per Sales Dollar	Earnings per Share	Dividends per Share	Price Range High	Low
Agro Feed							
1990	$ 527,701	$12,235	2.3%	$1.63	$1.00	$23	$23
1991	529,820	14,694	2.8	1.98	1.00	30	20
1992	545,998	16,817	3.1	2.26	1.00	38	30
1993	537,818	11,515	2.1	1.46	1.15	34	34
1994	575,512	12,832	2.2	1.63	1.20	39	31
Processors United:							
1990	$ 331,362	$ 4,006	1.2%	$2.02	$1.25	$22	$20
1991	350,610	5,641	1.6	2.90	1.25	37	21
1992	359,657	7,913	2.2	3.70	1.25	50	37
1993	373,818	6,541	1.8	3.03	1.40	47	32
1994	384,962	7,911	2.1	3.62	1.40	77	44
Parker Foods:							
1990	$ 438,261	$14,569	3.3%	$2.28	$0.80	$31	$23
1991	493,527	17,468	3.5	2.71	1.00	52	25
1992	530,571	17,784	3.4	2.74	1.20	52	42
1993	527,816	18,915	3.6	2.76	1.20	45	39
1994	581,042	19,908	3.4	3.03	1.35	45	39
National Foods:							
1990	$ 971,334	$43,399	4.4%	$1.81	$1.95	$25	$20
1991	1,008,897	48,397	1.99	2.00	2.00	40	24
1992	1,052,964	54,145	5.1	2.21	2.30	54	37
1993	1,087,076	61,071	5.6	2.48	2.60	75	62
1994	1,160,177	66,821	5.8	2.69	2.10	108	69
Consumer Products:							
1990	$1,432,319	$44,058	3.1%	$3.18	$1.80	$39	$33
1991	1,451,245	45,544	3.1	3.27	1.80	50	38
1992	1,605,725	49,362	3.1	3.51	1.95	54	46
1993	1,667,176	40,667	3.0	3.59	2.00	66	45
1994	1,790,834	50,211	2.8	3.51	2.00	79	59

[a]Fiscal year endings for the companies are: Agro Feed and Processors United Company, May 31; Parker Foods Company, September 30; National Food, Inc., March 31; and Consumer Products Corporation, December 31.

[b]In thousands. All data adjusted for stock splits and dividends.

the same period. At the time of the third quarter of fiscal year 1995, market analysts were anticipating that earnings for the year ending May 31, 1995, would just cover the $1.20 annual dividend and that in the longer run the stock price would recover to the 1994 levels.

Perhaps the most important single factor considered by management in choosing the method of reporting Feed Division liquidation losses was the anticipated effect upon stockholders and prospective investor attitudes toward the company. Throughout its entire history, AGF had maintained an ideal relationship with its stockholders, and the new management would not consider any reporting alternative which stockholders would be likely to interpret as improper or uninformative. Management was aware that the amount of net income reported for the fiscal year ending May 31, 1995, might have an effect upon the market price of the company's common stock. Not only was there a concern to preserve the position of present stockholders, but there was a strong possibility that in the near future, additional issues of common stock might be offered to facilitate further acquisitions for expansion in the area of convenience foods. Management was therefore anxious to avoid any reporting practice which might have a significant continuing adverse effect upon its relations in the stockholder and financial communities.

Questions

1. How should the liquidation of the Feed Division be reflected in the company's financial statements? _____

2. How should the company account for the other items on the audit committee's agenda? _____

3. Assume that AGF's 1995 profit after taxes before considering the "other agenda items" on the audit committee's agenda will be $9.5 million, prepare the company's 1995 income statement, starting with the line "Income from continuing operations." The $9.5 million includes the estimated 1995 operating losses of the Feed Division, but not the items included in **Exhibit 3.**

4. How do you think existing and potential investors might react to the 1995 income statement treatment of the items on the audit committee's agenda? _____

Chapter 12

Basic and Diluted Earnings per Share

The measurement of earnings per share can range from being simple to complex, depending on a company's capital structure. FASB Statement No. 128, "Earnings per Share" requires the periodic earnings per share of a company with a simple capital structure be determined by dividing its net income attributable to common stockholders for the period by the weighted average number of common shares outstanding during the period. The resulting figure known as "basic" earnings per share represents the common stockholders' equity in the company's net income. For companies with complex capital structures an additional earnings-per-share figure is required. Its computation involves some adjustments to net income and the weighted average number of shares outstanding to reflect potential dilution by convertible securities, warrants, and options. The resulting earnings per share is a statistical representation of the common stockholders' equity in net income after allowing for potential dilution of that interest by securities that could have claims on net income either directly or through the right to acquire common stock under certain conditions.[1] FASB Statement No. 128 calls this figure "diluted" earnings per share. Prior to FASB Statement No. 128, APB Opinion No. 15 required a similarly computed figure. It was referred to as "fully diluted" earnings per share.

   Earnings-per-share data are a key financial statistic for many statement users. Earnings-per-share data can be very useful, together with other data, in evaluating management's past performance and predicting future earnings potential. However, overreliance on published earnings-per-share figures has several pitfalls. First, the earnings-per-share data tend to be accepted without examining the details of the

---

Professor David F. Hawkins prepared this note as the basis for class discussion.
Copyright © 1995 by the President and Fellows of Harvard College. Harvard Business School teaching note 195–233.

   [1]It is important to note that the adjustments in complex capital structure situations are made for the sole purpose of calculating earnings per share. Neither the net income figure shown on the income statement nor the actual number of shares outstanding is affected by these adjustments.

income statement. This can lead to misleading inferences. Second, the emphasis on a single share-earnings figure tends to shift the attention of statement users and investors away from the enterprise's total operations and financial condition.

Dual Presentation: A Summary

After trying unsuccessfully for many years to deemphasize the significance of earnings per share in accounting reports, the Accounting Principles Board (APB) switched its position and required in Opinion No. 15 these data to be displayed on the earnings statement. The factors contributing to this decision were (a) the widespread use of these data; (b) the importance people attached to them; (c) the apparently misleading use of this figure by certain companies to boost their stock prices by issuing securities with common stock characteristics which did not enter into the earnings-per-share calculation; (d) the increasing use of warrants and convertible securities which had the potential effect of diluting earnings per share; and (e) the apparent unwillingness of other accounting authorities to deal forcefully with the inconsistencies, confusion, and abuses in this area. Subsequently, the FASB decided to issue a new earnings-per-share standard. The FASB's objective was to simplify the measurement of earnings per share and to support a concurrent earnings-per-share project of the International Accounting Standards Committee.

The APB in Opinion No. 15 required that companies present a primary earnings-per-share computation that would take into consideration all of a company's common stock and common stock equivalents. It also stated that when this primary earnings-per-share calculation was subject to future potential dilution from the conversion of senior securities, a second earnings-per-share figure should be published showing the full effect of this dilution. Henceforth, companies with complex capital structures had to present with equal prominence on the face of the income statement the company's primary earnings-per-share and fully diluted earnings-per-share amounts.

Primary earnings per share are the amount of net income attributable to each share of outstanding common stock and common stock equivalent. A common stock equivalent is any security which, because of its terms or the circumstances under which it was *issued,* is in substance equivalent to common stock.

The FASB Statement No. 128 replaced primary earnings per share with basic earnings per share.

Fully diluted earnings per share is the amount of current earnings per share reflecting the maximum dilution that would result from conversion of convertible securities and exercise of warrants and options that individually would decrease earnings per share and in the aggregate would have had a dilutive effect. All such issuances are assumed to have taken place at the beginning of the period (or at the time of issuance of the convertible security, if later).

The FASB Statement No. 128 replaced fully diluted earnings per share with diluted earnings per share, which is similar in concept and measurement to fully diluted earnings per share.

FASB Statement No. 128 requires the restatement of previously reported earnings per share data based on APB Opinion No. 15 to the new approach when included in comparative financial statement presentations.

Investors' Preference

Because the diluted earnings-per-share calculation reduces the earnings per share of a company to reflect potential dilution from all potentially dilutive sources, investors tend to use this figure in the case of companies with complex capital structures in preference to basic earnings per share. In addition, some investors claim that the diluted data are more indicative of a company's future earnings-per-share potential. However, some investors believe the FASB's measurement of diluted earnings per share is arbitrary and has little practical justification. Hence, they consider the resulting earnings-per-share data meaningless for the purpose of predicting long-term market values. They prefer to use other approaches to valuation, such as dividend and cash flow models.

Legal Considerations

The requirements for calculating earnings per share presented in FASB Statement No. 128 do not change in any way the legal rights of the various security holders. Thus, the long-term capital section of the balance sheet still reflects the legal relationships between the various classes of securities. Also, the interest expense related to convertible debt shown as an expense in the computation of net income remains unchanged regardless of how the related debt securities are treated for earnings-per-share calculation purposes.

Simple Capital Structures

In the case of companies with simple capital structures, a single presentation of basic earnings per share is appropriate. Such cases include companies whose capital stock consists only of common and preferred stock.

Illustration

Illustration A presents the disclosure of earnings-per-share data for a company with a simple capital structure. (This and subsequent illustrations assume that FASB Statement No. 128 was effective for all periods covered.) The numbers of shares assumed for **Illustration A** are as follows:

	1997	1996
Common stock outstanding:		
Beginning of year	3,300,000	3,300,000
End of year	3,300,000	3,300,000
Issued or acquired during year	None	None
Weighted average number of shares	3,300,000	3,300,000

ILLUSTRATION A   Examples of Simple Capital Structure Disclosure of Earnings per Share (in thousands, except per-share data)

	1997	1996
Income before extraordinary item	$ 9,150	$7,650
Extraordinary gain, less applicable income taxes	900	—
Net income	$10,050	$7,650
Earnings per common share:		
Income before extraordinary item	$2.77	$2.32
Extraordinary item	0.27	0.00
Net income	$3.04	$2.32

If the simple capital structure includes preferred stock, the preferred stock dividends are deducted from net income in the calculation of basic earnings per share.

Diluted Earnings per Share

The purpose of the diluted earnings-per-share presentation is to indicate on a prospective basis the maximum potential dilution of current earnings per share. Securities whose assumed conversion, exercise, or other contingent issuance would have an antidilutive effect are excluded from this computation. That is, securities whose assumed exercise would increase diluted earnings per share or reduce a loss per share.

Diluted earnings-per-share data are required to be shown on the face of the income statement for each period presented if shares of common stock (a) were issued during the period on conversions, exercises, etc., or (b) were contingently issuable at the close of any period presented. The above contingencies may result from the existence of (a) preferred stock or debt which is convertible into common shares, (b) options or warrants, or (c) agreements for the issuance of common shares upon the satisfaction of certain conditions (for example, the attainment of specified higher levels of earnings following a business combination). The computation should be based on the assumption that all such issued and issuable shares were outstanding from the beginning of the period (or from the time the contingency arose, if after the beginning of the period).

Potentially dilutive securities are included in the diluted earnings per share calculation in one of two ways. The "if converted" method is used in the case of convertible securities. The "treasury stock" method is used for options and warrants.

Previously fully diluted earnings-per-share amounts should not be retroactively adjusted for subsequent conversions of subsequent changes in the market prices of the common stock.

If Converted Method

The if converted method assumes that any security convertible into common stock is converted. Consistent with this assumption the net income figure in the numerator of the earnings per share calculation must be adjusted, if necessary, to reflect the elimination of any effect the convertible security had on the measurement of net income.

Computation Example

To illustrate the measurement of earnings per share in a complex capital structure using the if converted method, assume the ABC Company had a net income of $90,000 after interest and taxes paid at a 40% rate, but before preferred dividends of $40,000 and had the following long-term capital structure:

Convertible 12% bonds (convertible into 100,000 common shares)	$ 500,000
Convertible 10% preferred stock (convertible into 50,000 common shares)	400,000
Common stock (250,000 shares authorized, 50,000 outstanding)	2,000,000

The company's diluted earnings per share is calculated as follows:

$$\text{Diluted earnings per share} = \frac{\substack{\text{Profits after taxes} \\ \text{before} \\ \text{preferred dividends}} + \substack{\text{After-tax equivalent} \\ \text{of convertible} \\ \text{debt interest}}}{\substack{\text{Common shares} \\ \text{outstanding}} + \substack{\text{Common stock potentially} \\ \text{issuable to convertible} \\ \text{preferred stockholders} \\ \text{plus common stock} \\ \text{potentially issuable to} \\ \text{convertible debt holders}}}$$

$$= \frac{\$90,000 + \$36,000}{(50,000 + 50,000 + 100,000) \text{ shares}}$$

$$= \frac{\$126,000}{200,000 \text{ shares}}$$

$$= \$0.63 \text{ per share}$$

This last calculation reflects the elimination of the preferred dividends ($40,000) and the after tax interest cost ($60,000 × .6) after the assumed conversion of the convertible preferred and debt issues.

Treasury Stock Method

FASB Statement No. 128 requires options, warrants, and similar arrangements to enter into the fully diluted earnings-per-share calculations. Typically, whatever value these arrangements have is derived from their right to obtain common stock at a specific price during a specified time period. Accordingly, the *Statement* maintains that diluted earnings per share should reflect the assumption that these securities have been exercised.

The earnings-per-share effect of such securities is computed by the treasury stock method. This approach assumes (1) that the warrants and options are exercised at the beginning of the period (or at time of issuance, if later) and (2) that any proceeds received by the issuing company are used to purchase its common stock at an average market price during the period.[2]

The FASB recognized that the funds obtained by issuers from the exercise of options and warrants are used in many ways, with a wide variety of results that cannot be anticipated. Application of the treasury stock method in diluted earnings-per-share computations is not based on an assumption that the funds will or could actually be used in that manner implied by this method. Nevertheless, the FASB believed its assumed use of funds represented a practical approach to reflecting the dilutive effect that would result from the issuance of common stock under option and warrant agreements at an effective price below the current market price.

Finally, the number of incremental shares computed using the treasury stock method for any accounting period are assumed to be outstanding only for that period.

Computation Example

To illustrate the computation of diluted earnings per share using the treasury stock method, assume the following data:

Net income for year	$2,000,000
Shares outstanding	1,000,000
Warrants and options to purchase equivalent shares (outstanding for full years)	100,000
Exercise price per share	$ 15
Average price	$ 20

---

[2]For example, if a corporation has 10,000 warrants outstanding exercisable at $54 and the average market price of the common stock during the reporting period is $60, the $540,000 which would be realized from exercise of the warrants and issuance of 10,000 shares would be an amount sufficient to acquire 9,000 shares; thus, 1,000 shares would be added to the outstanding common shares in computing diluted earnings per share for the period.

Then diluted earnings per share would be computed as:

$$\left(\frac{\$20 - \$15}{\$20}\right) \times 100,000 = 25,000 \text{ incremental shares}$$

$$\frac{\$2,000,000}{1,000,000 + 25,000} = \$1.95$$

Weighted Average Computations

The denominator for the basic earnings-per-share calculation should be the weighted average number of outstanding common shares.

This number is determined by relating (a) the portion of time within a reporting period that a particular number of shares has been outstanding to (b) the total time in that period. Thus, for example, if 100 shares of a common stock were outstanding during the first quarter of a fiscal year and 300 shares were outstanding during the balance of the year, the weighted average number of outstanding shares would be 250, i.e., (100 + 300 + 300 + 300) divided by 4. The use of a weighted average is necessary so that the effect of changes in the number of shares outstanding is related to the operations during the portion of the accounting period affected.

If the company reacquires its shares, these shares should be excluded from the weighted average calculation from the date of their acquisition.

Computations of earnings-per-share data should give retroactive recognition in all periods presented to changes in the capital structure due to stock splits, stock dividends, or reverse stock splits.

When a business is acquired for stock, the transaction can be accounted for as either a purchase or a pooling of interests, depending on the particular circumstances. When a business combination is accounted for as a purchase, the new shares should be included in the computation of earnings per share only from the acquisition date. In the case of a pooling of interests, the computation should be based on the aggregate of the weighted average outstanding shares of the merged business, adjusted to the equivalent shares of the surviving business for all periods presented. These computations reflect the difference in accounting for income under the two methods of accounting for business combinations. (In a purchase, the income of the purchaser includes the income of the purchased company only from the date of acquisition. In a pooling of interests, the net incomes of the two companies are combined for all periods presented.)

Using the treasury stock method to include options and warrants in the per-share calculations can complicate the computation of the various quarterly, year-to-date and annual earnings-per-share figures. The following paragraphs set forth some of the rules that apply to the computation of these per-share figures when options and warrants are outstanding.

Dilutive options or warrants which are issued or which expire or are canceled during a period are reflected in both basic and diluted earnings-per-share computations for the time they were outstanding during the period.

A "period" is the time for which net income is reported and earnings per share are computed. However, when the treasury stock method is used and the reporting period is longer than three months, a separate computation is made for each three-month period.

A weighted average of shares is computed on the basis of average market prices during each three months included in the reporting period. Thus, if the period being reported upon is six months, nine months, or one year, a weighted average of shares is computed for each quarter. The weighted averages for all quarters are then added together, and the resulting total is divided by the number of quarters to determine the weighted average for the period.

Common stock issued upon the exercise of options or warrants is included in the weighted average of outstanding shares from the exercise date. The treasury stock method is applied for exercised options or warrants from the beginning of the period to the exercise date. Incremental shares are weighted for the period the options or warrants were outstanding, and shares issued are weighted for the period the shares were outstanding. For diluted earnings per share, however, the computation for the period prior to exercise is based on the market price of common stock when the options or warrants were exercised regardless of whether the result is dilutive or antidilutive. Incremental shares are weighted for the period the options or warrants were outstanding, and shares issued are weighted for the period the shares are outstanding.

No retroactive adjustment or restatement of previously reported earnings-per-share data is made if there is a change in the incremental number of shares determined by applying the treasury stock method. Computations for each quarter or other periods are independent.

Dividends-per-Share

Dividends-per-share presentations in comparative statements should reflect the actual dividends declared per share during the appropriate period adjusted for any subsequent stock splits or dividends. Following a pooling of interests, the dividends-per-share presentation for periods prior to the pooling creates a problem. In these cases, the typical practice is to disclose the dividends declared per share by the principal constituent.

Financial Analysis

Inexperienced statement users and equity investors tend to focus on the earnings-per-share statistics too much. This is a mistake. These summary data do not capture the whole story of a company's financial condition, results of operation, and cash flows. While the earnings-per-share data have some significance to equity investors, it is always wise to remember that it is only one of many pieces of data presented in financial statements that bear on the value of securities and the measurement of management's performance. These other data must be analyzed carefully in order to put the earnings-per-share data in its proper perspective.

Statement users should be aware of the following observations when using earnings-per-share data:

a. The same number of shares do not enter into the dividends-per-share and earnings-per-share calculations. Therefore, the earnings-per-share figure should not be divided into the dividends-per-share figure to compute payout ratios. Dividends per share is based on actual shares outstanding at the dividend date, whereas earnings per share may include all or some FASB Statement No. 128–type adjustments to the actual number of shares outstanding.

b. Earnings-per-share figures are seldom comparable when comparing companies because of differences in accounting, the probability that potentially dilutive shares will be actually turned into common shares, and levels of financial risk.

Diluted earnings-per-share data are used for most purposes where earnings-per-share figures are relevant. This is conservative. However, it can be misleading if it does not represent the current reality or expectations for the securities entering into the earnings-per-share calculation. Accordingly, experienced investors always identify the impact of potentially dilutive securities in the earnings-per-share calculations, check the current market status of the key securities leading to adjustments, and, if they believe the market and accounting views of these securities differ, the investor may readjust the earnings-per-share figures accordingly.

Lustra S.p.A. (A)

Peter Scala, president of Lustra S.p.A., Naples, Italy, quietly reflected on the contents of a letter he had sent the day before to his company's U.S. certified public accountant (**Exhibit 6**) in response to an earlier letter from the firm's U.S. certified public accountant (**Exhibit 5**). Scala's letter detailed his reaction to a significant accounting controversy that had arisen during the company's preparation for a planned U.S. issuance of its common stock. Of immediate concern to Peter Scala was what strategy he should adopt in reply to the auditor's anticipated response to his letter.

Background

Lustra was a distributor and retailer of fashion eyeware. The firm had been founded in 1965 by the late John Scala in Naples, Italy. In 1977, the company went public with an offering of common stock on the Milan Exchange. In 1982, Peter replaced his father as president. In 1987, Lustra opened two retail outlets in New York.

From 1965 to 1989, sales and profits had grown steadily each year. 1989 proved to be Lustra's best year with profits after tax of over $3.0 million (**Exhibit 1**).[1]

Professor David F. Hawkins prepared this case as the basis for class discussion rather than to illustrate either effective or ineffective handling of an administrative situation. This case is an adaptation of case materials prepared by Dennis P. Frolin and James F. Smith.

Copyright © 1991 by the President and Fellows of Harvard College. Harvard Business School case 192–028.

[1]All financial data have been restated to their U.S. dollar equivalent.

Financing Activities

Since 1977, Lustra had twice sought significant external financing in Italy to fund the company's expansion. **Exhibit 2** details the company's capital structure and common stock prices for 1988 and 1989.

In September 1985, a common stock issue with warrants added 200,000 common shares to Lustra's equity base. The warrants, issued one for each common share

---

EXHIBIT 1   Lustra S.p.A.—Financial Information

	1988	*1989*
Net sales (millions)	$102.30	$108.60
Gross margin (millions)	52.40	53.40
Profit after tax (millions)	3.00	3.05
Earnings per share	3.00[a]	3.05[a]

[a]Computations for Italian reporting purposes. Net income divided by average number of common shares outstanding.

EXHIBIT 2   Lustra S.p.A.—Partial Capital Structure and Common Stock Prices

	1988	*1989*
Common shares outstanding	1,000,000	1,000,000
Warrants outstanding	200,000	200,000
Exercise price $10 expiration date September, 2000, common shares reserved for exercise	200,000	200,000
Convertible debentures 9⅛%,		
Face value outstanding	0	$7,200,000
Maturity date, 2014, conversion price $20, common shares reserved for conversion	0	360,000
Common stock price—Milan exchange[a]		

	1988		**1989**	
	Close	*Average*	*Close*	*Average*
First quarter	6⅝	6	12¼	10
Second quarter	7	7⅞	17	15¼
Third quarter	8⅛	8	14½	17⅝
Fourth quarter	9⅞	5⅝	9	12⅛
Year		8		13

[a]The stock traded below $10 prior to 1988.

EXHIBIT 3   Lustra S.p.A.—9⅛% Convertible Debentures

Date	Event	Price	Average Italian Aa Equivalent Corporate Bond Yield
June 29	Issue priced and marketed	98	14.25%
July 5	First trade secondary market	97	14.50%

acquired, permitted the purchase of one additional share of common stock for $10 cash until September 2000.

In June 1989, the company issued subordinated convertible debentures with a face value of $7.2 million, a 9⅛% coupon rate of interest, and a life of 25 years. Each debenture was convertible after June 1991 into Lustra common stock at a conversion price of $20 per share. Thus, each $1,000 debenture was equivalent to 50 shares of common stock.

The relatively small size of the debenture issue resulted in somewhat limited distribution of the initial offering in a very thin and inactive secondary market. The debentures were offered and sold out on June 29 and the first trade in the over-the-counter secondary market occurred on July 5 (**Exhibit 3**).

In order to finance the expansion of Lustra's U.S. business, Peter Scala planned to sell Lustra stock in the United States.

1989 Annual Report

During preparations for the planned U.S. underwriting, Peter Scala was informed by his independent auditors, Peat, Waterhouse & Co., that the 1989 earnings-per-share computations that he had prepared for Italian financial statement purposes (**Exhibit 1**) were not acceptable under Accounting Principles Board (APB) Opinion No. 15. The senior in charge of the audit indicated that Lustra S.p.A. had failed to include as common stock equivalents the convertible debentures issued in 1989 and the outstanding common stock warrants issued in 1985. The requirements to treat both as common stock equivalents was explained as follows:

1. **9⅛ Percent Convertible Debentures.** The effective yield, based on its market price, was less than two-thirds of the then average Italian equivalent of the Aa corporate bond yield. Thus, the convertible qualifies as a common stock equivalent under APB Opinion No. 15's test of a common stock equivalent (i.e., the at issue yield was equal to or less than two-thirds of the straight debt rate for Aa corporate fixed income debt securities.) and must be counted in primary and fully diluted earnings per share on an "as if" converted basis.

2. **Common Stock Warrants.** The market price of the common stock during the year exceeds the exercise price of the warrant, hence, they are dilutive

and must be counted as outstanding during the year in the primary and fully diluted earnings-per-share figures using the "treasury stock" method of calculation. Under APB Opinion No. 15 the average or ending price of the common stock for each period, whichever is more dilutive, is used to determine the incremental shares included in the fully diluted earnings per share calculation. Only the average price is used in the measurement of primary earnings per share.

The audit senior proposed that the following earnings-per-share figures be published with the financial statements (**Exhibit 4**):

	1988	1989
Primary	$3.00	$2.63
Fully diluted	3.00	2.60

Exhibit 4   Lustra S.p.A.—U.S. Auditor's Calculation of Earnings per Share

	1988	1989
Primary		
Profit after tax (000 omitted)	$3,000	$3,050
Adjustments:		
Add back after-tax interest savings on convertible debentures (tax rate: 46%)	0	177
Profit after-tax (adjusted)	$3,000	$3,227
Common shares outstanding (000 omitted)	1,000	1,000
Adjustments:		
Add conversion of debentures	0	180
Add exercise warrants	0	47.6
Common shares outstanding (adjusted)	1,000	1,227.6
Earnings per share—primary	$ 3.00	$ 2.63
Fully Diluted		
Profit after tax (adjusted)	$3,000	$3,277
Common shares outstanding (adjusted)	1,000	1,227.6
Adjustments:		
Add additional shares outstanding upon exercise of warrants based on closing (not average) price	0	12.6
Common shares outstanding (adjusted)	1,000	1,240.2
Earnings per share—fully diluted	$ 3.00	$ 2.60

Warrants: treasury stock method

Primary: using average common stock price

1988—Antidilutive

EXHIBIT 4   (continued)

1989 Quarter	(000 omitted)		
	Exercise	*Purchase*	*Net Increment*
1	200	200	0
2	200	131.1	68.9
3	200	113.5	86.5
4	200	164.9	35.1
Total			190.5
Average			47.6

Fully diluted: using higher of average or closing quarterly or year end common stock price

1988—Antidilutive

1989 Quarter	(000 omitted)		
	Exercise	*Purchase*	*Net Increment*
1	200	163.3	36.7
2	200	117.6	82.4
3	200	113.5	86.5
4	200	164.9	35.1
Total			240.7
Average			60.2

Additional shares over primary (60.2 − 47.6)

Peter Scala's reaction to the audit senior's proposal was initially one of bewilderment, soon replaced by anger. The U.S. rules seemed to make no sense.

Peter Scala and his controller discussed the matter at length with Donna Christiansen, audit partner responsible for the Lustra audit. The result was a stalemate—Christiansen maintained that her hands were tied by APB Opinion No. 15, and Scala insisted that the rules were arbitrary and unfair and that he would have difficulty abiding by them. The meeting ended on strained terms. In the days following, Scala had several telephone conversations with Ms. Christiansen and with Mr. Mark Du-Mond, the partner-in-charge of the New York office of Peat, Waterhouse & Co. Three days later, Peter Scala received a letter from Mr. DuMond stating the position that Peat, Waterhouse & Co. intended to maintain in this matter (**Exhibit 5**).

On the following day, Peter Scala drafted a reply to Mr. DuMond (**Exhibit 6**).

Exhibit 5

February 6, 1990

Mr. Peter Scala
President
Lustra S.p.A.
Lustra Building, Via Saicar 551
Naples, Italy

Dear Peter:

This letter is written in follow-up to the telephone conversations that you had with Ms. Donna Christiansen and me earlier today concerning the computation of earnings per common share for the year ended December 31, 1989, for inclusion in your Security and Exchange filing in connection with your forthcoming public offering in the United States.

After giving careful consideration to all factors pertinent to the computation of earnings per common share as outlined in APB Opinion No. 15, it is the unanimous opinion of the National Accounting and Auditing Policy Committee of our firm that Lustra's convertible debentures (even though issued in Italy) and the company's warrants must properly be included as common stock equivalents in this computation. The Committee also noted that, even if the convertible debentures were *not* counted as common stock equivalents, thereby included in the *primary* earnings per share calculations, they would always be counted as converted in the *fully diluted* earnings per share calculation. Thus, in any case, the decline in earnings per share from 1988 to 1989 would be published on the face of the income statement.

It is our official position that if the earnings per common share included in the financial statements are not computed in accordance with APB Opinion No. 15, we will be unable to issue an unqualified opinion and must indicate that the computation is not within generally accepted accounting principles.

Sincerely,

Mark DuMond
Partner
PEAT, WATERHOUSE & COMPANY

/pbh

EXHIBIT 6

---

9 February, 1990

Mr. Mark DuMond
Partner
Peat, Waterhouse & Co.
One Lander Street
New York, NY 10021

Dear Mark:

I am very disappointed in the position you and your firm seem to have adopted on Lustra's per-share calculation.

In my opinion, the rules in question are arbitrary at best and they are unfair to Lustra because they present a distorted picture of the current year's operations. I have always believed that it was our obligation to present true and fair financial statements to our shareholders. Consequently, when we have found Italian accounting practices unsatisfactory, we have turned to the International Accounting Standards for our accounting guidance. There is no comparable accounting standard in effect in Italy or in the International Accounting Standards to APB No. 15. I now find it distressing to be forced to issue what I consider to be misleading statements in order to comply with your country's listing requirements.

With regard to the convertible debentures, I believe, inherent in the argument that these securities should be deemed converted to common shares for earnings per share computations is the assumption that conversion is imminent (or at least highly probable) in the foreseeable future. In point of fact, the rational investor will not convert to common shares until such time as the market price of the common exceeds the conversion price of $20 per share. Given the current market price of 9¼ and the downward price trend, it would appear that the probability of conversion in the foreseeable future is, in fact, nil. Further, if Lustra's earnings per share are computed as prescribed by APB Opinion No. 15, the resulting decrease in earnings per share will likely further depress the market price, thereby even further lessening the probability of conversion.

It is interesting to note that, if what you have identified to be the Italian equivalent of the average Aa corporate bond yield at the issue date of the convertible debenture issue had been slightly lower, your position would reverse; or, if Lustra's debenture interest rate had been slightly higher, your position would reverse. Furthermore, if you would have bothered to check the record, you would also see that, against the average Aa corporate bond yield for the full year, the convertible debenture issue would more than meet the corporate bond yield test and be excluded from the common stock equivalent category.

1989 was a year of interest rate turmoil. Interest rates changed numerous times. Under such conditions it hardly seems appropriate for the accounting treatment for a 25-year debenture to depend on the average interest rate in effect on a particular day, or even during a particular week.

Furthermore, when we sold the convertible debenture, we did not anticipate that one day we would seek financing in U.S. markets. If we had, I can assure you that we would have priced the convertible issue to remove it from the primary-earnings-per-share category. Now after the fact, to impose this U.S. accounting rule on us is unfair.

EXHIBIT 6   (continued)

Concerning the warrants, again inherent in the argument that the warrants should be deemed exercised for earnings-per-share computations is the assumption that actual exercise is imminent (or at least highly probable) in the foreseeable future. In point of fact, the rational investor will never exercise a warrant until it expires. Lustra's warrants expire in 2000, nearly 10 years hence. The fact that the market price of our common shares exceeded the warrant exercise price at various times during 1989 means absolutely nothing regarding the probability of exercise by the holder of the warrant; its only effect is to change the price of the warrant in the marketplace. We realize that the earnings-per-share impact of the warrants is relatively insignificant this year. The problem is in the future as our share price rises and the earnings-per-share impact becomes more significant.

I am also troubled by the fact that the financial statements we issue to our Italian investors will henceforth show different earnings than those reported to our U.S. investors. This discrepancy will cause confusion which, I believe, will not help our stock price in either country.[1] Also, your lower 1989 earnings-per-share figures will make it more difficult for us to sell securities in the United States. After all, who wants to invest in an IPO when the earnings are already sliding down? Maybe we will have to abandon our U.S. financing plan.

I have come to the conclusion that—as you say in American—"the bottom line" is this—in order to go ahead with our U.S. equity issue, we must conform to U.S. GAAP, including APB No. 15. Frankly, I am hesitant to go forward with the U.S. underwriting. Selling shares following a decline in earnings per share is not likely to enhance their value. Before our final decision on whether to proceed with the U.S. underwriting, please check the rules once again to see if it is truly necessary to report the figures you propose.

In the meantime, I hope you will assist me to understand the reasoning behind APB No. 15 so that I can in turn help my Board to understand why we must now report different earnings per share to our Italian and U.S. investors. Perhaps, when I understand APB No. 15 better, Lustra may even want to use it for our Italian reports; but I am not prepared to do this at this time.

Very truly yours,

Peter Scala
President
LUSTRA S.p.A.

---

[1]For U.S. listing purposes, Lustra S.p.A. had to adopt U.S. GAAP for financial statements issued to U.S. investors. Because of the nature of the business, the fact that it had grown without acquisitions and Peter Scala's insistence on high-quality accounting practices, the net income the company reported for U.S. and Italian listing purposes was essentially the same.

Questions

1. Review the auditor's determination of the 1989 E.P.S. for Lustra S.p.A. Do you agree with their results? _____

2. If you were Ms. Christiansen, how would you respond to Peter Scala's letter? _____ What is the rationale supporting APB Opinion No. 15? _____

3. Should Lustra adopt APB Opinion No. 15 for Italian reporting purposes? _____

4. Does it really matter what E.P.S. figure Lustra reports? _____ For instance, will the security market be influenced by this figure? _____

CASE
12-2

Lustra S.p.A. (B)

In late February 1990, Peter Scala decided not to issue and list Lustra S.p.A.'s common stock in the United States of America. The principal reason was a reluctance to go into the U.S. market with a declining earning-per-share trend that, in Peter Scala's mind, was simply the result of APB Opinion No. 15's "arbitrary and unrealistic" rules for computing earnings per share. Instead he decided to explore the possibility of listing the company's stock on the London Exchange as a preliminary step to raising equity capital in the United Kingdom at some future date.

Based on his experience with APB Opinion No. 15, Peter Scala decided to check quickly on the United Kingdom's earnings-per-share calculation and disclosure rules. Based on his research he concluded:

- Statements of Standard Accounting Practice (SSAP) 3 required listed companies to show earnings per share on the face of the income statement.
- Earnings per share was defined as the period's after-tax consolidated profit, deducting minority interest and preferred dividends but before taking into account extraordinary items based on the weighted-average share capital eligible for dividends. This figure was known as basic earnings per share.
- A second fully diluted earnings-per-share figure reflecting potential earnings-per-share dilution from warrants, opinions, or conversion rights should be disclosed, if applicable.

Peter Scala believed this last requirement would not be a problem, since he believed he could limit the potential dilution to an immaterial amount by the calculation methodology he elected to employ. Also Peter Scala believed U.K. investors did not use fully diluted earnings-per-share figures in their investment decisions.

During 1991 and 1992 the demand for fashion eyewear was hurt by the global recession. And despite a significant increase in new store openings, Lustra's sales and profits reflected this adverse development (see Exhibit 1). The company's poor financial results and the significant operating demands on Peter Scala's time led him to conclude that any listing decision should be postponed to the future.

Professor David F. Hawkins prepared this case as the basis for class discussion rather than to illustrate either effective or ineffective handling of an administrative situation.

EXHIBIT 1   **Lustra S.p.A.—Financial Information (millions, except earnings per share)[a]**

	1990	1991	1992
Net sales	£86.0	£92.0	£81.0
Profit on ordinary activities and attributable to ordinary shareholders	1.05	.7	.85
Extraordinary items	—	—	<1.45>
Profit for the financial year	£1.05	£ 0.7	£<0.60>
Earnings per share[b]	£1.05	£0.70	£0.85

[a]Converted to British pounds at the year end pound–lira exchange rate.

[b]Computation for Italian reporting purposes. Profit on ordinary activities and attributable to ordinary shareholders divided by average number of common shares outstanding.

Early in the fourth quarter of 1992 Peter Scala decided to restructure the company by closing a number of unprofitable stores, discontinuing a recently-started small chain of specialty stores, and disposing of some excess and slow-moving inventories. The after-tax losses associated with these three actions were:

1992 Extraordinary Items
(Millions of British pounds equivalent at year end pound–lira exchange rate)

Unprofitable store closings	£0.50
Discontinuance of specialty store business	.35
Inventory disposal	.60
Total extraordinary	£1.45

Lustra's chief financial officer told Peter Scala that the £1.45 million after-tax loss associated with these actions could be treated as an extraordinary item and as such excluded from the company's 1992 earnings-per-share calculation.[1]

In early January 1993, encouraged by the 1992 improvement in earnings per share, Peter Scala decided the time had come to get a London listing for the company's stock. The first step was to communicate his decision to Harold Denning, the senior partner of the London office of Peat, Waterhouse & Company, the company's auditors. At this time the 1992 audit was still in progress. Lustra's 1992 financial statements were due to be released in mid-March.

Peter Scala was surprised to learn from Harold Denning that under a new U.K. accounting standard (FRS3) Lustra would not show an improving earnings-per-share trend in 1992. Instead, 1992 earnings per share would not only be lower than the 1991 figure, they would be negative.

---

[1]There are no requirements covering extraordinary items or earnings-per-share computation and disclosure in the Italian civil code or in the accounting standards issued by the representative body of the Italian accounting profession.

The day after his conversation with Harold Denning, Peter Scala received a letter from Harold Denning explaining the new standard (**Exhibit 2**). Immediately after reading the letter, Peter Scala met with his chief financial officer to reassess his London listing decision.

Exhibit 2

10 January 1993

Mr. Peter Scala
President
Lustra S.p.A.
Lustra Building, Via Saicar 551
Naples, Italy

Dear Peter:

This letter is written to clarify my comments made to you yesterday regarding the format of your 1992 financial statements and earnings per share calculation should you decide to seek a London listing.

Since its formation in 1991 the Accounting Standards Board has undertaken a far reaching review of U.K. generally accepted accounting principles. This has resulted in major changes to the way companies present their accounts. In line with the recommendations of the Accounting Standards Board we urge you to adopt Financial Reporting Standard No. 3 (FRS3) at the earliest opportunity. This standard replaces SSAP3.

The objective of FRS3 is to highlight a range of important components of financial performance to aid users in their understanding of accounts and to assist them in forming a basis for their assessment of future results and cash flows. The format laid down in FRS3 for the profit and loss account will be demanded by investors to analyze your financial statements.

The basic FRS3 format we recommend for Lustra's 1992 profit and loss account in any listing submission is:

	Continuing Operations	Discontinued Operations	Total
Turnover	£XXX	£XXX	£XXX
Cost of sales	XXX	XXX	XXX
Trading profit (loss)	£XXX	XXX	XXX
Exceptional items	XXX	XXX	XXX
Operating profit (loss) on ordinary activities	£XXX	XXX	XXX
Minority interest	XXX	XXX	XXX
Profit (loss) for the financial year	£XXX	XXX	XXX
Profit (loss) per ordinary share	£XXX	£XXX	£XXX

As I explained to you during our phone conversation, FRS3 limits extraordinary items to very rare occurrences. As the illustrations in FRS3 clearly indicate, the extraordinary items your Italian GAAP based reports show do not qualify as an extraordinary item anymore in U.K. GAAP presentations.

Under FRS3 a business is classified as a discontinued operation if it is clearly distinguishable, has a material effect on the nature and focus of the Group's activities, represents a material reduction in the Group's operating facilities, and either its sale is completed, or if a termination, its former activities have

---

EXHIBIT 2   (continued)

---

ceased before the earlier of three months after the commencement of the subsequent period and the date on which the financial statements are approved. In line with these new requirements, we believe the charge associated with the discontinuance of your small specialty store business should be reported as a discontinued operation. To conform to FRS3, any prior periods presented will have to be restated to show the specialty stores as a discontinued business.

The store closing and inventory disposal losses are business activities that relate to your continuing business. As such FRS3 requires that these losses be included in the calculation of continuing operations related operating profit on ordinary activities.

FRS3 also deals with the calculation and disclosure of earnings per share data. It requires basic earnings per share to be calculated on the basis of profit for the financial year less preferred dividends, if any. Therefore, the basic earnings per share you would show under U.K. GAAP would be a negative amount rather than a positive amount as reported on your Italian GAAP statements.

When the FRS3 earnings per share calculation was proposed, it was bitterly opposed by the business and financial analysts communities. They believed it would lead to more volatile earnings and did not reflect the way investors view and use earnings per share data. As a compromise, the Accounting Standards Board agreed to permit companies to disclose an alternative earnings per share figure that the reporting company believed was a more useful one for investors. The requirements are that this alternative figure be presented with the official one, not be displayed in a more prominent way, and the method used to calculate it be fully disclosed.

We believe that you should consider reporting an alternative earnings per share figure on the face of your 1992 profit and loss account and in the accompanying notes. The presentation of the adjusted earnings per share figure would be accompanied by the following statement: "In the opinion of the directors, the adjustments give a better underlying picture of the Group's performance than the basic earnings per share figure."

Should you decide to proceed with a London listing, we will be delighted to assist you in the preparation of your listing materials. Please let me know your plans as soon as possible so that we can incorporate this matter into our current year end audit programme.

Sincerely,

Harold Denning
Managing Partner
Peat, Waterhouse & Company

HD/cbc

Questions

1. Determine Lustra's 1992 basic earnings-per-share presentation using FRS3.

2. If Lustra proceeds with a London listing application, what adjusted earnings-per-share figure, if any, should the company include in its 1992 financial report? _____ Why should the company present an adjusted 1992 earnings-per-share figure? _____ Explain the justification for your adjustment.

3. Does FRS 3 represent a significant improvement over SSAP3? _____ Should the International Accounting Standards Committee adopt earnings-per-share rules similar to SSAP3, FRS3, or Opinion No. 15? _____

4. How might FRS3 influence Lustra's decision to list on the London Exchange? _____

CASE 12-3

Lustra S.p.A. (C)

On March 15, 1997, Peter Scala, president, Lustra S.p.A. sent the following letter to Donna Christiansen, partner, Peat, Waterhouse & Company.

Dear Donna,

I read with great interest the FASB's new earnings per share standard. As I read the statement, I thought of our 1990 conversations dealing with the earnings per share figures we would have to report for 1988 and 1989 in our potential US listing documents. As you recall, I was not pleased with the Opinion 15 requirements. If you have the time, I would be interested in your views on the FASB's new standard. Also, I am curious as to what our 1989 earnings per share figures might have looked like under the FASB new standard. Would you recompute them for me using the FASB Statement No. 128?

I was delighted to see Mark when he passed through Naples earlier this month. We discussed the possibility that we might be able to get a New York listing using International Accounting Standards in the near future. Clearly, even in retirement he is still keeping active in accounting matters.

Very truly yours,

Peter

Professor David Hawkins prepared this case as the basis for class discussion rather than to illustrate either effective or ineffective handling of an administrative situation.

Questions

1. Recompute Lustra's 1989 earnings per share using FASB Statement No. 128.
2. Is the FASB's new standard a significant improvement over APB Opinion No. 15? Why? _____

PART SIX

Asset and Expense Reporting and Analysis

Income Taxes

Income taxes are a cost of doing business. The measurement of this cost for financial reporting purposes is complicated by the fact that tax laws and financial accounting standards related to income determination differ. As a result, differences may arise between a company's current taxable income and pretax book income and the tax and book basis of its assets and liabilities reported in the financial statements. Most of these differences are temporary in nature, since the differences will reverse and become taxable or deductible items in future tax returns.

In FASB Statement No. 109, "Accounting for Income Taxes," the FASB decided that the tax expense of a corporation should include two elements: the income tax obligation to or credit from taxing authorities based on the period's tax returns and a deferred tax component to provide for future taxes related to the temporary differences between book and tax reporting and tax credit and loss carryforwards, if any. The deferred tax component of the tax expense is the change during the period in the deferred tax asset and liability balances reported on the balance sheet. These balances are the tax equivalent of the temporary differences.

The income tax data included in financial statements can be very useful to statement users. These data provide an alternative measure of corporate profits that is typically determined by more cash-based and conservative accounting practices than those used to determine book income. The detailed notes explaining the elements of the deferred tax expense, assets, and liabilities and the reasons why the company's book tax rate and the statutory rate differ can provide insights into the quality of a company's earnings; reveal possible accounting manipulations; identify the contribution of tax rate management to the levels and change in reporting earnings; facilitate the deaccrual of income to a cash basis; and help readers estimate the effect of changes in the tax code on a company's earnings and cash flows.

Professor David F. Hawkins prepared this note as the basis for class discussion.
Copyright © 1995 by the President and Fellows of Harvard College. Harvard Business School teaching note 195–246.

Tax Expense Components

The tax expense of a corporation consists of two components—current taxes and deferred taxes.

The concept and measurement of the current tax component is straightforward. It is the company's obligation to make tax payments to or receive tax credits from taxing authorities based on the company's tax returns for the period covered by the income statement. For example, if a company's foreign and domestic tax returns for the year show a combined taxable income of $20 million and a tax payment obligation of $8 million, based on that taxable income, the current portion of the company's tax expense is $8 million. The accounting entry to record this tax obligation is ($ million):

```
Dr. Tax expense—current . . . . . . . . . . . . . . . . . . . . . . . . . . . . .    $8
    Cr. Taxes payable . . . . . . . . . . . . . . . . . . . . . . . . . . . . . . . .          $8
```

The concept and measurement of the deferred tax component of the tax expense is more complicated. The objective in accounting for deferred taxes is to recognize in current financial statements the future tax consequences of events that have been recognized in a company's financial statements or tax returns.

The accounting for the deferred tax component of the tax expense and the nature of this item has been a long standing accounting controversy. This income tax allocation controversy is a direct outgrowth of the federal governments use of income taxes as a positive or negative stimulus to the economy and to achieve social goals.

The tax deferred accounting issue arises when the government allows, for its purposes, a different pattern for recognizing revenues and expenses on tax returns from that employed in the financial accounting reports. This practice in turn raises a fundamental accounting question: Should the periodic income tax expense reported in financial reports be based on the taxable income reported to the taxing authorities (the current tax expense) or some other amount?

In deciding if the tax expense should be based on "some other amount," it is important to recognize that differences between the income reported in the financial statement and that reported on the tax return may be either (1) permanent or (2) related to temporary differences. *Permanent* differences arise from specific statutory concessions or exclusions of the tax code. For example, expenses required for financial reporting, such as premiums on officers' life insurance, may not be deducted in the computation of taxable income. There is general agreement that permanent differences should not enter into the measurement of a company's tax expense.

How temporary differences should or should not enter into the measurement of the tax expense is the focus of the "or some other amount" issue.

There are four general types of temporary differences. The individual transactions giving rise to these temporary differences originate in one period and reverse themselves in subsequent periods:

1. Revenues are included in taxable income later than in pre-tax accounting income, as when percentage of completion accounting is used in financial

reports and a modified version of this method that delays recognition of revenues is elected for tax purposes.

2. Expenses are deducted later in determining taxable income than in determining financial statement income, as in the case of warranty costs, which are deductible from taxable income only when incurred but must be accrued for book purposes when a sale is recognized.

3. Revenues are included earlier in taxable income than in pre-tax accounting income. For example, rent payments received in advance may be reported when received for tax determination, but in later periods when earned for financial reporting purposes.

4. Expenses or losses are deducted in determining taxable income earlier than in determining pre-tax book income, such as in the case of store-opening expenses that may be deducted immediately on a tax return, but amortized in the financial statement over several years.

Temporary differences can also arise when assets and liabilities acquired in business combinations have a tax basis different from their recorded book values.

The issue of how, if at all, to account for temporary differences which reverse or turn around in later periods that result in an equivalent reversal of the tax effects is further complicated by the fact that often the impact of the reversal of these differences is indefinitely postponed as new transactions give rise to temporary differences that offset the reversal. Consequently, a basic question develops as to whether the tax effect of temporary differences should be recognized in view of the possibility of indefinitely postponing the actual payment of the related tax. Also, since the tax implications of temporary differences are future amounts, there is an issue of should the current provision for these potential payments be their discounted dollar value.

Different Approaches

A number of widely different solutions, each with strong support, have been proposed over the years for handling temporary differences between book and tax income and the book value and tax basis of assets and liabilities. One concept is that the income tax expense of a period should equal the tax payable for the period. Advocates of this "flow-through" method argue that there is no tax liability created until a later period; thus, there is no need to create an additional tax expense applicable to the current book pre-tax income.

Others argue for the "deferred" method of reporting the tax income expense. This point of view holds that the tax expense reported in the financial statements should be essentially the same as if the book profit were the profit actually reported for tax purposes. Any difference between this tax calculation and the tax currently due to the Internal Revenue Service is recorded as potential tax liability or asset. Prior to FASB Statement No. 109 the FASB favored this approach.

In FASB Statement No. 109 the FASB adopted the "asset–liability" method. Under this approach, the deferred tax expense for a period is the change during the

ILLUSTRATION 1   **Accrual versus Installment Treatment of Pre-tax Profit**

	Accrual	*Installment*
1995	$90	$30
1996	—	30
1997	—	30
Total	$90	$90

period in the tax equivalent of the cumulative temporary differences. This tax value is computed using tax rates expected to be in effect when the temporary differences reverse. Also existing deferred tax balances are adjusted when tax laws change or a tax rate change becomes known.

Both the deferred and the liability methods are referred to as being "comprehensive tax allocation" approaches. Other less widely supported approaches have been suggested, such as the "partial allocation" method which would recognize in the determination of current income only those taxes deferred that are reasonably certain to be paid during, say, the next three to five years. Another approach, the so-called net-of-tax form of presentation, accepts comprehensive tax allocation, but would include deferred taxes as an element of the valuation of the asset and liability giving rise to the tax deferral.

Example.   The problem of recognizing temporary differences is illustrated in the following example. In early January 1995, retailer Smith sold a TV set for $360 on an installment sale basis. The installment sale contract called for no down payment and 36 payments of $10 per month plus interest on the unpaid balance. The retailer's gross margin was 25% of the sales price. (The interest and any carrying charges related to the installment payments can be ignored in this discussion.)

According to *APB Opinion No. 10,* the retailer must use the so-called accrual method or sale method to record the transaction rather than the installment method, since the circumstances of the sale were such that the collection of the sales price was reasonably assured. Therefore, Smith must recognize the full pre-tax profit of $90 at the time of the sale. If he had been able to use the installment approach, he would have shown a $2.50 before-tax profit at the time each $10 installment payment was received. The timing of the pre-tax profit recognition under the two methods is compared in **Illustration 1.**

First-Year Taxes

For calculating his tax payments, however, we will assume retailer Smith has the option of using either the accrual or the installment method. If Smith decides to

---

ILLUSTRATION 2   **Flow-Through Tax Accounting Illustrated**

	Pre-Tax Profit	Current Tax Expense[a]	Net Profit	Taxes Payable
1995	$90	$12	$ 78	$12
1996	—	12	(12)	12
1997	—	12	(12)	12
Total	$90	$36	$ 54	36

---

[a]40% of the 25% profit included in installments collected.

conserve his cash and use the installment method for tax purposes, he creates a tax deferral situation: he has recorded on his books the full $90 profit at the time of the sale, but for tax purposes he defers the actual payment of taxes on this profit until the time the installments are collected.

The after-tax profit consequences of using the accrual method for book purposes and the installment basis for tax purposes would depend on whether Smith uses the flow-through treatment for handling the tax deferral or the comprehensive allocation method. (Of course, in practice Smith would be required by FASB Statement 109 to use a comprehensive tax allocation approach in this situation. The purpose of this illustration is to show the differences between the flow-through and comprehensive approaches to tax expense accounting.)

The flow-through approach records for book purposes the current year's tax payment actually shown on the retailer's tax return. If we assume a 40% tax rate, its application in this case would lead to the incremental tax effect on profits shown in **Illustration 2.**

The accounting entries for the tax effects shown in Illustration 2 are:

Years 1, 2 and 3:
Dr. Tax expense—current   12
   Cr. Taxes payable   12

Given the pre-tax profit of $90 on the company's books in the year of sale and no anticipated future tax rate changes, the comprehensive allocation approaches lead to a book profit of $54 after taxes in 1995. This treatment puts the profit effect of the installment sale on the same basis as an equivalent cash sale. The difference between the $36 tax expense shown on the books and the actual tax of $12 paid to the Internal Revenue Service in 1995 is set up as a deferred tax account of $24 on the liability side of the balance sheet. The $24 amount is the tax equivalent ($60 × .4) of the change in the cumulative differences in the profit recognized for book purposes ($90) and tax purposes ($30). As shown in **Illustration 3** this account is reduced incrementally each subsequent year by the amount of taxes paid on the profit from the installment payments received during that year. So, in this example, the deferred tax account would be reduced by $12 each year over the remaining two-year installment payment period. Each of the $12 credits to the deferred tax expense shown on **Illustration 3** are the tax

---
ILLUSTRATION 3   Comprehensive Tax Allocation Accounting Illustrated

---

	Pre-Tax Profit	Current Tax Expense	Cumulative Book and Tax Profit Difference (Year End)	Deferred Tax Expense	Net Profit	Deferred Tax Liability	Taxes Payable
1995	$90	$12	$60	$24	$54	$24	$12
1996	0	12	(30)	(12)[a]	0	12	12
1997	0	12	(0)	(12)[a]	0	0	12

ILLUSTRATION 4   Flow-Through versus Comprehensive Tax Accounting: After-Tax Book Profits

---

	Flow-Through	Comprehensive	Differential
1995	$78	$54	$24
1996	(12)	—	(12)
1997	(12)	—	(12)
Total	$54	$54	$ 0

---

equivalent to the change in cumulative difference between the profit recognized for book and tax expenses. Income is not affected by these subsequent tax payments or installment collections.

The accounting entries for the tax effects shown in **Illustration 3** are:

Year 1:

Dr. Tax expense—current	12	
Tax expense—deferred	24	
Cr. Taxes payable		12
Deferred tax liability		24

Years 2 and 3:

Dr. Tax expense—current	12	
Deferred tax liability	12	
Cr. Taxes payable		12
Deferred tax—expense		12

A comparison of the results obtained from the flow-through and the comprehensive allocation methods, when Smith uses different book and tax income recognition timing, is shown in **Illustration 4.** (The cash flow effect of this sale depends upon whether the retailer sells for cash or on an installment basis and upon the method he uses in his tax return to recognize the profit from the sale. The financial accounting handling of the deferred taxes, if any, does not change his cash flow.)

ILLUSTRATION 5   **Flow-Through versus Comprehensive Tax Accounting: After-Tax Book Profits**

	Flow-Through	*Comprehensive*	*Differential*
1995	$ 78	$ 54	$24
1996	66	54	12
1997	(24)	—	(24)
1998	(12)	—	(12)
Total	$108	$108	$ 0

Second-Year Taxes

In addition to realizing a first-year profit differential of $24, the flow-through approach provides an opportunity to offset the $12 reduction in second-year profits (see Illustration 3). Smith can accomplish this by making a similar $360 TV set installment sale in 1996. Again, the after-tax profit differential between the flow-through and comprehensive allocation treatment would be $24. But he would offset this amount with the second-year $12 profit reduction associated with the 1995 sale. So the net differential in the second year would be $12. This effect is shown in **Illustration 5.**

If the retailer in the second example is using the comprehensive allocation approach and the tax rate is projected to stay at 40%, the deferred tax item appearing on the balance sheet at the end of the first year would be $24. This deferral would rise to $36 at the end of the second year (the $24 difference between the tax payment recognized by the second-year sale handled on an accrual versus an installment basis, less the $12 reduction for taxes related to the first-year sale's actual tax payments made during the second year). If Smith sells one $360 TV set each year on a three-year installment sales basis, his deferred tax liability will remain at $36. If he increases his installment sales volume, the deferred tax item will increase.

Deferred Tax Asset

So far we have looked only at recognizing the full book profits at the time of sale. Let us go back to the original one–TV-set sale and lay aside for a moment the APB's required accrual basis for recording installment sales for book purposes. If Smith, the retailer in this example, had handled his installment sale in a way exactly opposite to the previously assumed method—that is, if he reported the sale on an accrual basis for tax purposes and on an installment basis for book purposes—the sale would have the pretax effect on book profits and taxable income shown in **Illustration 6.** The first-year pre-tax profit on the installment method is $30, and the taxable income on the accrual method reported to the government is $90. In years 2 and 3, the book pre-tax profit is $30 each year. There is no profit reported on the tax return since it was all recognized in year 1. In **Illustration 7,** if comprehensive allocation is applied, the deferred tax item will show up on the asset side of the balance sheet, since the first-year profit recorded

ILLUSTRATION 6   **Book Pre-tax Profit versus Taxable Income**

	Book Pre-Tax Profit	*Taxable Income*
1995	$30	$90
1996	30	—
1997	30	—
Total	$90	$90

ILLUSTRATION 7   **Comprehensive Tax Allocation Accounting Illustrated**

	Pre-Tax Profit	*Current Tax Expense*	*Deferred Tax Expense*	*Net Profit*	*Deferred Tax Asset*	*Taxes Payable*
1995	$30	$36	$(24)[a]	$18	$24	$36
1996	30	—	12	18	12	—
1997	30	—	12	18	0	—

[a]Credit to tax expense.

for taxes would be greater than the profit recorded for financial accounting purposes (**Illustration 7**). In a sense, the company has overpaid, or prepaid, some taxes.

The accounting entries for the tax effect of the transaction presented in **Illustration 7** are:

Comprehensive Allocation

Year 1:

Dr. Deferred tax asset	24	
Tax expense—current	36	
Cr. Tax expense—deferred		24
Taxes payable		36

Years 2 and 3:

Dr. Tax expense—deferred	12	
Cr. Deferred tax asset		12

Flow-Through

Year 1:

Dr. Tax expense—current	36	
Cr. Taxes payable		36

Years 2 and 3:
No entry

ILLUSTRATION 8   **Flow-Through versus Comprehensive Tax Accounting: After-Tax Book Profits**

	Flow-Through	*Comprehensive*	*Differential*
1995	$ (6)	$18	$24
1996	30	18	(12)
1997	30	18	(12)
Total	$54	$54	$ 0

Illustration 8 shows after-tax book profit difference between the flow-through and comprehensive approaches to tax accounting if the installment method is used for book purposes and the accrual method is used for tax purposes.

FASB Statement No. 109

In FASB Statement No. 109 the FASB adopted the asset–liability approach to the recognition and measurement of a company's deferred tax liabilities and assets. The following basic principles are applied in accounting for income taxes by the Statement at the date of the financial statements:

1. A current tax liability or asset is recognized for the estimated taxes payable or refundable on tax returns for the current year.
2. A deferred tax liability or asset is recognized for the estimated future tax effects attributable to temporary differences and carryforwards.
3. The measurement of current and deferred tax liabilities and assets is based on provisions of the enacted tax law; the effects of future changes in tax laws or rates are not anticipated.
4. The measurement of deferred tax assets is reduced, if necessary, by the amount of any tax benefits that, based on available evidence, are not expected to be realized.

Balance Sheet Approach

Since FASB Statement No. 109 is a balance-sheet–oriented approach to deferred tax accounting, the Statement discusses deferred tax accounting primarily in terms of deferred tax assets and liabilities. Consistent with this approach, it defines periodic deferred tax expense or benefit as the change during the period in a company's deferred tax liabilities and assets. In the case of deferred tax liabilities and assets acquired in a business transaction during an accounting period, the related deferred tax expense or benefit is the change since the combination date.

Comprehensive Approach

FASB Statement No. 109 requires the deferred tax consequences to all temporary differences to enter into the measurement of deferred liabilities and assets. Consequently, it requires recognition of a deferred tax liability for all temporary differences that will result in taxable amounts in future years. Similarly, deferred tax assets must be recognized for all temporary differences that will result in deductible amounts in future years.

The transaction and accounting in **Illustration 3** is an example of a temporary difference that requires the recognition of a deferred tax liability. A temporary difference is created between the reported amount using sales accounting and the tax basis of the installment sales receivable, since for tax purposes some of the gain on the installment sale will be included in the determination of taxable income in future years. Because the amounts received from recovery of the receivable will be taxable, a deferred tax liability is recognized in the current year for the related taxes payable in future years.

The transaction and accounting in **Illustration 7** is an example of a temporary difference that requires recognition of a deferred tax asset. A temporary difference is created between the reported amount using installment accounting and the tax basis of the receivable, since none of the gain on the installment sale will be included in taxable income in future years. Because the amounts received upon recovery of the receivable are not taxable, a deferred tax asset is recognized in the current year.

Tax credit and tax loss carryforwards are also included in the measurement of deferred tax liabilities and assets.

Examples

FASB Statement No. 109 provides the following examples of differences between the tax basis of an asset or a liability and its reported amount in the balance sheet that will result in taxable or deductible amounts in some future period when the reported amount of assets are recovered and the reported amount of liabilities are settled:

1. *Revenues or gains that are taxable after they are recognized in financial income.* An asset (for example, a receivable from an installment sale) may be recognized for revenues or gains that will result in future taxable amounts when the asset is recovered.

2. *Expenses or losses that are deductible after they are recognized in financial income.* A liability (for example, a product warranty liability) may be recognized for expenses or losses that will result in future tax deductible amounts when the liability is settled.

3. *Revenues or gains that are taxable before they are recognized in financial income.* A liability (for example, subscriptions received in advance) may be recognized for an advance payment for goods or services to be provided in future years. For tax purposes, the advance payment is included in taxable

income upon the receipt of cash. Future sacrifices to provide goods and services (or future refunds to those who cancel their orders) will result in future tax deductible amounts when the liability is settled.

4. *Expenses or losses that are deductible before they are recognized in financial income.* The cost of an asset (for example, depreciable personal property) may have been deducted for tax purposes faster than it was depreciated for financial reporting purposes. Amounts received upon future recovery of the amount of the asset for financial reporting will exceed the remaining tax basis of the asset, and the excess will be taxable when the asset is recovered.

5. *A reduction in the tax basis of depreciable assets because of tax credits.* Amounts received upon future recovery of the amount of the asset for financial reporting will exceed the remaining tax basis of the asset, and the excess will be taxable when the asset is recovered.

6. *Business combinations accounted for by the purchase method.* There may be differences between the assigned values and the tax bases of the assets and liabilities recognized in a business combination accounted for as a purchase under APB Opinion No. 16, *Business Combinations.* Those differences will result in taxable or deductible amounts when the reported amounts of the assets and liabilities are recovered and settled, respectively.

Valuation Allowance

Deferred tax assets should only be recognized if, based on the weight of the available evidence, it is more likely than not in management's judgment that the deferred tax asset will be realized. "More likely than not" is defined in FASB Statement No. 109 as a probability of more than 50%. Deferred tax assets that are not likely to be recognized are recorded off the balance sheet in the so-called "valuation allowance" and disclosed in the tax note.

Management should review the adequacy of the valuation allowance at each measurement date. Any change in the valuation allowance should be included in income from continuing operations accompanied by the appropriate entry to the deferred tax asset account.

Management should consider tax planning strategies in determining the amount of valuation allowance required. Tax planning strategies include actions that are prudent and feasible that a company might take to prevent an operating loss or tax credit carryforward from expiring unused or result in the realization of deferred tax assets.

Enacted Change in Tax Laws or Rates

FASB Statement No. 109 requires that deferred tax liabilities and assets be adjusted in the period of the enactment for the effect of an enacted change in tax laws or rates. The effect is included in income from continuing operations.

Tax Allocations

The income tax expense or benefit for the accounting period must be allocated among continuing operations, discontinued operations, extraordinary items, and items charged or credited directly to owners' equity.

Exemptions

There are a number of exemptions to FASB Statement No. 109. The principal exemption is that a deferred tax liability does not need to be recognized for an excess of the amount for financial reporting over the tax basis of an investment in a foreign subsidiary or a foreign corporate joint venture that is essentially permanent in duration.

Display

In most cases deferred tax asset and liability balances are classified as current or noncurrent based on the classification of the related asset or liability for financial reporting.

Financial Analysis

The tax expense note accompanying the financial statement should always be carefully analyzed by statement users. It can be a valuable source of information. Statement users should always note the following:

1. *The percentage deferred taxes are of the total tax expense.* A high percentage might suggest liberal book accounting is being used, income is being recorded that may not be realized as cash until a much later period, or the company is relying on tax-shelter schemes to protect its income from taxes.

2. *The percentage book tax expenses are of the book pre-tax income and the dollar contribution to the change in earnings attributable to the change in the book tax rate.* A reduction in the book tax rate and/or a high contribution of tax savings due to a change in income tax rate may indicate that management is becoming more reliant on tax rate management as a source of net income. A low tax rate might indicate the company is vulnerable to tax code changes or its earnings are in low tax rate environments that might have restrictions on the use of profits earned in those locations. Low tax rates are generally considered low-quality earnings sources and a possible red flag. In making these calculations, equity-method income should be excluded. It can distort the tax rate percentage as it is included in pre-tax profits on an after-tax basis.

3. *Unusual change in the tax effect of individual temporary difference items.* A significant change may indicate a change in the level of activity related to the item or a shift in book or tax accounting methods and estimates.

4. *The company's past policy toward accruing potential U.S. taxes on overseas earnings.* The nonaccrual of potential U.S. taxes that would be due on repatriated foreign earnings could expose the company to a tax expense charge in a later period when the previously recorded overseas profits are repatriated.

5. *The current portion of the tax expense.* A decline in this figure is indicative of a lower level of profits reported to taxing authorities.

6. *One-time tax savings and sources of tax savings that are vulnerable to tax code changes.* The contribution of these items to net income might be nonrecurring and as such should be regarded as a low-quality earnings source.

7. *Capital gains.* Taxes attributable to capital gains might indicate that the company is selling assets at a gain to cover a decline in operating earnings.

8. *Valuation allowance changes.* Management may be manipulating the deferred tax asset valuation allowance to manage earnings rather than to reflect genuine changes in the company's prospects.

How deferred taxes should be regarded in financial analyses is a controversial topic. Some analysts argue that, in most cases, deferred tax liabilities are equivalent to permanent equity capital and should be lumped with owners' equity when computing debt-to-equity ratios. Others with this same view go even further. They would exclude deferred tax expenses from income in computing return on equity. In making this calculation, these individuals, for some unexplained reason, do not add the deferred tax liability back to owners' equity. This is a mistake. Many analysts, while recognizing that deferred tax liabilities are not the equivalent of debt and deferred tax expenses are not like most other expense items that must be paid in cash, accept the deferred-tax-accounting liability and expense classification for financial ratio purposes. This latter approach is generally followed when computing margin and return on investment ratio for management performance evaluation purposes. It is based on the belief that normalized earnings figures are better indicators of management performance over time than, say, income based on flow-through tax accounting. In contrast, in most financial structure analysis, all or some portion of the deferred tax liability is usually excluded from liabilities and/or included in equity. This treatment reflects the widespread acceptance among statement users of the quasi-equity nature of most deferred tax liabilities.

Grand Metropolitan PLC

Lyn Small, an associate analyst in the institutional equity research department of Holly and Manners, a large British merchant banking firm, received the following instructions from the firm's senior food and beverage analyst:

> Lyn, ever since Grand Metropolitan acquired Pillsbury there has been a strong interest in Grand Met in the U.S.A. We have received a request from one of our major American global equity accounts to give them an indication of what Grand Met's 1989 earnings might have been if the company had reported them on a U.S. GAAP basis. The client also wants our views on whether or not using the U.S. GAAP adjusted earnings-per-share figure is a useful way to look at Grand Met for equity valuation purposes.
>
> I'd like you to prepare a short memorandum responding to our client's request. The first section should show Grand Met's earnings on a U.S. GAAP basis. This earnings presentation should follow the U.S. GAAP presentation format. That is, it should identify earnings from continuing operations, discontinued operations, extraordinary items, unusual transactions and cumulative accounting changes, if any, as separate items. Deal with the valuation issue in the second part of your memo.

The Company

Grand Metropolitan's 1989 sales ("turnover") and net income were £9.3 billion and £1.1 billion, respectively.

Grand Metropolitan's business falls into three broad business segments—food, drinks and retailing.

Professor David F. Hawkins prepared this case as the basis for class discussion rather than to illustrate either effective or ineffective handling of an administrative situation.
Copyright © 1990 by the President and Fellows of Harvard College. Harvard Business School case 191–080.

In January, 1989, the food segment grew significantly with the acquisition of Pillsbury, a major U.S. food packaging and restaurant chain company. Previously Express Foods had dominated this segment. Negotiations were in progress to sell the food segment's Alpo Petfoods business.

The drinks segment included breweries and several wines and spirits subsidiaries, including Heublien and Almaden vineyards. Subject to government and shareholders' approval, the company's brewery operations were to be sold to Courage, a major United Kingdom brewery. This proposed transaction also involved the formation of a joint venture public house ("pub") company with Courage to operate the two company's tenanted pubs and most of their managed houses. Recently, Grand Metropolitan announced its intention to acquire a 20 percent interest in Remy & Cointreau Holdings.

The retailing segment is dominated by Burger King, a worldwide U.S.–based fast food chain. This segment also includes Pearle Eye-care, a property division, liquor stores and the company's managed houses. At the beginning of fiscal 1990, this segment's William Hill/Mecca betting business was sold.

Exhibit 1 reproduces a Grand Metropolitan "memo to file" Lyn Small had written shortly before the release of the company's 1989 annual report.

Exhibit 2 presents the Director's Report and Accounts section of Grand Metropolitan's 1989 annual report.

EXHIBIT 1   Lyn Small's "Memo to File"

To: File
From: Lyn Small
Re: Grand Metropolitan—Possible Client Presentation Ideas

Grand Met has moved quickly to reduce its absolute debt levels since the Pillsbury acquisition through asset sales. The benefit is a stronger balance sheet, the concentration of management on mainstream activities, high free cash flow and earnings growth well into the foreseeable future estimated at over 15% compound—all these factors combine to suggest a P/E of ? x at a ?% discount to the UK market is unjustified. On these grounds alone re-rating is now due. This is justified even before comparing Grand Met with similar U.S. consumer stocks selling at considerably higher cash flow multiples—and remember around 50% of Grand Met's profits are now dollar-denominated.

Since the last annual report the group has made the following significant acquisitions and disposals:

January	Acquisition of The Pillsbury Company.
	Disposal of Pillsbury Grain Merchandising.
March	Acquisition of S & E & A Metaxa.
May	Disposal of London Clubs.
	Acquisition of Mont La Salle Vineyards.
July	Disposal of S & A Restaurants.
August	Acquisition of Eyelab.
September	Disposal of Van de Kamp's.
	Disposal of Bumble Bee.
October	Acquisition of UB Restaurants.
December	Disposal of William Hill.

Current Price 567 p   52-week range, 658 p–498 p

EXHIBIT 2 Excerpts from Grand Metropolitan PLC's 1989 Annual Report

DIRECTORS' REPORT AND ACCOUNTS

GLOSSARY OF TERMS

In view of the different financial terms used in the international markets where GrandMet's shares are quoted, there follows a glossary of key financial terms used by GrandMet.

Gearing
The net debt (borrowings less cash) divided by the shareholders' equity (share capital, reserves and minority interests), expressed as a percentage.

Interest cover
The number of times the profit before interest and tax is greater than the net interest charge.

Earnings
The profit after tax and minority interest but before extraordinary items.

Earnings per share
Earnings (as above) divided by the weighted average number of shares in issue during the period.

P/E (price/earnings) ratio
The market price of the shares divided by the earnings per share.

Dividend yield
The dividend per share divided by the market price of the share expressed as a percentage.

Dividend cover
The number of times the dividend is covered by earnings (as above).

ACCOUNTING POLICIES

Accounting convention
The financial statements of the group are prepared under the historical cost convention modified by the revaluation of certain land and buildings. They have been drawn up to comply in all material respects with UK statements of standard accounting practice in force at the relevant time.

Basis of consolidation
The consolidated profit and loss account and balance sheet include the financial statements of the company and its subsidiaries made up to 30th September. The results of subsidiaries sold or acquired are included in the profit and loss account up to, or from, the earlier of the date consideration passes or the change of ownership becomes unconditional. As the company's results are included in the consolidated profit and loss account, a separate profit and loss account is not presented.

Overseas subsidiaries
The financial statements of some overseas subsidiaries do not conform with the group's accounting policies because of the legislation and accounting practices of the countries concerned. Appropriate adjustments are made on consolidation in order to present the group financial statements on a uniform basis.

Acquisitions
On the acquisition of a business, including an interest in a related company, fair values are attributed to the group's share of net tangible assets and significant owned brands acquired. Where the cost of acquisition exceeds the values attributable to such net assets, the difference is treated as goodwill and is written off direct to reserves in the year of acquisition.

EXHIBIT 2   (continued)

Intangible assets

Significant owned brands, acquired after 1st January 1985, the value of which is not expected to diminish in the foreseeable future, are recorded in the balance sheet as fixed intangible assets. No amortisation is provided on these assets but their value is reviewed annually by the directors and the cost written down as an exceptional item where permanent diminution in value has occurred.

Fixed assets and depreciation

Fixed assets are stated at cost or at professional valuation. Cost includes interest, net of any tax relief, on capital employed in major developments.

No depreciation is provided on freehold land or on freehold and long leasehold public houses (see below). Other leaseholds are depreciated over the unexpired period of the lease. All other buildings, plant, equipment and vehicles are depreciated to residual values over their estimated useful lives within the following ranges:

Industrial buildings	25 to 100 years
Plant and machinery	3 to 25 years
Fixtures and fittings	3 to 17 years

It is the group's policy to maintain all its public houses to a high standard in order to protect their trade. Because of this, such properties maintain residual disposal values in the aggregate at least equal to their book values and accordingly no provision for depreciation is made.

Leases

Where the group has substantially all the risks and rewards of ownership of an asset subject to a lease, the lease is treated as a finance lease. Other leases are treated as operating leases.

Future instalments payable by the group under finance leases, net of finance charges, are included within creditors with the corresponding asset values recorded as fixed tangible assets and depreciated over the shorter of their estimated useful lives or lease terms. Rentals payable are apportioned between the finance element, which is charged to the profit and loss account as interest, and the capital element, which reduces the outstanding obligation for future instalments.

Amounts receivable by the group under finance leases are included within debtors with income credited to the profit and loss account in proportion to the funds invested.

Operating lease payments by the group are charged to trading profit, receipts are treated as rental income. In both cases recognition for profit and loss account purposes is on a straight line basis over the life of the lease. Assets held by the group for letting under operating leases are included as fixed tangible assets.

Investments in related companies

A related company is one in which the group has a long term investment which is sufficiently substantial, usually from 20% to 50%, to enable the group to exercise a significant influence over the company in which the investment is made.

The group's share of the profits less losses of related companies is included in the consolidated profit and loss account and its interest in their net tangible assets is included in investments in the consolidated balance sheet.

Investments

Investments, other than in related companies, are valued individually at the lower of cost and net realisable value. Net realisable value is estimated by the directors in the case of unlisted investments and is market value in the case of listed investments.

Stocks

Stocks are valued at the lower of group cost and net realisable value. No interest is included but, where appropriate, cost includes production and other direct overhead expenses.

Foreign currencies

Transactions in foreign currencies are recorded at the rate of exchange at the date of the transaction or, if hedged forward, at the rate of exchange under the related forward currency contract. Assets and liabilities in foreign currencies, including the group's interest in the underlying net assets of related companies, are translated into sterling at the balance sheet exchange rates.

Profits and losses of overseas subsidiaries and related companies are translated into sterling at weighted average rates of exchange during the year with the year end adjustment to closing rates being taken to reserves.

Exhibit 2   (continued)

Gains or losses arising on the translation of the net assets of overseas subsidiaries and related companies are taken to reserves, less exchange differences arising on related foreign currency borrowings. Other exchange differences are taken to the profit and loss account.

Turnover
Turnover excludes inter-company sales and VAT but includes duty on beer, wines and spirits, together with rents and royalties receivable.

Research and development expenditure
Research and development expenditure is written off in the year in which it is incurred.

Post employment benefit costs
The group operates various pension plans and other post employment benefit plans. These are devised in accordance with the local conditions and practices in the countries concerned. Pension benefits are generally funded by payments to trustee administered funds; post employment medical benefits are, in general, unfunded.

The cost of providing pensions and other post employment benefits is charged against profits on a systematic basis, with pension surpluses and deficits arising allocated over the expected remaining service lives of current employees.

Differences between the amounts charged in the profit and loss account and payments made to the plans are treated as assets or liabilities. The unfunded post employment medical benefit liability is included in provisions in the balance sheet.

Taxation
The charge for taxation is based on the profit for the year and takes into account taxation deferred because of timing differences between the treatment of certain items for taxation and accounting purposes. However, no provision is made for taxation deferred, principally by accelerated taxation allowances on capital expenditure, if there is reasonable evidence that such deferred taxation will not be payable or recoverable in the foreseeable future.

Advance corporation tax recoverable by deduction from future corporation tax is carried forward within deferred taxation.[1]

Extraordinary items
Extraordinary items derive from events or transactions outside the ordinary activities of the business which are both material and expected not to recur frequently or regularly. They include profits and losses on disposals of significant investments and businesses.

---

[1]United Kingdom companies do not deduct withholding taxes from dividends paid. When dividends are paid the corporation makes an advance payment of corporate tax (ACT) equal to one quarter of the dividend paid to stockholders. ACT is treated as a payment on account of the company's liability for corporate taxes on profits for the period in which the dividend is paid. Under certain circumstances a surplus ACT can be created. It can be carried back or forward to offset corporate taxes. United Kingdom resident individual taxpayers receive a tax credit against their personal income tax liability equivalent to twenty-five percent of the dividend they receive.

CONSOLIDATED PROFIT AND LOSS ACCOUNT
for the year ended 30th September 1989

	Notes	1989 £m	1988 £m
Turnover	1	**9,298**	6,029
Operating costs	2	**(8,349)**	(5,387)
		949	642
Share of profits of related companies	3	**18**	12
Trading profit		**967**	654
Profit on sale of property		**80**	39
Reorganisation costs		**(35)**	25)
Interest	4	**(280)**	(93)
Profit on ordinary activities before taxation		**732**	575
Taxation on profit on ordinary activities	5	**(216)**	(155)
Profit on ordinary activities after taxation		**516**	420
Minority interests and preference dividends		**(8)**	(8)
Profit attributable to ordinary shareholders		**508**	412
Extraordinary items	6	**560**	290
Profit for the financial year		**1,068**	702
Ordinary dividends	7	**(167)**	(129)
Transferred to reserves		**901**	573
Movements in reserves			
Reserves at beginning of year		**2,964**	1,904
Exchange adjustments		**(81)**	(19)
Retained profit for year		**901**	573
Premiums on share issues, less expenses		**429**	7
Goodwill acquired during the year		**(1,909)**	(144)
Surplus on revaluation of property		**—**	643
Reserves at end of year		**2,304**	2,964
Earnings per share	8	**55.6p**	46.9p

CONSOLIDATED BALANCE SHEET
at 30th September 1989

	Notes	1989 £m	1989 £m	£m	1988 £m
Fixed assets					
Intangible assets	11		**2,652**		588
Tangible assets	12		**3,839**		3,280
Investments	13		**144**		206
			6,635		4,074
Current assets					
Stocks	14	**1,269**		761	
Debtors	15	**1,451**		873	
Cash at bank and in hand		**215**		138	
		2,935		1,772	
Creditors—due within one year					
Borrowings	17	**(362)**		(187)	
Other creditors	19	**(2,316)**		(1,301)	
		(2,678)		(1,488)	
Net current assets	15		**257**		284
Total assets less current liabilities			**6,892**		4,358
Creditors—due after more than one year					
Borrowings	17	**(3,494)**		(702)	
Other creditors	20	**(231)**		(163)	
			(3,725)		(865)
Provisions for liabilities and charges	21		**(325)**		(55)
			2,842		3,438
Capital and reserves					
Called up share capital	22		**506**		443
Reserves	23				
Share premium account		**436**		7	
Revaluation reserve		**(944)**		649	
Special reserve		**—**		282	
Related companies' reserves		**10**		16	
Profit and loss account		**2,802**		2,010	
			2,304		2,964
			2,810		3,407
Minority interests			**32**		31
			2,842		3,438

A J G Sheppard, *Director*
C Strowger, *Director*

BALANCE SHEET
at 30th September 1989

	Notes	1989 £m	1989 £m	£m	1988 £m
Fixed assets					
Investments	13		**737**		734
Current assets					
Debtors	15	**2,082**		1,215	
Cash at bank		**1**		11	
		2,083		1,226	
Creditors—due within one year					
Borrowings	18	**(42)**		(31)	
Other creditors	19	**(583)**		(513)	
		(625)		(544)	
Net current assets			**1,458**		682
Total assets less current liabilities			**2,195**		1,416
Creditors—due after more than one year					
Borrowings	18		**(156)**		(101)
			2,039		1,315
Capital and reserves					
Called up share capital	22		**506**		443
Reserves	23				
Share premium account		**436**		7	
Special reserve		**426**		426	
Profit and loss account		**671**		439	
			1,533		872
			2,039		1,315

A J G Sheppard, *Director*
C Strowger, *Director*

SOURCE AND APPLICATION OF FUNDS
for the year ended 30th September 1989

	Operations £m	Acquisition and disposals £m	1989 Total £m	1988 Total £m
Funds generated				
Group profit before taxation	732		732	575
Adjustments for items not involving cash movement:				
Depreciation	190		190	125
Profit on sale of property	(80)		(80)	(39)
Other items	—		—	5
	842		842	666
Sales of fixed assets and investments	306	1,313	1,619	749
Share issues, less expenses	492	—	492	9
	1,640	1,313	2,953	1,424
Funds applied				
Investments:				
Intangible fixed assets	—	1,853	1,853	—
Tangible fixed assets	464	877	1,341	345
Related companies and other fixed asset investments . . .	76	51	127	95
Goodwill	—	1,909	1,909	144
	540	4,690	5,230	584
Increase/(decrease) in working capital:				
Stocks	157	351	508	27
Debtors	(34)	661	627	62
Creditors and provisions	(84)	(1,186)	(1,270)	14
	579	4,516	5,095	687
Exchange adjustments	357	—	357	(38)
Tax paid	84	178	262	64
Dividends paid	129	—	129	104
	1,149	4,694	5,843	817
Decrease/(increase) in net borrowings	491	(3,381)	(2,890)	607
Movements in net borrowings				
Borrowings—due within one year			175	(143)
—due after more than one year			2,792	(440)
Cash at bank and in hand			(77)	(24)
Net movement shown above			2,890	(607)
Net borrowings at beginning of year			751	1,358
Net borrowings at end of year			3,641	751

NOTES

1 Sector analysis

	Turnover £m	Trading profit £m	1989 Capital employed £m	Turnover £m	Trading profit £m	1988 Capital employed £m
By activity:						
Continuing businesses:						
Food	2,872	245	2,468	1,253	84	310
Drinks	2,784	389	1,626	2,581	316	1,479
Retailing	2,040	230	2,266	1,040	143	1,842
	7,696	864	6,360	4,874	543	3,631
Discontinued businesses:						
Hotels	78	15	—	338	54	502
Betting and gaming	1,284	57	123	630	36	56
Other	240	31	—	187	21	—
	9,298	967	6,483	6,029	654	4,189
By geographical area:						
United Kingdom and Ireland ..	4,668	424	2,626	3,836	364	2,700
Continental Europe	471	66	330	221	46	384
United States of America	3,720	395	3,314	1,758	218	1,033
Rest of North America	174	20	145	54	14	50
Africa and Middle East	126	10	23	127	6	18
Rest of World	139	52	45	33	6	4
	9,298	967	6,483	6,029	654	4,189

The net £45m profit (1988—£14m) on sale of property less reorganisation costs relates to the following activities: food £(2)m, drinks £(10)m, retailing £14m and discontinued businesses £43m (1988—£(3)m, £(1)m, £6m and £12m respectively). Exports from the United Kingdom were £228m (1988—£197m).

The group interest expense is arranged centrally and is not attributable to individual activities or geographical areas. The analysis of capital employed by activity and geographical area is calculated on net assets excluding cash and borrowings.

The Pillsbury Company was acquired on 3rd January 1989. It contributed £1.456m turnover and £135m trading profit to the food sector and £834m turnover and £76m trading profit to the retailing sector. In addition the Pillsbury businesses which have subsequently been sold contributed £240m turnover and £31m trading profit.

The weighted average exchange rate used to translate the US dollar profits was £1 = \$1.66 for Pillsbury (nine months) and £1 = \$1.68 for other US companies (1988—£1 = \$1.77). The exchange rate used to translate the US dollar assets and liabilities at the balance sheet date was £1 = \$1.62 (1988—£1 = \$1.69).

2 Operating costs

	1989 £m	1988 £m
Raw materials and consumables	4,026	2,540
Other external charges	2,912	1,896
Staff costs	1,270	884
Depreciation of tangible fixed assets	190	125
Increase in stocks of finished goods and work in progress	(10)	(37)
Other operating income	(39)	(21)
	8,349	5,387

NOTES

Other external charges include operating lease rentals for plant and machinery of £28m (1988—£15m) and for other leases (mainly of properties) of £95m (1988—£70m). Auditors' remuneration was £4m (1988—£3m).

Operating costs include research and development expenditure of £25m (1988—£8m).

3 Related companies

	1989 £m	1988 £m
Share of trading profits before taxation	18	12
Taxation	(6)	(4)
Share of profits after taxation	12	8
Dividends received by the group	(4)	(6)
Retained by related companies	8	2

4 Interest

	1989 £m	1988 £m
On bank loans, overdrafts and other loans repayable wholly within five years	310	81
On 5.75% convertible unsecured loan stock	21	—
On finance leases	5	3
On all other loans	23	23
	359	107
Less: Interest receivable	(75)	(13)
Interest capitalised	(4)	(1)
	280	93

The increase in the interest charge arose primarily as a result of the acquisition of The Pillsbury Company.

5 Taxation

	1989 £m	1988 £m
UK corporation tax		
Payable at 35% (1988—35%)	97	111
Deferred	38	(2)
Overseas taxation		
Payable	16	60
Deferred	79	4
Taxation on the group's share of profits of related companies	6	4
	236	177
Less Provisions for taxation no longer required	(20)	(22)
	216	155

NOTES

6 Extraordinary items

	1989		1988
£m	£m	£m	£m

Extraordinary income/(charges):				
Business disposals and discontinuance				
Hotels		695		—
Gaming		48		—
US soft drinks operations		1		318
Other		(19)		38
		689		356
Other disposals and related provisions		(8)		30
		681		386
Tax (charge)/relief relating to extraordinary items				
UK corporation tax	3		(1)	
Overseas taxation	(127)		(92)	
Deferred taxation	3		(3)	
		(121)		(96)
		560		290

Extraordinary items include £4m (1988—£4m) interest paid and £nil (1988—£1m) dividends received in respect of the holdings in Irish Distillers Group plc (IDG) (1988—IDG and Société Martell & Co.).

7 Ordinary dividends

	1989	1988
	£m	£m
Interim of 6.75p per share (1988—5.5p)	58	47
Proposed final of 11.0p per share (1988—9.5p)	109	82
	167	129

Adjusted for the bonus element of the 1988 rights issue the 1989 interim dividend amounted to 6.6p per share (1988—interim 5.4p and final 9.3p).

8 Earnings per share

Earnings per share is calculated by reference to earnings of £508m adjusted by £14m (1988—£nil), being the after tax interest on the convertible loan stock, and the adjusted weighted average number of ordinary shares in issue during the year of 938,889,000 shares (1988—£412m and 878,791,000 shares after adjusting for the bonus element of the rights issue).

The 1988 rights issue took the form of 5.75% convertible unsecured loan stock and not equity for technical reasons. Since the stock was converted during the year earnings per share have been calculated as if it had been an equity issue.

NOTES

9 Employees

The average number of employees during the year was:

	Full time	Part time	1989 Total	Full time	Part time	1988 Total
Continuing businesses:						
Food	28,193	2,609	30,802	12,294	2,568	14,862
Drinks	15,297	304	15,601	15,563	462	16,025
Retailing	47,905	43,071	90,976	25,273	12,098	37,371
	91,395	45,984	137,379	53,130	15,128	68,258
Discontinued businesses:						
Hotels	2,590	58	2,648	12,271	277	12,548
Betting and gaming	6,938	2,673	9,611	5,591	1,565	7,156
Other	2,537	—	2,537	1,759	32	1,791
	103,460	48,715	152,175	72,751	17,002	89,753

The aggregate remuneration of all employees comprised:	1989 £m	1988 £m
Wages and salaries	1,150	784
Employer's social security costs	106	73
Employer's pension and other post employment benefits cost	14	27
	1,270	884

The group operates a number of pension plans throughout the world. The plans generally are of the defined benefit type funded by payments to trustee administered funds or insurance companies. In 1989 the method of accounting for pension costs has been changed to comply with the recently issued accounting standard on pensions.

Valuations by professionally qualified actuaries of all significant pension plans were carried out during the year. The actuarial method used for the significant valuations was the projected unit method. The major assumptions used by the actuaries were that the return on plan assets would be 9% per annum and wage and salary rates would increase at an average of 6%–7%. The market value of the principal UK plan assets at the date of the latest actuarial valuation totalled £756m. The market value of the plan assets of the major funds in the US was approximately £425m. The actuarial value of the assets of the significant plans was sufficient to cover approximately 129% of the benefits that had accrued to members after allowing for expected future increases in wages and salaries.

The group also operates a number of plans which provide employees with other post employment benefits principally in respect of US medical costs. The unfunded liability is assessed by professionally qualified actuaries and is included in provisions in the balance sheet.

NOTES

The following table shows the number of UK employees of the group, other than directors of the company, whose emoluments, excluding pension contributions, fell into the ranges shown:

	1989	1988		1989	1988		1989	1988
£30,001–£35,000	223	133	£ 85,001–£ 90,000	10	5	£140,001–£145,000	—	1
£35,001–£40,000	129	104	£ 90,001–£ 95,000	5	8	£145,001–£150,000	—	1
£40,001–£45,000	87	58	£ 95,001–£100,000	5	2	£150,001–£155,000	1	1
£45,001–£50,000	58	43	£100,001–£105,000	3	1	£160,001–£165,000	1	—
£50,001–£55,000	46	26	£105,001–£110,000	3	3	£180,001–£185,000	1	—
£55,001–£60,000	24	23	£110,001–£115,000	2	2	£185,001–£190,000	2	—
£60,001–£65,000	27	10	£115,001–£120,000	—	2	£190,001–£195,000	1	—
£65,001–£70,000	18	10	£120,001–£125,000	2	1	£315,001–£320,000	—	1
£70,001–£75,000	15	14	£125,001–£130,000	4	1		705	461
£75,001–£80,000	22	7	£130,001–£135,000	6	1			
£80,001–£85,000	10	1	£135,001–£140,000	—	2			

10 Directors
Emoluments

The total emoluments of the directors, including pension contributions, were £2,536,299 (1988—£1,969,337) including fees of £124,079 (1988—£127,914). The emoluments, excluding pension contributions, of the chairman were £506,438 (1988—£465,531).

The following table shows the number of other UK based directors whose emoluments, excluding pension contributions, fell into the ranges shown:

	1989	1988		1989	1988
£ 0–£ 5,000	1	—	£ 60,001–£ 65,000	1	—
£ 5,001–£10,000	1	1	£ 70,001–£ 75,000	—	1
£20,001–£25,000	1	1	£225,001–£230,000	—	2
£25,001–£30,000	1	—	£235,001–£240,000	1	—
£35,001–£40,000	—	1	£260,001–£265,000	2	—
£50,001–£55,000	—	1		8	7

In 1988 pensions of £19,755 were paid in respect of the services of former directors and a payment of £180,556 was made to a former director in settlement of the group's pension obligations.

A share price related cash bonus scheme is in operation which allows selected employees, including executive directors, to benefit from upward movements in the price of the company's shares over a period of between 6 and 10 years. The scheme is designed to encourage senior executives to align their long-term career aspirations with the long-term interests of the group. For this reason, in normal circumstances, no payments can be made under the scheme until the 6th year and full payment will only be made in the 10th year. Provision is made annually for future liabilities under the scheme.

NOTES

Shareholdings

The beneficial interests of the directors at 30th September 1989 in the share capital of the company were:

	Ordinary shares		Options	
	1989	*1988*	**1989**	*1988*
A J G Sheppard	**61,428**	10,000	**468,804**	338,457
G J Bull	**13,000**	11,500	**149,541**	118,307
R V Giordano (non-executive)	—	—	—	—
Sir John Harvey-Jones (non-executive)	—	—	—	—
Sir Colin Marshall (non-executive)	—	—	—	—
I A Martin	**10,000**	4,000	**185,640**	137,940
C Strowger	**5,285**	2,000	**133,496**	154,039
D E Tagg	**4,078**	2,000	**175,154**	104,853

G J Bull had a non-beneficial interest in 270,912 ordinary shares (1988—270,912).

The directors held the above options under the share option schemes approved by shareholders on 4th March 1982 and 5th March 1985, at prices between 239p and 540p per share exercisable by 1996.

Subsequent to the year end Mr D A G Simon was appointed. Mr. Simon held no interests in shares on the date of his appointment or on 7th November 1989. On 7th November 1989 each of the interests of the other directors was unchanged from 30th September 1989.

Other than the above, no director had any interest, beneficial or non-beneficial, in the share capital of the company or had a material interest during the year in any significant contract with the company or any subsidiary.

11 Fixed assets—Intangible assets

	Brands £m
Cost	
At 30th September 1988	588
Additions—Pillsbury	1,763
—Other	90
Exchange adjustments	211
At 30th September 1989	2,652

The brands are denominated in the currencies of their principal markets.

NOTES

12 Fixed assets—Tangible assets

	Land and buildings £m	Plant and machinery £m	Fixtures and fittings £m	Assets in course of construction £m	Total £m
Cost or valuation					
At 30th September 1988..............	2,561	773	403	59	3,796
Exchange adjustments	47	28	(1)	3	77
Additions	154	126	54	130	464
New subsidiaries	554	214	51	58	877
Disposals.........................	(494)	(141)	(117)	(9)	(761)
Transfers	19	58	19	(96)	—
At 30th September 1989..............	2,841	1,058	409	145	4,453
Depreciation					
At 30th September 1988..............	24	346	146	—	516
Exchange adjustments	1	6	—	—	7
Provided during the year	41	113	36	—	190
Disposals.........................	(10)	(48)	(41)	—	(99)
At 30th September 1989..............	56	417	141	—	614
Net book value					
At 30th September 1988..............	2,537	427	257	59	3,280
At 30th September 1989..............	2,785	641	268	145	3,839

	1989 £m	1988 £m
(i) The total at cost or valuation for land and buildings comprises:............		
At 1988 professional valuation	2,049	2,105
At 1985 professional valuation	7	368
At cost	785	88
	2,841	2,561

(ii) The net book value of land and buildings comprises freeholds of £2,743m (1988—£2,185m), long leaseholds of £166m (1988—£260m) and short leaseholds of £146m (1988—£92m).

(iii) Included in the net book value of freehold property is £1,395m (1988—£1,654m) in respect of public houses, and £350m (1988—£159m) of land unrelated to those properties. Depreciation is not charged on these amounts.

(iv) Included in the total net book value of tangible assets is £39m (1988—£34m) in respect of assets acquired under finance leases. Depreciation for the year on these assets was £6m (1988—£6m). There is also included £86m (1988—£nil) in respect of assets held for the purpose of leasing out under operating leases. The depreciation for the year on these assets was £1m (1988—£nil).

NOTES

(v) Historical cost figures for land and buildings, i.e., the original cost to the group of all land and buildings and the related depreciation, are:

	1989 £m	1988 £m
Historical cost	1,562	1,151
Depreciation	(78)	(675)
Net book value	1,484	1,086

(vi) Included in the historical net book value is £3m (1988—£6m) in respect of capitalised interest.

13 Fixed assets—Investments

Group	Investment in related companies £m	Loans to related companies £m	Other investments £m	Other loans £m	Total £m
At 30th September 1988	107	8	92	10	217
Exchange adjustments	2	—	11	2	15
Additions	29	1	52	45	127
Disposals	(72)	(7)	(116)	(9)	(204)
At 30th September 1989	66	2	39	48	155
Less: Provisions					
At 30th September 1988	—	—	10	1	11
Increase in year	1	—	—	7	8
Disposals	—	—	(8)	—	(8)
At 30th September 1989	1	—	2	8	11
Net book value					
At 30th September 1988	107	8	82	9	206
At 30th September 1989	65	2	37	40	144

The investment in related companies comprises cost of shares, less goodwill written off on acquisition, of £55m (1988—£91m) plus the group's share of post-acquisition retained profits and reserves of £10m (1988—£16m).

The net book value of listed investments is as follows:	1989 £m	1988 £m
Listed on UK stock exchanges	14	70
Listed on other stock exchanges	7	5
	21	75
Market value of listed investments	43	95

Listed investments in 1988 included a 25.1% holding in the ordinary shares of Irish Distillers Group, plc, a company incorporated and operating principally in Eire.

NOTES

Company	Shares in subsidiaries £m
Cost at 30th September 1988	734
Additions	175
Disposals..	(172)
Cost at 30th September 1989	737

Details of the principal group companies are given on pages 56 and 57.

14 Stocks

	1989 £m	1988 £m
Raw materials and consumables	363	214
Work in progress	245	177
Finished goods and goods for resale	661	370
	1,269	761

15 Debtors

	Group 1989 £m	Group 1988 £m	Company 1989 £m	Company 1988 £m
Trade debtors.......................................	883	625	—	—
Amounts owed by subsidiary companies	—	—	1,990	1,168
Amounts owed by related companies	3	10	—	—
Amounts receivable under finance leases	115	—	—	—
Other debtors.......................................	228	140	34	3
Prepayments and accrued income	94	52	3	1
Deferred taxation (see note 16).........................	128	46	55	43
	1,451	873	2,082	1,215

Included in group prepayments and accrued income is £18m (1988—£nil) in respect of pensions. The group debtors (and group net current assets) include £162m and a proportion of deferred taxation which fall due after one year (1988—£31m and a proportion of deferred taxation). The company deferred taxation comprises ACT recoverable.

16 Deferred taxation

	Capital allowances £m	Other timing differences £m	Total £m
At 30th September 1988...............................	(25)	28	3
Exchange adjustments	(5)	17	12
Acquisitions less disposals of subsidiaries	(64)	234	170
Transfers from profit and loss account....................	(4)	(108)	(112)
At 30th September 1989...............................	(98)	171	73
ACT recoverable (1988—£43m)			55
Deferred tax asset			128

NOTES

Provision for tax on capital gains payable on the disposal of revalued properties is made only when it is decided in principle to dispose of the asset. The tax liability on capital gains if all properties had been sold at their book values at 30th September 1989, and without taking advantage of the law relating to rollover relief, is estimated to be £325m (1988—£395m).

Other deferred taxation not provided, principally in respect of capital allowances, amounted at 30th September 1989 to £116m (1988—£150m). Deferred tax is not generally provided in respect of liabilities which might arise on the distribution of unappropriated profits of overseas subsidiaries and related companies.

17 Group borrowings

	1989 Bank loans and overdrafts £m	Other loans £m	Total £m	1988 Bank loans and overdrafts £m	Other loans £m	Total £m
Analysis by year of repayment						
After five years—by instalment	7	66	73	71	81	152
—other than by instalment	106	253	359	35	224	259
From two to five years	2,240	407	2,647	99	27	126
From one to two years	356	59	415	107	58	165
Due after more than one year	2,709	785	3,494	312	390	702
Due within one year	204	158	362	153	34	187
	2,913	943	3,856	465	424	889
Amounts repayable by instalment part of which fall due after five years	41	71	112	76	90	166

Borrowings under committed bank facilities are classified in the repayment analysis according to the maturity of the facility under which they are drawn. Commercial paper and cash advances issued in conjunction with a multi-option facility are classified within other loans according to the maturity of the committed bank credit forming part of that facility. In the above analysis the effect of currency swaps is taken into account when translating the group's borrowings into sterling.

Total borrowings comprise:	Year end interest rates %	1989 £m	1988 £m
Bank loans and overdrafts			
Drawn under multi-currency facilities expiring ultimately in the year to 30th September:			
1989		—	12
1990		—	99
1991	9.01–14.38	347	11
1992	9.17– 9.34	1,914	71
1994	7.05– 9.17	276	35
1995	9.25–14.27	135	74
Other loans, uncommitted loans and overdrafts		241	163
		2,913	465

NOTES

17 Group borrowings—(continued)

Total borrowings comprise:		*Year end interest rates %*	*1989 £m*	*1988 £m*
Other loans				
Guaranteed notes 1990	Sterling	10.875	50	50
Deutschemark bonds 1992	Deutschemark	6.625	45	—
Euro bonds 1993	US dollar	10.25	62	—
Notes payable 1995	US dollar	11.5	62	—
Redeemable loan notes 1998	Sterling	11.3125	55	—
1999 loan	US dollar		—	18
Extendible notes 1999	US dollar	12.0	62	—
Subordinated convertible bonds 2002	Sterling	6.25	100	100
Debenture stock 2008	Sterling	12.125	50	50
Sinking fund debentures 2015	US dollar	11.125	79	—
Commercial paper	Sterling/US dollar	8.36–14.03	270	113
Others	Various	Various	108	93
			943	424

£94m (1988—£108m) of borrowings due after more than one year and £7m (1988—£3m) of borrowings due within one year were secured on assets of the group.

The group had available unused committed bank facilities at 30th September 1989 of over £370m (1988—£850m).

The group has arranged interest rate swaps which have the effect of fixing the rate of interest at an average of 8.5% (1988—8.0%) on US dollar borrowings totalling £586m (1988—£562m) for a weighted average term of 3 years (1988—2½ years). In addition the interest rate on borrowings of £1,235m has been protected for 2 years by the purchase of interest rate caps at a rate of 9%. The interest rates shown in the table above are those contracted on the underlying borrowings before taking into account any interest rate swaps.

18 Company borrowings

	1989 £m	*1988 £m*
Analysis by year of repayment		
After five years	**100**	100
From two to five years	**1**	1
From one to two years	**55**	—
Due after more than one year	**156**	101
Due within one year	**42**	31
	198	132

Amounts falling due after one year include subordinated convertible bonds of £100m (1988—£100m) and a variable interest loan of £55m (1988—£1m).

NOTES

19 Other creditors—due within one year

	Group 1989 £m	Group 1988 £m	Company 1989 £m	Company 1988 £m
Trade creditors	702	370	—	—
Bills of exchange payable	66	51	—	—
Amounts owed to subsidiary companies	—	—	319	335
Amounts owed to related companies	10	13	—	—
Corporate taxation	360	229	71	43
Other taxation including social security	147	118	—	—
Net obligations under finance leases	11	5	—	—
Other creditors	233	64	2	—
Ordinary dividends payable	167	129	167	129
Accruals and deferred income	620	322	24	6
	2,316	1,301	583	513

20 Other creditors—due after more than one year

	1989 £m	1988 £m
Gross obligations under finance leases due:		
After five years	25	9
From two to five years	40	23
	65	32
Less: Future finance charges	(21)	(6)
	44	26
	33	52
Corporate taxation	154	85
Other creditors	231	163

21 Provisions for liabilities and charges

	Pensions and other post employment provisions £m	Acquisition provisions £m	Other £m	Total £m
At 30th September 1988	24	21	10	55
Exchange adjustments	7	12	—	19
New subsidiaries	89	413	54	556
Transfers from profit and loss account	7	—	17	24
Utilised and other movements	(25)	(257)	(47)	(329)
At 30th September 1989	102	189	34	325

NOTES

22 Called up share capital

The authorised share capital of the company is £660m (1988—£575m).

During the year 3,714,276 ordinary shares (aggregate nominal value £2m) were allotted under the share option schemes for an aggregate consideration of £13m (1988—3,124,113 shares, nominal value £2m, consideration £9m).

On 4th October 1988 a rights issue was made, for technical reasons, in the form of 5.75% convertible unsecured loan stock. The total consideration of £492m was payable in two equal instalments on 28th October 1988 and 2nd June 1989. The underlying basis for the issue of ordinary shares was one new ordinary share at 400p for every seven ordinary shares held. On 30th September 1989 the stock was converted into 122,942,119 ordinary shares.

The allotted and fully paid share capital at 30th September 1989 was as follows:

	1989 Shares	1989 £m	1988 Shares	1988 £m
Ordinary shares of 50p each	987,251,233	494	860,594,838	431
Cumulative £1 preference shares:				
4¾% (now 3.325% plus tax credit)	1,217,250	1	1,217,250	1
6¼% (now 4.375% plus tax credit)	3,278,454	3	3,278.454	3
5% (now 3.5% plus tax credit)	7,739,411	8	7,739,411	8
		506		443

The following potential issues to ordinary shares have not been dealt with in these financial statements:

(i) Under the share option schemes for executives, approved by shareholders on 11th January 1973 and 4th March 1982, directors and executives hold options to subscribe for up to 13,682,702 (1988—11,474,256) ordinary shares at prices ranging between 247p and 540p per share exercisable by 1995.

(ii) Under the savings-related share option scheme for employees, approved by shareholders on 5th March 1985, employees hold options to subscribe for up to 5,325,249 (1988—4,992,629) ordinary shares at prices between 239p and 503p per share exercisable between 1990 and 1996.

(iii) The holders of the 6¼% subordinated convertible bonds have the option of converting their bonds into ordinary shares at a price of 658p (1988—675p) per share exercisable up to and including 7th September 2002. These conversion rights could give rise to the issue of up to 15,197,568 (1988—14,814,814) ordinary shares.

(iv) The holders of £20m 9% unsecured convertible loan notes issued during the year have the option of converting their notes into ordinary shares at a price of 500p per share exercisable between 1992 and 1998. These conversion rights could give rise to the issue of up to 4,000,000 ordinary shares.

23 Reserves

	Share premium account £m	Revaluation and special reserves £m	Related companies' reserves £m	Profit and loss account £m	Total £m
Group					
At 30th September 1988	7	931	16	2,010	2,964
Exchange adjustments	—	1	—	(82)	(81)
Retained profit for the year	—	—	8	893	901
Premiums on share issues, less expenses	429	—	—	—	429
Goodwill acquired during the year	—	(1,909)	—	—	(1,909)
Transfer of goodwill on disposal	—	185	—	(185)	—
Other transfers between reserves	—	(152)	(14)	166	—
At 30th September 1989	436	(944)	10	2,802	2,304

NOTES

	Share premium account £m	Special reserve £m	Profit and loss account £m	Total £m
Company				
At 30th September 1988.............	7	426	439	872
Retained profit for the year...........	—	—	232	232
Premiums on share issues, less expenses	429	—	—	429
At 30th September 1989.............	436	426	671	1,533

Aggregate goodwill, net of disposals, of £2,676m (1988—£952m) has been written off against group revaluation and special reserves. The £1,909m of goodwill acquired during the year arose on the acquisition of The Pillsbury Company (£1,282m). The William Hill Organisation (£321m) and others (£306m).

In 1988, with the approval of shareholders and the Court, £426m was transferred from the share premium account to an undistributable special reserve in the company's balance sheet. In the group balance sheet the opening special reserve of £282m has been eliminated by goodwill written off.

The exchange adjustments include losses of £35m in respect of local currency borrowings by overseas companies and £321m in respect of other currency borrowings.

24 Contingent liabilities

The group has guaranteed borrowings of third parties and related companies which at 30th September 1989 amounted to £191m (1988—£172m) and has given performance guarantees to third parties of £23m (1988—£22m). The company has guaranteed certain borrowings of subsidiary companies which at 30th September 1989 amounted to £3,318m (1988—£494m) and has given performance guarantees to third parties of £nil (1988—£4m).

There are a number of legal claims or potential claims against the group, the outcome of which cannot at present be foreseen. Provision is made in these financial statements for all liabilities which are expected to materialise.

25 Commitments

(i) Capital expenditure authorised and commitments not provided for in these financial statements, all in respect of subsidiaries, are estimated at:

	1989 £m	1988 £m
Committed...	240	97
Authorised but not committed..	180	248

(ii) At 30th September 1989 the group had minimum annual commitments under non-cancellable operating leases as follows:

	Land and buildings £m	Other £m	1989 Total £m	Land and Buildings £m	Other £m	1988 Total £m
Operating leases which expire						
Within one year	4	6	10	2	4	6
From two to five years	18	16	34	13	9	22
After five years	73	3	76	37	1	38
	95	25	120	52	14	66

NOTES

26 Acquisition of The Pillsbury Company

	Pillsbury balance sheet at 31st December 1988 £m	Accounting policy realignment £m	Revaluation and acquisition adjustments £m	Fair value balance sheet at 3rd January 1989 £m
Fixed assets				
Intangible assets	326	1,437	—	1,763
Tangible assets	801	(38)	(19)	744
Investments	56	—	(5)	51
	1,183	1,399	(24)	2,558
Working capital				
Stocks	375	(2)	4	377
Debtors	416	—	147	563
Investments for resale	187	—	39	226
Creditors and provisions	(737)	(110)	(334)	(1,181)
Deferred tax	3	51	91	145
	1,427	1,338	(77)	2,688
Net borrowings	(746)	—	(3)	(749)
Shareholders' funds	681	1,338	(80)	1,939
Purchase price				(3,221)
Goodwill				(1,282)

The Pillsbury balance sheet at 31st December 1988 is a summarised version of the audited financial statements of The Pillsbury Company, which were filed with the Securities and Exchange Commission in the United States. The balance sheet has been converted at $1.79 = £1, the exchange rate at acquisition. The principal adjustments made to convert this balance sheet to fair values are as follows:

Accounting policy realignment
(i) Intangible assets are replaced by the purchase consideration attributable to significant brands acquired.
(ii) Tangible fixed assets are adjusted to reflect a higher minimum capitalisation level per addition.
(iii) Provisions are increased in respect of liabilities not previously included in the Pillsbury balance sheet, including post employment medical benefits.

Revaluation and acquisition adjustments
(i) Tangible fixed assets are adjusted to fair value based on external property valuations and internal reviews of other assets less provisions for closure where appropriate.
(ii) The investments for resale comprise those businesses which the group was committed to selling prior to acquisition—Steak & Ale Restaurant Corp. and Pillsbury Grain Merchandising. The acquisition adjustment is the profit on the sale of those businesses. Subsequently further businesses have been sold and the profit on disposal is included in the adjustment to debtors.
(iii) The acquisition adjustment to creditors and provisions represents the cost of restructuring the business and strategically realigning its operations to acceptable levels of efficiency.

27 Acquisition of The William Hill Organisation
On 16th December 1988 the group acquired The William Hill Organisation Ltd giving rise to a goodwill charge of £321m. This company was merged with the existing retail betting operations and the combined business was sold subsequent to 30th September 1989 at a substantial profit.

28 Approval of financial statements
These financial statements were approved by a duly appointed and authorised committee of the Board of Directors on 7th December 1989.

REPORT OF THE AUDITORS

to the members of Grand Metropolitan Public Limited Company

KPMG Peat Marwick McLintock

We have audited the financial statements on pages 36 to 54 in accordance with Auditing Standards.

In our opinion the financial statements give a true and fair view of the state of affairs of the company and the group at 30th September 1989 and of the profit and source and application of funds of the group for the year then ended and have been properly prepared in accordance with the Companies Act 1985.

Peat Marwick McLintock
Chartered Accountants
7th December 1989

PO Box 486
1 Puddle Dock
Blackfriars
London EC4V 3PD

Questions

1. How does Grand Metropolitan account or not account for deferred taxes? _____ How does this accounting and its effect on the balance sheet and net income differ from U.S. GAAP? What other accounting differences between U.K. accounting standards and U.S. GAAP can you identify? _____

2. Do you believe that the non–U.S. GAAP Grand Metropolitan accounting practices that you have identified result in useful information about the company for equity valuation and management performance evaluation purposes? _____ Would this accounting information have been more useful if it had been prepared using U.S. GAAP? _____

3. A number of Grand Metropolitan's businesses compete with domestic-based U.S. companies both in the United States and overseas. Does Grand Metropolitan's accounting practices give it a competitive advantage? _____

4. Adjust Grand Metropolitan's 1989 net income to a U.S. GAAP basis for the company's U.K. accounting practices that you believe account for most of the difference between its net income on a U.K. accounting and U.S. GAAP basis.

5. Do you believe that it is useful to convert Grand Metropolitan's net income to a U.S. GAAP basis for equity valuation purposes? _____

CHAPTER 14

Long-Lived Fixed Assets

A company's long-lived fixed assets ("fixed assets") include all of its physical assets with a life of more than one year that are used in operations but are not intended for sale as such in the ordinary course of business. Fixed assets can be classified in three different categories: (1) those subject to depreciation, such as plant and equipment; (2) those subject to depletion, such as natural resources; and (3) those not subject to depreciation or depletion, such as land. Fixed assets are normally carried at their original cost less any accumulated depreciation or depletion. Depreciation is the process of allocating the cost of fixed assets over the useful life of the asset so as to match the cost of an asset with the benefits it creates, and depletion is the process whereby the cost of wasting assets is matched with the revenues generated by the asset. Initially, the chapter focuses on the measurement of investments in fixed assets. The allocation of the cost of fixed assets to the income statement to determine periodic income is covered later in the chapter.

Fixed assets are shown on the balance sheet as follows:

Plant and equipment (original cost)	xxxx
Less: Allowance for depreciation	xxxx
Net plant and equipment	xxxx

Ordinarily, no mention is made of a fixed asset's market value.

Statement users should pay close attention to the fixed asset accounting employed by the companies they analyze. The net book value of plant and equipment is a major determinant of many companies' book value (assets less liabilities), which is a key value often used in equity valuations and debt covenants. The condition of a company's plant may determine in large measure its cost structure and ability to improve

---

Professor David Hawkins prepared this note as the basis for class discussion.
Copyright © 1995 by the President and Fellows of Harvard College. Harvard Business School teaching note 195–264.

its capital and employee productivity. The values assigned to fixed assets influence periodic income since they are the basis for future depreciation and depletion charges. Management decisions to capitalize or not capitalize fixed-asset–related expenditures can influence current profits. Finally, management can improve or depress current profits by lowering or raising the level of maintenance expenditures required to maintain the company's fixed assets.

Capitalization Criteria

Considerable judgment is sometimes required to determine whether or not an expenditure related to fixed assets should be capitalized or expensed as incurred. Generally, those fixed-asset–related expenditures are capitalized whose usefulness is expected to extend over several accounting periods, expand the usefulness of a fixed asset, or extend its useful life. Conversely, expenditures should be expensed when they neither extend the useful life of a fixed asset beyond the original estimates nor generate benefits beyond the current accounting period. Companies usually establish minimum cost limits below which all fixed-asset–related expenditures are expensed, even if they might otherwise be properly capitalized. The minimum amount selected should be set at a point which still results in fair financial reporting without placing an unreasonable burden on the accounting system.

Cost Basis

Unless otherwise indicated, the cost of a purchased fixed asset is the price paid for the asset plus all of the costs incidental to acquisition, installation, and preparation for use. Care must be applied to assure the inclusion of all material identifiable elements of cost, such as purchasing, testing, and similar items.

Fixed assets may be acquired by manufacture or by exchange. The cost of assets manufactured for use in the business generally includes the materials, labor, and manufacturing overhead directly related to the construction. How much, if any, of the general factory overhead is included in the construction cost depends on whether or not the plant constructing the asset is operating at or below capacity.

When the plant is operating at or near capacity, the use of the scarce productive facilities to construct an asset for internal use reduces the opportunity to produce regular items for sale. Because of this lost profit opportunity, a fair share of general manufacturing overhead is typically charged to an asset construction project, thereby relieving the income statement of costs that, in the absence of the construction, would have generated some offsetting revenue.

When below-capacity utilization conditions exist, it is debatable whether a fair portion of general manufacturing overhead should be charged to the cost of assets constructed for a company's own use. The arguments for charging a portion of general manufacturing overhead include: (a) the current loss from idle capacity will be overstated unless a cost for idle capacity used for construction is capitalized; (b) the construction will have future benefits, so all costs related to acquiring these benefits should be deferred; and (c) the construction project should be treated the same as regular products, which are charged with general manufacturing overhead.

The principal arguments opposing this point of view are: (a) the cost of the asset should not include general manufacturing overhead costs that would still have been incurred in the absence of the construction; (b) the general manufacturing overhead was probably not considered as a relevant cost in making the decision to construct the asset for the company's own use, since the costs would be incurred irrespective of whether or not the asset was constructed; (c) when part of the general manufacturing overhead is capitalized, the resulting increase in current income will be due to construction rather than the production of salable goods; and (d) it is more conservative not to capitalize general manufacturing overhead.

Increasingly, the practice of charging general manufacturing overhead to fixed assets constructed for a company's own use, on the same basis and at the same rate as regular goods produced for sale, is being adopted without regard to the prevailing capacity conditions. This trend reflects a movement away from conservatism for its own sake and a growing concern for proper allocation of costs to reduce distortions of periodic income due to undervaluation of assets.

Assets manufactured for a company's own use may cost less than their purchase price. This saving should not be recorded as profit at the time the asset is completed, since profits result from the use of assets, not their acquisition or construction. The advantage of the saving will accrue to the company over the life of the asset through lower depreciation charges than would have been incurred if the asset had been purchased.

Assets costing more to construct than their purchase price are sometimes recorded at their purchase price equivalent in the interests of conservatism. The difference between construction cost and purchase price is charged to income upon completion of the asset.

The cost of a nonmonetary asset, such as a building, acquired in exchange for another nonmonetary asset is the fair value of the asset surrendered to obtain it, and a gain or loss should be recognized on the exchange if the exchange is essentially the culmination of an earnings process. However, if the exchange is not the culmination of an earnings process, the accounting for an exchange of nonmonetary assets between an enterprise and another entity should be based on the book value of the asset relinquished with no gain or loss recognized on the exchange.

Trade-in allowances on exchanged assets are often greater than their market value. Consequently, the use of trade-in allowances to value a newly acquired asset may lead to misleading results, through an overstatement of cost and subsequent depreciation charges. Caution must be exercised in trade-in situations, since assets acquired through exchanges should not be recorded at a price greater than would have been paid in the absence of a trade-in.

The interest cost on funds financing construction must be capitalized as part of the fixed asset cost. *FASB Statement No. 34* established the standards for capitalizing interest costs as part of the historical cost of acquiring certain assets. Examples of the types of assets covered include assets intended for the enterprise's own use (such as facilities) or assets intended for sale or lease that are constructed as discrete projects (such as ships or real estate projects). This statement states:

> To qualify for interest capitalization, assets must require a period of time to get them ready for their intended use. . . . Interest cannot be capitalized for inventories that are routinely manufactured or otherwise produced in large quantities on a repetitive basis.
>
> The interest cost eligible for capitalization shall be the interest cost recognized on borrowings and other obligations. The amount capitalized is to be an allocation of the interest cost incurred during the period required to complete the asset. The interest rate for capitalization purposes is to be based on the rates of the enterprise's outstanding borrowings.
>
> If the enterprise associates a specific new borrowing with the asset, it may apply the rate on the borrowings to the appropriate portion of the expenditures for the asset. A weighted average of the rates on other borrowings is to be applied to expenditures not covered by specific new borrowings. Judgment is required in identifying the borrowings on which the average rate is based.
>
> Donated assets should be recorded at their fair market value.

Expenditures Subsequent to Acquisition and Use

After a fixed asset is acquired and put into use, a number of expenditures related to its subsequent utilization may be incurred. The manager must decide whether or not these expenditures should be capitalized as part of the asset cost or expensed as incurred. The general practice is to capitalize those expenditures that will generate future benefits beyond those originally estimated at the time the asset was acquired. However, if there is substantial uncertainty as to whether the benefits will ever be realized, such expenditures are charged to current income. Also, all expenditures related to fixed assets that are necessary to realize the benefits originally projected are expensed.

Maintenance and Repairs

Maintenance and repair costs are incurred to maintain assets in a satisfactory operating condition. When these expenditures are ordinary and recurring, they are expensed. Significant expenditures made for repairs which lead to an increase in the asset's economic life or its efficiency beyond the original estimates should be charged to the allowance for depreciation. This effectively raises the asset's book value. In addition, the asset's depreciation rate should also be changed to reflect the new use, life, and residual value expectations. Extraordinary expenditures for repairs that do not prolong an asset's economic life or improve its efficiency probably represent the cost of neglected upkeep of the asset, and as such should be charged to income as incurred.

Repairs made to restore assets damaged by fire, flood, or similar events should be charged to loss from casualty up to the amount needed to restore the asset to its condition before the damage. Expenditures beyond this amount should be treated like any other expenditure that prolongs the economic life of an asset.

When some assets are acquired, it is anticipated that unusually heavy maintenance costs, such as repainting, may be incurred at different points during their lives. In these situations, some managers establish an Allowance for Repairs and Maintenance account to avoid unusually large charges against income. This practice, which is permissible, charges income with a predetermined periodic maintenance expense based upon management's estimate of the total ordinary and unusual maintenance costs over the asset's life. The credit entry is to the liability account, Repairs and Maintenance Allowance. When the actual expenditures for the anticipated maintenance are incurred, the allowance account is charged with this amount. Since the allowance represents a future charge to current assets, it is sometimes treated as a current liability. In other cases, it is reported as a contra account to fixed assets, along with the allowance for depreciation account. Credit balances are deducted from original cost in determining book value. Debit balances are regarded as temporary additions, and as such increase book value. For income tax purposes, only the actual expenditures for maintenance are deductible. Therefore, the establishment of an allowance usually has deferred tax accounting implications also.

Betterments, Improvements, and Additions

Expenditures for betterments and improvements, such as replacing wooden beams with steel girders, usually result in an increase in an asset's economic life or usefulness. As such, these expenditures are properly capitalized and subsequently charged to the related asset's allowance for depreciation. Also, the asset's depreciation rate should be redetermined to reflect the economic consequences of the expenditure. Minor expenditures for betterments and improvements are typically expensed as incurred.

Additions to existing assets, such as a new wing to a plant, represent capital expenditures and as such should be recorded at their full acquisition cost and accounted for just like an original investment in fixed assets.

Land

Land is a nondepreciable asset. Its life is assumed to be indefinitely long. Land should be shown separately on the balance sheet.

The cost of land includes the purchase price, all costs incidental to the purchase, and the costs of permanent improvements, such as clearing and draining. Expenditures made for improvements with a limited life, such as sidewalks and fencing, should be recorded in a separate account, Land Improvements are written off over their useful lives.

If land is held for speculative purposes, it should be captioned appropriately and reported separately from the land used for productive facilities. The carrying costs of such land can be capitalized, since the land is producing no income and the eventual gain or loss on the sale of the land is the difference between the selling price and the purchase price plus carrying charges.

Wasting Assets

Mineral deposits and other natural resources that are physically exhausted through extraction and are irreplaceable are called "wasting assets." Until extracted, such assets are classified as fixed assets. The cost of land containing wasting assets should be allocated between the residual value of the land and the depletable natural resource. If the natural resource is discovered after the purchase of the land, it is acceptable to reallocate the original cost in a similar way.

Companies in the business of exploiting wasting assets on a continuing basis incur exploration costs to replace their exhausted assets. These exploration costs can be either expensed or capitalized. Because of the great uncertainty associated with exploration in the extractive industries, the typical practice is to capitalize only those costs identifiable with the discovery and development of productive properties and expense the rest as incurred.

There are two basic approaches to the capitalization of discovery and development costs. These are commonly called the "full cost" and "field cost," or "successful efforts," methods. In practice, these methods are applied in a variety of different ways.

The field cost method assigns the costs of discovery and development to specific fields of wasting assets, such as a specific oil or gas field in Oklahoma. If the exploration and development activities related to that field are unsuccessful, the costs are expensed. If the field proves to be successful, the costs are capitalized and written off against the production of the field on a units-of-production basis. If the costs exceed the value of the field's reserves, the costs are capitalized only to the extent they can be recovered from the sale of the reserves. Should a field be abandoned, any capitalized costs are written off immediately.

The full cost method assigns costs of discovery and development to regions of activity, such as the North American continent. These regions may include one or more fields in which the company is active. The full cost method follows the same capitalization-expense rules as the field method. However, since the area for measuring reserves is now a larger region, the costs of discovery and development in unsuccessful fields can be lumped together with the costs of successful efforts and written off against the total region's production.

Alternative Measurement Proposals

Historical cost is the only accepted base for measuring plant and equipment and related depreciation charges in published financial statements. A number of other approaches have been proposed by accounting authors. These include: making the carrying value of assets more responsive to their current market values, adjusting the historical cost base to reflect general price level changes, and the use of replacement costs as the basis for calculating annual depreciation charges.

Those who oppose the use of historical costs to value fixed assets do so principally on the ground that it does not, in their opinion, lead to useful financial statements. For many years, supporters of alternative approaches to the historical cost convention did not challenge the objectivity and feasibility of historical costs in comparison with other, alternative methods for measurement of fixed assets. In recent years, however, these two qualities have been increasingly questioned.

The proponents of historical cost argue that it is a useful basis and part of the discipline of management in that it holds managers responsible for the funds invested in fixed assets. Also, the users of financial reports are fully aware that historical costs do not represent value but merely unexpired costs. The weight of convention, experience, and acceptance is clearly on the side of historical costs; therefore, it is argued, the burden of proving any alternative basis more useful rests with those who oppose the use of historical costs to measure assets.

The essence of the price-level and market value approaches often proposed as alternatives to the historical cost method can be illustrated as follows. A farmer's sole asset is land purchased 15 years ago for $8,000. The current appraisal of the land's market value is $300,000. During the 15 years the farmer held the land, general price levels doubled.

A historical cost based balance sheet for this farmer would show assets of $8,000 and net worth of $8,000 (other items excluded). If price-level adjustments were made, the statement would show assets of $16,000 and a similar amount for net worth. The $16,000 is the current purchasing power equivalent of the original $8,000 × 200% inflation. If market values were used, the statements would show assets at $300,000 and net worth at $300,000, which would consist of $8,000 original investment and $292,000 appreciation by reason of holding the land in a rising market. If the price-level and market value approaches were combined, the assets would remain the same, but net worth would now consist of the $8,000 original investment, the $8,000 price-level gain, and the $284,000 appreciation in the market value of the land after adjusting for general price-level changes.

General price-level adjustment (constant dollar accounting) attempts to state historical costs incurred in different years in terms of a common monetary unit of equivalent purchasing power. It is not a valuation method. It simply adjusts nominal dollars spent or received in different periods to a common purchasing power equivalent. In countries with rapidly rising price levels, it is common practice to adjust the historical acquisition costs of fixed assets for general price-level changes. This results in a measurement of fixed assets and their related depreciation charges in terms of the general purchasing power invested and expiring. Under conditions of rapid inflation, few question the wisdom of this practice. However, for many years, it was argued that the annual rate of inflation in the United States had not been high enough to justify converting the historical costs invested in assets during prior years to equivalent dollars having the same purchasing power. In 1979, the FASB, after a period of above-average inflation, decided that general-price-level–adjusted statements may be more meaningful than historical-cost–based statements and required certain larger companies to provide supplemental disclosure of their price-level–adjusted data. Later, in

1985, the FASB rescinded this requirement to publish data adjusted for changes in the general price level. Price change accounting and recent developments in this area are covered in greater detail in another chapter.

The case for the market value approach to asset valuation is expressed as follows. Assets are recorded at cost initially, because this is the economic measure of their potential service value. After acquisition, the accounting goal should continue to be to express the economic value of this service potential. This is difficult to measure directly, but the current market price others are willing to pay for similar assets approximates this value in most cases. Therefore, to the extent that market values are available, they should be used to measure fixed asset carrying values and their subsequent consumption in the production of goods and services. Property values are more useful than historical costs to managers and stockholders because market values determine the collateral value of property for borrowing purposes, fix liability for property taxes, establish the basis for insurance, and reflect the amount an owner might expect to realize upon sale of the property.

The principal objection to market value is that it is often difficult to determine objectively. The proponents of market value answer this argument by indicating that the notion of market value has some important qualifications. For example, market values should be recognized only when the disparity between market value and cost is likely to prevail for a fairly long period. Furthermore, the market value of an asset should be recognized only on the basis of reliable evidence. The notion of market value probably has little relevance to nonstandardized equipment or special fixed assets for which no readily available market exists. Historical costs must suffice in these cases.

The market value approach has significant implications for the income statement. Market value advocates claim that management continually faces the alternative of using or disposing of assets. Income statements based on historical cost do not show how well management has appraised this alternative since in no way is the "cost" of the alternative forgone included in the statements. In a case where the market value of an asset is greater than its historical cost, historical-cost–based depreciation leads to an overstatement of the incremental benefit gained by using rather than selling, since the book depreciation basis is understated. The reverse is true when the market value is less than the book value. It is claimed that market-value–based depreciation would overcome this weakness. The incremental benefit of continuing to use the asset would be determined after a depreciation charge based on the "cost" of the income forgone by not disposing of the asset.

There is a difference of opinion among market value supporters as to how changes in the carrying value of the assets should be recorded. Some would treat the increases or decreases in stockholders' equity in much the same way as appraisal adjustments are recorded. Others propose including the changes as part of a comprehensive income determination.

The replacement cost approach advocates carrying assets at the cost of reproducing equivalent property, not identical property (as some critics of replacement cost assume). This approach is based on a concept of income which does not recognize profit until depreciation charges have provided adequately for the eventual cost of replacing the capacity represented in existing assets with an asset of more modern design. Based on this theory, traditional depreciation, which recovers original cost from revenues, fails to provide adequately for future replacement in periods of rising replacement costs, and so leads to an overstatement of distributable profits. As a result, excessive dividends, wages, and income taxes may be paid, to the detriment of the company's ability to maintain its current level of productive capacity.

The replacement cost approach is usually implemented by multiplying an asset's original cost by a price index specifically related to the changing cost of the asset involved. Sometimes a further adjustment is made to this figure to reflect technological changes since the date of the original asset's acquisition. The result approximates the replacement cost of an asset's equivalent capacity derived through an appraisal. Such price indexes are available and widely accepted for specific categories of assets. The replacement cost proponents argue that their method has the advantage of the objectivity associated with recording the original cost of the asset at acquisition, as well as minimizing the role of judgment in subsequent revaluations. Thus, the net result of their approach, they argue, is a more useful income figure without any sacrifice in objectivity.

In *FASB Statement No. 89,* the FASB provided guidance to companies working to report the current cost of their property, plant, and equipment. This valuation approach is similar in many respects to the replacement cost concept. The FASB defined current cost as "the current cost of acquiring the same service potential (indicated by operating costs and physical output capacity) as embodied by the asset owned." The service potential (or future economic benefit) of an asset is its capacity to provide services or benefits to the company using the asset.

Depreciation

The term *depreciation,* as used in accounting, refers to the process of allocating the cost of a depreciable tangible fixed asset to the accounting periods covered during its expected useful life. Some of the difficulties encountered by financial statement users in connection with depreciation result from failure to recognize the meaning of the term in this accounting sense. Outside the area of accounting, depreciation is generally used to denote a reduction in the value of property; misunderstandings are caused by attempts to substitute this concept for the more specialized accounting definition.

Depreciation was defined by the American Institute of Certified Public Accountants in its *Accounting Terminology Bulletin No. 1*:

> *Depreciation accounting* is a system of accounting which aims to distribute the cost or other basic value of tangible capital assets, less salvage (if any), over the estimated useful life of the unit (which may be a group of assets) in a systematic and rational manner. It is a process of allocation, not of valuation.
>
> *Depreciation for the year* is the portion of the total charge under such a system that is allocated to the year. Depreciation can be distinguished from other terms with specialized meanings used by accountants to describe asset cost allocation procedures. Depreciation is concerned with charging the cost of man-made fixed assets to operations (and not with determination of asset values for the balance sheet). Depletion refers to cost allocations for natural resources such as oil and mineral deposits. Amortization relates to cost allocations

for intangible assets such as patents and leaseholds. The use of the term *depreciation* should also be avoided in connection with valuation procedures for securities and inventories.

A good grasp of the nature of depreciation is important to statement users since depreciation enters into a number of common financial analysis ratios and techniques. For example:

1. Depreciation is added back along with other noncash income statement items to net income to derive "cash flow from operations" using the indirect method.

2. Capital expenditures are related to historical cost and current cost depreciation to judge the adequacy of a company's capital expenditure program.

3. The gross depreciable asset original cost balance is divided by the annual depreciation expense to determine the average depreciable life of a firm's plant and equipment.

4. The accumulated depreciation account is divided by the annual depreciation expense to estimate the average age of a company's plant and equipment.

5. Depreciation is an element of both the cost of goods sold and the general, administration and selling expense items; as such it influences gross margin and operating costs and profit percentages.

6. A company's book and tax depreciation accounting choices influence its deferred tax balances, tax payments, and earnings quality.

Computing Depreciation

Depreciation expense for a period of operations can be determined by a variety of means, all of which satisfy the general requirements of consistency and reasonableness. Depreciation accounting requires the application of judgment in four areas: (1) determination of the cost of the asset depreciated, (2) estimation of the useful life of the asset, (3) estimation of the residual value at the end of expected useful life, and (4) selection of a method of computing periodic depreciation charges.

Estimating the Useful Life of Fixed Assets

The estimated useful life of most fixed assets is expressed in terms of a period of calendar time. For example, a time basis for determining depreciation charges is suitable for general-purpose assets such as buildings. The useful life of an asset might be expressed in units other than time, however. For instance, the life of a motor vehicle could be estimated as 100,000 miles, while the life of a unit of specialized machinery could be estimated as 200,000 units of output or as 5,000 operating hours.

The estimated life of an asset should be the period during which it is of use to the business. Thus, the estimate should take into account such factors as the use of the asset, anticipated obsolescence, planned maintenance, and replacement policy. The period of useful life may be less than the entire physical life of the asset. For example, machinery with an expected physical life of 10 years under normal conditions will have a useful life for depreciation purposes of six years if company policy is to trade or dispose of such assets after six years or if technological improvements are expected to make the machine obsolete in six years.

Residual Value

Residual (or salvage) value of fixed assets represents estimated realizable value at the end of this useful life. This may be the scrap or junk proceeds, cash sale proceeds, or trade-in value, depending upon the company's disposition and replacement policies.

Depreciable cost is determined by subtracting residual value from the cost of the fixed asset. This depreciable cost is the amount allocated to the operating periods over the asset's useful life.

Depreciation Methods

Any depreciation method which results in a logical, systematic, and consistent allocation of depreciable cost is acceptable for financial accounting purposes. The procedures most commonly used are based upon straight-line, declining-balance, sum-of-the-years'-digits, and units-of-production (or service-life) depreciation methods. The commonly used depreciation methods are illustrated and discussed separately below. Several rarely used and comparatively complex depreciation methods which take into account the imputed earning power of investments in fixed assets will not be discussed. This group includes the annuity and sinking fund methods.

Straight-Line Depreciation

The most simple method of computing depreciation is the straight-line method. For purposes of illustration, a machine with a cost of $6,000 and estimated salvage value of $1,000 at the end of its expected five-year useful life is assumed. Depreciation expense for each year is computed thus:

$$
\begin{aligned}
&\text{Cost of machinery} \ldots\ldots\ldots\ldots\ldots \$6{,}000 \\
&\text{Less: Estimated residual value} \ldots\ldots\ldots \underline{1{,}000} \\
&\text{Depreciable cost} \ldots\ldots\ldots\ldots\ldots \$5{,}000
\end{aligned}
$$

$$
\frac{\text{Depreciable cost}}{\text{Estimated life}} = \text{Depreciation expense}
$$

$$
\frac{\$5{,}000}{5 \text{ years}} = \$1{,}000 \text{ per year}
$$

The straight-line method's strongest appeal is its simplicity. Until accelerated depreciation methods were permitted for income tax purposes, this method was used almost universally. Objections to the straight-line method center on the allocation of equal amounts of depreciation to each period of useful life. Identical amounts are charged in the first year for use of a new and efficient machine and in the later years as the worn machine nears the salvage market.

Accelerated Depreciation

Accelerated depreciation methods provide relatively larger depreciation charges in the early years of an asset's estimated life and diminishing charges in later years. The double-declining-balance method and the sum-of-the-years'-digits methods are the two best-known methods.

Double-declining-balance depreciation for each year is computed by multiplying the asset cost less accumulated depreciation by twice the straight-line rate expressed as a decimal fraction. Using the earlier example—machinery with a cost of $6,000 and a five-year estimated useful life, which is equal to 20% per year—depreciation is computed as follows:

First year:	$6,000 × 0.40	$2,400
Second year:	($6,000 − $2,400) × 0.40	1,440
Third year:	($6,000 − $3,840) × 0.40	864
Fourth year:	($6,000 − $4,704) × 0.40	518
Fifth year:	($6,000 − $5,222) × 0.40	311
Total		$5,533

Note that estimated residual value is not used directly in these computations, even though the asset has salvage value. Since the double-declining-balance procedure will not depreciate the asset to zero cost at the end of the estimated useful life, the residual balance provides an amount in lieu of scrap or salvage value. Ordinarily, however, depreciation is not continued beyond the point where net depreciated cost equals a reasonable salvage value. Also, it is common practice to switch from double-declining-balance depreciation to straight-line depreciation over the remaining life of an asset when the annual depreciation charge falls below what the charge would have been if straight-line depreciation had been used on the remaining cost of the asset.

Sum-of-the-years'-digits depreciation for the year is computed by multiplying the depreciable cost of the asset by a fraction based upon the years' digits. The years' digits are added to obtain the denominator (1 + 2 + 3 + 4 + 5 = 15), and the numerator for each successive year is the number of the year in reverse order.

The formula for determining the sum-of-the-years' digits is:

$$SYD = n \left(\frac{n + 1}{2} \right)$$

Again using the facts for the illustration of straight-line depreciation, annual depreciation computed by the sum-of-the-years'-digits method would be:

First year:	$5,000 × 5/15	$1,667
Second year:	$5,000 × 4/15	1,333
Third year:	$5,000 × 3/15	1,000
Fourth year:	$5,000 × 2/15	667
Fifth year:	$5,000 × 1/15	333
Total		$5,000

Accelerated depreciation methods provide larger depreciation charges against operations during the early years of asset life, when the asset's new efficient condition contributes to greater earnings capacity. Further, the increasing maintenance and repair costs in the later years of asset use tend to complement the reducing depreciation charges, thereby equalizing the total cost of machine usage. Therefore, it is claimed that accelerated depreciation methods more properly match income and expense than does the straight-line method.

Units-of-Production Depreciation

The units-of-production depreciation method is based upon an estimated useful life in terms of units of output, instead of a calendar time period. Units-of-production (or service-life) methods are appropriate in those cases where the useful life of the depreciable asset can be directly related to its productive activity.

Under the units-of-production method, depreciation is determined by multiplying the actual units of output of the fixed asset for the operating period by a computed unit depreciation rate. This rate is calculated by dividing the depreciable cost by the total estimated life of the asset expressed in units of output. A $6,000 machine is estimated to have a $1,000 salvage value after producing 100,000 units of output. The depreciation rate for the machine is:

$$\frac{\$5,000}{100,000 \text{ units}} = \$0.05 \text{ per unit}$$

And, the depreciation charge for a year in which 25,000 units are produced with this machine is $1,250 (25,000 units × $0.05 per unit).

The units-of-production depreciation method relates fixed asset cost directly to usage. It is argued this method best matches depreciation costs and revenues. However, the life of an asset is not necessarily more accurately estimated in units of output than in terms of time. Further, this depreciation method requires a record of the output of individual assets, which may not be readily available without significant additional effort and cost.

A hybrid straight-line and production method is sometimes used by companies in cyclical businesses. The straight-line portion is treated as a period cost and is the minimum depreciation charge. In addition, when production increases beyond a "normal" operating level, an additional depreciation charge is made to reflect the use of assets which are idle at normal production levels.

Accounting for Depreciation

Regardless of the method chosen for computing depreciation, the accounting entry required to record depreciation applicable to a period of operation is:

```
Dr. Depreciation Expense ........................................ XXX
    Cr. Accumulated Depreciation ................................        XXX
```

In addition, both account titles should indicate the type of fixed assets involved, that is, buildings, machinery, office equipment, and so on. This aids in proper handling of the accounts in the financial statements.

Depreciation expense can be listed in the income statement as a single item or according to the nature of the fixed asset giving rise to the depreciation. Depreciation expense on factory machinery is included in factory overhead and as such included in the cost of manufactured inventory, while depreciation on office equipment is included among the administrative expenses.

Accumulated Depreciation (sometimes called Allowance for Depreciation) is deducted from the related fixed asset account on the balance sheet. This account's credit balance increases as assets are depreciated in successive accounting periods. Of course, the allocation of fixed asset cost could be accomplished by crediting the amount of depreciation directly to the fixed asset accounts. This procedure is not recommended because it merges the cost of the fixed asset with estimated depreciation charges, and the users of financial statements would be denied information about fixed asset investment and depreciation policies.

Depreciation charges are continued systematically until the asset is disposed of or until the asset is depreciated to its salvage value. Fully depreciated assets remaining in service are carried in the accounts until disposition. From time to time, significant changes in a company's circumstances may require a switch from one depreciation method to another.

Group Depreciation

Depreciation is frequently computed for a group of assets owned by a business. In preceding illustrations, it was assumed that depreciation was calculated separately for each fixed asset; such procedures are called unit methods. If the asset units can be grouped together in some general category, such as machinery, delivery equipment, or office equipment, it may be desirable to compute depreciation for the total of each group. This practice minimizes detailed analyses and computations. Also, errors in estimates of useful life and salvage value tend to balance out for the group. Estimated useful life is established for the entire group of assets, and depreciation is computed on the basis of weighted-average or composite rates.

Both unit and group methods will theoretically achieve the same results of charging fixed asset costs to operations during the period of expected useful life.

Depreciation and Federal Income Tax

Federal income tax laws recognize depreciation as an expense in the computation of taxable income. There is no requirement that the same depreciation methods be used for both tax and financial reporting purposes. It is not uncommon for a business to adopt an accelerated depreciation method for tax purposes while using the straight-line depreciation method for financial reporting. Material differences in annual depreciation charges under this procedure will require appropriate deferred tax accounting in the financial statements.

Depreciation Schedule Revisions

Depreciation schedules are based upon management's best estimate of the future utilization of an asset at the time it is acquired. During the life of the asset, these estimates may prove to be improper due to circumstances that indicate the asset's useful life or the disposal value, or both, should be revised. Under these conditions, the approach specified in *APB Opinion No. 20* is to leave the book value as it is and alter the rate of future depreciation charges. The changes are made prospectively, not retroactively.

For example, assume a company depreciating an $11,000 asset on a straight-line basis over 10 years decided after five years that the asset's remaining useful life was only going to be two years, rather than five. In addition, the previous $1,000 estimate of the salvage value was now thought to be erroneous. The new salvage value was estimated to be zero. The prior depreciation schedule was $1,000 per year ([$11,000 − $1,000] ÷ 10). Therefore, after five years the book value of the asset would be $6,000 ($11,000 − [5 × $1,000]). Before the change in the estimated life and salvage value, the annual depreciation charge over each of the next five years would have been $1,000. Now, based on the revised estimates, the annual depreciation charge over the next two years will be $3,000 per year ([$6,000 − $0] ÷ 2).

Depreciation Method Changes

Companies change their depreciation method. Typically, the shift is from an accelerated to a straight-line depreciation method. A company may adopt the new accounting method for depreciable assets bought after a specific date, usually the beginning of the fiscal year in which the accounting change is initiated, or for all of its existing depreciable assets. In *APB Opinion No. 20* the APB recommended that when a company changes its depreciation accounting policy for all of its depreciable assets, the change should be recognized by including in the net income for the period of the change the cumulative effect, based on a retroactive computation, of changing to the new depreciation principle.

Additions

For depreciation purposes, an addition to fixed assets should be depreciated over its own economic life or that of the original asset, whichever is shorter.

Asset Write-Downs

Should it become clear to a company that it cannot recover through sale or productive use its remaining investment in a fixed asset, the asset should be written down to its net realizable value and current income charged with the write-down amount.

Written-Up Assets

The writing up of assets is not a generally accepted practice. However, it may happen under certain circumstances in the accounts of foreign subsidiaries. When appreciation is entered on the books, the subsidiary may be obliged to make periodic depreciation charges that are consistent with the increased valuation rather than the historical cost basis. The write-up is revised in the consolidation statement.

Accounting for Retirements

The accounting for asset retirement is fairly straightforward. At the time an asset is retired, its original cost is credited to the appropriate asset account and the related accumulated depreciation is charged to the accumulated depreciation account. Any gain or loss on the retirement after adjusting for the cost of removal and disposition should be recognized.

To illustrate, assume the Cleveland Company purchased a piece of equipment for $100,000. After two years, the company sold the equipment for $50,000. At the time of the sale the asset's book value was $60,000 and the related accumulated depreciation was $40,000.

The entries to record the purchase are:

```
Dr. Machinery ......................................... 100,000
    Cr. Cash ..........................................            100,000
```

The entries to record the subsequent sale are:

```
Dr. Cash ............................................. 50,000
    Accumulated Depreciation ............................. 40,000
    Loss of Sale of Machinery ............................ 10,000
    Cr. Machinery .......................................            100,000
```

If the group method of depreciation had been in use, there would have been no loss and Accumulated Depreciation would have been reduced by $50,000.

Capital Investment Decisions

Some fault current depreciation accounting on the ground that it does not lead to a measurement of return on investment which matches the economic concept of return on investment used by many companies in making asset investment decisions.

To illustrate, assume a company approves a proposed investment of $1,000, which is estimated to earn $250 *cash* per year after taxes for five years and therefore is expected to earn 8% on the amount, at risk, as indicated by **Illustration A.** The economic return on this investment is 8%, since the investor's principal is recovered over the life of the investment and each year the investor receives an 8% return on the principal balance outstanding.

Assuming a straight-line depreciation method, this investment will be reported for financial accounting purposes as shown in **Illustration B.** From this illustration it is clear that the financial reports in no year show a return of 8%. This problem is eliminated if the periodic cost-based depreciation of an asset is shown as the difference between the present value of the related future service benefits at the beginning and end of the accounting period discounted by the internal rate of return calculated in the purchase decision analysis.[1] In practice, it is difficult to measure the future service

---

[1]The internal rate of return is the discount rate which reduces the present value of the future benefits to the present value of the investment.

ILLUSTRATION A

Year	Total Earnings (a)	Return at 8% on Investment Outstanding (b)	Balance Capital Recovery (c) = (a) − (b)	Investment Outstanding End of Year (d)
0	—	—	—	$1,000
1	$250	$80	$170	830
2	250	66	184	646
3	250	52	198	448
4	250	36	214	234
5	250	19	231	3[a]

[a]Due to rounding.

ILLUSTRATION B

Year	Gross Assets	Average Net Assets[a]	Net[b] Income	Computed Return On Gross	Computed Return On Net
1	$1,000	$900	$50	5%	5.5%
2	1,000	700	50	5	7.1
3	1,000	500	50	5	10.0
4	1,000	300	50	5	16.7
5	1,000	100	50	5	50.0

[a]Beginning and ending book values divided by 2.
[b]Cash earnings, $250, minus depreciation, $200. Income taxes are included in the calculation of net earnings.

benefits accurately enough to apply this approach with confidence, so managers resort to using the various depreciation methods discussed above.

Depletion

Depletion is the process of allocating the cost of an investment in natural resources through systematic charges to income as the supply of the physical asset is reduced in the course of operations, after making provision for the residual value of the land remaining.

There are two depletion methods: the production method and percentage method. The production method is acceptable for accounting purposes, whereas the percentage method is not. It is used in certain circumstances for computing income tax payments, however.

The production method establishes the depletion rate by dividing the cost of the depletable asset by the best available estimate of the number of recoverable units. The unit costs are then charged to income as the units are extracted and sold. The unit can be the marketing unit (ounces of silver) or the extractive unit (tons of ore), although the marketing unit is preferred. It is permissible to adjust the depletion rate when it becomes apparent that the estimate of recoverable units used to compute the unit cost is no longer the best available estimate.

To illustrate the cost-based depletion method, assume a coal mine containing an estimated profitable output of 10 million tons of coal is developed to the point of exploitation at a cost of $1 million. Furthermore, during the first year of operations, 500,000 tons of coal are mined and 450,000 tons are sold. The depletion unit charge is the total development cost divided by the estimated profitable output, or 10 cents per ton, that is, $1 million/10 million tons. The total depletion charged to the inventory in the first operating year is $50,000, that is, total production (500,000 tons) times the depletion unit cost ($0.10). The depletion charged to income as cost of goods sold during this period is $45,000, that is, total production sold (450,000 tons) times the depletion unit cost of ($0.10). Consequently, $5,000 of the year's depletion charge is still lodged in the inventory account.

Depletion differs from depreciation in several respects: depletion charges relate to the actual physical exhaustion of an asset, and as such are directly included in inventory costs as production occurs. In contrast, depreciation recognizes the service exhaustion of an asset and is allocated to periodic income, except for depreciation related to manufacturing facilities, which is included in inventory costs on an allocated basis.

The percentage or statutory method, which is permissible for some tax purposes, computes depletion as a fixed percentage of the gross income from the property. The percentage varies according to the type of product extracted. The cost method is also permissible for determining income tax payments. Companies are not obliged to use the same depletion method for book and tax purposes. Over the years Congress has eliminated or reduced the use of percentage depletion for tax purposes for many oil- and gas-producing companies.

Depreciation Decisions

The accounting criteria for choosing one depreciation method rather than another in any particular situation are fuzzy.

The decision to use one of the depreciation methods over another should be made on the basis of a close examination of the asset's characteristics and the way management viewed these characteristics in its investment decision. Empirical and theoretical evidence suggests that most productive assets tend to become less and less valuable over time. Maintenance costs rise and the quality of the asset's service declines. Also, as technological advances are made, the quality of the existing equipment declines relative to alternative more modern equipment, even though quality does not deteriorate absolutely. Based on this evidence, it is believed by some that productive equipment depreciates on an accelerated basis is best in most cases, rather than, as was thought for a long time, on a straight-line basis. Similar studies indicate straight-line depreciation is a reasonable approximation of the depreciation rate of buildings and plant structures.

When an asset is utilized in a project whose future success is more uncertain than the typical situation, some managements believe it is prudent to use accelerated depreciation. Others object to this practice on the ground that the project is more likely to be viewed as unsuccessful because the high depreciation charges will lower profits in the early years. Thus the action taken to reflect the excessive risk involved would contribute to the worst fears of management being realized.

More often than not, depreciation accounting is used as an instrument of management's financial reporting policy. Management selects the depreciation method or mix of methods that contributes to the desired financial results it hopes to achieve over time. For example, in some cases accelerated depreciation methods have been used to hold earnings down and conserve funds by reducing stockholder pressure to increase dividend distributions. In other situations, straight-line depreciation has been utilized to smooth earnings. In times of depressed profits, some companies have switched from accelerated to straight-line depreciation to boost earnings with the hope that this will maintain the market price of the company's stock. The choice of service life can be used in a similar way to further the achievement of management's financial reporting objectives.

The different nature of assets argues for retaining the present wide range of permissible depreciation methods. However, the apparent use of depreciation as a tool of financial reporting policy, and the difficulty in practice of determining which method is the most appropriate for any given asset, have led some to conclude that depreciation methods should be standardized for similar categories of assets.

Asset Impairments

FASB Statement No. 121 deals with the accounting for impairment of long-lived assets and assets to be disposed of. While the standard should result in more realistic balance sheets, statement users should be wary of this rule. It leaves a lot up to management discretion in the timing of the recognition and in the measurement of impairment losses.

The Statement's fundamental conclusion is that a grouping of long-lived assets including fixed assets, intangible assets, capital leases and related goodwill, if any, is impaired when its book value is not recoverable, as measured by the projected cumulative undiscounted net cash flows (excluding interest) related to the asset. In this situation, FASB Statement No. 121 requires that a new cost basis for that asset be established at its fair value. The resulting asset write-down to fair value is charged to income as an impairment loss. If goodwill is included as part of the impaired asset group, the carrying value of the goodwill should be reduced before the other impaired asset carrying values are reduced to fair value. Companies are prohibited from restoring impairment losses if circumstances change.

In making the determination as to whether an asset is impaired, assets must be grouped at the lowest level for which there is an identifiable cash flow that is largely independent of the cash flows of other groups of assets. The term *asset* in FASB Statement No. 121 refers to a group of assets.

The grouping decision is potentially a very subjective one requiring considerable judgment. Varying interpretations of facts and circumstances may justify different groupings. For example, a hotel chain that shared advertising programs and reservation systems could justify a different and more inclusive grouping of its hotels for impairment

testing and measurement purposes than one that only owned and operated several autonomous and independent hotels. Alternatively, a bus company with a municipal contract
requiring operation of five routes could not test for impairment of the assets devoted to
one route. Since the company was required to operate all routes, the appropriate grouping
would be the assets devoted to the contract. In other cases, such as oil and gas producers,
the asset grouping may be defined by clear boundaries, such as geography.

According to the FASB Statement No. 121, fair value is to be determined as
follows:

> Fair value of assets shall be measured by their market value if an active market for them
> exists. If no active market exists for the assets transferred but exists for similar assets, the
> selling prices in that market may be helpful in estimating the fair value of the assets
> transferred. If no market price is available, a forecast of expected cash flows may aid in
> estimating the fair value of assets transferred, providing the expected cash flows are dis-
> counted at a rate commensurate with the risk involved.

The estimate of expected future cash flows should give weight to the likelihood
of possible outcomes and be based on reasonable and supportable assumptions and
projections.

The discount rate decision requires management judgment. The FASB suggests
that the hurdle rate used for internal capital budgeting decisions might be a useful
guide to estimating the discount rate.

After impairment is recognized, the new carrying value is charged to income over
the asset's remaining useful life.

In FASB Statement No. 121 the FASB concluded that an impairment loss was not
similar to an extraordinary item or a loss from discontinued operations. Therefore,
impairment losses are classified as components of earnings (losses) from continuing
operations.

FASB Statement No. 121 requires that assets to be disposed of be subjected to a
lower of cost or fair value to sell measurement.

Analysis of Fixed Assets

Companies usually file with the SEC in their 10-Ks more information on their various
fixed asset balances, additions, subtractions, and lives, as well as maintenance costs,
than they disclose in annual reports. These SEC filings are essential for a thorough
analysis of a company's fixed assets. With these data, statement users should attempt
to appraise the competitive quality of the company's fixed assets. Indications that a
company's fixed assets may be becoming less competitive are:

a. Lengthening of the average age of the company's plant and equipment,
   suggested by a drop-off in reported nominal or analyst-estimated inflation-
   adjusted capital expenditures for plant and equipment and an increasing
   estimate of the plant and equipment's average age in years, determined by

dividing the accumulated depreciation balance by the current year's depreciation expense.

b. Failure to maintain plant and equipment, indicated by a decline in maintenance expenditures relative to gross plant.

c. Uncompetitive facilities and equipment, suggested by an excess of analyst-estimated annual current cost or constant-dollar depreciation over current reported nominal annual capital expenditures.

It is difficult to establish absolute standards to evaluate the results of fixed asset studies. The analyst must make judgments on the relative results of fixed asset studies of companies in the same industry, the object company's own trend data, and management's description of its business strategy and the role of fixed assets in that strategy.

To understand in depth the quality of a company's earnings, the details of the fixed asset accounts should be analyzed to detect any gains or losses from the disposition of fixed assets. Losses may suggest the company is underdepreciating its assets, with the result that earnings from operations are overstated. A gain on the sale of an asset may appear in the details of the fixed asset accounts but be reported simply as other income in the income statement. The unwary reader relying solely on the income statement presentation might miss this onetime source of income and thus overestimate the company's income from operations.

Depreciation Analytical Considerations

Depreciation is a difficult item for analysts to deal with since depreciation accounting practices can vary considerably from company to company, are influenced by management judgments, and can be used to manipulate income. Faced with this situation, some statement analysts would prefer to exclude the distorting effect of depreciation from income when comparing the earnings performance of companies. This is a mistake. Depreciation is a cost of doing business and must be recovered like any other cost in order to earn a profit. Also, many of the differences between company depreciation accounting practices do reflect genuine differences in the nature of the companies' assets and their economic circumstances which justify, if not demand, different approaches to depreciation accounting.

Some financial analysts have claimed in the case of appreciating assets, such as real estate properties, that depreciation should not be charged against income. They argue that these assets are gaining value, not losing value. This point of view misses the cost allocation character of accounting depreciation, which has nothing to do with value. Also, it assumes assets appreciate forever. This is imprudent and does not reflect actual experience, which clearly indicates physical assets have definite lives and are subject to wear, tear, and exhaustion. If the business objective is to generate capital gains for investors through increases in the value of real estate, management's degree of achievement of this objective can be communicated through supplemental disclosures of the appraisal values of properties.

Depreciable asset accounting practices should be scrutinized carefully in earnings quality assessments and income source analyses. For example, a switch in depreciation method from accelerated to straight-line usually indicates that a company has trouble maintaining its earnings at a level high enough to support its former conservative approach to depreciation accounting. Another red flag indicating earnings problems and low-quality earnings is the use of unrealistically long depreciation lives. A depreciation red flag that can appear in profit analysis is a declining depreciation to sales ratio. This may indicate management is "milking" the company by not reinvesting in new assets and thereby not maintaining the operating quality of its plants and equipment. This practice is known as "riding down" the depreciation curve because as more assets become fully depreciated the level of depreciation to sales falls at an increasing rate. This usually results in the company becoming uncompetitive. Finally, in profit analysis, the depreciable-asset–related maintenance expense should be tracked relative to sales or total product costs (cost of goods sold plus change in inventory). Management may attempt to push profits up by cutting back on maintenance. This is another red flag indicating profitability problems and, if continued, reduced maintenance expenditures can lead to operating difficulties.

FASB Statement No. 121 write downs improve profits by eliminating depreciation and goodwill charges. Statement users should classify this source of profits as low quality. It is not sustainable, unrelated to operations, and does not have a related positive cash flow benefit.

Some statement users prefer to measure profits after adjusting depreciation for inflation. This approach to profit measurement and the role of inflation-adjusted depreciation on statement analysis is discussed in a later chapter. In times of above-average inflation rates, these inflation-adjusted data may produce more meaningful insights into how well a company is coping with inflation than the historical-cost–based depreciation data.

14-1 Electrical, Mining, and Industrial (EMI) Corporation

In fiscal year 1994, EMI changed its depreciation method and estimates. Soon after the receipt of the company's 1994 annual report by Strategic Investors, an institutional manager of corporate pension assets, Elizabeth Keller, a Strategic Investors equity analyst, was given the assignment to analyze the current and future financial statement impact of the company's depreciation accounting changes, illustrate the impact of these changes on the relevant accounts, and appraise the cash flow, financial ratio, managerial and equity valuation implications of the depreciation changes. Soon after she began her assignment, Elizabeth Keller noted that EMI's management had made what appeared to her to be a number of other one-time accounting, financial, and business structure decisions that had impacted the company's 1993–1994 financial statements (see Exhibit 1). The realization led her to conclude she should broaden her assignment to include in her analysis of EMI's depreciation changes the appraisal of how the depreciation changes related, if at all, to these other management decisions.

The Company

Mining and Industrial Corporation was founded in 1894 in Chicago, Illinois. Later, in 1918, to reflect the company's acquisition of several electrical equipment firms, the company name was changed to Electrical, Mining, and Industrial Corporation. In 1926 the company was listed on the New York Stock Exchange. Subsequently, in 1959, the company while retaining its full name for legal purposes, adopted its New York Stock Exchange symbol "EMI" as its name for business purposes.

Professor David F. Hawkins prepared this case as the basis for class discussion rather than to illustrate either effective or ineffective handling of an administrative situation. This case is based on materials previously prepared by Professor Krishna Palepu.

Exhibit 1   Selected Excerpts from 1994 Annual Report

Management's Discussion and Analysis Results of Operations

1994 Compared to 1993

Consolidated net sales of $399 million in fiscal 1994 increased $78 million or 24% over 1993. Sales increases were 62% in the Mining and Electrical Equipment Segment, and 10% in the Industrial Technologies Segment. Sales in the Construction Equipment Segment were virtually unchanged reflecting the continued low demand for construction equipment worldwide.

Effective at the beginning of fiscal 1994, net sales include the full sale price of construction and mining equipment purchased from Suma Steel, Ltd. and sold by the Corporation, in order to reflect more effectively the nature of the Corporation's transactions with Suma. Such sales aggregated $28.0 million in 1994.

The $4.0 million increase in Other Income reflected a recovery of certain claims and higher license and technical service fees.

Cost of Sales was equal to 79.1% of net sales in 1994 and 81.4% in 1993; which together with the increase in net sales resulted in a $23.9 million increase in gross profit (net sales less cost of sales). Contributing to this increase were improved sales of higher-margin replacement parts in the Mining Equipment and Industrial Technologies Segments and a reduction in excess manufacturing costs through greater utilization of domestic manufacturing capacity and economies in total manufacturing costs including a reduction in pension expense. Reduction of certain LIFO inventories increased gross profit by $2.4 million in 1994 and $15.6 million in 1993.

Product development, selling, and administrative expenses were reduced, due to the funding of R&D expenses in the Construction Equipment Segment pursuant to the October 1993 Agreement with Suma Steel Ltd., to reductions in pension expenses and provision for credit losses, and the absence of the corporate financial restructuring expenses incurred in 1993.

Net interest expense in 1994 increased $2.9 million due to higher interest rates on the outstanding funded debt and a reduction in interest income.

Equity in Earnings (Loss) of Unconsolidated Companies included 1994 income of $1.2 million reflecting an income tax benefit of $1.4 million not previously recorded.

The preceding items, together with the cumulative effect of the change in depreciation method described in Financial Note 2, were included in net income of $15.2 million or $1.28 per common share, compared with the net loss of $34.6 million or $3.49 per share in 1993.

The sales order booked and unshipped backlogs of orders of the Corporation's three segments are summarized as follows (in millions of dollars):

	1994	1993
Orders Booked		
Industrial technologies	$132	$106
Mining and electrical equipment . .	210	135
Construction equipment	109	109
	$451	$350
Backlogs at October 31		
Industrial technologies	$ 79	$ 71
Mining and electrical equipment . .	91	50
Construction equipment	23	20
	$193	$141

1993 Compared to 1992

Consolidated net sales of $321 million in fiscal 1993 were $126 million or 28% below 1992. This decline reflected, for the second consecutive year, the continued low demand in all markets served by the Corporation's products, with exports even more severely depressed due to the strength of the dollar. The largest decline was reported in the Construction Equipment Segment, down 34%; Mining and Electrical Segment shipments were down 27%; and the Industrial Technologies Segment, 23%.

Cost of Sales was equal to 81.4% of net sales in 1993 and 81.9% in 1992. The resulting gross profit was $60 million in 1993 and $81 million in 1992, a reduction equal to the rate of sales decrease.

The benefits of reduced manufacturing capacity and economies in total manufacturing costs were offset by reduced selling prices in the highly competitive markets. Reductions of certain LIFO inventories increased gross profits by $15.6 million in 1993 and $7.2 million in 1992.

EXHIBIT 1 (continued)

Product development, selling, and administrative expenses were reduced as a result of expense reduction measures in response to the lower volume of business and undertaken in connection with the Corporation's corporate recovery program, and reduced provisions for credit losses.

Net interest expense was reduced $9.1 million from 1992 to 1993, due primarily to increased interest income from short-term cash investments and an accrual of $4.7 million in interest income on refundable income taxes not previously recorded.

The Credit for Income Taxes included a federal income tax benefit of $5 million, based on the recent examination of the Corporation's income tax returns and refund claims. No income tax benefits were available for the losses of the U.S. operations in 1993.

Liquidity and Financial Resources

In April 1994, the Corporation issued in public offerings 2,150,000 shares of Common Stock, $50 million principal amount of 12% Senior Notes due in 1994, and 100,000 Units consisting of $100 million principal amount of 10% Subordinated Debentures due in 2004 and 2,000,000 Common Stock Purchase Warrants.

The net proceeds from the sales of the securities of $149 million were used to prepay substantially all of the outstanding debt of the Corporation and certain of its subsidiaries.

During the year ended October 31, 1994, the consolidated cash balances increased $32 million to a balance of $96 million, with the cash activity summarized as follows (in millions of dollars):

Cash provided by operations	$10
Cash returned to the Corporation upon restructuring of the Salaried Employees' Pension Plan	39
Debt repayment less the proceeds of sales of securities	(9)
Plant and equipment additions	(6)
All other charges—net	(2)
	$32

In the third quarter of 1994 the Corporation entered into a $52 million three-year revolving credit agreement with 10 U.S. and Canadian banks. While the Corporation has adequate liquidity to meet its current working capital requirements, the revolver represents another step in the Construction's program to strengthen its financial position and provide the required financial resources to respond to opportunities as they arise.

Exhibit 1   **(continued) Consolidated Statement of Operations (dollar amounts in thousands except per share figures)**

	Year Ended October 31,		
	1994	*1993*	*1992*
Revenues			
Net sales	$398,708	$321,010	$447,461
Other income, including license and technical service fees	7,067	3,111	5,209
	405,775	324,121	452,670
Cost of sales	315,216	261,384	366,297
Operating income	90,559	62,737	86,373
Less:			
Product development, selling and administrative expenses	71,196	85,795	113,457
Interest expense—net	12,625	9,745	18,873
Provision for plant closing	—	—	23,700
Income (loss) before provision (credit) for income taxes, equity items, and cumulative effect of accounting change	5,738	(32,803)	(69,657)
Provision (credit) for income taxes	2,425	(1,400)	(1,600)
Income (loss) before equity items and cumulative effect of accounting change	3,313	(31,403)	(68,057)
Equity items			
Equity in earnings (loss) of joint ventures and other companies	993	(3,397)	(7,891)
Minority interest in (earnings) loss of consolidated subsidiaries	(135)	170	(583)
Income (loss) before cumulative effect of accounting change	4,171	(34,630)	(76,531)
Cumulative effect of change in depreciation method	11,005	—	—
Net income (loss)	$ 15,176	$(34,630)	$(76,531)
Earnings (loss) per common and common equivalent share:			
Income (loss) before cumulative effect of accounting change	$ .35	$ (3.49)	$ (7.64)
Cumulative effect of change in depreciation method	.93	—	—
Net income (loss)	$ 1.28	$ (3.49)	$ (7.64)
Pro forma amounts assuming the changed depreciation method has been applied retroactively:			
Net (loss)		$(33,918)	$(76,695)
(Loss) per common share		$ (3.42)	$ (7.65)

(The accompanying notes are an integral part of the financial statements.)

EXHIBIT 1   **(continued) Consolidated Balance Sheet (dollar amounts in thousands except per share figures)**

	October 31,	
	1994	*1993*
Assets		
Current assets		
Cash and temporary investments	$ 96,007	$ 64,275
Accounts receivable	87,648	63,740
Inventories	144,312	153,594
Refundable income taxes and related interest	1,296	12,585
Other current assets	5,502	6,023
Prepaid income taxes	14,494	14,232
	349,259	314,449
Investments and other assets		
Investment in and advances to:		
Joint ventures, at equity in net assets	8,849	6,704
Other companies	4,445	2,514
Other assets	13,959	6,411
	27,253	15,629
Operating plants		
Land and improvements	9,419	10,370
Buildings	59,083	60,377
Machinery and equipment	120,949	122,154
	189,451	192,901
Accumulated depreciation	(93,259)	(107,577)
	96,192	85,324
	$472,704	$415,402
Liabilities and Shareholders' Equity		
Current liabilities		
Short-term notes payable to banks by subsidiaries	$ 9,090	$ 8,155
Long-term debt and capitalized lease obligations payable within one year	973	18,265
Trade accounts payable	37,716	21,228
Employee compensation and benefits	15,041	14,343
Accrued plant closing costs	3,260	6,348
Advanced payments and progress billings	20,619	15,886
Income taxes payable	1,645	3,463
Account payable to finance subsidiary	—	3,436
Other current liabilities and accruals	29,673	32,333
	117,217	123,457
Long-term obligations		
Long-term debt payable to:		
Unaffiliated lenders	128,550	139,092
Associated companies	—	5,400
Capitalized lease obligations	7,870	8,120
	136,420	152,612

EXHIBIT 1   (continued)

	October 31,	
	1994	*1993*
Deferred liabilities and income taxes		
Accrued pension costs	$ 57,611	$ 19,098
Other deferred liabilities	5,299	7,777
Deferred income taxes	6,385	134
	69,295	27,009
Minority interest		
Shareholders' equity		
Preferred stock, $100 par value—authorized 2,500,000 shares:		
Series A $7.00 cumulative convertible preferred shares; authorized, issued and outstanding 117,500 shares in 1994 and 100,000 shares in 1993	11,750	10,000
Common stock, $1 par value—authorized 25,000,000 shares; issued and outstanding 12,283,563 shares in 1994 and 10,133,563 shares in 1993	12,284	10,134
Capital in excess of par value of shares	114,333	88,332
Retained earnings	19,901	6,475
Cumulative translation adjustments	(10,896)	(5,022)
	147,372	109,919
	$472,704	$415,402

(The accompanying notes are an integral part of the financial statements.)

EXHIBIT 1   (continued) Consolidated Cash Flow Statement (dollar amount in thousands)

	Year Ended October 31,		
	1994	*1993*	*1992*
Operations:			
Income (loss) before cumulative effect of accounting change	$ 4,171	$ (34,630)	$ (76,531)
Cumulative effect of change in depreciation method . . .	11,005	—	—
Net income (loss)	15,176	(34,630)	(76,531)
Add (deduct)			
Depreciation	8,077	13,552	15,241
Unremitted (earnings) loss of unconsolidated companies	(993)	3,397	7,891
Deferred pension contributions	(500)	4,834	—
Deferred income taxes	6,583	(3,178)	1,406
Reduction in accumulated depreciation resulting from change in depreciation method	(17,205)	—	—
Other—net	(2,168)	(67)	2,034
	2,387	(16,092)	(49,959)
Accounts receivable	$ (23,908)	$ (5,327)	$ 42,293
Refundable income taxes and related interest	9,383	56,904	26,124
Trade accounts payable	16,488	(1,757)	(3,302)
Employee compensation and benefits	698	(15,564)	(3,702)
Other—net	(8,928)	(35,855)	(9,412)
Cash provided by operations	10,000	37,287	16,270
Investments:			
Plant and equipment additions	(5,546)	(1,871)	(10,819)
Advances to joint ventures and other companies	(2,882)	—	—
Other—net	269	1,531	848
Cash used by investments	(8,159)	(340)	(9,971)
Financing:			
Transactions in debt and capitalized lease obligations—			
Long-term debt and capitalized lease obligations:			
Proceeds from sale of 12% Senior Notes and 10% Subordinated Debentures, net of issue costs . . .	120,530	—	—
Other increases	1,474	—	25,698
Repayments	(161,500)	(760)	(9,409)
Restructured debt	—	158,058	—
Debt replacement, including conversion of receivable sale of $23,919, and short-term bank notes payable of $9,028	—	(158,058)	—
	(39,496)	(760)	16,289

Exhibit 1   (continued)

	Year Ended October 31,		
	1994	*1993*	*1992*
Net increase (repayment) in short-term bank notes payable	$ 2,107	$ (3,982)	$ (2,016)
Net increase (repayment) in debt and capitalized lease obligations	(37,389)	(4,742)	14,273
Issuance of:			
Common stock	21,310	—	449
Common stock purchase warrants	6,663	—	—
Salaried pension asset reversion	39,307	—	—
	29,891	(4,742)	14,772
Dividends	—	—	(2,369)
Cash provided (used) by financing	29,891	(4,742)	12,353
Increase in cash and temporary investments	$ 31,732	$ 32,205	$ 18,652

EXHIBIT 1   (continued)

Financial Notes

Note 1: Summary of Significant Accounting Policies

Consolidation   The consolidated financial statements include the accounts of all majority-owned subsidiaries except a subsidiary organized in 1992 as a temporary successor to a distributor, which is accounted for under the equity method, and a wholly-owned foreign subsidiary, which is carried at estimated net realizable value due to economic uncertainty. All related significant intercompany balances and transactions have been eliminated in consolidation.

Financial statements of certain consolidated subsidiaries, principally foreign, are included, effective in fiscal year 1994 on the basis of their financial years ending September 30, previously certain of such subsidiaries had fiscal years ending in July (see Note 2). Such fiscal periods have been adopted by the subsidiaries in order to provide a more timely consolidation with the Corporation.

Inventories   The Corporation values its inventories at the lower of cost or market. Cost is determined by the last-in, first-out (LIFO) method for inventories located principally in the United States and by the first-in, first-out (FIFO) method for inventories of foreign subsidiaries.

Operating plants, equipment and depreciation   Properties are stated at cost. Maintenance and repairs are charged to expense as incurred and expenditures for betterments and renewals are capitalized. Interest is capitalized for qualifying assets during their acquisition period. Capitalized interest is amortized on the same basis as the related assets. When properties are sold or otherwise disposed of, the cost and accumulated depreciation are removed from the accounts and any gain or loss is included in income.

Depreciation of plants and equipment is provided over the estimated useful lives of the related assets, or over the lease terms of capital leases, using effective in fiscal year 1994, the straight-line method for financial reporting and principally accelerated methods for tax reporting purposes. Previously, accelerated methods, where applicable, were also used for financial reporting purposes (see Note 2).

Discontinued facilities held for sale are carried at the lower of cost less accumulated depreciation or estimated realizable value, which aggregated $4.9 million and $3.6 million at October 31, 1994 and 1993, respectively, and were included in Other Assets in the accompanying Balance Sheet.

Pension plans   The Corporation has pension plans covering substantially all of its employees. Pension expenses of the principal defined benefit plans consist of current service costs of such plans and amortization of the prior service costs and actuarial gains and losses over periods ranging from 10 to 30 years. The Corporation's policy is to fund at a minimum the amount required under the Employee Retirement Income Security Act of 1974.

Income taxes   The consolidated tax provision is computed based on income and expenses recorded in the Statement of Operations. Prepaid or deferred taxes are recorded for the difference between such taxes and computed for tax returns. The Corporation, its domestic subsidiaries, and certain foreign subsidiaries file a consolidated federal income tax return.

Additional taxes are provided on the earnings of foreign subsidiaries which are intended to be remitted to the Corporation. Such taxes are not provided on subsidiaries' unremitted earnings which are intended to be permanently reinvested.

Reporting format   Certain previously reported items have been conformed to the current year's presentation.

Note 2: Accounting Changes

Effective November 1, 1993, the Corporation includes in its net sales products purchased from Suma Steel, Ltd., and sold by the Corporation, to reflect more effectively the nature of the Corporation's transactions with Suma. Previously only the gross margin on Suma-originated equipment was included.

During fiscal year 1994 such sales aggregated $28.0 million. Also, effective November 1, 1993, the financial statements of certain foreign subsidiaries are included on the basis of their financial years ending September 30 instead of the previous years ended July 31. This change had the effect of increasing net sales by $5.4 million for the year ended October 31, 1994. The impact of these changes on net income was insignificant.

EXHIBIT 1 (continued)

In 1994, the Corporation has computed depreciation expense on plants, machinery and equipment using the straight-line method for financial reporting purposes. Prior to 1994, the Corporation used principally accelerated methods for its U.S. operating plants. The cumulative effect of this change, which was applied retroactively to all assets previously subjected to accelerated depreciation, increased net income for 1994 by $11.0 million or $.93 per common and common equivalent share. The impact of the new method on income for the year 1994 before the cumulative effect was insignificant.

As a result of the review of its depreciation policy, the Corporation, effective November 1, 1993, has changed its estimated depreciation lives on certain U.S. plants, machinery and equipment and residual values on certain machinery and equipment which increased net income for 1994 by $3.2 million or $.27 per share. No income tax effect was applied to this change.

The changes in accounting for depreciation were made to conform the Corporation's depreciation policy to those used by manufacturers in the Corporation's and similar industries and to provide a more equitable allocation of the costs of plants, machinery and equipment over their useful lives.

Note 6: Transactions with Suma Steel, Ltd., and ELTA Industrial Systems Inc.

Suma Steel, Ltd., of Japan ("Suma"), has been a licensee of certain of the Corporation's products since 1965, and has owned certain EMI Japanese construction equipment patents and technology since 1991. As of October 31, 1994, Suma held 1,030,000 shares or 8.4% of the Corporation's outstanding Common Stock (see Note 13). Suma also owns 25% of the capital stock of EMI of Australia Pty, Ltd., a subsidiary of the Corporation. This ownership appears as the minority interest on the Corporation's balance sheet.

Under agreements expiring in December 2000, Suma pays technical fees on EMI mining equipment produced and sold under license from the Corporation, and trademark and marketing fees on sales of construction equipment outside of Japan. Net fee income received from Suma was $4.3 million in 1994, $3.1 million in 1993, and $3.9 million in 1992; this income is included in Other Income in the accompanying Statement of Operations.

In October 1993, the Corporation entered into a ten-year agreement with Suma under which Suma agreed to supply the Corporation's requirements for construction cranes for sale in the United States as it phases out its own manufacture of cranes over the next several years, and to make the Corporation the exclusive distributor of Suma-built cranes in the United States. The Agreement also involves a joint research and development program for construction equipment under which the Corporation agreed to spend at least $17 million over a three-year period and, provided it does so, Suma agreed to pay this amount to the Corporation. Sales of cranes outside the United States continue under the contract terms described in the preceding paragraph.

The Corporation's sales to Suma, principally components for mining and construction equipment excluding the R&D expenses discussed in the preceding paragraph, approximated $5.2 million, $10.5 million, and $7.0 million during the three years ended October 31, 1994, 1993, and 1992, respectively. The purchases from Suma of mining and construction equipment and components amounted to approximately $33.7 million, $15.5 million, and $29.9 million during the three years ended October 31, 1994, 1993, and 1992, respectively, most of which were resold to customers (see Note 2).

The Corporation owns 19% of ELTA Industrial Systems Inc. ("ELTA"), an electrical equipment company. The Corporation's purchases of electrical components from ELTA aggregated $11.2 million in 1994 and $6.1 million in 1993 and its sales to ELTA approximated $2.6 million in 1994 and $3.8 million in 1993.

The Corporation believes that its transactions with Suma and ELTA were competitive with alternative sources of supply for each party involved.

Note 7: Inventories

Consolidated inventories consisted of the following (in thousands of dollars):

EXHIBIT 1   (continued)

	October 31,	
	1994	*1993*
At lower of cost or market (FIFO method)		
Raw materials	$ 11,003	$ 11,904
Work in process and purchased parts	88,279	72,956
Finished goods	79,111	105,923
	178,393	190,783
Allowance to reduce inventories to cost on the LIFO method	(34,081)	(37,189)
	$144,312	$153,594

Inventories valued on the LIFO method represented approximately 82% of total inventories at both October 31, 1994 and 1993.

Inventory reductions in 1994, 1993, and 1992 resulted in a liquidation of LIFO inventory quantities carried at lower costs compared with the current cost of their acquisitions. The effect of these liquidations was to increase net income by $2.4 million or $.20 per common share in fiscal 1994, and to reduce the net loss by approximately $15.6 million or $1.54 per share in 1993, and by $6.7 million or $.66 per common share in 1992; no income tax effect applied to the adjustment in 1994 and 1993.

Note 8: Accounts Receivable

Accounts receivable were net of allowances for doubtful accounts of $5.9 million and $6.4 million at October 31, 1994 and 1993, respectively.

Note 9: Research and Development Expense

Research and development expense incurred in the development of new products or significant improvements to existing products was $5.1 million in 1994 (net of amounts funded by Suma Steel, Ltd.), $12.1 million in 1993, and $14.1 million in 1992.

Note 10: Foreign Operations

The net sales, net income (loss) and net assets of subsidiaries located in countries outside the United States and Canada and included in the consolidated financial statements were as follows (in thousands of dollars):

	Year Ended October 31,		
	1994	*1993*	*1992*
Net sales	$78,074	$45,912	$69,216
Net income (loss) after minority interest	828	(1,191)	3,080
Corporation's equity in total net assets	17,734	7,716	7,287

Note 11: Pension Plans and Other Postretirement Benefits

Pension expense for all plans of the Corporation and its consolidated subsidiaries was $1.9 million in 1994, $6.5 million in 1993, and $12.2 million in 1992.

Accumulated plan benefits and plan net assets for the Corporation's U.S. defined benefit plans, at the beginning of the fiscal years 1994 and 1993 with the data for the Salaried Employees Retirement Plan as in effect on August 1, 1994, were as follows (in thousands of dollars):

EXHIBIT 1   (continued)

	1994	*1993*
Actuarial present value of accumulated plan benefits:		
Vested	$52,639	$108,123
Nonvested	2,363	5,227
	$55,002	$113,350
Net assets available for benefits:		
Assets of the Pension Trusts	$45,331	$112,075
Accrued contributions not paid to the Trusts . . .	16,717	12,167
	$62,048	$124,242

The Salaried Employees' Retirement Plan, which covers substantially all salaried employees in the United States, was restructured during 1994 due to overfunding of the Plan. Effective August 1, 1994, the Corporation terminated the existing plan and established a new plan which is substantially identical to the prior plan except for an improvement in the minimum pension benefit. All participants in the prior plan became fully vested upon its termination. All vested benefits earned through August 1, 1994 were covered through the purchase of individual annuities at a cost aggregating $36.7 million. The remaining plan assets, which totaled $39.3 million, reverted to the Corporation in cash upon receipt of regulatory approval of the prior plan termination from the Pension Benefit Guaranty Corporation. For financial reporting purposes, the new plan is considered to be a continuation of the terminated plan. Accordingly, the $39.3 million actuarial gain which resulted from the restructuring is included in the Accrued Pension Costs in the accompanying Balance Sheet and is being amortized to income over a ten-year period commencing in 1994. For tax reporting purposes, the asset reversion will be treated as a fiscal 1995 transaction. The initial unfunded actuarial liability of the new plan, computed as of November 1, 1993, of $10.3 million is also included in Accrued Pension Costs.

In 1992 and 1993, the Pension Trusts purchased certain securities with effective yields of 9% and 8%, respectively, and dedicated these assets to the plan benefits of a substantial portion of the retired employees and certain terminated employees with deferred vested rights. These rates, together with 9% for active employees in 1994, 8% in 1993, and 7¼% in 1992, were the assumed rates of return used in determining the annual pension expense and the actuarial present value of accumulated plan benefits for the U.S. plans.

The effect of the changes in the investment return assumption rates for all U.S. plans, together with the 1994 restructuring of the U.S. Salaried Employees' Plan, was to reduce pensions expense by approximately $4.0 million in 1994 and $2.0 million in 1993, and the actuarial present value of the accumulated plan benefits by approximately $60.0 million in 1994. Pension expense in 1993 was also reduced $2.1 million from the lower level of active employees. Other actuarial gains, including higher than anticipated investment results, more than offset the additional pension costs resulting from plan charges on balance sheet accruals in 1994 and 1993.

The Corporation's foreign pension plans do not determine the actuarial value of the accumulated benefits or net assets available for retirement benefits as calculated and disclosed above. For those plans, the total of the plans' pension funds and balance sheet accruals approximated the actuarially computed value of vested benefits at both October 31, 1994 and 1993.

The Corporation generally provides certain health care benefits for U.S. retired employees through a defined contribution agreement. The retiree health care contributions are expensed as incurred. Such costs approximated $2.6 million in 1994 and $1.7 million in 1993.

Note 12: Income Taxes

Domestic and foreign income (loss) before income tax effects was as follows (in thousands of dollars):

Exhibit 1   (continued)

	Year Ended October 31,		
	1994	*1993*	*1992*
Domestic..........................	$1,578	$(35,412)	$(77,600)
Foreign	4,160	2,609	7,943
Total income (loss) before income tax effects, equity items and cumulative effect of accounting change	$5,738	$(32,803)	$(69,657)

Provision (credit) for income taxes, on income (loss) before income tax effects, equity items, and cumulative effect of accounting change consisted of (in thousands of dollars):

	1994	*1993*	*1992*
Currently payable (refundable):			
Federal	$ —	$(7,957)	$(9,736)
State	136	297	70
Foreign	2,518	3,379	5,376
	2,654	(4,281)	(4,290)
Deferred (prepaid):			
Federal	—	2,995	2,713
State and foreign	(229)	(74)	(23)
	(229)	2,881	2,690
Provision (credit) for income taxes	$2,425	$(1,400)	$(1,600)

During 1993 an examination of the Corporation's 1989–1991 federal income tax returns and certain refund claims was completed by the Internal Revenue Service and as a result, a current credit for federal income taxes of $8.0 million was recorded in 1993, $3.0 million of which was applied to the reduction of prepaid income taxes.

In 1994, tax credits fully offset any federal income tax otherwise applicable to the year's income, and in 1993 and 1992, the relationship of the tax benefit to the pre-tax loss differed substantially from the U.S. statutory tax rate due principally to losses from the domestic operations for which only a partial federal tax benefit was available in 1992. Consequently, an analysis of deferred income taxes and variance from the U.S. statutory rate is not presented.

Unremitted earnings of foreign subsidiaries which have been or are intended to be permanently reinvested were $19.1 million at October 31, 1994. Such earnings, if distributed, would incur income tax expense at substantially less than the U.S. income tax rate as a result of previously paid foreign income taxes, provided that such foreign taxes would become deductible as foreign tax credits.

At October 31, 1994, the Corporation had federal tax operating loss carryforwards of approximately $70.0 million, expiring in 2008 and 2009, for tax return purposes and $88.0 million for book purposes. In addition, the Corporation had for tax purposes, foreign tax credit carryforwards of $3.0 million (expiring in 1995 through 1999). For book purposes, tax credit carryforwards approximated $8.0 million. The carryforwards will be available for the reduction of future income tax provisions when and if it is determined that their realization for tax purposes is more likely than not.

The net deferred income tax liability balances were determined under FASB No. 109, "Accounting for Income Taxes," which was adopted effective January 1, 1992. The principal components of the deferred income tax liability balances are due to temporary differences between financial and tax reporting and relate to depreciation, consolidating eliminations for intercompany profits in inventories, and provisions, principally, for warranty, pension, compensated absences, product liability, and plant closing costs.

The company's principal products were a variety of different types of heavy equipment for use in the construction, mining, and manufacturing industries.

In 1992, due to weaknesses in many of the company's major markets around the world, the company reported significant losses, eliminated dividends, violated a number of its loan agreement covenants, and the company's auditors issued a "going concern" qualification to their opinion.

In response to the deteriorating situation EMI's board replaced the company's chairman and chief executive officer, who was a great grandson of the company's founder and a principal shareholder, with a new chief executive officer recruited from one of the company's major competitors. The new chief executive officer, Peter Lyman, immediately announced a turnaround plan with the goal of making the company profitable in the centennial year, 1994. The plan involved a drastic workforce reduction, aggressive replacement of aged equipment, elimination of bonuses and benefits, a wage freeze, liquidation of excess inventories, stretching of trade credits, closing and relocation of several plants, a reorientation of the company's business strategy, and a debt restructuring and recapitalization.

In December 1994, the company's board of directors established an Executive Incentive Plan for fiscal 1995 that would provide substantial incentive compensation to the company's senior management only if the company achieved certain after-tax profit goals.

On the day Elizabeth Keller received her assignment, EMI stock had a .95 beta (Value Line estimate) and traded at a price-to-earnings ratio slightly below the median price-to-earnings ratio of the construction and mining machinery industries sector.

In 1994, EMI earned a $5.7 million pretax operating profit, raised substantial new capital, paid off its restructured debt, and received a "clean" opinion from its public auditors.

Earlier, in the company's 1993 annual report Lyman had stated:

We approach our second century with the firm knowledge that we have turned the corner and that 1994 will see the positive results of our efforts to revitalize and reorient the company. We are confident that we will be operating profitably by year end 1994.

In the 1994 annual report Lyman stated:

The corporation recorded gains in each quarter during fiscal 1994. For the year ended October 31, net income was $15,176,000 or $1.28 per common share, which included $11,005,000 or 93¢ per share from the cumulative effect of a change in depreciation accounting. In 1993, the corporation reported a loss of $34,630,000 or $3.49 per share.

Sales for 1994 improved 24% over the preceding year, rising to $389.7 million from $321 million a year ago. New orders totaled $451 million, a $101 million increase over 1993. We entered fiscal 1995 with a backlog of $193 million, which compared to $141 million a year earlier . . .

As we move forward with confidence and optimism collectively we can take great pride in our accomplishments over the last three years. We have met our initial profit target and every day are attaining new and higher levels of market strength and leadership.

Questions

1. Explain the change in the company's accounting for depreciation. What other accounting changes can you identify? _____

2. Why do you believe the management changed, in its external financial reports, the company's accounting for depreciation? The company also changed its internal accounting for depreciation from an accelerated to a straight line basis in the same manner as the external reporting change. Why? _____ Why do you believe management made the other accounting changes you have identified? _____

3. What do the company's accounting changes signal to users of its financial statements? _____

CASE
14-2   United Kingdom Properties Trust

In late 1991, Sir George Henderson, chairman, United Kingdom Properties Trust ("Trust"), a publicly traded investment trust investing directly in income-producing commercial and residential properties located in the United Kingdom, was considering investing in the U.S. real estate market. In particular, he was trying to decide whether to acquire stock through an open market purchase in the Rouse Company ("Rouse"), a major U.S. property developer located in Columbia, Maryland.

An investment in Rouse would be a "first" for the Trust in two aspects. While the Trust's agreement permitted limited equity investments outside of the United Kingdom and in the past the Trust had made small direct investments in Canadian and Australian commercial properties, an investment in Rouse would be its first real estate investment in the U.S. market. Also, a Rouse investment would be the first time that the Trust had invested in the equity stock of a publicly traded development company. All of its prior equity investments had been made directly in specific properties.

Professor David Hawkins prepared this case as the basis for class discussion rather than to illustrate either effective or ineffective handling of an administrative situation.

Sir George was interested in the U.S. real estate market, and Rouse in particular, because he believed

- Compared to comparable U.K properties, quality U.S. properties were selling at significant discounts not justified by their long-run prospects.
- Given the relatively small size of the Trust's contemplated investment in the U.S. market, and the Trust's lack of U.S. real estate market experience, it was advisable to obtain the benefits of low entry costs, low monitoring costs, and investment diversification by acquiring stock in an established and successful real estate developer, rather than making a limited number of direct investments.
- Rouse's past performance indicated it was an experienced and successful real estate development company, and there were indications its stock was selling at a significant discount to its intrinsic value.
- Once the current oversupply of commercial and residential real estate in the United States began to disappear, the low level of future planned developments will cause an upward rental move accompanied by an increase in property values. The fact that property replacement costs were well in excess of current market values was viewed as support for this conclusion.
- Over the long run the exchange risk was low, if not favorable, to the U.S. dollar.

The Trust

United Kingdom Properties Trust was formed in 1978. By December 1990, the gross valuation of properties was £1,627 million, valuing income-producing properties on an open market basis and construction in progress at cost. One year earlier, the Trust's properties had been valued at £1,832 million. The decline in valuation from 1989 resulted from an overall decline in U.K real estate values.

At a 1990 meeting of security analysts, Sir George noted

The success of a property investment and dealing business can only be measured on a middle- to long-term basis. Even then, it is the performance of the overall business rather than of individual properties which matters most, since within a portfolio at any given time, there will be developments which have exceeded expectations and others which have not done so.

A volatile market is likely to continue for the foreseeable future. To meet this situation, property companies must be adequately funded. The strength of our balance sheet will enable us to ride out the depressed periods and to benefit from a return to normal trading conditions.

Chairman's Statement

In the Trust's 1990 annual report, Sir George stated in his Chairman's Statement

The Trust's core rental income has continued to grow, reflecting the underlying quality and strength of our portfolio. However, I regret to report that, due to adverse market conditions, significant provisions have been made against the book value of trading assets.

Conditions for property investment, development, and trading have worsened progressively during 1990 with declining tenant and investor demand and continuing high interest rates. The consequences are lower property values, very little growth in rental rates, and a surplus of property to let.

For some while, we have been limiting exposure to new development and programs have been reduced to reflect a lower level of potential demand for space. This is reflected in capital commitments for property expenditure which are below £100 million.

The pretax profit for 1990 amounted to £23 million compared with £82 million for the previous year. Included within the results is a property trading profit of £11 million.

Exceptional provisions of £63.8 million (1989 £nil) were made as a result of writing down where appropriate the value of trading assets to reflect net realizable values.

An external valuation of the Trust's investment properties was carried out on an open market basis as at 31 December 1990 by the Trust's retained valuers.

The gross value of investment properties as at 31 December 1990, taking into account the valuation, construction in progress at cost and exchange rates at that date, amounted to £1,627 million.

Diluted net assets per share as at 31 December 1990 amounted to 375p per share compared with 464p per share as at 31 December 1989, a decrease of 19.2 percent. The latest diluted net asset value per share approximates to the value prevailing at the end of 1988.

The external valuations were undertaken by Richard Hobbs and Thomas Parker who each valued part of the portfolio. This resulted in a valuation deficit of £205.4 million or 14.2 percent which reflects the generally adverse market conditions prevailing.

Director's Report

With respect to property valuation, the director's report in the Trust's 1990 annual reported noted

The Trust's investment property portfolio was valued externally as at 31 December 1990.

The net decline of £248.5 million in the value of the Trust's properties arising from the valuation has been debited to capital reserve. Allowing for capital expenditure, property disposals and differences on exchange, the net effect is that the book value of the Trust's land and buildings has declined to £1,627 million.

The assets of the Utilities Division were excluded from the valuation.

Trading properties held for resale and buildings under construction have been valued by the directors and, where appropriate, reflect the necessary adjustment to net realistic value.

Investment properties are accounted for in accordance with SSAP19.[1] Where the requirements of SSAP19 conflict with those of the Companies Act 1985, SSAP19 has been followed, as the directors believe this is necessary in order to present a true and fair view.

---

[1]Statement of Standard Accounting Practice ("SSAP") No. 19, "Accounting for Investment Properties," defines investment properties as completed properties held for their investment potential with any rentals negotiated at arm's length. They do not include properties owned and occupied by the reporting company for its own purpose or let to other group companies. The SSAP requires that investment properties not be subject to depreciation (except for properties held on lease, which must be depreciated at least over the last twenty years of its lease term) and be included in the balance sheet at their open-market value. Where investment properties represent a substantial portion of a company's

Accounting Policies

Under the heading "Accounting Policies" the Trust's 1990 annual report stated:

> These financial statements have been prepared in accordance with applicable Accounting Standards and on the basis of historical costs but incorporating property valuations.
>
> Completed investment properties and land held for or under development were valued as at 31 December by independent appraisers. These valuations have been prepared on the basis of open market value in accordance with the relevant guidance notes on the valuation of property assets applicable in the United Kingdom. Each property has been valued individually and not as part of a portfolio. No account has been taken of any intercompany leases or arrangements, nor of any mortgages, debentures, or other charges, and no allowance had been made for any expenses of realization, nor for any taxation which might arise in the event of a disposal. The figures also do not reflect any element of special purchaser value following a merger of interests or sale to an owner or occupier of an adjoining property.
>
> The valuations have been prepared on the basis of information provided to the valuers by the Trust relating to title, tenure, lettings, site and floor areas, planning consents, and other relevant information. Valuers were instructed to assume that no deleterious materials or techniques had been used in the construction of any of the buildings and not to carry out structural surveys.
>
> The surpluses and deficiencies arising attributable to the Trust are reflected in unrealized capital reserves. To the extent that projects have not been included in the valuation review, they are included at cost or at the directors' assessment of open market value. Buildings under construction are valued at cost.
>
> No depreciation is provided in respect of freehold investment properties or leasehold investment properties with over twenty years to run. The directors consider that this accounting policy results in the financial statement giving a true and fair view. Depreciation or amortization is only one of the many factors reflected in the annual valuation and the amount which might otherwise have been shown cannot be separately identified or quantified.
>
> No depreciation is charged where plant and equipment is provided in the Trust's premises for the use of its tenants, as it is covered by the full repairing covenant embodied in the respective leases. Other plant and equipment operated by the Trust in the normal course of business is depreciated on a straight-line basis over its estimated useful life: mainly ten to twenty-five years.
>
> Interest costs incurred in funding land for or under development and construction work in progress are capitalized during the period of development. A property is regarded as being in the course of development until substantially let or the expiration of a period varying from six months to two years from the issue of the Architect's certificate of practical completion, whichever is the earlier. Interest costs incurred in funding major construction programs for the Utilities Division are capitalized during the period of construction.
>
> Trading properties are held at the lower of cost, including finance costs, and net realizable value, less progress payments receivable. Cost includes direct expenditure and interest, less any relevant income.

---

total assets, the valuation can be carried out annually by persons holding a recognized professional qualification and having recent post-qualification experience in the location and category of the properties concerned; and at least every five years by an external auditor.

Investment Property Disclosure

The following investment properties information was disclosed in its Notes to the Trust's 1990 financial statement under the heading "Tangible Assets-Investment Properties (£m)."

At 1 January 1990	1,866.1
Additions	109.7
Disposables	(100.7)
Deficit on valuation	(248.5)
At 31 December 1990	1,626.6
Properties held at valuation:	
—cost	907.2
—valuation surplus	681.5
	1,588.7
Properties held at cost	37.9
	1,625.6

The Rouse Company

The Rouse Company of Columbia, Maryland, was a leading U.S. real estate development, management, and ownership organization. The company developed and acquired income-producing real estate and managed these properties for the long-term benefits of cash flow and residual value.

Rouse was the largest publicly held real estate developer in the United States. Rouse subsidiaries and affiliates operated 81 retail properties, 80 of which were located throughout the United States and one in Canada. The 81 retail properties totaled over 47 million square feet of space, including over 26 million square feet of space for 157 department stores with the remaining 21 million square feet for over 8,500 small merchants. Rouse was also the developer of the town of Columbia, Maryland, located between Baltimore and Washington, D.C.

Included in the 81 retail properties were 56 regional shopping centers representing 40 million square feet, 17 urban specialty marketplace/mixed-use centers with 6.8 million square feet and eight community centers in Columbia with approximately 599,000 square feet.

Among the urban specialty marketplace/mixed-use centers for which Rouse was widely known were: Faneuil Hall Marketplace in Boston; Harborplace and The Gallery at Harborplace in Baltimore; St. Louis Union Station in St. Louis; The Shops at Tabor Center in Denver; Bayside Marketplace in Miami; The Shops at National Place in Washington, D.C.; and South Street Seaport in New York City. These centers each averaged from 10 million to 18 million visitors a year.

In 1990, total retail sales of the merchants in Rouse's projects exceeded $4.6 billion.

In addition to its retail properties, Rouse subsidiaries and affiliates also operated 114 office, R&D and industrial buildings totaling 10.1 million square feet and four hotels.

The Rouse company had continued to develop Columbia, Maryland, which in 1990 was 24 years old and had approximately 70,000 residents, 2,300 businesses and industries providing 53,600 jobs, 19 public schools, 28,300 homes, and numerous medical, recreational, and cultural facilities. Under development in Columbia was a 600-acre corporate park and four residential neighborhoods.

Rouse was one of only a few U.S. publicly held development companies that regularly disclosed the current value of its income-producing properties. The company had started this annual practice in 1973 following a decision by the Securities and Exchange Commission (SEC) that Rouse and other companies could no longer publish cash-flow-per-share data in their annual reports. The Securities and Exchange Commission (SEC) based its decision on the grounds that disclosures of "cash flow per share . . . appear designed to decrease the credibility of conventional financial statements as a measure of business activity."[2]

In the previous year, 1972, Rouse had followed its past practice of including in its annual report two per share figures that management believed were key to judging real estate operations. The first was "Earnings before Noncash Charges." The second was "Net Cash from Operations." These data were highlighted because management wanted to disclose evidence of "economic appreciation."

In its 1973–1975 annual reports, Rouse continued to disclose gross cash flow data along with a new figure, "Value Added Above Cost." The value added above cost figure was computed by deducting the historical cost of the company's properties from the company's net cash flow available before debt service capitalized at a nine percent rate.

In its 1976 annual report, Rouse shifted away from a cash flow emphasis to a current value-based performance measurement. Earlier, the company's chairman, in a presentation to the Maryland Certified Public Accountants in 1975, had stated:

> If I have any complaint to make, it arises out of the fact that while the profession has ground away at some of the relative minutiae of our business' reporting techniques causing us to bite one bullet after another and to make accounting changes that have perplexed our public, it has continued to force us to produce financial statements that misrepresent the true financial position of the company and in a colossal way mislead the reader as to the true economics of our business.
>
> The answer for us must lie in some form of current value accounting.

Rouse's auditors supported the company's 1976 presentation of the current value of its properties as a supplement to the company's conventional historical-cost–based financial statements. The SEC, after insisting that deferred taxes should be accrued on any estimated gains on revaluation, agreed to permit the 1976 current value disclosure as long as the company consistently followed the disclosure practice in future years irrespective of the economic conditions.

---

[2]SEC Accounting Series Release No. 142, March 15, 1973.

Exhibit 1 presents, along with selected historical cost information, the current value data and related management comments, financial statement notes, supplemental disclosures, report of independent real estate consultants, and independent auditors' reports included in Rouse's 1990 annual report.

In addition to the data presented in **Exhibit 1,** the 1990 Rouse report included a listing of Rouse's properties that indicated the property's name, location, square footage, and date acquired.

Rouse Report

Before reaching a final decision on the Rouse investment, Sir George had his executive assistant, Patricia Logan, prepare a detailed research report on Rouse ("Rouse report").

EXHIBIT 1   The Rouse Company 1990 Annual Report (Selected Portions)

	1990	1989
Revenues		
Revenues	$ 529,570,000	$ 498,100,000
Earnings before depreciation and deferred taxes from operations[a]	50,290,000	57,084,000
Net earnings (loss)	(1,816,000)	9,733,000
Financial Position		
Total assets—cost basis	2,614,877,000	2,299,615,000
Total assets—current value basis	4,362,153,000	4,129,645,000
Shareholders' equity—cost basis	25,339,000	52,951,000
Shareholders' equity—current value basis	1,470,088,000	1,730,075,000
Statistical Highlights		
Weighted average number of common shares outstanding	48,019,000	47,910,000
Number of employees	5,612	5,337

[a]Earnings before depreciation and deferred taxes from operations represents revenues less operating, interest, and current income tax expenses and Preferred stock dividends.

Contents

Highlights

1

Letter to Shareholders

2

Financial Review

22

Management's Analysis

47

Exhibit 1   (continued) Letter to Shareholders

1990 was a challenging year for the company. The accidental deaths of our president, Mike Spear, his wife Judy, and their daughter Jodi, in an airplane crash were terrible tragedies. The company lost a leader with a long record of exceptional achievements, and many of us lost a valued colleague and three very good friends. We miss them immensely.

1990 was also a year marked by severe problems in the United States' economy, particularly for the real estate, retailing, and financial services industries. We believe The Rouse Company has adapted well to these difficult times and has in many ways grown stronger. And while our final results fell short of the goals we set in late 1989, the company experienced very solid performance, particularly considering the deterioration of our business environment.

Earnings Before Depreciation and Deferred Taxes from Operating Properties recorded an increase for the fourteenth consecutive year, up 10% to $66,050,000. Total Earnings Before Depreciation and Deferred Taxes declined to $50,290,000, from $57,084,000 in 1989, with the major reason being reduced earnings from the sale of land in Columbia. The decline in earnings from land sales and an increase in depreciation expenses were the primary causes of a Net Loss for 1990 of $1,816,000, compared with 1989's Net Earnings of $9,733,000.

At year end, Current Value Shareholders' Equity was $1.47 billion, or $30.10 per share, down $260 million and $4.70 per share, respectively, from year end 1989. These declines reflect troubled markets and cautious investors in the real estate industry rather than any fundamental change in the quality of the company's portfolio of properties.

During 1990, five new projects had very successful openings, and two projects were added through the acquisition/management program.

Finally, on February 28, 1991, the company's Board of Directors approved a quarterly dividend rate of $.15 per share. This rate represents no change from 1990, and reflects the Board's desire to act conservatively in these uncertain times.

Current Value Declines

Since the Rouse Company began reporting Current Value Shareholders' Equity in 1976, this important measure had increased each year through 1989, when it reached $1.73 billion, or $34.80 per share on a fully diluted basis. At year end, 1990 Cur-

rent Value Shareholders' Equity was $1.47 billion, or $30.10 per share on a fully diluted basis. This decline in value was due to the deterioration of the real estate and financial markets. By year end, some investors lacked capital to invest in real estate projects, and many of those who had funds were shifting their investment objectives away from real estate. Those remaining real estate–oriented investors with capital became very quality-conscious. Only trouble-free, large-scale projects in major markets attracted buying interest, and very few of these high quality projects were offered for sale.

The impact of these market realities has been to increase investors' yield requirements or, conversely, to lower the price investors are willing to pay for real estate properties, and this has been recognized in the company's current value process. While many of the company's major retail centers fall in the very high quality sector, and are still sought by investors, the company's portfolio also includes smaller retail centers, suburban office buildings, land, and three hotels. Properties in these latter categories are clearly worth less in today's market, even though most of ours performed well during 1990.

Since The Rouse Company's current value presentation is based on market appraisals of the value of each of the company's operating properties and of its land (primarily in Columbia), 1990's Current Value Shareholders' Equity declined as a result of these changes in the market. A subtlety of this environment is that very few major new projects of any type are being built or are in development today. This means that for the next two to five years, most of our retail centers will not face new competition. The end result will likely see investors once again aggressively seeking strong, quality projects, and the value "lost" in 1990 should be recovered, and possibly enhanced, in future years.

Operating Properties Perform Well

The company's portfolio of more than 200 operating properties performed well in a very difficult environment, with Earnings Before Depreciation and Deferred Taxes increasing by 10%, to $66,050,000.

Retail centers once again produced the major share of these results, $61,999,000, 11% above the $56,006,000 in Earnings Before Depreciation and Deferred Taxes generated in 1989. The primary reasons for this good growth were:

Exhibit 1   (continued)

☐ Retail sales of merchants in the company's centers increased by 3.2% (on a comparable space basis) despite the malaise in the general retail environment. This marked the fifth consecutive year that comparable space sales have increased in the range between 3.0% and 4.5%—lower than the prior decade, but stronger than department stores and other measures of national retail sales. The 8,500 merchants in our centers had a total sales volume for 1990 of approximately $4.6 billion.

☐ During 1990, over 2.6 million square feet of space was re-leased at average rental increases of over $6 per square foot. Occupancy levels in the company's centers continued strong, matching 1989's year end level of 93%.

☐ Major renovation and remerchandising programs have now been completed at a large number of centers, resulting in increased sales and revenues.

Office buildings, industrial buildings, major mixed-use projects, and some miscellaneous properties make up the balance of the operating properties portfolio. Though there were two major mixed-use project openings during the year—with some anticipated start-up losses—and a very difficult office leasing environment, results in 1990 were satisfactory. Earnings Before Depreciation and Deferred Taxes for Office, Mixed-Use and Other projects were $4,051,000, almost flat compared to $4,199,000 in 1989. In last year's Annual Report, our Letter to Shareholders forecast a decline, but the final results for 1990 were actually somewhat better than anticipated. . . .

New Development Outlook

The company has no major new projects scheduled to open in 1991, and only The Ryland Group Headquarters Building in downtown Columbia is targeted for 1992. While major retail centers are not overbuilt in most markets, there are very few existing development opportunities for economically viable retail centers across the country today. Office buildings and most other commercial real estate projects are substantially overbuilt in almost all markets, with large amounts of vacant space yet to be absorbed. In a foreseeably less exuberant economic environment, it will take several years to significantly reduce this substantial overhang.

The company anticipated this scenario several years ago and is well-positioned to weather this storm and await the upturn in this cycle. In the meantime, several of our existing retail centers have emerged as strong candidates for expansion in 1992 and 1993, and there are also a number of prospects for new retail centers in 1994, 1995 and beyond which we are pursuing. . . .

Summary and Outlook

Although the company did not achieve all of its objectives in 1990, it was nonetheless a year of solid performance. Continuing difficulties in the real estate, retailing, and financial industries, however, combining with a recessionary national economic environment, give cause for caution in 1991. The company's strategy during the coming year will be to focus on our existing portfolio of properties and to reinforce and nurture them. This is not the time to gamble, and consequently new opportunities will be scrutinized carefully and undertaken only on a very limited risk basis. We have also moved to strengthen our organization. . . .

The company enters 1991 in good financial health, with satisfactory liquidity for these troubled times. However, financial results for the year will probably be lackluster. Given the likelihood of weak consumer spending and increased pressure on office rental rates, our operating property portfolio may produce only modest gains during 1991. As previously mentioned, 1991 Columbia land sales and earnings will not exceed 1990's levels. Although our development organization has been appropriately reduced over the past three years, the dearth of new development projects has created some excess capacity. As a result, we expect our internal development expenses to remain at relatively high levels. Corporate expenses will be held down, but net corporate interest expense will increase, as both the level of funds available to invest and the yield on the invested capital decline as we deploy capital in our projects. As a result, we would expect Total Earnings Before Depreciation and Deferred Taxes to be below 1990 levels.

The future is not bleak, however, because as the American consumer regains confidence and the United States comes out of the recession, our financial results and asset values should rebound substantially, and opportunities for new commercial real estate projects will begin to occur. In the meantime, we remain confident of the company's ability to face today's challenges and to continue to create long-term values in real estate for our shareholders in the months and years ahead.

Mathias J. DeVito
Chairman of the Board
President and Chief Executive Officer

EXHIBIT 1

(continued)

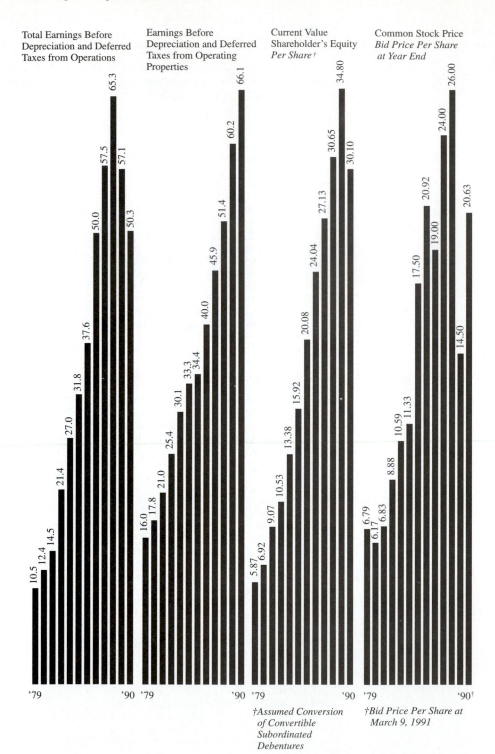

Total Earnings Before Depreciation and Deferred Taxes from Operations

Earnings Before Depreciation and Deferred Taxes from Operating Properties

Current Value Shareholder's Equity *Per Share*†

Common Stock Price *Bid Price Per Share at Year End*

†*Assumed Conversion of Convertible Subordinated Debentures*

†*Bid Price Per Share at March 9, 1991*

Exhibit 1   (continued)

The Rouse Company and Subsidiaries

MANAGEMENT'S STATEMENT ON RESPONSIBILITIES FOR ACCOUNTING, AUDITING AND FINANCIAL REPORTING

The information contained in the financial review section as well as other financial information contained in this annual report to shareholders has been prepared by management of the Company. Management has consulted with the Company's independent auditors, where appropriate, to secure their professional advice. Financial information elsewhere in this report is consistent with the data presented in the financial review section.

The cost basis financial statements have been prepared on the basis of the most appropriate generally accepted accounting principles in the circumstances. The primary objective of financial reporting is to provide users of financial statements with sufficient, relevant information to enable them to evaluate the financial strength and profitability of the Company. Consistent with this objective, this annual report includes current value basis financial statements and a measurement of operating results (Earnings Before Depreciation and Deferred Taxes from Operations) which supplements net earnings (loss).

The financial statements and other financial information require a certain amount of estimating and informed judgment. Management has made these estimates and judgments based on extensive experience and substantive understanding of events and transactions respecting the Company's past and prospective operations.

In fulfilling its responsibility for the reliability and integrity of financial information, management has established and maintains accounting procedures and related control systems. Management believes that these systems and controls provide reasonable assurance that assets are safeguarded; that transactions are executed in accordance with management's authorizations and recorded properly to permit the preparation of reliable cost basis financial statements in conformity with generally accepted accounting principles and current value basis financial information on the basis described in note 1 to the consolidated financial statements; and that any material errors or irregularities are prevented or detected within a timely period by employees in the normal course of performing their assigned duties. These systems and controls are supported by the Company's business ethics policy and are regularly tested by internal auditors. The independent auditors also review and test established internal control systems to the extent necessary to express an opinion on the financial statements.

The Audit Committee of the Board of Directors is composed of directors who are neither officers nor employees of the Company. The Committee meets periodically with management, the Company's internal auditors, the independent auditors and the independent real estate consultants to review the work and conclusions of each. The internal auditors and the independent auditors have full and free access to the Audit Committee and meet with it, with and without management present, to discuss auditing and financial reporting matters as well as the adequacy of internal controls. The Audit Committee recommends, and the Board of Directors appoints, the independent auditors.

Exhibit 1 (continued) Independent Auditor's Report

KPMG Peat Marwick
Certified Public Accountants
111 South Calvert Street
Baltimore, Maryland 21202

The Board of Directors and Shareholders
The Rouse Company

We have audited the accompanying consolidated cost basis balance sheets of The Rouse Company and subsidiaries as of December 31, 1990 and 1989, and the related consolidated cost basis statements of operations, common stock and other shareholders' equity and cash flows for each of the years in the three-year period ended December 31, 1990. We have also audited the supplemental consolidated current value basis balance sheets of The Rouse Company and subsidiaries as of December 31, 1990 and 1989, and the related supplemental consolidated current value basis statements of changes in revaluation equity for each of the years in the three-year period ended December 31, 1990. These financial statements are the responsibility of the company's management. Our responsibility is to express an opinion on these financial statements based on our audits.

We conducted our audits in accordance with generally accepted auditing standards. Those standards require that we plan and perform the audit to obtain reasonable assurance about whether the financial statements are free of material misstatement. An audit includes examining, on a test basis, evidence supporting the amounts and disclosures in the financial statements. An audit also includes assessing the accounting principles used and significant estimates made by management, as well as evaluating the overall financial statement presentation. We believe that our audits provide a reasonable basis for our opinion.

In our opinion, the aforementioned consolidated cost basis financial statements present fairly, in all material respects, the financial position of The Rouse Company and subsidiaries at December 31, 1990 and 1989, and the results of their operations and their cash flows for each of the years in the three-year period ended December 31, 1990, in conformity with generally accepted accounting principles.

As more fully described in note 1 to the consolidated financial statements, the supplemental consolidated current value basis financial statements referred to above have been prepared by management to present relevant financial information about The Rouse Company and its subsidiaries which is not provided by the cost basis financial statements and are not intended to be a presentation in conformity with generally accepted accounting principles. In addition, as more fully described in note 1, the supplemental consolidated current value basis financial statements do not purport to present the net realizable, liquidation or market value of the Company as a whole. Furthermore, amounts ultimately realized by the Company from the disposal of properties may vary from the current values presented.

In our opinion, the aforementioned supplemental consolidated current value basis financial statements present fairly, in all material respects, the information set forth therein on the basis of accounting described in note 1 to the consolidated financial statements.

EXHIBIT 1   (continued)

Landauer Associates, Inc.
335 Madison Avenue
New York, New York 10017
212-687-2323
Telex: 710-581-2012

LANDAUER
Real Estate Counselors

KPMG Peat Marwick and
The Board of Directors and Shareholders
The Rouse Company

We have reviewed estimates of the market value of equity and other interests in certain real property owned and/or managed by The Rouse Company (the Company) and its subsidiaries as of December 31, 1990 and 1989. The properties reviewed at December 31, 1990 include all the projects identified as "In Operation" on the "Projects of The Rouse Company" table on pages 56 through 60 of the Annual Report for 1990, property held for development and sale, and certain parcels of land in development operations. The properties reviewed at December 31, 1989 were the same, except for the properties which were opened, acquired or sold during 1990.

The total values of its equity and other interests estimated by the Company were $2,135,400,000 and $2,214,779,000 at December 31, 1990 and 1989, respectively.

Based upon our review, we concur with the Company's estimates of the total value of the property interests appraised. In our opinion, the aggregate value estimated by the Company varies less than 10% from the aggregate value we would estimate in a full and complete appraisal of the same interests. A variation of less than 10% between appraisers implies substantial agreement as to the most probable market value of such property interests.

The data used in our review were supplied to us in summary form by the Company. We have relied upon the Company's interpretation and summaries of leases, operating agreements, mortgages and partnership and joint venture agreements. We have had complete and unrestricted access to all underlying documents and have confirmed certain information by reference to such documents. We have found no discrepancies in the data and, to the best of our knowledge, believe all such data to be accurate and complete. The basic assumptions used by the Company and the individual value estimates prepared by the Company were, in our opinion, fair and reasonable. No assumption has been made with respect to a bulk sale of the entire holdings or groups of property interests. We have also physically inspected, within the past three years, substantially all of the properties which were reviewed.

We certify that neither Landauer Associates, Inc. nor the undersigned have any present or prospective interest in the Company's properties, and we have no personal interest or bias with respect to the parties involved. To the best of our knowledge and belief, the facts upon which the analysis and conclusions were based are materially true and correct. No one other than the undersigned assisted by members of our staff, performed the analyses and reached the conclusions resulting in the opinion expressed in this letter. Our fee for this assignment was not contingent on any action or event resulting from the analysis, opinions, or conclusions in, or the use of, this review. Our review has been prepared in conformity with the Uniform Standards of Professional Appraisal Practice.

James C. Kafes, MAI, CRE
Managing Director
February 18, 1991

Deborah A. Jackson
Senior Vice President
Director of Retail Valuation

EXHIBIT 1 **(continued) Consolidated Cost Basis and Current Value Basis Balance Sheets**
December 31, 1990 and 1989 (in thousands)

	1990		1989	
	Current Value Basis (Note 1)	*Cost Basis*	*Current Value Basis (Note 1)*	*Cost Basis*
Assets				
Property (Notes 4, 5, 8, and 14):				
Operating properties:				
Current value	$3,816,663		$3,483,703	
Property and deferred costs of projects		$2,414,784		$1,985,549
Less accumulated depreciation and amortization		287,365		243,579
	$3,816,663	$2,127,419	$3,483,703	$1,741,970
Development operations:				
Construction and development in progress	$ 66,023	$ 59,727	$ 203,762	$ 196,651
Pre-construction costs, net	16,304	16,304	11,415	11,415
	$ 82,327	$ 76,031	$ 215,177	$ 208,066
Property held for development and sale	$ 166,616	$ 125,387	$ 145,254	$ 73,671
Other property, net (Note 14)	20,234	9,727	19,651	10,048
Other assets	78,612	78,612	75,271	75,271
Accounts and notes receivable (Note 6)	85,153	85,153	84,766	84,766
Investments in marketable securities	41,758	41,785	68,526	68,526
Cash and cash equivalents	70,790	70,790	37,297	37,297
Total	$4,362,153	$2,614,877	$4,129,645	$2,299,615
Liabilities				
Debt (Note 8):				
Property debt not carrying a Parent Company guarantee of repayment . .	$1,591,680	$1,591,680	$1,266,786	$1,266,786
Parent Company debt and debt carrying a Parent Company guarantee of repayment:				
Property debt	$ 397,838	$ 397,838	$ 387,084	$ 387,084
Convertible subordinated debentures	230,000	230,000	230,000	230,000
Other debt	35,798	35,798	840	840
	$ 663,636	$ 663,636	$ 617,924	$ 617,924
Total debt	$2,255,316	$2,255,316	$1,884,710	$1,884,710
Obligations under capital leases (Note 14)	$ 88,779	$ 88,779	$ 86,059	$ 86,059
Accounts payable, accrued expenses and other liabilities	147,725	147,725	153,863	153,863
Commitments and contingencies (Notes 14 and 15)				
Deferred income taxes (Note 10)	400,245	97,718	249,938	97,032
Redeemable cumulative Preferred stock (Note 12)	—	—	25,000	25,000
Common stock and other shareholders' equity (Note 13)				
Common stock of 1¢ par value per share; 250,000,000 shares authorized;				
issued 48,130,184 shares in 1990 and 47,973,430 shares in 1989	481	481	480	480
Additional paid-in capital	85,521	85,521	80,447	80,447
Accumulated deficit	(60,663)	(60,663)	(27,745)	(27,745)
Revaluation equity (Note 1)	1,444,749	—	1,677,124	—
	$1,470,088	$ 25,339	$1,730,306	$ 53,182
Less receivables for common stock sold to officers	—	—	231	231
Total common stock and other shareholders' equity	1,470,088	25,339	1,730,075	52,951
Total	$4,362,153	$2,614,877	$4,129,645	$2,299,615

EXHIBIT 1 **(continued) Consolidated Cost Basis Statements of Earnings**
Years Ended December 31, 1990, 1989 and 1988 (in thousands)

	1990	*1989*	*1988*
Revenues	$529,570	$498,100	$460,778
Operating expenses	306,678	285,543	263,133
Interest expense (Note 8)	170,027	152,457	129,138
Depreciation and amortization (Note 4)	55,360	47,646	38,083
Gain on dispositions of assets and other provisions, net (Note 11) . .	2,752	5,377	2,791
Earnings before income taxes and extraordinary loss	$ 257	$ 17,831	$ 33,215
Income taxes (Note 10):			
Current—state	$ 302	$ 423	$ 1,098
Deferred—primarily federal	1,120	7,047	12,125
	$ 1,422	$ 7,470	$ 13,223
Earnings (loss) before extraordinary loss	$ (1,165)	$ 10,361	$ 19,992
Extraordinary loss from extinguishment of debt, net of related			
income tax benefit (Note 8)	$ (651)	$ (628)	$ —
Net earnings (loss)	$ (1,816)	$ 9,733	$ 19,992
Earnings (loss) per share of common stock after provision for			
dividends on preferred stock (Note 16):			
Earnings (loss) before extraordinary loss	$ (.07)	$ .16	$ .37
Extraordinary loss	(.01)	(.01)	—
Total	$ (.08)	$ .15	$ .37

EXHIBIT 1   (continued) Consolidated Cost Basis Statements of Cash Flows
Years Ended December 31, 1990, 1989 and 1988 (in thousands)

	1990	*1989*	*1988*
Cash flows from operating activities			
Rents and other revenues received	$ 503,196	$ 427,039	$ 375,518
Proceeds from land sales	16,040	34,970	59,105
Interest received	10,070	12,308	10,867
Operating expenditures	(310,139)	(248,860)	(239,475)
Land development expenditures	(17,330)	(17,007)	(21,956)
Interest paid	(166,780)	(148,411)	(127,078)
Net cash provided by operating activities	$ 35,057	$ 60,039	$ 56,981
Cash flows from investing activities			
Construction and development expenditures	$(132,209)	$(224,257)	$(178,633)
Expenditures for improvements to existing properties:			
Tenant leasing and remerchandising	(37,296)	(27,245)	(23,694)
Building and equipment–related	(34,016)	(30,823)	(31,887)
Expenditures for property acquisitions	(71,815)	(30,425)	(47,715)
Proceeds from sales of operating properties	1,166	2,599	6,761
Purchase of marketable securities	(29,270)	(59,336)	(43,625)
Proceeds from redemption or sale of marketable securities	56,039	64,435	20,122
Other	(1,131)	(2,076)	(6,291)
Net cash used in investing activities	$(248,532)	$(307,128)	$(304,962)
Cash flows from financing activities			
Proceeds from issuance of property debt	$ 319,439	$ 245,417	$ 293,923
Repayments of property debt:			
Scheduled principal payments	(22,722)	(18,525)	(16,793)
Other payments	(927,474)	(15,439)	(35,500)
Proceeds from issuance of other debt	35,000	—	3,500
Repayments of other debt	(1,362)	(16,214)	(625)
Redemption of preferred stock	(25,000)	—	—
Proceeds from exercise of stock options	213	1,295	775
Dividends paid:			
Common stock	(28,853)	(26,629)	(25,001)
Preferred stock	(2,273)	(2,593)	(2,109)
Net cash provided by financing activities	$ 246,968	$ 167,312	$ 218,170
Net increase (decrease) in cash and cash equivalents	$ 33,493	$ (79,777)	$ (29,811)

**EXHIBIT 1   (continued) Consolidated Current Value Basis Statements of
Changes in Revaluation Equity**
Years Ended December 31, 1990, 1989 and 1988 (in thousands)

	1990	1989	1988
Revaluation equity at beginning of year	$1,677,124	$1,424,683	$1,220,550
Revaluation equity attributable to interests in operating properties sold	(361)	(6,638)	(3,081)
	$1,676,763	$1,418,045	$1,217,469
Change in value of interests in operating properties in operation during entire year	(55,379)	283,247	203,943
Value of interests in operating properties opened or acquired....................................	3,251	37,551	10,967
Change in value of land in development operations and property held for development and sale, including effects of sales and transfers to operating properties	(31,169)	(13,289)	5,238
(Decrease) increase in value of interests in operating properties, property held for development and sale and land in development operations	(83,297)	307,509	220,148
Increase in value of other property, less accumulated depreciation	904	619	301
Decrease in value attributable to debt, exclusive of operating property debt	—	—	(689)
Increase in present value of potential income taxes, net of cost basis deferred income taxes	(149,621)	(49,049)	(12,546)
	$ (232,014)	$ 259,079	$ 207,214
Revaluation equity at end of year	$1,444,749	$1,677,124	$1,424,683

EXHIBIT 1   (continued)

The Rouse Company and Subsidiaries
Notes to Consolidated Financial Statements
December 31, 1990, 1989, and 1988

(1) Current value basis
financial statements

(a) Current value reporting

The Company's interests in operating properties, property held for development and sale and certain other assets have appreciated in value and, accordingly, their current values exceed their cost basis net book values determined in conformity with generally accepted accounting principles. These values are reported in the current value basis financial statements. Management believes that these financial statements more realistically reflect the underlying financial strength of the Company.

The current values of the interests in operating properties, including interests in unconsolidated real estate ventures, represent management's estimates of the value of these assets primarily as investments. These values will generally be realized through future cash flows generated by the operation of these properties over their economic lives. The current values of property held for development and sale represent management's estimates of the value of these assets under long-term development and sales programs.

The current value basis financial statements are not intended to present the current liquidation values of individual assets or groups of assets or the liquidation value of the Company or its net assets taken as a whole.

Shareholders' equity on a current value basis was $1,470,088,000 or $30.10 per share at December 31, 1990 and $1,730,075,000 or $34.80 per share at December 31, 1989. The per share calculations reflect the assumed conversion of the convertible subordinated debentures (see note 8).

(b) Bases of valuation

Interests in operating properties—The current value of the Company's interests in operating properties is the Company's share (based on its underlying ownership interest) of each property's equity value (i.e., the present value of its forecasted net cash flow and residual value, if applicable, after deducting principal and interest payments on the debt specifically related to the property) plus the outstanding balance of related debt. The current value of the Company's interests in unconsolidated real estate ventures is the present value of the Company's share of net cash flow, including incentive management fees and residual value of the respective real estate ventures.

The forecasts of net cash flow are based on an evaluation of the history and future of each property and are supported by market studies; analyses of tenant lease terms and projected sales performance; and estimates of revenues and operating expenses over projection periods of primarily eleven years.

The present values of forecasted net cash flows are determined using internal rates of return which vary by project and between years as investor yield requirements change. The resulting values recognize the considerable differences between properties in terms of quality, age, outlook and risks as well as the prevailing yield requirements of investors for income-producing properties.

Development operations—Properties under development are carried at the same amounts as in the cost basis financial statements (except for certain parcels of land). Management believes that such properties have values in excess of stated costs, but has taken the conservative position of not recognizing any value increment until these properties are completed and operating.

Property held for development and sale—The current value of property held for development and sale is based on the present value of forecasted net cash flows under development and sales programs. These programs set forth the proposed timing and cost of all improvements necessary to bring the properties to saleable condition, the pace and price of sales and the costs to administer the programs and sell the properties.

EXHIBIT 1   (continued)

Debt—Debt and obligations under capital leases specifically relating to interests in operating properties are earned at the same amount as in the cost basis balance sheets since the value of the Company's equity interest in each property is based on net cash flow after principal and interest payments. The current values of other debt and obligations under capital leases are carried at the same amount as in the cost basis balance sheets since the difference between the stated and estimated market interest rates for such obligations are not material.

Deferred income taxes—Because the current value financial statements presume that values will be realized over the long-term through operating cash flows and not through liquidation, the deferred income taxes on a current value basis is an estimate of the present value of income tax payments which may be made based on projections of taxable income through 2047. The projections of taxable income include projects presently under development and, for 1989, future unnamed development projects and reflect all allowable deductions permitted under the Internal Revenue Code. The increase in current value deferred income taxes for 1990 is due principally to refinements made to the calculation of such taxes by the Company. Such refinements include eliminating unnamed projects from the projections of taxable income and extending the period over which taxable income is projected for certain properties. In addition, taxable income projections were increased for periods subsequent to the periods used in the determination of equity values. The discount rates used to compute the present values of income taxes are based on the internal rates of return used to compute the current values of assets, adjusted to reflect the Company's assessment of the greater uncertainty with respect to the ultimate timing and amounts of income tax payments.

Other assets and liabilities—Substantially all other assets and liabilities are carried in the current value basis balance sheets at the lower of cost or net realizable value—the same stated value as in the cost basis balance sheets.

The application of the foregoing methods for estimating current value, including the potential income tax payments, represents the best judgment of management based upon its evaluation of the current and future economy and investor rates of return at the time such estimates were made. Judgments regarding these factors are not subject to precise quantification of verification and may change from time to time as economic and market factors, and management's evaluation of them, change.

The current value basis financial statements have been and will continue to be an integral part of the Company's annual report to shareholders, but consistent with previous practice, current value information will not be presented as part of the Company's quarterly reports to shareholders. The extensive market research, financial analysis and testing of results required to produce reliable current value information make it impractical to report this information on an interim basis.

(c) Revaluation equity
The aggregate difference between the current value basis and cost basis of the Company's assets and liabilities is reported as revaluation equity in the shareholders' equity section of the consolidated current value basis balance sheets.

EXHIBIT 1   (continued)

The components of revaluation equity at December 31, 1990 and 1989 are as follows (in thousands):

	1990	1989
Value of interests in operating properties	$2,010,158	$2,068,016
Value of property held for development and sale	119,016	135,154
Value of land in development operations	6,226	11,609
Total equity value	$2,135,400	$2,214,779
Debt related to equity interests	1,906,461	1,449,655
Total asset value	$4,041,861	$3,664,434
Depreciated cost of interests in operating properties and costs of property held for development and sale and land in development operations	(2,305,092)	(1,844,007)
Present value of potential income taxes related to revaluation equity, net of cost basis deferred income taxes	(302,527)	(152,906)
Other	10,507	9,603
Total revaluation equity	$1,444,749	$1,677,124

Logan's final Rouse report noted that Rouse had, since 1978

- Invested $1.5 billion in the development and acquisition of real estate.
- Raised $1.3 billion of nonrecourse property debt.
- Raised $230 million of convertible debt secured only by the Company's creditworthiness.
- Received an A-3 bond rating on its convertible debt from Moody's.
- Met all debt service obligations—on both nonrecourse first mortgage property debt and corporate debt.
- Paid out common stock dividends of $188 million.
- Achieved a 14.6% compound increase in share price.
- Provided an 18.9% compound total return to shareholders.

The Rouse report included a selected summary of Rouse-related historical cost (**Table A**) and current value data (**Table B**) for the period 1978–1990. These data were obtained from materials distributed by the Rouse management at a mark-to-market symposium.

The Rouse report also indicated that the company's stock at its late 1991 price of about $19 yielded 3.2 percent in the form of a tax-free return of capital and was judged by a recent Value Line report to have a 1.05 Beta (1.0 = market). According to the Rouse report, Value Line, while forecasting that Rouse may post flat earnings before depreciation and deferred taxes (EBDDT) in 1992, noted that Rouse views EBDDT as a better measure of performance than net earnings.

In Sir George's opinion, the most significant portion of the Rouse report was a chart comparing Rouse's stock price with its net assets measured on a current value basis over the period 1978–1991 (see **Exhibit 2**). Sir George believed it supported his view that the Rouse stock represented a sound investment for the Trust.

TABLE A   **The Rouse Company, GAAP Historical-Cost–Based Financial Information (dollars in millions, except per share amounts)**

	1978	*1982*	*1986*	*1990*
Total assets	$438	$633	$1,420	$2,615
Shareholders' equity	27	60	80	25
Debt/equity ratio	15/1	9/1	15/1	98/1
Net income:				
Amount	6	8	19	(2)
Per share	.15	.18	.35	(.08)
Share price	3.04	8.88	20.92	14.50
Share price/earnings ratio	20	49	60	n/a

Source: The Rouse Company.

TABLE B   **The Rouse Company, Current-Value–Based Financial Information (dollars in millions, except per share amounts)**

	1978	*1982*	*1986*	*1990*
Total assets	$622	$1,052	$2,533	$4,362
Shareholders' equity	196	475	1,116	1,471
Debt/equity ratio	2/1	1/1	1/1	2/1
Comprehensive income (loss);				
Including change in realized value of net assets:				
Amount	38	83	201	(234)
Per share	.96	1.86	4.32	(4.88)
Share price/"comprehensive income" ratio	3/1	5/1	5/1	n/a

Source: The Rouse Company.

EXHIBIT 2

The Rouse Company Stock Price versus Current Value

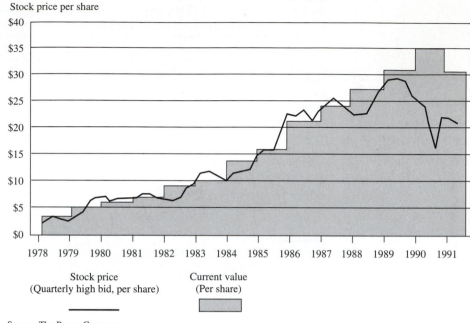

Stock price per share

Stock price
(Quarterly high bid, per share)

Current value
(Per share)

Source: The Rouse Company

Questions

1. Complete the assignment outlined in the case. Do you believe Rouse may be an "attractive" investment for United Kingdom Properties Trust? _____ What Rouse accounting information did you use in this analysis? _____

2. Explain Rouse's approach to measuring the current value of shareholders' equity.

3. Should U.S. GAAP allow Rouse to account on a current value basis? _____ Why? _____

4. How does the United Kingdom Properties Trust account for its properties? _____ How would it account for an investment in Rouse common stock? _____

Changing Prices

Inflation is a condition of overall rising prices. At some point, the rate of price increases requires that business performance, resources and obligations be measured by other than the historical-cost method to avoid distortions caused by the general inflation rate and the changes in specific prices paid for physical resources.

Accounting for changing prices is governed by FASB Statement No. 89, "Financial Reporting and Changing Prices." This statement encourages but does not require certain large, publicly held companies to supplement their annual primary financial statements with information about the effect of changing prices on income from continuing operations and selected assets and their related expenses. Due to the recent low U.S. inflation rate, most companies do not disclose this information.

While FASB Statement No. 89 is generally regarded as dealing with accounting during periods of inflation, it applies equally well to periods of deflation, when prices are falling.

Inflation-adjusted statements are very useful for evaluating how well a company is coping with inflation. By applying standard techniques in financial analysis to price-change data presented in these statements, the statement user can determine how well a company is doing in real terms. This view of a company during periods of inflation helps the statement user to avoid falling into inflation's trap of thinking the company is doing better than it is in reality.

Measures of Inflation

Economists measure inflation by selecting a sample of goods and services representative of the economy and recording their price movements. Each item in the sample is

Professor David F. Hawkins prepared this note as the basis for class discussion.

Copyright © 1995 by the President and Fellows of Harvard College. Harvard Business School teaching note 195–157.

weighted by its relative importance, measured by its volume of sales in relation to the sales of all items. Next, a base year is selected and the index number 100 is assigned to represent that year's composite price. The sample's composite price index for subsequent years can then be compiled and compared with the base year to measure changes in the price-level index.

The Consumer Price Index (CPI), prepared monthly by the Bureau of Labor Statistics of the U.S. Department of Labor, is a widely used indicator of general price level changes in the United States. The index is a weighted average of the prices paid for a variety of consumer products in various regions of the United States. Consumer Price Indices are also computed for different segments of the population. For example, there is an index for the goods and services consumed by urban dwellers (CPI-U). The CPI is often used in escalator clauses in wage and lease contracts.

A broader measure of changes in the overall level of prices is the Implicit Price Deflator for the Gross National Product (GNP). It is calculated by dividing GNP in current prices by GNP in constant prices. This index, published by the Office of Business Economics of the U.S. Department of Commerce, is used to convert the GNP from nominal prices to constant prices.

Another commonly used price index is the Wholesale Price Index, compiled by the Bureau of Labor Statistics. It measures price changes in primary producers' markets. Because of its limited coverage, this index is not considered a good measure of the general rate of inflation.

The CPI and the GNP Implicit Price Deflator often show different rates of inflation for the same period. These differences have led to controversy over which index is the more reliable measurement. The Implicit Price Deflator reflects broader price changes than the CPI, since it includes a wider range of goods and services. Apparently, however, it is less sensitive to short-run price changes.

The principal virtue of the CPI is that it is more easily understood by the general public. The principal criticism of it is that it does not adequately take into account changes in product quality. Nevertheless, quality is not ignored, and over the years, this index has generally proved to be a reasonable measure of the general rate of inflation.

In addition to the indices that measure general shifts in prices, government agencies and private companies publish a number of indices that measure the changes in the prices of specific items, such as construction, services, durables, electrical motors, and steel wire.

Business Considerations

During periods of high rates of inflation, managers try to offset inflationary cost increases by raising prices and improving productivity. In addition, they try to improve their asset and investment turnover ratios, because inflated prices usually result in lower liquidity, higher investments in working capital and higher interest costs.

Purchasing Power

In time of inflation, managers also try to minimize, if not eliminate, purchasing power losses on their monetary assets. The ways to do this are well known to business executives. The problem is to achieve them in practice.

Cash, accounts receivable, and similar monetary assets are all exposed to purchasing power losses in an inflationary economy. For example, a $10,000 check deposited in a bank on January 1 and left there for twelve months, would buy fewer goods on December 31 if prices rose during the year. Similarly, accounts and loans receivable held during the period would lose purchasing power.

Conversely, accounts payable, long-term debt, and similar monetary liabilities are exposed to purchasing power gains. If a liability is paid with dollars that have less purchasing power than those obtained by incurring the liability, a company is better off.

Consequently, most business executives during inflationary times seek to maintain a net monetary liability balance (i.e., monetary liabilities in excess of monetary assets), or at least operate at the minimum net monetary asset balance possible.

To the extent feasible, managers shift their resources from monetary to physical assets, such as inventory, plant, or equipment. They assume that raw materials and finished goods inventories are protected against inflation as long as their selling prices of finished goods keep pace with the rate of inflation. Similarly, fixed assets are protected to the extent that their resale or replacement value rises with inflation and their cost of replacement is recovered through increases in the prices of the goods and services produced with them.

Performance Measurement

During periods of high rates of inflation, financial measures of business performance expressed in nominal dollars (that is, actual dollars of the period) may give the impression that a business is doing better than it really is. To avoid being misled by these potentially illusory measurements, managers have found it essential to keep track of their results in "real" terms by eliminating the effects of inflation on the cash flows and values incorporated in the nominal accounting measurements.

Three kinds of accounting adjustments are used. These are the so-called current-cost, constant-dollar, and current-cost/constant-dollar adjustments.

Adjustments

Current-cost adjustments to historical-cost financial statements restate the historical costs of inventory and productive assets on hand and consumed to their current or specific cost equivalent. The current cost of inventory is the current cost to purchase the inventory. The current cost of property, plant, and equipment owned by a company is the cost of acquiring the same service potential (indicated by operating costs and output capacity) as embodied in the asset owned.

The current-cost view of performance assumes that a business does not earn a profit until it has earned enough to cover the current cost of replacing the assets consumed in the generation of income during the period. This approach to measuring performance tries to avoid the overstatement of profits that can result from including so-called "inventory and under depreciation profits" in income. These amounts are the difference between the historical-cost values and what it costs currently to replace the inventory sold or the asset giving rise to depreciation. If the prices of these items are rising, a portion of profits equivalent to the difference between the replacement cost and the historical cost of inventories and plant and equipment consumed during the account period must be reinvested in the business to maintain its physical inventories and productive capacity. If this portion of profits is distributed as dividends or used to reduce debt, the company's inventories and production capacity may shrink unless alternative funding is available. Adjusting the historical-cost carrying amounts of inventory and productive assets to a current-cost basis inevitably changes the carrying amount of total assets. To even both sides of the balance sheet, owner's equity is also adjusted by an amount equal to the net current-cost adjustment to assets.

To illustrate the current-cost approach to income measurement, assume a company's historical-cost statements report profits before taxes of $3,000 on sales of $12,000, after charging $3,000 to cost of goods sold, $2,000 to depreciation, and $4,000 to other costs. The company's tax rate is 50%. After analyzing the changes in the specific prices of the company's inventory, management decides that the current cost of the inventory sold was 10 percent higher than its historical cost at the time of sale. On the basis of another analysis, management concludes that the current cost of the assets giving rise to depreciation has risen since they were acquired, making the current-cost depreciation of these assets $1,000 higher than the $2,000 charged in the historical cost. (How this determination is made will be discussed later.) The current-cost method does not require restatement of sales and other costs. The company's historical cost and current-cost income statements are compared in **Illustration 1.**

The current cost of inventory depends on the type of inventory involved. The current cost of purchased inventory is the current cost of purchasing the goods

---

ILLUSTRATION 1

	Historical Cost Income Statement	Current Cost Adjustments	Current Cost Income Statement
Sales	$12,000		$12,000
Cost of sales	3,000	+$300	3,300
Gross margin	9,000		8,700
Depreciation	2,000	+$1,000	3,000
Other costs	4,000		4,000
Profit before taxes	3,000		1,800
Taxes	1,500		1,500[a]
Net income	$ 1,500		$ 300

[a]Since the current-cost step up in costs is not tax-deductible, the tax expense is based on the historical-cost pretax profit.

concerned. The current cost of manufactured inventory is the current cost of the resources, including allocated overheads, required to produce the inventory items.

In practice, companies using LIFO inventory accounting assume that the current cost of goods sold is equivalent to their LIFO-based cost-of-goods-sold figure, and the current cost of inventories on hand is equivalent to their FIFO value. This FIFO amount is estimated by adding back the so-called LIFO reserve to the LIFO inventory value.

Companies using FIFO inventory accounting often assume that their inventory's FIFO cost is equivalent to its current cost. FIFO companies have to adjust their historical-cost–based cost-of-goods-sold figures to a current-cost basis. Typically, this means an upward adjustment. If the current cost of the inventory items is falling, however, the current cost of goods sold will be lower than its historical-cost FIFO equivalent.

The current cost of property, plant, and equipment is the current cost of acquiring the service potential embodied in the owned asset. The service potential of an asset is equivalent to the estimated purchase price of a new improved asset minus an allowance for the operating disadvantages of the asset owned (higher operating costs or lower output potential) and an allowance for depreciation, calculated according to an acceptable accounting method. For public reporting purposes, fully depreciated assets are not adjusted to reflect their current costs. Also, in most circumstances, the current cost of owned assets must be reported whether or not the company intends to replace them. Sometimes, for internal current-cost measurement purposes, such as evaluating the performance of division managers, these external reporting requirements are not observed.

Two alternative, less complicated methods for estimating the current cost of owned assets are very frequently used. One is to estimate the purchase price of an asset of the same age and in the same condition as the asset owned. The other is to estimate the purchase price of a similar new asset minus an allowance for depreciation, calculated according to an acceptable accounting method.

The approach chosen to measure current cost should fit the situation, taking account of the availability and reliability of the evidence. Typically, the measurement approaches used can be divided into two categories: direct pricing methods, such as using current vendor invoices, and methods using indexes. Most companies seem to prefer a simple index approach similar to the one illustrated in the following example.

Illustration 2 shows the calculation of 1994 and 1995 current cost and current-cost depreciation for a company's plant. To calculate the 1994 and 1995 current cost for a building bought in 1993 for $10 million, assume the following: The building's straight-line depreciation is 5 percent per year. A reliable construction index indicates that the cost of constructing a similar building increased 10 percent in 1994 and 15 percent in 1995. In **Illustration 2B,** the 1995 current cost of the building ($11.39 million) does not equal its 1995 gross current cost ($12.65 million) minus the sum of the 1994 and 1995 current-cost depreciation ($1.18 million), because, unlike in the original cost minus accumulated depreciation approach to measuring a depreciable asset's net historical-cost book value, the current cost of a depreciable asset is calculated directly each year.

ILLUSTRATION 2   Current-Cost Calculation Example ($ millions)

A. Current-Cost Depreciation

Year	Historical Cost (Gross)	×	Construction Index Adjustment	×	Depreciation Rate	=	Current-Cost Depreciation
1994	$10.0	×	110/100	×	0.5	=	$.55
1995	$10.0	×	(110 × 115)/100	×	0.5	=	.63

B. Current Cost

Year	Current Cost (Gross)	×	Undepreciated Percentage	=	Current Cost
1994	$11.0[a]	×	95%	=	$10.45
1995	$12.65[b]	×	90	=	11.39

[a]$10 × 1.1.

[b]$10 × 1.1 × 1.15.

Current-cost accounting is not allowed for tax purposes. For public current-cost reporting purposes, therefore, the current-cost tax is based on the historical-cost taxable income. Consequently, a company's excess of current-cost expenses over its historical-cost expenses reduces net income by the same amount of the adjustment. Where current-cost income is greater than historical-cost income, the reverse is true.

Constant-dollar adjustments eliminate the effect of general inflation by restating dollar results or the dollar value of transactions occurring in different periods to a constant dollar or equivalent-purchasing-power basis. These adjustments are made to avoid treating dollars representing different purchasing-power outflows and inflows to the business as being equivalent.

The constant-dollar approach to measuring performance during inflationary periods is based on the managerial concept that a profit is not earned until the purchasing power invested in owners' equity is preserved.

To illustrate the constant-dollar approach, assume a company's sales in nominal dollars grew 10 percent, from $5 million to $5.5 million, during the last two years. If the inflation rate during this period was 20 percent, an astute manager, knowing that the dollar was losing purchasing power, would restate the sales figures to a constant-dollar or equivalent-purchasing-power basis to measure the real change in sales. To achieve this, the manager would first select one of the two years as a base against which the other's nominal sales purchasing power equivalent will be measured. Next, if the most recent year were selected, the prior year's sales would be adjusted to their base-year purchasing power equivalent. In this example, that would be $6 million ($5 million × 120/100).

When both years' sales are expressed in constant dollars, the real sales trend of the company becomes apparent. It is down 8.3 percent, from $6 million to $5.5 million.

This trend reflects the fact that the $5.5 million nominal sales earned during the most recent year would have bought 8.3 percent fewer goods and services during the current year than the prior year's actual nominal $5.0 million sales bought during the prior year. This general purchasing power comparison of sales reflects a financial point of view that believes sales do not grow in real terms unless the growth rate of nominal sales exceeds the general rate of inflation.

As we will see later, to remeasure profits in constant dollars requires adjusting many accounts besides sales.

The restatement for general-price-level changes required to generate constant-dollar statements of equivalent purchasing power is a statistical procedure independent of other accounting principles and procedures.

For the purpose of restating the balance sheet in the constant dollars, all items are classified as either monetary or nonmonetary. This distinction is important, since inflation affects the two classes differently. Monetary items are those normally carried in the accounts at current cash values, such as cash, accounts receivable, accounts payable, and long-term debt.[1] The remaining, nonmonetary items include inventory, plant and equipment, and capital stock.

The purchasing power of monetary items changes during periods of changing prices. Monetary assets held during periods of inflation lose purchasing power, whereas holding monetary liabilities leads to a gain in purchasing power. One of the principal objectives of restatement is to measure this net gain or loss.

Monetary items held at the balance sheet date do not need to be restated if the balance sheet date is also the same selected to measure purchase-power equivalents. They are automatically stated in constant dollars. Alternatively, if the average for the year dollar were selected for this restatement basis, these year-end balances would have to be restated to their mid-year purchasing-power equivalents. Similarly, monetary items reported in earlier-period balance sheets would have to be restated to this base-period equivalent. The Cruzeiro Corporation example presented in **Appendix A** demonstrates this restatement process and the calculation of monetary gains and losses.

Nonmonetary items are restated to the current equivalent of the purchasing power expended or received at the time they were recorded originally in the company's books. This is done by multiplying the item's historical-dollar cost by the price-level index at the time selected to measure constant-dollar equivalents divided by the price-level index at the time of the original transaction. The difference in the amounts shown for nonmonetary assets on the historical-cost–based statements and the constant-dollar statements is due entirely to a change in the measuring unit from historical cost to constant dollars. No actual profit or loss results from this process. The adjustment simply restates the original dollars involved in the transaction in terms of the constant dollars' purchasing-power equivalent. Restatement of nonmonetary items is also illustrated in **Appendix A.**

---

[1]A monetary asset is money or a claim to receive a sum of money the amount of which is fixed or determined without reference to future prices of specific goods or resources. A monetary liability is an obligation to pay a sum of money the amount of which is fixed or determinable without reference to future prices of specific goods or services.

Current-cost/constant-dollar adjustments are the third kind of modification managers make to historical-cost financial measurements during periods of high inflation. As its name implies, this method combines the current-cost and constant-dollar approaches. It is used to restate comparative current-cost statements to a constant-dollar basis. This is done by selecting one of the current-cost statements as the equivalent purchasing power base and then adjusting each item in the other current-cost statements to that base.

The current-cost/constant-dollar approach to measuring real performance reflects the belief of some managers that a business does not increase its real profits unless its change in current-cost profits exceeds the general rate of inflation.

For example, assume current-cost income statements for the last three years are presented, the inflation rate has been 10 percent per year over the period, and the most recent statement is selected as the purchasing power equivalent base. To adjust the current-cost statement for the most recent prior year to a current year's constant-dollar equivalent, one would multiply each item in the statement by 1.1, the rate of inflation between the two years (1.1×1.0). Similarly, the statement items for the year two years prior would be multiplied by 1.21 ($1.1 \times 1.1 \times 1.0$).

Illustration 3 shows how current-cost income statements are restated to a current-cost/constant-dollar basis. The assumed general rate of inflation during the period covered by the illustration is 10 percent per year. The 1993 and 1994 current-cost statements are restated to their 1995 purchasing-power equivalent simply by multiplying the statement amounts by the rate of inflation from the period covered by the statement to the base period. The 1995 current cost/nominal cost does not need to be restated since it is the base-period statement. The same procedure is used to restate comparative current-cost/nominal-cost balance sheets to a current-cost/constant-dollar basis.

A comparison of the 1994 and 1995 nominal and general-inflation–adjusted current-cost statements highlights the advantage of current-cost/constant-dollar state-

---

ILLUSTRATION 3   Current-Cost/Constant-Dollar Income Statement Restatement Example (millions)

	1993			1994			1995
	Current Cost/ Nominal Cost		Current Cost/ Constant Dollar	Current Cost/ Nominal Cost		Current Cost/ Constant Dollar	Current Cost/ Nominal Cost
Sales	$100	× 1.21[a] =	$121	$120	× 1.1 =	$133	$120
Cost of sales	80	× 1.21 =	97	96	× 1.1 =	106	106
	20		24	24		27	27
Taxes	15	× 1.21 =	18	18	× 1.1 =	20	18
Net income	$ 5		$ 6	$ 6		$ 7	$ 6

[a](1.10×1.10).

ments for evaluating corporate performance over time. The 1994 and 1995 current-cost/nominal-cost statements indicate that 1994 and 1995 profits were the same ($6 million). In contrast, the current-cost/constant-dollar statements for the same two years indicate that the 1995 profits ($6 million) declined from their real 1994 level ($7 million). This real profit decline reflects the fact that the 1995 nominal current-cost profits of $6 million were equivalent to more purchasing power than the 1994 $6 million profit.

Internal Measurements

Unless inflation rates are high, most managers do not use inflation accounting for internal management purposes. Among those few companies adjusting internal financial statements for changing prices, the current-cost approach to measuring managerial performance is preferred, primarily because it reflects the specific inventory and productive asset cost inflation the managers must cope with in their particular businesses. Also, in most situations it is relatively easy to apply.

The constant-dollar approach may be used if the current-cost method is not applicable, as is true for financial institutions that have few physical assets, or is difficult to apply, as would be true for a timber company with millions of acres of land and trees to value. Other managers prefer the constant-dollar method because they think it gives a more comprehensive picture than the current-cost approach of the impact of inflation on their company's resources, obligations, and operations.

The current-cost/constant-dollar approach is the least popular of the three, primarily because it is not well understood. Those few companies that use this method believe it is superior to the other two approaches because it reflects, over time, the effects of both specific and general price changes on their businesses.

Irrespective of which method they use, those companies that use price-change data internally believe it helps managers think in real terms and this in turn leads to better inflation management practices.

Accounting Requirements

Companies' primary financial statements are prepared initially in terms of historical costs. These statements assume that the dollar is a constant unit of measure. Inasmuch as the amounts shown in the statements result from many transactions occurring at different times, however, their purchasing power equivalents will not be the same if significant rates of inflation have occurred over the recording period. Also, the expenses charged for the consumption of inventories and productive assets may not reflect current replacement costs.

In countries with extreme inflation, it is generally agreed that it is desirable to restate historical-cost–based statements to some basis that reflects the impact on the reporting company of specific price changes and general inflation. In the United States, however, until the late 1970s inflation rates had been relatively low, and there was little support for proposals that financial statements be restated to reflect changing prices. As a result, the practice was not to adjust statements, although a few companies did voluntarily publish supplemental statements showing the impact of inflation on their businesses.

The above-average inflation during the late 1970s changed the situation. In 1979, the FASB in FASB Statement No. 33 required certain large, publicly traded companies to publish supplementary financial-statement data adjusted for changes in the purchasing power of the dollar as measured by changes in the Consumer Price Index for All Urban Consumers (CPI-U) and in the specific prices of the company's inventories and productive assets.

FASB Statement No. 33 was experimental. In 1985 the FASB reviewed this experiment and decided in FASB Statement No. 82 to amend FASB Statement No. 33 by dropping the general requirement to adjust supplemental statements for general-purchasing-power changes for those companies that present current cost/constant-dollar supplement statements. Next, in 1985, in FASB Statement No. 89, the FASB dropped the requirement that certain companies disclose current cost–constant purchasing power information.

Real Analysis

As might be expected, the usefulness of inflation-adjusted statements increases significantly during periods of high inflation. Typically, the inflation-adjusted data prepared using the current-cost/constant-dollar method are the most useful if growth rates are important to an analysis. If a single year is the focus of attention, current-cost data are preferred.

Not every company publishes inflation-adjusted data. In these cases, the statement users must develop their own estimated inflation adjusted statements from the data in the company's historical-cost statements. This can be done by using the constant-dollar method, illustrated in **Appendix A,** and estimates of the company's average fixed-asset and inventory ages.

The average age of a fixed asset can be estimated by dividing the most recent period's annual depreciation expense into the accumulated historical-cost depreciation balance. For example, if the annual depreciation expense is $5 million and accumulated depreciation expense is $50 million, the estimated average age of the plant is 10 years. If the general rate of inflation had been 300 percent over the last 10 years, the estimated constant-dollar equivalent of the $5 million historical-cost depreciation expense would be $15 million ($5 million × 3.0).

The estimated age of an inventory is its turnover period divided by two. For example, if a company's inventory turns over every six months (a turnover ratio of two times), the average age of its inventory is three months. If the year-end dollar is the purchasing-power base, the ending inventory will have to be restated for the inflation during the last three months of the year. This approach assumes a constant production rate.

The estimated constant-dollar statements users are able to develop using the method in Appendix A and asset-age approximations will be crude, but will be the best that can be achieved under the circumstances.

The principal value of price-change financial-statement data for statement users is that it allows them to determine how well companies are coping with inflation. These statements not only show the absolute real values of the various balances, they also provide inflation-adjusted data to compute the significant financial ratios, such as return on investment, dividend payout, and net income percentage, as well as the growth rates of net income, sales and dividends per share. For evaluation purposes, these real ratio values and growth rates should be compared with the company's performance during periods of low inflation and the most recent real ratio values and growth rates of comparable companies.

How to deal with net monetary gains or losses in financial statements is a controversial topic. Some statement users evaluating a company's ability to cope with inflation include net monetary gains and losses in price-change adjusted income. They believe that net monetary losses should be included in income because they represent a measurable loss to stockholders. Also, they believe that including in income interest earned on monetary assets without recognizing the purchasing-power losses on these assets that the inflation component of the interest is supposed to compensate creditors for incurring leads to an overstatement of income.

For the opposite reasons, some analysts include monetary gains in income. It is argued that net monetary gains benefit the stockholders. Also, they should be included in the income of net borrowers to offset the high interest rates creditors charge to compensate for the purchasing-power losses on their loans. Charging the debtor with the high interest rates and failing to give the debtor credit for a net purchasing-power gain ignores, it is claimed, the economic reality of the situation.

Those who do not include net monetary gains or losses in price change income argue that these are noncash items, and as such, do not improve a company's ability to cope with inflation. Furthermore, to include net monetary gains in income is potentially misleading. As an example, they cite the near-bankrupt company with excessive debt that may appear to be profitable simply because of its large monetary gains.

Irrespective of how net monetary gains and losses are treated for purposes of income management and financial analysis, statement users should not ignore them. For example, a large purchasing-power loss on a net monetary assets position that is not recovered through interest income or product pricing is usually a good indication that a company is having problems coping with inflation.

During periods of high inflation, the cost of productive assets may rise beyond the ability of some companies to finance replacement of their obsolete and worn-out assets. These companies may show high nominal profits because their depreciation charges are low in relation to their inflating revenue, but in reality they are falling behind their competitors by not buying more advanced, cost-effective productive assets.

Three simple ratios can be used to gauge whether a company is replacing its productive assets. The ratio of historical-cost depreciation to accumulated historical-cost depreciation can be used to approximate the average age in years of a company's depreciable assets. If this period is lengthening, the company may be slowing down its asset replacement. The ratio of historical-cost depreciation to current-cost depreciation and the ratio of capital expenditures for productive depreciable assets to current-cost depreciation over the same period as the expenditures are made can also be used for this purpose. In the latter two tests, a ratio of less than one may indicate inadequate asset-replacement expenditures.

Illiquidity is a major financial and operating problem for most corporations during prolonged periods of high inflation. This occurs because customers slow down payments, vendors demand faster payment, the costs of doing business often rise faster than selling prices increase, inventory investments rise, and the cost of credit increases significantly. Simple ratios, such as accounts receivables-to-sales, inventory turnover, payables-to-purchases, gross margin-to-sales, and fixed charges-to-operating income before fixed charges, using both nominal-dollar and current cost-statement data, can be employed to develop an understanding of a company's liquidity trends. In addition, comparative cash flow statements restated to their purchasing power flow equivalents can be very rewarding. These will show how well a company is able to finance its operations and asset replacements out of current operating cash flows, as well as the extent to which it is relying on outside financing. A trend toward increased reliance on expensive outside financing, coupled with a slowdown in productive depreciable asset replacement, should be interpreted as a sign of increasing inability to cope with inflation.

Controversial Method

To the extent that one approach to price-change accounting is favored over the other, current-cost accounting tends to have more support than constant-dollar accounting, but it is nevertheless a very controversial accounting method. Many who oppose current-cost accounting do so because they see it as a major step toward current-value accounting, which they oppose. Some claim current-cost accounting is subjective and open to income manipulation and as such can lead to unreliable and misleading income figures. Others believe that current-cost calculations fail to capture management's options when replacing assets.

Despite the many criticisms of price-change accounting, in 1986 the FASB decided in FASB Statement No. 89 to encourage current-cost supplemental disclosures. This was done in the belief that should the U.S. economy once again experience high rates of inflation, statement users and business managements would be well served by having in place an agreed-upon approach to making price-change–adjusted financial data readily available.

Appendix A

Cruzeiro Corporation Example

The unadjusted statements in local currency (LC$) of the Cruzeiro Corporation, a Latin American company in a highly inflationary economy, are presented in **Illustrations A–1** and **A–2.** They will be used to illustrate the full range of techniques for adjusting for general-price-level changes. This same approach would be used by a U.S. corporation preparing constant dollar statements. The general approach would be used also by a statement user trying to recast a company's historical-cost statements to a price change basis.

The following price index for the period 1985–1995 reflects the changes in the government's year-end wholesale price index. To speed up the restatement of past years to 1995 purchasing power equivalents, the index has been restated to show 1995 as the base year (1.0 = base period).

This restatement is achieved by dividing the price-level index for 1995 by the price-level index for the past year. For example, the price-level index for 1995 (1252) divided by the price-level index for 1994 (864) gives a factor of 1.45. These factors will be used to adjust the company's statements to a common purchasing-power equivalent.

December	Price Index	Factor
1995	1,252.0	1.00
1994	864.1	1.45
1993	566.5	2.21
1992	420.1	2.98
1991	309.9	4.04
1990	228.5	5.48
1989	220.0	5.69
1988	174.9	7.16
1987	150.3	8.33
1986	123.2	10.16
1985	100.0	12.52

The price-level factors for the last four months of 1994 and 1995 are:

	1994	1995
September	1.63	1.17
October	1.57	1.13
November	1.50	1.06
December	1.45	1.00

Illustration A–1   Cruzeiro Corporation—Comparative Balance Sheets as of December 31, 1994 and 1995

Assets	1994	1995	Liabilities	1994	1995
Cash	LC$ 10	LC$ 20	Accounts payable	LC$ 60	LC$ 92
Accounts receivable	100	150			
Inventory	120	185			
Plant and equipment (at cost)	260	280	Stockholders' equity:		
Less accumulated depreciation	(112)	(138)	Common stock	200	200
			Retained earnings	118	205
Total	LC$378	LC$497	Total	LC$378	LC$497

The company's unadjusted balance sheet at the beginning (December 31, 1994) and at the end (December 31, 1995) of calendar-year 1995 are not comparable, because the units of measurement in these balances are local currency of different dates and therefore of different purchasing power. To make these balance sheets comparable, we must adjust them to a common unit of measurement, namely, the local currency as of December 31, 1995.

Monetary assets and liabilities at the end of 1995 are already stated in local-currency purchasing power at the closing balance sheet date. The monetary assets and liabilities at the beginning of the year must be restated in year-end local currency, however, so that they may be compared with year-end balance-sheet figures. The restatement of December 31, 1994 monetary assets and liabilities is shown in **Illustration A–3**. The adjustment factor of 1.45 is based on the 45 percent increase in the general price level that occurred between December 31, 1994 and December 31, 1995.

The company's inventories are stated at their local currency cost at time of purchase. To make the beginning and year-end inventory figures comparable, it is necessary to restate them in end-of-year local currency. Assuming that inventories are valued by the first-in, first-out (FIFO) method and that they represent purchases made during the last months of each year, their restatement to the December 31, 1995 price level is accomplished as shown in **Illustration A–4**. The adjustment factors applied are based on increases in the price level from the date of purchase to December 31, 1995, as shown by the monthly price-level index.

Typically, the greatest distortion due to inflation is found in the property, plant, and equipment accounts. To adjust the property accounts and the related reserves for depreciation to the end-of-year price level, it is necessary first to analyze the accounts by dates of acquisition. In this example, we will assume all acquisitions were made at year-end for cash. The appropriate restatement factors are then applied to the cost and reserve balances as shown in **Illustration A–5**. Combining the above price-level adjustments with these calculations, the adjusted balance sheets as shown in **Illustration A–6**.

In addition, the 1995 cost of goods sold must be restated to year-end December 31, 1995 cruzeiros:

ILLUSTRATION A–2   Cruzeiro Corporation 1995 Income Statement

Sales	LC$900
Cost of goods sold	690
Gross margin	210
Depreciation	26
Other expenses	97
Net income	LC$ 87

ILLUSTRATION A–3   Net Monetary Assets

	Before Adjustment	Factor	After Adjustment
Cash	LC$10	1.45	LC$14
Receivables	100	1.45	145
Accounts payable	(60)	1.45	(87)
Net monetary assets	LC$50		LC$72

	Before Adjustment	Adjustment Factor	After Adjustment
Opening inventory	LC$120	(See Illustration A–4)	LC$180
Purchases	755	1.225	925
Closing inventory	(185)	(See Illustration A–4)	(199)
Cost of goods sold	LC$690		LC$907

ILLUSTRATION A–4   Inventories

	Before Adjustment	Adjustment Factors	After Adjustment
December 31, 1994 Balance			
Purchases			
October 1994	LC\$ 30	1.57	LC\$ 47
November 1994	40	1.50	60
December 1994...................	50	1.45	73
Year-end inventory	LC\$120		LC\$180
December 31, 1995 Balance			
Purchases			
September 1995	LC\$ 25	1.17	LC\$ 29
October 1995	45	1.13	51
November 1995	55	1.06	58
December 1995...................	60	1.00	60
Year-end inventory	LC\$185		LC\$199

ILLUSTRATION A–5   Plant and Equipment

	Before Adjustment		Adjustment Factor	After Adjustment	
	Cost	Depreciation		Cost	Depreciation
December 31, 1994 Balance					
Investments					
1989	LC\$180	LC\$ 90	5.69	LC\$1,024	LC\$512
1990	50	20	5.48	274	110
1993	20	2	2.21	44	4
1994	10	—	1.45	14	4
Plant and equipment	LC\$260	LC\$112		LC\$1,256	LC\$626
December 31, 1995 Balance					
Investments					
1989	LC\$180	LC\$108	5.69	LC\$1,024	LC\$614
1990	50	25	5.48	274	137
1993	20	4	2.21	44	9
1994	10	1	1.45	14	1
1995	20[a]	—	1.00	20	—
Plant and equipment	LC\$280	LC\$138		LC\$1,376	LC\$761

[a]Purchased December 31, 1995.

ILLUSTRATION A–6   **Comparative Balance Sheets, December 31, 1994 and 1995**

	Before Adjustment		After Adjustment	
	1994	*1995*	*1994*	*1995*
Cash.................................	LC$ 10	LC$ 20	LC$ 14	LC$ 20
Accounts receivable	100	150	145	150
Accounts payable	(60)	(92)	(87)	(92)
Net monetary assets	50	78	72	78
Inventory	120	185	180	199
Plant & equipment (at cost)	260	280	1,356	1,376
Less accumulated depreciation	(112)	(138)	(626)	(761)
Stockholders' equity	LC$318	LC$405	LC$982	LC$891
Reconciliation of stockholders' equity, beginning of year	—	318	—	902
Net income	—	87	—	(91)[a]
End of year	—	LC$405	—	LC$981

[a]Assume for the moment that this is a balancing figure. Derivation and proof are presented in **Illustration A–8**.

To simplify our calculations, purchases are assumed to be made evenly throughout the year. They have been adjusted by the average adjustment factor for the year $(1.45 + 1)/2 = 1.225$.

For the sake of convenience, 1995 sales and other expenses are also adjusted for the average adjustment factor for the year (this implicitly assumes these items were also evenly distributed throughout the year):

	Before Adjustment	*Adjustment Factor*	*After Adjustment*
Sales	LC$900	1.225	LC$1,103
Other expenses	97	1.225	119

To adjust for 1995 income statement to year-end 1995 local currency, we need to restate the 1995 depreciation expense. Using the adjusted data determined above, the 1995 depreciation expenses is:

	Before Adjustment	*After Adjustment*
Cost of plant and equipment at December 31, 1995 (see **Illustration A–5**)	LC$280	LC$1,376
Less December 31, 1995 addition not depreciated....................	20	20
Total	LC$260	LC$1,356
1995 depreciation (at 10% rate)	LC$ 26	LC$ 135

To complete the adjustment of the financial statements to common year-end local currency, it is necessary to calculate the loss for the year on the monetary items, and to restate each item in the conventional income statement.

Monetary assets (such as cash, receivables, and deposits) and liabilities (such as bank loans and accounts payable), are stated in fixed local-currency amounts. As the price level rises, monetary assets lose purchasing power, and liabilities become payable in local currency of decreasing purchasing power. The excess of monetary assets over liabilities represents the "exposure to inflation." The inflation loss may be computed on the basis of the average "exposure to inflation," as shown in **Illustration A–7**.

ILLUSTRATION A–7   Exposure to Inflation

| | Balance | |
	Beginning of Year	End of Year
Cash	LC$10	LC$20
Receivables	100	150
Accounts payable	(60)	(92)
	LC$50	LC$78
Add: Cash used to acquire property on December 31, 1995	—	20
	LC$50	LC$98

Average exposure, $\dfrac{50 + 98}{2}$ . . . .   LC$74

Loss on exposure to 45% inflation 74 × 0.45 . . . .   LC$33

The income statement before and after the price-level adjustments explained above is summarized in **Illustration**

A–8. In this example, the results of operations reported in accordance with generally accepted accounting principles indicated a profit, but a loss after general price-level adjustments. In addition, the balance sheet financial ratios are significantly different before and after the general-price-level adjustments are made.

ILLUSTRATION A–8   1995 Income Statement

	Before Adjustment	After Adjustment
Sales	LC$900	LC$1,103
Cost of goods sold	690	907
Gross margin	LC$210	LC$ 196
Depreciation	26	135
Other expenses	97	119
Loss on net monetary assets	—	33
Net income (loss)	LC$ 87	LC$ (91)

Discount Mart

Discount Mart was a two-year-old merchandising firm. During this period, the price-level index changed as follows:

Opening of business	150
First year, average	160
First year, end	175
Second year, average	190
Second year, end	200

The company business was such that all of its revenues and expenses were earned or incurred fairly evenly throughout the year. The only exceptions to this generalization were depreciation and that portion of the merchandise sold represented by the beginning inventory. Inventory was priced on a first-in, first-out basis. Dividends were declared and paid at the end of each year.

The company's plant and equipment was acquired on the first day of business and at the end of the first year. All of the plant and equipment was depreciated on a straight-line basis over a 10-year life. The land on which the plant was located was held under a long-term lease agreement.

At the beginning of the company's second year, management paid off in cash $50,000 of the company's $350,000 long-term liabilities. The remaining $300,000 was converted to capital stock.

Exhibit 1 presents the company's income statements on an historical basis for each of its first two years of operations. **Exhibit 2** shows the unadjusted statement of

Professor David F. Hawkins prepared this case as the basis for class discussion rather than to illustrate either effective or ineffective handling of an administrative situation.

EXHIBIT 1 **Discount Mart—Comparative Income Statement—Historical Basis (in thousands)**

	Year 1	Year 2
Sales	$800	$1,000
Operating expenses:		
Cost of goods sold	$470	$ 600
Depreciation.	30	40
Other expenses (including income tax)	280	300
Total operating expenses	$780	$ 940
Net profit from operations	$ 20	$ 60

EXHIBIT 2 **Discount Mart—Comparative Statement of Retained Earnings— Historical Basis (in thousands)**

	Year 1	Year 2
Retained earnings, beginning of year.	—	$15
Net profit from operations	$20	60
Total	$20	$75
Dividends to stockholders.	5	10
Retained earnings, end of year	$15	$65

retained earnings for the same periods. Discount Mart's balance sheets at the opening of business and at the end of each year's operations are presented in **Exhibit 3.**

At the end of the second year's operations, the management wanted the company's statements restated in current dollars to determine whether or not the company had experienced a monetary gain or loss to date. Management also wanted to know how much of this accumulated gain or loss related to the second year of operation.

EXHIBIT 3   **Discount Mart—Comparative Statement of Financial Position—Historical Basis (in thousands)**

	Opening of Business	End of Year 1	End of Year 2
Assets			
Cash, receivables, and other monetary items	$200	$195	$235
Inventories.	250	300	200
Plant and equipment.	300	400	400
Less: Accumulated depreciation	—	(30)	(70)
Total assets	$750	$865	$765
Liabilities and Stockholders' Equity			
Liabilities:			
Current liabilities	$100	$200	$100
Long-term liabilities	350	350	—
Total liabilities	$450	$550	$100
Stockholders' equity:			
Capital stock	$300	$300	$600
Retained earnings	—	15	65
Total stockholders' equity	$300	$315	$665
Total liabilities and stockholders' equity	$750	$865	$765

Question

Restate the company's statements for its first two years' operations in current dollars. (Note: If you are using the Cruzeiro Corporation example as a guide, the example does not include long-term liabilities whereas the Discount Mart case does.)

CASE
15-2

Teléfonos De México, S.A. de C.V.

In mid-1991, the government of the United Mexican States prepared to sell, as part of a worldwide offering of Teléfonos de México, S.A. de C.V. ("Telmex") L Shares owned by the government, 40 million American Depository Shares ("ADSs") representing 800 million Telmex L Shares. The ADSs would be evidenced by American Depository Receipts ("ADRs"). The government, which formerly controlled Telmex, had acquired the L Shares in December 1990, when Telmex issued a dividend of 1.5 L Shares for each of its Series AA and A Shares. The L Shares have the same rights as AA and A Shares, except that L Shares vote only in limited circumstances.

Prior to the government's offering, there had been no public market in the United States or elsewhere for the L Share ADSs or the L Shares. The A Shares were listed on the Bolsa Mexicana de Valores ("Mexican Stock Exchange") and ADSs, each representing one A Share, were quoted on the NASDAQ National List. It was anticipated that the initial public offering price for the L Share ADSs would be determined by reference to the market price for the A Shares and A Share ADSs.

While the proposed Telmex ADS offering created considerable interest and enthusiasm among U.S. investors, one concern some U.S. investors had was the possible adverse impact on Telmex of a continuation of Mexico's high inflation rate.

The Telmex case focuses on this concern. In particular, it deals with the Mexican inflation-related questions raised by a potential initial public offer buyer of the L Share ADSs, Charles Johnson, the manager of the Greentree Insurance Company's equity investment group.

After quickly reviewing the Telmex L Share ADS prospectus, Johnson raised the following questions:

- From the point of view of accounting theory, accounting practice, and communication of economic reality, how sound is Telmex's inflation accounting?

Professor David F. Hawkins prepared this case as the basis for class discussion rather than to illustrate either effective or ineffective handling of an administrative situation.

- What can potential investors learn about Telmex's ability to cope with inflation from a detailed analysis of Telmex's financial statements and other prospectus disclosures?
- To what extent does Telmex cover its nominal peso cash needs for operating, investing, and financing purposes from operations?

To help him answer these questions, Johnson had three members of his staff prepare memorandums which he intended to use as background material for a full equity investment group discussion of Telmex and Mexican inflation. The first memorandum was prepared by Cathy Foster, an investment officer with a strong accounting background. It covered Mexican inflation accounting **(Exhibit 1).** The second memorandum dealt with financial statement analysis in high inflation rate periods **(Exhibit 2).** It was prepared by Ted Hightower, a financial analyst, based on his prior experience as a manager of a Brazilian subsidiary of a major U.S. corporation. The third memorandum was prepared by Andrew Peters. It summarized information disclosed in the Telmex L Share ADS prospectus that Peters believed was relevant to Johnson's inflation concerns **(Exhibit 3).**

Question

Answer the questions raised by Johnson (see case).

EXHIBIT 1   Foster Memorandum

To: Charles Johnson
From: Cathy Foster
Re: MEASURING MEXICAN PESO
        PROFITS

The principal accounting difficulty encountered by non-Mexican readers of Mexican financial statements is the various unfamiliar price-change adjustments made to eliminate the distorting effects of inflation on the financial statement data. This memo assumes the reader is familiar with the fundamental concepts and practices of price-change accounting.

Current Cost/Constant Peso

The primary financial statements of Mexican companies are restated for the effects of changing prices. Prior to 1990, most restatements were limited to current cost adjustments for inventories, depreciable assets, and their related cost of goods sold

and depreciation expenses. Beginning in 1990, companies adopted the current cost/constant peso restatement approach.

Statement B-10

The guidelines for accounting for the effects of inflation on financial statements issued by Mexican companies are set forth in Statement B-10, as amended, issued by the Instituto Mexicano de Contodores Publicos ("IMCP"). Statement B-10, as amended, requires that:

- All financial statements be stated in pesos of purchasing power at the close of the most recent period.
- The company's net purchasing power gains or losses on monetary items be measured and included in the determination of the company's total financing costs.

EXHIBIT 1 (continued)

- Comparative prior-period financial statements be restated to the purchasing-power equivalent of the peso at the close of the most recent period; i.e., the last month of the current financial statement.
- Plant, property, and equipment, as well as construction in progress, be restated to its current cost using the specific cost method.
- Depreciation be based on the current cost of the related assets.
- The gain or loss from holding nonmonetary assets be included in owners' equity. The gain or loss is measured by the net difference between a fixed asset's restatement using specific prices and its restatement using the National Consumer Price Index.
- Investments in non-consolidated companies be recorded using the equity method based on the restated financial statements of the investee company.
- A provision for overvaluation of the peso, based on the economic theory of exchange rates known as technical parity, be included in the measurement of total financing costs.
- The specific cost method be used to measure inventories and their related cost of goods sold expense.
- The statement of financial position be stated in pesos of purchasing power as of the date of the most recent statement of financial position.
- Stockholders' equity accounts be restated to their constant purchasing power values.

Current Cost

Mexican companies determine the current cost of an asset by either direct appraisal or by the application of price indices appropriate for the particular asset to its original cost. The current cost of inventory is the cost to replace it as of the balance sheet date. The current cost of property, plant, and equipment is the cost as of the balance sheet date to acquire the same service potential as embodied by the asset. Cost of goods sold and depreciation expense reflect the current cost of the related asset as of the expense transaction date.

Total Financing Costs

The total net financing costs of Mexican companies consist of three elements: net interest expense, monetary gains and losses, and exchange loss.

Monetary Gains and Losses

The various asset and liability accounts shown on balance sheets can be divided into two categories—monetary and non-monetary items. Under Mexican accounting, the effect of the general inflation rate on a company's net monetary assets or liabilities during the accounting period is included in income along with net interest expense as a component of the company's net financing costs.

Monetary assets are money or a claim to receive a sum of money, the amount of which is fixed or determinable without reference to future prices of specific goods or services. Holding monetary assets during periods of inflation leads to purchasing power losses, since a peso will buy fewer goods and services at the end of the accounting period than at the beginning.

Monetary liabilities are obligations to pay a sum of money, the amount of which is fixed or determinable without reference to future prices of specific goods and services. During periods of inflation, monetary liabilities result in purchasing power gains, since the obligations are extinguished with pesos representing less purchasing power than the original peso measurement of the obligations.

Net monetary gains or losses are included as an element of financing cost to recognize that interest earned on monetary assets and interest paid on monetary liabilities include compensation to the lender for loss of purchasing power. Periodic net monetary gain or loss is determined by the following calculation:

$$\text{Monetary Gain/Loss} = \frac{\text{Average Net Monetary Position}}{\times \text{Period's Inflation Rate}}$$

The net monetary gain or loss for an accounting period is the sum of the monthly monetary gains and losses determined by this calculation.

There are caps and constraints on how much of a net monetary gain for a period may be credited to income. The limit is the sum of the interest income and expense and exchange fluctuation provisions. If the sum of these three items is a credit to income, no net monetary gains can be included in income. Furthermore, if the amount of the restatement of non-monetary assets for a period is negative (see holding gains and losses below), a net monetary gain is reduced by the negative amount. Any excess monetary gain remaining after the above limitations and requirements are applied is included directly in stockholders' equity.

Exhibit 1   (continued)

Technical Parity Adjustment

Mexican GAAP requires all exchange losses to be included in income. In certain circumstances, a portion of the recorded exchange differences is determined based on the economic theory of exchange rates known as technical parity. Any provision for exchange losses determined under this Mexican GAAP measurement procedure is included along with net interest expense and net monetary gains and losses as a third element of total financing costs. This exchange loss calculation is only applicable when the peso is overvalued based on the technical parity theory, and the reporting company has a net foreign currency liability position.

Technical parity is based on the economic theory that in the medium and long run, exchange rates tend to reflect the comparative relationship of the purchasing power of each currency in its own country. Mexican economists have determined that in 1977 the peso market rate of exchange for the U.S. dollar was equal to the technical parity between the two currencies. The average 1977 peso–dollar exchange rate was P22.58 to U.S. $1.00. Based on this conclusion, the formula for calculating technical parity at any point in time is:

$$\text{Technical Parity} = \text{P22.58} \times \frac{\substack{\text{\% Increase in Mexican} \\ \text{General Inflation Rate} \\ \text{Over 1977 Average}}}{\substack{\text{\% Increase in U.S.} \\ \text{Consumer Price Index} \\ \text{Over 1977 Average}}}$$

If the peso's market rate versus the U.S. dollar is below technical parity, the peso is considered to be overvalued. Furthermore, the expectation is that eventually the market rate will move toward technical parity. Therefore, if a company has net foreign currency liabilities and the peso is overvalued, a provision for the difference between the net position measured at the technical and market rates is recorded to reflect the expectation that the net position will most probably be settled in the future at the technical parity rate. The offsetting entry to this income charge is a contingent liability listed on the balance sheet as a non-current liability.

Technical parity between the peso and currencies other than the U.S. dollar is calculated by comparing the peso–U.S. dollar relationship and the other currency.

**Gains or Losses From Holding
Non-Monetary Assets**

In the case of non-monetary assets, a gain or loss for each accounting period is computed and included in owners' equity. This so-called "holding gain or loss" is the difference in the assets restated peso balance calculated using specific prices and using the general inflation rate. A holding gain results when an asset balance determined by the specific price method exceeds the restated asset balance based on general price movements. A holding loss occurs when the reverse is the case.

Constant Peso Accounting

Constant peso accounting is a method of accounting that states all historical peso prices in the same units of general purchasing power as measured by the Mexican National Consumer Price Index ("NCPI"), published by the Bank of Mexico. As of January 1, 1991, Bulletin B-10 requires restatement of all comparative financial statements to constant pesos as of the date of the most recent comparative balance sheet presented. Prior to this date, in comparative statement presentations each period's financial statements were expressed in terms of that period's ending peso purchasing power. No restatement of earlier statements was made for the period-to-period changes in the purchasing power of the peso.

The effect of the January 1, 1990 amendment to Bulletin B-10 was that beginning in 1990 annual reports, all prior-year financial statements presented for comparative purposes in 1990 annual reports had to be restated to the December 31, 1990 purchasing power of the peso. Since, for example, the earlier annual statements were already expressed in terms of each year's respective year-end peso purchasing power, the restatement to December 31, 1990 peso purchasing power was accomplished by multiplying each of the earlier year's financial statement data by the following restatement factor:

$$\frac{\text{Restatement}}{\text{Factor}} = \frac{\text{December 31, 1990 NCPI}}{\substack{\text{December 31 NCPI of Earlier} \\ \text{Statement's Annual Period}}}$$

Exhibit 1   (continued)

The NCPI at the respective dates used to restate the prior three years' statements to their equivalent December 31, 1990 peso purchasing power was as follows:

December 31, 1987	P10,647.2
December 31, 1988	16,147.3
December 31, 1989	19,327.9
December 31, 1990	25,112.7

Based on these NCPI levels, the restatement factors are:

December 31, 1990	1.00
December 31, 1989	1.30
December 31, 1988	1.56
December 31, 1987	2.36

Mexican accounting authorities do not consider it necessary or desirable to present information in nominal prices.

Shareholders' Equity

Prior to January 1, 1990, it was the common practice of Mexican companies to report the various components of stockholders' equity at their historical nominal values, and to present as a combined total the various equity accounts' restatement amounts. Beginning on January 1, 1990, the restatement increments must be allocated to the appropriate equity account. As a result, each equity account is reported at its restated amount.

Statement of Changes in Financial Position

The Statement of Changes in Financial Position published by Mexican companies reflects changes in the purchasing power equivalent of a company's cash balances, rather than its nominal cash balances.

The preparation of the Mexican Statement starts with the period's opening and closing balance sheets stated in constant pesos. The end product is a Changes In Financial Position Statement using a format very similar to the typical U.S. Cash Flow Statement prepared using the indirect method. That is, the principal subdivisions of the statement present resources provided (used) by operating activities, resources provided (used) by financing activities and resources provided (used) by investment activities. Each of these three subdivisions shows the net purchasing power flows ("resources") related to the activity described. The sum of these three balances equals the change in the reporting company's cash balance expressed in constant pesos during the accounting period.

When comparative changes in financial position statements are presented, the various periods presented are stated in pesos of purchasing power as of the most recent balance sheet date.

The information included in this memorandum is based on information provided to me by a friend in Price Waterhouse's Mexico City office and a reading of Statement 10-B.

Exhibit 2   Hightower Memorandum

To: Charles Johnson
From: Ted Hightower
Re: FINANCIAL STATEMENT ANALYSIS
IN HIGH INFLATION RATE PERIODS

The fundamental issues, techniques, and focus of financial statement analysis during high and low inflation rate periods is very similar. The principal difference between high and low inflation rate period financial statement analysis is two questions not normally raised during low inflation rate periods. These two questions are:

- How effective is the company's management of purchasing power flows?
- How well is the company performing in real terms?

Asking and answering these two questions is important since during periods of high inflation rates, the objective of management should be to enhance the real value of stockholders' equity and the level of real dividends. This is a difficult challenge. Current cost/constant currency unit statements can be useful to financial statement users seeking to measure how likely managers are to accomplish these tasks.

Purchasing Power Management

One of the paradoxes of inflation is that while the economy has too much money circulating, nobody seems to have enough money. As a result, high inflation rates are usually accompanied by purchasing power generation problems for individuals, corporations, and governments.

There are two ways to evaluate corporate purchasing power management during high inflation rate periods. One is to assess a company's capacity to generate units of purchasing power. The other is to identify its ability to generate units of currency. Of the two considerations, the latter is the more important. Units of currency pay bills. In contrast, purchasing power gains may be unrealized and, as such, cannot be used to meet current obligations. On the other hand, purchasing power losses reduce a company's ability to acquire goods and services.

Real Performance

During periods of high inflation rates, it is important to distinguish between nominal and real growth rates when measuring growth or rate of change.

Nominal growth rates can be misleading. They include the effect of general price inflation and, as such, can lead to a false sense of progress. Changes in inflation rates distort changes in growth rates from period to period.

Real growth rates should be used to measure growth. Real growth rates are nominal growth rates with the influence of general price inflation eliminated. Real growth rates are reliable measures of change from one period to another, since changes in inflation rates do not distort the rate of growth.

Real data should be used when computing the standard performance ratios, such as return on assets, capital and sales.

Desirable Company Attributes

It is important that investors in high inflation rate economies identify those firms with strong inflation-coping ability. In my view, in the long run, these firms should be the best investments.

Such firms can be identified using two approaches. One is to look at past success measured in real terms, such as growth in current cost/constant currency net income. The other is to rate them in terms of their inflation-advantageous characteristics, such as ability to raise prices. Typically, companies that rate high in terms of inflation-advantageous characteristics will also produce superior real results.

The characteristics of companies that are best able to cope with inflation are:

- Ability, opportunity, and willingness to finance greenfield investments.
- Ability to pass inflation risk onto others.
- Competitors who cope well with inflation.
- Control over critical input resources and distribution systems.
- Expenditures for future development currently tax-deductible.
- High real asset investment turnover rates.
- High real margins and returns on capital.
- Low capital requirements.
- Low labor dependence.
- Low requirement for most rapidly-inflating resources.
- Modern capital assets.
- Pricing flexibility.
- Timely real financial and cost data available for management decision-making and control purposes.
- Unused borrowing capacity.

EXHIBIT 2   (continued)

At a minimum, three operating capabilities are required to cope successfully with inflation. These are the ability to maintain productive capacity, improve productivity, and raise prices. Current cost restatement can be very helpful in assessing a company's ability and likely commitment to maintaining productive capacity. This approach to accounting reflects a view of income that believes a company does not earn a profit until it has provided for the replacement of the productive capacity consumed during the accounting period. Current cost depreciation and cost of goods sold accounting measure capacity consumption and the cost to replace it at prices on the transaction date. Failure to earn profits after considering the current cost to replace productive assets consumed and a ratio of capital expenditures to current cost depreciation of less than one may indicate a company is having trouble coping with inflation and may be falling behind in maintaining its productive capacity. Loss of competitive position often follows this deteriorating situation.

During periods of inflation, the rate of inflation can be offset by improving the productivity of labor, other costs, and capital. Therefore, in assessing management's real performance, it is useful to identify how successful it has been in improving the productivity of people and capital. Productivity is measured by comparing measures of inputs to outputs. Statement users can get a sense of whether or not a company is improving its productivity by comparing over time such ratios as asset turnover ratios, sales per dollar of employee cost, sales per employee and gross margin percentages. The current cost of assets and cost of goods sold should be used when computing ratios involving these items. Sales should be adjusted to a common purchasing power basis in sales per employee ratio comparisons.

An ability to raise prices is typically indicated by a constant or improving real gross margin percentage.

Data Base Management

Investing in Telmex will create a data base management problem. During periods of inflation, the money units from one period to another are not comparable. Each period's money unit represents different levels of purchasing power. In order to eliminate the effect of inflation in measuring growth rates, as each period's financial statement data is released, it must be restated to a common purchasing power base. Restatement of quarterly data to a common purchasing base is also needed so that the annual data is the sum of the quarterly data.

There are three ways to handle the restatement requirement. The purchasing power base may be some past period. If this is the case, only the current data needs to be restated. The problem with this practice is that the data base information will not be the same as presented in a Mexican company's published financial statements, since the company must use the current period's purchasing power as its restatement base.

Another approach is to select the current period as the common purchasing power base. In this case, as each new period's financial statement data is released, the existing data base must be restated to its current period purchasing power equivalent. Rolling forward data in this fashion can be costly, but the company data will be comparable to the comparative data issued by the company in its most recent financial statements.

A third way is to restate each inflation-adjusted financial report as issued to some foreign currency equivalent. In the case of the U.S. investors, this is usually done by simply translating the foreign currency statements as they are issued into U.S. dollar using the U.S. dollar exchange rate at the balance sheet. The resulting dollar figures may distort a company's actual growth rates, since the exchange rate changes may not be moving at the same rate as the inflation. Offsetting this potential disadvantage is the fact that once statement data has been translated into U.S. dollars, it does not have to be restated in subsequent periods.

Exhibit 3

To: Charles Johnson
From: Andrew Peters
Re: INFLATION-RELATED PROSPECTUS
         INFORMATION

Teléfonos de México, S.A. de C.V. ("Telmex") is a corporation organized under the laws of the United Mexican States. A majority of its directors and all of its officers reside in Mexico, and all or a substantial portion of the assets of these persons and of the Company are located in Mexico. Telmex publishes its consolidated financial statements in Mexican pesos. Pursuant to generally accepted accounting principles in Mexico ("Mexican GAAP"), financial data for all periods in the Consolidated Financial Statements are restated in constant pesos as of December 31, 1990.

The Company

Telmex is currently the only licensed supplier of fixed-link public telecommunications service in Mexico. The Mexican telephone system is the eighteenth-largest national telephone system in the world based on the number of lines in service at year-end 1988. Telmex owns all public exchanges, the nationwide network of local telephone lines, and the principal public long-distance telephone transmission facilities. It also provides telephone-related services such as directory services and cellular mobile telephone services. Based on total assets at December 31, 1990, Telmex is the third-largest company in Mexico and the largest company listed on the Mexican Stock Exchange.

The company operates under the communications law and regulations of Mexico and a license agreement referred to as a "concession," granted by the Mexican Ministry of Communications and Transportation. In 1990, the regulatory regime applicable to the Company underwent substantial changes, including the elimination of excise taxes on telephone charges; rate increases for local service and domestic long-distance service and rate reductions for international long-distance service; the adoption of new regulations; and the amendment of the Company's concession. The amendment to the concession changed the method of rate regulation to allow the Company to set rates freely subject to an aggregate "price cap"; set requirements for line growth, expansion of rural service and quality of service; and defined the scope of competition in telephone services, including requiring Telmex to interconnect with any competing long-distance carriers beginning in August 1996.

The Government, which previously owned a majority of the Company's capital stock, announced in 1989 its intention to privatize the Company. On December 20, 1990, it sold all of the AA Shares, representing 20.4% of the capital stock of the Company but 51% of the full voting shares, to a trust for the benefit of the Controlling Shareholders. The Controlling Shareholders consist of (i) a group of Mexican investors who collectively own 51% of the AA Shares; (ii) Southwestern Bell International Holdings Corporation, a subsidiary of the publicly held U.S. communications company Southwestern Bell Corporation, which owns 24.5% of the AA Shares; and (iii) France Cables et Radio, S.A., a subsidiary of the French state-owned telecommunications agency France Télécom, which owns 24.5% of the AA shares. Of the AA Shares beneficially owned by Mexican investors, the majority are owned by Grupo Carso, S.A. de C.V. and Seguros de Mexico, S.A., both of which are controlled by Mr. Carlos Slim Helú. The terms of the trust through which the AA Shares are held restrict transfers of beneficial ownership of AA Shares and generally require that the AA Shares be voted as a block.

Properties

The principal properties of the Company consist of transmission plant, including outside plant and trunk lines, and exchange equipment. Of the net book value of Telmex's total plant, property and equipment at December 31, 1990 (excluding construction in progress), exchanges represented 44%, outside plant represented 27.4%, long-distance transmission equipment represented 13.5%, and buildings and real property represented 8.3%.

The Company has experienced problems of poor service and high maintenance and operating costs due to the poor condition of portions of its outside plant. It is seeking to address these problems through a program of replacement of outside plant coupled with stricter controls on construction quality.

Employees

Telmex is one of the largest non-governmental employers in Mexico. At December 31, 1990, it had 65,195 employees. The workforce grew by more than 8% each year from 1984 to 1988, but it grew less than 1% in 1989 and 3.3% in 1990. The Company expects the rate of growth of its workforce to remain below the levels that prevailed through 1988.

Exhibit 3   (continued)

The Telephone Workers' Union of Mexico represented approximately 64% of the Company's employees at December 31, 1990, and approximately 18% of its employees were members of other unions. Most management positions are held by non-union employees. The Company and the union negotiate a new collective labor agreement every two years.

Research and Development

The Company operates a research and development center employing 168 engineers, which develops applications of new technology to the Company's telephone system. Estimated expenditures on research and development for the years ended December 31, 1988, 1989, and 1990 were P6,373 million, P10,988 million, and P16,601 million respectively.

Competition

The 1990 amendments to the Concession contain various provisions designed to introduce competition in the provision of telecommunications ser- vices. Certain customers of Telmex have established private telephone and data transmission services, partly as a result of dissatisfaction with the quality and scope of services provided by Telmex. The Company's plan to develop services that are attractive to commercial customers is intended to meet these concerns. In cellular mobile telephone services, Telmex faces competition from the other concessionaires in each service region, which have agreed to cooperate with one another to provide nationwide service.

Market Price Information

The table below sets forth, for the periods indicated, the reported high and low sale prices for A Shares on the Mexican Stock Exchange and the high and low bid prices for A Share ADSs published by NASDAQ. Sales prices on the Mexican Stock Exchange have been translated into U.S. dollars at the free exchange rate on each of the respective dates of such quotations. The prices set forth below have not been adjusted to reflect the L Share Distribution.

	Mexican Stock Exchange				NASDAQ	
	Pesos per A Share		U.S. $ per A Share		U.S. $ per A Share ADS	
	High	*Low*	*High*	*Low*	*High*	*Low*
1989:						
1st quarter	830	650	0.34	0.28	0.34	0.25
2nd quarter	1,550	770	0.62	0.32	0.59	0.31
3rd quarter	2,260	1,250	0.87	0.50	0.88	0.50
4th quarter	2,440	1,830	0.91	0.69	0.91	0.63
1990:						
1st quarter	3,420	2,420	1.23	0.89	1.22	0.88
2nd quarter	5,300	3,290	1.87	1.18	1.84	1.16
3rd quarter	5,575	4,090	1.93	1.40	1.94	1.34
4th quarter	5,675	4,280	1.92	1.47	1.94	1.44
1991:						
1st quarter	7,825	4,440	2.61	1.50	2.69	1.47
2nd quarter through April 5	8,300	7,750	2.77	2.54	2.75	2.56

Dividends

Telmex has paid cash dividends on its AA Shares and A Shares each year since 1958. Dividends paid in 1966 through 1989 were 12 pesos per share in nominal terms, and dividends paid in 1990 were 18 pesos per share in nominal terms. The Company also declared stock dividends, of one share for every four outstanding shares, in each year from 1983 through 1987, and in 1990 it issued the L Shares as a stock dividend.

EXHIBIT 3   (continued)

The table below sets forth the nominal amount of dividends paid per share in each year indicated, adjusted to give retroactive effect to the L Share Distribution, in pesos and translated into U.S. dollars at the free exchange rate on each of the respective payment dates.

Year Ended December 31,	Pesos per Share	$ per Share
1986	4.80	0.0072
1987	4.80	0.0032
1988	4.80	0.0021
1989	4.80	0.0019
1990	7.20	0.0025

The Board of Directors of the Company has announced that it will propose that in 1991 the Company pay a cash dividend of 25 pesos per share from 1990 earnings to the holders of AA Shares, A Shares and L Shares.

Mexican Economy

During the 1980s, Mexico experienced periods of slow or negative growth, high inflation, large devaluations of the peso and limited availability of foreign exchange. Limited availability of foreign exchange required the Government and all public-sector Mexican entities, including Telmex, to restructure portions of their foreign-currency–denominated indebtedness to commercial banks. The Company continued to report earnings throughout the period, but a recurrence of any of these conditions could adversely affect the Company's financial condition and results of operations.

Exchange Rates

Under the Mexican exchange control system established in 1982, Mexican residents and companies are entitled to purchase foreign currencies for certain purposes at a controlled rate of exchange (the "Controlled Rate") that is set daily by the Mexican central bank, the Bank of Mexico. For all transactions to which the Controlled Rate does not apply, foreign currencies may also be purchased, if they are available, at the domestic free-market rate, which is generally higher than the Controlled Rate.

The following table sets forth, for the periods indicated, the period-end, average, high, and low Controlled Rate and free rate for the purchase of U.S. dollars, expressed in pesos per U.S. dollar.

Year Ended Dec. 31	Controlled Rate[1] Pesos				Free Rate[2] Pesos			
	Period End	Average[3]	High	Low	Period End	Average[3]	High	Low
1986	924	634	372	924	920	658	445	920
1987	2,210	1,427	924	2,210	2,260	1,474	920	2,300
1988	2,281	2,276	2,210	2,281	2,330	2,325	2,260	2,330
1989	2,647	2,479	2,281	2,647	2,692	2,526	2,330	2,692
1990	2,948	2,827	2,647	2,948	2,959	2,861	2,692	2,959
1991 through April 8 . . .	2,987	2,985	2,948	2,987	3,000	2,998	2,959	3,000

[1]Source: Bank of Mexico.

[2]Source: Banco Nacional de Mexico.

[3]Average of month-end rates.

Selected Consolidated Financial Data

The selected consolidated financial data set forth below have been derived from the Company's audited consolidated financial statements for each of the years in the five-year period ended December 31, 1990, which have been reported on by Coopers & Lybrand, independent public accountants. The selected data have been restated in constant pesos as of December 31, 1990.

Exhibit 3   (continued)

SUMMARY CONSOLIDATED FINANCIAL INFORMATION

The Company's consolidated financial statements are prepared in accordance with Mexican GAAP, which differs in significant respects from U.S. GAAP. See Note 12 to Consolidated Financial Statements. In accordance with Mexican GAAP rules on inflation accounting, the Company's consolidated financial statements recognize certain effects of inflation and restate data for prior periods in constant pesos as of December 31, 1990. See Note 2 to Consolidated Financial Statements. The effect of these inflation accounting principles has not been reversed in the reconciliation to U.S. GAAP. See Note 12 to Consolidated Financial Statements.

	Year ended December 31,					
	1986	*1987*	*1988*	*1989*	*1990*	*1990*
	(in billions of pesos and millions of U.S. dollars, except per share and per ADS data)					
Income Statement Data[1]:						
Mexican GAAP						
Operating revenues	P5,039	P5,786	P6,179	P7,842	11,313	$3,838
Operating income	1,941	2,061	1,772	2,622	4,084	1,385
Net income[2]	685	917	2,726	1,816	3,308	1,122
Net income per share	85	95	269	174	313	0.11
Net income per ADS	1,854	1,906	5,373	3,482	6,270	2.13
Dividends per share	40	17	8	7	8	0.00
Dividends per ADS	794	344	161	137	162	0.06
U.S. GAAP[3]						
Operating income	1,681	1,906	1,409	1,727	3,097	1,051
Net income before extraordinary item			1,983	606		
Extraordinary item[4]			826	430		
Net income[2]	685	870	2,809	1,036	2,751	933
Net income per share before extraordinary item			195	58		
Net income per share	85	90	277	99	261	0.09
Net income per ADS before extraordinary item			3,909	1,163		
Net income per ADS	1,856	1,807	5,537	1,987	5,214	1.77

EXHIBIT 3 (continued)

	December 31,					1990
	1986	1987	1988	1989	1990	1990
	(in billions of pesos and millions of U.S. dollars)					
Balance Sheet Data:						
Mexican GAAP						
Property, plant and equipment, net . .	P14,089	P15,063	P16,303	P18,242	P20,635	$7,000
Total assets	18,113	20,371	21,298	24,103	28,429	9,644
Deferred income[5]	114	2,010	2,321	2,952	3,494	1,185
Total long-term debt	7,389	7,175	4,602	4,508	5,587	1,895
Total stockholders' equity	8,542	8,889	11,741	14,284	16,318	5,536
U.S. GAAP[3]						
Total stockholders' equity	9,635	9,935	12,871	14,635	15,590	5,289

(1) Per share and per ADS data have been restated to give retroactive effect to the issuance of the L Shares and have also been restated in constant pesos as of December 31, 1990. Nominal dividends per share and per ADS, restated to give retroactive effect to the issuance of the L Shares, would have been 4.80 pesos per share and 96.00 pesos per ADS for each year from 1986 through 1989, and 7.20 pesos per share and 144 pesos per ADS for 1990. Each ADS represents twenty L Shares.

(2) Net income for 1988 reflected an unusual combination of high inflation and limited devaluation of the peso against the U.S. dollar. Under Mexican GAAP, Telmex is required to report the effects of inflation on its monetary assets and liabilities. Because Telmex consistently had monetary liabilities in excess of its monetary assets, it had gains each year as the value of its liabilities declined in constant-peso terms due to inflation. These gains were substantially offset in 1986 and 1987, and more than offset in 1989 and 1990, by exchange losses incurred because most of Telmex's liabilities are denominated in foreign currencies. In 1988, however, the value of the peso against the U.S. dollar was held nearly constant for most of the year, and Telmex had a correspondingly small exchange loss. The combined effect of monetary gains and exchange losses in 1988 was a net gain of 1,729 billion pesos. Management does not expect a gain of this nature to recur.

(3) U.S. GAAP amounts reflect adjustments resulting principally from differences in the accounting treatment of pension benefits and deferred income taxes. See Notes 7 and 12 to Consolidated Financial Statements.

(4) Net income for 1988 and 1989 under U.S. GAAP reflects the effect of utilizing net operating loss carryforwards, which is an extraordinary item under U.S. GAAP. Such net operating loss carryforwards arose from monetary gains that are recognized for financial statement purposes but are not subject to tax.

(5) Beginning in 1987, deferred income principally represents proceeds from the sale of rights to receive a portion of future net settlement receivables from a foreign telecommunications carrier. See Note 8 to Consolidated Financial Statements.

EXHIBIT 3   (continued)

The principal differences between Mexican GAAP and U.S. GAAP as they relate to Telmex are the treatment of pension plan costs and deferred taxes. In addition, U.S. GAAP differ from Mexican GAAP, as they relate to Telmex, in the treatment of capitalization of interest on assets under construction, accrued vacation costs and the method of recognizing financing costs on deferred income. The effect of inflation accounting under Mexican GAAP has not been reversed in the reconciliation to U.S. GAAP.

Net income under U.S. GAAP for 1988, 1989, and 1990 was P2,809 billion, P1,036 billion, and P2,751 billion, respectively, as compared to that reported under Mexican GAAP of P2,726 billion, P1,816 billion, and P3,308 billion, respectively, or 3% higher in 1988, 43% lower in 1989, and 17% lower in 1990. Net income for 1988 and 1989 under U.S. GAAP reflects the effect of utilizing net operating loss carryforwards, which is an extraordinary item under U.S. GAAP, of P826 billion in 1988 and P430 billion in 1989. Net income before extraordinary item under U.S. GAAP was P1,983 billion in 1988 and P606 billion in 1989. Net income under U.S. GAAP in each year was adversely affected by significant pension plan charges beyond those required under Mexican GAAP, which were partially offset by related deferred income tax credits. The impact in 1989 and 1990 was more severe than in 1988 due to the adoption of Statement of Financial Accounting Standards No. 87, *Employers' Accounting for Pensions,* in 1989.

The Telmex consolidated balance sheets, income statements, and statements of changes in financial position included in the L Share ADS prospectus are attached to this memo. These consolidated financial statements are presented in conformity with accounting principles generally accepted in Mexico and consist of the accounts of Telmex and its subsidiaries.

The financial statements of all subsidiaries have been consolidated as of a date three months prior to the date of the consolidated financial statements. All material intercompany accounts and transactions have been eliminated in the consolidated financial statements.

EXHIBIT 3   (continued)

TELEFONOS DE MEXICO, S.A. DE C.V. AND SUBSIDIARIES

CONSOLIDATED BALANCE SHEETS

	Millions of Mexican Pesos and U.S. Dollars December 31,		
	1989	*1990*	*1990*
ASSETS			
Current assets			
Cash and cash equivalents (Note 3)	P 2,259,537	P 3,222,979	$1,093
Accounts receivable, net of allowance for doubtful accounts of P35,923 and P25,762 in 1989 and 1990, respectively:			
Subscribers	936,878	1,198,844	407
Amounts due from suppliers	155,690	223,050	76
Net settlement receivables	183,182	154,972	52
Other	196,918	413,196	140
	1,472,668	1,990,062	675
Prepaid expenses	266,693	261,898	89
Total current assets	3,998,898	5,474,939	1,857
Materials and supplies, principally for construction of telephone plant................................	1,862,602	1,797,714	610
Property, plant and equipment, net (Notes 2 and 4)	18,241,767	20,634,868	7,000
Other assets (Note 4)	—	521,182	177
Total assets	P24,103,267	P28,428,703	$9,644
LIABILITIES AND STOCKHOLDERS' EQUITY			
Current liabilities			
Current maturities of long-term debt (Note 9)	P 337,514	P 838,685	$ 284
Accounts payable and accrued liabilities (Note 5).........	659,627	854,000	290
Taxes payable (Note 6).............................	359,515	295,414	100
Total current liabilities	1,356,656	1,988,099	674
Accrued pension plan costs (Note 7)....................	1,002,088	1,040,892	353
Deferred income (Note 8)............................	2,952,121	3,494,471	1,186
Long-term debt (Note 9)	4,508,026	5,587,479	1,895
Total noncurrent liabilities	8,462,235	10,122,842	3,434
Total liabilities	9,818,891	12,110,941	4,108
Commitments and contingencies (Notes 9 and 10)			
Capital stock no par value (Note 11)			
Authorized 10,603 million shares			
Series AA			
Shares issued and outstanding: 2,370 million in 1989 and 2,163 million in 1990	6,120,656	5,575,308	1,891

EXHIBIT 3   (continued)

| | Millions of Mexican Pesos and U.S. Dollars December 31, | | |
	1989	*1990*	*1990*
Series A			
Shares issued and outstanding: 1,836 million in 1989 and 2,061 million in 1990, excluding 17 million held by a subsidiary in 1989 and 1990	4,809,087	5,356,668	1,817
Series L			
Shares issued and outstanding: 6,337 million in 1990, excluding 25 million held by a subsidiary in 1990	—	633,688	215
Capital stock issuance premium (Note 11)	1,913,313	1,980,455	672
Accumulated deficit from holding nonmonetary assets (Note 2)	(1,156,582)	(2,424,207)	(822)
Accumulated loss from monetary position (Note 2)	(1,919,302)	(1,919,302)	(651)
Retained earnings:			
Legal reserve (Note 11)	716,702	795,656	270
Unappropriated	3,800,502	6,319,496	2,144
Total retained earnings	4,517,204	7,115,152	2,414
Total stockholders' equity	14,284,376	16,317,762	5,536
Total liabilities and stockholders' equity	P24,103,267	P28,428,703	$9,644

The notes accompanying these consolidated financial statements are not reproduced.

Exhibit 3   (continued)

TELEFONOS DE MEXICO, S.A. DE C.V. AND SUBSIDIARIES

CONSOLIDATED STATEMENTS OF INCOME

	Millions of Mexican Pesos and U.S. Dollars (except per share amounts) For the year ended December 31,			
	1988	*1989*	*1990*	*1990*
Operating revenues:				
Long-distance service:				
International	P2,892,428	P3,295,152	P3,286,546	$ 1,115
Domestic	1,795,046	2,574,663	4,020,801	1,364
Local service	1,245,911	1,578,259	3,574,163	1,213
Other................................	245,196	393,643	431,301	146
	6,178,581	7,841,717	11,312,811	3,838
Expenses:				
Salaries and related costs (Note 7)	2,370,904	2,686,111	2,844,292	965
Depreciation (Note 2)	946,575	1,250,190	1,279,597	434
Other operating and maintenance.............	1,089,354	1,283,507	1,494,070	507
Telephone services tax (Note 6)	—	—	1,611,146	547
	4,406,833	5,219,808	7,229,105	2,453
Operating income	1,771,748	2,621,909	4,083,706	1,385
Financing costs (Notes 2 and 9):				
Interest income........................	(1,104,901)	(906,577)	(922,706)	(313)
Interest expense	1,084,534	861,338	874,190	296
Exchange loss	162,083	610,062	630,769	214
Gain from monetary position...............	(1,891,502)	(596,891)	(430,958)	(146)
	(1,749,786)	(32,068)	151,295	51
Income before provisions for income tax, workers' profit sharing and deferred income taxes	3,521,534	2,653,977	3,932,411	1,334
Provisions (Note 6):				
Income tax............................	747,480	571,050	351,700	119
Workers' profit sharing	136,335	267,350	273,064	93
Deferred income taxes	(87,865)	—	—	—
	795,950	838,400	624,764	212
Net income	P2,725,584	P1,815,577	P3,307,647	$ 1,122
Weighted average common shares outstanding	10,145	10,429	10,551	10,551
Earnings per common share (Note 1)	P268.66	P174.09	P313.49	$ 0.11

The notes accompanying these consolidated financial statements are not reproduced.

Exhibit 3   (continued)

TELEFONOS DE MEXICO, S.A. DE C.V. AND SUBSIDIARIES

CONSOLIDATED STATEMENTS OF CHANGES IN FINANCIAL POSITION

	Millions of Mexican Pesos and U.S. Dollars For the year ended December 31,			
	1988	*1989*	*1990*	*1990*
Operating activities:				
Net income	P2,725,584	P1,815,577	P3,307,647	$ 1,122
Adjustments to reconcile net income to resources provided by operating activities:				
Depreciation	946,575	1,250,190	1,279,597	434
Change in operating assets and liabilities:				
(Increase) decrease in:				
Accounts receivable	(224,502)	(102,573)	(517,394)	(175)
Prepaid expenses	(12,994)	(76,499)	4,795	2
(Decrease) increase in:				
Accrued pension plan costs	532,592	521,592	763,628	259
Pension plan payments	(419,102)	(339,444)	(724,824)	(246)
Accounts payable and accrued liabilities	251,571	(41,959)	194,373	66
Taxes payable	295,514	(364,953)	(64,101)	(22)
Advances from subscribers and other (Note 8)	(67,166)	202,098	(116,810)	(40)
Resources provided by operating activities	4,028,072	2,864,029	4,126,911	1,400
Financing activities:				
Proceeds from sale of net settlement receivables (Note 8)	737,547	913,527	1,367,527	464
Transfer of net settlement receivables (Note 8)	(358,873)	(484,843)	(708,367)	(240)
Reduction in current and long-term debt due to restatement in constant pesos	(2,685,001)	(595,596)	(765,251)	(260)
Proceeds from long-term debt	355,814	602,423	2,702,781	917
Payments on principal of long-term debt	(569,450)	(150,171)	(356,904)	(121)
Proceeds from issuance of capital stock	1,177,555	766,871	69,375	23
Dividends paid	(53,473)	(61,707)	(76,011)	(26)
Resources provided (used) by financing activities	(1,395,881)	990,504	2,233,150	757
Investing activities (Note 4):				
Investments in materials and supplies	(841,346)	(223,301)	(432,206)	(147)
Investments in property, plant and equipment	(2,992,121)	(3,169,792)	(4,443,231)	(1,507)
Investment in other assets	—	—	(521,182)	(177)
Resources used by investing activities	(3,833,467)	(3,393,093)	(5,396,619)	(1,831)
Net increase (decrease) in cash and cash equivalents	(1,201,276)	461,440	963,442	326
Cash and cash equivalents at beginning of period	2,999,373	1,798,097	2,259,537	767
Cash and cash equivalents at end of period	P1,798,097	P2,259,537	P3,222,979	$ 1,093

The notes accompanying these consolidated financial statements are not reproduced.

Intangible Assets

Intangible assets are expenditures for special rights, privileges, or competitive advantages which offer the prospect of increased revenues or earnings. They include expenditures for brand names, franchises, patents, and similar items that exist only on paper, but nevertheless can reasonably be expected to contribute to earnings beyond the current accounting period. The intangible asset "goodwill" is discussed in another chapter.

The accounting and analysis of intangible assets is complicated by the special characteristics of an intangible asset: its lack of physical qualities make evidence of its existence elusive, its value is often difficult to estimate, and its useful life may be indeterminate. If the intangible asset is purchased, identifiable, and can be given a reasonably descriptive name, such as a patent, the task is somewhat easier than if the intangible is an unidentifiable acquisition, such as goodwill, or an internally developed intangible asset.

A number of managers, accountants, and analysts believe conservatism should govern the accounting for intangibles. They adopt the general presumption that intangible asset costs should be written off as incurred, or, if capitalized, amortized over a relatively short period of time. Increasingly, however, there is a growing belief that conservatism alone is not sufficient justification for eliminating a valid business asset from the accounts. Rather, the financial reporting goal should be to provide as accurate a picture as possible of the economic realities of the business.

A business may acquire intangible assets from others or develop them itself. In theory, the accounting for these intangible items should be the same. In practice, however, acquired intangible assets are typically recorded as assets and amortized over two or more accounting periods. In contrast, internally developed intangibles are typically expensed as incurred, rather than capitalized.

The practice of expensing as incurred the costs of internally generated intangible assets is often justified on the ground that it is difficult to determine what future benefits might result from expenditures for a potential intangible asset as they are being made. Also, in companies that are continually making expenditures for internally developed intangibles, management considers this to be a regular, recurring expense of doing business and, hence, properly charged to income as incurred. In addition, it is sometimes difficult to determine the specific costs related to developing an intangible asset. Under these circumstances, the usual course of action is to expense the costs as incurred, on the ground that costs should be recorded as assets only when they can be specifically identified with an item that clearly meets an acceptable definition of an asset.

Authoritative Sources

The FASB has accepted the basic intangible asset accounting standards set forth in APB Opinion No. 17 of its predecessor, the APB. APB Opinion No. 17 states that intangible assets acquired from others should be recorded at cost. The cost to develop intangible assets that are not specifically identifiable and have indeterminable lines should be expensed as incurred. The cost to develop identifiable intangible assets may be capitalized as an asset if the period of expected future benefits can be determined and recovery is reasonably assumed. The asset should be charged to income in a systematic way over the expected benefits period.

APB Opinion No. 17 anticipates that the straight line method of amortization will be used, unless another systematic amortization method can be demonstrated. The amortization period cannot exceed 40 years.

The FASB has addressed the accounting for several specific intangible assets.

Research and Development.   FASB Statement No. 2 requires that all research and development costs be expensed as incurred. The FASB reached this conclusion because it believed:

1. There is normally a high degree of uncertainty about the future benefits of individual research and development projects.
2. There is a lack of causal relationship between expenditures for research and development and the benefits received.
3. The capitalization of research and development costs is not useful in assessing the earnings potential of a company or the variability of its earnings potential.

FASB Statement No. 2 requires that the total research and development cost charged to income in each period be disclosed in the notes for each period for which an income statement is presented.

Research and Development Arrangements.   Sometimes companies fund their research and development activities through arrangements with other enterprises. A typical arrangement may involve a partnership formed to fund under a contractual relationship the research activities of a corporation. If the research is successful, the corporation may for some form of compensation acquire the rights to its research from the partnership. If the research is unsuccessful the partnership may or may not receive a repayment of the funds advanced.

The accounting by the corporation for this type of arrangement turns on whether the enterprise is obligated to repay funds, regardless of the research and development outcome. According to FASB Statement No. 68 if the corporation is so obligated the arrangement must be accounted for as a borrowing transaction and the research and development costs expensed as incurred. If there is no obligation to repay funds, the corporation can record contract revenues to offset its research and development costs.

Computer Software.   FASB Statement No. 86 addressed the accounting for the cost of internally developed software to be sold, leased, or otherwise included. This Statement requires the costs incurred before the technological feasibility of a software package has been established to be expensed as incurred. Technological feasibility is achieved when "the enterprise has completed all planning, designing, coding, and testing activities that are necessary to establish that the product can be produced to meet its design specifications including functions, features, and technical performance requirements." Once this point in the development process is reached, the costs necessary to get the software ready for release to customers must be capitalized as an asset and amortized on a product-by-product basis over the product's expected useful life. The annual amortization cost is the greater of the amounts determined by either the straight line or gross revenue ratio methods.[1]

Role of Judgment

The appropriate accounting for intangible assets is very dependent on particular circumstances of each situation, perhaps more so than in any other area of accounting. Seldom does an exhaustive analysis of the facts lead to a clear-cut answer. Therefore, selecting the best approach usually requires the exercise of management judgment.

The public auditor faces the same judgmental situation in deciding what form the opinion statement will take. Sometimes the auditor's problem is aggravated when the auditor is not fully satisfied with management's treatment of the item, but is not absolutely convinced that the preferred alternative treatment is the only possible answer. In these situations, the auditor typically defers to management's judgment. Of course, if management's treatment seems clearly inappropriate and management insists on keeping that approach, the auditor will either insist on management adopting the recommended approach or terminate the audit arrangement.

Businesses change over time, and often their past accounting practices and estimates become inappropriate for their new conditions. This is particularly true of

---

[1]The gross revenue ratio method allocates the capitalized cost to each accounting period in the proportion that the actual periodic revenue bears to the product's estimated total revenues.

accounting for intangibles. However, it is seldom clear at what precise point in time a change in accounting policy or estimate is justified. Again, responsible management judgment must be exercised. Unfortunately, in most cases changes in accounting for intangibles appear to have been made long after the events justifying a change have occurred. Also, a decline in profitability is often the event that appears to prompt the decision to change accounting methods. Changes under these circumstances inevitably raise questions about the integrity of management's financial statements.

It is often difficult to determine whether or not an intangible asset expenditure will be recovered out of future revenues. Typically, this problem of uncertainty is resolved on the basis of conservatism, by expensing the cost as incurred. In the case of many well-established companies run by responsible managers, this treatment is often followed unnecessarily. The intangible asset is a valuable asset. This practice can result in an improper matching of costs and revenues and the omission of a valuable business asset from the balance sheet. On the other hand, marginal firms often resort to capitalizing intangible asset costs of dubious future value in order to boost earnings and net book values. Thus, in practice, the inappropriate treatment is often the one adopted.

Financial Analysis

Financial analysts are confronted with a number of problems when analyzing acquired and internally developed intangible asset values, costs, expenses, and accounting practices. For example, corporate management often use their intangible asset accounting policies as a vehicle to signal to statement user management's perception of how statement users ought to view their firm so as to better appreciate its corporate strategy, strategic achievements, and corporate strengths. The task of the statement user is to interpret the meaning of the signal, determine if it is genuine and to assess its implications. The transnational analyst must cope with a wide diversity of counting intangible asset accounting standards accounting practices which for analysis purposes often must be reconciled to a common standard. Evaluation of shifts in company intangible asset accounting practices from, say, expensing as incurred to capitalization must be made. The current value of intangible assets whose cost was expensed as incurred must be estimated to compute company breakup values. The reasonableness of capitalized intangible asset values must also be addressed.

Management Signals

A shift to capitalizing intangible asset costs from expensing as incurred, or extending the amortization period of an existing capitalization policy, is often intended by management to be a signal to statement users that management believes that the company has valuable intangible assets, management is confident that the future earnings streams associated with these intangible assets are identifiable and predictable, and a continuation of the old accounting policy would be misleading and possibly harmful to the company's valuation. If management is correct, the signal should be welcomed by statement users.

In practice, the interpretation by statement users of management's action is often the opposite to that intended by management. Statement users are wary of such management actions and, unless management makes a strong case that its actions are supportable by convincing evidence, investors tend to regard intangible asset accounting shifts away from expensing as incurred to capitalization and lengthening of amortization periods as accounting "red flags" signaling the company's operations are no longer strong enough to absorb the higher accounting costs associated with the old accounting practice. This statement user response is the product of an accumulation of statement user experience with companies that capitalized intangibles, reported higher profits, and then suddenly announced the capitalized intangibles were worthless and had to be charged immediately to income.

A policy to expense internally developed intangible assets as incurred and amortize purchased intangible assets over relatively short periods is often intended by management as a signal that while management is confident of the ultimate success of its intangible asset expenditures, management has a prudent and conservative view toward business and the company's underlying operations are strong enough to absorb the conservative accounting policy.

Statement users appear to be more comfortable with this signal, since it reflects the difficulty of determining the ultimate recoverability of intangible asset costs.

Coping with Diversity

Financial analysts often deal with the wide range of intangible asset accounting practices within some industries by adjusting company data to a common intangible asset accounting practice. This adjustment should reflect the analyst's accounting preferences and the nature of the intangible asset. For example, an analyst who believes all internally generated intangible asset costs should be expensed as incurred might adjust the financial statement data of a company that capitalized and subsequently amortized the cost of internally developed intangible assets as follows:

1. Adjust the periodic intangible asset amortization expense by the change during the period in the capitalized intangible asset balance. This adjustment converts the recorded expense to an expense as incurred basis.

2. Adjust net income by the change in capitalized intangible balance times one minus the company's tax rate. This step adjusts net income to the new accounting basis.

3. Eliminate the capitalized intangible asset balance at the end of the period. This step recognizes that if an expense as incurred policy had been followed there would not be capitalized cost.

4. Reduce owner equity at the end of the period by the capitalized intangible asset balance eliminated times one minus the tax rate. This step brings owners' equity in line with the elimination of the capitalized cost and the related book tax effect.

5. Adjust the appropriate balance sheet tax account to make the adjusted balance sheet balance. This is a "plug" adjustment.

Expense to Capitalize.   Typically, when a company changes from expensing to capitalizing internally developed intangible asset costs the impact on current profitability is disclosed. What is not disclosed is the effect on future income growth rates of this shift. To identify this future impact is the task of the analyst. While there are many possible variations of a shift from expensing to capitalization, depending on the direction and size of the annual expenditures, the following simple example presented in **Illustration A** should be sufficient to illustrate the effect the analyst must identify.

Assume:

The Viking Chemical Company has a very stable business. The management plans to continue its practice of spending $1 million per year to purchase patents over the next 10 years. In 1993, the company changed its accounting for purchased patents from expensing as acquired to capitalization and amortization over five years.

What will be the impact on profits of this decision over the next five years? **Illustration A** supplies the answer.

Valuation.   Rarely can statement users directly value or confirm a management valuation of an intangible asset using publicly available data. Typically, the best they can do is form an opinion of the intangible asset's general importance to a company's future profitability based on a thorough knowledge of such things as the company's products, product development skills, technological capabilities, and competitive environment. Forming such an opinion is often critical to understanding a company's potential breakup value, future profit stream, and ability to raise capital.

Outlined below are a few financial statement analysis hints. The key to understanding how appropriately a company has applied the intangible asset accounting rules is to have a thorough knowledge of the company's products, product development skills, technological capabilities, and competitive environment. In the end, these

ILLUSTRATION A   Capitalization Impact Illustration (in thousands)

	Old Policy: Expense Patents as Purchased	New Policy: Capitalize Patents as Purchased					
	1993	*1993*	*1994*	*1995*	*1996*	*1997*	*1998*
Profits before taxes and patent expenses	$4,000	$4,000	$4,000	$4,000	$4,000	$4,000	$4,000
Patent expenses	1,000	200	400	600	800	1,000	1,000
	3,000	3,800	3,600	3,400	3,200	3,000	3,000
Income taxes (50%)	1,500	1,900	1,800	1,700	1,600	1,500	1,500
Net income	1,500	1,900	1,800	1,700	1,600	1,500	1,500
Annual profit improvement	—	400	300	200	100	—	—
Deferred patent asset (balance sheet item)	—	800	1,400	1,800	2,000	2,000	2,000

are the factors that will determine whether or not a company's intangible asset accounting practices are sound.

The first analytical problem facing statement users is figuring out how much was spent during the accounting period on capitalized intangible assets. To compute the actual intangible asset cash expenditures in any one period, the analyst must add the change in the deferred costs to the deferred costs amortized in the period.

Two suggested financial analysis techniques are:

a. Keep track of the periodic capitalized intangible asset expenditures. An unusual increase in the balance may be a red flag signaling capitalization of costs beyond that permitted by the rules, or it may be the result of increased intangible asset acquisition and development activities. Seek more information.

b. Watch the percentage of amortized intangible asset costs relative to sales. A decline in this percentage may indicate stretching of the amortization period or a growing reliance on old products, ideas, patents, or rights.

In making the above calculations, one should keep in mind that not all intangible assets are developed internally. Intangible assets can be purchased from others. So, acquisition expenditures should be considered when evaluating trends in the ratios and balances described above.

Bitter experience has taught statement users to be wary of capitalized intangible assets. Some of the more troublesome aspects of capitalizing expenditures for intangibles are:

1. Capitalization may remove the discipline of expensing, which forces management to question the value of the incremental expenditures for intangible assets since they will depress current profits. Capitalizing rather than expensing as incurred can lead to overfunding of unsound projects long after they should have been terminated. Unfortunately, since earnings are not adversely impacted currently by imprudent funding, statement readers may fail to detect the poor management decision early enough to avoid a disappointing earnings surprise when the capitalized balances are written off in a lump sum.

2. Application of the intangible asset accounting rules requires considerable judgment on the part of managers, who may be tempted to stretch the rules when their companies experience difficult times by including in the capitalized balances costs that do not legitimately belong in the account and extending the amortization period by overestimating potential revenues. Outsiders seldom see though this maneuver in time to avoid unpleasant surprises.

3. When faced with a decision between internally developing or purchasing an intangible asset, some managers may lean toward the purchase alternative because it will be easier to justify capitalizing the cost of purchased intangibles. Sometimes, the desire to avoid lowering current profits by expensing as incurred the cost of internally developed intangible assets may lead to management's overpaying for the purchased intangible asset. This in turn may make future recoverability of the cost more difficult. Overpayment is hard to detect directly from an examination of financial statements.

4. Capitalization of intangible asset expenditures can encourage optimism on the part of managers and statement users. Capitalizing an expenditure signals that the expenditure is thought to be recoverable in the future. This signal can lead managers and statement users to focus too much on the expected benefits and to downplay, or even forget, that there may be many hazardous competitive and technological steps that must be overcome in the meantime. Capitalization is not synonymous with accomplishment. Statement readers who accept uncritically management's capitalization practices are well advised to remember this fact. To forget it can be costly.

Logic suggests that it is just as misleading to expense as incurred investments in intangible assets with a high probability of generating future benefits as it is to capitalize expenditures for intangible assets that are unlikely to produce future benefits. When statement users encounter a company that expenses as incurred its expenditures for intangible assets that it considers quite likely to produce future benefits, this practice should be considered a significant factor favoring a high-quality earnings rating for the company. In addition, since the anticipated future benefits will not be burdened by the amortization of prior period capitalized expenditures, the company's chances of being profitable in the future are enhanced.

These analyst attitudes, which are at variance with accounting theory, are the product of an accumulation of unpleasant investor experiences with companies that capitalized intangibles, reported profits, and then suddenly announced that the capitalized intangibles were worthless and had to be written off against income. This in turn has led to losses for investors. These same experiences have led some statement users to be wary of companies that capitalize intangibles; they associate the capitalization of intangible assets with low earnings quality and label this practice as an accounting "red flag."

SKA (Sweden)

I think it's pretty clear that what looks on the surface as though it's a bookkeeping decision may be one of our most important management decisions. And that's why we are here today.

Frank Johansson, president of the SKA (Sweden), a supplier to the Swedish defense industry, was addressing his executive group as they met to consider what had grown into a major corporate issue—namely, the accounting treatment of a special research and development (R&D) expenditure. The accounting of the costs would make the difference in reporting either continued losses or small profits for the company over the next three years. Because Swedish accounting rules permitted companies to capitalize R&D expenditures (see **Exhibit 1**) SKA's management team had been examining the accounting issue to uncover as many of the relevant considerations as possible. The meeting in progress was to try to resolve the question.

SKA was founded in 1980. The company's operations covered the development, manufacture, and sale of electronic equipment for military and civilian use. Some 300 shareholders owned SKA's stock which traded on the Stockholm Stock Exchange.

In its early years, SKA had rapidly expanded its sales and showed increasing earnings per share. The success was due principally to the company's development of a number of improved electronic components for military computer applications and aircraft defense systems. As a result, SKA was labeled a "growth company" and its stock sold at a substantial premium.

About 1985 SKA's sales and profits began to decline. The underlying reason was that the company's line of electronic gear was progressively being made obsolete by a

Professor David F. Hawkins prepared this case as the basis for class discussion rather than to illustrate either effective or ineffective handling of an administrative situation.

EXHIBIT 1   Swedish Accounting Principles: Research and Development Accounting

---

Under the Swedish Accounting Act, expenditures for technical assistance and for research and development (R&D) may be recognized as fixed assets if they will benefit the company in future years. The recorded asset should be amortized annually by an appropriate amount not less than 20% of its original value unless there are special circumstances in which amortization at a lower rate may be used in accordance with generally accepted accounting principles.

There is no uniformity in reporting practice in this area. The Swedish Accounting Standards Board recently issued a Recommendation on Accounting for Research and Development with the aim of conforming Swedish practice with international accounting practice (IAS 9). The general rule requires that research and development expenditures be expensed as incurred, unless the criteria set out below are satisfied:

- The R&D project and the expenditures attributed to it are clearly defined.
- The technical feasibility of the R&D project has been demonstrated.
- The products or process resulting from the R&D project is intended for sale or internal use.
- The expected revenue or cost savings resulting from the R&D project are known with reasonable probability.
- There are adequate resources to complete the project.

If capitalized, research and development costs must be amortized annually according to the rules stated in the Accounting Act, that is, at least 20% annually.

The financial statements, on their face or in notes, should disclose:

- The accounting policy for R&D.
- The R&D expenditures expensed in the current year and the amortization of R&D expenditures capitalized in previous years.
- The total R&D expenditures capitalized and the related accumulated amortization.

Source: Coopers & Lybrand, *International Accounting Summaries,* John Wiley & Sons, New York, 1992.

---

series of rapid changes in computer and military monitoring technology. Also, SKA's R&D group was unable to come up with any significant improvements in the company's existing products. Consequently, SKA's stock began to sell at an increasingly lower price earnings ratio.

Beginning in 1988 SKA reported losses to its stockholders. However, from the low point in 1989 these losses were reduced somewhat in 1990, and again in 1991, principally because the company had secured in those years several cost-plus-fixed-fee contracts related to the manufacture of experimental air-to-air missile guidance systems. But, despite the reduced losses, SKA's stock continued to be traded at a substantial discount from the stock prices of similar companies.

As a result of these repeated losses, the company management had been subjected to constant criticism by a dissident stockholder group since 1989. This group accused the management of being "unimaginative" and "incompetent." And, as the losses persisted, other stockholders became more and more sympathetic to the dissident group's demand for a "change of management."

In February 1992, encouraged by the trend toward profitable operations, Johansson

EXHIBIT 2   Selected Financial Data, 1980–1991 (all values in thousands)

Year	Gross Sales	R&D Expense	Earnings After Theoretical Tax[a]
1980	$ 8,000	$ 400	$ 100
1981	21,000	900	600
1982	33,000	800	2,000
1983	40,100	1,000	2,500
1984	42,000	950	2,600
1985	42,000	900	2,500
1986	40,000	1,000	1,800
1987	36,000	1,000	1,200
1988	35,500	800	(100)
1989	33,000	600	(600)
1990	36,100	1,000	(400)
1991	36,300	1,000	(10)

[a]The calculation of earnings after theoretical tax is based on recommendations issued by the Swedish Business Community's Stock Exchange Commission. Theoretical tax comprises those taxes (excluding profit-sharing tax) that would have been paid on earnings if no tax credits had been taken through special appropriations, such as untaxed reserves. Effective in 1992, the Swedish corporate tax rate was lowered to 30%. Also, the possibility to offset income by untaxed reserves was abolished. However, a tax equalization reserve was introduced in its place. Prior to 1992, the Swedish statutory corporate tax rate had been 52%.

promised the company's stockholders that SKA would show a small profit during 1992 and thereafter increased profits. This encouraging news was welcomed by the stockholders. Johansson's promise was reported to all the leading financial journals. And the price of the company's stock showed a slight improvement.

Exhibit 2 shows SKA's financial data for the years 1980–1991.

R&D Program

One month following Johansson's promise to the stockholders of future profits, SKA's management committee met and decided to undertake a stepped-up three-year R&D program, which hopefully would revitalize the company. This program grew out of a development by the company's R&D department of a simple pilot model of a computer component, which gave promise of revolutionizing computer memory capacity and allied systems for certain military applications. In this component, management decided, lay the chance for SKA to regain its lost market position.

However, one of SKA's competitors was known to be exploring the same principle of electronics on which SKA's laboratory model was based. Therefore, in the spring of 1992, SKA decided to accelerate the development of a patentable commercial product by increasing the company's R&D expenses from some $1,000,000 to $1,500,000[1] a year, of which $1,000,000 would be devoted to the new project. The remaining $500,000 would be used to continue R&D related to other products, most of

[1]To partially eliminate the effect of Swedish inflation on SKA's financial data, all Krona values have been restated to their U.S. dollar equivalent using year end exchange rates.

which the firm was already producing. Previously SKA had never spent more than $500,000 in total on any single R&D project.

Peter Pettersson, SKA's vice president for research and development, believed that even with the increased R&D expenditure, it would take nearly three years to develop the laboratory model into a sound commercial product. During the first year he proposed to conduct some further basic research on the electronic principles incorporated in the model. The actual development of commercial prototypes was scheduled to take place in the second and third years. Pettersson estimated the probability of success creating a commercial product at about seven chances out of ten.

Based on studies of the projected demand for military products during the period 1995 to 2000, Alan Fromm, SKA's vice president for sales, estimated that the new computer component and its allied systems' sales potential would be about $150 million between 1995 and 2001. This projection did not take into account any possible major negative impact on the global military market caused by the recent political and economic changes in Eastern Europe and the Soviet Union.

From its past experience with similar technological innovations, management expected that the competitive advantage of the component might be as short as two years, but more likely as long as four years. Thereafter as similar or better competitive components were developed by either SKA or other companies, it was anticipated that the component would experience declining sales for a period of two or three years.

Expense or Capitalize?

Shortly after the management committee had decided to go ahead with the new R&D program, Thomas Larsson, SKA's controller, circulated among top management a memorandum (See **Exhibit 3**) suggesting that the increase in R&D expenditures required offsetting cost cuts in other areas of the business.

Larsson's memorandum caused considerable consternation among management. As a result, Johansson called a meeting of his management group to discuss the memorandum and the expensing issue. The group consisted of Johansson, Pettersson, Fromm, and Larsson—as well as David Thor, vice president for finance, Philip Holter, vice president for purchasing, and Sebastian Jansson, vice president for employee and public relations.

After the prefatory remarks which Johansson made (as quoted at the beginning of the case), SKA's president asked the controller to expand on his memorandum.

> *Johansson:* Tom, why don't you discuss your memorandum a bit more extensively? Why do we have to write off *as they are incurred* these R&D costs related to the memory-storage project?
>
> *Larsson:* Well, first let me explain that *either* deferment or current expensing of R&D costs is an acceptable Swedish accounting practice. In fact, both practices at one time or another have been followed within our industry. However, the accounting profession has generally favored current expensing of such costs.
>
> Personally, I believe we should write off our R&D costs as incurred for several reasons: (1) the accounting treatment I propose is conservative; (2) it is

---

EXHIBIT 3 **Larsson's Memorandum**

TO: Frank Johansson
FROM: Thomas Larsson
RE: Need to Identify Promptly Cost Reduction Actions

Our decision to increase annual R&D expenses from the original planned level for $1 million to $1.5 million will have a significant impact on our anticipated reported profits for 1992–1994. It will turn the original profit projections (see below) into a loss.

**Original Projection
(as of January 1, 1992, 000s omitted)**

Year	Gross Sales	R&D Expenses	Earnings after Theoretical Tax[a]
1992	$37,500	$1,000	$ 50
1993	38,500	1,000	150
1994	38,500	1,000	150

[a]See Exhibit 2.

Better accounting practice and consistency with our earlier treatment of R&D costs calls for us to **expense** these additional R&D costs currently. If this is also your decision, we must cut costs in other areas of the business if we are to be profitable.

I recommend we meet as soon as possible to identify cost-cutting opportunities.

---

highly speculative that we will ever generate future revenues from these R&D costs; (3) if we defer them, we will be overstating our income during the next three years; and (4) we have always currently expensed our R&D costs, and consistency demands we treat these anticipated costs in the same way.

Johansson: Well, Tom, I think it is more than just an accounting question. I'm sure there are some additional considerations that we as management will have to evaluate. What thoughts do the rest of you have about Tom's proposed accounting policy to cover the handling of these R&D costs?

Pettersson: Speaking for the R&D group, I would reject out of hand Tom's statement that the project is highly speculative. As I've said before, I think our chances for success are seven out of ten. Those are pretty good odds to me.

One thing that worries me. The morale of the R&D group has been very low in recent years. They feel the losses of the last few years thanks to the wage freeze have resulted from *their* failure to come up with a new product. Now we have a red-hot prospect and everyone is happy. If you write off the costs and we continue to report losses to the stockholders, then the R&D group's morale might fall again during those periods when we have setbacks on the project. And make no mistake about it; this project, like all R&D projects, will have its discouraging moments.

On the other hand, if you capitalize the costs and carry them on the balance sheet as an asset, you will be telling the R&D groups that they have created something of value. And that is true. After all, we wouldn't spend all this money if we didn't think it was of some value to us, would we?

I'm for deferment of these particular costs. In fact, I'm for deferring all our R&D costs which will benefit future accounting periods.

Thor: I agree with Peter. From our point of view in finance, there is only one policy to follow—deferment.

If this R&D project is to be completed within three years and turned into a successful commercial venture, we will have to go to the public money markets for capital in 1994, the year before we get into commercial production. And, for the life of me, I don't see how we will get sufficient funds at a reasonable cost if we show losses for the entire period 1988 through 1993.

Now, I can't go along with Tom when he states that deferment would be overstating our income during the next three years. If we defer these costs, what we are really doing is matching our costs with our revenues. These R&D costs are clearly identifiable with the memory-storage project. And, just as clearly, sensible accounting would demand that the costs be matched with the memory-storage revenues. Therefore, since these revenues will not be realized until after 1994, the appropriate R&D costs should be deferred until 1994, and then expensed against the revenues from the project.

To write these R&D costs off as incurred would be misleading. We would understate our income over the next three years. And, because the post-1994 revenues would be relieved of these R&D costs, the post-1994 income would be overstated.

Of course, there would be full disclosure to our stockholders of our accounting policy covering R&D costs. The extraordinary costs related to the memory-storage project would be the only ones deferred. They would be clearly labeled as such on the balance sheet with an explanatory footnote. All other R&D costs would be expensed as incurred.

Johansson: How does this question look from the sales end, Alan?

Fromm: I go along with both Peter and David. If we are to finance this project, we will have to keep our sales volume up over the next few years. And the best way to do this is to continue to get cost-plus-fixed-fee contracts. However, the major defense contractors and the military don't like to let out contracts to unprofitable companies. Therefore, I can't see jeopardizing the whole project just to be "conservative" accounting-wise.

Holter: I know one thing—if we are to finance the bulk of this project for at least two years by ourselves, we will have to resort to such measures as drawing down our cash and stretching our accounts payable. And that means our current 2.2-to-1 ratio will decrease somewhat, irrespective of whether we expense or defer the R&D costs.

Currently, despite our losses we have been able to get reasonable trade credit because of our good current ratio. If, however, we have to reduce our current ratio to 1-to-1 or even less, and continue to report losses, I am sure our trade creditors will not be quite so generous. After all, they have seen far too many companies in the electronics business go under in recent years.

Admittedly, I don't understand all the fine accounting points, but just from the purchasing angle, I'm for deferment. Our current ratio will decline, but at least we will have profits to offset this disadvantage.

Johansson: Well, Seb, you are the last one. How do you see this issue from the employee and public relations point of view?

Jansson: Like Phil, I don't pretend to understand all the fine points of accounting. However, in contrast to the rest of you, I'm not as positive in my position with respect to the issue.

As you all know, over the last few years we have successfully put off the demands of some of our employees for higher hourly wages. Our principal argument has been that if wages were not frozen by the government we couldn't afford these increases in view of our losses. Now, if we defer the R&D costs, we are going to be showing profits. And under these conditions, I have no doubt that it will be harder to justify denying the employees a pay increase when the wage freeze ends.

In addition, I must point out that such wage increases would be an additional *out-of-pocket* expense. They would be an added drain on our resources at the very time we are scratching and scraping to get together enough money to finance the stepped-up R&D program.

As for the stockholders, I am sure they would like to see some profits. And, if we defer these R&D costs, there will be profits.

But if we expense the R&D costs, as Tom suggests, our stockholders are going to be unhappy over the losses. It's going to put you, Frank, in a difficult position since you promised them profits for 1992.

On balance, I guess I favor deferment. Perhaps we can put the employees off a year or two. Frankly, I don't know how we can expense R&D costs for three years and tell the stockholders we are confident of success. The dissident group will say, "Clearly, management by its own admission is throwing more money down the drain."

Johansson: Tom, one last point of information. What cost elements did you include in your R&D calculation?

Larsson: Only direct costs, which are mostly salaries and materials.

Johansson: As I understand it, Statistics Sweden's definition of R&D cost includes shares of administration and capital costs, among other items. Shouldn't we use their definition? I know the Association of the Swedish Pharmaceutical Industry has adopted this full cost approach.

Larsson: Maybe we should for footnote disclosure, but I would be hesitant to do so for asset measurement purposes. If we took the full cost approach, we would add 20 percent to the R&D cost. My concern is that the more you capitalize now, the more you may have to write off in the future if the project fails.

Johansson: It seems like the majority is for capitalization. Tom?

Larsson: If you are all so keen to defer these R&D costs, let me ask you some questions:

- Why shouldn't we have separate R&D accounts for *all* our projects?
- What do we do with that $3 million lump deferment if the component project fails?

- Aren't we just getting ourselves *into* more problems than we're getting *out* of?
- And, finally, over what period do you propose specifically to expense the capitalized costs after we go into production in 1994?

Fromm: On your last question, I believe we should plan to expense these deferred costs equally over the maximum period possible: that is, over the anticipated four years in which we expect to have a competitive advantage with the product, plus the subsequent three years of declining sales—that is, seven years in all.

In addition, we should also restate the comparative 1991 financial figures in our 1992 annual report. We should take out of the expenses charged against 1991 revenues the $300,000 we have already spent on the memory-storage project. These costs should be deferred also. Then we would show a small profit for 1991, which would be more realistic since the R&D costs rightly belong on the balance sheet. Both the 1991 and 1992 statements would then be truly comparable.

Larsson: Dave, you're trying to bookkeep us to profit!

Fromm: And you, Tom, are trying to bookkeep us to ruin.

Thor: Hold on, fellows, maybe there is another alternative. As some of you may recall, back in 1987 ASTRA[2] published an "article" in its 1987 annual report showing the company's book value and earnings assuming the company capitalized its R&D expenditures rather than expensing them as incurred. Maybe we could do something along the same lines. That is, use supplemental disclosure to let people know that we are really profitable.

Johansson: I think ASTRA's circumstances were a little different to ours, but David has raised an interesting possibility. What do you think, Tom?

Larsson: Who reads annual reports? People just look at the "Bottom Line." Nobody will see our "Article." No, I prefer to stick with expensing.

---

[2]AB ASTRA is a Swedish global pharmaceutical company.

Questions

1. Under what conditions, if any, should accounting standards require (permit) the capitalization of research and development expenditures? _____

2. As the president of SKA (Sweden), what accounting policy would you adopt to account for the R&D costs related to the computer memory project? _____ Would you expense or defer all, or some, of these costs? _____ If you elect to defer the R&D costs, what policy would you adopt to cover the eventual expensing of these deferred costs? _____ Why? _____

CASE
16-2

Stone & Sons Limited

The weak 1990 economy has forced us to curtail our expenditures on human resources. We will see further cuts in 1991. If we are to give a true and fair view of our situation and the economics behind our decisions, I believe we must incorporate our internal human resource accounting practices in the 1990 financial statements we send to shareholders.

Richard W. Stone, *Chairman of the Board, Stone & Sons Limited*

Stone & Sons Limited (Stone) manufactured and marketed in the United Kingdom a broad line of high-quality hand-made regimental and other men's ties and accessories. The company also exported private label ties to upscale men's stores located in the United States, such as The Exeter Shop in Harvard Square, Cambridge, Massachusetts. Stone's markets were characterised by intense price and style competition, which dictated that management have good internal controls. As part of its internal controls, Stone introduced in 1987 a "human asset accounting" concept.

Statement of Purpose

Richard Stone believed that corporations should have clear statements of purpose to guide their decision making. For example, in a 1986 United Kingdom Management Association lecture he stated:

> Divested of its legal and financial coverings, a company is but an idea or group of ideas upon which people act. To the extent that these ideas are consistent and clearly defined, they can be said to constitute a basic company purpose. Such a statement of purpose is vital to a growth-oriented company. It will provide direction as well as momentum, strength as well as incentive. In a dynamic economic and social environment, a company lacking a sound statement of purpose will not achieve the degree of progress that is most beneficial to its customers, shareholders and associates.

Professor David Hawkins prepared this case as the basis for class discussion rather than to illustrate either effective or ineffective handling of an administrative situation.
Copyright © 1993 by the President and Fellows of Harvard College. Harvard Business School case 193–182.

Stone's statement of purpose is reproduced below:

The basic purpose of the Stone & Sons Limited is to operate profitably a dynamic, progressive, growing, investor-owned company within the framework of high ethical standards of conduct which:

- Creates and sells quality products which serve the needs of people.
- Provides superior service to our customers who distribute, sell and display our products to the consumer.
- Creates a climate that stimulates, challenges and channels the human intelligence, ingenuity, and desire of our associates to the fulfillment of our purpose and provides them with a sense of achievement, equitable compensation plus participation in the results of success.
- Increases the value of all the assets (tangible and intangible) of the company and improves the stockholders' equity and/or return on investment over the long and short period of time.
- Makes a contribution to our society by demonstrating how people of all races, creeds and colors can work together cooperatively to the benefit of each and all.
- Strengthens the community, the country and the free enterprise system.

1987 Annual Report

The Report of the Chairman in the 1987 company's annual report stated under the subtitle "Organisation Assets":

As managers we are entrusted with the care of three types of assets: physical assets, organisation assets, and customer loyalty assets. Each manager is responsible for effective utilisation of these assets to create an earnings for the organisation while preserving the financial soundness of the business.

If people are treated abusively, short-term earnings will be derived at the expense of the company's organisation assets.

Managers now work with accounting data which reflect the condition of physical assets and changes in these assets over a period of time. The assets of human resources and customer loyalty do not appear in pound terms on the balance sheets. To employ effectively all three types of assets, and realise the objectives of Stone & Sons Limited, equally reliable accounting instruments are required to reflect the condition of organisation assets and customer loyalty and changes in these assets over time.

To fulfill these objectives we are now in the process of developing and installing as part of our internal control system a Human Resource Accounting system to measure in monetary terms the organisation assets and changes in these assets over time.

In later sections of the company's 1987 annual report "people—the human resources of the company" are referred to as that asset "without which all other assets become meaningless in terms of potential and future growth."

1988 Annual Report

Stone's commitment to human asset accounting for internal control purposes was further articulated throughout its 1988 annual report:

> We set ambitious goals for earnings growth in 1988. We achieved these goals in the principal result areas of the business, namely, (1) to generate earnings on total resources employed, (2) to protect and improve the value of the financial, physical, organisation, and customer loyalty resources of the company, and (3) to manage earnings to insure a sound financial position.
>
> The resources of the business are: (1) the financial resources available to the company; (2) the technological resources such as buildings, equipment, and production technology; (3) the human resources in terms of the skills and abilities possessed by the people who comprise the organisation; (4) the proprietary resources such as corporate name, brand names, copyrights, and patents; (5) the information resources of the business which provide reliable data upon which to make timely decisions.

The 1988 report went on to define the basic objectives of Stone's human resource accounting system as being:

1. To provide Stone & Sons Limited managers with specific feedback information on their performance in managing the organisational resources and customer loyalty resources entrusted to their care so that they can make proper adjustments to their pattern of operations to correct adverse trends or further improve the condition of these resources.
2. To provide Stone & Sons Limited managers with additional information pertaining to human resources to assist in their decision making.
3. To provide the organisation with a more accurate accounting of its return on total resources employed, rather than just the physical resources, and to enable management to analyse how changes in the status of the resources employed affect the achievement of corporate objectives.

The 1988 report clearly noted that Stone's human resource accounting system was a "first pioneering step" and that it lacked refinement. Additionally, Stone stressed that, "The human resource capital accounts are used for internal informational purposes only and are not reflected, of course, in the financial data presented in this report."

1989 Annual Report

Stone's 1989 annual report contained numerous references to the company's human resource accounting system similar to those included in the 1987 and 1988 annual reports.

1990 Board Report

Exhibit 1 presents a report on the status of Stone's human resource accounting system, presented to Stone's board of directors by Jane Bernado, Stone's chief financial officer, and Charles Gallagher, Stone's director for Human Resources, in March 1990.

EXHIBIT 1 Bernado and Gallagher Report, 15 March 1990

To: Board of Directors
From: Jan Bernado and Charles Gallagher
Re: Current Status of Human Resource
       Accounting System.

During the past year the Finance and Human Resources Departments continued to work jointly on the development of Stone's Human Resource Accounting System. The basic purpose of the system continues to be the development of a method of measuring in monetary terms the changes that occur in the human resources of a business that conventional accounting does not currently consider.

Basic Concept

Management can be considered as the process of planning, organising, leading, and controlling a complex mix of resources to accomplish the objectives of the organisation. Those resources, we believe, are: physical resources of the company as represented by buildings and equipment, financial resources, and human resources which consist of the people who comprise the organisation and proprietary resources which consist of trademarks, patents, and company name and reputation.

In order to determine more precisely the effectiveness of management's performance it is necessary to have information about the status of investments in the acquisition, maintenance, and utilisation of all resources of the company.

Without such information, it is difficult for a company to know whether earnings are being generated by converting a resource into cash or conversely whether suboptimal performance really has been generated by investments in developing the human resources which we expensed under conventional accounting practice.

Definition

Human Resource Accounting is an attempt to identify, quantify, and report investments made in resources of an organisation that are not presently accounted for under conventional internal and external accounting practice. Basically, it is an information system that tells management what changes over time are occurring to the human resources of the business. It must be considered as an element of a total system of management—not as a separate "device" or "gimmick" to focus attention on human resources.

Objectives

Broadly, the Human Resource Accounting Information System is being designed to provide better answers to these kinds of questions: What is the quality of earnings performance? Are sufficient human capabilities being acquired to achieve the objectives of the business? Are they being developed adequately? To what degree are they being properly maintained? Are these capabilities being properly utilised by the organisation?

As expressed in our 1988 Annual Report, our specific objectives in development of human resource accounting are . . . [see case for description].

Approach

The approach used has been to account for investments in securing and developing the organisation's human resources. Outlay costs for recruiting, acquiring, training, familiarising, and developing management personnel are accumulated and capitalised. In accordance with the approach conventional accounting employs for classification of an expenditure as an asset, only those outlays which have an expected value beyond the current accounting period deserve consideration as investments. Those outlays which are likely to be consumed within a twelve-month period are properly classified as expense items. The investments in human resources are amortised over their expected tenure with the company. Investments made for training or development are amortised over a much shorter period of time. The system now covers all management personnel at all locations of the corporation.

Research and development of the system began in late 1986 . . .

Applications

There are many potential applications for human resource accounting. Considering outlays for human resource investments which have a useful life over a number of years would have an impact upon the current year's earnings. Recognising investments in human resources and their useful lives, losses resulting from improper maintenance of those resources can be shown in monetary terms. Estimating the useful lives of investments also provides a basis for planning for the orderly replacement of human capabilities as they expire, supplementing conventional manpower planning. Finally, recognising investments in human resources will allow management to calculate return on investment on a more comprehensive resource base for a particular profit center.

EXHIBIT 1   (continued)

Financial Comparison

A comparison of Stone's 1989 financial results before and after capitalisation of human resource investments is attached to this report. The capitalised amounts reflect the following typical investment levels.

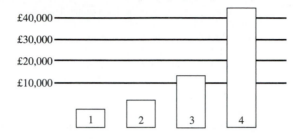

1. First Line Supervisor
2. Industrial Engineer

3. Middle Manager
4. Top Level Manager

Summary

From the standpoint of management, knowledge of the human resource investments, maintenance, and returns is necessary for proper decision making and planning long-range corporate growth. As industry becomes increasingly technical, and management becomes progressively more complex, we believe conventional accounting practice will begin to recognise human resource accounting in financial reporting.

At this stage, the Human Resource Accounting System at Stone's is best regarded as a potentially important tool of the overall management system. It is not an end in itself, and needs continuing refinement and development.

Selected Profit and Loss and Balance Sheet Accounts for the Year Ended 31 December, 1989

	Financial and Human Resources	*Financial Only*
Profit on ordinary activities before taxation	£ 1,344,222	£ 1,344,222
Human resources expenses applicable to future periods	173,569	—
	£ 1,517,791	£ 1,344,222
Taxation (Note 1)	531,227	470,478
Profit for the financial year	£ 986,564	£ 873,744
Total assets before investments in Human Resources	£13,069,832	£13,069,832
Net investment in human resources (Note 2)	986,094	—
Total assets	£14,055,926	£13,069,832
Less: Total creditors and provisions for liabilities and charges before provision for human resources	7,713,588	7,713,588
Less: Deferred taxation related to human resources (Note 1)	345,133	—
Total capital employed	£ 5,997,205	£ 5,356,244
Capital and reserves before provision for human resources	£ 5,356,244	£ 5,356,244
Provision for human resources	640,961	—
Total capital employed	£ 5,997,205	£ 5,356,244

Note 1 Deferred taxation is provided by the liability method based on full tax deduction for human resource expenditures. The current corporate tax rate of 35% is used to determine deferred taxation.

Note 2 Estimate of investment in managerial positions from first-level supervisors to chairman of the board. Reflects hiring and training costs as well as an estimated replacement cost for persons already employed when the human resource accounting system was introduced. Capitalised expenditures are amortised on a systematic basis. Capitalised expenditures are written off when an employee leaves the company or training becomes obsolete because of technological or other developments.

Richard Stone's Proposal

In November, 1990, Richard Stone proposed to the Stone Board of Directors that the financial statements included in the company's 1990 annual report be presented on a financial and human resource accounting basis.

Exhibit 2 presents selected excerpts from Stone's proposed 1990 Report of the Chairman.

Exhibit 3 presents summary financial data Stone presented to the Board to illustrate the 1990 financial statement consequences of Stone's proposal.

Exhibit 2   Selected Excerpts from Proposed 1990 Report of the Chairman

The best performance year in the history of the company was 1990.

Stone's consolidated turnover climbed to £28,164,181, a 14.2% gain over the £24,667,367 reported in 1989.

Earnings increased to £1,346,520 as against £986,564 for 1989. These earnings figures reflect Stone's new accounting policy of recognising the company's investment in human resources in its published financial statements.

Despite the difficult economic climate of 1990, the growing demand for Stone's products both in the United Kingdom and our principal export market the United States, coupled with significant internal operating improvements, generated record earnings for the company.

Stone's performance in 1990 demonstrated the responsiveness of the team management process within the organisation to the challenge of generally difficult business conditions. The concern, imagination, drive and energy of the people in the company brought us through 1990 a stronger, healthier and more vital organisation.

In reviewing 1990, on 22 January the company sold 110,000 additional shares of common stock through a private offering for net proceeds of approximately £1,630,000. The proceeds from the sale, in addition to aggressive and continuing efforts to improve asset management resulted in a sizeable improvement in our liquidity position . . .

The internal management of costs during the year greatly improved our operating effectiveness . . .

Development of the Human Resource Accounting System continued in 1990. The basic purpose of our effort, as originally reported, is to develop an information system that will measure changes occurring in the human resources of the business that conventional accounting does not currently consider. Our objective is to improve the effectiveness of management decision making and improve the profitability of the company over time.

Beginning with the 1990 annual report we have elected to adopt human resource accounting for external reporting purposes. We believe this presentation of our financial statements will reflect better than more conventional accounting the economic realities of our business and the company's approach to managing key organisation resources, such as our valuable human resource assets.

In planning for 1990, a year with considerable economic uncertainty, major investments in additional management personnel were curtailed and a somewhat more conservative position was taken on management development activities. Data provided by the Human Resource Accounting System highlighted write-offs which would occur in separating management personnel. Because the data gave high visibility to loss of prior investments, the reduction of management personnel was kept to a minimum.

The consequences of these decisions in 1990 was that write-offs and amortization related to management personnel exceeded slightly the level of investments made. Therefore, on the Income Statement the more conventional after-tax profit figure for 1990 was adjusted downward by £28,535.

The before-taxation movements in the company's human resources asset were:

New investments		
— Investments in developing existing managers	£157,462	
— Investments in acquiring new managers	96,405	
— Investment in training and familiarising new managers	67,483	321,500
Expired investment		
— Loss due to turnover	226,455	
— Amortization	138,795	365,250
Net change		£43,900

Until this year, the system covered only investments in management personnel throughout the corporation. In 1990, the Human Resource Accounting System was extended to include the factory and office people. The inclusion of factory and office people in the system resulted in a recorded investment of an additional three-quarters of a million pounds (£750,000). This number represents the investments made to acquire and train people to the expected level of effectiveness for their respective occupations, less the amortisation of this investment based upon expected tenure. Since the programme covering factory and office people was not completed until after mid-year, 1990 figures do not reflect this addition.

EXHIBIT 2   (continued)

In order to achieve the expected long-term value of accounting for all the resources of the business for balanced internal management control, additional development of data and operating applications are needed. As we gain the advantage of historical trends and can build more conclusive links between the human resource accounting information and more conventional results of the business, over time, we will gain better insights on preferred management strategies of allocating, maintaining and utilising the resources of the business. Much work still needs to be done to develop and extend practical applications of human resource accounting information to the decision-making process in operating units of the business. During 1991, our focus will be on the development of the operating applications.

Human Resource Accounting is only one part of our developing management system. When a company knows what return it receives, over time, from the total resource mix employed, and can re-late that performance to prior investments in the various resources, more effective management of the business will be possible. Much more development of Human Resource Accounting concepts is necessary before the full potential of this concept can be realised, but we believe it will certainly be worth the effort. We believe this process will be accelerated by our decision to incorporate human resource accounting in our published financial statements . . . .

We would like to express our sincere appreciation for the fine performance, support and loyalty of Stone people in all locations. They are the most vital resource of the company.

Our appreciation also goes to our many shareholders, customers and suppliers for their continuing enthusiasm and support of Stone.

Richard W. Stone
Chairman of the Board

EXHIBIT 3   **Richard W. Stone's Illustrative 1990 Financial Statements**
Limited Summary Profit and Loss and Balance Sheet Accounts for the Year Ended 31 December 1990

Conventional profit on ordinary activities before taxation	£ 2,115,470
Human resources expenses applicable to future periods	(43,900)
	£ 2,071,570
Taxation (Note 1)	725,050
Profit for the financial year	£ 1,346,520

Balance Sheet as of 31 December 1990

Total assets before investment in human resources	£13,982,171
Net investment in human resources	942,194
Total assets	£14,924,365
Less: Total creditors and provisions for liabilities and charges before provision for human resources	5,908,064
Less: Deferred taxation related to provision for human resources[1]	329,768
Total capital employed	£ 8,685,533
Capital and reserves before provision for human resources	£ 8,073,107
Provision for human resources	612,426
Total capital employed	£ 8,685,533

[1]Deferred taxation is provided by the liability method based on full tax deduction for human resource expenditures.

Questions

1. Comment on the following statement: A favorite cliché for any CEO's letter in the corporate annual report is "Our employees are our most important—our most valuable—asset," but when one turns from the CEO's letter to the remainder of the report, and in particular to the financial statements, there is, typically, never any other indication or acknowledgment of these "vital" human resources beyond that which may be subsumed in the *Goodwill* account. Richard Stone's proposal is a bold step to account for Stone & Son's human resources—an effort that perhaps has some fundamental conceptual problems.

2. Comment on this statement: The essential criterion for determining whether an expenditure is an "asset" or an "expense" relates to the notion of future service potential. Clearly, if a firm were to retain an upper management person under terms of a five-year contract, there would be this notion of future service potential and the person could quite properly be regarded as an asset.

3. In order to meaningfully reflect human assets in its financial accounting data, how would you suggest that Stone & Sons resolve some of the following issues? _____

   a. What is the acquisition cost for each human asset? _____ How much of this first cost, once quantified, is allocable to current expense or, vice versa, how much of it should be capitalized? _____

   b. Over what time period should the capitalized portion of the first cost be amortized? _____ Should the amortization interval be different for each person? _____ Will broad group accounts suffice (e.g., all division managers). _____

   c. How should continuing investments in people be treated in the financial statements (i.e., expensed or capitalized), and on the basis of what criteria should management make these judgments? _____

   d. Does the acquisition cost really capture and convey the value of the human asset? _____ Although historical-cost–based accounting records assets on the books of account at "cost," would it perhaps be better to use some more realistic and current measure of human resource "value"? _____ Some alternative methods for valuation might be:

1. *Capitalization of Salary:* Using this approach, one would make a pro forma projection of a person's salary and discount it to a present value at an appropriate discount rate. Aside from the difficulty of selecting an "appropriate" discount rate, a definition for *salary* will have to be developed. Is salary to include stock options, executive fringes, pensions, and so on, or rather simply just the plain cash disbursements across time? _____ In other words, what exactly is to be capitalized and at what rate? _____

2. *Replacement Costs:* This method would value human assets at the estimated costs to the firm of replacing them with others of "like talent and experience." This replacement cost concept would serve to adjust the balance sheet value of human resources to current price trends in the economy, thereby providing a more realistic value during, say, inflationary times. However, it would also be inconsistent with the historical cost approach to valuing assets and would thus lead to a balance sheet wherein different assets would be denominated in dollars of different years and therefore of different values. One possible solution to this dilemma would be to value all assets at replacement cost.

3. *Economic Value:* This approach to valuing the human resources of an organization involves discounting to a present value that portion of the firm's future earnings that is directly attributed to human resources. The matter of the appropriate discount rate has, again, to be resolved; but of more importance and difficulty is the problem of properly allocating the future earnings to the several factor inputs of production. People, patents, finance, capital goods, and so on, all contribute to a firm's output. Is it practical or even possible to attempt a reasonable partitioning of future earnings among these factor inputs, or would such an exercise degenerate into a totally arbitrary allocative process? _____

   e. Other problems remain: What attitude will the regulatory agencies adopt toward the inclusion of human resource assets and their concomitant amortization in the determination of allowable investment bases for public utilities? _____ Will government agencies recognize human resource assets as legitimate balance sheet items in determining proper fees and profits on their contract awards? _____ What are the legal implications of human resource assets? _____ Does a corporation really "own" its human resources? _____

4. Comment on the following: One view of Stone & Son's Human Resource Accounting system is that it represents

an effort to refine and improve its internal management practices and to make its financial accounting system and output data more responsive and relevant to the needs of its users. Another view might be that Stone & Sons has embarked on a course that will only add to the lack of objectivity and the problems that already plague generally accepted accounting principles.

CASE 16-3   Homearnings Reverse Mortgage Group (A)

Providian Corporation, a blue-chip financial services organization based in Louisville, Kentucky, had spent years developing its Homearnings Plan[sm], a home-equity conversion loan that allowed senior citizens to convert the equity in their home into tax-free advances. The reverse mortgage product was being sold by two of Providian's family companies, Commonwealth Life Insurance Company and Peoples Security Life Insurance Company. These companies along with the newly formed Homearnings Reverse Mortgage Group were part of Providian Capital Management (PCM).

Chuck Lambert, managing director of the Homearnings Reverse Mortgage Group, was preparing to meet with the senior staff of PCM to discuss the accounting policies for the reverse mortgage product. Because this product had features of both a mortgage loan and an insurance annuity, none of the existing technical accounting literature

Professor Amy Patricia Hutton prepared this case as the basis for class discussion rather than to illustrate either effective or ineffective handling of an administrative situation.

While the case facts faithfully reflect the spirit of the events occurring at the Homearnings Reverse Mortgage Group, they simplify complex issues to facilitate a general discussion. The case exhibits were created by the case author for illustrative purposes only.

Copyright © 1994 by the President and Fellows of Harvard College. Harvard Business School case 194–098.

prescribed exactly how to account for it. Chuck would have to interpret the existing literature and improvise to provide recommendations on how to account for this innovative financial product.

Cindy Brundage, director of finance at the Homearnings Reverse Mortgage Group, had been assisting Chuck with the interpretation of the existing technical accounting literature. She had discussed with Chuck pertinent highlights of the existing literature and their implications for the new reverse mortgage product.

Based on his discussions with Cindy, Chuck had decided to argue for capitalization of the costs incurred to develop the reverse mortgage product. However, he remained undecided on whether to recommend capitalizing or expensing the acquisition and origination costs associated with the reverse mortgage contracts. There were good arguments for either approach. Chuck was also undecided on how to handle the recognition of revenue for this new product.

The choice of accounting policies would determine the future stream of reported earnings of the Homearnings Reverse Mortgage Group. Overcapitalizing origination costs could paint too rosy a picture, while undercapitalization would result in too grim a picture. Likewise for the choice of revenue recognition policy, an overly aggressive policy could result in future write-offs, while an overly conservative policy would understate Homearnings' performance.

Chuck wanted the reported numbers to reflect the true performance of Homearnings on a timely basis. However, he worried that the accounting for this innovative product could make the reverse mortgage business seem unattractive. If in the short term Homearnings appeared unprofitable, management's excitement for this new product might wane and as a result Homearnings might receive less support from PCM during its critical start-up period. If in the longer term Homearnings continued to appear unprofitable, PCM's senior management might decide to discontinue the product line.

Background

In 1993, Providian Corporation was one of the five largest shareholder-owned life insurance organizations in the United States. With $22.9 billion in assets, over five million customers, and products and services offered in all 50 states, Providian was a leading provider of consumer financial services. Its stated mission was "to profitably assist individuals and families in achieving their financial objectives." Providian pursued this mission by providing products and services, including life insurance, consumer loans, and annuity and pension products, through a variety of distribution channels, including agents, direct marketing media, and investment professionals. Evidence of Providian's success included the fact that over its 23-year life the company had reported uninterrupted growth of annual operating earnings per share and dividends per share.

In the mid-1980s Providian's management began examining the compatibility of a reverse mortgage product with its overall corporate strategy. Management felt that the demographic trends indicated an emerging market for reverse mortgages. There were more than 30 million Americans over age 65. These citizens owned almost a trillion dollars of total home equity. Management envisioned that as an early entrant into the reverse mortgage market, the company could build expertise in structuring the product, develop brand recognition among senior citizens, and develop a distribution network that would target potential customers. In addition, Providian's guaranteed investment contract business offered a readily available source of funding for reverse mortgages. The reverse mortgage product could be designed as a floating-rate asset to match against this floating-rate liability product, which was indexed to long-term interest rates. Homearnings Plans℠ were priced to yield 240 basis points (2.4%) over 10-year U.S. Treasury bonds.

The Homearnings Plan℠

The Homearnings Plan℠ was a home-equity conversion loan that allowed homeowners to convert the equity or value in their home into tax-free advances. A homeowner had to be 62 or older and own a home with a lending value of $75,000 or more to qualify for the Homearnings Plan℠. Unlike a traditional mortgage, the Homearnings Plan℠ paid the homeowner money each month. Hence the name *reverse mortgage.* The Homearnings Plan℠ guaranteed monthly payments for as long as the homeowner lived in his or her home and guaranteed that repayment was not required until the homeowner died, moved, or sold the home. The Homearnings Plan℠ also protected the homeowner's other assets by limiting the mortgagor's obligation to the resale value of his or her home. Thus, a portion of a mortgagor's outstanding loan balance could be unrecoverable if either the mortgagor lived in their home longer than expected (tenure risk) or if their home's value appreciated less than expected (home appreciation risk). Providian Corporation assumed these risks each time its Homearnings Group wrote a reverse mortgage contract. (See **Appendix A** for a detailed example of a Homearnings Plan℠.)

Accounting for Reverse Mortgage Contracts

Accounting for Market and Line-of-Business Development

As of December 31, 1989, Providian had completed the basic market and line-of-business development activities necessary for sale of their reverse mortgage product. These activities included: product design and pricing, regulatory approval and licensing, registration of the Homearnings name for service mark protection, market research, and market development.

Recommendations were required on which development costs to capitalize and which to expense. Essentially, all references in the technical accounting literature indicated that capitalization of line-of-business development costs was appropriate if there was probable future economic benefit associated with these costs. Chuck believed that the reverse mortgage product line had extremely favorable prospects. His positive forecast was based on the many unique and very appealing features of the Homearnings product, Providian's ability to successfully combine the elements necessary to market and administer this complex product, their leadership position in the market, the lack of any strong competitors, the favorable market demographics and explosive growth potential, and the favorable profit margins priced into the Homearnings product.

In addition, there were several other tangible factors that pointed towards success for this product line, including: very favorable market research, a very positive response to initial advertising efforts (indicating that 70 thousand to 100 thousand people were interested in buying the Homearnings Plan^{sm}), extremely encouraging results in developing partnership marketing channels, and the closing of thirty-one contracts with eighty-five pending applications—while still very much in the development stage of the business. Based on these facts, Chuck was prepared to argue for capitalization of all development costs.

Product Accounting

At first glance, it seemed that the basic accounting for the reverse mortgage product was relatively straightforward. Traditional mortgage loan accounting could be applied; an asset would be accumulated as cash was paid out over the life of the contract and revenue would be recognized at a constant rate of return. However, recognizing that the Homearnings Plan^{sm} had features of both a mortgage loan and an insurance annuity, ongoing accounting for this product presented a dilemma—should it be accounted for as a mortgage loan or as an insurance contract?

Acquisition Costs.   With regard to acquisition or origination costs, the accounting literature prescribed very different treatments for insurance contracts and mortgage loans. Acquisition costs are all costs that varied directly with the production and sale of reverse mortgage contracts, including product marketing and solicitation costs, commissions, appraisals, and closing costs. For insurance contracts, Financial Accounting Standards Board Number 60 (FASB 60) permitted deferral of all "costs that vary with and are primarily related to the acquisition of" insurance business. Conversely, mortgage loan accounting, under FASB 91, indicated that acquisition costs "should be charged to expense as incurred because the nature of the solicitation is such that it is impracticable to identify the extent of successful and solicitation efforts on a timely, reliable basis."

Generally Accepted Accounting Principles' (GAAP's) differing treatments of acquisition costs for mortgage loan and insurance contracts seemed reasonable given the substantially different marketing efforts required to originate these contracts. Mortgage loans were a generic product offered on almost a commodity-type basis, and therefore product marketing and solicitation costs were relatively minor. However, insurance products were typically much more complex, requiring a very expensive marketing effort to explain the intricacies of the product and successfully place these higher-margin products. Thus, proper deferral of marketing costs was critically important for determining the profitability of insurance products. Accordingly, GAAP had always permitted deferral of product marketing and solicitation costs in the insurance industry.

Providian had designed its reverse mortgage product to be attractive primarily for the insurance protection it offered. The Homearnings Plan^sm could be viewed as an insurance annuity with the premium deferred until the end of the contract. Given the complexity of its benefit structure and pricing, a substantial marketing effort was required to sell this product. Thus, it seemed clear to Chuck that Homearnings was much more akin to an insurance policy than to a simple mortgage loan and therefore acquisition costs ought to be deferred. However, Chuck wondered if others, particularly Providian's auditor and the Security and Exchange Commission, would make the same call.

Revenue Recognition.   While capitalization of the acquisition costs under FASB 60 seemed appropriate for determining the profitability of the reverse mortgage product, revenue recognition under FASB 60 seemed inappropriate. FASB 60 permitted premium revenue to be recognized once payments were due from the policyholders. Thus, using *Insurance Accounting* under FASB 60, no revenue could be recognized during the life of the reverse mortgage contract. Revenue from reverse mortgage contracts could be recognized only at the end of the contracts when payments were due from the "policyholder."

Cindy proposed three alternatives to *Insurance Accounting* for reverse mortgage revenue recognition:

Investment Real Estate Accounting: Revenue from the reverse mortgage contracts would be recognized at the end of the contracts when the real estate assets were sold. Over the life of the contracts, as cash was paid out to the homeowner, Homearnings' asset, investment in real estate, would grow. To provide for potential declines in real estate values, a valuation allowance would be established.

Mortgage Loan Accounting: Revenue would be recognized at a constant rate of return over the life of the contract, using the contractual interest rate. Similar to the investment real estate accounting, an asset would accumulate as cash was paid out over the life of the reverse mortgage contract and a valuation allowance would be established to absorb realized gain or loss each period.

Pooling of Contracts Approach: Reverse mortgage contracts would be grouped into "pools" of sufficient size to insure an actuarially sound basis for making estimates of life expectancy and future expected home appreciation rates. Homearnings would use these estimates to make projections of future cash flows and from the projected cash flows estimate an effective yield (the internal rate of return). Investment income would be recognized by applying the effective yield to the net investment in the contracts. To provide for lower than predicted home appreciation rates, accumulated investment income would be reported net of a valuation allowance.

Chuck compared all four alternative approaches. It seemed to him that the investment in real estate approach was very similar to insurance accounting under

FASB 60. Both deferred revenue recognition until the end of the reverse mortgage contract. The pooling approach seemed very similar to mortgage loan accounting. Both recognized revenue over the life of the contract, just at different rates. Mortgage loan accounting used the contractual rate and the pooling approach used the effective yield. However, Chuck believed that the pooling of contracts approach was out of the running in the short term because Homearnings' portfolio of reverse mortgage contracts had not yet grown to a sufficiently large number to insure actuarially sound estimates.

Chuck tried to reason which one of the remaining methods was most appropriate. The Homearnings Plan[sm] was structured like a mortgage loan. The underlying secured asset was the borrower's residence, and the borrower had the right to prepay the loan at any time. Thus, mortgage loan accounting seemed appropriate. However, unlike a mortgage loan, repayment of the accumulated loan balance normally came solely from the proceeds from the sale of the borrower's residence. This aspect of the reverse mortgage product indicated that accounting for it as an investment in real estate was appropriate. On the other hand, since Homearnings had an open-ended commitment to make payments to the mortgagor until his or her death, the reverse mortgage contract lacked a fixed or certain maturity date and amount. This feature of the contract indicated that insurance accounting was more appropriate.

To gain a better understanding of the implications of these various policies for Homearnings' reported income, Cindy prepared three pro forma income statements. In the pro forma income statements Cindy assumed Homearnings would originate 1,000 reverse mortgage contracts each year. The first showed Homearnings' pro forma income over the next 20 years if Homearnings capitalized the acquisition costs and used mortgage loan accounting for revenue recognition (see **Exhibit 1**). To isolate the effect of expensing the acquisition costs, the second pro forma income statements assumed that Homearnings employed mortgage loan accounting for revenue recognition, but expensed the acquisition costs (see **Exhibit 2**). The final pro forma statements demonstrated the most conservative accounting methods, investment in real estate accounting for revenue recognition and expensing of the acquisition costs (see **Exhibit 3**).

It was apparent from the pro forma statements, that Chuck's recommendations, if accepted, would greatly influence stakeholders' perceptions of Homearnings' profitability. He worried that the proper accounting for reverse mortgage contracts might defer reported profitability too far into the future. If he chose the most conservative accounting methods, reported losses were projected for the next ten years (see **Exhibit 3**). Would the management of PCM and of Providian Corporation provide the support needed for this new product to be successful, if it appeared to be unprofitable for so long into the future?

Exhibit 1   Reverse Mortgages

Pre-Tax Pro Forma Statement of Income *

Accounting Methods:
capitalization of acquisition costs
mortgage loan accounting for revenue recognition
(000's)

						Year					
	1	*2*	*3*	*4*	*5*	*6*	*7*	*8*	*9*	*10*	*11*
Investment income	7,614	12,336	18,015	24,584	31,960	40,045	48,718	57,829	67,246	76,778	86,206
Non-origination costs	(2,408)	(2,508)	(2,449)	(2,119)	(2,429)	(2,718)	(2,985)	(3,230)	(3,454)	(3,655)	(3,836)
Amortization of acquisition costs	(484)	(877)	(1,184)	(1,404)	(1,624)	(1,844)	(2,064)	(2,284)	(2,504)	(2,724)	(2,460)
Amortization of development costs	(210)	(210)	(210)	(210)	(210)	(210)	(210)	(210)	(210)	(210)	0
Gain (Loss) before cost of funds	4,512	8,741	14,172	20,851	27,697	35,273	43,459	52,105	61,078	70,189	79,910
Costs of funds	(7,405)	(11,693)	(16,636)	(21,686)	(27,330)	(33,334)	(39,582)	(45,958)	(52,342)	(58,598)	(64,583)
Gain (Loss)	(2,893)	(2,952)	(2,464)	(835)	367	1,939	3,877	6,147	8,736	11,591	15,327
Net Cash Invested	(53,672)	(58,730)	(57,540)	(58,289)	(56,967)	(53,481)	(47,917)	(40,755)	(31,553)	(20,540)	(8,359)
Cum. Cash Invested	(135,496)	(194,226)	(251,765)	(310,055)	(367,022)	(420,502)	(468,419)	(509,174)	(540,727)	(561,267)	(569,626)
Max. Cash Invested	(569,626)										

				Year					
	12	*13*	*14*	*15*	*16*	*17*	*18*	*19*	*20*
Investment income	95,385	104,312	112,596	120,449	127,629	134,247	140,189	145,595	150,277
Non-origination costs	(3,997)	(4,138)	(4,261)	(4,366)	(4,456)	(4,532)	(4,595)	(4,647)	(4,689)
Amortization of acquisition costs	(2,287)	(2,200)	(2,200)	(2,200)	(2,200)	(2,200)	(2,200)	(2,200)	(2,200)
Amortization of development costs	0	0	0	0	0	0	0	0	0
Gain (Loss) before cost of funds	89,102	97,974	106,135	113,883	120,973	127,515	133,394	138,748	143,388
Costs of funds	(70,170)	(75,270)	(79,818)	(83,766)	(87,075)	(89,730)	(91,735)	(93,105)	(95,105)
Gain (Loss)	18,932	22,704	26,317	30,117	33,898	37,785	41,659	45,643	48,283
Net Cash Invested	(4,438)	174,859	30,409	43,391	55,688	67,062	77,645	87,355	96,310
Cum. Cash Invested	(565,189)	(547,730)	(517,240)	(473,849)	(419,161)	(351,099)	(273,454)	(186,098)	(89,788)

*Assumes 1,000 closings each year and expenses remain at pricing level prevailing in year 4.

EXHIBIT 2   Reverse Mortgages

Pre-Tax Pro Forma Statement of Income*
Accounting Methods:
expense acquisition costs
mortgage loan accounting for revenue recognition
(000's)

						Year					
	1	2	3	4	5	6	7	8	9	10	11
Investment income	7,614	12,336	18,015	24,584	31,960	40,045	48,718	57,829	67,246	76,778	86,206
Non-origination costs	(2,408)	(2,508)	(2,449)	(2,119)	(2,429)	(2,718)	(2,985)	(3,230)	(3,454)	(3,655)	(3,836)
Acquisition costs	(7,256)	(5,900)	(4,600)	(3,300)	(3,300)	(3,300)	(3,300)	(3,300)	(3,300)	(3,300)	(3,300)
Amortization of development costs	(210)	(210)	(210)	(210)	(210)	(210)	(210)	(210)	(210)	(210)	0
Gain (Loss) before cost of funds	(2,260)	3,718	10,756	18,955	26,021	33,817	42,223	51,089	60,282	69,613	79,070
Costs of funds	(7,405)	(11,693)	(16,636)	(21,686)	(27,330)	(33,334)	(39,582)	(45,958)	(52,342)	(58,598)	(64,583)
Gain (Loss)	(9,665)	(7,975)	(5,880)	(2,731)	(1,309)	483	2,641	5,131	7,940	11,015	14,487
Net Cash Invested	(53,672)	(58,730)	(57,540)	(58,289)	(56,967)	(53,481)	(47,917)	(40,755)	(31,553)	(20,540)	(8,359)
Cum. Cash Invested	(135,496)	(194,226)	(251,765)	(310,055)	(367,022)	(420,502)	(468,419)	(509,174)	(540,727)	(561,267)	(569,626)
Max. Cash Invested	(569,626)										

					Year				
	12	13	14	15	16	17	18	19	20
Investment income	95,385	104,312	112,596	120,449	127,629	134,247	140,189	145,595	150,277
Non-origination costs	(3,997)	(4,138)	(4,261)	(4,366)	(4,456)	(4,532)	(4,595)	(4,647)	(4,689)
Acquisition costs	(3,300)	(3,300)	(3,300)	(3,300)	(3,300)	(3,300)	(3,300)	(3,300)	(3,300)
Amortization of development costs	0	0	0	0	0	0	0	0	0
Gain (Loss) before cost of funds	88,088	96,874	105,035	112,783	119,873	126,415	132,294	137,648	142,288
Costs of funds	(70,170)	(75,270)	(79,818)	(83,766)	(87,075)	(89,730)	(91,735)	(93,105)	(95,105)
Gain (Loss)	17,918	21,604	25,217	29,017	32,798	36,685	40,559	44,543	47,183
Net Cash Invested	(4,438)	174,859	30,409	43,391	55,688	67,062	77,645	87,355	96,310
Cum. Cash Invested	(565,189)	(547,730)	(517,240)	(473,849)	(419,161)	(351,099)	(273,454)	(186,098)	(89,788)

*Assumes: 1,000 closings each year and expenses remain at pricing level prevailing in year 4.

EXHIBIT 3   Reverse Mortgages

Pre-Tax Pro Forma Statement of Income*
Accounting Methods:
expense acquisition costs
investment in real estate accounting for revenue recognition
(000's)

	Year										
	1	2	3	4	5	6	7	8	9	10	11
Investment income	0	0		0	0	0	0	0	0	0	129,493
Non-origination costs	(2,408)	(2,508)	(2,449)	(2,119)	(2,429)	(2,718)	(2,985)	(3,230)	(3,454)	(3,655)	(3,836)
Acquisition costs	(7,256)	(5,900)	(4,600)	(3,300)	(3,300)	(3,300)	(3,300)	(3,300)	(3,300)	(3,300)	(3,300)
Amortization of development costs	(210)	(210)	(210)	(210)	(210)	(210)	(210)	(210)	(210)	(210)	0
Gain (Loss) before cost of funds	(9,874)	(8,618)	(7,259)	(5,629)	(5,939)	(6,228)	(6,495)	(6,740)	(6,964)	(7,165)	122,357
Costs of funds	(7,405)	(11,693)	(16,636)	(21,686)	(27,330)	(33,334)	(39,582)	(45,958)	(52,342)	(58,598)	(64,583)
Gain (Loss)	(17,279)	(20,311)	(23,895)	(27,315)	(33,269)	(39,562)	(46,077)	(52,698)	(59,306)	(65,763)	57,774
Net Cash Invested	(53,672)	(58,730)	(57,540)	(58,289)	(56,967)	(53,481)	(47,917)	(40,755)	(31,553)	(20,540)	(8,359)
Cum. Cash Invested	(135,496)	(194,226)	(251,765)	(310,055)	(367,022)	(420,502)	(468,419)	(509,174)	(540,727)	(561,267)	(569,626)
Max. Cash Invested	(569,626)										

	Year								
	12	13	14	15	16	17	18	19	20
Investment income	129,493	129,493	129,493	129,493	129,493	129,493	129,493	129,493	129,493
Non-origination costs	(3,997)	(4,138)	(4,261)	(4,366)	(4,456)	(4,532)	(4,595)	(4,647)	(4,689)
Acquisition costs	(3,300)	(3,300)	(3,300)	(3,300)	(3,300)	(3,300)	(3,300)	(3,300)	(3,300)
Amortization of development costs	0	0	0	0	0	0	0	0	0
Gain (Loss) before cost of funds	122,196	122,055	121,932	121,827	121,737	121,661	121,598	121,546	121,504
Costs of funds	(70,170)	(75,270)	(79,818)	(83,766)	(87,075)	(89,730)	(91,735)	(93,105)	(95,105)
Gain (Loss)	52,026	46,785	42,114	38,061	34,662	31,931	29,863	28,441	26,399
Net Cash Invested	(4,438)	174,859	30,409	43,391	55,688	67,062	77,645	87,355	96,310
Cum. Cash Invested	(565,189)	(547,730)	(517,240)	(473,849)	(419,161)	(351,099)	(273,454)	(186,098)	(89,788)

*Assumes: (i) 1,000 closings each year, (ii) mortgagors sell their home 10 years after origination of the contract, and (iii) expenses remain at pricing level prevailing in year 4.

Questions

1. Describe the economics of the Homearnings' reverse mortgage product. What would Homearnings have to do well to succeed in the reverse mortgage business? _____ What were the risks and rewards to Providian Corporation each time the Homearnings Group underwrote a reverse mortgage contract? _____

2. How do the accounting issues discussed in the case relate to these risks and rewards? _____ What would be the best choices of accounting procedures if management wanted to faithfully reflect the risks and rewards of this new product? _____

3. What other considerations were likely to influence management's final policy choices? _____

Appendix A: A Sample Homearnings Plan^{sm}

Consider Mrs. Angeline Logar, a 75 year-old widow, who decided to obtain a reverse mortgage on her $100,000 home. Assuming a 10% nominal interest rate and a 5.6% annual home appreciation rate for Mrs. Logar's home, Homearnings offered to pay Mrs. Logar $500 per month for as long as she lived in her home. Under the terms of the contract, Mrs. Logar could remain in her home as long as she wished; would retain full ownership of her home; and would have no payments due as long as she lived in her home. Providian agreed to pay all acquisition, closing, and origination costs. In exchange, Mrs. Logar agreed to pay a borrower's fee totaling $10,000, $3,000 plus 7% of the initial home value. Collection of this fee plus accrued interest was deferred until the end of the contract.

While the amount of the annuity paid to Mrs. Logar was fixed ($500 per month), its length was not. Under certain conditions either Providian or Mrs. Logar could terminate the contract. Providian could terminate the contract if for any reason Mrs. Logar was absent from her home for 60 consecutive days. Mrs. Logar could terminate the contract at any time by simply selling her home and using the proceeds to repay her loan.

Suppose at the age of 83 Mrs. Logar decided to sell her home. **Figure A1** illustrates Homearnings' cash payments to (negative) and from (positive) Mrs. Logar. Homearnings paid Mrs. Logar $500 per month for 96 months. In the 97th month Mrs. Logar sold her home for $154,636 and used $95,273 of the proceeds to repay her loan obligation. Mrs. Logar's loan obligation was the sum of the 96 monthly payments, the borrower's fee, and accrued interest.

Schedule A1 provided Mrs. Logar's accumulated loan balance over the next 20 years. The accumulated loan balance in year N is equal to the future value of an annuity of $500 per month for N × 12 months plus the future value of the $10,000 borrower's

FIGURE A1

Homearnings' Cash Flows if Mrs. Logar Sold Her Home at the Age of 83

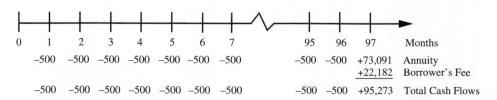

SCHEDULE A1   Mrs. Angeline Logar's Homearnings Plan

Year of the Contract	Mrs. Logar's Age	Accumulated Loan Balance	Estimated Selling Price	Original Home Value
0	75	$ 10,000	$100,000	$100,000
1	76	17,330	105,600	100,000
2	77	25,427	111,514	100,000
3	78	34,373	117,758	100,000
4	79	44,255	124,353	100,000
5	80	55,172	131,317	100,000
6	81	67,232	138,670	100,000
7	82	80,554	146,436	100,000
8	83	95,272	154,636	100,000
9	84	111,531	163,296	100,000
10	85	129,493	172,440	100,000
11	86	149,335	182,097	100,000
12	87	171,255	192,295	100,000
13	88	195,471	203,063	100,000
14	89	222,222	214,435	100,000
15	90	251,774	226,443	100,000
16	91	284,421	239,124	100,000
17	92	320,487	252,515	100,000
18	93	360,328	266,655	100,000
19	94	404,342	281,588	100,000
20	95	452,965	297,357	100,000

fee N years into the future. An interest rate of 10% is assumed. The estimated selling price of her home over the next 20 years is also shown in column four of **Schedule A1**: The selling price of Mrs. Logar's home was expected to appreciate 5.6% each year (the national average rate of appreciation during the period 1955 to 1985).

If Mrs. Logar decided to sell her home at the age of 83, its value would still be greater than the accumulated loan balance. However, if Mrs. Logar continued to live in her home, eventually the accumulated loan balance would exceed the estimated selling price of her home. **Figure A2** plots the schedules of the accumulated loan balance and the

FIGURE A2

*Pro Forma Schedules for Mrs. Logar's Homearnings Plan*sm

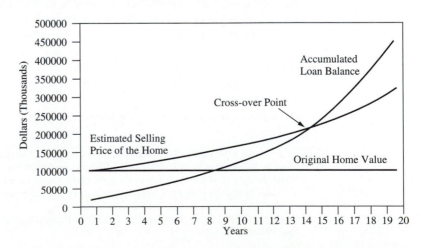

estimated selling price provided in columns three and four of **Schedule A1.** The "cross-over point" indicates when the loan balance first exceeds the estimated selling price of the home. This occurs in the 14th year of the contract, at the end of which the estimated selling price would be $214,435 and the accumulated loan balance would be $222,222.

Since Homearnings' claim on Logar's assets is limited to the value of her home, after the cross-over point a portion of the outstanding loan balance would be unrecoverable. To illustrate, suppose Mrs. Logar lived in her home until the age of 95. The outstanding balance of her loan would be $452,965 and the value of her home would be only $297,357 (see **Schedule A1**). Under the terms of the reverse mortgage contract, Mrs. Logar (or her estate) would be required to repay $297,357, the value of the home. Thus, Homearnings would lose $155,608 as a result of Mrs. Logar outliving the life expectancy projected for her age group. Mrs. Logar could stay in her home beyond the cross-over point as a result of either longer-than-average tenure or lower-than-expected home appreciation.

CASE
16-4

Homearnings Reverse Mortgage Group (B)

Our strategy was to enter the reverse mortgage market early and build a presence that would lead to a competitive advantage as this new market emerged. We made the decision to enter the reverse mortgage market to create economic value for our shareholders. Ultimately, the creation of economic value flows through the financial statements, but the timing of when the economic value flows through the financial statements is governed by the accounting rules. And the SEC's new rules do not allow the reported numbers to reflect the economic value we are creating at Homearnings.

Joe Tumbler, *president of Providian Capital Management, Providian Corporation*

Professor Amy Patricia Hutton prepared this case as the basis for class discussion rather than to illustrate either effective or ineffective handling of an administrative situation.

While the case facts faithfully reflect the spirit of the events occurring at the Homearnings Reverse Mortgage Group, they simplify complex issues to facilitate a general discussion. The case exhibits were created by the case author for illustrative purposes only.

Joe Tumbler, president of Providian Capital Management (PCM), was commenting on the Security and Exchange Commission's (SEC's) memorandum dated July 14, 1992. The memorandum would require the Homearnings Reverse Mortgage Group, a start-up group within PCM, to change its current accounting policies for its reverse mortgage product. The required accounting change would have a dramatic effect on the reported profitability of this new group.

With no clear precedent to follow, the Homearnings Group had been using a hybrid of mortgage loan and insurance accounting to account for its reverse mortgage product. Employing customary mortgage loan accounting, Homearnings had been accumulating an asset on its balance sheet as cash was paid out over the life of the reverse mortgage contract and revenue had been recognized each year at a constant rate of return. Applying customary insurance accounting, Homearnings had been capitalizing the origination costs of reverse mortgages and expensing them over the life of the contract to provide for matching of revenues and expenses.

The SEC's memorandum sent to Providential Corporation, Providian's main competitor in the reverse mortgage business, required immediate expensing of origination costs and disallowed customary mortgage loan accounting for reverse mortgage contracts. The memorandum recommended accounting for reverse mortgage contracts as an investment in real estate, which deferred the recognition of revenue until the end of the contract. However, the SEC's memorandum did permit earlier revenue recognition via the pooling of contracts method if a company originated a large number of reverse mortgage contracts, such that the cash flows associated with the contracts could be reliably estimated. Companies employing the pooling of contracts method were required to use the SEC's formula for calculating investment income, which assumed a zero home appreciation rate. (See **Exhibit 1** for a brief summary of the SEC's pooling of contracts method.) Despite the fact that the SEC's memorandum dealt only with *the accounting* for reverse mortgage contracts, two days after the publication of the memorandum Providential's stock price plummeted from $18 to $6. And within a few days, six shareholder lawsuits alleging securities violations were filed against Providential Corporation and its management.

EXHIBIT 1   A Summary of the SEC's Pooling of Contracts Method

All origination and acquisition costs are to be expensed as incurred.

Reverse mortgage contracts are to be grouped into "pools" of sufficient size to insure an actuarially sound basis for making estimates of life expectancy. Lenders are to use these estimates of life expectancy to make projections of future cash flows. When projecting estimated cash inflows, lenders may incorporate actual increases (and have to incorporate actual decreases) in property values that have occurred to date, but are not permitted to project future increases (i.e., lenders are required to assume a zero home appreciation rate).

Using their projections of future cash flows, lenders are to estimate an effective yield (the internal rate of return) and recognize investment income by applying the effective yield to the net investment in the contracts. At each reporting period, lenders are required to re-estimate future cash flows (including actual cash flows to date) and to recompute the effective yield. The accumulated investment income is to be adjusted at the close of each period to the amount that would have been recognized to date had the revised effective yield been applied since the inception of the pool. To provide for potential declines in real estate values, a valuation allowance is to be established.

In recent months, the marketing and accounting issues surrounding the reverse mortgage business had begun to appear more difficult than Joe had originally anticipated. The origination costs associated with this innovative financial product were not falling as quickly as planned. It was turning out to be exceptionally difficult to lower the cost of originating a product that was very complicated, was sold to elderly customers, and involved mortgaging the customer's home. And, under the SEC's new accounting rules, these high costs would be a current expense with little or no revenue to offset them. As a result, Homearnings would report a loss of $11 million in 1993 and would not report its first profit for nine years. (See **Exhibit 2** Homearnings' pro forma income statements under the SEC's new accounting rules.)

As a result of these developments, Joe began to wonder whether Providian Corporation ought to be in the reverse mortgage business. The Homearnings Plan was a very appealing product and met what was likely to become a growing need among senior citizens. It allowed elderly homeowners to convert their home equity into cash without selling their homes. Providian had received considerable positive press coverage for servicing elderly homeowners' need for cash. Furthermore, the reverse mortgage product fit well with Providian's overall corporate strategy and was priced to yield high margins, 240 basis points (2.4%) over 10-year U.S. Treasury bonds.

Providian had been among the first to enter the reverse mortgage business. Joe understood that scouts take the arrows; but he was beginning to wonder whether Homearnings had taken enough arrows. He was particularly concerned with the magnitude of Homearnings' reported losses under the unfavorable accounting regulations. And, he wondered if the economic value of the product had changed: acquisition costs were above plan and future home appreciation rates might not be as high as originally expected. Joe asked Chuck Lambert, the managing director of Homearnings Reverse Mortgage Group, to suggest several possible plans of action.

Questions

1. See case.

EXHIBIT 2 Reverse Mortgages

Pre-Tax Pro Forma Statement of Income*

Accounting Methods:
expense acquisition costs
pooling of contracts approach for revenue recognition
(000's)

Year

	1	2	3	4	5	6	7	8	9	10	11
Investment income	7,188	11,631	16,956	23,101	29,974	37,494	45,501	53,890	62,480	71,139	79,653
Non-origination costs**	(3,789)	(3,889)	(3,830)	(3,500)	(3,810)	(4,099)	(4,366)	(4,611)	(4,835)	(5,036)	(3,836)
Acquisition costs	(7,256)	(5,900)	(4,600)	(3,300)	(3,300)	(3,300)	(3,300)	(3,300)	(3,300)	(3,300)	(3,300)
Amortization of development costs	(210)	(210)	(210)	(210)	(210)	(210)	(210)	(210)	(210)	(210)	0
Mark to market adjustment	+/-	+/-	+/-	+/-	+/-	+/-	+/-	+/-	+/-	+/-	+/-
Gain (Loss) before cost of funds	(4,067)	1,632	8,316	16,091	22,654	29,885	37,625	45,769	54,135	62,593	72,517
Costs of funds	(7,405)	(11,693)	(16,636)	(21,686)	(27,330)	(33,334)	(39,582)	(45,958)	(52,342)	(58,598)	(64,583)
Gain (Loss)	(11,472)	(10,061)	(8,320)	(5,595)	(4,676)	(3,449)	(1,957)	(189)	1,793	3,995	7,934
Net Cash Invested	(53,672)	(58,730)	(57,540)	(58,289)	(56,967)	(53,481)	(47,917)	(40,755)	(31,553)	(20,540)	(8,359)
Cum. Cash Invested	(135,496)	(194,226)	(251,765)	(310,055)	(367,022)	(420,502)	(468,419)	(509,174)	(540,727)	(561,267)	(569,626)
Max. Cash Invested	(569,626)										

Year

	12	13	14	15	16	17	18	19	20
Investment income	87,891	95,763	103,085	109,872	115,998	121,571	126,494	130,782	134,504
Non-origination costs	(3,997)	(4,138)	(4,261)	(4,366)	(4,456)	(4,532)	(4,595)	(4,647)	(4,689)
Acquisition costs	(3,300)	(3,300)	(3,300)	(3,300)	(3,300)	(3,300)	(3,300)	(3,300)	(3,300)
Amortization of development costs	0	0	0	0	0	0	0	0	0
Mark to market adjustment	+/-	+/-	+/-	+/-	+/-	+/-	+/-	+/-	+/-
Gain (Loss) before cost of funds	80,594	88,325	95,524	102,206	108,242	113,739	118,599	122,835	126,515
Costs of funds	(70,170)	(75,270)	(79,818)	(83,766)	(87,075)	(89,730)	(91,735)	(93,105)	(95,105)
Gain (Loss)	10,424	13,055	15,706	18,440	21,167	24,009	26,864	29,730	31,410
Net Cash Invested	(4,438)	174,859	30,409	43,391	55,688	67,062	77,645	87,355	96,310
Cum. Cash Invested	(565,189)	(547,730)	(517,240)	(473,849)	(419,161)	(351,099)	(273,454)	(186,098)	(89,788)

*Assumes 1,000 closings each year and expenses remain at pricing level prevailing in year 4.

**Includes adjustments for the cumulative effect of the accounting change on prior years.

Inventory

Selection of a method for pricing inventories represents an important management decision. The procedure chosen will have a major impact on the measurement of net income and net working capital. Competent statement users always pay close attention to inventories, primarily because they are a major asset of many firms, the management judgments and decisions that enter into their pricing can have a significant impact on financial results, and the state of a firm's inventories is often a good indicator of its economic health.

Inventory Pricing

Inventories include all tangible items held for sale or consumption in the normal course of business for which the company holds title, wherever they might be located. Typically, inventories can be placed in one of four categories: finished goods, goods in process, raw materials, and manufacturing supplies. There are several generally accepted methods for pricing inventories. The significant problems in inventory valuation result from the difficulties involved in allocating costs between periods and products, and the failure of selling prices and costs to move together.

Typically, inventories are shown in the current asset section of the balance sheet, immediately after accounts receivable.

Periodic and Perpetual Inventory Systems

Inventory value is determined by multiplying the quantity of inventory on hand by the price per unit. There are two systems for determining inventory quantity: the periodic

Professor David F. Hawkins prepared this note as the basis for class discussion.
Copyright © 1995 by the President and Fellows of Harvard College. Harvard Business School teaching note 195–192.

and the perpetual inventory systems. Irrespective of the system used, it is necessary periodically to inspect inventories physically.

The periodic inventory system involves a periodic determination of beginning inventory, purchases for the period, and ending inventory. These totals are determined by actual count. For these counts the cost of goods sold (COGS) may be determined by deduction. The basic formula is:

Beginning inventories + Purchases − Ending inventories = Cost of goods sold

The perpetual inventory system involves keeping a running record of all the additions to and subtractions from the inventory.

Pricing Bases

Depending on the circumstances, the basis for pricing inventories may be cost; cost or market, whichever is lower; or selling price. The major objective underlying the selection of a pricing basis in a particular case should be the fairest determination of periodic income.

Cost Methods.   Cost is the principal basis for pricing inventories. *Accounting Research Bulletin No. 43,* chapter 4, states:

> The primary basis for accounting for inventories is cost . . . as applied to inventories, cost means in principle the sum of the applicable expenditures and charges directly or indirectly incurred in bringing an article to its existing condition and location.

The inventory prices of manufacturing and merchandising companies reflect the different functions of these two classes of business activity. Manufacturing companies convert raw materials into finished goods. Consequently, their inventory prices reflect the cost of raw materials, direct labor, and factory overhead. Those costs associated with the product are referred to as product costs and are charged against revenues when the products are sold. All other costs, such as general administration and selling costs, are classified as period costs and are charged to the period in which they were incurred. Typically, a merchandising business does not incur conversion costs. As a result, its inventory prices are the prices it paid for the products it sells.

Every well-run business maintains some record of its costs. These costs may be collected and recorded on the basis of either individual jobs (a job cost system) or the various production processes (a process cost system). The costs assigned to the various finished and partially finished products may be predetermined standard costs or actual costs. If a standard cost system is used, the common practice is to assign any small difference between actual and standard costs to costs of good sold (COGS). If the variance is relatively large, however, some effort may be made to allocate the variance between the COGS and ending inventory accounts. In practice, a number of methods are used to allocate overhead costs to products. Most cost systems use a standard manufacturing overhead rate that allocates a fixed amount of overhead per unit to finished or partially finished goods, based on the amount of, say, direct labor dollars embodied in the product cost. Other common bases for allocating overhead are machine-hours, direct labor hours and activities.

The exclusion of all factory overheads from inventory costs does not constitute an accepted accounting procedure for financial or tax accounting. Some argue that the inclusion of fixed factory overhead in inventory prices (and the cost of goods sold) is misleading, since it tends to make profit a function of production rather than sales: a buildup of inventory means more overhead will be charged to inventory and less to the current accounting period. These people advocate "direct costing," a procedure that includes in the product price only variable manufacturing costs. Fixed manufacturing costs are treated as period costs and are charged against income during the period in which they are incurred. Irrespective of the method used in financial reports, direct costing can be used for internal accounting purposes.

Often more than one product is produced from the same raw material. In the case of common products and by-products, raw material costs are typically allocated between the products on the basis of relative sales value, although various other methods are permissible as long as the results are not misleading. Often, for example, if the by-products represent a relatively minor portion of total production, the "by-product cost method" is used. Under this method, the by-product is initially valued at selling price less disposition costs. As a result, the profits and losses of the company are recorded on the sale of the primary product.

Inventory Methods.   A number of generally acceptable methods based on historical costs are used to determine the price of inventories.

Illustration A will be used to demonstrate a number of these cost-based methods (how the actual unit costs were determined will be ignored in these examples).

Specific identification.   The specific identification procedure associates the actual costs with the particular items in inventory. For example, if by inspection the ABC

ILLUSTRATION A   ABC Company

	Units	Unit Cost	Total
Beginning inventory	2	$10	$20
Purchases:			
#1	1	11	11
#2	1	10	10
#3	1	12	12
#4	1	13	13
Cost of goods available for sale			$66
Total quantity available for sale	6		
Total sold during period	4		
Ending inventory	2		

Company determined that its ending inventory consisted of purchases 1 and 3, the ending inventory would be valued at $23. Consequently, the cost of goods for the period would be $43 (total goods available for sale less ending inventory). While this method may relate revenues and costs directly, it is impractical for most businesses. It is sometimes used, however, for "big ticket" items, such as autos.

Last invoice price.   The last invoice price method values the ending inventory at the most recent invoice price paid. Under this method, the two units in the ABC Company's ending inventory would be priced at $26 (2 × $13) and the cost of goods sold expense would be $40. For those companies with a rapid turnover of inventory and where older inventory items are used first, this method gives inventory prices that closely approximate those determined by the specific identification method. This method is not widely used.

Simple average.   The simple average method prices the ending inventory as follows:

$$\frac{\text{Sum of invoice prices per unit}}{\text{Number of invoices}} \times \text{Number of units in ending inventory}$$

For ABC Company, this method would lead to an ending inventory value of $22.40 if the beginning inventory value per unit were included as an "invoice price." As a result, the cost of goods sold would be $43.60. The principal weakness of this procedure is that it gives equal weight to the invoice prices of large and small purchases. Like some of the other methods discussed in this section, however, it is used by small businesses because of its simplicity.

Weighted average.   The weighted average method assigns to the ending inventory the average cost of the units available for sale during the period. The weighted average cost of ABC Company's ending inventory is $22, and the COGS expense for the period is $44:

Cost of goods available for sale	$66
Total units available for sale	6
Average cost	$11
Ending inventory price (2 units × $11)	22

Moving Average.   The moving average method computes the average unit price of the inventory after each purchase. The use of a moving average reduces the extent of the possible lag between inventory price and selling prices associated with the weighted average method. With a perpetual inventory system, the cost of goods sold of ABC Company is $42.22 and the value of the ending inventory is $23.78 (see **Illustration B**).

ILLUSTRATION B

	Physical Units			Dollar Costs		
Date	*Additions to Stock*	*Reductions in Stock*	*Balance*	*Additions to Stock*	*Reductions in Stock*	*Balance*
April 1	—	—	2	—	—	$20.00
6	1	—	3	$ 1	—	31.00
7	—	2	1	—	$20.66	10.34
15	1	—	2	10	—	10.34
16	1	—	3	12	—	32.34
25	—	2	1	—	21.56	10.78
27	1	—	2	13	—	23.78

First-in, First-out.   The first-in, first-out (FIFO) method assigns to inventory the costs that reflect the most recent purchases. For ABC Company, the price of the ending inventory using the FIFO procedure is $25 (i.e., the sum of the costs of purchases 3 and 4—see Illustration A). As a result, the COGS expense is $41.

Last-in, First-out.   The last-in, first-out (LIFO) method assumes the most recent purchase costs are related to current revenues. As a result, the ending inventory reflects the oldest costs.

   LIFO inventories consist of a series of "cost layers." The initial layer includes the quantities and related prices existing when LIFO was adopted. The ending inventory is the base-cost layer plus the older layers of inventory required to equal the quantity of goods at the balance sheet date. For ABC Company, if LIFO had been adopted before the beginning of the period, the initial cost layer would be two units at $10 (i.e., the beginning inventory). The next layer would be purchase 1. Under the LIFO method, ABC's ending inventory determined by a periodic inventory system is $20[1] and the resulting COGS expense is $46. Since unit reduction in inventory equaled purchases, the two units in the ending inventory are valued at the $20 shown for the two units in the beginning inventory. (In practice, LIFO inventory accounting is more complex than suggested by the ABC Company example. These complexities will be discussed later.)

   A company can adopt the LIFO method for income tax purposes only if it also uses this method in its published financial statements. If ABC Company used LIFO accounting, its taxable profits would be less than under FIFO since the LIFO COGS would be higher ($46) than the FIFO figure ($41).

---

[1]**Illustration B** shows that on April 7 ABC Company reduced its inventory to one unit, which is less than the LIFO layer of two units at the beginning of the year. The same thing occurred on April 25. Since the value of LIFO inventory is determined at year-end, if the depleted LIFO layers are replaced by year-end the fact that the company "dipped into" its LIFO basis during the year has no impact on the cost of goods sold.

LIFO inventory accounting can be applied to raw materials, finished goods, or some component of finished goods. It may be used to account for some inventories and not others. Or, it may be used to account for one item or a collection of items grouped into so-called dollar value pools. Pools are often formed around natural business unit inventories, product lines, or geographic locations.

LIFO versus FIFO.   The LIFO and FIFO methods are among the most popular inventory pricing procedures. In practice, each is considered an equally acceptable alternative. Their impact on working capital and net income, however, can differ significantly. For example, in the ABC situation, the LIFO procedure led to an ending inventory valued at $20, whereas the FIFO method resulted in an ending inventory valued at $25. The cost of goods sold for the period also reflected the different procedures: LIFO led to a COGS expense of $46, versus $41 with FIFO. The extent of the cost difference in this illustration should not be considered typical. It highlights, however, the relationship between the inventory pricing procedure, the inventory value, and the COGS expense.

The adoption of LIFO as an acceptable inventory method caused considerable controversy. The advocates of LIFO argued that this procedure stated the cost of goods sold in current dollars. As a consequence, they note, cost and revenues would be matched in terms of relatively similar dollars, irrespective of the direction of the trend in prices. This result, the LIFO advocates argued, overcame a major weakness of FIFO, namely, that in periods of rising prices it leads to overstatement of profits, since a portion of these profits have to be used to replace the consumed inventories at higher costs. Similarly, in periods of falling prices, the LIFO proponents stated, FIFO leads to understatement of profits, since inventories produced or bought during an earlier period of higher prices are matched with current lower selling prices.

Those who opposed LIFO argued that it leads to an unrealistic balance sheet presentation of inventory. Except in some rare situations, LIFO does not correspond to the actual flow of goods, or necessarily result in an improved matching of costs and revenues. If a LIFO inventory consisting of very old cost layers were depleted, the LIFO opponents argued, the current profits would be misleading, since current revenues would be matched in part against the old, unrealistic costs.

While not necessarily agreeing that LIFO was a sound accounting method, a number of people became reconciled to LIFO because it represented a partial recognition of price-level changes for the purpose of determining income. Others accepted LIFO because of the tax advantage it gave users in periods of inflation. FIFO users may recognize these tax and income measurement advantages of LIFO, but still be reluctant to adopt it because of uncertainty about the impact on their stock prices of reporting lower profits under LIFO. The efficient-market theory suggests this concern is naive, on the grounds that the market sees through the LIFO-based profits to the underlying economic reality, which in periods of inflation is more favorable to LIFO companies, since they pay less taxes than FIFO companies. The results of specific research on this question are inconclusive.

Typically, LIFO companies do not use LIFO accounting for their overseas inventories, since in most foreign countries this accounting method is not available for tax purposes. In addition, only a part of the company's domestic inventories may be accounted for by the LIFO method. When more than one inventory method is used, the proportion of inventory accounted for by each principal method should be disclosed.

Retail Method.   The retail inventory method is used as an approximation of the cost-or-market method (see below) by retailers and others who keep their inventory records on a selling-price basis. Application of this method requires that records be maintained of purchases from and returns to manufacturers, showing cost and selling prices; and of customer sales and returns, showing selling prices. The cost of the ending inventory is calculated as follows:

1. Add the purchases during the period at cost to the opening inventory at cost.
2. Add the purchases at retail to the opening inventory at retail.
3. Subtract the first of these totals from the second. The difference is the so-called cumulative mark-on in dollars. Calculate this amount as a percentage of the total retail price of the goods available for sale during the period (determined in 2 above).
4. Subtract actual sales from the total retail price of goods available for sale to obtain computed inventory at retail.
5. Multiply the ending inventory at retail by the mark-on percentage (computed in 3 above) and subtract from inventory at retail to determine inventory at cost.

The retail method is widely used in the retail business, since it reduces the clerical work and permits cost to be omitted from price tags.

The following procedure is used to state inventories on a LIFO basis:

1. Inventory at retail value is calculated for all items in a department at inventory date.
2. The total department inventory at retail is reduced to a base-year value by applying the appropriate indices published by the Bureau of Labor Statistics for this purpose. This base-level value is then separated into LIFO layers attributable to each year.
3. A layer is added if ending inventory is greater than beginning inventory. If it is less, the more recent layers in beginning inventory are moved to cost of goods sold.
4. Each layer in ending inventory is reduced to **cost** by using the average gross margin in that department appropriate to the year the layer was acquired.
5. The result is ending inventory at LIFO cost.

Selling Price.   Another basis for pricing inventories is selling price. According to *Accounting Research Bulletin No. 43,* Chapter 4:

Only in exceptional cases may inventories properly be stated above cost. For example, precious metals having a fixed monetary value with no substantial cost of marketing may be stated at such monetary value; any other exceptions must be justified by inability to determine appropriate approximate cost, immediate marketability at quoted market price, and the characteristic of unit interchangeability. When goods are stated above cost this fact should be fully disclosed.

If the selling-price basis is used, the cost of disposition should be deducted. The principal arguments for the application of selling price basis are: first, the inventory is readily marketable at known market prices; and second, production is the critical business activity, rather than selling. In general, the inability to determine cost is the weakest argument for pricing inventories on a selling-price basis.

Cost or Market, Whichever Is Lower

A basic rule of accounting is that losses should be recorded as charges to income as soon as they are discovered. This rule takes precedence over the matching-costs-with-revenue rule. So, any inventory losses should be recognized currently to the extent that they can be determined, and the cost of inventory in excess of its utility should be charged to income and not carried forward as an asset. The lower-of-cost-or-market rule applies to such situations and provides a guide to the proper accounting treatment. Accounting Research Bulletin No. 43, Chapter 4 states:

> A departure from cost basis for pricing the inventory is *required* when the utility of goods is no longer as great as their cost. Where there is evidence that the utility of goods, in their disposal in the ordinary course of business, will be less than cost, whether due to physical deterioration, obsolescence, changes in price levels, or other causes, the difference should be recognized as a loss of the current period. This is generally accomplished by stating such goods at a lower level commonly designated as *market.*

The lower-of-cost-or-market rule is based on the assumption that costs and selling prices move together. Thus, a decrease in the replacement cost of an inventory item signals a potential selling price decline and a decline in utility of the inventory on hand. If the sales price does not decline and the inventory on hand will be sold at the normal margin, however, there will be no loss of utility. Conversely, if selling prices decline but the replacement cost does not, a lower than normal margin will be earned. This is also a signal that the utility of the inventory has decreased.

The word *cost* in the rule means the cost of replacing the inventory on hand by purchase in the open market or reproduction in the company's own factories. The purchase price includes all the costs of bringing the goods to their usual location. The reproduction cost includes all the direct and indirect costs associated with manufacturing the goods.

The term *market* has a specific technical meaning in the context of this rule. It is an indication of the utility of the inventory as measured by the relationship between replacement cost, selling price, and normal margin. As used in the rule, *market* also means current replacement cost, but with two provisions:

1. Market should not exceed realizable value (estimated selling price less costs of completion and disposal); and
2. Market should not be less than net realizable value reduced by an allowance for an approximately normal profit margin. This figure is often referred to as the "market floor."

Thus, determining market requires comparing three values: replacement cost, net realizable value, and the market floor. If net realizable value is lower, it is market: if replacement cost is lower, it is market *unless* its use would result in a larger than normal profit margin; in that event, the market floor is market.

Inventory Analysis

The inventory turnover calculation is the basic financial analysis tool used to evaluate inventory management. It measures the number of times management's investment in inventory is turned over each year. As discussed in earlier chapters, inventory turn over is measured by dividing the annual cost of sales by the average FIFO (or FIFO-equivalent) inventory for the period. The resulting turnover figure can then be converted to the average length of time an item spends in inventory by dividing the turnover rate into 365 days. The average age of the inventory is the turnover ratio expressed in days divided by 2. The brief inventory analysis discussion included in the earlier chapter should be read in conjunction with the inventory analysis presented here.

Another quantitative approach to analyzing inventories is to compute as percentages the relation of raw materials, work-in-process and finished goods to total inventory. This calculation should be tracked over time. Any major shifts in the relationships should be noted and their causes identified and evaluated. For example, an increase in the finished goods percentage might indicate poor sales forecasting, a slowdown in customer orders, or a failure to react promptly to a downturn in business. The higher finished goods might also result from a change in manufacturing policy to reduce production costs by lengthening production runs, which then requires holding product in inventory in anticipation of future orders. Such a strategy may increase the company's capital needs and level of risk and should be closely monitored by statement analysts.

It is difficult to determine what the appropriate turnover ratio and distribution of inventory between raw materials, work-in-progress and finished goods should be for a company. In general, a high turnover ratio is preferable to a low one, but if the turnover rate is too high the company may be subject to stockouts or incur excessive production costs due to short production runs. Some clues as to how high or low an inventory turnover should be for a particular company, as well as the appropriate composition of its inventory, are the comparable ratios of other companies in the same industry, particularly the ratios of those companies with a reputation for having good management.

During periods of above-average inflation it is important that statement users eliminate from the income of FIFO companies the so-called inventory profit, which is the difference between the replacement cost of the inventory items sold and their original cost. This portion of profits must be used in replacing the inventory sold in order to maintain inventory levels. In addition, on the balance sheet, statement users must restate the inventory of LIFO companies to its current value. This restatement is required to measure correctly the amount of capital committed to finance inventories.

The inventory note is helpful in trying to reconcile the effect of the LIFO–FIFO choice on income and inventory values when examining a single company or comparing many companies. The data related to inventories can be used to adjust a LIFO company's income and inventory value to a FIFO basis. Here are the disclosure rules that make these analyses of the income statement and balance sheet effect of different inventory accounting possible:

a. When a company shifts from FIFO to LIFO accounting, the impact of the change on earnings in the year of change must be disclosed.

b. If a company already on LIFO for some of its inventories decides to extend the use of LIFO to other inventories, the effect of the LIFO extension on earnings must be disclosed.

c. LIFO companies must disclose in their notes to the financial statements for each period presented the difference between the LIFO and FIFO values of their inventories. This disclosure, which is sometimes called the "LIFO reserve," is useful in two ways: first, this amount can be added to the LIFO inventory value shown on the face of the statement to obtain an approximation of the company's FIFO inventory value. Second, the change in LIFO reserve from one year to another is equivalent to the before-tax effect on earnings of using LIFO rather than FIFO accounting.

d. Sometimes LIFO companies at year-end dip into, or "invade," one of their LIFO inventory's old cost layers. Typically, this boosts earnings, since current revenues are matched with costs from a period when unit costs were considerably lower than the current replacement cost. The effect on earnings of LIFO layer invasions must be disclosed.

Inventory practices vary from company to company and involve management judgment. Statement users must be wary of interim statement COGS figures. They may be little more than estimates based on the dubious assumption that the budgeted gross margin is being earned or that a LIFO company's management projection of year-end price levels is reliable. In addition, the percentage of manufacturing overhead costs management includes in interim and annual inventory (and cost of goods sold) can range from the bare minimum required for tax purposes to the maximum permitted by accounting rules. Statement users should always attempt to determine the costing practice used by the company being examined. A company that treats most of its manufacturing overhead as a period cost will tend to have more operating leverage than a company that classifies most of its manufacturing overhead as a product cost. Auditors are often present when year-end inventory is counted, but they do not always participate in counting all of the inventory. Also, they rely heavily on management representations that the inventory is saleable. Under these conditions, a combination of an inept audit and a dishonest management can easily result in nonexistent, obsolete, damaged and nonsaleable inventory's being recorded as good inventory and cost of goods sold being understated. It is almost impossible for the statement user to detect this type of fraud directly. Fortunately, in these situations there are usually enough "red flags" to alert the astute statement user that the company may be in trouble.

Often the price movements of only a few of the cost elements in a LIFO company's cost of goods sold are responsible for the bulk of the inflation component of that expense item. For example, the price of copper drives the inflation component of an electrical manufacturer's LIFO COGS. Statement users should always identify the item that drives the LIFO-based costing and track its movements. The company's COGS and LIFO reserve should reflect these price changes. If they do not, either the company has changed the way it does business or the reader has detected a "red flag" suggesting closer examination of the company is warranted.

Companies with inventory problems sometimes attempt to hide their difficulties by shipping product to customers prematurely or extending generous credit terms to customers accepting early delivery. Accelerating sales may result in a book entry reducing inventory, but the so-called product sales should be regarded as the equivalent of moving inventory from the vendor's plant to the customers' plants. The vendor still has an inventory problem since the customer will not pay for the goods until the normal payment date. Statement users can detect this practice, which usually occurs near the end of the accounting period, by an unusual build-up of accounts receivables.

Companies that manage inventories well usually do well in other aspects of management. The converse is true for companies that have poor inventory management. Statement users should respond favorably to companies that manage their inventories effectively. This is a critical management skill that can make a major contribution to the efficient use of capital and manufacturing facilities as well as to the effective execution of a company's product marketing program. Actions that lead to efficient inventory management include: short manufacturing cycles, integration of vendor and customer production plans, optimum inventory lot size scheduling, receipt of vendor shipments as close to use as possible, favorable vendor payment terms, infrequent stockouts, and reliable sales forecasts.

Summit Distributors (A)

Kathy Hutton, chief executive officer of Summit Distributors, was concerned with the poor economic outlook for the coming year. Continued deterioration of the economy could place the future viability of Summit Distributors in jeopardy. After a decade of steady growth in earnings per share (EPS), the company had experienced a 32% decline in EPS for 1990 and a 40% decline for 1991 (see **Exhibit 1**). Furthermore, the 1992 operating budget forecasted the company's first loss in over two decades.

Because of the deterioration of general economic conditions in the United States and elsewhere, Summit began a program of selling, liquidating, or otherwise disposing of unprofitable domestic and foreign operations. In the fiscal year 1992, a provision for losses of $3.7 million was expected for disposal and restructuring of domestic operations, and a provision for losses of $2.4 million was expected for disposal of foreign operations. The forecasted losses would cause retained earnings to decline from $11.6 million in 1991 to $5.6 million by the end of 1992.

Summit Distributors was in danger of default on financial covenants in its loan agreement with Prime Trust Bank. Financial covenants included in the lending agreement specified limits on certain financial ratios, and if these limits were violated, the required payments could be accelerated or the capital stock of Summit's subsidiaries could be seized. Kathy was in the process of evaluating several possible courses of action, including accounting changes proposed by Dave Flanders, the company's new chief financial officer. The proposed accounting changes would strengthen the company's balance sheet and could postpone default for at least another year. The most

Research Associate Marc H. Zablatsky prepared this case under the supervision of Professors Amy Patricia Hutton and William J. Bruns, Jr., as the basis for class discussion rather than to illustrate either effective or ineffective handling of an administrative situation.

Exhibit 1 Consolidated Statement of Operations. For the years ended August 31 (in thousands of dollars)

	1991	1990	1989
Net sales and revenues	$149,582	$116,706	$97,411
Cost of sales	112,831	86,190	72,541
Gross profit	$ 36,751	$ 30,516	$24,870
Selling, general and administrative expenses	31,754	24,479	19,111
Operating income	$ 4,997	$ 6,037	$ 5,759
Other (income) and expense:			
Interest expense	2,470	1,777	1,257
Provision for losses on dispositions	(375)	250	—
Other, net	(98)	20	(50)
	$ 1,997	$ 2,047	$ 1,207
Income (loss) from continuing operations before provision for income taxes	3,000	3,900	4,552
Provision for (benefit from) income taxes	1,242	2,020	2,135
Income (loss) from continuing operations	$ 1,758	$ 1,970	$ 2,417
Loss from discontinued operation, net of applicable income taxes of $166	(234)	—	—
Net income (loss)	$ 1,524	$ 1,970	$ 2,417
Earnings-per-common and common-equivalent share:			
Primary	$1.21	$2.03	$2.98
Fully diluted	$1.19	$1.73	$2.26

significant accounting change proposed was a shift in inventory valuation methods from last-in-first-out (LIFO) to first-in-first-out (FIFO).

Industry Outlook

Summit Distributors sold and distributed industrial supplies to fabricators, manufacturers, and distributors throughout the United States. The company sold approximately 30,000 different industrial-supply products. Major markets for the company's products included construction, energy, metal fabrication, general manufacturing, and utilities. Industrial-supply products were consumed in fabrication and manufacturing processes and in maintenance activities. Customers typically ordered $200 to $800 worth of supplies to meet their immediate needs.

The industrial-supply industry was highly fragmented, and most products were available from multiple suppliers. Since purchase amounts were relatively small, price differences were generally not the dominant competitive factor. Competition was based mainly on service, such as reliability in meeting delivery requirements of customers, the variety and quality of products distributed, and the accessibility of sales personnel. To compete successfully, Summit had to maintain significant inventories at many strategically located warehouses.

EXHIBIT 1   **(continued) Consolidated Statement of Financial Position for years ended August 31 (in thousands of dollars)**

	1991	1990	1989
Assets			
Current Assets:			
Cash and Marketable securities	$ 1,450	$ 2,447	$ 1,941
Accounts and notes receivable, less allowances for doubtful			
accounts of $884 in 1991, $782 in 1990, and $670 in 1989	19,651	15,036	14,345
Inventories (Note 5)	28,354	24,074	19,558
Refundable Federal income taxes	—	—	—
Other current assets and deferred income tax benefit	1,462	872	800
Total Current Assets	$50,917	$42,429	$36,644
Property, Plant and Equipment			
Land	93	93	63
Buildings and leasehold improvements	736	736	559
Machinery and equipment	6,358	4,521	3,820
	$ 7,187	$ 5,350	$ 4,442
Less—accumulated depreciation	3,296	2,734	2,127
Total Property, Plant and Equipment	$ 3,891	$ 2,616	$ 2,315
Other Assets	1,538	3,036	1,830
Total Assets	$56,346	$48,081	$40,789
Liabilities and Shareholders' Equity			
Current liabilities:			
Current portion of long-term debt (Note 6)	$ 572	$ 410	$ 577
Accounts and notes payable	13,848	10,730	11,857
Accrued liabilities	5,376	4,553	3,328
Income taxes payable	498	68	733
Other current liabilities	150	105	105
Total Current Liabilities	$20,444	$15,868	$16,600
Other Obligations:			
Long-term debt, net of current portion (Note 6)	18,127	15,980	10,449
Minority interests	332	337	335
Other noncurrent liabilities	774	711	781
Total Other Liabilities	$19,233	$17,028	$11,565
Shareholders' Equity:			
Preferred stock, $1.00 par value, 93,442 shares outstanding			
having a preference on involuntary liquidation of a total			
of $4,671	93	41	41
Common stock, $.50 par value, 1,048,014 shares issued in 1991	524	491	449
Capital in excess of par value	5,631	3,690	3,442
Retained earnings	11,647	10,965	9,413
Common stock in treasury at cost (126,470 shares in 1991) . . .	(1,226)	0	(721)
Total Shareholders' Equity	$16,669	$15,187	$12,624
Total Liabilities and Shareholders' Equity	$56,346	$48,081	$40,789

EXHIBIT 1   (continued)

Selected Notes to Consolidated Financial Statements

Note 5. Inventories

Inventories are stated at the lower of cost or market. Approximately 79, 74, and 70% of total inventories in 1991, 1990, and 1989, respectively, were valued using the last-in-first-out (LIFO) method. The remaining inventories were valued using the first-in-first-out (FIFO) method. Inventory costs include the cost of items purchased for resale as well as supplies. For inventories valued using the LIFO method, the excess of current cost over LIFO cost was $4,440 at August 31, 1991; $3,623 at August 31, 1990; and $2,412 at August 31, 1989.

Note 6. Long-Term Debt

At August 31, 1991, 1990, and 1989, the following long-term debt was outstanding:

	1991	1990	1989
Revolving credit notes payable to banks at interest rates of ¼% above prime, convertible to a term note on March 1, 1994	$10,150	$ 8,600	$ 3,700
11¼% senior subordinated debentures, with sinking fund requirements due $300 annually through 1999, and $450 annually 2000 through 2002, with final payment due May 2003	5,100	5,400	5,700
9½% convertible subordinated notes due in three equal annual installments commencing in 1998	2,000	2,000	
9% convertible subordinated notes due in three equal annual installments commencing 1992	—	—	960
Other notes at interest rates from 5½% to 21% due at various dates through 2003	1,449	390	666
	18,699	16,390	11,026
Current portion	(572)	(410)	(577)
	$18,127	$15,980	$10,449

The company has a credit agreement with Prime Trust Bank which provides for $20,000 of revolving credit commitments maturing March 1, 1994, if not extended as provided by the agreement. The Company pays commitment fees of approximately ½% per annum on the unused portion of the revolving credit line. The credit agreement also provides for the bank to make a 5-year loan at an interest rate of ½% above the prime rate to the Company at the maturity of the revolving credit commitment, in a principal amount up to the revolving credit commitment of the banks in effect on such date. At August 31, 1991, the unused portion of the revolving credit line was $9,850. The capital stock of 11 subsidiaries is pledged as collateral for the revolving credit commitment.

Under terms of the credit agreement, the Company, among other things, must:

a. maintain a minimum consolidated tangible net worth, as defined, of $12,000;

b. maintain minimum consolidated working capital, as defined, of $16,000, and a consolidated current ratio of at least 1.5 to 1; and

c. maintain a loan outstanding balance not to exceed the sum of 80% of consolidated accounts receivables and 50% of consolidated inventory, as defined.

The Company's various lending agreements, among other things, also provide for restrictions and limitations on purchases, sales, and collateralization of assets; additional financing, loans, and advances; investments; guarantees of indebtedness of others; acquisitions; and issuance of capital stock. The total payments of dividends on common shares plus

EXHIBIT 1   (continued)

purchases of treasury stock in any one year is restricted; at August 31, 1991, approximately $1,378 of retained earnings were available for these purposes during fiscal 1992.

Note 7. Income Taxes

The provisions for (benefit from) income taxes for the years ended August 31, 1991, 1990, and 1989, are composed of the following:

	1991	*1990*	*1989*
Current			
U.S. provision (benefit)	$1,085	$1,412	$2,145
Foreign provision	235	296	230
State provision	278	243	139
	$1,598	$1,951	$2,514
Deferred			
U.S. provision (benefit)	(363)	5	(392)
Foreign provision (benefit)	7	64	13
	(356)	69	(379)
	$1,242	$2,020	$2,135

With customers ordering industrial supplies only for their immediate use, performance of Summit Distributors and its competitors was closely tied to the fortunes of the industries they served. When specific sectors of the economy experienced a downturn, distributors, who were essentially just-in-time suppliers, felt the squeeze almost immediately. Along with the downturn in demand for industrial products, a decline in demand for industrial supplies was expected for fiscal 1992.

Financial Covenants with Bank

Kathy Hutton was very concerned with how Prime Trust Bank would respond if the company violated its financial covenants. The company had a strong relationship with Sandy Petronka, Summit's lending officer at Prime Trust. Whenever there had been a need for additional working capital for growth, Sandy had been willing to increase the limit on Summit's line of credit. However, the decline in Summit's performance had put strains on the company's future financial flexibility.

Under Summit Distributors' loan covenants, the company was required to: (a) maintain a minimum consolidated tangible net worth of $12 million; (b) maintain minimum consolidated working capital of $16 million and a current ratio exceeding 1.5 to 1; and (c) maintain an outstanding loan balance not to exceed the sum of 80% of accounts receivables and 50% of inventory. (**Exhibit 1** includes selected notes to the company's financial statements. Note 6 contains details on the loan covenants.)

If Summit Distributors violated one of these loan covenants, Prime Trust would have the right to accelerate maturity of the debt or seize collateralized assets. If this happened, the company's only hope would be to reorganize under Chapter 11 of the Bankruptcy Reform Act of 1978. Prior to an actual default, Kathy could approach

Sandy Petronka and attempt to renegotiate the financial covenants. Kathy anticipated that Sandy and Prime Trust's credit-watch committee would request at least a 50–basis-point increase in the interest rate on the outstanding loan (50 basis point is equivalent to 0.5%). However, as Dave Flanders had pointed out, the cost of default could be considerably higher. Other lenders had been known to require increased collateralization of assets, restrict future borrowing, require additional covenants, force the sale of assets to pay down the debt, or even demand warrants or common stock of the company be issued to them. Kathy was not sure what actions Sandy Petronka and the credit-watch committee might take, how she should react, and what costs the company might incur as a result.

Situation Facing Kathy Hutton

As of August 31, 1991, the company reported tangible net worth of $16.7 million (**Exhibit 1**). If nothing were done to improve the balance sheet, the current forecast for 1992 would place Summit in default of the minimum tangible net worth covenant by year's end (see **Exhibit 2** for status of loan covenants). Kathy Hutton expected the economy to turn around in 1993, and she believed Summit was well positioned to return to profitability with the economic upswing. Kathy had to admit, however, the immediate future looked bleak.

Dave Flanders had suggested a number of accounting changes permitted under generally accepted accounting practices. These accounting changes would improve the company's balance sheet and help Summit avoid default during the coming year. The largest proposed accounting change would require a return to the FIFO-inventory-valuation method. Since 1988, Summit Distributors had employed the LIFO-inventory-valuation method for financial and tax reporting. With the trends of rising prices for industrial supplies, LIFO had resulted in income being reported lower than it would have been reported if FIFO or the average-cost method of inventory valuation had been used. To demonstrate his point that by merely changing the inventory-valuation method default on the loan covenant could be postponed for at least one

EXHIBIT 2   Financial Covenants

	Forecast 1992	1991	1990
Consolidated tangible net worth (minimum balance $12,000) . . .	$ 9,828	$16,669	$15,187
Consolidated working capital (minimum balance $16,000)	$23,788	$30,473	$26,563
Consolidated current ratio (minimum ratio 1.5 to 1)	2.70	2.49	2.67
Outstanding loan balance not to exceed the sum of			
80% of A/R and	$10,050	$15,721	$12,029
50% of inventories	10,187	14,177	12,037
	$20,237	$29,898	$24,066

EXHIBIT 3   Dave Flanders' Calculations: Balance-Sheet Effects of Switching to the FIFO-Inventory-Valuation Method (in thousands of dollars)

Assets = Liabilities + Owners' Equity

		Retained Earnings:	
Inventories	+4,802	Lower COGS	+362
		Higher current taxes	−62
Deferred taxes	+238	Increased deferred taxes	238
		Restoration of LIFO reserve	4,440
Refundable taxes	−825	Taxes on LIFO reserve	−763
	+4,215		+4,215

---

year, Dave had quickly jotted down the balance-sheet effects of switching to FIFO (see **Exhibit 3**)

Dave briefly explained his calculations to Kathy. For 1992, the projected LIFO reserve was $4,802,000, and therefore a switch to FIFO would increase the reported inventory amounts and taxable income by $4,802,000. Retained earnings and net worth would increase by $4,215,000, enough to delay or avoid default. As Kathy glanced at Dave's back-of-the-envelope calculations, she was initially pleased by the apparent ability to avoid default. However, as she examined the calculations more closely, she noticed that refundable taxes declined by $825,000 and deferred taxes increased by only $238,000, as a result of the switch to FIFO. Dave explained that under either method Summit would report a loss for 1992. The good news was that the loss would allow Summit to claim a refund of taxes paid in earlier years. However, since the switch to FIFO in financial reports would require the same switch in the company's income tax returns (including amendments to tax returns in earlier years) and would result in less of a loss than LIFO, the current refund would be $825,000 less under FIFO than it was forecasted to be under LIFO.

Kathy sat back in her chair and began listing the pros and cons of adopting the FIFO-inventory method. She had received some input from her chief financial officer but wondered how other parties that could be affected by her decision viewed the current crisis, and how they would view a return to the FIFO-inventory method. Kathy especially wondered how Prime Trust Bank viewed Summit's current circumstances.

Questions

1. If you were Kathy Hutton, what would you do? _____

2. If you were Dave Flanders, would you recommend staying with the LIFO-inventory-valuation method or switching to FIFO? _____ Why? _____ What are the cash-flow ramifications of the accounting change? _____

3. If there were no cash-flow consequences associated with the accounting change, would you change your answers to questions 1 or 2? _____

4. How does the decision facing Kathy Hutton impact Summit Distributors' other constituencies, such as Prime Trust Bank, shareholders, auditors, and the company's internal financial reporting group? _____

5. Dave Flanders had not been employed by the company four years earlier. However, he was aware that at that time the company had switched inventory-valuation methods for most inventory from FIFO to LIFO. The company's 1988 annual report justified the change as follows:

The Company believes the LIFO method of accounting will result in a more representative presentation of the Company's financial position and results of operations.

Does the fact that Summit Distributors switched methods four years ago change your answers to questions 1 or 2? _____

6. When companies change accounting methods, managers and auditors are required to justify the change. Their justification must explain why the new method is *preferable* to the old method. What are the potential justifications for Summit's managers changing to FIFO from LIFO? _____

CASE 17-2 # Daniel Dobbins Distillery, Inc.

In early August 1988, David Dobbins, president and chief operating officer (COO) of Daniel Dobbins Distillery, Inc., of Oakwoods, Tennessee, sat in his office pondering the results of the previous day's meeting of the board of directors and wondering whether he should submit the 1988 financial statements (**Exhibits 1** and **2**) to the Ridgeview National Bank of Nashville, Tennessee, in support of a recent loan request for $3 million, or whether he should wait until after next month's board meeting to clarify some of the preceding day's discussion. A great deal of controversy had arisen over the 1988 reported loss of $814,000 and how this result should be reported to the bank. The controversy revolved principally around the accounting treatment of various expenses reported in the "other costs" section of the operating statement. Mr. Dobbins knew that a decision had to be reached on these matters quickly, because the company

This case was prepared as the basis for class discussion rather than to illustrate either effective or ineffective handling of an administrative situation.
Copyright © 1989 by the President and Fellows of Harvard College. Harvard Business School case 189–065.

EXHIBIT 1   Daniel Dobbins Distillery, Inc., Balance Sheet as of June 30, 1987, and 1988 ($ thousands)

	1987	1988
Current Assets		
Cash	$ 2,548	$ 632
Accounts receivable—trade (less allowance for doubtful accounts of approximately $330,000)	2,854	3,662
Inventories:		
Bulk whiskey in barrels at average production cost (no excise tax included)	9,013	10,061
Bottled and cased whiskey, 175,000 gallons in each year at an average cost of $22.50 per gallon (including excise tax)	3,938	3,938
Inventory in process	202	202
Raw materials and supplies	800	472
Prepaid expenses	881	777
Total current assets	$20,236	$19,744

	Cost		Accumulated Depreciation		Net	
	1987	1988	1987	1988	1987	1988
Fixed Assets						
Cash surrender value of officers' life insurance					$ 64	$ 70
Land	$ 60	$ 60			60	60
Building[a]	3,820	4,220	$1,600	$1,706	2,220	2,514
Factory equipment	144	144	52	76	92	68
Warehouse equipment........................	70	128	48	68	22	60
Trademarks and brands.......................	16	16			16	16
Total assets					2,474	2,788
					$22,710	$22,532

	1987	1988
Current Liabilities		
Notes payable:		
Short-term to banks	$ 2,200	$ 3,000
Current maturities of long-term debt	460	966
Accounts payable	1,720	838
Accrued liabilities	398	230
Federal excise taxes payable	820	—
Total current liabilities	$ 5,598	$ 5,034
Noncurrent Liabilities		
Notes payable (9½%) secured by deed of trust on warehouse property (less current maturities of $460,000 for 1987 and $966,000 for 1988)	7,000	8,200
Stockholders' Equity		
Common stock held principally by members of the Dobbins family	**3,600**	**3,600**
Earnings retained in the business	6,512	5,698
Total liabilities and capital..................	$22,710	$22,532

[a]In June 1988, payment was made for work that had been performed during the year in adding to and improving the warehousing space in the building owned by Dobbins Distillers.

EXHIBIT 2 Daniel Dobbins Distillery, Inc., Statement of Income for the Years Ended June 30, 1987, and 1988 ($ thousands)

	1987		1988	
Net Sales:				
Sale of whiskey to wholesalers	$42,000		$42,000	
Cost of Goods Sold:				
Federal excise taxes—on barrels sold	31,605		31,605	
Cost of product charged to sales:				
Bulk whiskey inventory July 1, of each year—172,000 barrels	9,013		9,013	
Plus: Cost of whiskey produced to inventory (43,000 barrels in 1987 and 63,000				
barrels in 1988 at an average cost of $52.40/50 gallon barrel in both years)	2,253		3,301	
	11,266		12,314	
Less: Bulk whiskey inventory June 30 of respective year (172,000 and 192,000				
barrels, at average production cost)	9,013	2,253	10,061	2,253
Cased goods and in process July 1, of respective year	4,140		4,140	
Cased goods and in process June 30, of respective year	4,140	—	4,140	—
		$33,858		$33,858
Other Costs Charged to Cost of Goods Sold:				
Cost of barrels used during year at $63.00 per barrel	2,709		3,969	
Occupancy costs: factory building	265		297	
rented building	272		572	
Warehouse labor and warehouse supervisor	188		334	
Labor and supplies expense of chemical laboratory	136		166	
Depreciation: factory equipment	24		24	
warehouse equipment	12		20	
Cost of government supervision and bonding facilities	6		14	
Cost of bottling liquor (labor, glass, and miscellaneous supplies)	458	4,070	458	5,854
Total cost of goods sold		$37,928		$39,712
Gross profit from operations		$ 4,072		$ 2,288
Less: Selling and advertising expenses	1,568		1,874	
Administrative and general expense	1,000	2,568	1,228	3,102
Net profit (loss)		$ 1,504		$ (814)

had reached a point where additional working capital was needed immediately if it was to remain solvent.

Company History

Daniel Dobbins began distilling whiskey in 1880. Daniel had come to Oakwoods, Tennessee, from Scotland the preceding year and had decided to carry on in the family tradition of beverage manufacture. He purchased a tract of land on a high knoll adjacent to a small stream fed by a limestone spring and began to distill bourbon whiskey in an old barn behind his home. His business grew from a trickling in 1880 to a million-dollar firm by 1911. He attributed this growth to the high-quality, distinctive bourbon whiskey that he produced. The quality of "Old Trailridge," Dobbins's only brand of whiskey, was claimed to be the result of the unusual iron-free spring water used in the distillation process and the specially prepared fire-charred white oak barrels used in the aging process.

From 1911 to 1933, the years of prohibition in Tennessee, the distilling equipment lay dormant, and it was not until late in 1934 that the company began to operate once again in a newly constructed building. Sales rose from $500,000 in 1935 to nearly $5 million in 1941, when the plant was converted to U.S. defense production of commercial alcohol.

In 1973, David Dobbins, great-grandson of Daniel, took over as COO of the company and nearly doubled sales revenue during the next 10 years. Mr. Dobbins felt that the company had grown because of the stress it placed on marketing a distinctive, high-quality, high-price product and because of its continued concentration on only one brand of fine bourbon whiskey—Old Trailridge. The company's advertising stressed the uniqueness of the cool, bubbling spring water used in the distillation of Old Trailridge and pointed to its use of "specially prepared and cured fire-charred white oak barrels." This promotion had been very effective in establishing a brand image of Old Trailridge in the consumer's mind that connoted full-bodied mellowness, camaraderie, and old-fashioned backwoods quality.

In 1987, the company produced just over 1% of the whiskey distilled in the United States and thus was one of the smaller distillers in the industry. Since the mid-1980s, the company's production had been stable; the financial statements for 1987 (**Exhibits 1** and **2**) were typical of the results of the preceding several years. After a surge in demand in the 1970s, no special effort had been made to gain a larger share of the market, but at a board meeting in December 1987, a decision had been made to expand production to try to capture a larger than proportionate share of the increase in whiskey consumption that Mr. Dobbins had forecasted, based on an industry research report. This report showed that the consumption of straight bourbon whiskey was increasing as the baby boom generation matured. Based on this report and other industry forecasts, Mr. Dobbins had forecasted a doubling of straight whiskey consumption from 1987 to 1995. In view of this assumption, and because bourbon whiskey had to be aged for at least four years, the board had decided to increase the production of whiskey in 1988 by 50% of the 1987 volume (see Exhibit 2) in order to meet the anticipated increase in consumer demand for straight bourbon whiskey from 1991 through 1995.

The Manufacturing Process

Old Trailridge was a straight bourbon whiskey and thus, by law, had to be made from a mixture of grains containing at least 51% corn and be aged in new (not reused) charred white oak barrels. The process began when the ground corn was mixed with pure limestone spring water in a large vat. To this mixture was added a certain amount of ground barley malt and rye. It was then heated slowly until the starches were converted to sugars, thus completing the "mashing" process. This mash was then pumped into a cypress fermenting vat where yeast and certain other ingredients were added. This mixture was allowed to ferment for several days until the yeast had converted the sugars into alcohol, at which time the fermenting process was complete and the mash was pumped into a distillation tower (or still) where the alcohol was separated from the "slurry," or spent mash, through a series of distillation tanks and condensers. The distilled liquor was then mixed with limestone spring water to obtain the desired proof (percent of alcohol by volume where one degree of proof equals .5% alcohol).

At this point the whiskey was a clear liquid with a sharp, biting taste and had to be mellowed before consumption. For this process, it was pumped into 50-gallon barrels and moved to an aging warehouse. The cost accumulated in the product prior to its entry into barrels, including all direct and indirect materials and labor consumed in the production process, was approximately $1 per gallon (see **Exhibit 2**). The volume of production had been the same for each of the years 1984 to 1987, and all costs during this period had been substantially the same as the 1987 costs shown in **Exhibit 2.**

Maturing or Aging Process

In order to mellow the whiskey, improve its taste, and give it a rich amber color, the new bourbon whiskey had to be matured or aged for a period of time of not less than four years under controlled temperature and humidity conditions. The new whiskey reacted with the charred oak and assimilated some of the flavor and color of the fire-charred oak during the period of aging.

Since the quality of the aging barrel was an important factor in determining the ultimate taste and character of the final product, Dobbins had his 50-gallon barrels manufactured under a unique patented process at a cost of more than $60 per barrel. The barrels could not be reused for aging future batches of bourbon whiskey but could be sold to used barrel dealers for $1 each at the end of the aging period.

The filled barrels were next placed in open "ricks" in an aging warehouse rented by Dobbins or in that half of the factory building converted into warehousing space. The increased production in 1988 necessitated the leasing of an additional warehouse at an annual rental cost of $200,000. The temperature and humidity of the warehouse space had to be controlled, since the quality of the whiskey could be ruined by its aging too fast or too slowly, a process determined by temperature and humidity conditions.

Every six months, the barrels had to be rotated from a high rick to a lower rick or vice versa (because of uneven temperatures at different locations in the warehouse) and sampled for quality and character up to that point in the aging process. A small amount of liquid was removed from representative barrels at this time and sent to the sampling laboratory for quality inspection (usually performed by skilled tasters). If the quality of the whiskey was not up to standard, certain measures were taken, such as adjusting the aging process, to bring it up to standard. At this time, each barrel was also checked for leaks or seepage, and the required repairs were made.

At the end of the four-year aging period, the barrels were removed from the ricks and dumped into regauging tanks where the charred oak residue was filtered out and volume was measured. On the average, the volume of liquid in a barrel declined by 30% during the aging period because of evaporation and leakage. Thus, a barrel originally filled with 50 gallons of new bourbon would, on the whole, produce only 35 gallons of aged bourbon. The regauging operation was supervised by a government liquor tax agent, since it was at this point that federal excise tax of $21 per gallon was levied on the whiskey removed from the warehouse. Once the bourbon had been removed from the aging warehouse, it was bottled and shipped to wholesalers with the greatest speed possible because of the large amount of cash tied up in taxes on the finished product. During both 1987 and 1988, the company sold 30,000 regauged barrels of whiskey, equivalent to about 43,000 barrels of original production.

Excerpts from Board of Directors' Meeting— August 3, 1988

David Dobbins: I'm quite concerned over the prospect of obtaining the $3 million loan we need in light of our 1988 loss of $814,000. We have shown annual profits since 1974, and our net sales of $42 million this year are the same as last year, and yet we incurred a net loss for the year. I think I understand the reason for this, but I'm afraid that the loan officers at the Ridgeview National Bank will hesitate in granting us a loan on the basis of our most recent performance. It appears that we are becoming less efficient in our production operation.

James Doud (Production Manager): That's not quite so David. You know as well as I do that we increased production by 50% this year, and with this increased production our costs are bound to increase. You can't produce something for nothing.

Darlene Thompson (Controller): Well, that's not quite so, Jim. Granted that our production costs must rise when production increases, but our inventory account takes care of the increased costs of deferring these product costs until a future period when the product is actually sold. As you can see by looking at our 1988 profit and loss (P&L) statement, our cost of goods sold did not increase in 1988, since the volume of sales was the same in 1988 as in 1987. The largest share of the increase in production costs has been deferred until future periods, as you can see by looking at the increase in our inventory account of more than $1 million. I believe that the real reason for our loss this year was the large increase in other costs, composed chiefly of warehousing costs. The "Occupancy Costs" category in our P&L is really the summation of a group of expense accounts, including building depreciation or rent, heat, light, power, building maintenance, labor and supplies, real estate taxes, and insurance. In addition, warehouse labor cost also rose substantially in 1988. Even administrative and general expenses went up, due primarily to higher interest expense on the additional money needed to finance our increase in inventory.

David Dobbins: Well, what's our explanation for the large increase in warehousing costs, Jim?

James Doud: As I said before, Dave, we increased production, and this also means an increase in warehousing costs, since the increased production has to be aged for several years. You just can't age 50% more whiskey for the same amount of money.

David Dobbins: But I thought Darlene said that increased production costs were taken care of in the inventory account. Isn't that so, Darlene?

Darlene Thompson: Well, yes and no, David. The inventory account can only be charged with those costs associated with the direct production of whiskey, and our warehousing costs are handling or carrying costs, certainly not production costs.

James Doud: Now just a minute, Darlene, I think that some of those costs are just as valid production costs as are direct labor and materials going into the distillation of the new bourbon. The manufacturing process doesn't stop with the newly produced bourbon; why it isn't even marketable in that form. Aging is an absolutely essential part of the manufacturing process, and I think the cost of barrels and part of the warehouse labor should be treated as direct costs of the product.

David Dobbins: Great, Jim! I agree with you that warehousing and aging costs are an absolutely essential ingredient of our final product. We certainly couldn't market the bourbon before it had been aged. I think that all the costs associated with aging the product should be charged to the inventory account. I think that most of the "other costs" should be considered a cost of the product. Don't you agree, Darlene?

Darlene Thompson: Sure, Dave! Let's capitalize depreciation, interest expenses, your salary, the shareholders' dividends, our advertising costs, your secretary's salary—why, let's capitalize all our costs! That way we can show a huge inventory balance and small expenses! I'm sure Ridgeview and the Internal Revenue boys would be happy to cooperate with us on it! Why, we'll revolutionize the accounting profession!

David Dobbins: I think you're being facetious, Darlene. Be reasonable about this. I'm afraid I really don't see why we couldn't charge all of those costs you mentioned to the inventory account, since it seems to me that they are all necessary ingredients in producing our final product. What distinction do you draw between these so-called "direct" costs you mentioned and the aging costs?

Darlene Thompson: By direct costs, I mean those costs that are necessary to convert raw materials into the whiskey that goes into the aging barrels. This is our cost of approximately $1 per gallon and includes the cost of raw materials going into the product such as grain, yeast, and malt; the direct labor necessary to convert these materials into whiskey; and the cost of any other overhead items that are needed to permit the workers to convert grain into whiskey. I don't see how aging costs can be included under the generally accepted accounting definition of the inventory cost of the product.

David Dobbins: I think we'd better defer further discussion of this entire subject until our meeting next month. In the meantime, I am going to try to get this thing squared away in my own mind. I have never really thought that financial statements had much meaning, but now I am not at all sure that they aren't truly misleading documents!

Well, let's turn next to the question of . . .

Questions

1. In your opinion, what costs should be included in Dobbins's inventory? _____

2. Assuming Dobbins decided to charge barrel costs (but not other warehousing and aging costs) to inventory, what 1988 income statement and balance sheet items would change, and what would the new amounts be? (Assume no change to in-process inventory.) _____

3. If Dobbins's suggestion of including all warehousing and aging costs in inventory were accepted, how would the 1988 financial statements be affected? (Same assumption as for Question 2.) _____

4. What method of accounting would you recommend that Dobbins use in preparing the annual financial statements to be submitted to Ridgeview National Bank? _____

CHAPTER 18

Business Combinations

A business combination occurs when two or more businesses are joined together as one entity to continue the same business activities each had carried on previously. Business combinations include all changes in corporate ownership that are termed mergers, purchases, consolidations, pooling of interests, amalgamations, uniting of interests, legal mergers and acquisitions. The financial accounting issues raised in recording and reporting business combinations centers upon the valuation of the assets brought together in a business unit and the treatment of goodwill, if any. The two methods used to record business combinations are (1) the purchase method and (2) the pooling of interests method.

Purchase Method

Under the purchase method of recording a business combination the purchase cost is the fair value of the consideration given or received, and the assets and liabilities of the acquired entity are recorded at their fair value to the extent acquired on the books of the acquirer. This approach treats the acquisition as if the acquirer had bought the net assets of another business and established a new cost basis for these acquired assets.

Purchase Method Illustration

The accounting for purchases can be illustrated by a relatively simple example of a business combination.

Professor David F. Hawkins prepared this case as the basis for class discussion rather than to illustrate either effective or ineffective handling of an administrative situation.
Copyright © 1994 by the President and Fellows of Harvard College. Harvard Business School teaching note 194–086.

Company A acquired Company B intending to continue the operations of both companies as a single unit. Company B's financial position at the date of acquisition was as follows:

	Book Value	Fair Value[a]
Net current assets	$100,000	$100,000
Fixed assets	400,000	700,000
Total	$500,000	$800,000
Capital stock	$300,000	
Retained earnings	$200,000	
Total	$500,000	

[a]The price that could be reasonably expected in a sale between a willing buyer and seller, other than in a forced or liquidation sale.

Company A paid $900,000 cash for Company B. The accounting entry in Company A's records is:

```
Dr. Net current assets . . . . . . . . . . . . . . . . . . . . . . . . . . . . . . . . . . .   100,000
    Fixed assets . . . . . . . . . . . . . . . . . . . . . . . . . . . . . . . . . . . . . . .   700,000
    Excess of purchase price over net assets acquired  . . . . . . . . . . . . .   100,000
        Cr. Cash . . . . . . . . . . . . . . . . . . . . . . . . . . . . . . . . . . . . . . .             900,000
```

This transaction is clearly a purchase of Company B by Company A. The previous owners of Company B received cash and retained no ownership in the new business unit. Consequently, assuming its fixed assets are all depreciable assets, subsequent operations will be charged with depreciation based on fixed asset costs of $700,000, which is the fair value of the assets acquired. The excess of the purchase price over the fair value of the net assets acquired is typically called goodwill.

Goodwill

It is difficult to give a precise definition of the nature of goodwill, since every business situation gives rise to a different mutation. However, in most situations it can be considered, in the technical sense, as simply being the cost paid for a business in excess of the fair value of its net tangible and intangible assets and representing an expectation of earnings in excess of a normal return on these assets. It is only through such a transaction that goodwill can be recognized on the books of a company. Goodwill is an integral part of a business and cannot be regarded as an asset which is salable independent of the business.

Goodwill is first recorded as an asset and subsequently charged to operations over a period of years to be benefited by the goodwill not to exceed 40.

Sometimes companies are purchased for a price less than their net book value. In these so-called bargain purchase cases, a "negative goodwill" item is created. If, after adjusting the book value of the assets acquired and liabilities assumed to their fair values, the sum of the market or appraisal values of the assets acquired less liabilities still exceeds the purchase cost, the values assigned to noncurrent assets acquired (except marketable securities) should be reduced proportionately by the negative goodwill balance. If a negative goodwill balance still remains, it is recorded and amortized systematically as a credit to income over the period estimated to be benefited, so long as the period is not in excess of 40 years.

Only from Acquisition Date

It is important to note that in a business combination accounted for as a purchase, income from the acquired company will be included in Company A's income statement only from the date of acquisition, and Company B's retained earnings at acquisition are not carried over to Company A.

Principal Issues

The principal accounting issues to be decided in mergers required to be accounted for by the purchase method are:

1. Which company is the acquirer?
2. How much did the acquirer pay for the purchase?
3. What adjustments are required to the book values of the individual assets acquired and liabilities assumed so that these values on the acquirer's book reflect their net realizable value or fair market value?
4. How should any differences between the purchase price and those adjusted book values be handled in the accounts of the acquired?

APB Opinions No. 16 and *No. 17,* which were issued concurrently, discuss these issues.

Acquirer Characteristics.   A corporation which distributes cash or other assets or incurs liabilities to obtain the assets or stock of another corporation is clearly the acquirer. In most cases involving exchanges of stock, the APB concluded that presumptive evidence of the acquiring corporation in combinations effected by an exchange of stock is obtained by identifying the former common stockholder interests which either retain or receive the larger portion of the voting rights in the combined corporation, unless other evidence clearly indicates that another corporation is the acquirer.

Purchase Price Determination.   The responsibility for determining the purchase price rests with the acquiring company. The general principles governing this determination are:

1. Assets acquired by exchanging cash or other assets are recorded at cost, which is the amount of cash disbursed or the fair value of the assets distributed.

2. Assets acquired by assuming liabilities are recorded at cost, which is the present value of the amounts to be paid.

3. Assets acquired by issuing stock are recorded at the fair value of the stock or the fair value of the consideration given up for the stock.

The difficulty of determining the "fair value" of noncash assets or stock given up by the acquirer has led to the rule that their cost may be determined either by the fair value of the consideration given or by the fair value of the property acquired, whichever is more clearly evident.

Book Value Adjustments.   The acquiring company is responsible for making any required adjustment to the book values of assets acquired and liabilities assumed as a result of the purchase. *APB Opinion No. 16* presented some guidelines for this assignment of the purchase price. They are:

1. Marketable securities should be recorded at their current net realizable values.

2. The amounts shown for receivables should be the present value of amounts to be received, determined at appropriate current interest rates, less allowances for uncollectibility and collection costs, if necessary.

3. Inventories:
   a. Finished goods and merchandise should be recorded at their selling price less the sum of (1) cost of disposal and (2) a reasonable profit allowance for the selling effort of the acquiring corporation.
   b. Work in process must be valued at the estimated selling price of finished goods less the sum of (1) costs to complete, (2) costs of disposal, and (3) a reasonable profit allowance for the completing and selling effort of the acquiring corporation based on profit for similar finished goods.
   c. Raw materials have to be restated to their current replacement cost.

4. Plant and equipment (a) to be used must be stated at current replacement cost for similar capacity unless the expected future use of the assets indicates a lower value to the acquirer; (b) to be sold or held for later sale rather than used must be adjusted to its current net realizable value; and (c) to be used temporarily should be presented at its current net realizable value recognizing future depreciation for the expected period of use.

5. Intangible assets which can be identified and named, including contracts, patents, franchises, customer and supplier lists, and favorable leases, should be recorded at their appraised value.

6. Other assets, including land, natural resources, and nonmarketable securities, must be presented at their appraised value.

7. The amounts shown for accounts and notes payable, long-term debt, and other claims payable should be the present values of amounts to be paid determined at appropriate current interest rates.

8. Similarly, the amounts recorded for liabilities and accruals—for example, accruals for pension cost, warranties, vacation pay, deferred compensation—must be present value of amounts to be paid determined at appropriate current interest rates.

9. Other liabilities and commitments, including unfavorable leases, contracts, and commitments, and plant closing expense incident to the acquisition, should be recorded at the present value of amounts to be paid determined at appropriate current interest rates.

10. A deferred tax asset or liability should be recorded for any temporary differences between the book and tax basis of assets or liabilities resulting from the purchase accounting.

Additional rules are: an acquiring corporation should record periodically as a part of income the accrual of interest on assets and liabilities recorded at acquisition date at the discounted value of amounts to be received or paid (see **Illustration A**). An acquiring corporation should not record as a separate asset the goodwill previously recorded by an acquired company and should not record deferred income taxes recorded by an acquired company before its acquisition. An acquiring corporation should reduce the acquired goodwill retroactively for the realized tax benefits of loss carryforwards of an acquired company not previously recorded by the acquiring corporation.

ILLUSTRATION A   Implementation of *APB Opinion No. 16,* Purchase Accounting Using Discounted Values

	Book Value	Basis of Valuation	Value for Purchase Accounting
Current assets:			
Cash	$ 10,000	Actual	$ 10,000
Accounts receivable (net)	90,000	Discounted 1 year @ 8%[a]	83,340
Fixed assets	400,000	Fair value	700,000
	$500,000		$793,340
Accounts payable	$ 10,000	Actual	$ 10,000
Long-term debt	90,000	Five years @ 8%	61,290
	$100,000		$ 71,290
Net value of purchases	$400,000		$722,050
Net charge/credit to income:			
In year 1: Income (accounts receivable, 90,000 − 83,340)			$ 6,660
Expense (long-term debt[b])			4,860
Net credit to income			$1,800

---

[a]Assume for the purposes of the example, that accounts receivable are due one year from this date ($90,000 × 0.926).
[b]Present value of debt @ 8%, payable in four years ($90,000 @ 0.735) $66,150
Present value of debt @ 8%, payable in five years ($90,000 @ 0.681) 61,290
Change in present value of debt . . . . $ 4,860

Pooling of Interests Method

Under the pooling of interests method, all assets of the newly combined group are valued at the same amounts at which they were previously carried in the accounts of the individual predecessor businesses. Underlying this method is the presumption that no new business entity has been created. Instead, it is assumed that ownership groups have merely contributed assets (or pooled resources) to carry on operations in an organization which is substantially a continuation of the preceding entities. Therefore, there is no reason to change asset values from those carried by the predecessor businesses.

Pooling of interest accounting must be used if certain criteria are met.

Pooling of Interests Illustration

Using the example presented earlier, assume that Company A issued its own capital stock with a par value of $200,000 and a fair value of $900,000 in payment for Company B, instead of paying $900,000 cash. In this transaction, the choice of the pooling of interests method can be strongly supported. The new entity is owned jointly by all stockholders of the previously separate corporations. The total assets and liabilities and retained earnings are undiminished and unchanged by the combinations. The stockholders of two corporations have merely pooled assets and liabilities and retained pro rata ownership in the new entity.

The combination would be entered on Company A's records as follows:

Dr. Net current assets	100,000	
Fixed assets	400,000	
Cr. Capital stock		200,000
Capital in excess of par value		100,000
Retained earnings		200,000

It should be noted that subsequent operations of the combined companies will be charged with depreciation based upon the original $400,000 book value of Company B's fixed assets. Also, no goodwill is recognized and no related problems of subsequent amortization or write-off are encountered. Further, the retained earnings of Company B are carried over into the combination, and the paid-in capital accounts are adjusted to reflect any differences between the par value of Company B stock and the par value of stock issued by Company A.

Company A's statement of results of operations for the accounting period in which Company B was acquired will include the combined results of operations of the constituent interests for the entire annual accounting period in which the combination was effected.

APB Opinion No. 16

APB Opinion No. 16 governs accounting for business combinations. The APB issued *APB Opinion No. 16* to clarify criteria for using the purchase and pooling methods to account for business combinations. It concluded that both methods were acceptable in accounting for business combinations, but not as alternatives under the same conditions. A business combination meeting specified conditions *required* the pooling of interest method. All other combinations were *required* to use the purchase method.

Pooling of interests was defined in *APB Opinion No. 16* as the presentation as a single interest of two or more common stockholder interests that were previously independent, and the combined rights and risks represented by those interests. The use of this method showed that the combining stockholder groups neither withdrew nor invested assets, but simply exchanged voting common stock in a ratio that determined their respective interests in the combined corporation.

The pooling of interests method could only be used if the transaction met all of the conditions specified in the opinion. In fact, if all of these conditions were met, the pooling of interest method had to be used. These basic conditions fall under three categories:

1. With respect to the combining companies
   a. Each of the combining companies is autonomous and has not been a subsidiary or a division of another company within two years before the plan of combination is initiated.
   b. Each of the combining companies is independent of the other companies. (Independence existed if neither of the combining companies held as intercorporate investments more than 10% in total of the outstanding voting common stock of the other combining company.)
2. With respect to the manner of combining of interests
   a. The combination is effected in a single transaction or is completed in accordance with a specific plan within one year after the plan is initiated.
   b. A corporation offers and issues only common stock with rights identical to those of the majority of its outstanding voting common stock in exchange for substantially all of the voting common stock interest of another company at the date the plan of combination is consummated.
   c. None of the combining companies changes the equity interests of the voting common stock in contemplation of effecting the combination, either within two years before the plan of combination is initiated or between the dates the combination is initiated and consummated; changes in contemplation of effecting the combination may include distributions to stockholders and additional issuances, exchanges, and retirements of securities.
   d. Each of the combining companies reacquires shares of voting common stock only for purposes other than business combinations, and no company reacquires more than a normal number of shares between the dates the plan of combination is initiated and consummated.
   e. The ratio of the interest of an individual common stockholder to those of other common stockholders in a combining company remains the same as a result of the exchange of stock to effect the combination.
   f. The voting rights to which the common stock ownership interests in the resulting combined corporation are entitled are exercisable by the stockholder; the stockholders are neither deprived nor restricted in exercising those rights for a period of years.
   g. The combination is resolved at the date the plan is consummated, and no provision of the plan relating to the issue of securities or other considerations is pending.

3. With respect to the absence of planned transactions
   a. The combined corporation does not agree directly or indirectly to retire or reacquire all or part of the common stock issued to effect the combination.
   b. The combined corporation does not enter into other financial arrangements for the benefit of the former stockholders of a combining company, such as a guaranty of loans secured by stock issued in the combination which in effect negates the exchange of equity securities.
   c. The combined corporation does not intend or plan to dispose of a significant part of the assets of the combining companies within two years after the combination, other than disposal in the ordinary course of business of the formerly separate companies and to eliminate duplicated facilities or excess capacity.

Ninety Percent Test

The primary source of technical problems in applying these criteria is the definition of "substantially all of the voting common stock" which must be exchanged (see **2b.** above). The text of *APB Opinion No. 16* states that substantially all of the voting common stock means "90% or more." That is, at the date the combination is consummated, one of the combining companies (issuing corporation) issues voting common stock in exchange for at least 90% of the outstanding voting common stock of the other company (combining company).

For the purposes of computing the 90% figure, shares of the combining company are excluded if they were (1) acquired before and held by the issuing corporation and its subsidiaries at the date the plan of combination is initiated, regardless of the form of consideration; (2) acquired by the issuing corporation and its subsidiaries after the date the plan of combination is initiated other than by issuing its own voting common stock; or (3) outstanding after the date the combination is consummated.

An investment in the stock of the issuing corporation by a combining company may prevent a combination from meeting the 90% criterion, even though the investment of the combining company may not be more than 10% of the outstanding stock of the issuing corporation. To determine whether or not an investment by the company being acquired in the stock of the issuing corporation precludes use of the pooling method, this stock investment must be expressed as an equivalent number of shares of the combining company, because the 90 percent-of-shares-exchanged criterion is expressed in terms of shares of stock of the combining company.

In a combination of more than two companies, the percentage of voting common stock is measured separately for each combining company.

Accounting Mechanics

The pooling of interests method requires that the recorded assets and liabilities of the separate companies be combined at their historical cost basis. However, since the separate companies may have recorded assets and liabilities under differing methods of accounting, it is permissible to adjust the amounts to the same basis of accounting if the change would otherwise have been appropriate for the separate company. Such a change in accounting method to make the accounts conform should be applied retroactively, and financial statements for prior periods should be restated.

The stockholders' equities are also combined as part of the pooling of interests, including the capital stock, capital in excess of par value, and retained earnings or deficits. If the par value of the total outstanding stock exceeds the capital stock of the separate combining companies, the excess is deducted first from contributed capital, then from retained earnings.

If treasury stock is used to effect a combination, this treasury stock should first be treated as retired, and the stock issued in the combination then treated as if it were previously unissued shares.

The treatment of stock of the combining companies held by another company depends on whether the holder is the issuing company or another combining company. If the investment of a combining company is in the common stock of the issuing company, it is, in effect, returned to the resulting combined corporation and should be treated as treasury stock. In contrast, an investment in the common stock of another combining company (not the issuing company) is an investment in stock that is exchanged in the combination for the common stock issued. This stock is in effect eliminated in the combination, and would be treated as retired stock.

Reporting Requirements

A corporation that uses the pooling of interests method of accounting for a combination should report results of operations for the period in which the combination occurs as though the companies had been combined as of the beginning of the period. Thus, the results of operations combine results of the separate companies from the beginning of the period to the date the combination is consummated, and represent combined operations from that date to the end of the period. The effects of intercompany transactions on current assets, liabilities, revenues, and cost of sales for the periods presented, and on retained earnings at the beginning of the periods presented, should be eliminated to the extent possible.

The combined corporation should disclose in notes to its financial statements the revenue, extraordinary items, and net income of each of the separate companies from the beginning of the period to the date of combination. In addition, balance sheet and financial information presented for prior years should be restated on a combined basis to furnish comparative information. Such data should clearly indicate the nature of the information.

Expenses incurred in effecting a business combination accounted for as a pooling of interests should be deducted in determining the net income of the combined corporation for the period in which the expenses are incurred. These expenses include such items as registration fees and costs of furnishing information to stockholders.

Continuing Controversy

Over the years, the accounting for business combinations has been one of the most controversial areas in financial accounting. Most of the controversy centers on the legitimacy of pooling of interests accounting, the criteria for a pooling of interests, and the treatment of goodwill.

Some critics of business combination accounting maintain that business combinations in which a continuing entity survives are in essence purchase transactions and that the pooling of interests method is not appropriate in such combinations. Furthermore, they conclude that in those relatively rare combinations where no constituent company clearly emerges as the continuing entity, a new business has in effect been created. In these cases, the accounting should be similar to that for a new company: the assets and rights should be recorded at fair market value and no goodwill recognized. Based on these conclusions, they have recommended that the pooling of interests method be discontinued as an acceptable accounting practice.

Those holding this view argue that by treating as purchases most combinations that qualify for pooling of interests, financial statements would be more useful to investors. First, the fair market value of separate assets and property rights would be disclosed. Second, assigning fair market, rather than book, values to acquired assets would result in more realistic depreciation charges. Third, the amount paid for goodwill would be fully disclosed. Some go further and suggest that goodwill should be charged directly against the retained earnings of the acquiring corporation as an advance payment by the current stockholders for excess future earnings.

Others with similar views recommend that the pooling of interests concept be dropped and replaced by a "fair-value pooling" concept. They argue that the fair-value pooling treatment should be applied to those business combinations in which (a) the constituent companies to the combination approximate each other in size; (b) it is difficult to determine which constituent acquired the other; and (c) the facts of the transaction clearly indicate that the combined entity is a new enterprise. All other combinations they would treat as purchases.

The fair-value pooling method proposed would record the assets of the new combined entity at their fair market value. Normally, because it is essentially a new enterprise, the combined entity would not begin operations with any retained earnings. However, if it was required to for legal or regulatory purpose, the combined entity may record as retained earnings that portion of the constituent companies' retained earnings that is legally available for dividends.

A number of accountants and business executives disagree with these conclusions. They argue that pooling of interests and purchase accounting are appropriate methods for accounting for business combinations and that many combinations are in effect pooling of interests. The challenge, they believe, is to identify the proper circumstances when each approach is appropriate.

Some argue that combinations effected by cash are in substance different from those affected by stock and a different method of accounting should be applied to each. Acquisitions for cash, they argue, should be treated as purchases, since one company gains control over the assets of another. An exchange of shares means that both groups of stockholders continue their ownership interest and genuine pooling of interests takes place, a fact which the accounting should reflect. While agreeing with this basic position, those who consider continuity of ownership interest as the key criterion for pooling believe purchase accounting is appropriate for combinations if either a material minority interest in a subsidiary company exists after acquisition of the subsidiary or if a material amount of preferred stock, either voting or nonvoting, has been used for the acquisition.

Others question the practicality of the fair-value pooling concept for combinations which in essence create "a new enterprise." In their opinion, the tests for determining whether or not a new enterprise has in fact been created are not clear and, hence, not operational.

Financial Analysis

Business combination accounting creates many problems for statement users when evaluating companies individually or on a comparative basis. The comments below relate to these questions statement users should always ask when they encounter a business combination: What are the accounting implications of the acquisition terms and payments? Were these terms and payments developed in order to obtain a specific accounting outcome? Is goodwill over or undervalued?

The accounting for business combinations can influence a company's current and future growth rate. Statement users must distinguish this source of growth. It may be a onetime earnings boost that can not be sustained by future operations. For example, a company with flat earnings acquiring another company with flat earnings for cash in a purchase transaction will include in its statements the acquiree's profits from the date of acquisition. The addition of these profits will cause the acquiring company's profits to rise relative to the period before acquisition. However, if the operating profits of both companies remain flat, the combined companies' profits will also be flat after the acquisition. Or, alternatively, an acquisition for stock of a company with a lower price-to-earnings ratio than the acquiring company, accounted for as a pooling of interests, will cause the acquiring company's earnings per share to rise. Again, unless the underlying operating earnings are rising, this earnings-per-share growth will be a onetime event impacting the earnings in the year of acquisition and the subsequent year. All too often, companies with weak underlying operations seeking growth through acquisitions find themselves so dependent on this source of growth that they increasingly acquire overpriced marginal companies to maintain their growth rate. Eventually, the weight of these marginal acquisitions causes the corporate structure to crumble. Statement users must be wary of such companies, particularly since their stock is often "hyped" by the promoter to maintain its price-to-earnings ratio to facilitate future acquisitions.

Pooling of interests accounting can change the acquiring company's past growth record, since the combining company's past results are combined for accounting purposes as if the two companies had always been one. Statement users must be careful not to relate the acquiring company's past stock prices to the pooled results. These stock prices reflect the prepooling statements. In addition, the past pooling historical results may not be a good indicator of future growth rates. The acquired company's management might not be retained, and the combined companies may work less successfully together than they did as individual companies because of such factors as corporate culture differences.

Goodwill is a difficult item for statement users to evaluate. It relates to the potential value of the acquirer of acquired entities that typically lose their identity once merged by the acquiring company into its consolidated statements. This makes it difficult for statement users to evaluate whether the goodwill balance is overstated, understated, or being amortized over a reasonable period of time. Unpleasant memories of unexpected goodwill write-downs have led many experienced statement users to favor companies that write off goodwill over relatively short periods of time, and to be suspicious of companies adopting long write-off periods. Negative goodwill is seldom regarded as a positive income item since it has no positive cash flow attached to it and often arises from the purchase of troubled companies who must sell out for less than their net book value.

Combination accounting can be abused by unscrupulous managements to mislead unwary statement users. The best protection for statement users is to know the relevant accounting rules, carefully analyze the accounting results required by the acquisition deal, and be wary of managements that appear to be using business combination accounting to puff up current results, rewriting history to imply greater future growth possibilities, and sacrificing future cash flow for improved short-term accounting results.

Comptrex Associates, Inc.

In connection with the issuance of Comptrex Associates, Inc.'s (CAI) first quarter 1991 financial statements, and an anticipated public sale of its stock, the company's certified public accountants were asked to give their views on how CAI should account for an acquisition agreement entered into on January 30, 1991, by which CAI acquired all of the assets and assumed all of the liabilities of Axtra Services Corporation (ASC). As part of the same transaction, CAI acquired from Lewis Clarke and Thomas Chen, the sole stockholders of ASC, all of the computer software program packages that had been marketed by ASC under license from Clarke and Chen. To pay for the ASC acquisition, CAI issued an aggregate of 1,385,356 shares of common stock (representing approximately 42.0% of CAI's outstanding common) to ASC. Based on CAI's most recent closing bid prices in the over-the-counter market, the value of the deal was estimated to be approximately $18 million. The number of shares issued in the combination was based on the net earnings of ASC for the year ended December 31, 1990. ASC subsequently distributed the CAI shares to its sole stockholders, Clarke and Chen.

In connection with the ASC acquisition, CAI and Clarke and Chen entered into certain separate agreements:

1. Clarke and Chen and CAI's two principal executives, Peter Koster and Larry Leonard, agreed to vote their CAI common stock for a one-year period from February 27, 1991 for the perpetuation of the current members of CAI's board of directors or their successors as designated by CAI's board.

2. Clarke and Chen also agreed, subject to certain conditions as to minimum price ($8.00 per share), to sell at least 50% of their CAI common stock acquired in the combination prior to February 27, 1993.

Professor David F. Hawkins and Professor Norman J. Bartczak of Columbia University prepared this case as the basis for class discussion rather than to illustrate either effective or ineffective handling of an administrative situation.

3. CAI granted Lewis and Chen the right to have CAI prior to December 31, 1992, use its best efforts to register for public sale the CAI common stock acquired by them in the combination. However, CAI and Clarke and Chen agreed that if prior to the effectiveness of such registration statement the Securities and Exchange Commission (SEC) would not allow the accounting treatment of the acquisition transaction to be recorded on a pooling of interests basis for financial reporting purposes, then the acquisition transaction would be rescinded.

4. CAI granted Clarke and Chen the right to include their shares in any appropriate registration statement filed by CAI before February 27, 1995 unless they previously exercised their right described above. Clarke and Chen agreed to pay their pro rata share of the expenses associated with such registrations.

5. CAI agreed with Clarke and Chen that should they not sell any shares of CAI common stock in a public offering, CAI would lend to Clarke up to $1,400,000 and to Chen up to $600,000, for two years at 12% interest per annum to provide for the payment of federal tax liabilities incurred as a consequence of the combination. Such loans would be secured by a portion of the CAI common stock held by Clarke and Chen.

6. CAI further agreed to provide unsecured loans of up to $1,000,000 each to Clarke and Chen repayable 10 years from the date of loan, at 6% interest per annum, to satisfy possible additional tax liabilities incurred as a consequence of the combination.

7. Both Clarke and Chen agreed not to compete with CAI during the terms of their agreements and for certain periods thereafter.

Earlier in March 1991, CAI had informed its public accountants that it intended to file a registration statement with the SEC covering a secondary public offering and sale of 1,050,000 shares of CAI common stock to be offered and sold by means of a firm commitment underwriting of which 1,033,930 shares would be owned by Clarke and Chen. Included in the registration statement would be an unaudited supplemental combined balance sheet for CAI and ASC at December 31, 1990 and unaudited supplemental combined statements of income for CAI and ASC for the five fiscal years ended April 30, 1990 and the results of combined operations for CAI and ASC for the eight month period ended December 31, 1989 and 1990 as if the acquisition transaction had occurred at the beginning of the 1986 fiscal year (see **Exhibits 1** and **2**). The registration statement would also include recent CAI and ASC financial statements (see **Exhibits 3** through **6**). For financial reporting purposes, CAI intended to account for the acquisition of ASC on a pooling of interests basis in these unaudited combined financial statements. The use of pooling of interests for financial reporting purposes had no effect on the tax status of the acquisition, i.e., as structured for tax purposes, the acquisition was a taxable transaction to Clarke and Chen whether or not CAI used pooling of interests or purchase accounting for financial reporting purposes.

Company Backgrounds

CAI was incorporated in Delaware in 1983. CAI provided a broad range of computer consulting services and marketed proprietary computer software packages. Its customers included principally insurance companies, banks, oil, petrochemical and pharmaceutical companies, manufacturing and computer manufacturing companies, and government agencies. CAI's largest customer accounted for approximately 18% of CAI's revenues in fiscal 1990.

EXHIBIT 1   Comptrex Associates, Inc. Unaudited Supplemental Combined Statement of Income, 1986–1990

The following Unaudited Supplemental Combined Statements of Income represent a combination of the Consolidated Statements of Income of CAI and subsidiaries for the five fiscal years ended April 30, 1990 and the results of their operations for the eight-month periods ended December 31, 1989 and 1990, with the Statements of Income of ASC for the five fiscal years ended April 30, 1990 and the results of its operations for the eight-month period ended December 31, 1989 and 1990 as if the combination occurred at the beginning of the 1986 fiscal year.

	(Dollars in thousands) Years Ended April 30,					8 Months Ended December 31,	
	1986	1987	1988	1989	1990	1989	1990
Revenues	$2,479	$6,120	$10,336	$15,120	$19,227	$11,883	$13,351
Operating costs and expenses							
Direct costs	1,339	3,320	6,252	8,769	11,348	7,163	7,441
Selling, general and administrative expenses	574	1,318	2,146	3,264	4,446	2,767	3,509
	1,913	4,638	8,398	12,033	15,794	9,930	10,950
Operating income	566	1,482	1,938	3,087	3,433	1,953	2,401
Other income (deductions)							
Interest income	21	25	38	65	175	97	328
Interest expense	(7)	(9)	(5)	(3)	(6)	(6)	—
Gain on sale of subsidiary	—	—	—	53	—	—	—
Unrealized decline in market value of investments and other	—	1	(1)	1	(26)	(12)	(1)
	14	17	32	116	143	79	327
Income before income tax	580	1,499	1,970	3,203	3,576	2,032	2,728
Income taxes	272	714	848	1,513	1,816	1,032	1,346
Net income	$ 308	$ 785	$ 1,122	$ 1,690	$ 1,760	$ 1,000	$ 1,382
Earnings per common share							
Primary	$ .13	$ .33	$ 42	$ .59	$ .63	$ .36	$ .46
Fully diluted	$ .12	$ .30	$ .40	$ .59	$ .63	$ .36	$ .46
Average number of shares outstanding							
Common stock and common stock equivalents	2,376,016	2,376,874	2,675,038	2,847,298	2,806,770	2,805,520	3,028,372
Assuming full dilution	2,647,936	2,648,794	2,829,478	2,847,298	2,806,770	2,805,520	3,028,372

EXHIBIT 2   Comptrex Associates, Inc. Unaudited Supplemental Combined Balance Sheet December 31, 1990 ($ in thousands)

The following unaudited supplemental combined balance sheet represents a combination of the consolidated balance sheet of CAI with the balance sheet of ASC at December 31, 1990. Stockholders' equity has been adjusted to reflect pooling of interests accounting.

Assets
Current Assets

Cash and interest-bearing deposits	$ 5,220
Short-term investments at lower of costs or market	228
Accounts receivable	
Trade	3,993
Other	222
Prepaid expenses	66
Total current assets	9,729

Equipment and Leasehold Improvements—at Cost

Furniture and equipment	619
Leasehold improvements	31
	650
Less accumulated depreciation and amortization	253
	397

Other Assets

Deferred costs	22
Other assets	111
	133
	$10,259

Liabilities
Current Liabilities

Accounts payable	$ 220
Accrued liabilities	958
Income taxes	
Current	378
Deferred	676
Total current liabilities	2,232

Stockholders' Equity

Common stock—authorized, 5,000,000 shares of $.10 par value, issued and outstanding, 3,264,353 shares	326
Capital in excess of par value	3,894
	4,220
Retained earnings	3,807
	8,027
	$10,259

EXHIBIT 3   Comptrex Associates, Inc. Consolidated Statement of Income, 1986–1990 ($ in thousands)

	Years Ended April 30,					8 Months Ended December 31,	
	1986	*1987*	*1988*	*1989*	*1990*	*1989*	*1990*
						(Unaudited)	
Revenues (note 2)	$2,093	$3,165	$5,776	$8,790	$11,813	$ 7,110	$9,401
Operating Costs and Expenses							
Direct costs	1,260	1,800	3,586	5,030	6,679	3,784	5,310
Selling, general and administrative	539	1,005	1,672	2,740	3,559	2,343	2,927
	1,799	2,805	5,258	7,770	10,238	6,127	8,237
Operating income	294	360	518	1,020	1,575	983	1,164
Other Income (Deductions)							
Interest income.....................	21	18	15	37	104	56	260
Interest expense	(7)	(7)	(5)	(3)	(6)	(6)	—
Gain on sale of subsidiary	—	—	—	53	—	—	—
Unrealized decline in market value							
of investments	—	—	—	—	(32)	(15)	(23)
	14	11	10	87	66	35	237
Income before income taxes	308	371	528	1,107	1,641	1,018	1,401
Income taxes	144	180	208	492	840	521	710
Net income.....................	$ 164	$ 191	$ 320	$ 615	$ 801	$ 497	$ 691
Earnings per common share							
Primary	$ .17	$ .19	$ .25	$ .42	$ .56	$ .35	$ .42
Fully diluted	$ .13	$ .15	$ .22	$ .42	$ .56	$ .35	$ .42
Average number of shares outstanding, adjusted for stock splits and stock dividend Common stock and common stock							
equivalents	990,660	991,518	1,289,682	1,461,942	1,421,414	1,420,164	1,643,016
Assuming full dilution	1,262,580	1,263,438	1,444,122	1,461,942	1,421,414	1,420,164	1,643,016

EXHIBIT 4   Comptrex Associates, Inc. Balance Sheets ($ in thousands)

	April 30, 1990	December 31, 1990 (Unaudited)
Assets		
Current Assets		
Cash and interest bearing deposits	$1,424	$4,890
Short-term investments—at lower of cost or market	241	228
Accounts receivable		
Trade	1,898	2,594
Other	9	222
Prepaid expenses	16	53
Total current assets	3,588	7,987
Equipment and Leasehold Improvements—at Cost		
Furniture and equipment	227	256
Leasehold improvements	16	16
	243	272
Less accumulated depreciation and amortization	93	124
	150	148
Other Assets		
Deferred costs	35	22
Other assets	32	57
	67	79
	$3,805	$8,214
Liabilities		
Current Liabilities		
Accounts payable	$ 268	$ 179
Accrued liabilities		
Salaries, bonuses, and vacation	368	385
Payroll taxes	20	36
Profit-sharing plan	179	120
Royalties	38	24
Other	73	210
Income taxes	340	276
Total current liabilities	1,286	1,230
Commitments		
Stockholders' Equity		
Common stock—authorized, 5,000,000 shares of $.10 par value; issued and outstanding, 949,276 shares at April 30, 1990 and 1,878,997 at December 31, 1990	95	188
Capital in excess of par value	350	4,031
	445	4,219
Retained earnings	2,074	2,765
	2,519	6,984
	$3,805	$8,214

EXHIBIT 5   Axtra Services Corporation Statement of Earnings and Retained Earnings, 1986–1990 ($ in thousands)

	Twelve-Month Period Ended April 30,					8 Months Ended December 31,	
	1986	1987	1988	1989	1990	1989	1990
	(Unaudited)					*(Unaudited)*	
Revenue	$386	$2,955	$4,560	$6,330	$7,414	$4,773	$3,950
Operating costs and expenses							
Direct costs	79	1,520	2,666	3,739	4,669	3,379	2,131
General and administrative	7	113	274	324	687	291	449
Allocated portion of officers' salaries	28	200	200	200	200	133	133
	114	1,833	3,140	4,263	5,556	3,803	2,713
Operating income	272	1,122	1,420	2,067	1,858	970	1,237
Other income (deduction)							
Interest income	—	7	23	28	71	41	68
Interest expense	—	(2)	—	—	—	—	—
Miscellaneous	—	1	(1)	1	6	3	22
	—	6	22	29	77	44	90
Earnings before income taxes	272	1,128	1,442	2,096	1,935	1,014	1,327
Income taxes							
Current	12	184	28	239	318	(255)	(462)
Deferred	116	64	75	212	41	197	167
Pro forma	—	286	537	570	617	569	931
	128	534	640	1,021	976	511	636
Net earnings before distributions to stockholders and pro forma tax provision	$144	$ 594	$ 802	$1,075	$ 959	$ 503	$ 691
Net earnings before distributions to stockholders and pro forma tax provision	$144	$ 594	$ 802	$1,075	$ 959	$ 503	$ 691
Distributions to stockholders	—	(450)	(491)	(695)	(690)	(671)	(1,377)
Commissions							
Salaries, net of salaries charged to operations (included in operating costs and expenses)	—	(172)	(628)	(492)	(651)	(458)	(388)
Tax provision pro forma	—	286	537	570	617	568	931
Dividends	—	—	(10)	(50)	(70)	(70)	—
Retained earnings at beginning of period	—	144	402	612	1,020	1,020	1,185
Retained earnings at end of period	$144	$ 402	$ 612	$1,020	$1,185	$ 892	$1,042

EXHIBIT 6 Axtra Services Corporation Balance Sheets ($ in thousands)

	April 30, 1990	*December 31, 1990*
Assets		
Current Assets		
Cash and interest-bearing deposits	$ 897	$ 330
Accounts receivable—trade	1,403	1,399
Advance distributions to stockholders	150	—
Prepaid expenses and other	24	13
Total current assets	2,474	1,742
Equipment and Leasehold Improvements—at Cost		
Furniture, equipment, and apartment	383	363
Leasehold improvements	15	15
	398	378
Less accumulated depreciation and amortization	99	129
	299	249
Other Assets	16	54
	$2,789	$2,045
Liabilities		
Current Liabilities		
Accounts payable	$ 110	$ 41
Accrued liabilities		
Salaries and commissions	188	161
Profit-sharing contributions	75	—
Payroll taxes and other	28	22
Distribution due to stockholders	75	—
Income taxes		
Current	619	102
Deferred	508	676
Total current liabilities	1,603	1,002
Commitments	—	—
Stockholders' Equity		
Common stock—authorized, 500 shares of no par value; issued and outstanding, 10 shares	1	1
Retained earnings	1,185	1,042
	1,186	1,043
	$2,789	$2,045

CAI marketed its computer consulting services to customers who often required outside assistance with the software portions of their computer systems for (i) certain technical expertise not available internally; (ii) projects which cannot be completed on time using internal manpower; and (iii) short-term needs which do not justify permanent increases in personnel. In addition, the demands placed upon the computer installations of large companies required them to operate in the most efficient manner possible. To accomplish this, many data processing departments used packaged computer programs such as CAI's software packages.

ASC had been engaged in a business substantially similar to CAI. ASC provided computer consulting services and marketed five proprietary computer software packages. Like CAI, ASC licensed the use of its software products under long- and short-term agreements. Such agreements typically call for the payment of either monthly or annual licensing fees. During the past five calendar years the number of software packages under licensing agreements from ASC had increased from approximately 25 to 600 packages. For the 12 months ended April 30, 1990, ASC derived 34% of its revenues and 79% of its operating income from the licensing of its software products.

The following chart sets forth the amounts of revenues and operating income derived by CAI and ASC from computer consulting services and computer software during the fiscal year ended April 30, 1990.

	CAI	ASC (dollars in thousands)	Combined
Revenues:			
Consulting services....................	$10,638	$4,862	$15,500
Software	1,175	2,552	3,727
Total revenues	$11,813	$7,414	$19,227
Operating income:			
Consulting services....................	$ 1,341	$ 385	$ 1,726
Software	234	1,473	1,707
Total operating income	$ 1,575	$1,858	$ 3,433

The following table shows revenue and operating income attributable to CAI's computer consulting services and software packages for the periods indicated and includes the revenue and operating income of ASC for those periods:

	Years Ended April 30,					December 31,	
	1986	*1987*	*1988*	*1989*	*1990*	*1989*	*1990*
			(dollars in thousands)			*(unaudited)*	
Revenue							
Computer consulting	$2,153	$4,649	$ 8,963	$13,019	$15,500	$ 9,781	$10,776
Software package	326	1,471	1,373	2,101	3,727	2,102	2,575
Total revenue	$2,479	$6,120	$10,336	$15,120	$19,227	$11,883	13,351
% of Revenue							
Computer consulting	86.8	76.0	86.7	86.1	80.6	82.3	80.7
Software package	13.2	24.0	13.3	13.9	19.4	17.7	19.3
Operating Income							
Computer consulting	$ 315	$ 879	$ 1,855	$ 2,378	$ 1,726	$ 1,121	$ 1,183
Software package	251	603	83	709	1,707	832	1,218
Total operating income	$ 566	$1,482	$ 1,938	$ 3,087	$ 3,433	$ 1,953	$ 2,401
% of Operating Income							
Computer consulting	55.7	59.3	95.7	77.0	50.3	57.4	49.3
Software package	44.3	40.7	4.3	23.0	49.7	42.6	50.7

Questions

1. As best you can, prepare a set of combined financial statements for ASC and CAI using the purchase accounting method for the acquisition. How do these financial statements differ from those prepared using the pooling of interest accounting methods for acquisitions? _____

2. Do you believe the SEC will object to CAI's use of the pooling of interests method to account for its acquisition of ASC in the registration statement

accompanying any public sale of CAI's stock? _____

3. What are the earnings and cash flow implications of the alternative accounting treatments for the acquisition? _____ Why does CAI's management care which method is used? _____

4. Putting aside US-GAAP, do you believe pooling of interests accounting is appropriate for the CAI-ASC merger? _____

CASE
18-2   Medaphis Corporation

Jane Edward, a recent hire of Investment Management Company, an institutional manager of corporate and private pension money, was given the following task by her immediate supervisor.

> Jane, I would like your opinion on the Medaphis Corporation. For most of last year, we could have bought this stock for under $30 a share. Now, it is in the low $60s. All I have is the company's 1994 annual report. Here it is. (See **Exhibit 1** for selected excerpts.) Do the best you can with it, and give me your opinion on the company's strategy, accounting policies and practices, and key financial ratios. The focus of my interest is, "Should we be interested in this stock, and if so, in what way—short or long?" Based on your preliminary analysis, we might or might not invest more time in analyzing this stock. I'm sorry I don't have any more data for you to work on at this time.

EXHIBIT 1   Selected Excerpts from Medaphis Corporation's 1994 Annual Report

---

Questions and Answers

Q: What is the mission of Medaphis Corporation?

A: The mission of Medaphis is to provide an unequaled level of measurable quality and productivity in the delivery of business management services which respond to the wants, needs and values of healthcare providers.

Q: How is the Company structured?

A: Medaphis Corporation has four operating subsidiaries: Medaphis Physician Services Corporation, Medaphis Hospital Services Corporation, Gottlieb's Financial Services, Inc. and Imonics Corporation (formerly Gateway Conversion Technologies, Inc.). There are approximately 325 offices nationwide and we currently operate in 46 states. The acquisition of Atwork on March 17, 1995 expanded Medaphis' market to include all fifty states plus Canada, Australia, the United Kingdom and Europe. Medaphis currently employs approximately 8,000 people.

Q: What were the significant events for Medaphis during 1994?

A: During 1994, Medaphis completed eleven acquisitions. In November, we acquired AdvaCare, Inc. for $32.3 of Medaphis common stock plus the assumption of $69.3 million of liabilities. This was our largest acquisition for the year. Additionally, Medaphis obtained a new senior credit facility of $150,000,000 to refinance existing indebtedness, future acquisitions and general corporate purposes. In March 1995, the senior credit facility was amended and, among other things, increased to $250,000,000.

Professor David F. Hawkins prepared this case as the basis for class discussion rather than to illustrate either effective or ineffective handling of an administrative situation.

EXHIBIT 1   (continued)

Q: What were significant changes, trends or events in the healthcare industry during 1994?

A: The healthcare market is changing quickly. The wants and needs of Medaphis' existing and prospective customers are transforming as rapidly as the healthcare environment they occupy. To maintain their lifestyle despite declining reimbursement trends, doctors and hospitals are placing steadily higher value on increased effectiveness and efficiency in the conversion of medical services into cash. Further, to compete effectively while maintaining profitability, healthcare providers now must capture and use comprehensive cost utilization and outcome information about their medical service transactions. Most of this information is generally inaccessible today.

Q: How is Medaphis responding to those events?

A: The Company's services and products assist healthcare providers in addressing their two largest and most pressing business problems: how to effectively get paid for the work they perform and how to efficiently manage their costs of healthcare delivery. The Company's billing, accounts receivable and other business management services have historically assisted its clients in addressing the inefficiencies embedded in the healthcare revenue cycle through the conversion of medical services into cash. Medaphis has begun to address the tremen-

dous cost inefficiencies in healthcare through the addition of the scheduling systems of Atwork, which are designed to help healthcare providers control labor costs and maintain efficiency, and the systems integration and workflow engineering skills of Imonics Corporation.

Q: Describe Medaphis' acquisition strategy.

A: Medaphis is a transaction processing company in an industry that we believe is ripe for consolidation. We are leading the consolidation effort so that we can broaden our customer base, enhance operating efficiencies and extend and concentrate our service offerings. The sellers have wonderfully run businesses that are our fragmented, local competition. Their revenues, except for a few regional competitors, range from $1–$10 million and their owners are looking to exit.

Q: Describe Medaphis' convertible debentures.

A: The convertible debentures bear interest at 6 1/2 percent payable semiannually on January 1st and July 1st. The maturity date is January 1, 2000 and the debentures are convertible into common stock at a conversion price of $28.00 per share. The underlying stock is currently not registered; however, the stock will be freely tradable under Rule 144(k) on and after January 1, 1996, when the no-hard-call period terminates.

Selected Consolidated Financial Data (in thousands, except per share data)

Year Ended December 31	1994	1993	1992	1991	1990
Statement of Income Data					
Revenue..........................	$253,490	$169,518	$ 97,385	$55,643	$41,646
Salaries and wages	142,656	95,387	55,753	31,448	23,763
Other operating expenses	61,941	43,461	27,560	16,169	12,410
Depreciation.......................	6,660	4,988	2,999	2,134	1,622
Amortization	6,818	4,327	1,502	532	804
Interest expense, net	6,276	6,407	1,350	2,019	1,537
Income before extraordinary items and cumulative effect of accounting change	17,429	9,153	5,799	3,175	1,445
Net income	$ 17,429	$ 9,153	$ 6,140	$ 3,175	$ 1,063
Weighted average shares outstanding	15,206	11,465	10,278	7,022	6,463
Per Share Data					
Income before extraordinary items and cumulative effect of accounting change	$ 1.15	$ 0.80	$ 0.57	$ 0.45	$ 0.22
Net income	$ 1.15	$ 0.80	$ 0.60	$ 0.45	$ 0.16

EXHIBIT 1   (continued)

December 31	1994	1993	1992	1991	1990
Balance Sheet Data					
Working capital	$ 57,482	$ 50,222	$ 24,449	$37,315	$ 8,591
Intangible assets	367,677	173,178	106,900	22,158	10,497
Total assets	524,600	288,456	170,171	79,180	30,652
Long-term debt	145,730	6,054	11,762	19,470	10,817
Convertible subordinated debentures	63,375	63,375	60,000	—	—
Stockholders' equity	227,940	169,651	73,726	48,756	14,252

Medaphis is a leading provider of business management services to physicians and hospitals. The Company's services and products assist healthcare providers in addressing their two largest and most pressing business problems: how to get paid for the work they perform and how to effectively manage that work. The Company's billing, accounts receivable and other business management services have historically assisted its clients in addressing the inefficiencies currently embedded in the healthcare revenue cycle through the conversion of medical services into cash. In addition, the Company's business management services have historically assisted its clients in addressing certain of the cost inefficiencies associated with the delivery of healthcare services. To further enhance its ability to address the cost inefficiencies associated with the delivery of healthcare services, the Company acquired Automation Atwork ("Atwork") on March 17, 1995. Atwork's scheduling systems are designed to help healthcare providers control labor costs and maintain efficiency by automating certain scheduling and management functions, which can be highly labor intensive.

Medaphis' business is impacted by trends in the U.S. healthcare industry. As healthcare expenditures have grown as a percentage of U.S. gross national product, public and private healthcare cost containment measures have applied pressure to the margins of healthcare providers. Historically, some payers have willingly paid the prices established by providers while other payers, notably the government and managed care companies, have paid far less than established prices (in many cases less than the average cost of providing the services). As a consequence, prices charged payers willing to pay established prices have increased in order to recover the cost of services purchased by the government and others but not paid by them (i.e., "cost shifting"). Increasing complexity in the reimbursement system and assumption of greater payment responsibility by individuals have caused healthcare providers to experience increased receivables and bad debt levels and higher business office costs. Providers overcome these pressures on profitability by increasing their prices, by relying on demographic changes to support increases in the volume and intensity of medical procedures, and by cost shifting. As providers experience limitations in their continued ability to shift costs in these ways, the amount of reimbursement received by Medaphis' clients may be reduced and Medaphis' rate of growth in revenues, assuming present management fee levels, may decline. However, management believes Medaphis may benefit from providers' attempts to offset declines in profitability through seeking more effective and efficient business management services such as those provided by Medaphis.

The U.S. healthcare industry continues to experience tremendous change as both federal and state governments as well as private industry work to bring more efficiency and effectiveness to the healthcare system. Medaphis continues to evaluate governmental and industry reform initiatives in an effort to position itself to take advantage of the opportunities created thereby.

As of December 31, 1994, Medaphis provided business management services to approximately 13,300 physicians and 650 hospitals.

Results of Operations

The following table shows the percentage of certain items reflected in the Company's statements of income to revenue.

Exhibit 1   (continued)

Year Ended December 31,	*1994*	*1993*	*1992*
Revenue	100.0%	100.0%	100.0%
Salaries and wages	56.3	56.3	57.2
Other operating expenses	24.4	25.6	28.3
Depreciation	2.6	2.9	3.1
Amortization	2.7	2.6	1.5
Interest expense, net	2.5	3.8	1.4
Income before income taxes, extraordinary item and cumulative effect of accounting change	11.5	8.8	8.5
Income taxes	4.6	3.4	2.5
Income before extraordinary item and cumulative effect of accounting change	6.9	5.4	6.0
Extraordinary item	—	—	(2.2)
Cumulative effect of accounting change	—	—	2.5
Net Income	6.9%	5.4%	6.3%

Revenue. Revenue increased 49.5% to $253.5 million in 1994 as compared with $169.5 million in 1993 and increased 74.1% in 1993, as compared with 1992. Revenue growth results from (i) acquisitions and (ii) increases in the number of clients and changes in clients' year over year cash collections ("internal growth"). The Company has consummated 18 business combinations during the period from January 1, 1992 through December 31, 1994. Revenue increases related to acquisitions and internal growth were 87% and 13%, respectively, in 1994 and 85.2% and 14.8%, respectively, in 1993.

The Company's selling activities generated new client relationships with estimated annualized revenue of approximately $46 million and $33 million in 1994 and 1993, respectively. The Company's clients' year over year cash collections were flat in 1994 as compared with 1993 and increased 2% in 1993 as compared with 1992.

Salaries and Wages. Salaries and wages represented 56.3% of revenue in 1994 and 1993 as compared with 57.2% in 1992. The operating leverage achieved by the Company in 1994 was offset by the costs associated with recent acquisitions. The decrease in 1993 resulted primarily from completing the conversion of the three acquisitions consummated in the first quarter of 1992 to the Company's systems and procedures, and operating leverage arising primarily from the four acquisitions completed in 1992.

Other Operating Expenses. Other operating expenses decreased to 24.4% of revenue in 1994 from 25.6% in 1993 and 28.3% in 1992. These decreases resulted primarily from the benefits of economies of scale realized by the growth in the Company's business, particularly reduced postage, travel, rent, insurance and telephone costs, as a percentage of revenue.

Depreciation. Depreciation expense was $6.7 million in 1994, $5.0 million in 1993, and $3.0 million in 1992. These increases reflect the Company's investment in property and equipment to support growth in its business, including acquisitions.

In July 1994, the Company began a comprehensive re-engineering and consolidation project. As part of this project, Management anticipates consolidating the processing function currently being performed in approximately 300 local business offices into approximately 10 regional processing centers. In addition, new computer equipment and proprietary software will be installed throughout the Company. The project will result in an anticipated increase in depreciation expense and amortization expense of approximately $1.5 million and $1 million, respectively, in 1995 with further increases anticipated in 1996. Management anticipates this project will be completed by the end of 1996.

EXHIBIT 1   (continued)

Amortization.   Amortization of intangible assets associated with the Company's acquisitions was $6.8 million in 1994, $4.3 million in 1993, and $1.5 million in 1992. The increases are primarily due to increased amortization of goodwill and client lists resulting from acquisitions. Management estimates that intangible assets acquired in connection with 1994 acquisitions will increase amortization expense by approximately $6 million in 1995. As noted above, Management anticipates that its re-engineering and consolidation project will result in an additional increase in amortization expense in 1995 and 1996.

Interest.   Net interest expense was $6.3 million in 1994, $6.4 million in 1993 and $1.3 million in 1992. The increase in 1993 as compared with 1992 was primarily due to the issuance of approximately $63.4 million of 6½% convertible subordinated debentures in December 1992 and January 1993 to finance an acquisition as well as borrowings under the Company's Senior Credit Facility. Management anticipates an increase in interest expense during 1995 as a result of increased interest rates and increased borrowings under the Senior Credit Facility to finance 1994 acquisitions.

Income before Income Taxes, Extraordinary Item, and Cumulative Effect of Accounting Change.   The Company's income before income taxes, extraordinary item and cumulative effect of the change in accounting for income taxes was increased to 11.5% of revenue in 1994 as compared with 8.8% of revenue in 1993 and 8.5% of revenue in 1992. The increases are primarily a result of operating leverage and changes in interest expense.

Income Taxes.   The Company's effective income tax rate was 40.2%, 38.8%, and 29.5% for 1994, 1993, and 1992, respectively. The increase in the Company's effective tax rate in 1994 resulted primarily from a change in the valuation allowance in 1993. The increase in the Company's effective tax rate in 1993 as compared with 1992 resulted primarily from a change in the valuation allowance in 1992 relating to the anticipated future realization of certain net operating loss carryforwards. The Company's adoption of Statement of Financial Accounting Standards No. 109 resulted in a cumulative benefit during 1992 of $2.5 million.

Extraordinary Loss on Prepayment of Debt.   On May 28, 1992 the Company completed a second public offering of its common stock. The net proceeds to the Company were approximately $18.1 million. These proceeds were used to prepay substantially all of the Company's outstanding long-term indebtedness. An extraordinary loss of $2.1 million (net of an income tax benefit of $1.0 million) was recorded in 1992 relating to the write-off of unamortized deferred financing costs and debt issue discount.

Net Income.   Net income was $17.4 million in 1994, a 90.4% increase over the $9.2 million achieved in 1993, which represented a 49.1% increase over the $6.1 million reported in 1992. As a percentage of revenue, net income increased to 6.9% in 1994 from 5.4% in 1993 due to economies of scale realized in other operating expenses and lower interest expense as a percentage of revenue being offset by a higher effective tax rate in 1994. Net income decreased as a percentage of revenue to 5.4% in 1993 from 6.3% in 1992 due to economies of scale realized in salaries and wages and other operating expenses being offset by a higher effective tax rate in 1993 and increased amortization and interest resulting from acquisitions.

Net Income per Common Share.   The weighted average shares outstanding were 15,206,000 in 1994, 11,465,000 in 1993, and 10,278,000 in 1992. The increases were primarily the result of 1.5 million shares of common stock sold in May 1992 as part of the second public offering and 3.2 million shares of common stock sold in December 1993 in the Company's third public offering. Even with the significant increases in the weighted average shares outstanding, net income per common share increased 43.8% to $1.15 in 1994 as compared with $0.80 in 1993, and net income per common share increased 33.3% in 1993 as compared with $0.60 in 1992.

Outlook.   During July 1994, the Company began a comprehensive re-engineering and consolidation project in order to enhance its ability to provide more effective and efficient business management services to its clients. This project is designed to further enhance the Company's long-term operating efficiency and client service capability. The Company will consolidate its billing and accounts receivable processing

Exhibit 1   (continued)

function, which is currently operated out of approximately 300 local business offices, into approximately 10 regional processing centers. It is currently anticipated that this project will continue through 1996. As a result of this project, the Company announced in January 1995 that it would record restructuring and other charges of approximately $25 million ($15 million, net of tax) in the first quarter of 1995, consisting primarily of lease buy-out and termination payments, involuntary severance benefits and impairment losses associated with the disposition of property and equipment. In addition, on March 17, 1995, the Company exchanged four million shares of its common stock for all of the outstanding common shares of Atwork. This transaction will be accounted for as a pooling of interests in the first quarter of 1995. As a result of the merger, the Company incurred approximately $6 million of merger-related costs that will be reflected in its operating results in the first quarter of 1995. The Company will also record a tax benefit of approximately $2.3 million in the first quarter of 1995 related to the Atwork merger. This tax benefit relates primarily to the change in the tax status of Atwork.

Recent Acquisitions.   On April 29, 1994, the Company acquired substantially all of the assets and certain of the related liabilities of the New York and California operations of the Managed Practice Division of Datamedic Corporation (the "Datamedic Business") for approximately $5.0 million in cash. The Datamedic Business performs billing and accounts receivable management services for physicians and had revenue of approximately $5.0 million in 1993.

On June 1, 1994, the Company acquired the outstanding capital stock of Lerner-Eureka, Inc., which owned all of the issued and outstanding capital stock of Northwest Creditors Service, Inc. ("NCS") for approximately $6.6 million in cash. NCS provides billing and accounts receivable management services primarily to hospitals and physicians and had revenue of approximately $6.0 million for the year ended March 31, 1994.

On June 3, 1994, the Company acquired the outstanding capital stock of Consolidated Medical Services, Inc. ("CMS") for approximately $4.8 million in cash. CMS provides billing and accounts receivable management services primarily to physicians and had revenue of approximately $3.8 million in 1993.

On July 11, 1994, the Company acquired Medical Management Resources, Inc. ("MMR") in a merger transaction for approximately $11.0 million in cash. MMR provides billing and accounts receivable management services to physicians and had revenue of approximately $6.7 million in 1993.

On July 27, 1994, the Company acquired the assets and assumed certain liabilities of Physician Billing, Inc. ("PBI") for approximately $13.0 million in cash. PBI provides billing and accounts receivable management services to emergency room physicians and had revenue of approximately $10.5 million in 1993.

On August 1, 1994, the Company acquired Omni Medical Systems, Inc. ("Omni") in a merger transaction for approximately $1.6 million in cash. Omni provides billing and accounts receivable management services to physicians and had revenue of $1.9 million in 1993.

On September 30, 1994, the Company acquired Central Billing Services, Inc. ("CBS") and related affiliates in a merger transaction for approximately $19.7 million in cash and common stock, plus a potential earn-out payment of $1.8 million in cash based on future earnings. CBS provides bad debt, Medicaid eligibility and electronic claims processing services primarily to hospitals and had revenue of approximately $15.0 million in 1993.

On September 30, 1994, the Company acquired Marmac Management, Inc. ("MMI") in a merger transaction for approximately $2.3 million in cash. MMI provides business management services to anesthesiologists and had revenue of approximately $2.3 million in 1993.

On November 30, 1994, the Company acquired AdvaCare, Inc. ("AdvaCare") in a merger transaction for approximately $101.6 million. The consideration paid for AdvaCare consisted of common stock and cash which was used to repay certain outstanding indebtedness of AdvaCare assumed in the acquisition. AdvaCare provides business management services, principally medical reimbursement management services, to healthcare providers and had revenue of approximately $66.7 million for the year ended September 30, 1994.

On December 7, 1994, the Company acquired the outstanding capital stock of John Rex, Inc. ("Anescor") for approximately $6.0 million in cash. Anescor provides billing and accounts receivable management services primarily to anesthesiologists and had revenue of approximately $4.9 million in 1993.

EXHIBIT 1   (continued)

On December 30, 1994, the Company acquired Imonics Corporation [formerly Gateway Conversion Technologies, Inc. division of Broadway & Seymour, Inc. ("BSI")] and in connection therewith, licensed certain software from BSI and entered into an agreement under which BSI will provide software maintenance services for the 18 succeeding months, for aggregate consideration of approximately $32.2 million. Imonics provides products, software development and support and systems integration services and had revenue of approximately $21.4 million in 1994.

On January 23, 1995, the Company acquired substantially all of the assets and assumed certain of the related liabilities of a healthcare decisions support company located in Burlington, Vermont ("Decisions Support") for approximately $2.0 million in cash and common stock. Decisions Support is involved primarily in the development of healthcare decision support systems and had no significant revenue in 1994.

On March 6, 1995, the Company acquired the outstanding capital stock of Medical Management, Inc. ("MMP") for $8.0 million in cash. MMP provides billing and accounts receivable management services to anesthesiologists.

Each of the foregoing acquisitions was recorded using the purchase method of accounting and, accordingly, the purchase price has been allocated to the assets acquired and liabilities assumed based on their estimated fair market value at the date of the acquisition.

On March 17, 1995, the Company acquired Atwork by exchanging four million shares of common stock for all of the outstanding common stock of Atwork. Atwork provides scheduling and management systems and services to hospitals and emerging integrated healthcare delivery systems and had revenue of approximately $28.3 million in 1994. This transaction will be accounted for using the pooling of interests method of accounting in the first quarter of 1995.

Liquidity and Capital Resources

The Company had working capital of $57.5 million at December 31, 1994, including $4.5 million of cash and cash equivalents.

Management believes additional working capital is not required to meet its current liquidity needs before acquisitions and internal growth of the business. The Company produced $26.9 million of operating cash flow ($42.1 million of operating cash flow before increases in working capital required to fund internal growth) in 1994. If current operating levels are maintained, Management believes that the Company should produce cash flow from operations adequate to meet its existing liquidity requirements. Any excess will be available to help fund the working capital requirements of internal growth and the re-engineering and consolidation project.

At December 31, 1994, $120.7 million of borrowings were outstanding under the $150 million Senior Credit Facility. On March 17, 1995, the Senior Credit Facility was amended to, among other things, increase the borrowing capacity to $250 million, extend the expiration date to March 1997 and improve the interest rate options available to the Company. Amounts available for borrowing under the Senior Credit Facility may be used for future acquisitions, expansion of the Company's business, and general corporate purposes. Additionally, Management believes under current market conditions the Company may use its ability to issue debt or equity securities to service or refinance existing long-term debt.

The Company estimates that each one million dollars of internal revenue growth requires no more than $400,000 of additional capital. If the current rate of internal revenue growth continues at historical operating margins, the Company estimates that its cash flow from operations will be adequate to meet its capital requirements for internal growth. Internal growth may also be funded by the Company's Senior Credit Facility. Management estimates that, at historical operating margins, any borrowings that are incurred for internal growth purposes can be repaid within two years by operating cash flow. Management also believes the Senior Credit Facility will be sufficient to meet any seasonal cash requirements.

During July 1994, the Company began a comprehensive re-engineering and consolidation project. As part of this project, the Company anticipates consolidating the processing function currently being performed in approximately 300 local business offices into approximately 10 regional processing centers. The Company anticipates obtaining computer equipment for approximately $25 million and $11 million in 1995 and 1996, respectively, and incurring software development costs of approximately $14 million and $8 million, respectively. Additionally, the Company anticipates incurring

Exhibit 1   (continued)

lease buy-out and termination payments, involuntary severance benefits, and other cash expenditures of approximately $25 to $30 million during 1995 and 1996 relating to this project. These costs are expected to be financed through future operating cash flows, the Company's Senior Credit Facility, and capital lease financing.

Substantially all of the Company's capital expenditures have related either to acquisitions of healthcare business management services operations or to the expansion, improvement, or maintenance of existing facilities. The Company has financed its growth through cash flows from operations, the issuance of debt and equity securities and borrowing. Management believes anticipated cash flow from operations, borrowing capacity under the Senior Credit Facility, and the Company's ability to issue debt or equity securities will provide adequate capital resources to support the Company's anticipated long-term financing needs.

Consolidated Statements of Income (in thousands, except per share data)

Year Ended December 31	1994	1993	1992
Revenue	$253,490	$169,518	$ 97,385
Salaries and wages	142,656	95,387	55,753
Other operating expenses	61,941	43,461	27,560
Depreciation	6,660	4,988	2,999
Amortization	6,816	4,327	1,502
Interest expense, net	6,276	6,407	1,350
Total Expenses	224,351	154,570	89,164
Income before income taxes, extraordinary item and cumulative effect of change in accounting for income taxes	29,139	14,948	8,221
Income taxes	11,710	5,795	2,422
Income before extraordinary item and cumulative effect of change in accounting for income taxes	17,429	9,153	5,799
Extraordinary loss on prepayment of debt, net of income tax benefit	—	—	(2,139)
Cumulative effect of change in accounting for income taxes	—	—	2,480
Net Income	$ 17,429	$ 9,153	$ 6,140
Income per common share:			
Income before extraordinary item and cumulative effect of change in accounting for income taxes	$ 1.15	$ 0.80	$ 0.57
Extraordinary loss on prepayment of debt	—	—	(0.21)
Cumulative effect of change in accounting for income taxes	—	—	0.24
Net Income	$ 1.15	$ 0.80	$ 0.60
Weighted average shares outstanding	15,206	11,465	10,278

See notes to consolidated financial statements.

Medaphis Corporation

Consolidated Balance Sheets (in thousands, except per share data)

December 31	1994	1993
Assets		
Current Assets:		
Cash and cash equivalents	$ 4,489	$ 28,114
Trust cash	2,428	1,473
Accounts receivable, billed	43,422	26,504
Accounts receivable, unbilled	55,788	31,772
Other	7,497	2,579
Total Current Assets	$113,624	$ 90,442
Property and equipment	39,704	22,351
Intangible assets	367,677	173,178
Other	3,595	2,485
	$524,600	$288,456
Liabilities and Stockholders' Equity		
Current Liabilities:		
Accounts payable	$ 5,573	$ 3,194
Trust payable	2,428	1,473
Accrued expenses	43,381	32,859
Current portion of long-term debt	4,760	2,694
Total Current Liabilities	$ 56,142	$ 40,220
Long-term debt	145,730	6,054
Other obligations	9,927	630
Deferred income taxes	21,486	8,526
Convertible subordinated debentures	63,375	63,375
Total Liabilities	296,660	118,805
Stockholders' Equity:		
Common stock, voting, $.01 par value, 30,000 authorized; issued and outstanding 15,019 in 1994 and 13,658 in 1993	150	137
Common stock, nonvoting, $.01 par value, 600 authorized; none issued	—	—
Paid-in capital	214,005	173,158
Retained earnings (deficit)	13,785	(3,644)
Total Stockholders' Equity	227,940	169,651
	$524,600	$288,456

See notes to consolidated financial statements.

Consolidated Statements of Cash Flows (in thousands)

Year Ended December 31	*1994*	*1993*	*1992*
Cash Flows from Operating Activities			
Net income	$ 17,429	$ 9,153	$ 6,140
Adjustments to reconcile net income to net cash provided by operating activities:			
Depreciation and amortization	13,478	9,315	4,501
Deferred income taxes	11,198	5,534	2,204
Extraordinary loss relating to prepayment of debt	—	—	2,139
Cumulative effect of change in accounting for income taxes . .	—	—	(2,480)
Changes in assets and liabilities, excluding effects of acquisitions:			
Increase in accounts receivable, billed	(7,388)	(3,909)	(860)
Increase in accounts receivable, unbilled	(6,561)	(5,687)	(2,951)
Increase (decrease) in accounts payable	1,295	(113)	(227)
Increase (decrease) in accrued expenses	(2,869)	1,934	705
Other, net	309	122	(614)
Net Cash Provided by Operating Activities	$ 26,891	$16,349	$ 8,557
Cash Flows from Investing Activities			
Acquisitions, net of cash acquired	(151,815)	(68,563)	(89,570)
Purchases of property and equipment	(9,399)	(3,090)	(2,634)
Software development costs	(6,384)	—	—
Net Cash Used for Investing Activities	($167,598)	($71,653)	($92,204)
Cash Flows from Financing Activities			
Proceeds from issuance of common stock	1,528	86,772	18,830
Proceeds from borrowings	120,459	69,099	70,300
Payments of long-term debt	(4,905)	(75,963)	(29,200)
Net Cash Provided by Financing Activities	$117,082	$79,908	$59,930
Cash and Cash Equivalents			
Net change	(23,625)	24,604	(23,717)
Balance at beginning of year	28,114	3,510	27,227
Balance at End of Year	$ 4,489	$28,114	$ 3,510

See notes to consolidated financial statements.

Consolidated Statements of Stockholders' Equity (in thousands)

Years Ended December 31, 1994, 1993 and 1992	Common Shares	Common Stock Amount	Paid-in Capital	Retained Earnings (Deficit)	Total Stockholders' Equity
Balance at January 1, 1992	7,854	$ 79	$ 67,614	$(18,937)	$ 48,756
Issuance of common stock	1,473	15	17,204	—	17,219
Exercise of stock options and warrants	878	8	1,603	—	1,611
Net income	—	—	—	6,140	6,140
Balance at December 31, 1992	10,205	$102	$ 86,421	$(12,797)	$ 73,726
Issuance of common stock	3,221	33	85,444	—	85,477
Exercise of stock options	232	2	1,293	—	1,295
Net income	—	—	—	9,153	9,153
Balance at December 31, 1993	13,658	$137	$173,158	$ (3,644)	$169,651
Issuance of common stock in acquisitions	1,054	10	38,786	—	38,796
Exercise of stock options	307	3	1,962	—	1,965
Other	—	—	99	—	99
Net income	—	—	—	17,429	17,429
Balance at December 31, 1994	15,019	$150	$214,005	$ 13,785	$227,940

See notes to consolidated financial statements.

Notes to Consolidated Financial Statements

1. Summary of Significant Accounting Policies

Consolidation. The consolidated financial statements include the accounts of Medaphis Corporation and its subsidiaries (the "Company"). All significant intercompany transactions have been eliminated.

Concentration of Credit Risk. The Company provides business management services to physicians and hospitals throughout the United States. The Company historically has not experienced any significant losses related to individual customers or groups of customers in any geographical area.

Revenue Recognition. Fees for the Company's services are primarily based on a percentage of net collections of clients' patient accounts, and revenue is recognized as such services are performed. Accounts receivable, billed, principally represents amounts invoiced to clients. Accounts receivable unbilled, represents amounts recognized for services rendered but not yet invoiced and is based on the Company's estimate of the fees that will be invoiced when collections on patient accounts are received.

Cash and Cash Equivalents. Cash and cash equivalents include all highly liquid investments with an initial maturity of no more than three months.

Trust Cash. Trust cash and the corresponding trust payable represent amounts collected on behalf of certain clients which are held in trust until remitted to such clients.

Property and Equipment. Property and equipment, including equipment under capital leases, is stated at cost. Depreciation is computed using the straight-line method over the estimated useful lives of the assets, generally four to ten years for furniture and fixtures, five years for data processing equipment, and 20 years for buildings.

Intangible Assets. Intangible assets are composed principally of goodwill and client lists. Goodwill represents the excess of the cost of the businesses acquired over the fair value of net identifiable assets at the date of the acquisition and is amortized using the straight-line method over 25 to 40 years. Client lists are amortized using the straight-line method over their estimated useful lives, generally 7 to 20 years.

(continued)

The Company continually monitors events and changes in circumstances that could indicate carrying amounts of intangible assets may not be recoverable. When events or changes in circumstances are present that indicate the carrying amount of intangible assets may not be recoverable, the Company assesses the recoverability of intangible assets by determining whether the carrying value of such intangible assets will be recovered through undiscounted expected future earnings after interest charges associated with the business acquired. No impairment losses were recorded by the Company in 1994, 1993 or 1992.

Software Development Costs. Intangible assets include software development costs incurred in the development or the enhancement of software utilized in providing the Company's business management services. Software development costs are capitalized upon the establishment of technological feasibility for each product or process and ceases when the product or process is available for general release to customers or is put into service. Capitalized software development costs were approximately $6.4 million in 1994 and $0 in 1993 and 1992.

Software development costs are amortized using the straight-line method over the remaining estimated economic life of the assets, which is generally 4 to 5 years. As such assets had not been released or placed in service, the Company did not record any amortization expense related to software development costs in 1994.

Postemployment Benefits. The Company adopted Financial Accounting Standards Board No. 112 ("FASB 112"), "Employers' Accounting for Postemployment Benefits," effective January 1, 1994. The financial statement impact of adopting FASB 112 was not material.

In January 1995, Management approved an involuntary severance benefit plan (the "Plan") in conjunction with its re-engineering and consolidation project (see note 13). Accordingly, the Company recorded a liability of approximately $4.9 million in the first quarter of 1995 to reflect the expense for employees' rights to benefits that had accumulated at that date.

Income per Common Share. Income per common share is based on the weighted average number of shares of common stock and common stock equivalents outstanding during the period. Common stock equivalents represent the dilutive effect of the assumed exercise of certain outstanding stock options. Fully diluted income per common share is not presented as it is not materially different from primary income per common share. The Company's convertible subordinated debentures were not considered common stock equivalents at issuance and are included in the computation of fully diluted income per common share.

Income Taxes. Deferred income taxes are recognized for the tax consequences of "temporary differences" between financial statement carrying amounts and the tax bases of existing assets and liabilities. The measurement of deferred tax assets and liabilities is predominantly determined by reference to the tax laws and changes to such laws. Management includes the consideration of future events to assess the likelihood that tax benefits will be realized in the future.

The Company adopted Statement of Financial Accounting Standards No. 109, "Accounting for Income Taxes," effective January 1, 1992.

2. Business Combinations

From January 1, 1992 through December 31, 1994, the Company acquired either substantially all of the assets or all of the outstanding capital stock of each of the following businesses (in thousands):

(continued)

Company Acquired	Consideration	Acquisition Date
Imonics Corporation (Gateway Conversion Technologies, Inc.) . . .	$ 32,200	December 1994
John Rex, Inc. ("Anescor")	6,000	December 1994
AdvaCare, Inc.	101,600	November 1994
Marmac Management, Inc.	2,300	September 1994
Central Billing Services, Inc.	19,700	September 1994
Omni Medical Systems, Inc.	1,600	August 1994
Physician Billing, Inc.	13,000	July 1994
Medical Management Resources, Inc.	11,000	July 1994
Consolidated Medical Services, Inc.	4,800	June 1994
Northwest Creditors Service, Inc.	6,600	June 1994
Managed Practice Division of Datamedic Corporation	5,000	April 1994
Practice Management Division of CyCare Systems, Inc.	24,000	November 1993
Gottlieb's Financial Services, Inc.	31,000	September 1993
Medical Management of New England, Inc.	14,200	July 1993
CompMed, Inc.	63,300	December 1992
The Management Company of Virginia, Inc.	7,300	March 1992
Bauld Investment Corporation	12,800	February 1992
SMS/Medical Associates, Inc.	5,500	January 1992

Each of these acquisitions have been recorded using the purchase method of accounting and, accordingly, the purchase price has been allocated to the assets acquired and liabilities assumed based on their estimated fair value as of the date of acquisition. The allocation of the purchase price of the 1994 acquisitions is preliminary and will be adjusted when the necessary information is available. The operating results of the acquired businesses are included in the Company's consolidated statements of income from the respective dates of acquisition.

The following unaudited pro forma financial information presents the results of the Company for the years ended December 31, 1994 and 1993, as if the acquisitions referenced above and Atwork (see below) had occurred on January 1, 1993. The pro forma information does not purport to be indicative of the results that would have been obtained if the operations had actually been combined during the period presented and is not necessarily indicative of operating results to be expected in future periods (in thousands, except per share data). The pro forma net income (loss) and net income (loss) per common share reductions in 1994 and 1993 compared to historical results for those years resulted primarily from restructuring and other special charges incurred by AdvaCare, Inc.

	1994	1993
Revenue	$379,785	$356,050
Net income (loss)	15,511	(28,933)
Net income (loss) per common share	.77	(1.86)

On March 17, 1995, the Company exchanged four million shares of its common stock for all of the outstanding shares of common stock of Automation Atwork and its affiliates ("Atwork"). Atwork is a leading provider of scheduling and management systems and services to hospitals and integrated healthcare delivery systems. This transaction will be accounted for as a pooling of interests. A summary of revenue, net income, and net income per common share of the Company, Atwork and Combined is as follows (in thousands, except per share data):

(continued)

	1994	1993	1992
Revenue:			
Medaphis	$253,490	$169,518	$ 97,385
Atwork	28,323	20,574	15,547
Combined	$281,813	$190,092	$112,932
Net Income:			
Medaphis	$ 17,429	$ 9,153	$ 6,140
Atwork	4,248	72	(1,738)
Combined	$ 21,677	$ 9,225	$ 4,402
Net income per common share:			
Medaphis	$ 1.15	$ .80	$ .60
Combined	$ 1.13	$ .60	$ .31

3. Property and Equipment

Property and equipment consists of the following (in thousands):

	1994	1993
Land	$ 2,873	$ 1,073
Buildings	4,826	4,097
Furniture and fixtures	11,121	5,790
Data processing equipment	34,460	19,987
Other	2,100	1,099
	$55,380	$32,046
Less accumulated depreciation	15,676	9,695
	$39,704	$22,351

4. Intangible Assets

Intangible assets consist of the following (in thousands):

	1994	1993
Goodwill	$302,955	$139,264
Client lists	51,942	40,357
Other (principally software development costs and acquired software)	27,321	1,280
	382,218	180,901
Less accumulated amortization	14,541	7,723
	$367,677	$173,178

5. Accrued Expenses

Accrued expenses consist of the following (in thousands):

	1994	1993
Compensation and employee benefits	$17,825	$13,198
Accrued costs of businesses acquired	17,151	14,223
Interest	2,317	2,153
Other	6,088	3,285
	$43,381	$32,859

(continued)

6. Long-term Debt

Long-term debt consists of the following (in thousands):

	1994	1993
Borrowings under Senior Credit Facility	$120,714	$ —
Capital lease obligations, weighted average effective interest rates of 9.1% and 9.2%	11,612	6,808
Deferred purchase price relating to acquisitions	15,672	—
Other notes payable	2,492	1,940
	$150,490	$8,748
Less current portion	4,760	2,694
	$145,730	$6,054

At December 31, 1994, the Company had a $150 million revolving credit agreement ("Senior Credit Facility") which was composed of a $145 million revolving credit line and a $5 million cash management line with a six-bank syndicate to finance future acquisitions, working capital, and other general corporate needs. The Company had the option of making "LIBOR"-based loans or "base rate" loans under the Senior Credit Facility. LIBOR-based loans bore interest at LIBOR for the then current interest period plus amounts varying from 1¼% to 2¼% based on the Company's financial performance. Base rate loans bear interest equal to prime. At December 31, 1994, the Company had LIBOR-based loans outstanding at interest rates ranging from 7.8% to 8.1%. The Senior Credit Facility contains, among other things, financial covenants which require the Company to maintain certain financial ratios. The Company was in compliance with all covenants as of December 31, 1994.

On March 17, 1995, the Company amended the Senior Credit Facility. The Amended Senior Credit Facility has a $240 million revolving credit line and a $10 million cash management line, which expires in March 1997. The Amended Senior Credit Facility can be extended one year at each anniversary date through March 2000 with the consent of the banks. Borrowings under the Amended Senior Credit Facility are secured by the stock of the Company's subsidiaries.

The Company had obligations outstanding at December 31, 1994 to the former owners of Imonics Corporation (formerly Gateway Conversion Technologies, Inc.), Anescor and Gottlieb's Financial Services, Inc. These amounts have been or will be refinanced under the Senior Credit Facility as they come due. Accordingly, these amounts have been classified as long-term debt at December 31, 1994.

The Company used the net proceeds from its second public offering in May 1992 to prepay indebtedness incurred under a previous credit agreement. Subsequent to this prepayment, the agreement was terminated. An extraordinary loss of approximately $2.1 million was recorded in 1992 relating to the write-off of unamortized deferred financing costs and debt issue discount (net of an income tax benefit of approximately $1.0 million).

The Company's capital leases consist principally of leases for data processing equipment. As of December 31, 1994 and 1993, the net book value of equipment subject to capital leases totaled $9.1 million and $4.3 million, respectively.

The aggregate maturities of long-term debt (effecting for the Amendment to the Senior Credit Facility) and capital lease obligations are as follows (in thousands):

1995	$ 4,760
1996	3,988
1997	140,148
1998	1,483
1999	22
Thereafter	89

7. Convertible Subordinated Debentures

The Company issued $63.4 million of 6½% convertible subordinated debentures to finance the acquisition of CompMed, Inc. The debentures are due on January 1, 2000. The debenture holders may convert the debentures into shares of the Company's common stock at a conversion price of $28.00 per share. The Company has the option to redeem the debentures after January 1, 1996 at a redemption premium of 3.71% in 1996 declining annually to .93% in 1999. The fair value of these convertible subordinated debentures was $108 million at December 31, 1994, based on a market quote.

(continued)

8. Lease Commitments

The Company leases office space and equipment under noncancelable operating leases which expire at various dates through 2001. Rent expense was $8.9 million, $6.2 million, and $3.7 million for the years ended December 31, 1994, 1993, and 1992, respectively.

Future minimum lease payments under noncancelable operating leases are as follows (in thousands):

1995	$8,121
1996	7,168
1997	3,889
1998	2,200
1999	1,356
Thereafter	948

9. Income Taxes

Income tax expense is comprised of the following (in thousands):

	1994	1993	1992
Current:			
Federal	$ —	$ —	$ —
State	257	159	249
Deferred:			
Federal	10,134	5,391	2,597
State	1,319	702	529
Valuation allowance	—	(457)	(953)
	$11,710	$5,795	$2,422

A reconciliation between the amount determined by applying the federal statutory rate to income before income taxes and income tax expense is as follows (in thousands):

	1994	1993	1992
Income tax expense at federal statutory rate . . .	$10,199	$5,173	$2,795
State taxes, net of federal deficit . . .	1,548	827	348
Items not deductible for tax purposes .	535	252	232
Valuation allowance	—	(457)	(953)
Other	(572)	—	—
	$11,710	$5,795	$2,422

Deferred taxes are recorded based upon differences between the financial statement and tax bases of assets and liabilities and available tax credit carryforwards. The components of deferred taxes as of December 31, 1994 and 1993 are as follows (in thousands):

	Assets/(Liabilities)	
	1994	*1993*
Acquisition base differences	$ (6,469)	$ 918
Net operating loss carryforwards	40,326	19,961
Valuation allowance . . .	(10,476)	(1,542)
Accounts receivable, unbilled	(19,537)	(12,539)
Depreciation and amortization	(6,419)	(3,473)
Other deferred tax liabilities	(18,911)	(11,851)
	$(21,486)	$ (8,526)

The valuation allowance relates primarily to the uncertainty of the reliability of net operating loss carryforwards. The change in the valuation allowance during 1994 relates primarily to the valuation allowance related to net operating loss carryforwards established in the AdvaCare, Inc. purchase price allocation.

As of December 31, 1994, the Company had federal net operating loss carryforwards for income tax purposes of approximately $106 million which expire at various dates between 1999 and 2009. The Internal Revenue Code imposes substantial limitations under certain circumstances on the use of net operating loss carryforwards upon the occurrence of an "ownership change." The Company has experienced three prior ownership changes which established a maximum annual limitation of $3.4 million of income against which net operating losses incurred prior to the most recent ownership change may be offset. However, because the limitation operates in a cumulative manner and in previous years the Company did not utilize net operating losses up to the maximum annual limitation, the Company has approximately $60 million in cumulative unutilized net operating losses available in 1995.

(continued)

10. Common Stock

On December 2, 1993, the Company completed a third public offering of its common stock in which 3,450,000 shares were sold at $28.00 per share. The Company sold 3,221,000 shares of its common stock and 229,000 shares of common stock were sold on behalf of certain of the Company's stockholders. The net proceeds to the Company were approximately $85.5 million.

On May 28, 1992, the Company completed a second public offering of its common stock in which 2,300,000 shares of its common stock were sold at $12.75 per share. The Company sold 1,473,000 shares of its common stock and 827,000 shares of common stock were sold on behalf of certain of the Company's stockholders. The net proceeds to the Company, including proceeds relating to the exercise of 674,000 warrants by certain of the Company's stockholders, were approximately $18.1 million.

11. Common Stock Options and Stock Awards

The Company has a Non-Qualified Stock Option Plan and a Non-Qualified Stock Option Plan for Key Employees of Acquired Companies ("Non-Qualified Stock Options Plans"). Stock options outstanding at December 31, 1994 under these plans permit employees to purchase up to 2,591,000 shares of the Company's common stock. Granted options expire 11 years after the date of grant and are generally exercisable based on a five-year vesting period. Options outstanding at December 31, 1994 were granted at prices ranging from $2.27 to $156.02 per share, of which 731,000 were exercisable at that date. Options were exercised during 1994 with grant prices ranging from $2.27 to $24.88 per share. As of December 31, 1994, 532,000 shares were available for future grants under these plans.

Activity related to the Non-Qualified Stock Options Plans is summarized as follows (in thousands).

	1994	1993	1992
Options outstanding as of January 1	2,046	888	669
Granted:			
To employees	492	495	296
Relating to acquisitions	416	771	—
Canceled	(61)	(27)	(60)
Exercised	(302)	(81)	(17)
Options outstanding as of December 31	2,591	2,046	888

The Company has a Senior Executive Non-Qualified Stock Option Plan which permits certain of the Company's executive officers to purchase up to an aggregate of 275,000 shares of the Company's common stock at $4 per share. All options available for grant under this plan have been granted, expire January 16, 2001, and are currently exercisable. As of December 31, 1994, 115,000 options issued under this plan have been exercised (none during 1994).

On August 12, 1994, the disinterested members of the Company's Board of Directors approved the Medaphis Corporation Restricted Stock Plan (the "Restricted Plan") for executive officers. The Restricted Plan authorized the award of 124,500 shares of $0.01 par value of common stock to certain of the executive officers of the Company. The restricted stock vests ratably over a four-year period from the date of award. Vesting may be accelerated if certain performance goals are achieved. The Restricted Plan will be voted upon by the shareholders of the Company at the annual meeting of stockholders in April 1995.

12. Employee Benefit Plans

The Company has a 401(k) plan whereby employees, upon meeting certain eligibility requirements, can make specified contributions to the plan, a percentage of which are matched by the Company. The Company's contributions to the plan were $1.1 million, $253,000, and $200,000 for the years ended December 31, 1994, 1993, and 1992, respectively.

(continued)

The Company maintains a noncontributory money purchase pension plan which covers substantially all employees which are retained by the Company primarily to service specific physician clients. Contributions are determined annually by the Company not to exceed the maximum amount deductible for federal income tax purposes. The Company's contribution to the plan was $700,000 in 1994 and $1.1 million in 1993.

13. Re-engineering and Consolidation
During July 1994, the Company began a comprehensive re-engineering and consolidation project in order to enhance its ability to provide more effective and efficient business management services to its clients. In January 1995, the Company approved a restructuring plan and an involuntary severance policy in anticipation of the consolidation of the production function from approximately 300 local business offices into approximately 10 regional processing centers. This project is expected to be completed by the end of 1996.

The Company plans to record restructuring and other charges related to the re-engineering and consolidation project of approximately $25 million during the first quarter of 1995. The costs consist primarily of lease buy-out and termination payments, involuntary severance benefits, and impairment losses associated with the disposition of property and equipment.

14. Cash Flow Information
Supplemental disclosures of cash flow information and noncash investing and financing activities were as follows (in thousands):

	1994	1993	1992
Noncash investing and financing activities:			
Liabilities assumed in acquisitions	$108,781	$23,799	$18,341
Additions to capital lease obligations	5,356	2,352	2,314
Common stock issued in conjunction with acquisitions	38,796	—	—
Cash paid for:			
Interest	6,185	3,956	1,450
Income taxes	290	360	394

15. Quarterly Financial Information (unaudited) (in thousands, except per share data)

	Quarter Ended			
	March 31	June 30	September 30	December 31
1994				
Revenue	$53,260	$57,866	$64,484	$77,888
Net income	$ 3,550	$ 4,031	$ 4,818	$ 5,032
Net income per common share	$ 0.24	$ 0.27	$ 0.32	$ 0.32
Weighted average shares outstanding	14,993	14,831	15,049	15,819
1993				
Revenue	$37,312	$39,272	$42,454	$50,480
Net income	$ 1,842	$ 2,102	$ 2,447	$ 2,752
Net income per common share	$ 0.17	$ 0.19	$ 0.22	$ 0.22
Weighted average shares outstanding	10,989	11,001	11,311	12,408

Independent Auditors' Report

To the Board of Directors and Stockholders of Medaphis Corporation:

We have audited the accompanying consolidated balance sheets of Medaphis Corporation and subsidiaries as of December 31, 1994 and 1993 and the related consolidated statements of income, stockholders' equity, and cash flows for each of the three years in the period ended December 31, 1994. These financial statements are the responsibility of the Company's management. Our responsibility is to express an opinion on these financial statements based on our audits.

We conducted our audits in accordance with generally accepted auditing standards. Those standards require that we plan and perform the audit to obtain reasonable assurance about whether the financial statements are free of material misstatements. An audit includes examining, on a test basis, evidence supporting the amounts and disclosures in the financial statements. An audit also includes assessing the accounting principles used and significant estimates made by management, as well as evaluating the overall financial statement presentation. We believe that our audits provide a reasonable basis for our opinion.

In our opinion, such consolidated financial statements present fairly, in all material respects, the financial position of Medaphis Corporation and subsidiaries at December 31, 1994 and 1993 and the results of their operations and their cash flows for each of the three years in the period ended December 31, 1994 in conformity with generally accepted accounting principles.

As discussed in Note 1 to the consolidated financial statements, the Company changed its method of accounting for income taxes in 1992.

Deloitte & Touche LLP

Atlanta, Georgia
February 7, 1995
(March 17, 1995 as to notes 2 and 6)

Questions

1. Complete the assignment described in the case.

PART SEVEN

Long-Term Financial Commitment Reporting and Analysis

Financial Instruments

Financial instruments are cash and contracts that result both in a financial asset for one party and a financial liability or evidence of ownership interest in an entity for another party. Bonds and financial derivatives are common examples of financial instruments. Initially this chapter's accounting and analysis discussion focuses on financial instruments in the form of long-term debt issued under formal agreements, such as bonds, which usually have at least a five-year term. The accounting and analysis for other forms of debt are similar. The accounting for derivative financial instruments and other financial instruments is covered following long-term debt discussion.

Characteristics of Long-Term Debt

Long-term debt issued by corporations to raise funds from credit sources represents a promise (1) to repay the sum of money at a specified future date and (2) to compensate the lender for the use of the lender's money through periodic interest payments. The full details of the contract between the company and the bondholders are contained in the bond indenture, which is held by a representative of the bondholder, who is known as the trustee under the indenture. In bankruptcy, the claims of the bondholders rank ahead of those of stockholders.

Long-term debt is issued in a variety of forms. It may be secured or unsecured; if unsecured, it is termed a debenture. Secured debt often takes its name from the character of the collateral pledged. For example, bonds secured by marketable securities are known as collateral trust bonds. Mortgage bonds or notes are secured by all or some of the fixed assets of the borrower. Securities backed by chattel mortgages may be called equipment trust certificates. Within the various categories of long-term debt, some

---

Professor David F. Hawkins prepared this note as the basis for class discussion.
Copyright © 1996 by the President and Fellows of Harvard College. Harvard Business School teaching note 197–001.

debt instruments, such as subordinated debentures, may rank lower than others in their claims upon the company's assets in bankruptcy.

There are also variations in the method and timing of the repayment of the principal amount of long-term debt. The basic bond is repayable in a lump sum at a specific future date. The sinking fund bond is a modification of this form. Its indenture requires the borrower to make periodic cash payments into a sinking fund. This cash, plus the accumulated interest on it, is used to retire the bonds at maturity. A more common type of sinking fund bond indenture calls for payments to a trustee, who uses the funds accumulated for making periodic bond retirements. This practice increases the probability that the lender will be repaid.

Serial bonds are another type of bond with provisions designed to reduce risk to the bondholders. These bonds are repayable in a series over the life of the issue instead of a single maturity date.

Callable bonds give the borrower the option, after a certain period of time, to redeem all or some of the debt prior to maturity for the payment of a specified call premium beyond the principal amount. The call provision gives the borrower greater flexibility in the design of its capital structure in that as interest rates fall old bonds may be replaced with less expensive new ones.

Long-term debt indentures contain a number of provisions. Some provisions may restrict the dividend payments of the borrower. These restrictions often limit the use of additional short- or long-term debt, or require that the borrower stay within certain debt-to-equity and working capital ratio limits. Other provisions may include the right to convert the bonds to other securities, such as stock.

Typically, the borrower's obligation to pay interest is fixed. It is not conditional upon company earnings, except for income and participating bonds. The payment of interest on income bonds is conditional upon the borrower's earning income: if the income is not sufficient to pay interest, no payments need be made. The interest obligation may or may not be cumulative (i.e., unpaid interest from one year becomes a lien against future earnings). These bonds usually result from corporate reorganizations, when it is necessary to give old security holders a less desirable form of security so that new senior securities can be sold. Participating bonds entitle the holder to share in earnings with the stockholders in a pro rata or limited way, in addition to the bondholder's usual fixed interest.

Other forms of long-term debt include zero coupon bonds, variable interest rate bonds, and bonds convertible at the option of the issue into different financial instruments or, in some cases, the issuer's assets. A zero coupon bond does not pay periodic interest. Rather, it is issued at a deep discount from its face value, which is the amount the issuer promises to redeem the bond for at its maturity date. A variable interest rate bond, as its name implies, pays periodic interest that varies according to the current level of interest rates.

Financial Consideration

The long-term capital requirements of corporations are usually satisfied through the issuance of a combination of stocks and bonds and the retention of earnings. Compared to stocks, bonds have some attractive features. The interest payments are deductible as a business expense in determining taxable income, whereas dividends are not. The owner-ship interest is not diluted when bonds are issued. The earnings on the funds obtained through a bond issue may be greater than the related interest charge, with the result that the earnings per share of the stockholders increase since no additional equity shares are issued. This effect is called "financial leverage."

The major disadvantage of bonds is the fixed requirement to repay principal and to pay interest periodically. If a corporation fails to meet these obligations, the bond-holders may assume control of the company or force it into bankruptcy.

Valuation

The price of a bond is the present value of its future stream of interest payments plus the present value of the maturity principal payment. The discount rate applied to these future payments is the investor's required rate of return for the class of bond acquired.

The most simple bond to value is a consol-type bond, which is a bond that never matures and pays interest at a fixed amount. Its value is the present value of an infinite series of equal interest payments, namely:

$$V = \frac{I}{K_r}$$

where:

V = Price of the bond.
I = Constant annual interest in dollars paid every year in perpetuity.
K_r = Investor's required rate of return.

To illustrate, assume that the investor's required rate of return is 10% and the perpetual annual interest payment is $2 per year, paid at the end of each year.[1] The value of this bond is $20 ($2 divided by .10).

For a bond with a specific maturity date, which most bonds have, the price of the bond today is:

$$V = \frac{I_1}{(1 + K_r)^1} + \frac{I_2}{(1 + K_r)^{2}\cdots} + \frac{I_n + M_n}{(1 + K_r)^n}$$

where:

V = Price of the bond.
I = Annual interest paid in dollars.
n = Number of years to maturity.
M = Maturity principal payment.
K_r = Investor's required rate of return.

To illustrate, assume a $1,000 bond has five years to mature. The annual interest payment is $80 and the investor's required rate of return is 8% (.08). The price of the bond today is:

---

[1]In practice, bond interest is paid semi-annually.

$$V = \frac{\$80}{(1 + .08)^1} + \frac{\$80}{(1 + .08)^2} + \frac{\$80}{(1 + .08)^3} + \frac{\$80}{(1 + .08)^4} + \frac{(\$80 + \$1000)}{(1 + .08)^5}$$

$$= \$74.07 + \$68.59 + \$63.51 + \$58.80 + \$735.03$$

$$= \$1000.44$$

or using present value labels[2]

$$V = \$80(.926) + \$80(.857) + \$80(.794) + \$80(.735) + \$1080(.681)$$

$$= \$74.08 + \$68.56 + \$63.52 + \$58.80 + \$735.48$$

$$= \$1000$$

The price of a bond will respond to changes in interest rates. It is generally thought that the longer to the maturity time of any given security the greater is the likelihood of a price change in response to a change in interest rates. For this reason, it is considered riskier to hold longer-term securities; thus, they typically, but not always, have higher yields or rates of return than do short-term bonds.

If the price of a bond is known, its yield to maturity is the discount rate that, when applied to the future cash payments, gives a present value equal to the current price.

The Present Value **Tables A and B** included at the end of this book or the present value applications included in most hand-held calculators can also be used to approximate bond yields and bond prices. For example, assume the Viking Chemical Company issued $1 million worth of 10%, $1,000 principal bonds repayable in 10 years and the current market interest rate for comparable bonds was 12%, the company would receive $887,000 from the buyers of the bonds, or $887 per bond. Assuming interest is paid annually, this sum represents the present value of 10 annual payments of $100,000 plus payments of $1 million 10 years hence, all discounted at 12%. If a bondholder held the Viking bonds to maturity, the return on the investment of $887 per bond would be 12%. The computation of market value at issue is shown in **Illustration A**.

The market price of a bond can vary during its life as the level of interest rates shifts or the quality of the company's credit changes. For example, assume that after five years pass, the market rate for bonds similar to the Viking Chemical Company's bonds falls to 8% very soon after the fifth interest payment. Since the Viking bonds pays a 10% nominal rate, the market price for this issue of bonds will rise to $1,080,300, which is $1,080.30 per bond. Anyone buying the bonds in the market for this price would get a yield of 8% on this investment if the bonds were held over the remaining five years to maturity. Assuming annual interest payments, the present value calculations are shown in **Illustration B**.

When bonds are purchased between interest dates, the purchase price includes the accrued interest.

---

[2]Value in brackets is the present value of a dollar discounted at 8% received in years hence. (See Present Value Table A)

ILLUSTRATION A   Cash Flow

Years	Item	Times PV Factor (12%)[a]	Equals Present Value
1–10	Annual interest payments, $100,000	5.650	$565,000
10	Repayment of principal, $1 million	0.322	322,000
Market value			$887,000

---

[a]See Present Value Tables A and B. The PV factor 5.650 is the present value of an annuity of $1 per year for 10 years discounted to the present (Table B). The PV factor 0.322 is the present value of a dollar received 10 years hence discounted at 12% (Table A).

ILLUSTRATION B   Cash Flow

Years	Item	Times PV Factor (12%)[a]	Equals Present Value
1–5	Annual interest payments, $100,000	3.993	$ 399,300
10	Repayment of principal, $1 million	0.681	681,000
Market value			$1,080,300

---

[a]See Present Value Tables A and B. The PV factor 3.993 is the present value of an annuity of $1 per year for five years discounted to the present 8% (Table B). The PV factor 0.681 is the present value of a dollar received five years hence discounted at 8% (Table A).

Investment Risk

All bonds have an investment risk associated with them. This risk can come from four sources: (1) *Default risk* arises from the possibility that the firm's future resources will be insufficient to meet part or all of the bond interest and principal payments. (2) *Interest rate risk* comes from possibilities that unexpected changes in interest rates will adversely affect the market value of the bond. That is, a change in prevailing interest rates can affect the opportunity cost of holding a fixed interest security. (3) *Purchasing power risk* is the possibility of loss in real terms sustained by bondholders during inflationary periods when the purchasing power of money decreases. (4) *Marketability risk* relates to the ease with which the investor may dispose of the bond.

Although investments in U.S. government obligations involve some interest rate and purchasing power risks, they are generally described as risk-free investments, since the investor is certain that the issuer will make the required payments and a market will always exist for the bonds.

The required rate of return from a security is the minimum expected rate of return necessary to induce investors to buy or hold the security. The required rate is the sum of the riskless rate of interest (usually defined as the current yield on short-term U.S. Treasury securities) plus a risk premium. The investor's expected rate of return can be thought of as the rate of return in event of default times the probability of default, plus the promised yield to maturity at purchase, times 1 minus the default probability (see calculation below). When this value is also the minimum rate of return required by the investor, this value less the riskless rate of return is the investor's risk premium for assuming this bond's risk of default. It is the probability portion of this concept that bond ratings reflect, since an agency's rating indicates its assessment of the bond's relative default and marketability risks. The following equation describes the required rate of return for the investor:

$$K_r = R_f + \rho$$

where:

K_r = Investor's required rate of return.
R_f = Riskless rate of return.
ρ = Risk premium.

The investor's required rate of return is always less than a bond's promised return at the time of purchase. At the time a bond is purchased, it promises a certain yield to maturity. This is the highest rate of return or yield that the investor can expect from this particular bond purchase. However, because there is some probability that any bond may default, the investor's expected or required rate of return from the bond purchase will be less than the maximum promised yield. Thus, when the required or expected yield is calculated as stated above, there is a difference between the maximum promised yield and the investor's expected or required rate of return. This difference is called the default premium.

This default premium plus the investor's required rate of return less the riskless interest rate is often referred to as the premium yield. To illustrate: Assume that a bond's promised yield to maturity at purchase is 10%, the probability of default is 5 chances out of 100, and the rate of return in case of default is 0%. Thus, the investor's expected return is 9.5%, i.e., $[.10 (1 - .05)] + (.00 \times .05)$. If the investor's required rate of return is 9.5%, this bond is acceptable to the investor. Thus, in this case, the default premium is .5% (10% − 9.5%). If the riskless rate of return is 6%, the investor's risk premium is 3.5% (9.5% − 6.0%).

Rating Agencies

The two major bond-rating services are Moody's Investors Service, Inc., and Standard & Poor's Corporation. These two companies rate public and private corporate bond issues, commercial paper, preferred stock, and some large debt offerings of foreign companies and government. Other rating agencies are Duff and Phelps, and Fitch's.

The information provided by the rating agencies is one of the factors that the marketplace uses to determine interest rates. Since many institutional investors can only own bonds above a certain rating, the rating also determines who will or will not buy the issue. A bond rating may also influence the value of a company's common equity, since some common stock rating services take bond ratings into account when they rate stocks.

A committee of the rating agency is responsible for ratings. Initially, in the case of corporate bonds, the company seeking a rating for a new issue makes a presentation to the rating agency. Based on these and other data, such as company visits, a bond analyst employed by the rating agency prepares a report on the company that measures the probability of trouble or loss for the investor, especially from default and poor marketability of the bonds. In this report, the analyst assesses the likelihood of earnings declining or turning negative; the likelihood of a company's survival during a recession period; the likelihood that the issuer will be able to repay the principal borrowed and pay the interest owed, and to do these two things at the times agreed upon. The analyst may suggest a rating to the rating committee.

The rating agencies charge a fee for ratings requested by companies. Many companies contract with the agencies to do a preliminary rating and then, depending on what it is, the company may or may not bring the issue to the marketplace.

Bond Ratings

A bond rating represents the likelihood that the issuer will pay principal and interest on time. For the most part, the higher a rating is, the lower is the required rate of return by investors. **Illustration C** lists the principal ratings using Moody's notation and an

ILLUSTRATION C   Bond Ratings

Rating[a]	*Investment Characteristic*
Aaa	Bonds which are rated Aaa are judged to be of the best quality. They carry the smallest degree of investment risk. Interest payments are protected by a large or by an exceptionally stable margin and principal is secure.
Aa	Bonds which are rated Aa are judged to be of high quality by all standards. They are rated lower than the best bonds because margins of protection may not be as large or fluctuation of protective elements may be of greater amplitude or there may be other elements present which make the long-term risks appear somewhat larger than Aaa securities.
A	Bonds which are rated A possess many favorable investment attributes. Factors giving security to principal and interest are considered adequate but elements may be present which suggest a susceptibility to impairment sometime in the future.
Baa	Bonds which are rated Baa are considered as medium-grade obligations. Interest payments and principal security appear adequate for the present, but certain protective elements may be lacking or may be characteristically unreliable over any great length of time.
Ba	Bonds which are rated Ba are judged to have speculative elements. Often the protection of interest and principal payments may be very moderate and thereby not well safeguarded during both good and bad times over the future.
B	Bonds which are rated B generally lack characteristics of a desirable investment. Assurance of interest and principal payments or of maintenance of other terms of the contract over any long period of time may be small.
Caa	Bonds which are rated Caa are of poor standing. There may be present elements of danger with respect to principal or interest.
Ca	Bonds which are rated Ca represent obligations which are speculative in a high degree.
C	Bonds which are rated C are the lowest rated class of bonds, and can be regarded as having extremely poor prospects of ever attaining any real investment standing.

[a]Standard & Poor's comparable ratings are designated by capital letters and a different notation scheme (i.e., AAA for Aaa, BBB for Baa and CCC for Caa).

interpretation of their significance to investors. Within most of these grades, the rating agencies also have degrees of rating indicated by plus or minus signs in the case of Moody's and 1, 2, and 3 by Standard and Poors.

Moody's has commented on their ratings and their significance as follows:

> The quality of most bonds is not fixed and steady over a period of time . . . a change in rating may thus occur at any time in the case of an individual issue. Such rating change should serve notice that Moody's observes some alteration in the investment risks of the bond or that the previous rating did not fully reflect the quality of the bond as now seen.
>
> Bonds carrying the same rating are not claimed to be of absolutely equal quality . . . the symbols cannot reflect the fine shadings of risks which actually exist . . . (ratings) have no value in forecasting the direction of future movements of market prices. Market price movements in bonds are influenced not only by the quality of individual issues but also by changes in money rates and general economic trends, as well as by the length of maturity, etc. During its life even the best quality bond may have wide price movements, although its high investment status remains unchanged.
>
> Since rating involves a judgment about the future, on the one hand, and since they are used by investors as a means of protection, on the other, the effort is made when assigning ratings to look at "worst" potentialities in the "visible" future rather than solely at the past record and the status of the present. . . . They are not statistical ratings but an appraisal of long-term risks, such appraisal giving recognition to many nonstatistical factors.

The difference in risk associated with bonds of varying qualities is also reflected in the yield spreads. To illustrate this difference, at any one time the average industrial bond yields may be as follows:

Aaa	8.35%	A	9.00%
Aa	8.55%	Baa	10.30%

The dividing line between what is considered to be an investment-grade bond and a noninvestment-grade bond is a rating equivalent to Moody's Baa and Standard & Poor's comparable triple B rating. Anything higher is considered a relatively safe investment, while anything lower is not. Many unrated and less-than-investment-quality bonds are referred to as "junk bonds."

In published lists of ratings, Moody's rating generally precedes that of Standard & Poor's—i.e., for a triple A rated bond the listing would read "Aaa/AAA."

Rating Considerations

In general, five areas are examined in rating a bond:

1. The bond's indenture.
2. The issuer's asset protection.
3. Future earning power.
4. Financial resources.
5. Management.

Indenture

The indenture is the legal document stating the terms of the contract between the bondholder and the issuing company. The following questions are considered in examining the indenture:

1. Are there restrictions on any subsidiaries to issue their own debt? This is important since this debt would have priorities on the assets of the subsidiary in case of any default or bankruptcy.

2. May the issuing company issue new debt which might subordinate the bonds now being rated or have a prior claim on the company's assets? Certain standards and key ratios should be met before a company should be able to issue additional debt.

3. Is a sinking fund required to help ensure repayment of principal to the bondholders? Such a requirement may require the issuer to retire a portion of the bond's principal before maturity. Or, alternatively, cash is paid by the issuer to a trustee prior to maturity. These funds are then used to retire the debt at maturity.

4. Is there a mortgage or lien on the company's income or assets?

5. Do the requirements of the indenture put too many constraints on the company? In other words, can the issuing company remain flexible enough to meet changing conditions?

6. Is the bond being issued a senior or subordinated debt? This is an important consideration to the bondholder, for in the event of bankruptcy and liquidation, senior debt will be repaid first.

7. What might be the impact of current and future regulations (e.g., ERISA, OSHA, etc.) on the claims of creditors and bondholders?

In most cases, the indenture will set out a financial framework within which the borrower must operate, defined by a minimum level of working capital, net worth, capitalization, liquidity, interest coverage, etc. Aside from considering the appropriateness of these constraints, the rating agency is concerned with indenture restrictions relating to intercompany and/or parent–subsidiary transactions. The entity being financed could, for example, be required to upstream profits or pay dividends which affect the ultimate security of the debt in question.

Increasingly, the structure of the indenture has been used as a creative tool for the issuer. For example, Standard and Poor's notes that the indenture can "separate out" the most liquid assets to be reserved for collateral against debt repayment, the objective of which is to further secure the issue and, hence, boost the rating and reduce the cost of the issue. This paper manipulation, however, could trigger a default on another obligation which could, in turn, result in default on the issue being rated. The bond rating agencies must, therefore, analyze the terms of the legal framework for their impact on the ultimate ability of the borrower to service and repay all of its lenders.

In summary, it must be noted that in determining the final rating, the indenture is far less important than the company's financial resources, earning power, asset protection, and management.

Asset Protection

In the event of default, bondholders look to the company's assets for protection from loss. Therefore, it is important to determine to what degree the debt of a company is covered by asset values. In addition to some key financial ratios, the following points are considered in assessing the degree of asset protection:

1. The composition of the company's working capital. The greater the proportion of liquid assets, the better is the position of the company.
2. The nature and value of inventories.
3. The status of a company's plant and equipment (age, efficiency, needed improvements, etc.).
4. Book value of assets and the adequacy of depreciation charges.
5. Leasing commitments and other obligations that might not appear on the face of the balance sheet.

The ratios often used to measure asset protection are:

$$\frac{\text{Pro forma long-term debt}[3]}{\text{Net property, plant, and equipment}}$$

$$\frac{\text{Working capital}}{\text{Pro forma long-term debt}}$$

$$\frac{\text{Pro forma long-term debt}}{\text{Equity}}$$

$$\frac{\text{Net tangible assets}}{\text{Pro forma long-term debt}}$$

Future Earning Power

Investors would prefer to invest in a company that will be able to cover payment of debt from earnings rather than resort to liquidation of assets to cover it in the case of default. The following are considered in determining the issuer's future earning power:

1. The issuer's industry and its position in it.
2. The trends in the industry, such as market share, costs of operations, and tax and depreciation practices.
3. The adequacy of the issuer's financial controls.

In studying future earning power, the fixed charges coverage ratios are extremely important. They are designed to measure how adequately creditors can be protected by funds from operations in case a company incurs losses. The key coverage ratio is:

---

[3]Existing debt plus proposed debt being rated.

$$\frac{\text{Earnings before interest, taxes, depreciation and amortization charges (EBITDA)}}{\text{Total interest charges}}$$

EBITDA is often referred to as "operating cash flow." This is erroneous. EBITDA is not a cash flow measurement. Nevertheless EBITDA is used to measure the stability and continuation of a company's cash flow in evaluating long-term solvency. The more stable this cash flow is over time, the lower will be the interest coverage ratio that investors will accept.

$$\frac{\text{Earnings before interest and taxes (EBIT)}}{\text{Total interest charges}}$$

This is the most simple and most frequently used times-interest-earned ratio. If it is used to compute the coverage ratio for a senior debt issue, only the interest related to the senior debt is used in the denominator.

Financial Resources

Cash and other working capital resources are examined so as to judge the ability of a company to withstand a dip in the economy or other adverse conditions and still be able to meet its debt payments. Asset quality and dividend and debt policies are also carefully examined. For example, an overly generous dividend may jeopardize a company's ability to protect itself financially in the future. The extent to which a company relies on external financing, both long- and short-term, may seriously affect future performance and ability to sustain itself against economic uncertainties.

Management

The rating agencies go beyond financial ratio analysis and look at the management of a company. Here their main concerns are the depth of management; management's philosophies, policies, and goals; and the quality of financial planning and projections. The rating agencies examine a company's acquisition policy and practice, particularly to see if the management is expanding into fields in which it has little expertise or knowledge. A company's research and development and its advertising practices are also compared to those of other companies in the same industry.

Issuer's Accounting

When bonds are issued, they are recorded by the issue at their face value in the long-term liability account. Any difference between the proceeds of the sale and the face value of the bond is put into the liability account Bond Premium or the asset account Bond Discount. The premium or discount balance is then written off to the Bond Interest account over the life of the issue.

The accounting entry to record an issue of one thousand $1,000 bonds at their face value is:

```
Dr. Cash ........................................  1,000,000
    Cr. Bonds Payable .................................            1,000,000
```

If these bonds had been issued at a price of $1.1 million (a premium of $100,000), the entry would have been:

```
Dr. Cash ........................................  1,100,000
    Cr. Bonds Payable ................................            1,000,000
       Bond Premium ..................................              100,000
```

If these bonds had been issued at a price of $900,000 (a discount of $100,000) the entry would have been:

```
Dr. Cash ........................................    900,000
    Bond Discount ....................................    100,000
    Cr. Bonds Payable .................................           1,000,000
```

The costs associated with issuing bonds include underwriting fees, taxes, printing, and engraving. These issuing costs are accounted for as a deferred cost and amortized over the life of the issue.

Amortization of Bond Premium and Discount

When bonds are issued at a premium or discount, the bond's nominal interest rate specified in its indenture is not the issuer's effective interest rate for the issue. Accounting requires the effective interest rate be charged to income. This is accomplished by adding to the issue's nominal interest payment an appropriate portion of the related premium or discount account. The compound-interest method is used to determine the periodic amortization charge. The compound-interest method reduces the discount or premium account by the amount needed to make the periodic interest expense equal to the effective rate of interest.

Illustration D demonstrates the compound-interest method, using a $1 million, five-year, 10% bond issued at a discount to yield 12%.

Using the amounts in **Illustration D** for each annual interest period, the first-year accounting entries for recording periodic interest payment and adjustment to the bond discount account are:

```
Dr. Bond Interest Expense ................................  111,300
    Cr. Cash .............................................           100,000
       Bond Discount .....................................            11,300
```

The entries for amortizing bond premiums are similar, except the amortization charge is debited to the bond premium account.

Extinguishment before Maturity

Corporations sometimes reacquire their debt securities through exercise of their call provision or by purchase in the open market. Bonds acquired by call are usually called at a periodic interest date, after paying and recognizing in the accounts the interest due for the period. Repurchase of debt securities occurs most frequently when interest rates rise and the market value of low nominal rate bonds declines. This provides the

ILLUSTRATION D   Discount Amortization, Compound-Interest Method ($1 million five-year bonds, nominal rate 10% payable annually, sold at $927,500 to yield approximately 12%)

	A	B	C	D	E
					Bond Carrying Value[a] − (PV of Future Interest + Principal Payments Discounted at 12%)
Interest Payment Periods	Cash Interest Payment	Effective Interest Expense (12% of E)	Bond Discount Amortization (B − A)	Unamortized Bond Discount Balance (D − C)	
0	—	—	—	$72,500	$ 927,500
1	$100,000	$111,300	$11,300	61,200	939,700
2	100,000	112,764	12,764	48,436	952,200
3	100,000	114,264	14,264	34,172	996,000
4	100,000	115,920	15,920	18,252	982,300
5	100,000	118,252	18,252	—	1,000,000

[a]Carrying value on the balance sheet if the bond discount is treated as a valuation account rather than as an asset.

corporate issuer with the opportunity to reacquire these discounted debt obligations at less than their principal value. Once acquired, the debt security may be retired or used to satisfy sinking fund requirements.

The FASB in *FASB Statement No. 4* required that the gains and losses from the extinguishment of debt be classified as an extraordinary item. This conclusion does not apply to gains or losses from cash purchases of debt made to satisfy one year's sinking fund requirements. *FASB Statement No. 64* permits these gains or losses to be recorded as ordinary income.

The reacquisition price of debt is the amount paid on early extinguishment, including any call premium and miscellaneous costs of reacquisition. If early extinguishment is achieved by a direct exchange of new securities, the reacquisition price is the total present value of the new securities.

To illustrate the accounting entries, assume that bonds with a principal value of $100,000 and a related discount of $3,000 are retired after paying a call premium of $2,000. The entries to record the call and retirement are:

```
Dr. Bonds Payable ......................................... 100,000
    Loss on Bond Extinguishment ............................   5,000
Cr. Cash ..............................................              102,000
    Bond Discount .....................................                3,000
```

For a similar issue that had originally been sold at a premium of $3,000, the accounting entries to record the call and retirement are:

```
Dr. Bonds Payable ......................................... 100,000
    Bond Premium ........................................   3,000
Cr. Cash ..............................................              102,000
    Gain on Bond Extinguishment .........................            1,000
```

Extinguishment of Liabilities

Under FASB Statement No. 125 a debtor shall derecognize a liability if and only if it has been extinguished. A liability has been extinguished if either of the following conditions is met:

    a. The debtor pays the creditor and is relieved of its obligation for the liability. *Paying the creditor* includes delivery of cash, other financial assets, goods, or services or reacquisition by the debtor of its outstanding debt securities whether the securities are canceled or held as so-called treasury bonds.

    b. The debtor is legally released from being the primary obligor under the liability, either judicially or by the creditor.

Troubled Debt Restructuring

For the purposes of accounting, a "troubled" debt restructuring implies that the creditor, for economic or legal reasons related to the debtor's financial difficulties, has granted a concession that it would not otherwise consider, such as a modification of the terms of the debt or accepting an equity interest in the debtor to satisfy a debt obligation.

    A debtor that transfers its assets or an equity interest to a creditor in restructuring of troubled debt situations recognizes an extraordinary gain from this restructuring to the extent that the carrying amount of the payable settled exceeds the fair value of the assets or equity interest transferred to the creditor. In many cases the debtor will also have to recognize a gain or loss on the transfer of the assets. No gain or loss is recognized on the transfer of equity.

    If the terms of the debt agreement are modified in a troubled debt restructuring, the debtor accounts for the modification prospectively. The carrying amount of the payable remains unchanged unless the sum of the future cash payments exceeds the carrying amount of the payable. The new effective interest rate for computing interest expense is the discount rate that equates the present value of the debtor's restructured future cash payments with the carrying amount of the payable. If the sum of the future cash payments is less than the carrying amount of the payable, the carrying amount is reduced to the sum of the future cash payments, and all future payments are accounted for as reductions of the restructured payable. The reduction in value is recognized as an extraordinary gain on restructuring of payables in the period of the restructuring.

    Debtors must disclose in financial statements the nature of any debt restructuring.

Convertible Debt

In order to make bonds more attractive to buyers, some issues give the bondholder the right under certain conditions to convert bonds into stock. The conversion terms can vary: the conversion ratio may specify a certain number of shares of stock to be issued for each bond, or it may simply indicate that stock of an equivalent par value to the bond's value may be issued. Sometimes the conversion right can be exercised only after a specific period of time.

Convertible debt is accounted for by the issuer as if it was debt without a conversion privilege. No value is assigned to its equity character of the issue.

Conversion

When bonds are converted, the first step is to correct the current balances by recording any accrued interest and by adjusting, if necessary, the unamortized bond discount or premium accounts. The next step is to record the conversion.

Conversions are recorded on a market value basis. The newly issued security is recorded at either its market value or the market value of the bonds, whichever is more readily determinable; the appropriate bonds payable account is reduced by the par value of the bonds converted; and any difference between par value of the bonds and the market value assigned to the new securities is reported as a gain or loss on conversion. This method assumes that the conversion terminates the bond transaction and begins a new one for the stock. Therefore, the relevant value associated with this transaction is the amount that would be received today if the bonds were sold, or if the stock was sold rather than exchanged. If the market values of the bonds and equity differ, the market value of the bonds is the preferred measure of the new equity created.

To illustrate, the Ronald Company offers bondholders 20 shares of $5 par value stock in exchange for each $1,000, 6% bond they hold. The market value of the stock is $60 per share, and of the bonds, $1,200 per bond. All accrued interest has been paid, and the balance of the unamortized premium account is equivalent to $20 per bond. Holders of 600 bonds exercise their conversion right. The accounting entries are:

Market Value Method (based on bonds' market value of $72,000)

Dr. Bonds Payable (600 bonds @ $1,000)	600,000	
Bond Premium (600 × $20)	12,000	
Loss on Bond Conversion.	108,000	
Cr. Common Stock (12,000 shares × $5 par value).		60,000
Capital in Excess of Par Value ([600 × $1,200] − $60,000)		660,000

Debt Issued with Stock Warrants

The interest rate of bonds issued with warrants giving the bondholders the right to buy the issuer's common stock is typically lower than the rate for similar quality bonds without warrants. Therefore, the issuer is able to get a higher price for bonds by adding stock warrant features. This difference in the proceeds is in effect a payment by the bondholder for a future "call" on the stock of the issuer. The proceeds minus this amount can be considered as the imputed cost of the straight bond portion of the security.

In the case of convertible debt and debt issued with stock warrants where the debt must be converted to obtain the advantage of the warrants, the APB recommended in *APB Opinion No. 14* that no portion of the proceeds from the issuance be accounted for as attributable to the conversion feature. The APB stated that the inseparability of the debt and conversion feature was the primary difficulty, rather than the practical problems of valuing the conversion feature.

If the debt was issued with detachable stock warrants, the APB stated that the portion of the proceeds allocable to the warrants should be accounted for as a credit to paid-in capital. Since the face value of the debt obligation remains unchanged, the offsetting entry is to the discount or premium on debt accounts, depending upon the relationship between the proceeds of the issue and the face amount of the obligation. This has the effect of recording the discount or premium that would have been re- corded if the issue had been sold as straight debt.

Warrants are often traded, and their fair market value can usually be determined by their market price at the issue date. This value is the basis for allocating the proceeds of the issue between the debt obligation and warrants. If no market exists for the warrants, the market value for the debt without warrants must be estimated.

Classification of Short-Term Debt Expected to Be Refinanced

FASB Statement No. 6 specifies that short-term obligations expected to be refinanced on a long-term basis could be classified as noncurrent liabilities rather than current liabilities only if a company's intent to refinance its short-term obligation was sup- ported by an ability to consummate the refinancing, demonstrated in either of the following ways: (1) After the date of an enterprise's balance sheet, but before the balance sheet is issued, a long-term obligation or equity security has been issued for the purpose of refinancing the short-term obligation on a long-term basis. Or, (2) before the balance sheet date, the company has entered into a financing agreement permitting the company to refinance the short-term obligation on a long-term basis on terms that are readily determinable. In addition, all of these conditions must be met: (a) The agreement does not expire during the 12 months (or operating cycle, if longer); and (b) during this period the agreement is noncancellable by the prospective lender, except for violation of a provision with which compliance is objectively determinable or measurable; (c) prior to the issuance of the statements, the agreement has not been violated and no information exists that suggests that it will be violated; and (d) the lender is financially capable of honoring the agreement.

Classification of Obligations That Are Callable

Many loans have provisions that if the borrower fails to meet certain requirements, such as a specified working capital level, the loan is callable by the lender immediately. When a company violates one of these covenants that makes a loan callable by the creditor, the loan should be reclassified as a short-term obligation unless the lender signs a written waiver of the call privilege for at least a year from the balance sheet date.

Inappropriate Interest Rates

In *FASB Statement No. 21* the APB set forth its views regarding the appropriate accounting when the face amount of a note does not reasonably represent the present value of the consideration given or received in the exchange. Such a transaction may occur when property is exchanged for a long-term, non-interest-bearing note, or for a note with artificially low interest.

In these circumstances, unless the note is recorded at its present value, the sale price and profits to the seller in the year of the transaction and the purchase price and cost to the buyer are misstated, and the interest income and interest expense in subsequent periods are also misstated. The present value of the note is determined by discounting all future payments at an imputed interest rate, which is the appropriate rate that would have resulted if an independent borrower and an independent lender had negotiated a similar transaction under comparable terms and conditions with the option to pay cash upon purchase or to give a note in the amount of the purchase bearing the prevailing rate of interest to maturity. One guide to the appropriate rate is the prevailing rate for similar instruments of issuers with similar credit ratings.

The discount or premium resulting from the application of *APB Opinion No. 21* is not an asset or liability separable from the note that gives rise to it. Therefore, the discount or premium is reported in the balance sheet as a direct deduction from or addition to the face amount of the note.

The discount or premium is amortized and reported as interest in the income statement over the life of the note.

Impaired Loans

A loan is impaired when it is probable that the creditor will not collect all of the principal and interest specified in the loan agreement. The accounting for loan impairments is covered by FASB 114.

FASB 114 permits creditors to use one of three methods to measure impairment losses. These are:

1. The excess of the creditor's investment in the loan over the present value of the future cash flows associated with the loan, using as the discount rate the effective rate in the original loan agreement.
2. The excess of the creditor's investment in the loan over an observable market price for the loan.
3. The excess of the creditor's investment in the loan over the fair value of the loan's collateral.

The impairment loss is accounted for as a bad debt expense and a valuation allowance adjustment to creditor's investment in loans.

Transfers of Financial Assets

Under *FASB Statement No. 125* a transfer of financial assets (or all or a portion of a financial asset), such as a securitization or sale of accounts receivable, in which the transferor surrenders control over those financial assets must be accounted for as a sale and a gain or loss recognized to the extent that consideration other than **beneficial interests** in the transferred assets is received in exchange. The transferor has surrendered control over transferred assets if and only if all of the following conditions are met:

a. The transferred assets have been isolated from the transferor—put presumptively beyond the reach of the transferor and its creditors, even in bankruptcy or other receivership.

b. Either (1) each transferee obtains the right—free of conditions that constrain it from taking advantage of that right—to pledge or exchange the transferred assets or (2) the transferee is a qualifying special-purpose entity and the holders of beneficial interests in that entity have the right—free of conditions that constrain them from taking advantage of that right—to pledge or exchange those interests.

c. The transferor does not maintain effective control over the transferred assets through (1) an agreement that both entitles and obligates the transferor to repurchase or redeem them before their maturity or (2) an agreement that entitles the transferor to repurchase or redeem transferred assets that are not readily obtainable.

If the transfer of financial assets does not meet the criteria for a sale, the transferor must account for the transfer as a secured borrowing with pledge of collateral.

Buyer's Accounting

Bonds may be purchased at their face value or at a price which represents either a premium or discount from the face value. The accounting entry in the bondholder's books to record the purchase of one thousand $1,000 bonds at their face value bonds is:

Dr. Investment in Bonds	1,000,000	
Cr. Cash		1,000,000

Interest Income

When bonds are bought at their face value, the bondholder records the periodic interest received by a simple debit to Cash and credit to Interest Income. If the purchase involved a premium or discount and the bondholder intends to hold the bonds as a long-term investment, the accounting is more complex.

The carrying value of a bond bought at a discount gradually rises to par at maturity. Rather than wait until the maturity date to recognize all of this gain over cost, it is customary to record in the bondholder's accounts the increase as it accrues as part of interest income. Thus, the interest income includes the interest payment received plus the change in the carrying value of the bond. This treatment assumes that the discount is analogous to a prepayment of interest by the issuer. It also assumes that the bond will be held to maturity.

ILLUSTRATION E   Calculation of Carrying Value Change at End of Year 1

Years	Item	Times PV Factor (6%)	Equals Present Value
1–9	Annual interest payments, $50,000	6.802	$340,100
9	Principal repayment, $1,000,000	0.592	592,000
	Present value on first payment date		$932,100
	Present value at purchase date		926,000
	Change in bond investment		$ 6,100

The carrying value of a bond purchased at a premium slowly declines to par at maturity. The accounting treatment for recognizing this change in carrying value is the reverse of the bond discount situation. However, the carrying value at any point in time should not be greater than the redemption value at the issuer's next optional redemption date.

The change in the carrying value is the difference between the present value of future interest payments and the redemption payment at maturity at the current interest payment date, and the date of the prior interest payment. The discount rate used to compute these present values is the yield to maturity rate implicit in the purchase price. If the bondholder's balance sheet date does not match the interest payment date, the accrued interest to date is the difference between the carrying values at the two dates bounding the current accounting period.

To illustrate the calculation of change in carrying value, assume that $1 million of 10-year exempt bonds paying 5% annually is bought at a discount for $926,000 to yield 6% to maturity. **Illustration E** reflects the carrying value *after* one year. At the end of this year, the first annual interest payment of $50,000 is received.

The accounting entries to record interest income are:

Dr. Cash	50,000	
Investment in Bonds.	6,100	
Cr. Interest Income		56,100

More precise present value tables than those used in Present Value Tables A and B would have led to the following calculation:

Purchase price of bond	$926,399
Present value of bond at end of year 1	938,983
Increase in bond value.	$5,584
Nominal interest payments.	50,000
Interest expense	$55,584
Verification of interest expense: $926,399 × 6% = $55,584	

A similar entry at the end of each period will result in a level effective rate of interest income being recognized on the carrying value of the bond.

Troubled Debt Restructuring

FASB Statement No. 15's rules on troubled debt restructuring apply to lenders also.

A credit to receiving an equity interest in assets from a debtor in full satisfaction of a restructured troubled debt must account for the item received at its fair market value. Any excess of the recorded investment in the debt over the fair market value received is recorded as a loss in the period of restructuring to the extent it exceeds related loss provisions previously established.

The effects of a modification of the terms of a debt receivable are accounted for prospectively. The amount of the recorded investment in the receivable at the time of restructuring is adjusted only if it is less than the future cash proceeds specified by the new terms. The new effective interest rate is the discount rate that equates the new future cash receipts with the recorded investment in the receivable. If the undiscounted future cash flow is less than the amount of the recorded receivable investment before restructuring, the recorded receivable is reduced to the amount of the future cash flows, and the write-down is charged to current income. All future cash received is accounted for as a recovery of investment, and no interest income is recognized for the period between the restructuring and the maturity of the receivable.

Creditors should disclose the nature of any troubled debt restructuring.

FASB Statement No. 115

FASB Statement No. 115, "Accounting for Certain Investments in Debt and Equity Securities," addresses the accounting and reporting for investments in equity securities that have readily determinable fair values and for all investments in debt securities. Those investments are to be classified in three categories and accounted for as follows:

- Debt securities that the enterprise has the positive intent and ability to hold to maturity are classified as *held-to-maturity securities* and reported at amortized cost.

- Debt and equity securities that are bought and held principally for the purpose of selling them in the near term are classified as *trading securities* and reported at fair value, with unrealized gains and losses included in earnings.

- Debt and equity securities not classified as either held-to-maturity securities or trading securities are classified as *available-for-sale securities* and reported at fair value, with unrealized gains and losses excluded from earnings and reported in a separate component of shareholders' equity.[4]

---

[4]At the time this chapter was prepared the FASB had proposed a new display referred to as Statement of Financial Performance. This display would include net income plus other comprehensive income which together would sum to comprehensive income. If adopted, the unrealized gains and losses

Transfers of a security between categories of investments should be accounted for at fair value. At the date of transfer the security's unrealized gains or losses are accounted for as follows:

a. For a security transferred from the trading category, the unrealized holding gain or loss at the date of the transfer will have already been recognized in earnings and must not be reversed.

b. For a security transferred into the trading category, the unrealized holding gain or loss at the date of the transfer is recognized in earnings immediately.

c. For a debt security transferred into the available-for-sale category from the held-to-maturity category, the unrealized holding gain or loss at the date of the transfer is recognized in a separate component of shareholders' equity.

d. For a debt security transferred into the held-to-maturity category from the available-for-sale category, the unrealized holding gain or loss at the date of the transfer continues to be reported in a separate component of shareholders' equity but is amortized over the remaining life of the security as an adjustment of yield in a manner consistent with the amortization of any premium or discount. The amortization of an unrealized holding gain or loss reported in equity offsets or mitigates the effect on interest income of the amortization of the premium or discount for that held-to-maturity security.

The sale or transfer of a held-to-maturity security may raise a question as to management's intent to hold to maturity and require reclassification of the entire portfolio of held-to-maturity to another category. Exceptions to this rule include sale of securities close to maturity and securities whose issuer's creditworthiness has deteriorated significantly.

Derivative Financial Instruments

For the purpose of accounting a derivative financial instrument is a forward, futures, option, or swap contract, or other financial instrument with similar characteristics. These contracts create rights and obligations that have the effect of transferring between the parties of the contract one or more of the financial risks inherent in an underlying financial instrument. The underlying primary financial instrument is not

---

on available-for-sale securities would be included in this display. FASB Concepts Statement No. 6 defines comprehensive income as: " . . . the change in equity (net assets) of a business enterprise during a period from transactions and other events and circumstances from nonowner sources. It includes all changes in equity during a period except those resulting from investment by owners and distributions to owners." Other comprehensive income is comprehensive income less the traditional net income. At the end of each accounting period, other comprehensive income would be transferred to a section of owners' equity with the same account name. Net income would continue to be transferred to retained earnings.

transferred from one party to the other at the inception of the contract and may or may not be transferred on maturity of the contract.

Forward contracts are the most straightforward of the four basic derivative instruments. A forward contract obligates its holder to buy (sell) a specific asset at a specified date at a price specified in the contract. No asset transfer is made at the origination date or during the contract. Assets are transferred only at the maturity date. Forward contracts are custom designed and are written with brokers. They are not traded on exchanges.

Futures contracts are similar to forward contracts except that the contract is an exchange traded instrument rather than an agreement with a broker; the market participants maintain a margin account; at the end of each day rather than at the end of the contract period, the value of the contract is conveyed; and, the margin account is adjusted daily to reflect the day's gain or loss on the contract. Conceptually, futures contracts are like a series of one-day forward contracts. Each day the forward contract is settled and a new one is written.

An **option** gives the owner the right to buy an asset at a specific price (a call option) or to sell an asset at a specific price (a put option). In contrast to a forward or futures contract, only the contract writer is obligated to act. The contract owner or holder is not obligated. Unlike futures, options are not settled with cash until exercised or expired.

A **swap contract** obligates two counterparts to exchange specified cash flows at specified intervals. For example, the most common form of a swap, the interest rate swap, is structured as follows: Two parties agree to exchange interest-rate–determined cash flows based upon an agreed upon notional principle. One party pays to the other a market-determined, floating-rate–based cash flow. The other party pays to the first party a specified fixed-rate–based cash flow. The notional principle is used solely to determine the exchanged cash flows. It is not paid to or received by either party.

Under a new approach being proposed by the FASB at the time this chapter was prepared, all derivatives would be recorded on the balance sheet at fair value. Depending on the reason for holding the derivative, unrealized gains and losses on derivatives due to fair value changes would be accounted for as follows:

a. *Hedge Accounting for Fair Value Hedges of Existing Assets and Liabilities*
   The change in the fair value of a derivative designated as a hedge of a fair value exposure of an existing asset or liability would be recognized in earnings in the period of change, along with the change in the fair value of the hedged item attributable to the risk being hedged (a separation-by-risk approach).

b. *Hedge Accounting for Cash Flow Hedges of Existing Assets and Liabilities*
   The change in fair value of a derivative designated as a hedge of the cash flow exposure of an existing asset or liability would be reported in other comprehensive income until it is recognized in earnings.[5] The accumulated change in fair value would be recognized in earnings in the same period or periods as the earnings impact of the hedged item.

[5]See footnote 4 for an explanation of other comprehensive income.

c. ***Hedge Accounting for Cash Flow Hedges of Forecasted Transactions***
The change in fair value of a derivative designated as a hedge of the cash flow exposure of a forecasted transaction would be reported in other comprehensive income until it is recognized in earnings. The accumulated change in fair value would be recognized in earnings in the same period or periods as the earnings impact of the forecasted transaction. If the forecasted transaction is the acquisition of an asset or is related to the incurrence of a liability, the accumulated change in fair value would be recognized in earnings in the same period as the earnings impact of the asset required or liability incurred.

d. ***Hedge Accounting for Foreign Currency Net Investments***
The change in fair value of a derivative designated as a hedge of a foreign currency net investment would be reported in other comprehensive income and recognized in net income in the same period as the gain or loss on the net investment is realized.

Disclosure Standards

The FASB has issued a number of Statements dealing with financial-instrument–related disclosures. Three Statements that significantly expanded financial instrument disclosures are discussed below.

FASB Statement No. 105, "Disclosure of Information about Financial Instruments with Off-Balance-Sheet Risk and Financial Instruments with Concentrations of Credit Risk," requires all entities to disclose the following information about financial instruments with off-balance-sheet risk of accounting loss by class, business activity (such as trading or other purposes) or other category that is consistent with the entity's management of those instruments:

- The face, contract, or notional principal amount.
- The nature and terms of the instruments and a discussion of their credit and market risk, cash requirements, and related accounting policies.
- The *accounting loss* the entity would incur if any party to the financial instrument failed completely to perform according to the terms of the contract and the collateral or other security, if any, for the amount due proved to be of no value to the entity.
- The entity's policy for requiring collateral or other security on financial instruments it accepts and a description of collateral on instruments presently held.

This Statement also requires disclosure of information about significant concentrations of credit risk from an individual counterparty or groups of counterparties for all financial instruments.

FASB Statement No. 107, "Disclosure about Fair Value of Financial Instruments," requires all entities to disclose the fair value of financial instruments, both assets and liabilities recognized and not recognized in the statement of financial position, for which it is practicable to estimate fair value. If estimating fair value is not practicable, this

Statement requires disclosure of descriptive information pertinent to estimating the value of a financial instrument. The fair value information must be presented without combining, aggregating, or netting the fair value of derivative financial instruments with the fair value of nonderivative financial instruments and be presented together with the related carrying amounts in the body of the financial statements, a single footnote, or a summary table in a form that makes it clear whether the amounts represent assets or liabilities. The Statement requires that a distinction be made between financial instruments held or issued for trading purposes (including dealing and other trading activities measured at fair value with gains and losses recognized in earnings) and financial instruments held or issued for purposes other than trading.

FASB Statement No. 119, "Disclosures about Derivative Financial Instruments and Fair Value of Financial Instruments," requires disclosures about derivative financial instruments—futures, forward, swap, and option contracts, and other financial instruments with similar characteristics. This Statement requires disclosures about amounts, nature, and terms of derivative financial instruments that are not subject to FASB Statement No. 105 because they do not result in off-balance-sheet risk of accounting loss. It requires that a distinction be made between financial instruments held or issued for trading purposes (including dealing and other trading activities measured at fair value with gains and losses recognized in earnings) and financial instruments held or issued for purposes other than trading.

For entities that hold or issue derivative financial instruments for trading purposes, this Statement requires disclosure of average fair value and of net trading gains or losses. For entities that hold or issue derivative financial instruments for purposes other than trading, it requires disclosure about those purposes and about how the instruments are reported in financial statements. For entities that hold or issue derivative financial instruments and account for them as hedges of anticipated transactions, it requires disclosure about the anticipated transactions, the classes of derivative financial instruments used to hedge those transactions, the amounts of hedging gains and losses deferred, and the transactions or other events that result in recognition of the deferred gains or losses in earnings. This Statement also encourages, but does not require, quantitative information about market risks of derivative financial instruments, and also of other assets and liabilities, that is consistent with the way the entity manages or adjusts risks and that is useful for comparing the result of applying the entity's strategies to its objectives for holding or issuing the derivative financial instruments.

Financial Analysis and Decision Models

In recent years, considerable research has been done on the role of data generated through financial analysis in statement users' decision-making processes. Much of this work has focused on the usefulness of financial data in predicting bankruptcy and bond ratings.

A number of researchers have attempted to predict bond ratings, simulate the rating-agency rating process, or predict bond rating changes by creating purely statistical models of rating agency decision-making activities. These researchers have developed models utilizing a limited number of variables while recognizing that in actual practice a multitude of quantitative and qualitative variables are examined by the rating agencies before a bond rating is assigned. Nevertheless, these studies suggest strongly that regardless of judgmental considerations, a reliable gauge of a potential agency rating can be determined from certain financial data.

These studies lead to several guideline conclusions for issuers and others interested in simple approaches to predicting bond ratings.

1. The variables that determine perhaps 50% to 70% of a bond rating are the following:

   - Subordination status of issue;
   - Size of issuer;
   - Degree of financial leverage;
   - Interest coverage adequacy; and
   - Stability of issuer's dividends and earnings.

2. Variables such as asset protection, short-term liquidity, and marketability are probably less important.

3. Management, industry, general economic condition, future prospects, and other qualitative factors account for perhaps 30% to 50% of a bond rating.

4. Complicated extrapolations or transformations of financial and other data are probably not worth the effort and may even make communication of results more difficult.

5. Probably much of the financial ratio analysis that is used to help predict or determine bond ratings is redundant. One measure of size, leverage, profitability, or stability is probably enough. As long as a relatively standard definition of the variable is used, it may not matter which definition is chosen for analytical purposes.

6. High-quality bond ratings are typically associated with low earnings variability, a history of meeting obligations, good market acceptance, a preferred claim on assets, and a prudent leverage rate, which in turn implies a high fixed charges coverage ratio.

Models that employ financial data to predict *corporate insolvency or bankruptcy* due to severe financial and/or operational difficulties fall into two broad classes: univariate models that use a single variable to predict failure, and multivariate models with several variables used simultaneously in the prediction process.

The univariate approach research indicates that the financial ratios of failed firms differ from those of solvent firms, and that the nonliquid asset ratios are better predictors of failure than the liquid asset ratios, such as the current ratio, quick ratio, and net working capital to total assets. Furthermore, the nonliquid asset ratios that seem to be the best predictors of failure are the cash flow to total debt including preferred stock, net income to total assets, and total debt to total assets ratios. In addition, the "mixed ratios," which are those with income or cash flow in the numerator and assets and liabilities in the denominator, are better predictors of failure than the short-term solvency ratios are.

The multivariate approach research predicts a quantitative measure of solvency status. Scores below a critical level indicate a firm is very likely to slip from the nonfailed to failed firm category. The score is derived from a linear combination, developed through mathematical techniques, of some characteristics that best discriminate between failed and nonfailed firms.

For example, one researcher, Altman, that used this approach developed the following discriminate function for small manufacturing firms:

$$Z = 0.012X_1 + 0.014X_2 + 0.033X_3 + 0.006X_4 + 0.010X_5$$

where:

X_1 = Working capital/Total assets (a liquidity measure).
X_2 = Retained earnings/Total assets (a measure for reinvested earnings).
X_3 = Earnings before interest and taxes/Total assets (a profitability measure).
X_4 = Market value of equity/Book value of total liabilities (a measure for the firm's financial structure or leverage).
X_5 = Sales/Total assets (a measure for the sales-generating ability of the firm's assets).

The ratios are expressed in absolute terms, for example, a working capital to asset ratio of 10% is noted at 10.0 and a sales to total asset ratio of 2.0, or 200%, is noted as 200.0.

A Z score below 1.81 indicates potential bankruptcy. A score above 2.99 suggests a company will remain viable. And, scores between 1.81 and 2.99 indicate a gray area where a firm may or may not be approaching bankruptcy.

The variables included in a successful prediction equation may not be the most significant for predicting bankruptcy when measured independently (as in the univariate research). For instance, the equation above was derived by testing 22 potential variables. Among these variables, X_5 was the least significant when measured individually. However, the multivariate approach derives the most successful prediction equation for replicating the interactions among the variables. This is the principal difference between the multivariate and univariate models.

Cash Flow Focus

The importance of cash to a company's viability supersedes all other considerations. The ability to generate cash and to obtain cash from sources outside the entity is the "bottom line" of most analyses focusing on a company's financial viability. Those responsible for assessing a company's ability to meet its maturing financial obligations should never lose sight of this fact.

Franklin Corporation

On June 30, 1988, Franklin Corporation issued 11%, convertible first mortgage 10-year bonds having a maturity value of $3 million. The bonds were issued at a price to yield 10%.

The Franklin bonds were dated June 30, 1988, and required semiannual interest payments. They were redeemable after June 30, 1993, and before June 30, 1995, at 104; thereafter until maturity they were redeemable at 102. They were also convertible into $10 par value common stock according to the following schedule:

Before June 30, 1993: 60 shares of common stock for each $1,000 bond.

July 1, 1993 to June 30, 1996: 50 shares of common stock for each $1,000 bond.

After June 30, 1996: 40 shares of common stock for each $1,000 bond.

The following transactions occurred in connection with Franklin's bonds:

July 1, 1994: Bonds having a maturity value of $500,000 were converted into common stock.

December 30, 1995: Bonds having a maturity value of $500,000 were reacquired by Franklin Corporation by purchase on the market at 99¼ and accrued interest. The reacquired bonds were canceled immediately.

June 30, 1996: Franklin Corporation called the remaining bonds for redemption. In order to obtain the cash necessary for the redemption and for business expansion, a $4 million issue of 20-year, 8% sinking fund debenture bonds were issued at a price to yield 8%. The new bonds were dated June 30, 1996, and also called for semiannual interest payments.

Professor David F. Hawkins prepared this case as the basis for class discussion rather than to illustrate either effective or ineffective handling of an administrative situation.
Copyright © 1996 by the President and Fellows of Harvard College. Harvard Business School case 197–022.

Present Value of $1

Periods	3%	3.5%	4.0%	4.5%	5.0%	5.5%
10	0.744	0.709	0.676	0.644	0.614	0.585
20	0.554	0.503	0.456	0.415	0.377	0.343
40	0.307	0.253	0.258	0.172	0.142	0.117

Present Value of $1 per Period

Periods	3%	3.5%	4.0%	4.5%	5.0%	5.5%
10	8.530	8.317	8.111	7.913	7.222	7.538
20	14.877	14.212	13.590	13.008	12.462	11.950
40	23.115	21.355	19.793	18.402	17.159	16.046

Questions

1. Determine the amount of the proceeds from the June 30, 1988, bond issue. Illustrate the December 31, 1988 balance sheet disclosure(s) related to this indebtedness. (Use tables above.)

2. Determine the amount of "interest expense" to be deducted in arriving at the net income for the year ending December 31, 1989.

3. Describe the balance sheet and income statement effects of the July 1, 1994, conversion, including dollar amounts involved.

4. Describe the balance sheet and income statement effects of the June 30, 1996, redemption, including dollar amounts involved.

CASE

19-2

First Securities, Inc.

First Securities, Inc., a leading regional investment banking firm, was negotiating bond underwritings with five of its clients: Orion, Inc., Midwest Mining Company, Simmons Corporation, Sunshine Foods, Inc., and Beekhus Industrial Company. Summary sheets prepared for the executive committee presenting each company's business, existing debt, the nature of its proposed issue, selected balance sheet data, and key financial ratios are presented in **Exhibits 1** through **5**. The final piece of information to be added to each summary sheet before being presented to the committee is the anticipated bond rating the issue might receive from the major rating agencies.

Professor David F. Hawkins prepared this case as the basis for class discussion rather than to illustrate either effective or ineffective handling of an administrative situation.
Copyright © 1997 by the President and Fellows of Harvard College. Harvard Business School case 197–029.

Questions

1. Rank the five cases in order of the quality of their long-term debt (highest at top of list).
2. What debt rating would you assign to each of the five companies' long-term debt? _____ (Use Moody's classification scheme.)

Exhibit 1   Orion, Inc.

Orion, Inc., is a multinational diversified manufacturer of consumer and industrial products. More than 90 percent of its operations are in four basic industries: chemicals and coatings, pulp and paper, foods, and consumer products, including typewriters and appliances. The company's long-term debt consists of the following: a subsidiary 25-year, 5½ percent, unsecured sinking fund debenture; three 20-year sinking fund debentures at 5¾ percent, 7¼ percent, and 9¼ percent, respectively, secured only by the creditworthiness of the company; some 5½ percent convertible subordinated debentures; and other miscellaneous subsidiary debt and lease obligations. The various indentures restrict the company from incurring further senior debt unless, immediately thereafter,

consolidated net tangible assets will be at least 250 percent of consolidated senior funded debt and 200 percent of consolidated funded debt. Indentures also restrict the company from paying cash dividends or acquiring stock after a certain date in excess of consolidated net income and net proceeds from stock sale after such date, plus a specified amount.

The company proposes to issue a $50 million, 20-year, sinking fund debenture. The sinking fund requirement, which is designed to retire 91 percent of the issue prior to maturity, begins six years from the issue date and will retire annually not less than $3,250,000 and not more than $6.5 million of the principal.

Selected Accounts (thousands of dollars)	1992	1991	1990	1989	1988
Net sales	$1,331,897	$1,287,454	$1,202,248	$ 980,281	$ 917,817
Cost of goods sold	968,179	956,550	876,106	708,946	671,894
Selling and administrative expenses	291,816	269,898	264,270	227,481	215,141
Gross income	71,079	61,061	60,870	43,278	31,066
Interest on long-term debt	15,173	12,722	9,848	10,452	11,802
Other interest	2,225	6,270	3,173	1,541	1,673
Provisions for all taxes	25,170	16,828	22,503	13,786	7,964
Net income	30,395	27,886	27,646	18,299	10,327
Dividends	$ 6,182	$ 4,579	$ 3,892	$ 915	—
Depreciation	38,168	33,055	30,334	27,210	23,845
Cash and temporary investments	$ 45,077	$ 21,009	$ 6,640	$ 9,391	$ 17,164
Notes and accounts receivable (net)	171,358	169,664	189,024	152,931	134,315
Products, materials, supplies	240,372	214,034	213,353	177,975	160,586
Total Current Assets	$ 465,993	$ 415,777	$ 425,908	$ 356,560	$ 328,330
Land, buildings, machinery & equipment	518,281	507,831	433,712	400,194	369,100
Less: Depreciation reserve	266,989	248,952	226,475	212,832	192,262
Other assets and deferred charges	22,805	29,422	13,538	8,785	3,181
Intangibles					5,518
Total Assets	$ 740,090	$ 704,078	$ 646,683	$ 552,707	$ 515,149
Total Current Liabilities	$ 178,140	$ 164,146	$ 193,941	$ 126,619	$ 104,033
Long-term debt	210,389	214,472	152,906	149,439	162,024
Debt of foreign subsidiaries	—	—	—	—	—
Minority interest	—	—	—	—	—
Deferred taxes	12,751	11,586	16,583	17,158	13,457
Common stock (par $5)	45,809	45,784	45,782	45,782	45,753
Capital surplus	111,377	111,351	111,349	111,349	111,321
Retained earnings	156,457	132,244	108,937	85,183	67,799
Total stockholders' equity	313,643	289,379	266,068	242,314	224,873
Reacquired shares	—	—	—	—	—
Total	$ 740,090	$ 704,078	$ 646,683	$ 552,707	$ 515,149
Number of common shares at year-end	9,161,885	9,156,885	9,156,485	9,156,485	9,150,640
Lease expenses	$ 53,800				
$\dfrac{\text{Pro forma long-term debt}}{\text{Net property, plant, and equipment}}$	1.04	.82	.74	.80	.92
$\dfrac{\text{Working capital}}{\text{Pro forma long-term debt}}$	1.11	1.17	1.52	1.54	1.38
$\dfrac{\text{Pro forma long-term debt}}{\text{Equity}}$	.83	.74	.58	.62	.72
$\dfrac{\text{Net tangible long-term assets}}{\text{Pro forma long-term debt}}$	2.75	3.15	4.14	3.64	3.13
$\dfrac{\text{Cash flow}}{\text{Long-term debt}}$	.326	.284	.379	.305	.148
$\dfrac{\text{Total interest charges + Income before tax}}{\text{Total interest charges}}$	4.09	3.22	4.68	3.61	2.31

EXHIBIT 2   Midwest Mining Company

Incorporated in 1922, Midwest Mining Company manufactures refractory products which are heat-resistant clay and basic mineral products whose prime function is to provide structure of or linings of facilities where high temperatures are required. These products are used by major customers in the steel, glass, nonferrous metals, rock products, ceramics, waste disposal, and petroleum industries to contain high temperature processes and reactions. They have subsidiaries worldwide.

Long-term debt currently consists of the following: domestic banks, revolving credit—$36 million; foreign banks, notes payable, 8.8 percent aver-

age interest—$17,690,000; construction loan—$13.7 million; other mortgages and notes payable, average interest 5.1 percent—$4,573,000; capitalized leases, 5.6 percent average interest—$1,605,000. Loan agreements with various banks and insurance companies provide that the company maintains certain levels of working capital, limits total liabilities, capital expenditures, and foreign investments and restricts payment of dividends. The company proposes to issue a $25 million, 30-year, unsecured debenture for which no sinking fund is provided.

Selected Accounts (thousands of dollars)	1992	1991	1990	1989	1988
Net sales	$326,589	$329,023	$320,098	$228,229	$179,402
Cost of goods sold	315,863	317,292	303,096	221,298	177,292
Selling and administrative expenses					
Gross income	10,726	11,731	17,002	6,931	2,110
Interest on long-term debt	7,746	4,815	3,898	4,553	2,453
Other interest					
Provisions for all taxes	1,984	5,976	7,308	2,070	1,811
Net income	893	9,271	10,125	6,202	(2,508)
Dividends	$670	$1,431	$832	$340	$145
Depreciation	12,038	9,984	8,246	8,982	8,483
Cash and temporary investments	$7,362	$8,268	$9,089	$11,537	$10,259
Notes and accounts receivable (net)	62,523	49,400	69,442	44,021	36,816
Products, materials, supplies	79,343	73,522	60,298	45,133	38,628
Total Current Assets	$151,782	$134,440	$140,962	$102,956	$87,834
Land, buildings, machinery & equipment	276,615	246,404	207,541	201,677	193,340
Less: Depreciation reserve	144,247	135,419	128,181	131,075	125,062
Other assets and deferred charges	12,464	10,461	10,795	7,698	13,293
Intangibles	—				
Total Assets	$296,614	$255,886	$231,117	$181,256	$169,405
Total Current Liabilities	$86,376	$65,972	$68,333	$43,864	$38,534
Long-term debt	66,616	48,452	29,859	22,732	22,152
Debt of foreign subsidiaries	—	—	—	—	—
Minority interest	—	—	—	333	301
Deferred taxes	6,165	7,435	4,095	1,810	2,510
Common stock (par $5)	19,020	19,020	19,020	19,020	19,020
Capital surplus	18,485	18,485	18,485	18,485	18,485
Retained earnings	70,426	70,133	63,386	52,053	45,806
Total stockholders' equity	108,204	108,572	102,374	91,262	85,314
Reacquired shares	—	—			
Total	$296,614	$255,886	$231,117	$181,256	$169,405
Number of common shares at year-end	3,804,009	3,804,009	3,804,009	3,804,009	3,804,009
Lease expenses	$1,560				
$\dfrac{\text{Pro forma long-term debt}}{\text{Net property, plant, and equipment}}$	.69	.44	.38	.32	.32
$\dfrac{\text{Working capital}}{\text{Pro forma long-term debt}}$	.71	1.41	2.43	2.60	2.23
$\dfrac{\text{Pro forma long-term debt}}{\text{Equity}}$	.85	.45	.29	.25	.26
$\dfrac{\text{Net tangible long-term assets}}{\text{Pro forma long-term debt}}$	3.24	5.28	7.74	7.97	7.65
$\dfrac{\text{Cash flow}}{\text{Long-term debt}}$	.194	.397	.615	.668	.496
$\dfrac{\text{Total interest charges} + \text{Income before tax}}{\text{Total interest charges}}$	1.38	2.44	4.36	1.52	.86

EXHIBIT 3   Simmons Corporation

Simmons Corporation is a multinational company engaged primarily in the manufacture and distribution of cosmetics and fragrances; it is the market leader in cosmetics and fragrances sold at retail. As of December 31, 1992, the company had outstanding a $21,223,000, 4¾ percent Eurodollar subsidiary convertible debenture and a $50 million unsecured, 4¾ percent convertible subordinated debenture. The company has agreed to certain restrictions provided by indentures, which to date have been met, on levels of working capital, dividend payments, debt ratio, acquisition of its own stock, and creation of liens on or sales and leasebacks of certain properties in connection with the notes and the company's revolving credit agreement with its banks.

The company wishes to issue a $100 million, 10-year debenture. There is no provision for a sinking fund and the issue is secured only by the creditworthiness of the company. Restrictions are similar to those described above. The proceeds will be added to working capital to be available for general corporate purposes.

Selected Accounts (thousands of dollars)	1992	1991	1990	1989	1988
Net sales	$955,600	$775,614	$635,263	$522,351	$451,833
Cost of goods sold	349,544	282,356	234,392	190,305	163,015
Selling and administrative expenses	431,599	357,556	300,410	246,358	219,596
Gross income	187,015	146,351	113,052	95,926	75,132
Interest on long-term debt	10,760	8,565	3,301	3,035	2,935
Other interest	9,379	9,532	10,671	6,199	5,400
Provisions for all taxes	71,933	56,641	44,943	38,338	28,179
Net income	81,473	64,254	54,005	46,729	39,830
Dividends	$23,757	$18,720	$16,735	$13,942	$13,028
Depreciation	11,532	9,306	8,003	6,849	6,105
Cash and temporary investments	$268,452	$245,988	$108,312	$105,911	$81,766
Notes and accounts receivable (net)	165,254	154,978	149,729	140,804	128,471
Products, materials, supplies	180,625	166,063	177,519	118,378	106,639
Total Current Assets	$640,249	$591,287	$456,388	$374,599	$325,582
Land, buildings, machinery & equipment	202,294	153,258	134,997	110,832	104,578
Less: Depreciation reserve	63,647	52,587	43,129	31,518	27,937
Other assets and deferred charges	14,792	19,482	17,686	17,127	18,714
Intangibles	79,953	57,008	46,377	40,800	41,647
Total Assets	$873,641	$768,448	$612,319	$511,840	$462,584
Total Current Liabilities	$230,462	$177,739	$182,473	$125,202	$107,233
Long-term debt	182,430	183,227	96,910	109,208	116,567
Debt of foreign subsidiaries	—	—	—	—	—
Minority interest	—	—	—	—	—
Deferred taxes	4,530	4,700	4,893	4,228	2,916
Common stock (par $1)	30,154	14,960	14,244	13,293	13,166
Capital surplus	72,301	77,729	69,282	60,242	52,838
Retained earnings	355,776	301,704	247,128	202,228	173,504
Total stockholders' equity	458,231	394,393	330,654	275,763	239,508
Reacquired shares	2,012	2,611	2,611	2,561	3,640
Total	$873,641	$768,448	$612,319	$511,840	$462,584
Number of common shares at year-end	30,054,873	29,781,302	29,531,766	28,115,274	27,787,386
Lease expenses	$14,724				
$\dfrac{\text{Pro forma long-term debt}}{\text{Net property, plant, and equipment}}$	2.04	1.82	1.05	1.38	1.52
$\dfrac{\text{Working capital}}{\text{Pro forma long-term debt}}$	1.45	2.26	2.83	2.28	1.87
$\dfrac{\text{Pro forma long-term debt}}{\text{Equity}}$	.616	.465	.293	.396	.487
$\dfrac{\text{Net tangible long-term assets}}{\text{Pro forma long-term debt}}$	2.81	3.88	5.84	4.31	3.61
$\dfrac{\text{Cash flow}}{\text{Long-term debt}}$	.510	.401	.640	.491	.394
$\dfrac{\text{Total interest charges + Income before tax}}{\text{Total interest charges}}$	9.29	8.10	8.09	10.4	9.01

Exhibit 4   Sunshine Foods, Inc.

Sunshine Foods, a multinational company engaged primarily in the manufacture or processing and distribution of various lines of food products, directly owns a large number of plants. The company already has three sinking fund debentures outstanding at 4⅞ percent, 6⅞ percent and 8⅜ percent, respectively, secured by the creditworthiness of the company. The indentures require that the company may not mortgage or pledge any property without equally securing the debentures, and the company may not merge into another corporation if its property would be subject to a mortgage without equally securing its debentures.

Sunshine Foods has been in business for 54 years and has a strong management. The company is one of the industry leaders and its products are known and respected for high standards of quality. It proposes to issue a $100 million, 30-year, sinking fund debenture, secured in the same manner as the existing debentures. The annual sinking fund requirement is $5 million of principal, retiring 95 percent of the issue prior to maturity. The proceeds of this issue will be used to reduce short-term debt and for general corporate purposes.

Selected Accounts (thousands of dollars)	1992	1991	1990	1989	1988
Net sales	$4,976,643	$4,857,378	$4,471,427	$3,601,534	$3,196,789
Cost of goods sold	3,990,939	3,920,605	3,647,233	2,827,058	2,457,717
Selling and administrative expenses	691,762	649,994	613,596	569,930	541,790
Gross income	306,850	304,307	225,556	216,932	207,872
Interest on long-term debt	15,854	16,794	14,318	8,872	8,388
Other interest	9,751	15,246	24,962	8,085	3,441
Provisions for all taxes	142,386	128,678	82,222	94,443	95,408
Net income	135,650	139,551	94,627	103,428	88,335
Dividends	$58,919	$53,305	$52,160	$49,330	$49,741
Depreciation	57,821	52,376	49,150	46,690	43,727
Cash and temporary investments	$37,301	$33,482	$36,240	$33,987	$68,012
Notes and accounts receivable (net)	310,654	304,690	300,666	260,978	207,592
Products, materials, supplies	763,353	706,624	793,045	558,612	464,269
Total Current Assets	$1,111,308	$1,044,796	$1,129,951	$853,576	$739,873
Land, buildings, machinery & equipment	56,006	12,215	8,219	8,987	8,320
Less: Depreciation reserve	1,123,432	1,062,628	977,601	914,008	892,562
Other assets and deferred charges	517,837	478,699	453,208	434,395	433,087
Intangibles	15,047	11,444	13,509	13,178	11,186
Total Assets	33,848	34,133	34,366	35,544	27,319
Total Current Liabilities	$1,821,854	$1,686,517	$1,710,438	$1,390,897	$1,245,193
Long-term debt	$518,201	$485,557	$582,443	$410,839	$313,974
Debt of foreign subsidiaries	217,697	215,533	237,474	138,610	130,765
Minority interest	3,060	—	—	4,408	4,700
Deferred taxes	2,979	2,831	2,430	2,298	2,060
Common stock (par $2.50)	44,798	32,299	26,575	19,717	17,504
Capital surplus	73,628	73,628	73,628	73,628	73,505
Retained earnings	49,337	49,324	49,910	49,958	49,543
Total stockholders' equity	952,682	885,951	799,706	757,239	703,142
Reacquired shares	1,085,647	1,008,903	923,244	880,826	826,270
Total	69,741	70,427	73,232	73,162	57,526
Number of common shares at year-end	$1,821,854	$1,686,517	$1,710,438	$1,390,897	$1,245,193
Lease expenses	27,800,258	27,784,009	27,717,615	27,719,643	28,045,696
$\dfrac{\text{Pro forma long-term debt}}{\text{Net property, plant, and equipment}}$	.52	.37	.45	.28	.29
$\dfrac{\text{Working capital}}{\text{Pro forma long-term debt}}$	1.87	2.59	2.31	3.19	3.26
$\dfrac{\text{Pro forma long-term debt}}{\text{Equity}}$	.293	.214	.257	.157	.158
$\dfrac{\text{Net tangible long-term assets}}{\text{Pro forma long-term debt}}$	5.63	7.67	7.06	9.78	9.31
$\dfrac{\text{Cash flow}}{\text{Long-term debt}}$	.609	.890	.605	1.08	1.01
$\dfrac{\text{Total interest charges + Income before tax}}{\text{Total interest charges}}$	12.0	9.5	5.7	12.8	17.6

EXHIBIT 5 Beekhus Industrials Company

Beekhus Industrials is a 73-year-old company with two foreign subsidiaries. It is the world's largest manufacturer of vulcanized fiber and the 13th largest steel company in the United States. The company is engaged primarily in the production of steel, a highly competitive industry.

    The company has a 25-year, 5 percent, unsecured sinking fund subordinated debenture outstanding, as well as $9 million, ¼ percent above prime, revolving credit notes and a $975,000 industrial development lease at varying rates. Among the restrictions imposed by the company's debt agreements, payment of cash dividends, purchase redemption, or retirement of Beekhus capital stock, the steel company's capital stock, or of any subordinated indebtedness is limited to an aggregate amount not to exceed $30 million plus 60 percent of aggregate consolidated net earnings of the company.

    It proposes to issue a $50 million, 30-year, sinking fund debenture. The sinking fund would commence 20 years from the issue date, retiring by redemption the lesser of 2½ percent of outstanding debentures on the October 1 before each November 14 or $1,250,000. In addition, the company must make cash sinking funds payments during the last five years to retire by redemption the lesser of 5 percent of outstanding debentures each year or $2 million.

Selected Accounts (thousands of dollars)	1992	1991	1990	1989	1988
Net sales	$443,682	$323,948	$517,908	$379,486	$326,840
Cost of goods sold	383,377	277,178	380,290	324,491	281,385
Selling and administrative expenses	25,539	20,215	23,661	16,189	13,203
Gross income	21,400	14,678	102,131	27,374	21,260
Interest on long-term debt	4,851	3,343	3,052	2,672	2,449
Other interest	7,293	7,375	7,521	6,686	6,950
Provisions for all taxes	4,074	2,319	46,839	9,649	4,042
Net income	23,870	7,011	47,203	12,132	8,761
Dividends	$21,695	$13,923	$6,335	$—	$—
Depreciation	13,366	11,877	11,826	11,432	10,992
Cash and temporary investments	$23,501	$44,151	$102,562	$24,058	$4,950
Notes and accounts receivable (net)	54,858	44,166	47,522	48,165	45,082
Products, materials, supplies	72,938	75,926	69,956	53,134	59,507
Total Current Assets	$153,388	$166,247	$223,886	$127,108	$111,168
Land, buildings, machinery & equipment	304,321	289,420	283,501	266,668	260,324
Less: Depreciation reserve	164,453	154,687	152,545	143,722	137,858
Other assets and deferred charges	58,134	12,402	3,936	2,138	2,386
Intangibles	—	—	—	—	—
Total Assets	$351,390	$313,382	$358,778	$252,192	$236,020
Total Current Liabilities	$81,274	$64,038	$107,090	$59,156	$48,857
Long-term debt	103,930	95,007	91,510	83,652	82,768
Debt of foreign subsidiaries	—	—	—	—	—
Minority interest	25,432	25,618	25,750	18,713	17,404
Deferred taxes	13,891	11,993	21,317	13,598	12,319
Common stock (par $1)	906	6,284	1,609	1,630	1,257
Capital surplus	62,592	34,655	23,896	26,778	27,809
Retained earnings	58,602	68,997	75,909	35,041	30,024
Total stockholders' equity	122,100	109,936	101,414	63,449	59,090
Reacquired shares	—	—	—	—	—
Total	$351,390	$313,382	$358,778	$252,192	$236,020
Number of common shares at year-end	13,311,510	12,183,761	11,649,464	14,375,425	12,319,293
Lease expenses	$4,763				
Pro forma long-term debt / Net property, plant, and equipment	1.10	70.5	69.9	68.0	67.6
Working capital / Pro forma long-term debt	.47	1.08	1.28	.81	.75
Pro forma long-term debt / Equity	1.26	.864	.902	1.32	1.40
Net tangible long-term assets / Pro forma long-term debt	2.28	3.30	3.92	3.01	2.85
Cash flow / Long-term debt	.252	.199	.569	.282	.239
Total interest charges + Income before tax / Total interest charges	1.76	1.37	9.66	2.93	2.26

CASE
19-3

Bishay Industries

On March 18, 1990, Michael Frye met with his boss, Gerry Bloomfield, to discuss the possibility of adding the stock of Bishay Industries, a Canadian cosmetics company, to their firm's investment portfolio. Their firm, Turnaround Investment Ventures (TIV), was a small investment service specializing in assessing turnaround situations. As an initial screen for turnaround candidates, TIV used a computer program which monitored the financial performance of companies that were in loss positions or had suffered substantial earnings setbacks. Companies which met a set of quantitative criteria were printed out and sent to the appropriate TIV analyst to be considered for further detailed analysis.

One of the criteria of the computer program was known as the "Z-Score Screen." This screen used a set of weighted ratios from a model developed by Professor Edward Altman to ascertain the "bankruptcy profile" of a firm (see chapter on "Financial Instruments" for a description of the Altman model).

Using balance sheet items as of the end of the period and the closing share price, Michael Frye obtained the following Z-scores for Bishay Industries for the fiscal years ended October 31, 1986, 1987, 1988, and 1989.

End of Fiscal Year	Z-Score
1986	3.71
1987	3.16
1988	0.75
1989	0.84

Although Bishay's Z-Score was still in the "bankruptcy zone" at the end of fiscal 1989, Mr. Frye wondered if the slight increase in the Z-Score might be signaling the beginning of a turnaround. Mr. Frye noted that in July 1989, Bishay had recruited a new president, Alec Faber. Also, during 1989 operating losses had been reduced by $4.6 million from those reported in fiscal 1988.[1] Mr. Frye noted further that on July

---

Professors David F. Hawkins and Norman J. Bartczak, Columbia University, prepared this case as the basis for class discussion rather than to illustrate either effective or ineffective handling of an administrative situation.

[1]Dollar amounts are Canadian dollars.

EXHIBIT 1   Board of Directors and Stock Price Information

Board of Directors

Name	Bishop Common Stock Beneficially Owned: March 1, 1970
Leo Betis	109
Peter F. Brody	100
Wilbur E. Jewell	800
Alec R. Faber	50,000
Justin N. Field	100
Anthony Franklin	a
A. Sam Git	a
William C. Jaushen	2,100
Len Karp	a

[a]Realty Investors Corporation of New York, of which Messrs. Franklin, Git, and Karp are directors and/or officers, owns 883,334 shares of Bishay's common stock.

29, 1989, Bishay Industries completed an $8.8 million refinancing transaction. The financing package included: (1) the sale of $3 million of 7%, 12-year secured notes with warrants to purchase 800,000 shares to a group of four insurance companies; and (2) $3 million in equity capital through the private sale of one million common shares, at a price below market value, to several funds, corporations, and private investors. Two million, eight hundred thousand dollars of the package represented revision and consolidation of existing senior indebtedness. In addition, the transaction relieved Bishay of the obligation of making amortization payments during the next three and one-half years on its present senior and subordinated long-term debt. Finally, Mr. Frye knew that other cosmetics companies, in general, appeared to be rather highly valued by the marketplace. Bishay Industries was incorporated in Toronto in January 1982 as the result of the merger of two small regional cosmetic firms. Exhibit 1 lists the company's board of directors.

Company Background

Until 1988, the years since incorporation proved to be moderately successful for Bishay. Bishay's sales grew by approximately 10% compounded annually from 1982 through 1987. However, its net income was relatively volatile over this period; $19,000 in 1982; $416,000 in 1983; $1,654,000 in 1984; $136,000 loss in 1985; $1,011,000 in 1986; and $192,000 in 1987. Bishay's stock price mirrored this volatility and ranged as follows: $13.63–$4.75 in 1982; $6.13–$3.75 in 1983; $12.13–$4.25 in 1984; $11.75–$6.63 in 1985; $9.88–$5.88 in 1986; and $18.13–$7.25 in 1987.

Fiscal 1988 was a disastrous year for Bishay Industries. On sales of $24.5 million, down 26% from 1987, Bishay incurred a net loss of $7.6 million. Industry sources were puzzled at the dramatic downturn in Bishay's fortunes. Bishay explained its 1988 results to its shareholders as follows:

To Our Shareholders:

It is in the nature of a highly competitive consumer industry, such as ours, that success depends on the coordination of product development and manufacturing, marketing, and financial planning. Whenever these functions fail to mesh perfectly, adverse effects on sales and profits are inevitable.

When it became evident during the past year that Bishay Industries was suffering from severe setbacks of this nature, your board made a full appraisal of the apparent causes and began remedial steps to counteract them.

Our examination revealed that Bishay's product line was excellent and that we had every reason to be optimistic about new products being developed in our research laboratories. But it also disclosed severe weaknesses in our past marketing program and policies as well as inadequate capital funds and resources to maintain and expand production and distribution needs.

The financial results in this report reflect these fears with surprising, though disappointing precision. The overall loss of $7,605,378, after a tax credit of $771,628, can be traced in large part to a decline in sales from $33,052,406 in 1987 to $24,466,643 in 1988, with no compensating reduction in the cost of sales or overhead.

More than one quarter of the loss, or about $2 million, resulted from merchandise inventory being reevaluated in relation to its ultimate salability as well as additional reserves and write-offs. And while it is best, in such cases, to accept the consequences of such drastic write-offs, it is important at the same time to buttress this step with a fresh look at the marketing program.

With these facts at hand, your board of directors began to realign the company's management in several channels—notably in financial and sales planning. In this program, it received substantial encouragement by Realty Investors Corporation of New York, a broadly diversified listed company.

The company's financial position was strengthened by the acquisition by BEC in November 1988 of 375,000 shares of Bishay common stock in exchange for 125,000 shares of BEC common stock. The exchange ratio has since been renegotiated to provide for the issuance of a total of 500,000 shares of Bishay common stock of which 125,000 are subject to approval by our shareholders. Moreover, our directors have granted BEC a 10-year option, subject to shareholders' approval, to purchase an additional 200,000 shares of Bishay common stock at $14 per share.

Strengthened in this way, your board of directors obtained the financial, management, and administrative counseling of A. Sam Git, who is highly regarded in business and banking circles and has a proven record in administrative and financial management. Subsequently, on January 30, 1989, Mr. Git was elected vice chairman of the board and chief executive officer of our company. As chief executive, he succeeds Morton Dell, the former president who retired but will be available if needed as a consultant.

At the same time, the board elected Peter Brody and William Jaushen to be directors, filling vacancies left by the resignations of Mr. Dell, Charles Brown, and Milton J. Lens. Both Mr. Brody and Mr. Jaushen have broad experience as executives of consumer-oriented industries.

The new management team was recently augmented by the appointments of a new executive vice president for marketing and sales and a new controller.

At the time Realty Investors acquired its Bishay shares, its management stated that it was making the investment as part of its own diversification program as well as to strengthen Bishay's financial management. To implement this plan, your board was pleased last December to elect three executives of Realty Investors as directors.

The management changes, which have been and will be combined with newly instituted cost and production controls, coordinated and imaginative marketing policies, and management's studied determination to recast the company's financial structure, augur well for the future of Bishay Industries and its products. In addition, an extensive program has been instituted to tighten our production cost controls, to reduce overhead substantially, to reduce inventories and relate marketing programs to profit controls, all of which will serve to improve the company's performance. As, over the coming 12 months, the company eliminates some of its unprofitable product lines, we can look forward to a narrowing gap between overall sales volume, which may decline, and financial results from operations, which should rise.

In view of all this, I trust you share with our new management and directors the conviction that Bishay Industries has taken on a new vitality which should reflect itself in substantial growth and profitability in the years ahead.

On June 9, 1989, Bishay Industries reported the following interim results for the quarter and six months ended April 30, 1989:

	(Dollars in Thousands)	
	1989	*1988*
Quarter April 30:		
Sales	$3,173.3	$7,766.5
Net loss	442.1	607.7
Six Months:		
Sales	$6,903.8	$14,916.0
Net loss	1,285.2	870.0

At the annual shareholders' meeting on June 26, 1989, shareholders approved an increase of Realty Investors Corporation's ownership of Bishay to 20% from 16.3%. As part of the agreement and in return for Bishay stock, Realty arranged a $1 million short-term bank loan to Bishay.

Bishay holders also approved a new stock option plan that offered 50,000 Bishop shares to A. Sam Git, chief executive officer of Bishay, and 2,000 shares to Brody and Jaushen, at a price of $3 a share. The day before the meeting, Bishay common closed at $6.75. It closed at $6.625 on June 27, 1989. According to Bishay's proxy statement, the reason for the plan was to encourage certain new employees to "become more personally involved in its success" and to encourage them to remain with Bishay.

On July 14, 1989, Bishay announced the election of Faber as president and chief executive officer. Mr. Faber succeeded A. Sam Git as chief executive officer. Mr. Git continued as chairman of Bishay.

Mr. Faber was recruited from a major cosmetic firm, where he had worked for 19 years, during which time he held the positions of vice president and controller, vice president and general manager—operations, and, most recently, group vice president—subsidiaries.

Under the terms of an employee agreement with Bishay, until October 31, 1989,

Bishay agreed to pay Mr. Faber a salary at the rate of $80,000 per year. From November 1, 1989 through October 31, 1990, his salary rate would be $95,000 per year. In addition, Bishop agreed to pay Mr. Faber a bonus of 2% of net pretax profits from operations ("pretax profits") up to $2 million, plus 1-1/2% up to the next $2 million, 1% up to the next $2 million, and 1/2% of any pretax profits in excess of $6 million for the fiscal year ended October 31, 1990. For fiscal years ending October 31, 1991, 1992, 1993, and 1994, Mr. Faber's salary would be $100,000 per year. In addition, he would receive a bonus of 2-1/2% of pretax profits up to $2 million for the fiscal year ended during each of those years, plus 2% of pretax profits up to the next $2 million, 1-1/2% up to the next $2 million, 1% up to the next $2 million, and 1/2% of any pretax profits in excess of $8 million.

Mr. Faber was also given a stock option to purchase 50,000 shares of Bishay's common stock at a price of $0.10 per share subject to certain restrictions. Mr. Faber exercised this option in September 1989 and paid $5,000 for 50,000 shares of Bishay's common.

As mentioned previously, on July 29, 1989, Bishay announced the completion of an $8.8 million refinancing transaction.

On September 15, 1989, Bishop reported the following interim results:

	(Dollars in Thousands)	
	1989	*1988*
Quarter July 31:		
Sales	$2,645.8	$4,957.2
Net loss	566.0	1,817.1
Nine Months:		
Sales	$9,549.6	$19,873.6
Net loss	1,851.2	2,687.4

On March 4, 1990, Bishay reported the following results for the fiscal year ended 1989 and for the first quarter ended January 31, 1990:

	(Dollars in Thousands)	
	1989	*1988*
Year Ended October 31:		
Sales	$12,277.3	$24,466.6
Loss	3,445.3	8,377.0
Tax credit	—	771.6
Net loss	3,445.3	7,605.4
Quarter Ended January 31:		
Sales	$ 3,250.0	$ 3,730.5
Net loss	380.0	843.0

Bishay's annual report to shareholders for fiscal 1989 was issued on March 17, 1990 (see **Exhibit 2**). Bishay's 1989 financial statements were given a "clean opinion" by the company's auditors.

Stock Price

	Bishay Industries			Realty Investors		
	High	*Low*	*Close*	*High*	*Low*	*Close*
1988: Quarter Ended:						
March 31	$15.75	$ 8.625	$ 9.375	$22.00	$10.00	$17.00
June 30	13.25	9.25	11.75	28.125	15.75	24.50
September 30	13.125	9.25	11.875	32.75	24.625	31.00
December 31	15.00	11.00	13.125	37.75	29.625	32.50
1989: Quarter ended:						
March 31	14.625	7.75	9.00	35.00	27.125	30.125
June 30	10.25	6.50	6.75	30.50	19.50	21.00
September 30	7.625	5.25	6.00	22.25	14.00	14.25
December 31	8.325	5.325	5.875	16.50	9.50	10.25
1990: Period ended:						
March 18	7.75	5.25	6.00	12.625	9.25	10.125

EXHIBIT 2 **Bishay Industries, Inc. and Subsidiaries—Selected Excerpts from 1989 Annual Report (Eight-Year Financial Summary)**

Fiscal Year-End October 31	1989	1988	1987	1986	1985	1984	1983	1982
Income:								
Net sales	$12,277	$24,467	$33,052	$31,085	$27,964	$28,065	$23,214	$20,478
Earnings (loss) before interest and taxes	(2,596)	(7,508)	767	2,309	150	2,488	744	133
Interest expense	897	637	415	398	411	429	328	114
Net earnings (loss)	(3,445)	(7,605)	192	1,011	(136)	1,654	416	19
Retained earnings (deficit)	(9,131)	(5,685)	1,920	2,472	2,002	2,125	551	135
Earnings (loss) per share	($1.23)	($3.85)	($0.10)	$0.52	($0.07)	$0.85	$0.21	$.01
Financial Position:								
Current assets	$8,694	$11,074	$17,677	$14,163	$13,960	$12,423	$10,387	$10,185
Current liabilities	4,515	10,192	9,135	4,779	5,906	9,307	6,547	6,881
Working capital	4,179	882	8,542	9,384	8,054	3,116	3,840	3,304
Plant and equipment, net	2,635	2,927	2,692	2,125	2,054	2,050	2,114	2,434
Total assets	16,291	18,522	22,162	17,383	17,274	15,714	13,028	13,295
Long-term debt	9,365	5,949	6,066	5,839	6,123	1,193	1,258	1,486
Stockholders' equity	2,355	2,296	6,961	6,765	5,245	5,214	5,223	4,927
Common shares outstanding at year-end	3,602,791	2,347,791	1,962,795	1,962,257	1,962,257	1,942,787	1,942,787	1,951,440

Exhibit 2   (continued)

Dear Shareholder:

The fiscal year ended October 31, 1989, was one of consolidation of company facilities and operations, reassessment and repositioning of corporate sales and marketing strategy, as well as recruitment of a new management team at Bishay Industries. As noted in the previous annual report, A. Sam Git was elected chief executive officer (and subsequently board chairman) of Bishay on January 30, 1989. He immediately instituted a twofold program to strengthen the company's weakened financial position, namely availing the company quickly of every possible economy that could prudently be employed with no injury to the future and recasting the company's financial structure. Both of these goals were met.

These planned economies were instrumental in reducing our operating losses by approximately $4.6 million from those sustained in the preceding fiscal year. The refinancing and recasting, completed July 29, was in the amount of $8,780,000 and resulted in the infusion of approximately $2.5 million of new working capital after repaying short-term obligations, including satisfaction of bank loans. Additionally, Bishay was relieved of making amortization payments during the next three and one-half years on its present senior and subordinated notes.

In order to maximize the impact of the new financial structure and develop meaningful programs as a foundation for profitable future growth, the board directed the recruitment of a president with a proven record of accomplishment in the consumer package goods industry, preferably in cosmetics. On July 14, I was elected to that position.

At this time, there were certain new priorities which had to be established and certain goals which had to be met. The most important priority concerned the development of new relationships with our suppliers; the most urgent goal was reestablishment of our position at the store level. The company was successful in accomplishing both, aided by creditor confidence in new management and the knowledge that Bishay products enjoyed consumer acceptance.

Concurrently, the company decided to increase significantly the depth of its top management team, placing special emphasis on sales and marketing experience as well as research and development talent, since these are the heart of our business. We have also strengthened the company's financial and operational divisions, emphasizing tighter controls and improved decision-making procedures. Great efforts are still being made to reduce costs throughout the company while maintaining or upgrading the efficiency of operations and rendering the best possible service to Bishay's customers.

We have recruited a group of new executives and special consultants representing a century of experience in the cosmetic and package goods field. These people are young, aggressive, and ambitious, and they bring to our company the expertise required to move us forward. All members of the new Bishay team, including the president, have held important positions in well-known companies. They have joined us because they are dedicated to and confident of the revival of a new and exciting Bishay, whose future will be secured by orderly growth and profit-oriented operations.

Within several months, a nationwide network for sales and distribution of our products, sorely lacking in recent years, was developed. This network is being subjected daily to reassessment and improvement. Our products are steadily gaining greater consumer acceptance. Of equal importance is the growing confidence shown in Bishay Industries itself by retail buyers and distributors of cosmetics and toiletries in every branch of the trade. The company is pressing vigorously toward its goals through a policy of service reliability, resourceful marketing methods, active research and development of new products, and new, exciting packaging designs for both existing and emerging product lines.

The company is now determined to bring to the trade and consumer the highest quality and fashion in cosmetics. Our current product lines, plagued by poor shelf space in the past few years, are being actively extended and completed. Our Hand Soft products, now enjoying wide acclaim, will shortly become a complete line in every sense of the word and hopefully will appear on the shelves of every major outlet in America.

Exhibit 2   (continued)

New White toothpaste has just been selected for use by the 1992 Canadian Olympic team and a new package and marketing program was designed to capitalize fully on this opportunity. Our SD natural hair coloring restorer for men will receive new advertising support and serve as the foundation of a complete new SD family of hair products and related cosmetics and toiletries for men. Our private label hand care collection is being expanded rapidly into a sophisticated and complete line which we plan to launch with a label of its own, to include many items in the nail enamel, nail care, and treatment lines. Moreover, Bishay has ready for marketing or on the drawing boards a large number of new products or similar type-products for which we envision early and successful market penetration.

We think the progress manifested this year will benefit our shareholders, whose personal endorsements and continued purchases of our products have been of great help.

Finally, on a financial note, I am pleased to report our working capital at the end of the year was $4.2 million, an increase of $3.3 million over last year's figure.

Eхнівт 2 (continued) **Bishay Industries, Inc., and Subsidiaries—Consolidated Balance Sheets, October 31, 1989, 1988, 1987, 1986, and 1985**

	1989	1988	1987	1986	1985
Assets					
Current assets:					
Cash	$ 1,295,274	$ 153,826	$ 1,062,257	$ 1,300,974	$ 1,102,712
Short-term investments, at cost (approximates market)	600,000	—	—	500,000	—
Receivables, less allowances for doubtful accounts, sales return, and discounts, 1989, $825,000; 1988, $721,000; 1987, $523,000; 1986, $278,000; 1985, $298,000 (Note 2)	2,573,449	3,180,357	6,475,439	6,036,844	5,964,774
Income taxes refundable	—	771,628	—	—	796,030
Inventories (Notes 2 and 3)	4,023,158	6,584,697	9,522,598	6,033,012	5,761,635
Prepaid expenses	202,139	383,111	616,410	291,814	334,734
Total current assets	$ 8,694,020	$11,073,619	$17,676,704	$14,162,644	$13,959,885
Investment in common stock of Realty Investors Corporation (Notes 2 and 4)	3,050,000	3,050,000	—	—	—
Plant and equipment, at cost (Notes 2 and 5)	3,971,096	4,336,751	3,798,347	3,053,364	2,832,924
Less: Accumulated depreciation	1,336,220	1,409,909	1,106,119	927,973	778,761
Plant and equipment, net	$ 2,634,876	$ 2,926,842	$ 2,692,228	$ 2,125,391	$ 2,054,163
Investment in excess of net assets of purchased subsidiary, at amortized cost (Note 1)	416,529	357,250	366,410	—	—
Trade names and other intangibles, at amortized cost (Notes 2 and 6)	449,875	570,257	776,504	418,335	453,874
Unamortized debt discount and issue expenses (Note 8)	667,023	396,220	428,702	461,184	182,792
Deferred charges and other assets (Notes 1 and 11)	378,824	147,500	221,585	215,555	623,217
Total assets	$16,291,147	$18,521,688	$22,162,133	$17,383,109	$17,273,931

Exhibit 2 (continued)

	1989	1988	1987	1986	1985
Liabilities					
Current liabilities:					
Current maturities of long-term liabilities	$ 115,043	$ 511,045	$ 296,188	$ 283,962	$ 69,680
Trade payables:					
Notes	1,257,352	366,329	—	—	—
Accounts	2,131,352	4,967,547	5,564,120	3,182,102	3,234,282
Loans payable, principally to banks	97,288	3,037,817	1,981,573	—	1,750,000
Accrued liabilities	914,128	1,308,974	1,292,884	1,312,891	851,755
Total current liabilities	$ 4,515,163	$10,191,712	$ 9,134,765	$ 4,778,955	$ 5,905,717
Long-term liabilities, less current maturities:					
Notes payable to institutional lenders (Note 8):					
Senior notes, 7%	5,782,500	2,540,000	2,770,000	3,000,000	3,000,000
Subordinated notes, 6-1/2%	2,000,000	1,867,000	2,000,000	2,000,000	2,000,000
Mortgages payable, 6% to 6-3/4%	1,105,355	1,163,781	1,021,236	839,231	1,123,194
Other notes payable, noninterest bearing and at rates 5% to 9%	477,621	377,863	274,967	—	—
Total long-term liabilities	$ 9,365,476	$ 5,948,644	$ 6,066,203	$ 5,839,231	$ 6,123,194
Deferred royalty income	55,773	85,329	—	—	—
Commitments and contingent liabilities (Note 9)					
Stockholders' Equity					
Preferred stock, par value $1 per share, authorized 200,000 shares; none issued					
Common stock, par value $.10 per share, authorized 5 million shares; issued, 1989, 3,616,201 shares; 1988, 2,361,201 shares; 1987, 1,976,205 shares; 1986, 1,900,196 shares; 1985, 1,827,627 shares (Notes 4, 8, 10 and 11)	361,621	236,121	197,621	190,020	182,763
Additional paid-in capital	11,184,206	7,805,723	4,904,007	4,162,966	3,120,314
Retained earnings (deficit)	(9,130,747)	(5,685,496)	1,919,882	2,472,282	2,002,288
	$ 2,415,080	$ 2,356,348	$ 7,021,510	$ 6,825,268	$ 5,305,365
Less: Treasury common stock, 13,410 shares at cost	60,345	60,345	60,345	60,345	60,345
Total stockholders' equity	$ 2,354,735	$ 2,296,003	$ 6,961,165	$ 6,764,923	$ 5,245,020
Total liabilities and stockholders' equity	$16,291,147	$18,521,688	$22,162,133	$17,383,109	$17,273,931

See notes to financial statements.

683

EXHIBIT 2 (continued) Bishay Industries, Inc., and Subsidiaries—Consolidated Statement of Operations for the Years Ended October 31, 1989, 1988, 1987, 1986, and 1985

	1989	1988	1987	1986	1985
Sales	$ 13,939,126	$ 28,770,764	$ 36,629,184	not reported	not reported
Less: Sales returns and allowances	1,661,843	4,304,121	3,576,778	not reported	not reported
Net sales	$ 12,277,283	$ 24,466,643	$ 33,052,406	$ 31,084,567	$ 27,963,108
Cost of goods sold	8,016,862	17,507,289	17,908,964	16,632,955	15,139,340
Gross margin	$ 4,260,421	$ 6,959,354	$ 15,143,442	$ 14,451,612	$ 12,823,768
Advertising, promotion, selling, and administrative expenses	6,700,111	13,882,973	13,889,595	11,712,896	12,244,121
	$ (2,439,690)	$ (6,923,619)	$ 1,253,847	$ 2,738,716	$ 579,647
Other deductions (income):					
Discounts allowed	226,219	414,901	540,966	548,779	490,020
Interest expense	896,678	637,486	415,175	398,005	410,832
Other, net	(69,730)	168,887	(54,255)	(118,701)	(60,416)
	$ 1,053,167	$ 1,221,274	$ 901,886	$ 828,083	$ 840,436
Earnings (loss) before provision for federal income taxes	(3,492,857)	(8,144,893)	351,961	1,910,633	(260,789)
Provision (credit) for federal income taxes:					
Provision for taxes	—	—	160,000	900,000	—
Prior years' provision no longer required	(47,606)	—	—	—	—
Tax credit arising from carryback of tax losses	—	(771,628)	—	—	(125,179)
Deferred tax benefits written off	—	232,113	—	—	—
Net income (loss)	$ (3,445,251)	$ (7,605,378)	$ 191,961	$ 1,010,633	$ (135,610)
Net earnings (loss) per share	$ (1.23)	$ (3.85)	$ 0.10	$ 0.52	$ (0.07)

See notes to financial statements.

EXHIBIT 2 (continued) Bishay Industries, Inc., and Subsidiaries—Consolidated Statement or Stockholders' Equity for the Years Ended October 31, 1989, 1988, 1987, 1986, and 1985

	Common Stock	Additional Paid-in Capital	Retained Earnings (Deficit)	Treasury Common Stock	Total Stockholders' Equity
Balance, November 1, 1985	$182,763	$ 3,120,314	$ 2,002,288	$(60,345)	$5,245,020
Net earnings			1,010,633		1,010,633
4% stock dividend paid in January 1987 (72,569 shares)	7,257	533,382	(540,639)		
Amount attributable to warrants to purchase common stock issued to holders of long-term notes		320,000			320,000
Tax benefit resulting from abandonment of trade names written off prior to merger entered into to form the company		206,630			206,630
Other		(17,360)			(17,360)
Balance, November 1, 1986	$190,020	$ 4,162,966	$ 2,472,282	$(60,345)	$6,764,923
Net earnings			191,961		191,961
4% stock dividend paid in January 1988 (75,493 shares)	7,549	736,812	(744,361)		
Exercise of stock options (520 shares)	52	4,229			4,281
Balance, November 1, 1987	$197,621	$ 4,904,007	$ 1,919,882	$(60,345)	$6,961,165
Net loss			(7,605,378)		(7,605,378)
Issuance of 385,000 shares in exchange for 125,000 shares of common stock of Realty Investors Corporation (Note 4)	38,500	3,011,500			3,050,000
Deferred federal income tax benefits written off		(109,784)			(109,784)
Balance, October 31, 1988	$236,121	$ 7,805,723	$(5,685,496)	$(60,345)	$2,296,003
Net loss			(3,445,251)		(3,445,251)
Issuance of 125,000 shares as additional consideration in exchange for 125,000 shares of common stock of Realty Investors Corporation and applicable costs (Note 4)	12,500	(22,680)			(10,180)
Net proceeds from sale in July 1989 of 1 million shares (45,000 additional shares issued as compensation for brokerage services)	104,500	2,989,358			3,093,858
Issuance of 35,000 shares in connection with an agreement covering the acquisition of a purchased subsidiary (Note 1)	3,500	99,310			102,810
Portion of proceeds from sale of senior notes allocated to warrants issued (Note 8)		167,495			167,495
Discounted market value of 50,000 shares sold under Restricted Stock Purchase Plan (Note 11)	5,000	145,000			150,000
Balance, October 31, 1989	$361,621	$11,184,206	$(9,130,747)	$(60,345)	$2,354,735

See Notes to financial statements.

EXHIBIT 2   **(continued) Bishay Industries, Inc. and Subsidiaries—Consolidated Statement of Changes in Financial Position for the Year Ended October 31, 1989**[a]

Working capital at beginning of year		*$881,907*
Source of funds:		
Net proceeds from sale of common stock	$3,098,858	
Net proceeds from issuance of senior notes	2,870,197	
Issuance of long-term notes in payment of trade accounts payable	405,621	
Deferment of amortization of senior and subordinated notes	363,000	
Other, net.	35,049	
Total funds provided		6,772,725
		$7,654,632
Application of funds:		
Net loss	$3,445,251	
Depreciation. $185,950		
Amortization of intangible assets and deferred items 227,238	(413,188)	
	$3,032,063	
Portion of long-term liabilities transferred to current liabilities	98,116	
Purchase of trade names, trademarks, and contract rights	258,382	
Deferred product development costs incurred	87,214	
Total funds applied		3,475,775
Working capital at end of year		$4,178,857

---

[a]Note: In 1989 Canadian companies published a changes in financial position statement rather than a cash flow statement as required by U.S. GAAP.

EXHIBIT 2   (continued) Bishay Industries, Inc. and Subsidiaries Notes to
Consolidated Financial Statements

1. Principles of Consolidation and Changes in Accounting Policy

The consolidated financial statements include the accounts of the company and its active subsidiaries, all of which are wholly owned. All significant intercompany transactions have been eliminated.

Under terms of an amendment to an agreement covering the acquisition in May 1987 of a subsidiary, Bishay Imports, the company issued in August 1989, 35,000 shares of its common stock for release from all obligations under such acquisition agreement. The discounted market value of the shares issued was added to the cost of investment in excess of net assets of this purchased subsidiary. As of November 1, 1988, the company adopted the policy of amortizing such excess by ratable charges to income over a period of 10 years. Previously, this account was amortized over a 40-year period. The effect of this change was to increase the net loss for 1989 by $46,300 ($.02 per share).

Also, as of November 1, 1988, the company adopted the policy of deferring certain costs incurred in connection with the development of its products. Previously, such costs had been charged to income as incurred. Deferred product development costs are being amortized over three years. As a result of this change, the net loss for 1989 was decreased by $72,700 ($.03 per share). . . .

2. Assets Pledged as Collateral

Assets pledged as collateral for the senior notes comprise all receivables and inventories (and the proceeds from these items), 125,000 shares of common stock of Realty Investors Corporation and all trademarks and trade names of the company and related rights. Land and buildings with a cost of $2,253,000 are pledged as collateral for mortgages payable.

3. Inventories

Inventories which are stated at the lower of cost (first-in, first-out) or market comprise the following:

	1989	1988	1987	1986	1985
Finished goods and work in process ..	$2,337,222	$4,974,351	$6,218,868	$3,897,929	$3,539
Raw and component materials	3,435,936	3,610,346	3,303,730	2,135,083	2,222
	$5,773,158	$8,584,697	$9,522,598	$6,033,012	$5,761
Less: Valuation reserve............	1,750,000	2,000,000	Not separately disclosed		
Inventories, net	$4,023,158	$6,584,697	$9,522,598	$6,033,012	$5,761

4. Exchange of Stock and Stock Option

Under the terms of an agreement dated October 31, 1988 (amended in March 1989) with Realty Investors Corporation of New York, the company exchanged 500,000 shares of its common stock (375,000 shares in 1988 and 125,000 shares in 1989) for 125,000 shares of Realty Investors common stock. An additional 10,000 shares of the company's common stock were issued in 1988 in payment of the related brokerage fee. The 125,000 shares of Realty Investors stock were recorded as an investment at the aggregate market price of such shares at the time of the exchange negotiations, less a 20% discount and estimated registration costs, as such shares were registered at no cost to the company. The discounted market value of the shares issued for the brokerage fee was recorded as an additional cost of the investment in Realty Investors stock. Under the terms (as amended) of the exchange agreement, a 10-year option was granted to Realty Investors to purchase 200,000 shares of the company's common stock at $14 per share.

Exhibit 2   (continued)

The Realty Investors common stock is pledged with the institutional lenders as collateral for long-term notes payable (see Note 8). The lenders may at their election, with certain restrictions, sell this stock and apply the proceeds to the payment of the notes. Based on the per-share market price of Realty Investors common stock on March 6, 1990, the indicated market value of the company's investment in such stock amounted to approximately $1 million. At October 31, 1989, such stock investment is shown at its original recorded amount since the company considers the decline in the market value of these shares, which it acquired as a long-term investment, to be temporary and neither the company nor, absent special circumstances, the lenders, have any present intention to sell such stock. No provision for any contingent loss which may be sustained in connection with this investment has been made in the accompanying financial statements.

5. Plant and Equipment and Depreciation Policy

Plant and equipment comprise the following:

	1989	*1988*	*1987*	*1986*	*1985*
Land	$ 470,125	$ 470,125	$ 359,455	$ 359,455	$ 359,455
Buildings, equipment, and improvements	1,783,033	1,782,610	1,551,605		
Machinery and equipment . . .	1,134,521	1,221,032	1,010,605	2,693,909	2,473,469
Office furniture, fixtures, and equipment	508,254	605,705	599,828		
Leasehold improvements	75,163	257,279	276,854		
	$3,971,096	$4,336,751	$3,798,347	$3,053,364	$2,832,924

The provision for depreciation, determined by the straight-line method, amounted to approximately $186,000, $230,000, $182,000, $150,000, and $137,000 for 1989, 1988, 1987, 1986, and 1985, respectively. In addition, provision was made in 1988 for approximately $110,000 estimated obsolescence applicable to equipment and leasehold improvements at four beauty salons which were disposed of during 1989.

6. Trade Names and Amortization Policy

The costs of certain trade names and contract rights are being amortized by the straight-line method over their estimated useful lives of 5 to 40 years. Provision for amortization amounted to approximately $69,000, $98,800, $36,400, $40,000, and $30,000 for 1989, 1988, 1987, 1986, and 1985 respectively. (See Note 14.)

7. Income Taxes

At October 31, 1989, unused carryforward losses approximating $7,430,000 (which excludes a $1,750,000 inventory valuation reserve) and $392,000 were available to reduce possible future Canadian and U.S. taxable income, respectively. The losses expire $3,960,000 in 1993 and $3,470,000 in 1994. The U.S. losses expire $233,000 in 1993 and $159,000 in 1994.

In 1988, $232,000 of deferred tax benefits arising from allowances for sales returns and discounts were charged to income since realization was not assured.

8. Notes Payable to Institutional Lenders

On July 29, 1989, the company borrowed $3,012,500 by issuance of additional principal amount of senior notes and warrants to purchase shares of common stock. In addition, the interest rate of the then outstanding senior notes was increased and the repayment terms and covenants of such senior notes and the subordinated notes were revised. At October 31, 1989, such notes payable to

---

EXHIBIT 2   (continued)

---

institutional lenders aggregated $7,782,500. The notes are payable in aggregate annual installments as follows:

1990	$ —
1991	—
1992	—
1993	908,500
1994	775,500
1995	775,500
1996	775,500
1997	775,500
1998	775,500
1999	775,500
2000	775,500
2001	775,500
2002	133,000
2003	537,000
	$7,782,500

The terms of the notes require maintenance at all times of consolidated net working capital of not less than $5 million, consolidated net worth (as defined) of $3 million, and consolidated net worth (as defined) plus subordinated debt of $5 million. Current indebtedness for loans from banks or commercial factors must not exceed $2 million and indebtedness for loans from others must not exceed $1.5 million at any time. Restrictions are also placed on cash dividends and the purchase or redemption of stock is limited to 25% of consolidated net earnings subsequent to October 31, 1989.

On March 17, 1990, the institutional lenders and the company entered into an agreement which amended the notes and established the following requirements: (1) Sale by the company to Realty Investors Corporation (or others) of securities (junior subordinated debt, preferred stock, or common stock) for not less than $1 million by August 31, 1990, and (2) minimum consolidated net working capital of $3.5 million, minimum net worth (as defined) of $1.5 million, and minimum net worth (as defined) plus subordinated debt of $3.5 million until the date of the aforementioned sale of securities or by August 31, 1990, whichever first occurs. Thereafter, each of the foregoing requirements are in-

creased by $1 million to November 1, 1990, whereupon the former requirements in effect at October 31, 1989, become applicable. Net worth (as defined) is to include the junior subordinated debt which may be outstanding.

The institutional lenders have unconditionally and irrevocably waived the working capital and net worth conditions of default, which conditions existed as of October 31, 1989 and to March 17, 1990. At October 31, 1989, net working capital amounted to $4,179,000, net worth (as defined) was $2,193,000, and net worth (as defined) plus subordinated debt aggregated $4,193,000. The lenders had previously waived their right to declare the principal amount of notes to be due and payable with respect to the conditions of default which existed under terms of the original notes which were replaced or amended in July 1989.

Warrants to purchase 891,429 shares of common stock were outstanding at October 31, 1989. The warrants were issued to the institutional lenders in connection with the issuance of the long-term notes and are exercisable in respect to (a) 800,000 shares to $4 per share to June 1, 1984, and at $5 per share thereafter to June 1, 1989, and (b) 91,429 shares at $10.50 per share at any time up to May 15, 1995. The portion of the proceeds of the notes attributable to the warrants was treated as debt discount and is being amortized in equal installments over the term of the notes.

9. Commitments and Contingencies

The company and its subsidiaries are obligated as lessees under various leases for operating and warehouse facilities and equipment. Aggregate rentals under all leases amounted to approximately $461,000 for 1989 and $642,000 for 1988. With respect to property leases expiring more than three years after October 31, 1989, rentals aggregate approximately $60,000 on an annual basis and $530,000 over the lives of such long-term leases.

Under the terms of a license agreement, the company is obligated to pay minimum royalties of $50,000 annually for a period of 10 years beginning with November 1, 1989, for the manufacture of licensed products.

A claim has been asserted against the company for advertising services and costs which the

Exhibit 2   (continued)

claimant alleges were incurred on behalf of the company. Management is of the opinion that the company has a meritorious defense to this claim. The company believes that the disposition of this matter will not have a material effect on consolidated financial position and no provision has been made with respect to such contingent liability.

10. Stock Options

At October 31, 1989, options to purchase shares of common stock were outstanding under Employee Stock Option Plans. The options were granted at either 95% or 100% of the market price on the date of grant. The options become exercisable in installments during the three years following the date of grant and generally expire five years after grant. During 1989, options were granted to 33,500 shares at market prices ranging from $5.63 to $12.94 per share, and options for 56,626 shares were canceled or terminated. No options were exercised during the year. At October 31, 1989, there were 29,556 shares under option at prices ranging from $5.63 to $15.75 per share (of which 4,181 shares were exercisable) and 27,768 shares were reserved for future grants.

See Note 4 for information with respect to a stock option for 200,000 shares granted to Realty Investors Corporation. Options to purchase 32,448 shares at $5.43 per share which were outstanding at October 31, 1988, under 1984 agreements with former officers, terminated in February 1989.

11. Restricted Stock Purchase Plan

In June 1989, the stockholders approved a Restricted Stock Purchase Plan under which a total of 150,000 shares of common stock may be offered, until June 30, 1989, to key employees, officers, and directors of the company and its subsidiaries. The prices at which shares may be sold under the plan may not be less than the par value of the shares as determined over the five trading days preceding the offer. Restrictions as to the sale or disposition of shares sold under the plan lapse, in general, over a period of four years following the date of sale.

In August 1989, 50,000 shares were sold under this plan to an officer at par value. The excess ($145,000) of the discounted market value at the date of the sale over the sale price has been recorded as deferred compensation and is being charged ratably to income over the period from the date of the sale to the dates on which the restrictions lapse.

12. Retirement Plan

The company has a noncontributory, trusteed retirement plan for eligible salaried employees. The plan provides for annual retirement benefits at normal retirement age 65 based on average annual compensation in excess of certain social security coverage for years of credited service and also provides for the payment of death benefits. The provision for pension costs charged to operations, which have not been funded, amounted to approximately $75,000, $80,200, $67,200, $56,500, and $30,200 for 1989, 1988, 1987, 1986, and 1985, respectively. At October 31, 1989, the unfunded reserve liability was estimated to be $179,000. The portion applicable to past service costs is being amortized over a 20-year period.

13. Per-Share Data

Net earnings (loss) per share was computed using the weighted average number of shares outstanding during each year (1989, 2,804,406 shares; 1988, 1,976,205 shares; 1987, 1,962,387 shares; 1986, 1,962,257 shares; 1985, 1,952,522 shares). Outstanding warrants and stock options to purchase common stock have not been considered in computing net earnings (loss) per share since no dilution would result from their exercise.

14. Subsequent Events

On November 3, 1989, the company acquired at a cost of $500,000 an option from a wholly owned subsidiary of Realty Investors Corporation to purchase for $1 million all of the stock of its subsidiary. The company elected not to exercise this option and the $500,000 was returned to the company during February 1990, with interest at the rate of 12% per annum.

Subsequent to October 31, 1989, the company decided to reconvey trademarks which it originally acquired for a maximum conditional obligation of $300,000. The unpaid balance of this obligation ($266,200) will be satisfied by such reconveyance or unilateral termination. Retroactive effect has been given to such termination in the October 1989 consolidated balance sheet and accordingly, $33,800 has been charged to operations for 1989.

Questions

1. Would you recommend that Turnaround Investment Ventures buy the Bishay stock? _____ Why? _____

2. How useful was the Altman Z-Score in your decision? _____

3. Do you believe Bishay is heading for bankruptcy? _____

4. If you believe that Bishay is heading for bankruptcy, how long from March 1990 do you think it will be before the company files for bankruptcy? _____

Leases

Leases are used to finance the use of assets. The principal lessee accounting question raised by lease financing is: Are assets and liabilities created on the lessee's books by entering an agreement to lease property? From the lessor point of view, accounting for leases raises several questions: How should the lease revenues and costs be allocated to the appropriate accounting periods? What is the appropriate description and classification of leased assets and lease contracts in the balance sheet and income statement?

The ability to analyze lease accounting and lease arrangements is a critical financial analysis skill. Many of the unpleasant earnings surprises that investors experience result from companies using lease accounting that does not reflect the realities of the situation. To make a determination that the lease accounting employed is appropriate requires that statement users understand lease accounting, diligently read the details of the lease arrangement, carefully project lease-related cash flows, and penetrate the legal form of the lease arrangement to identify its substance.

Leasing Practice

A lease agreement conveys the right to use property in return for a series of specified future rental payments over a definite period.

There are a great many different leasing agreements in practice. A typical lease contract contains provisions covering the following areas:

1. The duration of the lease, which can run from a few hours to the expected economic life of the asset.

Professor David Hawkins prepared this note as the basis for class discussion.
Copyright © 1995 by the President and Fellows of Harvard College. Harvard Business School teaching note 195–156.

2. The options open, if any, to renew the lease or purchase the property at the end of the lease's term. In some cases, these renewal or purchase options can be exercised for a nominal consideration.

3. The duties of the lessor to service the leased property. The service duties may range from none to complete maintenance.

4. The restrictions, if any, on the lessee's business activities, such as paying dividends or entering new bank loans.

5. The penalties for early termination of the lease. Often, the cost of termination is the lessor's unrecovered costs plus a penalty payment.

6. The consequences of default. Usually, the lease agreement requires the lessee to pay immediately all future payments in the event of default. However, in practice this provision may be difficult to enforce since the lessor has an obligation to attempt to mitigate any losses.

7. The obligation of the lessor to provide the lessee with "quiet enjoyment" of the leased property.

There are a number of advantages and disadvantages to leasing assets. One of the advantages claimed by leasing companies is that certain lease obligations can be structured so that they do not have to be listed among a company's liabilities, whereas comparable loan obligations must be recorded. Consequently, by financing asset acquisitions with leases of this type, rather than borrowing, a company can report a better debt-to-equity ratio. Some of the other advantages cited by leasing companies include: shifting the risk of ownership, such as technological obsolescence, onto the lessor; freeing of lessee capital to finance working capital needs; possible tax advantages in certain cases that make leasing cheaper on an aftertax basis than owning and 100% financing.

Typically, the cost of a lease is slightly higher than the cost of a direct borrowing to finance acquisition of an asset. However, in some cases, because of the tax treatment of leased assets, the lessor may be willing to lease at a cost lower than the lessee's marginal borrowing rate. For example, the availability to the lessor of depreciation write-offs may make the aftertax return from leasing higher than the return from straight loans. In return for these tax advantages, the lessor may give the lessee a lease at a cost that is less than the lessee's debt cost.

In law, leases are a form of executory contracts. That is, both parties have obligations they must meet over some specified future time period.

Lease Accounting

FASB Statement No. 13 and its various amendments and interpretations deal with the accounting for leases. *FASB Statement No. 13* defines a lease as "an agreement conveying the right to use property, plant, or equipment (land and/or depreciable assets) for a stated period of time." The *Statement* covers agreements that meet this definition, even though they are not identified as leases, such as a heat supply contract for nuclear fuel, which under current accounting rules is treated as a depreciable asset.

The *Statement* does not apply to rights to explore for or to exploit natural resources, nor does it apply to licensing agreements.

FASB Statement No. 13's approach to lease accounting is based on the belief that (a) the characteristic of the leasing transaction should determine the appropriate lessee and lessor accounting and (b) accounting for a lease by both parties to the lease should be similar.

Lessee's Statements

The FASB concluded in *FASB Statement No. 13* that any lease agreement that substantially transfers all of the benefits and risks of ownership to the lessee should be accounted for as an acquisition of an asset and the incurrence of an obligation. Such leases are called "capital leases." All other leases are regarded as rentals and are called "operating leases."

Capital Leases.   *FASB Statement No. 13* requires that leases meeting any *one* of the following four criteria be accounted for by lessees as "capital leases":

1. Title is transferred to the lessee by the end of the lease term.[1]

2. The lease contains a bargain purchase option.[2]

3. The lease term is at least 75% of the leased property's estimated economic life.[3]

4. The present value of the minimum lease payments[4] is 90% or more of the fair value of the leased property[5] less any related investment tax credit retained by the lessor. (If the beginning of the lease term falls within at least 25% of the total estimated economic life of the leased property, including earlier years of use, this criterion need not be used for the purpose of classifying the lease.)

---

[1]The lease term is the fixed noncancelable term of the lease plus all periods, if any, covered by bargain renewal options but not extending beyond the date a bargain purchase option becomes exercisable. A bargain renewal option is a provision that allows the lessee, at the lessee's option, to renew the lease for a rental that at the inception of the lease is expected to be substantially less than the fair rental of the property at the date the option becomes exercisable.

[2]A bargain purchase option is a provision that allows the lessee, at the lessee's option, to acquire the leased asset for a price that at the inception of the lease is expected to be substantially less than the fair market value of the property at the date the option becomes exercisable.

[3]The estimated economic life is the estimated remaining useful life of the leased property with the purpose for which it was intended at the inception of the lease, without limitation by the term of the lease.

[4]The minimum lease payment includes: (1) the minimum rental payments over the lease term, excluding estimated executory costs, such as maintenance costs; (2) any guarantee of the residual value at the expiration of the lease terms; (3) any payment required for failure to renew or extend the lease at the expiration of the lease terms; and (4) the payment called for by a bargain purchase option. If the lease contains a bargain purchase option, only the rental payments plus the bargain purchase option would be included in the minimum payment computation.

[5]The fair value of the leased asset is the price at which the property could be sold.

ILLUSTRATION A   Lambert Diversified Products, Inc., Balance Sheet

---

	December 31, 1997	*December 31, 1996*
Assets		
Leased property under capital leases less accumulated depreciation	XXX	XXX
Liabilities		
Current:		
Obligations under capital leases	XXX	XXX
Long-term:		
Obligations under capital leases	XXX	XXX

A capital lease is recorded initially by the lessee as an asset (capital lease asset) and a liability (obligation under capital lease). The amount of the asset and liability is the present value of the rental and other minimum lease payments or the fair value of the leased property. The present value discount rate is the interest rate implicit in the lease, if the lessee knows this implicit rate and it is less than the lessee's incremental borrowing rate. If these two conditions are not met, the lessee's incremental borrowing rate should be used. The capitalized amounts are then accounted for like any other asset that is amortized and interest-bearing debt that is reduced over its term. That is, the asset is depreciated in a manner consistent with the lessee's normal depreciation policy over the lease term or, if the lease meets the first or second of the capital lease criteria listed above, over the leased asset's estimated economic life. The interest expense on the recorded liability is recognized in proportion to the remaining unpaid balance of the obligation.

Illustration A presents the balance sheet classification for capital leases required by *FASB Statement No. 13.*

As noted above, when capitalized lease obligations are recorded on the face of financial statements, an asset account, Leased Property under Capital Leases, and a liability account, Obligations under Capital Leases, are shown. Subsequently, as the leased property right is "depreciated" and the rental payments made, the two balance sheet accounts are reduced. The asset account is amortized in the same manner as owned property is depreciated. This treatment recognizes the fact that depreciation schedules reflect the characteristics of the property, not the means used to finance its acquisition. The liability account is extinguished by the principal repayment amount implicit in the rental payment. The remaining portion of the rental payment is charged to the income statement as an interest expense.

Typically, rental payments are level. Therefore, in the case of long-term leases, the liability account would be extinguished slowly at first, since the bulk of the rental payment would be interest on the unpaid balance of the obligation. Toward the end of the lease, the opposite would occur, because the unpaid balance and related interest charges would be smaller.

Operating Leases.   Leases that do not meet any of the four capital lease criteria listed above are classified as "operating leases." No related assets or liabilities are recorded at the time the lessee enters into such lease agreements, and the rentals for these leases are charged to operations. Should the rental payments be unequal amounts over the lease term, the rental cost should be recognized on the straight-line basis, unless some other systematic method that reflects the benefits derived from the leased asset is more appropriate.

Accounting Entries.   To illustrate the accounting entries by a lessee, assume that the lessee signs a 10-year lease payable in annual amounts of $1,000. The implicit pretax interest rate of the lease financing is 10%.

If the transaction is regarded as an operating lease, the lessee simply records the rental payment for the lease as a cost as the obligation to pay is satisfied or accrues. The annual cost entry is:

Dr. Equipment Rental Cost	1,000	
Cr. Cash		1,000

If the lease obligation is a capital lease, the following entries would be made to recognize an asset and a related liability at the time the lease was signed by the lessee:

Dr. Capital Lease–Equipment	6,145	
Cr. Obligation under Capital Lease		6,145

The account balances are the present value of the future lease payment obligations (in this case, $1,000 a year for 10 years discounted at 10% per year).[6]

The first rental payment would be recorded as follows:

Dr. Obligation under Capital Lease	385	
Interest Expense (10% of $6,145)	615	
Cr. Cash		1,000

An additional entry each year should be made to recognize the Capital Lease–Equipment asset's depreciation charge:

Dr. Depreciation Expense–Equipment		
(10% of $6,145)	615	
Cr. Accumulated Depreciation–Equipment		615

---

[6]The present value of a stream of payments or receipts is the amount that would have to be invested today to generate that cash flow at a given rate of interest. For example, $6,145 invested today at 10% would return $1,000 per year for 10 years to the investor. At the end of that time, the investment would be recouped and the return would be 10%. Thus, the present value of $1,000 per year for 10 years discounted at 10% is $6,145.

If the lease rental included executory costs, such as maintenance and real estate taxes paid by the lessor, these amounts would be deducted from the gross rental for the purpose of making the present value capital lease calculation. Only the net rental is capitalized. In this illustration, there are no executory costs. If executory costs are included in the lease rental, a separate accounting entry is made to reflect these costs annually as they are paid. The entry is:

Dr. Lease Executory Cost	XXX	
Cr. Cash		XXX

The Accumulated Depreciation–Equipment account is shown on the balance sheet as a contra account to the Capital Lease–Equipment account.

The following year, the interest expense would be less, since the balance of the rental obligation had been reduced by $385 during the first year. The second-year entries are:

```
Dr. Obligation under Capital Lease ............................... 424
Interest Expense (10% of $6,145 − $385) ......................... 576
   Cr. Cash ............................................              1,000
```

In subsequent years, more of the $1,000 lease payment will go toward reducing the balance of the obligation under capital leases as the annual interest on the declining balance of this account gets smaller. At the end of the lease period, the capital lease obligation liability account will be reduced to zero by the last lease payment.

Over the life of the lease, the sum of the annual depreciation and interest expenses will equal the total net lease rental payments. Thus, the total cost of a lease is the same irrespective of whether it is classified as a capital or operating lease. However, the sum of the annual lease-related interest expense and asset depreciation charges for a capital lease will be greater than the annual rental expense for an operating lease in the early years of a lease term. In the later years of the lease, the reverse is true.

Lessor's Statements

Three Types.   *FASB Statement No. 13* classifies leases from the lessor's point of view in three categories, namely: direct financing leases, sales-type leases, and operating leases. The accounting for each category is different.

Criteria.   A lease that satisfies *one* of the four lessee capital lease criteria is classified from the point of view of the lessor as being either a direct financing or a sales-type lease, provided it also meets *both* of these criteria:

1. Collectibility of the payments required from the lessee is reasonably predictable.
2. No important uncertainties surround the amount of costs yet to be incurred by the lessor under the lease.[7]

A lease meeting the two criteria listed above is classified as a sale-type lease when the fair value of the leased property at the inception of the lease is greater or less than its carrying amount on the books of the lessor. Otherwise, it is classified as a direct financing lease. Leases that do not meet these two criteria are classified as operating leases.

---

[7]Important uncertainties might include commitments by the lessor to guarantee performance of the leased property in a manner more extensive than the typical product warranty or to effectively protect the lessee from obsolescence of the leased property. However, it is not intended that the necessity of estimating executory expenses such as insurance, maintenance, and taxes to be paid by the lessor shall constitute an important uncertainty.

Sales-type leases normally arise in situations where a company uses leases as a means to market products. Direct financing leases usually result when the lessor's primary mission is to finance the acquisition of property by a lessee.

Operating Leases.   The accounting for operating leases by lessors is fairly straightforward. Revenue is recognized as each rental receipt is received or accrued. Costs related to the leased asset, such as depreciation and executory costs like maintenance, are expensed as incurred. Thus, the lease profit is the difference between the lease rentals received and the related depreciation and executory costs. Under the operating lease method, the leased asset is shown as an asset, less its accumulated depreciation. No receivable recognizing the lessee's future obligation to pay rental is recorded.

Illustration B illustrates the operating method with different depreciation schedules. The illustration assumes that equipment costing the lessor $10,000 is leased for a five-year period with 60 noncancelable monthly payments of $225 each. The unguaranteed residual value is zero. At the end of five years, the lessee has the option of renewing for one year at a time for a nominal annual rental of $100. In the illustration, it is assumed that five renewal payments are received and at the end of 10 years, the equipment is abandoned by the lessor. The total payments for the 10 years is thus $14,000, and the lessor's total gross profit is $4,000. Assuming 95% of the equipment cost is amortized during the initial term of the lease, the question is: How much of the $4,000 gross profit should be recognized each year? Columns (c) and (e) of Illustration B show how the annual gross profit (or loss) varies with the depreciation method selected.

Direct Financing Leases.   When a lease falls in the direct financing category, the lessor's net investment in the lease is recorded as an asset on the lessor's balance sheet. The net investment consists of the sum of the minimum lease payments and the unguaranteed residual value, if any, less the unearned lease income. Unearned income

---

ILLUSTRATION B   **Operating Method**

| | | Sum-of-the-Years' Digits | | Straight-Line Depreciation | |
| | *Lease Payments Received (a)* | *Depreciation Expense (b)* | *Gross Profit or Loss (c) = (a) − (b)* | *Depreciation Expense (d)* | *Gross Profit or Loss (e) = (a) − (d)* |
Year					
1	$ 2,700	$ 3,167	$ (467)	$ 1,900	$ 800
2	2,700	2,533	167	1,900	800
3	2,700	1,900	800	1,900	800
4	2,700	1,267	1,433	1,900	800
5	2,700	633	2,067	1,900	800
6	100	100	0	100	0
7	100	100	0	100	0
8	100	100	0	100	0
9	100	100	0	100	0
10	100	100	0	100	0
Total	$14,000	$10,000	$4,000	$10,000	$4,000

ILLUSTRATION C   Financing Method

Year	Months in Year[a]	Gross Profit
1	60–49	$1,251
2	48–37	975
3	36–25	700
4	24–13	425
5	12–1	149
6	0	100
7	0	100
8	0	100
9	0	100
10	0	100
Total		$4,000

[a]The sum of 60 months' digits is 1,830. During the first year, the sum of the 49th through the 60th month is 654/1,830, so 35.7% of the income is recognized during the first year.

is determined by subtracting the cost or carrying value of the leased property from the gross investment. Unearned income is amortized over the lease term so as to produce a constant periodic rate of return on the net investment.

Illustration C shows the application of this financing method to the example presented above. In **Illustration C** the deferred gross income is recognized over the initial lease period on the sum-of-the-months'-digits basis.[8] This technique approximates more refined interest calculations. The income over the renewal periods is equal to the option period payments of $100 per year.

Accounting Entries.   Using the same example as **Illustration B**, which assumes that a company purchases an asset for $10,000 and then leases it, the operating method recognizes the income as the cash is received as payments or accrued from the $2,700 annual lease rental charge. The leased asset owned by the lessor is depreciated in this case on a straight-line basis of $1,900 per year. The gross profit is the difference between these amounts.

```
Dr. Cash ...........................................  2,700
     Cr. Rental Income .......................................       2,700

Dr. Depreciation Expense ....................................  1,900
     Cr. Allowance for Depreciation ...............................       1,900
```

---

[8]Rather than actually working out what the unpaid principal amounts to each month, which would require splitting each lease payment into an interest portion and a principal repayment portion, the total amount of gross profit is simply spread over the life of the lease on a declining scale. This is a reasonable approximation of the result obtained by using a more accurate method based on compound interest, even though it does tend to recognize income slightly earlier than a true compound-interest–based method.

Based on the gross profit schedule in **Illustration C** and the aggregate lease payments and asset cost in **Illustration B**, the direct financing method recognizes at the time the lease is signed the following asset and liability accounts:

Dr. Lease Payments Receivable 14,000
    Cr. Deferred Profit on Leasing 4,000
        Cost of Leased Asset 10,000

The profit is recognized as each $2,700 payment is received:

Dr. Cash 2,700
    Cr. Lease Payments Receivable 2,700

Dr. Deferred Profit on Leasing 1,251
    Cr. Current Profit on Leasing 1,251

The amount of the last entry is the first-year sum-of-the-months'-digits figure shown in **Illustration C**.

Therefore, at the end of the first year, the receivable from leasing would be $11,300 and the remaining deferred profit $2,749 ($4,000 − 1,251). At the end of the second year, the lease receivable would be $8,600 ($11,300 − 2,700) and the deferred profit account $1,774 ($2,749 − 975).

Sales-Type Leases. As part of their regular marketing programs, a number of companies are willing to lease, rather than sell, their products to customers. In these cases, the company receives the normal sales profit margin as well as a return on the lease financing. Depending on the circumstances, the sales profit on leased assets should be recognized either at the time the lease agreement is signed or over the lease period.

According to *FASB Statement No. 13,* if a transaction qualifies as a sales-type lease, it should be accounted for by the lessor as follows. The present value of the minimum lease payments receivable from the lessee is reported as sales. The carrying amount of the leased property plus any initial direct costs, less the present value of any unguaranteed residual value, is charged to cost of sales. The difference between the sales and cost of sales amounts is the seller's gross profit. The financing aspect of the sales-type leases is then accounted for similarly to a direct financing lease.

A manufacturer using leasing as a marketing aid under the lease conditions illustrated in **Illustration B** and **C** might have the following breakdown for a $10,000 sale on a 10-year lease contract basis of a product that cost the manufacturer $8,000 to produce:

Cost........................	$ 8,000
Manufacturing profit	2,000
Selling price..................	$10,000
Deferred leasing profit	4,000
Lease payments receivable	$14,000

If the sales-type lease conditions listed above were met, the $2,000 profit from manufacturing would be recognized immediately, and the financing profit from leasing the equipment would be recognized over the life of the lease.

Under the *direct financing method* to calculate the periodic income, the accounting entries would be:

1. Immediate (to recognized manufacturing profit):

Dr. Lease Payments Receivable	14,000	
Cr. Sales		10,000
Deferred Profit on Leasing		4,000
Dr. Cost of Goods Sold	8,000	
Cr. Inventory		8,000

2. As the first payment is received or accrued (to recognize leasing revenue using the sum-of-the-years'-digits method):

Dr. Cash	2,700	
Cr. Lease Payments Receivable		2,700
Dr. Deferred Profit on Leasing	1,251	
Cr. Current Profit		1,251

The subsequent leasing profit entries would follow the schedule shown in **Illustration C**. If there is substantial risk in the lease, recognition under the *operating method* would be required. The accounting entries would be the same as for **Illustration B**, except the depreciation expense would be based on the manufacturer's cost of $8,000, not the $10,000 basis used in **Illustration B**.

Initial direct costs. Leasing costs such as commissions and legal fees can be directly associated with consummating particular leases. In the case of direct financing leases, these costs are accounted for as part of the investment in the direct financing lease. Initial direct costs associated with sales-type leases are included in the cost of goods sold. Initial direct costs related to operating leases are deferred and allocated over the expected lease term in proportion to the recognition of rental income.

Sale and Leaseback

The sale and leaseback is a financing device whereby the owner of a property sells it and simultaneously leases it back from the buyer. The lease portion of the transaction presents no accounting problem; it is treated like any other lease. A seller lessee accounting problem arises when there is a gain or loss on the sale of the asset, however.

FASB Statement No. 13 treats a sale and leaseback as a single transaction. It requires seller-lessees to classify leases arising from sale-and-leaseback transactions as capital or operating leases. In either case, any loss on the sale should be recognized as such at the time of the sale. Gains are deferred. The actual treatment of this deferred gain depends on the lessee's classification of the lease. If it meets any one of the criteria for a capital lease, any gain on the sale of the leaseback property must be deferred and amortized over the lease term in proportion to the amortization of the capital lease asset. The deferred gain is presented on the balance sheet as a deduction from the capital lease asset. When the lease is an operating lease, any gain on the sale of the asset is amortized in proportion to the rental payments over the expected lease term.

If the lease meets the bargain purchase or asset transfer criteria for a capital lease, the purchaser-lessor should record the transaction as a purchase and a direct financing lease; otherwise, the purchaser-lessor should record the transaction as a purchase and an operating lease.

Financial Analysis

Statement users should always be wary of the possible use of lease accounting to improperly record sales or to avoid recording debt on the balance sheet. Some manufacturer-lessor companies using leasing to finance the sale of their products deliberately write the terms of their leases to ensure that sales accounting is required. This is accomplished by including what appear to be bargain renewal options in the lease agreement. In these cases, the analyst should focus on the question: Will the lessee renew? If the answer is no, or there is doubt in the analyst's mind, the analyst should restate the company's statements to reflect sales made through operating lease arrangements. Typically, the company's earnings will be significantly lower and will probably better reflect the actual situation. Similarly, in order to avoid reporting additional debt on their balance sheets, some lessees arrange with their lessors to structure the form of their lease agreements in such a way that the lease is classified as an operating lease when in substance it is a capital lease. All off-balance-sheet lease financing should be closely scrutinized to see if in fact it is in essence a form of debt.

Here are some questions statement users should ask about lease arrangements and lease accounting.

1. Does the lease accounting accurately reflect the economic and business substance of the lease?
2. What are the cash flow implications of the lease arrangement to the lessee and lessor?
3. How does the lessor's pattern of periodic income differ from the related cash inflows?
4. What is the probability that the lessee may default on its lease payments or the lessor fail to meet the lease obligations? What are the consequences of default?
5. What is the real nature of the lease-related assets and liabilities recognized and not recognized on the financial statements?
6. To what extent have lease accounting rules influenced the lease deal? How might possible lease accounting rule changes affect this type of lease arrangement?
7. What role does on- and off-balance-sheet lease financing play in the company's total capital structure, policy, and plans? Is this a prudent use of leasing?

8. Are the lessor's revenue recognition rules realistic for sales accomplished through lease financing arrangements?

9. What happens to the lease-related assets and obligations in the event of the lessee or lessor experiencing financial difficulties?

10. What is the probability that the lessee will extend the lease beyond the initial term? What impact will this have on the lessee and lessor?

11. What residual values will revert to the lessor at the end of the lease term? Are these valuable?

In most financial analyses, capital leases and many operating leases—particularly those that involve assets that are critical to the firm's operations or have long lease terms—are regarded as a form of debt. The lessee is the borrower and the lessor the creditor. As a result, lease payments are included in fixed charges—coverage ratios and lease obligations are regarded as part of the debt component of the debt-to-equity ratio. Because the lease payment includes two elements, an interest charge and a principal repayment, often only some portion, such as a third, of the total rentals is included in interest-coverage ratios. Also, since lessors have an obligation to mitigate their damages should a lessee default, some analysts exclude as much as two-thirds of the lease obligations from the debt portion of the debt-to-equity ratio calculation.

Teltronica S.A.

"The irony of life is that what one person thinks is conservative another feels is misleading," said Miguel Oriol, the chairman of Teltronica S.A., a Spanish vendor of telephone interconnect equipment. "We want to tell our financial story as it is, show Telco, our principal vendor, we are profitable, the banks we are solvent, and reflect to prospective customers we will continue to be in business. Everyone seems to believe that accounting for long-term leases on the equivalent of an operating basis is the conservative approach, but I don't think that this method accurately portrays the operations of this company and I think it deludes our present investors."

Oriol made the above comment in late July during an executive committee meeting devoted to determining the way in which the company would report its earnings for the first half of 1990. Although the selection of an accounting method for the interim report would not preclude the use of alternative methods at year-end, the executive committee felt strongly that switching methods six months from now would damage the company's credibility in the investment community.

Spanish Lease Accounting

In 1990, Spanish company law, financial reporting, and auditing requirements were in a state of flux. Following its full admission into the European Community (EC) in 1986, Spain was obligated to conform its company laws and financial reporting practices to the appropriate EC Directives. While much progress had been made in this direction with

Professor David F. Hawkins prepared this case as the basis for class discussion rather than to illustrate either effective or ineffective handling of an administrative situation. This case is based on materials prepared by Professor Dennis Frolin.
Copyright © 1993 by the President and Fellows of Harvard College. Harvard Business School case 194–010.

the adoption of the Plan General de Contabilidad (PGC: General Chart of Accounts) in 1990, the PGC rules were vague on the treatment of leased assets.[1] It was believed this action was deliberately taken in the interest of simplicity and in the expectation that the Instituto de Contabilidad y Auditoría de Cuentas (ICAC: Institute of Accounting and Auditing of Accounts) would eventually issue detailed rules. It was also believed managements would adopt appropriate lease accounting practices so as to comply with the PGC's "true and fair" financial reporting requirement. As a result, the accounting law did not distinguish between financing and operating leases.

Nonmandatory guidance provided by Asociación Española de Contabilidad y Administración (AECA), a voluntary body of a number of professional accountants and representatives from business and the academic world, suggested the following criteria for capitalization of a lease by lessees:

1. A purchase option must exist in the leasing contract at a price that, at the commencement of the contract, appears to be significantly less than the expected market value of the asset at the time the option may be exercised.
2. The duration of the contract should be equal to the economic useful life of the leased asset.

AECA has given little guidance to lessees as to how to account for a finance lease.[2]

Company Background

Teltronica was incorporated in late 1987 in anticipation of the "liberalization" of the market for phone equipment. The company began operating in 1988. It marketed business telephone systems to organizations primarily in the greater Madrid, Barcelona, and Seville metropolitan areas. Teltronica's product line included technologically advanced telephone switching equipment located on the customer's premises and connected to the national telephone company's (Telefónica de España) trunk lines, telephone instruments, and telephone-type intercom systems.

Strategy

Teltronica viewed the advanced electronic interconnect market as a classic situation in which penetration would initially occur in small- to medium-sized firms and then move to the larger companies. Accordingly, Teltronica had primarily concentrated its sales effort on smaller companies.

Teltronica was also formed with the expectation of going public as soon as possible to raise the capital necessary to offer a lease program which, according to Oriol,

---

[1]Prior to 1990, Spain did not have a body of generally accepted accounting principles. The general belief was that tax reporting rules were the only appropriate ones for public financial statement presentation purposes.

[2]*1991 International Accounting Summaries* (New York: John Wiley & Sons, 1991).

is essential for successful marketing of telephone equipment. A lease program effectively counters argument to customers that small interconnect companies will sell you the equipment and then walk away. However, lease programs require substantial capital because of the investment required in equipment and installation and the delayed return of cash in the form of rental payments spread, in the case of Teltronica leases, over three to nearly ten years.

To implement its financial strategy, Teltronica looked to the financial markets. In January 1989 the company sold 200,000 shares of common stock to the public at 10,000 Spanish pesetas (Pta) a share. These funds and the close connections the company maintained with the banking community—four of the six company officers were formerly employed in financial positions—allowed Teltronica to maintain a cash balance of nearly Pta 50,000,000. According to Oriol:

> A customer often has a vision—often implanted by a rival salesperson—that small interconnect firms are going to sell the equipment and disappear. When they see 50 million pesetas in cash on the balance sheet, the sale is half made. In 1988 and 1989 the company entered into an arrangement with a major bank to "sell" them customer leases at "LIBOR plus 2½%" with a minimum of requirements—a compensating-type cash balance amounting to 3% of the aggregate unpaid balance of these contracts that can be accessed by the bank to cover credit losses beyond a certain limit. This amounted to an effective interest rate of about 11% a year in 1990.

Teltronica's relationship with Telco, a large Scandinavian company, provided it with a strong product line and increased financial strength. The Telco plant in Madrid maintained inventories for Teltronica and Telco had agreed to guarantee a forthcoming Teltronica five-year bank loan to fund its rental program. The Telco product line was complete, ranging from small telephone systems to huge computer-controlled switching systems. Teltronica believed Telco's superior quality accounted for Telco being one of the largest telecommunications companies in the world. For its part, Telco regarded Spain as one of its major markets.

The Market

The Spanish telecom network had experienced strong expansion in recent years. Teltronica offered equipment to customers in this market for purchase or for lease. The leasing terms normally ranged from three to ten years with the provision that the customer had the right to buy the equipment at the end of the lease at its then market value.

Teltronica installed the equipment free, generally including one-year free service, and offered service on a low fixed-rate contract or a time-and-materials basis for the life of the lease. As Luis Robles, director of marketing, put it, "We are happy to use our service contract as a loss leader; installing equipment is the key to this business, and you'd be amazed how well customers respond to a guaranteed rental rate and essentially free service."[3] The reliability of the equipment is attested to by the fact that maintenance expenses ran some 2% of operating expense.

Customer choice between outright purchase and leasing had been changing (see **Exhibit 1)**. The shift toward leasing was due in part to Teltronica sales efforts and the

---

[3]Teltronica's lease payments were indexed to the general inflation rate. For the sake of simplicity this aspect of the Teltronica lease agreement is ignored in this case.

EXHIBIT 1   Mix of Equipment Placements

Year	Outright "Cash" Sale	Lease Placements Retained	Lease Placements Sold to Banks
1988	20%	—	80%
1989	30	10%	60
1990 (first half)	40	25	35
1991 (estimate)	40	40	20
1995 (estimate)	33	67	—
1997 (estimate)	25	75	—

nature of the economy, but it was also attributable to the larger systems Teltronica was selling. According to Oriol:

> It is much easier for the communications manager to get top-level approval—or to even avoid going to the top altogether—on a telephone equipment rental contract than for a capital expenditure. After all, companies have to have telephone service and they always rented it. If you ask a manager what his phone system is worth, he has a hard time deciding even a guesstimate. "We get it from Telefónica free, don't we?" is a typical response. We are flexible, however, and we will try to accommodate the customer in any way that is appropriate—cash purchase, lease funding—you name it. In fact, to survive we must be flexible because we anticipate facing an increasingly competitive market fueled by rapid advances in technology, new relaxed relationships between Telefónica and the state, a more open market, and a reenergized National Telecommunications Plan and future European Community directives encouraging more competition that will be incorporated in the Telecommunications Act.

The Economics

Teltronica's rates for telephone equipment were approximately 20% under those of the national telephone company. In spite of the flexibility in payment terms available, most customers either purchased for cash or took a lease, tending toward five years in length, that provided for a series of monthly payments with an extra one in the first month and another in the last. Thus a five-year lease would have 59 equal payments plus a double payment in the first month and an extra one at the end. Teltronica used a 16-plus percent interest rate to calculate the monthly payments which, with the two extra payments, approximated the 18% interest charged by banks to finance competitors' interconnect installations. This rate was caused both by the high current interest charges and the dropouts experienced in the interconnect business. Using interest tables, the monthly factor for five years was 0.0245. This times the cash selling price yielded the monthly payment.[4] For a system with a cash selling price of Pta 3,200,000 and a five-year lease (see **Exhibit 2**), the comparative rate would be Pta 78,400 per

---

[4]The factor is calculated as that number that equates a stream of rental payments at the end of each month for five years with the present lump-sum cash price at an interest rate of 16.34%.

Exhibit 2   Typical Contract

Cash sales price . . . . Pta 3,200,000
Cost equipment . . . .   Pta 1,500,000
Cost installation   260,000

Lease terms:
  Pta 3,200,000 × 0.0245 = Pta 78,400 per month for 5 years

Cash flow—contract effective 1/1/90. Rents are received on the first day of each month.

Year	January	February	March	...	December	Total Payments
1990	Pta 156,800	Pta 78,400	Pta 78,400	...	Pta 78,400	Pta 1,019,200
1991	78,400	78,400	78,400	...	78,400	940,800
1992	78,400	78,400	78,400	...	78,400	940,800
1993	78,400	78,400	78,400	...	78,400	940,800
1994	78,400	78,400	78,400	...	156,800	1,019,200
	Total					Pta 4,860,800

Present value of cash stream to equal cash price of Pta 3,200,000 is about 18¾%. Cost of the equipment, installation, and selling commission (Pta 320,000) is recovered in two years and two months.

---

month (0.0245 x Pta 3,200,000) versus Pta 94,000 per month for the national telephone company. The average cost of sales to Teltronica had been 55% including installation.[5] Teltronica paid a sales commission of 10% of the cash sales price. The Pta 3,200,000 system cited above, if sold for cash, would produce a direct contribution of Pta 1,120,000 calculated as follows:

Sales revenue		Pta 3,200,000
Cost of sales:		
Equipment	1,500,000	
Installation	260,000	1,760,000
Sales commission		320,000
Direct contribution		Pta 1,120,000

In 1989, Teltronica increased its sales to Pta 157,000,000 from Pta 106,100,000 in 1988. During the year, the company's owners became divided over whether or not Teltronica should go into manufacturing. The issue was resolved at a stockholder's meeting with a subsequent buyout of the former president. The year 1989 saw Teltronica with an operating loss due in part to the dissension that existed and in part to the write-off of the manufacturing project's study costs.

---

[5]The average cost of equipment was going down—45% (excluding installation fee) in 1990 and 30% estimated in a few years. This was because Teltronica was selling both new and used equipment. While Teltronica acquired very little used equipment, the company anticipated reacquiring equipment through conversions of customers to larger systems and reinstalling this equipment elsewhere at essentially zero cost.

The 1989 customer installations were mostly in the form of leases, which Teltronica turned around and "sold" at an average of 9¾% interest annually, and the provision of the 3% recourse account. These advantageous terms were due to Teltronica's solid financial position and a history of lease placements with essentially a no-default record. Teltronica recorded the cash received from the bank as sales revenue in the same way it did cash from customers. If in the **Exhibit 2** example a lease was signed and then sold to the bank, sales revenue would be recorded at Pta 3,868,500 and the direct contribution is Pta 1,788,500 as calculated below:

Sales revenue (discounted at 0.008125 per month)	Pta 3,868,500
Cost of sales—equipment	1,500,000
—installation	260,000
Sales commission	320,000
	Pta 1,788,500

The few leases not "sold" were accounted for on a monthly operating basis. In addition, customers were continually adding instruments and features to the systems they purchased or leased. Each year this business totaled approximately 10% of the installed equipment base and produced a 40% profit on sales.

The First Six Months of 1990

In the first half of 1990, Teltronica increased the number of placements and the peseta value of each over the same 1989 period. While the number sold for cash increased, Teltronica also began to increase the number of leases it held and thus to reduce the number of leases sold. In effect, Teltronica was using its own cash and its general credit to finance its sales, and this was expected to continue as Teltronica's financial structure increased its capacity to finance leases. This shift in the nature of the sales arrangement and management's prediction of its future trend—see **Exhibit 1**—called for a reconsideration of the method for recording "lease placements retained."

The Executive Committee Meeting

In preparation for the executive committee meeting, Juan Chanda, vice president of finance, projected that equipment placements, priced on a cash sales basis, would be about Pta 200 million in 1990—divided between cash sales, retained leases, and leases sold on a 40–30–30 basis. When asked what he forecasted Teltronica's profit would be, Juan Chanda replied, "that depends," an answer that required the following explanation:

There is no problem when we record a cash sale. We show the cash price as revenue, the costs of equipment, installation, and sales commission as expenses and the difference is a profit contribution—and we get the cash.

In the past, when we signed a customer to a lease, we would take it to its bank and get cash for it. Thus we have always recorded as sales revenue the cash the lease provided without having to worry about interest income. Then we deducted the equipment and commission costs and showed a profit—one higher than cash sales because of the 16% to 18% interest rate built into our leases. When we kept an occasional lease we used the U.S.-style operating method. In the past this problem just wasn't worth worrying about.

This year we are beginning to keep as many leases as we sell to the bank, and we will be keeping all of them in a few years. Thus Miguel (the chairman) wanted us to review the way we record profit on the leases we keep, since we don't immediately get much in the way of cash.

Part of the accounting problem we face is that current company law doesn't give us much in the way of guidance as to how to account for leases. The AECA's nonmandatory guidelines are not much help either. Also, personally I don't accept the current practices of most other Spanish companies. Their methodology is just plain wrong for finance leases and out of step with good practice in other countries. Since the current PGC was so heavily influenced by the French Plan Comptable Général you might think it would be useful to look to it for guidance, but French lease accounting standards are just as vague as ours.

In the end, Miguel (Oriol) believes Teltronica should account for leases in a way that best reflects its circumstances and interests. With this goal in mind, he believes Teltronica should be looking overseas to the U.S.A. practice or the International Accounting Standards Committee's pronouncements for guidance. He believes future Spanish lease accounting developments will be influenced by these standards, particularly since the EC Directives do not specify any required accounting treatment for leases.

One way we might consider is to record profit on the so-called *operating method* in which we would show only the lease payments we receive each year as revenue, write off the sales commission as an immediate expense, and depreciate the cost of equipment and installation over its useful life.

A second way is known as the *financial method*. This method treats a lease as really being a sale. With the finance method you determine the selling price by calculating the present value of the lease payments. We could make the sales revenue on a lease equal to the cash sales price by discounting the lease at the 18¾% rate we charge our customers. Then we treat all the costs as we do with a cash sale and we would show the same operating profit whether we leased or sold—and our "financial profit" would show the 18¾% interest revenue.

The third alternative is also the *financial method* but doing what we do now—discounting the lease at the 11% bank rate. With this method, the sales revenue on a leased placement is greater than on a cash sale.

If you look at the first sheet in front of you (**Exhibit 3**) you will see for our lease example the profit pattern we would report if it was a cash sale and if it was a lease under each accounting alternative.

Following Chanda's explanation of the accounting alternatives a rather heated discussion ensued:

Enrique Magnet (director of leasing): The way I look at it is that we are in two businesses: marketing and banking. We make a profit on both, and we have the market savvy and the cash to do both. I can't see why we should get one marketing profit on a sale and another one on a lease. My salespeople get the same 10%. The critical element in this business is installing our equipment. How it is financed is a secondary consideration. We check the customer's credit, and if it is OK, we will make any deal he wants in order to make a sale. If we think rental is the only way to overcome any skepticism about our equipment and us, we will rent to him and I'll write the lease to best meet the

Exhibit 3   Alternative Accounting for Leases

Cash sales price	Pta 3,200,000
Cost (including installation of Pta 260,000)	1,760,000
Sales commission	320,000

	1990	1991	1992	1993	1994	Total
Cash Sale						
Revenue	Pta 3,200,000	—	—	—	—	Pta 3,200,000
Cost of equipment	1,760,000	—	—	—	—	1,760,000
Commission	320,000	—	—	—	—	320,000
Profit before taxes	Pta 1,120,000	-0-	-0-	-0-	-0-	Pta 1,120,000
Operating Lease						
Revenue	Pta 1,019,200	Pta 940,800	Pta 940,800	Pta 940,800	Pta 1,019,200	Pta 4,860,800
Cost of equipment depreciation,						
10 years including installation	176,000	176,000	176,000	176,000	176,000	880,000
Commission	320,000	—	—	—	—	320,000
Profit before taxes	Pta 523,200	Pta 764,800	Pta 764,800	Pta 764,800	Pta 848,200	Pta 3,660,800
Financial Lease (18¾%)						
Revenue	Pta 3,200,000	—	—	—	—	Pta 3,200,000
Cost of equipment	1,760,000	—	—	—	—	1,760,000
Commission	320,000	—	—	—	—	320,000
Interest income	531,800	453,500	353,800	233,700	88,000	1,660,800
Profit before taxes	Pta 1,651,800	Pta 453,500	Pta 353,800	Pta 233,700	Pta 88,000	Pta 2,780,800
Financial Lease (11%)						
Revenue	Pta 3,763,100	—	—	—	—	Pta 3,763,100
Cost of equipment	1,760,000	—	—	—	—	1,760,000
Commission	320,000	—	—	—	—	320,000
Interest income	368,400	302,200	228,200	145,800	53,100	1,097,700
Profit before taxes	Pta 2,051,500	Pta 302,200	Pta 228,200	Pta 145,800	Pta 53,100	Pta 2,780,800

customer's objectives. To me a sale is a sale, and I say show the same profit on every transaction.

Mariano Brieva (director of operations): I don't agree, Enrique. There is something different about a lease. The customer doesn't own the equipment— we do—and it is good for 20 or more years. Further, we don't get the cash the first year so how can we take the profit? Let's use the operating method but depreciate the leases we keep over 25 years. In five years we know we are going to get back a perfectly useable, solid telephone system which you tell me, Enrique, we can lease out at at least 75% of a new one—and that could be 125% of the old price. I think our business is renting out equipment for three- to ten-year periods; let's show our profit that way—and you can't call me conservative since my method will show more total profit in five years than yours will.

Miguel Oriol (chairman): One thing, Juan, about the financial method is that you never lose sight of sales on an annual basis. With the operating method there is a guaranteed income stream, and thus people can rest on previous efforts and it takes you a while to see the slowdown. You see it right away when you present value the lease.

Juan Chanda: In a way, Miguel, our problem is to decide if we are in the equipment or the banking business. The accounting rules in the future may offer some basic guidelines to help decide, but today we have to choose— along with our auditors. Generally, we should look at the nature of our leasing activity, the terms of the lease relative to its useful life, the renewal and purchase options of the lease, the probability that these options will be exercised, and who has the risks and rewards of ownership. This last factor relates to who "really" worries about the equipment. For example, if the equipment became totally obsolete, who is stuck with it; or if a major repair was necessary, who pays the bill; or if the rates that Telefónica charges for this sort of equipment are doubled, who benefits from the rate increase?

If we want to treat these leases on a financing basis, the accounting must reflect the interest rate used to generate the sales revenue; one suggestion is that the rate normally used by the person leasing the equipment is appropriate.

Enrique Magnet: That would be the 18% we charge them.

Luis Robles (director of marketing): Oh come on, Enrique, you know the only reason we can charge 18% is that the competition charges so much and the public have been conditioned to believe that telephone rental is the only way to go. LIBOR plus a few points depending on their credit rating would be a better estimate.

I like 11%. It makes Teltronica profits look the best. We use the fact that we are a public company in our sales presentations. Customers in this industry have seen enough "red ink." Our customers are sophisticated, yet I am afraid they would not be able to perceive that Teltronica is running an efficient organization if its profits are way down as they would be under the operating method. I don't think our salespeople have the expertise necessary to explain the differing effects of accounting. Let's show our profits on the financial basis and use 11%. Isn't that the rate at which we sell our leases to the bank? Don't we want to be consistent and isn't that what our auditors keep talking about?

Mariano Brieva: I don't know what accountants talk about but I think our investors and even our customers should be sophisticated enough to realize the possible distortions that can occur in reporting on an operating basis. Don't we face a problem if we use the financing method? What happens to profits when you have a change in the mix of lease arrangements?

Juan Chanda: I have made up some projected financials under four methods for 1990. Maybe it's time for me to hand them out (**Exhibit 4**). You will notice that I kept our accounting for cash sales constant. The only difference is in the way we handle the leases. The income statements are based on the same assumptions underlying the cash-flow figures on the next page (**Exhibit 5**) and reflect the fact that 35% of the leases we will retain have come in the first six months—the rest will come in from now until December. As for our cash flows in future years, they will be increased by 1991 sales and so on. We haven't had enough unsold leases in the past to make any difference.

Personally, I believe we should adopt the operating method for *all* leases—the stock market is really lousy right now; good earnings won't help us and bad earnings won't hurt us. If we adopt the operating method, we will have built up a nice off-balance-sheet profit reserve which can help us out in future years and it hasn't cost us a thing.

Mariano Brieva: Wait a minute, Juan, I want the operating method but not on the leases we sell. We haven't any defaults on our sold leases to speak of, and in this case the one or two we have had the equipment was worth more than the balance of the contract. I say it would be a real crime to hide that money

EXHIBIT 4   Estimated Pretax Profit for 1990 (00,000 omitted)

	Operating Method		Financial Method	
	All Leases (A)	*Retained Leases* (B)	*18¾%* (C)	*11%* (D)
Revenue				
Cash sales	Pta 800	Pta 800	Pta 800	Pta 800
Retained leases	70	70	610	770
Sold leases	70	770	610	770
Total sales revenue	Pta 940	Pta 1,640	Pta 2,020	Pta 2,340
Cost of Sales				
Cash sales	Pta 440	Pta 440	Pta 440	Pta 440
Retained leases	33	33	330	330
Sold leases	33	330	330	330
Total cost of sales	Pta 506	Pta 803	Pta 1,100	Pta 1,100
Sales gross margin	Pta 434	Pta 837	Pta 920	Pta 1,240
Financial Profit				
From banks[a]	—	30	200	30
Interest income	—	—	47	25
Total gross margin	Pta 434	Pta 867	Pta 1,167	Pta 1,295
Less				
Sales commission	200	200	200	200
General and administrative expense	650	650	650	650
Net profit before taxes	Pta (416)	Pta 17	Pta 317	Pta 445

[a]The difference in present value of the leases sold to the bank calculated at Teltronica rate, 18¾% or 11%, and the bank rate, which averaged 9¾%.

Exhibit 5   Estimated Cash Flow from 1990 Equipment Placements (000,000 omitted)

Year	Cash Sales	Leases Kept	Leases Sold
1990	Pta 800	Pta 70	Pta 800
1991		150	
1992		140	
1993		135	
1994		130	
1995		120	
1996		120	
1997		120	
1998		100	
1999		80	

from profits. We are in a cash-flow business; let's record the profits when we get the money.

Enrique Magnet: Juan, the operating method is just too conservative; I like the thinking behind the numbers in column C (**Exhibit 4**). They show our profits when we earn them, when we put the equipment in, and that is the story of our business. The gross profit is due to operations, and it doesn't change with differing financial terms; the financial profit is shown separately where it should be.

Luis Robles: Well, I like the financial method too; but one thing I don't like about your proposal, Enrique, is all the financial profit it shows. I say use the prices we charge as the sales revenue and show Telco we are great equipment salespersons and not just efficient bankers. If we didn't have a price list you couldn't use the 18% but would take the rate we borrow at to produce the sales figure—that's what column D (**Exhibit 4**) shows and that is what is right.

Miguel Oriol: Juan, I think these income statements, the cash-flow streams, and the examples of what happens in each year are helping us to put the problem in the proper perspective. I don't think the operating method fairly reflects this company for its current accounting period because it doesn't show the future effects of today's transactions—the company's sales. In effect, future stockholders will be buying earnings subsidized by previous losses. That's not even conservative; that is unfair. The present stockholders are also deluded into making decisions based on a distorted picture of operations. Juan, I appreciate your strategic view; Luis, I understand your wanting to see figures that reflect sales efforts; and Enrique and Mariano, I understand your concerns for cash and for equipment placements. What we want to do is to show this business as it is. Now let's take a look at the options again and see how they match up to the way we really operate Teltronica.

Questions

1. What appears to be Teltronica's business strategy? _____

2. Which revenue recognition method should Teltronica adopt? _____

3. What business, accounting and other relevant considerations should be used in selecting this method? _____

4. How well does the method you selected meet these criteria? _____

5. How does the method you selected compare with the lessor accounting pronouncements of the FASB? _____

CASE
20-2

Security Plus, Inc.

On October 14, 1993, Security Plus, Inc., issued the following press release:

For Immediate Release

Holyoke, Mass, October 14, 1993—Security Plus, Inc. (AMEX: SPI), announced today that as a result of Electronics City's proposed plan to institute its own in-house security alarm systems, replacing in the future the service Security Plus provides, that Electronics City has indicated it does not presently plan to exercise its "bargain renewal options" under the approximately 2,500 leases in effect between the companies.

According to James W. Cutler, chairman of the board and president, "Security Plus and Electronics City are attempting to determine the best course of action for both companies. Negotiations have commenced to determine if Electronics City wishes to purchase our equipment or continue to lease it through existing contracts that expire from 1995 through 1998. Security Plus may be required to write off the effect of the three-year renewal period; however, in the event of a sale of the systems to Electronics City, the net investment in the leases would be written off against the proceeds."

Professors David F. Hawkins and Norman Bartczak of Columbia University prepared this case as the basis for class discussion rather than to illustrate either effective or ineffective handling of an administrative situation.

Mr. Cutler added, "Security Plus has its equipment in 2,500 company-owned Electronics City stores. Presently, Electronics City represents approximately 9% of Security Plus's monthly recurring billing, but amounts to only 2% to 3% of total annual revenues. This number is expected to decrease to 5% of monthly recurring billing and 1% of total annual revenues upon completion of the proposed Alarmco acquisition scheduled to close in 1993. In the meantime, we are confident that the possible loss of this business will not have a significant effect on Security Plus's future earnings."

The stock market reacted very unfavorably to Security Plus's press release. On volume of 316,200 shares, Security Plus's common stock closed at $18 per share on October 14, off $3.25 (15.3%) from its close of $21.25 on October 13. The stock continued to drift downward subsequent to the October 14 announcement, closing at a 1993 low of $13.75 a share on October 27.

On October 27, 1993, Security Plus issued the following press release containing its estimate of the economic effect of Electronics City's action:

For Immediate Release

Holyoke, Mass., October 27, 1993—Security Plus, Inc. (AMEX: SPI), announced today that due to Electronics City's intention of not renewing its three-year bargain renewal options under their alarm system leases with the Company, Security Plus has revised their earnings estimates for the year ended December 31, 1993.

According to James S. Cutler, chairman of the board and president, "If Electronics City elects to purchase the alarm systems presently in use, the unusual and nonrecurring charge may be immaterial. However, if they do not purchase the equipment, Security Plus's earnings for 1993 will be adversely effected [sic] by approximately $.30 per share. (Prior to the Electronics City action, Security Plus had been projecting earnings per share of $1.28 for all of 1993, and net income of $4.3 million on revenues of $41.0 million.) This would result in Security Plus reporting earnings of approximately $1 per share for 1993, an increase of 25% over 1992 earnings of $.80 per share.

Mr. Cutler concluded, "Our previous estimates for 1994 of $80 million in total revenues and $2 earnings per share remain unchanged."

On November 15, 1993, Security Plus issued its third-quarter report to shareholders announcing record revenues and earnings for the company. On volume of 37,600 shares, Security Plus's stock closed at $14.50 per share on November 15, up $.25 from its close on November 14.

Company Background

Security Plus, Inc. (SPI) was incorporated on December 30, 1987. SPI designs, installs, services, and monitors from a remote location electronic security systems used primarily to protect businesses against burglaries and fires. Upon receiving an alarm signal, SPI's monitoring personnel summon the appropriate police or fire department and notify the customer. SPI's systems sometimes are also used to monitor such conditions as electric power interruptions, freezer temperature suitability, water pressure adequacy, and flooding. SPI also markets closed circuit television systems, card access systems, remote environmental control systems for buildings, and medical emergency alert systems.

SPI specifies and procures, but does not manufacture, the components of its systems and has no plans to engage in such manufacturing. Some system assembling of the various components is typically conducted by SPI's installation personnel.

A substantial majority of SPI's systems are leased by commercial enterprises, typically retail establishments. The remainder are leased or have been sold, mainly to residential and governmental customers. Substantially all users of SPI's systems are required to contract for both monitoring and maintenance. SPI's security system agreements normally combine a lease of the alarm system (or a portion of the system) with an agreement for monitoring and report services. The minimum term for "sales-type" leases is typically a fixed noncancelable term of five years with three-year bargain renewal periods, while the minimum terms for SPI's "operating" leases is typically three years. In the case of commercial and other lease customers, SPI generally retains ownership of all alarm system equipment and can thereby retain certain tax benefits.

On January 29, 1992 SPI became a public company following an initial public offering of 725,000 shares.

Exhibit 1 lists the SPI stock holdings of the company's management and directors.

EXHIBIT 1   Management and Stock Ownership, Directors and Executive Officers

Name	Position	As of 12/31/92 Remuneration	At 6/30/93 Shares Owned
Donald R. Brown Age 37	Consultant[a]	$206,500	1,074,605[a]
James W. Stuart Age 39	Director and vice president– technical operations	100,000	689,065
James W. Cutler Age 31	Director, chairman of the board, and president[b]	100,000	163,830[a]
E. Davis Shay Age 39	Director and secretary, partner— Coots, Henke, & Wheeler	N/A	525
John W. Biddle Age 43	Director, president—Biddle Investment Capital Corporation	125,000[c]	5,500
Joseph Gray Age 41	Vice president–national sales	154,632[d]	N/A
James Clark Age 33	Vice president–operations	88,424	N/A
J. Jeffrey Kessler Age 29	Controller and chief accounting officer	<50,000	N/A

[a]Until October 4, 1993, Mr. Brown was chairman of the board and president. On or about October 4, 1993, Mr. Brown sold 202,868 shares to Mr. Cutler and granted Mr. Cutler an option to purchase 405,737 of Mr. Brown's shares until October 3, 1995. In addition Mr. Brown granted Mr. Cutler a proxy to vote 210,000 of Mr. Brown's shares. These transactions, along with similar transactions between Mr. Stuart and Mr. Cutler, give Mr. Cutler control over approximately 35% of SPI's common stock.

[b]Until October 4, 1993, Mr. Cutler was vice president–finance, treasurer (principal financial officer), and assistant secretary.

[c]Represents consulting fees paid to Mr. Biddle.

[d]Mr. Gray is compensated on a commission basis.

Leasing Policies

As a result of its acquisition in mid-1993 of Houston-based McCane Protection, Inc., SPI currently has a mix of approximately 50% operating leases and 50% sales-type capital leases. This represents a significant shift from SPI's previous mix of 10% operating leases and 90% capital leases. According to SPI, "this shift will continue with its pending Alarmco acquisition." However, SPI also points out that "the capitalization of leases will remain a major measure of company growth as 'capital lease sales' are reported in the financial statements. Most new customers' system leases are reported as sales with all costs reflected against the sales revenue. Therefore, sales figures are an accurate pulse that measures true growth."

Under the operating lease method of accounting the amounts billed to lessees are recorded as revenue as earned and the cost of the equipment is depreciated over 10 years. According to SPI, this will result in a steady stream of contractual revenues being reflected as "service and monitoring fees" which, based upon the present level of operating leases, will amount to approximately $8 million in the next 12 months. In 1996, SPI's leases, which were accounted for as sales-type leases in 1988 will become operating leases if they are renewed by the lessees. In each subsequent year, the sales-type capital leases entered into eight years earlier, if renewed, will also become operating leases.

SPI normally requires customers leasing systems to enter into a lease for a term of at least five years (60 months), with a "bargain renewal" option for at least one additional three-year (36-month) period. The renewal period is a bargain renewal in part because the initial rental rate for each renewal period will be at least 10% less than the rate at the expiration of the preceding term. According to SPI, it "is required to account for these long-term leases as 'sales-type leases' under the 'capital lease' method of accounting since the lease term exceeds 75% of the estimated economic life of the equipment (10 years). That method of accounting attempts to reflect the economic reality of certain leases which, in part because of the length of their term relative to the useful economic life of the equipment, more closely resemble sales than leases."

Under the sales-type capital lease method of accounting, the aggregate payments due under a long-term lease (including the bargain renewal period) are deemed to consist of a "sales price," interest on such sales price (as if the "sale" were financed by SPI), and monthly provisions for service and monitoring payments. In accordance with this method of accounting, SPI records as revenue from the "lease sale," at the inception of the lease, an amount equivalent to the "sales price" of its systems, which consists of the present value of the aggregate payments attributable to such system due over the 96 months of the lease. This is calculated by aggregating the present value of the 96 monthly installments (net of estimated costs of servicing and monitoring), each discounted at the rate implicit in the lease (which normally has approximated 2% over the prevailing prime rate as of the inception of the lease). Once the present value is recognized as revenue, the amount recorded is unaffected by any subsequent change in the prime rate. The balance of the payments under the lease contract (net of servicing and monitoring costs) not immediately recognized is recorded as unearned interest and recognized as interest income monthly over the life of the lease. For example, if the implicit rate were 13%, approximately 63% of the aggregate rentals (net of servicing and monitoring costs) would be recorded at the inception of the lease, with the remainder being recorded over the term of the lease. If the implicit rate were less than 13%, a greater portion of the aggregate net rentals would be recorded at the inception of the lease and, conversely, if the implicit rate were greater than 13%, more of the aggregate net rentals would be recorded over the term of the lease. The portion of the lease payments representing income for servicing and monitoring the system is recognized as revenue monthly over the term of the lease contract. All direct costs of the system, including cost of goods sold and selling and installation expense (but excluding financing costs), are expensed at the time of reporting the lease sale. Although SPI's long-term leases are accounted for as sales-type leases, no sale of the equipment is involved and SPI retains ownership of all systems subject to such leases, thereby also availing itself of the tax benefits and residual values related to the equipment.

The hypothetical example presented in **Exhibit 2** illustrates the impact (before indirect expenses) of a typical sales-type lease transaction at the inception of the lease,

---

EXHIBIT 2   Illustrative Example of Sales-Type Lease Transaction

Balance sheet (impact at lease inception):

Cash (installation fee)			$ 600
Total minimum lease payments receivable (96 months			
at $60 per month)		$ 5,760	
Amounts allocated to service and monitoring (96 months			
at $10 per month)		(960)	
Minimum lease payments receivable[a]		$ 4,800	
Allowance for doubtful accounts (1.25% of the total			
minimum lease payments receivable)		(72)	
Net minimum lease payments receivable		$ 4,728	
Estimated residual value of leased property[b]		100	
Unearned interest income:[c]			
Equipment portion[a]	$(1,793)		
Residual value portion[b]	(64)		
		(1,857)	
Net investment in sales-type lease			2,971
Accounts payable (direct expenses)			(1,800)
Addition to net assets before indirect expenses			$ 1,771

Income statement (impact at lease inception)

Installation fee	$ 600	
Present value of $4,800 minimum lease payments[a]	3,007	
Equipment sales lease		$ 3,607
Reduction of cost of equipment sold (present value of the		
$100 residual value of leased property)[b]		36
Provision for doubtful accounts		(72)
Income before expenses		$ 3,571
Direct expenses		1,800
Income before indirect expenses		$ 1,771

---

[a]"Minimum lease payments receivable" ($4,800) has a present value of $3,007 calculated by discounting at 13% (1.08% per month) on an "annuity due" basis (payments due at the beginning of each month). The difference between $4,800 and $3,007 is the financing cost ($1,793) of the equipment portion of the lease to the subscriber and unearned interest income to SPI.

[b]The present value, discounted at 13% annual interest (calculated monthly as above), of the $100 estimated residual value of the leased equipment is $36. The difference between $100 and $36 is also unearned interest income to SPI.

[c]"Unearned interest income" is recognized monthly to produce a constant periodic rate of return on the "net investment in the sales-type lease."

assuming a $600 installation fee, a $60 monthly lease payment of which $10 per month is allocated to the executory costs related to service and monitoring, a 96-month lease term (initial 60-month term plus 36-month bargain renewal period), a residual value of the leased property of $100, an implicit interest rate of 13% and direct expenses of $1,800. All direct costs of the system, including cost of goods sold and all selling installation expenses, but excluding financing costs, are expensed at the time of recognizing each lease sale.

SPI attempts to recover increases in financing costs, maintenance, and other expenses through periodic increases in lease charges. Although SPI is generally permitted under the terms of its leasing and service agreements to make such increases, customers have the right to cancel their agreements in lieu of accepting such increases. The installation charges that generally would be incurred by a customer in changing companies tend to discourage such cancellations, as long as SPI's service has been satisfactory. Although SPI has experienced cancellations in response to rate increase notices, to date such cancellations have been minimal. SPI currently provides an allowance for doubtful accounts of 1.25% of its lease contract receivables. In the event of a default or cancellation by a lessee, SPI writes off the remaining net investment in the lease against the allowance.

Acquisitions

According to SPI,

> Acquisitions are an integral part of SPI's growth strategy. SPI is continually evaluating possible acquisition candidates as a means of economically expanding into new market areas and increasing its business in existing markets. Acquisitions in geographic areas targeted as new regional centers expand SPI's potential customer base, facilitate its marketing efforts to new subscribers in the area, and allow SPI to service such customers more quickly and profitably than in an area where SPI has no start-up base. Following such an acquisition, SPI will typically increase the sales force. Subsequently acquisitions in the same area are also desirable, principally because they result in lower operating costs per customer due to the economies of scale inherent in greater utilization of the monitoring and servicing capability of the central station. In the future, SPI also intends to expand into areas not targeted as new regional centers through the acquisition of numerous small alarm companies located throughout the country. SPI believes that, because the protective service industry historically has been fragmented, there are numerous attractive candidates available.

Through December 31, 1992, SPI acquired certain assets and customer lists of 12 companies in the central station alarm business. Following each acquisition, SPI salesmen called upon the acquired company's customers to convert them to SPI's standard long-term lease contract. By one year after an acquisition, usually 70% to 85% of the acquired customers have executed long-term contracts.

From January 1, 1993 through November 15, 1993, SPI made the following acquisitions:

Company	Location	Date Acquired	Acquisition Price	Monthly Billings
Crime Alarm Systems	Ft. Lauderdale	March 21, 1993	$ 297,000	$ 10,000
Alarm, Inc.	Houston, Texas	May 2, 1993	3,645,000	120,000
McCane Protection	Houston, Texas	June 7, 1993	16,000,000	670,000

SPI currently plans to follow its previous practice and convert the customers of Crime Alarm Systems and Alarm to long-term contracts. However, SPI does not presently intend to convert the existing customers of McCane, or the customers obtained in future acquisitions, to long-term contracts. As was noted earlier, SPI expects that this change in practice will substantially increase its base of operating leases that generate level recurring revenues over their terms.

SPI expects to close the acquisition of Alarmco, a West Coast firm, for $21.4 million in cash in December. Alarmco has $17 million in annual revenues and pre-tax income of $5.2 million. Its 11 operating locations serve 23,000 accounts in California, Nevada, Washington, and Texas. At present, SPI expects to finance the bulk of the Alarmco purchase from the remaining funds available to it from its $30 million revolving bank credit. The acquisition of Alarmco will increase SPI's accounts to 49,000 from its present 26,000.

Exhibit 3 presents selected excerpts from SPI Third Quarter, 1993, Report to Stockholders.

Exhibit 4 presents selected excerpts from the company's 1992 annual report.

Competition

Much of the protective service industry has historically been fragmented with numerous small companies competing for customers in local areas. In addition, several major firms such as American District Telegraph (ADT) offer security systems to more than 60% of the security market located throughout the country. SPI must thus compete not only with local alarm businesses present in its markets but also with larger national companies, many of which charge less for their systems than SPI charges. However, SPI believes that its marketing efforts and the quality of its systems make it one of the predominant competitors in each of its primary market areas.

Although technological advances have not historically been a significant competitive factor, the protective alarm industry may be susceptible to changes in technology which could adversely affect SPI's competitive ability. Furthermore, none of SPI's systems is covered by patents (which is not unusual in the protective alarm industry) and the technology utilized in SPI's systems is available to competitors. Nevertheless, SPI believes that it can continue to compete favorably. Because SPI purchases all the component devices used in its systems, it believes it can upgrade its systems as new technology emerges and becomes available through existing or new vendors. Moreover, SPI's existing customers have either purchased their systems outright or, more

EXHIBIT 3   Security Plus, Inc., Selected Excerpts from Third Quarter 1993 Report to Shareholders

I am honored to have been elected chairman of the board and president of Security Plus on October 4, 1993. It gives me great pleasure to report our third-quarter results for 1993 which show record revenues and earnings.

Revenues for the three months ended September 30, 1993, were up by 84% to $10,765,068 compared to $5,855,454 for the same period in 1992. Net income increased by 73% to $1,226,671 or $.34 per share versus $710,780 or $.26 per share for the same period a year ago.

The nine-month results in 1993 also showed new record levels with revenues of $26,826,118 (up 65%) and net income of $2,954,101 (up 50%) compared to $16,293,749 and $1,973,216, respectively, for the same period in 1992. Earnings per share were $.95 for the nine months in 1993 compared to $.74 in 1992, with weighted average shares outstanding increased significantly by the 1,210,000 share offering of common stock on July 21, 1993.

Your company experienced strong retail sales growth from its Houston, Texas, market in the third quarter. We expect this trend to continue in subsequent quarters.

Negotiations with Electronics City regarding the sale of the alarm systems leased from Security Plus are continuing and are expected to conclude during the fourth quarter. Therefore, the effect of the previously announced nonrecurring charge (resulting from Electronics City's intention not to renew its bargain renewal options under its leases with Security Plus) has not been recorded in the third quarter.

The Alarmco acquisition is on schedule for an early December closing. The purchase of Alarmco represents our first entry into the California/West Coast market which is one of the three primary growth areas targeted by Security Plus, along with Texas and Florida.

As we enter into our second Five-Year Plan, the outlook has never been better for continued growth and greater profitability.

We appreciate your loyalty and continued support.

James W. Cutler
Chairman and President

	Nine-Month Period Ended September 30		Three-Month Periods Ended September 30	
	1993	*1992*	*1993*	*1992*
Revenues				
Equipment sales—lease	$16,071,766	$10,769,020	$ 5,552,450	$3,811,850
Equipment sales—direct	1,034,943	856,002	518,697	314,058
Service and monitoring fees on sales-type leases	1,781,467	1,042,562	665,976	409,077
Interest earned on sales-type leases	3,436,406	2,712,881	1,314,938	1,014,197
Monitoring fees on operating leases	3,587,515	288,575	2,152,775	154,392
Other	914,021	624,709	560,232	151,880
	$26,826,118	$16,293,749	$10,765,068	$5,855,454
Expenses				
Cost of equipment sold	$ 2,094,913	$ 2,200,075	$ 908,315	$ 756,800
Salaries and wages	6,946,166	3,692,844	2,862,160	1,434,393
Administrative and general	6,001,797	2,993,830	2,809,044	1,049,232
Provision for doubtful accounts	1,404,771	1,094,338	60,657	461,462
Taxes, other than on income	625,142	297,565	271,045	97,270
Interest	2,918,759	2,309,868	1,107,126	716,934
Depreciation	648,253	305,474	279,836	117,339
Amortization of intangible assets	934,216	539,539	286,214	191,244
	$21,574,017	$13,433,533	$ 8,584,397	$4,824,674

EXHIBIT 3   (continued)

Income before provision for income taxes . . .	$ 5,252,101	$ 2,860,216	$ 2,180,671	$1,030,780
Provision for state and federal income taxes—deferred	2,298,000	887,000	954,000	320,000
Net income	$ 2,954,101	$ 1,973,216	$ 1,226,671	$ 710,780
Earnings per share	$ .95	$ .74	$ .34	$ .26

	September 30, 1993	December 31, 1992
Assets		
Cash and temporary cash investments	$ 6,221,891	$ 5,716,571
Net investment in sales-type leases	39,212,764	26,082,236
Nonnegotiable certificate of deposit	3,200,000	4,000,000
Inventory	2,253,507	1,369,021
Property and equipment net	6,485,510	2,114,656
Purchased rights to customer lists, net	6,478,346	4,117,386
Excess of purchase price over fair value of acquired assets	10,607,480	—
Other	4,163,300	2,045,128
	$78,622,798	$45,444,998
Liabilities		
Notes payable	$12,821,478	$ 4,170,698
Convertible subordinated debentures	20,000,000	20,000,000
Notes payable—shareholders	3,200,000	4,000,000
Deferred income taxes	3,694,000	1,396,000
Other	2,667,212	1,892,315
	$42,382,690	$31,459,013
Shareholder's Equity		
Common stock, $1 par value, 15 million and 5 million shares authorized, respectively	$ 4,009,414	$ 2,798,868
Additional paid-in capital	27,104,199	9,014,723
Retained earnings	5,126,495	2,172,394
	$78,622,798	$45,444,998

Exhibit 4   Security Plus, Inc., Selected Excerpts from 1992 Annual Report

Selected Financial Data	Years Ended December 31				
	1992	*1991*	*1990*	*1989*	*1988*
Revenues:	$22,756,586	$14,671,120	$5,838,116	$2,882,746	$ 685,631
Income before provision for					
federal and state taxes	3,568,394	1,022,311	1,649,310	867,673	159,275
Net income[a]	2,172,394	1,392,311	926,310	508,673	97,275
Net income per share[a,b]	$ .80	$ .70	$ .46	$ .25	$ .05
Weighted average shares					
outstanding[b]	2,729,679	2,000,000	2,000,000	2,000,000	2,000,000
Total assets	45,444,998	25,427,255	9,777,314	3,709,176	611,061
Debt obligations	28,170,698	18,602,277	6,529,007	2,491,047	393,197
Total liabilities	31,459,013	20,711,872	7,073,242	2,654,414	485,972
Shareholders' equity	13,985,985	4,715,383	2,704,072	1,054,762	125,089

[a]A pro forma provision for federal income tax has been deducted as if the company had been a taxable corporation for the years 1989 through 1991, during which it was a Subchapter S corporation.

[b]Reflects the 2,000-for-1 stock split effected December 14, 1991.

To our shareholders:

In just five years, Security Plus ranks among the fastest growing companies in the expanding security alarm industry. From 500 customers and total assets of $100,000 in 1988, Security Plus has grown to over 12,000 customers in 48 states and Puerto Rico and total assets of $45 million at year-end 1992. For the year ended December 31, 1992, Security Plus reported a revenue increase of 55%, rising to $22.8 million from $14.7 million. Net income for the year climbed to $2.2 million, equal to $.80 per share, compared to $1.4 million, equal to $.70 per share in 1991. Per share figures include a 35% increase in common shares outstanding for . . .

Balance Sheet Strengthened

In addition to our initial public offering last year of $7.25 million, we completed a $20 million public placement of convertible debentures in November of 1992. At year-end we had negotiated a line of credit for up to $30 million with a new group of banks. We are relying on this new line of credit to add greater flexibility to our acquisition program and allow us to finance the strong increase we are expecting in the leased sales of our equipment in our major markets.

During the year, we also reduced our debt-to-equity ratio to 1.73 to 1, compared to 3.10 to 1 in 1991. At the same time, book value per share increased 118% to $5.12 compared to $2.35 a year ago.

Looking Ahead

Major goals were achieved in 1992, but management expects 1993 to be the greatest year in Security Plus's history.

We expect that our customer base will double resulting in increased revenue . . . is planning a nationwide network of working affiliates of approximately 200 independent security businesses. And, finally, we are pleased to report that the financial resources are in place to finance our planned growth for 1993.

Respectfully submitted

Donald R. Brown
President

Exhibit 4   (continued) Statement of Financial Position, December 31, 1990, 1991, 1992

	1992	*1991*	*1990*
Assets			
Cash and temporary cash investments, at cost which			
approximates market (note 4)	$ 5,716,571	$ 1,208,051	$1,045,900
Net investment in sales-type leases (note 3)........	26,082,236	14,101,116	5,591,852
Accounts receivable	677,820	963,780	465,300
Nonnegotiable certificates of deposit (note 7)	4,000,000	4,000,000	
Inventory (note 1)	1,369,021	1,083,554	374,600
Property and equipment, net (note 5)	2,114,656	1,384,554	881,530
Purchased rights to customer lists, net	4,117,386	2,294,225	1,405,700
Unamortized debt expense (note 6)	1,040,382	—	
Deferred charge, costs incurred on stock offering			
(note 9)		342,432	
Other assets	326,926	49,543	12,100
Total assets	$45,444,998	$25,427,255	$9,777,314
Liabilities			
Accounts payable—trade	$ 747,754	$ 901,727	$ 341,900
Accounts payable—other	183,136	269,536	
Accrued interest and other expenses	961,425	938,332	202,200
Notes payable (note 6)	4,170,698	14,602,277	6,529,000
Convertible subordinated debentures (note 6).......	20,000,000	—	
Notes payable—shareholders (note 7)	4,000,000	4,000,000	
Deferred income taxes	1,396,000	—	
Total liabilities	$31,459,013	$20,711,872	$7,073,242
Shareholders' Equity			
Common stock, no par value, stated value $1 per			
share, 5 million shares authorized; issued and			
outstanding—2,798,868 shares in 1992, 2 million			
shares in 1991 and 1990 (note 9)	$ 2,798,868	$ 11,160	$ 11,100
Additional paid-in capital	9,014,723	4,704,223	1,418,600
Retained earnings (note 9)	2,172,394	—	1,274,200
Total shareholders' equity....................	$13,985,985	$ 4,715,383	$2,704,072
Total liabilities and shareholders' equity	$45,444,998	$25,427,255	$9,777,314

Exhibit 4   (continued) Statement of Income, Years Ended December 31, 1990, 1991, 1992

	1992	1991	1990
Revenues			
Equipment sales—lease....................	$15,148,186	$10,311,476	$4,354,852
Equipment sales—direct	1,020,362	958,456	342,449
Service and monitoring fees	2,107,214	1,943,620	594,234
Interest earned on leases	3,571,040	1,436,573	524,311
Other, including $775,778 interest income on temporary cash investment in 1992	909,784	20,995	22,270
	$22,756,586	$14,671,120	$5,836,116
Expenses			
Cost of equipment sold	$ 2,954,977	$ 2,569,900	$ 878,199
Salaries and wages.........................	5,654,615	3,830,023	1,219,014
Administrative and general	3,941,100	2,654,000	1,067,107
Provision for doubtful accounts................	1,453,354	560,167	110,680
Taxes, other than on income	504,364	269,426	78,326
Interest	3,403,097	1,938,694	566,901
Depreciation	489,561	290,363	136,531
Amortization of purchased rights to customer lists	787,124	547,236	132,858
	$19,188,192	$12,659,809	$4,188,806
Income before provision for income taxes	$ 3,568,394	$ 2,011,311	$1,649,310
Provision for income taxes—deferred	1,396,000	—	—
Net income	$ 2,172,394	$ 2,011,311	$1,649,310
Provision for income taxes—pro forma		619,000	723,000
Pro forma net income........................		$ 1,392,311	$ 926,310
Earnings per share	$ .80	$ .70	$ .46

Notes to Financial Statements

1. Summary of Significant Accounting Policies

Security Plus, Inc. (the company) provides electronic alarm systems, including service and monitoring, to commercial and residential customers.

Sales-type leases:

Sales-type lease receivables include equipment sales, service, and monitoring and are generally due in monthly or quarterly installments over a term of five years with a bargain renewal option for an additional three years. The bargain renewal option allows the lessee the option to renew at 10% less than the rental rate in effect at the expiration of the initial lease term. The company believes there is reasonable assurance that its customers will exercise the bargain renewal option based upon the scheduled rent reduction, an industry average customer life of 10 to 13 years, and the "penalty" the customer would incur in the form of an installation fee to change to different equipment. The leases have been accounted for as sales-type leases under the provisions of *Financial Accounting Standards Board (FASB) No. 13* since the lease term exceeds 75% of the estimated economic life of the equipment (10 years).

Income recognition:

Income is recognized on equipment sales when the equipment is delivered and installed. Income from service and monitoring is recognized as income on a straight-line basis over the term of the contract. Unearned interest income on lease contracts receivable is amortized to income over the lease term so as to produce a constant periodic rate of return on the net investment in the lease.

Exhibit 4   (continued)

Operating leases:

    Rentals and monitoring fees relating to operating leases, generally related to companies acquired, are recorded as billed. Such customers are generally billed monthly.

Inventory:

    The inventory of equipment held for sale or lease and related repair parts is stated at the lower of cost (first-in, first-out method) or market.

Property and equipment:

    Property and equipment are recorded at cost. Depreciation is computed on the straight-line method over the estimated useful lives as follows:

Vehicles . . . .   3 years
Furniture and equipment and computer
   equipment . . . .   5–10 years
Purchased alarm systems . . . .   8 years

Leasehold improvements are amortized over the lease term (five years).

    The cost, less related accumulated depreciation, of purchased alarm systems under contracts converted to sales-type leases is charged to cost of equipment sold at the date of conversion. The cost of systems remaining under operating leases is depreciated on the straight-line method over the remaining estimated useful lives of the equipment.

Purchased rights to customer lists:

    The excess of cost of purchased alarm system companies over the fair value of the tangible assets acquired is ascribed to the unexpired portion of existing lease contracts and the customer list. Such costs are amortized over 96 months. The company uses the sum-of-the-years'-digits method during the initial two-year period during which many of the customers are expected to be converted to long-term sales-type leases, and the straight-line method thereafter. The accumulated amortization was $1,531,316, $744,192, and $196,956 at December 31, 1992, 1991, and 1990, respectively.

Bonus arrangements:

    The company has not established bonus or incentive compensation plans. The board of directors awarded a discretionary bonus of $50,000 in 1991.

Federal and state income taxes:

    During 1991 and 1990, the company was not subject to income taxes because of an election under Subchapter S of the Internal Revenue Code. Under Subchapter S, the shareholders consented to the inclusion of the effects of the company's operations in their own federal and state income tax returns. The provision of income taxes—pro forma is the approximate expense which would have been incurred in 1991 and 1990 assuming the company had no Subchapter S election.

    Deferred income taxes are provided on income and expenses recognized in different periods for financial reporting purposes than for income tax purposes. The deferred income tax liability results principally from the reporting of the sales-type leases as operating leases for tax purposes.

2. Acquisitions

During 1990, the company expanded its customer base through the acquisition of certain assets of two alarm system companies. In May 1990, certain assets (primarily a customer list plus inventory and equipment at Miami, Florida) were purchased from Harrey's Wholesale Hardware, Inc. for cash ($71,000) and a 6%, $200,930 note (present value of $127,612 with interest imputed at 21%). In November 1990, the assets of Alarm Corporation, doing business as Best Alarm Services Company (Best), an alarm system company located near Washington, D.C., were purchased for $1.3 million cash and a $1,136,452 note including interest at 6% (present value of $704,118, with interest imputed at 18%).

    During 1991, the company acquired certain assets of two additional alarm system companies, both of which had been operated as divisions of larger corporations. In March 1991, the company purchased the customer list and some other assets of Seaboard System, Ltd. (Seaboard), a division of Quality Drug Stores, Incorporated, located near Washington, D.C., for $300,000 in cash and a $450,000 note including interest at 6% (present value of $377,792 with interest imputed at 17.5%). The note was repaid in February 1992 from the proceeds of the public stock offering. In July 1991, the assets of the Miami Alarms Division Electronic Systems Corporation (Electronic) were purchased for $500,000 cash, a $600,000, 15% promissory note and a $575,000, 6% convertible promissory note. Electronic exercised its option following the

EXHIBIT 4   (continued)

company's public stock offering to convert one half of the principal amount of the $575,000 note into 38,766 shares of common stock and to receive the remainder in cash.

In January 1991, the company acquired certain assets and right to its customer list from P.J. Enterprises, Inc. (doing business as Bur-tell), for cash ($440,000), and a deferred payment of $110,000, including interest at 9% due in February 1993. The company is negotiating an adjustment to the final settlement of the purchase price due to termination of purchased customers. The $110,000 deferred payment is not expected to be required and therefore has not been recorded as a liability. The majority of the $440,000 has been allocated to purchased rights to customers lists with the balance allocated to installed alarm equipment. Any further adjustment in the purchase price will be added to or subtracted from purchased rights to customer lists.

In June 1992, the company acquired certain assets of Controls, Inc., a McLean, Virginia, alarm company, for approximately $400,000 in cash. The company filed suit against the seller for breach of certain terms of the acquisition contract and in March 1993 agreed to accept $25,000 as full settlement of the dispute. The adjustment will reduce the purchased rights to customer lists to which the majority of the purchase price is assigned.

On August 2, 1992, the company acquired certain assets of Security Systems, Inc., a central station alarm business in the Fort Lauderdale, Florida, area. The purchase price, which is subject to adjustment, was payable in cash ($300,000 at the closing and $200,000 on the adjustment date 14 months after the closing) and by issuing 35,102 shares of common stock having a market value of $14.25 per share. In addition, the company is obligated to pay additional cash or issue additional shares of common stock if, during the 90-day period commencing August 2, 1994, the highest average of the mean between the closing bid and asked prices of the company's common stock for any five consecutive trading days during such period is not at least $19.25 per share. The purchase price ($1,153,169) includes the common stock at the contingent price of $19.25 per share and is net of imputed interest of $22,544 on the $200,000 deferred payment.

In December 1992, the company acquired certain assets of North American Systems, Inc. (NASI), a central station alarm company in the Fort Lauderdale, Florida, area. The purchase price, which is subject to downward adjustment, was payable in cash ($430,000 at the closing and $37,000 on the adjustment date 10 months after closing). The purchase price was primarily allocated to purchased rights to customer lists.

Also in December 1992, the company acquired certain assets of Burglar Alert Systems, Inc. (BAS), a central station alarm and monitoring business in the Fort Lauderdale, Florida, area. The purchase price, which is subject to adjustment, was payable in cash ($590,000 at the closing). The purchase price was primarily allocated to purchased rights to customer lists.

The purchase price of each of the above acquisitions, discounted in certain circumstances at the prevailing interest rate at the time of acquisition to reflect the present value of the notes payable, exceeded the fair value of the tangible assets acquired as follows:

Selling Entity	Adjusted Purchase Price	Fair Value of Tangible Assets	Amount Allocated to Value of Purchased Rights to Customer Lists
Harrey's	$ 198,612	$ 50,380	$ 148,232
Best	2,004,118	848,605	1,155,513
Seaboard	677,792	21,800	655,992
Electronic	1,553,795	709,625	844,170
Bur-tell	439,340	93,343	345,997
Controls	400,000	95,395	304,605
Security Systems	1,153,169	224,000	929,169
NASI	466,748	100,150	366,598
BAS	711,097	68,250	642,847

Exhibit 4   (continued)

All of the above acquisitions have been accounted for by the purchase method and, accordingly, results of operations have been included in the statements of income since the respective dates of acquisition.

If Electronic (the significant 1991 acquisition) had been acquired on January 1, 1990, and had been included in the results of operations for 1990, along with the pro forma results of Best as if Best had been acquired on January 1, 1990, the unaudited pro forma results would have been:

Revenues $8,921,000
Net income   243,000
Net income per share 12

If Bur-tell, Security Systems, and NASI had been acquired on January 1, 1991, and had been included in the results of operations for 1991, along with the pro forma results of Electronic as if it had been acquired on January 1, 1981, the results would have been:

Revenues $17,155,000
Net income   668,000
Net income per share 34

If Security Systems and NASI had been acquired on January 1, 1992, and had been included in the results of operations for 1992, the unaudited pro forma results would have been:

Revenues $23,253,000
Net income   1,983,000
Net income per share 73

In management's opinion, the pro forma financial information is not necessarily indicative of the results that would have occurred or of future results of operations of the combined companies. Net income and net income per share are reduced in 1991 and 1990 by a pro forma provision for income taxes (see note 1).

The effect of the Harrey's results cannot be determined because the assets acquired represented a division without separate financial statements, and subsequent to the acquisition of the alarm division, all financial records of the company were destroyed in a fire. Based on the limited information available, management does not believe the effect of the Harrey's acquisition, if known, would be material to the company. The results of operations of Seaboard, Controls, and BAS are not material to the company; therefore, the pro forma results do not give effect to the operations of these companies.

3. Net Investment in Sales-Type Leases

The net investment in sales-type leases consists of the following:

	1992	1991	1990
Total minimum lease payments receivable	$56,652,947	$32,460,161	$12,814,727
Amounts allocated to service and monitoring	(11,788,453)	(6,387,817)	(2,861,869)
Minimum lease payments receivable	$44,864,494	$26,072,344	$ 9,952,858
Allowance for doubtful accounts	(570,000)	(325,000)	(130,000)
Net minimum lease payments received	$44,294,494	$25,747,344	$ 9,822,858
Estimated residual value of leased property	1,024,600	559,000	180,000
Unearned income	(19,236,858)	(12,205,228)	(4,411,006)
	$26,082,236	$14,101,116	$ 5,591,852

Uncollectible accounts charged to the allowance in 1992, 1991, and 1990 were $1,208,354, $365,167, and $20,680, respectively.

Interest has been imputed on lease receivables based on an amount normally approximating 2% in excess of the prime lending rate at the inception of the respective leases which management believes

approximates the implicit interest rate based on the creditworthiness of the lessees. In each of the next five years, approximately $7.3 million of the $56.5 million total minimum lease payments receivable matures with the balance of $20.1 million due after five years.

EXHIBIT 4   (continued)

The residual value of the leased equipment is based on its estimated fair value at the end of the lease term.

The company has one major customer which accounted for revenues of $4,817,000, $2,985,000, and $1,060,000 in 1992, 1991, and 1990, respectively.

5. Property and Equipment

Property and equipment consist of the following:

	1992	*1991*	*1990*
Vehicles	$ 589,772	$ 578,543	$ 294,110
Leasehold improvements	253,609	9,106	—
Computer equipment	664,674	145,826	51,700
Furniture and equipment.........................	1,128,737	810,738	454,720
Purchased alarm systems on operating leases	370,300	273,300	250,000
	$3,007,092	$1,817,513	$1,071,530
Accumulated depreciation........................	892,436	432,959	190,000
	$2,114,656	$1,384,554	$ 881,530

Furniture and equipment and computer equipment include gross assets acquired under capitalized leases of $485,351 at December 31, 1992; the related amount of accumulated depreciation was $48,535. Amounts at December 31, 1991, and 1990, were insignificant.

6. Debentures and Notes Payable

In 1992, the company issued $20 million in convertible subordinated debentures due November 1, 2007, with interest payable semiannually at 10%. The debentures can be converted to common stock at a price of $18 per share or redeemed at the option of the company at a range of prices from 110% in 1994 to par value in 2006. If not earlier converted or redeemed, the debentures will require sinking fund payments of $2 million each year beginning November 1, 1998.

The cost of issuing the debentures has been deferred and is amortized to interest expense over the expected life of the debentures. . . .

The acquisition loans are generally collateralized by the assets purchased, and substantially all the notes are guaranteed by certain corporate offi-cers. Certain lines of credit also require compensating balances as described in note 4.

The principal portion of notes payable due in the next five years is as follows:

Due	*Amount*
1993	$2,692,000
1994	572,000
1995	446,000
1996	203,000
1997	172,000
	$4,085,000
After five years	86,000
	$4,171,000

The loan agreements restrict payment of cash dividends, issuance and retirement of capital stock, incurrence of certain indebtedness, and advances to officers and stockholders without the consent of the lenders.

Exhibit 4   (continued)

---

7. Related Party Transactions and Commitments

On December 31, 1991, the principal shareholders of the company loaned the company $4 million. The amount is payable in annual installments of $800,000 with interest at prime plus one-half of 1% commencing January 1993. The note may be repaid before maturity at the option of the company or upon demand by the principal shareholders. A non-negotiable certificate of deposit of the same amount is collateral to the loan and will be redeemed in amounts equal to the note payments required. The shareholders have also pledged their shares of the company stock as collateral.

8. Income Taxes

The election under Subchapter S of the Internal Revenue Code was automatically terminated retroactive to January 1, 1992, by the public offering on January 29, 1992. If the company had been a taxable corporation for the years 1989 to 1992, deferred income taxes at December 31, 1991, would approximate $2,160,000 resulting from the reporting of lease income on the operating methods for income tax return purposes and the capital lease method for financial reporting purposes. The reversal of this temporary difference will result in a provision for income taxes, and currently payable income taxes, greater than that at customary income tax rates in the absence of sufficient originating timing differences. The tax losses passed through to the shareholders for the years 1989, 1990, and 1991 (which would have been available as a corporate net operating loss carryover if not for the Subchapter S election) totaled approximately $6 million.

The company has not recognized deferred tax assets arising from net operating loss carryforwards of $4,572,000 at December 31, 1992, which expires as follows: $72,000—1993, $4.5 million—2007.

9. Shareholders' Equity

In December 1991, the company increased its authorized common stock to 5 million shares and declared a 2,000-for-1 stock split. All per-share amounts have been retroactively restated to give effect to the split.

Pursuant to the rules of the Securities and Exchange Commission regarding termination of a Subchapter S election, all retained earnings accumulated to December 31, 1991, have been transferred to additional paid-in capital. . . .

13. Subsequent Events

In January 1993, the company completed a new revolving credit and term loan agreement as of December 31, 1992, with seven participating banks for up to $30 million. The agreement provides for the company to pay interest only on the revolving credit loans to June 30, 1994, at which time they may be converted into four-year term loans. Under the terms of the agreement, the company is required to maintain specified levels of net worth, debt-to-equity ratios, and working capital. The agreement calls for interest on the revolving loans at the rate of 1% above prime, 1½% above prime on the term loans, and fees of one quarter of 1% on the total commitment plus one-half of 1% on the unused commitment. Borrowing under the agreement may be prepaid without premium or penalty. The loan is collateralized by certain lease contracts, equipment, other personal property, and insurance policies on certain officers. The loan agreement requires the maintenance of compensating cash balances equal to the sum of 10% of the commitment under the line of credit during the commitment period and 10% of the aggregate principal amount of the term loans thereafter.

On March 14, 1993, the company entered into an agreement to acquire certain assets of Alarm, Inc., a Houston, Texas, alarm company for approximately $3.5 million in cash, 60% at closing (expected to be in April 1993) with the remainder placed in escrow to be paid within 10 months.

On March 21, 1993, the company acquired certain assets of Crime Alarm Systems, Inc., a Southeastern Florida alarm company, for approximately $300,000 (approximately $150,000 in cash at closing and approximately $150,000 payable in March 1994), the allocation of which has not been determined.

The company also entered into an agreement on March 25, 1993, to acquire all of the common stock of another alarm service company in Houston for an aggregate of approximately $16 million in cash. Completion of this acquisition is subject to an audit of the financial statements of the Houston company, an appraisal of their assets and the availability of adequate funds to complete the transaction.

frequently, leased such systems for a long-term period, thus placing much of the risk of obsolescence on customers.

The total market for private security equipment and services is estimated to be about $15 billion for 1993. A Cleveland-based research firm had estimated the market to grow between 10% and 15% a year for the next 10 years.

Questions

1. Do you agree with Security Plus's use of "capital lease" accounting? _____

2. Why is Security Plus changing its mix of leases between capital and operating leases? _____

3. What do you think is Security Plus's potential as an equity investment as of November 15, 1993? _____

CHAPTER
21

Retiree Benefits

A retiree benefit plan is an agreement between an employer and its employees whereby the employer agrees to provide employees for services rendered prior to retirement certain retiree benefits, such as a pension and health care coverage. The principal accounting issues associated with these arrangements are how to measure the cost of the plan to the employer during the employee's service period and the employer's current obligation to provide these future benefits.

The accounting for retiree benefits is complex. The accounting for pension plans is covered by FASB Statement No. 87, "Employer's Accounting for Pensions." The accounting for other retiree benefits, such as health care and life insurance, is specified in FASB Statement No. 106, "Employers' Accounting for Postretirement Benefits Other than Pensions." For the purpose of this note many of the complexities of the Statements will be omitted.

Pension Plans

A full understanding of pension cost accounting and the analytical issues related to it requires an appreciation of the actuarial valuation techniques, funding instruments, agencies, and methods involved in determining the financial provisions for pension benefits.

The three most popular types of corporate pension plans are defined contribution plans, profit sharing plans, and defined benefits plans. An employer may maintain a single-employer pension plan or participate in a multiemployer plan, to which two or more unrelated employers contribute. Some companies use more than one type of pension plan to satisfy their pension obligations.

Professor David F. Hawkins prepared this note as the basis for class discussion.
Copyright © 1996 by the President and Fellows of Harvard College. Harvard Business School teaching note 197–021.

733

A defined contribution plan provides for each participant an individual account to which the employer is obligated to make periodic contributions. The employee's ultimate pension payments depend solely on the amount contributed to the account and the gains or losses earned. The employer is only liable for contributions to the plan, not for benefits payable to the retired employees.

A profit sharing plan is similar to a defined contribution plan. As its name implies, the employer agrees to assign a portion of the company's profits to the employee's pension fund. The amount contributed may or may not be set by formula.

A defined benefit pension plan specifies that the employer will provide to each retired employee a specified pension payment, usually based on factors such as age, years of service, and salary.

Unless specified otherwise, this chapter deals with single-employer defined pension plan accounting and analysis.

Valuation

Actuarial valuation is the process of determining the amounts needed to finance a pension plan. The process relies on three principal concepts. First, the valuation is for a closed group of employees. Second, the ultimate cost of the plan is primarily the present value, as of the valuation date, of expected future benefit payments. Third, the valuation is merely an approximation, because of uncertainties inherent in the actuarial assumptions underlying the calculations. After it is determined, the valuation of a pension plan is sometimes separated into two portions: (a) retroactive pension costs or benefits assigned on account of services rendered in years prior to the inception or current modification of the pension plan; and (b) pension benefits or costs based on service after its inception or current modification. In making the actuarial valuation, however, these costs are not considered separately.

Assumptions

When they estimate the cost of pension plans, actuaries must make a number of assumptions regarding uncertain future events. For example, they have to make estimates of the expected rate of return on the pension fund's assets, the fund's administrative expenses, and the amounts and timing of future benefits. The future benefit estimates, in turn, may involve estimates of future employee compensation levels, cost-of-living indexes, mortality rates (both before and after retirement), retirement ages, employee turnover, vesting privileges, and Social Security benefits.

Clearly, it is most unlikely that the actuarial assumptions will occur as projected, so it is necessary to review and change the actuarial assumptions from time to time. If the original assumptions turn out to have been optimistic, there will be an actuarial deficiency.

The net adjustment for actuarial gains and losses is handled by actuaries in one of two ways when revising valuations and contribution patterns. The so-called immediate method applies to net actuarial gain to reduce the employer's next contribution. This method is not used for net losses. The spread method spreads a net gain or loss over present and expected future contributions. Some actuaries use the immediate method for handling net gains and the spread method for losses.

Benefit Formulas

The three most popular formulas for determining employee pension payments are the flat benefit, career-average-pay, and final pay formulas. Flat benefit formulas base benefits on a fixed amount per year of service. A career-average-pay formula bases benefits on the employee's compensation over the entire period of service with the employer. Final pay formulas base employee benefits on the employee's compensation over a specified number of years near the end of that employee's service period, or else on the period of highest compensation.

Funding Instruments and Agencies

Typically, employers make some financial provision for the current and future benefits they are obligated to pay under their pension plans. Among a variety of funding instruments, the most popular are contracts with life insurance companies (insured plans) and trust agreements (trust fund plans).

Insured plans cover a number of possible arrangements. For example, individual policies providing death and retirement benefits may be issued to a trustee for each employee. A similar arrangement is a group annuity contract issued to the employer. Both of these arrangements specify the premiums and benefits.

Other popular insured funding arrangements are deposit administration contracts and immediate participation guaranteed contracts. Essentially, both of these plans require the employer to open an account with an insurance company and to make regular contributions to this account. The insurance company agrees to add interest to the account at a specified rate. When the employee retires, the insurance company issues an annuity providing the stipulated benefits and the annuity premium is withdrawn from the employer's account.

Trust fund plans require the employer's contributions to be made to a trustee who invests the funds and pays retirement benefits according to the terms of the trust agreement. Trustees may be an individual, a bank, or a group of individuals. The terms of trust agreements may give the trustee full power to select investments, or the trustee may be subject to general direction by the employer.

Employee Retirement Income Security Act

The Employee Retirement Income Security Act (ERISA) sets minimum eligibility, funding, and vesting requirements. In addition, the law imposes a liability on the employer to reimburse this fund for any insurance benefits that are paid if the company's plan fails.

The amount of this liability is limited to 30% of the employer's net worth. ERISA also sets regulatory reporting standards for employers and pension trusts.

Income Tax Considerations

Most pension plans are designed so that the employer contributions are deductible for tax purposes during the year contributed. There are several other tax aspects which should be noted. First, the tax treatment of pension costs follows cash, rather than accrual, accounting. Second, the earnings of qualified trust plans are tax free. Third, employer contributions to the fund are not taxable income to employees until distributed as retirement benefits.

Vesting

In most pension plans at some point in time an employee's interest in the employee's pension rights becomes vested. Vested benefits are benefits for which the employee's right to receive a present or future pension benefit is no longer contingent on remaining in the service of the employer. These benefits are referred to as vested benefits.

Pension Accounting

Pension accounting is based upon four fundamental concepts. These are:

1. **Accrued cost.** The cost of an employer's pension plan should be accrued over the covered employee's service period.
2. **Net cost.** There is one pension cost and it aggregates at least three elements: (a) the compensation cost of pension benefits promised employees; (b) the interest cost resulting from the deferred payment of those benefits; and (c) the results of investing in assets to fund the promised benefits.
3. **Delayed recognition.** Certain changes in the pension obligation and plan assets are not recognized as they occur but are gradually and systematically spread over subsequent periods.
4. **Offsetting.** The plan assets and obligations can be netted against each other since the employer has considerable control over these items and the substantial risk and rewards associated with them are in large part borne by the employer.

Key Terms

There are four key terms that financial statement users, accountants, and managers must appreciate before they can understand pension accounting rules. These terms are:

1. **Net periodic pension cost.** The amount recognized in an employer's financial statements as the cost of the pension plan for a period. The Statement uses the term *net periodic pension cost* (rather than "expense") because part of the cost recognized in a period may be capitalized along with other costs as part of an asset such as inventory.

2. **Fair value of plan assets.** The amount that a pension plan could reasonably expect to receive for its investments in a current exchange between a willing buyer and a willing seller, that is, other than in a forced liquidation sale. This is the method used to value the pension plan assets.

3. **Accumulated benefit obligation.** The actuarial present value of vested and nonvested benefits attributed by the pension benefit formula to service to date, and to *current* and *past* compensation, if applicable. The accumulated benefit obligation is considered by the FASB as representative of a pension plan's obligation should the plan cease to exist. The accumulated benefit obligation does not include an assumption about future compensation levels.

4. **Projected benefit obligation.** The actuarial present value of all benefits attributed by the pension benefit formula to employee service rendered to date using *current* and *past* compensation and assumptions as to *future* compensation if the company's pension benefit formula is based on such future compensation levels. If a company's pension benefit formula does not incorporate assumptions about future compensation, the accumulated benefit obligation and the projected obligation have the same value.

It is important to be aware of the distinction between the latter two terms, because net periodic pension cost is based in part on the projected benefit obligation, and pension liability calculations incorporate the accumulated benefit obligation.

Net Periodic Pension Cost

A company's net periodic pension cost is the net of these six components:

1. **Service cost.** This component is the actuarial present value of benefits attributed by the pension benefit formula to services rendered by employees during the accounting period. The service cost component is a portion of the projected benefit obligation. The service cost figure is provided by the plan's actuaries and is unaffected by the funded status of the plan.

2. **Interest cost.** Measuring the projected benefit obligation as a discounted present value requires accrual of an interest cost over time at rates equal to the assumed discount rate. The interest cost component is equivalent to the increase in the projected benefit obligation due to the passage of time during the accounting period. The discount rate should be based on the current prices for settling the pension obligation. This rate is determined at the beginning of each annual accounting period. In making this determination, employers may also look to rates of return on high-quality fixed income

investments currently available and expected to be available during the period until the pensions are paid.

3. **Return on plan assets.** This component of net periodic pension cost reduces the net cost by the assumed investment income from the plan assets based on assumed rates of return. This is an actuarial calculation and is not based on the plan's actual returns. The expected return on plan assets is determined based on the expected long-term rate of return on plan assets and the market-related value of the plan assets. Actual returns in excess of or less than those assumed are treated as gains or losses.

4. **Amortization of unrecognized net gain or loss.** As a minimum, amortization of the unrecognized cumulative net gain or loss resulting from a change in either the projected benefit obligation or the plan assets (because of experience different from that assumed or a change in actuarial assumptions) is included as a component of net periodic pension cost if, as of the beginning of the year, that unrecognized net gain or loss exceeds 10% of the projected benefit obligation or the fair value of plan assets, whichever is greater. If amortization is required, the minimum amortization is the excess over the 10% test divided by the service period of the active employees expected to receive benefits under the plan. The amortization of any unrecognized net gain or loss may either increase or decrease the net periodic pension cost.

5. **Amortization of unrecognized prior service costs.** The cost of providing retroactive benefits (that is, prior service cost) arising at the initiation or amendment of a plan are amortized over time rather than recognized in full at the time of the plan's initiation or amendment. The cost of retroactive benefits is the increase in the projected benefit obligation at the date of the amendment. This cost is amortized by assigning an equal amount to each future period of service of each employee active at the date of the plan's initiation or amendment who is expected to receive benefits under the plan.

6. **Amortization of obligation or gain.** At the time FASB Statement No. 87 became effective, the FASB had to devise a way for companies to move to the Statements' new pension accounting rules. For a defined benefit plan, an employer had to determine for the beginning of the fiscal year in which FASB Statement No. 87 was first applied, the amounts of (a) the projected benefit obligation; and (b) the fair value of plan assets plus previously recognized unfunded accrued pension cost or less previously recognized prepaid pension cost. The difference between those two amounts, whether it represented an unrecognized net obligation (and loss or cost) or an unrecognized net asset (and gain), is amortized on a straight-line basis over the average remaining service period of employees expected to receive benefits under the plan, except that, (a) if the average remaining service period is less than 15 years, the employer may elect to use a 15-year period; and (b) if all or almost all of a plan's participants are inactive, the employer must use the inactive participants' average remaining life

expectancy period. That same amortization must also be used to recognize any unrecognized net obligation related to a defined contribution plan.

Accounting Illustrated

Two examples of FASB Statement No. 87's approach to pension accounting are presented. Example (A) is fairly straightforward, since the company funds its periodic cost and has an overfunded plan (relative to its accumulated benefit obligation). Assume the following:

A company's net periodic pension cost is $100,000. It funds all of this cost. The fair value of the plan's assets is greater than the company's accumulated benefit obligation. The accounting entries are:

```
Dr. Net Periodic Pension Cost (to record the cost) . . . . . . . . . . . . . . .  100,000
    Cr. Cash (to reduce cash) . . . . . . . . . . . . . . . . . . . . . . . . . . . . . . . .          100,000
```

The above illustration did not result in a pension-related asset or liability being recorded. In the following situation where there is a difference between the pension expense and the contributions to the fund, a pension-related asset or liability would be recorded.

1. An unfunded accrued pension cost (liability) is recorded if the pension cost is greater than the contribution. The liability is equal to the excess of the cumulative pension cost over the cumulative contributions.

2. A prepaid pension cost (asset) is recorded if the contribution to the fund is greater than the pension cost. The asset is equal to the excess of the cumulative contributions over the cumulative pension cost.

3. An additional liability is recorded if the accumulated benefit obligation is greater than the fair value of the plan assets. The liability is the difference between the two balances adjusted for any prepaid pension cost (asset) or accrued pension cost (liability). If a prepaid pension cost balance exists, the additional liability is the excess of the accumulated benefit obligation over the fair value of the plan assets plus this asset. If an accrued pension cost balance exists, the additional liability is the excess less this liability.

4. If an additional liability is recorded, an offsetting intangible asset is recognized. Should the additional liability be greater than the unrecognized prior service cost, the intangible asset recorded is equal to the unrecognized prior service cost and the excess is recorded as a separate component of owners' equity (a reduction).

Example (B) is more complex. It is only one of the many possible situations that FASB Statement No. 87 deals with. It is an example of situation (4) above. In this example the company only funds part of its periodic pension cost and has an underfunded plan (relative to the company's accumulated benefit obligation).

A company's net periodic pension cost is $100,000. It funds $50,000 of this cost. The resulting accounting entries based on accrual accounting are:

```
Dr. Net Period Pension Cost (to record the expense) ............... 100,000
    Cr. Cash (to reduce cash) ..................................         50,000
        Unfunded Accrual Pension cost (liability created by underpayment) .    50,000
```

The company has a $560,000 accumulated pension obligation and the fair value of its plan assets is $500,000. The company's unrecognized prior service cost is $5,000. To bring the balance sheet pension liability up to the $60,000 difference between the accumulated benefit obligation ($560,000) and the plan asset ($500,000), and to record the intangible asset [which can be no more than the unrecognized prior service cost ($5,000)] and the adjustment to owners' equity, the accounting entries are:

```
Dr. Intangible (to record the intangible asset) ....................   5,000
    Owners' Equity (to reduce owners' equity) ...................  55,000
    Cr. Additional Pension Liability (to bring the total pension liability
        up to $60,000) .......................................          60,000
```

The employer's intangible asset, pension liability, and owners' equity balances would be adjusted at the end of each accounting period to reflect the current status of the accumulated benefit obligation, plan assets, unrecognized prior service cost, and unfunded accrued pension cost balances. These balance sheet adjustments would not directly enter into the computation of net periodic pension cost. Also, because of valuation changes in the elements entering into the liability calculation the liability might disappear from the balance sheet in one period and reappear in another.

Other Plans

FASB Statement No. 87 also covers the accounting for annuity contract funded pension plans, defined contribution plans, or multiemployer plans. Typically, the net periodic pension cost of these plans is the actuarially determined payment required to meet the employer's periodic funding obligations.

Settlements and Curtailments

FASB Statement No. 88 covers employers' accounting for settlements and curtailments of defined benefit plans. Settlement is an irrevocable action that relieves the employer (or the plan) of primary responsibility for an obligation and eliminates significant risks related to the obligation and the assets used to effect the settlement. A curtailment is a significant reduction in, or an elimination of, defined benefit accruals for present employees' future services. In general gains or losses from these actions are recognized immediately in income.

Postretirement Benefits

In addition to pension payments, many employers provide postretirement health care, life insurance, and other benefits to retired employees.

From the accounting point of view, the accounting for the postretirement benefits is almost identical to the FASB's pension accounting rules. Also, the types of judgments that management must make to measure postretirement benefit obligations and costs are similar to those involved in pension obligation cost measurement. Relative to pension estimates, postretirement benefit estimates involve considerably more uncertainty. Also, management has more flexibility. Statement users need to examine management's postretirement benefit estimates carefully to avoid being misled.

FASB Statement No. 106

FASB Statement No. 106 is based on the conclusion that benefits promised to active employees upon retirement are a form of deferred compensation and, as such, should be accounted for over the employee's active work life. The FASB believed that the cost of future postretirement benefits should be accrued beginning at the date that an employee is hired and continue through the time that the employee becomes fully eligible for the benefits.

The measurement of an employer's expected postretirement benefit obligation at a particular date is the actuarial present value of the postretirement benefits attributable to current and retired employees expected to be paid by the employer taking into account the expected future cost and timing of these benefits, employee cost sharing and coinsurance, and available government programs. While it may be difficult to measure the current cost of these future benefits, the FASB believed that it was better to record a reasonable approximation of them than to ignore their existence in situations where they are material.

Scope

FASB Statement No. 106 applies to *all* postretirement benefits expected to be provided by an employer to current and former employees. The Statement covers written as well as unwritten postretirement plans and practices. The Statement also applies to plan settlements, curtailments and special termination benefit offers.

The Statement covers both defined benefit and defined contribution postretirement plans. The defined contribution plan accounting is relatively straightforward. To the extent that the employer contributions are made during an employee's active work life, the periodic postretirement cost is equal to the required contribution. If the employer funds the employee's plan after the employee retires, the employer must accrue the estimated cost during the employee's service period. The accounting for defined postretirement plans is more complex. It is covered in the rest of this chapter.

Obligation

The expected postretirement benefit obligation is the actuarial present value as of a date of the benefits expected to be paid to or for an employee, the employee's beneficiaries, and any covered dependents pursuant to the terms of the postretirement benefit plan. The expected postretirement benefit obligation for an employee is measured using assumptions about the employee's expected retirement date and the employee's future compensation (if the benefit formula is based on future compensation levels).

The determination of the actuarial present value of an employer's postretirement benefit obligation as of a particular date requires the employer to make a number of estimates of future values and trends. There can be considerable diversity in these estimates due to differences in employee profiles, benefit plans, and management judgments. Management's estimate of the postretirement benefit obligation determines in large measure the size of its annual accrual based postretirement benefit cost. The key assumptions made in the measurement of postretirement benefit obligations are:

1. Under certain circumstances management may assume future modifications will be made to the existing plan when forecasting future postretirement benefit costs. Assuming aggressive future plan modifications that result in fewer benefits, lower coverage caps, and higher employee participation can lower the postretirement benefit obligation significantly.

2. The expected type and timing of future benefits projected by management. For example, assuming low levels of long-term healthcare benefits can reduce postretirement benefit cost materially.

3. Medical coverage provided by government authorities and other providers of healthcare benefits reduces an employer's healthcare obligation to employees. Assumptions must be made about primary and supplemental coverage availability.

4. The projected inflation rate of healthcare cost assumption is the most critical management judgment entering into the measurement of postretirement benefit obligations and costs. Low healthcare cost inflation rate assumptions can reduce significantly the obligation and cost values.

5. The period over which benefits are expected to be provided should be based on the same mortality tables used for pension measurement purposes. The use of aggressive mortality tables lowers both the pension and postretirement benefit health obligation and cost.

6. The discount rate applied to reduce the projected level of future benefit costs to their present value. A combination of a high discount rate and a low cost inflation rate will dramatically reduce the actuarial present value of a company's postretirement health obligations.

Net Periodic Postretirement Benefit Cost

The net periodic postretirement benefit cost consists of the following components:

1. **Service cost.** The portion of the expected postretirement benefit obligation attributed to employee service during the accounting period. This figure is obtained from an actuary.

2. **Interest cost.** The increase in the postretirement benefit obligation to recognize the effects of the passage of time. The interest rate is the rate used to determine the actuarial present value of the postretirement benefit obligation.

3. **Actual return on plan assets.** Funds plans can reduce the periodic postretirement benefit cost by the actual return on the plan's assets measured at their fair value during the period. The actual return on plan assets component is the change in the fair value of the plan's assets for a period including the decrease due to expenses incurred during the period (such as income tax expense incurred by the plan, if applicable), adjusted for contributions and benefit payments during the period.

4. **Amortization of unrecognized prior service cost.** Plan amendments may increase or decrease benefits expected to be paid to current and future retirees. These changes in expected benefits will in turn change the company's postretirement benefit obligation. That portion of the change in postretirement benefit obligation related to periods of employee service prior to the plan amendment are referred to as prior service costs. At a minimum, these costs should be amortized on a straight-line basis over the employee's years of service to the full eligibility date.

5. **Gains and losses.** Gains and losses are changes in the amount of postretirement benefit or plan assets resulting from experience different from that assumed or from changes in assumptions. Any reduction in the obligation is first used to reduce any existing unrecognized prior service cost, then to reduce any unrecognized transition obligation (see below). The excess, if any, is amortized on the same basis as prior service costs.

6. **Unrecognized transition obligation or asset.** At the time FASB Statement No. 106 was adopted, the net difference between the benefit plan's assets and obligation was determined. The net amount was either a transition obligation or asset. Companies could elect to recognize their transition asset or liability immediately upon adoption of the new standard as a credit or charge to earnings. If this alternative was elected, this item ceases to be a consideration in future postretirement cost measurements. Alternatively, companies could have elected to delay recognition of their transition asset or obligation. If this alternative was selected, the transition asset or obligation was amortized on a straight-line basis over the average remaining service period of active plan participants. If this period was less than 20 years, a 20-year amortization period could have been used.

Accounting Illustrated

The accounting entries for postretirement benefit costs are illustrated below using a company that switched from cash accounting[1] to FASB Statement No. 106 accounting for postretirement benefits. Two examples are presented. The first illustrates immediate recognition in income of the postretirement benefit obligation at date of adoption of the new accounting. The second illustration assumes that the company delayed recognition in income of its postretirement benefit obligation using a 20-year amortization period.

Immediate Recognition

At the time the company adopted accrual postretirement benefit accounting, it had an unrecognized postretirement benefit obligation of $115.7 million. In that year the company's FASB Statement No. 106 cost is $12 million and it paid $5.3 million in cash to provide postretirement benefits to its retirees. The company's obligation is unfunded. The accounting entries to record the initial year's postretirement benefit costs are ($ in millions):

1. Record pre-adoption years cumulative difference between accrual and cash based accounting for postretirement health costs as of beginning of first year

   Dr. Earnings—Cumulative effect 115.7
       Cr. Postretirement benefits liability 115.7

2. Record first year postretirement benefits expense on an accrual basis.

   Dr. Earnings—Annual expense   12
       Cr. postretirement benefits liability   12

3. Pay first year postretirement benefit cash cost.

   Dr. postretirement benefits liabilities 5.3
       Cr. Cash 5.3

The $12 million accrual charge consists of only two of the six components of the postretirement cost measurements listed above. The two components are the service and the interest components. Since this is the first year of the new accounting, no provision is required for plan gains and losses and prior service costs. The return on plan assets component is zero because the plan is unfunded. The transition component is not included in the annual cost measurement. It is reported separately as a cumulative accounting change charge.

Delayed Recognition

The principal difference between the delayed and immediate recognition alternatives is that in the former, the initial $115.7 million postretirement obligation is amortized over a 20-year period. As a result, in contrast to the immediate recognition alternative,

---

[1]Prior to the adoption of FASB Statement No. 106 most companies accounted for their postretirement benefit costs on a "pay-as-you-go" or cash basis.

the annual postretirement benefit cost is higher and the postretirement benefit liability is lower. The accounting entries to record the initial year using FASB Statement No. 106 are ($ in millions):

1. Record the postretirement benefit expense on an FASB Statement No. 106 basis including a $5.8 million transition obligation amortization charge ($115.7/20).

Dr. Earnings—annual expense	17.8	
Cr. Postretirement benefits liability		17.8

2. Pay retirement benefit cash cost.

Dr. Postretirement benefits liability	5.3	
Cr. Cash		5.3

In the delayed recognition example, the annual postretirement benefit cost consists of the service, interest, and transition obligation components.

Curtailments and Settlements

In general, curtailment and settlement gains and losses are immediately recognized in income.

Multiemployer Plans

The postretirement benefit cost of companies participating in multiemployer plans is the annual cash contribution required to be made to the plan.

Deferred Compensation Contracts

FASB Statement No. 106's coverage goes beyond postretirement plans. It also covers deferred compensation contracts. It requires deferred compensation contracts to be fully accrued by the date the employee reaches full eligibility for the deferred compensation benefit.

Financial Analysis

The analysis of net periodic retiree benefit costs and obligations can be difficult for statement users. The subject is complex; much of the information needed to fully evaluate the appropriateness of a company's policies, estimates, and actuarial assumptions may not be disclosed; and estimates and actuarial assumptions employed can vary between companies. Nevertheless, statement users must do the best they can with the available data, since a company's retiree benefit accounting and funding practices can significantly influence the level and quality of its earnings.

There is considerable controversy as to how statement users should view under-funded retiree benefit plans. Some regard it as an acceptable form of off–balance-sheet financing. They recognize that while companies have an obligation to meet their retiree obligations as they mature, they seldom need to fully fund their plans to meet maturing obligations. Also they argue that a company may be able to earn more on funds not contributed to retiree benefit plans than the plan could have earned on these funds. This in turn improves the employee current and future positions.

Others view underfunded retiree benefit plans as a negative when evaluating a corporation's financial position. They seem to regard an underfunded pension plan as a "red flag." In their view if management is unable to fund fully, there must be some unfavorable reason why it cannot. This concern is often justified, particularly if a company is under pressure from employees to fund retiree benefit plans.

The relative degree of financial risk that analysts should attach to underfunded pension obligations can be measured by comparing the unfunded obligation with the owners' equity in the company. The higher this ratio of unfunded obligation to own-ers' equity, the greater the financial risk. In addition, the higher the percentage of unfunded vested obligation is of this total unfunded obligation, the greater is the level of financial risk, since vested benefits are pension benefits that accrue to an employee irrespective of whether the employee continues in the service of the employer.

Many retiree benefit plans are overfunded. Typically statement users regard overfunding positively. It reduces the need for companies to fund the plan currently. This allows the company to retain more cash for other corporate purposes.

Statement users should always pay close attention to the assumptions made in the measurement of retiree benefit obligations. Relatively small changes in the discount rate, expected return on plan assets, and the rates used to project variables, such as future salaries and healthcare cost inflation, can significantly influence the size of the obligation and the related costs. Statement users should always compare a company's assumptions in these areas to the assumptions made by managers of comparable com-panies. Adoption of relatively optimistic assumptions by management may indicate a lower quality of earnings relative to comparable companies.

International Paper (A)

The headline read, "New Rule on Benefits Approved—Accounting Change Trims Earnings to Reflect Future Costs."[1] Bob Butler, senior vice president and chief financial officer of International Paper (IP), put down the newspaper clipping on his desk and sighed. It was late November 1991, and Butler well remembered the first time he saw the story, more than a year ago. The action of the Financial Accounting Standards Board (FASB) had not come as a complete surprise to him. The proposed rules had been the subject of a major debate ever since they had been released in an exposure draft 20 months earlier. Still, the final approval by a four-to-three vote over the strenuous opposition of many employers was a shock. Everyone agreed that the cost of "other postemployment benefits" (OPEB), particularly health care benefits for retirees and their dependents, was a significant liability for many U.S. companies. The current accounting practice of expensing these benefits as they were paid was clearly an inadequate way to recognize the obligation. Yet estimates of the liability that FASB would require employers as a whole to accrue ranged from $670 billion to over $2 trillion. Moreover, unlike pensions, virtually no OPEB plans were prefunded, so this liability would not be offset by assets that employers had set aside previously to pay for OPEB.

The uncertainty in the OPEB liability for employers as a whole was reflected at the level of individual employers. Many firms lacked the data even to estimate the size of their OPEB liabilities. Their medical claims payments for active workers and retirees were not separated. Even if they were separated, often there existed no breakdown in claim payments by age, type of payment, or other categories, which were all necessary to make projections about future payment patterns. However, IP was in a better

---

This case was prepared by Research Associate Charles A. Nichols III under the supervision of Professor Mary E. Barth as the basis for class discussion rather than to illustrate either effective or ineffective handling of an administrative situation.
Copyright © 1992 by the President and Fellows of Harvard College. Harvard Business School case 193–060.
[1]Milt Freudenheim, "New Rule on Benefits Approved," *New York Times*, Oct. 18, 1990, D1.

position than many other companies. Faced with rising health care costs, in 1987, IP had recognized early on the expected costs of its OPEB plans and had acted to curtail sharply the level of OPEB for its nonunion workforce. As a result, IP had better control over its OPEB costs, and under the new rules, the company would accrue a much smaller liability than it otherwise would have accrued.

IP still had a decision to make about when to adopt the new rules. IP was planning a public offering of common stock to refinance some of its debt. Butler was trying to anticipate the potential effect on the offering of electing to adopt the new rules in advance or electing to wait until after the offering when adoption became mandatory. Although he had a clear sense of IP's OPEB liability, he was not sure whether IP's investors did.

Company Background

IP was the largest integrated pulp and paper company in the world, ranking 32d among the Fortune 500 Industrial Companies. It was founded in 1898 by the consolidation of 18 companies in New England and New York in order to achieve lower manufacturing costs through economies of scale. During the 1920s and 1930s, IP built and operated a hydroelectric plant on the Hudson River, an enterprise it later sold. Expansion in the 1940s and 1950s came about through acquisition of firms in related industries, such as container and carton manufacturing. An unsuccessful diversification strategy in the 1960s was followed by a period of divestment in the 1970s and a greatly needed program of modernization in its core business plants.

The current chairman, John A. Georges, 60, came to IP from a 28-year career at E. I. du Pont de Nemours & Co. Georges, trained as a chemical engineer, was appointed chief operating officer in 1981 and chairman in 1985. In his corporate strategy, Georges focused on the need for IP to be a low-cost producer in the competitive markets for pulp and paper products. Making use of both plant modernization and acquisitions, he shifted IP's product mix toward better quality papers and high-technology products that were higher value-added and less cyclical than its previously existing products.

Under Georges' leadership in the 1980 to 1990 period, IP spent $8 billion in modernization programs, transforming itself from a high- to a low-cost producer in its major product lines. In addition, through the middle of 1989, the company paid $3 billion to acquire both foreign and domestic firms. Many of its acquisitions had been financed with short-term debt to take advantage of the low short-term interest rates. Currently the company was planning through a Securities and Exchange Commission registration to issue stock and use the proceeds to strengthen its balance sheet by paying down debt, particularly high-cost debt.

In the middle 1980s, as part of his strategy to make IP a low-cost producer, Georges instituted severe cost-cutting measures. Among other actions, these measures included the elimination of one-third of the corporate staff as well as reductions in the company's retiree health benefits for nonunionized employees. In mid-1987, IP informed these workers that only those who had retired before 1983 would continue to receive benefits as before. Those who had retired in 1983 and later had their premiums for coverage increased, and current employees were informed that their own premiums as retirees would be even higher. Finally, new nonunion hires beginning in October 1987 would receive no retirement health care coverage at all. Premiums for those receiving coverage were set at a higher level for those retirees under age 65, reflecting both a higher rate of claims for this group and the lack of coverage under Medicare, a U.S. federal government program that paid for a significant portion of medical expenses for retired people.

IP continued to review OPEB costs and in 1992 planned to cap annual OPEB medical expenditures per claimant at the level of $3500 to $4000, anticipating that this cap would have a significant effect on expenditures in three to four years.

Exhibit 1 presents a summary of IP's financial position and operating results for the period 1986–91.

EXHIBIT 1   International Paper: Six-Year Financial Summary
($ millions, except per-share amounts and stock prices)

	1991[a]	1990	1989	1988	1987	1986
Operating Results						
Net sales	$12,703	$ 12,960	$ 11,378	$ 9,587	$ 7,800	$ 5,540
Costs and expenses,						
excluding interest	11,750	11,737	9,768	8,224	6,952	5,030
Earnings before income taxes	663	946	1,405	1,198	681	454
Net earnings	415	569	864	754	407	305
Financial Position						
Working capital	$ 404	$ 784	$ 366	$ 781	$ 657	$ 296
Plants, properties and						
equipment, net	7,848	7,287	6,238	5,456	5,125	4,788
Timberlands	743	751	764	772	780	783
Total assets	14,941	13,669	11,582	9,462	8,710	7,848
Long-term debt	3,351	3,096	2,324	1,853	1,937	1,764
Common shareholders' equity	6,154	5,632	5,147	4,557	4,052	3,664
Per Share of Common Stock						
Net earnings	$ 3.76	$ 5.21	$ 7.72	$ 6.57	$ 3.68	$ 2.89
Cash dividends	1.68	1.68	1.53	1.28	1.20	1.20
Common shareholders' equity	53.08	51.34	47.35	41.14	36.35	35.04
Common Stock Prices						
High	78¼	58⅜	58¾	49⅜	57¾	40
Low	50½	43½	45⅛	36½	27	24⅜
Year-end		53½	56½	46⅜	42¼	37½
Financial Ratios						
Current ratio	1.1	1.2	1.1	1.5	1.4	1.2
Total debt to capital ratio . . .	38.4	36.1	33.9	25.8	31.6	31.2
Return on equity	6.9	10.5	17.8	17.0	10.0	8.3
Return on capital employed	5.4	8.0	13.4	13.8	10.2	8.4
Capital expenditures	$ 1,197	$ 1,267	$ 887	$ 645	$ 603	$ 576
Number of employees	70,500	69,000	63,500	55,500	45,500	44,000

Source: International Paper.

[a]Preliminary and excluding potential effects of FASB 106 if adopted early for 1991.

OPEB Background

OPEB covered a broad range of benefits other than pensions, which were offered to retirees by their former employers. Financially, the most significant of these benefits was health insurance for retirees and their dependents, both for the period before they became eligible for the federal Medicare program at age 65 and also as a supplement to Medicare coverage afterwards.

Employers first provided OPEB as a part of collectively bargained union contracts during World War II, when wage-and-price controls made it impossible to offer increased cash compensation. In the postwar period through the 1960s and early 1970s, employers regarded OPEB as a fringe benefit. It was relatively inexpensive and could serve as a cost-effective incentive to attract new employees or as a reward for existing ones. Universally, employers accounted for OPEB costs on a pay-as-you-go basis. That is, the expense recorded in the financial statements was just the disbursements for benefits in the fiscal period.

OPEB was a widely provided benefit. A 1991 survey reported that 88% of corporations and 62% of public employers offered health benefits to retirees.[2]

The rapidly rising costs of medical care beginning in the 1970s changed the character of OPEB. Annual expenditures for retiree medical benefits became a significant expense, requiring footnote disclosure in the financial statements. In the early 1980s, FASB began a project on accounting for OPEB. An exposure draft was issued early in 1989, and in 1990, the final rules were published in Financial Accounting Standards Board 106 (FASB 106), "Employers' Accounting for Postretirement Benefits Other than Pensions."

FASB 106

FASB 106 required employers to account for the cost of OPEB on an accrual basis. In general, the total benefits had to be prorated by years of service, and charges for the cost of these prorated benefits had to be made against income during the active life of employees. The cost had to be fully accrued by the time employees were vested in the benefit, which was usually the point at which they were eligible for early retirement. An interest-bearing liability corresponding to the income statement charges had to be accrued in the balance sheet, and firms needed to record an expense for the accrual of interest on this liability. FASB 106 contained guidelines for the treatment of the "transition obligation," the unfunded amount of the OPEB liability relating to employee service before the adoption of the new rules. Companies also had to make footnote disclosures of the components of OPEB-related entries in the financial statements, as well as of other information pertaining to OPEB (see **Appendix** for details).

Calculating OPEB liabilities required making assumptions for decades into the future about uncertain demographic and economic variables. These variables included discount rates, retirement ages, medical expense claim costs and medical inflation

---

[2]Pensionforum, "Attacking a Health Care Goliath," *Institutional Investor* 25 (June 1991): 145.

rates, and employee termination and mortality rates. In recognition of the great uncertainties surrounding the calculation of the liability and current charges for OPEB, FASB required companies to disclose the effect of a 1% increase in the health-care–cost trend rate on the calculations. This disclosure was in part FASB's response to many critics of the proposed rules. While agreeing that a liability did exist for OPEB, these critics argued that the uncertainties surrounding it were so great that it could not be reasonably estimated. However, FASB noted that with additional experience, estimates would become more accurate. Furthermore, whatever the limitations of any particular calculation of the liability, an estimate was clearly preferable to recording nothing at all for it, as occurred under the previously existing practice.

In FASB 106, FASB attempted to follow as closely as possible the accounting principles for pensions laid down in the 1980s in FASB 87. However, OPEB presented significantly greater uncertainties for estimating future liabilities. The promise made by a company to pay a pension under a defined benefit plan was measured in a specified dollar amount. In contrast, OPEB promises were generally in terms of medical services covered, the costs of which were not fixed. Coverage of spouses and dependents of employees, common under OPEB plans, could extend significantly the coverage period and therefore the cost of these plans.

FASB 106 was effective for fiscal years beginning after December 15, 1992, for most employers and after December 15, 1994, for all employers. As usual, FASB encouraged earlier adoption of the new standard. FASB 106 was expected to produce significantly increased liabilities in company financial statements. Industry reaction to the FASB exposure draft was almost universally negative, but in spite of these protests, the final rules were substantially the same.

Responses to FASB 106

Many companies were concerned with the size of the liability they would have to recognize once the accounting rules in FASB 106 became effective. Moreover, with health-care–cost trend rates currently in the double digits and well above the general inflation rate, many business leaders believed that what their OPEB plans promised was more than they could reasonably afford to pay. In recent years, many companies had cut back benefits to reduce costs, or increased required contributions from or cost-sharing of expenses with employees or retirees. A Fortune 500/CNN Moneyline CEO poll in 1989 reported that among responding Fortune 500 and Service 500 companies, approximately 40% had recently asked or were expecting to ask retirees to pay more for OPEB.[3] The 1991 survey[4] noted that 49% of OPEB providers had redesigned their plans to reduce their accounting impact or cost burden, while 54% of those who had not done so were considering it.

Other responses included reducing the cost or usage of medical services, for example, through the use of health maintenance organizations, second surgical opin-

---

[3]Fortune 500/CNN Moneyline CEO Poll, "No More Health Care on the House," *Fortune,* Feb. 27, 1989, 71–72.

[4]Pensionforum, "Attacking a Health Care Goliath," 145.

ions, or programs to promote healthy lifestyles. Some companies also tried to discourage early retirement, so as to reduce the period of time spent by former employees in retirement before Medicare eligibility.

In extreme cases, the large liabilities associated with OPEB could push a financially weak company into bankruptcy: 15% of the corporate respondents to the *Institutional Investor* survey reported that the required FASB 106 accruals would wipe out or greatly reduce their net worth; 10% noted that their earnings would be greatly reduced, while 47% expected a moderate reduction in earnings. Even financially sound U.S. corporations were concerned about the effect of FASB 106 on their international competitiveness. However, in response to concerns that FASB 106 would unfairly penalize U.S. corporations in international markets by saddling them with costs that their competitors were not required to accrue, FASB noted that OPEB represented a real cost that had to be recognized. Foreign companies did not incur this cost because their countries generally provided national health insurance for all residents. The United States and South Africa were alone among industrialized countries in lacking such social insurance.

Thus, because of the high costs of OPEB and its correspondingly large financial statement impact, relatively few companies elected to adopt FASB 106 early and recognize the liability before it was necessary. There was also the faint hope that FASB might make last minute changes in the standard.

Bob Butler's Choices

When, Butler wondered, should IP recognize its own OPEB liability? Some of the largest and most prestigious U.S. corporations, such as Bell Atlantic, General Electric, and IBM, were expected to adopt FASB 106 early, reporting multibillion dollar OPEB liabilities in their financial statements. There were advantages to being included among such blue-ribbon companies. In addition, IP's earnings in 1991 were already likely to be depressed due to the recession and to cyclical conditions in the pulp and paper industry. Perhaps it would be best to "clear the decks" in 1991, so that IP's future earnings would not be distorted by the recognition of a transition obligation. But then there was the SEC registration to worry about. . . .

The decision would be made by the chairman. But Georges would soon be asking for an analysis and recommendations from Butler.

EXHIBIT 2   Illustration of Calculation of FASB 106 Financial Entries

Assumptions
- No advance funding of liability
- No coverage of retiree dependents
- No withdrawal from employment before retirement
- 1991 net medical expense costs (including administration expense) payable at the end of the calendar year:
    - Before attainment of age 65: $3000
    - After attainment of age 65 (net of Medicare reimbursement): $1500
- Medical expense inflation rate:

1992–1996:	15%
1997:	14%
1998:	13%, declining 1% per year to
2006 and later:	5%

- After-tax interest rate:

1991:	8%
1992:	7%
1993:	6%
1994 and later:	5%

Full eligibility for benefits: age 60
Assumed retirement: age 62
Annual mortality rates:
- Preretirement: 0%
- Postretirement: 10%, except
                     100% in year beginning with age 84.

Example: Employee age 47 on January 1, 1991. Hired at age 25.
- On January 1, 1991:
    - Accumulated postretirement benefit obligation (APBO): $23,975
    - 1991 service cost: $1,090
- On December 31, 1991:
    - 1991 interest cost on OPEB liability: $2,005
- On January 1, 1992:
    - APBO: $27,070

Questions

1. Based on the assumptions given in Exhibit 2, what would be the 1991 accumulated postretirement benefit obligation (APBO), service cost, and interest cost for an employee now age 56 and hired at age 37? _____ How would they change if:
    - The interest rate were increased by 1% in every year? _____
    - The health inflation rate were increased by 1% in every year? _____
    - The retirement age were increased to 65? _____ To 68? _____
    - The benefit accrual period were extended to the expected retirement age? _____ (Note: Under FASB 106, this method is not permitted.)

    Hints for calculation:
    - First, project the probability in each future year of being employed. Then from these probabilities and

the death and retirement rates, project probabilities of survival in retirement.

- Second, project the claim cost to the company per retiree in each future year, reflecting Medicare reimbursement and health care inflation rates.
- Third, determine the expected cash flow of claim payments in each future year from the results of the first and second steps. Discount these flows with interest to determine FASB 106 expected postretirement benefit obligation (EPBO) figures for each future year.

To simplify the calculation, certain assumptions were ignored. What are these assumptions, and what would you expect to be the effects on the illustration if they were explicitly included in the calculation? _____

2. How did IP respond to the OPEB crisis? _____ What responses might companies in general make to the situation? _____
3. What are the advantages and disadvantages of the approach taken by FASB in accounting for OPEB? _____ What other approaches might have been taken? _____
4. When should IP adopt the provisions of FASB 106 for its financial statements, and how should it treat the OPEB transition obligation? _____ Why? _____
5. What do you think would be the effect of early adoption on the upcoming stock? _____ Why? _____

Appendix
Summary of the Major Provisions of FASB 106

The following summary is not meant to be complete but rather to outline significant elements of the OPEB accounting rules.

FASB's general approach was to follow the pension accounting guidelines laid down in FASB 87. Three basic aspects of pension accounting used in applying accrual accounting to OPEB are:

- Delayed recognition of plan changes, gains, and losses, with disclosure of unrecognized amounts;
- Reporting only of net cost in financial statements, with disclosure of periodic cost, accrual of interest, and return on plan assets (if any); and
- Offsetting of plan liabilities and assets in the financial statements.

Key Terms

Actuarial Present Value (APV). The present discounted value of a future contingent payment, taking into account both the time value of money and the probability of payment.

Expected postretirement benefit obligation (EPBO). The APV of benefits paid by the employer's plan.

Accumulated postretirement benefit obligation (APBO). The APV of benefits attributed to service rendered to date.

Transition obligation. The difference between the APBO and the fair value of plan assets (if any) on the date as of which the rules of FASB 106 are adopted by a company. (This amount is a "transition asset" if the value of assets exceeds the APBO.)

Net periodic postretirement benefit cost (NPPBC). Composed of the following elements:

- **Service cost.** The APV of benefits attributed to services rendered during the period;
- **Interest cost.** Interest accruing on the APBO;
- **Actual return on plan assets** reduced by applicable taxes on this return;
- **Amortization of unrecognized prior service cost**;
- **Amortization of transition obligation** if not totally recognized as of the adoption of FASB 106; and
- **Amortization of previous gains and losses.**

Calculation Rules

Substantive plan. The basis for determining benefits is the "substantive plan," which may be different from the written plan. For example, if the employer has established a pattern of increasing benefits in response to increases in medical costs, such a pattern must be projected in determining the benefits for purposes of FASB 106.

Explicit assumptions. FASB 106 requires the use of explicit assumptions, "each of which individually represents the best estimate of a particular future event." However, approximate methods are permitted, "provided the results are reasonably expected not to be materially different" from the use of exact methods. The following are the principal assumptions that are required for the calculation:

- **Discount rate**;
- **Retirement age** or distribution of ages;
- **Factors affecting the amount and timing of future benefit payments**, such as per-capita claims costs by age, sex, geographical area, etc., health-care-cost trend rates, Medicare reimbursement rates. (However, FASB 106 notes that future changes in laws concerning medical costs covered by governmental programs such as Medicare "shall not be anticipated"); and
- **Factors affecting the probability of payment**, such as employee turnover, projected number of employee dependents (for plans covering dependents), and mortality.

In certain cases, other assumptions may be required:

- **Participation rates** (for plans requiring employee contributions); and
- **Salary progression** (for plans providing benefits based on pay).

Attribution of benefits to years of employee service. In general, FASB 106 requires that "an equal amount of the expected postretirement benefit obligation . . . shall be attributed to each year of service in the attribution period." The attribution period normally begins on the date of hire and ends on the date at which the employee is fully eligible for benefits (the "full eligibility date"). This rule was opposed by many companies, including IP, on the grounds that on average employees would retire later than the full eligibility date, and that full accrual of benefits before this expected retirement date was too rapid.

Recognition of cost of increased benefits attributed to prior service. In general this cost is amortized on a straight-line basis to the full eligibility date.

Recognition of transition obligation. FASB 106 gives companies the option of recognizing the transition obligation immediately in the financial statements or of amortizing it on a straight-line basis over the average remaining service period of active plan participants or over 20 years if longer. However, recognition of the cost of OPEB must be at least as rapid as under a pay-as-you-go approach.

Amortization of gains and losses. These arise from experience variances or changes in assumptions. Within certain guidelines, FASB 106 permits any systematic method of amortization.

Required Disclosures

Description of the substantive plan including the employer's funding policy for the plan.

Components of the NPPBC.

Reconciliation of the funded status of the plan with the employer's statement of financial position, showing the following components separately:

- **Fair value of plan assets**, if any;
- **APBO**, separately shown for retirees, other fully eligible employees, and other active plan participants;
- **Unrecognized prior service cost**;
- **Unrecognized net gain or loss**; and
- **Unrecognized transition obligation (or asset).**

Health-care–cost trend rate together with the effects of a 1% increase in this rate on the service and interest components of the NPPBC and on the APBO.

Other key assumptions including the discount rates, salary progression rates (if applicable), expected long-term rate of return on plan assets, and applicable tax rates on this return.

Amount of employer's securities included in plan assets.

Amortization methods for gains and losses.

Effective Date

In general, FASB 106 is effective for fiscal years beginning after December 15, 1992. As usual, FASB encouraged earlier adoption.

CASE
21-2

International Paper (B)

Georges decided to have International Paper (IP) adopt early the provisions of Financial Accounting Standards Board 106 (FASB 106), for fiscal year 1991 beginning January 1, 1991. The full transition obligation was recognized immediately. Accordingly, quarterly results for 1991 were restated. As of January 1 IP recorded an obligation of $350 million ($215 million after tax) to reflect the cumulative effect of the adoption of FASB 106, and income in 1991 was reduced by $25 million ($16 million after tax) for additional expenses related to the new accounting rules.

In January 1992 a successful public offering of 9.2 million shares of common stock brought IP $650 million in proceeds, which were used to repay long-term and short-term borrowings. A simultaneous debt offering also raised $250 million.

Bob Butler noted that part of the success of the offerings was due to IP's policy of close contact with key analysts and ratings agencies about the company's decision to adopt FASB 106 early.

Exhibit 1 shows excerpts from IP's 1991 financial statements and accompanying notes.

This case was prepared by Research Associate Charles A. Nichols, III under the supervision of Professor Mary E. Barth as the basis for class discussion rather than to illustrate either effective or ineffective handling of an administrative situation.

EXHIBIT 1A   International Paper: 1991 Consolidated Statement of Earnings (in millions, except per share amounts for the year ended December 31)

	1991	1990	1989
Net Sales	$12,703	$12,960	$11,378
Costs and Expenses			
Cost of products sold—Note 11	9,341	9,263	7,918
Depreciation and amortization	700	667	559
Distribution expenses	569	528	411
Selling and administrative expenses—Note 11	945	934	789
Taxes other than payroll and income taxes	135	133	91
Reduction in force charge	60		
Business improvement charge		212	
Total Costs and Expenses	11,750	11,737	9,768
Earnings before Interest, Income Taxes and Cumulative Effect of Accounting Change	953	1,223	1,610
Interest expense, net	315	277	205
Earnings before Income Taxes and Cumulative Effect of Accounting Change	638	946	1,405
Provision for income taxes	239	377	541
Earnings before Cumulative Effect of Accounting Change	399	569	864
Cumulative effect of change in accounting for postretirement benefits (less deferred income tax benefit of $135)—Note 11	(215)		
Net Earnings	184	569	864
Preferred dividend requirements			19
Earnings Applicable to Common Shares	$ 184	$ 569	$ 845
Earnings per Common Share			
Earnings before cumulative effect of accounting change	3.61	5.21	7.72
Cumulative effect of change in accounting for postretirement benefits—Note 11	(1.95)		
Earnings per Common Share	1.66	5.21	7.72

Source: International Paper 1991 Annual Report.

Exhibit 1B   International Paper: 1991 Consolidated Balance Sheet (in millions at December 31)

	1991	1990
Assets		
Current Assets		
Cash and temporary investments, at cost, which approximates market	$ 238	$ 256
Accounts and notes receivable, less allowances of $74 in 1991 and $57 in 1990	1,841	1,798
Inventories	1,780	1,638
Other current assets	272	247
Total Current Assets	4,131	3,939
Plants, Properties and Equipment, Net	7,848	7,287
Timberlands	743	751
Investments	383	103
Goodwill	816	687
Deferred Charges and Other Assets	1,020	902
Total Assets	$14,941	$13,669
Liabilities and Common Shareholders' Equity		
Current Liabilities		
Notes payable and current maturities of long-term debt	$ 1,699	$ 1,087
Accounts payable	1,110	1,094
Accrued payroll and benefits	216	195
Accrued income taxes	102	150
Other accrued liabilities....................................	600	629
Total Current Liabilities	3,727	3,155
Long-Term Debt...	3,351	3,096
Deferred Income Taxes	1,044	1,135
Minority Interest and Other Liabilities	1,080	651
Commitments and Contingent Liabilities		
Common Shareholders' Equity		
Common stock, $1 par value	118	117
Paid-in capital	1,264	1,243
Retained earnings	4,592	4,581
Total	5,974	5,941
Less: Common stock held in treasury, at cost	235	309
Total Common Shareholders' Equity	5,739	5,632
Total Liabilities and Common Shareholders' Equity	$14,941	$13,669

Source: International Paper 1991 Annual Report.

Exhibit 1C   International Paper: Note 11 to 1991 Financial Statements

The Company provides certain retiree health care and life insurance benefits covering substantially all U.S. salaried and certain hourly employees. Employees are generally eligible for benefits upon retirement and completion of a specified number of years of creditable service. The Company does not pre-fund these benefits and has the right to modify or terminate certain of these plans in the future.

In the fourth quarter of 1991, the Company adopted the provisions of the Financial Accounting Standards Board's Statement No. 106, "Employers' Accounting for Postretirement Benefits Other Than Pensions," changing to the accrual method of accounting for these benefits effective January 1, 1991. Prior to 1991, postretirement benefit expense was recognized when claims were paid. The Company restated 1991 first-quarter operations to record a pre-tax charge of $350 million ($215 million after taxes or $1.95 per share) as the cumulative effect of an accounting change at that date. This change also increased 1991 pre-tax postretirement benefit expense by $25 million.

Postretirement benefit expense was $42 million, $12 million and $12 million in 1991, 1990 and 1989, respectively. The components of expense in 1991 were as follows:

In millions	*1991*
Service cost–benefits earned during the period	$10
Interest cost of accumulated postretirement benefit obligation	32
Net postretirement benefit cost	$42

The accumulated postretirement benefit obligation, included in Minority Interest and Other Liabilities at December 31, 1991 in the accompanying balance sheet, comprises the following components:

In millions	*1991*
Retirees	$201
Fully eligible active plan participants	84
Other active plan participants	137
Total accumulated postretirement benefit obligation	422
Unrecognized net loss	(17)
Accrued postretirement benefit obligation	$405

Future benefit costs were estimated assuming medical costs would increase at a 15% annual rate, decreasing to a 6% annual growth rate ratably over the next 13 years and then remaining at a 6% annual growth rate thereafter. A 1% increase in this annual trend rate would have increased the accumulated postretirement benefit obligation at December 31, 1991 by $52 million, with an immaterial effect on 1991 postretirement benefit expense. The weighted average discount rate used to estimate the accumulated postretirement benefit obligation was 8.0%.

Source: International Paper 1991 Annual Report.

Question

As a potential investor in IP, how would you react to the company's OPEB accounting decision, disclosures, and assumptions? _____

PART EIGHT

Stockholders' Equity Reporting and Analysis

CHAPTER 22

Stockholders' Equity

The stockholders' equity section of the balance sheet discloses the sources and nature of equity capital, including the types of stock authorized and outstanding and any related statutory or contractual limitations. Also included are a number of other accounts that relate to the stockholders' equity in the firm, such as adjustments for treasury stock, translation gains and losses, unrecognized losses on long-term equity stock investments, certain loans to officers, and deferred compensation related to employee stock-incentive plans. Stockholders' equity is sometimes referred to as "owners' equity" or "net worth." **Illustration 1** shows the stockholders' equity portion of a major U.S. corporation's balance sheet.

Financial statement users should understand the accounting, legal, and financial distinctions between the various accounts that constitute the stockholders' equity section of the balance sheet. Statement users aware of these distinctions are not likely to make the common mistake of treating stockholders' equity as a single account. This error can be costly, particularly when several classes of common stock are involved with very different voting rights and claims on residual assets, when management has engaged in extensive stock buyback transactions, when numerous stock splits and stock dividends have been declared, or when company actions have changed the company's legally-deferred unrestricted capital.

Under these circumstances, a detailed analysis of stockholders' equity is required to appreciate the relative rights of each class of stockholder, the relationship between stock buyback transactions and reported return on equity and earnings per share, and the composition of stockholders' equity which in some jurisdictions may limit a company's ability to pay cash dividends. In addition, statement users need to understand stockholders' equity accounting in order to know how to compute and interpret the common financial statistic "book value per share."

Professor David F. Hawkins prepared this note as the basis for class discussion.

Copyright © 1991 by the President and Fellows of Harvard College. Harvard Business School teaching note 191–143.

ILLUSTRATION 1   Stockholders' Equity Portion of a Major U.S. Corporation's Balance Sheet ($ millions)

	December 31, 1991	December 31, 1990
Stockholders' equity		
Preferred stock, $1.00 par value, authorized 50,000,000 shares; issued—none	—	—
Common stock, $1.00 par value, authorized 200,000,000 shares; issued 34,501,924 shares	34.5	34.5
Paid-in capital	572.1	572.8
Retained earnings	242.4	155.0
Treasury stock, 628,251 shares on December 31, 1991, and 799,841 shares on December 31, 1990, at cost	(15.5)	(19.6)
Unearned portion of restricted stock issued for future service	(8.0)	(11.3)
Cumulative foreign currency adjustment	(71.1)	(68.3)
Guarantees for long-term stock-savings plan	(15.0)	(18.0)
Investment valuation allowance	(10.8)	(9.2)
Stockholder notes receivable	(3.1)	(2.9)
Total stockholders' equity	725.5	633.0

Financial statement users should always be aware of the limitations of the stockholders' equity account. It does not measure the market value of a firm. Rather, it is simply the difference between the accounting measurement of a company's individual assets and liabilities. In jurisdictions where corporations are permitted to pay dividends up to the point where the fair value of assets equals liabilities, it is a poor indicator of dividend-paying potential. Also, because of the introduction of many innovative forms of securities, the traditional distinction between debt and equity is breaking down. Financial reporting has not kept pace with this development. As a result, statement users must look beyond the stockholders' equity section to the notes and listing of liabilities to ensure that they have identified all of a company's actual-and-near-equity.

The stockholders' equity section of non-U.S. corporate balance sheets often includes accounts not normally found in the measurement of U.S. stockholders' equity. For example, the stockholders' equity in non-U.S. corporations may include a portion of the equity in controlled subsidiaries held by minority interests (U.S. corporations exclude this account from stockholders' equity); upward revaluation gains related to adjusting fixed asset and intangible asset carrying values to their fair or appraised value (U.S. corporations carry these assets at cost); and direct one-time charge-offs for good will acquired (U.S. corporations carry goodwill as an asset that is charged to income over periods of up to 40 years). Other differences in stockholders' equity reported by companies in other countries may result from different accounting policies, such as the use of the cost method rather than the equity method to report unconsolidated investee companies. Because of these classifications and accounting differences, statement users should examine the components of stockholders' equity and possibly adjust stockholders' equity to a comparable basis when performing transnational financial analysis involving a consideration of stockholders' equity, either directly or as an element of specific financial ratios.

Stockholders' Equity

Holders of common stock have a residual ownership interest in a company after recognizing the preferred stockholders' preferred position. Common stockholders elect directors, share in the profits of the business after preferred dividends are paid, and in liquidation, share in the residual value of the assets of the company after the claims of all creditors and preferred stockholders have been settled. Often, common stockholders have the option to purchase any new common shares issued by their company in proportion to their holdings. This is called a "preemptive" right.

Common Stock Accounts

The common stockholders' investment in a company is typically shown in three parts: Common Stock—par value, Paid-in Capital, and Retained Earnings.

Common Stock—Par Value.   The stockholders' equity account shows the par, or stated, value of the common shares issued. It is customary to disclose the number of shares authorized by the board of directors, and the number issued. The par value of a share bears no relationship to actual value; it is simply an amount assigned to each share of common stock. This practice satisfies a legal requirement and indicates the limit of the stockholders' liability for the company's debts. To limit legal liability and lessen certain stock-transfer taxes, the par value is usually set as low as possible. Some states permit companies to issue no-par stock, which is assigned a value and recorded on the books at this stated value, which is usually very low.

Paid-in Capital.   Typically, shares are issued at a price in excess of their par, or stated, value. In such cases, the excess amount is shown in the paid-in capital account. In addition, the value of any capital the company received which did not involve issuing shares, such as donated assets, is included in this account. Other transactions (described later) that could affect the capital in excess of par values account include: treasury stock transactions, stock dividends, and stock splits. The adjustments to the paid-in capital account associated with accounting for "pooling of interests" and the financial analysis significance of these adjustments have been discussed in an earlier chapter dealing with business combination accounting.

Accounting Entries.   The accounting entries for a new stock issue are fairly straightforward. For example, assume the Lawson Corporation issued at $25 per share 10,000 new common shares with a par value of $5 per share. The underwriting costs were $15,000. Consequently, the net proceeds to the company from the issue were $235,000. The practice is to show the increase in common stock accounts net of the direct underwriting costs associated with the stock issue paid to third parties. None of these transactions, including the underwriting costs, affect net income.

The accounting entries are:

```
Dr. Cash . . . . . . . . . . . . . . . . . . . . . . . . . . . . . . . . . . . . . . . . . . . . . 235,000
    Cr. Common Stock—Par Value . . . . . . . . . . . . . . . . . . . . . . . . . . .          50,000
        Paid-in Capital . . . . . . . . . . . . . . . . . . . . . . . . . . . . . . . . . . .      185,000
```

Retained Earnings. Retained earnings represent the accumulated earnings of the company less dividends and, in some cases, other adjustments. If there is no paid-in capital available, the retained earnings account may properly be charged with those items normally absorbed by the paid-in capital account. Also, under some circumstances, such as the declaration of a stock dividend, a portion of the retained earnings account may be transferred to the paid-in capital account (see below).

Preferred Stock

Preferred stock is a form of equity capital. Owners of preferred stock have certain privileges ahead of the common stockholders, such as preference in dividends or liquidation. Preferred stock dividends are usually fixed in amount and can be noncumulative or cumulative. Usually, no dividend can be paid on the common stock until preferred dividends previously earned but not declared are paid. Preferred shares may be classified as participating. That is, the owners can participate beyond their preference dividend in dividend distributions with the common stockholders once a specified level of dividends has been paid to the common stockholders. In liquidation, after the claims of creditors have been settled, preferred stockholders have a preferred fixed claim on assets relative to the common stockholders. Typically, preferred stock does not carry voting rights. Most preferred stock is redeemable under certain conditions at the corporation's option, according to a specified price schedule that usually includes a special redemption premium. Sometimes, preferred stockholders are granted the privilege of converting their holdings into shares of common stock. The conversion ratio and conditions vary from issue to issue, but the company's intent is usually the same: to make the preferred stock more attractive to potential purchasers.

Treasury Stock

Treasury stock is a company's own stock that has been issued and subsequently reacquired by the company but not yet retired formally. Treasury stock is shown as a deduction at cost from equity capital, rather than as an asset, because legally a company can reacquire its own stock only with unrestricted capital. Treasury stock does not have voting privileges, does not enter into the computation of earnings per share, and does not receive dividends.

When treasury stock is retired, the common stock account is reduced by the stock's par, or stated, value. The number of shares authorized remains unchanged, but the number of shares issued is reduced by the number of shares retired. Any difference between the retired treasury stock's cost and the amount charged to the common stock account is deducted from the paid-in capital account applicable to the retired class of shares. If the paid-in capital account is inadequate to absorb the full excess of cost over par value, any remaining excess is charged to retained earnings.

When treasury stock that has not been retired is resold, the paid-in capital account is adjusted to reflect any difference between the stock's cost and selling price. Losses on sales of treasury stock in excess of cumulative net gains from sales or retirements of the same class of stock are charged to retained earnings. Such transactions do not give rise to corporate profits or losses.

"Greenmail"

A "greenmail" transaction occurs when treasury stock is acquired at above fair value. Typically, these transactions are entered into either to end or to reduce the ability of large stockholders to pressure a takeover of the issuing company. In such cases, the accounting presumption is that the price premium was paid to obtain a benefit beyond the simple acquisition of treasury stock. As a result, the excess of price over fair value is charged to income and not as a reduction of stockholders' equity.

Dividends

Dividend distribution to stockholders can be in the form of cash, additional stock, or property. Depending on the jurisdiction, dividends may be limited to the accumulated earnings of the company or up to the point at which the fair value of the company's assets equals its liabilities. Debt covenants often place limits on dividend payments. Any restrictions as to dividend distributions should be fully disclosed.

Legal Obligation

The board of directors' declaration of dividends legally binds the company to pay them, unless the stockholders rescind the decision. Therefore, at the time dividends in cash or property are declared, retained earnings is charged with the dividend amount, and a current liability account, dividends payable, is established. When the dividends are distributed, the liability account is reduced accordingly.

Stock Dividends and Splits

Stock dividends and splits are treated differently for accounting purposes, although they are generally regarded, from the viewpoint of financial practice and tax regulations, as being essentially the same because, in either case, stock dividends and splits leave the stockholders' proportional share of equity unchanged.

Stock Dividends.   Accounting practice treats a stock dividend on the issuing company's books as if it were a dividend to the recipient, principally because many recipients appear to regard it as such. The Committee on Accounting Procedure (CAP) believed that where these circumstances exist, the company must "in the public interest" account for the transaction by transferring from retained earnings to the permanent equity capital accounts (i.e., the common stock and paid-in capital) an amount equal to the "fair value" of the additional shares issued. For example, to account for the issuance of 10,000 shares with a par value of $5 and a fair value of $25 as a stock dividend, the following entries would be required:

Dr. Retained Earnings	250,000	
Cr. Common Stock—Par Value		50,000
Paid-in Capital		200,000

Typically, the declaration date is used for determining the fair market value of stock dividends.

Stock Splits.   Where the number of additional shares issued as a stock dividend is so great that it has, or might reasonably be expected to have, the effect of materially reducing the market value per share, CAP believed there was no likelihood of dividend income implications or possible other constructions that stockholders might attribute to stock dividends. In such circumstances, the nature of the transaction clearly indicates it is a stock split. Consequently, CAP did not require retained earnings to be capitalized, except to the extent required by law.

For example, assume a company splits its stock two for one, issues 100,000 new shares, and reduces its par value per common share from $5 to $2.50. Under such circumstances, no accounting entries would be required. The common stock account would remain unchanged. The stockholders' equity section of the balance sheet would now show twice as many authorized and outstanding shares as before the split, and a par value per share of half the original value.

20 to 25 Percent Rule.   The problem of determining at what point a stock dividend becomes so large as to constitute a stock split was resolved by Accounting Research Bulletin (ARB) No. 43, as follows:

> Obviously, the point at which the relative size of the additional shares issued becomes large enough to materially influence the unit market price of the stock will vary with individual companies and under differing market conditions, and hence, no single percentage can be laid down as a standard for determining when capitalization of earned surplus in excess of legal requirements is called for and when it is not. However, on the basis of a review of market action in the case of shares of a number of companies having relatively recent stock distributions, it would appear that there would be few instances involving the issuance of additional shares of less than, say, 20 percent or 25 percent of the number previously outstanding where the effect would not be such as to call for the procedure [described for accounting for stock dividends].

Stock-Based Compensation

FASB Statement No. 123, "Accounting for Stock-Based Compensation," sets forth the FASB's preferred alternative approach to the one used in the past by most corporations to account for stock based compensation. Most companies where stock-based compensation is used extensively did not switch to the FASB's preferred alternative, and few investors use for equity valuation purposes the new stock-based compensation disclosures mandated for those companies that did not switch.

The FASB's decision to approve alternative ways to account for essentially the same transaction makes it imperative that statement users understand fully the allowed alternative approaches so they can understand when comparing companies the impact on earnings when different approaches to stock-based compensation accounting have been elected by the reporting companies.

Summary

FASB Statement No. 123 introduced a new preferred accounting standard for stock option transactions entered into in fiscal years beginning after December 15, 1995.

FASB Statement No. 123 allows companies to select one of two allowed approaches to accounting and reporting of stock-based employee compensation plans. They are the:

   a. Intrinsic value method; and

   b. Fair value method.

The FASB encourages companies to adopt the fair value method, but it is not required. They can use the intrinsic value method prescribed in APB Opinion No. 25, "Accounting for Stock Issued to Employees," which is the pre-FASB Statement No. 123 standard dealing with stock-based compensation plans. If a company uses the APB Opinion 25 approach, it must disclose the pro forma impact on income and earnings per share of using the fair value method.

Intrinsic Value Method Explained

The pre FASB Statement No. 123 stock based compensation standard prescribed by APB Opinion 25 is based on the intrinsic value method. Under this approach, compensation cost is the excess, if any, of the quoted market price of the stock at the measurement date over the employee's exercise price. The measurement date is the first date that *both* the number of options to be granted and the exercise price are known.

In the case of most fixed stock option plans, (i.e., plans where the number of optioned shares and the exercise price is known at the grant date), the grant date is the measurement date. Typically, at this time, there is no intrinsic value or excess of exercise price over market price. Consequently, no compensation cost is recognized. In contrast, a compensation cost is sometimes recognized for other types of stock compensation plans under the intrinsic value method. Typically, these are plans with variable, usually performance-based, features, where either the option price or the number of option shares is not determinable until some date beyond the grant date.

Any compensation cost recognized under the intrinsic value method is amortized to income as a charge over the period the corporation benefits from the employee's service.

Fair Value Method

Under the fair value based method, stock-based compensation cost is measured at the grant date based on the value of the award, and is recognized as a charge to earnings over the employee's service period, which is usually the vesting period.

In the case of stock options, the fair value is determined using an option-pricing model. Once the fair value is determined at the grant date, it is not subsequently adjusted for changes in the price of the underlying stock or its volatility, the life of the option, dividends on the stock, or the risk free interest rate.

Other Plans

FASB Statement No. 123 does not require a compensation cost to be recognized for employee stock purchase plan discounts if three conditions are met. They are: (a) the discount is relatively small; (b) substantially all full time employees participate on an equitable basis; and, (c) the plan does not incorporate any stock option features.

The compensation cost of stock awards required to be settle in cash as determined by increases in the employer's stock price is the amount of the change in the stock price in the periods in which the changes occur.

The fair value of nonvested or restricted stock awarded to an employee is measured at the market price of a share of nonrestricted stock at the grant date. If there will be restrictions imposed on the employee after vesting, the fair value estimate should take these restrictions into account.

Intrinsic Value Method Explained

Under APB Opinion 25—the intrinsic value standard—stock option plans are classified as either "compensatory" or "noncompensatory." The distinction is important. As the category labels suggest, when options are granted, a compensation expense is recognized in one case, but not in the other.

Four Tests   Noncompensatory option plans are considered to be a vehicle for companies to raise capital. For a plan to be classified as noncompensatory, it must meet all of the following tests:

  a. Be open to most employees after meeting minimal employment qualifications;
  b. Grant options on a substantially equal basis to participating employees:
  c. Have a reasonable exercise period for options granted; and
  d. Have an exercise price approximately equal to the market price on the grant date.

If a plan fails to meet any of the above criteria, it is classified as a compensatory plan. That is, it is considered to be a plan to compensate employees beyond their regular remuneration.

Noncompensatory Plan   The accounting for a noncompensatory plan is simple. Accounting entries are made only if the employee exercises the option to acquire stock.

The entry is made at the exercise date. It is a debit to cash for the amount received by the issuer, a credit to common stock for the par value of the stock issued, and a credit to the capital in excess of par value ("paid-in-capital") for the excess of the purchase price over the stock's par value.

To illustrate, assume an option is granted for 1,000 shares at an exercise price of $25 per share (par value $1), which is also the market price at the grant date. Consequently, no compensation is recognized since the plan is assumed to meet all of the other tests to qualify as a noncompensatory plan. The option period is five years. At the end of the five-year option period, the employee exercises the option. The current market price of the stock is $50. The accounting entries are:

Assets		Owners' Equity	
+ Cash	$25,000	+ Common Stock	$1,000
		($1 par value)	
		+ Paid in Capital	24,000
	$25,000		$25,000

The nonrecognition of compensation is based on the reasoning that if the employee had exercised the option on the grant date, the price paid would be the same as if the stock had been purchased on the open market.

Compensatory Plan   Classification of an option plan as compensatory does not necessarily mean that compensation will ultimately be recorded by the issuing corporation. Under a compensatory plan, a compensation cost to the issuing corporation will only result if the market price of the optioned shares exceeds the exercise price on the so-called measurement date. The measurement date is the first date that both the number of options to be granted and the exercise price is known. At that date, the compensation cost is the excess of the market price over the exercise price. This excess is then amortized over the period the corporation receives benefits from the employees' services.

Compensatory plans can be grouped into one of two broad groups:

a. Fixed plans; and
b. Variable plans.

A *fixed* compensatory plan is a plan that fails the tests for a noncompensatory plan, but specifies the number of optioned shares and the exercise price at the grant date.

The accounting for a fixed compensatory plan is fairly straightforward. Any excess of the optioned stock's market price over its exercise price at the grant date is compensation. If compensation cost must be recognized, the accounting entry on the grant date is as follows: Two offsetting accounts in the stockholders' equity section of the balance sheet are established. A positive balance equal to the compensation cost is recorded as "Common stock options outstanding." Offsetting this account is a balance of equal amount labeled "Deferred stock option compensation." The net of the two accounts is a zero balance. Subsequently, the deferred stock option compensation balance is amortized on a straight line basis as a charge to earnings over the period the corporation receives the benefit of the employees service. If the options outstanding are exercised at the exercise date, the common stock options outstanding account is eliminated and the balance added to the paid in capital account. The issuance of the stock is accounted for in the same manner as described above in the noncompensatory example.

To illustrate, assume an option is granted for 1,000 shares at an exercise price of $25 per share ($1 par value), which is $10 per share below the $35 per share market price of the shares at the grant date. In this case, a $10 per share compensation cost related to the granted options must be recognized. The option period is five years. At the grant date, the accounting entries are:

Owners' Equity	
+ Common stock options outstanding	$10,000*
+ Deferred stock option compensation	(10,000)**

*$10/share × 1,000 shares.
**A debit or negative balance.

At the end of the first year, the compensation expense is recognized as follows (similar entries are made in periods 2–5):

Owners' Equity		*Income Statement*	
– Deferred stock option compensation	$2,000**	+ Compensation expense	$2,000*

*$\dfrac{\$10,000}{5 \text{ yrs}}$ = $2,000 = annual expense and annual reduction in deferred stock option compensation balance
**A credit entry or reduction of a debit or negative balance

At the end of the fifth year, the deferred stock option compensation balance has all been expensed to income (see above). If the option is exercised, the accounting entries are:

Assets		*Owners' Equity*	
+ Cash	$25,000	– Common stock options outstanding	($10,000)
		+ Common stock ($1 par value)	1,000*
		+ Paid in capital	34,000**
	$25,000		$25,000

* $1 × 1,000
** 1,000 × ($25 – $1) + $10,000

A *variable* compensatory plan—and there are a number of different versions—is one where *either* the number of options or the option price is unknown at the grant date.

The accounting for a variable plan is complex and can involve considerable uncertainty. This results from the accounting requirement to record the potential compensation cost at the grant date even though the measurement date is subsequent to the grant date. In the usual situation where the option price is unknown and the number of optioned shares is known, this problem is solved at the end of each accounting period by assuming the period end stock price adjusted by the terms of the option agreement relating to the exercise price is the exercise price. Each period, the difference between the market price and the exercise price becomes the current estimate of the compensation cost per share. This amount will vary from period to period as the optioned stock's market price changes.

To illustrate, assume an option is granted for 1,000 shares at an exercise price equal to 80% of the company's stock price at a future date when the company's return on equity reaches 20%. The option can be exercised any time after that date, but must be exercised no later than five years after the grant date. At the end of the first year, the stock's market price is $25. At the end of the second year, the stock price rises to $30. In year 3, the 20% return on equity goal is reached. The year 3 yearend stock price is $40.

At the end of the first year, the estimated total compensation cost is calculated as follows:

Yearend market price of stock	$25
Estimated option price ($25 × .8)	− 20
Estimated compensation cost per share	$ 5
Total optioned shares	× 1,000
Estimated total compensation cost	$5,000
(as of end of year 1)	

At the end of the second year, the estimated total compensation cost is calculated as follows:

Yearend market price of stock	$30
Estimated option price ($30 × .8)	− 24
Estimated compensation cost per share	$ 6
Total optioned shares	× 1,000
Estimated total compensation cost	$6,000
(as of end of year 2)	

Each period, the current estimate of the compensation cost must be amortized over the employees' service period, which may be unknown at the grant date. Typically, if the service period is unknown, the amortization period is assumed to be the vesting period, which is assumed to be the period from the grant date to the first date the stock can be exercised. Based on this estimate of the vesting period, at the end of each period the current estimate of total compensation cost is multiplied by the percentage the expired service period bears to the estimated service period. From this sum, the compensation expense recognized to date, if any, is subtracted. The residual, if any, is the current period's compensation expense. The offset is to the common stock options outstanding account.

The year 1 compensation expense is calculated at the end of year 1 as follows:

Total estimated compensation cost (as of end of year 1—see above)	$5,000
Divided by amortization period in years	5
Equals year 1 compensation expense	$1,000

The accounting entry at the end of year 1 is:

Owners' Equity		Income Statement	
+ Common stock options outstanding	$1,000	+ Compensation expense	$1,000

At the end of the second year, the compensation expense is calculated as follows:

Total estimated compensation cost (as of end of year 2—see above)	$6,000
Percentage that should be amortized by end of year 2 (.4 = 2 yrs/5 yrs)	× .4
Amount that *should* be amortized to date	$2,400
Amortized to date	(1,000)
Year 2 compensation expense	$1,400

The accounting entries at the end of year 2 are:

Owners' Equity		Income Statement	
+ Common stock options outstanding	$1,400	+ Compensation expense	$1,400

By the end of year 3, the return on equity goal is met.

Consequently, the measurement date has arrived. The exercise price (80% of $40 = $32) and the compensation cost [$(40 − 32) × 1,000 = $8,000] is known for the first time.

At this point, the accounting for the variable compensatory option plan during years 4 and 5 becomes the same as that used for a fixed compensatory option plan.

The transition to the fixed-plan-type accounting requires the measurement of the year 3 compensation expense. It is calculated as follows:

Yearend market price of stock	$ 40
Actual option price ($40 × .8)	− 32
Actual compensation cost per share	$ 8
Total optioned shares	× 1,000
Actual compensation cost	$8,000
Percentage that should be amortized by end of year 3 (.6 = 3 yrs/5 yrs)	× .6
Amount that *should* be amortized to date	$4,800
Amortized to date	(2,400)
Year 3 compensation expense	$2,400

The accounting entries to recognize the year 3 compensation expense are:

Owners' Equity		*Income Statement*	
+ Common stock options outstanding	$2,400	+ Compensation expense	$2,400

A second set of accounting entries are also made to recognize the shift to fixed plan style accounting. The entries are:

Owners' Equity	
Common stock options outstanding (Beginning Balance)	$4,800
+ End of year 3 addition to adjust to actual compensation cost	3,200
	$8,000
+ Deferred stock option compensation	(3,200)*

*A debit or negative balance.

As noted above, the accounting over the remaining two years is identical to that illustrated in the fixed compensatory plan example.

Fair Value Method Explained

The FASB believes that the fair value method is the preferred accounting for stock options because:

   a. Stock options represent compensation and that the amount of associated cost can be determined with sufficient reliability using accepted option pricing models for recognition in financial statements.
   b. Fixed and variable stock option plans are treated equally.
   c. It is consistent with the accounting treatment of equity instruments in other situations.
   d. The information provided is relevant and useful to statement users.

Option Pricing Model Used   The objective of the fair value method's measurement process is to estimate the fair value of a stock option based on the optioned stock's price at the grant date. The fair value of stock options granted by public companies can be estimated using an option-pricing model that takes into account as of the grant date the following (illustrative example values):

   a. The exercise price per share ($50)
   b. Expected life of the option (6 years)
   c. The current price of the underlying ($1 Par Value) stock and its expected volatility ($50 and 30%)
   d. Expected dividend yield on the stock (2.5%)
   e. The risk-free interest rate for the expected term of the option (7.5%)

To illustrate, using the above values, the Black-Scholes option-pricing model modified for dividends indicates a fair value of $17.15 for each option at the grant date. For further illustration purposes, assume 1,000 options are granted with a three-year vesting period and all of the options are exercised at the first vested date.

Adjustments Needed   The fair value of a stock option determined using an option-pricing model meeting the above specifications must be adjusted to reflect FASB Statement No. 123's requirement that the total compensation cost recognized is the fair value of all options that *actually vest.* To accomplish this, the Statement allows an entity either to estimate at the grant date the number of options expected to vest or to recognize compensation cost each period based on the number of options not yet forfeited.

   To illustrate the grant date adjustment alternative, assume the 1,000 options are granted and management estimates a 3% forfeiture rate per year over a three-year vesting period. Using the $17.15 fair value per option figure calculated above, the expected fair value of the options at the grant date is $15,652 (1,000 × .97 × .97 × .97 × $17.15).

Compensation Cost Recognition   Under the fair value method, the compensation cost for future services is recognized over the periods which the related employee services are provided. The offsetting entry to the compensation expense is a corresponding credit to paid in capital—stock options. Previously recognized compensation cost is not reversed if a vested employee stock expires unexercised.

To illustrate, the year 1 compensation cost is $5,217 ($15,652/3). The accounting entries are:

Owners' Equity	*Income Statement*

+ Paid in capital—$5,217
   stock options
	+ Compensation $5,217
	   expense

In the absence of a change in estimate or experience different from that initially assumed, the same accounting entries would be made to recognize compensation cost over the remaining two years of the vesting period.

Exercise Date Accounting   At the time the option is exercised, the accounting for the issuance of the stock is straightforward.

Assuming the forfeiture assumption is realized, the issuance of 913 shares of stock (1,000 × .97 × .97 × .97) upon exercise of the option is as follows:

Assets		*Owners' Equity*	
+ Cash	$45,650*	− Paid in capital stock options	$(15,651)**
		+ Common stock ($1 Par Value)	913
		+ Paid in Capital	60,388
	$45,650		$45,650

*913 shares × $50
**$5,217 × 3

Expired Options   If options expire unexercised, the previously recognized compensation cost is not reversed. When this occurs, the paid-in-capital—stock options account is closed to the paid-in-capital account.

Disclosure Requirements

Irrespective of whether FASB Statement No. 123 or APB Opinion 25 is used to account for employee stock options, a company is required to disclose certain information. The principal required disclosures relate to the company's plan, plan experience, and option valuation.

FASB Statement No. 123 requires disclosure of the intrinsic value (security price and exercise price) and time value estimates and option price model used to compute the value of options granted and compensation cost.[1] A typical disclosure for a public company of the time value related assumptions might read as follows:

> . . . The fair value of each option grant was estimated on the date of grant using the Black-Scholes option-pricing model with the following assumptions for 1996, 1997, and 1998, respectively: risk-free interest rates of 6.5, 7.6, and 7.4 percent; dividend yield of 1.5 percent for all years; expected lives of 6, 6, and 7 years; and volatility of 24, 26, and 29 percent.

Statement users should examine and test for reasonableness these disclosed estimates, since their impact on the fair value of options differs greatly. For example, an increase in the expected volatility assumption can have a very significant positive impact on the value of the stock option. An increase in the expected dividend yield assumption can lead to a significant decrease in an option's value. An increase in the risk-free interest rate assumption will have a significant positive impact on an option's value. And, an increase in the term of the option can have a very significant positive impact on an option's value.

Statement No. 123 requires a special disclosure by companies that continue to use Opinion 25. These companies must present pro forma tax effects, net income, and earnings per share figures based on the Statement No. 123's fair value method. These pro forma figures need not be disclosed in interim statements unless a complete set of financial statements is presented.

Stock Purchase Loans

Sometimes corporations lend money to employees to acquire the company's common stock. The unpaid balance of these loans is reported as a deduction from stockholders' equity.

Employee Stock Ownership Plans

Employee stock ownership plans (ESOPs) are a tax advantage vehicle for corporations to sell common stock to employees. The typical ESOP works as follows: A company forms an ESOP to acquire and hold stock for its employees. It borrows funds that are in turn lent to the ESOP for the purpose of purchasing common stock in the company. The loan is at an advantageous rate because the lender receives certain tax advantages for making an ESOP loan. The company and ESOP loans have similar terms. The ESOP pays off its loan through dividends paid on the stock and tax-deductible contributions from the company. The company funds its contributions primarily through reduced employee compensation and benefits. For financial statement purposes, the company's ESOP-related borrowing is listed as a company liability and its loan to the ESOP is shown as a reduction in stockholders' equity. Such accounting is also practiced if the employer guarantees a direct loan to the ESOP, rather than borrowing the funds and then re-lending them to the ESOP.

---

[1]An option's value consists of two components—its intrinsic value and its time value.

Other Accounts

Two other accounts that frequently appear in the stockholders' equity section of the balance sheet are cumulative translation adjustments and valuation allowances for marketable equity securities. Cumulative translation adjustments are the cumulative gains or losses arising from the translation of the foreign currency statements of foreign subsidiaries into U.S. dollars in situations where the U.S. dollar is designated as the functional currency for statement translation purposes. The valuation allowance records the amount by which the current market value of marketable equity securities classified as long-term assets is below their original cost.[2] Many financial analysts ignore the balance sheet accounting treatment of these two accounts and include them in quality-of-earnings assessments. The accounting and financial analysis significance for these two items are discussed in other chapters.

Stockholders' Equity Analysis

The analysis of shareholders' equity typically focuses on the determination of book value, which is equivalent to stockholders' equity with or without certain adjustments. Many financial authors relegate book value to a low level of importance (or even a meaningless statistic) in the hierarchy of financial ratio data. Such assignment is a mistake because there are many practical applications in which book value plays an important role. In such situations, the question of what book value figure is relevant depends on the analyst's purpose. Also, in the case of complex capital structure situations, there may be controversy over the appropriate way to calculate the relevant book value per share figure.

Stockholders' Book Value

In companies with only common shares outstanding, the stockholders' book value is equal to stockholders' equity. If there is preferred stock outstanding, however, the common stockholders' book value is equal to their equity less the preferred stock. If preferred stock dividends are in arrears, they are excluded from book value. The preferred stock value used in making this calculation is its liquidation value, which may differ from its par value or call value. If more than one class of common stock is outstanding, book value should be allocated to each class in accordance with the rules governing preference in liquidation.

Adjusted Book Value.　　Typically, a firm's book value is equivalent to its stockholders' equity as determined by generally accepted accounting principles. In certain cases, this figure may be adjusted.

---

[2]The FASB has proposed that these "other accounts" be reported in stockholders' equity under the caption "Accumulated other comprehensive income."

In some situations, a distinction is made between book value and tangible book value, which is owners' equity after eliminating intangible assets from the asset side of the basic accounting equation (stockholders' equity = assets − liabilities). Tangible book value is of interest to creditors concerned with estimating net collateral values represented by "hard" assets that may have some value in liquidation.

Sometimes in loan covenants, all or a portion of the deferred tax liability is considered equivalent to equity and, as such, is included in the definition of stockholders' equity for determining permissible debt-to-equity ratio limits.

In liquidation analysis, book value is usually based on the estimated liquidation values of a company's individual assets rather than its balance sheet values.

Accounting book values are frequently adjusted to a market value equivalent in selling situations, when the company's accounting book value is significantly below its book value based on the current market value of its assets and liabilities, including such items as trademarks, patents, and liabilities, such as contingencies, which may not be listed on the balance sheet.

Book Value per Share.   As its name implies, book value per share is equal to book value divided by the number of common shares outstanding at the end of the accounting period. Some analysts argue that it would be more conservative to include dilutive senior convertible debt issues, options, and warrants in the book value per share calculation. That would also adjust book value for any capital additions assumed to arise from debt conversions.

Accounting Difference Adjustments.   Comparisons of company book values can be misleading unless certain adjustments are made for differences in accounting policies and real values. Conservative accounting practices such as accelerated depreciation, LIFO inventory accounting, and rapid amortization of intangibles tend to depress book values relative to those of companies using more liberal accounting methods. Accounting adjustments, such as adding back LIFO reserves to inventory, should be made when comparing book values of companies with different approaches to accounting. In the case of some companies, there may also be a significant difference between the book and market values of assets that enter into the book value calculation. These value differences should be considered when making intercompany book value comparisons.

Not Going Concern Value.   Rarely will the book value of a company be equivalent to its market value as a going concern. Therefore, book value is often regarded as having little value for most commercial and financial purposes. Despite this view, book value figures are used in a variety of situations. Many private companies, in the absence of a market-determined stock price, use book value per share as the equivalent of their stocks' value when pricing shares for buyback agreements and stock option awards. Some utility regulators use book value as a basis for determining allowable rates of return. Stock prices are often quoted as a multiple of book value, as a way to communicate the relative value of stocks. Book value is also used frequently in defining debt covenants. Finally, many business acquisition agreements include provisions for purchase price adjustments if the acquired company's book value is less than a certain figure after any possibly required adjustments to its assets and liabilities based on post-acquisition audit.

Other Information

Beyond using the stockholders' equity section of the balance sheet to compute book value, it should be examined for such matters as possible debt covenant violations; accounting adjustments that did not go through income, such as translation gains or losses; changes in the relative standing of various classes of equity holders; restrictions on dividend payments; possible dilution from holders of convertible debt, options, and warrants; and possible value to others in liquidation, merger, or acquisition.

It is particularly important to note whether or not stock purchase rights have been distributed to stockholders as part of an anti-takeover plan. These rights entitle the holder to purchase additional common stock in the company should an outsider acquire or tender for a substantial amount of the company's stock. These rights may reduce the company's takeover value and eliminate the possibility of its stock being bid up in an unfriendly takeover attempt.

Buybacks

The effect of stock buybacks should be analyzed carefully. They can increase a company's return on equity and earnings per share, but such improvements may hide a deteriorating operating situation. In the absence of future buybacks, the improved return on equity may deteriorate over time, and the gain in earnings per share will not persist beyond a few years. In stock buyback situations, analysts should always compute the company's key ratios before and after the buyback effect for the year it takes place and for several years thereafter to separate the effect of the buyback from those of the company's other activities.

Changing Nature of Debt and Equity Distinction

In recent years, the distinction between debt and equity has become blurred as the financial structure of corporations changed as new securities incorporating novel options, such as puts, were issued and derivative securities and swaps arrangements became commonplace. In the absence of clear guidelines, these changes in business financing have raised a number of accounting issues as to how to account for hybrid securities combining both debt and equity characteristics, such as convertible debt with warrants. Currently, the Financial Accounting Standards Board is moving toward new standards to cover these nontraditional forms of equity and debt. The breakdown of the well-defined distinction between debt and equity has also challenged existing public policy, legal, taxation and bankruptcy positions that assumed a clear separation of stockholder and creditor interests. Adaptations to the new realities of corporate financial structures are being made in these areas. The emergence of hybrid securities is also changing financial theory and financial analysis. Theories about the optimal ratio of debt to equity threaten to be replaced by theories specifying the optimal form of securities. Similarly, the utility of common ratios such as debt-to-equity and net-income-to-owners'-equity for financial analysis purposes is also being questioned.

Those that issue and use financial statements must be alert to the many changes flowing from the recent innovations in corporate financial structures. In particular, statement users should not blindly accept the accounting distinction between debt and equity. They must examine all elements of a company's financial structure to determine what in reality constitutes its equity from both the legal and financial points of view; incorporate these determinations in their financial ratio analyses; and assess how this view of the company differs from one based on the conventional reporting of its debt and equity. This assessment should include a consideration of stockholder and creditor claims and rights, financial risk, potential to adopt alternative capital structures, takeover defense value, tax status, and level of security-market understanding of the true debt-to-equity situation.

Nutra Foods

"Here's the entire mess," said Ed McCowan, as papers of various sizes and colors fluttered from the large manila envelope and spread over the desk of Dan Conner, CPA.

I bought 40 shares of Nutra Foods common last year in May. Since then I've received proxy statements, notices of stock splits, stock certificates, quarterly financial statements, and a few dividend checks. When this thick annual report came in yesterday's mail, I called you. I knew what to do with those little dividend checks, but to tell the truth I don't know what the rest of this means. I thought the annual report would explain things, but I don't see any relationship between my 40 shares and the numbers in the report.

If that wasn't enough, this morning I read in the paper that Nutra expects to borrow $3 million for 15 years at 10%. The deal is expected to close in the next 30 days. The company anticipates using the cash to buy back from a founding stockholder's estate 100,000 shares, which would be at approximately $30 per share at current prices. What will this do to my stock? How does this impact the company?

"It appears that you saved everything, Ed," said Dan Conner. "Let's see if we can list things as they happened from the beginning." He made these notes on a desk pad as he selected papers from the assortment before him:

May 5, 1994	Bought 40 common at 38 plus commission	$1,539.60
July 20, 1994	Received cash dividends, 40 at 25 cents	10.00
October 20, 1994	Received cash dividends, 40 at 25 cents	10.00
October 25, 1994	Received two shares, common stock dividend	
January 20, 1995	Received cash dividends, 42 at 25 cents	10.50
March 15, 1995	Received 21 shares, 3 for 2 stock split	
April 20, 1995	Received cash dividends, 63 at 20 cents	12.60

Professor David F. Hawkins prepared this case as the basis for class discussion rather than to illustrate either effective or ineffective handling of an administrative situation.
Copyright © 1995 by the President and Fellows of Harvard College. Harvard Business School case 196–038.

Exhibit 1   Nutra Foods Corporation Comparative Balance Sheets, April 30, 1995 and 1994

	1995	1994
Assets		
Current assets:		
Cash	$ 996,020	$ 1,124,588
Receivables (net)	5,076,894	5,084,087
Inventories, at the lower of cost (FIFO basis) or market	10,440,509	8,708,578
Total current assets	$16,513,423	$14,917,253
Prepaid expenses	133,434	230,002
Plant and equipment:		
Land	$ 290,349	$ 346,319
Buildings and leasehold improvements	4,200,760	4,719,515
Machinery and equipment	3,916,508	4,275,927
Automotive equipment	601,393	586,030
Construction in progress	2,033,324	—
	$11,042,334	$ 9,927,791
Less: Accumulated depreciation and amortization	5,038,251	4,532,823
Net plant and equipment	$ 6,004,083	$ 5,394,823
Total assets	$22,650,940	$20,542,078
Liabilities and Stockholders' Equity		
Current liabilities:		
Bank loans	$ 2,192,500	$ 1,350,000
Current maturities of long-term debt	170,790	163,478
Accounts payable and accrued liabilities	2,187,440	1,770,026
Income taxes	1,014,527	936,889
Dividends payable	126,811	102,554
Total current liabilities	$ 5,692,068	$ 4,322,947
Long-term debt, noncurrent portion	3,660,223	3,831,013
Deferred income taxes and other expenses	273,850	174,225
	$ 9,626,141	$ 8,328,185
Stockholders' equity:		
Cumulative 4% preferred stock, par value $100; authorized 15,000 shares, issued 8,995 shares less 198 shares in treasury	$ 879,700	(See **Exhibit 2**)
Common stock, par value $5; authorized 1 million shares, issued 590,552 shares, (4,482 shares in treasury, see below)	2,952,760	″
Capital in excess of par value	2,853,702	″
Retained earnings:		″
Reserve for plant expansion	1,466,676	″
Unappropriated[a]	4,997,457	″
	$13,150,295	″
Less: Treasury stock, common (4,482 shares at cost)	125,496	″
Total stockholders' equity	$13,024,799	$12,213,893
Total liabilities and stockholders' equity	$22,650,940	$20,542,078

[a]Under terms of the long-term debt agreement, $2,330,808 of retained earnings at April 30, 1995, is restricted against payment of cash dividends on or purchase of common stock.

EXHIBIT 2   Common Stock, Capital in Excess of Par Value, and Retained Earnings for the Year Ended April 30, 1995

| | Common Stock | | Capital in Excess of Par Value | Retained Earnings | |
	Shares	Par Value		Restricted for Plant Expense	Unappropriated
Balance at May 1, 1994	375,130	$1,875,650	$3,197,277	$3,500,000	$2,742,831
Add:					
Net income for the year	—	—	—	—	1,376,871
Gain on sale of 600 shares common treasury stock	—	—	17,716	—	—
Discount on 245 shares of preferred stock purchased	—	—	4,003	—	—
Reduction in reserve for plant expansion	—	—	—	(2,033,324)	2,033,324
Total	375,130	$1,875,650	43,218,996	$1,466,676	$6,153,026
Add or (deduct):					
Transfer to common stock in connection with 3-for-2 stock split	196,690	893,450	(983,450)	—	—
Cash dividends:					
Preferred ($4 per share)	—	—	—	—	(35,386)
Common ($0.95 per share)	—	—	—	—	(408,367)
5% stock dividend, recorded at fair market value of $38 per share	18,732	93,660	618,156	—	(711,816)
Balance at April 30, 1995	590,552	$2,952,760	$2,853,702	$1,466,676	$4,997,457

"Now, let's look at the quotations in today's *Wall Street Journal* and see how you've made out over the past year. Here it is on the Pacific Coast Exchange. The June 10 closing price was $28½. Now we'll look at the April 30, 1995, annual report and see what it tells us."

The Company

Nutra Foods Corporation was established in California to acquire and operate three small vegetable canning plants. Operations were expanded to include canning of fruits and frozen fruit processing. In 1995, the company operated a number of small canning and processing plants throughout the Midwest and on the West Coast.

Nutra's operations had always been profitable. Earnings per share of common reached a historic high of $2.27 in the fiscal year ended April 30, 1995. Net income for the year was $1.3 million on sales of almost $59 million. Stockholders' equity at April 30, 1995, exceeded $13 million. The company's comparative balance sheets at the close of the two most recent years are shown in **Exhibit 1.** The 1995 movements in the common stock and retained earnings accounts are shown in **Exhibit 2.**

Most of the funds needed to finance the company's growth had been provided internally. Modest cash dividends had been paid quarterly without interruption since

1986, when the common stock was split 3 for 1. In 1982, after a public offering of preferred and common stock, a policy of supplementing the regular cash dividends with stock dividends to common stockholders was adopted. Five percent stock dividends were declared in each year thereafter except for 1985 and 1986, when stock dividends were 20% and 10% respectively. The 4% preferred stock was gradually being retired as it became available in the market at an attractive price. Some funds had been obtained by the use of long-term debt, and future expansion was to be financed more extensively in this way.

The price of Nutra's common stock had risen steadily since the mid-1980s. For example, the price had ranged from a low of $12¾ to a high of $18⅝ in the year 1989 and reached an all-time high of $43½ in 1994.

Questions

1. Evaluate Ed McCowan's investment at June 10, 1995.

2. Examine the stockholders' equity section of Nutra Foods' balance sheet to:
   a. Determine how each item was originally created.
   b. Explain changes during the year ended April 30, 1995.

3. Contrast Nutra's methods of reporting preferred treasury stock and common treasury stock.

4. What is the effect of Nutra's acquisition of treasury stock upon investor McCowan's holdings? _____

5. Suggest improvements Nutra might make in reporting stockholders' equity information on its balance sheet.

6. How does the issuance of stock options to the management change in the company's net worth account at (a) date of issuance, (b) date options are first exercisable, and (c) date exercised? _____ Assume options to buy 2,000 shares are first exercisable in 1995. (These were issued originally at a price equal to the then current market price of $20.) What would be the accounting entry for these options if they were exercised during 1995, when the market price of Nutra stock was $26? _____ How did the company originally account for the granting of these options? _____

7. How will the proposed 100,000-share purchase impact Nutra's balance sheet, income statements, and key ratios? _____ Use **Exhibits 1** and **2** data to illustrate your answer. What might be the impact on McCowan's investment if he holds onto his Nutra stock? _____

PART NINE

Special Reporting and Analysis Issues

Foreign Activities

Managers of international companies must deal with financial statements from different foreign subsidiaries which are stated in terms of more than one local currency. This is a major difference between managing domestic and global operations. Typically, the parent company manager overcomes this difficulty by translating the foreign subsidiary statements into the reporting currency of the parent company. If the exchange rate between the domestic and foreign currency has changed since the last balance sheet date, translation gains and losses will be generated by this procedure. In addition, if a company has payables or receivables which are denominated in a foreign currency and the exchange rate changes, an exchange gain or loss related to these items must be recognized in some way on the company's statements.

The financial reporting consequences of transnational corporations operating in a number of different currencies vary depending on the reporting company's circumstances, accounting policies and management's actions to mitigate or benefit from changes in exchange rates. This chapter covers:

- The accounting for realized and unrealized currency gains and losses on foreign currency-denominated transaction-related assets and liabilities.
- The methods used to restate financial statements expressed in one currency into another currency.

The chapter also covers some of the managerial and financial analysis aspects of these accounting practices. Accounting for currency risk management is covered in another chapter.

Statement issuers and users must understand the various accounting approaches to incorporating financial statements, and the effects of operating in different currencies.

Professor David F. Hawkins prepared this note as the basis for class discussion.

Depending on the accounting method used, exchange rate shifts may have very different impacts on the earnings and ratios of the reporting entity. If statement issuers and users do not have a good grasp of foreign currency accounting, they will not appreciate the interplay between accounting methods, exchange rate shifts, and financial statement values. Also, meaningful comparisons between companies using different accounting approaches will be more difficult to make, and erroneous conclusions based on ratio analysis and reported income may be reached. Managers who do not fully understand foreign currency accounting may fail to manage appropriately currency risks and to appreciate the influence of foreign currency accounting on employee behavior.

It is difficult to determine exactly how exchange rate movements will impact a company's financial statements and cash flows. Nevertheless, managers and analysts must form opinions as to the general direction and approximate impact. Beyond the financial statement consideration, they must also be able to identify the operating and financial actions a company might take to mitigate adverse consequences and to take advantage of opportunities created by exchange rate changes. When evaluating the financial statements of transnational entities, statement users must also develop an appreciation of the political, legal, and environmental factors that can influence the flow of cash from the overseas operations to their parent, as well as shape the future development of the company's overseas opportunities.

Exchange Rates

An exchange rate is the price of one unit of a country's currency expressed in one unit of another country's. For example, A$1 (Australian) is the price of US$.85. Conversely, one would have to pay A$1.18 to purchase US$1.00. Since each country has its own currency, there is a multiplicity of exchange rates. The exchange rates for the major countries involved in international trade are published daily in leading newspapers.

At any moment, more than one exchange rate may exist between two currencies. For example, the "spot," or immediate currency delivery rate or price is usually different from the forward rate or price for delivery in, say, 90 days. The common reasons for this difference are that the market expects future spot rates to change because of economic, political, interest rate, or inflation rate developments. Sometimes, countries use different rates for financing different types of goods and services. Also, in some cases, a black market rate may exist alongside the official government rate.

The supply and demand for foreign currencies is influenced by international movements involving goods, services, and investments, as well as currency speculation. For example, when U.S. residents export goods or services, they receive payment in U.S. dollars. To obtain these dollars, the foreign importers must exchange some of their currency. Thus, U.S. exports increase the supply of foreign currency and the demand for U.S. dollars in the foreign exchange market. The reverse situation exists when U.S. residents import goods or services.

In a free market, the exchange rate for a given currency will tend to stabilize at the point where the supply and demand for that currency are in balance. This balance can be influenced by a variety of factors. Since a country's exports and imports often reflect its internal cost–price structure, changes in the domestic purchasing power of different currencies may influence their relative exchange rates. The exchange in free markets is also influenced by the fact that not all imports and exports are bought on price alone. For example, consumer preferences for certain imports and inelastic demand situations can complicate the adjustment mechanism. If any discrepancies between foreign exchange markets exist, arbitrage by foreign currency traders will soon eliminate them.

The major trading countries support a worldwide system of exchange rates that permits rates to fluctuate freely. To minimize the possibility that freely fluctuating rates could cause distortions in a country's balance of payments and internal economy, governments use a number of devices that increase the supply or decrease the demand for their currencies to keep their exchange rates fairly stable and at a desired level. These include selling or adding to foreign exchange reserves, establishing foreign exchange controls, imposing import controls, subsidizing exports, and reducing or expanding foreign aid programs.

Restrictions on the free exchange of currencies can lead to a currency being overvalued. In these cases, it becomes desirable to shift funds from the overvalued currency to the more normally valued ones. To halt this flight from the overvalued ("soft") currency to the normally valued ("hard") currencies, its government can declare the soft currency inconvertible, or not subject to exchange. Countries can make their currencies inconvertible for all people; for residents but not foreigners; for some but not all other currencies; or for certain types of transactions only.

At times, governments with serious adverse balance of payments problems are unable to maintain their currency's exchange rate. The classic solution to this problem is to let the currency devalue. It is hoped that this step will improve the balance of trade by making it more expensive for citizens to import goods and less expensive for foreigners to buy exports. Successful devaluation requires an increase in exports and, since local prices of imported goods will rise, an anti-inflationary domestic fiscal policy must be instituted. Trade is only one part of the international payments system. Currency speculation, foreign investments, and military aid may also affect the payments balance.

Foreign Currency Transactions

A foreign currency transaction is a transaction involving a currency other than the entity's reporting currency.

At the initial transaction date, the practice is to measure and record foreign currency transactions in the reporting currency using the transaction date exchange rate between the reporting and other currency. For example, if a U.S. corporation incurs an obligation to pay an Australian corporation A$10 million and the current exchange rate is A$1/US$.85, the U.S. corporation would record a US$8.5 million obligation.

If a foreign currency, denominated receivable or payable is settled prior to the end of the reporting period, and the related exchange rate has changed in the interim, the reporting company will record in income a realized currency exchange transaction gain or loss. For example, if the reporting company settled the above A$10 million obligation following an appreciation of the U.S. dollar to US$.80 to the A$1.00, the U.S. company would pay US$8 million to buy the Australian currency to settle this obligation and record a US$.5 million gain. If the reporting currency has appreciated relative to the foreign currency, a loss is recognized on foreign currency receivables. A gain is recognized on foreign currency payables. The reverse is true when the reporting currency devalues.

Period end foreign currency receivable and payable balances are restated to their reporting currency equivalent. Any unrealized exchange gains or losses are recorded in current income.

Consolidated Statements

To include the local currency-denominated financial statements of foreign operations in the consolidated statements prepared for the parent's stockholders, it is necessary to express the overseas subsidiary's statements in the consolidated statement reporting currency equivalent, determined in accordance with generally accepted accounting principles. No actual cash changes hands in this process. It is simply a worksheet adjustment. For example, if the current spot rate is US$.85/A$1, to convert the balance sheet account Cash in Australian Dollars to U.S. dollars, the cash balance on the Australian statement is multiplied by .85.

As explained later, some items in the foreign-currency–denominated financial statements may be restated to the consolidated statement reporting currency using the exchange rate at the time of the transaction giving rise to the item, and others may be restated using the exchange rate as of the balance sheet date. If there has been a change in exchange rates, when each item is converted to the reporting currency the consolidated statements will probably be out of balance. Depending on the restatement methodology, the balancing item is either a translation or remeasurement gain or loss. This gain or loss can arise only from the process of translation.

Stable Exchange Rate

There are few conceptual problems involved in restatement from one currency to another when the exchange rate between the parent company's reporting currency and the overseas currency has been stable over a long period of time. To convert the amounts shown on the foreign currency statements to their parent company's reporting currency equivalents, the exchange rate is applied directly to the amounts shown on the local currency statements. Since the same rate will most likely be applied to each item in the statements, the equality of the right and left sides of the balance sheet is maintained, as is the relationship between current financial statements and those for prior periods.

Fluctuating Exchange Rate

When there has been a change in the exchange rate, the selection of the appropriate approach to converting statements from one currency to another becomes more difficult. These difficulties arise because not all of the items on the financial statements are affected by the devaluation or appreciation in the exchange rate in the same manner.

For example, in the case of a devaluation of the pound from, say, US$1.50/£1 to US$1.40/£1, the equivalent dollar value of the pound currency cash balances of a British subsidiary of a U.S. company will decline. The pound will now buy fewer dollars. However, the dollar equivalent value of the foreign-pound–denominated inventory might remain unchanged, because management may be able to raise its selling prices sufficiently to offset the devaluation effect. This is usually possible if the devaluation is the result of locally inflating price levels.

Recognizing that different items are affected differently by exchange rate changes, accountants group assets into categories which reflect their responsiveness to exchange changes. Then, depending on the translation model used, the exchange rate used to translate statement items is either the current or the historical rate. The current rate is the exchange rate prevailing on the date of the balance sheet. The historical rate is the rate of exchange existing on the date the original transaction took place. For example, in the case of fixed assets, the historical rate would be the rate prevailing at the time the company acquired the asset. To simplify the translation process, average rates for the reporting period are often used to translate recurring income items, much as sales.

FASB Statement No. 52

Translation requirements are set forth in FASB Statement No. 52.

FASB Statement No. 52 refers to the primary currency in which an entity does business as its functional currency. The designation of each foreign entity's functional currency is an important management decision. It determines the method used to restate the foreign-currency–denominated financial statements into the consolidated entity's reporting currency, which is the U.S. dollar for U.S. firms, and the disposition of any translation or remeasurement gain or loss.

The objective of this standard is to implement foreign currency translation standards that (a) provide information that is generally compatible with the expected economic effects of an exchange rate change on a company's cash flow and owners' equity and (b) reflect in consolidated statements the financial results and relationships as measured in the primary currency in which each entity included in the consolidated results conducts its business.

Depending on how a company's situation is assessed in terms of these two objectives, the effect of translation on the consolidated statements can vary significantly. For example, if the operating unit's local currency is designated as its functional currency, the current-rate method is used to translate the statements to dollars and any translation adjustments are direct adjustments to owners' equity. Alternatively, if the U.S. dollar is considered the unit's functional currency, the remeasurement method is used to convert the foreign currency statements into their dollar equivalents. In this case, any remeasurement adjustments are included in the determination of income.

The current-rate and remeasurement approaches to translation outlined in FASB Statement No. 52 reflect the board's conclusions about how its two translation accounting goals can best be met:

   a. The effect of changing currency prices on the carrying amounts of all
   foreign assets and liabilities should be recorded currently after recognizing
   situational differences.

   b. The economic effects of exchange rate changes on an overseas operating unit
   that is relatively self-contained and integrated within a foreign country relate
   primarily to the net investment in that unit. Translation adjustment gains or
   losses that arise from consolidating such foreign operations do not change the
   parent's cash flows. Consequently, in these cases, the current-rate translation
   method should be used; the local currency should be designated as the
   functional currency; and translation adjustments should not be included in the
   consolidated U.S.-dollar–denominated income, but rather be made directly to
   owners' equity.

   c. The economic effects of an exchange rate shift on a foreign operation that
   is essentially an extension of the parent's domestic operations relate
   primarily to individual assets and liabilities and affect the parent's cash flow
   directly. Accordingly, the functional currency of such a business should be
   the U.S. dollar; the remeasurement approach should be used to translate;
   and translation adjustments should be included in net income.

Functional Currency

A foreign entity's functional currency is the currency of the primary economic environment in which the entity operates. Normally, that is the currency of the country in which the business primarily generates and spends cash.

   As indicated above, the local currency should be the functional currency for operations that are relatively self-contained and integrated within a particular foreign country. Alternatively, the FASB concluded that the parent company's reporting currency should be the functional currency for overseas businesses that are primarily a direct extension or integrated component of the parent company's operations.

   In practice, determining the functional currency of an operation can be difficult. Many operations do not clearly fall into one or the other of the two operating situations described by the board. To assist managements in making functional currency determinations, the FASB identified a number of economic facts to consider. These are listed in **Illustration A.** The considerations listed indicate whether the functional currency should be the local currency or the parent company's currency. The FASB did not assign any priorities to these indicators. Also, if management regards factors other than those listed by the board as relevant to the functional currency decision, they can be considered also.

   The functional currency determination need not be made on a legal-entity basis. It may be made on an operation-by-operation basis. For example, an entity may have distinct, self-contained operations in several countries, and each may have its own functional currency. In some cases, the facts may indicate that a company's functional

ILLUSTRATION A Functional Currency Indicators

Indicator	Foreign Currency	Parent's Currency
Cash Flow	Cash flow related to the foreign entity's individual assets and liabilities are primarily in the foreign currency and do not directly affect the parent company's cash flows.	Cash flows related to the foreign entity's individual assets and liabilities directly affect the parent's cash flows on a current basis and are generally available for remittance to the parent company.
Sales Price	Sales prices for the foreign entity's products are not primarily responsive on a short-term basis to changes in exchange rates but are determined more by local competition or local government regulation.	Sales prices for the foreign entity's products are primarily responsive on a short-term basis to changes in exchange rates; for example, sales prices are determined more by worldwide competition or by international prices.
Sales Market	There is an active local sales market for the foreign entity's products, although there may also be significant amounts of exports.	The sales market is mostly in the parent's country, or sales contracts are denominated in the parent's currency.
Expenses	Labor, materials, and other costs for the foreign entity's products or services are primarily local costs, even though there may be some imports.	Labor, materials, and other costs for the foreign entity's products or services, on a continuing basis, are primarily costs for components obtained from the country in which the parent company is located.
Financing	Financing is primarily denominated in foreign currency, and funds generated by the foreign entity's operations are sufficient to service existing and normally expected debt obligations.	Financing is primarily from the parent or other dollar-denominated obligations, or funds generated by the foreign entity's operations are not sufficient to service existing and normally expected debt obligations without the infusion of additional funds from the parent company. Infusion of funds from the parent for expansion is not a factor, provided funds generated by the foreign entity's expanded operations are expected to be sufficient to service that additional financing.
Intercompany Transactions and Arrangements	There is a low volume of intercompany transactions, and the relationship between the operations of the foreign entity and the parent company is not extensive. The foreign entity's operations may rely on the parent's or affiliates' competitive advantages, however, such as patents and trademarks.	There is a high volume of intercompany transactions and the relationship between the operations of the foreign entity and the parent company is extensive. In addition, the parent's currency generally would be the functional currency if the foreign entity were a device or shell corporation for holding investments, obligations, intangible assets, etc., that could readily be carried on the parent's or an affiliate's books.

currency is the currency of a foreign country other than the one in which the entity is located.[1]

Once an entity's functional currency has been determined, the designation should be used consistently, unless significant changes in the entity's economic circumstances suggest clearly that another currency should be designated.

Current-Rate Method

The current-rate method uses the current exchange rate to translate all elements of financial statements, except owners' equity. For assets or liabilities, the exchange rate at the balance sheet date is used. Income statement items are translated at the exchange rate at the time they are recognized for income determination purposes. A distinctive feature of the current-rate method is that translation adjustments are made directly to owners' equity.

The current-rate method is used when the functional currency is other than the parent company's reporting currency.

In practice, companies translate recurring revenue and expense items at the average exchange rate for the period. This is a less expensive approach than attempting to translate each transaction at the exchange rate on the transaction day. If a significant transaction occurs, however, such as a material gain on the sale of an asset, the transaction date exchange rate should be used for translation purposes.

The cumulative translation adjustments included directly in equity under the current-rate method are reported under that title, "Equity Adjustments from Foreign Currency Translation." Companies must keep track of the sources of the amounts carried in this account, because if an entity, or part of an entity, responsible for a portion of the accumulated translation adjustment is sold or liquidated, the related translation adjustment is included in the computation of the gain or loss on the transaction.

A Current-Rate Illustration: Overseas Incorporated.   **Illustration B** presents the worksheet for translating a foreign subsidiary's local currency balance sheet and income statement into dollars using the current-rate method. Later, in **Illustration D,** the same foreign currency statements are used to illustrate the remeasurement method.

The example assumes the company started business on January 1, 1993; plant is bought at the beginning of the year; sales, purchases of raw materials, and expenses are spread evenly throughout the year; inventory is priced at its average cost for the year (relevant only for **Illustration D**); plant is depreciated on a straight-line basis over 10 years; and no dividends are paid. On January 1, 1993, the exchange rate was four local units to US$1. During the year, the currency steadily devalued relative to the

---

[1]If the foreign entity's functional currency is a currency other than the parent company's reporting currency or the entity's reporting currency, a two-step translation process is used. First, the remeasurement process is used to remeasure the reporting currency statements in their functional currency equivalent. Then, these functional currency statements are translated into the parent company's reporting currency using the current-rate method, and any translation adjustment gain or loss resulting from this second step is included in owners' equity.

ILLUSTRATION B   Foreign Statement Translation Example Using Current-Rate Method—Overseas Incorporated

	1993 Financial Statements (local currency)	*Translation Factors*	*1993 Financial Statements (U.S. dollars)[a]*
Assets			
Cash and receivables	40	.125	5
Inventory	32	.125	4
Plant	80	.125	10
Less: accumulated depreciation	(8)	.125	(1)
Total assets	144		18
Liabilities			
Current liabilities	56	.125	7
Long-term debt	24	.125	3
Total liabilities	80		10
Owners' Equity			
Capital stock	20	.25	5
Beginning retained earnings	0	—	0
Plus net income	44	(see below)	7
			22
		Equity adjustment from currency translation (plug figure, 18–22) ..	(4)
Total liabilities and owners' equity	144		18
Income Statement			
Sales	401	.167	67
Less: cost of sales	196	.167	33
Gross margin	205	.167	34
Depreciation	8	.167	1
Other expenses	153	.167	26
Net income	44		7

[a]Rounded to nearest dollar.

dollar so that on December 31, the exchange rate was eight local units to US$1. The average rate for the year was six local units to the US$1.

The rate for translating Overseas Incorporated's capital stock in **Illustration B** is four local currency units to the dollar. Thus, the dollar equivalent of these local currency balances in this account can be obtained by multiplying the foreign currency balance by 0.25 (US$1/4 local currency units). Since the exchange rate changed evenly throughout the year, a factor of 0.167 (US$1/6 local currency units) can be used to translate the revenues and expenses that occurred evenly throughout the year. On the last day of the year, the exchange rate is eight local currency units to the dollar. Consequently, a factor of 0.125 (US$1/8 local currency units) can be used to convert those year-end balance sheet accounts that must be translated at the balance sheet date exchange rate.

When Overseas Incorporated's foreign currency statements are translated into U.S. dollars, the balance sheet translation process leads to a translation adjustment loss of four U.S. dollars, since the company had an excess of translated liabilities and owners' equity ($22) over translated assets ($18). Because the current-rate method is used, the translation adjustment loss is not included in the income statements. It is shown only on the translated statements as an adjustment to owners' equity.

The FASB believes that for reasonably self-contained foreign operations, the translated financial statements of the parent company should carry over to the consolidated dollar statements the local currency statement's profit or loss position and financial relationships, such as the current ratio and gross margin percentage. As shown in **Illustration B,** the current rate achieves this goal mechanically by (a) multiplying the local currency amounts by a constant factor equivalent to the current exchange rate between the local currency and the dollar and (b) including translation adjustments, if any, in owners' equity.

Remeasurement

The remeasurement process is used whenever an entity's functional currency is other than its local currency. When the U.S. dollar is the functional currency, the remeasurement process is used to restate the overseas entity's local-currency–denominated financial statements in U.S. dollars.

The remeasurement process is similar to the current-rate method except for these important differences:

   a. The remeasurement adjustment is included in net income.

   b. Some balance sheet and related income statement accounts are remeasured using historical exchange rates. **Illustration C** lists those accounts that are remeasured using historical exchange rates.

A Remeasurement Illustration: Overseas Incorporated.   The remeasurement process is demonstrated in **Illustration D,** using the same Overseas Incorporated data previously presented in **Illustration B.** The principal differences between the remeasurement and current-rate examples are:

   a. The remeasurement process uses an historical exchange rate to restate inventory, plant, accumulated depreciation, cost of sales, and depreciation, whereas the current-rate method translates the three balance sheet items at the balance sheet date exchange rate and the two expense items at the average rate for the period to which the expense items apply.

   b. The remeasurement process includes the remeasurement exchange gain in the determination of net income, whereas the foreign currency translation loss arising from the current-rate method is a direct adjustment to owner's equity.

ILLUSTRATION C   **Selected Accounts Reported at Cost Remeasured Using Historical Exchange Rates**

Balance Sheet Items
Marketable securities and investments carried at cost
Inventories carried at cost
Prepaid expenses such as insurance, advertising, and rent
Property, plant, and equipment
Accumulated depreciation on property, plant, and equipment
Patents, trademarks, licenses, and formulas
Goodwill
Other intangible assets
Deferred charges and credits, except deferred income taxes and unamortized policy acquisition costs for
  life insurance companies
Deferred income
Common stock
Preferred stock carried at issuance price

Income Statement Items
Cost of goods sold
Depreciation of property, plant, and equipment
Amortization of intangible items such as goodwill, patents, licenses, etc.
Amortization of deferred charges or credits, except deferred income taxes and policy acquisition costs
  for life insurance companies

Since Overseas Incorporated's reporting currency is the same as its functional currency, remeasurement is equivalent to translation.

Economic Hedges

Companies use hedging transactions to neutralize the effect of exchange rate movements on their net investments in foreign entities. These hedges are referred to as "economic hedges" in FASB Statement No. 52. If the functional currency is the local currency, the effects of the hedge are included directly in owners' equity. If the functional currency is the U.S. dollar, the hedge adjustments are included in income. This treatment follows the reporting of translation and remeasurement gains and losses.

Highly Inflationary Economies

FASB Statement No. 52 requires that the financial statements of overseas entities in highly inflationary economies be remeasured using the parent's reporting currency as their functional currency, which in the case of a U.S. parent corporation is the U.S. dollar. A highly inflationary economy is defined as one that has a cumulative three-year inflation rate of approximately 100% or more. This definition should be applied with judgment.

**ILLUSTRATION D   Foreign Statement Remeasurement Example—
Overseas Incorporated**

	1993 Financial Statements (local currency)	Translation Factors	1993 Financial Statements (U.S. dollars)[a]
Assets			
Cash and receivables	40	.125	5
Inventory	32	.167	5
Plant	80	.25	20
Less: accumulated depreciation	(8)	.25	(2)
Total assets	144		28
Liabilities			
Current liabilities	56	.125	7
Long-term debt	24	.125	3
Total liabilities	80		10
Owners' Equity			
Capital	20	.25	5
Beginning retained earnings	0	—	0
Plus net income	44	Income before remeasurement gain or loss (see below)[b]	6
	144		21
		Remeasurement gain (plug figure, 28–21)[b] . . .	7
Total liabilities and owners' equity	144		28
Income Statement			
Sales	401	.167	67
Less: cost of sales	196	.167	33
Gross margin	205		34
Depreciation	8	.25	2
Other expenses	153	.167	26
		Income before remeasurement gain or loss	6
		Remeasurement gain (see above)	7
Net income	44	Net income	13

[a]Rounded to nearest dollar.
[b]Included in reported owners' equity as retained earnings (6 + 7 = 13).

The FASB adopted its special rule for entities operating in highly inflationary economies because the use of the current-rate method to translate assets and liabilities in such economies might produce unrealistic results. For example, assume a subsidiary in a highly inflationary economy acquired a building on January 1, 1993, for the local currency equivalent of US$2 million. During the year, the local currency devalued 100% against the dollar and the local annual inflation rate was 100%. If the building asset valued in local currency were translated into U.S. dollars using the year-end exchange rate, its carrying value on the consolidated U.S. dollar statements would be reduced from the beginning-of-the-year value of US$2 million to US$1 million because of the devaluation of the local currency. This result is unrealistic, since the value of the building in local currency probably doubled because of inflation. As a result, its actual U.S. dollar equivalent value may still be approximately US$2 million. Remeasurement using the historical rate will report this figure.

In addition, using the current-rate method to translate the local currency depreciation expense for the building would result in decreasing dollar equivalents as the local currency devalued. Using the historical exchange rate, as required by the remeasurement process, to remeasure the local-currency cost of the building and related depreciation stabilizes the dollar equivalents.

The FASB decision to require financial statements of foreign entities in highly inflationary economies to be remeasured using the reporting currency reflects the board's view that a currency that has largely lost its utility as a store of value cannot be a functional unit of measurement. While the board's solution to the problem of unstable units of measurement is not completely satisfactory, it is a pragmatic solution that reduces potential inflationary distortions without introducing general price-level accounting into the basic financial statements.

Measurement and Motivation

The business decisions managers of overseas entities make in response to exchange rate shifts may be biased by the internal accounting method used to measure their profit performance.

Typically, companies measure the performance of their overseas operating units in terms of the parent's reporting currency. They want to encourage the overseas managers to make decisions that enhance the reporting currency value of the parent's shareholders' interests. Some companies use the overseas unit's local currency profit to measure overseas managers. This can be a misleading indication of managerial performance. For example, rising local currency profits may be inadequate to offset local currency devaluation relative to the parent's reporting currency. As a result, the contribution of the overseas unit to consolidated results may be declining, while the overseas managers may be rewarded for higher local profits.

Not all companies use the same approach to measure the parent company's reporting currency profit performance of their overseas managers. Many use the identical accounting for both internal and external accounting purposes. Some use a modified version of their parent company country's equivalent to FASB Statement No. 52.

Others use methods that depart significantly from the required external reporting standard. The selection of the appropriate internal measurement for overseas managers depends on the scope of the overseas managers' authority over balance sheet items, the company's overseas operating and financial objectives, and the cost of maintaining alternative accounting systems for foreign operations.

Local managers in economically unstable countries are often held responsible for translated profits after translation gains and losses. This measure of performance puts pressure upon them to take, with the cooperation of the parent company, whatever steps are possible to reduce their exposure to exchange gains and losses. In highly inflationary economies, many of these same steps also protect against inflation eroding the parent company stockholders' investment.

The interest a manager shows in taking particular steps to reduce exposure to currency risk may be biased somewhat by the translation method used. For example, the remeasurement method biases a manager toward shifting funds from cash to inventories because inventories are translated at the historical rate, and hence, are not exposed to currency risk. On the other hand, cash is translated at the current rate, which means it is exposed to currency risk losses. The current-rate method translates both cash and inventories at the current rate. So, the local manager is biased by this method toward being indifferent between holding cash or inventories. They both are exposed to devaluation losses. Of course, to the extent the local manager believes local prices for products will rise, after, say, devaluation, the manager will be biased toward preferring to hold inventory rather than cash. The manager can recapture some of the devaluation loss through these higher prices.

Regardless of how the overseas manager is measured or what generally accepted accounting principles governing foreign currency translation are in force, someone in the organization must be responsible for seeing that the economic value of the parent company stockholders' investment is protected against adverse exchange rate shifts and fully enhanced by favorable currency movements. This requires continuous planning, expert knowledge of world economics and currency movements, and an aggressive approach to financial management on a worldwide basis. This is not an easy task.

Statement Analysis

Currency exchange rate shifts are critical to the economic value of companies whose profitability is very dependent on their overseas operations, such as the major global pharmaceutical companies. In these situations, the principal purpose of statement analysis is often to gain insight into how the interaction of the translation method with past and anticipated changes in exchange rates impact the actual and perceived economic value of these companies, particularly as it is reflected in their stock prices.

The principal analytical challenge facing those examining the financial statements of multinational corporations is to estimate how exchange rate shifts influence operating income before considering any translation gain or loss or remeasurement adjustments. This is an important determination because if the parent company reporting currency strengthens against a foreign subsidiary's local currency, the parent company reporting currency equivalent of each unit of the overseas company's local currency profits declines. The opposite occurs when the parent company's reporting currency weakens.

Estimating the amount of the change is considerably more difficult. It can seldom be done with a high degree of accuracy or confidence. The geographical segment data showing the source of profits by geographical regions may be helpful in this task. First, it can be used to determine how material the foreign operations are to the consolidated entity's financial results. This determination can be made by expressing the segment data related to overseas operations as a percentage of total sales, income, and assets. Second, if the analyst knows how the parent company reporting currency has moved against the currencies of these regions included in the overseas segments or the currency of the country within each segment providing the majority of the segment's profit, a rough estimate of the impact of exchange rate shifts can be made. Any import–export data in the notes may be used in a similar manner.

The choice of the translation method can influence many of the common financial ratios of multinational companies. For example, if the functional currency of the overseas subsidiary is the parent company reporting currency and the remeasurement method is used, some overseas assets and liabilities are remeasured using historical exchange rates. The use of different rates in the remeasurement process can change the underlying local currency ratios of companies with extensive overseas property, plant, and equipment investments and slow-moving inventories. For example, the assets will be remeasured using old rates. Sales will be remeasured using current rates. If the sales in local currency are steady and the local currency is appreciating relative to the parent company's reporting currency, the remeasured asset turnover rates will improve. The pretranslation local currency ratios of companies whose functional currency is not the parent's reporting currency are not influenced by the translation process when converted to parent company reporting currency equivalent, since the current rate is used to translate all of the income statement, asset, and liability values.

Translation and remeasurement adjustments reflect the impact of changing exchange rates on owners' equity. Whether or not for security valuation purposes these should be included in income is a controversial issue. Financial analysts appear to accept the economic rationale underlying the translation and remeasurement concepts. They include remeasurement adjustments in income and exclude translation adjustments from income. Nevertheless, while doing this they are mindful of the fact that stockholders are better off when translation adjustment gains occur and worse off when translation adjustment losses are incurred. How this awareness enters, if at all, into the equity valuation process is unclear at this time.

Income earned overseas may not be freely available for parent company stockholders or the financing of global operations. An appraisal of foreign operations should always include an assessment of the ability of a foreign company to repatriate earnings to its parent and affiliates. Income that is unavailable to the parent and other affiliates is of lower quality than income freely available for global use.

Finally, statement users should be aware of the fact the contribution of overseas profits to consolidated income can be managed in part by management decisions to accrue or nonaccrue prior to repatriation any potential parent company country taxes on overseas profits repatriations. Usually the nonaccrual of potential parent country taxes on unrepatriated foreign profits is justified on the grounds that management intends to leave the profits overseas. This may or may not be an accurate statement.

Controversial Subject

Foreign currency statement translation is a controversial accounting topic. However, to keep this controversy in perspective it is useful to remember the comment made by a senior financial officer of a major U.S. corporation upon reading FASB Statement No. 52 for the first time. "This is the worst translation method I have ever seen, except for every other one."

A. B. Deutz GmbH

Machinery International, a U.S. multinational corporation, sold advanced computer-controlled production equipment on a worldwide basis. The company had manufacturing facilities and sales offices in a number of foreign countries. Thomas Matthews, the corporate financial vice president, was reviewing the method used to translate into U.S. dollars the deutsche mark (DM) financial statements of the company's German subsidiary, A. B. Deutz GmbH (Deutz).

In 1991, Deutz's statements were remeasured to U.S. dollars using FASB No. 52 and the U.S. dollar as the functional currency. This method had been considered appropriate in 1988 when Deutz had been acquired by Machinery International. Prior to its acquisition, Deutz's principal business had been acting as Machinery International's German distribution agent for Machinery International products produced in the U.S. Deutz also operated a small, underutilized manufacturing facility. During the years since its acquisition, Deutz had expanded its manufacturing facilities and direct sales operations.

Given the changes in Deutz's activities, Matthews was now considering whether Deutz's functional currency ought to be changed from the U.S. dollar to the deutsche mark. To help resolve this issue, Matthews decided to ask his assistant, Jim Taylor, to prepare 1991 pro forma statements for the German subsidiary using the deutsche mark as the functional currency and to compare the results with its budgeted 1991 U.S. dollar statements, prepared using the U.S. dollar as the functional currency (see **Exhibits 1, 2,** and **3**). Accordingly, Matthews instructed Taylor as follows:

> I am beginning to think our German subsidiary's functional currency for U.S. consolidated shareholder reports should be the deutsche mark. The subsidiary does a lot of

This case was prepared by Professor David F. Hawkins as the basis for class discussion rather than to illustrate either effective or ineffective handling of an administrative situation.
Copyright © 1993 by the President and Fellows of Harvard College. Harvard Business School case 193–164.

Exhibit 1 Statement of Financial Position, December 31, 1990

		Functional Currency: U.S. Dollar		Functional Currency: Deutsche Mark	
		Exchange Rate	U.S. Dollars	Exchange Rate	U.S. Dollars
Assets					
Current Assets:					
Cash	DM575,000	.510	$ 293,250		
Certificate of deposit	1,960,784	.510	1,000,000		
Accounts receivable	1,685,000	.510	859,350		
Inventories	1,600,000	.534	854,400		
Total current assets	5,820,784		3,007,000		
Property and Equipment	2,250,000	.529	1,190,250		
Less: Accumulated depreciation	260,000	.529	137,540		
Property and Equipment (net)	1,990,000		1,052,710		
Total assets	**DM7,810,784**		**$4,059,710**		
Liabilities and Stockholders' Equity					
Current liabilities: Accounts payable	DM1,745,625	.510	$ 890,269		
Due to parent	2,941,176	.510	1,500,000		
Total current liabilities	4,686,801		2,390,269		
Long-term debt	2,000,000	.510	1,020,000		
Deferred income taxes	45,000	.510	22,950		
Stockholders' equity:					
Capital stock	600,000	.529	317,400		
Paid-in capital	200,000	.529	105,800		
Retained earnings	278,983	(Various)	203,291		
Equity adjustment from translation					
Total stockholders' equity	1,078,983		626,491		
Total liabilities and stockholders' equity	DM7,810,784		$4,059,710		

Exhibit 2 Statement of Financial Position, December 31, 1991

		Functional Currency: U.S. Dollar		Functional Currency: Deutsche Mark	
		Exchange Rate	U.S. Dollars	Exchange Rate	U.S. Dollars
Assets					
Current Assets:					
Cash	DM530,000	.450	$ 238,500		
Certificate of deposit	2,222,222	.450	1,000,000		
Accounts receivable	1,400,000	.450	630,000		
Inventories	1,500,000	.435	652,500		
Prepaid expenses	75,000	.415	31,125		
Total current assets	5,727,222		2,552,125		
Property and Equipment	2,400,000	(Various)	1,252,500		
Less: Accumulated depreciation	410,000	(Various)	215,750		
Property and Equipment (net)	1,990,000		1,036,750		
TOTAL ASSETS	DM7,717,222		$3,588,875		
Liabilities and Stockholders' Equity					
Current liabilities:					
Accounts payable	DM1,570,000	.450	$ 706,500		
Due to parent	3,333,333	.450	1,500,000		
Total Current Liabilities	4,903,333		2,206,500		
Long-term debt	1,600,000	.450	720,000		
Deferred income taxes	60,000	.450	27,000		
Stockholders' equity:					
Capital stock	600,000	.529	317,400		
Paid-in capital	200,000	.529	105,800		
Retained earnings	353,889	(Various)	212,175		
Equity adjustment from translation					
Total stockholders' equity	1,153,889		635,375		
Total liabilities and stockholders' equity	DM7,717,222		$3,588,875		

Exhibit 3 Statement of Income, 1991

	Functional Currency: U.S. Dollar			Functional Currency: Deutsche Mark	
		Exchange Rate	*U.S. Dollars*	*Exchange Rate*	*U.S. Dollars*
Sales	DM7,800,000	.457	$3,564,600		
Other income	31,250	.457	14,281		
	7,831,250		3,578,881		
Cost of goods sold	6,200,000	(Various)	2,989,600		
General and administrative	650,000	.457	297,050		
Depreciation	150,000	(Various)	78,210		
Interest	220,000	.457	100,540		
	7,220,000		3,465,400		
GROSS PROFIT	611,250		113,481		
Transaction gain (loss)	(130,719)	(Various)[a]	76,574		
Income before income taxes	480,531		190,055		
Income taxes—Current	290,625	.457	132,816		
—Deferred	15,000	.457	6,855		
	305,625		139,671		
Net income	174,906		50,384		
Retained earnings at beginning of year	278,983		203,291		
	453,889		253,675		
Less dividends paid	100,000	.415	41,500		
Retained earnings at end of year	DM353,889		$ 212,175		

[a]Includes US$ equivalent ($59,738) of net DM loss on net US$ obligation position ($500,000) and remeasurement gain.

business in Germany as well as the rest of Europe on its own account. In addition, it acts as a foreign sales branch for some of our U.S. divisions. It takes orders for them in local currency prices, bills and collects directly from their European customers, and provides a local warehouse service to facilitate prompt delivery of the U.S. division's products. Also, it manufactures a critical subassembly that is shipped to our U.S. and Latin American plants.

I have not pushed the numbers yet, but intuitively I know, changing the functional currency will make a difference to the subsidiary's 1991 financial statements.

Here is Deutz's actual deutsche mark December 31, 1990 balance sheet (**Exhibit 1**), its projected December 31, 1991 balance sheet (**Exhibit 2**), and its budgeted 1991 income statement (**Exhibit 3**). I am also giving you the version of these statements using the U.S. dollar as the functional currency. I want you to translate Deutz's deutsche mark statements into their U.S. dollar equivalent assuming Deutz's functional currency is the deutsche mark. Our international accounting section can give you all the data you will need.

Following Matthews' instructions, Taylor met with the head of the international accounting section. Here are the notes Taylor took during that meeting:

1. The year-end exchange rates are: Actual 1990, DM1.96 = US$1 (or DM1 = US$.51); projected 1991, DM2.22 = US$1 (or DM1 = US$.45).

2. The projected average 1991 exchange rate is DM2.19 = US$1 (DM1 = US$.457).

3. The exchange rate at September 30, 1988, the date on which acquisition capital stock was recorded, long-term debt was issued, and the initial property and equipment were recorded, was DM1.89 = US$1 (DM1 = US$.529).

4. The average exchange rate during the production period for 1990 year-end inventory was DM1.87 = US$1 (DM1 = US$.534). The company uses FIFO inventory accounting.

5. The 1990 and 1991 certificate-of-deposit and due-to-parent items are U.S.-dollar–denominated instruments with U.S. dollar values of $1 million and $1.5 million, respectively. The net impact of the DM130,719 loss exchange rate change on these items is recorded in the transaction gain (loss) account listed on the subsidiary's local currency 1991 income statement before remeasurement into U.S. dollars.

6. Assume the beginning retained earnings on the December 31, 1990 translated balance sheet is $203,291, assuming the functional currency is the deutsche mark. This assumption is to simplify the task.

7. The projected exchange rate at June 30, 1991, is DM2.41 = US$1 (DM1 = US$.415), the date on which prepaid expenses are projected to be incurred, additional property and equipment purchased, and dividends declared.

8. The German subsidiary's 1991 cost of goods sold in deutsche marks was calculated as follows:

Inventories at January 1, 1991 . . . . DM1,600,000
Cost of 1991 production   6,100,000
                                                                    DM7,700,000
Less inventories at December 31, 1991   1,500,000
Cost of 1991 goods sold DM6,200,000

The 1991 production is scheduled to be spread evenly throughout the year. The estimated exchange rate for the last quarter of 1991 is DM2.30 = US$1 (DM1 = US$.435).

9. The 1991 DM150,000 depreciation expense included DM10,000 related to depreciable assets purchased on June 30, 1991 (see note 7, above).

10. The transaction gain (loss) account line in the 1991 income statement is a "plug" number when remeasuring the 1991 deutsche mark income statements, assuming the U.S. dollar is the functional currency.

11. All of the items on the 1991 dollar statement of income and retained earnings can be computed directly from the deutsche mark income statement when the deutsche mark is designated as the functional currency.

12. Use the equity-adjustment-from-translation line in the 1991 U.S. dollar balance sheet as a "plug" number when assuming the deutsche mark is the functional currency.

Internal Performance Measurement

Typically, Machinery International used the same translation method used for external reporting purposes to measure subsidiary performance for internal reporting purposes. The key internal subsidiary performance measurements were U.S.-dollar–based return on sales, return on equity, return on assets and profits.

From time to time over the last few years, Harold Schmitt, Deutz's chief executive officer, had indicated to Matthews that he believed the designation of the U.S. dollar as Deutz's functional currency for translation purposes placed Deutz at a competitive disadvantage relative to his German-based competitors with overseas operations. In particular, he objected to recognizing remeasurement losses in income.

According to Schmitt, no specific requirements existed in German law or accounting principles as to which translation method should be used. The only requirement was that whatever method was used, it be used in a consistent manner. Consistent with this standard, Deutz's German-based competitors had elected to use the current–non-current translation method and to record gains and losses resulting from the translation of foreign-currency–denominated financial statements as a direct adjustment to equity section reserves. In addition, Schmitt noted that some German companies that used other translation methods deferred translation losses on long-term debt to the extent that gains had previously been deferred.

While Matthews was not prepared to make Deutz an exception to the company-wide requirement that each subsidiary's performance be measured for internal purposes using the same translation method used in external reports, he believed he should give some consideration to Schmitt's possible reaction to a change in Deutz's functional currency should Matthews decide to make the switch from the U.S. dollar to the deutsche mark. Matthews' initial conclusion was that Schmitt would welcome a functional currency change to the deutsche mark.

Questions

1. How did the DM130,719 transaction loss arise (see **Exhibit 3**)? _____ Show how this loss was calculated.

2. Complete **Exhibits 1, 2,** and **3.**

3. What differences do the choice of functional currency make in the German subsidiary's dollar statement results and its key financial ratios? _____ Explain the reasons for these differences.

4. If Machinery International changes Deutz's functional currency for financial reporting purposes, it intends to use the same approach for measuring the performance of the Deutz management. As a Deutz senior manager, how might you react to the new performance measurement approach, assuming the deutsche mark is the functional currency? _____

Disaggregated Business Disclosures

A number of publicly traded companies have diversified into more than one industry as well as expanded their operations overseas, principally through acquisitions and mergers. To help statement users understand these diversified companies better, FASB Statement No. 14, "Financial Reporting for Segments of a Business Enterprise," was adopted. It required that diversified companies in their annual financial statements disclose supplemental financial information related to their principal industry segments, different country operations, export sales, and major customers.[1] For each reported industry segment and geographical grouping, the diversified company disclosed sales, operating profit or loss, and the carrying amount of identifiable assets. These disaggregated disclosure requirements did not apply to nonpublic companies.

In-mid 1997, the FASB proposed to amend FASB Statement No. 14 to require that an organization's segment data for external reporting be the management or organization unit data that the senior decision maker used for resource allocation purposes. This units of management approach would replace FASB Statement No. 14's industry and geographic disclosure requirements.

While the segment data available to statement users is skimpy, it is nevertheless very useful for developing an understanding of how a business generates its sales, earns its income, and invests its capital. It can also reveal the impact of changes in the value of the dollar relative to other currencies on a multinational business. Proficient segment analysis involves identifying changes in the segment mix over time, appraising the segment results against comparable industry trends, and determining how a particular company's

---

Professor David Hawkins prepared this note as the basis for class discussion rather than to illustrate either effective or ineffective handling of an administrative situation.

Copyright © 1995 by the President and Fellows of Harvard College. Harvard Business School teaching note 195–235.

[1]Business segments under FASB Statement No. 14 were based on the "risks and rewards" approach to defining business segments. That is, each segment consisted of business activities that had similar risk and reward characteristics.

segment diversification affects its level of operating and financial leverage and risk. To interpret segment disclosure data in a meaningful manner, analysts must be aware of various ways these data are prepared, the potential shortcomings of the data, and the accounting rules governing these required disclosures. The challenge of segment analysis is to do a lot with a little data. This requires going beyond the data presented to perform an analysis that gives that analyst an edge over rivals.

Management Unit

The FASB's 1997 project on disaggregated business disclosures was a joint undertaking with the Canadian Institute of Chartered Accountants and the International Accounting Standards Committee. The result was a proposal by the FASB changing the existing disaggregated disclosure requirements to disclose industry segment data to one that reflects the way the business is managed. This so-called management units approach would required disclosure of operating unit data. The FASB concluded that operating segments are those organizational units that are regularly reviewed by the senior decision maker for resource allocation purposes.

The FASB believes that this new approach will:

1. Give statement users a better understanding of the reporting company by giving them financial results on the same basis as used internally by the management.
2. Reduce the cost of preparing and communicating annual and quarterly segment information.
3. Provide greater consistency between the segment note and other disaggregated disclosures presented elsewhere in the annual report.
4. Reduce considerably the number of companies presenting only single-segment data.

The FASB has further concluded that intersegment sales and transfers would be accounted for at prices used internally.

Like FASB Statement No. 14, the board's proposal would also require business disclosures by geographic area.

Beyond the segment data required by FASB Statement No. 14, the FASB decided to require disclosure of certain additional segment information, for example, significant noncash items included in segment income or loss, the amount of current year expenditures included in segment assets, and the following conditional disclosures about certain segments:

1. Revenues by groups of related products and services (for segments that are not based on products and services).
2. Revenues by location of customers, assets, and capital expenditures by location of the assets (for segments that are not based on geographic areas).

The FASB also decided to require disclosure of segment revenues, segment profit or loss, and material changes in segment assets in interim financial statements issued to shareholders of public companies.

Illustration A presents an example of the type of information that would be required to be disclosed by the FASB's management units proposal.

ILLUSTRATION A   Units of Management Disaggregated Business Disclosure Example

Diversified Company has five operating segments: Auto Parts, Motor Vessels, Software, Electronics, and Finance. The Auto Parts segment produces replacement parts for sale to auto parts retailers. The Motor Vessels segment produces small motor vessels to serve the offshore oil industry and similar businesses. The Software segment produces application software for sale to computer manufacturers and retailers. The Electronics segment produces integrated circuits and related products for sale to computer manufacturers. The Finance segment includes all of the company's financial operations including financing customer purchases of products from other segments and real estate lending operations in several states.

The accounting policies of the segments are the same as those described in the Summary of Significant Accounting Policies except that pension expense for each segment is recognized and measured on the basis of cash payments to the pension plan.

Diversified Company evaluates performance based on profit or loss from operations before income taxes not including nonrecurring gains and losses and foreign exchange gains and losses. Liabilities and interest expense are a part of the operations of the Finance segment, but other liabilities and interest expense are maintained in the corporation headquarters records and are not a part of segment operations.

Diversified Company accounts for intersegment sales and transfers as if the sales or transfers were to third parties, that is, at current market prices.

Diversified Company's operating segments are strategic business units that offer different products and services. They are managed separately because each business requires different technology and marketing strategies. Most of the businesses were acquired as a unit, and the management at the time of the acquisition was retained.

	Auto Parts	Motor Vessels	Software	Electronics	Finance	Totals
Revenues from external customers	$3,000	$3,000	$7,000	$12,000	$5,000	$30,000
Intersegment revenues	—	—	3,000	1,500	—	4,500
Segment profit	200	70	900	2,300	500	3,970
Interest revenue	—	—	—	—	4,000	4,000
Interest expense	—	—	—	—	3,000	3,000
Research and development	—	200	200	300	—	700
Depreciation and amortization . . .	200	100	50	1,500	1,100	2,950
Other significant noncash item: Cost in excess of billings on long-term contracts	—	200	—	—	—	200
Segment assets	2,000	5,000	3,000	12,000	57,000	79,000
Expenditures for segment assets	300	700	500	1,700	600	3,800
Segment liabilities	—	—	—	—	45,000	45,000

ILLUSTRATION A **(continued)**

	Auto Parts	Motor Vessels	Software	Electronics	Finance
Revenues	**$3,000**	**$3,000**	**$7,000**	**$12,000**	**$5,000**
United States	2,000	2,000	4,000	7,000	3,000
Canada	900	300	1,000	2,000	1,000
Japan	—	—	1,000	1,000	500
Others	100	700	1,000	2,000	500
Assets	**$2,000**	**$5,000**	**$3,000**	**$12,000**	*
United States	1,500	4,800	1,000	3,000	*
Taiwan	500	—	1,000	5,000	*
Japan	—	—	500	3,000	*
Others	—	200	500	1,000	*
Capital expenditures	**$300**	**$700**	**$500**	**$ 1,700**	*
United States	150	600	100	1,200	*
Others	150	100	400	500	*

*One of Diversified Company's customers that purchases products from the Software and Electronics segments accounts for approximately $5,000 of the Company's revenues.

Oil and Gas Reserves

Oil- and gas-producing companies and diversified companies with significant activities in these businesses are required by FASB Statement No. 25 to disclose their reserve quantities, costs incurred, and capitalized costs.

Investor Surveys

In surveys of financial analysts and investment advisors conducted as part of the continuing research effort to determine what constitutes useful segment disclosure, in the case of diversified companies, there is widespread agreement that it is necessary to appraise the major segments of a business on a segment-by-segment basis before considering them in combination, particularly where the sales and profits of different segments are affected differently by economic conditions.

Information concerning business segments that analysts consider most useful is: contribution, net income and operating income, sales or gross revenues, and total or net assets devoted to the operations of the segment. Most analysts apparently do not feel it is necessary for the independent auditor's opinion to cover these data. A large number of analysts have expressed a desire for a standard approach to defining reporting components on some product basis, such as the Standard Industrial Classification.

The minimum point at which it becomes necessary to report separately for a component, in the opinion of most analysts surveyed, is when it accounts for between

10% and 14% of whatever base the analyst eventually selects as being the most relevant for understanding the company. Some of the bases suggested are: sales, net income, assets employed, net income before allocation of common costs, and total expenses. The analyst surveys also indicate the number of components reported upon should not exceed 11, in most cases.

Corporate Viewpoint

The response of companies to the exposure draft of the FASB's proposal indicated that most managements support the basic concept of full and fair disclosure. However, many of them have expressed a strong conviction that the content and format of segment disclosure should be on a voluntary basis and appropriate to the company's interests. Forced disclosure of profits and revenues by business segments, they argued, might be:

1. Harmful, since it could be used against the company by customers, competitors, labor unions, and governmental agencies.
2. Misleading, if it led to uniform rules for reporting the results of operations by segments that did not permit the reports to reflect the unique characteristics of a company.
3. Misinterpreted, because the public could not appreciate the limitations of the somewhat arbitrary basis for most cost allocations.

It is clear from the surveys that most companies collect data for management purposes on the basis of organizational units. However, this is done in a variety of ways for different management control purposes.

Companies seem to be split almost equally between those with a close relationship between organizational units and product lines and those with little relationship between organizational units and product lines. The majority of companies prepare fairly complete income statements and balance sheets by organizational units, whereas the remainder prepare partial income statements and balance sheets of one sort or another for organizational units. Typically, the amount of information collected by product lines is significantly less than that available for organizational units.

Common Costs

A difficult problem in trying to determine the profits of business segments is how to handle common or joint costs, those that are jointly shared by more than one business segment. For example, the headquarters accounting staff may keep the accounts for each of the company's components. The costs of this department are common to all of the company's operations. There is usually no clearly discernible way to associate these costs with the particular parts of a business. They must be allocated on some reasonable, but nevertheless arbitrary, basis if they are assigned to other parts of the business.

Irrespective of the degree to which common costs are allocated, a variety of cost allocation bases are used. Some companies spread common costs on the basis of segment sales or profits. Others use component asset or investment as the basis. Some allocate common costs on the basis of specific segment expense items, whereas others do it through negotiations with the managers of the operation affected by the allocations. Some use a basis combining several of these methods. In addition, many companies use more than one method for allocating costs among the different components of their company.

Transfer Prices

Transfer prices are prices charged for goods and services that are transferred between units in the same company. The transfer price is revenue to the selling unit and a cost to the buying unit. These prices are not subjected to the pressures of arm's-length bargaining that exist in the marketplace, and hence lack the objectivity usually associated with sales to those outside the company. The costs and revenues created by these internal transfers are eliminated in the preparation of consolidated statements, since the transfers are offsetting within the corporate entity. In segment reports, however, these transfers are not eliminated. Thus, the sales and costs of the individual segments may total more than those reported for the entire company on a consolidated basis.

A variety of transfer pricing practices exists in practice, often in the same company. Transfer prices range from the equivalent of market prices to direct costs. Some companies base prices on established pricing formulas. Others leave the establishment of the price of internally transferred products or services to negotiations between the units involved.

A number of factors influence the setting of transfer prices. In some situations, the prices of goods moved into states that levy taxes on inventories are deliberately set at a low value in order to minimize taxes. Some companies use their transfer price system as a management control device. The pricing approach used will vary with the different motivational objectives top management hopes to achieve through its control system. Transfer prices between foreign and domestic operations are sometimes used as a device to repatriate cash from foreign operations, rather than through cash dividends which may be restricted by exchange controls.

Analytical Value and Techniques

Statement users must be wary of how they use operating segment data. It can be very misleading unless the statement user has a firm grasp of the definition of the reporting bases, the nature of joint cost allocations, the methods used to price intercompany transfers, and the appropriateness of these items to the company and to its industry. Also, because management has flexibility to define their own management units that in turn are the disaggregated reporting units, the disaggregated data of one company may be of little use in making comparisons with the disaggregated data of other companies.

The goal of disaggregated disclosure analysis is to appreciate better the operating and financial risk of the company, the sources of its profits, and its future prospects.

With above limitations in mind, the analyst can use these data to enhance a company analysis in these ways:

1. Identify the historical relationship between intracompany and external sales by disaggregated reporting unit to see if the units are becoming more or less dependent on external customers for sales.

2. Compute the relative contribution to total company sales and profits of each disaggregated reporting unit's noncompany sales and profits, to identify shifts in the relative importance of units.

3. Use an index number or compound growth rate analysis over time to identify and compare the growth rates of disaggregated reporting units, sales, and profits, and the sources of changes in the total company's growth rates.

4. Calculate the operating profit percentage margin and operating profit return on assets for each disaggregated reporting unit to identify the relative profitability of units and their relationship to total company profitability over time.

5. Compute the trends in each disaggregated reporting unit's total assets using an index number and absolute annual dollar change approaches to understand better the capital allocation decisions of management and the capital requirements of each unit and the total company.

6. Compare the relative percentage distribution of assets by disaggregated reporting units over time to appreciate the changing character of the company's asset base.

7. Use index number, absolute annual dollar changes, annual percentage distribution, and capital expenditure to depreciation expense ratio-type analyses to gain a better understanding of the company's distribution of expenditures for property, plant, and equipment by disaggregated reporting units so as to identify which units are being favored, the capital expenditure requirements of each unit, the adequacy of the capital expenditures by unit, and the sources of the total company's capital expenditure needs.

8. Calculate asset turnover ratios for each disaggregated reporting unit to determine how efficiently each unit's assets are utilized and the various units' impact on total company asset utilization efficiency.

9. Combine the asset turnover, operating profit margin, and return on asset calculations to identify how turnover and margin performance influence each disaggregated reporting unit's return on assets and to explain the influence of units on changes in the total company's return assets.

The above ratio-type data should be evaluated and tested against management's stated goals, strategies, and its own analysis of disaggregated reporting unit results. In addition, it should be related to the various disaggregated reporting units' relevant industry trends and forecast, exchange rate trends and predictions, general domestic and foreign economic conditions, industry and product life cycle stages, as well as

relevant domestic and foreign political developments to determine the past and prospective influence of these environmental factors on disaggregated reporting unit and
total company performance, requirements, challenges, and opportunities.

The text of many annual reports is organized by major organizational units. These
narrative reviews should be read in conjunction with the disaggregated reporting unit
financial results and discussions included in the notes to the financial statements. In
addition, analysts should review the disaggregated reporting-unit–related discussions
included in the annual 10-K and quarterly 10-Q SEC company filing. These materials
tend to be more frank and objective than the more optimistic presentations usually
included in the text of annual reports.

The major customer and industry disclosures should never be neglected. The
condition of these customers and industries may determine in large measure the future
condition of the reporting company. Always check the financial condition, operating
results, and prospects of these major customers, as well as the prospects of the industries served by the company.

More than any other area of financial analysis, disaggregated reporting unit analysis requires the analyst to reach out beyond the present data to other sources. The
astute analysts know this and by doing so hope to gain an edge over rivals who are less
competent, energetic, and diligent. To appreciate disaggregated disclosure data fully
requires an understanding of the relevant disaggregated reporting unit, industry, geographical environment, and operating characteristics. Seldom is sufficient insight in
these areas provided by management in its periodic reports.

CASE
24-1

Value Investment Management

Anne Bright, a food analyst for Value Investment Management, a pension fund management firm, was assigned the task of analyzing the business segment data in the 1994 Quality Products Company's annual report. As its name suggests, Value Investment Management was a so-called "value investor." Here are some excerpts from the conversation in which Ms. Bright's supervisor, Joan Bennett, the director of research, gave her the assignment:

> Ann, Quality's management announced that the company had achieved the highest return on equity in its history. Management even included a Du Pont analysis to show how they did it. Here it is (**Exhibit 1**). I want you to tell me how the various business segments might have contributed to the company's success.
>
> I am impressed with several aspects of the annual report. First, in the introduction, the management clearly stated their financial and operating objectives (**Exhibit 2**).
>
> Second, on the cover, management showed how it viewed the major segments and where each was expected to go in the future. This was communicated by a chart depicting each of Quality's four lines of business[1] in relative size based on sales plotted on real

---

Professor David F. Hawkins prepared this case as the basis for class discussion rather than to illustrate either effective or ineffective handling of an administrative situation.

Copyright © 1995 by the President and Fellows of Harvard College. Harvard Business School case 195–236.

[1]The segments and their principal product lines are:

United States Grocery Products: Ready-to-eat and hot cereals; snacks; mixes, syrups, and corn products; frozen pizza and breakfast products; canned chili; dry, semimoist, and canned dog foods; semimoist and canned cat foods; pork and beans; beverages; and institutional and food service products.

International Grocery Products: Food and pet food products in Canada, Europe, Latin America, and the Pacific; and household products in Latin America and the Pacific.

Childway: Crib and playpen, preschool, audiovisual, dolls, trucks, action figures, plush toys, arts and crafts, construction sets, juvenile furnishings, educational software, and children's apparel.

Specialty Retailing: Mail order crafts; retail and mail order specialty tools and gifts; retail and mail order men's and women's clothing; retail prescription and nonprescription eyewear products.

EXHIBIT 1   **Return on Equity from Continuing Operations, 1989–1994**

		Fiscal Year					
		1989	*1990*	*1991*	*1992*	*1993*	*1994*
Asset turnover		1.65	1.78	1.71	1.76	1.78	2.04
Return on sales	×	4.37%	4.14%	4.18%	4.38%	4.41%	4.03%
Return on assets	=	7.21%	7.37%	7.15%	7.7%	7.85%	8.22%
Leverage factor	×	2.20	2.25	2.33	2.36	2.31	2.41
Return on equity	=	15.9%	16.6%	16.7%	18.2%	18.1%	19.8%

EXHIBIT 2   **Quality Food's Financial Objectives and Operating Strategies**
Returns and Growth: A Balance

In last year's annual report, the message was, "We're doing what we said we would." We still are. This 1994 annual report reviews our progress this year in detail and provides insight into future directions.

Our mission, as always, is to maximize return on investment for Quality Foods' shareholders, both today and consistently in future years. The method is to balance these two major objectives—our number one and number two financial objectives—return on investment and growth.

Financial Objectives	*Operating Strategies*
1. Improve return on equity to 19+ percent over time.	**1.** Be a leading marketer of strong consumer brands of goods and services.
2. Achieve "real" earnings growth averaging 5% per year over time.	**2.** Achieve profitable, better-than-average real volume growth in worldwide grocery and toy businesses.
3. Increase Quality's dividend consistent with earnings growth in "real" terms.	**3.** Improve profitability of low-return businesses or divest.
4. Maintain a strong financial position as represented by Quality's current bond and commercial paper ratings.	**4.** Establish a meaningful position in specialty retailing businesses which will enhance overall corporate growth.
The prime financial goal of a corporation must be to enhance the value of the investment for its shareholders. The investor is looking for returns in the form of dividends and appreciation of stock while the company maintains its financial strength. It is with this in mind that Quality has enunciated its financial objectives.	Our action of the past year were consistent with our operating strategies.
Our financial objectives provide the benchmark for measuring our progress toward achieving our financial goals.	The acquisition of Baldwin Brands, the recovery at Childway, and the aggressive new product activity by U.S. Grocery will contribute to profitable, better-than-average, real growth in grocery and toy businesses (*Strategy 2*) while maintaining Quality's position as leading marketer of strong consumer brands (*Strategy 1*). The Optical Value acquisition will enable us to build a stronger position in specialty retailing (*Strategy 4*). In addition, we closed the sale of our Chemicals Division (*Strategy 3*).

Exhibit 3

*Balancing Profitability
with Growth*

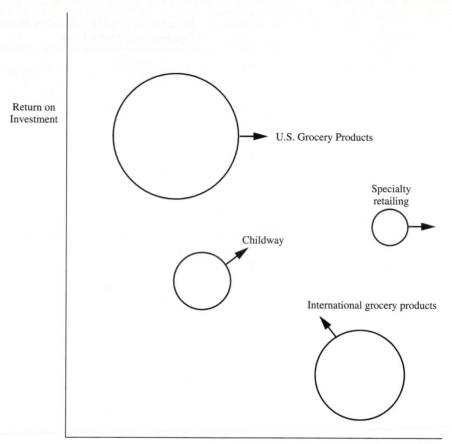

growth and return on investment axes. The chart also indicated where each business has
been and where management believed each is going in the future (**Exhibit 3**). Incidentally,
Quality's organization structure is identical to its business segments. That is, each segment
is headed by an executive vice president.

Third the report's text and financials present an unusual amount of segment and product
data (partially reproduced in **Exhibit 4**). The real-growth and return on investment chart
presentation is repeated for each major business segment.

Quality was featured recently in a *Fortune* article. Its thrust was that under Mr. Smith,
Quality's chairman and chief executive officer, the once sleepy cereal company, founded in
1898, was introducing glitzy new products, whittling costs, and managing finances adroitly.
The article also noted that the food processing industry was only growing at a mere 2% a
year. Smith is described as a master marketer. No doubt that's one of the major reasons
Quality's advertising and merchandising expenditures for its existing businesses have gone
from $212 million in 1989 to $573 million in 1994.

EXHIBIT 4   **Selected Excerpts from Quality Products' Annual Report**
Financial Highlights (millions of $ except share and percent data)

	Year Ended June 30,		
	1994	*1993*	*% Change*
From continuing operations:			
Net sales	$3,344.1	$2,611.3	28.1%
Operating income	326.0	286.1	13.9
Income after taxes	138.7	119.3	16.3
Return on average common equity	19.8%	18.1%	
Per common share:			
Income from continuing operations	6.71	5.83	15.1
Dividends declared	2.20	2.00	10.0
Book value	35.57	32.07	10.9
Common stock:			
Common shareholders' equity	720.1	639.4	12.6
Average number of common shares outstanding (in thousands)	20,103	19,752	1.8
Number of shareholders	26,785	27,943	(4.1)
Capital expenditures	120.1	124.2	(3.3)

Letter to Shareholders

To our Shareholders and Employees:

This was a year in which Quality made substantial progress towards reaching our corporate objectives. We are pleased to report that our fiscal 1994 results show the highest return on equity in company history, and double-digit "real" earnings growth. This performance was led by excellent volume gains in our U.S. grocery products business, aided by a host of successful new product introductions, and the largest acquisition in our history, Baldwin Brands. Our results also reflect the strong recovery of Childway's domestic business from last year's depressed levels. Strength in these areas more than made up for weakness in our edible oils business in Italy, which was the major cause of an overall earnings decline in our international grocery products business.

Here Are the Highlights

- Earnings per share from continuing operations reached $6.71 per share, 15% better than last year's figure. When the effect of inflation is subtracted, "real" earnings growth was 12%. Contributing to this advance were earnings of $.65 cents a share from the newly acquired Baldwin Brands operations and a $.19 per share gain on a debt-for-debt exchange.

- Return on shareholders' equity for the year reached a record high of 19.8%, compared to 18.1% last year.

- Sales increased 28% to $3.34 billion.

- The company raised the annual dividend on its common stock by 10% to $2.20 per share, for fiscal 1994, our 17th consecutive year of dividend increases.

- Early in the fiscal year, Quality completed the largest acquisition in our history, Baldwin Brands, Inc. By year end, all Baldwin operations had been successfully integrated into the company.

- Our U.S. grocery products business introduced the largest number of new products in company history.

- Childway recovered from depressed fiscal 1993 results, benefiting from an excellent Christmas buying season, strong order volume for its 1994 toy line, and reduced costs.

- In November, the company acquired Optical Value, a specialty retail eyewear, based in New York and New Jersey.

- This spring, we completed the sale of Chemical Division for $45.3 million in cash and securities.

EXHIBIT 4   (continued)

Summary of the Year's Activities

U.S. Grocery Products Sales for the year totaled $1.7 billion, 37% better than last year's performance, with the Baldwin business contributing $288 million. Total operating income was $210.9 million, a major improvement over the prior year, boosted by $32.2 million in operating income from Baldwin. Excluding Baldwin, operating income was $178.7 million, down modestly from last year. Our overall operating income growth was restrained by our planned, substantial increase in advertising and marketing expenditures to support the greatest number of new product introductions in our history and to extend the franchise of Baldwin's Qwik Quenche thirst quencher.

Excluding Baldwin, "real growth" in sales totaled 11%, representing unit volume growth as well as a shift to more profitable items in the mix of products we sold. Unit volume rose 3% without Baldwin, reflecting exceptional gains in grain-based snacks aided by the introduction of Quality Granola bars and two new flavors in our highly successful Quality Tasty Granola. Unit volume gains also came from food service, Instant Quality Oatmeal, syrups, dry dog food brands, frozen breakfast items, and ready-to-eat cereals. Both Qwik Quenche thirst quencher and Baldwin's pork and beans, acquired with Baldwin, achieved better-than-expected volumes during their first year as part of Quality.

International Grocery Products Sales rose 3% to $905 million, while operating income declined 21% to $46.9 million. The decline resulted mainly from a major shortfall in our corn oil business in Italy, but also included $6.6 million in nonrecurring charges related to the restructuring of our European and Pacific operations. The United Kingdom, Brazil, and the Benelux countries showed solid operating income and volume gains. Our Latin American businesses performed well in a difficult economic environment, thanks to tight management of working capital and fixed investment.

Childway The division improved significantly over last year, with sales of $383 million up 14%, and operating income of $43.6 million, a 47% gain. Reduced manufacturing and overhead costs worldwide complemented very strong U.S. and Canadian sales. New product introductions were particularly successful, led by the Childway child's camera. During the year, Childway also entered three nontoy areas—juvenile furnishings, educational computer software for children, and children's clothing, the last two through licensing agreements. While Childway's European business has not yet experienced the improvement of the domestic area, the same strategies which contributed to the recovery of the U.S. business are being applied in Europe.

Specialty Retailing The Specialty Retailing Group recorded sales of $157 million, a 22% gain, and operating income of $16.8 million, 6% above last year. Operating income in fiscal 1993 included a favorable $1.8 million prior year inventory adjustment at Saville Clothiers. Sales were bolstered by the Optical Value acquisition, the acceleration of new store openings for Saville Clothiers and Creekstore, and a particularly strong recovery at Saville. Operating income was adversely affected by increased expenditures associated with the opening of the new Creekstore and Saville stores.

Financial

In December, the company issued a new, zero-rate installment note in exchange for two outstanding issues of private placement debt. This debt-for-debt exchange provided a one-time, pre-tax gain of $5.7 million, or $.19 per share after taxes. Net financing costs—the net total of interest expense and foreign exchange gains or losses—rose $1.6 million. Interest expense for the year was $59.9 million or $18 million above last year, due to higher levels of domestic borrowing related to the Baldwin acquisition and higher interest rates in Latin America. The higher interest rates in Latin America were offset by foreign exchange gains of $9 million.

A Perspective on Quality

As we have stated on the inside of this report, we believe Quality will maximize value for its shareholders by achieving a balance between consistent, competitive returns on investment from year to year and solid, profitable growth over the long term. The balance we seek is embodied in the financial objectives and operating strategies which we have been consistently communicating over the last four years and which appear on the inside cover of this report. Our financial objectives provide the benchmark for measuring our progress towards the balance between returns and growth. Our operating strategies outline the steps we will take to make that progress.

EXHIBIT 4   (continued)

This year the Baldwin acquisition, the Childway recovery, and U.S. Grocery's new product activity all will contribute to profitable, above-average, "real" growth in our grocery and toy businesses, while maintaining Quality's position as a leading marketer of strong consumer brands. Our acquisition of Optical Value will help us grow in the highly profitable specialty retailing business while the sale of our Chemical Division was consistent with our strategy of divesting low-return businesses.

In the future, we will continue to emphasize investment in U.S. Grocery Products and Specialty Retailing, support a steady stream of new products, and accelerated store openings, respectively. We will also continue to grow through acquisition. We expect Childway to continue its profitable growth, with the new diversified businesses, such as juvenile furnishing and licensing ventures, making an increasingly important contribution. Given the great expansion in International Grocery Products over the last few years and the state of many foreign economies, we will focus on improving International's profitability, through capital controls and improved overheads, while supporting aggressive marketing programs in opportunity areas.

September 9, 1994
William D. Smith
Chairman and Chief Executive Officer

Six-Year Analysis

Sales

Over the last five years, Quality's sales from existing businesses have increased annually at a compound rate of 13.7%. When we adjust for inflation, sales grew at a compound rate of 10% per year.

Sales for U.S. Grocery Products grew at an annual rate of 14.9% over the last five years, aided by the fiscal 1994 acquisition of Baldwin, new product introductions, price increases, and the favorable effect on sales of selling proportionately more value-added products. Excluding Baldwin, sales grew annually at 11% in nominal terms (not adjusted for price increases).

For International Grocery Products, sales increased at an average rate of 12% for the period fiscal 1989 through fiscal 1994, aided by acquisitions, internal new product development, substantial unit volume growth, and a weakening dollar.

Childway's sales increased at a lesser rate than the grocery areas from fiscal 1989 through fiscal 1994, reflecting, in large part, the softness of the U.S. toy market during fiscal 1993 and the continuing problems of weak economic conditions. However, Childway has shown a strong rebound in fiscal 1994 from the depressed level in fiscal 1993.

Specialty Retailing's sales totaled $157 million in fiscal 1994, up dramatically from a small base of $18.1 million in fiscal 1989, due to several acquisitions and, more recently, an acceleration in retail store expansion. In fiscal 1994, the acquisition of Optical Value added $7 million (seven months' sales) to the group sales.

Operating Income

Operating income from existing businesses increased at a compound annual rate of 14% from fiscal 1989 to fiscal 1994. Adjusting for inflation, operating income from existing businesses grew approximately 10% per year, compounded.

Over the last five years, operating income growth has been particularly strong for U.S. Grocery Products. Excluding Baldwin, the base business showed a compound operating income gain of 13% per year. This growth has been achieved through improved product mix and by steadily reducing our overheads as a percent of sales, with compound annual price increases of about 7%.

Operating income growth for International Grocery Products have been 7.2% per year, compounded, over the last five years. While acquisitions and international expansion of the businesses have contributed growth, weak economies worldwide over the past several years, and fiscal 1994's Italian operating income decline have limited our progress.

Childway's operating income growth of 6.4% per year, compounded, over the last five years reflects the earnings difficulty experienced in fiscal 1993. Fiscal 1994 operating income reflected a strong recovery over fiscal 1993.

Starting from a small base of $2.2 million of operating income in fiscal 1989, and again, aided by acquisitions, Specialty Retailing operating income has grown to $16.8 million in fiscal 1994.

Exhibit 4 (continued)

Fiscal Year	C.G.R.[a]	(Dollars in Millions)					
		1994	1993	1992	1991	1990	1989
Sales	14.9%	$1,719.7	$1,258.9	$1,197.1	$1,056.6	$944.0	$858.1
Operating income	16.6	210.9	183.8	142.5	129.1	106.1	98.0
Identifiable assets	16.4	769.8	483.8	457.6	450.2	395.3	361.5
Return on sales		12.3%	14.6%	11.9%	12.2%	11.2%	11.4%
Return on assets		33.6	39.0	31.4	30.5	28.0	28.2

[a]Five-year compound growth rates.

Advertising and Merchandising Expenditures (A&M)

Marketing investment is necessary to build and maintain our customer franchises. In fiscal 1994, overall A&M from existing businesses increased 32%, or $140 million, to $574 million. Most of this increase occurred in U.S. Grocery Products. The numerous new product entries in U.S. Grocery Products lifted its expenditures, excluding Baldwin, 28%, or $66 million, to $305 million.

While these expenditures constrain profit growth initially, they support the development of strong, long-lived brand franchises which will provide growth and returns for shareholders over the long term. Since fiscal 1989, A&M has increased 22% per year, compounded, and now represents approximately 18% of sales from existing businesses, from a fiscal 1989 level of 13% of sales.

Capital Expenditures

Capital investment is also essential for future growth. In fiscal 1994, capital spending totaled $118.4 million. These expenditures primarily support our three largest lines of business; in fact, more than 90% of the fiscal 1994 expenditures were in the worldwide grocery and toy businesses and over half of the total was devoted to U.S. Grocery alone.

U.S. Grocery Products

U.S. Grocery Products is Quality's largest business segment. This fiscal year it accounted for 54.3% of Quality's sales and 66.3% of Quality's operating income from existing businesses. U.S. Grocery Products employs assets totaling $769.8 million, 47% of total identifiable assets from existing businesses. U.S. Grocery Products is also Quality's most profitable business segment. Over the last six years, the return on assets (operating income as a percent of average identifiable assets) have averaged 32%, and the return on sales (operating income as a percent of sales) have averaged 12%.

While for each business segment, U.S. Grocery Products, International Grocery Products, Childway, and Specialty Retailing, we show the return on sales and assets, these returns are not directly comparable among segments because of differing business dynamics and because they are computed on a historical cost, not current cost, basis. However, the trend of these returns is important and indicates the recent progress of each segment.

Fiscal 1994 Progress

Sales up 37% This fiscal year, sales for U.S. Grocery Products reached $1,719.7 million, a 37% increase over last year. Baldwin, which was acquired during fiscal 1994, had sales of $288.3 million included in U.S. Grocery Products sales and accounted for about two-thirds of the increase. Excluding Baldwin, sales increased 14%, with price increases accounting for about 4% of the gain. The remaining 10% increase in sales, therefore, was a "real" gain, reflecting both unit volume growth and a favorable shift in the mix of products sold.

Operating Income up 15% Operating income rose 15% to $219.9 million. Baldwin contributed $32.2 million to U.S. Grocery Products' operating income. Excluding Baldwin operating income of $178.7 million was down modestly from last year, reflecting the 28% planned increase in advertising and merchandising expenditures which supported the largest number of new product introductions in Quality's history. Excluding Baldwin, the anticipated incremental marketing investment totaled $66 million and represents an investment in future growth.

Exhibit 4 (continued)

Return Remains Solid Return on sales (operating income as a percent of sales) remained strong at 12.3%, despite record levels of advertising and merchandising expenditures which are expected to be maintained during our current and projected period of very aggressive new product activity. The return on sales hit a record level in fiscal 1993, when commodity costs were low and new product activity was just beginning to accelerate.

The operating income return on assets (operating income as a percent of average assets) at 33.6% in fiscal 1994 is strong, although below last year's return for the same reasons noted above.

"Real" Growth Trends

As noted, excluding Baldwin, real growth in sales in fiscal 1994 totaled 11%, representing both unit volume growth and the favorable shift in the mix of products sold. Excluding Baldwin, overall unit volume was up 3%, reflecting gains in the snacks, hot and ready-to-eat cereals, food service, syrup, frozen breakfast, and dry dog food categories. The Baldwin products also increased unit volume year-to-year in fiscal 1994. Categories declining in tonnage this year include pancake, pizza, corn products, and canned and semimoist pet foods. Market shares increased with the majority of product categories.

Quality has achieved significant unit volume gains in "growth" categories, which include instant oatmeal, ready-to-eat cereals, granola snacks, dry dog food, and food service. Over the last five years, growth categories advanced from 34% of total volume to 48%. Compound growth in these categories was 7.1% per year over that period. In addition, products in these categories tend to offer greater value to the consumer and typically carry above-average margins.

"Mature" categories, usually characterized by stable or declining unit volume and high return on investment, include standard oats, mixes, syrup, corn goods, frozen foods, and canned and semimoist pet foods. Tonnage in mature categories has declined 4.6% per year from fiscal 1989 to 1994, and went from 66% to 52% of our total volume. That increase mainly reflects industry declines in canned and semimoist pet food and also reflects the impact on tonnage of the relatively heavy weight of the canned products. However, despite the volume loss for mature categories, their profitability did increase over the same period.

U.S. Grocery Products: Unit Volume Growth, "Mature" versus "Growth" Categories, Fiscal 1989–1994

	Percent of Total U.S. Grocery Products Tonnage		
	Fiscal 1989	*Fiscal 1994*	*5-Year Compound Growth Rates*
Mature categories	66%	52%	−4.6%
Growth categories	34	48	+7.1

Mature: Standard oats; mixes, syrup and corn goods; frozen foods; canned and semimoist pet foods; chili.
Growth: Instant oatmeal; ready-to-eat cereals; snacks; dry dog food; food service.

Net unit volume has been flat over the last five years because of declines in mature categories which have represented more than half of the total tonnage. However, by continuing our emphasis on investment in growth categories in the future, we believe we can achieve overall unit volume gains similar to those achieved this fiscal year.

Unit volume is only one measure of real growth. Real growth can also be derived by selling more value-added products. This is the favorable effect of a shift in product mix which accounted for approximately 7% of the fiscal 1994 sales gain.

EXHIBIT 4   (continued)

Over the past five years, sales have increased 11% per year, compounded (excluding Baldwin). As noted, unit volume growth was flat over this period and price increases averaged 7% per year. Thus, real sales have increased 4% per year.

Real growth is also reflected in operating income gains. Operating income growth is derived from gross margin improvement, affected by real growth in sales, from both unit volume and product mix, and favorable commodity costs. It is also derived from product productivity improvements,

which means that overhead costs decline as a percent of sales. At the same time, an increase in marketing investment as a percent of sales can inhibit growth in operating income.

This year's operating income growth for U.S. Grocery Products was totally due to the contribution of Baldwin, otherwise restrained by the planned increase in marketing expenditures. However, over the past five years (excluding Baldwin), U.S. Grocery operating income growth averaged 13% per year.

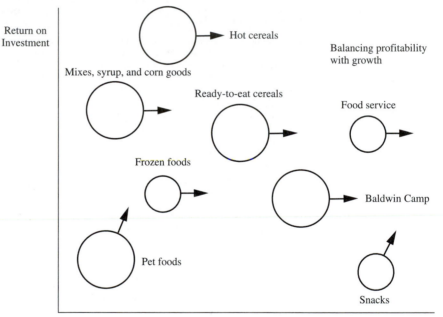

Balancing Return on Investment with Growth

Volume, mix, and productivity improvements are fundamental to U.S. Grocery's strategy to build growth while maintaining good returns. The earlier chart illustrates each of U.S. Grocery Product's categories in terms of their relative return on invested capital and real growth rates. As the chart indicates, U.S. Grocery is comprised of a number of very profitable categories, such as hot cereals, corn goods, and mixes, which have good returns on

investment but are not growth categories. At the same time, higher growth, but with initially lower returns while marketing investments are made in initial years, will be derived from new product categories, such as grain-based snacks. Growth in U.S. Grocery has been, and will continue to be, achieved by identifying segments of opportunity and effectively developing and marketing new products to fill these needs.

EXHIBIT 4   (continued)

New Product Activity

The level of new product activity in snacks, hot and ready-to-eat cereals, and pet foods this year represents the beginning of a steady stream of new products to meet consumer needs in profitable growth segments of the grocery business. This requires investments in research and development, advertising and merchandising, and capital expenditures.

For fiscal 1994, advertising and merchandising expenditures (including Baldwin) rose over 47%. Excluding Baldwin, advertising and merchandising expenditures were up 28%. These marketing investments must be made when the products are initially introduced in order to generate interest by consumers to try the new brands. In fiscal 1994, the timing of these introductions was such that the majority of the marketing spending occurred in the second and third quarters. This quarterly variation in marketing spending for new products will vary from year-to-year depending on the timing of new product introductions and any related seasonality.

Capital expenditures in support of U.S. Grocery growth objectives increased 18% to $69 million and represented about half of the company's capital spending.

Foods Division

Quality's largest single profit center, the Foods Division, increased 46% in fiscal 1994, with the Baldwin acqusition alone increasing sales by 33%.

Fiscal Year	C.G.R.[a]	1994	1993	1992	1991	1990	1989
Hot cereals	12.9%	$ 219.6	$194.2	$183.9	$158.5	$126.3	$119.5
Ready-to-eat cereals	13.3	280.7	258.5	235.2	20.4	171.3	150.6
Mixes, syrup, and corn goods . .	6.4	195.7	197.7	199.0	187.7	152.7	143.3
Snacks	NA	125.8	61.1	23.0	—	—	—
Baldwin Brands	NA	288.3	—	—	—	—	—
Frozen foods	5.6	104.0	104.0	99.3	89.9	89.7	79.2
Other foods	9.5	79.6	69.5	74.4	70.0	59.6	50.6
Total Food Division	19.0%	$1,293.7	$885.0	$814.8	$710.1	$609.6	$543.2

[a]Five-year compound growth rates.

Food Service Division

With the continuing growth of away-from-home food consumption, the food service field represents an attractive growth area for Quality. The Food Service Division, with fiscal 1995 sales of $121 million, continued to show significant profitable growth this year, particularly from its expanded Qwik Quenche marketing program.

Fiscal Year	C.G.R.[a]	1994	1993	1992	1991	1990	1989
Sales	2.0%	$305.0	$277.4	$319.2	$297.9	$292.8	$276.2

[a]Five-year compound growth rates.

Pet Foods Division

Quality's pet food products include a broad line of dog and cat foods.

Fiscal Year	C.G.R.[a]	1994	1993	1992	1991	1990	1989
Sales	25.6%	$121.0	$96.5	$63.1	$48.6	$41.6	$38.7

[a]Five-year compound growth rates.

EXHIBIT 4   (continued)

International Grocery Products

Fiscal Year	C.G.R.[a]	1994	1993	1992	1991	1990	1989
Sales	12.0%	$905.0	$877.6	$869.9	$845.1	$726.4	$513.8
Operating income	7.2	46.9	59.1	52.1	49.5	37.2	33.2
Identifiable assets	11.8	459.0	482.5	432.6	409.8	348.7	262.8
Return on sales		5.2%	6.7%	6.0%	5.9%	5.1%	6.5%
Return on assets		10.0	12.9	12.4	13.1	12.2	14.5

[a]Five-year compound growth rates.

International Grocery Products is Quality's second largest business segment, representing 28.6% of sales in fiscal 1994 and 14.7% of operating income. This segment employs assets totaling $459 million, 28% of total identifiable assets from existing businesses. In fiscal 1994, the operating income return on average assets was 10%, and the operating income return on sales was 5.2%.

Balancing Return on Investment with Growth

The chart illustrates by geographic area the strategic direction for International Grocery Products in terms of growth and return on invested capital.

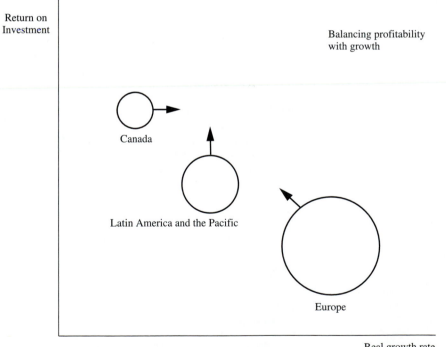

EXHIBIT 4   (continued)

Fiscal Year	C.G.R.[a]	1994	1993	1992	1991	1990	1989
Sales	15.7%	$552.4	$511.9	$450.1	$449.3	$412.7	$266.0

[a]Five-year compound growth rates.

Europe

Quality's European Grocery sales are about evenly divided between pet foods and human foods. Despite sharp volume declines in Italian oils, volume for Europe was up nicely. This increase was aided by the major European pet food acquisition in mid-fiscal 1993 and by strong volume gains in the United Kingdom. All European subsidiaries, except in Italy, contributed to the volume increase.

Fiscal Year	C.G.R.[a]	1994	1993	1992	1991	1990	1989
Sales	6.9%	226.8	$245.1	$303.2	$292.9	$219.7	$162.8

[a]Five-year compound growth rates.

Canada

Fiscal Year	C.G.R.[a]	1994	1993	1992	1991	1990	1989
Sales	8.2%	$125.8	$120.6	$116.6	$102.9	$94.0	$85.0

[a]Five-year compound growth rates.

Childway

Childway is Quality's third largest business segment. This fiscal year it accounted for 12.1% of Quality's sales and 13.7% of Quality's operating income. Childway employs assets totaling $318.1 million, 19.4% of total identifiable assets from existing businesses. In fiscal 1994, the total income return on average assets was 14%, and the return on sales (operating income as a percent of sales) was 11.4%.

Fiscal Year	C.G.R.[a]	1994	1993	1992	1991	1990	1989
U.S. Sales	8.3%	$282.4	$232.1	$261.2	$250.4	$259.4	$189.2
International sales	3.0	101.0	103.8	112.1	116.4	104.5	87.1
Total sales	6.8	383.4	335.9	373.3	366.8	363.9	276.3
Operating income	6.4	43.6	29.6	50.0	46.0	50.3	31.9
Identifiable assets	6.0	318.1	305.8	315.4	296.2	305.4	237.2
Return on sales		11.4%	8.8%	13.4%	12.5%	13.8%	11.5%
Return on assets		14.0	9.5	16.4	15.3	18.5	14.7

[a]Five-year compound growth rates.

Exhibit 4   (continued)

Real Growth

Since one-quarter to a third of the toy line each year represents new toys, all with different price points, and other toys are discontinued, it is virtually impossible to measure unit volume growth. In addition, for the international business, it can be misleading to use dollar sales growth, either nominal or adjusted for inflation, as a measure of real growth because dollar sales include the effect of our currency translation. For the U.S. business (both toys and diversified products), however, nominal sales less average price increases is the best measure of real growth.

Over the past five years, nominal U.S. sales growth was 8%, compounded, with Childway prices increasing at a compound rate of about 7% per year. Thus, real sales growth has been 1% per year during this period, which includes the depressed fiscal 1993 results. However, sales growth for fiscal 1994 rebounded to a "real" rate of about 20%. Similarly, operating income has not increased in real terms over the last five years (again, including the depressed results in fiscal 1993); however, for fiscal 1994, "real" operating income growth was over 40%.

With the encouraging progress made in fiscal 1994, looking ahead, we believe 5% real growth in both sales and operating income is a reasonable target.

Balancing Return on Investment with Growth

Continued improvement in fiscal 1994 financial trends is at the heart of Childway's objectives and plans for the future. We aim to build value for Quality's shareholders by achieving the optimal balance between real growth and return on investment. That means getting consistent volume and income growth overall, while improving returns.

The chart below illustrates Childway Europe, U.S. and Canada, and the Diversified Products area in terms of their relative return on investment and growth potential. As the chart indicates, in Europe we must significantly improve our returns, while in the United States and Canada we must build on the progress made in 1994. Diversified Products, a new juvenile furnishing area for Childway, is in a developmental stage, and returns will improve as the businesses in that area mature. Childway will continue to grow by strengthening its share of the preschool toy market, furthering expansion into toys for school-age children, and diversifying into nontoy areas.

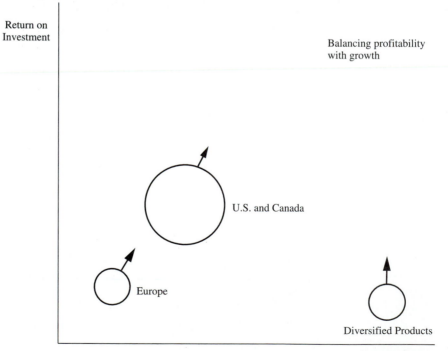

EXHIBIT 4   (continued)

Specialty Retailing

The smallest of Quality's four lines of business, Specialty Retailing is composed of four companies: Saville (men's clothiers), Creekstore (specialty foods), Hammonds (mail order), and Optical Value (eyewear chain).

Fiscal Year	C.G.R.[a]	1994	1993	1992	1991	1990	1989
Sales	54.0%	$157.0	$128.6	$117.8	$ 55.4	$ 47.9	$ 18.1
Operating income	50.2	16.8	15.8	11.6	5.5	4.8	2.2
Identifiable assets	89.9	91.4	65.2	52.2	14.4	12.5	3.7
Return on sales		10.7%	12.3%	9.8%	9.9%	10.0%	12.2%
Return on assets		21.5	26.9	34.8	40.9	59.3	56.4

[a]Five-year compound growth rates.

Balancing Return on Investment with Growth

The chart below illustrates Quality's four specialty retailing businesses in terms of their relative profitability and growth potential.

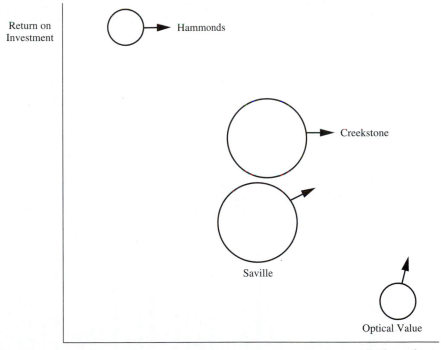

Eхнiвт 4 (continued) Eleven-Year Selected Financial Data (millions of dollars except share and percent data)

Year Ended June 30[a] Fiscal Statistics[b]	5-Year Compound Growth Rate	10-Year Compound Growth Rate	1994	1993	1992	1991	1990	1989	1988	1987	1986	1985	1984
Current ratio			1.5	1.5	1.5	1.6	1.8	1.8	2.0	2.0	2.0	2.4	1.8
Working capital	4.8%	5.6%	$316.8	$261.9	$266.6	$252.4	$265.9	$250.7	$223.1	$233.2	$215.5	$208.7	$184.5
Working capital turnover[c]			11.6	9.9	9.9	9.2	8.5	7.5	6.6	6.4	6.5	6.6	6.8
Property, plant, and equipment—net	7.6	8.6	730.6	616.3	618.4	633.3	572.8	507.4	458.0	406.7	373.6	358.2	319.3
Depreciation expense	15.6	11.7	70.0	52.3	46.3	42.3	37.1	33.9	30.2	29.0	30.4	27.4	23.1
Total assets	9.8	8.8	1,806.0	1,463.7	1,476.7	1,454.1	1,334.2	1,131.5	1,008.8	924.3	854.9	765.1	776.4
Long-term debt	4.9	1.6	200.1	152.8	162.2	165.2	151.7	157.5	159.4	151.8	148.7	158.3	171.4
Redeemable preference stock			38.5	41.3	45.4	46.7	50.0	50.0	50.0	50.0	50.0	50.0	—
Common shareholders' equity	7.0	7.9	720.1	639.4	630.5	612.6	582.9	513.6	461.5	434.3	386.0	350.1	335.2
Book value per common share	6.5	8.2	35.57	32.07	32.17	31.98	28.85	25.94	23.13	20.75	18.62	16.91	16.19
Return on average common shareholders' equity			19.8%	18.1%	18.2%	16.7%	16.6%	15.9%	15.3%	16.8%	12.1%	6.4%	11.6%
Gross profit as a percent of sales			38.0	39.6	36.6	34.2	33.8	33.9	33.7	32.1	31.2	25.2	25.4
Advertising and merchandising as a percentage of sales													
Research and development as a percent of sales			17.2	16.6	14.7	13.8	12.7	12.3	11.7	10.3	9.8	8.5	6.7
Income as a percent of sales			4.1	4.6	4.6	4.4	4.4	4.6	4.9	5.1	3.6	1.8	3.3
Long-term debt ratio[d]			20.9	18.3	19.4	20.0	19.3	21.8	23.8	23.9	25.1	28.0	33.4
Total debt ratio[e]			35.5	33.5	34.1	36.8	33.1	30.7	33.0	30.8	30.8	31.5	45.9
Common dividends as a percent of income available for common			32.9	34.3	31.2	32.0	30.8	30.7	31.2	27.7	29.2	75.5	42.2
Number of common employees			26,785	27,943	29,552	30,418	30,818	31,567	31,853	31,830	24,747	25,064	22,320
Number of employees worldwide			28,400	25,200	26,000	30,900	31,400	31,400	29,600	27,800	23,900	25,100	25,400
Market price range of: Common stock—High			$64-5/8	$51-3/4	$43-1/2	$37-3/4	$34-1/2	$27-1/2	$26	$27-3/4	$28-3/8	$24-3/8	$24-3/8
—Low			42-3/4	35-1/4	31-1/4	25-7/8	23-1/2	22	20	20-7/8	15	11	19-3/4

[a] Financial data presented, where appropriate, reflects pro forma amounts assuming retroactive application of the fiscal 1989 accounting change for deferred taxes.

[b] Income-related statistics have been restated to exclude results of chemicals, video games, and restaurants, which are reported as discontinued operations. Balance sheets and related statistics for fiscal 1993 and prior years have not been restated for these discontinued businesses.

[c] Net sales divided by average working capital.

[d] Long-term debt divided by long-term debt plus total equity including redeemable preference stock.

[e] Total debt divided by total debt plus total equity including redeemable preference stock.

EXHIBIT 4 (continued) Sales and Operating Income by Industry Segment[a] (millions of $ except share data)—Year Ended June 30, 1989–94.

Sales

Year Ended June 30[a] Fiscal Statistics[b]	5-Year Compound Growth Rate	1994	1993	1992[b]	1991[b]	1990[b]	1989[b]
U.S. Grocery Products	14.9%	$1,719.7	$1,258.9	$1,197.1	$1,056.6	$ 994.0	$ 858.1
International Grocery Products	12.0	950.0	877.6	869.9	845.1	726.4	513.8
Childway	6.8	383.4	335.9	373.3	366.8	363.9	276.3
Specialty Retailing	54.0	157.0	128.6	117.8	55.4	47.9	18.1
Total existing businesses	13.7	3,165.1	2,601.0	2,558.1	2,323.9	2,082.2	1,666.3
Other[c]	NA	179.0	10.3	18.1	61.2	111.4	101.1
Total sales and operating income	13.6	3,344.1	2,611.3	2,576.2	2,385.1	2,193.6	1,767.4

Operating Income

Year Ended June 30[a] Fiscal Statistics[b]	5-Year Compound Growth Rate	1994	1993	1992[b]	1991[b]	1990[b]	1989[b]
U.S. Grocery Products	16.6%	$210.9	$183.8	$142.5	$129.1	$106.1	$ 98.0
International Grocery Products	7.2	46.9	59.1	52.1	49.5	37.2	33.2
Childway	6.4	43.6	29.6	50.0	46.0	50.3	31.9
Specialty Retailing	50.2	16.8	15.8	11.6	5.5	4.8	2.2
Total existing businesses	14.0	318.2	288.3	256.2	230.1	198.4	165.3
Other[c]	NA	7.8	(2.2)	4.9	1.9	7.6	8.3
Total sales and operating income	13.4	326.0	286.1	261.1	232.0	206.0	173.6
Less: General corporate expenses	9.6	15.0	16.9	7.3	12.1	11.5	9.5
Interest expense—net	34.5	59.9	41.9	45.9	31.9	24.8	13.6
Foreign exchange (gain) loss—net	NA	(9.0)	7.4	1.0	.8	(1.9)	4.9
Income from continuing operations	11.1	138.7	119.3	117.3	104.3	95.6	82.1
Income from continuing operations per common share	11.5	6.71	5.83	5.81	4.96	4.51	3.89

NA = not applicable.

[a]Sales between industry segments were not material and are not separately set forth.

[b]Restated to exclude restaurant, chemicals, and U.S. games business segments which are reported as discontinued operations.

[c]Fiscal 1994 includes the operations of Baldwin which were sold or are to be sold, fiscal 1993 and earlier years include the Brazilian toy operations sold in fiscal 1993.

EXHIBIT 4 (continued) Quality Products Industry Segment Information (millions of $)

	Identifiable Assets				Capital Expenditures				Depreciation and Amortization			
	1994	1993	1992	1991	1994	1993	1992	1991	1994	1993	1992	1991
U.S. Grocery Products	$ 769.8	$ 483.8	$ 457.6	$ 450.2	$ 68.5	$ 58.2	$ 30.1	$ 41.2	$33.4	$23.0	$21.5	$19.1
International Grocery Products	459.0	482.5	432.6	409.8	29.1	45.2	60.0	58.7	21.1	17.6	14.4	13.9
Childway	318.1	305.8	315.4	296.2	13.7	17.1	21.3	21.2	12.9	12.5	11.5	9.6
Specialty Retailing	91.4	65.2	52.2	14.4	7.1	3.5	2.1	1.6	2.8	1.9	1.6	.5
Total existing businesses	$1,638.3	$1,337.3	$1,257.8	$1,170.6	$118.4	$124.0	$113.5	$122.7	$70.2	$55.0	$49.0	$43.1
Other[a]	34.3	—	12.8	20.1	1.7	.2	.6	4.1	4.0	.1	.3	1.6
Corporate[b]	134.2	126.4	206.1	263.4	—	—	—	—	—	—	—	—
Total consolidated	$1,806.8	$1,463.7	$1,476.7	$1,454.1	$120.1	$124.2	$114.1	$126.8	$74.2	$55.1	$49.3	$44.7

[a]Fiscal 1994 includes the operations of Baldwin Brands which were sold or are to be sold; fiscal 1993 and earlier years include the Brazilian operations sold in fiscal 1993.

[b]Corporate identifiable assets include the net assets of discontinued operations, corporate cash and marketable securities, and miscellaneous receivables.

EXHIBIT 4 (continued) Quality Products Geographic Area Information (millions of $)

	Sales[c]				Operating Income				Identifiable Assets			
	1994	1993	1992	1991	1994	1993	1992	1991	1994	1993	1992	1991
United States	$2,164.0	$1,623.5	$1,580.7	$1,367.2	$ 249.5	$ 210.6	$ 183.7	$ 163.0	$1,113.1	$ 783.6	$ 748.7	$ 694.7
Canada	160.3	151.3	148.3	135.6	12.4	10.7	8.7	7.2	60.0	58.8	52.3	53.1
Europe	614.4	581.0	525.8	533.0	22.0	34.8	30.5	31.6	325.3	346.7	282.2	252.4
Latin America & Pacific	226.4	245.2	303.3	388.1	34.3	32.2	33.3	28.3	139.9	148.2	174.6	170.4
Total existing businesses	$3,165.1	$2,601.0	$2,558.1	$2,323.9	$ 318.2	$ 288.3	$ 256.2	$ 230.1	$1,638.3	$1,337.3	$1,257.8	$1,170.6
Other[a]	179.0	10.3	18.1	61.2	7.8	(2.2)	4.9	1.9	34.3	—	12.8	20.1
Corporate[b]	—	—	—	—	—	—	—	—	134.2	126.4	206.1	263.4
Total consolidated	$3,344.1	$2,611.3	$2,576.2	$2,385.1	$ 326.0	$ 286.1	$ 261.1	$ 232.0	$1,806.8	$1,463.7	$1,476.7	$1,454.1

[a] Fiscal 1994 includes the operations of Baldwin Brands which were sold or are to be sold; fiscal 1993 and earlier years include the Brazilian operations sold in fiscal 1993.

[b] Corporate identifiable assets include the net assets of discontinued operations, corporate cash and marketable securities, and miscellaneous receivables.

[c] Represents sales to unaffiliated customers only; sales between geographic segments are not material.

EXHIBIT 4   (continued)

Note 2: Acquisitions and Dispositions
Acquisitions

During the first quarter of fiscal 1994, the company acquired Baldwin Brands, pursuant to a tender offer. The tendered shares, combined with shares acquired previously and also those purchased under agreements with certain Baldwin Brands shareholders, resulted in Quality's owning 77% of Baldwin's common stock. All remaining shares were acquired pursuant to a merger which was approved by Baldwin shareholders in September 1993 and became effective October 31, 1993. The purchase price was approximately $238 million. Results of operations have been consolidated since the acquisition date.

Presented below are the consolidated results as reported for fiscal 1994 compared to pro forma combined results of Quality and Baldwin for fiscal 1993. Fiscal 1994, as reported, is indicative of a full year of combined operations, since 11 months of Baldwin results since acquisition are included in consolidated Quality reporting. The pro forma combined results for fiscal 1993 assumes the acquisition had occurred at July 1, 1992. The pro forma data was prepared making those adjustments necessary due to the reevaluation of the acquired assets of Baldwin and certain other adjustments required as a result of the acquisition. The adjustments do not include nonrecurring expenses which resulted directly from the acquisition.

	(Millions of $ except share data)	
	FY 1994 as Reported	*FY 1993 Pro Forma Combined*
Revenue	$3,344.1	$2,994.5
Income from continuing operations	138.7	126.2
Net income	138.7	63.7
Per common share:		
Income from continuing operations	$ 6.71	$ 6.15
Net income	6.71	2.98

Question

Complete Ann Bright's assignment. How have the various business segments contributed to the company's record 1994 return on equity? _____ How has the management changed the character and mix of the company's various business segments since 1989? _____ Does the segment data support management's appraisal of the company's achievement and prospects? _____

CHAPTER 25

Interim Period Reports

The same financial analysis techniques that statement users apply to annual statements can be used to interpret interim reports. The difficulty in applying these techniques is that the financial data presented in interim reports may be partial, condensed, not explained in detail by accompanying notes, unaudited, and very dependent on management judgments. As a result, the statement user often has less confidence in the results of his or her analysis of interim reports than in the conclusions drawn from analysis of annual statements.

To overcome some of the limitations of interim reports, statement users should always refer to the company's last annual report to refresh their understanding of the company's accounting principles, examine past year-end adjustments to gain an appreciation of the reliability of management's interim reporting judgments, and use interim period data cautiously.[1]

Many of the issues involved in interim reporting are the same as those encountered in annual reporting. However, a number of reporting practices are peculiar to interim reporting. This note concentrates on these latter issues, which are dealt with primarily in APB Opinion No. 28.

Inherent Problems

The determination of the results of operations for periods of less than a full year presents inherent difficulties for the management trying to prepare a meaningful statement and the investor seeking to use the interim data.

Professor David F. Hawkins prepared this note as the basis for class discussion.
Copyright © 1995 by the President and Fellows of Harvard College. Harvard Business School teaching note 195–231.

[1]Interim statements presume that the interim report user is familiar with the company's annual report accounting policies, which were disclosed in the latest annual report.

Too Short

The most common difficulty is that information for any period less than a full year may have limited usefulness because the reporting period is too short to reflect adequately the nature of a company's business. For example, the revenues of some businesses fluctuate widely among interim periods because of seasonal or random factors. In other businesses, heavy costs incurred in one interim period may benefit another period. In other situations, costs and expenses related to a full year's activities may be incurred at infrequent intervals throughout the year. In this case, costs may be allocated to products in process or to the interim periods to avoid distorting the interim results.

Limited Time

Another reporting problem inherent in interim reporting is that in the limited time available, it is impractical to develop the complete information needed to present the report. As a result, many costs and expenses are estimated in interim reports. For example, it may not be practical to perform extensive reviews of individual inventory items, costs on individual long-term contracts, and precise income tax calculations. As a result, the interim data are tentative, and subsequent refinement or corrections of these estimates may distort the results of operations of later interim periods. Similarly, the effects of disposal of a segment of a business and extraordinary, unusual, or infrequently occurring events and transactions will often be more pronounced on the results of operations for an interim period than they will be on results for the annual period.

Alternative Objectives

There is considerable controversy as to what the principal objective should be for interim financial reporting. The two principal alternative objectives follow from their proposers' views of the nature of the interim period. One group believes that each interim period should be viewed as the basic accounting period. This approach is called the "independent theory." In contrast, those who propose the alternative objective maintain that each interim period should be viewed as an integral part of the annual period; this is referred to as the "dependent theory."

Those who support the basic accounting period position tend to think of an accounting period as such, irrespective of its length, and to believe that the events and transactions of each accounting period should be reported. From this position, they conclude that the results of operations for each interim period should be determined in essentially the same manner as if the interim period were an annual accounting period. Under this view, deferrals, accruals, and estimations at the end of each interim period would be determined by following essentially the same principles and judgments that the company applies to annual reports. For example, if an expenditure was expensed in the annual statement, it should be expensed in any interim report, irrespective of the amount of the expenditure and its relationship to the annual amount or the revenues of other interim periods within this year.

Those who hold that interim financial data are an integral part of the annual period believe it is essential to provide investors with timely information on the progress the enterprise is making toward its annual results of operations. Therefore, the usefulness of interim data rests on the predictive relationship that it has to the annual period results. Thus, each interim period should be regarded as an integral part of the annual period rather than a discrete period standing on its own.

Under this view, deferrals, accruals, and estimations at the end of each interim period are affected by judgments made then as to the results of operations for the balance of the annual period. Thus, for example, a portion of an estimated annual expenditure that might be expensed for the entire annual period might be accrued or deferred at the end of an interim period as management allocates the estimated annual expense between interim periods on a basis that reflects time, sales volume, or production activity.

APB Opinion 28

APB Opinion No. 28 and its subsequent amendments adopted the integral part point of view based on the dependent theory. The opinion recognized that, in general, each interim report should be based on the accounting policies used in the preparation of the latest annual statements, unless some accounting policies have been changed in the current year. However, it went on to conclude that certain modifications of these annual report practices may be required in interim reports so that the reported results may correspond better to the results of operations for the annual period. What follows is a summary of the opinion's recommendations.

Revenues

Revenues earned during an interim period should be recognized on the same basis as followed for the full year. For example, if the revenue from long-term contracts is accounted for under the percentage-of-completion method in annual statements, the same approach should be used in interim reports. If future losses on such contracts become evident during an interim period, the projected losses should be recognized in full in the interim period, however.

Product Costs

Costs that are associated directly with or allocated to the products and services sold are called product costs. These costs for both annual and interim reporting purposes should be charged to the period in which the related revenue is recognized. Examples of product costs include material costs, direct production wages and related fringe benefits, variable manufacturing overheads, warranty expenses, and similar expenses whose total level tends to vary with or relate closely to business volume.

Most product costs are included in the income statement as an element of the cost-of-goods-sold figure. This item in interim reports should be regarded as a very tentative expression of the expense, since the inventory valuation procedures used to measure it are typically based on perpetual inventory records and estimates of future inventory replenishment costs, rather than physical counts and actual prices. Inventory records are seldom accurate; and the future cost estimates of executives are seldom correct due to random factors, a desire to be conservative, a need to inflate current profits, or poor forecasting information and skills.

For interim reporting purposes, companies should generally use the same inventory pricing methods as those followed to determine annual results. However, some exceptions may be appropriate for interim reporting. For example, some companies use estimated gross profit rates to determine the cost of goods sold during interim periods. Under this procedure, management simply assumes a margin percentage—usually the margin achieved in prior annual periods or budgeted for the current annual period—and applies it to the sales of the period to determine the period's dollar gross margin. This approach in times of inflation can produce misleading results if a company does not keep close track of its cost increases and is slow to raise prices.

Other companies that use the LIFO method may, at an interim date, encounter a temporary liquidation of the LIFO base period inventories, which are expected to be replaced by the end of the annual period. If these base period costs are allowed to flow through to the income statement, profits would be inflated and not representative of the annual results.

In such cases, the inventory at the interim reporting date should not give effect to the LIFO liquidation. The cost of sales for the interim reporting period should be based on the expected cost of replacement of the liquidated LIFO base. Again, in periods of inflation or commodity shortages, this estimate may be difficult to make.

Many companies use standard cost accounting systems for determining inventory and product costs. These companies should generally follow the same procedure in reporting purchase price, wage rate, usage, or efficiency variances from standard cost at the end of the interim period as followed at the end of the fiscal year. However, if the cost variances associated with an interim period are planned and are expected to be absorbed by the end of the annual period, they may be deferred and not recognized in the interim period in which they occur. The decision as to what is "planned" and "unplanned" rests with the reporting management.

Whether to apply the lower-of-cost-or-market rule in reporting inventories for interim periods also requires judgment on management's part. If a company has inventory losses from market price declines at an interim period date, the loss should be recognized in the interim period in which it occurs if management believes the loss is permanent. On the other hand, if a market decline at an interim date can reasonably be expected to be restored in the current fiscal year, the temporary decline need not be recognized at the interim date. Should management decide to recognize an inventory loss in one interim period and if the market price later recovers in the same fiscal year, the gain can be recognized in the later interim period in which it occurs.

Other Costs

All businesses have costs and expenses that are not allocated or associated directly with product and service revenues. These other costs include such items as advertising expenditures, vacation pay, maintenance costs, and property taxes. According to APB Opinion No. 28, these other costs may be expensed as incurred or allocated among interim periods based on an estimate of time expired, benefit received, or other activity associated with the period. In line with its overall objective for interim statements, the opinion expressed a preference for allocating these other costs between periods, but it did not preclude the option to expense as incurred.

To guide management in interim accounting for costs and expenses other than product costs, the opinion set forth these standards:

1. Procedures adopted for assigning specific expense items to an interim period should be consistent with the bases followed by the company for that item in reporting results of operations at an annual reporting date.
2. When a specific cost item charged to expense for annual reporting purposes benefits more than one interim period, the item may be allocated as an expense between those interim periods that benefit from the expenditure.
3. Costs and expenditures incurred in an interim period that cannot be identified with the activities or benefits of other interim periods should be charged to the interim period in which they are incurred.
4. Costs should not be assigned arbitrarily to an interim period.
5. Gains and losses that arise in any interim period similar to any that would not be deferred at year-end should not be deferred to later interim periods within the same year.

APB Opinion No. 28 presents a number of examples of the preferred accounting for costs other than product costs. Here are some of these examples:

Many companies schedule their major repair work during the annual plant vacation shutdown period, typically in the summer months. These repairs benefit the whole year's operations and relate to the use of the plant during the year. In these cases, it is appropriate to estimate the cost of these repairs at the beginning of the year and then allocate the cost over the entire year for interim reporting purposes. This means that prior to the actual repair work, a portion of the expenditure may be charged to each interim period on an accrual basis. This is achieved through a debit to the repair expense account and a credit to a reserve for repair expenditure, which is a liability account. When the anticipated expenditure is made, the reserve is charged. Any excess expenditure above the reserve amount is deferred. Then, over the year's remaining interim periods, the difference between the actual repair expenditure and the amount of the accumulated reserve (an asset called deferred repair expense) is amortized by a debit to expense and credit to the deferred asset account, according to the allocation basis adopted at the beginning of the year.

Quantity discounts are often allowed customers based upon annual sales volume. In order to relate this discount to the sales of each interim period, an amount for anticipated year-end discounts should be charged to each interim period based on the relationship between interim period sales to customers and customers' estimated annual sales and discounts.

The accounting entry to record anticipated discounts at the time sales are made is:

Dr. Discounts and Allowances XXX
    Cr. Reserve for Discounts and Allowances   XXX

Later, as discounts are earned by customers, the reserve for allowances is eliminated and any discounts in excess of this reserve are charged to sales over the remaining portion of the annual period.

Property taxes, interest, and rents are usually payable as of a certain day. Typically, these costs are accrued or deferred at annual reporting dates to record a full year's charge. Similar procedures should be adopted at each interim reporting date to provide for an appropriate cost in each period.

In some sales programs, it is necessary to stock dealers with products before launching an advertising program. If a subsequent advertising program is clearly implicit in the sales arrangement, the anticipated program costs may be accrued and assigned to interim periods in relation to sales recorded prior to the time the advertising service is rendered.

The amounts of certain costs and expenses are frequently subjected to year-end adjustments, even though they can be reasonably approximated at interim dates. Examples of such items include inventory shrinkage, allowance for quantity discounts, and discretionary year-end bonuses. To the extent possible, year-end adjustments should be estimated at the beginning of the year and the estimated costs assigned to interim periods so that the interim periods bear a reasonable portion of the anticipated annual amount.

APB Opinion No. 28 recommends that the tax rate applied to each interim period's pre-tax income for determining tax expense should be the best estimate of the effective tax rate expected to be applied to the full fiscal year's pre-tax profits. This requires that the interim period rate reflect anticipated investment tax credits, foreign tax rates, capital gains rates, and other similar tax planning alternatives. Since a management estimate is required to implement the opinion's recommendation, the quality of the estimate may vary depending on (a) the company's ability to reach its interim profit goals and (b) management's willingness to use accounting techniques to raise or lower its interim profits.

Advertising costs should be expressed when incurred. Direct mail selling costs may be deferred until the sales responses are received if the company can reliably estimate the response rate.

Extraordinary and Unusual Items

Immaterial extraordinary items can be included as part of the calculation of income before extraordinary items. In the case of interim reports, a question arises as to whether the interim period profit before extraordinary items or the estimated annual profit before extraordinary items should be the basis on which to measure materiality.

APB Opinion No. 28 recommends that the year-end profit estimate be used.[2] Thus, an extraordinary item that is very material relative to interim earnings results, but immaterial relative to the annual profit estimate, may be included in the interim period's income before extraordinary items. To let the statement reader be made aware of the inclusion of such items in income, the opinion recommends that all "unusual" events and items be disclosed.

The effects of disposal of a segment of a business should be reported separately in interim statements.

Other kinds of events that should be disclosed to provide the statement user with a proper understanding of interim financial reports include unusual seasonal results and business combinations.

Extraordinary items, gains, or losses from a business segment disposal and unusual or infrequently occurring items should not be prorated over the balance of the fiscal year.

Role and Limitations

Often, by the time a company's annual data are available, its stock price has already anticipated them many months earlier. This discounting is in large measure influenced by the interim period reports that precede the annual reporting date. As a result, there are many who believe that interim financial data are more important to the securities market than annual period data.

Fundamental investors use interim data in two ways. Some use them to predict the annual results. Others use them to check to see if the reporting company is on a track that will validate the investor's prior prediction of its annual results.

While statement users use interim data in this fashion, they should not lose sight of three facts that will limit the usefulness of these disclosures. First, because of the shortness of the period, interim data are less reliable than annual data as a measure of corporate health. Second, the interim disclosures are meager. Third, managements can—and do—create interim earnings through accounting judgments in order to meet statement users' expectations.

Another problem that may limit the usefulness of the first two interim reports of each year is the interim reporting strategy many managements have typically followed in the past. Some managements like to understate their first- and second-quarter results so that (1) they can keep some profits in reserve should problems occur later in the year, and (2) they can finish with a strong fourth quarter. If companies have followed this strategy in the past, they may be able to top the previous year's first- and second-quarter results by simply not understating current results as they may have done in prior years. In these cases, any improvement over last year would not be real progress, but just the result of a change in interim reporting strategy.

---

[2]The year-end profit estimate is the suggested test of materiality for all interim statement items.

Champion International

Champion International was a publicly traded multinational diversified U.S. company. In 1993 Champion was known as a "growth" stock. During 1992 a number of major institutional investors had acquired relatively large holdings of the stock, and the stock's price had risen rapidly in a stock market environment that valued "growth" highly and was characterized as "an earnings momentum" market.

Champion was about to issue its first-quarter 1993 financial statements to shareholders. The company's quarterly statements to shareholders included condensed financial statements following presentation instructions outlined by the Securities and Exchange Commission [SEC] for filing quarterly report 10-Q. An auditor's opinion was not included since an independent audit was not required when issuing quarterly reports. Also, only limited footnotes were provided. Besides the financial statements, Champion's quarterly reports included a brief discussion and analysis of the company's operations and financial condition by management. Excerpts from Champion's first-quarter 1992 report to shareholders are shown in **Exhibit 1.**

Board Meeting

The following board of directors' discussion of the first-quarter 1993 statements for Champion took place in early April 1993. The final statements were due to be released later in the month:

Professor David F. Hawkins prepared this case as the basis for class discussion rather than to illustrate either effective or ineffective handling of an administrative situation.

EXHIBIT 1   Champion International
Excerpt from Champion International's 1992 First-Quarter Report, "Growth through Diversification"

To Our Shareholders, Customers, and Employees:

The record sales and earnings of this quarter exceed any first quarter in Champion's history. In fact, sales and earnings are exceeded only by the fourth quarter of the preceding year. This was a remarkable performance given the depressed state of the global economy.

Consolidated net income of Champion International for the three-month period ended March 31, 1992, was equal to 52 cents a share. This compared to 46 cents a share, in the first quarter last year.

This growth represents both a continuation of the basic demand for Champion's products and Champion's program of diversification through acquisition. Our three principal operating sectors, Consumer Products, Paper Products, and Industrial Systems, all showed growth throughout the quarter due to our successful global search for compatible and reinforcing acquisitions.

As the cover of this quarterly report indicates, your management is committed to "growth through diversification." We expect that this global strategy will enable Champion to sustain its current growth record. . . .

David X. Morris
President and Chief Executive Officer
April 29, 1992

Lawrence (vice president–finance): The figures for the first quarter don't look good. However, I believe we have it in our power to push them over the same period results for the last year, if we want to do so.[1]

Franklin (outside director): What do you mean by that?

Lawrence: Let me explain. Last year, we earned 52 cents per share for the first quarter, which was the best we had ever done to date for that period. This year with interim accounting practices that I prefer, we have only 47 cents per share, before any adjustments to my conservative accounting decisions that you may wish to make.

Morris (president): In view of the 47 cents per share number, I decided to take the unusual step of bringing the question of what accounting practices are appropriate for our first quarter report to the full board. Frankly, I think it is imperative that we report a good first quarter. Last year, our earnings were a record high and our fourth quarter was extremely strong. In fact, it was our best quarter ever. . . .

Powers (outside director): Yes, I know. But didn't we pull a lot of income into the last quarter from this year to get those results? For example, we cut advertising, accelerated foreign dividend receipts, picked up an export incentive[2]

---

[1]Lawrence had been hired as the company's new vice president-Finance, early in 1993.

[2]Champion's Southwest Asian subsidiary exported through an export incentive corporation (EIC). These were special corporations permitted by the local tax code to encourage exports. EIC's were required to pay taxes immediately on only part of their EIC profits. The payment of taxes on the remainder of the profits was deferred as long as the untaxed profits were used for export purposes. Should these profits subsequently be used for nonexport purposes, the deferred tax payments became payable. Prior to 1992,

tax savings for the first time, deferred maintenance, recognized income on planned 1993 shipments advanced to 1992 delivery. It seems to me that what we did was to "rob Peter to pay Paul." Now we have to pay the price.

Morris: I admit we pushed a bit, but the fact is, the stock market reacted favorably to our strong finish to last year and our stock price has really started to climb. In fact, since mid-January our price-earnings ratio has gone from 21 times to 24 times this year's estimated earnings, which the market estimates will be higher than last year. I don't think we can afford to lose this stock price momentum.

I am convinced that if we report earnings for this quarter that are substantially below last year's first-quarter results, we will see our price-earnings ratio decline. This is a very "nervous" stock market we are in. The Dow is high, but it is subject to wide fluctuations on a weekly basis.

Braun (vice president–marketing): Why are the first-quarter earnings less than last year? What are the causes and dollar value? What options do we have? I for one want to keep our stock's price-earnings ratio up.

Lawrence: Here is an analysis of the differences between this year and last year: First, because we deferred maintenance on a worldwide basis from last year to this year, our first-quarter maintenance costs are up by two cents a share over last year. Also, since the first quarter is normally the heaviest maintenance month of the year, we have an extra two cents per share charge above what the average will be for the next three quarters, which have fairly equal maintenance expenditures. I have charged the extra four cents maintenance to the first quarter.

Second, our EIC tax deferrals in this quarter ran at the rate of three cents per share. This is our Southwest Asian subsidiary's peak export period. It is over one-third of the year's projected EIC tax saving of eight cents, which we can flow through to income. Last year's fourth quarter was the first time we had material EIC tax savings. In that case, we credited all of the savings to that quarter's income. Now, I believe we should spread our EIC tax savings equally over the full year on a quarter by quarter basis. So, I picked up two cents for this quarter and deferred one cent. Actually the EIC tax impact on earnings is a "plus" from last year at this time.

Braun: Do we have to spread the EIC benefit?

Lawrence: No. We can pick up the EIC earnings as earned. However, I felt "spreading" was the preferred approach.

Powers: It all depends on how you define "preferred."

Lawrence: Next, we have the costs of relocating the Southern Paper Sioux Springs offices. These came to three cents a share. Actually, we had planned to

---

for book purposes, Champion fully accrued its potential EIC taxes. In the fourth quarter of 1992 Champion switched to flowthrough-type tax accounting for its EIC (i.e., only recorded the taxes actually paid on the grounds that it would never have to pay the deferred tax payments). Since the impact on annual profits of the accounting change was "immaterial," the new accounting policy was not disclosed in 1992 financial reports.

do that last year, but put it off to its first quarter this year because we didn't want to hurt last year's earnings. I included all of that cost in the first quarter.

Morris: I talked to Bill (Lawrence) about these charges which are depressing earnings and he tells me that it is good accounting to recognize costs and defer revenues. I suspect he is correct, but do we necessarily have to do this for interim reports? Bill, you have some more items don't you?

Lawrence: Yes. This first quarter includes a dividend of four cents per share we got from our Brazilian subsidiary in March. Because of "control problems," we account for this subsidiary on the cost basis, we only pick up income from it as it is received in dividends in the United States.

Morris: Last February, I felt we were going to have consolidated first-quarter earnings problems, so I put extra pressure on Brazil to repatriate some dividends. As you know, our Brazilian subsidiary has legal problems over whether our investment in Brazil is properly registered. This in turn limits our ability to get dividends out of Brazil.

Cohen (vice president–personnel): What do the dividends from cost-basis investments look like this year?

Morris: Well I think we can get about 10 cents per share's worth in the last quarter, but between now and then I am not very hopeful. Incidentally, 10 cents is all we budgeted for foreign dividends from cost-basis investee companies this year.

Frankly, while domestic and export sales and profits are on track from regular operations, our overseas operations are down. In fact, that is the major reason for our problems. In particular, our new Italian company, Grazzini, which we picked up late last year and included in the consolidated results on a pooling of interests basis, is a real "lemon." I have to admit we were in a big hurry to acquire it. We wanted its full-year profits to be included in the full year's results. As you know, its profits were up some 200 percent over the previous year.

Peter (Pike), why don't you explain the situation to us?

Pike (vice president–international): Well, the company is still delivering operating profits, but its inventories and receivables turned out to be overstated. Once our internal auditors got in last January and examined what we had bought, they found a lot of obsolete and damaged inventories. Also, the receivables' bad debt reserves were too low. In addition, some equipment was still carried on the books, but it couldn't be found. Then some other equipment should be written off. It is junk.

All this amounts to a six cents per share write-off. . . .

Lawrence: I charged it to operating income.

Morris: Of course, we have filed a lawsuit in the Italian courts against the Grazzini brothers to recover these amounts.

Braun: What do you think our chances are of collecting?

Morris: Very slim. However, I thought it was worth the effort. Maybe to protect their name they may settle out of court. They are not dishonest. They're just poor bookkeepers.

Outside of the Grazzini problem, I expect our foreign operations will deliver their budgeted share of this year's earnings per share by December 31.

Braun: Bill (Lawrence), how did you charge the major advertising program we had in March?

Lawrence: I figured we spent about two cents a share above our average monthly budget. The principal cost was the "unusual" TV show and related radio and paper advertising. All of this was charged to March.

Braun: The benefits will come in April, May, and June, won't they? In fact, so far this month our sales are up just as we planned. It seems to me that—to quote you from an earlier meeting—"proper matching of costs and revenues" should require us to defer this "extra" two cents per share to the second quarter.

Cohen: It looks like Congress later this summer is going to adopt an investment tax credit retroactive to January 1 this year. Should we be taking that into account in some way in the first quarter?

Lawrence: If the investment tax credit is adopted—and the probability looks high—I have figured it will be worth about 12 cents per share for 1993 of which about 1 cent would be earned in the first quarter. The first quarter is typically our lowest capital expenditure period.

Morris: Can we pull some of these anticipated investment tax credits into the first quarter? After all our quarterly tax rate is supposed to reflect the anticipated annual rate.

Lawrence: I'm not sure. If we did that we might have to take a second look at our recognition of EIC benefits in the first quarter.

Morris: This year we have had to adopt new postretirement benefit and income tax accounting rules. My understanding is that the impact of these new rules is immaterial.

Lawrence: That's correct.

There are two more items I wanted to mention. First, I have picked up in the first quarter one-third of the third-quarter advertising costs related to this year's special fall campaign. I'll pick up another third in each of the next two quarters. This special program, which is in addition to our normal advertising costs, is going to cost about six cents per share above our regular advertising costs, which are run fairly evenly throughout the year.

Second, due to the change in the dollar relative to many overseas currencies, we had an exchange gain of four cents per share on our hedging of anticipated 1993 foreign-currency–denominated transactions. I did not include this in the first-quarter results. In my opinion, by year-end we could end up with currency losses on open transaction hedges. So, I feel it is wise to defer this gain as a possible offset against future losses.

Powers: I thought Statement 52 prohibited deferral of hedging again and losses on anticipated transactions?

Lawrence: That's true in most circumstances, but the amount is immaterial so the rules don't apply. I think conservatism should apply in this case.

Morris: Thank you, Bill (Lawrence).

Well, here's our problem. The security analysts are predicting we will make nearly 60 cents for the first quarter. We don't have that kind of performance now based on Bill's initial conservative figure. However, I feel that if we don't report 60 cents, our price-earnings ratio will drop. If this happens, I am fearful that our merger negotiations with Apex in Cleveland and Contrelli in Italy will collapse or not produce the earnings-per-share impact we expected. We need the earnings of both of these companies and at least one more merger to meet the analyst's consensus profit forecast for this year. As I reported to the finance committee last month, these two mergers under negotiation will be for stock and will be accounted for as a pooling of interests. . . . The Apex price-earnings ratio based on our offering price is 20 times this year's projected earnings. . . . The Contrelli family is interested in us because they feel we are a growth stock. . . .

Well, what first quarter earnings per share figure should report to the public?

Questions

1. What earning per share figure should Champion International report as its first-quarter operating result? _____

2. How do you believe the various accounting issues raised in the case should be resolved? _____

Contingencies

For the purposes of contingency accounting and disclosure, a contingency is defined as an existing condition, situation, or set of circumstances involving uncertainty as to the possible gain or loss to an enterprise that will ultimately be resolved when one or more future events occur or fail to occur. The resolution of the uncertainty may confirm the acquisition of an asset or reduction of a liability, or the loss to impairment of an asset or incurrence of a liability. The accounting for contingencies is covered primarily by *FASB Statement No. 5*.

The accounting process requires many estimates in accounting for ongoing and recurring business activities. In most cases, the uncertainty inherent in these estimates does not necessarily give rise to a contingency as that term is used in *FASB Statement No. 5*. For example, depreciation accounting requires that estimates be made to allocate the known cost of an asset over the period of use by the enterprise. The fact that an estimate is involved does not make depreciation a contingency, since the eventual expiration of the asset is not uncertain. Also, accrued amounts that represent estimates of amounts owed for services received but not yet billed are not contingencies, since there is nothing uncertain about the fact that obligations have been incurred.

FASB Statement No. 5 presents these examples of loss contingencies: collectibility of receivables; warranty obligations; risk of loss or damage of enterprise property by fire, explosion, or other hazards; threat of expropriation of assets; pending or threatening litigation; actual or possible claims and assessments; risk of loss from catastrophes assumed by property and casualty insurance companies; guarantees of indebtedness of others; obligation of commercial banks under standby letters of credit; and agreements to repurchase receivables (or to repurchase the related property) that have been sold. In these examples, the likelihood that a future event or events will confirm the loss or impairment of an asset or incurrence of a liability can range from probable to remote.

Professor David Hawkins prepared this note as the basis for class discussion.

FASB Statement No. 5

The key provisions of *FASB Statement No. 5* are:

1. An estimated loss from a loss contingency shall be accrued by a charge to income only if *both* of the following conditions are met:
   a. Information available prior to the issuance of the financial statements indicates that it is probable[1] that an asset had been impaired or a liability had been incurred at the end of the most recent accounting period for which statements are being presented. Implicit in this condition is the expectation that one or more future events will probably occur that confirm the fact of the loss.
   b. The amount of the loss can be reasonably estimated.
2. Contingency gains usually are not recorded prior to realization, but may be disclosed in the notes prior to realization.
3. Reserves are not permitted for catastrophe losses, general or unspecified business risks, and self-insurance except for some self-insurance for employee-compensation–related costs which are excluded from the scope of *FASB Statement No. 5*.
4. Disclosure sufficient to "not make the statements misleading" should be made of the nature and estimated loss for both accrued loss contingencies and loss contingencies that are not accrued, but represent at least a reasonable possibility of a loss.
5. Classification of a portion of retained earnings as "appropriated" for loss contingencies is permitted as long as it is shown within the stockholders' equity section of the balance sheet, but losses cannot be charged to an appropriation of retained earnings, and no part of such appropriation can be transferred to income.

It is important to note that a loss contingency can only be accrued if the two specific conditions mentioned earlier, 1.*a* and *b,* are met. According to the FASB:

> The purpose of those conditions is to require accrual of losses when they are reasonably estimable and relate to the current or a prior period. The requirement that the loss be reasonably estimable is intended to prevent accrual in the financial statements of amounts so uncertain as to impair the integrity of those statements. The board has concluded that disclosure is preferable to accrual when a reasonable estimate of loss cannot be made. Further, even losses that are reasonably estimable should not be accrued if it is not probable that an asset has been impaired or a liability has been incurred at the date of an enterprise's financial statements because those losses relate to a future period rather than

---

[1] *FASB Statement No. 5* defines the terms *probable, reasonably possible,* and *remote* as follows:
Probable: The future event or events are likely to occur.
Reasonably possible: The chance of the future events or events occurring is more than remote but less than likely.
Remote: The chance of the future event or events occurring is slight.

the current or a prior period. Attribution of a loss to events or activities of the current or prior periods is an element of asset impairment or liability incurrence.

Later, the FASB in *Interpretation No. 14* clarified how to deal with situations where the first condition, 1.a above, has been met and a range of loss can be reasonably estimated, but no single amount within the range appears at the time to be a better estimate than any other amount within the range. In these cases, the FASB decided the minimum amount in the range should be accrued.

Accounting Entries

When a company accrues an estimated loss for a contingency, this is reported by making (1) a charge to income prior to the occurrence of the event that is expected to resolve the uncertainty and (2) a related credit entry to a contingency reserve for a similar amount, which is listed among the liability accounts. Then, when the event occurs that confirms the loss, the reserve is used to absorb the loss. If appropriate, a provision for the related tax effect of the actual loss is also made at the time the anticipated loss is accrued. For example, assume a company anticipated that it may have to pay $100,000 damages as the result of a claim brought against the company in the courts. In the period in which the management becomes aware of this probable contingency loss, it will charge the anticipated $100,000 loss, less the related tax effect, to income and set up a $100,000 litigation reserve as a liability. In a later accounting period, when a court decision confirms the loss and the successful litigant is paid, the actual loss is charged to the balance sheet contingency reserve and cash is reduced by a similar amount. If the amount of the claim is less than the related reserve, the excess reserve is credited to income. If the claim paid is greater than the reserve, the excess is charged to income.

The accounting entries to establish the reserve and the related deferred tax asset[2] are:

```
Dr. Litigation expense  . . . . . . . . . . .  100,000
    Cr. Litigation reserve  . . . . . . . . . .              100,000
Dr. Deferred tax assets . . . . . . . . . . .   40,000
    Cr. Deferred tax expense. . . . . . . .               40,000
```

The entries to record the payment of the $100,000 litigation loss are:

```
Dr. Litigation reserve  . . . . . . . . .  100,000
    Cr. Cash  . . . . . . . . . . . . . . . . .              100,000
Dr. Taxes payable  . . . . . . . . . . . .   40,000
    Cr. Deferred tax assets  . . . . . . .               40,000
```

It is important to note that the accrual for accounting purposes of a loss related to a contingency does not create or set aside funds which can be used to lessen the possible financial impact of the loss. The creation of a contingency reserve by a charge

---

[2]A deferred tax asset is created because the loss is recognized for book purposes only. The loss cannot be deducted for tax purposes until it is actually incurred. The example assumes a 40% tax rate.

to income is simply an accounting provision. The accrual, in and of itself, provides no financial protection that is not available in the absence of the accrual.

Loss Contingencies Subsequent to the Balance Sheet Date

Information concerning a loss contingency which becomes known subsequent to the date of the financial statements, but before their issuance, may satisfy the two accrual criteria. Whether or not this post-financial statement date information requires accrual of a loss contingency as of the statement date depends on when the related asset was impaired or liability was incurred. If the post-statement date information indicates that events leading to the loss occurred or were in process during the period preceding the financial statement date, then an accrual for a loss contingency should be made at the financial statement date. If the event giving rise to the contingency loss occurred after the financial statement date, no accrual at the balance sheet date should be made. However, disclosure of this post-financial statement event is required if nondisclosure would make the financial statements misleading.

Accounts Receivable and Warranty Obligations

The FASB believed that the uncollectibility of receivables and product warranties constituted contingencies and as such are within the scope of *FASB Statement No. 5.*

Accordingly, potential losses from uncollectible receivables must be accrued at the time of sale when both of the contingency loss accrual criteria have been met. These criteria may be considered in relation to individual receivables or to groups of similar types of receivables. If the reasonable estimation criterion cannot be satisfied, it is doubtful if the sale or accrual method of income recognition is appropriate. Therefore, consideration should be given to using the installment method, the cost recovery method, or some other appropriate method for income recognition.

Similarly, if the two accrual criteria are met, losses from warranty obligations must be accrued at the time of sale. The criteria can be applied to either individual sales or groups of similar sales made with warranties. If accrual is precluded because the reasonable estimate criterion cannot be met, consideration should be given to delaying the recognition of the sale until the warranty period expires or the contingency criteria can be satisfied.

Self-Insurance

Some businesses choose not to purchase insurance against the risk of loss that may result from injury to others, damage to the property of others, or business interruption. Exposure to future risks of this kind creates a contingency. However, the FASB concluded that mere exposure to risks of these types does not mean that an asset has been impaired or a liability has been incurred in the current or some prior period. As a result, the accrual of a loss contingency is not warranted.

Some companies do not carry insurance against the risk of future loss or damage to its property by fire, explosion, or other hazards. The occurrence of these events is random, and until they occur no asset has been impaired or a liability incurred. Therefore, it is inappropriate to accrue for this type of contingency loss prior to its occurrence.

Litigation, Claims, and Assessments

FASB Statement No. 5 states that the following factors, among others, must be considered in determining whether accrual and/or disclosure is required with respect to pending or threatened litigation and actual or possible claims and assessments:

> *a.* The period in which the underlying cause of the pending or threatened litigation or of the actual or possible claim or assessment occurred.
>
> *b.* The degree of probability of an unfavorable outcome.
>
> *c.* The ability to make a reasonable estimate of the amount of loss.

An accrual may be appropriate for litigation, claims, or assessments whose underlying cause occurred before the date of the financial statement and where an unfavorable outcome is probable and a reasonable estimate can be made of the loss. In the case of unasserted claims and assessments, a judgment must first be made as to whether the assertion of a claim is probable. If such a claim is probable, an accrual can be made if an unfavorable outcome is probable and the amount of the loss can be reasonably estimated. If there are several aspects of litigation, each of which gives rise to a possible claim, then the accrual criteria should be applied to each possible claim to determine whether an accrual should be made for any part of the claim.

Threat of Expropriation

FASB Statement No. 5 defines the threat of expropriation of assets as a contingency. Thus, the two accrual criterion must be met before an accrual for the loss can be made. The imminence of an expropriation may be indicated by a public or private declaration of intent by a government to expropriate assets of the enterprise or actual expropriation of assets of other enterprises.

Catastrophe Losses

At the time a property and casualty insurance company issues an insurance policy covering the risk of property loss from catastrophes, a contingency arises. *FASB Statement No. 5* prohibits property and casualty insurance companies from accruing estimated losses related to future catastrophes, since over the short run, the actuarial predictions of the rate of occurrence and the amounts of loss "are subject to substantial deviations."

Indirect Guarantees of Indebtedness

Indirect guarantees and other similar loss contingencies where the possibility of loss may be remote should be disclosed. The disclosure should include the nature and amount of the guarantee.

Contingency Gains

Examples of contingencies that may result in the acquisition of assets, or in gains, are claims against others for patent infringements, price redetermination upward, and claims for reimbursement under condemnation proceedings. Contingencies of this type which may result in gains should not be reflected in the accounts since to do so might be to recognize revenue prior to its realization. Adequate disclosure should be made of gain contingencies, however.

Restructuring

Corporate restructurings involve future costs, such as employee termination benefits, asset write-offs, relocation of operations, and discontinuance of business activities. *FASB Statement No. 5* is relevant to accounting for corporate restructurings, but its guidance is not specific enough. Accordingly, it has been supplemented by subsequent pronouncements.

FASB Statement No. 30 deals with accounting for unusual events and discontinued businesses. *FASB Statement No. 30* is covered in another chapter.

FASB Statement No. 112 provides guidance as to when *FASB Statement No. 5* applies to employee termination benefits. If the answer to any of the following four questions is no, accrual of employee termination costs is required upon the occurrence of the loss event. The questions are:

1. Do the rights of termination benefits arise from service?
2. Do the rights vest or accumulate?
3. Are the termination payments probable?
4. Are the termination payments estimable?

If the answer is yes to all these questions, *FASB Statement No. 5* does not apply and the termination benefits must be accrued over the employee's service life. Subsequent to the issuance of *FASB Statement No. 112,* the Emerging Issues Task Force (EITF) concluded that the following criteria must be met in order to recognize involuntary employee termination costs and a related liability:

1. Prior to the date of the financial statements, management having the appropriate level of authority to involuntarily terminate employees approves and commits the enterprise to the plan of termination and establishes the benefits that current employees will receive upon termination.
2. Prior to the date of the financial statements, the benefit arrangement is communicated to employees. The communication of the benefit arrangement includes sufficient detail to enable employees to determine the type and amount of benefits they will receive if they are terminated.
3. The plan of termination specifically identifies the number of employees to be terminated, their job classification or functions, and their location.
4. The period of time to complete the plan of termination indicates that significant changes to the plan of termination are not likely.

With respect to restructuring costs and other than employee termination benefits, *FASB Statement No. 5* contingency loss accounting should only be applied to an exit plan that results in the incurrence of costs that have no future economic benefit.

EITF reached a consensus that a commitment date for an exit plan occurs when all of the following conditions are met:

1. Prior to the date of the financial statements, management having the appropriate level of authority approves and commits the enterprise to an exit plan.
2. The exit plan specifically identifies all significant actions to be taken to complete the exit plan, activities that will not be continued, including the method of disposition and location of those activities, and the expected date of completion.
3. Actions required by the exit plan will begin as soon as possible after the commitment date, and the period of time to complete the exit plan indicates that significant changes to the exit plan are not likely.

EITF also reached a consensus that only costs resulting from an exit plan that are not associated with or that do not benefit activities that will be continued would be eligible for recognition as liabilities at the commitment date. A cost meeting that requirement should be recognized at the commitment date if the cost is not associated with or is not incurred to generate revenues after the exit plan's commitment date and it meets either criterion (1) or (2) below:

1. The cost is incremental to other costs incurred by the enterprise in the conduct of its activities prior to the commitment date and will be incurred as a direct result of the exit plan. The notion of incremental does not contemplate a diminished future economic benefit to be derived from the cost but rather the absence of the cost in the enterprise's activities immediately prior to the commitment date.
2. The cost represents amounts to be incurred by the enterprise under a contractual obligation that existed prior to the commitment date and will either continue after the exit plan is completed with no economic benefit to

the enterprise or be a penalty incurred by the enterprise to cancel the contractual obligation.

EITF agreed to define costs that meet the criteria in the previous three paragraphs as exit costs.

Environmental Remediation Costs

Companies must accrue future environmental remediation costs that meet *FASB Statement No. 5*'s recognition criteria. An American Institute of Certified Public Accountants' Statement of Position dealing with environmental remediation liabilities recommends that companies record, in addition to their own remediation obligations, a proportionate share of the cleanup costs allocated to other potentially responsible parties; the remediation accrual include direct remediation costs plus the cost of employees devoting time to the cleanup; the remediation accrual be based on current environmental laws and regulations; and, technologies expected to be used in the cleanup.

Objections

The FASB received a number of objections to its accounting for contingencies proposal. One objection was that it was a retreat from conservatism. The FASB did not agree that this was the case, since its proposal did not require virtual certainty before an accrual. In the absence of a probable occurrence of the contingency event and a reasonable estimate of the loss, the FASB believed accrual for unlikely events and uncertain amounts impaired the integrity of financial statements.

Another objection was that the matching concept required that estimated losses from certain types of contingencies that irregularly occur over a long period of time should be accrued in each accounting period. The FASB noted that the matching concept associated cost with revenues on a cause-and-effect basis and as such did not support the objection raised.

Other opponents claimed *FASB Statement No. 5* would lead to greater earnings volatility, which would lead to lower equity prices. The FASB felt that the use of accounting reserves to reduce inherent earnings volatility was misleading. In order to reduce earnings volatility, some critics of the FASB recommendations claimed, companies would be forced to purchase unnecessary insurance to cover contingencies.

The FASB recognized that insurance reduces or eliminates risks. In contrast, accounting reserves do not reduce risks. Accordingly, the FASB rejected the contention that the use of accounting reserves could be an alternative to insurance against risk. The FASB believed that it could not sanction the use of an accounting procedure to create the illusion of protection from risk when, in fact, protection does not exist. Furthermore, the FASB argued that earnings fluctuations are inherent in risk retention and they should be reported as they occur.

Financial Analysis

Because of the uncertainty involved, financial statement analysts find it difficult to predict, interpret, and evaluate corporate contingency loss accounting decision. Another complicating factor is that the statement user does not have access to sufficient data to form an independent appraisal of the management judgments that underlie their accounting treatment of contingencies. Usually, the best that statement users can do is to form gross assessments of the reasonableness of management's judgments based on available public information related to the causes of the contingency and its impact on others, if any; the analysts' own understanding of the situation gained by analysis of current and pass statements; and the statement user's confidence in management based upon its exercise of judgment in other situations.

Fortunately, in most situations the statement user is somewhat protected against under-reserving for contingency losses by the tendency of managers faced with the necessity under *FASB Statement No. 5* to record major contingency losses to over-reserve for anticipated losses. Their motivation is to avoid future surprises and to create possible future "earnings banks" should the anticipated loss be less than the reserved amount. If this happens, management simply eliminates the excess reserve and related deferred tax asset, and credits the net amount to income.

In contrast, statement users are less protected by managers' motivation when management must simply disclose a potential contingency loss. In these cases, the tendency of management is either to delay disclosure in the hope that things will improve, or if required to disclose, to minimize the potential adverse impact. In these cases statement users usually must go to information sources beyond the financial reports, such as court records and trade journals, to obtain the information required to assess the situation more accurately.

As noted earlier, it is important for statement users to remember that creation of a reserve for a contingency loss and the recognition of the related expense does not create a fund to pay for the loss, reduce the risk associated with the contingency's occurrence and adverse impact, eliminate the need to take action to deal with the situation, or create a taxable loss. Financial resources must still be found to fund any cash losses created by the contingency. The contingency event's related probabilities are independent of the accounting treatment. Management must still deal administratively with the problem, although the recording of the reserve may make this task easier since it can be done without concern for its impact on future earnings per share. Finally, tax code only allows a contingency loss to be deducted for tax purposes when the actual loss has been incurred. As a result, statement users should always remember that the tax treatment of the loss is uncertain at the time a contingency loss reserve is established, since it is dependent on the extent of the actual loss and the company's future tax status.

Frequently, companies report significant profit gains in the period following the accounting recognition of a contingency loss, and management proclaims that the company's situation has turned around. This can be an illusion. It may not represent the actual situation, since the actual contingency losses will be occurring during this period and they are being charged to the reserve rather than income. The improved profits do not signal better times. To avoid falling into the trap of believing management's optimistic interpretations, statement users should keep track of contingency loss reserves established in earlier periods and use this knowledge to put current earnings into their proper perspective. Finally, in those situations, management may reverse unused reserves resulting from earlier over-reserving to give an added boost to the apparent profit recovery. This is a cashless profit source that should be valued at zero and regarded as low-quality earnings.

The announcement that a company is recording a contingency reserve often comes as a surprise to many statement users. Because of the nature of many contingencies, such as loss from a fire, this is understandable. However, many others can be anticipated through normal financial analysis techniques. For example, a massive write-off of uncollectible accounts receivable might be expected when a company's accounts receivable to sales ratio deteriorates significantly. Similarly, losses due to the company's being called upon to make good on the guarantee of the indebtedness of another company in financial difficulties might be anticipated if a financial analysis of the borrower's statements indicates it is experiencing increasing financial difficulties. Statement users wishing to minimize accounting surprises should always ask themselves as they review the results of their financial analyses, "Are there any indications that a material loss contingency might have to be recognized in the near future?"

Global Industries, AG

This case presents selected excerpts related to accounting for contingencies from two meetings of the Supervisory Board of Global Industries, AG, a German multinational conglomerate listed on the Frankfurt Stock Exchange.

The first meeting occurred in September 1994. It was a regular quarterly meeting of the Supervisory Board. This meeting involved a review of the company's pro forma December 31, year-end financial results.

The second meeting took place in February 1995. It was a special meeting devoted in part to discussing the implication for the 1994 and possibly 1995 financial results of some events that had occurred subsequent to the close of the 1994 fiscal year, but before the financial statements for the year had been issued.

According to German GAAP, accruals or provisions may be recorded for uncertain liabilities and loss contingencies. The application of this accounting standard is heavily influenced by the overarching financial reporting requirement that the prudence concept be observed. This concept requires that all anticipated risks and losses be recognized. It prohibits recognition of unrealized profits. The concept also requires an item-by-item approach to valuation.

During the last decade, the company earnings per share had grown at a 10% per year rate with little year-to-year variation from this trend. Management was proud of this record. Management wished to continue this growth rate and to satisfy what it perceived to be a preference of debt and equity investors for a stable pattern of earnings, which management believed indicated less uncertainty or risk than fluctuating earnings.

One of the functions of Global Industries Supervisory Board was to review the appropriateness of the company's financial reporting practices. As part of this

Professor David F. Hawkins prepared this case as the basis for class discussion rather than to illustrate either effective or ineffective handling of an administrative situation.

responsibility, the Supervisory Board participated with management in setting the company's financial reporting policies. This was an unusual practice for German companies. Typically, accounting policy decision making was the prerogative of the Management Board. However, because of some recent unexpected bankruptcies of major German companies, the Supervisor Board had voted to involve itself in this process.

Global International's estimated 1994 net income was DM 150 million. The company's net assets were in excess of DM 1 billion.

September Meeting

The following are selected excerpts from the September 1994 meeting.

Breval (chairman, Supervisory Board): I asked the financial office to prepare a list of company's current accounting for contingencies practices. At this meeting I think we should discuss what changes, if any, we believe should be made to these practices. I have asked Fanz Schneider, the company president, and Martin Ebner, the company's chief financial officer, to sit in on this meeting. They can supply us with whatever additional data we need to form our conclusions.

The first item on my list is possible accounts receivables losses from bad debts. Currently we accrue for these losses based on our past experience, the experience of other companies in the same business, and our appraisal of our customer's financial condition. These accruals are close to the maximum allowed by the tax code. So far, from the total company point of view, our actual write-off experience has been below the projections underlying our accruals. I do not think we need to change our policy on accounting for losses related to accountability of receivables.

Blocher (member, Supervisory Board): How has our experience been for groups of similar receivables rather than for the company as a whole?

Brevel: As you might expect, there are many variations. However, I couldn't locate any group of receivables where actual experience suggests that our loss reserves are not prudent estimates.

Wier (member, Supervisory Board): What about those Plastic Group's receivables we discussed last month? As I recall, the Group had some DM 50 million of outstanding receivables and some 50% of them are overdue, most of which are with smaller companies. In the past, we seemed to have a good feel for the credit risks in this business, but I don't think that is true anymore. The current recession in our industry adversely changed the economics of many of our customer's businesses and the demand for their end products. The recession has hit the smaller companies very hard. Let's be frank. We raised the bad debt reserve on these receivables from 2% to 4% of receivables but we don't really know if that is adequate. I heard from an associate of mine at the bank that Tempo (the major competition of the Plastic Group) has a 7% reserve. Personally, I think that is a more realistic figure.

Ebner (chief financial officer): You're right, but when I prepared the figures, I included the Plastic Division receivables in the total Chemical Group's receivables. When you consider that the group's receivables are slightly over DM 150 million, the problems you raise with the Plastic Division receivables becomes less material.

Weir: From that perspective you are correct.

Schneider (chief executive officer): While on the subject of the Plastic Group, you might be interested to know that at the last Management Board meeting I got approval of my plan to increase our share of the plastic market by offering on a very aggressive basis more generous credit terms for our product. The small- to medium-sized companies need financial help. We will use our financial strength to tie them to us through long-term purchase contracts under which they will pay us the amount due for each shipment as follows: 25% 30 days after delivery, 25% 60 days after delivery, 25% 90 days after delivery, and the remainder within 120 days of delivery.

We are prepared to invest DM 30 million in this effort. This is a large sum and there is no doubt that this approach to building market share carries some financial costs, but I think it will pay off. However, just to be on the safe side I plan to establish a bad debt reserve equal to 5% of the receivables created by this marketing plan.

Brevel: That sounds prudent.

The next item on my list is losses related to warranty obligations. Currently, we have not been accruing for this contingency. The practice has been to charge warranty costs as incurred. This practice has been justified in the past because the amounts involved are immaterial and the difference between cash and accrual accounting was not very great. The company has had a study underway since last January looking into the question of whether we should begin accruing for warranty obligations. Martin (Ebner), what is the status of that study?

Ebner: As you will recall, the proposal to consider accruing warranty costs came from my office for several reasons. First, warranty costs are becoming very substantial. Second, they are beginning to vary considerably from our budget figures. This in turn made it harder to smooth earnings. My proposed solution is to switch to the accrual approach. In this way, we could smooth out the recognition of this cost item over the years.

The study group has not reached any conclusion yet. However, I know that the warranty costs for this fiscal year will be DM 2.5 million higher than budgeted. We don't seem to have very good control over this cost item.

Brevel: We should defer any discussion on this item until the study group's report is completed. Let's move on.

The next item is our exposure to significant catastrophe losses in our Property Insurance Group (a Netherlands Antilles–based property and casualty insurance company in which Global Industries held a 40% equity interest). As you may recall, to protect itself against significant losses, Property has been buying considerable amounts of reinsurance. The Management Board (of Global Industries) believes this strategy is getting too expensive. The Management Board asked me to let them know how we feel about letting Property retain a little more risk, which would reduce their reinsurance premiums.

Weir: In my opinion catastrophes are certain to occur and as such are not contingencies. Also, on the basis of experience and the application of appropriate statistical techniques, I have got to believe that catastrophe losses can be predicted over the long term with reasonable accuracy. Then, some portion of the premium is intended to cover losses that usually occur infrequently and at intervals longer than both the term of the policies in force and the financial accounting and reporting period. As a result, it seems to me that proper matching of costs and revenues requires that catastrophe losses should be accrued when the revenue is recognized—or at least a portion of the premiums should be deferred beyond the terms of the policies in force to periods in which the catastrophes occur—to match catastrophe losses with the related revenues.

Schneider: I agree with you. However, I do want to make two points. First, irregularly occurring catastrophes will cause erratic variations in earnings. This runs counter to our whole earnings strategy. Second, Property Insurance was a prime insurer that did not buy very much reinsurance to protect itself against catastrophe losses before it used the substantial catastrophe reserve that it had built up to absorb some very big losses. As I recall, the size of this reserve was one of the reasons we bought into the company. Now, to keep earnings stable the company has to buy much more reinsurance than it did previously. These premiums hurt the company's cash flow. However, it is necessary to do this in order to make the risk characteristics of its earnings stream comparable to those of casualty companies that reinsure. I believe we should seriously consider aggressively building up catastrophe reserves as soon as possible and cut down on the extent of our reinsurance.

Ebner: One more small point. Reinsurance premiums reduce income before the catastrophe occurs. Thus, if you buy reinsurance or accrue for a catastrophe loss, the effect on income is the same—income is reduced prior to the catastrophe.

Brevel: Let's move on to the litigation loss reserves. In the past, we have accumulated a reserve for litigation losses. No additions were made to the reserve last year, but additions were made in every prior year for the last 10 years.

Blocher: Was the reserve set up with specific litigation in mind?

Ebner: No. You could think of it as a general-type reserve.

Blocher: What have been our charges to the reserve in recent years?

Ebner: There have been no material charges over the last two years. Three years ago, we made a DM 1.2 million charge to it to settle out of court a patent infringement claim. Today the balance of the reserve is DM 10 million.

Blocher: What litigation are we involved in now, and what is its status?

Schneider: We have three major litigation problems at present. A number of female employees in our U.S. subsidiaries have joined together and are suing us on behalf of themselves and other women employees for DM 5 million. They claim the company's promotion practices have discriminated against women. They want to be paid the differences between the wages they believe they would have received if they had been promoted on the same basis as men and what they now get. The suit was filed in January of this year. At this time our U.S. legal counsel is unable to express an opinion that the outcome will be favorable. Should we lose, it is hard to determine what the ultimate settlement will be. This type of litigation is fairly new.

The second suit is a claim against us for failure to perform on a major glass division contract to install all of the windows in a new 50-story office tower. The project's completion was delayed for nearly a year due to our inability to solve some glass technology and installation engineering problems that arose when the windows kept blowing out. This suit was filed over a year ago. It is for DM 10 million in damages. The plaintiff is claiming for the cost of lost rentals, lost tenants, and damages done to surrounding property.

Our lawyers have advised us to settle out of court as they believe the plaintiff will be successful. Also, the glass division's marketing department does not want to have a court trial. They thought it would be bad publicity. The Management Board agreed. So Franz instructed our counsel to enter into negotiations. So far we have agreed to pay DM 1 million for lost rentals. The other claims are still being negotiated. It seems most likely that the lost tenants' claims will be settled for about DM 1 million, but we have no idea at this time what the figure will be for damage to surrounding property. That is somewhat dependent on the outcome of suits by surrounding property owners for damages against the tower owners. We are not involved in those suits, but the tower owners feel that we are the cause of any losses that they may have.

Our business insurance should cover up to 50% of the product liability litigation settlement.

The third suit is not in litigation. At the time of the patent infringement problem I mentioned earlier, we discovered that our Chemical Group may inadvertently be violating some patents held by others. These patent holders have not given any indication that they are aware of our possible infringement of their patent. If they should ever sue it would be for a large sum, which counsel estimates in the range of DM 15 million to DM 25 million. Of course, our chemical engineers have been busy trying to develop alternatives to these patents, but so far we have not been able to make a breakthrough. In the meantime, we have had to continue using these patented processes since they are critical to our chemical division's operations.

Weir: What do you think are the chances that we might get sued?

Schneider: I have no idea. However, our patent lawyers tell me that if we get sued, our chances of a favorable outcome are not good. Based on their assessment of the possible claimants, similar cases, and our use of the patented process, they believe an out-of-court settlement in the order of DM 5 million to DM 10 million might be possible.

Weir: Well, I think we ought to continue to build our litigation reserve. If these litigation losses occur, it would play havoc on our earnings stream.

Blocher: What other contingency reserves do we have?

Ebner: We have a number of miscellaneous reserves that total about DM 30 million. These involve accruals built upon the years through charges to earnings for unexpected major repairs, future operating losses, unexpected negative year-end closing adjustments, and self-insurance.

February Meeting

In mid-February 1995, the Supervisory Board met to review with senior management two events involving possible contingency losses that had occurred since the end of the company's fiscal year (December 31, 1995). The February meeting was a special Supervisory Board meeting.

Since the company's 1994 statements had not yet been published, there was a question as to whether or not the 1994 results should reflect these subsequent events.

The first event was the possible expropriation of the company's assets in an African country. Sections of the discussion related to this agenda item are presented below:

Schneider: General Mantuto has just announced that his government intends to nationalize the country's mining industry. Presumably this will include our mining subsidiary, International Mining S.A., and its related transportation subsidiary, International Transportation S.A. Ever since the general took power last year with the army's backing, we have been expecting such an announcement, since the nationalization of this country's raw material resources and communications network was a central part of his party's political rhetoric. In early January when the government took over the local telephone company, which was a subsidiary of a U.S. company, it became clear that the general meant what he said.

Blocher: Do you expect any losses?

Schneider: Yes. The government has indicated that it would issue government 30-year bonds bearing a 3% interest rate as compensation for the physical properties of the expropriated companies. Compensation would be based on the tangible asset's book value. The finance department estimates we would have a loss somewhere between DM 15 million and DM 17 million, after taking into account insurance coverage, the intangible assets that would have been written off, and the real value of the bonds.

Blocher: This turn of events will require us later in fiscal 1995, should the expropriation occur, to recognize our losses.

Ebner: Well, there is another possibility. It might be argued that our assets were impaired when the general took over the government and that his recent

---

EXHIBIT 1

To: Supervisory Board
From: Karl Ebner
Regarding: Accounting for Restructuring

Operations has proposed the following restructuring actions. The accounting issue is listed with each proposed action.

- The restructuring plan includes the ceasing of operations currently performed in the Essen facility that we lease under an operating lease. Global will incur a lease cancellation penalty fee to terminate the lease. How should the termination fee be treated?

- The Jersey City plant will be closed and made permanently idle as part of a New Jersey exit plan. The plant will operate for one year after the commitment date. After the plant ceases operations, all employees will be terminated except for a certain number of employees retained until work is completed to close the plant. How should the costs of employees (salaries and benefits) and other costs to be incurred after operations cease and that are associated with the closing of the plant be treated? The plant is a leased facility and the lessor will not permit Global to sublease the space. How should the lease costs be treated?

- As part of the restructuring plan, Global will exit certain lines of business. Global will subcontract all warranty work on products to an outside contractor after the commitment date. The estimated cost of subcontracting the warranty work exceeds the cost that Global would have incurred if the work had been performed as part of the ongoing operations. How should the increase in the cost for the warranty work on products sold before the commitment date be treated? How about for products sold after the commitment date?

- The restructuring plan includes a reduction in the German-based administrative personnel that requires costs (both internal and external) to develop computer software that will enable the remaining personnel to work more efficiently. How should the cost of developing the new software be treated?

- The New Jersey exit plan includes the cost of outside consultants to identify future corporate goals, strategies, and necessary organizational structures for East Coast USA operations. How should the costs of the consultants be treated?

- The restructuring plan includes costs to retrain and relocate existing employees in both German and foreign locations. How should the retraining and relocation costs be treated?

- The New Jersey exit plan includes the consolidation of the Elizabeth facility into a facility in Singapore. How should the costs to pack and move inventory and equipment from the U.S. location to the successor location in Singapore be treated?

- The New Jersey exit plan includes closing the Trenton plant. Global will operate the facility for nine months from the commitment date to complete outstanding orders. Unfavorable overhead variances will result from the fixed nature of certain manufacturing costs and the smaller number of units in production. How should these costs be treated?

The accounting staff is working on the accounting issues listed. The major issue is which costs should be reported as a one-time restructuring cost and which costs should be charged over time to future revenues. The staff's recommendations will be discussed at the next meeting of the Management Board. I expect to present the accounting plan to the Supervisory Board soon after that meeting.

---

expropriation announcement was simply additional evidence with respect to conditions that existed before December 31, 1994. This interpretation might allow us to charge the loss to 1994 fiscal year.

Regardless of whether we take the loss in 1994 or 1995 it will not hurt earnings. We will charge it to our existing reserves for litigation, restructuring, major repairs, year-end adjustment, and self-insurance.

The second event involving a potential contingency loss was the unexpected announcement in late January by one of the Plastic Group's largest customers that it was filing for bankruptcy. This customer owed Global

Industries DM 3.4 million. Based on materials filed with the bankruptcy court, Industries' lawyers believed that the company would recover no more than 5% of the amount owed. Here are excerpts from the meeting related to this event:

Blocher: How did we let this customer get so much credit from us?

Schneider: Our new marketing approach using trade credit was very effective. This particular customer was buying all of its plastic requirements from us.

Blocher: Did you know they were in financial trouble when you offered them our new terms?

Schneider: No. However, since the bankruptcy announcement I have gone back and looked at the company's December 31, 1993, financial statements. They clearly indicate bankruptcy was likely, since the days of trade credit used were way out of proportion to the industry averages. I asked our credit people how they let this happen. They indicated that prior to our new credit terms program this customer bought very little from us, so no credit analysis had been made. Then, once the new program was offered to them, they bought over DM 4 million of plastics from us in the period between September 1 and December 31. This rapid buildup of business caught the credit staff by surprise. Then, I suspect marketing was not anxious to push for a credit check, since the Plastic and Chemical Groups were having trouble making their profit goal. This was profitable business. Our contribution margin was close to 50%.

As a result of my inquiries into how these sales were made, I will be making some personnel changes.

Brevel: What was the status of the plastic customer receivables as of January 31?

Schneider: The balance was about DM 65 million of which DM 30 million are on the new marketing program terms.

Ebner: Before we move onto another agenda item, I would like to leave with each of you a memorandum I prepared. (See **Exhibit 1.**) It lists a number of restructuring moves the operations staff has prepared. Each of these actions will require an accounting decision. My staff is working on these issues. This memorandum is for information purposes. I will present our recommended accounting actions at a later date.

Questions

1. How should Global Industries account for contingency losses in fiscal years 1994 and 1995? _____

2. Do you agree with the comments related to recognition and measurement of contingency losses expressed in the case? _____

3. If Global Industries was subject to U.S. GAAP, how would it have to account for the contingency losses discussed at the two Supervisory Board meetings? _____

4. How should Global Industries account for the restructuring costs associated with the restructuring actions listed in **Exhibit 1**? _____

5. If Global Industries was subject to U.S. GAAP, how would it have to account for the restructuring costs associated with the restructuring actions listed in **Exhibit 1**? _____

CHAPTER 7

International Accounting Standards and Transnational Financial Analysis

Outside of the U.S.A. stock exchange listed corporations, stock exchange listing regulators and national accounting standard setters throughout the world are increasingly adopting accounting practices and principles that conform to all or most of the International Accounting Standards (IAS) issued by the International Accounting Standards Committee (IASC). This is good news to U.S. direct transnational equity investors. It increases their universe of potential foreign equity investments, since financial reports that conform to IAS are typically understandable to U.S. readers competent in U.S. generally accepted accounting principles (U.S. GAAP). It also reduces their need to learn accounting practices and principles on a country-by-country basis; lowers their financial data, analytical, and monitoring costs; and increases their confidence in making investment decisions.

Non-U.S. corporations that conform to all or part of the IASC's standards may still use a wide range of accounting conventions, since the IASC in some cases has approved more than one way to account for similar transactions. This is an analytical and valuation problem, but it can be mitigated through earnings-focused reconciliation of accounting numbers, quality of earnings assessments, and cash flow analysis. Cash flow analysis standing alone is very useful when confronted with the need to continually screen and analyze a large number of foreign stocks where the cost of earnings reconciliation and earnings quality analyses would be prohibitively high. In the case of stocks that are priced on a local market basis, it is also useful to use local valuation methodologies incorporating the data in the company's financial report as issued and interpreted by local investors.

Professor David F. Hawkins prepared this note as the basis for class discussion. Reprinted by permission. Copyright © 1991 Merrill Lynch, Pierce, Fenner & Smith Incorporated.

International Accounting Standards

International Accounting Standards are set by the International Accounting Standards committee located in London, England. The Committee was formed in 1973 as a result of an agreement among a number of national accounting bodies to work for a greater harmonization of accounting principles throughout the world. While IASC pronouncements do not override local accounting regulations, many countries have adopted them as issued and other countries refer to them as authoritative guides to proper accounting in areas not covered by local standards.

As of mid-1997, the IASC has issued 33 accounting standards. These are summarized and compared to U.S. GAAP in **Appendix A.**

Some IASC standards permit a range of accounting principles for reporting essentially the same transaction. This diversity is the result of the IASC's recognition that there are legitimate differences of opinion as to what constitutes proper accounting, and that statutory requirements in some countries require that specific accounting principles be used. As a result, it is possible for corporations using dissimilar accounting principles to meet all or most of the IASC's accounting standards. In addition, other accounting differences can arise because corporations meet most but not all of the IASC's standards. Also, accounting diversity can arise because the IASC standards do not cover all areas of accounting.

In those situations where IAS permits free choice alternative accounting treatments, the IASC has designated its preferred benchmark accounting method and an allowed alternative treatment. These designations are summarized in **Illustration A.** Companies using allowed alternative accounting must reconcile this treatment to the benchmark standard.

Transnational Financial Analysis

In a global economy financial statement users are increasingly faced with the need to read, analyze, and understand financial statements issued by companies located in many countries. This activity is known as transnational financial statement analysis. In this setting the task of the analyst is complicated because the analysts must deal with financial statements that are often based on unfamiliar accounting rules, expressed in a foreign language and currency, and present financial data in an unfamiliar format. Underlying these differences may be cultural, tax, and legal conditions particular to the reporting company's country that influence a company's attitudes toward financial reporting principle and disclosure decisions.

Formats

Statement formats can vary considerably from country to country. For example, some income statement formats show expenses by function (wages) while others classify expenses by type (production wages, selling wages, etc.). Some balance sheets show

APPENDIX A Comparison of International Accounting Standards and U.S. Generally Accepted Accounting Principles[a]

International Accounting Standard No.	Topic	International Accounting Standard: Summary	U.S. Generally Accepted Accounting Principle
1.	Disclosure of Accounting Policies	Financial statements should include a clear and concise disclosure of all significant accounting policies.	Similar.[b]
2. (Rev.)	Valuation and Presentation of Inventories in the Context of the Historical Cost System.	Inventories should be valued at the lower of historical cost or net realization value. FIFO and average cost methods preferred. LIFO methods permitted as an allowed alternative if disclosure of FIFO values.	Similar.
3. and 27.	Consolidated Financial Statements	Consolidated statements including all controlled investee companies should be presented for a group of related enterprises.	Similar.
4.	Depreciation Accounting	Depreciation should be allocated on a systematic basis to each accounting period.	Similar.
5.	Information to be Disclosed in Financial Statements	All material information should be disclosed that is necessary to make financial statements clear and understandable.	Similar.
6. and 15.	Information Reflecting the Effects of Changing Prices	Enterprises are encouraged to disclose in supplementary statements fixed asset, depreciation, cost of sales and monetary item data using an accounting method reflecting the effects of changing prices.	Similar, but current cost/constant dollar method specified.
7. (Rev.)	Cash Flow Statements	A cash flow statement should be included as an integral part of the financial statements. Interest and dividends may be classified as operating or financing items.	Similar. Interest is an operating item. Dividends are a financing item.
8. (Rev.)	Unusual and Prior Period Items and Changes in Accounting Policies	Unusual items should be included in income and separately disclosed. Prior period items and adjustments resulting from changes in accounting policies should be treated as an adjustment to opening retained earnings. The allowed alternative is to include in current income. Accounting estimate changes should be accounted for in the period of the change and future effected periods. Extraordinary items should be rare.	Similar.
9. (Rev.)	Accounting for Research and Development Activities	Research costs should be charged as incurred. Development costs of a project must be capitalized if specific criteria are met. Otherwise expense as incurred.	Similar with respect to research. Only software development costs can be capitalized.
10.	Contingencies and Events Occurring After the Balance Sheet Date	The amount of a contingency loss should be accrued by a charge to income if (a) it is probable that future events will confirm that an asset has been impaired or a liability incurred at the balance sheet date; and (b) a reasonable estimate of the amount of the resulting loss can be made. Contingent gains should not be accrued in financial statements. Balance sheets should be adjusted to reflect post-balance-sheet events that provide additional evidence of the enterprise's condition as of the balance sheet date.	Similar.
11. (Rev.)	Accounting for Construction Contracts	The percentage of completion method must be used. When outcome cannot be measured reliably, cost recovery method must be used.	Similar. Use completed contract method when outcome is uncertain.
12. (Rev.)	Accounting for Taxes on Income	The liability method should be used. Comprehensive tax-allocation-based standard.	Similar.

APPENDIX A (continued)

International Accounting Standard No.	Topic	International Accounting Standard: Summary	U.S. Generally Accepted Accounting Principle
13.	Presentation of Current Assets and Current Liabilities	Each enterprise should determine whether or not to present current assets and current liabilities in its financial statements.	Similar.
14.	Reporting Financial Information By Segment	Enterprises whose securities are publicly traded should report sales or other operating revenues, results, assets, and the basis for intersegment pricing by the industry and geographical segments considered significant by the enterprise.	Similar with more explicit segment definitions.
16. (Rev.)	Accounting for Property, Plant and Equipment	The gross carrying amount of an asset included in property, plant and equipment should be historical cost. Revalued amounts is the allowed alternative. The selection of assets for revaluation should be on a systematic basis. An increase in the net carrying value of property, plant and equipment should be credited to stockholders' equity.	Historical cost only permitted.
17.	Accounting for Leases	A lease is classified as a finance lease if it transfers substantially all the risks and rewards incident to ownership. A lease is classified as an operating lease if substantially all the risks and rewards incident to ownership are not transferred. In the case of lessees, a finance lease gives rise to a depreciation charge for the asset as well as a finance charge for each accounting period. In the case of lessor, an asset held under a finance lease should be recorded at an amount equal to the net investment in the lease. Finance income should be recognized over the lease period based on a pattern reflecting a constant periodic rate of return on either the lessor's net investment outstanding or the net cash investment outstanding in respect of the finance lease. Profits or losses should be recognized on sale-type leases in accordance with the policy normally followed by the enterprise for outright sales. Operating leases rental income should be recognized over the lease term.	Similar with more explicit criteria for determining when a lease is a financing or capital lease. The finance income associated with a financing lease is based on the lessor's net investment outstanding.
18. (Rev.)	Revenue Recognition	Revenue from sales or service transactions should be recognized when the enterprise has performed as evidenced by the transfer of the significant risk and rewards of ownership to the buyer and no significant uncertainties existed with respect to collection, future obligation, and returns.	Similar.
19. (Rev.)	Accounting for Retirement Benefits in the Financial Statements of Employers	In a defined benefit plan, the cost of retirement benefits should be determined using appropriate and comparable assumptions and an accrued benefit valuation method. (Pension costs based on services rendered to date.) In a defined contribution plan, the employer's contribution applicable to a particular accounting period should be charged against income in that period.	Projected benefit valuation method required for measuring net periodic pension costs. (Pension cost based on services rendered to date and expected future salary levels.) Defined contribution plan similar. In addition, enterprises must record a liability equivalent to the extent their plan is underfunded.
20.	Accounting for Government Grants and Disclosure of Government Assistance	Government grants should be recognized in income over the period necessary to match them with the related costs which they are intended to compensate on a systematic basis provided there is reasonable assurance that the enterprise will comply with the grant's conditions and that the grant will be received.	Similar.

APPENDIX A (continued)

International Accounting Standard No.	Topic	International Accounting Standard: Summary	U.S. Generally Accepted Accounting Principle
21. (Rev.)	Accounting for the Effects of Changes in Foreign Exchange Rates	The method of translating the financial statements of foreign operations is determined by the operating and financial characteristics of the operations. In the case of foreign operations determined to be an integral part of the parent's operations, nonmonetary assets and liabilities are translated at the exchange rate when the relevant transaction or revaluation occurred. Income statement items are translated at exchange rates that correspond with the dates of underlying transactions. Exchange differences arising from these procedures are taken into income of the period. In the case of foreign entities that operate substantially in the local currency, both monetary and nonmonetary assets and liabilities are translated at the balance sheet date's exchange rate. Exchange differences arising from these procedures' effect on the parent's opening net investment in the foreign entity are taken to stockholders' equity. Income statement items are translated either at an average or transaction date exchange rate. Any exchange differences arising from the use of different exchange rates in the income statement and balance sheet translations are taken into income.	Similar.
22.	Accounting for Business Combinations	A business combination should be accounted for under the purchase method, except in the rare circumstances when it is deemed to be a uniting of interest in which case the pooling of interest method is appropriate. A business combination is considered to be uniting of interest when the basis of the transaction is principally an exchange of voting stock, the combining enterprises are combined in one entity, and there is a continual mutual sharing of risks and rewards by the combining shareholders. Positive goodwill arising in a purchase transaction should be amortized to income on a systematic basis over five years or up to 20 years if justified by circumstances. Negative goodwill should be allocated over individually acquired depreciable nonmonetary assets in proportion to their fair values. The allowed alternative treatment for negative goodwill is systematic amortization to income.	Similar, except that 12 specific tests must be met before pooling of interest accounting can be used. Positive goodwill may be charged to income over a period not to exceed 40 years.
23.	Capitalization of Borrowing Costs (Rev.)	An enterprise that has incurred borrowing costs and incurred expenditures on assets that take a substantial period of time to get them ready for their intended use or sale should adopt a policy of expensing borrowing costs as incurred. Capitalizing borrowing costs is an allowed alternative treatment.	Interest capitalization required.
24.	Related Party Disclosures	Related party relationships where control exists should be disclosed even though there have been no transactions between related parties. Transactions between related parties should be disclosed.	Similar.

International Accounting Standard No.	Topic	International Accounting Standard: Summary	U.S. Generally Accepted Accounting Principle
25.	Accounting for Investments (Rev.)	An investment is an asset held by an enterprise for the creation of wealth through distribution for capital appreciation or for other benefits to the investing enterprise such as those obtained through trading relationships. Investments classified as current assets should be carried at either market value or the lower of cost and market value. Investments classified as long-term assets should be carried at either cost, revalued amounts, or, in the case of equity securities, the lower of cost and market value determined on a portfolio basis. Increases in the carrying amount of long-term investments arising from revaluations should be credited to stockholders' equity as a revaluation surplus. Any subsequent writedowns arising from revaluations should be distributed to stockholders' equity. Further writedowns below cost should be charged to income. Future writeups may be credited to income to the extent of past income charges. Changes in the carrying amount of current investments carried at market value should be either consistently included in income or accounted for as surplus revaluations.	Investments for trading purposes are measured on a market-to-market basis with changes in carrying value included in income. Investments intended to be held to maturity are accounted for at cost. All other investments are presumed to be held for sale and are accounted for at market with changes in carrying value included in stockholders' equity.
26.	Accounting for Reporting by Retirement Plans	Retirement benefit plan investment should be carried at fair value. The plan report should show the net assets available for benefits and, in the case of defined benefit plans, the actuarial present value of promised benefits (distinguished between vested and nonvested benefits) using either current or project salary levels. Other disclosures required include the nature of the plan, changes in plan net assets available for benefits, and a summary of significant accounting policies.	Similar.
28.	Accounting for Investments in Associates	An "associate" is an enterprise over which the investor has significant influence. Significant influence is defined as holding 20% or more of the voting stock of the investee company. An investment in an associate should be accounted for in consolidated financial statements under the equity method. An investment in an associate that is included in statements of an investor that does not issue consolidated statements should be accounted for using either the equity or cost method, whichever would be appropriate if the investor issued consolidated statements; or, alternatively at either cost or revalued amounts under the accounting policy for long-term investments.	Similar, except that revaluation accounting not permitted.
29.	Financial Reporting in Hyperinflationary Economies	The financial statements of an enterprise that reports in the currency of a hyperinflationary economy, whether they are based on a historical cost or a current cost approach, should be stated in terms of the general price level index at the balance sheet date. Gains or losses on the enterprise's net monetary position should be included in net income. The statement does not establish an absolute rate at which hyperinflation is deemed to arise. A cumulative inflation rate over three years approaching or exceeding 100% is suggested as an indication of hyperinflation.	No comparable rule.

APPENDIX A (continued)

International Accounting Standard No.	Topic	International Accounting Standard: Summary	U.S. Generally Accepted Accounting Principle
30.	Disclosure in the Financial Statements of Banks and Similar Financial Institutions	Disclosure of principal types of income and expenses, assets and liabilities, contingencies and commitments, maturities of assets and liabilities, concentration of assets and liabilities, and general banking risks required.	Similar.
31.	Financial Reporting of Interests in Joint Ventures	Jointly controlled entities can be reported in the consolidated statements of a venturer using either the proportionate consolidation or the equity methods.	Equity method. Proportionate consolidation not permitted.
32.	Financial Instruments: Disclosure and Presentation	Disclosure required about financial that includes terms and conditions, accounting policies, fair values, and exposure to interest rate risk and credit risk.	Similar.
33.	Earnings Per Share	Basic and diluted earnings per share disclose required.	Similar.

[a]A number of new and revised IAS are scheduled to be released in late 1997 and early 1998. Before using Appendix A, the status of these IASs should be determined.
[b]"Similar" should be interpreted to mean "similar in concept and thrust, but not necessarily in all of the details."

ILLUSTRATION A   Benchmark and Allowed Alternative Treatments

Issue	*Benchmark Treatment*	*Allowed Alternative Treatment*
Fundamental errors and changes in accounting policy	Adjust opening retained earnings	Include in income of the current period
Property, plant & equipment	Measure at cost	Measure at revalued amounts
Retirement benefit costs	Use accrued benefit valuation model	Use projected benefit valuation model
Exchange differences on the acquisition of an asset resulting from severe currency devaluation	Recognize in income of the current period	Recognize as part of the cost of the asset
Negative goodwill	Allocate to reduce the carrying value of nonmonetary assets, then treat any remaining balance as for the allowed alternative	Treat as deferred income and recognize in income on a systematic basis as for positive goodwill
Minority interest arising on a business combination	Measure at pre-acquisition carrying amounts	Measure at postacquisition fair value
Assignment of cost to inventories	Use FIFO or weighted average cost formulas	Use LIFO formula
Borrowing costs	Recognize in income of the current period	Recognize as part of the cost of the asset

---

assets by increasing order of liquidity while others list assets in the reverse order. Classification of items within financial statements can also differ. For example, current liabilities in Germany may be liabilities maturing over the next four years whereas one year is the cutoff point in the U.S.A. Transnational financial analysts deal with the multiformat problem by either learning to work with different formats, recasting foreign financial statements to their domicile country's format or recasting all financial statements to a standard format developed by the analyst.

Language

Few statement users have the multilanguage skills required to feel comfortable dealing with financial statements presented in languages other than their own. Some companies recognized this problem and publish their financial reports in several languages. In some cases statement users employ translators. Translations can be helpful, but often the translation is prepared by accountants who know accounting but are not good translators or by translators who are not accountants. In either case this can lead to confusing and misleading translations. Statement users must be alert to this problem. Other solutions include using accounting lexicons to translate foreign account terms or limiting the analysis to the financial statement data in standard investor reference books. These two solutions often result in the analyst using summary data without a full understanding of the company's true condition or the accounting policy decisions.

Different Terminology

Transnational financial analysts must become familiar with accounting terminology differences. Some of these differences are easy to deal with as one term can be directly substituted for the other. For example, turnover is the British equivalent for what is called sales in the U.S.A. Other differences are more difficult to handle. For example, the term *exceptional* in a French financial report might mean the item is either an unusual or an extraordinary item. In these cases, close reading of the financial statement is required to determine the exact meaning of the term.

Currencies

Typically companies issue financial statements expressed in the currency of the parent company's country. Financial ratios are unaffected by the reporting currency, except in the case where a company for the convenience of foreign readers restates its reporting currency financial statements into other currencies. These so-called convenience statements are prepared by multiplying all items in the statements by the period-end exchange rate. Analysts using these data must be careful to not be misled by distortions in period-to-period comparisons and trend analyses caused by changes in exchange rates. If the analysts want to use convenience reports to analyze trend data, then the data must be scaled to eliminate the exchange rate effect. This can be done by using a consistent exchange rate over time. The best way to avoid being misled by convenience statements is to use the original reports to calculate trend data. This approach has the added advantage of giving the analyst the same view of the reporting company as its management, who is most probably measuring itself and managing the company based on the original statements.

Accounting Principles

There is considerable diversity of accounting standards around the world. For example, some countries, such as the Republic of Ireland, permit revaluation of property, others, such as the U.S.A., insist on valuing property at its original purchase price, while others, such as Mexico, require the cost of property be adjusted for inflation. Some countries, such as the United Kingdom, allow purchased goodwill to be charged directly to owner's equity, while others, such as Sweden, require it to be recorded as an asset and then charged to income over time.

How these differences are handled in financial analyses depends on the intended use of the analysis and the analysis comfort level in dealing with different accounting models and rules. If the analyst is analyzing different companies within a single country or a single company over time, in most cases a satisfactory financial ratio analysis can be prepared using the financial statements data as reported regardless of the accounting rules employed. Accounting diversity becomes a major problem in comparative analysis of financial statements from different countries with dissimilar accounting standards. In this situation the analyst usually recasts the financial statement data to make it comparable using a common accounting basis, such as the analyst's home country accounting standards or an accounting model of the analyst's own creation. Since restatement to a common basis is often difficult to accomplish and inevitably leads to at best rough approximations of comparable data, analysts tend to focus on reconciling only those accounting differences responsible for material differences in the original comparative data.

Disclosure

The extent of financial disclosure by corporations can vary considerably between countries and within some countries between listed and private companies. When confronted with the need to analyze a company with a low level of financial disclosure, such as a Swiss company, the analyst has little choice than to seek the missing information from noncompany sources, such as local investment bankers, competitors, retired employees and others familiar with the company. This will increase the financial analysis cost, but it may give the analyst a valuable advantage over less diligent analysts who are simply content to analyze the limited financial data provided by the company.

Tax Code

In some countries, such as Germany, the tax code requires in a large number of instances identical accounting be used in financial statements if certain tax accounting rules are elected for tax reporting purposes. In other countries, such as the U.S.A., companies are not bound except in a limited number of cases by such tax code requirements. Transnational analysts must be aware of situations where tax return accounting elections may have a significant distorting influence on financial statements. The financial statements may not reflect the economic realities of the reporting company, since the goal of tax management is usually to minimize taxable income and tax accounting rules are adopted by governments to achieve revenue, social and economic objectives.

Legal

In many countries corporate reporting practices are governed by company legislation. Typically, this legislation provides some overarching requirements for financial reporting and, in some cases, may specify specific accounting practices. For example, the United Kingdom's 1985 Companies Act requires that financial statements provide a "true and fair" view of the company's state of affairs and of the profit or loss. Such legislation may provide companies with an opportunity to depart in their financial reports from their local generally accepted accounting principles. Such departures may be very useful to statement users, since the data may represent management's best judgment of the company's true state of affairs. In contrast, in other cases, such as the statutory reporting requirements of France, company legislation spells out in great detail and severely restricts company accounting principle elections and classification practices. These requirements have been imposed on corporations to facilitate national economic planning by the government and are not likely to lead to useful financial reports for other purposes. Fortunately, listed French corporations have more flexibility in the presentation of consolidated financial statements for public reporting purposes.

Cultural

A country's accounting culture or traditions can influence the way in which local accounting standards are employed in practice. For example, German accounting has a long history of being creditor-oriented with the result that prudence is encouraged in financial reports. That is, assets tend to be understated, liabilities tend to be overstated and disclosure clearly limited. In contrast, United Kingdom accounting has for a long time been geared more to the information needs of public equity investors who want transparent financial reports that reflect the current economic realities of the reporting company. Given these different perspectives on accounting, it is very likely that a German company and a British company could apply the same accounting standard to an identical transaction and end up with very different accounting results. Transnational financial analysts need to be aware of these accounting cultural differences so that they do not fall into the trap of assuming the same accounting rule necessarily leads to comparable accounting data.

Coping with Accounting Diversity

U.S. transnational equity investors competent in U.S. GAAP should be able to identify and appreciate the significance of nearly all of the accounting differences between companies that meet all or most of the IASC's accounting standards, as well as the accounting similarities and differences between these foreign accounting practices and U.S. GAAP. A careful reading of the notes accompanying the foreign company's financial statements will reveal most of these similarities and differences. Some of the differences can be quantified, but most will have to be evaluated on a quality of earnings basis. Cash flow analysis can also be used to deal with accounting diversity.

There are several different approaches to dealing with international financial reporting diversity.

One approach is to restate to the extent possible earnings figures to some comparable basis. This basis could be another company's accounting principles, U.S. GAAP, benchmark IASC standards, or an accounting model developed by the investor to fit the investor's equity valuation methodologies.

Another approach is to assess the quality of the company's earnings against some scale developed by the investor. Then this determination becomes a factor to be considered in the investor's judgment as to the appropriate price/earnings ratio or discount rate to apply to the earnings as reported.

Since in practice it is almost impossible to restate earnings completely, the restatement approach is often combined with a quality of earnings assessment. In this case, the partially restated earnings figure is used for valuation purposes. When making quantitative adjustments to financial statements or quality of earnings assessments due to accounting differences, care must be taken to make sure that the differences are not justified by differences in circumstances. If they are justified by circumstances, no adjustment or lowering of the earnings quality rating should be made.

A third way to deal with international financial reporting diversity is to apply on a worldwide basis the well-accepted financial analysis practice of focusing on cash flows when confronted by unresolvable accounting diversity and unfamiliar accounting practices. Several definitions of cash flow should be used. In addition to net income plus depreciation, these should include earnings before interest, taxes, depreciation and amortization charges, and a cash from operations figure comparable to the one presented in cash flow statements.

A fourth approach to coping with international accounting diversity is to adopt the foreign corporation's financial report as issued, analyze it from the perspective of a local investor, and apply local valuation methodologies. This approach has much to recommend it, since prices in many local capital markets are set by local residents.

Serious transnational equity investors use all four approaches. In addition to income adjustments and income quality assessments, asset and liability accounting and values and dividend considerations should also be included in any analytical response to international accounting diversity.

Learn the Range of Differences

U.S. direct transnational equity investors should be familiar with the range of different IAS and global accounting practices that can materially impact net income and the other financial statement data relevant for foreign equity valuation purposes. Being aware of these differences alerts investors to what to look for when analyzing statements. It also speeds up their analysis, reconciliation, and assessment of accounting differences.

The recommended approach for most U.S. investors to dealing with international accounting differences is to focus on the range of accounting practices used overseas without particular regard for which countries permit or use which alternatives. In the past, investors have tried to become familiar with international accounting differences by studying and learning the foreign accounting rules on a country-by-country basis. This approach is acceptable for transnational investors who invest in only a few countries or in the non-IAS conforming countries, but it is not recommended for U.S. transnational equity investors who operate on a global basis. The country-by-country accounting knowledge is too difficult and costly to acquire.

Lowering the Cost of Information

For U.S. investors, the cost associated with gathering, interpreting, and using IAS and local-GAAP–based foreign financial reports is higher than performing the same task on comparable U.S.-domiciled corporations. This higher transnational information cost can be reduced by focusing on the foreign stock with the larger market values within this group of corporations. The information gathering, analysis, and tracking costs associated with these stocks is usually considerably lower than the information cost associated with medium and smaller market value foreign stocks. A "big cap" focus has the following benefits:

a. The universe of these corporations is large enough to construct well-diversified transnational equity portfolios.

b. Almost all of the accounting principles used by any one of these corporations in their consolidated financial statements will be familiar to U.S. investors, since the accounting used will either be IAS similar to current U.S. GAAP, U.S. GAAP used in the recent past but not now acceptable, or well-publicized alternatives considered and rejected by the FASB in its deliberations.

c. Statement users can rely on the financial presentations to the extent indicated by the auditor's report, since these corporations are usually audited by either a major national or multinational auditing firm using auditing practices of the highest quality.

d. There is seldom a language barrier. Most of these corporations issue timely English language versions of their financial reports.

e. Investors can readily confirm their judgments on these corporations, since most of them are covered by at least one leading institutional equity research firm located either in the United States or abroad.

f. The valuation methodologies appropriate for these companies are most likely to be ones familiar with U.S. investors since the stocks of these companies are more likely to be valued in many capital markets, rather than primarily on a local capital market basis.

It should be recognized that while a large company focus may reduce the informational costs of transnational investing, it also can introduce a big cap investment bias. Depending on the investor's resources, tolerance for risk, and return objective, this may or may not be a desirable result.

Pushing Costs Even Lower

The cost of direct transnational financial analysis can be lowered further by investors and analysts adopting a systematic approach to converting foreign company financial statement data to conform to the accounting form and inputs required by the investor or analyst for equity valuation purposes.

The process for restating the financial statements of non-U.S. companies to a U.S. GAAP basis is done in two principal steps. The first involves an examination and classification using a standard form of the firm's accounting policies. The second requires the completion of a standard worksheet to convert the company's reported net income and cash flow figures to a U.S. GAAP basis.

When preparing restatements, it is important to remember that a complete restatement to a U.S. GAAP basis is seldom possible. The best point of view to adopt is that "close is good enough." This perspective is acceptable, since accounting reports prepared according to U.S. GAAP are themselves only approximations of the "truth." A corollary of this point of view is "focus on the material differences." This perspective does not mean that the areas of nonreconciliation should be ignored. Their significance must be assessed. This can be accomplished, for example, as part of the quality of earnings appraisal incorporated in the price-earnings ratio assessment.

Another important point to keep in mind when preparing U.S. GAAP restatements is to use restatement approaches that minimize the cost of restatement without introducing material distortions. Often, more precision can be achieved by using costly restatement methods, but the added precision may not be worth the added cost. The best approach to restatement is "keep it simple."

Step 1: Classify Accounting Policy

The first restatement step is to examine the non-U.S. company's accounting policies to identify non-U.S. GAAP accounting practices and to record their differences in a systematic written format that focuses attention on the material items for restatement.

The value of the following recommended approach to accounting policy analysis is that it forces the analyst to study the foreign companies' accounting policies carefully; it alerts the analyst to problem areas; it provides a permanent record to keep track of accounting changes; and, it speeds up the accounting policy review and comparison in future years. All the analyst needs to do is focus on changes in accounting policy. This reduces future analytical costs significantly.

The accounting policy appraisal should be reduced to writing using a three-column format. The first column lists the items being accounted for. The next column shows the foreign company's accounting policy used to recognize and measure each item. The third column indicates the comparable U.S. GAAP accounting principles.

Within the recommended three-column accounting policy record format, the various accounting policies are divided into six categories. Assigning accounting policies to these categories focuses attention on the significant areas for restatement; provides a permanent record of the analyst's rationale for restating some items and not others; and further reduces the cost of future accounting policy reviews. The six categories and their significance for restatement are listed below. The assumption made is that income is the focus of analytical interest.

Similar to U.S. GAAP.   These accounting policies are similar to U.S. GAAP and produce results roughly equivalent to U.S. GAAP. They do not require restatement. In making this classification, "similar" should be interpreted to mean "similar in concept and thrust to U.S. GAAP, but not necessarily in all of the details."

No Material Difference.   These are accounting policies where the effect of the difference between U.S. GAAP and the company's accounting policy is typically immaterial in its effect on account balances. For restatement purposes, reported account balances should be regarded as being approximately equivalent to U.S. GAAP–determined values.

Similar Outcome.   These are non–U.S GAAP accounting policies whose application leads to similar financial statement results as those that would result from the use of U.S. GAAP. In some cases, U.S. GAAP is restricted to one method, but in practice many outcomes result from its application. Pension accounting is a good example. All U.S. companies follow the same method but in any one situation management can apply this method to obtain a wide range of pension expenses depending on the assumptions made. If the results of the non-U.S. company's accounting policy produce results that probably fall within the range of reasonable outcomes possible from applying U.S. GAAP, accept the foreign accounting practice as being equivalent to U.S. GAAP.

Balance Sheet Effect Only.   Non–U.S. GAAP accounting policies that only have balance sheet effects belong in this category. If the analyst's focus is on income, these differences should be put aside and examined later when the analyst's attention turns to balance sheet items.

Different Circumstances.   Accounting policies belong in this category for which there is no U.S. GAAP equivalent. Typically, this non–U.S. GAAP accounting reflects circumstances of a foreign company that are different from those encountered by U.S. companies. Where there are differences between a foreign company and U.S. companies and there is no U.S. GAAP covering the foreign company's circumstances, accept the foreign company's treatment of the particular situation as long as the accounting reflects the reality of the circumstances. If the foreign company's accounting does not reflect the particular circumstances, if possible, restate the accounting results using an accounting approach of your choice that does reflect the circumstance. The stock market probably is already making a similar adjustment.

Material Differences.   These are non–U.S. GAAP accounting practices that may result in material financial statement differences between the application of the company's accounting policy and its U.S. GAAP equivalent. The restatement should focus on these accounting differences. The accounting policies in this category will usually be accounting for consolidated results, business combinations, discontinued operations, provision for reserves and pensions, leases, depreciation, extraordinary items, deferred taxes, and intangible assets.[1]

Step 2: Complete the Worksheet

The next step in transnational financial analysis is to complete the worksheet designed to reflect the typical transnational financial statements analyst's cash flow and profit information objectives. The worksheet consists of two major sections, each of which is

---

[1]If the analyst is reconciling to an accounting model other than U.S. GAAP, the same classification approach can be used with the exception that the analysts' model becomes the standard for classification and restatement purposes.

ILLUSTRATION B   Basic Restatement Worksheet Calculation Flow Chart

---

Reported Results	*Estimated U.S. GAAP Equivalent*
Reported net income	Estimate U.S. GAAP net income
↓	↑
Reported operating profit after taxes	Estimate U.S. GAAP operating profit after taxes
↓	↑
Reported operating profit before taxes	Estimate U.S. GAAP operating profit before taxes
↓	↑
Reported operating profit before interest, taxes, depreciation and amortization (EBITDA) →	Estimate U.S. GAAP operating profit before interest, taxes, depreciation and amortization

---

broken down in turn into comparable profit and cash flow subsections. **Illustration B** presents the worksheet's basic flow chart.

The worksheet's first major section shows the company's profit and cash flows based on its reported results. These data are important. They give the analyst a view of the company as its home country investors may see it for valuation purposes. Sometimes it is a more relevant perspective for valuation purposes than the U.S. GAAP perspective. These data also provide a benchmark for measuring the extent of the profit and cash flow differences resulting from using non-U.S. GAAP rather than U.S. GAAP accounting.

The second major section of the worksheet presents the U.S. GAAP equivalent of the profit and cash flow items shown in the first major section.

Both major subsections are broken down into comparable subsections, each of which presents the typical principal profit and cash flow information objectives of financial statement analysts.

The restatement objective of most equity investors' attempts to convert non–U.S. company financial statement data to a U.S. GAAP basis is to determine the U.S. GAAP equivalent of the foreign company's:

- *Profits related to continuing operations.* These data are important since equity values reflect in large measure a company's expected continuing stream of profits. Operating profits best measure this expectation.
- *Cash flow related to continuing operations.* Cash flow data is regarded by many as the best measure of corporate performance to use when comparing companies across national boundaries. It is a legitimate valuation basis and easier to compute than earnings on a comparable accounting basis. Cash flow data is used by transnational investors who rely heavily on computer-driven approaches.
- *Net income.* This all-inclusive figure when viewed over time captures the company's overall profit trends and performance.

As indicated on **Illustration B,** the basic worksheet format reflects these analytical information objectives and practices as it moves from the company's reported net income to its EBITDA cash flow based on reported data; then, to the company's EDITDA cash flow's U.S. GAAP equivalent; next, to the company's operating profit on a U.S. GAAP basis, and ends with the company's net income on a U.S. GAAP equivalent. This basic worksheet format can be expanded to fit additional profit and cash flow information objectives. For example, the calculation of after-tax cash flow, such as net income plus depreciation, could be shown as a separate step in the flow. Also, a line showing operating data excluding unusual items might also be added.

Allocating any difference between the operating profits of continuing operations and net income on a U.S. GAAP basis to discontinued operations, extraordinary items, and cumulative accounting changes on a U.S. GAAP basis is seldom a restatement objective or practice of equity investors. Since equity values reflect a company's future continuing stream of earnings and this is best reflected by operating profits, the added information value of calculating the U.S. GAAP equivalent of foreign company's gains and losses from discontinued operations, extraordinary items, and cumulative accounting changes is very low. Simply knowing the net difference between operating profits and net income on a U.S. GAAP basis is sufficient in most cases.

U.S. GAAP Model Preferred

Transnational financial statement analyses of foreign companies are usually performed on both the company's financial results as reported and on an adjusted basis that conforms to an accounting model that the analyst believes is appropriate for the analytical purpose. The U.S. GAAP accounting model is preferred by most U.S. equity analysts as the accounting basis for the adjusted version of a foreign company's financial statements. This is a sensible approach since

- U.S. investors and analysts are comfortable working with U.S. GAAP financial statements;
- U.S. GAAP is designed to be useful to investors making investment decisions;
- The accounting and cash flow–related equity valuation multiple that U.S. investors are most familiar with uses U.S. GAAP–determined accounting data;
- The number of U.S. GAAP adjustments and their cost is reduced since U.S. GAAP conforms to IAS, and IAS conforming statements typically provide sufficient data to make most of the desired U.S. GAAP adjustments; and
- The financial ratio standards U.S. analysts are most familiar with are based on U.S. GAAP accounting data.

While the U.S. GAAP model is preferred by most U.S. investors and is useful for many analytical purposes, its use should not be automatic. Alternatives to using a U.S. GAAP–based accounting model may in some circumstances be more relevant to the analytical purpose. Also, in some cases, restatement may not be necessary. Whenever an analytical purpose requires a transnational financial statement analysis, always ask and answer the question: "Should the foreign company's financial statements be restated to an alternative accounting basis and, if so, what should that basis be?"

Daimler-Benz AG

In order to be a true Global Player we also have to be active in the world's financial markets. Thus in addition to making extensive use of the Euromarket we have listed our shares on all German and three Swiss stock exchanges as well as most recently in Tokyo, London, Paris, and Vienna. However, the world's largest and most important exchange, the New York Stock Exchange, remained a blank spot for us.

The reasons for this are buried in the different accounting systems . . .

Any accounting system that wants to be accepted by international investors must satisfy such aspects as reliability (existing legal system, audited statements, true and fair view, timeliness) and understandability (language, notes, comments). In addition investors are demanding comparability of the various financial figures across companies in different countries' though this may not be so easy to achieve as every accounting system is a vital part of a countries' environmental context and is heavily influenced by the relevant social, legal, and economic structures. Finally, any accounting system should be fairly inexpensive to install, i.e., the benefits should outweigh the costs . . .

Thus Daimler-Benz had to come up with its own way. We started by critically asking where the obstacles were. The calculations and publication of two results could not pose a major problem . . . (Germany) enterprises published a second income figure, the so-called DVFA result which is usually reported on a per share basis. Furthermore U.S. accounting principles are by and large becoming the world's accounting language whereas the German system seems to be heading for a reclusive island status.

Dr. Gerhard Liener, *Chief Financial Officer, Daimler-Benz AG[1]*

Professor David Hawkins prepared this case as the basis for class discussion rather than to illustrate either effective or ineffective handling of an administrative situation.

Copyright © 1993 by the President and Fellows of Harvard College. Harvard Business School case 194–027.

[1]"Entering the U.S. Accounting World: A View from the First German Player," International Capital Markets Conference, IIR Limited, London, United Kingdom, June 29, 1993.

Daimler-Benz Corporation

On September 17, 1993, Daimler-Benz American Depositary Shares were approved for listing on the New York Stock Exchange. They trade under the symbol "DAI."

Daimler-Benz is the largest industrial group in Germany in terms of sales. Daimler-Benz AG is the holding company of four corporate units: Mercedes-Benz, AEG, Deutsche Aerospace and debis. Mercedes-Benz, the world renowned passenger car and commercial vehicle manufacturer, continues to be the largest corporate unit within the Daimler-Benz Group. However, the primary business areas of the Group today also include the manufacture and distribution of products in the fields of rail systems, automation, energy distribution, aeronautics and aerospace, propulsion systems, defense systems, and information technology services. In addition, the Daimler-Benz Group is engaged in a variety of supporting businesses, such as applied microelectronics and selected financial services, and in certain other fields such as domestic appliances and medical systems.

For the year ended December 31, 1992, the Daimler-Benz Group had revenues of DM 98.5 billion and net income of DM 1.5 billion. As of that date the Daimler-Benz Group operated in 54 countries through 831 subsidiaries, affiliates, and related companies in which Daimler-Benz holds a minority investment. Located in Germany there were 336 such entities. As of December 31, 1992, The Daimler-Benz Group had 376,467 employees, 80% of whom were employed in Germany.

Daimler-Benz believes that as of June 1993 it had approximately 400,000 stockholders. The Deutsche Bank owned 28.3% of the company. Other large ownership portions were held by the government of Kuwait and several major German banks and insurance companies.

Background

On November 28, 1890, Gottlieb Daimler incorporated Daimler-Motoren-Gesellschaft AG, a German stock corporation in Cannstatt, near Stuttgart, Germany, for the purpose of manufacturing internal combustion engine vehicles. In 1901, Emil Jellinek, the Austro-Hungarian Consul-General at Nice, took a concession for the sale of Daimler cars and persuaded the company to name its new model after his 10-year-old daughter, Mercedes. In 1902, Daimler registered the name "Mercedes" as a trademark, and in 1911 it registered the three-pointed star. In 1926, Daimler-Motoren-Gesellschaft AG merged with Benz & Cie., Rheinische Automobil-und Motorenfabrik Aktiengesellschaft, Mannheim, a corporation formed by Karl Benz, who had invented the automobile in 1886. The new corporation resulting from this merger was named Daimler-Benz Aktiengesellschaft.

In an effort to reduce its dependence on the cyclical market conditions of the world's motor vehicle industry and to expand its technological leadership in the automotive area the Group started to implement a diversification strategy in the mid-1980s seeking to expand into the areas of space technology, aviation, and electronics. These diversification efforts began in 1985 when Daimler-Benz acquired the remaining 50% equity interest in Motoren- und Turbinen-Union Munchen GmbH (MTU-M), a company primarily engaged in the manufacture of turbines and large diesel engines. This was followed by the

---

EXHIBIT 1   A Summary of the Daimler-Benz Group Structure

Mercedes-Benz	*AEG*	*Deutsche Aerospace*	*Debis*
	Automation	Aircraft	Systemhaus
Passenger Car Division	Electrotechnical Systems and Components	Space Systems	Financial Services
Commercial Vehicle Division	Rail System	Defense and Civil Systems	Insurance
	Domestic Appliances	Propulsion Systems	Trading
	Microelectronics	Additional Business Fields	Marketing Services
			Debitel
1992 Revenues[a] DM 66.5 billion	1992 Revenues[a] DM 11.6 billion	1992 Revenues[a] DM 17.3 billion	1992 Revenues[a] DM 8.0 billion
Employees at end 1992 22,482	Employees at end 1992 60,784	Employees at end 1992 81,872	Employees at end 1992 8,258
Headquarters Stuttgart	Headquarters Frankfurt	Headquarters München	Headquarters Berlin

Source: Daimler-Benz AG Form 20-F, September 17, 1993.
[a]Prior to elimination from consolidation.

acquisition of a majority of the voting stock of the German aerospace company Dornier GmbH (Dornier) later in 1985 and in 1986 the acquisition of a majority of the voting stock of AEG Aktiengesellschaft, one of the three leading companies in the German electro-engineering industry. In 1988, Daimler-Benz increased its shareholding in AEG Aktiengesellschaft to its current level of 80.2%. At the end of 1989 Daimler-Benz acquired a majority of the voting stock of Messerschmitt-Bölkow-Blohm GmbH (MBB), the German participant in the European Airbus program.

These acquisitions were followed by a corporate reorganization beginning in 1989 in which Daimler-Benz AG became the holding company for the newly formed corporate units Mercedes-Benz, AEG, and Deutsche Aerospace. The current structure of the Daimler-Benz Group was completed in 1990 when debis, the fourth corporate unit of the Group, was formed to consolidate the Group's information technology and financial services activities. (See **Exhibit 1.**)

Daimler-Benz AG coordinates, controls, and monitors the four corporate units in all matters of strategic interest to the Group as a whole. It is Group policy that although strategic and financial decisions are made centrally, managerial and operational control remains with each of the four corporate units. The holding company is responsible for the ongoing development of the Group's business portfolio and for the Group's goals and operating results. It is the responsibility of the corporate units to manage themselves to achieve the goals and target operating performance objectives established by the holding company for the corporate units and the Group.

The year 1992 was difficult and competitive for many industries worldwide, as the low level of demand for consumer and capital goods continued in most industrial countries. The global economy remained adversely affected by the slow economic recovery in the United States and the recessionary trends and economic downturns in Western Europe and Japan, the economic and social crisis in the Central and Eastern European countries, and the uncertain conditions in the new Commonwealth of Independent States (CIS).

Sharply reduced export opportunities exacerbated the problems facing German manufacturers as a result of the drastic decline in domestic demand which began in mid-1992. Beginning in early 1992, the German economy decelerated substantially as a consequence of the growing public deficit caused by the high costs of German unification. High interest rates have curbed investment activities in Germany and the rise in the value of the mark within the European Monetary System (EMS) has made the price of German products in the European Community (sometimes referred to as the EC) considerably less competitive. As a result of these and certain other factors, net income of Daimler-Benz Group declined to DM 1.45 billion in 1992, as compared to DM 1.95 billion in 1991.

The Daimler-Benz Group has responded proactively to these adverse operating conditions. The Group actively manages its portfolio of businesses and will continue to commit resources to those areas which consistently contribute acceptable rates of return. Conversely, the Group will rationalize or dispose of businesses which do not or cannot demonstrate a consistent pattern of acceptable rates of return or which require a disproportionate share of management resources. For example, in 1991 the Group disposed of AEG KABEL Aktiengesellschaft (AEG KABEL) after determining that it was not part of the long-term strategic plan and AEC Olympia after determining, as had others in the industry, that office automation was not a growth opportunity. In some areas steps are being taken to improve short- and medium-term profitability and to increase flexibility to adapt to changes in operating environments. These measures include cost reduction in all corporate units and divisions of the Group, enlarging core capabilities, streamlining the organizational structure with smaller central offices and fewer levels of management, internationalizing production structures, and broadening of sourcing. Comprehensive cost-reduction measures in the Group have already resulted in a reduction in the work force by approximately 19,000 people (mainly at Mercedes-Benz) in 1992 and the Group is continuing this rationalization process in 1993. During the third quarter of 1993 Daimler-Benz announced a program to further reduce its work force significantly. There will be a charge to earnings in the second half of 1993 in respect of the estimated cost of the program. The Company currently estimates that the charge will be in the range of DM 1.5 billion. It is expected that by the end of 1993 the total reductions achieved through dispositions and work force reduction programs will be approximately 12.5% of the work force which was in place at the end of 1990.

Exchange Rates

The following table sets forth, for the periods and dates indicated, the average, high, low, and period-end Noon Buying Rates for marks expressed in marks per $1.00.

Year Ending December 31,	Average[a]	High	Low	Period End
1988	1.7569	1.9197	1.6333	1.7735
1989	1.8808	2.0295	1.6875	1.6895
1990	1.6166	1.7225	1.4708	1.4970
1991	1.6610	1.8350	1.4512	1.5170
1992	1.5618	1.6777	1.3907	1.6197
1993[b]	1.6471	1.7405	1.5675	1.6595

[a]The average of the Noon Buying Rates for each business day during the relevant period.
[b]Through September 1, 1993.

On September 16, 1993, the Noon Buying Rate was DM 1.6065 per $1.00.

Dividends

Dividends are jointly proposed by the Supervisory Board and the Board of Management of Daimler-Benz AG based on the unconsolidated financial statements of the Company. The following table sets forth the annual dividends paid per Ordinary Share in marks, and the dollar equivalent, for each of the years indicated.

Year Ending December 31,		Dividend paid per Ordinary Share of DM 50 Par Value
1988	DM 12	$6.14[a]
1989	12	7.28
1990	12	6.68
1991	13	8.43
1992	13	8.06

[a]Translated into dollars at the Noon Buying Rate on the dividend payment date, which typically occurred during the second quarter of the following year.

U.S. GAAP Financial Reports

On September 17, 1993 Daimler-Benz published U.S. GAAP–based financial data for the first time. According to Dr. Liener:

> Nevertheless, drawing up U.S.-style accounts is still a formidable task especially the first time around. A big challenge was the drafting of an information package with which we were requesting all the necessary data from our subsidiaries as not all information was available at our headquarters. In the future though this package will simply be the SEC appendix to our annual forms which we mail out anyhow. The relevant SEC accounts

which will be presented in a reconciled format are then drafted by the central accounting department at Daimler-Benz. This will also be the only place where the know-how regarding U.S. GAAP is necessary. I am convinced that within a very short time the preparation of our U.S. accounts will become a mere routine.

This brings me back to the issue of benefits and costs. Once the whole process has been institutionalized within our country, the effort and thus the costs will decrease dramatically. But even the expenses for the original listing—though reaching several million DM—will be far outweighed by the benefits.[2]

Daimler-Benz included financial data based on German and U.S. GAAP in its September 17, 1993 Form-20F. A summary of Daimler-Benz's 1988–1992 financial data is presented in **Exhibit 2.** The company's six months ended June 30, 1992–1993 financial data is summarized in **Exhibit 3.** Selected notes to the company's 1991–1993 annual and first six-month interim consolidated financial statements are presented in **Exhibits 4** and **5,** respectively.

DVFA Earnings

Two earnings for figures are quoted for listed German companies—earnings measured by German GAAP and earnings estimated by the DVFA method. The DVFA method is a series of adjustments to the German GAAP income of German companies made by financial analysts through negotiations with the reporting company to facilitate the comparison of German company earnings. DVFA stands for the initials in German of the German Association of Financial Analysts and Investment Advisors.

The principal DVFA method adjustments to German GAAP earnings are:

- Eliminate extraordinary items—which in German GAAP includes many more items than U.S. GAAP—from net income. A DVFA method objective is to determine what a company could have earned if the extraordinary items had not occurred.
- Eliminate the effects of excessive provision and pension entries that hide or boost income. In making this adjustment the analysts often must rely on management for the information.
- Eliminate depreciation expense due to special and accelerated tax valuation. Since a goal of DVFA is to put German firms on the same footing and all German firms have the same tax depreciation schedules, no depreciation adjustment is made for regular tax conforming book depreciation that might be shorter than the economic lives of the related assets.
- Eliminate capitalized goodwill charges.
- Eliminate any minority interest in consolidated income.

[2]"Entering the U.S. Accounting World: A View From the first German Player," International Capital Markets Conference, IIR Limited, London, United Kingdom, June 29, 1993.

EXHIBIT 2 **Summary Interim Financial Data (in millions, except per ordinary share and ADS amounts)**

	Six Months Ended June 30,		
	1993[a]	1993 (Unaudited)	1992[b]
Income Statement Data			
Amounts in Accordance with German GAAP			
Revenues	$24,407	DM 41,638	DM 48,137
Total output	25,742	43,916	50,982
Results from ordinary business activities	184[c]	313[c]	2,128
Net income	98[c]	168[c]	1,073
Earnings (loss) per ordinary share	1.47[c]	2.51[c]	24.86
Earnings (loss) per ADS[d]	0.15[c]	0.25[c]	2.49
Approximate Amounts in Accordance with U.S. GAAP			
Net income (loss)	$ (556)	DM (949)	DM 965[e]
Earnings (loss) per ordinary share	(11.94)	(20.37)	20.73[e]
Earnings (loss) per ADS[d]	(1.19)	(2.04)	2.07[e]
Balance Sheet Data			
Amounts in Accordance with German GAAP			
Total assets	$51,730	DM 88,251	—
Long-term borrowing	5,809[f]	9,911[f]	—
Stockholders' equity	11,101	18,938	—
Approximate Amounts in Accordance with U.S. GAAP			
Total assets	$55,394	DM 94,503	—
Stockholders' equity	15,376	26,231	—

Source: Daimler-Benz AG Form 20-F, September 17, 1993.

[a]Amounts in this column have been translated solely for the convenience of the reader at an exchange rate of DM 1.706 = $1.00, the Noon Buying Rate on June 30, 1993.

[b]Deutsche Aerospace Airbus was consolidated beginning in 1992. See Note 3 to the Consolidated Financial Statements set forth in Item 18.

[c]Includes the positive effect of approximately DM 1,800 ($1,054) of accounting changes relating to provisions. Excluding such items, results from ordinary business activities, net income, earnings (loss) per ordinary share and earnings (loss) per ADS whould have been approximately (DM 1,527) ($895), (DM 1,672) ($980), (DM 36.98) ($21.68), and (DM 3.70) ($2.17), respectively.

[d]Each ADS (American Depository Share) represents one-tenth of an ordinary share.

[e]Includes the cumulative effect of a change in accounting for postretirement benefits other than pensions of DM 52 ($32), net of tax of DM 33 ($20), or DM 1.12 ($0.69) per ordinary share (DM 0.11 per ADS).

[f]The Group acquired a majority interest in Fokker in May 1993 and will begin consolidating Fokker by the end of 1993. At June 30, 1993, Fokker had long-term debt of DM 1,471 ($862) which would increase consolidated long-term borrowings of the Group under U.S. GAAP.

EXHIBIT 3   Summary Financial Data (in millions except ordinary share and ADS amounts)

	Year Ended December 31,					
	1992a	1992b	1991b	1990b	1989	1988
Income Statement Data						
Amounts in Accordance with German GAAP						
Revenues	$57,766	DM 98,549	DM 95,010	DM 85,500	DM 76,392	DM 73,495
Total output	59,132	100,879	98,566	88,340	80,552	75,637
Results from ordinary business activities	1,485	2,533	4,027	4,221	10,096c	5,197
Extraordinary resultd	—	—	(544)	—	—	—
Net income	851	1,451	1,942	1,795	6,809c	1,702
Earnings per ordinary share	17.85	30.46	40.21	36.18	38.55e,f	39.58
Earnings per ADSg	1.79	3.05	4.02	3.62	3.86	3.96
Dividends declared	354	604	603	557	555	504
Approximate Amounts in Accordance with U.S. GAAP						
Net income	$791h	DM 1,350h	DM 1,886	DM 884	—	—
Earnings per ordinary share	17.00	39.00h	40.52	18.99	—	—
Earnings per ADSg	1.70	3.90h	4.05	1.90	—	—
Balance Sheet Data						
Amounts in Accordance with German GAAP						
Total assets	$50,518	DM 86,184	DM 75,714	DM 67,339	DM 62,737	DM 51,931
Long-term borrowings	4,408	7,520	7,039	4,676	3,533	3,370
Stockholders' equity	11,559	19,719	19,448	17,827	16,966f	11,323
Approximate Amounts in Accordance with U.S. GAAP						
Total assets	$53,102	DM 90,592	DM 87,186	—	—	—
Stockholders' equity	16,181	27,604	26,745	—	—	—

Source: Daimler-Benz AG Form 20-F, September 17, 1993.

aAmounts in this column are unaudited and have been translated solely for the convenience of the reader at an exchange rate of DM 1.706 = $1.00, the Noon Buying Rate on June 30, 1993.

bDeutsche Aerospace Airbus was consolidated beginning in 1992. Assuming Deutsche Aerospace Airbus had been consolidated since acquisition at the end of 1989, revenue and long-term debt in 1991 and 1990 would have been DM 99,892 and DM 7,044 and DM 89,648 and DM 4,727, respectively. See Note 3 to the Consolidated Financial Statements set forth in Item 18. Under U.S. GAAP, Deutsche Aerospace Airbus would have been consolidated since acquisition.

cIncludes nonrecurring expenses of DM 1,370 and nonrecurring income credit of DM 6,500 related to restructuring costs and changes in Group accounting methods principally relating to pensions and inventories of the Group.

dExtraordinary result would be included as part of results from ordinary business activities under U.S. GAAP. Details of the extraordinary items in 1991 are given in Note 14 to the Consolidated Financial Statements set forth in Item 18.

eExcludes the effect of nonrecurring items discussed in footnote (d) above. Including such items, earnings per ordinary share would have been DM 150.71.

fIncludes the effects of the issuance of approximately 4,200,000 ordinary shares in December 1989.

gEach ADS represents one-tenth of an ordinary share.

hIncludes the cumulative effect of a change in accounting for postretirement benefits other than pensions of DM 52 ($30), net of tax of DM 33 ($19), or DM 1.12 ($0.66) per ordinary share (DM 0.11 per ADS).

EXHIBIT 4   **Selected Notes to Consolidated Financial Statements (in millions of DM, except per share amounts)**

---

1. Summary of Accounting Policies

The consolidated financial statements of Daimler-Benz Aktiengesellschaft and subsidiaries (Daimler-Benz or "the Company") have been prepared in accordance with the German Commercial Code, which represents generally accepted accounting principles in Germany (German GAAP) and comply with the significant accounting policies described hereunder. Generally accepted accounting principles in Germany vary in certain significant respects from generally accepted accounting principles in the United States. Application of generally accepted accounting principles in the United States would have affected the results of operations for each of the years in the three-year period ended December 31, 1992 and stockholders' equity as of December 31, 1992 and 1991 to the extent summarized in Note 2 to the consolidated financial statements. All amounts herein are shown in millions of Deutsche marks (DM) and for the year 1992 are also represented in U.S. dollars, the latter being unaudited and presented solely for the convenience of the reader, at the rate of DM 1.706 = US$1, the Noon Buying Rate of the Federal Reserve Bank of New York on June 30, 1993.

The Company's consolidated accounting principles and valuation methods have been consistently applied for all periods presented. Certain reclassifications have been made to the prior year amounts to conform to the 1992 presentation.

Consolidation methods All material companies in which Daimler-Benz has legal or effective control are fully consolidated. In 1992 Daimler-Benz AG consolidated 278 (1991: 255) domestic and foreign subsidiaries and joint venture companies, including 26 companies for the first time. Certain joint venture companies related to the Eurocopter Group are accounted for using the pro rata method of consolidation (see Note 3). Ten subsidiaries and one joint venture company were deleted from consolidation in 1992. Deutsche Aerospace Airbus GmbH and its subsidiaries were fully consolidated beginning January 1, 1992 (see Note 3).

For the year ended December 31, 1992, 248 subsidiaries are not consolidated as their effect on the financial position and results of operations are not material. The effect of such nonconsolidated subsidiaries to the 1992 consolidated assets, revenues, and net earnings of Daimler-Benz was approximately 2%, 1%, and nil, respectively. In addition, 11 companies administering pension funds whose assets are subject to restrictions have not been included in the consolidated financial statements.

Significant investments in which Daimler-Benz has an ownership interest in the range of 20% to 50% are generally accounted for using the equity method. Investments in which Daimler-Benz has an ownership interest of less than 20% are accounted for at cost.

These financial statements include references to affiliated, associated and related companies. Affiliated companies include entities in which Daimler-Benz has majority ownership or an interest of 20% to 50% and which are not consolidated or accounted for on an equity method, respectively, as their effect would not be material. Associated companies represent entities in which Daimler-Benz owns between 20% and 50% and are accounted for using the equity method. Related companies include entities which have a significant ownership interest in Daimler-Benz or an entity in which a member of Daimler-Benz management is a board member.

The effects of intercompany transactions have been eliminated.

Total cost method The income statement has been presented according to the total-cost (or type-of-expenditure) format as commonly used in Germany. According to this format, production and all other expenses incurred during the period are classified by type of expenses. Sales of the period, and the increase in inventories and capitalized in-house output is disclosed at Total Output.

Foreign currencies Foreign currencies receivables and payables are recorded at historical rates unless the use of the exchange rate at balance sheet date would result in a lower receivable or a higher payable balance. This results in unrealized losses being recognized currently and unrealized gains being deferred until they are realized.

Exhibit 4   (continued)

The balance sheets of foreign subsidiaries have been translated to DMs on the basis of historical exchange rates for noncurrent assets at the period end exchange rates for all other assets and liabilities. Expense and income items are generally translated at average exchange rates. Depreciation, amortization, and profit and loss from the disposal of noncurrent assets are translated at historical rates. Net income is translated at period end rates. The differences resulting from the translation of net income between average rates and period end rates is reflected in other operating income in the case of gains or other operating expenses in the case of losses. The accounts of foreign companies operating in hyperinflationary economies have been translated using period end rates.

Revenue recognition Revenue is recognized when title passes or services are rendered net of discount, customer bonuses, and rebates gained. For certain long-term contracts revenue is recognized upon the attainment of milestones or on the completed contract method. Revenue from financial receivables is recorded on the interest method. Operating lease income is recorded when earned.

Property, plant, and equipment Property, plant, and equipment is valued at acquisition or manufacturing cost and subsequently reduced by scheduled depreciation charges over the assets' useful lives as follows: Buildings, 17 to 50 years; site improvements, 8 to 20 years; technical facilities and machinery, 3 to 20 years; and facilities, factory, and office equipment, 2 to 10 years. Buildings are generally depreciated on a straight line basis. Equipment is depreciated using an accelerated depreciation method until such time that the straight line method yields a larger expense, then the straight method is utilized. Depreciation on additions during the first and second half of the year are calculated using full-year or half-year rates, respectively. Low value items are expensed in the year of acquisition. Opportunities for special tax deductible depreciation are utilized for both book and tax purposes and such amounts are not material.

Leased equipment Leased equipment is valued at acquisition cost and depreciated over the assets' useful lives, generally five years, using an accelerated depreciation method until such time that the straight line method yields a larger expense, then the straight line method is used.

Intangible assets Intangible assets other than goodwill are valued at acquisition cost and are amortized over their respective useful lives (3 to 10 years). Goodwill derived from acquisitions is generally amortized over 5 to 15 years. Goodwill related to the restructuring of the group is charged to retained earnings. Goodwill resulting from strategic alliances is split; the portion relating to the expansion of the group is written off over its relevant useful life. The remainder is charged directly to retained earnings.

Pension costs Provision for pensions and similar obligations are actuarially determined and are based on discounted amounts.

Inventory valuation Raw materials, manufacturing supplies, and goods purchased for resale are valued at the lower of cost, determined on an average of first-in, first-out method, or market. Finished goods are valued at the lower of manufacturing cost, determined on an average or first-in, first-out method, or net realizable value and comprise direct material and labor applicable manufacturing overheads including depreciation charges. Obsolescence provisions are made to the extent that inventory risks are determinable.

Income taxes Deferred tax assets are generally recognized for the elimination of intercompany profits. Other deferred taxes are calculated on the liability method but are recognized only to the extent that consolidated deferred tax liabilities exceed consolidated deferred tax assets. Deferred tax assets are not recorded for operating loss carryforwards.

Product-related expenses Expenditures for advertising and sales promotion and for other product-related expenses are charged to expense as incurred. Provision for estimated costs related to product warranty are made at the time the products are sold. Research and development costs are expensed as incurred. Company funded research and development costs amounted to DM 4,914, DM 4,722, and DM 4,717 in 1992, 1991, and 1990, respectively.

Securities Securities have been valued at the lower of cost or market value at the balance sheet date.

EXHIBIT 4   (continued)

Interest costs All interest costs are charged to the income statement as incurred.

Receivables and other assets Non-interest–bearing receivables are reduced to their present value at the balance sheet date, and are valued taking into account all known risks. A lump-sum allowance for doubtful accounts on a country-specific basis is deducted from the receivables in recognition of the general risk inherent in receivables.

Liabilities Liabilities are shown at their repayment amounts.

Earnings per share Earnings per share are calculated based upon net income after deduction for amounts applicable to minority shareholders and dividends paid on preferred stock and dividing by the number of ordinary shares outstanding.

2. Significant Differences between German and U.S. Generally Accepted Accounting Principles

The Daimler-Benz consolidated financial statements comply with generally accepted accounting principles (GAAP) in Germany as prescribed by the German Commercial Code, which differ in certain significant respects from those applicable in the United States. The significant differences that affect the consolidated net income and stockholders' equity of Daimler-Benz are set out below.

a. Appropriated retained earnings—provisions, reserves, and valuation differences

According to German GAAP, accruals or provisions may be recorded for uncertain liabilities and loss contingencies. The amount of such accruals or provisions represents the anticipated expense to the Company. Accruals for potential losses on open production orders take into consideration all internal costs, including indirect selling and administrative expenses. Application of German GAAP may also lead to higher accrual balances and reserves for possible asset risks than are allowed under U.S. GAAP. To the extent that German provisions, reserves, and valuations are more conservative than the corresponding U.S. GAAP values, such differences can be viewed in a manner similar to appropriated retained earnings. Under U.S. GAAP, in accordance with Financial Accounting Standards

Board (FASB) No. 5 "Accounting for Contingencies," an accrual for a loss contingency is recorded by a charge to income if it is both probable that an asset has been impaired or a liability has been incurred and the minimum amount of loss can be reasonably estimated. Unspecified liabilities reserves for future losses, costs or risks do not meet the conditions for accrual under FASB No. 5.

The adjustments to Stockholders' Equity of DM 9,931 and DM 6,984 would have reduced other provisions at December 31, 1992 and 1991 by DM 8,105 and DM 5,402, respectively. The remainder of the adjustments would have increased inventories and other receivables under U.S. GAAP. The significant increase in the 1992 adjustment to Stockholders' Equity as compared to the 1991 adjustment, after taking into account the adjustment to 1992 net income, resulted from the first-time consolidation of Deutsche Aerospace Airbus beginning in 1992.

b. Long-term contracts

Daimler-Benz generally accounts for revenues and costs on long-term contracts using the completed contract method with recognition of performance milestones where practicable. Under U.S. GAAP, revenues and costs on long-term contracts are recognized using the percentage-of-completion method of accounting.

c. Goodwill and business acquisitions

In accordance with German GAAP, goodwill may be charged directly to shareholders' equity or capitalized and amortized over its useful life generally ranging between 5 and 15 years. Prior to 1988, net assets acquired as part of a business combination were valued at historical cost. Net assets acquired after 1987 have been recorded at their estimated fair value. Under U.S. GAAP, the difference between the purchase price and fair value of net assets acquired as part of a business combination is capitalized as goodwill and amortized through the income statement over its estimated useful life which may not exceed 40 years. For the purpose of the reconciliation to U.S. GAAP, goodwill is being amortized through

EXHIBIT 4   (continued)

the income statement over estimated useful lives ranging between 15 and 40 years.

d. Business dispositions

German GAAP requires the accounting for the disposition of a business based upon the date of a signed contract. Under U.S. GAAP, a gain on the sale of a business is reflected in the period in which a closing occurs with the exchange of consideration. The gain on the sale of AEG KABEL which was recognized in 1991 for German GAAP purposes is recognized in 1992 under U.S. GAAP. In addition, applying the differing accounting principles between German and U.S. GAAP results in differing book values of the underlying businesses. As a result, the German and U.S. GAAP accounting gain or loss on a business disposition may be different.

e. Pensions

Daimler-Benz provides for pension costs and similar obligations including postretirement benefits based on actuarial studies using the entry age method as defined in the German tax code. U.S. GAAP, as defined by FASB No. 87, "Employers' Accounting for Pensions" is more prescriptive particularly as to the use of actuarial assumptions and requires that a different actuarial method (the projected unit credit method) be used. In addition the Company adopted FASB No. 106 "Employers' Accounting for Postretirement Benefits other than Pensions" as of January 1, 1992. The application of this standard, to provide fully for the transitional liability is included in the net income reconciliation as a cumulative effect adjustment net of income taxes.

f. Foreign currency translation

The Company's foreign currency accounting policies are disclosed in Note 1. Under U.S. GAAP, in accordance with FASB No. 52, "Foreign Currency Translation," assets and liabilities denominated in a foreign currency are recorded at period end rates with any resulting unrealized gain or loss recognized in the income statement. The balance sheets of foreign companies are translated at period end exchange rates and income statements are translated using an average rate during the period.

The assets and liabilities of foreign companies operating in hyperinflationary countries are remeasured into the functional currency (DM) by translating monetary items at current rates and nonmonetary items at historical rates, with all resulting translation gains and losses being recognized in income.

g. Financial instruments

The Company enters into contracts using financial instruments to cover certain foreign currency risks related to future transactions. In accordance with the German Commercial Code a reserve is set up for unrealized losses relating to such financial instruments whereas unrealized gains are not recognized until realized. Under U.S. GAAP, there are prescriptive rules that govern the application of hedge accounting. Financial instruments that do not qualify for hedge accounting are marked to market with any resulting unrealized gains or losses recognized in the income statement.

h. Deutsche Aerospace Airbus GmbH (DA)

As discussed in Note 3, under German GAAP DA was not consolidated as part of the Daimler-Benz Group for periods prior to 1992. Under U.S. GAAP DA would have been consolidated to reflect Daimler-Benz's 80% ownership interest during 1991 and 1990. The adjustments to net income included in the reconciliation to U.S. GAAP represent the U.S. GAAP earnings of DA.

i. Other

Other differences in accounting principles include adjustments for LIFO inventory, treasury stock, and the minority shareholders' interest in U.S. GAAP adjustments.

j. Deferred taxes

Under German GAAP deferred tax assets are generally recognized for the elimination of intercompany profits. Other deferred taxes are calculated on the liability method but are recognized only to the extent that consolidated deferred tax liabilities exceed consolidated deferred tax assets. Under U.S. GAAP as prescribed by FASB No. 109 "Accounting for Income Taxes" deferred taxes are provided for all temporary differences using the liability method based on enacted tax rates.

The deferred tax adjustment included in the following reconciliation to U.S. GAAP also includes the income tax effects of the above U.S. GAAP adjustments, where appropriate.

Exhibit 4   (continued)

In addition, the 1991 extraordinary items under German GAAP would be recorded as part of ordinary income under U.S. GAAP.

Reconciliation to U.S. GAAP

The following is a summary of the significant adjustments to net income for the years 1992, 1991, and 1990 and to stockholders' equity at December 31, 1992 and 1991, which would be required if U.S. GAAP had been applied instead of German GAAP. The translation of 1992 amounts from Deutsche marks into U.S. dollars is unaudited and has been made solely for the convenience of the reader at the June 30, 1993 rate of DM 1.706 = US$1.

	Notes	1992	1992	1991	1990
Net income as reported in the consolidated income statements under German GAAP		$ 851	DM 1,451	DM 1,942	DM 1,795
Less: Income and loss applicable to minority shareholders		(20)	(33)	(70)	(111)
Adjusted net income under German GAAP		831	1,418	1,872	1,684
Add: Changes in appropriated retained earnings—provisions, reserves, and valuation differences	(a)	454	774	64	738
		1,285	2,192	1,936	2,422
Other Adjustments Required to Conform with U.S. GAAP					
Long-term contracts	(b)	(33)	(57)	(32)	(14)
Goodwill and business acquisitions . . .	(c)	(45)	(76)	(270)	(251)
Business dispositions	(d)	198	337	(490)	0
Pensions and other postretirement benefits	(e)	56	96	(66)	(153)
Foreign currency translation	(f)	(55)	(94)	155	46
Financial instruments	(g)	(257)	(438)	86	35
Earnings of Deutsche Aerospace Airbus	(h)	—	—	636	(512)
Other	(i)	52	88	57	69
Deferred taxes	(j)	(379)	(646)	(126)	(758)
Net income in accordance with U.S. GAAP before cumulative effect of a change in accounting principle		822	1,402	1,886	884
Cumulative effect of change in accounting for postretirement benefits other than pensions as of January 1, 1992, net of tax of DM 33	(e)	(31)	(52)	—	—
Net income in accordance with U.S. GAAP		791	1,350	1,886	884
Earnings per share in accordance with U.S. GAAP		$ 17.00	DM 29.00[a]	DM 40.52	DM 18.99
Earnings per American Depository Share in accordance with U.S. GAAP[b]		$ 1.70	DM 2.90[a]	DM 4.05	DM 1.90

Exhibit 4   (continued)

	Notes	1992	1992	1991	1990
Stockholders' equity as reported in the consolidated balance sheet under German GAAP		$11,559	DM 19,719	DM 19,448	
Less: Minority interest		(720)	(1,228)	1,214)	
Adjusted stockholders' equity under German GAAP		10,839	18,491	18,234	
Add: Appropriated retained earnings— provisions, reserves, and valuation differences	(a)	16,660	28,422	25,218	
Other Adjustments Required to Conform with U.S. GAAP					
Long-term contracts	(b)	77	131	188	
Goodwill and business acquisitions . . .	(c)	1,097	1,871	2,737	
Business dispositions	(d)	—	—	(490)	
Pensions and other postretirement benefits	(e)	(711)	(1,212)	(1,082)	
Foreign currency translation	(f)	(200)	(342)	(624)	
Financial instruments	(g)	340	580	134	
Deutsche Aerospace Airbus	(h)	—	—	1,124	
Other	(i)	(1,001)	(1,708)	(1,746)	
Deferred taxes	(j)	(81)	(138)	1,286	
Stockholders' equity in accordance with U.S. GAAP		16.181	27,604	26,745	

[a]Includes the negative effect of the change in accounting for postretirement benefits other than pensions of DM 1.12 per share (DM 0.11 per American Depository Share).

[b]Earnings per American Depository Share are calculated on the basis of 10 American Depository shares for every Ordinary Share.

New U.S. Accounting Standards—Not Yet Adopted

FASB No. 112 "Employers Accounting for Post-employment Benefits" establishes an accounting standard for employers who provide benefits to former or inactive employees after employment but before retirement. The Statement was issued in November 1992 and is effective in 1994.

FASB No. 114 "Accounting by Creditors for Impairment of a Loan" addresses the accounting by creditors for the impairment of certain loans. The Statement was issued in May 1993 and is required to be adopted in 1995.

FASB No. 115 "Accounting for Certain Investments in Debt and Equity Securities" prescribes accounting for investments in equity securities that have readily determinable fair values and all investments in debt securities. The Statement was issued in May 1993 and is effective in 1994.

Daimler-Benz has not yet addressed the impact of each of the above Statements on its financial position or results of operations or determined the period in which each will be adopted.

9. Retirement Plans

The Company operates various defined benefit pension plans all based upon years of service. Some pension plans are based on salary earned in the last year of employment and some are fixed DM-amount plans depending on ranking (both wage level and hierarchy).

Pension costs are actuarially determined on the basis of an assumed interest rate of 6% using the entry age actuarial cost method, and are in accordance with the regulations of the 1992 Pension Reform Act passed by the German government. Pension and other similar expenses charged to the income statement were DM 1,539, DM 1,511, and DM 1,347, for 1992, 1991, and 1990, respectively.

EXHIBIT 4   (continued)

Most plan obligations are accrued for the financial statements. External pension funds are also used for the nonexecutive pension plans and contributions are generally made to the extent that they are tax deductible in accordance with German income tax law. The pension accruals in the financial statements relate to the plans financed directly by the Company and any underfunded portion of the external pension funds. When the assets of the separate pension plan funds are added to the provisions for pensions and similar obligations in the balance sheet at December 31, 1992, 1991, and

1990 of DM 12,217, DM 10,790, and DM 10,831, respectively, the Company's pension obligations are fully funded.

Pension Plans

For purposes of disclosure in accordance with U.S. GAAP, the following information for the Company's material pension plans is provided in accordance with the requirements of FASB 87.

The funded status of the Company's major retirement plans under FASB No. 87 is as follows:

| | **December 31,** | | | |
| | 1992 | | 1991 | |
	Assets Exceed Accumulated Benefits	*Accumulated Benefits Exceed Assets*	*Assets Exceed Accumulated Benefits*	*Accumulated Benefits Exceed Assets*
Actuarial present value of benefits:				
Vested	211	15,008	180	13,136
Nonvested	23	635	20	560
Accumulated benefit obligation	234	15,643	200	13,696
Effect of projected future salary increase	92	2,312	80	1,809
Projected benefit obligations	326	17,955	280	15,505
Plan assets at fair value	497	4,505	430	4,083
Projected benefit obligations in excess of (less than) plan assets	(171)	13,450	(150)	11,422
Unrecognized net gains (loss)	161	(521)	159	60
Prior service cost not yet recognized	(13)	—	(12)	—
Pension liability (prepaid pension cost)	(23)	12,928	(3)	11,482

Plan assets consist primarily of investments in equity and fixed interest securities and real estate.

Assumed discount rates and rates of increase in remuneration used in calculating the projected benefit obligations together with long-term rates of return on plan assets vary according to the economic conditions of the country in which the retirement plans are situated. The average rates used in the principal retirement plans for FASB No. 87 purposes were as follows:

	1992	*1991*	*1990*
Discount rate	7.5% to 9.0%	7.5% to 9.0%	7.0% to 10.0%
Long-term rate of increase in remuneration	3.0% to 6.5%	2.75% to 6.5%	2.75% to 6.5%
Expected long-term rate of return on assets	7.0% to 8.5%	7.0% to 8.5%	7.0% to 8.5%

Exhibit 4   (continued)

The net periodic pension cost for the major retirement plans under FASB No. 87 comprised:

	1992	*1991*	*1990*
Service cost: present value of benefits earned during the year	594	524	492
Interest cost on projected benefit obligation	1,245	1,156	1,074
Actual loss/(return) on assets	(359)	(354)	(293)
Net amortization and deferral	(1)	33	(24)
Curtailment loss	—	12	14
Net periodic pension cost	1,479	1,371	1,263
Other plans	29	27	21
Total	1,508	1,398	1,284

Other Postretirement Plans

Certain of the Company's U.S. operations provide postretirement medical benefits to their employees. For U.S. GAAP purposes, the Company adopted the provisions of FASB No. 106, "Employers' Accounting for Postretirement Benefits other than Pensions," as of January 1, 1992. The Company elected to immediately recognize the cumulative effect of the change in accounting for postretirement benefits of DM 85 (DM 52, net of income taxes).

The following table presents the plan's funded status reconciled with amounts recognized in the Company's consolidated balance sheet at December 31, 1992.

Accumulated postretirement benefit obligation:	
Retirees	71
Fully eligible active plan participants	32
Other active plan participants	128
	231
Plan assets at fair value	50
Accumulated postretirement benefit obligation in excess of plan assets included in provisions for pensions and similar obligations	181

Net periodic postretirement benefit cost for 1992 includes the following components:

Service costs	10
Interest cost	17
Actual return on plan assets	(2)
Net period postretirement benefit cost according to U.S. GAAP	25

For measurement purposes, a weighted average 11% annual rate of increase in the per capita cost of covered benefits (i.e., health care cost trend rate) was assumed for 1993; the rate was assumed to decrease gradually to 6% by the year 2005 and remain at that level thereafter. The effect of increasing the assumed health care cost trend rates by one percentage point in each year would increase the accumulated postretirement benefit obligation as of December 31, 1992 by DM 39 and the aggregate of the service and interest cost components of net periodic postretirement benefit cost for the year ended December 31, 1992 by DM 6.

The weighted average discount rate used in determining the accumulated postretirement benefit obligation was 8% at December 31, 1992. The expected long-term rate of return on plan assets, after estimated income taxes, was 5% at December 31, 1992.

Exhibit 4   (continued)

14. Extraordinary Results

	1992	1991	1990
Extraordinary income	—	490	—
Extraordinary expense	—	(1,034)	—
	—	(544)	—

The extraordinary income results from the gain on the sale of AEG KABEL Aktiengesellschaft and its subsidiaries. Extraordinary expenses are in connection with the withdrawal from the office and communication technology business of AEG. Under U.S. GAAP such amounts would be included in operating profit.

15. Income Taxes

Income before income taxes is attributable to the following geographic locations:

	Year Ended December 31,		
	1992	1991	1990
Germany	989	2,232	2,609
Foreign	1,048	749	1,000
	2,037	2,981	3,609

The provision for income taxes (credit) follows:

	Year Ended December 31,		
	1992	**1991**	**1990**
Corporate tax at German federal statutory rate	1,019	1,491	1,805
Credit for dividend distribution	(189)	(189)	(174)
Foreign tax rate differential	(164)	(103)	(136)
Municipal trade taxes, net of federal tax benefit..................	198	247	300
Nondeductible expenses	289	68	70
Temporary differences	(256)	(398)	(409)
Losses for which no tax benefit was recorded	—	—	140
Net operating loss utilization	(415)	—	—
Other	104	(77)	218
Provision for income taxes	586	1,039	1,814
Effective rate	29%	35%	50%

German Corporate tax law applies the imputation system to the income taxation of a corporation and its shareholders. Upon distribution of retained earnings in the form of a dividend, shareholders receive an income tax credit for taxes previously paid by the corporation.

In general, corporate income is initially subject to a federal tax rate of 50% (prior to 1989, the corporate tax rate was 56%). Upon distribution of retained earnings to shareholders, the corporate tax rate is adjusted to 36% by receiving a refund from the government for taxes previously paid on income in excess of 36% (the distributed earnings rate). This refund is passed on to the shareholder through a gross up of the dividend from the corporation. For financial reporting purposes under German and U.S. GAAP, the Company provides for current and deferred federal income taxes in Germany using a 50% rate. Upon the distribution of a dividend, income tax expense is reduced by the tax refund due from the government.

EXHIBIT 4   (continued)

Under U.S. GAAP, the effective income tax rate would approximate 48%, 38%, and 74% in 1992, 1991, and 1990, respectively. The principal reason for the differences to the German GAAP effective rate is that all temporary (timing) differences between book and tax income are tax effected under U.S. GAAP. If the Company used the distribution earnings tax rate of 36% for U.S. GAAP purposes to account for current and deferred federal income taxes in Germany, the effective income tax rate would approximate 51%, 30%, and 69% in 1992, 1991, and 1990, respectively.

Deferred income tax assets and liabilities at December 31, 1992 and 1991 are summarized as follows:

	1992	1991
Deferred tax assets relating to:		
Intangible assets	617	675
Fixed assets	1,523	1,755
Inventories	702	809
Pension provisions	938	713
Other provisions	2,602	2,749
Liabilities	360	386
Net operating loss and credit carryforwards	1,993	1,153
Other	215	171
	8,950	8,411
Deferred tax liabilities relating to:		
Liabilities and provisions	(19)	(85)
Other	(279)	(134)
	(298)	(219)
	8,652	8,192
Net deferred tax asset before valuation allowance	(7,323)	(6,596)
Deferred tax asset per balance sheet	1,329	1,596

At December 31, 1992, the Company had net operating losses (NOLs) and tax credit carryforwards available to certain subsidiaries amounting to approximately DM 3,700. The majority of the NOLs have an unlimited carryforward period under German tax law, but are limited in their use to the subsidiary which generated the loss. Other NOLs have extended carryforward periods.

Deferred tax liabilities have not been recognized on unremitted earnings of subsidiaries intended to be indefinitely reinvested (DM 4,373, DM 3,958, and DM 3,519 at December 31, 1992, 1991, and 1990, respectively). Determination of the amount of unrecognized deferred tax liabilities is not practicable.

	At December 31,	
	1992	1991
Sales financing	6,364	4,503
Finance leases	917	710
	7,281	5,213
Unearned income	(944)	(802)
Allowance for credit losses . .	(171)	(156)
	6,166	4,255

Sales financing and finance lease receivables consist of retail installment sales contracts secured by automobiles and commercial vehicles. Contractual maturities applicable to receivables from sales financing and finance leases maturing in each of the five years following December 31, 1992 are as follows: 1993, DM 3,003; 1994, DM 1,817; 1995, DM 1,393; 1996, DM 731; 1997, DM 274; and thereafter, DM 63.

Under U.S. GAAP, amounts due after one year would be classified as noncurrent assets.

Source: Daimler-Benz Form-20F, September 17, 1993.

EXHIBIT 5   **Selected Notes to Unaudited Interim Condensed Consolidated Financial Statements (in millions of DM except per share amounts)**

---

1. Presentation of Condensed Consolidated Financial Statements

The condensed consolidated financial statements of Daimler-Benz Aktiengesellschaft and subsidiaries (Daimler-Benz or "the Company") are unaudited and have been prepared in accordance with the German Commercial Code, which represents generally accepted accounting principles in Germany (German GAAP). Generally accepted accounting principles in Germany vary in certain significant respects from generally accepted accounting principles in the United States (U.S. GAAP). Application of generally accepted accounting principles in the United States would have affected the results of operations for the six-month periods ended June 30, 1992 and 1991 and stockholders' equity at June 30, 1993 and December 31, 1992 to the extent summarized in Note 2 to the condensed consolidated financial statements. All amounts herein are shown in millions of Deutsche marks (DM) and for the six months ended June 30, 1993 are also presented in U.S. dollars, the latter being presented solely for the convenience of the reader, at the rate of DM 1.706 = US$1, the Noon Buying Rate of the Federal Reserve Bank of New York on June 30, 1993.

The information included in the condensed consolidated financial statements is unaudited but reflects all adjustments (consisting only of normal recurring adjustments) which are, in the opinion of management, necessary for a fair statement of the results for the interim periods presented. The condensed consolidated financial statements should be read in conjunction with the consolidated financial statements and notes included elsewhere in this Registration Statement.

In May 1993 the Company purchased a controlling interest in Fokker N.V., the Dutch airplane manufacturer, for cash of DM 492. At June 30, 1993 the Company's investment in Fokker has been presented in financial assets. The balance sheet and results of operations of Fokker will be consolidated by the end of the second half of 1993.

Accounting changes During the six-month period ended June 30, 1993, the Company changed, under German GAAP, its method of application of valuation measures as well as accounting policies to move certain of the Company's German accounting policies towards U.S. GAAP with respect to the determination of certain accrued expenses, including accrued sales commissions, accrued internal expenses for such items as major repairs, restructuring and year-end closing costs, accrued anniversary payments, accrued maintenance expenses, and accrued apprentice training costs. The net effect of these changes was an increase in the results from ordinary business activities of approximately DM 1,800 for the six-month period ended June 30, 1993.

2. Significant Differences between German and U.S. Generally Accepted Accounting Principles

The Daimler-Benz condensed consolidated financial statements are unaudited and are prepared in accordance with German GAAP which differs in certain significant respects from U.S. GAAP. The principal differences that affect the consolidated net income and stockholders' equity of Daimler-Benz are explained in Note 2 to the consolidated financial statements for the years ended December 31, 1992, 1991, and 1990 included elsewhere in this Registration Statement.

The following is a summary of the significant adjustments to net income for the six-month periods ended June 30, 1993 and 1992 and to stockholders' equity at June 30, 1993 and December 31, 1992, which would be required if U.S. GAAP had been applied instead of German GAAP. The translation of 1993 amounts from Deutsche marks to U.S. dollars is made solely for the convenience of the reader at the June 30, 1993 rate of DM 1.706 = US$1.

EXHIBIT 5   (continued)

	Six Months Ended June 30,		
	1993	*1993*	*1992*
Net income as reported in the consolidated income statement under German GAAP	$ 98	DM 168	DM 1,073
Less: Income and losses applicable to minority shareholders . . .	(30)	(51)	84
Adjusted net income under German GAAP	68	117	1,157
Add: Changes in appropriated retained earnings—provisions, reserves, and valuation differences	(950)	(1,615)	(169)
	(882)	(1,498)	998
Other adjustments required to conform with U.S. GAAP:			
Long-term contracts	18	30	70
Goodwill and business acquisitions	(19)	(33)	(35)
Business dispositions	—	—	337
Pension and other postretirement benefits	(79)	(135)	80
Foreign currency translation	(4)	(7)	161
Financial instruments	(172)	(293)	(199)
Other	43	67	(130)
Deferred taxes	539	920	(255)
Net income (loss) in accordance with U.S. GAAP before cumulative effect of a change in accounting principle	(556)	(949)	1,017
Cumulative effect of change in accounting for postretirement benefits other than pensions as of January 1, 1992, net of tax of DM 33	—	—	(52)
Net income (loss) in accordance with U.S. GAAP	(556)	(949)	965
Earnings (loss) per share in accordance with U.S. GAAP	$(11.94)	DM (20.37)	DM 20.73[a]
Earnings (loss) per American Depository Share in accordance with U.S. GAAP[b]	$ (1.19)	DM (2.04)	DM 2.07[a]

[a]Includes the negative effect of the change in accounting for postretirement benefits other than pensions of DM 1.12 per share (DM 0.11 per American Dispository Share).

[b]Earnings per American Dispository Share are calculated on the basis of 10 American Dispository shares for every Ordinary Share.

EXHIBIT 5   (continued)

	June 30,		December 31,
	1993	*1993*	*1992*
Stockholders' equity as reported in the consolidated balance sheets under German GAAP	$ 11,101	DM 18,938	DM 19,719
Less: Minority interest	(739)	(1,260)	(1,228)
Adjusted stockholders' equity under German GAAP	10,362	17,678	18,491
Add: Appropriated retained earnings—provisions, reserves, and valuation differences	4,875	8,316	9,931
	15,237	25,994	28,422
Other adjustments required to conform with U.S. GAAP			
Long-term contracts	94	161	131
Goodwill and business acquisitions	1,081	1,844	1,871
Pensions and other postretirement benefits	(789)	(1,347)	(1,212)
Foreign currency translation	119	203	(342)
Financial instruments	168	287	580
Other	(980)	(1,672)	(1,708)
Deferred taxes	446	761	(138)
Stockholders' equity in accordance with U.S. GAAP	$ 15,376	DM 26,231	DM 27,604

The adjustments to stockholders' equity of DM 8,316 and DM 9,931 would have reduced other provisions at June 30, 1993 and December 31, 1992 by DM 5,945 and DM 8,105, respectively. The remainder of the adjustments would have increased inventories and other receivables under U.S. GAAP.

Source: Daimler-Benz Form 20-F, September 17, 1993.

Daimler-Benz's 1990–1992 DVFA income was:

1992	DM 1,379 million[a]
1991	DM 2,580 million[a]
1990	DM 2,230 million

[a]The DVFA method adjustment to Daimler-Benz's German GAAP income in 1992 (1991) were: +DM 160 (+86) million for depreciation and amortization; –DM 88 (+573) million for provisions; –DM 33 (–70) million minority interest income; and –DM 111 (–171) million for other items. 1991 DVFA adjustments included a +DM 220 million extraordinary item.

Following Daimler-Benz's listing on the New York Stock Exchange it was believed that the company planned to end the practice of reporting its earnings per share determined by the DVFA method.

Questions

1. As a global manager what do you believe are the strengths and weaknesses of the Germanic model? _____

2. What are the principal differences between German GAAP, DVFA and U.S. GAAP? _____

3. What are the principal differences between German GAAP and IAS? _____

4. What accounting practices account for the principal difference between Daimler-Benz's German and U.S. GAAP reported profits for the first six months of 1993? _____

5. Do you agree with the view that in the future Daimler-Benz's U.S. GAAP results will be more useful than the company's German GAAP and DVFA figures to value the company's equity securities? _____ (In early 1994 the Deutsche Bank plans to reduce its holdings in Daimler-Benz from 28% to 25% by selling 15 million Daimler-Benz shares through an exclusive U.S. underwriting.)

6. Does German GAAP give German companies a competitive advantage relative to U.S. corporations? _____

Present Value Tables

TABLE A: Present Value of $1

Table A shows the present value of $1 received n years hence at i annual rate of return on the original investment. For example, to find the amount that would have to be invested today (the "present value") to receive $1 10 years hence if the annual rate of return earned was 10 percent, follow these steps: First, go across the top of the table to the 10 percent column. Next, go down this column until the 10 years line is reached. The factor 0.386 is found at this location in the table. This factor indicates that an investment of approximately 39 cents today at 10 percent annual interest will grow to $1 in 10 years.

Years Hence	1%	2%	4%	6%	8%	10%	12%	14%	15%	16%	18%	20%	22%	24%	25%	26%	28%	30%	35%	40%	45%	50%
1	0.990	0.980	0.962	0.943	0.926	0.909	0.893	0.877	0.870	0.862	0.847	0.833	0.820	0.806	0.800	0.794	0.781	0.769	0.741	0.714	0.690	0.667
2	0.980	0.961	0.925	0.890	0.857	0.826	0.797	0.769	0.756	0.743	0.718	0.694	0.672	0.650	0.640	0.630	0.610	0.592	0.549	0.510	0.476	0.444
3	0.971	0.942	0.889	0.840	0.794	0.751	0.712	0.675	0.658	0.641	0.609	0.579	0.551	0.524	0.512	0.500	0.477	0.455	0.406	0.364	0.328	0.296
4	0.961	0.924	0.855	0.792	0.735	0.683	0.636	0.592	0.572	0.552	0.516	0.482	0.451	0.423	0.410	0.397	0.373	0.350	0.301	0.260	0.226	0.198
5	0.951	0.906	0.822	0.747	0.681	0.621	0.567	0.519	0.497	0.476	0.437	0.402	0.370	0.341	0.328	0.315	0.291	0.269	0.223	0.186	0.156	0.132
6	0.942	0.888	0.790	0.705	0.630	0.564	0.507	0.456	0.432	0.410	0.370	0.335	0.303	0.275	0.262	0.250	0.227	0.207	0.165	0.133	0.108	0.088
7	0.933	0.871	0.760	0.665	0.583	0.513	0.452	0.400	0.376	0.354	0.314	0.279	0.249	0.222	0.210	0.198	0.178	0.159	0.122	0.095	0.074	0.059
8	0.923	0.853	0.731	0.627	0.540	0.467	0.404	0.351	0.327	0.305	0.266	0.233	0.204	0.179	0.168	0.157	0.139	0.123	0.091	0.068	0.051	0.039
9	0.914	0.837	0.703	0.592	0.500	0.424	0.361	0.308	0.284	0.263	0.225	0.194	0.167	0.144	0.134	0.125	0.108	0.094	0.067	0.048	0.035	0.026
10	0.905	0.820	0.676	0.558	0.463	0.386	0.322	0.270	0.247	0.227	0.191	0.162	0.137	0.116	0.107	0.099	0.085	0.073	0.050	0.035	0.024	0.017
11	0.896	0.804	0.650	0.527	0.429	0.350	0.287	0.237	0.215	0.195	0.162	0.135	0.112	0.094	0.086	0.079	0.066	0.056	0.037	0.025	0.017	0.012
12	0.887	0.788	0.625	0.497	0.397	0.319	0.257	0.208	0.187	0.168	0.137	0.112	0.092	0.076	0.069	0.062	0.052	0.043	0.027	0.018	0.012	0.008
13	0.879	0.773	0.601	0.469	0.368	0.290	0.229	0.182	0.163	0.145	0.116	0.093	0.075	0.061	0.055	0.050	0.040	0.033	0.020	0.013	0.008	0.005
14	0.870	0.758	0.577	0.442	0.340	0.263	0.205	0.160	0.141	0.125	0.099	0.078	0.062	0.049	0.044	0.039	0.032	0.025	0.015	0.009	0.006	0.003
15	0.861	0.743	0.555	0.417	0.315	0.239	0.183	0.140	0.123	0.108	0.084	0.065	0.051	0.040	0.035	0.031	0.025	0.020	0.011	0.006	0.004	0.002
16	0.853	0.728	0.534	0.394	0.292	0.218	0.163	0.123	0.107	0.093	0.071	0.054	0.042	0.032	0.028	0.025	0.019	0.015	0.008	0.005	0.003	0.002
17	0.844	0.714	0.513	0.371	0.270	0.198	0.146	0.108	0.093	0.080	0.060	0.045	0.034	0.026	0.023	0.020	0.015	0.012	0.006	0.003	0.002	0.001
18	0.836	0.700	0.494	0.350	0.250	0.180	0.130	0.095	0.081	0.069	0.051	0.038	0.028	0.021	0.018	0.016	0.012	0.009	0.005	0.002	0.001	0.001
19	0.828	0.686	0.475	0.331	0.232	0.164	0.116	0.083	0.070	0.060	0.043	0.031	0.023	0.017	0.014	0.012	0.009	0.007	0.003	0.002	0.001	
20	0.820	0.673	0.456	0.312	0.215	0.149	0.104	0.073	0.061	0.051	0.037	0.026	0.019	0.014	0.012	0.010	0.007	0.005	0.002	0.001	0.001	
21	0.811	0.660	0.439	0.294	0.199	0.135	0.093	0.064	0.053	0.044	0.031	0.022	0.015	0.011	0.009	0.008	0.006	0.004	0.002	0.001		
22	0.803	0.647	0.422	0.278	0.184	0.123	0.083	0.056	0.046	0.038	0.026	0.018	0.013	0.009	0.007	0.006	0.004	0.003	0.001	0.001		
23	0.795	0.634	0.406	0.262	0.170	0.112	0.074	0.049	0.040	0.033	0.022	0.015	0.010	0.007	0.006	0.005	0.003	0.002	0.001			
24	0.788	0.622	0.390	0.247	0.158	0.102	0.066	0.043	0.035	0.028	0.019	0.013	0.008	0.006	0.005	0.004	0.003	0.002	0.001			
25	0.780	0.610	0.375	0.233	0.146	0.092	0.059	0.038	0.030	0.024	0.016	0.010	0.007	0.005	0.004	0.003	0.002	0.001	0.001			
26	0.772	0.598	0.361	0.220	0.135	0.084	0.053	0.033	0.026	0.021	0.014	0.009	0.006	0.004	0.003	0.002	0.002	0.001				
27	0.764	0.586	0.347	0.207	0.125	0.076	0.047	0.029	0.023	0.018	0.011	0.007	0.005	0.003	0.002	0.002	0.001	0.001				
28	0.757	0.574	0.333	0.196	0.116	0.069	0.042	0.026	0.020	0.016	0.010	0.006	0.004	0.002	0.002	0.002	0.001	0.001				
29	0.749	0.563	0.321	0.185	0.107	0.063	0.037	0.022	0.017	0.014	0.008	0.005	0.003	0.002	0.002	0.001	0.001	0.001				
30	0.742	0.552	0.308	0.174	0.099	0.057	0.033	0.020	0.015	0.012	0.007	0.004	0.003	0.002	0.001	0.001	0.001	0.001				
40	0.672	0.453	0.208	0.097	0.046	0.022	0.011	0.005	0.004	0.003	0.001											
50	0.608	0.372	0.141	0.054	0.021	0.009	0.003	0.001	0.001	0.001												

TABLE B: Present Value of $1 Received Annually for n Years

Table B shows the present value of $1 received annually for each of the next n years if i annual rate of return is earned on the remaining balance of the original investment throughout this period. For example, to find the amount needed to be invested today to receive $1 for each of the next 20 years if 10 percent can be earned on the investment, follow these steps: First, go across the top of the table in the 10 percent column. Next, go down the column to the 20 years line. The factor 8.514 is shown at this spot. This factor tells us that a 10 percent investment of $8.51 today will return to the investor $1 for each of the next 20 years. At the end of that time, the investor will have recovered all of the original investment plus a return of 10 percent. Therefore the present value of $1 per year for 20 years discounted at 10 percent is $8.51.

Years (n)	1%	2%	4%	6%	8%	10%	12%	14%	15%	16%	18%	20%	22%	24%	25%	26%	28%	30%	35%	40%	45%	50%
1	0.990	0.980	0.962	0.943	0.926	0.909	0.893	0.877	0.870	0.862	0.847	0.833	0.820	0.806	0.800	0.794	0.781	0.769	0.741	0.714	0.690	0.667
2	1.970	1.942	1.886	1.833	1.783	1.736	1.690	1.647	1.626	1.605	1.566	1.528	1.492	1.457	1.440	1.424	1.392	1.361	1.289	1.224	1.165	1.111
3	2.941	2.884	2.775	2.673	2.577	2.487	2.402	2.322	2.283	2.246	2.174	2.106	2.042	1.981	1.952	1.923	1.868	1.816	1.696	1.589	1.493	1.407
4	3.902	3.808	3.630	3.465	3.312	3.170	3.037	2.914	2.855	2.798	2.690	2.589	2.494	2.404	2.362	2.320	2.241	2.166	1.997	1.849	1.720	1.605
5	4.853	4.713	4.452	4.212	3.993	3.791	3.605	3.433	3.352	3.274	3.127	2.991	2.864	2.745	2.689	2.635	2.532	2.436	2.220	2.035	1.876	1.737
6	5.795	5.601	5.242	4.917	4.623	4.355	4.111	3.889	3.784	3.685	3.498	3.326	3.167	3.020	2.951	2.885	2.759	2.643	2.385	2.168	1.983	1.824
7	6.728	6.472	6.002	5.582	5.206	4.868	4.564	4.288	4.160	4.039	3.812	3.605	3.416	3.242	3.161	3.083	2.937	2.802	2.508	2.263	2.057	1.883
8	7.652	7.325	6.733	6.210	5.747	5.335	4.968	4.639	4.487	4.344	4.078	3.837	3.619	3.421	3.329	3.241	3.076	2.925	2.598	2.331	2.108	1.922
9	8.566	8.162	7.435	6.802	6.247	5.759	5.328	4.946	4.772	4.607	4.303	4.031	3.786	3.566	3.463	3.366	3.184	3.019	2.665	2.379	2.144	1.948
10	9.471	8.983	8.111	7.360	6.710	6.145	5.650	5.216	5.019	4.833	4.494	4.192	3.923	3.682	3.571	3.465	3.269	3.092	2.715	2.414	2.168	1.965
11	10.368	9.787	8.760	7.887	7.139	6.495	5.397	5.453	5.234	5.029	4.656	4.327	4.035	3.776	3.656	3.544	3.335	3.147	2.752	2.438	2.185	1.977
12	11.255	10.575	9.385	8.384	7.536	6.814	6.194	5.660	5.421	5.197	4.793	4.439	4.127	3.851	3.725	3.606	3.387	3.190	2.779	2.456	2.196	1.985
13	12.134	11.343	9.986	8.853	7.904	7.103	6.424	5.842	5.583	5.342	4.910	4.533	4.203	3.912	3.780	3.656	3.427	3.223	2.799	2.468	2.204	1.990
14	13.004	12.106	10.563	9.295	8.244	7.367	6.628	6.002	5.724	5.468	5.008	4.611	4.265	3.962	3.824	3.695	3.459	3.249	2.814	2.477	2.210	1.993
15	13.865	12.849	11.118	9.712	8.559	7.606	6.811	6.142	5.847	5.575	5.092	4.675	4.315	4.001	3.859	3.726	3.483	3.268	2.825	2.484	2.214	1.995
16	14.718	13.578	11.652	10.106	8.851	7.824	6.974	6.265	5.954	5.669	5.162	4.730	4.357	4.033	3.887	3.751	3.503	3.283	2.834	2.489	2.216	1.997
17	15.562	14.292	12.166	10.477	9.122	8.022	7.120	6.373	6.047	5.749	5.222	4.775	4.391	4.059	3.910	3.771	3.518	3.295	2.840	2.492	2.218	1.998
18	16.398	14.992	12.659	10.828	9.372	8.201	7.250	6.467	6.128	5.818	5.273	4.812	4.419	4.080	3.928	3.786	3.529	3.304	2.844	2.494	2.219	1.999
19	17.226	15.678	13.134	11.158	9.604	8.365	7.366	6.550	6.198	5.877	5.316	4.844	4.442	4.097	3.942	3.799	3.539	3.311	2.848	2.496	2.220	1.999
20	18.046	16.351	13.590	11.470	9.818	8.514	7.469	6.623	6.259	5.929	5.353	4.870	4.460	4.110	3.954	3.808	3.546	3.316	2.850	2.497	2.221	1.999
21	18.857	17.011	14.029	11.764	10.017	8.649	7.562	6.687	6.312	5.973	5.384	4.891	4.476	4.121	3.963	3.816	3.551	3.320	2.852	2.498	2.221	2.000
22	19.660	17.658	14.451	12.042	10.201	8.772	7.645	6.743	6.359	6.011	5.410	4.909	4.488	4.130	3.970	3.822	3.556	3.323	2.853	2.498	2.222	2.000
23	20.456	18.292	14.857	12.303	10.371	8.883	7.718	6.792	6.399	6.044	5.432	4.925	4.499	4.137	3.976	3.827	3.559	3.325	2.854	2.499	2.222	2.000
24	21.243	18.914	15.247	12.550	10.529	8.985	7.784	6.835	6.434	6.073	5.451	4.937	4.507	4.143	3.981	3.831	3.562	3.327	2.855	2.499	2.222	2.000
25	22.023	19.523	15.622	12.783	10.675	9.077	7.843	6.873	6.464	6.097	5.467	4.948	4.514	4.147	3.985	3.834	3.564	3.329	2.856	2.499	2.222	2.000
26	22.795	20.121	15.983	13.003	10.810	9.161	7.896	6.906	6.491	6.118	5.480	4.956	4.520	4.151	3.988	3.837	3.566	3.330	2.856	2.500	2.221	2.000
27	23.560	20.707	16.330	13.211	10.935	9.237	7.943	6.935	6.514	6.136	5.492	4.964	4.524	4.154	3.990	3.839	3.567	3.331	2.856	2.500	2.222	2.000
28	24.316	21.281	16.663	13.406	11.051	9.307	7.984	6.961	6.534	6.152	5.502	4.970	4.528	4.157	3.992	3.840	3.568	3.331	2.857	2.500	2.222	2.000
29	25.066	21.844	16.984	13.591	11.158	9.370	8.022	6.983	6.551	6.166	5.510	4.975	4.531	4.159	3.994	3.841	3.569	3.332	2.857	2.500	2.222	2.000
30	25.808	22.396	17.292	13.765	11.258	9.427	8.055	7.003	6.566	6.177	5.517	4.979	4.534	4.160	3.995	3.842	3.569	3.332	2.857	2.500	2.222	2.000
40	32.835	27.355	19.793	15.046	11.925	9.779	8.244	7.105	6.642	6.234	5.548	4.997	4.544	4.166	3.999	3.846	3.571	3.333	2.857	2.500	2.222	2.000
50	39.196	31.424	21.482	15.762	12.234	9.915	8.304	7.153	6.661	6.246	5.554	4.999	4.545	4.167	4.000	3.846	3.571	3.333	2.857	2.500	2.222	2.000

Source: From tables computed by Jerome Bracken and Charles J. Christenson. Copyright © 1961 by the President and Fellows of Harvard College. Used by permission.

Subject Index